on Gres

British Cookery

Editor	Lizzie Boyd
Research Directors	Professor John Fuller, FHCI, FRSH
	Professor John Beavis, BA (Econ.) FCA, FHCIMA
Researchers	Catherine Braithwaite
	Linda Malone
	D.W. Kennedy
	Bridget McGregor
	J.S.L. McKee
Recipe Testing	Scottish Hotel School, University of Strathclyde
Colour Illustrations	Barry Hicks, British Tourist Authority

BRITISH COOKERY

A COMPLETE GUIDE TO CULINARY PRACTICE IN THE BRITISH ISLES

Based on research undertaken for the British Farm Produce Council
and the British Tourist Authority by the University of Strathclyde

REVISED EDITION

CROOM HELM LTD   BRITISH FARM PRODUCE COUNCIL   BRITISH TOURIST AUTHORITY

Published by Croom Helm Ltd.,
2-10 St. John's Road, London SW11

ISBN 0-85664-352-1

The suitability of each recipe is
indicated by H (Hotel/Commercial)
and F (Family/Domestic)

Printed and bound in Great Britain by
Redwood Burn Limited
Trowbridge & Esher

Contents

Foreword

Time was when the British were renowned throughout Europe for their good living, for splendid native dishes and for their uninhibited enjoyment of fine food and drink.

Unhappily we passed into an era when the culinary arts sank into a decline. Except among a small minority, at best it was regarded as eccentric, at worst as decadent, to evince an interest in the good things of the table. Food became for too many merely something which one was obliged to transfer at regular intervals from plate to mouth.

Happily, today there is a great and ever-growing interest in food. Much of this renewed interest among the British may be attributed to the influence of travel. One of the major joys of travel is sampling the food of other lands.

So today food is one of the chief tourist attractions of a country. The general standard of food available in the eating places of Britain is high and the variety offered is wide. But as real standards rise so emphatically, so can we all become increasingly self-critical in a constructive sense.

One area where complacency would be out of place is the disappearance over the years of many old British dishes. No doubt there were bad ones which rightly have been forgotten. But there are many good ones and they are the object of this book.

So with our old friends, the British Farm Produce Council, with whom we have been associated on many occasions in promoting British food, we commissioned a study by the University of Strathclyde. This book is the outcome of our work together.

In revealing something of the splendours of our native kitchen and by distilling within two covers the wisdom of centuries, we hope this book will make its own contribution towards the restoration of the best of the traditional fare enjoyed by our forebears to the tables of Britain's hotels and restaurants.

Alexander Glen, KBE, DSC,
Chairman, British Tourist Authority

June 1976

From these islands come the finest foodstuffs in the world. The nation's farmers and growers see to that. Their skill, ingenuity and sheer hard work in every sort of weather provide the basic raw material for our meals, whether we eat them in hotel, restaurant or at home.

But for too long the formal training and instruction of those engaged in the catering industry has been influenced by the "French Cuisine" — not that that is without significance.

The idea of "Eating British" has been neglected, largely because there was no established training manual.

It was to fill that gap that the British Farm Produce Council and the British Tourist Authority decided to ask the University of Strathclyde to undertake research. From that exhaustive investigation and its subsequent editing there has emerged something that will become a standard work for universities, training colleges and schools of every sort concerned with the realms of catering, home economics and, indeed, education in its broadest sense.

It is my belief that this manual, codifying, as it does, recipes and methods that have been passed from generation to generation in cottage and mansion in every corner of the United Kingdom, will have a profound influence in the years to come, ranking with "Escoffier" and "Larousse".

Charles M. Jarvis
Chairman, British Farm Produce Council

June 1976

A Brief History of British Cookery

National food characteristics have been forming since the beginnings of life on these islands, but the mid-eleventh century has been chosen as the starting point for a short discourse on the outstanding features of British cookery. Such features are necessarily linked to individual dishes, their origins and developments throughout the centuries; they are also related to new types of foods — and hence new dishes — which have been introduced during the twentieth century, their subsequent integration and their effects on older dishes. Emphasis has been laid on the social life of the British people since this is intimately connected with the necessities of eating and drinking.

Wherever possible, information and conclusions have been based on contemporary sources in the form of manuscript recipes, recipe books and literary works. It cannot, however, be assumed that such accounts are necessarily accurate or totally unbiased or that they present a complete picture of cooking and eating habits at the different levels of society. It is hoped that this glimpse into the past will prove sufficiently revealing to reconstruct many of the basic features on which the traditions of British cookery rest.

THE MIDDLE AGES (1066-1534)

A critical point in the evolution of British cookery came in 1066, with the Normans. The Romans had extended and developed the culinary knowledge of the early Britons, but much was lost in the period after they left: culinary refinements could not be expected of the fierce and warlike Saxons and Danes. Quantity rather than quality was important. The Normans were more refined and brought to Britain the habits, manners and cooking of France and Italy.

During the Norman, medieval and Tudor periods the foundations of traditional British cooking were laid. Chaucer (c. 1340-1400) is considered a fairly credible and accurate writer of his period; his descriptions illuminate the contrast between the luxurious fare of the rich and the spartan food of the poor. They also pinpoint varying degrees of prosperity in different parts of the country. From William Langland's descriptions in *Piers Plowman* (fourteenth century) it seems clear that quantity, quality and variety of diet changed according to season, with people indulging themselves after harvest time to compensate for when they were trying to eke out the remains of the previous harvest. Dishes common during periods of dearth — Beans and Bacon, Pease Pudding and Staffordshire Peas — are indications of the peasants' ingenuity in supplementing scarce or expensive animal protein foods with vegetable ones. When the harvest failed, rabbits, birds and other game were trapped and wild herbs and roots were gathered.

The yeoman farmer fared well in comparison with the peasant since his luxuries were supplied by his own farmyard while the farm labourer lived on cheese and oaten cakes. Bacon was by far the most common meat and since eggs were usually plentiful they were combined in these early centuries to establish the bacon and egg habit now so inherent in the British tradition. Another simple combination in the peasants' diet was curds and cream. A hunk of bread, lump of cheese, onions for flavour, and ale must also have been one of the most common meals considering the lack of cooking facilities. Pottages with bread were probably the main dish in winter months, and the contents would depend on the wealth of the household. Vegetables were usually the main ingredient — onions, garlic, leeks and cabbage, peas, beans and oats with a selection of herbs from the garden or woods. From the many descriptions of food provided by the lord for his serfs during harvesting it is apparent that the variety of foods was limited. Two meals were usually provided: dinner consisting of a loaf, pottage ("a grewell without flesh"), meat and/or fish, and perhaps cheese and ale. At supper, bread with cheese and ale, sometimes only water, constituted a meal.

Simple, repetitive and based almost entirely on natural produce, the everyday food of the peasant makes sharp contrast with the fare prepared in the kitchens of royalty and nobility. William I is thought to have transplanted in bulk his kitchen from Normandy, and it seems natural that his barons did likewise. Sufficiently revealing is the fact that manuscript recipes of the fourteenth century were strongly influenced by the French, both in terminology and methods. The dishes described were elaborate combinations rather than simple dishes implying that these cooks were required to develop artistic qualities.

A significant feature of medieval recipes is the constant use of spices and condiments. Returning crusaders of the eleventh, twelfth and thirteenth centuries brought back tales of more advanced civilisations with an abundance of spices, dates, figs, almonds, sherberts and sweetmeats. These foods became a necessity, even among those who had never left England; they added interest and variety to the rich man's food, were useful during the long banquets to revive flagging appetites, and were often used, discreetly or otherwise, by the cook to camouflage meat or fish that was tainted or heavily salted and unpalatable.

Contemporary accounts refer to feasts and banquets, characteristic of the medieval love of grandeur, pomp and pageantry with a glitter and splendour only to be paralleled in the Tournament. The inauguration of Archbishop Nevill during the reign of King Edward IV (1461-83) was documented in great detail. The actual bills of fare, since a feast of this size would have extended over several days, were interspersed throughout other details in the account. The bill of fare was divided into courses: one or two dozen dishes were brought out and set on the table for the first course and these were subsequently removed and replaced by another collection of dishes which formed the second course. Similarly with the third, fourth, fifth and sixth courses. Most courses included an elaborately decorated confection, known as a "suttletie"; this frequently represented a relevant feature of the occasion. The following is the dinner at the Archbishop Nevill feast and represents a typical collection of medieval dishes.

THE FIRST COURSE

A suttletie of Saint George
Viante Cipress Potage
Partridge in brasill
Pestels (*haunches*) of Venison rost
Swan rost
Capons of gease

Teales roast
Pyke in harblet (*herbs*)
Woodcocks baked
Partriche leiche (*sliced*)
A Dolphin in foyle (a suttletie)
Hart for a suttletie

THE SECOND COURSE

Brent Tuskin to Potage
Crayne Potage
Cony rost (rabbit)
Herenshaw rost (young herons)

Breame in harblet
Venison baked
A Dragon (a suttletie)
A Porke Payne (*with bread*)

Curlewe rost

Lech (a sweet with wine, sugar, dates and spices),
Damaske (*perfumed water*) and Sampson
(a suttletie)

THE THIRD COURSE

Dates in compost (*preserve*)
Pecocke with gylt neb
Reyes rost
Rabits rost

Larks rost
Tenche in gelly
Venison baked
Petypanel a march payne (almonds, rose water
and sugar baked like small loaves)

Partridge rost
Redshanks rost
Plovers rost
Quayles and Styntes rost

A suttletie, a Tart
Leche Lumbard gylt, partie jelly and a suttletie
of Saint William with his coat of armour betwixt
his hands

Item Wafers and Ipocras (*highly spiced liquor*) when dyner was done.

Here followeth the serving of Fyshe in order

THE FIRST COURSE

First potage
Almond Butter
Red Herrynges
Salt Fysch
Luce salt
Salt Eel
Kelyng, Codling and Hadock boyled

Thirlepoole rost
Pyke in harblet
Eels baked
Salmon chynes broyled (*chops, grilled*)
Turbot baked
And fritters fryed

THE SECOND COURSE

Fresh Salmon jowles (*head and shoulder cut*)
Salt Sturgion
Whytynges
Pylchers
Eels
Makerels
Places fryed
Barbelles
Conger rost
Troute

Lamprey rost
Bret
Turbot
Roches
Salmon baked
Lynge in gelly
Bream baked
Tenche in gelly
Crabbes

THE THIRD COURSE

Jowles of freshe Sturgion

Small Perches fryed

Great Geles

Broyled Conger

Cheums

Breames

Rudes

Lamprones

Smells rost

Shrympes

Small Menewes

Thirlepoole baked

And Lopster

The exact nature of the dishes is difficult to establish since the documented recipes are often lacking in information. This applies in particular to the vast number of recipes which were a kind of "soft mess", without any indication as to whether they were soups or stews. The dishes which were obviously soups would have been fairly simple, such as "Cabbages in Pottage", cooked in broth, with onions, whites of leeks, saffron, salt and mixed spices. Stews, or those which can be clearly defined as such, usually contained meat, ground fine in the mortar with bread and sometimes thickened with egg. "Mortrews of Pork and Hens" is a typical example: the meat was boiled, the flesh removed and ground, grated bread, yolks of eggs, pepper, ginger, sugar, saffron and salt added and the mixture stiffened (presumably by heating to thicken the egg) after which the whole was floured with powdered ginger. The term "mortrews" was applied generally to any dish containing pounded meat. Pork, veal, poultry and game are the most common meats in the recipes, beef and mutton are rarely mentioned.

Many dishes which have survived the passage of time started out as quite different items. Mixtures of sweet and savoury ingredients were common and the original terminology was often retained. The medieval "Blanc-mang" is a good example of this development. Described in *The Forme of Cury* (a roll of ancient English cookery, compiled about 1390 by the master cooks of Richard II), the meat from a boiled capon was ground finely, simmered with the capon stock and served with red aniseed and almonds fried in oil. Presumably, at some stage the meat and rice were omitted, cream was added, additional flavourings of lemon and brandy were mixed with milk and cream and set with isinglass to become the popular cold sweet of the eighteenth and nineteenth centuries.

The pie was associated with a collection of ingredients under a pie crust, and the pudding was also related to a mixture of various items, this time boiled in the stomach bag of an animal, from the fifteenth century onwards known as a "haggas". The pudding cloth and eventually the pudding basin were later developments, but traces of the original pudding concept have survived in the form of haggis and black and white puddings.

The variety of fish available and the diverse methods of preparing it emphasise its importance in the medieval diet since for a large part of the year its consumption was compulsory by law. Hard salted, dried and smoked fish in the form of red herrings, speldings and salt pickled herrings were used by the majority of the population on "fish days". Small fish were served whole, while large fish were cut in pieces or "crimped". They were often boiled in wine and water, vinegar and water or ale and water as typified in a recipe for "Cypre of Salmon": Cook almonds; stew salmon; mix almonds with salmon broth; remove bones from the fish and grind the flesh small; add to the broth along with milk, rice, powder fort, sugar and salt; colour with alkenet; do not make thick.

The principal vegetables were onions, leeks, garlic, peas, beans and cabbages with occasional mention of turnips, parsnips, beetroot, skirrets (water parsnip), funges (mushrooms) and spinach. They seem to have been used more in soups than served as individual dishes. Herbs were widely used — one salad recipe recommends no less than twelve herbs and vegetables (parsley, sage, garlic, young onions (shallots), onions, leeks, borage, mint, fennel, cress, rosemary, purslain). It is unlikely, however, that salads were widely eaten at this time in Britain as oil was not readily available.

Sweet dishes, apart from the "suttletie",varied from strawberries and cream to fritters, tarts, fruit pies, custards, flans and stewed fruits. A popular dish was "tartys in applis", stewed fruit with spices, figs, raisins and pears, coloured with saffron and baked in a pie crust. Dates, figs, raisins and currants were used a great deal and honey to sweeten; almonds were a favourite ingredient in many types of dishes; marzipan is a modern remnant of the medieval obsession with almonds.

During this period baking of cakes was limited to bread doughs mixed with honey, spices, currants and raisins according to taste. Cakes were for special occasions. Christmas had its celebration cake, the origins of which go back to pre-Christian days. The most magnificent festival in the Anglo-Saxon calendar was in honour of the god Thor, named "Yule" or "Yeol", at which cakes sweetened with honey were dedicated to the god as peace offerings. Twelfth Night Cake celebrated the season of Twelvetide or Epiphany; it was a large flat cake made of flour, sugar, honey, ginger, pepper and probably dried fruit; sometimes also eggs. Hidden in it were a pea and a bean and whoever found the bean in his piece of cake was king for the evening, his queen being the one who found the pea.

Gingerbread was quite different from the modern version; it was made with breadcrumbs and dried out until hard, more like a biscuit than a cake. The gingerbread booth or stall was an essential feature of annual fairs with ornamented gingerbread in the form of crowns, kings, queens, cocks, etc., resplendent with gilt and decorated with bows and streamers of brightly coloured ribbons. Gingerbread shapes were many and varied and must have included the gingerbread man as well as letters and numbers which were used for teaching children to read and count.

THE GROWTH OF NATIONAL CHARACTERISTICS (1534-1700)

The sixteenth century was an important turning point in the development of British cookery. Historical events indirectly set the course of cookery in Britain, most significantly with the rejection by Henry VIII in 1534 of papal control. As a result monasteries were dissolved, and the break with Rome and other Catholic countries meant an end to many foreign influences. Britain developed a natural individuality and insularity which indirectly affected eating habits.

Equally important was the protest in the 1560s against the episcopal organisation of the newly formed Church of England. The influence of this Puritan movement on cookery is difficult to assess fully, but sufficiently revealing is the fact that not only were all feasts and feastings abandoned, including Christmas, but the use of wines and spices was also discouraged. To the Puritans any sensual pleasures were corrupt and materialistic, and they have been charged with the destruction of some of the traditional splendour of British fare. More damaging, however, was their lack of encouragement and interest in culinary affairs. While in France, the foundations of classical French cuisine were laid under the guidance and enthusiasm of Louis XIV, British cookery under the Puritan influence was virtually at a standstill, showing little refinement or development from its medieval period.

Britain, envious of the reputation which France was developing in the culinary field, reacted in two ways: firstly by cautiously adopting some of the French recipes of which British cooks approved and secondly, in rivalry with France, by managing to produce more cookery books than any other country of the period. In 1660 Charles II was restored to the throne after his exile in France. He came back not only with a taste for champagne, which he popularised in this country, but also with lavish tastes in food.

James II in his brief reign (1685-8) perpetuated his brother's passion for the French style while later William and Mary had natural leanings towards the Dutch style of cooking. Thus, with no monarch to set the fashion in British cookery, it foundered. In sophisticated circles it was propped up by French and Dutch styles while the population at large was left to lead the way, not with *haute cusine*, but with their ordinary roast and boiled meat, numerous varieties of puddings and pies and simple everyday combinations. The use of natural produce rather than imported was inevitable, and the earlier familiar combinations again appear: beans and bacon, bacon and eggs, curds and cream, pork and pease pudding, cheese and oatcakes, bread and cheese, onions and ale. Relief from this monotony was found in the variety of foods available at fairs, in cook shops, taverns, inns and from street vendors.

Contemporary accounts of the food eaten at fairs suggest that besides the general guzzling, certain foods were specifically associated with certain fairs. The colourful gingerbread booth and the huge open fire with its ceremonial roast ox turning on the spit could be found at any big fair; the Stourbridge Fair in Cambridge specialised in other foods – fresh herrings were the principal dish at the banquet which concluded the procession through the town. Roast goose was also traditionally associated with this fair as were roast and boiled pork. On Horse Fair Day (14 September), Colchester oysters and fresh herrings were always on the bill of fare. The Michaelmas Fair at Bedford was renowned for its sale of baked Warden pears; in Wellingborough, the special dish at St Duke's Fair was Rock and Dough Flake.

St Bartholomew's Fair was particularly well supplied with food and the smell of roast pig was said to be everywhere; greedy spectators standing round the roast were sold hot slices of the meat as it was carved. The fair was usually the only opportunity many people had to enjoy the flavour of roast meat, and for some it was probably one of the few occasions when they tasted meat at all. Apples were another favourite at "Bartlemy"; the small windfall apples skewered on sticks and dipped in a thick honey mixture were the forerunners of toffee apples. At West Country fairs, roast goose or lamb pie washed down with Devonshire cider were standard fare, and at St Giles Fair in Barnstaple, said to be the most typical of West Country fairs, spiced ale mixed by the senior beadle from a secret recipe was served with toast and cheese.

Townspeople had access to a regular type of fare from the cook shops, "pastelers", pie bakers, taverns, inns and ale houses which offered roast or boiled meat puddings and pies, bread, cheese and broth, everything accompanied by ale or beer. Thirst-provoking foods, such as pickled anchovies and herrings, slices of ham, prawns and toasted cheese were also popular; for sweets there were jellies, syllabubs and sweet pastries from the pastry cooks. They usually also had a variety of meats, such as beef, mutton, veal, pork and lamb, roasting on spits before the fire. Many cook shops also supplied pies of all kinds; the cheaper cook shops produced dubious pies often made from tainted meat, but highly spiced to disguise the taste. Even cheaper were the humble "dives" in rooms below ground; inadequate ventilation coupled with the nauseating cooking smells made them particularly unpleasant places, serving boiled shin of beef, boiled tripe and cow heel, and sausages with bread or a savoury pudding and beer.

While the cook shops provided food and drink of all kinds, the early taverns, also known as public houses or taprooms, were first associated with the retailing of wine. Later on, food was served at taverns although the pattern of eating was different; a daily meal was served for a fixed price and at a stated time. Because of the regularity of this meal it came to be known as an "ordinary"; in London, fashionable taverns served a sophisticated type of "ordinary" for the rich, costing about a guinea. More modest establishments promoted a plainer type of fare; at the Cheshire Cheese Tavern in London "The Pudding" was legendary. Made on Wednesdays and Saturdays in winter, it was described as ranging from fifty to eighty pounds in weight.

"It is composed of a fine light crust in a huge basin, and there are entombed therein beef-steaks, kidneys, oysters, larks, mushrooms, and wondrous spices and gravies the secret of which is known only to the compounder. The boiling process takes about sixteen to twenty hours . . ."

Finally there were the inns which provided lodging and entertainment for travellers. The fare was similar to that of the cook shops and taverns depending on the nature of the establishment; country inns were often farmhouses as well and as such naturally promoted the local produce. Well established country traditions of curing hams, of preserving and storing sauces, of local pies and pasties and all types of country preserves flourished at country inns.

Of the basic foods, cheese was particularly important. In rich pastoral areas local cheeses were served at the inn or sold in nearby towns, their fame spreading beyond the neighbourhood. Cheeses from the Leicestershire pastures were widely known for their fine quality, but most famous of them all was the Stilton. Originally created from a recipe belonging to a local family, it is thought to have been made commercially for the first time by the family's housekeeper, Mrs Orton, after she had left the family and married. About 1730 Cowper Thornhill, inn keeper at the Bell Inn at Stilton, began to buy it from her in large quantities; the cheese was first known as Quenby Cheese, but later became known as Stilton because of its association with the village.

The West Country produced another blue-veined cheese — the Blue Vinney. Other local cheeses maintained the old traditions of flavouring and colouring cheeses with herbs; bruised leaves steeped in milk or chopped herbs were mixed through the curds. Particularly famed was Sage Derby cheese; it was commonly believed that sage digested fat, and it was used with pork and duck and added to cheeses with a high fat content. Many other local cheeses became well known, such as the hard-pressed Cheddar, Gloucester, Dunlop, Lancashire, Derby, Cheshire and Leicester cheeses together with the semi-hard Caerphilly, White Wensleydale and White Stilton.

Cookery Writers

During the sixteenth and seventeenth centuries cookery writers wrote for the aristocracy and the wealthy. There were no cookery books to influence the majority of the population which continued to depend on instructions handed down from generation to generation by word of mouth. Robert May, the first professional English cook to write a cookery book, moved in aristocratic circles all his life and was motivated by strong foreign influences. There is little standard British cookery to be found in his cookery book, much of which is devoted to his love of creating allegorical "suttleties". He does, however, give instructions on some simple British basics of roasting and broth making as well as some recipes for "Sheeps Haggas Pudding" and for bacon and eggs.

Gervase Markham probably did more than anyone else at this period to encourage and develop a national cooking tradition with his book *The English Housewife*, published in 1615. His admonition to the housewife called on her to "let the provision of her meals be esteemed for the familiar acquaintance she hath with it than for the strangeness and variety it bringeth from other countries". His recipes show herbs as an integral part of broths and salads; the "simple sallet" uses greens, oil, vinegar and sugar, while the compound one, the forerunner of the "Grand Sallet" later known as "Salamagundy", includes almonds, raisins, currants, dates, olives, sugar, oranges and lemons as well as sage, spinach, capers, red cauliflower, cucumber, cabbage, lettuce, oil and vinegar.

The extensive use of fruits, vegetables, herbs and flowers reflects the fact that in the seventeenth century the wealthy spent lavishly on their gardens, houses and farms. From contemporary descriptions there is abundant evidence of well stocked gardens in which grew various types of lettuce, mustard, cucumbers, celery, mint, parsley, sage, scurvy grass, purslain, samphire, fennel, basil, sorrel, spinach, tansy, thyme, onions, peas, artichokes, asparagus, turnips and parsnips. Nettles were usually eaten raw or boiled in spring potages, red beets were boiled and used for "winter sallets". Radishes, leeks, salsify and hops had medicinal uses; rosemary flowers were used in vinegar or in a glass of "sherris sack" (sherry), marjoram was used in broths, while garlic was thought to be

> "more proper for our Northern Rustics, especially living in moist places or such as use the sea. Whilst we absolutely forbid its entrance into our salleting, by reason of its intolerable rankness, and which made it as detested of old, that the eating of it was part of the punishment for such as commited horrid crimes to be sure it is not fit for ladies palates nor those who court them". (John Evelyn, 1678)

DEVELOPMENT AND CHANGE (1700-1800)

The changes which influenced the pattern of eating in the eighteenth century were many and varied but in contrast with previous periods were influenced by material rather than political factors. Agricultural improvements brought a better quality of fresh meat all the year round and the quality of flour also improved. The poor man's diet of black bread and salt meat was gradually being exchanged for one of fine wheaten loaves and fresh meat. The quantity and variety of fruits and vegetables supplied to urban markets was rapidly increasing, particularly around London. The potato, well established in Ireland by 1700, was becoming popular in the North of England and in Scotland and Wales. Sugar came down in price and of the non-alcoholic drinks, tea had taken the lead over coffee and chocolate. Finally the import of cheap cereals from the colonies was beginning to have an effect on the diet.

Such changes in available commodities were bound to have considerable effects on the existing pattern of eating and particularly on the mass of the population. In the past, foreign commodities had been either too expensive or too scarce, but now tea, sugar and potatoes became cheap while existing commodities of meat, vegetables, fruits and cereals were more plentiful.

Good supplies of fresh meat contributed to well-established roasting traditions; the demand was high and from the very poor upwards prosperity was determined by the amount of meat in the diet. Meat became synonymous with manliness for the English whose fictitious character John Bull was supposed to have thrived on it, and the Marlborough wars were said to have been won by sturdy Englishmen fed on roast meats. Beef was the most popular meat and acquired for itself such a reputation that the "Roast Beef of England" has passed into legend.

While the popularity of meat established itself as the most desirable type of food there seems to have been a certain amount of disdain, in certain classes of the community, for vegetables. Town people associated vegetables with penury, and despite increasing supplies from market gardens, the development of vegetable dishes in towns was limited. In country areas, however, the situation was different, and vegetables were still regarded as useful ingredients in traditional broths and stews. In addition, the savoury pudding formerly eaten with meat was being replaced with vegetables.

The acceptance of the potato by the North, Scotland, Ireland and Wales long before the South of England creates a comparison which affects the development of certain foods and subsequent dishes. The whole pattern of life in these areas had been different to the customs and habits of the South for many centuries; geographically they were remote from the South, where trade had established a freer interchange of ideas as well as commodities, their soil was poorer with more highland areas than in the South, and their climate was wetter. In addition, these regions had suffered severely from political unrest in some form or other, leading to economic disadvantages.

Ireland, the first area in Britain to grow the potato, is also the one which allowed it to become most firmly established in its eating pattern. It was introduced when Ireland was most receptive to a saviour from the widespread and increasing deterioration, cultural, social and economic, which overtook the Irish nation from the sixteenth century onwards. All the elements which favour a potato-controlled economy were there: the impoverished smallholding peasantry, poor communications, lack of monetary resources and a particularly suitable soil and climate for growing. That the potato became the staple item of food for the mass of the population is seen in its extensive use in Irish dishes.

The arrival of the potato in Lancashire and the North of England, and its acceptance in these parts before other areas of England, had a significant effect on the diet. The social and economic factors in these areas also favoured the potato, and the large number of Irish in these areas must have had a considerable influence. While in the South of England wheat was the principal cereal, the staple cereals in the North were oats and barley, and areas which were denied fine wheaten bread welcomed the potato.

Scotland and Wales were both areas with an impoverished peasantry, bad communications and a lack of monetary resources; their soil and climate were more suitable for potatoes, oats and barley than wheat. In spite of these factors neither Scotland nor Wales allowed the potato to dominate their diet as the Irish had done although in Scotland the potato flourished to a greater extent in the Highlands and Islands than in the Lowlands. In Wales, a few traditional dishes began to include the potato. Generally, potatoes in these areas complemented oatmeal and barley and were also combined with dairy produce which was an important feature of the diet.

The early savoury pudding developed into sweet, rich suet puddings cooked in a cloth. Endless varieties emerged, notably the plum pudding together with other heavy, rich and often indigestible puddings. Cheap and plentiful sugar and cereals from abroad were having an influence on established sweet dishes. The Hasty Pudding was an ideal basic from which many variations developed. Sage, vermicelli, millet and rice were increasingly used as farinaceous thickening agents in sweet puddings; the potato was also used for this purpose. These new thickenings and the concept of the Hasty Pudding were responsible for developments in the milk pudding tradition.

The popularity of tea was a result of a number of factors. The conquest of India, beginning in 1730, made the British owners of a potential tea growing country; tea was said to be more compatible with the English character than coffee or chocolate. The East India Company which had the monopoly of the tea trade reduced prices and increased supplies and by the end of the century began extensive propaganda for tea. Although beer was still the universal drink, it was confronted in the eighteenth century with this serious rival and disappeared in the next century as an essential element of standard British fare.

The transition from beer to tea may have been gradual, but was at least evident. Other more subtle alterations to standard British dishes of roast and boiled meat, puddings and pies, bread, cheese and simple combinations were more obscure. Variations developed from new, increased and improved supplies but they were built into the existing pattern without altering the basic elements which were still the essential part of British cookery.

Cookery writers who attempted to express the new impetus in British cooking traditions contrast with those of the previous century. Women seized the pen and the potential market for the works of cookery writers extended beyond the aristocracy of the land, as housewives required written instructions for their domestic servants and cookery schools needed manuals; but above this many more people could for the first time afford to buy books as they became cheaper. It was at this point that the first best-selling cookery book was written: *The Art of Cookery Made Plain and Easy* (1747) by Hanna Glasse. She was not a professional cook, but her cookery book was a best seller for almost a hundred years. *The Complete House-wife* by Mrs E. Smith had appeared earlier, in 1728, but did not achieve the same popularity as Mrs Glasse. Mrs Smith *was* a professional cook, and although her dishes were for the upper rather than the lower sections of the community, she shared Mrs Glasse's disdain for French dishes. Her respect for natural produce, and for the English palate, earned her recipes a significant position in the history of English food. Similarly Ann Peckham in *The Complete English Cook; or Prudent Housewife* (1773), concentrates on national food rather than foreign.

In Edinburgh, Susanna MacIver had her *Cookery and Pastry* published in 1787. Her recipes were intended for the wealthy and it was apparent that French influences were important to her. Although few differences in basic cooking appear between North and South of the Border, Mrs MacIver includes several national and Scottish dishes not found in other cookery books of the time. That a recipe for Scotch Barley Broth is not included seems strange, even more so since John Farley, who was cook at the London Tavern about this time, gives a comprehensive recipe in his *London Art of Cookery* (1785). This enigma illustrates the fact that cookery books do not necessarily portray an accurate picture of the food eaten at a certain time and place.

Factual records of meals during the eighteenth century must, however, be based on truth. While cookery books give recommendations for fashionable dinner parties, examples of everyday food are found in the pages of *Parson Woodforde's Diary* (1765-1803) and in the descriptions of meals in Sir Frederick Eden's treatise on *The State of the Poor* (1797). Parson Woodforde was a countryman among the moderately wealthy while Sir Fredrick Eden's diets were a description of the workhouse food of the very poorest sections of the community. Despite the staggering contrast their examples illustrate standard British dishes and consolidate the general features which were emerging at this time.

Parson Woodforde's meals (see the following extract) are testimony to the general features of natural food in the eighteenth century. Meat takes precedence over everything else, puddings and pies are well represented, vegetables and made dishes are at a minimum. The simpler types of standard dishes lacking in his meals are found in the workhouse food to complete the picture of broths or pottages, bread, cheese, beer and simple combinations which formed the diet of the poor. Not only the workhouse poor, but people of limited means existed on this type of diet with variety and quantity depending on circumstances.

A number of workhouse diets from different regions are included to illustrate the contrast between North and South: potatoes, oatmeal and milk form the basis in the North, while in the South bread is more of a staple item with limited amounts of potatoes, oatmeal and milk. Evidence of cheap imported cereals can be found in the incidence of rice pottage, rice milk, rice pudding, etc. Beer was still the most common beverage for the poor, but Parson Woodforde drank tea and coffee as well as chocolate.

From *The Diary of a Country Parson* (The Reverend James Woodforde)

Date	Meat and Vegetables	Fish	Sweets	Miscellaneous
1787				
8 May	Fillet of Veal Leg of Lamb Boiled Loin fryed Fine Tongue Asparagus	Skaite	Plumb Pudding Tarts Trifle Cheesecakes	
22 May	Chine of Mutton Rosted Ham and 3 Chickens	Maccarel	Apricot and Gooseberry	Oranges Almonds

	2 Pigeons Rosted		Tarts	Raisins
	Asparagus		Rasp Jam	Nuts
	Cucumber		Tartlets	Apples
28th	Boiled Leg of Lamb		Apricot and	Oranges
	Small Roasting Pig		Gooseberry	Nuts
			Tarts	
June 2nd	Knuckle of Veal	Some Fish		
	Bacon			
	Small Piece of Rost		Tarts	
	Pork			
11th	Boiled Beef and Lamb		Gooseberry	
			Tarts	
12th	3 Chicken Boiled		Baked Plumb	
	Tongue		Pudding of the	
	Piece of Rost Beef		Custard kind	
	Asparagus			
21st	Saddle of Mutton Rosted	Maccarel	Blamange	
	Ham and Chicken		Custards	
	Some Young beans		Lemon Cream	
	Young ducks Rosted		Tarts	
	Green peas			
	Rabbit fryed			
	Asparagus			
23rd	Calf's Pluck (heart,		Gooseberry	
	liver, lights)		Tarts	
	Boiled Beef			
	Calf's Liver			
	Hash Mutton			
	Fat Young Goose and Peas			

From *The State of the Poor* by Sir Fredrick Eden (1797)

WILTSHIRE (Bradford)

DAY	BREAKFAST	DINNER	SUPPER
Sunday	Onion broth made of water, onions, oatmeal and the fat of meat broth	Meat and vegetables	Bread and cheese
Monday	Onion broth	Bread and cheese	As Sunday
Tuesday	Onion broth	As Sunday	As Sunday
Wednesday	Onion broth	As Monday	As Sunday
Thursday	Onion broth	As Sunday	As Sunday
Friday	Onion broth	As Monday	As Sunday
Saturday	Onion broth	As Monday	As Sunday

GLOUCESTERSHIRE (Bristol)

DAY	BREAKFAST	DINNER	SUPPER
Sunday	Water gruel	Soup made of bullock's head	Bread and cheese
Monday	As Sunday	Pease soup	As Sunday
Tuesday	As Sunday	Meat and potatoes	As Sunday
Wednesday	Broth	Bread and cheese	As Sunday
Thursday	As Sunday	As Tuesday	As Sunday
Friday	As Wednesday	As Monday	As Sunday
Saturday	As Sunday	Bread and cheese	As Sunday

NORFOLK (Yarmouth)

DAY	BREAKFAST	DINNER	SUPPER
Sunday	Bread and butter	Suet pudding	Bread and cheese
Monday	Bread and treacle	Boiled meat, dumplings and vegetables	As Sunday
Tuesday	Bread and broth	Pease soup and bread	As Sunday
Wednesday	As Sunday	Milk or gruel and bread	As Sunday
Thursday	As Monday	As Monday	As Sunday
Friday	As Tuesday	As Tuesday	As Sunday
Saturday	As Sunday	As Wednesday	As Sunday

NOTTINGHAMSHIRE (Newark)

DAY	BREAKFAST	DINNER	SUPPER
Sunday	Milk pottage	Bread puddings, beef, bread, broth and roots	Bread and cheese or butter, beer
Monday	As Sunday	Bread and pease pottage	As Sunday
Tuesday	As Sunday	Boiled meat, broth, roots and bread	As Sunday
Wednesday	As Sunday	Frumety of wheat, milk	As Sunday
Thursday	As Sunday	As Tuesday	As Sunday

| Friday | As Sunday | Suet pudding | As Sunday |
| Saturday | As Sunday | Dumplings with sauce of vinegar, sugar and water | As Sunday |

MONMOUTHSHIRE (Monmouth)

DAY	BREAKFAST	DINNER	SUPPER
Sunday	Milk pottage	Meat and vegetables	Bread and beer
Monday	Broth	Bread and cheese	As Sunday
Tuesday	As Sunday	As Sunday	As Sunday
Wednesday	As Monday	As Monday	As Sunday
Thursday	As Sunday	As Sunday	As Sunday
Friday	As Monday	As Monday	As Sunday
Saturday	As Sunday	As Monday	As Sunday

LANCASHIRE (Lancaster)

DAY	BREAKFAST	DINNER	SUPPER
Sunday	Milk pottage	Bread, broth, beef and vegetables	Milk pottage
Monday	As Sunday	Broth, bread, hashed meat	As Sunday
Tuesday	As Sunday	As Sunday	As Sunday
Wednesday	As Sunday	As Monday	As Sunday
Thursday	As Sunday	As Sunday	As Sunday
Friday	As Sunday	As Monday	As Sunday
Saturday	As Sunday	Hash made from meat left unconsumed in the week, butter and milk	As Sunday

YORKSHIRE (Sheffield)

DAY	BREAKFAST	DINNER	SUPPER
Sunday	Water pottage, gravy and bread	Beef, bread, broth and potatoes or cabbage, beer	Broth and bread

Monday	As Sunday	Puddings and sauce, beer	Bread and beer
Tuesday	As Sunday	As Sunday	As Sunday
Wednesday	As Sunday	As Monday	As Monday
Thursday	As Sunday	As Sunday	As Sunday
Friday	As Sunday	As Monday	As Monday
Saturday	As Sunday	Cheese, bread, beer	Milk pottage, bread

CUMBERLAND (Carlisle)

On Christmas Day, the Paupers are allowed roast mutton, plum pudding, best cheese and ale.

DAY	BREAKFAST	DINNER	SUPPER
Sunday	Hasty pudding, milk or beer	Broth, beef, bread, beer	Bread and broth
Monday	As Sunday	Potatoes mixed with milk and butter; broth, bread, beer	Hasty pudding or boiled milk and bread
Tuesday	As Sunday	Boiled milk and bread	Hasty pudding, milk or beer
Wednesday	As Sunday	As Sunday	As Sunday
Thursday	As Sunday	As Monday	As Monday
Friday	As Sunday	Two slices boiled beef, soup	As Sunday
Saturday	As Sunday	Boiled milk and bread	Bread, cheese, beer

CHANGE CONSOLIDATED (1800-1900)

Most major changes in standard British cooking during the nineteenth century can be traced to one cause — the Industrial Revolution. Between the critical years of 1760 and 1830, inventions in textile machinery, developments in the iron industry and the improvement of the steam engine combined to produce the age of the machine. The term "revolution" was applied to the effects which machines had on the whole structure and life of the country. The repercussions on our cooking are so varied and confused that they do not submit readily to generalisations. However, facts, such as the rural exodus, the growth of towns, the growth in size and complexity of the food industry, the developments in purchased and imported foods, and the rising middle classes all act as signposts.

There seems little doubt among historians that rural life suffered at the expense of the machine. A social pattern was disrupted and along with other things the national diet changed. In the past, many labourers had land for a cow so that they had as good food as their own industry could provide from their own land and few commodities had to be bought with money. Changes in agriculture in keeping with the growing urban population ended this domestic period of economic organisation; people were driven off the land, mainly by the enclosures, and a rural exodus to the towns and to colonies abroad took place in the Highlands of Scotland where self-sufficient crofters were literally burned out of their homes to make way for the sheep which were in demand by wool merchants and growing urban markets.

Depopulation of rural areas and decline in the conditions of the remaining rural population meant a loss of existing traditions. The staple food items of the past changed, not dramatically at first but as the century progressed changes were gathering momentum. The workhouse poor of 1793 who existed on the bare minimum were more fortunate than the labouring classes of 1863. The workhouse usually provided a selection of vegetables, a reasonable supply of meat in the form of broths, pottages, soups and stews. By 1863 the picture was quite different. The remnants of this tradition contained neither vegetables nor meat. It was simply bread and milk with hot water from the tea kettle, salt to flavour and sometimes added dripping or butter.

The first national food enquiry in Britain was carried out by Edward Smith in 1863 and shows amongst other things that potatoes, along with bread, butter and tea formed the staple food. The milk and oatmeal tradition in the North was dying out. Milk was now sent to the growing towns; without milk, oatmeal dishes were unpalatable and gradually disappeared. Despite this decline the North of England, according to Smith's conclusions, still fared better than the South; oatmeal dishes survived in these areas, as well as in Wales, and are still evident today.

The increasing population of industrial workers cut off from the land had to abandon many of their traditions. Directly affected by bad housing, poor cooking facilities, little or no time to prepare food, only the bare essentials were possible for those on low incomes. Social historians have sought to prove the good and bad effects of the Industrial Revolution on the community and from their findings we may generalise that where the standard of living declined so did the food.

While the standard of living may have fluctuated from town to town the dependence on ready-made foods and food retailers was now universal. The problems of feeding a growing urban population gave new impetus to the food industry and developments were aimed at new methods of preservation since the storage and marketing of large quantities of highly perishable food were impracticable. Years of experimentation and failure were to pass before dried, tinned and frozen foods were successfully brought to the table. At the same time as the development of this new source of food supply came improvements in the processing of bread, butter and milk. Technical achievements led to finer flour; a Frenchman invented a margarine less perishable than butter, and experiments in processing milk soon enabled manufacturers to produce tins of condensed, evaporated and dried milk.

Street Vendors

The food industry provided necessary commodities at a time when the people most needed them. Urban life was often identical with insufficient cooking equipment, expensive fuel and a non-existent water supply; the housewife was faced with an impossible task and welcomed time and labour saving products. In the past, cook shops, dives, street vendors, taverns, inns and ale houses had provided plain British fare. Now their horizons were widened beyond the roast meats, mustard, bread and beer; new traditions were born, and old ones either developed or declined. Prepared foods and cooked provisions became essential to the mass of the population. Breakfast, dinner and supper were obtained from itinerant or stationary vendors who plied their trade in hot eels, pea soups, oysters, fried fish, pies, trotters, puddings, whelks, baked potatoes and hot green peas. London is a particularly rich source of information about the trade in these goods.

Hot eels, as they were cried in the streets, were usually combined with the sale of hot pea soup as the two required the same sort of equipment — soup kettle, ladle, basins or cups and spoons for serving, and a charcoal or coal fire. The eels were cut up into pieces, boiled in water and the liquid thickened with flour and flavoured with chopped parsley and mixed spices. The best hot eel men would add a little bit of butter and the whole was ladled from the soup kettle into cups and served with vinegar and pepper. Pea soup, which was made from beef bones, split peas and celery with salt, pepper and mint to flavour, was a winter trade. In summer the trade in hot eels continued, with pickled whelks substituted for pea soup.

Cold fried flounders may not have much appeal today but the trade was a brisk one in nineteenth-century London. So also was the baked potato trade which began to develop in the streets about 1835. Cooked at the bakehouse, kept hot and served with butter and salt, a couple of potatoes sufficed as a complete meal. Customers were from all classes, but the working classes were the greatest purchasers. "The next course of some boiled feet of some animal" was another growing trade in mid nineteenth-century London. Sheep or lamb trotters were the most common. The trade had started in a small way about the turn of the century but had developed considerably after 1835 when the glue and size makers abandoned the use of trotters and sold them instead at greater profit as food for the poor.

Hot peas were carried in oval tin pots wrapped up with thick cloths to keep in the heat and the peas were served by the ladleful into basins and eaten with salt, vinegar and pepper. The cry was "hot-pea-cod" (pea shell) which implies that the pods were drawn through the teeth to extract the peas.

The pie tradition still flourished, with highly spiced and peppered fillings so that the exact flavour of the meat was not discernible. Gingerbread in various forms was also common, but the trade was on the decline and had to take its place among other fancy cakes and buns. The oyster stall was another old institution; eaten with white bread and butter and seasoned with pepper and vinegar the consumption of oysters was high in the first half of the century and the heartiest customers were the working classes, usually on Saturday nights. The trade declined about 1850 and eventually became obsolete.

Although gingerbread and oysters were on the decline, new developments took their place. In the 1830s the sale of boiled currant puddings began; preparations of milk such as curds and whey were sold in the parks during summer and rice milk was also common.

Finally, if he had a penny to spare, the London street boy finished up with a glass of ginger beer or elder cordial, a salad or baked apple. The variety in the pastry and confectionery line included fruit pies, mince pies, plum duff or puddings, as well as muffins, crumpets, hot-cross buns, Chelsea buns and an infinite variety of tarts, cakes, biscuits, gingerbread and what was known as "sweet-stuff" which included several kinds of rocks, lozenges, candies, medicinal confectionery, cough drops and horehound. Nor were ginger beer and hot elder cordial the only drinks available. About 1830 street sales of tea, coffee and cocoa developed: as coffee was cheap at this time and could be easily adulterated with chicory, the sale in coffee was extremely profitable. Coffee stalls also sold bread and butter, currant cake, ham sandwiches, watercress and boiled eggs.

Apart from new commodities, such as pineapples and brazil nuts, one of the most novel foods introduced at this time was ice cream. It was already quite common among the wealthy classes, but not until the summer of 1850 did it become available in the streets and its reception was not very favourable.

The increased variety of food was reflected not only in the street stalls but also in shops. Institutions appeared such as the tripe shop and the pork butcher where, besides bacon, ham, pies and sausages, such regional delicacies as faggots, black puddings, brawn and haslet could be had. The "hot eel and pea soup men" complained bitterly of their loss in sales to the "penny pie" shops. However, the hot eels joined up with the penny pie shops to become known as "eel and pie shops" still common in some parts today. More significantly, the "cold fried flounder" joined up with potatoes (fried rather than baked to begin with) which developed the combination which spread throughout the country in the form of "fish and chip shops".

Home Cooking

In the home, circumstances dictated the variety of dishes cooked. It may be assumed, however, that the days of roast meat turning on the spit were over in the new industrial towns. Even the days of the peasant-type broth were on the decline except in periods of scarcity when soup kitchens, poorhouses and benevolent ladies provided "washy messes" for the starving. A deep-rooted association of poverty with soup seems to have stunted the soup traditions in the growing industrial towns of the nineteenth century.

An illustration of the change in standard dishes and the amount of cooking done in the home of every-day meals is carefully documented by B. Seebohm Rowntree in *Poverty – A Study of Town Life* (1901). His study was an exposé of the amount and degree of poverty which existed in York at the turn of the century. It classified families by their income, Class I having a total weekly earnings of under 26s per week, Class II earning 26s and over, while Class III were in the servant keeping class representing families who were comfortably off but who lived simply.

Rowntree was primarily concerned with the adequacy of the diet from a nutritional point of view and the economic selection of food. Since his survey is limited to York, generalisation cannot be made without some qualifications. York was certainly among the growing industrial towns, but not on the same scale as the towns in the North West and the Midlands whose industry was more widespread and consequently involved women and children to a much greater extent. However, the following examples illustrate both the types of foods purchased and the types of meal provided by the three categories.

Class I   Working Class Family

The meals provided for this family (parents and two children) show clearly the dependence on bread, butter and tea with other quickly prepared foods, little or no cooking being of paramount importance.

Day	Breakfast	Dinner	Tea	Supper
Friday	Bread and butter, tea	Toast, tea, bread and butter	Bread and butter, tea	
Saturday	Bread, bacon, coffee	Bacon, potatoes, pudding, tea	Bread and butter, shortcake, tea	Tea, bread, kippers
Sunday	Bread and butter, shortcake, coffee	Pork, onions, potatoes, Yorkshire pudding	Bread and butter, shortcake, tea	Bread and meat
Monday	Bread, bacon, tea	Pork, potatoes, pudding, tea	Bread and butter, boiled eggs, tea	Bread and butter, bacon, tea
Wednesday	Bread, bacon, tea	Bacon and eggs, potatoes, bread, tea	Bread and butter, tea	
Thursday	Bread and butter, coffee	Bread, bacon, tea	Bread and butter, tea	

Tradition is preserved in the only incidence of time spent on preparing a whole meal: the Sunday dinner of pork, onions, potatoes and Yorkshire pudding. Even at such a low level of existence this family was considered fortunate since Rowntree's survey documented evidence only from those families who were teetotal. The temptations of drink and betting combined with possible unemployment, sickness or death reduced even further the standard of living and consequently the food.

Class II   Lower Middle Class Family

This example is based on the family of a clerk with a weekly income of 35s; the house contained five rooms and a scullery.

Day	Breakfast	Dinner	Tea	Supper
Tuesday	Boiled eggs, bread and butter, tea	Cold pork, mashed potatoes, jam roll, sauce	Toast and butter, teacakes, tea	Porridge, brown bread and butter, cocoa
Wednesday	Fried bacon, eggs, bread and butter, tea	Boiled mutton, onion sauce, potatoes, vegetables, pudding, tea	Bread and butter, scones, teacakes, tea	Porridge, fried fish, bread, cocoa
Thursday	Boiled eggs, bread, butter, scones, tea	Haricot mutton, lemon pudding, tea and cakes	Luncheon tongue, bread and butter, tea	Porridge, cocoa
Friday	Fried eggs, bacon, bread and butter, tea	Stuffed hearts, potatoes, jam pudding	Pickled mackerel, bread and butter, tea	Porridge, bread and butter, cocoa
Saturday	Potted meat, bread and butter, teacakes, tea	Tomatoes, sausages, potatoes, pastry, tea	Boiled eggs, bread and butter, brown bread, teacakes, tea	Porridge, fried fish, bread, cocoa
Sunday	Cold tomatoes, sausages, boiled eggs, bread and butter, tea	Stuffed pork, new potatoes, cauliflower, Yorkshire pudding, tea	Bread and butter, teacakes, raspberry sandwich, tea	Cold meat, pickled beetroot, bread, cocoa
Monday	Fried bacon, bread and butter, brown bread, cakes, tea	Spare-rib pie, potatoes, oats pudding, tea	Potted meat, bread and butter, teacakes, tea	Porridge, cocoa

Greater variety of foods, particularly among the manufactured foods, is evident here in the form of tinned meat and fish, increased purchases of cheap jam and niceties such as vanilla and lemon essence. Traditional foods, however, still exist in boiled mutton and onion sauce, haricot mutton, Yorkshire pudding and pickled mackerel.

Class III   Middle Class Family

The middle classes had existed prior to the nineteenth century, but they were an insignificant section of society and as such had no influence in establishing the basic British dishes since they tended to copy those above them rather than those below. By the end of the nineteenth century, however, the middle classes had increased in wealth, power and numbers, and their diet became more significant.

Rowntree's middle class examples were from families whose male heads were engaged in professions or in the control of business undertakings. This class perpetuated much of the past, according to their degree of wealth, indulged themselves in any food they fancied, had servants to prepare it and the necessary equipment and fuel to cook it. It is generally accepted, however, that experimentation and development in dishes was confined to the very wealthy. Plain family dinners were quite a different thing as can be seen from the following.

Day	Breakfast	Dinner	Tea	Supper
Monday	Porridge, fried bacon and bread, toast, bread and butter, marmalade, treacle, tea, coffee, milk, cream	Boiled mutton, carrots, turnips, potatoes caper sauce, roly-poly pudding, rice pudding, oranges, tea	Bread and butter, teacake, cake, milk, tea	Fish, bread and butter, biscuits, cake, oranges, cocoa
Tuesday	Porridge, fried bacon and eggs, bread and butter, toast, marmalade, coffee, tea, milk, cream	Mutton, carrots, turnips, capers sauce, potatoes, hayneck, lemon or tapioca pudding, tea	Bread and butter, marmalade, milk, cream, tea	Cutlets, stewed plums, bread, biscuits, cheese, cocoa
Wednesday	Frame food, fried eggs, bacon and bread, toast, white and brown bread, butter, marmalade, coffee, tea, milk, cream	Rissoles, poached eggs, potatoes, bread pudding, bread and butter, tea	Bread and butter, teacakes, milk, tea	Baked haddock, stewed plums, biscuits, hot milk
Thursday	Bacon and eggs, toast, white and brown bread, butter, marmalade, tea, coffee, milk, cream	Roast mutton, greens, potatoes, chocolate mould, rhubarb and orange tart, bananas, coffee, cream	Bread and butter, teacake, seed cake, marmalade, milk, tea	Fish cakes, stewed rhubarb, biscuits, bread and butter, hot milk
Friday	Porridge, fried bacon and eggs, white and brown bread and butter, marmalade, tea, coffee, milk, cream	Haricot mutton, carrots, potatoes, tapioca pudding	White and brown bread and butter, cake, tea, milk	Boiled chicken, white sauce, bacon, potato chips, stewed rhubarb, bread and butter, cocoa
Saturday	As Friday	Haricot mutton, cold chicken, sausages, boiled rice, stewed rhubarb	Bread and butter, teacake, tea, milk, cream	Chicken, potatoes, bread and butter, cheese and milk
Sunday	Porridge, eggs, bread and butter, milk, coffee, tea, cream	Mutton, cauliflower, bread sauce, potatoes, rhubarb, custard, blancmange, oranges, biscuits	Potted meat, sandwiches, bread and butter, cake, marmalade, tea, milk	Potted meat, cornflou mould, bread and butter, cake, rhubarb custard, cheese, hot milk

These meals show the importance of traditional dishes, perhaps unfashionable among influential circles but still forming the basis of the daily food for the middle classes. Roasting traditions and accompaniments are still strong; the nineteenth century was renowned for its large joints and Mrs Beeton would not consider anything less than 10 lb, while a 20 lb joint was quite common in large households of the rich. The pattern of eating depended on a certain amount of ingenuity in using up the left-overs. The greater part of the Sunday roast might have to be eaten for the rest of the week, as is indicated in the meals. There was truth, therefore, in the old jingle:

> Hot on Sunday, cold on Monday, hashed on Tuesday,
> minced on Wednesday, curried on Thursday, broth
> on Friday and cottage pie on Saturday.

Savoury puddings, apart from the universal Yorkshire, do not seem popular although the sweet puddings, pies and tarts display variety, Fruits and vegetables are more varied, oranges make their entrance while fish dishes are practically non-existent. Cakes and teabreads are essential, with bread, butter and sandwiches as tea dishes. Purchased foods show more sophistication with such things as bottled cherries and gooseberries, glacé cherries, peel, jelly squares, cornflour and marmalade — which do not appear in any of the previous budgets — appearing regularly. Dependence on prepared meats is not inconsiderable, with potted meats, shrimps, pork pies, boiled ham, chicken and tongue moulds much in evidence.

The conclusions to be drawn are that the most firmly welded features of established dishes were not lost completely. Country and regional traditions appear to have suffered heavily although they were not entirely lost. To compensate, however, new eating habits were to be found in developing urban areas. The preference for a plain style of cooking was still evident even if tempered with many newly adopted features. Nevertheless, the British have a tendency to cling to old customs and usages and only cautiously accept new ideas to incorporate within existing traditions.

Cookery Writers

The changing pattern of life throughout the nineteenth century made earlier cookery books obsolete thus creating the need for fresh directions. The French influence in cookery instructions was considerable. Every writer with any pretensions knew and used basic French terms, and at this period more than any other since the Norman conquest there was an amalgam of cooking methods.

While the great French masters — Careme, Ude, Francatelli, Soyer, Escoffier and others — published cookery books with detailed information on the classical French cuisine for professional chefs, British writers were not in complete agreement on how much these French influences should invade their traditional British fare. Many writers aimed at improving British cookery by adopting the latest methods, not only from France, but also from other countries including Italy, Spain, Germany, Russia and Scandinavia. In their search for something new many writers realised the variety in their own country and adopted many national English, Scottish, Irish and Welsh dishes as well as lesser-known regional dishes such as Bakewell Tart, Devonshire Cream and Junket, Bath Buns, Everton Toffee, Scotch Eggs, Cock-a-Leekie, Athole Brose and Shrewsbury Cakes.

While the eighteenth century had produced only one outstanding best seller, the nineteenth century produced several. Among these Mrs Rundell's *Domestic Cookery*, Dr Kitchener's *Cook's Oracle*, Meg Dod's *Cook's Manual*, Eliza Acton's *Modern Cookery*, Alexis Soyer's *Modern Housewife* and, as the climax to these and all others, Mrs Beeton's *Home Management*.

The cookery book, the legend we affectionately know today as "Mrs Beeton", was a compilation of all past developments presented in one book. She openly admitted her indebtedness to the past as well as to many of her contemporaries on whom she had drawn for contributions and advice. Her strength lay in an ability to compile material and a sensitivity to present needs. The encyclopedia of domestic subjects, interspersed with about one thousand recipes, was a three-inch thick volume thus surpassing all her predecessors in sheer size alone. Despite the quantity nothing is lacking in quality: thorough treatment of basic methods, a wide collection of foreign dishes, an integration of French methods and dishes and a representation of national and regional dishes, old and new, combine to make up the total.

THE TWENTIETH CENTURY

Distinctive national features of British cookery may have suffered severely during the nineteenth century, but the suffering was minimal compared with the damage sustained in the twentieth century. The social and economic disruptions of two World Wars, and a developing food technology which has completely revolutionised eating habits have taken their toll on our heritage, the long-term consequences of which can only be determined in the centuries to follow. At this point, it is pertinent to establish the features that have survived the passage of time to the extent that they are recognisable elements of British cooking today.

A recurring feature from the seventeenth century onwards is simplicity and ability to use fine quality raw materials and cook them in such a way that their perfection is retained and their flavour preserved. It is not so much what is done to them as what is not done. To the British, beef is not an ingredient for a dish, it is beef, to be cooked so as to show it in all its glory. Continental cooking tends to regard ingredients as a means to an end, composing dishes from a variety of raw materials with the aim of developing flavours and introducing new subtleties. It is not so with British food where the food is almost an end in itself. We ask the cook to add nothing to it, and that not too much should be taken away. We want our beef to taste of beef, to savour the sweet tenderness of our lamb, we like our chickens to taste fresh and we prefer our game to be gamey. In fact, we prefer the flavour of natural things.

British cookery relies on homely-style dishes since our cooking is at its best when the ingredients have been home grown, home reared and home made. Our national, unsophisticated dishes and all the variety of puddings, pies, tarts, broths, hot-pots and stews which are so well integrated into the British way of cooking have a basic plainness and a certain solidity about them.

A powerful influence in any country, and no less so in Britain, is the regional and national food, tried and tested over the centuries, suiting the climate, using the best products of the area and so expressing the heritage of the people. Even if the trend today is towards standardisation, wide differences still exist, revealing characteristic dishes of an area. To the casual observer it may seem that there is little culinary difference between the regions of the British Isles: shortbread, barley broth, marmalade and scones are as well known south of the border as Yorkshire pudding, mint sauce and pork pies are north of it. Despite this, however, distinguishing features have emerged throughout the centuries, influenced by culture, geography, social and economic reasons and prejudices.

Despite long years of poverty and want, detrimental to a wide and varied gastronomic repertory, Ireland has produced many distinctive dishes which, although they may not constitute a large national choice, express the basic characteristics of the people and their heritage.

The Welsh like the Irish have a limited number of dishes which can accurately be called national. Differences lie in the ingredients used rather than cooking methods, leeks, laver and Welsh mutton being the most outstanding. The Welsh have accepted and copied many English dishes, and there are fewer differences here than in Scotland and Ireland.

Finally, mention must be made of our attitude to festive eating and the almost ritual foods which have become so much part of our traditions. With all our virtues and vices in the matter of food, we have from earliest times been noted for our hospitality and for our joy of feasting to such a degree that great and small events must have their celebration meal. Long forgotten pagan rites of the Celts, Romans, Vikings and even earlier peoples have left their mark on such traditions as Hallowe'en, Hogmanay, Hot Cross Buns and Simnel Cakes. The Harvest Festival, All Souls, Shrove Tuesday, Ash Wednesday, Passion Sunday, Easter and other observances like Guy Fawkes, Burns' Night, St David's Day, St Patrick's Day and many others are all bound up inextricably with what we eat.

Therefore, we lack neither variety nor interest in our cooking, and history has shown how our food has developed individual character not only from a mixed ancestry but also from the many social, political and economic factors which have had their effects on the food of the people. Despite the complex collection of dishes which have resulted through many centuries they all rely heavily on perfect raw materials. That these materials be prepared and presented with care is essential if we are to preserve that perfection of simplicity which is British cooking at its best.

MEALS AND MEAL TIMES

Certain types of dishes because of their suitability have developed an association with certain meals. The meal, therefore, has influenced the traditions of the dish, and when meals change so do the dishes. It is necessary to trace the developments in meals and meal times throughout the centuries in order to establish the history of certain customs and the types of dishes which have evolved as a result.

Meals are determined by the pattern of life, and today we would have little in common with the type of pattern to be found in Norman, medieval and Tudor times. Then most people spent the day working or playing in the open. Only a small minority worked indoors; the houses were unpleasant, dark, draughty and damp. Many of the meals were therefore cooked and eaten outside, and this helped to encourage large appetites stimulated also by heavy manual work. The meal times were affected by the fact that the day began at sunrise and that artificial lighting was primitive and expensive. Dinner — the largest meal of the day — began early: in Norman times at about 9 a.m., in the Middle Ages about an hour later. In Tudor times it had settled down to twelve o'clock noon.

The simple dinner of the peasant consisted of one course — broth — bread being the staple food, ale the universal drink. At the other extreme the feast could consist of anything up to sixteen courses, each with a variety of meat, fish, vegetable and sweet dishes and always with a "suttletie".

Breakfast, eaten at 6-7 a.m. consisted of a mug of ale, salted or pickled herrings, cold meat, pottage and cheese. Supper was more substantial, varying according to the wealth of the household. Originally it was a "sop" of bread dipped in soup or gravy, but later it became similar to breakfast, eaten between 5 and 7 p.m. In Norman times, the last meal of the day was livery, often eaten in bed at about 8 or 9 p.m. and consisting of cheese, bread, spiced or plain ale and perhaps cakes. This meal was also referred to as "rere" supper and was mainly taken by people who kept late hours.

There was little apparent change in seventeenth-century meals and meal times, although the beginnings of change must have been initiated. It was during the eighteenth and nineteenth centuries that daily life changed dramatically, bringing about many alterations in meals and meal times. Most significant was the increase in refinement and comfort through the increased wealth of the country. More people could heat and light their homes, enabling them to stay up later at night and to rise later in the morning.

Breakfast was the first meal to be affected by these changes: it became a lighter meal, taken at about 9 or 10 a.m. and consisting of toast and butter with the new beverages of tea or coffee instead of ale. The dinner hour moved from 2 to 3 p.m. and by the end of the century, 4 p.m. was the usual hour. As the dinner hour advanced, so the custom developed of taking a snack in late morning of Madeira and cake or a glass of sherry and biscuits. After dinner, port was served to the gentlemen while the ladies took tea. From the tea habit developed the popularity of the London tea gardens of Vauxhall, Ranelagh and Marylebone where people drank tea in the afternoon without actually calling it afternoon tea. Later this developed into tea and cakes at about 5 p.m. Supper at 10 or 11 p.m. was fairly substantial, consisting of cold or hot meats, sweets and fruit served with mulled wine or hot nightcaps — not so very different from the Norman "rere" supper.

By the nineteenth century life was becoming hectic as the Industrial Revolution advanced: business men were having breakfast earlier, and the habit of taking something more substantial than Madeira and cake in the middle of the day developed. This new meal came to be described as lunch or luncheon. This was served between 1 and 2 p.m. and might consist of steaks, mutton chops, veal cutlets or kidneys. At home, luncheon might be something from the sideboard dressed with cold joints, potted and collared meat, bread, butter, cheese and biscuits.

Breakfasts

With earlier breakfasts hot dishes were introduced and these were both extensive and substantial. Grilled fish, chops, rump steaks, kidneys, sausages, bacon rashers, poached, boiled, baked, scrambled eggs and omelets were accompanied by hot toast and fancy breads, butter, preserves and tea or coffee. In summer, bowls of fresh fruit were popular. Traditional cold meats, cheese and collared or potted meats continued to be eaten although the habit was declining and by the end of the nineteenth century little remained of these as breakfast dishes.

Afternoon Teas

The long gap between lunch and dinner in middle and upper class society was partly responsible for afternoon tea becoming a national habit during the nineteenth century. Fashionable society, the upper and middle classes, took tea about 4 p.m.; this would usually consist of very thinly sliced bread and butter, Madeira, seed or Dundee cake, cucumber sandwiches in summer and buttered toast, Sally Lunns, toasted muffins or crumpets in winter. Meanwhile, the working population, and in particular those in rural areas of the North of England and Scotland, continued to eat dinner at midday. They began to call their evening meal high tea; it was a substantial meal with a main course, bread, butter, tea and cakes. In this way numerous regional dishes — cakes, pies, potted meats, fish pastes and many savoury dishes which had been so much a feature of the past — were perpetuated. Sometimes the meal was simply termed tea in which case there was no main dish, but fare similar to a substantial afternoon tea was served.

Dinners and Suppers

A later dinner hour gradually established itself in the late nineteenth century. Fashionable dinner parties would start between 7 and 8 p.m., while the working classes called their main meal in the middle of the day dinner. The wealthy, which now included the rising middle classes, called their midday meal lunch and they dined at night.

From earliest times the British custom at feasts, banquets or intimate dinner parties was to place cooked dishes at strategic positions on the table prior to the guests' entrance. The first impression of the table and its array of dishes was vitally important to the success of a dinner. Long hours of preparation were spent not only on the dishes, but on table decorations, and detailed plans were drawn up to illustrate the position of every item.

The system of serving several dishes in each course was maintained by the Victorians and encouraged the types of dishes characteristic of British cooking at this time. Large joints of roast and boiled meat and large fish were particularly suitable since they overcame one of the main disadvantages of the system: that of other dishes becoming cold while one was eaten. If a guest sampled a plate of soup in the first course, fried soles would be cold, whereas whole boiled turbot in the same course, roast turkey or haunch of venison in the next course would have retained the heat.

This style of meal also encouraged the innovation of "made" dishes, since it was considered important by every middle-class housewife to present a good show of dishes, to fill every space on the table. To this end she required an extensive repertory of made dishes, often turning to foreign dishes.

In a never abating desire to impress, dishes became more elaborate and the plainness which had been a characteristic of British cooking declined. The crystal, silver or glass dish with a long ornate stem that showed off the elaborately decorated food became an essential piece of equipment. Moulds of the most intricate shapes were used for both savoury and sweet jellies, and even the plum pudding was turned out of an elaborate mould. Boiled puddings, cakes, blancmanges, charlottes and creams were moulded and often decorated in the most bizarre fashion.

The Victorians lost much of the plain cooking style which was their heritage and often failed to achieve the desired refinement. Their style of dinner affected the style of dishes which caused changes in the service referred to as the Russian style or *à la Russe* in which the dishes were put up on a sideboard and handed round to the guests, each dish being considered a separate course.

Soups were now served first, fish dishes second and meats third. The fourth course, however, reverted to the old style of mixing all types of dishes together although the principal dishes were sweets and puddings. The final course of desserts and ices also reverted to the old style, all the dishes being placed on the table at the same time and the overall appearance and positioning was of utmost importance.

Restaurant Meals

The growth in the number of meals taken in restaurants that has occurred in the twentieth century encouraged certain dishes because of their suitability. The restaurant originated in Paris in 1765 when Monsieur Boulanger started selling a variety of hot soups as quick restoratives or *restaurantes* in his shop. The public outcry by cook-shop owners who took court action against him gave him useful publicity, particularly as he won his case. More than a hundred years passed before Britain adopted the habit with Whiteley's Restaurant in London in 1873. Until then, the coffee houses (later clubs), inns, taverns and cook-shops had sufficed. From 1873 onwards, however, the restaurant flourished and influential French chefs began working throughout the country. The most influential and respected French chef of the time was Auguste Escoffier (1847-1935), who was instrumental in changing the style of eating and who also devised the pattern which is still in use today.

The old array of dishes set on the table was finished. So was the conglomeration of dishes served at each course. Refinement became more evident in the bill of fare which was now termed *menu* and which was built up of a succession of courses, each comprising only one or two select dishes. In 1899, Escoffier, with the aid of a huge staff, introduced for the first time the *à la Carte* menu at the Carlton Hotel. The types of dishes which developed from this system were in stark contrast to the past; quickly prepared dishes of all kinds flourished, and the custom of one dish with numerous garnishes and sauces developed.

Plain roast meats with their traditional accompaniments were no longer the focal point of the meal although they still retained a degree of importance. A repertory of basic sauces and garnishes from which numerous varieties could be developed was essential and Escoffier established the new system with French rather than British dishes.

Gradual changes throughout the centuries have shaped our meals and their contents. The slow disappearance of cold meat and the corresponding increase in hot dishes has completely changed the original concept of the breakfast meal. Lunch changed rather more quickly from a meal of Madeira and cakes to one of cooked and reheated dishes; afternoon tea was transformed from after-dinner tea to the variety of cakes and tea-breads, potted meats and cold dishes that is high tea. The rate of change in the most important and most complex meal of the day, dinner, is more difficult to determine. While plain whole roasts as the nucleus may for the time being have given way to more complicated made dishes, the meal will influence the traditions of the dishes and determine its durability, in the future as in the past.

KITCHENS AND KITCHEN TOOLS

The conditions and the tools with which the cook is equipped have a great influence on any type of cooking. Social, economic and geographical factors throughout the centuries have influenced conditions in the kitchen and determined cooking methods and eating habits. In areas where only certain facilities for cook-ing have been available and fuel has been scarce, certain types of dishes have developed, while in other areas with good facilities and plentiful fuel, different methods and eating habits have resulted.

In order to establish the development of cooking methods it is necessary to identify the evolution of kitchens and kitchen tools from the foundations which were laid in medieval times. At one end of the social scale was the cottager whose kitchen and tools were obviously more limited and primitive than those to be found in the lord's castle. His home consisted of a single room, blackened by smoke from the wood fire in the centre. Round the fire were clustered cooking utensils, simple pots and pans of earthenware or brass and perhaps an iron cauldron, ladles, spoons, a few bowls, earthenware mugs and pitchers; rough tools were carved from beech or oak.

The situation at the other end of the social scale was quite different. The largest and most important room in the castle was the great hall where originally all the cooking as well as eating and sleeping was done. In this communal room the hearth was a stone slab set in the centre of the floor. The open fire used wood which did not produce too much smoke, charcoal being particularly favoured. Whether all the smoke reached the hole in the roof through which it was supposed to escape is debatable; the fire was later removed to the side of the room to a raised hearth known as a reredos. This was still used during Henry VIII's reign (1509-47), but by the time of Elizabeth I (1558-1603) there is evidence that chimneys were becoming more common. But it was not until the seventeenth century that wall fireplaces took over from the central hearth and the necessity of having the hall open at the roof ceased. Eventually a partition was built to seal it off from the main hall or cooking was carried out in a separate building connected to the hall with a passage.

Spit-Roasting

Essential to the medieval cook was the huge wrought-iron spit which rested on iron dogs at either side of the hearth. It was capable of turning a whole carcass, a task which must have been monotonous and uncomfortable with no mechanical device. To protect himself from being roasted, the cook erected a fire screen, usually circular in shape and made of dampened straw. Pieces of food would be skewered on to this screen and toasted before the fire. From this developed the upright toaster which remained in use until the late nineteenth century. During the Tudor period, canine turnspits were substituted for human ones. The dogs were put in a wheel cage from which they turned the spit with their paws.

Beneath the roast was a long metal pan, the original dripping pan. By the end of roasting time this was full of hot fat and meat juices and was used for frying small pieces of food. At some point it must have been discovered that the result was greatly improved if the food was coated in batter before frying to give a crisp finish. This method of cooking, mentioned in fifteenth century manuscripts, was sometimes described as a "froise" or "fraise" from which we get Bacon Froise; it seems likely that Toad-in-the-Hole also developed in this way. Yorkshire Pudding was originally cooked below the roasting meat with the meat juices dripping into it.

During roasting, meat was not only basted with fat and meat juices from the dripping pan, but was also dredged with spices and chopped herbs. Towards the end the joint was thickly dredged with flour, boiling liquid was trickled over until the flour was partly cooked, and the joint was then turned before the fire for a final crisping. This was known as "frothing" and appropriate liquids were used — red wine for venison, red currant juice for hare, beer for rabbit, and for mutton water in which mint leaves had been boiled.

The type of spit depended on the meat, and a wide variety of spits were made for specific purposes. The most common type had a claw-shaped prong which gripped the meat firmly. Some had holes in the iron which were threaded with twine and the meat was tied on to the spit while splints were used to tie fish and soft meats to prevent them from breaking.

Massive iron cauldrons hung over the open fire on a hook were used for boiling. Although they may have been used to boil large quarters of meat and make pottages and stews, it is possible that bag puddings of cereals, beans and peas as well as earthenware pots with meat and fish were hung in the boiling water so that a whole meal could be cooked in one cauldron.

Baking

Baking was usually carried out in a communal bakehouse attached to the castle where people of the village were obliged to bring their bread and other dishes for baking. The brick oven, introduced by the Romans, was a simple construction set in a stone or brick foundation. The oven cavity was lined with fire bricks in a beehive shape with a small wooden door opening on to the floor of the oven which was at waist level. To heat it a large quantity of wood shavings was placed in the centre, faggots of wood on top, then larger pieces of log. This was set alight and kept burning for two hours; the fire was then spread over the floor of the oven to heat it evenly. When the fire was completely burnt out the charcoal and ash were swept out. A wet mop known as a "huzzy" was used to remove the last particle of dust and to leave a little steam in the oven. The oven was left until the heat was even and the bread was packed in. The door was closed and left shut for about 2 hours until the contents were judged cooked.

Various other types of primitive ovens existed, some on the principle of the brick oven, others based on the hearth stone. Bread or pastry was placed on the hot stone and covered with an iron pot around which was packed burning fuel. This was particularly successful where peat was common as it retained heat and could be easily packed round the pot. Where fuel was too scarce for using with this pot oven, small cakes or bread were placed on the hot hearth stone and turned once during baking. Hence the origins of hearthstone cakes and the beginnings of griddle baking.

Griddle baking was widely practised by the poor in areas where wood or coal was either expensive or scarce or peat the only fuel available. In the North of England, in parts of Wales, in the West Country and particularly in Scotland there is evidence of this in the wide variety of griddle-baked specialities in these areas. In Yorkshire, Lancashire, Cheshire and Staffordshire the bakestone was used, a development from the hearth stone and an indication that even as late as 1912 baking on a stone surface was still common. The bakestones were thin slabs of stone, fashioned into rectangular shapes which fitted into the oven like a shelf. Cast-iron bakestones are still widely used in Wales.

Kitchen and Eating Tools

The kitchen floor was usually stone or brick. An open drain ran through it until about the middle of the thirteenth century when it was first covered and carried underground. The work table was of massive hewn oak planks resting on trestles, while on the walls hung long-handled ladles, strainers, graters, spoons, skimmers, pot sticks, slices for turning meat in the frying pan, and a variety of knives and meat hooks for removing the quarters of meat from the boiling cauldrons. One of the most important tools was a pestle and mortar, a pepper mill, mustard quern and salt box.

In the larders, where much of the preparation, especially of pastry, was done, there were smaller tables, dressing boards, spice cupboards, chests for oatmeal, a kneading trough, a boulting trough for meal, and shelves with pots and pans.

Wooden bowls were used for mixing ingredients; cullenders (colanders) had holes in the bottom. Oak chopping boards were used for chopping and cutting. Food was served on long tables, for the most part movable constructions of boards on trestles, covered with linen cloths on which were set out cups and jugs of earthenware, and wooden platters. Among the rich there was much display of silver and gold plate. Meat was eaten on trenchers — thick slices of bread which became sodden with gravy and were afterwards given to the poor. Later the trenchers were made of wood, then pewter and eventually pottery or porcelain.

Diners brought their own cutlery consisting of a set of spoons, a knife and a spike. Forks were unknown in Britain in Norman and medieval days, but were arousing interest as a curiosity by Elizabethan times.

Cooking Fuels

Changes in the social structure, the distribution of wealth, and particularly industrial changes had their effects on the kitchen and the tools available. Developments in coal mining and improved transport facilities made coal more common as a domestic fuel while concurrent developments in iron smelting were eventually to revolutionise the whole system of cooking. Wood was the common fuel in most districts throughout the medieval period. The forests were massive compared with today, and it was only with the population increase in the eighteenth century that the diminishing woodland became insufficient to supply fuel needs.

Peat or turf was not generally used except in certain areas. It was common in Cornwall and Devon and in the Western Isles and the Highlands of Scotland. In some areas even peat was scarce, and on Iona and Muck there was none at all. In such cases dung, seaweed, barley, straw and broom were used and if all these failed, depopulation was the inevitable result. In England, peat was common in the Fens and in parts of Yorkshire, particularly on the moors, and in the marshes of Wales. Ireland used a great deal of peat. In all these areas the system of cooking shows basic differences from the predominantly wood areas.

The warm glow of the peat fire was not sufficiently hot for spit roasting. Instead the pot simmered, stewed and boiled permanently on the hearth, while the pot oven and griddle baked. Twice as much peat as wood was required to heat the fire bricks in a brick oven in order to retain enough heat, and although it was used to some extent where peat was plentiful it was not an economic proposition. As compensation, however, peat had qualities which were used to advantage in the drying and smoking of meat and fish. The delicate aroma from peat permeated the food giving it a distinctive flavour, and areas where peat was common have characteristic dishes as a result, illustrated in the development of the Finnan haddock at the fishing villages of Findon and Boddam on the Aberdeenshire coast in the seventeenth century.

While wood and peat could be burnt satisfactorily in the open hearth the same was not possible with coal which required an upward draught and a chimney to remove the dirty smoke. It was not until the chimney and iron grate became common that coal was used in any significant quantity. Neither was coal possible as a general fuel until the introduction of cheap transport facilities. Only in areas near to coal-fields was it sufficiently cheap for general use. Where coal was plentiful its use necessitated some alterations in kitchen equipment and required an iron grate raised from the ground. Whether from economy or from the fact that a large coal fire would have given out too intense a heat, the coal fire tended to be narrower than the open wood fire and subsequently the long horizontal spit became obsolete. Instead roasting was done with a perpendicular spit, known as "Silas Marner", swinging and turning the food. In its simplest form the hanging spit was a length of twisted cord with the meat tied or hooked on at one end; the other end was attached to a hanger on the mantlepiece.

Complicated clockwork systems to revolve the meat were devised, complete with jack, roasting screener and drip tray. By about 1800 these units were incorporated into one called a roasting screen and jack with a door at the back of the screen for inspection and a removable drip tray in the base. The change in the type of spit did not alter the basic roasting process, although it did mean that the size and number of the roasts cooked at one fire was limited.

While the iron basket grate could be put in the old wood fire hearth it was not so easy to adapt the brick oven. It remained, therefore, in its original state for much longer and was in common use well into the nineteenth century. For the purpose of boiling water, a separate fire was introduced with a built-in boiler. Thus three separate fires were used in the kitchen until they merged into one in the form of the kitchen range, literally a range of three fireplaces with the oven at one side, the boiler at the other and on top of each an iron hob. The front of the fire had an iron grid to support the fire, and the roasting screen and jack continued to be used for all roasting.

It was not until 1830 that the railways began moving supplies of coal to areas previously without it. About the same time great advances were made in the manufacture of iron and steel. With these the stage was set for new developments in the kitchen range.

Spit and Oven Roasting

The venerable Mrs Beeton mentions only in passing the use of the oven for roasting and roasting at the open fire on a spit, without giving any guidance or comment on either method. Much controversy existed at that time over roasting methods, and there was only a slow acceptance of the continental oven-roasting. The British appetite was for strongly flavoured meat, and by roasting in front of the fire more water was evaporated than in baked meat, the size of the roast was reduced and the flavour concentrated.

There was no dramatic changeover from spit to oven at any particular point, but the old and new methods carried on alongside one another throughout the nineteenth century. The open ranges of the old pattern gradually disappeared as new houses were built and the rising generation began to accept the scientific theories. A significant point was reached with the introduction of gas as a cooking fuel in 1849 and the subsequent development of the Bunsen burner in 1855. The original roasting traditions were modified to suit the new gas and electric ovens. Two world wars, rationing and general scarcity helped to consolidate this change. Today, the old spit-roasting method has been revived in rotary spits fitted to modern cookers, but while the old tradition has not been lost altogether it is unlikely to alter the now common practice of oven-roasting.

Kitchens

While cooking arrangements in medieval times reflected two distinct classes, lord and cottager, a new class structure had evolved by the beginning of the nineteenth century. Each class developed its own habits, evident in different types of kitchens which had significant effects on cooking methods and eating habits. Old traditions were lost, others developed in the expanding towns of the industrial Midlands and the North of England. The new houses being built were cheap and had cramped living accommodation. People worked long hours, and most women and girls worked in the factories alongside men and boys. Young girls lost the chance of learning domestic skills while their mothers cut down wherever possible on cooking and baking and abandoned altogether brewing, preserving, pickling and potting.

The kitchen, which also served as the dining room and bedroom, was furnished with a fire in an iron grate with a hob at either side. The kettle with hot water for constant tea making hung over the fire. Other cooking equipment was limited, sometimes only to one large iron pot. This was used for the stews and hotpots so traditional in these areas and could be left cooking slowly all day while the family were at work. There was probably also a frying pan for quick-fried dishes, and some homes may have had a griddle. Ovens were rare. Some towns were not well supplied with coal, and in such places fuel was expensive. The poor sometimes had only enough fuel for two or three hot meals a week. This problem was to some extent overcome by taking pies, puddings, hot-pots, stews and roasts to the cook shop for baking. The pottery workers in Staffordshire used the ancient system of baking meat, fish or game encased in clay in the factory kiln. To save the expense of using new clay, dishes of suitable shape were made with tight-fitting lids.

The fact that the kitchen, together with other social factors, shaped developments in the eating habits of the working classes can be illustrated by the dishes that have evolved as a result. A wide variety of cheap, boiled or stewed dishes is epitomised by the Welsh meat and vegetable broths, familiarly known as *cawls*, the Lancashire hot-pot and its variations, and by boiled trotters, boiled beans and bacon, tripe and cow heel, bacon ribs with onions and collared pork. Quickly reheated dishes, such as black pudding, faggots and chitterlings are all common to the industrial areas of the North of England.

Victorian Middle-Class Kitchens

Home was a symbol of wealth and success to the rising middle classes of the mid-nineteenth century. In the terraced houses of the period the kitchen was usually placed in a small part of the basement beneath the dining room and connected to it by a lift. A table and chairs usually sat in the centre of the room, a dresser at the side held the dinner service, cutlery and dishes. A huge black iron range with ovens, boilers and a continuous hot plate lined one side of the kitchen. It consumed vast quantities of coal while coping with all the cooking, baking and roasting necessary for a large household. An impressive array of copper or iron pots lined the walls; particularly significant was the selection of pots for a specific purpose, such as a fish kettle, the stock-pot, the turbot kettle, potato steamer, omelet pan and copper preserving pan. Other equipment was becoming increasingly popular, such as the *bain marie* and a wide variety of fancy moulds for jellies and blancmanges, fancy cutters for vegetables and fluted and plain patty pans for cheese-cakes, tarts and mince pies. Labour-saving devices, however, were still comparatively unknown although the mincing machine had been invented.

Kitchens were well equipped, labour was cheap and the middle classes were steadily growing more and more affluent. This was the era of lavishly extravagant dinner parties when French cuisine and domestic arts flourished; baking was done at home, vast amounts of bottling, preserving, jam making and pickling as well as the making of wines and cordials were common. A well-stocked larder was essential to the middle classes in the days before canned or frozen foods were available.

In the country, development was much slower, the tendency was to retain the old customs, and it is not surprising to find a farmhouse kitchen of about 1900 little influenced by the effects of industrialisa-tion of the previous century or the wealth of the time. An old-style, wide, deep open hearth burning logs was the focal point; on separate ratchets hung pots; kettle, frying pan, a large pot with a stew or a piece of meat would simmer gently at the side, while skillets sat on the hearth at the fringe of the fire. Sometimes the fireplace was sufficiently deep to have seats on either side in the chimney corner or "ingle neuk", later high-backed wooden angular settles gave protection from draughts drawn in by the wide chimney. The rest of the furniture in this living room consisted of a large dresser and a long table with benches on either side. The stone flagged floor and low black ceiling beams added to the homely atmosphere.

In this type of kitchen, cooking methods depended principally on the boiling and stewing tradition with the permanent pot on the hearth. Baking was done in the original brick oven, built into the wall and used not only for bread, cakes, pies and pasties but also for the wide variety of preserved, pickled and potted items that were common in farming families.

The Kitchen in the Twentieth Century

From around 1920, architects began to give more consideration to the position of the kitchen. It was no longer condemned to the basement; the sink was placed at a window and thought was given to the overall design; by the late 1940s the kitchen was fitted with shelves round the walls above the working surface and the necessary equipment stored away in cupboards and drawers underneath. Gas and electric cookers had greatly improved; ovens were better insulated, hot plates and burners more efficient.

Progress improved and transformed kitchen tools and introduced an ever expanding list of electric beaters, blenders for chopping, pulverising and sieving, pressure cookers, electric equipment for peeling, slicing, chopping and shredding vegetables, and thermostatically controlled frying pans.

A single century has seen the greatest improvements ever in cooking facilities. Exactly how much these improvements have affected cooking methods is difficult to assess as so many other factors have been influential, but existing methods of boiling, stewing, grilling, frying and roasting are easier to regulate with more reliable and satisfactory results.

The past produced a variety of cooking methods, from the medieval cook's ability with the spit roast to the cottager baking on the hearthstone, from the Victorian cook with her abundance of facilities, supplies and servants to the factory worker limited to the very simplest form of cooking and the farmer's wife perpetuating old traditional methods. Each section has evolved a pattern of eating based on immediate conditions that are continually fluctuating. Coal replaced wood and peat as a fuel, gas replaced coal, and electricity has made its claims on the gas market. The spit and cauldron were replaced by the coal and wood range, which in turn has been superseded by gas and electric cookers which may eventually be replaced by some future development. Despite changing conditions, however, the cooking methods which influence the whole range of dishes peculiar to an area or class have a habit of resisting change. They are perpetuated in the boiling, stewing and griddle baking traditions of Scotland, Ireland, Wales and the North of England and in the roasting traditions of England. These methods, with their far-reaching consequences, have developed distinct features which, even if the influences of environment no longer exist to the same degree, are still handed down to us as a heritage to be cherished and preserved.

FOOD RESOURCES

Most national and regional variations in food habits rest on three factors: the prevailing social and economic conditions, the subsequent effect on utilisation of the land, and the climate and geography of the land. Under the feudal system in the Middle Ages, transport facilities were poor, industry primitive, and people had to depend on their land for practically all their needs. Today there is a complete reversal of this situation, and land is irrelevant to the mass of the population not directly concerned with agriculture.

After the Norman landing in 1066, the existing methods of land use were continued by the Norman barons installed as overlords. The manorial or feudal system was based on the relation of the lord to vassal and the holding of the land in feud. Vassals held their land from the lord, who in turn held it from the king in return for homage and military service. The economic unit was the manor, and villeins and serfs held land from the lord of the manor, rendering in return labour services and dues.

This highly organised unit depended on the land for its needs. Cultivated land was of two types, the manorial (sometimes called demesne) land — the produce of which belonged to the lord — and the common land, the produce of which belonged to the cottagers and on which they worked in their spare time. In addition to cultivated land, the Domesday Book indicates vast areas of waste land which included forest, marshland and bog, and areas devastated by war. These areas played an integral part in the feudal system since they provided common turbary (peat-cutting), pasture and wood. The extent of forest available was decided by the Normans. Manor houses and monasteries had herb gardens, orchards and sometimes vineyards, and the peasants often had a plot of land near their homes for herbs, fruits and vegetables.

Agriculture and Field Systems

Some diversity of food becomes apparent through examination of the pattern of field systems which were directly affected by the nature of the land. In the lowlands of the English plain, where the climate and soil were most suitable for corn crops, extensive arable farming was practised using the two- or three-field system. Under this one field was left fallow every year and the other one or two fields were productive. The most important crops were wheat and rye for bread, sometimes grown together as "maslin", but during the Middle Ages the cultivation of wheat gradually increased at the expense of rye. Oats, peas and beans were grown for human and animal consumption, spring barley for ale. Oats were comparatively rare in the Midlands and South of England, but they were extensively cultivated in the North.

The uplands of the West and North practised a different method of farming based on the in-field, out-field system, also known as the Celtic System. This was characterised by a shorter growing season, heavy rainfall, more pasture land than arable, and dispersion of settlement. Round each was an enclosed arable area, called the in-field, the rest of the arable land was the out-field with abundant natural pasture beyond. The crops grown consisted chiefly of oats, and bigg which was a northern form of barley. Pastoralism was the predominant occupation in these areas and in some of the West Lowlands as well. Oxen were reared as work animals and as such were prized for length of limb, heavy weight of bone and good development of muscle; cows were reared for milk. Only unproductive, diseased or very old sheep were killed for meat as the most important product was the fleece. Milk from ewes was commonly used in upland counties of Wales as late as the nineteenth century.

Eventually man learned to control and direct nature, but during the Middle Ages, the physical influences of nature dictated the use which man could make of the land. The pattern of diversity which emerges throughout the country is therefore directly affected by the geographical nature of the area. In the lowlands of England extensive arable land encouraged the development of a peaceful agricultural community centred on developing towns. The eastern areas of East Anglia and Kent were different since they had been influenced by the invasions of Jutes and other Scandinavians, and also because there were large areas of fenland. In the North and West, poor soil, wet climate and highland meant a more precarious existence; scattered communities, often tribal societies, lived freely and in a primitive state.

Transportation

Self-sufficiency in agriculture during the early medieval period also prevailed in industry; the same type and range of goods were produced and consumed in the same region, and specialist craftsmen in wood, leather and metal work were to be found in every village. Regional specialisation in industry was limited to lead and tin. Transportation was difficult; roads were affected by the type of soil as well as the weather; bridges were sometimes good, sometimes precarious, but river crossings were usually by ferry or ford. Sea and river transportation presented obstructions such as weirs, mills and low bridges; the natural course of rivers seldom took the straightest route, but river transportation, albeit slow, was also cheap, and river barges were used extensively. Sea transport was hazardous in the small frail medieval sailing vessels with no compass, imperfect steering controls and primitive sails.

The vicissitudes of medieval transport discouraged trade which was generally limited to iron for ox and horse shoes, sickles, scythes and plough-shares, pots and cooking utensils, and to salt, all important for the preservation of meat and fish. Wine, spices and foreign textiles were imported for the manor house only.

Markets and Fairs

A certain amount of internal transfer of supplies took place in the manorial system where the manors were held in groups and the deficiencies of one manor were made up from the surpluses of another. The lords also sold produce, principally corn, to the developing urban community and wool was sent to the major clothing districts. Sales were transacted at weekly town markets or the annual fairs. Local trade centred on a weekly market at which surplus produce from the land, such as dairy produce, meat, vegetables, poultry and wood, was sold to townspeople while the town produce in the form of craftsmen's goods, bread, cooked meats, candles, articles of leather, wood and metal, cloth and linen were sold in return.

The annual fair must have been an impressive spectacle for medieval people, most of whom spent their lives in a laborious monotony with few outside distractions. Fairs originated during celebrations connected with religious festivals, and by 1400 A.D. about two or three dozen, of varying sizes, were held. While town markets provided for the surrounding areas, fairs catered for the whole county. They dealt with the wholesale trade of raw materials — corn for the miller, flour for the baker, iron, gold, silver and other metals for the smiths, wool for the clothmaker in exchange for the craftsmen's products. Also traded were large quantities of winter stores, such as salt, barrels of salt fish and wine. Other non-perishable foodstuffs of a better quality could be bought more cheaply at the fairs than at the local markets. Finally, the fair was the main outlet for luxuries from abroad, silks, velvets, glass, jewellery, Flemish linens, French and Rheinish wines, spices, almonds from the Levant, fine furs from the Baltic, tar from Norway.

Some fairs developed specialities according to their geographical position and peculiar traditions and it would be necessary for large households to send a steward on a succession of trips to procure household necessities from more than one fair. He would travel to Yarmouth for fish, to St Bartholomews for English cloth, Stourbridge for luxury fabrics and St Giles, Winchester, for wines and spices.

Foreign Trade

The early beginnings of foreign medieval trade developed from an exchange of French wines for English corn. In 1200 A.D., the Angevin Empire, which was ruled over by the kings of England, included more than half the land of France. Bordeaux was the outlet for the wine-growing province of Aquitaine, and a trade route developed from this port to England. This continued almost uninterrupted over the next 250 years. By the beginning of the fifteenth century the greatest percentage of imported wine was still coming from France to major medieval English ports although this was to decline with the loss of French territories. Wine from the Levant, Portugal and Spain was also arriving at Southampton and Rheinish wine at London, Yarmouth, Lynn, Boston, Hull and Newcastle.

Spices were imported on Venetian galleys to Southampton and London, along with dates, figs, raisins and vegetable oils. Flemish vessels brought fish to London and Southampton while the Irish ports of Waterford, Cork, Kinsale, Limerick, Galway and Sligo sent fish, especially salmon, but also herring and cod, to Bristol. Onion seeds, garlic, corn and hops came with the Flemish vessels to Southampton.

On the South Coast, the port of Southampton dominated. It was the main outlet for the Hampshire basin and had all the essential qualities of a medieval port. Foreign traders, including Venetians, Florentines, Genoese and Catalans were well established by 1450, bringing with them luxury produce from the Mediterranean and the Levant. Exeter and Bristol were the other two important ports in the South West, also trading with the western part of Europe and the Mediterranean.

The development of the East Coast ports came with the breakdown of feudalism and the growth of native enterprise. The battle for control of the traffic across the seas against the Hansards, Dutch, Brabantins, Flemings, French and Italians waged throughout the later centuries of the Middle Ages. Food imports to the East Coast ports were mainly of wine, fish, corn, onion seeds and hops.

The port of London grew during this period and became the most important factor in the economic life of the capital and whole country. Its position gave it access to trade with south-west Europe and the Mediterranean as well as northern Europe, the Baltic and Low Countries and it became a powerful rival to the East Coast ports which declined in the later Middle Ages. Western ports, however, increased in importance as they were independent enough to survive without London.

Among the overlords and the aristocracy the position of ports which handled foreign trade was significant to the diversity of their food. Poor internal transport facilities meant a limited radius of transfer, and while the historic hinterland of the South, the South Western and the Eastern ports of England enjoyed numerous types of foreign produce, other distant areas were less affected by these influences.

In most parts of the North of England, Scotland and Wales, primitive societies existed with little desire for the refinements of foreign produce. In addition to the disadvantages of their position these areas had poor agricultural land and a wetter, colder climate than the south. The backwardness and insularity was transmitted to their food and made them almost wholly dependent on their limited natural resources.

Agrarian Changes

The phasing out of feudalism was gradual, and took place over several centuries. The lords slowly lost their hold over the cottagers, villeins and serfs and money payments were substituted for compulsory work. Cottagers and the villeins began to rent their land from the lord and became the new class of yeoman farmers, while the lords became landed proprietors. Those who did not rent land became landless labourers, no longer bound to the soil and their lord, but free to work where and when they pleased.

The consequences of the Black Death in 1348-9 A.D., which reduced the population by almost half, hastened this change as land was left without sufficient labour to work it. The lords were compelled to hire labour and where this was unattainable, rented out the demesne land to a tenant or turned areas of their estates into sheep runs which required little manual labour compared with crops. This swing from arable to sheep farming continued until the middle of the sixteenth century with much of the land untilled, cottages and villages deserted and famine common among the poor.

The ensuing agrarian changes which took place during this period were greatly affected by a movement to enclose the land which had previously been open fields of cultivated common lands, often in the hands of peasants who were not utilising the land to its best advantage. Enclosure was an economic improvement for the country as a whole although it was stoutly resisted and was seen as a devastation of the traditional way of life. Common lands were swallowed up in new farms, and the peasant who lost his strips of land suffered; at the same time progressive utilisation of waste land with subsequent diminution of common pasture, turbary and woods contributed to the process of change.

This complete or partial disintegration of the open-field system undermined the structure of manorial life and paved the way for social and economic changes which were to establish the foundations for the revolution in agriculture which dramatically changed the whole system of our food supplies. The eighteenth and nineteenth centuries mark the change-over from self-sufficient agriculture to farming for profit. There was a general awakening to new ideas, to inventions, improvements and experiments which stimulated a spirit of agricultural enterprise not economically possible in the past.

The leaders of the agricultural movement were men like Jethro Tull (1674-1741), Charles Townshend (1674-1738), Robert Bakewell (1725-95), Thomas William Coke of Holkham, Earl of Leicester (1752-1842) and Arthur Young (1741-1820). Jethro Tull pioneered new techniques in ploughing and sowing, and Charles Townshend, the second Duke of Townshend, encouraged the cultivation of turnips as winter fodder for cattle. He is also credited with the introduction in Norfolk of the system known as the four course system which abandoned fallow land.

Robert Bakewell, a farmer from Dishley near Loughborough, concentrated his attention on the improvement of cattle, and Thomas William Coke of Holkham followed up and consolidated Townshend's ideas. In 1793, the government set up the Board of Agriculture and elected Arthur Young as secretary. He travelled throughout the country encouraging farmers to try out new farming methods. The efforts of these five men revolutionised food supplies with improved quality and quantity. The new methods, however, created new regional variations, coinciding with differences in soil and climate.

In Norfolk the system which most suited the soil and climate was associated with arable turnip husbandry and winter feeding of stock whose manure was necessary for the maintenance of land fertility to allow continued cultivation. On the clay soils of the English plain, turnip husbandry was impossible and grass was prevalent. In western districts with a wetter climate and poorer soil, grass was grown and improved arable rotations based on new methods were practised.

For economic and geographical reasons, Scotland was slow to adopt new methods. The most progressive areas were those bordering on England: Berwickshire and East Lothian were the first areas to practise the new husbandry as their light fertile soil and dry climate were particularly suitable. The Southern uplands and the Highlands specialised in sheep, while Galloway and Ayrshire raised cattle.

Regional Dishes and Food Supplies

The distribution of natural food resources in the British Isles and the surrounding areas have greatly influenced regional dishes as can be seen from the following tables. Although raw materials were limited in variety and quantity, ingenuity bred by necessity created many unique dishes. Original and frequent use of oatmeal, potatoes and dairy produce in particular created an amazing variety of combinations. Individual variation makes Scotland and Wales excel in oatmeal dishes, Ireland in potato and Wales in many local dishes based on buttermilk.

In comparison with the Celtic countries, England was generally better endowed. Agriculturally the land was more fertile, the population density higher and life more stable and prosperous. Trade and transport facilities developed more rapidly, and people were more receptive to change and development. All these factors were conducive to a diversity which is consolidated by extensive use of beef, dairy produce, pork, lamb and mutton, poultry and game, fruit and vegetables in regional dishes.

LONDON

Boodle's Cake
Boodle's Orange Fool
Brumbrays
Chelsea Buns
Crystal Palace Pudding
Deptford Pudding
Dowlet Pie
East Ham Eel Pie
Eel Pie Island Pie
Eels and Mash

Fried Veal Cutlets
Goose Pie
Hot Cross Buns
Kensington Rolls
Jellied Eels
Lobster Pie
London Double Crust Pie
London Buns
Loving Cup
Parsnip Sauce

Pea Soup
Pigeons in Pimlico
Raspberry Lockets
Saffron Wigs
Steak, Kidney and Oyster
    Pudding and Pie
Syllabub
Whelks
Whitebait

SOUTH EAST

Surrey
Artichokes with Cheese
Broad Bean Pudding (Windsor)
Herb Pie
Jugged Hare

Mutton Pie with Mushrooms
Roast Chicken

Kent
Biddenden Biscuits

Cheese Pasties
Cherry Pancakes
Cherry Preserves
Cherry Pudding
Flead Cakes

Fruit Batters
Huffkins
Kentish Cake
Kentish Farmhouse Chicken
Kentish Fruit and Cream
Kentish Well Pudding
Morello Cherry Jam
Oast Cakes
Pigeon Pudding
Rabbit Pudding
Tonbridge Brawn
Tunbridge Wells Cakes
Twice Laid

Whitstable Oysters

Sussex
Apple Pie
Arundel Mullets
Ashdown Partridge Pudding
Ashdown Pickles
Blanket Pudding
Brighton Rocks
Chichester Pudding
Chiddingly Hot-Pot
Goger Cakes
Goose or Chicken Pudding

Hastings Gurnet Pudding
Huckle-my-Buff
Ifield Vicarage Hog's Pudding
Lardy Johns
Pulborough Eels
Pumpkin Pie
Southdown Lamb and Mutton
Summer Pudding
Sussex Plum Duff
Sussex Pond Pudding
Sussex Pudding
Sussex Sole in Cider
Tomato Pie

RURAL SOUTH

Hampshire
Brown George Pudding
Friar's Omelet
Gipsy Bread
Grape Wine
Hampshire Drops
Hampshire Roll
Kidney in Onions
Lardy Cakes
Mothering Sunday Wafers
Minced Ham
Osborne Pudding
Pickled Green Cabbage
Stuffed Liver
Syllabub
Vectis Pudding

Berkshire
Bacon and Egg Pie
Bacon Pudding
Critton Pies
Ginger Apples
Jugged Steak
Poor Knights of Windsor
Windsor Bean Pudding

Oxfordshire
Apricot Stuffed Ham
Banbury Apple Pie
Banbury Cakes
Brown Betty
Carrot Pudding
Cider Cake
Deddington Pudding Pie
Lardy Cakes

New College Pudding
Oxford Brawn Sauce
Oxford Johns
Oxford Pudding
Oxford Sauce
Oxford Sausages
Spatchcocked Eels
Spiced Oxford Cake

Buckinghamshire
Aylesbury Duck
Aylesbury Game Pie
Buckinghamshire Bacon Badger
Blackberry and Apple Cream
Cherry Turnovers
Gammon and Apricot Pie
Mutton Pie
Rabbit Pie
Roast Leg of Mutton

WEST COUNTRY

Gloucestershire
Bristol Cake
Cheese and Ale
Cheese (single and double)
Elvers with Bacon
Gingerbread

Halibut Bristol
Newent Apple Cobs
Oldbury Tarts
Pheasant Soup
Rabbit and Hare Brawn
Royal Pie

Severn Elvers
Speechhouse Pudding
Tewkesbury Saucer Batter

Wiltshire
Bradenham Ham

Bradenham Chaps
Chicken and Ham Pie
Devizes Pie
Lardy Cake
Rhubarb and Mixed Peel Jam
Salisbury Steaks
Truckles (Wiltshire Cheese)
Wiltshire Ham
Wiltshire Porkies

Somerset
Apple Pudding
Apple Sauce Cake
Bath Buns
Bath Chaps
Bath Ground Rice Pudding
Bath Olivers
Bath Polonies
Cheddar Cheese
Crockie Pie
Easter Cakes
Elvers Cakes
Exmoor Lamb
Faggots
Frumenty
Potato Cakes
Pickled Walnuts
Priddy Oggies
Rook Pie
Sally Lunn Buns
Samphire
Somerset Casserole
Somerset Stew
Syllabub

Dorset
Apple Cake
Apple Mincemeat
Blue Vinney Cheese
Dorset Scalloped Crab
Pickled Pork

Roast Mutton
Tench with Herbs

Devonshire
Apple Cake
Apple Curranty
Apple In-and-Out
Ashburton Open Pasty
Baked Devonshire Onions
Beef and Egg Pie
Brixton Punch
Cider
Clotted Cream
Devon Cured Ham
Devon Flats
Devonshire Chicken
Devonshire Tart
Exeter Stew
Herring, Soused
Honiton Fairings
Junket
Lamb's Fry
Leeky Stew with a Nackerjack
Mazzard Tart
North Devon Black Cake
Pears, Stewed
Potato Cakes
Revel Buns
Salt Beef Olives
Scones
Steak and Kidney Pie
Squab Pie
Torbay Soles
Vegetable Stew
Widecombe Fair Gingerbread
Yeast Cake

Cornwall
Black Cake
Broccoli Pasty
Burnt Cream

Chicken and Parsley Pie
Clotted Cream
Conger Eel Pie
Cornish Eel Pie
Cornish Pasty
Cornish Red Gurnet
Cornish Toad-in-the-Hole
Cornish Splits
Crab Soup
Eggiot
Fairings
Figgie Hobbin
Fish Pie
Herby Cake
Herby Pie
Junket with Cream
Kettley Broth
Kiddley Broth
Leek and Potato Pie
Likky Paste or Pie
Mackerel
Mahogany
Milk Punch
Muggety Pie
Mullet Pie
Negus Oggie
Pilchard Hot-Pot
Pilchard Pie
Pitchy Cake
Potato Cakes
Punch
Rumfustian
Rum Booze
Sampson
Saffron Cakes
Sennen Cove Conger Stew
Sour Sauce Pastry
Squab Pie
Stargazy Pie
Sultana Cake
Wholemeat or Great Pasty

EAST ANGLIA

Norfolk
Autumn Partridge Pot
Biffins
Black Cap Pudding
Bloaters
Dressmaker Tripe
Guinea Fowl, Fried
Herrings
Kippers
Pig's Fry
Pork Cheese
Roman Rabbit

Suffolk
Brotherly Love
Buns
Cheese
Chitterling Turnovers
Guinea Fowl, Fried
Jugged Hare
Lowestoft Poached Herrings
Rusks
Sweet Cured Pig's Chaps
Syllabub (Cream)

Essex
Colchester Pudding
Dunmow Flitch
Epping Sausages
Gooseberry Pudding
Ham Cake
Samphire Pickle
Whitebait

Hertfordshire
Beef
Cider Sauce
Gooseberry Pudding
Hertfordshire Stew
Pope Lady Cakes
Mutton with Ham and Pickled
    Walnuts
Veal and Kidney Pie
Watercress

Bedfordshire
Apple Florentine Pie
Bread Cheese Cakes
Cattern Cakes
Clanger

Tandra
Wigs
Yule Bread

Huntingdonshire
Fidget Pie
Gooseberry Pie
Goose Giblet Pie
Pork and Onion Dumplings
Scallops, Fried
Stilton Cheese
Veal and Oranges

Cambridgeshire
Ale Cup
Cambridge Sauce
Chestnut Jam
Cream Darioles
Grassy Corner Pudding
Lardy Cake
Milk Punch
Newmarket Pudding
Pork Sausages
The Dean's Cream
Vegetable Marrow Soup

NORTH MIDLAND

Lincolnshire
Apple Pudding
Brawn
Chine, Stuffed
Clee Saucer Cheesecakes
Grantham Gingerbread
Geese
Ham, Cured
Haslet
Pig's Fry
Pork Pies
Pheasant Casserole

Rutland
Plum Shuttles
Rutland Rabbit and Mushroom
    Pudding
Slipcote Cheese
Valentine Buns

Derbyshire
Apple Bread
Bakewell Pudding
Batter Pudding
Bilberry Pie

Chesterfield Rabbit Stew
Derbyshire Oatcakes
Derby Cakes
Derbyshire Cheese
Lamb, Boiled
Herb Cheese
Medley Pie
Pork Pies
Red Whortleberry Jelly
Savoury Pudding
Tripe with Cow Heel and Sausages
Venison Sauce

Nottinghamshire
Batter Pudding with Apples
Belvoir Castle Buns
Coffee Biscuits
Gotham Pudding
Mansfield Toffee
Raised Fruit Pie
Rook Pie
Venison, Potted
Welbeck Pudding

Leicestershire
Black Treacle Roll
Bosworth Jumbles
County Sauce
Leicestershire Cheese
Lutterworth Tea Tart
Market Harborough Pork Pie
Medley Pie
Melton Mowbray Pork Pie
Partridge Casserole
Quorn Bacon Roll
Whetstone Cakes

Northamptonshire
Beef, Potted
Cheesecakes
Chocolate Pudding
Farmhouse Pudding
Hough and Dough
Northamptonshire Pudding
Pork and Onion Pudding
Seblet Cakes
Veal, Potted
Venison Pasty

MIDLANDS

Staffordshire
Chicken Hot-Pot
Faggots
North Staffordshire Swallows
Rabbit Pie
Staffordshire Beefsteaks
Syllabub
Yeomanry Pudding

Worcestershire
Apple Pudding, Baked
Cider
Lamperns, Potted
Malvern Apple Pudding
Malvern Batter Pudding
Pershore Ham
Spring Onion Tart

White Ladies Pudding
Worcestershire Sauce

Warwickshire
Chine of Pork, Roast
Coventry God Cakes
Crayfish and Bacon Savoury
Jellied Chitterlings
Leamington Sauce
Marrow Cream
Pig's Pudding
Warwick Chops and Chestnuts

Shropshire
Fidget Pie
Heart and Kidney Pudding
Kingston Jam

Sage Cheese
Shrewsbury Biscuits
Shropshire Pie
Shropshire Salmon Pie
Veal, Savoury

Herefordshire
Cider Cake
Cider Sauce
Grayling with Thyme
Herefordshire Cured Ham
Love in Disguise
Tripe in Cider
Whortleberry and Crowberry
  Pudding
Wye Salmon

WALES

Aberffrau Cakes
Anglesey Dark Cake
Apple Pudding
Beef, Spiced
Berffro Cakes (Cacen Iago also
  known as James' Cakes)
Caerphilly Cheese
Carmarthen Yeast Cake

Cheese Cakes
Cheese Pudding
Chicken and Leek Pie
Cinnamon Cakes
Cockle Pie
Cow Heel Brawn
Currant Bread
Duck, Boiled Salt

Egg Whey
Faggots
Flummery
Glamorgan Sausage
Gower Oyster Soup
Herring Casserole
Laver Bread

Laver Sauce
Leek and Bacon Pasty
Leek Pie
Leek Porridge
Lobscouse
Mackerel with Fennel Sauce
Marrow Tart
Onion Cake
Pembrokeshire Pie
Plank Bread
Plank Pastry with Apples

Potatoes and Meat in the Oven
Potatoes and Swedes with Liver
Prune Sauce
Rice Pudding
Salmon in a Soup Plate
Salmon, Grilled
Snowdon Pudding
Teisen Lap
Teisen Dinca
The Miser's Feast
Welsh Cakes

Welsh Hot-Pot
Welsh Lamb Pie
Welsh Leek Broth
Welsh Mutton Cawl
Welsh Mutton Ham
Welsh Pancakes
Welsh Pikelets
Welsh Rarebit
Welsh Stew
Welsh Stwns
Welsh Venison

NORTH WEST

Lancashire
Bacon Ribs and Onions
Beef Sausages
Blackburn Cracknels
Black Pudding
Bolton Hot-Pot
Braggot
Brawn
Bun Loaf
Cheese
Chip Butties
Chitterlings
Chorley Cakes
Cow Heel Brawn
Cow Heel Pie
Cow Heel and Steak Pie
Everton Toffee
Faggots
Goosenargh Biscuits
Hindle Wakes Fowl
Hot-Pots
Lancashire Foot
Lancashire Nuts
Lancashire Potato Pie
Lancashire Spiced Loaf
Lobscouse
Manchester Collared Pork
Manchester Pudding

Morecambe Bay Shrimps
Oldham Parkin
Plum Cake
Poor. Man's Cake
Potato Pie
Preston Parkin
Sheep's Trotters with Oatmeal
Sly Cake
Sorrel Turnover
Sparerib Pie
Tripe and Cow Heel
Tripe and Onions
Trotters, Boiled
Turnips, Carrots and Brown Gravy
Wet Nelly

Cheshire
Cheese
Cheshire Soup
Cheshire Chicken Brawn
Chester Buns
Chester Cake
Chester Fingers
Chester Pudding
Cow Heel and Steak Pie
Pig's Brain and Kidney
Potato Cakes

Yorkshire
Apple Cheese and Butter
Apple and Honey Pudding
Batley Cake
Batter Pudding
Bedale Plum Cake
Beef Sausages
Bilberry Pie
Bloater Paste
Cheese
Christmas Pie
Crayfish
Curd Tarts
Doncaster Butterscotch
Eccles Cakes
Faggots
Harrogate Sponge
Grouse, Buttered
Harrogate Sponge
Ilkley Cake
Kipper Paste
Leeds Parkin
Meat and Pot Pie
Mint Pasty
Old Yorkshire Stuffing
Orange Jelly
Ormskirk Gingerbread
Oven Bottom Cake

Pontefract Cakes
Pork Chaps
Pork Pie
Rice Pudding with Suet
Runnel Pudding
Salmon with Cucumber
Sausage Roll
Savoury Pudding
Scones

Sheffield Biscuits
Starforth Gingerbread
Sweet Lamb Pie
Tea Cakes
Treacle Tart
Veal and Ham Pie
Wakefield Gingerbread
Wakefield Rabbit
Wandsford Steak

Whitby Lamb
Wilfra Tarts
Wine Pudding
York Biscuits
York Ham
Yorkshire or Buck Rarebit
Yorkshire Fritters
Yorkshireman's Goose
Yorkshire Veal and Oysters
Yorkshire Yule and Spice Cake

NORTH

Cumberland

Apple Pudding
Bean Salad
Clipping Time Pudding
Cow Heel Brawn
Cumberland Raised Pie
Cumberland Shipped Herring
Currant Cakes
Ham
Herb Pudding
Lobscouse
Muffin Pudding
Mutton Ham
Mutton Pies or Saucer Pies
Northcountry Sweet Pie
Northcountry Tart
Pork Sausage
Potato Hot-Pot
Rum Butter
Rum Nicky
Scrap and Currant Pasty
Sloe Jelly
Sparerib Pie
Trout, Potted

Westmorland

Apple Pasty with Elderberries
Beer Cake
Bilberry Pie
Fig Sue
Grasmere Gingerbread
Grasmere Shortcake
Herb Pudding
Lister Pudding
Pasty
Sweet Lamb Pie
Three Deckers
Westmorland Cake

Northumberland

Alnwick Stew
Brown Caraway Bread
Celery Cheese
Craster Kippers
Felton Spice Loaf
Griddle Cakes
Leek Pudding
Marrow Jam
Mitton of Pork

Newcastle Pudding
Newcastle Potted Salmon
Pan Haggarty
Peas and Beans in Butter
Pressed Pig's Cheek
Salmon, Pickled
Singin' Hinnies
Whitley Goose

Durham

Bacon Cakes
Beef Stew
Chitterlings
Cousin Jim
Curd Cheesecakes
Durham Cutlets
Durham Pikelets
Hot-Pot
Lunch Cake
Panackelty
Panjotheram
Pot Pie
Pressed Pig's Cheek
South Tyne Yeast Cake
Stanhope Firelighters

SCOTLAND

Auld Man's Milk
Baps
Bacon Stovies

Barley Bannocks
Bawd Bree
Black Puddings

Blackberry Jam
Boiled Bacon with Oatmeal Dumplings
Bramble and Apple Fool

Caledonian Ice Cream
Caledonian Liqueur
Champ
Chappit Tatties
Clootie Dumpling
Cookies
Cock-a-Leekie
Crunchan or Cream Chowdie
Crowdie or Cruddy Butter
Crowdie Potato Cakes
Crulla
Cussieston Cake
Curds and Cream
Custard for a Centre Dish
Deer
Deer Horns
Drambuie Cream
Dulse
Dunfillan Pudding
Feather Fowlie
Fitless Cock
Friars Chicken
Grouse
Gudewife's Soup
Gundy
Haggis

Hallowe'en Cake
Hardboiled Egg Sauce
Hatted Kit
Hot Pint
Honey Cakes
Hotch Potch
Hunters Nuts
Inky Pinky
Kail Brose
Lentil and Oatmeal Broth
Lorraine Soup
Marmalade Batter Pudding
Peg Merriles Soup
Minced Collops
Mutton Ham
Mutton Pies
Oatcakes
Oatmeal Pancakes
Oatmeal Posset
Old Scots Brown Soup
Old Scots White Soup
Rhubarb Tart with Oatmeal Pastry
Rowan Jelly
Ruthven Cake
Scotch Broth
Scotch Eggs
Scots Flummery

Scots Gingerbread
Scots Kidney Soup
Scots Nettle Broth
Scots Noyau
Scots Potato Pies
Scotch Rarebit
Scots Trifle
Scots White Collops
Seed Cake
Shortbread
Skink
Skirlie
Sloe and Apple Jelly
Soda Scones
Sowans
Stoved Howtowdie
Sweet Haggis
Tablet
Toddy
Tripe Pie
Urney Pudding
Veal Flory
Venison Collops
Venison Pasty
Whim Wham
White or Mealie Puddings
Yellow Milk

BORDERS

Berwick Cockles
Carluke Balls
Champ
Eyemouth Pale Finnans
Hawick Balls

Jeddart Snails
Peebles Sour Plooms
Rumbledethumps
Selkirk Bannock

Tattie Pot or Mutton and Potato Pie
Teviotdale Pie
Tweed Kettle
Tweedshire Potted Salmon

CENTRAL LOWLANDS

Apples and Elderberries
Auld Reekie Plum Cake
Ayrshire Galantine
Ayrshire Shortbread

Barley Kail
Barley Pudding
Beef Ham
Corstorphine Cream

Dunlop Cheese
Edinburgh Fog
Edinburgh Gingerbread
Edinburgh Rock

Edinburgh Tart
Fife Bannocks
Fife Broth
Glasgow Magistrates
Glasgow Pales
Glasgow Punch

Glasgow Toffee
Glasgow Tripe
Green Kail
Helensburgh Toffee
Kilmenny Kail

Kingdom of Fife Pie
Lowland Game Pie
Largo Potato Soup
Macallum
Rutherglen Cream

HIGHLANDS

Athole Brose
Blairgowrie Foam
Carageen Mould
Colcannon
Culloden Collops
Highland Bake

Highland Beef Balls
Highland Slim Cakes
Inverness Gingerbread
Inverness Gingernuts
Iona Whelk Soup
Limpet Stovies
Loch Fyne Toasts

Nettle Broth
Nettle Soup
Ormidale Steak Pie
Perthshire Bramble Mist
Pocha Buidha
Portree Plum Cake

NORTH EAST

Aberdeen Sausage
Angus Farmers' Fruit Cake
Angus Fish Soup
Angus Potatoes
Angus Toffee
Angus Vegetable Soup
Arbroath Smokies
Balmoral Tripe
Banffshire Potatoes

Buchan Potatoes
Butteries
Cullen Skink
Dundee Biscuits
Dundee Cake
Fochabers Gingerbread
Glister Pudding
Grampian Grouse Pudding
Ham and Haddie

Kailkenny
Kirrie Loaf
Montrose Cakes
Montrose Pales
Pease Meal Brose
Skirlie
Softies
Strathmore Cream of Green Pea
   Soup

ORKNEY AND SHETLAND

Brides Bonn
Breonie
Burston
Clapshot

Cod Sounds
Haddock
Hakka Muggies
Krappen

Liver Krolls
Orkney Cheese
Roe Cakes
Slot
Sour Skons

OUTER HEBRIDES

Carageen Mould
Crappit Heids

Cropadeau
Greisegaen

Marag
Seaweed Soup

CHANNEL ISLANDS

Ormer Stew

NORTHERN IRELAND

Almond Cheesecakes
Apple Cheesecakes
Bacon and Cabbage
Bacon Broth
Balnamoon Skink
Barm Brack
Ballyindland Rolls
Beef, Spiced
Belem Tarts
Belfast Ham
Boxty Bread and Pancakes
Brown Fadge
Buttermilk Scones
Carageen Jelly
Carageen Mould
Champ
Chocolate Cake
Cockle Soup
Cockelty Pie
Colcannon
Crubins

Crubin Pea Soup
Eels
Farm Broth
Farmhouse Bread
Grunt Soup
Hallowe'en Cake
Irish Boiled Cake
Irish Brawn
Irish Coffee
Irish Delight
Irish Herring Soup
Irish Leek Broth
Irish Potted Herring
Irish Rarebit
Irish Rink Cake
Irish Soda Bread
Irish Stew
Irish Shortcakes
Irish Slim Cakes
Kidney Broth
Kidneys in Suet

Ling and Potatoes
Nectar
Nettle Brothan
Nettle Soup
Oaten Bread
Pig's Face
Pig's Haggis
Plum Cake
Potato and Apple Cake
Potato Pudding
Pratie Cakes
Pratie Oaten
Red Herrings
Sausages and Onions in Milk
Salmon, Smoked
St Patrick Cakes
Sloke
Treacle Bread
Wattle Soup
White Puddings
Yellow Man

Basic Cookery Methods

The national cooking of any country will always incorporate certain characteristics that are basic and fundamental to a complete understanding of its cookery. The following section is intended as identification and classification of the basic characteristics that constitute British cookery.

The object of cooking is, basically, that of making a raw material edible through subjecting it to heat. A variety of methods of heat transfer has developed over the centuries, side by side with an even greater variety of raw materials, and these trends will doubtless continue in the future. However, roasting, baking, frying, grilling, boiling, poaching, steaming, stewing and braising are the most commonly practised methods in traditional British cooking.

The instructions and information contained in this section are confined to the basic methods of cooking, an understanding of which is fundamental in the preparation and execution of particular dishes.

STOCKS, COOKING AND PICKLING LIQUIDS

These terms all refer to flavoured liquids for use in soups, sauces, pies, puddings and in many boiled, stewed, poached and braised dishes. They may result simply from the boiling process: the liquid in which meat, vegetables or fish has been cooked is strained and used as a foundation for another dish. More often stocks are prepared in advance and classified according to the basic ingredient.

The thickness or viscosity of the finished stock depends on the type and amount of bones used; bones from young animals, poultry and some fish, being more gelatinous, give a thicker stock than bones from old animals.

Fresh, thoroughly cleaned ingredients should be used; salt liquids from salted meats, salt and starch should never be added to the stock. Remove vegetables at the end of the cooking time as they re-absorb the flavour from the liquid.

Stock should be thoroughly cooled and stored in a cool place to prevent it going sour.

THICKENINGS AND BINDING AGENTS

These are liaisons used to give body and consistency to liquid foods. The following variations are used to thicken sauces, soups, stews, puddings and pies.

White Roux

Depending on required consistency use 3 oz flour and 3 oz butter to thicken 4-8 pt of liquid. Melt the butter in a pan, sift in the flour, mixing well with a wooden spoon; cook for 2-3 minutes to remove the starchy taste of the flour. Gradually stir in the liquid; boil up to thicken.

Brown Roux

To thicken 4-8 pt of soup depending on consistency required, melt 3 oz butter or dripping, sift in 2 oz flour and mix well with a wooden spoon. Cook gently over low heat, stirring regularly until the roux turns a light brown colour. Add the liquid to the roux gradually, away from the heat; boil up to thicken.

Egg and Cream

This is especially used to thicken cream soups and sauces, using 2 egg yolks and 5 fl oz cream to thicken 2-4 pt of liquid depending on richness required. Beat the egg yolks well, combine with cream, strain. Add a little of the hot liquid to the eggs and cream and return to the pan. Do not boil the liquid after the liaison is added or the eggs will curdle. Heat through to thicken and serve immediately.

Potato Starch Thickening

Blend 1½ oz potato starch in ¾ pt cold water to a smooth paste and use to thicken 4 pt of soup. Strain into the boiling liquid and simmer until cooked through. Left-over mashed or creamed potatoes may be used as a thickening agent.

Cornflour and Arrowroot

Blend cornflour or arrowroot with a little cold liquid; add a few tablespoons of the hot cooking liquid, stir and return to the pan. Boil up to cook the starch and thicken the soup.

Sago, tapioca and ground rice (semolina) can also be used as a thickening agent, sprinkled on top of the boiling liquid and cooked for 10-15 minutes to thicken.

Kneaded Butter

Depending on the consistency required, use 4 oz butter and 3 oz flour to thicken 4-8 pt of liquid. Mix the butter and flour together with a broad-bladed knife; add in small knobs to the boiling liquid just before serving.

Butter

Butter on its own, cut in small pieces, can be added to a sauce immediately before it is served; blend in without stirring.

Blood

To prevent the blood curdling, blend 1 teaspoon vinegar into 1 pt blood; when required for use mix in 5 fl oz water. Add a little of the hot liquid to the blood and return it to the pan. Do not boil the liquid after the blood is added or it will curdle. Heat through to thicken.

Brown Stock

This is made with meat and roasted bones and a selection of vegetables and herbs. It is used as a liquid in soups, in brown sauces, stews and for braising.

2 lb bones
2 lb shin or neck of beef
6 pt water
¾ lb chopped and browned carrots
¾ lb chopped and browned onions
2 sliced leeks
2 oz chopped celery
1 faggot of herbs
9 peppercorns
3 cloves
Oven: 325°F; gas mark 3; 1-2 hours

Remove excess fat from the bones and meat and cut into large pieces. Break the bones into small pieces to release maximum flavour. Put the bones in a roasting tin and sprinkle with pieces of fat; brown thoroughly in the oven. Drain off the fat, rinse out sediments in the pan with boiling water and simmer. Put the bones, meat and sediments in a large pan with the cold water.

Bring slowly to simmering point, skim off fat and scum as they rise to the top and simmer gently for 1 hour, skimming when necessary until the stock is clear. Add the vegetables, herbs, peppercorns and cloves.

Simmer the stock for 4-5 hours to give maximum extraction, skimming when necessary and removing the tide mark from time to time. Strain and use as required.

White Stock

This is made with bones that are not browned, white meat — veal, rabbit, chicken or mutton — and vegetables and herbs. Used as a liquid in soups, white sauces and stews and for poaching poultry.

2 lb bones
2 lb white meat (veal, rabbit, chicken or mutton)
1 calf's foot (optional)
6 pt water
¾ lb chopped carrots
¾ lb chopped onions
2 sliced leeks
2 oz chopped celery
1 faggot of herbs
9 peppercorns
3 cloves

Follow the method for brown meat stock, omitting browning of the bones and vegetables.

Fish Stock

This is prepared with the bones and trimmings of fish; the only aromatics used are onion, celery, parsley, lemon and faggot of herbs. Dry white wine may be added. Fish stock is used in fish soups, in the preparation of fish sauces and for stewing and poaching fish.

4 lb white fish (bones, heads and trimmings)
4 oz grated onions
1 oz chopped celery
1 oz chopped parsley stalks
½ lemon
6 pt water
6 peppercorns
1 faggot of herbs
2 oz butter
Dry white wine (optional)

Place all the ingredients except the water and wine in a pan; sweat, covered, in the butter without colour. Add the water and wine and bring to the boil, skimming thoroughly as the scum rises.

Simmer for 20 minutes, skimming when necessary. Strain through a fine sieve or muslin and as required.

Game Stock

Prepared with the bones, meat and trimmings of any kind of game, browned in fat, with vegetables and herbs. It is used for game soups, stews and sauces.

2 lb game trimmings
2 lb game meat
6 pt water
¾ lb chopped and browned carrots
¾ lb chopped and browned onions
2 sliced leeks
2 oz chopped celery
1 faggot of herbs
9 peppercorns
3 cloves

Follow the method for brown meat stock.

Pickling Liquid

An infusion of vinegar and water, with onions, herbs and spices.

5 fl oz malt vinegar
5 fl oz water

2 oz sliced or grated onions
4 bay leaves
¾ oz pickling spice
1 tablespoon sugar
Sprig each, sage, marjoram and thyme

Bring all the ingredients to the boil, cover and leave for 15 minutes. Use the pickling liquid for baked fish and strain before serving.

Cooking Liquid for White Fish

A quickly prepared liquid flavoured with parsley, bay leaf, onions and lemon juice.

4 pt boiling water
1 bay leaf
1 oz parsley stalks
4 oz sliced onions
6 peppercorns
½ pt milk
½ tablespoon salt
Juice of 1 lemon

Add all ingredients to the boiling water; simmer for 10 minutes, strain and use as required.

Cooking Liquid for Lobster, Shellfish, Trout and Salmon

A more strongly flavoured liquid.

4 pt water
5 fl oz malt vinegar
12 ground peppercorns
6 oz sliced carrots
1 bay leaf
1 sprig thyme
1 oz parsley stalks
½ lb sliced onions
1½ tablespoons salt

Bring the vegetables and other ingredients to the boil; simmer for 10 minutes, strain and use as required.

Vegetable Stock

This is the strained liquid from boiled vegetables and is used mainly in vegetarian cookery.

SAUCES

These are designed to provide a liquid accompaniment to foods. There are numerous sauce preparations, all differing from each other in flavour, consistency and texture, as well as in their initial preparations. Sauces used in British cookery are based on savoury brown, white and butter sauces and on sweet white sauces from which a variety of combinations are made.

Brown Sauce

Made with bones, bacon, carrots, onions and mushrooms browned in fat, tomato purée, brown stock and thickened with a brown roux. Used with a wide variety of additional flavourings.

2 lb beef bones
3 oz dripping
1 oz diced bacon
4 oz diced carrots
4 oz diced onions
2 oz mushroom trimmings
3 oz flour
½ oz tomato purée
4 pt brown stock
Salt and pepper

Oven: 325°F; gas mark 3; 1-2 hours

Place the bones with fat in a roasting tin and brown in a slow oven. Melt the dripping in a pan and fry the bacon and vegetables until light brown. Stir in the flour and continue cooking until the roux is brown. Add the tomato purée. Gradually stir in the stock, bring slowly to the boil and add the browned bones. Strain off the fat from the roasting tin, scrape out the sediments and add to the pan. Simmer for 1½-2 hours, season; strain and use as required.

White Sauce

Made with milk and flavoured with herbs, bay leaf and an onion studded with cloves; thickened with a white roux. Strained, seasoned and used with additional flavourings.

1 faggot of herbs
1 bay leaf
1 onion stuck with cloves
2 pt milk
3 oz butter
3 oz flour
Salt and pepper

Simmer the faggot of herbs, bay leaf and onion in the milk for 10 minutes. Melt the butter in a pan, stir in the flour and cook for 2-3 minutes without colour.

Add the milk gradually and bring slowly to the boil, stirring continuously; simmer for approximately 10-15 minutes until the flour has cooked and the sauce thickened; season. Strain and use as required.

Gravy

Made with the sediments from any roast meat, mixed with stock; reduced and sometimes thickened. Served with roast meat.

Pan sediments
1 pt brown stock
½ oz flour, cornflour or arrowroot (optional)
Salt and pepper

Carefully pour off most of the fat from the roasting tin, leaving the sediments. Add the stock and stir well to scrape up the residues. Bring to the boil and reduce to the required consistency.

Alternatively, blend the thickening agent with a little water. Add to the reduced stock, stir and reboil to thicken. Season and serve.

Butter Sauce

Water thickened with white roux and butter, flavoured with lemon. Used on its own or with additional flavourings.

1½ oz butter
1½ oz flour
2 pt boiling water
1 teaspoon lemon juice
½ lb butter

Work equal amounts of butter and flour to a smooth paste. Add to the boiling water in small pieces, stirring constantly. Stir in the lemon juice. Remove from the heat and whisk in the remaining butter.

For a sweet butter sauce, add 3 oz sugar.

Sweet White Sauce

Made with flavoured milk and a white roux, sweetened with sugar and used with additional flavourings for dessert sauces.

2 pt milk
1 bay leaf
½ lb butter
2 oz flour
4 oz sugar

Bring the milk to the boil with the bay leaf; cover and leave to infuse for 10 minutes.

Melt 2 oz of the butter, stir in the flour and cook for 2-3 minutes without colour. Stir in the sugar and gradually add the strained milk, stirring continuously; simmer for 10 minutes, then blend in the remaining butter until smooth.

FORCEMEATS AND STUFFINGS

The purpose of a forcemeat or stuffing is to provide an internal basting to prevent the meat from drying out during cooking. A forcemeat also adds to and absorbs the flavours of the meat. Some type of fat is used in most stuffings, and all the ingredients are usually minced, chopped or liquidised until finely divided and thoroughly mixed. A binding agent is used to hold the ingredients together, breadcrumbs and eggs being the most common.

Forcemeats may also be used as garnish for eggs, fish, poultry, game, meat and vegetables. The most commonly used forcemeats are based on veal, pork and herbs.

Veal Forcemeat

½ lb minced fillet of veal
4 oz uncooked, finely chopped ham or gammon
4 oz fresh white breadcrumbs
2 tablespoons finely chopped parsley
Salt and pepper
1 beaten egg

Mix the veal, ham, breadcrumbs and parsley thoroughly; season with salt and pepper and bind with the egg.

Pork Forcemeat

6 oz chopped onions
1 oz lard
1 lb pork sausage meat or minced shoulder pork
2 tablespoons finely chopped parsley
1 teaspoon chopped mixed herbs

1 oz fresh breadcrumbs (optional)
Salt and pepper

Fry the onion in the lard until soft, but not brown; add the sausage meat, parsley, herbs and breadcrumbs if used. Season to taste.

Sage and Onion Stuffing

4 oz chopped onions
3 oz pork dripping or suet
½ lb white breadcrumbs
1 teaspoon finely chopped sage
5 fl oz stock
Salt and pepper
1 beaten egg

Fry the onions in the dripping until soft, add the breadcrumbs, sage and stock. Combine thoroughly, season with salt and pepper and bind with the egg.

EGGS

Eggs are probably the most commonly used ingredient in cooking. They are used as thickenings for soups, sauces and stews, as binding agents, in cakes, pastries, breads and in many sweets and puddings. Boiled, poached, fried and scrambled, they serve as garnishes and as the basis for many savouries.

Boiled Eggs

1-2 eggs per person

Place the eggs in a large pan of boiling water, bring back to the boil, and according to size allow 3-3¾ minutes for softboiled eggs, 10-12 minutes for hardboiled eggs.

Remove from the water and serve at once or plunge into cold running water. Shell and use as required.

Fried Eggs

1-2 eggs per person
2 oz butter and oil

Melt the butter and oil in a frying pan and heat. Break the eggs carefully, slide them into the pan and cook for 3-5 minutes until set.

Baste with the fat to form a thin white film over the yolks. Drain and serve.

Plain Omelet

2-3 eggs
Oil or clarified butter
Salt and pepper

Heat enough oil or clarified butter in an omelet
pan to glaze the surface. Beat the eggs lightly with
a fork and season. Pour off surplus fat from the
pan, add the eggs and shake the pan briskly,
using the fork to keep the eggs moving and to
loosen them round the sides of the pan.

Fold one side into the centre, tap the
opposite side of the pan sharply and fold this
side to the centre. Tilt the pan and turn out the
omelet.

Poached Eggs

1-2 eggs per person
1 teaspoon vinegar

Bring a pan of water to the boil and add the
vinegar. Break the eggs into the water and cook
gently, using two spoons to gather the whites
round the yolks. Simmer until the whites are
just set, after 3-5 minutes.

Lift from the pan with a perforated spoon,
trim the edges and serve on hot buttered toast,
dusting with pepper. Cheese, mushroom or
tomato sauce may also be served.

Scrambled Eggs

1-2 eggs per person
Salt and pepper
½ oz butter
1 tablespoon cream

Break the eggs into a basin, beat thoroughly and
add the seasoning. Melt half the butter in a heavy-
based pan and add the eggs; cook over gentle
heat, stirring continuously until the eggs are
lightly cooked.

Add the remaining butter, adjust seasoning and
cook until soft; add the cream. Serve on hot
buttered toast.

FISH

All types of fish should be cooked on the day of
purchase. Basic cooking methods include boiling,
poaching and steaming, grilling, frying and baking.
Whichever cooking method is used, all fish should
first be prepared according to kind, scaling when
necessary and gutting; this is done by removing
the entrails, blood and slime along the belly on
round fish and from behind the head on flat fish.
On small fish, such as smelts and sprats, the
entrails are squeezed out after cutting off the
heads.

Depending on the method, fish may be cooked
whole, with or without skin and bone, or cut into
portions or fillets.

All shellfish must be boiled fresh irrespective
of how they are to be used, with the exception of
oysters. After boiling, poisonous parts should be
removed, such as the beards on mussels, "dead
men's fingers" on crabs and lobsters, and the
stomach bags and intestines.

BOILING

Most suitable for this method are large whole
fish, middle, tail or head and shoulders of large
fish, and shellfish. Prepare whole fish by cutting
off the fins and trimming round the tail. Remove
the eyes and scales, scraping from tail towards
the head. Loosen the gills with a sharp knife,
make a slit in the belly and pull out the entrails,
blood and roes.

Wash and dry the fish thoroughly; leave whole
or cut into steaks or cutlets. Prepare a basic
cooking liquid for fish (see Stocks). Put the
cooled liquid in a fish kettle and bring slowly to
simmering point; add the fish and take care to
keep the liquid at a simmer, not boiling. Count
timing from the moment the liquid begins to
simmer again after the fish has been added.

Cold Service

Leave the fish in the cooking liquid until cold;
cooking times are reduced to allow for the latent
heat in the liquid.

4 lb fish − 10 minutes (total)
6 lb fish − 12 minutes
8 lb fish − 15 minutes
10 lb fish − 18 minutes
14 lb fish − 20 minutes

Hot Service

Remove and drain after cooking, peel off skin
and serve at once.

4 lb fish — 5 minutes per lb
6 lb fish — 4½ minutes per lb
8 lb fish — 4 minutes per lb
10 lb fish — 3½-4 minutes per lb
14 lb fish — 3-3½ minutes per lb

Boiled Lobster and Crab

Rinse under cold running water, drop into a large pan of boiling salted water and cover with a tight-fitting lid. Simmer for about 20 minutes, leave to cool in the liquid, then remove the flesh from shell and claws.

POACHING

Fillets, steaks and small whole fish are suitable for poaching. Prepare whole fish by removing fins, eyes, scales and entrails. Wash and dry whole fish, fillets and steaks thoroughly. Fillets may be left flat, folded in two or rolled, depending on size and thickness.

Butter a shallow, ovenproof dish, sprinkle with finely chopped shallots and lay the fish on top. Season with salt and pepper. Pour fish stock or milk into the dish to reach half-way up the fish; cover with buttered paper. Cook in the oven at 350°F; gas mark 4, allowing 8-10 minutes per lb.

Drain the fish, set on a serving dish and pour over the strained cooking liquid or use this to make a sauce.

Jugged Kippers

Place the whole kippers, head down, in a jug or lay them in a roasting tin. Pour boiling water into the jug, up to the tails and leave in a warm place for 5-10 minutes. Drain and use as required.

Alternatively, remove heads and fins from the kippers and trim the tails. Place in a pan, cover with boiling water and simmer for 6 minutes. Drain and serve.

STEAMING

Thin fillets or small steaks are the most suitable; wash and dry well, place the fish on a greased plate, brush with melted butter and season. Add a little milk, cover with another plate and set over a pan of boiling water. Steam for 20-25 minutes.

Steamed Kippers

Remove heads and fins and trim tails. Place in a large pan, add enough water to come half-way up the kippers. Cover with a tightly fitting lid.

Bring the water to the boil and reduce the heat and simmer for 30 minutes. Drain and serve with mustard butter.

GRILLING

All types of small whole fish, steaks, cutlets and fillets are suitable. Large whole fish and cuts are not suitable because of their size.

Grilled Whole Fish (Herring, Mackerel)

Prepare the fish by removing heads and fins; trim the tails and scrape off the scales. Sprinkle the inside with salt and make three shallow incisions, diagonally, on both sides of the fish. Coat with seasoned flour and brush with melted butter or oil. Set on a greased grill and cook under gentle heat for about 6 minutes, turning once.

Grilled Fillets and Steaks (Herring, Mackerel, Finnan Haddock)

Wash and dry the fish, brush with melted butter or coat with seasoned flour or egg and breadcrumbs. Grill for about 3 minutes on each side.

Grilled Lobster

Return the boiled lobster meat to the cleaned shells, brush with melted butter and sprinkle with salt and pepper. Grill under moderate heat for 10-12 minutes and serve with melted butter or a shrimp sauce.

Grilled Cured Fish

Bloaters: scrape lightly with a knife and wipe clean with a cloth. Loosen the backbone or remove this altogether and cut each bloater into two fillets and lay these together again, skin sides out. Grill for 6 minutes, turning once, and serve with pats of butter. Kippers: remove heads and fins and trim tails; grill, skin side up, for 5 minutes. Alternatively, grill jugged kippers for 2 minutes on each side, or pairs of kippers for 10 minutes, turning once.

Serve grilled fish with the pan juices, parsley butter, lemon slices and chopped parsley.

FRYING

Fillets, steaks, cutlets and small whole fish are suitable for shallow-frying in hot butter or oil. Thin fillets and tiny whole fish, such as whitebait, smelts and sprats, can also be deep-fried in boiling fat.

Prepare the fish, washing and drying fillets, steaks and cutlets, cleaning whole fish such as herrings, mackerel and plaice, and coat with seasoned flour, egg and breadcrumbs or seasoned oatmeal.

Shallow-Frying

Heat a heavy-based pan and melt butter and oil in the proportions of one quarter butter to three quarters oil. Put the coated fish in the hot fat and fry until tender, turning once only. Allow about 10 minutes for whole fish, steaks and cutlets, slightly less for fillets; the latter should be fried first on the side at which they will be served.

Small whole herrings can be fried in a layer of salt, sprinkled over a heavy-based pan, with no extra fat. Mackerel, whole or filleted, are often coated with seasoned oatmeal, and smoked haddock (pales) are often fried with bacon and a little water in a covered pan.

Deep-Frying

Coat the prepared fish with seasoned flour, dip in beaten egg, then coat with breadcrumbs, pressing these in well. Alternatively, dip the fish, coated with seasoned flour, in a batter and allow any surplus to drain off. Pre-heat a pan or deep-fryer and wire basket with oil or fat; allow this to reach a temperature of 375°F before immersing the fish, a few at a time. Fry until crisp and golden, depending on size and thickness; fillets require about 3-5 minutes. Drain on absorbent paper.

Serve fried fish garnished with lemon quarters or slices, sprigs of parsley and pats of butter. Accompany with the pan juices from shallow-fried fish, or with melted butter, parsley, mustard or onion sauce.

BAKING

All types and cuts of fish are suitable for baking — cuts of whole fish (middle, tail, head and shoulders), smaller cuts, such as steaks and cutlets, and fillets.

Prepare whole fish and larger cuts by cutting off the fins, trim round the tail. Take out the eyes and scrape off the scales, from tail to head. Loosen the gills and the entrails through an opening in the belly or behind the head. Pull out the gills and entrails, wash thoroughly giving particular attention to the backbone. Dry with a clean cloth.

Wash and dry fillets with a clean cloth, fold in two, roll or leave flat depending on size.

Whole fish and large cuts may be stuffed with forcemeat, secured with wooden skewers. Fillets can be spread with a stuffing and rolled up.

Melt a generous amount of butter in a shallow baking dish, put in the fish, baste with the butter and season. Sprinkle with lemon juice and cover with buttered paper.

Bake in the oven at 350°F, gas mark 4, basting frequently. Timing depends on size and thickness; kippers only need 10-15 minutes, but in general allow about 30 minutes for whole fish, 15-20 minutes for steaks and fillets. Baked smokies (haddock) are grilled first, the backbones removed and the smokies liberally spread with butter and baked for 5 minutes.

MEAT

Several cooking methods are applied to meat, depending on the type, size and tenderness of the cut and on presentation. Roasting, grilling and frying, braising and stewing, boiling and poaching are all applicable, but the British roasting traditions are probably unique.

ROASTING

In its original sense roasting meant cooking meat by prolonged exposure to the heat of a fire. This was the most logical process in the days of huge open fires when food was held and revolved at or above the fire by means of a spit. This roasting method based on heat transfer by radiation changed during the nineteenth century with the development of the enclosed fire. Meat cooked in the oven by dry convected heat retained the original term of roasting, despite protestations from traditionalists who maintained that roasted meat could only be cooked at or before an open fire. Correctly, oven-cooked roasts are baked, but the two terms are now interchangeable.

GRILLING

This implies cooking an item of meat on the bars of a grid beneath a source of radiant heat. Originally, the food was placed on the fire or on a grid-iron (grill) over the fire. This was known as broiling, but later became known as grilling from the piece of equipment used. As the radiant heat now comes from above rather than below open bars are unnecessary, and the food may be placed on a metal tray instead.

FRYING

This means cooking an item of food in fat in a pan over a source of heat. Food was originally fried in its own fat or in the dripping fat which collected from the spit roast. Shallow- or pan-frying is applied to food cooked in a minimum of clarified meat fat, oil, butter or margarine; the food is usually turned during cooking so that the characteristic browning is achieved evenly on both sides.

Deep-frying is applied to food immersed completely in clarified fat or oil, thereby producing a crisp, brown end product. Deep-frying of raw meat is not usually practised as the temperature at which normal deep-frying is carried out produces unsatisfactory products. Frying of meat is therefore synonymous with shallow-frying in the basic cooking methods.

BRAISING

This is principally used for less tender cuts of meat and may be regarded as a combination of roasting and stewing methods. The meat is sealed by shallow-frying in fat, then partially covered with a liquid and cooked slowly under cover in the oven.

POT ROASTING

This cooking method is done in an enclosed pot and again is used chiefly for less tender cuts of meat. It was originally used for cuts of meat not large enough to roast by the traditional method. It is usually first browned in fat and the meat then cooks in its own juices.

STEWING

Applied to any food which is cooked slowly in a small amount of liquid in an enclosed pot.

BOILING

The cooking of meat by total immersion in a liquid kept at or just below boiling point.

POACHING

Chiefly used for fish, eggs, but also for certain cuts of some white meat. The food is cooked very slowly with a minimum of liquid and should never fully reach boiling point.

STEAMING

Applied to any food cooked in the moist heat of steam. The food may be placed in a perforated container over a pan of boiling water, or enclosed in a steamer or between plates and cooked by the heat of steam. Steaming is also applied to food cooked in a bowl or basin in a pan of boiling water.

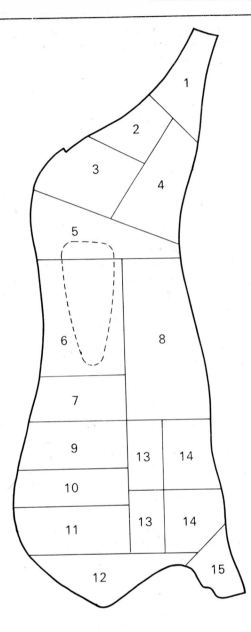

BEEF

Dissection of Beef

1.　Shin

2.　Silverside

3.　Topside

4.　Thick Flank

5.　Rump

6.　Fillet, Sirloin

7.　Wing Ribs

8.　Thin Flank

9.　Fore Ribs

10.　Middle Ribs

11.　Chuck Ribs

12.　Neck

13.　Flat Ribs

14.　Brisket

15.　Fore Shin

ROASTING (BEEF)

Suitable cuts are fillet and sirloin, and wing, fore and middle ribs.

Preparation

Sirloin on the bone. Trim off any surplus fat and remove the fillet. Saw through the chine bone and remove the tough sinew. Tie up the joint if necessary.

Baron of beef. This is two sirloins joined at the spine and with the rumps attached. Trim off any surplus fat and remove the fillet.

Boned sirloin. Remove the bones, excess fat and sinew. Leave flat or roll up and tie firmly with string.

Fillet. Trim the fillet by removing sinews and fat. It may be divided into three portions as it is of uneven thickness. The top or widest part is usually used for steaks, the middle part may be roasted whole, while the end piece or tail can be cut into steaks or chunks.

Lard the fillet for roasting with ¼ in strips of fat bacon.

Wing ribs. Cut through the chine bone, leaving it attached.

Fore ribs. Remove the nerve and tough sinew.

Middle ribs. Saw through the rib bones on the underside. Trim off any excess fat and tie firmly with string.

Bastings and Dredgings

Before cooking, sprinkle with a mixture of freshly ground black pepper and powdered English mustard; salt should never be used. Alternatively, sprinkle with a mixture of flour and breadcrumbs.

Method of Roasting

Melt fat or dripping in a roasting tin and seal the meat. Set it on a bed of chopped bones and place in a hot oven at 400°F, gas mark 6, for 20-25 minutes.

Reduce the heat to 325°F, gas mark 3, and baste frequently. Allow approximately 15-20 minutes per lb. Beef should traditionally be served underdone.

When cooked, remove the meat from the tin, pour off any surplus fat, add brown stock to the pan residues and bring to the boil. Simmer gently to reduce the gravy slightly. Season, strain and skim and serve with the roast.

Accompaniments

Yorkshire pudding, horseradish sauce, mustard, roast potatoes and parsnips.

GRILLING (BEEF)

Rump, fillet, sirloin and wing ribs are suitable for grilling as boned steaks.

Preparation

Sirloin. Cut boned sirloin into steaks, usually ½-1 in thick slices.

Fillet. Large steaks are cut from the top part which may give two or three portions. Slightly smaller steaks, ¾-1 in thick, are cut from the middle, each serving one portion.

Wing rib. This cut may be boned like a sirloin

(see Roasting) and cut into steaks, ½-1 in thick.

Rib bones. These may be grilled if there is enough meat left on them.

Rump. Trim the boned rump of excess fat and sinew. Cut thick slices across the grain and divide into two or three even-sized steaks.

Brush all steaks with melted fat or oil and season with pepper.

Method of Grilling

Place the steaks on a pre-heated, greased grid and cook under a hot grill, basting and turning. The degree of cooking depends on preference for rare, underdone, medium or well-done.

Cooking time depends on the thickness and tenderness of the steaks. To test for readiness, press the surface. The more underdone the steak, the greater the springiness and the more evidence of blood.

Devilled Beef Bones. Rib bones may be brushed with a mixture of mustard, cayenne pepper, salt, vinegar and Worcestershire sauce prior to and during grilling.

Accompaniments

Traditionally served with the pan juices and garnished with a pat of plain butter or parsley butter on top; grilled mushrooms are also usual.

FRYING (BEEF)

Suitable cuts for shallow-frying are steaks or slices cut from the fillet, sirloin and wing ribs. They are prepared as for grilling.

Method of Frying

Pre-heat a pan containing a minimum of fat and/or oil. Put in the meat and turn once during cooking. The time depends on the thickness and tenderness of the steak, on individual preference and on the amount of heat used. By pressing the surface of the steak, the degree of cooking can to some extent be determined: the greater the springiness and the more evidence of blood, the rarer the steak.

Remove the steaks to a serving dish, boil up the pan juices for a few minutes to concentrate them; drain off excess fat and pour the juices over the meat.

Accompaniments

Traditionally served with fried onions, creamed potatoes or chips.

BRAISING AND POT ROASTING (BEEF)

Less tender, large cuts of beef, such as topside, silverside, thick flank, rump and middle and chuck ribs, are best braised or pot roasted. Middle and chuck ribs should be boned and the tough sinews removed; tie firmly with string to retain shape.

The other cuts may be left in one piece and tied to keep shape during cooking; alternatively divide them into steaks.

Method of Braising

Fry diced fat pork in a deep, heavy-based pan to extract the fat. Add diced carrots, celery and onions and cook until light brown. Add the meat and seal on all sides. Sprinkle with flour.

Pour in enough brown stock to come three quarters of the way up the meat, add a faggot of herbs and pepper; bring to the boil. Cover with a tight-fitting lid and place in the oven at 350°F, gas mark 4.

Baste and turn the meat during the cooking; allow approximately 35 minutes per lb plus an extra 35 minutes.

To serve, remove the meat from the pan. Reduce the liquid to the required consistency, strain, skim and season. The meat may be served whole or in slices, garnished with glazed carrots, turnips, sliced onions, button onions, peas, French beans or mushrooms.

Methods of Pot Roasting

1.   Dredge the meat with seasoned flour, brown on all sides in beef dripping and place on a trivet or shallow wire grid. Add about 5 fl oz hot water or stock, cover with a tight-fitting lid and cook very gently, allowing 30-35 minutes per lb plus an extra 35 minutes.

To serve, remove the meat and reduce the sauce to the required consistency; season and serve with the meat.

2.   Dredge the meat with seasoned flour and brown in dripping as before. Leave the meat in the pan, dispersing with the trivet, and cover tightly with a lid. Cook over gentle heat, allowing the same time as above, but turning the meat frequently to prevent burning.

3.   Vegetables may be pot-roasted with the meat. For a 4 lb boned beef joint allow roughly 1½ lb diced carrots, onions and celery. Fry the vegetables lightly in butter and add a faggot of herbs and pepper.

Brown the meat (dredged with seasoned flour) separately in dripping and place on top of the vegetables. Add enough brown stock to come level with the top of the vegetables and cover the meat with larding bacon.

Put a lid on the pan and cook as above, over gentle heat. To serve, lift out the meat and arrange the vegetables round it; reduce the pan liquids to make a gravy.

STEWING (BEEF)

The most suitable cuts for stewing include the less tender joints such as shin and fore shin, topside, silverside and thin flank, chuck and flat ribs and the neck. All should be boned, the tough sinews and excess fat removed and the meat diced.

Method of Stewing

There are numerous variations of stews based on the method of simmering diced meat and vegetables in water; colour, flavour and method of thickening are therefore variable.

Dust the meat with seasoned flour and fry until brown in melted dripping; add sliced onions and continue frying until lightly browned.

Add brown stock and bring to the boil. Add carrots cut into strips and an equal amount of sliced turnips. Cover and simmer for 2-2½ hours or until the meat is tender; or cover and place in a moderate oven at 350°F, gas mark 4, for 2-2½ hours.

BOILING (BEEF)

Large cuts of shin and fore shin, silverside, thin flank and brisket are the most suitable for boiling.

Preparation

Fore shin and shin. May be boned out or left on the bone; used for stocks and broths.

Silverside. May be pickled or fresh; left whole.

Thin flank. Remove excess fat, trim and roll up and tie to shape with string.

Brisket. May be used pickled or fresh. Remove excess fat, trim and roll up and tie with string.

Method of Boiling

Put the meat in a large pan with enough water to cover. Add salt with fresh beef. Bring to the boil and remove any scum that rises to the surface. Add a faggot of herbs and two or three onions studded with cloves.

Reduce the heat, cover and simmer. Allow 30 minutes per lb, and 30 minutes extra for joints of 3 lb and under; 45 minutes per lb for joints over 3 lb. About 45 minutes before the end of cooking time, add chopped leeks, diced carrots and diced turnips; suet or parsley dumplings may be added for the last 20 minutes.

To serve, remove the beef and serve garnished with vegetables and dumplings, or use the broth and vegetables for soup.

Boiled Salt Beef

Rub a boned topside or silverside joint all over with salt, a little brown sugar and about 1 oz of saltpetre. Set aside in a covered bowl for a week, turning from time to time; the meat will keep for 8 weeks in the salt. Soak the meat overnight in fresh water, rinse, put in a pan with fresh warm water and proceed as for fresh boiled beef, allowing 1 hour per lb.

Boiled Spiced Silverside

4 lb salted silverside
6 oz chopped onions
½ lb sliced carrots
2 oz chopped celery
4 oz sliced turnips
8 cloves
4 oz brown sugar
½ teaspoon dry mustard
1 teaspoon ground cinnamon
Juice of ½ orange

Soak the meat overnight, put in a large pan with the vegetables, cover with water and bring slowly to the boil; remove scum, cover with a lid and simmer until tender, allowing 1 hour per lb.

Leave to cool in the liquid, drain and put into a roasting tin with cloves stuck into the meat. Mix together the remaining ingredients and spread over the meat. Bake in the centre of the oven at 400°F, gas mark 6, for 45 minutes, basting from time to time.

Serve hot or cold.

Pressed Beef

4 lb salted brisket or pickled flank
4 oz onion stuck with cloves
6 oz sliced carrots
1 oz chopped celery
1 faggot of herbs
12 peppercorns

Soak the meat for 1 hour, immerse in sufficient water to cover and add the spices, herbs and vegetables. Bring to the boil and simmer for 3-4 hours until the meat is almost in shreds and the stock has almost boiled away. Remove faggot, peppercorns and studded onion.

Drain and press under a heavy weight for 24 hours. Serve cold with salads and pickles.

ROASTING (VEAL)

The leg, loin and best end of veal are the most suitable cuts for roasting.

Preparation

Leg. Remove the aitch bone, trim off top of knuckle bone and any excess sinew. Tie with string to retain shape.

Loin and best end. Remove chine bone and back sinew; trim meat and fat from the tips of rib bones.

Boned loin and best end. Remove chine bone, back sinew and rib bones; trim the flap, roll up and tie with string.

Forcemeats may be used with boned loin and best end.

Basting and Dredging

A skin of fat pork is usually placed on top of the meat or a piece of caul or flead wrapped round it.

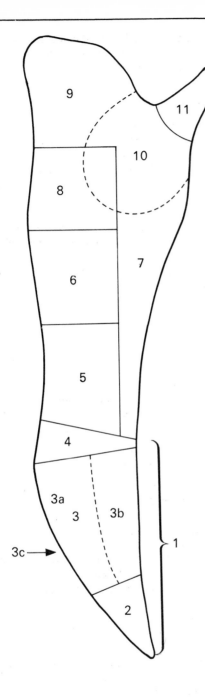

VEAL

Dissection of Veal

1. Leg
2. Knuckle
3. Round
3a. Cushion
3b. Thick Flank
3c. Undercushion
4. Rump
5. Loin
6. Best End
7. Breast or Tendons
8. Low Cutlets
9. Neck
10. Shoulder
11. Knuckle

Method of Roasting

Melt a little fat in a roasting tin and seal the meat; place on a bed of chopped bones; season. Cook in a hot oven at 400°F, gas mark 6, for 15-20 minutes; reduce the heat to 325°F, gas mark 3, and allow approximately 25-30 minutes per lb.

Baste frequently. Veal is traditionally served cooked through rather than underdone.

When cooked, remove the meat; pour off any surplus fat and retain the residue: add brown stock blended with arrowroot and bring to the boil. Simmer the gravy gently to reduce. Season, strain, skim and serve with the roast.

Accompaniments

Traditionally stuffed with lemon stuffing. Originally served with a piece of boiled bacon or ham; but baked or grilled bacon may be used instead; and roast or mashed potatoes.

FRYING (VEAL)

Veal is seldom grilled, but slices from the leg and cutlets from the loin and best end are suitable for frying.

Preparation

Leg. Bone the leg out to smaller cuts, remove all sinew and cut into collops across the grain. Beat these slices flat and thin.

Loin and best end. Trim the joint, remove the surplus breast flap; cut into cutlets.

Method of Frying

Pre-heat a pan with oil and/or clarified butter. Fry collops and cutlets as they are or coated with seasoned flour, egg and breadcrumbs: turn once during cooking.

Cooking time for the collops is 2-3 minutes on each side; cutlets require approximately 8-10 minutes.

Accompaniments

Serve with the pan juices, fried bacon and mushrooms.

POT ROASTING AND BRAISING (VEAL)

Suitable cuts for pot roasting include the leg, loin, best end, low cutlets, neck and shoulder cuts. Prepare the leg, loin and best end as for roasting, and cut the neck piece into cutlets for braising. Follow the basic methods for pot roasting of beef.

STEWING (VEAL)

Breast, neck and shoulder are the best cuts for stews; they should be boned and cut into dice, although the neck piece may also be cut into 2 in chunks on the bone.

Method of Stewing

Put the meat in a pan with 2 studded onions, a faggot of herbs and seasoning. Add white stock to cover, bring to the boil and skim. Reduce the heat, cover and simmer for approximately 1-1½ hours. Drain off the cooking liquid, remove the faggot and onion.

Make a white roux with butter and flour, add the liquid and some milk. Bring to the boil and simmer. Beat 1 oz butter into the sauce and add the meat.

Serve with grilled bacon rolls and crisp sippets of toast.

BOILING (VEAL)

The knuckle of veal and the neck are used whole in the preparation of broths, soups and stocks. Breast of veal is usually boned, spread with a veal forcemeat, rolled up and tied into shape.

Method of Boiling

Put the meat in a pan with enough boiling white stock to cover. Bring to the boil and add a faggot of herbs. Reduce the heat, cover and simmer, allowing 20 minutes per lb.

To serve, lift out the meat; make a parsley sauce with the cooking liquid. Serve with boiled potatoes, carrots and turnips. The meat may also be pressed and served cold with salads.

ROASTING (LAMB AND MUTTON)

Lamb and mutton are seldom pot roasted or braised, but practically all the cuts – leg, chump, saddle, best end, flank, shoulder – are ideal for oven roasting.

Preparation

Leg. On the bone. Shorten and trim the leg bone, remove aitch bone and trim off excess fat if necessary; tie into shape with string. Chop the

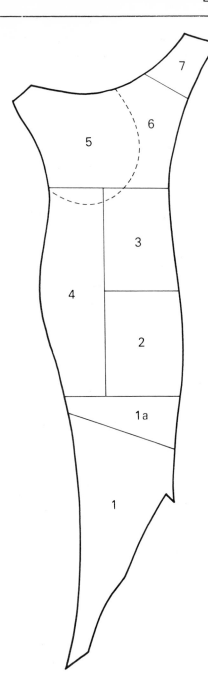

LAMB AND MUTTON

Dissection of Lamb and Mutton

1.   Leg

1a. Chump

2.   Saddle

3.   Best End

4.   Flank (Breast)

5.   Shoulder

6.   Neck

7.   Scrag End

bones and use as a bed for roasting.

Boned. Remove the aitch and leg bones; roll up and tie with string. Chop the bones and use as a bed for roasting.

Best end. Remove the whole chine bone and skin, excess fat, back sinew and the tip of the blade bone. Trim meat and fat from the tips of the rib bones. Score the fat lightly in a diamond pattern.

Saddle. Remove skin, kidneys and excess fat and sinew, especially from the surface of fillets. Trim the flaps at the sides and tuck in. Tie into shape and score the fat lightly in a diamond pattern.

Flank. Bone and remove excess fat and skin. Roll up and tie with string.

Shoulder (boned). Trim the knuckle bone, leaving a few inches of trimmed bone. Bone out the long upper arm bone and the shoulder blade bone. Roll up and tie with string.

Crown roast. Use two pieces of best end each with six or seven cutlets. Remove the chine and blade bones and trim away the meat from the top ½ in of the ribs. Bend the cutlets round into the shape of a crown, with the skin side towards the centre. Tie or sew the two pieces together firmly. Fill the centre with a stuffing, cover exposed ends of bone with foil or buttered paper to prevent burning.

Whirligig. This is similar to crown roast, but with the skin side of the meat turned to the outside. Use saddle instead of best end of neck.

Guard of Honour. Use the same cuts and amount of meat as for crown roast and prepare in the same way, but instead of shaping the meat into a circle, the two pieces are sewn together along the long sides and the trimmed bones interlaced over the top. The space between the arch is stuffed with forcemeat.

Forcemeats

These are used with boned leg, flank, shoulder, crown roast and guard of honour.

Bastings and Dredgings

Anchovies. Used with shoulder of lamb.

4 finely chopped anchovy fillets
1 clove garlic
Pepper and salt
½ pt brown stock
½ pt port
1 teaspoon mushroom ketchup

Insert the slivers of garlic under the top skin and dust the outside with black pepper. Roast the meat until half cooked; add the anchovies, stock, port, ketchup, salt and pepper. Baste frequently.

Apple juice. For joints stuffed with apple cider and ginger stuffing.

Ground ginger
Ground pepper
Butter
Apple juice

Rub the joint with ginger and ground pepper. Place apple juice and butter in the pan with the roast and baste frequently.

Brown sugar. With saddle of lamb.

2 oz brown sugar
1 glass red wine

Dredge the joint with sugar. Pour the red wine into the pan with the roast and baste frequently.

Buckinghamshire paste. Used for saddle of lamb.

2 tablespoons Worcestershire sauce
1 teaspoon anchovy essence
1 tablespoon made mustard
2 finely chopped onions

Mix all the ingredients and put in the pan with the roast; baste frequently.

Caul or lamb's flead. With leg of lamb.

Wrap the caul (flead or leaf) around the meat to act as a basting during cooking; used especially with the lean, but delicate Welsh mountain sheep.

In Cheshire, Shropshire and Staffordshire and other counties bordering Wales, lamb is often sold already wrapped in caul.

Guinness. For rolled, stuffed breast of lamb.

Pour ½ pt Guinness into the pan with the roast; baste frequently.

Herbs. For any roasting joint.

Sprinkle chopped mint, thyme, rosemary or marjoram over the joint before cooking.

Mint and lemon. For leg of lamb.

4 oz melted butter
1 teaspoon chopped mint
Juice of 1 lemon

Put all the ingredients in the pan with the roast and baste frequently.

Orange juice. For any roasting joint, add the juice of one orange to the pan juices and baste.

Port and treacle. For leg of mutton.

1 tablespoon port
1 teaspoon treacle, apple or red currant jelly
1 clove garlic

Make a small incision close to the knuckle bone, pushing a wooden skewer down the leg bone as far as it will go. Pour the mixed wine and treacle down the hole and stop the hole with garlic. Leave to soak overnight before roasting.

Method of Roasting

Melt fat in a roasting tin and seal the meat. Season. Set on a bed of chopped bones and carrots and place in the oven at 400°F, gas mark 6, for 20-30 minutes. Reduce the heat to 325°F, gas mark 3; baste frequently.

Allow approximately 20-25 minutes per lb plus an extra 20 minutes. Lamb and mutton are traditionally served cooked through rather than underdone. Leave to stand for 10-15 minutes before carving.

When cooked, pour off the surplus fat, retaining the residue; add brown stock and bring to the boil. Simmer gently to reduce the gravy. Season, strain and skim. Serve with the roast.

Accompaniments

Fat lamb and mutton roasts are traditionally served with red currant jelly while the leaner roasts are served with rowan jelly. Salt marsh mutton is served with laver sauce or pickled samphire, young lamb with mint sauce or jelly, boiled new potatoes and spring vegetables. Mutton is accompanied with onion or capers sauce, red currant jelly, roast potatoes and haricot beans, turnips, onions and parsnips.

GRILLING (LAMB AND MUTTON)

Cutlets and chops from the chump, saddle and best end are excellent for both grilling and frying.

Preparation

Best end cutlets. Cut even-sized cutlets between each bone of a prepared best end.

Saddle chops. Cut into large chops across the saddle including the kidney.

Loin chops. Chop through the centre of the backbone, along the length of the spine of the saddle. Trim and skin each loin. Stand the loin upright and cut into chops.

Method of Grilling

Place on a pre-heated, greased grid. Cook under a hot grill, basting and turning the chops or cutlets. Cooking time depends on thickness and tenderness; allow approximately 5 minutes on each side for a medium-sized tender cutlet which should be cooked through.

Accompaniments

Fresh green peas cooked with mint, plain butter or parsley butter, mashed potatoes.

FRYING (LAMB AND MUTTON)

Use the same cuts as for grilling and prepare the cutlets and chops similarly. Cutlets may be coated with seasoned flour, egg and fresh white breadcrumbs.

Method of Frying

Pre-heat a pan containing a minimum of fat and/or oil. Put in the meat and turn once during cooking. Time depends on thickness and tenderness of the meat, but allow approximately 7 minutes on each side. Serve with the pan juices.

Accompaniments

Parsley butter, green peas cooked with mint, mashed potatoes.

STEWING (LAMB AND MUTTON)

All cuts of lamb and mutton with the exception of best end are used for brown and white stews.

Preparation

Leg. Cut in slices (gigot chops).

Chump. Cut in slices (chump chops).

Saddle. Cut into chops.

Flank. Remove skin, excess fat and hard edge. Cut into strips of two bones, then across to make approximately 2 in squares.

Shoulder. Bone as for roasting and cut into small dice.

Neck. Remove excess fat and gristle; cut between the bone into cutlets and trim.

Scrag end. Cut down through the middle, remove fat and gristle and cut, with the bones, into 2 in pieces. It may also be boned and cut into dice.

Methods of Stewing

For brown lamb or mutton stews follow stewing methods for beef.

White Stew. Put the meat in a pan with layers of 1 lb sliced onions and 2 lb sliced potatoes. Season and place a faggot of herbs in the middle. Add 1 pt white stock and bring to the boil.

Reduce the heat and simmer for approximately 2-2½ hours or until the meat is tender. Alternatively cover and cook for 2-2½ hours in the oven at 350°F, gas mark 4.

To serve, sprinkle with chopped parsley.

BOILING (LAMB AND MUTTON)

Mutton rather than lamb is used for boiling, leg, flank, shoulder and scrag end being the most suitable cuts; the last is chiefly used for broths, the other cuts are prepared as for roasting.

Method of Boiling

Put the meat in a large pan with enough water to cover. Bring to the boil and remove any scum that rises. Add a faggot of herbs and two or three onions studded with cloves. Reduce the heat, cover and simmer. Allow 20-25 minutes per lb plus an extra 20-25 minutes.

Diced carrots and turnips may be added for the last 45 minutes of cooking. To serve, remove the meat and place on a serving dish; garnish with the vegetables and serve with a capers sauce.

ROASTING (PORK)

The leg, loin, spare rib and shoulder (hand and spring) are suitable pork cuts for roasting.

Preparation

Leg. Remove the aitch bone and trotters, trim off excess fat, score the rind, diagonally or in a diamond pattern. Tie to shape if necessary.

Loin. Trim away excess fat and remove the back sinew; saw through chine bone; score the rind as for leg and tie with string.

Boned loin. Remove the fillet and bone the loin; trim off excess fat and remove back sinew. Place the fillet or stuffing in the centre and roll up; score the rind as for leg and tie with string. Chop the bones and use as a bed for roasting.

Spare rib. Remove all excess fat and sinew; tie in a few places with string.

Forcemeats

Herb and fruit stuffings are used with boned loin.

Bastings

For all roasting joints.

Onion and mustard.

4 oz finely chopped onions
1 teaspoon dry mustard
Salt and pepper

Rub the outside of the joint with oil or lard, then coat with the mixture.

Mix any of the following combinations and use to coat roasting joints after brushing with oil or melted lard.

Breadcrumbs and pig's brain
2 oz boiled and chopped pig's brain
2 oz white breadcrumbs
1 tablespoon sugar
1 oz butter
Flour and breadcrumbs
2 oz flour
2 oz white breadcrumbs
Salt and pepper
Herbs and breadcrumbs
2 teaspoons each, chopped parsley, marjoram and thyme
1½ oz white breadcrumbs
Lemon and orange peel
Grated rind of 1 orange and 1 lemon
¾ oz white breadcrumbs
Egg yolks and spices
1 egg yolk beaten with pinch of nutmeg, ginger and pepper
1½ oz white breadcrumbs
1 oz sugar
Coriander and fennel
1 teaspoon each, coriander and fennel seeds pounded with

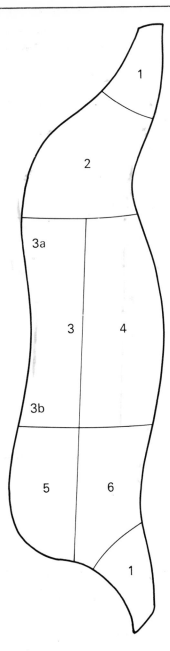

PORK

Dissection of Pork

1. Trotters

2. Leg

3. Loin

3a. Saddle

3b. Best End

4. Belly

5. Spare Rib

6. Shoulder

1 teaspoon cinnamon
1 oz sugar
¾ oz flour
    Lemon juice
Rub the joint with half a lemon until the juice is
absorbed by the meat.

Method of Roasting

Place the meat in a roasting tin on a bed of chopped
bones. Melt a little dripping and pour over the
meat. Set in the oven at 425°F, gas mark 7, for 20
minutes. Reduce the heat to 350°F, gas mark 4.

Allow approximately 25 minutes per lb plus
an extra 25 minutes. Pork must be served
thoroughly cooked. When cooked, remove
the meat to a tray, pour off surplus fat,
retaining the residue; add some brown stock
and chopped root vegetables and bring to the
boil. Simmer gently to reduce the gravy and

thicken slightly with arrowroot. Season, strain, skim and serve with the roast.

Accompaniments

Worcestershire sauce. Add 1 tablespoon sauce to the prepared gravy.

Sultanas and sherry. Soak 2 oz sultanas in 2½ fl oz sherry and 1 oz sugar for 2 hours. Heat in a pan, stirring until the sugar has dissolved; add to the prepared gravy.

Cream and prune juice. Stuff the joint with chopped prunes, and add 2 tablespoons double cream to the prepared gravy.

Wine and spices. Boil 5 fl oz white wine, 6 cloves, 2 oz sugar and ½ teaspoon cinnamon to a syrup and add to the prepared gravy.

Vinegar, butter and egg yolk. Blend the yolks of 4 hardboiled eggs with 1 oz butter and 2½ fl oz vinegar; add to the prepared gravy.

Sage and onion. Chop 4 oz onions and 10 sage leaves; infuse in the brown stock for 30 minutes before making the gravy.

Apple sauce and sage and onion stuffing are traditional with roast pork. The gravy of pan juices may be variously flavoured.

GRILLING (PORK)

Loin chops cut from the saddle and cutlets from the best end as well as the trotters are suitable for grilling. They are traditionally served with apple sauce.

Preparation

Loin. Remove the skin, excess fat and sinew; cut between the bones in approximately ½-1 in chops from the saddle piece, cutlets from the best end. Trim and remove excess bone. Brush with oil or melted fat and season.

Trotters. Clean, split in two lengthways; boil and cool; remove the meat in one piece.

Method of Grilling

Chops, cutlets. Place on a pre-heated, greased grid; cook under a hot grill, turning the chops or cutlets during cooking. The time depends on thickness and tenderness; allow approximately 7-10 minutes on each side for a medium-sized tender chop or cutlet.

Trotters. Brush with oil and mustard; season and sprinkle with breadcrumbs. Cook under a hot grill, skin side up until golden brown.

FRYING (PORK)

Loin chops and cutlets as well as trotters are suitable for both frying and grilling and are prepared in a similar manner. Serve hot with apple sauce or fried apple rings.

Method of Frying

Pre-heat a pan containing the minimum amount of fat and/or oil. Put in the meat and turn once during cooking. Time depends on thickness and tenderness of the meat, but allow about 7 minutes on each side. Serve with the pan juices.

STEWING (PORK)

Loin chops, boned, and diced belly and shoulder of pork are suitable for stewing by the same methods as for beef.

BOILING (PORK)

Several pork cuts are suitable for boiling. Thoroughly cleaned, scrubbed trotters are split or left whole; the leg trimmed of aitch bone, trotters and excess fat; the belly, usually brined, is left in one piece, and the shoulder is usually boned and tied into shape with string.

Method of Boiling

Put the meat in a large pan with enough water to cover; bring to the boil and remove the scum as it rises. Add a faggot of herbs and two onions studded with cloves. Reduce the heat, cover and simmer, allowing 20 minutes per lb, plus an extra 20 minutes. To serve, lift out the meat and serve with apple sauce and boiled potatoes.

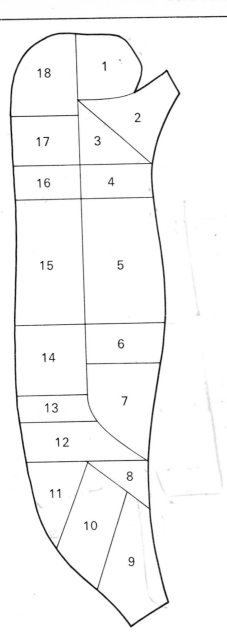

BACON AND GAMMON

Dissection of Bacon

1. Small Hock ⎫
2. Fore Slipper ⎬ Fore Hock
3. Butt ⎭
4. Top Streaky
5. Prime Streaky
6. Thin Streaky
7. Flank
8. Gammon Slipper
9. Gammon Hock
10. Middle Gammon
11. Corner Gammon
12. Long Back
13. Oyster
14. Short Back
15. Back and Ribs
16. Top Back
17. Prime Collar
18. End Collar

GRILLING AND FRYING (BACON AND GAMMON)

The principal cooking methods for bacon and gammon are grilling and frying, stewing and boiling, the latter sometimes with a baked finish. All cuts from the bacon pig are suitable for grilling.

Preparation

Gammon. Remove the rind from the slices, ½ in thick and cut from the middle of the gammon across the grain; trim. Snip round the edges of the fat to prevent them curling up.

Bacon rashers. Remove the rind and gristle from rashers cut across the grain.

Method of Grilling

Gammon steaks. Place on a pre-heated, greased grid and cook under a hot grill for approximately 7 minutes on each side.

Rashers. Grill both sides for about 2-3 minutes.

Method of Frying

Shallow-fry to the required degree of crispness in a small amount of fat, turning once.

Accompaniments

Serve with grilled tomatoes, mushrooms and fried eggs. Fried bread is also served with fried gammon and bacon.

STEWING (BACON)

Fore hock and end collar are usually boned and rolled and cooked in one piece. They may, however, like top streaky, prime streaky and flank, be diced; the latter three are also cut into rashers for stewing.

Method of Stewing (Bacon)

Whole piece. Soak the bacon overnight if salty. Put in a pan and cover with water, bring to the boil; add a bay leaf and a few peppercorns. Reduce the heat, cover and simmer for 30 minutes.

Meanwhile, fry a few chopped onions, diced carrots and diced parsnips in lard to an even brown colour; add the vegetables and continue simmering for 1½-2 hours or until tender.

To serve, lift out the meat and place on a serving dish; surround with the vegetables.

Diced rashers. Arrange in layers in a pan with chopped onions, sliced potatoes, seasoning and a bay leaf. Cover with water and bring to the boil. Reduce the heat and simmer for 1½-2 hours.

BOILING (BACON)

For boiling, the most suitable cuts are whole gammon and ham, whole gammon hock, a whole piece of top back and ribs and boned and rolled fore hock, prime collar and end collar. Flank, in one piece, is mainly boiled for use in broths.

Method of Boiling

Put the meat in a large pan with enough water to cover, bring to the boil and remove the scum as it rises. Add a bay leaf and a few peppercorns; reduce the heat, cover and simmer, allowing 20 minutes per lb plus 20 minutes.

To serve, remove the meat, strip off the skin and serve hot or cold.

Gammon; ham. Soak in cold water overnight if very salty. Rinse and place in a large pan, cover with fresh cold water and bring to the boil; remove scum.

Reduce the heat, cover and simmer for 20-25 minutes per lb. Leave to cool in the cooking liquid, then remove rind and excess fat. Brush with English mustard and sprinkle with freshly fried breadcrumbs. Clean the knuckle bone and cover with a frill.

Finishes

Strip the skin off the ham or gammon while still warm and dust with a coating of browned crumbs. Crisp in a hot oven for 10-15 minutes.

Slash through the fat in a diamond pattern and stick a clove in each; this decoration is used with a brown sugar glaze.

Leaf patterns cut from the removed skin can be "nailed" back on to the fat with cloves.

Arrange daisy patterns from hardboiled egg white and yolk on breadcrumbs with sprigs of parsley.

Stamp out small rounds of bread with a pastry cutter, fry and colour in the oven and arrange on the fat of a skinned ham.

POULTRY AND GAME

All the basic cooking methods of roasting, grilling, frying and boiling are applicable to poultry, game birds and furred game. These food items, how-ever, differ from meat in the methods of preparation which include hanging, plucking, drawing and trussing, irrespective of the chosen cooking method.

ROASTING (POULTRY AND GAME BIRDS)

All types of poultry — chicken, duck, goose, guinea fowl and turkey — are suitable for roasting. The most commonly available game birds are grouse, partridge, pheasant, pigeon, ptarmigan, quail, snipe, wild duck and woodcock.

Preparation

Plucking. Hold the bird in one hand; pulling the feathers against the way they are lying, give a sharp jerk, taking care not to break the skin.

Begin plucking under one wing, working over the back, then under the other wing. Work over the breast and down to the tail and lastly pull out pinion feathers.

Drawing. Singe the bird by holding it over a small gas flame or by moving a lighted taper over it, being careful not to blacken or scorch the skin. Cut the skin round the legs, above the foot, break the bone at this point and draw out the sinews.

Cut the neck skin along the back and remove the crop and windpipe. Cut the neck off close to the body, leaving a long piece of neck skin. Push the fingers into the neck opening and loosen heart and lungs.

Enlarge the vent opening, push the fingers round the skeleton and loosen the intestines, being careful not to break them. With two fingers of one hand secure the gizzard and pull out all the internal organs.

Separate the edible offals — heart, liver and gizzard. Split the heart and soak in cold water; remove the gall bladder from the liver. Split the gizzard and discard the lining and contents. The gizzard, neck, feet and heart are used to make stock for gravy to be served with poultry and game; it may also be used as a foundation for soup. Gizzard of duck cannot be opened and both knobs should be cut off.

Stuffing and trussing. To stuff a bird, loosen the skin at the neck end, remove the wishbone and insert the stuffing over the breast flesh and fill the loose neck skin with as much as it will hold. Fold the skin over.

Stuff the body cavity three quarters full. Make a slit in the skin above the vent hole and pull the tail (parson's nose) through. Fold the wings back to hold the neck skin in position.

Place the bird on its back; draw the legs forward and press them towards the breast. Pass the trussing needle through the body near the thigh joint, then through the wings and over the neck flap. Tie the loose ends firmly. To secure the legs, pass the needle through the loose skin above the legs, below the tip of the breast bone and return the needle below the legs through the back. Pull the two loose ends firmly and tie.

Sprinkle with salt and pepper, cover breast with slices of fat bacon or bird fat, or brush with melted butter. Cover with buttered greaseproof paper or wrap in foil.

Duck and goose. These should not be stuffed at the neck end nor be covered with bacon or fat. Prick the breast and rub it with salt.

Game birds. Most game birds are drawn and trussed as already described, but the legs are usually crossed when trussing.

Small game birds which roast in a short time are usually barded, which consists of tying thin slices of bacon or salted pork fat over the breast. Barding is unnecessary in the case of pheasants and poultry and other game which have sufficient natural fat.

Woodcock and snipe. Only the intestines and the gizzards are removed prior to cooking; the heart, lungs and liver are left in the bird. Do not cut off the head or feet, but press the legs close to the body, crossing them at the knee joints, turn the head under the left wing and pass the long bill through the thighs and body, the bill acting as a skewer. These birds may also be left undrawn as the trail or intestines is considered a delicacy in fresh birds.

Hanging. Game birds are usually hung in order to develop the flavour. The period for hanging game depends on the age and type of bird, the time spent in transit, the weather and personal preference. They are hung by the neck, before plucking, in a cool, dry, airy place.

Pheasants may be hung for 6-14 days, partridges for 7-8 days, grouse for 3-4 days while water birds, such as wild duck, teal and widgeon, should hang for only 2 days otherwise a rancid flavour develops. In warm humid weather allow a shorter hanging period.

Forcemeats

Game birds are not stuffed, with the exception of pigeon which may have a barley stuffing. Poultry may be stuffed with a number of different forcemeats, but the traditional stuffings are herb for chicken, sage and onion for duck and goose, raisin for guinea fowl and chestnut and sausage meat for turkey.

Method of Roasting

Chicken, capon, turkey, guinea fowl, pigeon. Melt fat in a roasting tin and seal the bird on all sides. Season and place in a hot oven, 375°F, gas mark 5. For poussin, allow 10 minutes on each side. Finish with the breast upwards for 10-15 minutes.

For roasting chicken, allow 15-20 minutes on each side. Finish with the breast upwards for 15-20 minutes. For turkey and capon reduce the heat to 325°F, gas mark 3, and allow 20 minutes per lb.

For guinea fowl and pigeon allow approximately one hour total roasting time.

To test for readiness, pierce the thigh with a needle; if the juice is free of blood and the leg and drumstick come away easily from the body when gently pulled, roasting is complete.

When cooked, lift out the bird and remove the trussing string; pour off any surplus fat, retaining the residue and add giblet stock. Bring to the boil and simmer to reduce the gravy. Season, strain and skim. Serve with the bird.

Duck, goose, duckling, gosling. Brush the bird lightly with fat, prick the breast and seal in a roasting tin. Season; place in the oven at 375°F, gas mark 5, and allow 20-25 minutes per lb plus an extra 20 minutes. Turn frequently. When cooked, remove the string from the bird and keep warm. Pour off surplus fat, retaining the residue and add giblet stock; bring to the boil and simmer to reduce the gravy. Season, strain and skim. Serve with the bird.

Game birds. Melt fat in a roasting tin and seal the birds on all sides. Season. Place in a hot oven, at 400°F, gas mark 6, then 350°F, gas mark 4.

Roasting times for young game birds.

Grouse	30 minutes
Partridge	30 minutes
Pheasant	45 minutes
Pigeon	60 minutes
Ptarmigan	45 minutes
Quail	45 minutes
Snipe	45 minutes
Wild Duck	45 minutes
Woodcock	30 minutes

When cooked, remove string from the bird; pour off any surplus fat, retaining the residue and add game stock. Bring to the boil and simmer to reduce the gravy. Season, strain and skim. Serve with the bird.

Accompaniments

Chicken and guinea fowl. Traditionally served with bread sauce, bacon rolls, small pork sausages, roast potatoes, watercress, peas.

Turkey. Bread sauce, cranberry sauce, bacon rolls, Brussels sprouts, roast potatoes and baked sausages which when draped in an unbroken link across the breast is known as an "alderman in chains".

Goose. Apple sauce, bread sauce, boiled potatoes, greens.

Gosling. Watercress, green gooseberry sauce or sorrel sauce.

Duck. Apple sauce, peas, roast potatoes.

Game birds. Bread sauce, fried crumbs, chip potatoes, watercress, green salad, slice of fried or toasted bread on which to serve the bird.

GRILLING (POULTRY AND GAME BIRDS)

Chicken is the most suitable poultry for grilling, such as small poussins and joints of chickens. Game is seldom grilled although young pigeons may be treated as chicken.

Preparation

Prepare the bird as for roasting but do not truss it. Remove the backbone by inserting a knife through the chicken from tail to the neck and cutting along one side of backbone, open the chicken out and chop the bone away.

Lay the chicken flat and remove rib bones and any congealed blood. Break the leg and insert through the skin below the breast tip.

Marinate in oil, lemon juice, salt and pepper for 10-15 minutes.

Method of Grilling

Place on a pre-heated, greased grid. Cook under a hot grill, basting and turning. Allow approximately 15 to 20 minutes on each side.

Accompaniments

Halfway through grilling brush with a mixture of mustard, cayenne, Worcestershire sauce and vinegar in proportions depending on individual taste. Cover with white breadcrumbs and melted butter. Finish the grilling and serve with devil sauce.

Before grilling is complete, sprinkle with white breadcrumbs; pour over melted butter and finish grilling, basting frequently. Serve with grilled bacon, tomatoes and mushrooms.

FRYING (POULTRY AND GAME BIRDS)

Chicken joints such as leg joints, quartered, halved or whole split birds are commonly used for frying; game birds may be similarly prepared and cooked.

Preparation

Prepare as for roasting, but do not truss. Remove the feet above knuckle bone and take off leg joints by cutting the skin where the leg joins the body; cut into the ball joint and socket, press out the leg and cut through joints to give the thigh and drumstick.

Clean the knuckle from each end of the bone; on the drumstick cut the meat carefully back from the knuckle end and chop off the exposed bone halfway up the drumstick, leaving about 1½ in of bone. Push the meat back into shape and pull the skin in place.

Cut the white meat into four equal pieces. First remove the small wings, then separate the breast from the back of carcass and cut diagonally into two portions; trim the winglets at both ends. Season and dust with seasoned flour.

Method of Frying

Pre-heat a pan with oil and/or butter and add the joints; dark meat usually takes longer to cook than white meat. Cook quickly until golden brown on all sides, turning several times. Reduce the heat or transfer to a moderate oven. Cover and finish frying in 10-15 minutes. Serve with the pan juices, fried bacon and tomatoes.

BOILING (POULTRY AND GAME BIRDS)

Other types of poultry, e.g. fowl, duck, small turkeys and pigeons, are suitable for boiling. Prepare the birds as for roasting, including stuffing if liked.

The same types of poultry are suitable for stewing by the same methods as hare and rabbit.

Method of Boiling

Put in a large pan and cover with cold water. Bring to the boil and remove the scum; add a faggot of herbs, an onion studded with cloves, 1 oz chopped celery and ½ lb whole peeled carrots.

Reduce the heat, cover and simmer, allowing 20-30 minutes per lb, depending on size and age of the bird.

Lift out the bird and keep warm. Strain the cooking liquid and use in the preparation of an accompanying sauce. The bird may also be left in the cooking liquid until cool and served cold.

STEWING (POULTRY AND GAME)

Any type of poultry and game bird may be stewed, older tougher birds being more suitable than young ones; they may be jointed or left whole. Both rabbit and hare are suitable as well as the neck and shoulder of venison. The leg and back joints of hare are well covered with meat and excellent for stewing. Bone and dice venison meat from neck, shoulder and flank.

ROASTING (VENISON)

The haunch, loin and saddle of venison are usually roasted while the less tender cuts are used for stewing (see above).

Preparation

Haunch. Remove the aitch bone; trim off excess fat and, if necessary, tie with string to shape. Chop the knuckle and aitch bones and use as a bed for roasting.

Loin, saddle. Trim off excess fat and remove the kidneys; trim the flaps at the sides, tuck in and tie into shape.

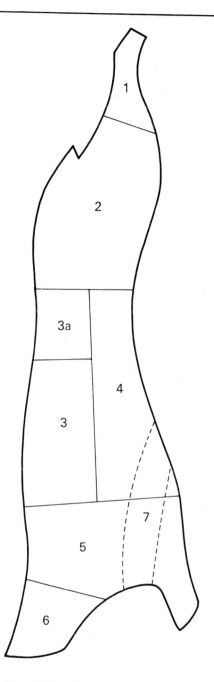

VENISON

Dissection of Venison

1. Hough

2. Haunch

3. Loin

3a. Saddle

4. Flank

5. Fore Shoulder

6. Neck

7. Brisket

Larding. Chill a piece of pork fat until firm and cut into strips 2 in long and just over 1/8 in wide. Thread a strip of fat into a larding needle and make a small stitch in the joint. Repeat until the whole joint is studded with fat. Pork fat may also be tied with string on to smaller pieces of meat and saddle of venison.

Lard the joint before marinating it.

Marinade. As roast venison can be dry and sometimes tough it is usually marinated prior to cooking. Joints for roasting should preferably be young; older animals are difficult to roast.

½ pt red wine or dry white wine
½ pt wine vinegar
½ pt oil

12 peppercorns
2 bay leaves
1 sliced lemon
2 sprigs thyme
Salt

Mix all the ingredients together in a large bowl
and leave for 1 hour before use. Add the meat,
set in a cool place and turn frequently. Marinate
for at least 24 hours. Strain the marinade and use
in cooking. Alternatively, use any of the following marinades.

1 pt wine vinegar
½ pt oil
Herbs and seasoning as above

Juice of 3 lemons
½ pt oil
Herbs and seasoning as above

½ pt claret
Juice of 3 lemons
Herbs and seasoning as above

Huff Paste. Large cuts, such as the haunch, which
require longer cooking are sometimes covered with
huff paste.

2½ lb flour
1 oz salt
5 oz lard
1 pt water

Rub the lard into the flour and salt and mix with
water to a fairly stiff dough. Leave for 1 hour
before use. Roll out to a large round shape, no
thicker than ¼ in; remove the haunch from the
marinade and wrap the paste round it; keep the
joins on the underside and seal well.

The joint may also be wrapped in foil or well
oiled greaseproof paper, or in paper before wrap-
ping in huff paste.

Method of Roasting

Melt fat in a roasting tin and seal the meat unless
it is encased in huff paste or foil. Place on a bed
of chopped bones. Season and pour over the
strained marinade. Place in a hot oven at 400°F,
gas mark 6, for 15-20 minutes, then reduce to
325°F, gas mark 3.

Allow approximately 20 minutes per lb; baste
frequently. When cooked, pour off any surplus
fat, retaining the residue and add game stock.

Bring to the boil and simmer gently to reduce
the gravy slightly. Season, strain and skim; serve
with the roast.

Accompaniments

Roast venison is traditionally served with roast or
boiled potatoes, rowan or red currant jelly, green
vegetables.

ROASTING (HARE AND RABBIT)

Saddle and baron of hare and rabbit are the most
suitable cuts for roasting. The other, tougher cuts
are more suitable for stewing and jugging (see
Stewing, Poultry and Game).

Preparation

Hare and rabbit are usually jointed after the
initial preparations which include paunching
and skinning. In addition, hares are first hung
from the hind legs for 4-5 days in hot weather,
10-14 days in cold weather. Rabbits are not
hung.

Paunching hare. Make an incision in the
middle of the belly to open the abdominal cavity,
from the legs to the ribs. Split the pelvic bone to
separate the legs and facilitate the removal of the
intestines. Place these in a basin reserved for this
purpose.

Break the thin skin which separates the intestines from the liver, heart and lungs and lift them
out. Remove the blood which is found in the
thoracic cavity and put it into a china basin with
a little vinegar to keep it fluid. Set the liver, lungs
and heart aside for later use.

Paunching rabbit. Rabbit is skinned soon after
killing and should not be hung.

Lay the rabbit on its back, slit the belly open
with a sharp knife or scissors, cutting through the
pelt first and laying it open. Remove the
intestines and set the kidneys, heart and liver
aside. Wipe with a damp cloth but do not wash,
or the pelt will become difficult to handle.

Skinning hare and rabbit. Cut the skin round
the first joint of the hind legs, cutting off the
paws completely. Push the hind legs up to the
belly, holding on to the pelt which will come
away easily.

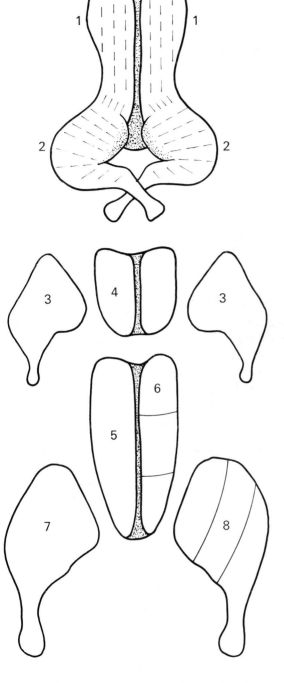

HARE AND RABBIT

Dressed joints

1. Saddle (larded)

2. Legs

3. Shoulders

4. Low Back

5. Back (fillet)

6. Back (cut into three)

7. Leg

8. Leg (cut into three)

Ease the pelt over the rump, snipping the tail bone if it resists pressure. Cut off the front paws at the first joint and pull the front legs through the pelt. The head should be cut off as part of the pelt.

Jointing hare and rabbit. Place the skinned animal on its belly, with the hindquarters to the front. Cut around the two arcs where the hindquarters join the pelvis. Turn over and cut along the insides of the legs, exposing the ball and

socket joints of the thigh bones. Sever the ligaments holding them together and remove the
legs which should look like elongated hams. Cut
round at right angles immediately above the hip
bones and twist the pelvis off. Discard.

Cut up and in below the lower ribs on each
side; take off the back in the same way. Run the
knife under the shoulder blades and remove the
front legs, attached only with muscle. Take the
feet off the hind legs by cutting the ligaments.

Method of Roasting

Remove the head and forelegs; cut the ribs short,
or leave in place and stuff the cavity. Lard with
pork fat as for venison.

Melt butter in a roasting tin and seal the meat.
Season. Place in a hot oven at 425°F, gas mark 7;
baste every 10 minutes. Allow approximately
45-50 minutes in total. Remove the hare to a
serving dish and keep warm.

Pour off surplus fat, retain the residue and
add 2½ fl oz game stock and 5 fl oz double
cream, Madeira or sherry; heat through and
pour over the hare. Garnish with grilled bacon
and serve with rowan or red currant jelly,
potatoes and green peas.

PREPARATION AND COOKING OF VEGETABLES

Prepare vegetables immediately before use as
exposure to air destroys the vitamins. Avoid
soaking any but close-hearted vegetables in water.
Prepare green vegetables by shredding and root
vegetables by slicing to hasten cooking. Serve all
vegetables immediately they are cooked.

BOILING

Root vegetables. Put into sufficient boiling water
to cover; 1 oz salt to 2 pt water. Cover and
simmer steadily until tender. Drain thoroughly
and finish according to recipe.

Green vegetables. Put into a large pan with
only 1 in boiling, salted water and boil rapidly,
with the lid on, until tender, after 10-20 minutes.
Avoid overcooking. Drain and serve according to
particular recipe.

STEAMING

Root vegetables may be cooked by this method,
but are inclined to discolour unless there is a good
volume of steam; steaming should not be used for
green vegetables.

Place the prepared vegetables in a steamer or
over a pan of boiling water and cover. When
cooked, toss in butter and chopped parsley or
coat with a white sauce.

STEWING

Root vegetables may be cooked by this method,
but not green vegetables as the green colour would
deteriorate.

Prepare the vegetables and cut into suitably
sized pieces. Put in a pan with a little stock or
water — about 2½ fl oz to 1 lb vegetables — and
1 oz butter. Add seasoning.

Cook slowly until tender; time varies according
to age of the vegetable and size of the pieces.
Serve in the cooking liquid, reducing it if necessary. Alternatively, use the liquid as a base for a
sauce and make up as required.

Vegetables may also be stewed in a pan or
casserole placed in the oven; this method takes a
little longer than on top of the stove.

FRYING

Most vegetables may be fried; they should be
cooked previously with the exception of potatoes,
onions, mushrooms and tomatoes. Coat the cut-
up vegetables with egg and breadcrumbs or batter
and fry in shallow or deep fat.

BAKING

Prepare vegetables and put in a roasting tin with
a little salt and melted dripping. Bake in a
moderate oven until tender, turning them often.
Drain well and serve very hot.

GRILLING

This method is suitable for mushrooms and
tomatoes. It is unsuitable for vegetables with a
high cellulose content, such as carrots and

turnips. Dot with butter or dripping and cook under a medium hot grill.

ASPARAGUS

Preparation Trim the stems into equal lengths and scrape the white part lightly, from the tip downwards. Tie the stems in bundles with soft string. Allow 8-12 thin stems and 6-8 thick stems per portion.

Cooking Stand the bundles upright in sufficient boiling water to cover the stems, with the tips above the water; add a little salt and a lump of sugar. Cook until tender, for 5-8 minutes although this varies with the age and size of the asparagus. Drain thoroughly and remove the string.

Serving Asparagus are eaten with the fingers and served hot with melted butter, English butter sauce or a cream sauce. Serve them cold with an oil and vinegar dressing, mayonnaise or cream sauce. Provide finger bowls.

BEANS, FRENCH

Preparation Select bright green and small beans; a fibrous string along the length of the pod is a sign of age.

Top and tail young beans and leave whole. String the smooth side and slice off the ribbed side of older beans; cut into strips. Allow ¼-½ lb per portion.

Cooking Cook rapidly in a little boiling, salted water; young beans for 6-8 minutes, older beans for 15 minutes. Drain well.

Serving Serve hot with melted butter and chopped parsley (optional) or a cream sauce.

BEANS, RUNNER

Preparation Choose small beans with smooth skin; rough skin and obvious fibrous threads are a sign of age. Remove tops and tails and the fibrous thread; cut into diagonal slices. Very young beans may be left whole. Allow ¼-½ lb per portion.

Cooking Cook rapidly in a little boiling, salted water for 10-15 minutes, depending on age.

Serving Serve with melted butter together with young boiled carrots.

BEANS, BROAD (WINDSOR BEANS)

Best when young and green; a black line on the bean is a sign of age and toughness. Immature and small beans may be cooked whole with mint. Shell the beans just before using: blanch and drain. Open the bean skins by pressing gently with the thumb and forefinger. Allow ½-¾ lb per portion (purchased weight).

Cooking Put in a little boiling, salted water with a little parsley or winter savory and cook until tender, 8 minutes when young, longer when older. Drain well.

Serving Serve with melted butter and parsley, cream sauce or plain cream, parsley or onion sauce.

Variation Boil the beans in the liquid used to boil a bacon joint and serve with the bacon.

BEETROOT

Preparation Choose tender, deeply coloured beetroot, free of fibres; large roots tend to be coarse. Can be bought ready boiled. Wash carefully, taking care not to break the skins or the beetroot will bleed. Allow 4-6 oz per portion.

Cooking Put into boiling, salted water and cook until tender; time varies according to age and size, from 30 minutes to 3 hours. Test for readiness by pressing with a finger; when ready the skin should come off quite easily. Avoid testing with a fork or the beetroot will bleed. Drain, peel and cut into thick slices.

Serving Hot. Toss in melted butter and sprinkle with chopped parsley or coat with a white sauce, cream sauce or white sauce flavoured with grated horseradish.

Cold. Cut into slices or cubes and arrange on a dish; pour over equal quantities of water and vinegar mixed with a little sugar.

BROCCOLI

Preparation Broccoli should have firm curds, sprouting broccoli should look fresh and snap easily. Prepare and cook large-headed broccoli as for cauliflower. Wash sprouting broccoli well and chop roughly or divide into sprigs. Allow 4 oz per portion.

Cooking   Cook in boiling, salted water for about 8-10 minutes. Drain thoroughly.
Serving   Hot. Toss in melted butter with pepper and a little paprika or serve with a cheese sauce. Sprouting broccoli may be served like asparagus, boiled in bundles and served with melted butter.

Cold. Serve with oil and vinegar or mayonnaise.

BRUSSELS SPROUTS

Preparation   Remove any damaged outer leaves; trim stalks and make a cross in the base; wash and soak in cold salted water for 10 minutes. Allow 4 oz trimmed weight per portion.
Cooking   Cook rapidly in a little boiling, salted water with the lid on for 6-8 minutes. Drain well.
Serving   Hot. Toss in butter with seasoning and lemon juice or serve with a cream or cheese sauce or with chopped fried bacon, tossing the sprouts in the bacon fat. May also be served with boiled chestnuts, tossed in butter; alternatively, par-boil the sprouts and fry lightly in butter.

Cold. Serve with lemon juice or an oil and vinegar dressing.

CABBAGE, WINTER

Preparation   Select firm-headed cabbages with crisp leaves. Remove coarse outer leaves; cut the cabbage into quarters and remove the stalk. Wash thoroughly under running water; soak in cold, salted water for 5-10 minutes to remove any grit or insects. Shred finely. Allow 4 oz per portion.
Cooking   Put in a little boiling, salted water and boil rapidly for 10 minutes (savoy) and 7-10 minutes (drumhead or white Dutch). Drain thoroughly.
Serving   Toss in butter and seasoning or coat with cream or a white cream sauce, or a white sauce flavoured with horseradish.

CABBAGE, SPRING

Preparation   Choose fresh, crisp leaves and stems free of blemishes and of a good, dark green colour. Remove any coarse outer leaves; cut the cabbage into quarters and remove the hard stalk; wash thoroughly under running water; shred fairly finely. Allow ½ lb per portion.

Cooking   Put in a little boiling, salted water and boil rapidly, with the lid on, for 6-8 minutes. Drain thoroughly.
Serving   Serve with melted butter tossed with the drained cabbage over heat.

CABBAGE, RED

Preparation   Select cabbages of a good purple-red colour. Prepare as for winter cabbage. Allow ½ lb per portion.
Cooking   Boil as for winter cabbage, but do not use iron saucepans as they will cause the cabbage to lose its colour; the addition of lemon juice or vinegar helps to preserve the colour.
Serving   Serve with melted butter.

CARROTS

Preparation   Spring carrots should be no bigger than ½ inch in diameter; main crop carrots are larger but should be tender with no woody cores. All should be well shaped, bright, with smooth skins. Carrots are sold washed and unwashed.

Spring carrots. Cut the green tops off young carrots, scald and rub off the skins; leave whole. Wash and scrape or peel main crop carrots; cut into slices, dice or strips. Allow 4-6 oz per portion.
Cooking   Put in boiling, salted water, with a little sugar and mint added, and cook rapidly until tender; young carrots after 15-20 minutes, main crop carrots after 30-40 minutes. Drain well.
Serving   Toss in melted butter and sprinkle with chopped parsley or coat with a white or cream sauce or with double cream.

Carrots may be mashed, particularly if old, with butter or cream and sprinkled with finely chopped parsley.
Variations   Cook the carrots in enough water or white meat stock to cover, with 1 oz butter and a little sugar to 1 lb carrots. Add seasoning and simmer slowly until tender, spring carrots for 30-40 minutes, main crop carrots for 45-50 minutes. Serve with the cooking liquid reduced to a glaze.

About 1 oz honey may be added to the cooking liquid, and chopped tarragon or chervil or spring onions towards the end of cooking time.

CAULIFLOWER

Preparation   Remove any coarse outer leaves, wash and soak in salted water with a little lemon juice or vinegar for 30 minutes to bring out any insects. Trim the stalk and hollow it out at the base to let the heat penetrate and reduce cooking time; alternatively, divide the head into individual sprigs. Allow 4-6 oz per portion.

Cooking   *Whole.* Put in boiling, salted water with a squeeze of lemon juice to preserve the white colour, stem downwards. Cook quickly until the stem is soft; the time varies according to size, but approximately 10-15 minutes.

Sprigs. Put in boiling, salted water with lemon juice and cook quickly until tender, after 4-7 minutes.

Never overcook cauliflower as this causes an unpleasant change in flavour and colour. Cauliflower should still be slightly crisp after cooking. A mixture of milk and water may be used for cooking. Drain well.

Serving   Serve whole, hot cauliflower with a white sauce, Dutch, parsley sauce, or cheese sauce with a sprinkling of cheese and lightly browned under the grill.

Serve hot cauliflower sprigs with melted butter, lemon juice and chopped parsley; cold with salad sauce or mayonnaise.

CELERIAC

Preparation   Choose clean, undamaged roots; smaller ones are likely to be most succulent. Peel the root thinly and cut into slices or dice. Allow 4-6 oz per portion.

Cooking   Boil in a small quantity of salted water until tender, the time depending on size of the pieces. Drain well.

Serving   Coat with melted butter and chopped parsley, or with mustard butter, white sauce, cheese sauce, or hardboiled egg sauce.

Variations   Celeriac may be cooked and served as stewed celery.

Alternatively, cut into slices and par-boil; drain and coat with seasoned flour, egg and breadcrumbs, or dip in coating batter; fry in deep fat until golden brown and crisp.

CELERY

Preparation   Choose firm, crisp stems with as little green as possible. Allow ½ head per portion or 2-3 sticks if large. Remove the green top and roots. Separate the stalks and wash well; scrub them to remove sand and if necessary scrape. Cut into lengths of about 4 in and tie in bundles.

Cooking   Cook in a little boiling, salted water until tender, after about 10 minutes; drain well.

Serving   Hot. With melted butter, chopped parsley and a little lemon juice; coat with a white sauce, egg or cheese sauce.

Cold. Coat with a salad sauce.

Variations   Stew slowly in a small quantity of stock or milk and water with 1 oz butter and seasoning. Serve with the cooking liquid or in a sauce made from this; sprinkle with chopped parsley.

Alternatively, boil the celery until nearly cooked but still firm enough to be handled. Drain on a cloth and season. Coat with flour, egg and breadcrumbs or dip in coating batter, and fry in deep fat until golden brown and crisp.

Fresh celery   Leave attractive leaves on the stalks; separate and clean the stalks and stand them in a jug of cold water in a refrigerator to allow them to become crisp.

Serve with unsalted butter, sea salt and cheese and biscuits.

CUCUMBERS

Preparation   Choose straight, large, firm cucumbers which look fresh and show no signs of wilting, especially at the stalk end. Chiefly used as a salad vegetable, washed and dried and cut into slices or small dice.

Cooking   Slice the cucumber into 1 in long pieces, remove any seeds and cook the cucumber gently in 1 oz butter and a little salt and sugar. If cooked very slowly it can be simmered in its own juice without turning the heat down.

Serving   Serve in the cooking liquid or coat with a white sauce made from a mixture of the cooking liquid and milk.

GLOBE ARTICHOKES

Preparation and Cooking   Avoid artichokes with sharp brown tips to the leaves as this is a sign of age. Allow one artichoke per person.

Wash the heads; using a stainless steel knife, trim off the lower leaves and trim the stalk so that the artichokes will remain upright on the serving dish. Cut off the pointed top and trim the points of the leaves with scissors. Rub the cut surfaces with lemon juice to prevent discolouring. Tie a slice of lemon on top and bottom. Put in boiling, salted water and cook for 30-40 minutes. To test for readiness, pull at one end of the leaves which should come away easily. Drain well upside down. Remove string and pull out the inner choke.
Serving Serve hot with melted butter or cold with an oil and vinegar dressing or mayonnaise.

JERUSALEM ARTICHOKES

Preparation Jerusalem artichokes are naturally a warty, ugly-looking vegetable, but avoid any that are too mis-shapen, small, dirty or bruised. Scrub the artichokes, and using a stainless steel knife or potato peeler, peel them quickly and immediately plunge them into cold water with a squeeze of lemon juice or vinegar to prevent discoloration. Alternatively, par-boil first, which makes peeling easier. Allow 6-8 oz per portion.
Cooking Put in boiling, salted water with a squeeze of lemon juice and boil quickly until soft, after 20-30 minutes. Drain thoroughly.
Serving Toss with melted butter and chopped parsley or coat with a rich white sauce, cheese sauce or parsley sauce.
Variations Par-boil or peel the artichokes, coat with seasoned flour, egg and breadcrumbs or dip in a coating batter. Fry in deep fat or oil until crisp and golden, drain and serve with mace.

Alternatively, cook peeled artichokes around roasting meat, adding them to the hot fat and allowing 30 minutes to cook.

KALE OR KAIL

Preparation Choose fresh, crisp looking leaves of a good dark colour. Wash thoroughly in several lots of water; strip the leaves from the stalks unless the kale is very young and tender; cut into strips. Allow 4-6 oz per portion.
Cooking Cook in a little salted, boiling water for 20-25 minutes; drain thoroughly.
Serving Excellent with strong red meats and

salted meat; serve the kale tossed in melted butter and seasoned with pepper or coat with a cheese sauce; serve with oatcakes or bannocks, or with a sprinkling of toasted oatmeal.

KOHL-RABI OR KOHLRABI

Choose unblemished, firm roots; avoid those with side roots and large specimens which tend to be woody. Remove any green leaves and wash the roots carefully; peel and cut into slices or dice. Allow 4 oz per portion.
Cooking Cook in boiling water until tender, after 20-30 minutes. Drain thoroughly.
Serving Toss in melted butter and chopped parsley or coat with a white or cream sauce. The leaves may be boiled with the roots and used as a garnish.
Variation Heat enough butter to cover the bottom of a pan, add the kohl-rabi, cut in neat pieces, season and cover with a lid. Stew gently until tender after approximately 45 minutes. Serve with the cooking liquid and sprinkle with parsley.

LAVER

Preparation Gather the laver as fresh as possible and wash well, first in sea water, then in fresh water to remove all traces of sand.
Cooking Boil down to a stiff jelly for about 2-3 hours, in sea water if possible. Drain well. This is "laver bread" and can be kept fresh for several weeks if packed into small pots and covered with a layer of clarified butter or suet.

According to Welsh connoisseurs laver should never be cooked in an iron pot as this affects the flavour.

LEEKS

Preparation Choose fresh looking, white stems with well trimmed leaves showing no signs of discoloration. Remove the roots and the coarse outer leaves. Slit the leeks in half nearly down to the white part and leave, green head downwards, in cold water or in a colander with running cold water to remove sand and dirt trapped in the leaves. If small leave whole, if large cut in half lengthways. Allow two large or three small leeks per portion.

Cooking Cook in a little boiling, salted water until tender; time depends on size, but approximately 10-20 minutes for whole leeks and less if halved or quartered. Drain thoroughly.

Serving Serve coated with melted butter and chopped parsley or freshly ground black pepper or coat with a white sauce, cream or cheese sauce or fresh cream.

Variation Simmer slowly with a small amount of salted water, 2 oz to five large leeks. Serve with the cooking liquid or a white sauce made from this, or a cream or cheese sauce.

MARROWS AND COURGETTES

Preparation Choose young marrows no more than 9-12 in long and 3-4 in thick as these have more flavour, and the seeds are hardly formed. The skin should be green, tender and have a dull shine. Very small marrows of 3-4 in are known as courgettes. Wash the marrow, cut into quarters, remove the seeds and peel. Cut into neat pieces. For stuffing, peel and split lengthways.

Cooking Melt sufficient butter in a pan to cover the base, add the marrow (cut into pieces) and toss in butter for a few minutes. Add a little stock, put on the lid and cook gently until tender, for about 15 minutes. Chopped onions, parsley and black pepper may be added. Drain well and put into a serving dish to keep hot.

Serving Use the cooking liquid to make a rich white sauce or cheese sauce. Alternatively, mix double cream with the liquid and pour over the marrow.

Variation Peel the marrow and cut into rings, remove the seeds; cook in the fat round roasting meat. Drain and serve with the meat.

Courgettes Wash the baby marrows, trim both ends but do not peel. Leave whole or cut into slices, crossways. Larger courgettes may be halved lengthways, the seeds scooped out and the cavities filled with a savoury mixture or cream sauce.

Boil in salted water until tender, after 10-15 minutes, or steam whole courgettes for 15-20 minutes, slices for about 10 minutes. Alternatively, brush halved courgettes with melted butter, season and bake in a moderate oven for 25 minutes.

Courgette slices may also be stewed in butter like marrow.

Toss boiled courgettes in butter and sprinkle with chopped parsley.

MUSHROOMS

Preparation Button and cup mushrooms are white or pale brown with pink gills and firm flesh, excellent for garnish, while the larger flat mushrooms have dark coloured gills and a more pronounced flavour. Wipe buttons and cups, clean and trim away any ragged edges; cut off and discard the lower part of the stalk and use the rest of the stalk for stocks and stews. Treat flat mushrooms similarly, but peel off the skin if blemished.

Cooking Melt butter in a frying pan and add the seasoned mushrooms; fry gently until tender, after 5 minutes.

Serving Serve with the pan juices poured over and sprinkle with chopped parsley.

Variations Place in an ovenproof dish, brush with butter and season. Bake in a moderate oven at 350°F, gas mark 4, for 20 minutes.

For grilling, brush the mushrooms with melted butter and place on a greased grill pan, rounded sides upwards. Grill for 4-5 minutes. Turn the mushrooms over, put a small piece of butter and a sprinkling of salt on each and return to the grill for another 4-5 minutes. Sprinkle with pepper.

ONIONS

Preparation Choose firm onions with papery skins, slice off root base and top and remove outer skins. Allow 4-6 oz per portion.

Cooking Cook large onions of similar size whole in boiling water and cook steadily until tender, after 30-45 minutes, depending on size. Drain well.

Serving Serve with melted butter and chopped parsley or cheese sauce and a sprinkling of grated cheese.

Variations Prepare small whole onions and put in a pan with a little water and a piece of butter and seasoning. Cook gently until tender. If the liquid reduces too much before the onions are cooked, add a little more water. Serve with the pan liquids poured over and sprinkle with chopped parsley.

Fried onions Peel the onions and slice thinly. Melt dripping in a pan and fry onions in hot fat until brown and crisp. Drain and serve. Alternatively, coat the onion rings in seasoned flour and fry in deep fat.

PARSNIPS

Preparation Select straight, fresh roots without
any soft brown patches. Wash and peel thinly
and cut into quarters lengthways or leave whole
if small. Allow 6-8 oz per portion.
Cooking Cook in boiling salted water until tender,
after about 20 minutes. Drain well.
Serving Toss in melted butter and chopped
parsley or a sprinkling of nutmeg, or serve with a
white sauce. Alternatively, mash and mix with
butter or double cream, black pepper and a little
salt, chopped parsley and a pinch of cinnamon.
Variations Simmer 1 lb parsnips in 2½ fl oz
white stock and 1 oz butter; add seasoning and
cook gently for about 40 minutes or until tender.
Serve in the cooking liquid and sprinkle with
chopped parsley. Roast parsnips are traditional
with roast beef; put them in a roasting tin with
melted dripping and salt, baste frequently until
cooked or add the parsnips to the roasting tin
with a joint of meat. Alternatively, par-boil the
parsnips, cut them lengthways in finger-wide
pieces and fry in fat until tender and brown.

POTATOES

Preparation *New potatoes*. Choose firm, unblemished potatoes, scrub with a stiff brush to
remove earth and most of the skin, scrape off
the remainder and remove any eyes with a knife.
Wash well. Alternatively, cook and serve the
potatoes in their skins. Allow 4-6 oz per
portion.
    Maincrop potatoes. Choose firm potatoes,
without green patches, according to purpose;
in general, red potatoes are floury and suitable
for mashing, baking and soups. White potatoes
have a waxy texture and are suitable for boiling,
frying, slicing for stews and cold salads. Scrub
with a brush and remove skin with a sharp knife,
dig out eyes and cut into even pieces, Allow
6-8 oz per portion.
Cooking Put into boiling, salted water and
cook for 20-25 minutes or until tender, according
to age. Drain well. A sprig of mint may be added
to new potatoes.
Serving Toss in melted butter and chopped
parsley or oatmeal.

Variations
    Mashed potatoes (maincrop). Rub boiled
potatoes through a sieve, return to the pan and
add boiling milk and butter; heat until smooth
and creamy. Season.
    Creamed potatoes (maincrop). As mashed
potatoes, spooned into serving dish and covered
with cream.
    Fried potatoes (new and maincrop). Cut into
slices about ¼ in thick and fry in hot fat until
brown on both sides; drain. May be par-boiled
before slicing and frying.
    Roast potatoes (maincrop). Peel and cut
into even pieces, coat in melted fat or dripping,
sprinkle with salt and cook in roasting tin in
oven at 400°F, gas mark 6, until golden brown.
    Baked potatoes (maincrop). Wash potatoes,
prick with a fork and rub with buttered paper;
sprinkle salt on a baking sheet and set potatoes on
top. Bake in the oven at 400-425°F, gas mark
6-7, for 1-1½ hours, depending on size. Score the
top with a cross, press the sides of the potato to
open it slightly, top with butter and garnish
with parsley.

PEAS, GARDEN

Green Pea Vendors These were a feature of the
streets in Victorian London: vendors carried
large pans of hot peas cooked in their pods, and
customers removed the peas by drawing them
from the pod through the teeth. Salt, pepper,
butter and vinegar were provided as accompaniments. Rural festivals of pea scaldings used to
take place, when the peas were cooked and
eaten as described at the time of the first crop.
Preparation The first pea crops are known as
sugar peas and are usually cooked and served
whole in the pods. The pods should be flat, tender
and succulent with no blemishes and with very
small and tender peas. Maincrop peas should have
juicy pods, well filled with small to medium-
sized peas; the pods when pressed should give
with a gentle pop.
    Top and tail sugar peas and remove the fibrous
strings; wash the pods well. Split maincrop pods
and remove the peas. Allow 4 oz sugar peas per
portion, 4-6 oz maincrop peas.
Cooking Plunge sugar peas into salted boiling

water and cook for 5-8 minutes or until tender. Drain and toss in melted butter. Cook maincrop peas in sufficient salted water to cover and add a pinch of sugar and a sprig of mint; cook rapidly for 5-10 minutes. Drain and serve tossed in melted butter.

SALSIFY AND SCORZONERA

Preparation Select long tapering salsify roots with white skin and flesh, free of wrinkles or blemishes. Scorzonera is similar, but with black skins. Scrape salsify roots well, cover at once with water and lemon juice to prevent discoloration. Wash scorzonera roots, but do not peel or cut until after cooking. Allow 4-6 oz per portion.
Cooking Cook in boiling salted water or a mixture of milk and water until tender, after 40-45 minutes. Drain thoroughly and peel scorzonera.
Serving Cut the roots into conveniently sized pieces and coat with melted butter, a rich white sauce, anchovy sauce or cheese sauce.
Variations For salsify pie, cover the cooked salsify with mashed potatoes and bake in a hot oven until the top is brown.

SAMPHIRE

This fleshy green plant grows wild on sea marshes, sand dunes and shingle in East Anglia and South and West Wales; it is seldom seen outside the market towns around the Norfolk coast. The fleshy green leaves are gathered in summer. Wash the leaves well and wipe clean with a cloth.
Cooking Put in boiling water and cook for 10 minutes or until tender. Drain and serve as an accompanying vegetable, tossed in melted butter.

SEA KALE

Preparation Choose straight stems of ivory colour, sometimes with a tinge of purple, and crisp green leaves. Cut off any broken or discoloured leaves and trim most but not all of the roots as they help to keep the stems in place. Wash carefully and tie in bundles if necessary. Cook as soon as possible after picking, as exposure to air causes discoloration. Allow 5 oz per portion.

Cooking Put in boiling salted water to which a good squeeze of lemon juice has been added; cook until tender, after 20-30 minutes. Drain well.
Serving Serve hot with melted butter and lemon juice and with toast if served as a first course. Alternatively, serve the hot stems in a rich white, cream or cheese sauce.

For a cold first course, serve sea kale as asparagus or in oil and vinegar with roast turkey, pheasant or chicken.

SPINACH

Preparation Choose clean, fresh green leaves and wash thoroughly in several lots of water. Remove coarse stalks and midribs. Allow ½ lb per portion.
Cooking Put the leaves, dripping wet, into a pan, add a pinch of sugar, cover and cook gently for 5-8 minutes. Drain thoroughly.
Serving Chop the spinach finely and return to the pan with butter and a sprinkling of pepper. Heat through, pile on a dish and serve immediately. Alternatively, rub through a wire sieve, add butter and heat through. Pile on toast and serve separately or as an accompanying vegetable. For creamed spinach, add melted butter, a pinch of sugar and nutmeg and lemon juice to the cooked spinach. Heat through, add double cream and pile on fried bread or toast or serve with sippets.

SPINACH BEET

This is a variety of sugar beet, grown for its stems and leaves. The green leaves may be cooked separately in the same way as spinach or it may be cooked together with the stems. Most commonly, the white stems and leaf ribs are cooked separately rather as asparagus, when it is referred to as blett or blite. It used to be a common vegetable in rural areas and it is still grown on the East coast, particularly in Lincolnshire.
Preparation Select fresh green leaves with thick stems and midribs. Separate the white ribs and the stems from the leaves and cook the leaves as spinach. Wash the stems and tie in bundles of equal size with a piece of mint in each. Allow 4 oz per portion.
Cooking Put in boiling water and boil rapidly for 30 minutes; drain thoroughly.
Serving Serve one bunch per portion and coat

with melted butter and chopped parsley. Alternatively, chop the stems roughly and coat with a cream sauce.

TOMATOES

Preparation Tomatoes should be firm to the touch and of a good round or oval shape, of good red colour with a matt rather than shiny skin. Avoid blotchy, cracked or greenish specimens. Wash, remove calyx and cut in halves crossways for cooking purposes. Also used fresh in salads and for garnishes.
Baking Season with salt and pepper, dot with butter and arrange in a greased baking dish; cover with buttered paper or a lid. Bake in moderate oven at 350°F, gas mark 4, for 10 minutes depending on size and firmness of the tomatoes.
Grilling Dot with butter and place on a heated grill, cut side down, for 2-3 minutes, turn, dot with more butter and grill for 2-3 minutes.
Frying Season the tomatoes and fry in a little butter, placing the cut side down first, turn and fry on the other side.

TURNIPS AND SWEDES

Preparation Choose young turnips of uniform size and firm flesh. Maincrop turnips and swedes should be free from holes, sponginess and soft brown smelly patches. Remove leaves and fibrous roots from young turnips; leave whole. Remove roots and wash away clinging dirt from maincrop turnips and swedes; peel thinly and cut off any rough or woody parts, chop into large chunks. Allow 4 oz of turnips and swedes per portion.
Cooking Cook young turnips in rapidly boiling salted water for 20-30 minutes; drain and peel off the skins. Cook maincrop turnips and swedes in salted boiling water or white stock for 30-40 minutes or until soft; drain.
Serving Toss young turnips in melted butter and chopped parsley or coat with a white sauce. Serve chopped turnips and swedes in butter and chopped parsley or coat with a white sauce, cream sauce or mustard sauce. Alternatively, mash maincrop turnips and swedes, add butter, pepper and cream or a little cinnamon or ground mace and lemon juice. In Scotland mashed turnips are known as "Turnip Purry" or "Bashed Neeps" and are the traditional accompaniment to haggis.

Variation Par-boil turnips and arrange round a roasting joint; baste frequently and serve with roast meat.

WATERCRESS

Preparation Choose bunches of fresh green leaves showing no signs of wilting. Remove any roots, blemished leaves and thick stems. Separate into small sprigs, wash and drain. Normally used raw in salads or as garnish to meat and fish dishes.

PULSES AND RICE

Preparation and Cooking (dried peas, beans and lentils) Wash well in cold water and remove any bits that float to the top of the water. Soak peas and beans in cold water for at least 24 hours; lentils can be cooked without soaking.

Put in a pan with plenty of fresh cold water as much water is absorbed during cooking and softening. Add no salt at this stage as this makes the pulses hard. Bring to the boil, cover and simmer gently until soft; do not overcook or they become pulpy. The cooking liquid can be used for soups. Add salt to taste. Allow 1-2 oz dry weight per portion of pulses.
Variation For extra flavour, use stock as the cooking liquid or boil ham, bacon, pork or beef with the pulses. Onions, garlic, carrots, celery, leeks, bay leaf or a faggot of herbs may be added to the cooking liquid.

Cooking Times for Pulses		
Soaked:	Dried peas	1-1½ hours
	Split peas	1 hour
	Haricot beans	45 minutes
	Butter beans	1 hour
Unsoaked:	Lentils	25 minutes

Haricot Beans

Haricot is the name used for a number of different types of dried beans, such as small white beans (the dried seeds of a variety of French beans) and red beans sometimes called kidney beans. Haricot beans also include the small green beans known as flageolet in France and pea bean in America and the large white beans, usually referred to as butter beans or Lima beans.
Serving Serve haricot beans with melted butter

and chopped parsley, or season lightly with black pepper, cayenne, paprika, or curry powder. Alternatively, serve with a cheese sauce or with chopped bacon, fried until crisp — toss the beans in the bacon fat.

Lentils

There are two types of lentils, the German lentil, purplish green and flat, and the Egyptian lentil, like a small split pea, reddish yellow in colour.
Serving Drain the cooked lentils and toss in melted butter and sprinkle with chopped parsley. Alternatively, boil and drain the lentils, rub shallots and serve with pork chops, knuckle of bacon or any kind of sausage. Dress cooked, drained and cooled lentils with oil and vinegar and serve as a starter.
Variations Boil the lentils and drain; add minced onions fried in butter, season with salt and pepper and shape into small cakes. If the mixture is too wet, mix in dried breadcrumbs; dredge with flour and fry in hot oil.

For a purée, boil and drain the lentils, rub through a fine sieve or blend in a liquidiser. Fry a little chopped onion, chopped parsley, carrot and celery in butter and liquidise; mix into the lentils and serve with roast duck or other poultry.

Dried Peas

These are available either as whole green peas or yellow split peas with the outer skins removed.
Serving Toss in melted butter.

Rice

Wash the rice in cold water, drain and put in a large pan of boiling salted water with a few drops of lemon juice. Boil for 12-15 minutes, test the rice with the finger and thumb and, if soft, drain and pour boiling water through the rice to rinse it. Drain on a cloth to absorb any excess moisture.

BATTERS

These are basically made up of flour and liquid and beaten to a pouring consistency; they may be enriched with eggs, cream or oil. Batters which are required for coating food are classed together as coating batters since they are stiffer than the other types. Plain and rich batter mixtures, which are used for sweet and savoury puddings and pancakes, are generally of a thinner consistency than coating batters.

All batters should be made in a cool place and should be allowed to rest before use to allow the starch granules to soften. They should never be overcooked.

Plain Batter Mixture (for savoury puddings)

½ lb plain flour
Pinch salt
3 eggs
¾ pt milk

Mix the flour and salt together; drop the eggs into the centre of the flour with one third of the milk and mix to a smooth paste. Beat the mixture well and gradually add the rest of the milk. Cover and rest for at least 1 hour in a cold place.

Use as required for savoury batter puddings, such as Yorkshire Pudding.

Rich Batter Mixture (for sweet puddings)

6 oz plain flour
Pinch salt
4 eggs
1 pt milk
2 oz sugar

Separate the eggs. Sift the flour and salt and mix the egg yolks thoroughly into the flour until there are no lumps. Gradually add the milk to make a creamy mixture, beating constantly. Leave the batter to rest for 1 hour.

Beat the egg whites to a stiff froth and just before the batter is used, gently fold in the egg whites. Use the batter to make sweet batter puddings, fritters or pancakes.

Plain Coating Batter

½ lb plain flour
Pinch salt
2 eggs
½ pt milk

Sift the flour and make a well in the centre;
add the salt, break in the eggs and add half the
milk. Beat the mixture until smooth. Gradually
add the remaining milk and beat until well
mixed. Rest for 30 minutes before use.

Coating Batter with Egg Whites

½ lb plain flour
Pinch salt
2 tablespoons oil
½ pt water
4 egg whites

Sift the flour and salt into a bowl and make a well
in the centre. Pour in the oil and half the water.
Beat until smooth, then gradually add the remaining water. Leave to rest for 30 minutes.

Whisk the egg whites stiffly and fold into the
batter just before using. The mixture must be
used at once in order to obtain maximum
benefit from the aeration.

Yeast Batter

½ lb plain flour
½ pt warm water
¼ oz fresh yeast
1 tablespoon oil
1 oz sugar
Pinch salt

Dissolve the yeast in a little of the warm water.
Whisk all other ingredients together until smooth.
Add the yeast and mix. Cover with a damp cloth
and prove for 1 hour. Use for fritters.

Beer Batter

½ lb plain flour
Pinch salt, sugar and cinnamon
1 egg
2 tablespoons oil
½ pt beer

Sift the flour, sugar, salt and cinnamon. Beat the
egg and add to the flour, stirring gently. Add the
oil and beer. Leave the batter to rest for at least
30 minutes, then use as ordinary batter.

Fritters can be made from this batter with the
addition of 1 oz currants.

PASTRY

In cookery, the term pastry or paste is applied
to any mixture consisting of flour and fat (or oil)
moistened with a liquid and kneaded to a dough.
Variations are a result of different types and
proportions of flour, fat and liquid, as well as a
result of different methods of incorporation of
the ingredients.

British pastry variations fall within the following categories: shortcrust, suet crust, puff
pastry, rough puff pastry, flaky pastry, Cornish
pastry, hot water or raised pie pastry, flead pastry
and huff paste.

Flour
The type of flour used for pastry is wheat, which
in addition to starch, water, fat, sugars and mineral
matter also contains an elastic protein substance
called gluten. When mixed with water, wheat
flour forms an elastic cohesive mass. The amount
of gluten in flour varies according to the type of
wheat; flour is classified as "strong" or "hard",
"general purpose" and "soft" or "weak". Strong
flour has the highest gluten content producing a
dough with more elasticity than one made with
general purpose flour, while soft flour has least
gluten and therefore least elasticity.

In the preparation of pastry, the type of
flour is important, and this is particularly the
case with puff, rough puff and flaky pastry which
should be made with strong flour. All other types
of pastry may be made with a strong flour or
general purpose flour.

Fat
The type of fat used may be lard or dripping,
suet, oil, butter or margarine. When a crumbly,
brittle texture is required as in short pastry the
least suitable fat is margarine although it may be
mixed with lard which will produce a "short"
result. Lard has a greater shortening effect
than butter, while margarine has less shortening
effect than either lard or butter. The fat should
be evenly dispersed throughout the pastry or
bubbles and blisters will occur in the finished
product.

TRADITIONAL JAM TART DESIGNS FROM THE NORTH OF ENGLAND

Red cross

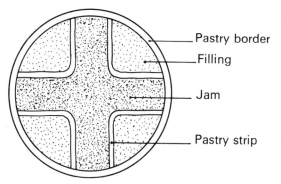

- Pastry border
- Filling
- Jam
- Pastry strip

Red currant jelly is used for the cross, curd for the filling

Star shape

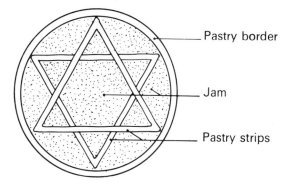

- Pastry border
- Jam
- Pastry strips

Each section of the star is filled with a different jam or curd

Lattice design

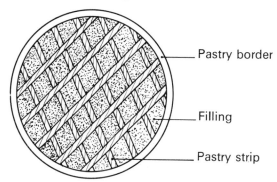

- Pastry border
- Filling
- Pastry strip

Traditional design for treacle tarts, with interwoven pastry strips

Gable tart

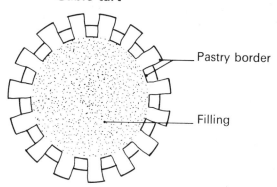

- Pastry border
- Filling

Alternate sections of the pastry border are folded towards the centre

Diagonal cross

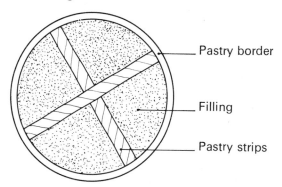

- Pastry border
- Filling
- Pastry strips

Different jam flavours and colours make up four separate portions

Spiral tart

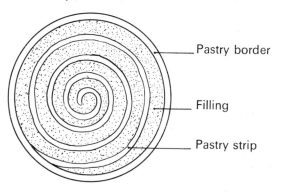

- Pastry border
- Filling
- Pastry strip

The pastry coil decoration varies in thickness and number of loops

All pastries except hot water pastry should be worked and stored in a cool place to prevent the fat melting.

Liquid
All the liquid should be added at one time and must be evenly distributed throughout. The consistency of the finished pastry can be described in the following order of stiffness: very stiff (close textured, the hardest consistency), stiff, fairly stiff, stiff and elastic, and elastic (open textured, softest consistency).

Kneading
Pastry should be kneaded only if it is necessary to develop the gluten in puff, rough puff and flaky pastries. Other pastries should be handled and kneaded as little as possible. The more gently it is mixed the lighter the product.

All pastry should be rested before use in order to allow the gluten which has been stretched to relax and become less rubbery. The pastry when subjected to heat will otherwise contract and distort the intended shape.

Savoury Shortcrust Pastry

1 lb plain flour
4 oz margarine or butter
4 oz lard
¼ oz salt
3 fl oz cold water

Cut up the fat and rub into the flour until this resembles fine breadcrumbs; add the salt. Sprinkle the cold water over the flour and mix well to a very stiff consistency. Work the mixture until smooth; do not overwork. Allow it to rest for at least 30 minutes before use. Roll out as required.

Sweet Shortcrust Pastry

1 lb plain flour
4 oz margarine or butter
4 oz lard
4 oz caster sugar
3 fl oz milk

Follow the method for savoury shortcrust pastry.

Rich Shortcrust Pastry

1 lb plain flour
½ lb butter
4 oz caster sugar
2 egg yolks and water (to make 4 fl oz)
Pinch salt

Cut the butter into the flour and rub in until it resembles fine breadcrumbs; add the salt. Mix the sugar, egg yolks and water and add to the flour mixture. Mix thoroughly to a very stiff consistency, but do not overwork.

Allow the pastry to rest in the refrigerator for 30 minutes before use. Roll out as required.

Spiced Shortcrust Pastry

1 lb plain flour
½ lb butter
4 oz caster sugar
¾ oz cinnamon
2 eggs

Rub the butter into the flour to a crumbly mixture; mix the sugar, cinnamon and eggs and add to the mixture. Follow the method for rich shortcrust pastry.

Cheese Shortcrust Pastry

1 lb plain flour
4 oz margarine or butter
4 oz lard
Salt, pepper and cayenne
½ lb grated cheese
3 egg yolks and water (to make 4 fl oz)

Follow the method for rich shortcrust pastry, adding the cheese after the fat.

Oatmeal Pastry

½ lb plain flour
½ lb fine oatmeal
3 oz margarine or butter
3 oz lard
Pinch salt
2 tablespoons water

Follow the method for savoury shortcrust pastry, adding the oatmeal with the flour.

Savoury Suet Pastry

1 lb plain flour
1 oz baking powder (optional)
¼ oz salt
½ lb finely chopped suet
½ pt water

To prepare the suet, remove the papery skin; chop finely, using a little flour to prevent sticking.

Mix all the ingredients, adding cold water to give a stiff elastic consistency. May be used as required — boiled, steamed or baked, but cannot be stored.

Sweet Suet Pastry

1 lb plain flour
½ lb shredded or chopped suet
6 oz caster sugar
1 oz baking powder (optional)
½ pt milk

Prepare the suet as for savoury suet pastry. Mix all the dry ingredients, add the milk and mix to a stiff elastic consistency. Use as required, steamed, boiled or baked; do not store.

Puff Pastry

1 lb plain flour
¼ oz salt
1 lb butter
½ pt ice cold water
1 teaspoon lemon juice

Sift the flour and salt and rub in 4 oz of the butter. Make a well in the centre and add the water and lemon juice; knead well to a smooth dough the shape of a ball. Rest the dough in a cool place for approximately 30 minutes.

Cut a cross halfway through the dough and pull out the corners to form a star shape; roll out the points of the star leaving the centre thick. Knead the remaining butter to the same texture as the dough. Shape into a square. Place the butter on the centre square and fold over the flour flaps.

Roll out thickly keeping the edges square, and then rest the dough in a cool place for 5-10 minutes. Roll out to approximately 24 in by 8 in; fold the short ends to the centre, fold in half again to form a square and allow it to rest in a cool place for approximately 20 minutes.

Give the pastry a quarter turn to the right (or left) and repeat the rolling-out procedure; rest the dough for 20 minutes. Continue rolling out and resting twice more, making five rollings altogether; leave to rest again after shaping.

Use as required. May be stored in the refrigerator for 1 week, dusted with flour and covered.

Rough Puff Pastry

1 lb plain flour
¼ oz salt
1 teaspoon lemon juice
¾ lb butter
½ pt cold water

Sift the flour and salt, cut the fat into ½ oz pieces and add to the flour. Add lemon juice and water and mix to an elastic dough. Turn out and work lightly into a square shape.

Roll the dough into an oblong strip, fold in three and seal the edges; give a quarter turn, roll out again and rest it for 5-10 minutes in a cool place. Repeat this twice more and if necessary a fourth time until the fat is evenly distributed; rest the dough between each rolling out.

Allow the dough to rest again after shaping. Use as required. May be stored, covered, in the refrigerator for 1 week.

Flaky Pastry

1 lb plain flour
¼ oz salt
¾ lb butter
1 teaspoon lemon juice
½ pt cold water

Divide the butter into four equal portions. Add the salt to the sifted flour and rub in a quarter of the fat. Mix with lemon juice and water to an elastic dough.

Turn out and work lightly into a square shape. Roll into an oblong shape. Place one quarter of the fat in small pieces on the top two thirds of the pastry. Fold up the bottom third which is not covered with fat and fold down the upper third on top. Seal the edges and give a quarter turn to the right (or left).

Repeat this twice more, each time adding one quarter of fat and resting the dough for 20 minutes in a cool place. Roll out twice more, giving five rollings in all. Rest before using; may be stored in a refrigerator for 1 week.

Cornish Pastry

1 lb plain flour
Pinch salt
4 oz suet
½ pt water
4 oz lard

Flake or chop the suet finely and mix with the
sifted flour and salt. Mix to a stiff paste with cold
water. Roll out and add the lard in small pieces as
for flaky pastry, using a quarter at a time. Roll
out three more times. Use for covering meat pies.

Hot Water Crust or Raised Pie Pastry

1 lb plain flour
¼ oz salt (for savoury pies)
4 oz lard
½ pt hot water

Sift the flour and salt into a warm bowl and
make a well in the centre. Boil the lard in the
water until melted and pour into the flour; mix
quickly with a wooden spoon.

Knead the dough by hand while the mixture
is still warm, until all the flour is worked in and
the pastry is smooth and free from cracks.
Use while still warm and before it hardens.
It cannot be stored at this stage although it may
be stored after moulding to the desired shape.

Raising a Hot Water Pie Crust

By hand. This is the traditional method, but
requires a certain amount of skill. Roll out three
quarters of the pastry and shape into a thick
round; with the thumbs work the pastry out from
the centre to make a round hollow. Thin out the
sides a little, then place the filling in the pie.
Work the sides up along the filling, shaping the pie
at the same time. It is important to do this as
quickly as possible since the hot water pastry
tends to harden on cooling and becomes difficult
to mould. When the pie is a good round shape, wet
the inner top edges, place on the lid rolled out
from the remaining pastry and press down well.

Pinch the rim with the fingers or snip with
scissors to make a decoration; make a small hole
in the lid. Make decorations from the pastry
trimmings into leaf and flower shapes and set
these around the hole in the pastry.

Pin a double thickness of greaseproof paper
round the pie to help keep the shape. Set it on a
baking sheet and bake as directed.

Using a mould. A floured or oiled 2 lb jam jar
or a special wooden pie mould may be used.
Mould most of the pastry round the mould to the
desired height and thickness. Then roll it sideways
to smooth the outside and leave the dough to set
before removing the mould. Fill the pie and
decorate as before.

Using a tin. A greased rectangular loaf tin, a
deep-sided 6 in cake tin with a loose base or a tin
mould specially designed for raised pies may be
used. Moulds are sold in traditional shapes and
designs with fluted edges and the two sides are
held together by hinges. Remove a third of the
pastry and keep it covered. Roll out the remainder,
¼ in thick and large enough to line the sides and
bottom of the tin. Add the filling. Roll out the
reserved pastry for the lid, cover, seal, trim and
decorate the pie as already described.

Flead Pastry

1 lb leaf flead
1 lb plain flour
¼ oz salt
½ pt cold water

Flead is the inner membrane of the pig's insides,
a thin fine skin full of particles of pure lard.
Remove the fat from the membrane and rub one
quarter of the flead into the flour; add the salt
and water and mix to a stiff elastic dough. Knead
well and roll out into an oblong shape. Follow
the method of incorporating the remaining fat as
for flaky pastry and use as required.

Huff Pastry

2½ lb flour
5 oz lard
1 oz salt
1 pt water

Rub the lard into the sifted flour; add the salt
and water. Mix together to make a fairly stiff
dough. Leave to rest for 1 hour. Use as required.

Pastry Covers and Linings

TYPE AND SIZE OF DISH	PASTRY	INGREDIENTS	APPROXIMATE TOTAL WEIGHT OF PASTRY
2-2½ pt deep-pie dish, top covering (for savoury and sweet pies)	Puff pastry	6 oz flour 6 oz butter 3 fl oz water	1 lb
	Savoury shortcrust pastry	6 oz flour Salt 1½ oz margarine 1½ oz lard ¾ fl oz water	½ lb
	Sweet shortcrust pastry	6 oz flour Salt 3 oz butter 1 oz sugar ¾ fl oz water	½ lb
	Rich shortcrust pastry	4 oz flour 2½ oz butter 1½ oz sugar 1 egg yolk	½ lb
8-9 inch pie plate, top and base covering	Savoury shortcrust pastry	½ lb flour Salt 2 oz margarine 2 oz lard 1½ fl oz water	¾ lb
	Sweet shortcrust pastry	½ lb flour 4 oz butter 1 oz sugar 1 fl oz water	¾ lb
	Rich shortcrust pastry	6 oz flour 3½ oz butter 2 oz sugar 1 egg	¾ lb
3-4 pt deep pie dish, top covering only (savoury pies)	Puff pastry	½ lb flour Salt ½ lb butter ¼ pt water Lemon juice	1¼ lb
	Savoury shortcrust pastry	½ lb flour 2 oz margarine 2 oz lard 1½ fl oz water	¾ lb

TYPE AND SIZE OF DISH	TYPE OF PASTRY	INGREDIENTS	APPROXIMATE TOTAL WEIGHT OF PASTRY
8-9 inch pie plate, base covering only	Savoury shortcrust pastry	6 oz flour Salt 1½ oz margarine 1½ oz lard ¾ fl oz water	½ lb
	Sweet shortcrust pastry	6 oz flour Salt 3 oz butter 1 oz sugar ¾ fl oz water	½ lb
	Rich shortcrust pastry	4 oz flour 2½ oz butter 1½ oz sugar 1 egg yolk	½ lb
8 inch flan ring, top and base covering	Savoury shortcrust pastry	10 oz flour 5 oz butter 1 fl oz water	1 lb
	Sweet shortcrust pastry	10 oz flour 5 oz butter 2½ oz sugar 1 fl oz water	1 lb
	Rich shortcrust pastry	½ lb flour 5 oz butter 3 oz sugar 1 egg yolk	1 lb
9 inch flan ring, top and base covering	Savoury shortcrust pastry	¾ lb flour Salt 3 oz margarine 3 oz lard 2 fl oz water	1¼ lb
	Sweet shortcrust pastry	¾ lb flour 6 oz butter 3 oz sugar Milk	1¼ lb
	Rich shortcrust pastry	10 oz flour 5½ oz butter 2 oz sugar 2 egg yolks	1¼ lb

TYPE AND SIZE OF DISH	TYPE OF PASTRY	INGREDIENTS	APPROXIMATE TOTAL WEIGHT OF PASTRY
9 inch flan ring, base covering only	Savoury shortcrust pastry	½ lb flour Salt 2 oz margarine 2 oz lard 1½ fl oz water	¾ lb
	Sweet shortcrust pastry	½ lb flour 4 oz butter 1 oz sugar 1 fl oz water	¾ lb
	Rich shortcrust pastry	6 oz flour 3½ oz butter 2 oz sugar 1 egg	¾ lb
Pasties and turnovers	Puff pastry	6 oz flour 6 oz butter 3 fl oz water	1 lb
	Savoury shortcrust pastry	½ lb flour Salt 2 oz margarine 2 oz lard 1½ fl oz water	¾ lb
	Sweet shortcrust pastry	½ lb flour 4 oz butter 1 oz sugar 1 fl oz water	¾ lb
	Rich shortcrust pastry	6 oz flour 3½ oz butter 2 oz sugar 1 egg	¾ lb
2 pt pudding basin	Savoury suet crust pastry	½ lb flour 4 oz suet Salt ½ oz baking powder 5 fl oz water	1 lb
	Sweet suet crust pastry	½ lb flour 4 oz suet 3 oz sugar ½ oz baking powder 5 fl oz milk	1 lb

TYPE AND SIZE OF DISH	TYPE OF PASTRY	INGREDIENTS	APPROXIMATE TOTAL WEIGHT OF PASTRY
3-4 pt pudding basin	Savoury suet crust pastry	1 lb flour ½ lb suet Salt ½ pt water 1 oz baking powder	2 lb
	Sweet suet crust pastry	1 lb flour ½ lb suet 6 oz sugar 1 oz baking powder ½ pt milk	2 lb

PUDDINGS, FRUITS, SWEETS AND DESSERTS

In its original form a pudding was a savoury item consisting of an accumulation of ingredients stuffed into the stomach bag or the intestines of an animal and boiled in water. The pudding term has extended to such an extent that it can now mean any mixture, boiled, steamed, baked or fried and its meaning and application are indefinite.

Sweet puddings were originally an extension of the savoury pudding concept, but are now an established feature with definite variations. Sweet puddings most closely connected with the original are those which are boiled in a cloth or steamed in a pudding basin, followed by baked puddings.

In addition, there are other sweet puddings which have developed as distinct variations, and in this group are found those based on milk or cream and which are thickened with either a farinaceous substance, with eggs, gelatine, rennet, cream or by freezing. The following items comprise this classification:

Boiled or steamed puddings. Termed boiled if they are made in intestines, stomach bag, or cloth; termed steamed if they are made in a pudding bowl or basin. May be sweet or savoury.

Milk puddings. A sweet pudding made with milk; thickened with some form of grain.

Custard puddings. A sweet or savoury pudding made with milk; thickened with eggs.

Gelatine puddings. These are made with some kind of sieved fruit or juice set in gelatine.

Syllabub. An infusion of sherry or wine, brandy, lemon juice and rind, and sugar; mixed with whipped double cream; served in tall glasses

so that the liquid and cream separate and the liquid is either spooned or drunk through the cream.

Junket (or curds and cream). A sweet pudding made with fresh milk and flavourings, set with rennet; served with cream .

Ices. Made with some kind of fruit pulp or juice or a cream-based custard; set by freezing.

BOILED OR STEAMED PUDDINGS

Savoury (Using stomach bag or intestines)

Stomach bag and intestines should be free from holes and should be thoroughly washed and scraped before use. Steep overnight in cold water. Half-fill as the filling needs room for expansion. Sew up securely.

Prick the outside of the bag or intestine surface with a fork or skewer to prevent bursting: it may also be pricked during cooking. Simmer in sufficiently boiling water to cover. It is not necessary to cover with a lid during the cooking.

Savoury and Sweet (Pudding cloth)

Use a cloth of closely woven cotton or linen. Scald before use and dust the inside with flour. To fill, place the cloth in a large basin so that the edges overlap. Pour the mixture in so that it takes the round shape of the basin. Draw the edges together and tie securely, allowing enough air space for the expansion of the pudding.

Place in a large pan of boiling water — enough almost to cover the pudding. Cover with a tight fitting lid and simmer. Check the water level occasionally throughout the cooking and fill up with boiling water as necessary.

Savoury and Sweet (Pudding basin)

Cover the filled bowl securely with greaseproof paper and a cloth tied on top of this. If the top covering should break the condensed steam makes the pudding soggy and heavy-textured.

Place the basin in a large pan of boiling water with enough water to come at least halfway up the sides of the basin. Cover with a tight fitting lid and simmer. Check the water level throughout cooking time and fill up with boiling water as necessary.

MILK PUDDINGS

These are made from milk and grain which may be whole — rice, barley or ball tapioca — or from partially ground grains, such as semolina, ground rice, sago or seed pearl tapioca or from powdered grain, e.g. cornflour, arrowroot or wheat flour.

Adding Eggs to Milk Puddings. Beat a whole egg and add to the pudding when cooked and cooled for 5-10 minutes. Do not boil. Separate egg and beat in the yolk; beat the white stiffly and fold in. Bake in a hot oven until well risen and brown on top.

Alternatively, separate the egg and beat the yolk into the cooked pudding. Make a meringue from the white and pile on top of the pudding. Bake very slowly for about 20 minutes or until light brown on top.

Average Portions

1½ oz grain
1 pt milk
1 oz sugar
½ oz butter
Flavourings

Whole Grain Milk Puddings

Bake slowly in an ovenproof dish for 2-3 hours or boil over low heat until all the milk is absorbed,

after 1 hour. Alternatively, boil and finish off in a hot oven with an egg to give a brown surface.

Partially Ground Grain Milk Puddings

Sprinkle the grains gradually into hot milk; stir until boiling and cook for approximately 10 minutes. Alternatively, add an egg to the boiled mixture and bake in a hot oven until brown on top.

Powdered Grain Milk Puddings

Blend the grains with part of the measured milk. Heat the remainder of the milk and pour over the mixture. Return to the pan and bring to boiling point, stirring all the time. Cook gently for 2-3 minutes. It may also be moulded and turned out when cold.

Alternatively, add an egg to the boiling mixture and bake in a hot oven until brown on the top.

CUSTARD PUDDINGS

Plain Custard Pudding

4 eggs
1 pt milk
3 oz sugar
Flavouring

Oven: 325°F; gas mark 3; 45-50 minutes

Heat the milk, pour it over the beaten eggs and sugar and blend; strain and add flavouring. Pour into a buttered dish; place in a roasting tin with hot water and bake in centre or lower part of oven until set. Do not boil the custard. The texture should be smooth and free from holes. Leave to cool. Turn out and serve.

Rich Custard Pudding

4 eggs
¾ pt milk
5 fl oz double cream
3 oz sugar
Flavouring

Oven: 325°F; gas mark 3; 45 minutes

Heat the milk and cream; pour over the beaten

eggs and sugar; mix and strain. Add flavouring. Pour the mixture into a buttered dish, set in a roasting tin of hot water and bake until set. Turn out and serve hot or cold.

Rich Custard Sauce

8 egg yolks
¾ pt milk
5 fl oz double cream
3 oz sugar
Flavouring

Heat the milk and cream; pour over the beaten eggs and sugar; mix and strain. Add flavouring. Heat in a double saucepan, stirring continuously until it thickens and coats the back of a wooden spoon. Pour into a dish or mould and allow to set, or serve as a sauce.

GELATINE PUDDINGS

Fruit Jelly (Lemon)

1¼ pt water
½ pt lemon juice
Thinly cut rind of 4 lemons
½ lb caster sugar
2 cloves
2 egg whites
2 oz gelatine (dissolved in a little water)
5 fl oz sherry or water

Place the rind, sugar, cloves, egg whites, water and lemon juice in a pan and bring slowly to the boil; strain. Place the gelatine in a cup with a little water, set in a pan of boiling water and dissolve. Whisk the dissolved gelatine into the mixture.

Simmer gently for 10 minutes, then add the sherry or water. Allow to cool; pour into a wetted mould and leave to set.

When set, dip the mould quickly into hot water and turn out.

Fruit Mould (Rhubarb)

1½ lb rhubarb
2 tablespoons water
Juice of 1 lemon
1 oz gelatine
6 oz sugar
Colouring (optional)

Wash and cut up the rhubarb, add the water and stew to a pulp. Add the lemon juice, measure and make up the pulp to 1 pint. Dissolve the gelatine in a little warm water and mix with the rhubarb. Add the sugar, stir well and pour into a mould.

Leave to set, turn out and serve with custard or whipped cream.

Stewed Fresh Fruit

2 lb prepared fresh fruit
½ lb sugar
½ pt water (1 pt for hard fruits)

Put the prepared fruit with the sugar and water into a pan and cook gently until soft.

Alternatively, make a syrup with the sugar and water and simmer for 2 minutes; add the fruit and cook gently until tender. This method is recommended for fruits which break down easily in cooking.

The prepared fruit may also be put in a casserole with the sugar and water or the prepared syrup and cooked in the oven at 350°F, gas mark 4, for 30-60 minutes, covered with a tight fitting lid.

Stewed Dried Fruit

1 lb dried fruit (prunes, apricots, peaches, figs, apples, pears)
1 pt water
½ lb Demerara sugar
1 strip lemon peel

Wash the fruit thoroughly, add the water and soak for 12 hours. Put the fruit in a pan with the water and add the sugar and lemon peel. Simmer until the fruit is soft.

Remove the fruit to a serving dish; boil up the juice to a syrup and pour over the fruit. Serve hot or cold.

The soaked fruit may also be cooked with the other ingredients in an ovenproof dish in the oven for 1 hour.

CREAM SWEETS

Syllabub

1½ pt double cream
10 oz sugar

Rind and juice of 3 lemons
½ pt sherry or wine
5 fl oz brandy

Dissolve the sugar in the lemon juice; add the rind, sherry and brandy. Warm slightly to dissolve the sugar and infuse the flavours, then decant into a bowl.

Whip the double cream and blend into the mixture. Pour into tall glasses. The cream will separate so that the liquid is either spooned or drunk through the cream as in Irish Coffee.

Junket

2 pt milk
1 oz sugar
1 tablespoon rennet (double quantity if pasteurised milk is used)

Warm the milk to blood heat and add the sugar; pour into a glass dish. Stir in the rennet and allow to set at room temperature for approximately 30 minutes. Serve with cream and sprinkle the top with grated nutmeg.

ICES

Fruit Ices

½-¾ pt fruit pulp
Lemon juice
½ pt double cream, lightly whipped
Rich custard from 3 egg yolks, ½ pt single cream, 1½ oz sugar
6-8 oz caster sugar
Food colouring (optional)

Blend the fruit pulp with a squeeze of lemon juice, the cream and custard and add sugar and colouring; stir well. Pour the mixture into an ice tray; half freeze.

Transfer the mixture to a bowl and beat until broken up but not soft. Return the mixture to the tray and freeze until firm.

Water Ices

1 pt water
½ lb caster sugar
5 fl oz lemon juice, grated rind of 2 lemons
2 egg whites

Put the water, lemon rind and sugar in a pan and boil for 10 minutes. Strain the lemon juice which should measure 5 fl oz. When the syrup is cold, strain, add the lemon juice and freeze. When half frozen, add the beaten egg whites and continue freezing until firm.

Custard Cream Ices

1 pt double cream, lightly whipped
Rich custard from 3 eggs or 6 yolks, 1 pt single cream, 3 oz sugar
10-12 oz caster sugar
Flavouring

Prepare the custard and leave to cool. Add the sugar, flavouring and whipped cream.

Have the refrigerator set at its coldest and pour the cream mixture into clean and dry freezing trays. When half frozen, remove the cream to a bowl and beat until broken down but not soft. Return to the trays and continue freezing until firm.

YEAST-BAKED GOODS

Bread is made from a fermented yeast dough using wheat flour; it may be shaped into loaves, rolls or buns of any size and shape. The plain dough may be enriched with fat, sugar and eggs.

YEAST

Yeast may be obtained fresh or dried. Fresh yeast can be kept for four or five days in a polythene bag or covered plastic container in a cool place. If stored in a refrigerator it will keep for a month, or if stored in an ice box or freezer it will keep for much longer, provided it is wrapped in plastic or foil.

Dried yeast is useful as it can be stored with other dry ingredients in the larder. It will keep for about six months.

Yeast is a minute single-celled plant visible only under the microscope. It feeds on carbohydrates — starches and sugars. Given the right conditions for growth, such as food, moisture and warmth, yeast produces carbon dioxide as a waste product. The carbon dioxide acts as a raising agent making the dough spongy and light. Time is needed for this to take place and the dough is therefore left while this takes place, as evident in the dough rising.

Fresh yeast is mixed with sugar and part of the warmed liquid. *Dried yeast*, which is used in half the quantity of fresh yeast, is mixed with a quarter of the measured liquid and warmed to blood heat. Boiling water kills the yeast. Pour the water into a cup or container and sprinkle on the yeast, whisking with a fork. Leave for 10-15 minutes in a warm place or until the surface of the liquid is covered with bubbles and the yeast granules have dissolved. Stir the mixture and use as required. If milk is used instead of water, a little sugar dissolved in the milk before the yeast is added helps it to work more quickly.

FLOUR

A strong flour with a high gluten content should be used to give the best results (see pastry); self-raising flour is not suitable.

OTHER INGREDIENTS

Salt is necessary for flavour, but too much retards the action of the yeast and may kill some of it. Sugar is required by yeast as a food; too much sugar will kill some of the yeast cells and delay fermentation.

Fat added to a mixture enriches the dough and helps to prevent the bread from going stale. It also reduces the elasticity of the dough and retards the action of the yeast which may result in a smaller rise.

Water alone gives a better texture to plain bread while milk improves the food value and helps to give a browner crust. Egg yolks improve the gluten, giving a better rise and also help to prevent the bread from going stale.

White Bread

3 lb strong plain flour
½-1 oz cooking salt
1 oz fresh or ½ oz dried yeast
½ tablespoon sugar
1½ pt warm water
1 oz lard or 1 fl oz oil

Oven: 450°F; gas mark 8; 15 minutes, reducing to
       375°F; gas mark 5; 1 hour (for two 2 lb
       loaves or 35 minutes for three 1 lb loaves)

Mix the flour and salt together, the bowl, flour and liquid being warmed to blood heat. The temperature should remain constant to activate the yeast; intense heat will kill the yeast while at low temperatures it becomes inactive.

Cream the yeast with the sugar until liquid or blend dried yeast with ¾ pt of the warmed liquid. Rub the fat into the flour or add oil to the liquid. Mix the yeast into the flour, using the fingers stretched open, until all the flour has been absorbed. The dough should feel firm but soft at this stage.

Knead the dough, on a floured surface, to strengthen it and distribute the yeast. The dough may at first feel soft and sticky, but do not add any more flour. Kneading is a process in which the dough is pulled, stretched and squeezed and folded in a rhythmic manner; the fingers will come clean and the dough feel elastic when ready. Kneading can be done at slow speed in an electric mixer using dough hooks until the mixture leaves the bowl clean.

Lightly flour the mixing bowl and return the kneaded dough to it. Cover the bowl with a damp cloth or a large oiled polythene bag and leave in a warm place until the dough has risen and doubled in size, about 1 hour.

While the dough is rising, grease the loaf tins; from the basic recipe three loaves can be made in 1 lb tins or two loaves in 2 lb tins.

The dough is now knocked back, a process whereby the bubbles formed by the yeast are knocked out. The large gas bubbles would make holes in the dough if baked. The action of the yeast will have softened the dough and kneading is again necessary to strengthen it so that the dough regains its elasticity and firmness. The mixer can be used at a slow speed.

The dough is ready for shaping according to various recipes. Put the tins on baking sheets in a warm place and leave for 15-20 minutes. The dough will recover and puff up to twice its size as the yeast becomes lively again and proves itself. The dough must not be allowed to form a skin as a dry surface will impede rising. It is therefore important to cover it lightly with an oiled polythene bag or a damp cloth above the dough.

Bake in a hot oven at first to kill the action of the yeast, then reduce the heat after 15 minutes. When baked the bread should be well risen and golden brown and when tapped underneath with the knuckles should sound hollow. Cool it on a wire tray.

Brown Bread

3 lb plain flour (a mixture of brown and white)
1½ pt warm water
1oz fresh or ½ oz dried yeast
1 oz salt
½ tablespoon sugar
2 oz lard or 2 fl oz oil

Follow the instructions for white bread. Shape into baps, cobs, rolls, tin loaves or bake in clay flower pots. For a soft crust, brush with oil before proving; for a crisp crust, brush with salt and sprinkle with water and crushed wheat before baking.

For flower-pot loaves, grease the pots well before use; it is advisable to grease and bake the pots empty several times.

Enriched Bread

1 lb plain strong flour
¼ oz salt
½ oz fresh or ¼ oz dried yeast
½ tablespoon sugar
4 fl oz warm milk and water
2 oz butter
1 beaten egg

Oven: 450°F; gas mark 8; 10 minutes
       375°F; gas mark 5; 35 minutes

Put the flour and the salt in a warm bowl and keep warm. Cream the yeast and sugar. Warm the milk and butter to blood heat; add the egg. Add this mixture and the creamed yeast to the flour and knead to an elastic dough.

Cover the mixture and allow to rise; knock back, shape and prove. Bake.

Bread Rolls

White bread dough mixture, using 1½ pt milk and water

Oven: 425°F; gas mark 7; 20-30 minutes

Make up as for white bread. After knocking back, divide and shape the dough as follows:

Plain round. Roll into a ball using the palm of the hand.

Cottage roll. Divide the dough into two thirds and one third portions. Roll into balls. Put one on top of the other, damping to make them stick; use a floured finger to make a hole through the centre of the roll.

Plait. Divide into three portions; roll each into a long sausage. Damp the ends and secure while plaiting loosely; seal the ends together.

Horseshoe. Roll into a sausage shape and curve into a horseshoe.

Winkle. Make into a 9-10 in roll, and form into a coil or shell shape.

Knot. Make a roll about 9-10 in long and tie into a loose knot.

Ring. Make into a 7-8 in roll; secure the ends to form a ring.

Bridge roll. · Shape into small rolls under the palm of the hand, tapering the ends slightly.

Clover leaf. Divide into three equal pieces and roll each into a ball; place in the tin so they just touch each other.

Place on a lightly floured baking tray to double in size. Brush with milk or, if a soft top is preferred, with fat or cooking oil, or brush with beaten egg and sprinkle with poppy or caraway seeds. Bake.

SCONES, BUNS AND CRUMPETS

Scones

1 lb self-raising flour (or 1 lb plain flour and 1 oz baking powder, a little more milk may be necessary; or 1 lb plain flour and 2 teaspoons bicarbonate of soda and 4 teaspoons cream of tartar)
1 teaspoon salt
4 oz butter
4 oz sugar
2 eggs
5 fl oz milk

Oven: 425-450°F; gas mark 7-8 ; 8-10 minutes

Sift the flour, raising agents and salt. Rub in the fat until the mixture resembles fine breadcrumbs; add any other dry ingredients. Make a well in the centre and add the beaten eggs and the liquid. Bring the flour in from the edges by stirring round the edge of the liquid, tossing the flour lightly in. Never stir in the centre. The dough should have a soft elastic consistency.

Shape as required, handling as little as possible; do not roll out with a rolling pin, but flatten with the knuckles to ½-¾ inch in thickness. Brush with milk or beaten egg or dust with flour. Place on a greased baking sheet and bake.

Buns

1 lb plain flour
1 oz baking powder
Pinch salt
6 oz butter
6 oz caster sugar
2 eggs
3/8 pt milk

Oven: 425°F; gas mark 7; 15-20 minutes

Sift the flour, baking powder and salt. Rub in the butter until the mixture resembles fine breadcrumbs and add any other dry ingredients. Add the beaten eggs and milk and mix to a fairly stiff consistency.

Shape as required and brush with beaten egg or milk; place on a greased baking tray and bake.

CRUMPETS AND PANCAKES

These are cooked on a griddle (or girdle). Put the griddle over very low heat for about 30 minutes before it is required to ensure an even distribution of heat. Grease with a piece of suet wrapped in a cloth. To test the heat, hold the palm of the hand over the griddle, about 1 in from the surface. It should not be burning hot, but should give off a bearable heat.

Alternatively, dust the griddle with a little flour which should turn brown in a few minutes, not burn immediately. Keep the heat constant throughout to prevent uneven browning.

Crumpets (or Pikelets)

1¼ lb plain flour
1 oz salt
1 pt warm water
½ oz yeast

Dissolve the yeast in part of the water; sift the flour and salt and mix in water. Add the yeast; cover and leave in a warm place until the dough rises. Thin down to Yorkshire pudding consistency with half a cup of warm water. Leave for 3 minutes.

Cook the crumpets in greased crumpet rings on a hot plate or griddle. Fill the rings halfway up with batter and turn. When dry on top and lightly browned underneath, remove the crumpet rings. These are 3½ in wide and about 1 in deep.

Pancakes (Scottish)

1 lb plain flour
1 oz baking powder
¾ pt milk
2 eggs
5 oz sugar
2 fl oz oil or melted butter
Pinch salt

Mix the milk, eggs, sugar, oil or melted butter together in a bowl. Sift the flour, baking powder and salt and mix to a soft dropping consistency.

Drop the mixture in spoonfuls on to a heated griddle. Cook until the surface begins to bubble, then turn and cook on the other side. Cool in a towel; serve with butter.

CAKES, GINGERBREAD AND BISCUITS

Rich cakes have a high proportion of eggs, sugar and butter to flour so that enough air can be enclosed to rise it by beating the sugar and butter and then beating the eggs into the mixture; chemical raising agents are therefore not necessary. Rich cakes have a fine crumb, good flavour and colour and good keeping qualities.

In plain cakes, the proportion of eggs, sugar and butter to flour is less than in rich cakes and they need a chemical raising agent. As the amount of fat to flour is small it is usually rubbed into the mixture rather than creamed. Plain cakes are coarse-textured, with poorer keeping qualities than rich cakes.

In sponge cakes, equal quantities of eggs and sugar are beaten together until thick and full of air bubbles, the flour is then folded in. No chemical raising agent is necessary. The result is a very light, fine-textured cake.

GINGERBREAD

Gingerbread cakes are made to the principles of rich or plain cakes, but with the addition of gingerbread ingredients, such as spices, honey, black treacle or golden syrup. The sweetening is often melted with the fat and sugar and incorporated in this way rather than by the creaming or rubbing-in methods common in cakes.

Gingerbread biscuits are thin and hard, spiced and sweetened with golden syrup, sugar, honey or treacle. Gingerbread parkins are made with oatmeal instead of wheat flour.

BISCUITS

These are hard and usually with a low moisture content compared with other baked goods; they may be rich or plain.

FLOUR

Use self-raising flour, omitting the raising agents, or a general-purpose or soft plain flour (see pastries) with the prescribed raising agents. It is not necessary to use flour with a high gluten content. Excessive handling or mixing should be avoided as this develops the gluten and gives a tough texture to the end product.

FATS

Butter or margarine are the most suitable fats for cake making, particularly butter because of its flavour. Lard or vegetable cooking fats may be used in conjunction with butter or margarine, but used on their own do not have the same flavour or colour.

SUGAR

Caster sugar is the most suitable for all types of cakes and biscuits, but soft brown sugar or Demerara sugar may be used for gingerbreads and granulated sugar for plain cakes.

RAISING AGENTS

Baking powder may be used for all types of cakes, bicarbonate of soda and cream of tartar with fresh milk. If buttermilk is used, the amount of cream of tartar is reduced as buttermilk provides some of the acidity. This is used for some types of scones and teabreads. Air is used as a raising agent in sponge cakes by including whisked eggs.

PREPARATION OF FRUIT AND NUTS

Dried fruit can be bought packaged and cleaned, otherwise wash in a sieve in cold water, drain and dry in a cloth, then spread on greaseproof paper and dry in a warm place. Alternatively, place the fruit in a clean towel, cover with flour and rub well; sieve to remove the flour.

Scrape the sugar off candied peel and cut into fine shreds or chop; if hard, soak in boiling water for a minute or two. Wash and dry glacé cherries and toss in flour.

To blanch almonds, place in a pan with cold water to cover; bring to the boil, strain and rinse in cold water. Slide off the skins. Heat hazelnuts through in the oven or under a slow grill, shaking occasionally to turn them; rub in a clean cloth and the papery skins will come off.

CONSISTENCY

In order to give an approximate indication of the required finished consistency, the following terms have been used: very stiff (close-textured, hardest consistency), stiff, fairly stiff, stiff elastic, elastic (open-textured, softer consistency), soft elastic, dropping (a stiff pouring consistency which will drop easily from a spoon), and soft dropping.

PREPARATION OF TINS

Plain cakes. Brush with melted fat or oil.

Rich cakes. Line the sides and base of the tin with greaseproof paper.

Cut a piece of greaseproof paper long enough to reach round the tin and deep enough to extend about 2 in above the top edges. Cut another piece to fit the base of the tin. Fold up the bottom edge of the long strip about 1 in creasing it firmly, and snipping the folded portion at intervals with scissors. Place the strip in position round the inner edge of the tin, then put in the bottom piece which will keep the snipped edge of the band in position. If the cake is to be baked for more than 2-3 hours, tie two or three layers of greaseproof paper round the outside and have several layers of greaseproof paper on the base. This prevents excessive browning round the outside edges of the cake, and also prevents the cake drying out too quickly.

Sponge sandwich cakes. Grease and flour the tins; they may also be lined with greaseproof paper.

Swiss rolls. Cut a piece of greaseproof paper 2 in longer and wider than the tin; place the tin on it and in each corner make a cut from the corner of the paper to the corner of the tin. Grease both paper and tin and line with the paper so that it fits closely, overlapping at the corners.

Gingerbread. Grease tins for plain cakes and line with greaseproof paper for rich cakes.

TESTING FOR READINESS

Large cakes. Should be well risen, firm to the touch and lightly browned. Test by inserting a warm skewer or knitting needle into the centre of the cake: the skewer should come out perfectly clean without any uncooked mixture adhering.

Small cakes. Should be well risen, lightly browned and when pressed gently with the finger-tips should give very lightly to the pressure, then rise again immediately, retaining no impression.

COOLING

Leave the cake for a few minutes before turning out of the tin on to a wire rack. If the cake is small, remove any greaseproof paper. If large, the paper may be left on until the cake is cold.

STORING

Store in airtight tins. Leave rich cakes for at least 24 hours before cutting. Large rich cakes may be wrapped in greaseproof paper if they are to be kept for any length of time. Alternatively, wrap cakes in greaseproof paper and kitchen foil instead of storing in tins. Never store cakes and biscuits in the same tin.

Rich Cake

9 eggs
1 lb butter
1 lb caster sugar
1 lb plain flour

Oven: 350°F; gas mark 4; 2 hours

Line a 10 in cake tin with greaseproof paper.

Beat the eggs in a large bowl set over a pan of hot water; warm the butter and sugar slightly and cream until light and fluffy. Gradually beat in the warmed eggs; add a little of the measured flour if there is any sign of the mixture curdling.

Stir in the sifted flour and mix to a soft dropping consistency; add any additional ingredients. Pour into the prepared tin, level the top and bake.

Plain Cake

1 lb plain flour
1 oz baking powder
6 oz butter
6 oz caster sugar
Pinch salt
2 eggs
½ pt milk

Oven: 350°F; gas mark 4; 2 hours

Sift the flour and baking powder; rub in the fat until the mixture resembles fine breadcrumbs, add the sugar and any other dry ingredients.

Mix to a dropping consistency with the beaten eggs and milk and pour into a greased cake tin; make a shallow well in the centre of the mixture to prevent the cake from rising unevenly.

Sponge Cake

3 eggs
3 oz caster sugar
3 oz plain flour

Oven: 375°F; gas mark 5; 20 minutes

Grease two sandwich tins, 6-7 in wide, and dust lightly with flour. Put the eggs and sugar in a warm bowl, stand it over a pan of hot water and whisk the mixture until light and creamy; it should be stiff enough to hold the shape of a trail from the whisk.

Remove the bowl from the heat and sift half the flour over the mixture; fold it in very lightly with a metal spoon. Add the remaining flour in the same way. Pour the mixture immediately into the tins and bake. When cool, sandwich with jam and dust the top with icing sugar.

Gingerbread Cake

Approx. total weight 3 lb		*1½ lb*	*¾ lb*
Plain flour	1 lb	½ lb	4 oz
Butter or lard	½ lb	4 oz	2 oz
Caster sugar	½ lb	4 oz	2 oz
Black treacle	6 oz	3 oz	1½ oz

Eggs	4	2	1
Ground ginger	½ oz	¼ oz	1/8 oz
Bicarbonate of soda	½ oz	¼ oz	1/8 oz
Milk			

Oven: 375°F; gas mark 5; 1½-2 hours

Melting method. Melt the butter, sugar and treacle very slightly. Sift all the dry ingredients and pour in the treacle mixture; stir well. Add the beaten eggs and any other ingredients and mix with enough milk to give a soft consistency. Pour into a greased tin and bake.

Creaming method. Cream the butter and sugar until light and fluffy; beat in the eggs and dissolve the treacle in milk.

Stir in the sifted dry ingredients and mix to a soft consistency with the treacle and milk; add any other ingredients. Pour into a greased tin.

Rubbing-in method. Rub the fat into the flour, add sugar, ginger and bicarbonate of soda. Dissolve the treacle in milk, add with any other ingredient to give a soft consistency. Pour the mixture into a greased tin and bake.

Gingerbread Biscuits (Ginger Nuts)

½ lb plain flour
¼ oz baking powder
¾ oz ground ginger
3 oz caster sugar
4 oz lard
4 oz golden syrup
½ beaten egg

Oven: 350°F; gas mark 4; 15 minutes

Sift the flour, baking powder and ginger and add the sugar. Melt the lard and syrup and add to the flour; mix to a stiff paste with the egg.

Roll into walnut-sized balls and place well apart on a greased baking tray. Bake.

Gingerbread Parkin

½ lb plain flour
½ lb butter
½ lb caster sugar
½ oz ground ginger
2 lb medium oatmeal
½ teaspoon bicarbonate of soda
2 lb golden syrup
2½ fl oz milk

Oven: 350°F; gas mark 4; 45-60 minutes

Rub the butter into the flour and add the sugar, ginger, bicarbonate of soda and oatmeal. Melt the syrup in the milk and pour into the dry ingredients; mix to a fairly stiff consistency.

Put the mixture into a well greased square 8 in tin, 2 in deep, and bake. When cold, cut with a fork through the slab to make a line of holes; pull the pieces apart along these lines.

Plain Biscuits

10 oz butter
4 oz caster sugar
1 lb plain flour
2 eggs
1/8 oz salt

Oven: 325°F; gas mark 3; 30 minutes

Cream the butter and sugar until light and fluffy; beat in the eggs and then mix in the sifted flour and salt to a stiff consistency. Alternatively, rub the butter into the flour, add the other ingredients and mix with the eggs to a stiff consistency.

Knead well, roll out, prick with a fork and shape as required. Bake.

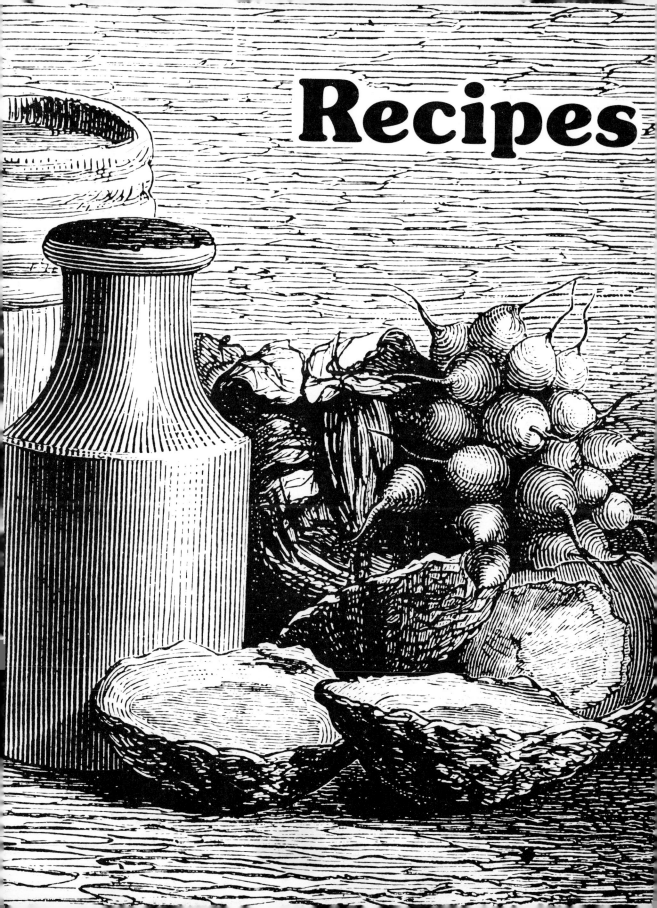

Recipes

Soups, Broths and Pottages

The word soup has developed from "sop", a term originally applied to bread dipped or soaked in water or wine before being eaten or cooked. Broth was the liquid in which a piece of meat (or fish) had been boiled, with the additional flavours of herbs, spices and vegetables. A pottage was a thick concoction of the broth to which were added chopped-up pieces of meat; this all-in-one meal was served hot in a small basin or bowl, made from metal, earthenware or wood and known as a "pottager".

Today, the term soup is applied to a more sophisticated version of the broth and may be Strained or sieved or made into a cream soup with the addition of fresh cream. A pottage usually refers to a thick sieved soup or a thick broth.

Broths, soups and pottages often have additional thickening in the form of a starchy substance, such as potatoes, oatmeal, barley, sago, rice, tapioca, arrowroot or cornflour. The thickening may also be in the form of a white or brown roux to which the liquid is gradually added, or flour and butter may be kneaded together and added to the simmering liquid. To enrich the soup a mixture of eggs and cream, known as a liaison, is sometimes added just before serving.

Soups are divided into the following categories:
1. Fish Soups
2. Game and Poultry Soups
3. Meat Soups
4. Vegetable Soups
5. Miscellaneous Soups

FISH SOUPS

These range from the once traditional Irish herring soup, consisting of a grilled salt or red herring placed in a soup bowl and covered with boiling water and a good helping of boiled potatoes, or the equally spartan whelk soup from the Island of Iona (seasoned whelk stock thickened with oatmeal and minced onions) to the luxurious lobster soups.

Grunt soup was another Irish speciality reflecting hard pecuniary circumstances: cleaned grunts (the young of the perch) were cooked until tender in water or milk and water, boned and skinned and added to the cooking liquid together with chopped chives and seasonings; the thickened broth was served with boiled potatoes.

Angus Fish Soup (10 portions) H Angus

An economical soup that makes use of the trimmings from a previous haddock dish.

16 fresh haddock heads
2 pt water
6 oz sliced carrots
½ lb chopped turnips
4 oz chopped celery
½ lb chopped onions
6—8 sprigs of parsley
Salt and pepper
1½ oz flour
1½ oz butter
1½ pt milk
Pinch of thyme
1 heaped tablespoon finely chopped parsley
Mushroom ketchup (optional)
2 egg yolks
5 fl oz cream
Garnish: chopped parsley

Clean and rinse the heads and place in a saucepan with the water. Bring to the boil and skim carefully. Add the carrots, turnips, celery, onions and parsley sprigs; season with salt and bring to the boil, cover and simmer for 20 minutes.

Make a white roux from the flour and butter and gradually stir in the strained stock. Bring to the boil and simmer, adding the milk, thyme, chopped parsley and mushroom ketchup if used.

Blend the liaison of egg yolks and cream and add to the soup; do not let it come to the boil. Adjust the seasoning and serve garnished with freshly chopped parsley.

Clam Soup (8 portions) F and H Northern Ireland

Made from fresh clams which are particularly good in late summer and early autumn.

3 doz clams
3 pt fish stock
1 pt milk
2 lb peeled and chopped potatoes
2 oz butter
2 oz flour
1 oz chopped chives
Salt and pepper
Accompaniment: sippets

Wash and scrub the clams and boil in a pan with enough fish stock to keep them from burning. As soon as the shells open, remove the clams from the pan and extract the meat from the shells.

Chop the meat finely; strain the liquid and make up to 3 pints with more stock. Pour the liquid back into the pan and add the milk and potatoes; bring to the boil and simmer until tender. Add the clam meat, butter and chives and cook for a further 12 minutes.

Blend the flour with a little milk, stir into the soup and simmer until it has thickened. Season with salt and pepper. Serve the soup with sippets.

Cockle Soup (8 portions) F Northern Ireland

Reminiscent of Iona whelk soup, but enriched with butter and a liaison of eggs and cream.

6 lb well-washed cockles
½ lb chopped onions
6 oz butter
2 tablespoons chopped parsley
½ lb chopped celery
4 pt boiling water
2 pt milk
4 oz cornflour
2 egg yolks
5 fl oz double cream
Salt and pepper

Garnish: 4 oz diced, blanched celery; 5 fl oz whipped cream

Sweat the onions in butter over low heat until golden; add the parsley and celery and cook for 5 minutes covered with a lid. Add the cockles and water, cover and simmer until the cockles open.

Strain and remove the cockles from the shells. Add the milk to the stock and simmer for 20 minutes. Blend the cornflour with a little milk and add to the soup. Bring to the boil and simmer for 10 minutes.

Add the cockles to the soup and blend in the liaison of egg yolks and cream. Heat through, but do not allow to reach boiling point. Adjust seasoning and just before serving lightly stir in the diced celery and whipped cream.

Crab Soup (8 portions) H Cornwall

A thick fish pulp soup, enriched with cream.

1 large cooked crab
4 oz long grain rice
2 pt milk
1 oz butter
Salt, pepper and nutmeg
2 pt chicken stock
1 teaspoon anchovy essence
5 fl oz cream

Place the rice, milk and butter in a pan, with salt, pepper and nutmeg to taste. Bring to the boil and simmer until the rice is tender. Add the brown crab meat, setting the white meat from the claws aside. Rub the mixture through a sieve or blend it in a liquidiser. Return to the pan, add the chicken stock, anchovy essence and the white crab meat.

Adjust seasoning and stir in the cream; heat the soup through without boiling.

Cream of Scallop Soup (8 portions) H

The English version of Crème de Coquilles St. Jacques.

24 scallops
4 pt fish stock
Salt and pepper
1 bay leaf
2 cloves
2 oz finely chopped onions
2 oz butter
2 oz flour

½ pt double cream
2 egg yolks

Slide the scallops from the shells, remove the beards
and chop the white meat and pink coral roughly.
Put the meat and coral into a pan with the fish
stock, salt and pepper, bay leaf, cloves and onions;
simmer gently for 20 minutes.

Make a white roux from the butter and flour,
and gradually stir in the strained scallop stock.
Bring to the boil and correct seasoning.

Blend the cream and egg yolks, add to the soup
and heat through without boiling. Stir in the diced
scallop meat and coral just before serving.

Cullen Skink (8 portions) F North East Scotland

Skink is an old Scots and Irish term for a broth;
originally it simply meant a drink of liquor.

1 large Finnan haddock
4 oz finely chopped onions
1 pt milk
Salt and pepper
3–4 oz mashed potatoes
5 fl oz cream
1 oz butter
Garnish: finely chopped parsley.

Skin the haddock and place in a pan with sufficient
boiling water to cover. Bring to the boil; add the
onion and simmer until the haddock is cooked.
Lift out the fish and remove the bones. Return
the bones to the stock and simmer for 1 hour.
Flake the fish.

Strain the stock, put in a clean pan and bring to
the boil. Boil the milk separately and add to the
stock together with the flaked fish. Add salt to
taste and simmer for few minutes. Stir in the
potatoes, cream and butter. Correct seasoning.
Heat through and serve, garnished with parsley.

Eel Soup (8 portions) F and H

For centuries eels have been a favourite fish in the
West Country; they feature particularly in Cornish
recipes.

1½ lb eels
2 oz butter
3 oz flour
3 pt fish stock
1 faggot of herbs

4 oz sliced onions
10 peppercorns
3 blades of mace
Salt
5 fl oz cream
Accompaniment: sippets or soft rolls

Soak the eels in salt and water. Cut off and discard the heads and tails; pull off the skins. Melt
the butter and cook the eels, covered, for 10
minutes over gentle heat without browning. Lift
out the eels and keep them warm.

Stir the flour into the butter to make a roux
and gradually add the fish stock. Replace the eels
and add the herbs, onions, peppercorns, mace and
salt to taste. Cook, covered, over low heat until the
eels are tender; strain. Flake the fish off the bones
and add the flaked eel to the strained soup,
correct seasoning and blend the cream into the
soup. Heat through without boiling. Serve with
sippets or soft rolls.

Gower Oyster Soup (8 portions) F Wales

Until the early 19th century, oysters were everyday
fare. In this recipe from the Welsh peninsula of
Gower, oysters are served in mutton stock.
16 oysters
2 oz butter
2 oz flour
4 pt mutton stock or broth
flavoured with onions, mace and black pepper

Make a light brown roux from the butter and
flour; add the stock gradually, stirring
continuously. Bring to the boil and leave to
simmer for 15 minutes. Clean the oysters, remove
from the shells and place in soup bowls. Strain
the broth, pour over the oysters and serve.

Lobster Soup (8 portions) H

This rich and creamy shellfish soup probably has
its origin in the opulent Edwardian era.

1 large cooked lobster
2 oz butter
2 oz diced celery
4 oz finely chopped onions
2 oz diced carrots
2 fl oz brandy or white wine
2 oz flour
2 pt fish stock

2 sprigs thyme and parsley
1½ pt milk
2 egg yolks
5 fl oz double cream
Anchovy essence (optional)
Accompaniment: sippets

Melt the butter and cook the celery, onions and carrots over gentle heat, covered, until light brown. Dice the lobster meat and pound the shell roughly; add the pounded shell to the vegetables, together with the brandy or wine. Simmer for 10 minutes. Stir in the flour and gradually add the stock. Add the herbs and simmer for a further 30 minutes.

Heat the diced lobster meat in the milk. Strain the soup into the lobster and milk and blend thoroughly. Make up a liaison of the egg yolks and cream, blend into the soup and heat through without boiling.

The soup may be flavoured to taste with anchovy essence just before serving, accompanied by small bread sippets. Finely diced cucumber is sometimes used as a garnish to lobster soup.

Mussel Soup (8 portions) H and F

The native mussel is in season from September to March; for this soup it may be substituted with the more expensive oyster.

3¾ lb mussels
4 oz chopped onions
1 sprig parsley
½ pt cider
2 oz butter
6 oz sliced leeks
2 oz diced celery
1 pt fish stock
1 pt milk
Pepper, salt, nutmeg
2 egg yolks
5 fl oz double cream
Garnish: parsley

Scrub the mussels thoroughly and scrape off the beards; discard any with broken or half-open shells. Put the mussels in a large pan, with the onions, parsley and cider; cover with a lid and simmer for 5—10 minutes.

As soon as the shells open, remove the pan from the heat. Strain and reserve the stock. Remove the mussels from the shells.

Melt the butter and cook the leeks and celery,

covered, for 5 minutes without colouring. Add the heated fish stock and milk, season to taste with pepper, salt and nutmeg and simmer for 20 minutes. Stir in the reserved mussel stock and the mussels; blend the liaison of egg yolks and cream and add to the soup. Heat through without boiling; correct seasoning, sprinkle with finely chopped parsley and serve.

Oyster Stew Soup (4 portions) H

Oysters should never be subjected to fierce or prolonged cooking, or the delicate flesh becomes leathery and tough.

1¼ lb fresh or tinned oysters
1 oz butter
½ lb finely chopped onions
5 fl oz white wine
1 pt double cream
2 egg yolks
Salt and pepper

Melt the butter and cook the onions, covered, until golden; add the white wine and half the shelled and cleaned oysters, roughly chopped, together with the liquid. Cook gently for 10 minutes, add the rest of the oysters and ¾ pint of cream. Simmer for a few minutes to heat through without boiling.

Blend the egg yolks with the remaining cream; add to the soup and heat through without boiling. Season to taste with salt and pepper; serve.

Partan Bree (8—10 portions) H Scotland

"Partan" is the Gaelic word for crab, and "Bree", is a corruption of "brigh" meaning broth or juice.

2 large boiled crabs
6 oz long grain rice
2 pt milk
2 pt chicken or veal stock
Salt and pepper, anchovy essence
½ pt double cream

Remove all the meat from the boiled crabs, keeping the brown and white meat separate. Cook the rice in the milk mixed with the stock until tender; strain. Sieve or liquidise the rice and brown crab meat.

Reheat the rice and brown crab meat mixture, add the strained milk and stock to the desired consistency, then season with salt, pepper and anchovy essence. Add the chopped white crab meat, stir in the cream and heat the soup through without boiling. Correct seasoning before serving.

Salmon Soup (8 portions) F and H North England

An economical fish soup which can be made from the tail piece of a salmon, with other fish trimmings.

½ lb fresh, cooked salmon
¾ lb salmon trimmings
½ lb bones of sole
2 oz diced carrots
4 oz diced turnips
2 oz chopped celery
4 oz chopped onions
Salt and pepper
2½ lb potatoes
1 tablespoon finely chopped parsley
2 oz white breadcrumbs

Put the salmon trimmings in a pan together with the sole bones, carrots, turnips, celery and onions. Add enough water to cover, bring to the boil and add salt; skim and boil for 1 hour, covering the pan with a lid.

Strain the stock; leave to cool, then remove all fat from the surface. Boil and mash the peeled potatoes and stir into the soup. Reheat and add the salmon, chopped into ¼ in dice. Stir in the parsley, simmer for 10 minutes, then correct seasoning.

Serve the soup sprinkled with breadcrumbs.

GAME AND POULTRY SOUPS

Today, these soups are made from good quality game and meat and cleared stock unlike earlier days, when the Fife crofters supped on Kilmenny Kail, cooked on an old rabbit and water, to which were added shredded kail and chopped pickled pork; oatcakes were the traditional accompaniment. An even leaner soup was obtained from boiling an old, scrawny goose in plenty of water with a few carrots and lettuce. This would give two meals: a thinnish soup and the boiled goose served with onion sauce.

Bawd Bree (10—16 portions) F and H Scotland

This is a Scots hare broth, "Bawd" being the

Gaelic word for hare. Rowan jelly is sometimes added to the soup tureen before the soup is poured in.

1 hare
1 hough (shin) bone
6 oz diced turnips
6 oz diced carrots
½ lb chopped onions
6 oz chopped celery
Faggot of herbs
Salt and cayenne
2 oz flour
2 oz bacon fat or dripping
2 oz lightly toasted fine oatmeal
2½ fl oz mushroom ketchup
½ pt port (optional)

Prepare the hare the day before it is required; skin and clean and discard all the intestines, setting the liver aside. Hold the hare over a basin to catch all the blood, then wash to remove all the hairs. Cut off the best parts of the flesh from the back, shoulders and rump; break up the remainder and place in a deep dish, cover with cold water and leave overnight.

The next day strain the water into a pan, add the hare carcass and the hough bone; bring slowly to the boil, add the prepared vegetables, faggot of herbs and salt; simmer under cover for 2—3 hours. Remove the hare carcass and hough making sure that all bones are taken out, together with the faggot of herbs. Strain the soup and rub the vegetables through a sieve; stir this pulp back into the soup.

Flatten the pieces of hare meat, season and coat in the flour; fry until crisp in hot bacon fat. Parboil the hare liver, chop this and the fried hare pieces finely; add to the soup, with the lightly toasted oatmeal and simmer for 30 minutes. Strain the reserved blood into a small bowl, blend in the remaining flour and a few spoonfuls of the hot soup. Add this mixture to the soup, stirring continuously. Keep just below boiling point for 10 minutes, skim, add the mushroom ketchup and port wine and season to taste with salt and cayenne.

Brown Venison Soup (8 portions) F and H

Probably originating in Scotland, this is a thick game broth suitable for a cold winter's day.

1½ lb breast of venison

1½ oz butter
½ pt blood
4 pt water
6 oz finely chopped onions
1 whole carrot
Salt and black pepper
5 fl oz port
1 oz flour
1 oz butter

Strip off the meat and chop up the bones. Cut the meat into 1 in cubes and put in a pan with the butter and bones; cover tightly with a lid and cook gently for 1 hour, stirring once or twice. Remove the bones when brown.

Mix the blood and cold water and bring to the boil stirring constantly; add the bones. Stir in the venison meat, onions, carrot, salt and pepper. Simmer for 2–2½ hours depending on the tenderness of the meat. Remove the carrot, all bones and some of the meat cubes.

Add the port wine and bring to the boil; knead the flour and butter together, add to the soup and stir for a few minutes until the flour is cooked and the soup has thickened. Correct seasoning and serve the soup topped with the reserved meat.

Clear Highland Game Soup (8—10 portions) H Scotland

The best flavour is obtained from well-hung game. A similar clear game soup is made in Gloucestershire from pheasant and served with forcemeat balls made from minced pheasant and diced celery.

6 lb game bones
2 onions, halved
1 oz butter
1 shin of beef, minced
1 set of game bird giblets, minced
6 oz chopped celery
4 oz chopped white of leeks
6 oz sliced carrots
1 bay leaf
6 parsley stalks
Salt
6 peppercorns
5 fl oz port wine
Garnish: cooked game meat

Brown the bones in a roasting tin in the oven; cook the onions in the butter until light brown. Put the bones, onions, beef, giblets, celery, leeks, carrots, bay leaf, parsley stalks, salt and

peppercorns in a large pan; pour over enough water to just cover. Bring to the boil and leave to simmer for 4–5 hours, without stirring.

Strain the soup through a double layer of muslin, skim carefully to remove all traces of fat and if necessary, clarify the soup through egg foam so that it is quite clear.

Reheat the soup, add the port and correct seasoning. Serve the soup garnished with diced cooked game meat.

Cock-a-Leekie (8 portions) F Scotland

One of the oldest and best loved dishes of Scotland, cock-a-leekie was traditionally made with an old, tough cock and cooked over a low peat fire overnight for next day's supper.

1 fowl
6 pt beef stock
Faggot of herbs
Salt and pepper
1¾ lb leeks
1 doz prunes, soaked overnight

Truss the cock and place in a deep pan with the stock; bring to the boil and skim before adding the herbs, salt and pepper. Prepare the leeks, wash and cut in four lengthways, chop into 1 in long pieces, keeping the green separate from the white. Add the white of the leeks to the soup and simmer for 2–3 hours.

Add the prunes and green of leeks 30 minutes before serving. Lift out the cock, remove skin and bones and cut the meat into small pieces; put the meat in a soup tureen, correct seasoning and pour the soup over the meat.

Cream of Rabbit Soup (8 portions) F

A popular soup throughout the British Isles; it can be made from even an old rabbit provided it is simmered until tender.

1 rabbit, whole or jointed
1 lb shin of beef
½ lb chopped onions
4 oz chopped carrots
3 oz chopped celery
Faggot of herbs
3 cloves
10 peppercorns
2 oz butter
2 oz flour

5 fl oz port
2 egg yolks
5 fl oz double cream
Salt and pepper
Accompaniment: sippets

Wash the skinned and cleaned rabbit and put in a large pan with the shin of beef, cover with water and bring gently to the boil; simmer for 1 hour. Lift out the rabbit; strip off the best meat, chop it finely and rub through a sieve or blend in a liquidiser. Return the remainder of the rabbit to the pan and add the vegetables, faggot of herbs, cloves and peppercorns.

Bring to the boil and simmer for 2 hours, skim and strain. Make a white roux from the butter and flour; add the rabbit pulp. Gradually stir in the stock, bring gently to the boil and simmer for 15 minutes; add the port. Blend the liaison of egg yolks and cream; stir into the soup and heat through without boiling. Correct seasoning and serve the soup with sippets.

Feather Fowlie Soup (8 portions) F Scotland

Thought to have originated at Holyrood and said to have been a favourite dish of Mary, Queen of Scots.

1 chicken, about 3½ lb
4 oz sliced ham
1 oz chopped celery
4 oz chopped onions
6 oz sliced carrots
Faggot of herbs
3½ pt white stock
2 egg yolks
5 fl oz cream
1 tablespoon finely chopped parsley
Salt and pepper

Joint the fowl and soak the pieces in lightly salted water for 30 minutes. Rinse thoroughly; put in a pan with the ham, celery, onions, carrots, faggot of herbs and the stock. Bring to the boil, skim and simmer gently for 1½ hours. Strain into a basin, leave until cold, then remove all grease from the surface of the soup.

Simmer the soup in a clean pan, uncovered, for 20 minutes; remove from the heat. Remove the skin from the best chicken pieces and mince the meat finely. Blend the egg yolks and cream, add this liaison to the soup and heat through without boiling. Stir in the parsley and minced chicken.

Season with salt and pepper and serve.

Giblet Soup (8 portions) F

An economical broth which can be enriched by adding lean beef to the giblets and by garnishing with macaroni rings.

2 sets goose giblets or 4 sets duck giblets
4 pt carcass stock
3 oz butter
3 oz flour
1 tablespoon finely chopped parsley
1 teaspoon chopped chives
1 teaspoon chopped marjoram
5 fl oz Madeira
Salt and cayenne pepper
Accompaniment: sippets

Clean and scald the giblets and add to the strained stock. Bring to the boil and simmer until the giblets are tender. Remove the giblets and strain the soup.

Make a light brown roux from the butter and flour and gradually stir in the soup. Stir in the parsley, chives, marjoram and Madeira; season to taste with salt and cayenne pepper. Add the diced giblets and heat the soup through. Serve with toasted sippets.

Friar's Chicken Soup (8 portions) F Scotland

Dating back to at least the 18th century, this broth is traditionally served with the carved chicken in the soup. Some old recipes recommend the addition of ground mace or cinnamon and sometimes substitute the chicken with rabbit.

1 young chicken
2 lb knuckle of veal
4 pt water
Salt and white pepper
1 heaped tablespoon chopped parsley
3 eggs
Garnish: finely chopped parsley

Put the veal into a large pan, cover with water and simmer for 2 hours. Strain. Remove the skin from the chicken, cut it into small joints and add to the boiling stock; season with salt and pepper and continue cooking. Add the parsley 30 minutes before the soup is ready.

When the chicken is tender, stir in the well-beaten eggs away from the heat. Serve the soup sprinkled with parsley.

Lorraine Soup (8 portions) H Scotland

Developed from Feather Fowlie Soup, this is said to have been introduced by Mary of Lorraine, mother of Mary, Queen of Scots.

5 pt Old Scots White Soup (see recipe)
½ lb skinned breast and white meat of cold roast
    fowl
2 oz white breadcrumbs
4 hardboiled egg yolks
Grated rind of 1 lemon
Pinch grated nutmeg
3 oz butter
3 oz flour
10 oz ground almonds
Salt and pepper
1¼ pt cream

Mince the chicken meat and blend with the breadcrumbs and egg yolks; stir into 1 pt of the soup. Add lemon peel and nutmeg; bring to the boil and simmer for 30 minutes.

    Make a white roux from the butter and flour and gradually stir in the remaining soup, bring to the boil and cook for a few minutes. Stir in the almonds and the chicken, breadcrumb and egg yolks mixture; season with salt and pepper. Add the cream and heat the soup through but do not boil. Correct seasoning and serve.

Meg Merilies Soup (12 portions) F and H Scotland

Also known as Poacher's Soup, this rich game broth from the early 19th century is served with forcemeat balls and is a complete meal in itself.

½ hare
6 pt water
¾ lb chopped onions
Small bunch sweet herbs
Salt and pepper
1 oz rice flour
1 partridge or moor fowl
1 oz butter
4 oz diced carrots
4 oz diced turnips
Forcemeat balls: ½ quantity of fat bacon to liver

and meat; 1 anchovy, chopped; grated rind of ½ lemon; 1 beaten egg; salt and pepper; ½ lb breadcrumbs; grated nutmeg

Cut the hare into pieces, preserving the blood and setting aside the best meat and liver to make forcemeat balls. Wash the hare and set the water aside. Put the remainder of the hare in a pan with the water, onions, sweet herbs, salt and pepper; bring to the boil and simmer for 2 hours.

    Put the hare blood and the water in which the hare was washed in another pan and stir in the rice flour. Bring to the boil, stirring continuously, then add to the soup. Skin the partridge, cut into four pieces and brown in the butter. Add the partridge to the soup together with the carrots and turnips.

    Make up the forcemeat balls by mincing the meat and liver of the hare with the fat bacon; mix in all the other ingredients. Shape the forcemeat into marble-sized balls, fry in the butter until light brown, drain and add to the soup for the last 30 minutes of cooking. Lift out the hare and partridge pieces, remove all bones and dice the meat. Return the meat to the soup, heat through and serve.

Old Scots White Soup (16 portions) F Scotland

Dating from the 16th century, this smooth creamy soup is also known as Soup à la Reine. It is traditionally poured over rounds of crusty bread.

1 knuckle of veal
1 boiling fowl
4 oz lean bacon
3 oz chopped carrots
4 oz chopped onions
½ lb chopped turnips
½ head chopped celery
2 blades of mace
1 sprig lemon thyme
12 white peppercorns
Salt and pepper
6—8 pt water

Wipe the knuckle of veal with a damp cloth and place in a pan with the fowl and bacon. Add the chopped vegetables, herbs, peppercorns and water; bring to the boil and skim. Season with salt and pepper, then simmer gently for 2 hours, skimming occasionally.

    Strain and serve hot over rounds of bread or garnished with vermicelli. Alternatively, leave the soup to cool and set to a jelly. Before reheating, skim off the surface fat and remove any sediments. Reheat and simmer for 30 minutes.

Scots Hare Soup (10—16 portions) F
Scotland

Similar to Bawd Bree, this hare broth makes a nourishing family meal on a winter's day.

1 hare
4 oz butter
3 oz flour
8 pt water
6 oz chopped carrots
6 oz chopped celery
1½ lb finely chopped onions
Salt and pepper
½ lb rice (optional)

Skin the hare, reserving the blood. Cut into pieces and wash thoroughly, then cut off the fleshy parts from the hind legs and the back. Put the remainder in a pan with 1 oz of butter and brown gently for a few minutes; cover and cook over low heat for 30 minutes, stirring occasionally.

Make a brown roux from the remaining butter and the flour. Mix the blood with the water, strain and gradually stir into the roux; add the reserved hare meat. Bring to the boil; add the browned hare pieces, the carrots, celery and onions. Season with salt and pepper. Simmer for 2—2½ hours or until the hare is tender.

Remove the bones, strip off the hare meat, dice and return to the soup; correct seasoning and serve. Rice may be added to the strained soup and cooked for about 20 minutes to make a more substantial broth.

Turkey Soup (18 portions) F and H

Of unknown origin, this soup makes good use of a turkey carcass; duck or goose can also be used in which case the chestnuts should be omitted and the soup garnished with chopped parsley.

1 turkey carcass
5 pt white stock
2 bay leaves
Faggot of herbs
4 oz butter
2 oz flour
4 oz chopped celery
½ lb halved mushrooms
1 lb skinned and boiled chestnuts
Salt and pepper
2 fl oz Madeira

Break up the carcass, remove any meat and set aside. Put the bones in a pan, add the stock, bay leaves and faggot of herbs. Bring to the boil; simmer for 3 hours, then strain.

Make a light brown roux from half the butter and the flour; gradually stir in the stock and bring to the boil. Add the celery and simmer gently for 20 minutes.

Fry the mushrooms lightly in the remaining butter and add to the soup. Rub the chestnuts through a sieve or blend in a liquidiser, add to the soup with the diced turkey meat; season with salt and pepper and stir in the Madeira.

MEAT SOUPS

The classic British meat soups reflect centuries of inventiveness on the part of thrifty housewives who knew how to turn a piece of bacon or a few mutton scraps with plenty of water into sustaining broths. Barley Kail, cooked on a piece of hough, thickened with barley and kail and served with oatcakes were as familiar in Scotland during earlier days as the Fife Broth of pork ribs, potatoes and barley. Calf's Head Soup, however, symbolises another form for austerity. It was cooked with a cow heel or calf's head and was extremely popular after the Civil War in the 17th century when the Puritan followers of Cromwell formed the Calf's Head Club. Here, Calf's Head Soup was eaten as a symbol of scorn towards the recently beheaded King Charles I.

Bacon Broth (8 portions) F

A thick vegetable broth given additional flavour with bacon and beef.

1½ lb bacon, soaked and diced
1 lb diced shin or leg of beef
2 oz butter
1 lb sliced white cabbage
6 oz chopped parsnips
6 oz chopped carrots
6 oz sliced swedes
4 pt water
Salt and pepper
1 lb diced potatoes
6 oz sliced leeks
2 oz oatmeal

Melt the butter in a pan and cook the meat and vegetables, except the potatoes and leeks for 5–10 minutes under cover, without colouring. Pour over the water, season with salt and pepper; bring to the boil and simmer for about 3 hours; skim occasionally.

Add the potatoes 30 minutes before the end of cooking and add the leeks for the last 10 minutes. Bring the soup back to the boil. Mix the oatmeal to a paste with a little water, stir into the soup and boil until thickened. Correct seasoning.

Barley Broth (12 portions) H and F Scotland

First recorded in 19th century cookery books, various forms of barley broth were probably known in Scotland long before.

2 lb boiling beef
5 pt white stock
Salt and pepper
4 oz barley, soaked overnight
½ lb dried peas, soaked overnight
3 oz chopped onions
5 oz chopped leeks
2 oz shredded cabbage
2 oz diced celery
3 oz diced carrots
3 oz diced turnips
3 oz diced potatoes
Garnish: parsley

Put the meat in a large pan with the stock, salt, barley and peas. Bring slowly to the boil and skim. Simmer for 1 hour. Add the vegetables and simmer for 1½ hours. If the meat is cooked through before the broth has thickened it may be taken out and kept warm; dice and replace in the broth to heat through just before serving.

Skim as much fat as possible from the surface of the soup; correct seasoning. Serve garnished with finely chopped parsley.

Brown Windsor Soup (8 portions) H

A thick brown soup, popular on Victorian and Edwardian bills of fare.

½ lb shin of beef, cut into 1 in cubes
½ lb mutton, cut into 1 in cubes
2 oz butter
6 oz sliced onions
4 oz sliced carrots

2 oz flour
4 pt brown meat stock
Faggot of herbs
Salt and cayenne pepper
2 oz boiled rice (optional)
5 fl oz Madeira

Melt the butter in a pan and fry the meat and vegetables until lightly browned. Sprinkle in the flour and cook until brown. Gradually stir in the stock; bring the soup to the boil, add the faggot of herbs and simmer for 2 hours or until the meat is tender.

Season to taste with salt and cayenne pepper. Lift out the meat and remove bones and skin. Return the meat to the soup and rub through a sieve or blend in a liquidiser. Reheat the thick soup and add the rice and Madeira. Correct seasoning and serve.

Cabbage Broth I (8 portions) F

Tomatoes and paprika give a delicate pink colour to this broth.

1 lb pickled diced pork
2 oz bacon fat
2 lb shredded cabbage
4 oz chopped onions
4 oz sliced tomatoes
4 pt ham stock
2 oz flour
½ pt milk
Salt and paprika

Melt the bacon fat in a pan and cook the pickled pork, cabbage, onions and tomatoes, under cover, for 10–15 minutes without browning. Add the stock and simmer for 30–45 minutes or until the meat is tender.

Blend the flour with half the milk, stir into the broth and heat until thickened. Add the remainder of the milk, season to taste with salt and paprika and serve.

Cabbage Broth II (10–16 portions) F

This is a more substantial cabbage broth, subtly flavoured with garlic and cloves.

¾ lb diced salt pork or bacon
4 oz diced carrots
4 crushed garlic cloves
8 crushed peppercorns
2 oz butter

8 pt white stock
4 oz haricot beans, soaked overnight
2 onions studded with cloves
Faggot of herbs made from marjoram, thyme,
    parsley, bay leaf
¾ lb diced potatoes
2 lb diced cabbage
Salt
Garnish: finely chopped parsley

Cook the pork, carrots, garlic and peppercorns
in the butter under cover without browning. Add
the stock, haricot beans, onions and faggot of
herbs. Bring to the boil and simmer for 1 hour.

Add the potatoes and cabbage and simmer for
a further 30–45 minutes; remove the faggot of
herbs. Add salt to taste, sprinkle with parsley
and serve.

Hessian Soup (16 portions) F

An English economy broth, given slight substance
by the addition of a small piece of beef.

1 lb sliced lean beef
1 oz butter
8 pt water
1 lb split peas, soaked overnight
2 oz long grain rice
¾ lb sliced potatoes
6 oz chopped celery
4 oz chopped leeks
4 oz chopped onions
1 tablespoon chopped parsley
Pinch thyme
1 bay leaf
A few dried mint leaves
Salt and pepper
Accompaniment: fried sippets

Brown the meat in the butter for 5 minutes, then
put in a large pan with the water; bring to the boil
and simmer for 30 minutes skimming frequently.

Add the peas, rice, potatoes, celery, leeks,
onions and herbs; season with salt and pepper.
Simmer the soup for 2–3 hours or until it has
reduced to about 6 pints. Remove the bay leaf;
rub the soup through a sieve or blend in the
liquidiser; correct seasoning and serve with sippets.

Hotch-Pot (12 portions) F Scotland

Hotch-Pot is derived from the French term *hocher*

which means shaking together, plus pot. Hotch-
potch, hodgepot and hodgepodge are corruptions
of the word, indicating a mixture of ingredients.

3 lb neck of lamb or mutton
5 pt water
Salt and pepper
6 oz diced turnips
6 oz diced carrots
6 oz chopped salad onions
4 oz cauliflower
½ finely chopped lettuce
4 oz green peas
4 oz broad beans
Garnish: chopped parsley

Put the meat in a large pan, add the water and
salt and bring to the boil; skim carefully. Add the
turnips, carrots and onions, lower the heat and
simmer for 3–4 hours.

Soak the cauliflower and lettuce in cold salted
water for 30 minutes; break the cauliflower into
sprigs and add with the lettuce to the soup 30
minutes before the end of cooking. Add the peas
and beans to the soup for the last 12 minutes.

Lift out the meat, remove skin and bones, dice
the meat and return to the soup. Correct
seasoning and serve garnished with parsley.

Irish Bacon Broth (8 portions) F Ireland

A typical Irish farmhouse broth, the bacon in
good times being served as part of the broth, while
in leaner days it was served as a separate course.

2–3 lb bacon
4 oz split peas, soaked overnight
4 oz barley, soaked overnight
3 oz chopped cabbage
¾ lb sliced leeks
4 oz chopped carrots
3 oz chopped turnips
1 oz flour
2 oz brown sugar.

Soak salty bacon in cold water overnight. The
next day, put the bacon in a pan with 6 pints
of water, the peas and barley; bring to the boil,
skim and simmer for 1 hour. Add the vegetables
and simmer for 1 further hour or until the bacon
is tender.

Lift out the bacon and remove the skin. Dredge
with the mixed flour and sugar and put under the
grill or in the oven until brown and crisp on top.

Dice the bacon and return to the broth; heat through before serving.

Irish Farm Broth (8 portions) F Ireland

Another Irish farmhouse broth, more substantial than Bacon Broth. Traditionally, the meat is cubed and distributed in soup bowls before the broth is poured over; a boiled floury potato tops each bowl.

2 lb beef or mutton
10–12 pt water
½ lb barley, soaked overnight
1 lb dried peas or 2½ lb fresh peas
Salt
½ lb sliced onions
½ lb sliced carrots
4 oz diced swedes
With beef: 4 oz shredded cabbage
            2 lb chopped leeks
            2 lb diced potatoes
With mutton: 3 oz sliced carrots
              1 tablespoon chopped parsley
              ½ lb diced turnips
              2 oz chopped celery

Put the beef or mutton in a large pan with the water, barley and dried soaked peas; season with salt. Bring to the boil, skim and simmer, covered, for 1½ hours. Add the onions, carrots, swedes and fresh peas, if used; also the leeks and potatoes with beef, or the carrots, turnips and celery with mutton. Simmer for a further 30 minutes, then add the cabbage to beef broth, parsley to mutton.

Simmer for 20 minutes, then lift out the meat and cut into cubes. Correct seasoning before pouring the broth over the meat.

Kidney Broth (8–10 portions) F Ireland

A strongly flavoured everyday broth thickened with barley.

1 lb hough or shin of beef
6 pt water
1 lb ox kidney
2 oz diced carrots
1½ lb chopped leeks
½ lb chopped onions
4 oz barley, soaked overnight
Salt and pepper

Place the hough in a pan with the water and bring slowly to the boil. Clean the kidney and cut it into small pieces; add to the broth with the vegetables and barley.

Season with salt and pepper and simmer for 2½–3 hours. Lift out the hough, and serve the broth and meat as separate courses.

Kidney Soup (8 portions) F

Probably developed from Kidney Broth in more favourable economic conditions, this is a smooth, well-flavoured thick soup.

½ lb shin of beef
1 lb ox kidney
2 oz butter
4 oz coarsely chopped onions
1 dessertspoon chopped parsley
4 pt brown meat stock
Salt and pepper
1 oz flour
1 tablespoon tomato paste

Cut the beef and kidney into small pieces. Melt half the butter in a heavy-based pan and brown the meat and kidney, onions and parsley. Add the stock, salt and pepper and bring to the boil; skim well, cover and simmer for 3 hours, skimming occasionally.

Strain the soup and set part of the kidney pieces aside. Pass the remaining meat through a sieve or blend in a liquidiser. Melt the rest of the butter, stir in the flour to a brown roux and gradually blend in the strained liquid, meat and tomato paste. Bring to the boil and correct seasoning. Serve the soup topped with the reserved kidney pieces.

Largo Potato Soup (8 portions) F Scotland

Originating in Fife, this mutton broth is usually served on its own, the meat forming a separate course.

1 lb neck of mutton
4 pt water
4 oz finely chopped carrots
1¼ lb finely chopped onions
Salt and pepper
2 lb sliced potatoes
Garnish: chopped parsley

Wipe the mutton with a damp cloth, place in a pan with the water; bring to the boil and skim. Add the carrots and onions and season with salt and pepper. Simmer gently for 2 hours, skimming well.

Add the potatoes 30 minutes before the end of cooking time. Lift out the meat and serve separately or dice part of the meat and add to the soup. Correct seasoning; serve the soup garnished with parsley.

Lentil and Bacon Broth (8 portions) F

An English broth, often the mainstay of the poor. A similar recipe occurred in Ireland, where the broth was further thickened with 2 oz of oatmeal added with the potatoes.

½ lb diced bacon
¾ lb golden lentils, soaked overnight
1 crushed clove garlic
1 clove
1 tablespoon finely chopped parsley
Salt and pepper
1 lb diced potatoes
Accompaniment: sippets

Put the lentils in a pan with the water in which they were soaked, add the bacon, garlic, clove and parsley: season with salt and pepper. Cover and simmer for 1 hour or until lentils and bacon are cooked. Add the diced potatoes and cook for a further 20 minutes. Remove the clove; correct seasoning and serve the broth with sippets.

Old Scots Brown Soup (8 portions) F
Scotland

In spite of its similarities to Old Scots White Soup, this soup shows a definite preference for sweetness as is evident in the use of sago and the accompanying caraway sticks.

1½ lb shin of beef
1½ oz butter
6 oz roughly chopped carrots
6 oz roughly chopped onions
6 oz roughly chopped turnips
1 pt brown stock
3 pt water
1½ oz fine sago
Salt and pepper
Pinch dry mustard
2½ fl oz sherry
Accompaniment: carvie sticks

Cut the beef into cubes. Melt the butter and fry the meat and vegetables, turning frequently until brown. Add the stock and water; bring to the boil,

skim. Cover and simmer gently for 3½ hours.

Skim and strain into a clean pan; add the sago and bring to the boil. Simmer gently for a few minutes until the sago is cooked. Season with salt, pepper and mustard. Add the sherry and serve at once with carvie sticks.

Oxtail Soup (8 portions) H and F

This classic 19th century English soup has numerous variations. It is sometimes clarified and served clear, and in its more usual thick form it may contain both red currant jelly and tomato paste for colouring.

2½ lb oxtail
2 oz flour
3 oz butter
6 oz chopped onions
6 oz chopped carrots
1 oz chopped celery
4 pt brown stock
Faggot of herbs
Salt and pepper
1 teaspoon lemon juice
5 fl oz claret or sherry

Cut the oxtail into pieces, wash and dry well and dust with flour. Fry the meat and vegetables in 1 oz of the butter for 5—10 minutes or until lightly brown. Add the stock and herbs, salt and pepper; simmer, covered, for 3 hours, skimming occasionally.

Remove the meat and herbs and pass the remainder through a sieve or blend in a liquidiser. Remove all bones and dice the meat.

Make a brown roux from the remaining butter and flour. Gradually stir in the sieved soup, bring to the boil and simmer for a few minutes. Add the lemon juice, claret or sherry and serve the soup topped with the oxtail meat.

Powsowdie (16 portions) Scotland

Also known as Sheep's Head Broth, "pow" meaning head and "sowdie" sodden or boiled, and once a popular Sunday dinner dish. Sometimes the sheep's head and trotters were substituted with the skinned and split head of a stag or hind.

1 large fat sheep's head and trotters, singed
6 oz barley
½ lb dried peas, soaked overnight

2–3 lb mutton scrag or trimmings
½ lb diced carrots
2 chopped celery heads (optional)
6 oz diced turnips
¾ lb chopped onions
Salt and pepper
1 tablespoon finely chopped parsley

Steep the head and trotters overnight in warm
water. Remove the glassy part of the eyes, scrape
the head and trotters and brush until clean and
white. Split the head with a cleaver and lay aside
the brains. Clean the nostrils; split the trotters
and cut out the tendons. Wash the head and
trotters again and steep in warm water for at least
2 hours.

Put the barley and peas in a pan with the head,
trotters, scrag of mutton and enough water to
cover. Bring to the boil and skim as the scum
rises. Simmer for 1 hour, then add the carrots,
celery and turnips. The more slowly the head is
boiled, the better both broth and meat will be.
Simmer for another 2–3 hours, depending on
the age and size of the head. Add the onions and
continue simmering over very low heat for 1 hour
to finish the soup. Season with salt and pepper
and add the parsley just before serving.

The trotters and the head are served separately,
garnished with carrots, and turnips or fresh green
peas and a white sauce made from part of the
broth thickened with a roux.

Tripe Soup (6–8 portions) F

This has possibly originated in Lancashire, home
of many of the classic tripe dishes.

1 lb prepared cooked tripe
½ lb finely chopped onions
2 pt water
1½ oz butter
1½ oz flour
¾ pt milk
Salt
Garnish: chopped parsley

Cut the tripe into ½ in cubes, put in a pan with the
onions and add the water. Simmer for 30–40
minutes. Make a white roux from the butter and
flour; gradually stir in the milk and tripe and
onion soup. Season with salt. Bring to the boil,
then simmer for 5 minutes. Correct seasoning and
serve the soup garnished with parsley.

Buttermilk Soup (8 portions) F

Typical of much farmhouse fare, this broth is based
on the ready-to-hand ingredients of lamb (or
mutton) and buttermilk.

2 lb neck or shoulder of lamb
½ lb sliced onions
½ lb sliced turnips
2 oz sliced celery
1 sprig parsley
Salt and pepper
4 pt water or mutton stock
2 oz butter
2 oz flour
½ pt warm buttermilk

Put the lamb in a large pan, with the vegetables,
parsley sprig, salt and pepper. Add water or stock.
Bring to the boil and simmer over gentle heat
until the lamb is tender, skimming regularly. Strain
the soup and remove any fat from the surface.

Make a white roux from the butter and flour
and gradually add the buttermilk, stirring until
smooth; bring to the boil and simmer for a few
minutes. Gradually stir the buttermilk mixture into
the broth and simmer for 10 minutes. Correct
seasoning; serve the meat separately.

Welsh Leek Broth (8 portions) F Wales

Also known as Cawl Cennin, "cawl" meaning broth.
Traditionally, any left-over cawl was reheated and
served for breakfast the following day and was
then called Cawl aildwyn, twice-heated broth.

1 lb salt bacon
5 oz diced potatoes
6 oz diced carrots
1½ lb leeks, cut into 1 in pieces
6 oz shredded cabbage
4 pt white stock
2 oz oatmeal
Garnish: chopped parsley

Place the piece of bacon and prepared vegetables
in a pan and sweat for 5–10 minutes, under
cover, without colouring. Add the stock, bring to
the boil and simmer for 1 hour. Strain the broth
and return to the pan; blend the oatmeal with a
little water, stir into the broth and simmer until
thickened. Serve the broth as a first course,
followed by the bacon and vegetables, sprinkled
with parsley.

VEGETABLE SOUPS

From Norman days right up to the early 18th century, the daily main meal for the ordinary man consisted of a simple pottage or broth, eaten with bread. Vegetables were the main ingredients with imaginative use of cultivated herbs; in times of famine wild roots, berries and herbs scrounged from the countryside formed the basis for the daily soup. Mustard soup — thickened white stock flavoured with onion juice and mustard — occurs as early as 1375. Gerard and Markham (16th and 17th centuries) discourse at length on the excellent flavouring qualities of marigold, used for example in the Cornish Kiddley Broth, a simple pottage of bread squares, finely chopped shallots ("scifers"), seasoning, chopped marigold flowers and boiling water. Kettley broth — then standard breakfast for Cornish farm labourers — was even plainer and consisted simply of a bowl of bread with salt, pepper and a little bacon fat, covered with boiling water.

Compared with these austerity pottages, the later nettle broths of Ireland and Scotland, thickened with oats or barley, and seaweed soups seem almost luxurious. Today, vegetable soups are made from the finest ingredients and stocks, the majority of them being enriched with thick cream and eggs and often heavily garnished.

Artichoke Soup (8 portions) H

Also known as Palestine Soup from the basic ingredient of Jerusalem artichokes, this creamy soup can also be made from baby marrows.

2 lb Jerusalem artichokes
1 oz butter
½ lb sliced onions
4 oz diced celery
4 pt chicken or white stock
1 pt milk
Salt and pepper
5 fl oz double cream
2 egg yolks
Garnish: thin lemon slices, whipped cream
   flavoured with cayenne, toasted hazel nuts
   crushed and pounded.

Scrub the artichokes and place them in cold water with a tablespoon of vinegar to keep them white while scraping or peeling. Slice the artichokes; melt the butter in a pan and add the artichokes, onions and celery.

Cook the vegetables, covered, for 5—10 minutes without colouring them. Pour in the stock and simmer until the artichokes are tender. Rub the soup through a fine sieve or liquidise, return to the pan and add the milk and salt and pepper to taste.

Blend the cream and egg yolks, add to the soup and heat through without boiling. Serve the soup in individual bowls, garnish with lemon slices, whipped cream and hazel nuts.

Asparagus Soup, Creamed (8 portions) H

A popular summer soup, economically made from tough asparagus stalks and trimmings.

1 lb asparagus stalks and trimmings
3 oz butter
3 oz flour
1 pt milk
2 pt chicken or white stock
Faggot of herbs
Salt and pepper
1 tablespoon sugar
5 fl oz double cream
2 egg yolks
Garnish: cooked asparagus tips

Cut the asparagus into small pieces and put in a heavy-based pan with the butter; cook, covered, until golden. Stir in the flour and gradually add the milk and stock, stirring continuously.

Add the herbs, salt and sugar; bring to the boil and simmer for 1 hour. Remove the herbs and rub the soup through a sieve or blend in a liquidiser.

Blend the cream and egg yolks, add to soup and reheat without letting the soup come to the boil. Correct seasoning and serve the soup topped with asparagus tips.

Balnamoon Skink Soup (8 portions) F Ireland

Skink is an old Irish and Scots term for broth, in this case subtly flavoured with summer vegetables and herbs.

2 oz diced celery
4 diced lettuce leaves
4 oz fresh green peas
2 pt chicken stock
1 dessertspoon chopped chives

2 oz chopped salad onions
Sprig thyme
1 bay leaf
Salt and pepper
5 fl oz double cream
2 egg yolks

Put the prepared vegetables in a large pan with the
chicken stock, chives, thyme, bay leaf, salt and
pepper: simmer for 30 minutes or until the
vegetables are tender. Remove the thyme and bay
leaf.

    Blend the liaison of cream and egg yolks, add
to the soup and heat through without boiling.

    Correct seasoning and serve.

Beetroot Soup, Creamed (8 portions) F and H

Reminiscent of Russian Borshch but without sour
cream, this is easily and quickly made from fresh
beetroot.

1½ lb fresh beetroot
2 pt chicken stock
2 oz butter
2 oz flour
1 pt hot milk
Salt and pepper
2½ fl oz double cream
1 egg yolk

Boil the beetroot in water until tender; drain.
Carefully peel off the skin of the beetroot, chop
and liquidise with the chicken stock.

    Make a white roux from the butter and flour,
gradually stir in the beetroot mixture and the
milk; season with salt and pepper. Bring the soup
back to the boil; blend in the liaison of cream and
egg yolk. Heat through. Correct seasoning and
serve at once.

Brown Vegetable Soup (8 portions) F

This has been developed from an old Scottish
recipe for a meat and vegetable broth, with the
meat served in the soup.

¾ lb chopped potatoes
6 oz chopped carrots
4 oz chopped turnips
1 lb chopped onions
1 oz dripping
1 oz flour
4 pt brown meat stock

Salt and pepper
Garnish: chopped parsley

Melt the dripping and fry the chopped vegetables
until lightly browned. Stir in the flour. Gradually
stir in the stock, season with salt and pepper and
bring to boiling point. Simmer for 1½–2 hours,
skimming occasionally.

    Pass the soup through a sieve or blend in a
liquidiser; heat the soup through and serve
garnished with finely chopped parsley.

Celery Soup, Creamed (8 portions) H and F

A delicate vegetable broth, lightly enriched with a
little cream.

1¼ lb celery
1½ oz butter
1½ oz flour
3 pt white stock
Salt, pepper and nutmeg
1 tablespoon caster sugar
½ pt milk
2½ fl oz double cream
Accompaniment: sippets

Trim the green parts off the celery, wash and chop
roughly; blanch in salted water and drain. Melt the
butter and fry the celery lightly, under cover, for a
few minutes without colouring. Add the flour and
cook for 2–3 minutes, gradually stir in the stock;
season with salt, pepper, sugar and nutmeg.
Simmer, covered, for 30 minutes; skim if
necessary.

    Pass the soup through a sieve or blend in a
liquidiser, add the milk; bring back to the boil,
then remove from the heat and stir in the cream.
Serve with sippets.

Cheshire Soup (8 portions) F Cheshire

This cheese-flavoured potato soup is a quick
stand-by or a satisfying luncheon dish.

4 pt white stock
1 lb diced potatoes
½ lb chopped leeks
Salt and pepper
6 oz grated carrots
2 oz oatmeal
2 oz grated Cheshire cheese

Put the stock in a large pan, add the potatoes and
leeks; season with salt and pepper and bring to the

boil. Simmer for 15 minutes. Add the grated carrots and sprinkle in the oatmeal; simmer for a further 10 minutes or until thickened. Stir in the cheese just before serving.

Crécy Soup (8 portions) H

Named after the French cookery term, *a la Crécy*, which always implies the inclusion of carrots. A variation of this soup, the Buchanan Carrot soup, is further seasoned with curry or cayenne and may also contain boiled rice or pearl barley.

1½ lb roughly chopped carrots
4 oz roughly chopped turnips
4 oz roughly chopped onions
2 oz roughly chopped celery
6 oz diced potatoes
2 oz chopped ham
1 oz butter
1 teaspoon tomato purée
1 oz flour
4 pt white meat stock
Faggot of herbs
Salt and pepper
½ pt cream or milk
Garnish: chopped watercress
Accompaniment: sippets

Lightly fry the vegetables and ham in the butter under cover for 5–10 minutes without browning. Add the tomato purée and flour and gradually stir in the stock; add the faggot of herbs. Season the soup with salt and pepper; bring to the boil and simmer for 1½–2 hours, skimming if necessary.

Remove the faggot and rub the soup through a sieve or blend in a liquidiser. Return the soup to the pan and bring back to the boil. Add the cream or milk and heat through without boiling. Serve garnished with watercress and accompanied with fried sippets.

Cucumber Cream Soup (8 portions) H and F

This delicate summer soup can also be flavoured with chopped sorrel or chervil instead of the onion, and thickened with a cream and egg liaison rather than a roux.

2¼ lb finely chopped cucumber
2 oz finely chopped celery
1 oz finely chopped onions
1½ pt milk
2 oz butter

2 oz flour
Salt and pepper
½ pt double cream

Place the prepared cucumber in a double boiler, with the celery, onions and milk. Cook for 20 minutes or until the cucumber is tender.

Make a white roux from the butter and flour; gradually stir in the cucumber and milk mixture. Season with salt and pepper and simmer for a further 10 minutes, stirring frequently. Rub the soup through a sieve or blend in a liquidiser; add the cream and heat through without boiling. Correct seasoning and serve.

Irish Potato Soup (8 portions) F Ireland

This farmhouse-type soup combines the favourite Irish soup ingredients: potato and bacon.

2 lb sliced potatoes
1 oz butter or bacon fat
½ lb sliced onions
½ pt milk
3 pt white meat stock
Salt and pepper
5 fl oz single cream
Garnish: diced bacon, chopped parsley and chives

Melt the butter and gently cook the potatoes and onions, under cover, for 5–10 minutes without browning. Add the milk and stock; season with salt and pepper and simmer for 1 hour.

Rub the soup through a sieve or blend in a liquidiser. Stir in the cream and heat through without boiling; correct seasoning. Serve the soup with diced, fried bacon and parsley and chives.

Laver Soup (8 portions) F Wales and Ireland

Laver, an edible seaweed of which the red variety is considered superior to the green, is sold washed and boiled to a pulp, ready for use.

6 oz laver
6 oz butter
½ lb chopped onions
½ lb chopped potatoes
4 oz chopped carrots
4 pt mutton or fish stock
Salt and pepper, caster sugar

Melt the butter and cook the vegetables, covered, for 5–10 minutes or until slightly brown. Add the laver and stock; simmer for 20 minutes.

Rub the soup through a sieve or blend in a liquidiser; season with salt, pepper and sugar. Reheat the soup, correct seasoning and serve.

Leek and Potato Soup (8 portions) F

Reminiscent of the Welsh Leek and Potato Pie, this is a substantial, everyday soup.

1¼ lb leeks
2 oz butter
1 lb diced potatoes
3 pt white stock
1 oz flour
5 fl oz milk
Salt, pepper, mace

Trim the leeks and wash them thoroughly; cut into three lengthways and across into 1 in pieces. Melt the butter and fry the leeks until lightly coloured, under cover. Add the diced potatoes and cook for a few minutes without colouring. Sprinkle lightly with salt, add the stock and bring to the boil; simmer for 25 minutes.

Blend the flour with the milk and stir into the soup; simmer until thickened. Season with salt, pepper and mace before serving.

Leek Soup, Creamed (8 portions) F and H
Wales

A richer and smoother soup than the everyday leek and potato and enriched with cream.

1¼ lb leeks
2 oz butter
¾ lb roughly chopped onions
1 roughly chopped head of celery
3 pt mutton stock
1 oz roughly chopped parsley
Salt and pepper
5 fl oz double cream
Garnish: diced meat (optional)
Accompaniment: sippets

Clean the leeks thoroughly, chop them roughly and set a little of the green aside for garnish. Melt the butter and cook the vegetables, under cover, without browning them. Add the stock, bring to the boil and simmer for 1 hour, skimming if necessary.

Rub the soup through a sieve or blend in a liquidiser. Reheat the soup, stir in the parsley, green of leek and diced meat if used. Season with salt and pepper. Stir in the cream, correct seasoning and serve with sippets.

Marrow Soup, Creamed (8 portions) F and H

The Cambridge version of this creamed vegetable marrow soup also uses 2 oz celery, 3 oz turnips and 4 oz carrots.

2 lb vegetable marrow
3 oz butter
4 oz finely chopped onions
2 oz flour
4 pt white stock
Salt, pepper, ground ginger
5 fl oz double cream
Accompaniment: sippets

Peel the marrow, cut in half and scoop out the seeds; cut the flesh into 1 in cubes. Melt the butter in a heavy, deep pan and cook the onions and marrow, under cover, for 5–10 minutes without colouring. Stir in the flour and gradually stir in the stock; simmer gently for 40 minutes.

Rub the soup through a sieve or blend in a liquidiser. Reheat the soup and season with salt, pepper and ginger; stir in the cream but do not let the soup reach boiling point. Serve with sippets.

Mulligatawny Soup (8 portions) H and F

This highly spiced East Indian soup was extremely popular among the British Colonials and was brought to England in the 19th century. The soup was then sometimes served clear without any vegetables, but is today usually made as a thick soup.

4 oz sliced onions
4 oz sliced carrots
4 oz sliced turnips
2 oz sliced apples
2 oz chopped ham
2 oz butter
1 oz flour
1 dessertspoon curry powder
1 teaspoon curry paste
1 teaspoon tomato paste
1 tablespoon chopped chutney
4 pt brown stock
Faggot of herbs
1 blade of mace

1 clove
Salt and pepper
5 fl oz double cream
Garnish: boiled rice

Fry the onions, carrots, turnips, apples and ham in the butter until lightly brown. Mix in the flour, curry powder and paste, tomato paste and chutney. Gradually stir in the stock, add the faggot, mace and clove. Bring the soup to the boil, skim and cook over low heat for 30–40 minutes.

Remove the faggot, mace and clove and rub the soup through a sieve or blend in a liquidiser. Reheat the soup, add salt and pepper to taste and stir in the cream, but do not let the soup come to the boil. Serve the soup topped with hot, fluffy, boiled rice.

Mushroom Soup, Creamed (8 portions) H and F

Field mushrooms, freshly gathered, give the best flavour to this creamed soup; use the stalks as well as the caps and wipe them clean without peeling unless badly bruised.

1 lb chopped mushrooms
4 oz finely chopped onions
3½ oz butter
1½ pt chicken stock
2½ oz flour
1½ pt milk
Salt and pepper
2 egg yolks
5 fl oz double cream

Cook the mushrooms and onions under cover, in 1 oz of butter for 5 minutes; set aside some of the mushrooms for garnish. Add the stock and simmer for 40–45 minutes. Rub the soup through a coarse sieve or blend in a liquidiser.

Make a white roux from the remaining butter and the flour. Gradually stir in the milk and the mushroom pulp. Simmer for a few minutes; season with salt and pepper. Blend the egg yolks and cream and add this liaison to the soup; heat through without boiling and stir in the reserved mushrooms. Correct seasoning and serve.

Onion Soup, Creamed (8 portions) H and F

While the traditional French Onion Soup is clear and served with the onion rings floating in it, the British Onion Soup is a fairly thick soup, made smooth with the addition of cream.

1½–2 lb sliced onions
3½ oz butter
6 oz chopped potatoes
4 oz chopped celery
3 pt white stock
1½ oz flour
Salt and pepper
5 fl oz double cream

Melt 2 oz of the butter and cook the onions, potatoes and celery, under cover, for 5–10 minutes until the onions are transparent. Add the stock and simmer for 1 hour. Rub the soup through a fine sieve or blend in a liquidiser.

Make a white roux from the remaining butter and the flour; gradually stir in the onion pulp. Bring to the boil and simmer for a few minutes. Season the soup with salt and pepper, blend in the cream and serve.

Parsnip Soup (8 portions) F

One of the most popular root vegetables with roast meats, parsnips can also be used for a nourishing, early-winter soup.

1½ lb chopped parsnips
1 oz butter
4 oz chopped onions
2 oz chopped celery
3 pt white stock
1 oz cornflour
1 pt milk
Salt and pepper
Juice of 1 lemon (optional)
Accompaniment: sippets

Melt the butter and cook the vegetables, under cover, for 10 minutes without colouring. Add the stock and simmer for 40 minutes or until the vegetables are tender.

Rub the soup through a sieve or blend in a liquidiser. Reheat the soup; blend the cornflour with milk and stir into the soup. Season with salt and pepper and simmer for a few minutes. Sharpen with lemon juice and serve the soup with sippets.

Pea Soup (8 portions) F and H

Frozen peas may be used for this soup, but the finest flavour is obtained from freshly picked garden peas. In some versions, chicken stock replaces the white stock, and a little chopped lettuce, cucumber, leek or spinach is added for extra colour. For special occasions, cooked asparagus tips can be used for garnish.

1½ lb peas (podded)
2 oz butter
2 pt white stock
Salt and pepper
Sprig mint
Caster sugar
Garnish: small boiled peas, chopped mint
Accompaniment: sippets

Melt the butter in a pan and cook the peas gently, under cover, for 5 minutes. Add the stock, salt, pepper and sprig of mint; bring to the boil and simmer for 10 minutes or until the peas are perfectly tender.

Rub the soup through a sieve or blend in a liquidiser. Reheat the soup, correct seasoning and add sugar to taste. Serve the soup topped with small, freshly boiled peas and sprinkle with chopped mint; accompany with sippets.

Pea Soup, Creamed (8 portions) H

Fresh peas and mint constitute the traditional summer flavours of British cooking. Strathmore Creamed Pea Soup omits flour altogether and a liaison of two egg yolks with the cream is used to thicken the soup.

1½ lb fresh green peas (podded)
4 oz butter
2 oz flour
2 pt white stock
Salt and pepper
Sprig mint
Caster sugar
5 fl oz double cream
Garnish: small boiled peas, chopped mint
Accompaniment: sippets

Melt 2 oz of the butter in a pan, add the peas and cook gently, under cover, for 5 minutes. Blend in the flour and gradually stir in the stock; season with salt and pepper and add the sprig of mint. Bring to the boil and simmer for 10 minutes or until the peas are tender.

Rub the soup through a sieve or blend in a liquidiser. Return the soup to the heat; correct seasoning and add sugar to taste. Stir in the cream, but do not let the soup reach boiling point. Serve the

soup garnished with small cooked peas and chopped mint.

Potato Soup (8 portions) F

A homely, thick soup made from cooked or uncooked potatoes and thinned as required with milk.

3 lb chopped potatoes
2 oz finely chopped onions
2 oz butter
4 pt white stock
Salt and pepper
Milk
Accompaniment: sippets

Cook the onions and potatoes in half the butter until light brown. Add the stock, salt and pepper and simmer gently for 30 minutes or until the potatoes are soft. Strain the soup through a coarse sieve; reheat and add milk to the desired consistency. Serve with sippets.

Salsify Soup (8 portions) H

The long tapering roots of salsify were once gathered from the countryside, but today it is a scarce and expensive, cultivated vegetable, valued for its piquant flavour.

1 lb salsify
4 pt chicken or white stock
Juice of ½ lemon
½ lb chopped onions
Salt and celery salt
12 peppercorns
Pinch cayenne
2 oz butter
2 oz chopped watercress
2 egg yolks
5 fl oz double cream
Garnish: watercress

Prepare the salsify by scrubbing until smooth and white; put whole in a large pan together with the boiling stock and lemon juice; cook over gentle heat for 20 minutes. Add the onions, salt, celery salt, peppercorns, cayenne and butter and continue cooking until the salsify is soft. Add the watercress, retaining some for the garnish.

Rub the soup through a sieve or blend in a liquidiser. Return the soup to the pan and heat through. Blend the egg yolks with the cream and add this liaison to the soup; do not let it reach boiling point. Garnish with chopped watercress and serve.

Saxe-Coburg Soup (8 portions) F

This soup is named after Queen Victoria's eldest son who in 1901 became Edward VII of the House of Saxe-Coburg.

1 lb blanched, chopped Brussels sprouts
2 oz butter
1 chopped onion
2 oz chopped ham
2 oz flour
1 tablespoon sugar
1 pt milk
4 pt white stock
Salt and pepper
Accompaniment: sippets

Melt the butter in a large pan and cook the Brussels sprouts, onion and ham, under cover, for 5–10 minutes. Mix in the flour and sugar and gradually stir in the boiled milk and the stock. Bring the soup to the boil and simmer for 15 minutes or until tender.

Rub through a sieve or blend in a liquidiser. Return the soup to the heat, season to taste with salt and pepper and bring back to the boil. Serve with sippets.

Sorrel Soup (8 portions) F and H

The wild sorrel plant is said to have been introduced by Mary, Queen of Scots, from France although some authorities maintain that sorrel soup originated in Poland. Use a stainless steel knife for chopping the leaves to avoid stains.

½ lb sorrel leaves
2 oz butter
3 pt white stock
½ lb grated potatoes
Salt and pepper
5 fl oz double cream
Garnish: chopped sorrel leaves

Wash the sorrel leaves and remove any tough stalks and veins; retain some of the leaves, chopped finely, for garnish. Melt the butter and cook the roughly chopped sorrel, under cover, until the leaves have softened. Add the stock, grated potatoes and salt; simmer for 1 hour.

Rub the soup through a sieve or blend in a liquidiser. Return the soup to the pan and heat

through; season with salt and pepper and stir in the cream. Serve garnished with chopped sorrel.

Spinach Soup (8 portions) H and F

Until spinach was introduced in the 16th century, sorrel leaves formed the basis for this creamy summer soup.

1 lb spinach
3 oz butter
6 oz chopped onions
2 oz flour
4 pt white stock
Salt and pepper
Sprig rosemary
2 egg yolks
5 fl oz cream
Garnish: whipped cream

Wash the spinach, remove any stalks and coarse veins and chop the leaves roughly. Melt the butter and cook the spinach and onions, under cover, for 10 minutes without colouring. Stir in the flour and gradually add the stock; season with salt and pepper, add the rosemary and simmer for 1 hour.

Remove the rosemary. Blend the egg yolks with the cream and add this liaison to the soup; heat through but do not let the soup reach boiling point. Garnish with whipped cream.

Summer Vegetable Soup (8 portions) H and F

An early-summer or late-spring soup made from the last of the previous season's leeks and the first summer vegetables.

1 lb fresh green peas
4 chopped lettuce hearts
6 oz chopped leeks
1½ lb chopped cucumber
2 oz butter
Small bunch chervil, parsley and mint
4 pt white stock
Salt and pepper
2 egg yolks
5 fl oz double cream
Garnish: boiled peas

Melt the butter in a large pan and cook the peas, lettuce, leeks and cucumber, under cover, for about 10 minutes without colouring. Add the herbs and the stock and simmer until the vegetables are tender.

The soup may be rubbed through a sieve or blended in a liquidiser, but this is not obligatory. Season the soup with salt and pepper; blend the egg yolks with the cream and add to the soup. Heat through without boiling and correct seasoning. Serve garnished with small boiled peas.

Tomato Soup (8 portions) H and F

Also known as love apple, the tomato was introduced to Europe from South America. Invaluable for flavouring a number of dishes, the tomato is possibly most appreciated by the British when used for a soup.

1½ lb fresh tomatoes
4 oz butter
½ lb sliced carrots
2 oz chopped bacon trimmings
4 oz flour
4 pt white stock
Faggot of herbs
Salt and pepper, caster sugar
Accompaniment: sippets
5 fl oz double cream (optional)

Melt the butter in a large pan and cook the carrots and bacon, under cover, for 5—10 minutes. Stir in the flour and cook this roux for 2—3 minutes. Remove the pan from the heat and add the chopped tomatoes, the stock and faggot of herbs. Return to the heat, bring to the boil and add salt, pepper and sugar. Simmer for 1 hour, skimming when necessary.

Rub the soup through a sieve or blend in a liquidiser. Heat the soup through, correct seasoning and serve with sippets. For cream of tomato soup, blend in the cream, without boiling, just before serving.

Watercress Soup, Creamed (8 portions) H

Delicate of colour and flavour, this is an ideal summer soup to be served hot or chilled.

¾ lb watercress
4 oz butter
4 oz sliced onions
½ lb chopped celery leaves
4 oz flour
3 pt milk
3 pt white stock
Salt and pepper
½ pt double cream

Wash the watercress, remove stalks and any yellowed leaves, blanch the remainder and chop finely, setting some of the leaves aside for garnish. Melt the butter and cook the onions, celery leaves and watercress, under cover, for 5 minutes. Stir in the flour. Remove the pan from the heat and gradually stir in the milk; add the stock.

Simmer for 15 minutes, then strain through a sieve. Reheat the soup, season with salt and pepper and blend in the cream. Serve the soup garnished with watercress.

White Windsor Soup (8 portions) F

Totally unlike Brown Windsor Soup (see Meat Soups), this is a thick soup, suitable as a first course for a winter supper or lunch.

2 oz butter
2 lb chopped potatoes
6 oz chopped onions
6 oz chopped celery
4 pt white meat stock
Faggot of herbs
Salt and pepper
1 pt milk
2 oz fine sago or cornflour, blended with a little milk
Garnish: finely chopped watercress
Accompaniment: sippets

Melt the butter in a large pan and cook the potatoes, onions and celery, under cover, for 5—10 minutes without colouring. Add the stock, herbs, salt and pepper and simmer until all the vegetables are tender.

Rub the soup through a sieve or blend in a liquidiser; return to the pan and add the milk. Bring the soup to the boil, and stir in the blended sago or cornflour. Heat the soup through and correct seasoning. Serve garnished with watercress and accompanied with sippets.

LENTIL SOUPS
Alexandra Soup (8 portions) F

Dried pulses — peas, beans, lentils — form the main ingredients of many traditional soups and are particularly useful in the winter months when fresh vegetables are scarce.

4 oz barley, soaked overnight
4 oz lentils, soaked overnight
3 pt white stock

2 oz butter
4 oz chopped onions
1 pt tomato pulp
Salt and pepper
Milk (optional)

Scald the barley and wash the lentils; put in pan with the stock, butter and chopped onions. Bring to the boil and simmer for 1½ hours. Add the tomato pulp and cook for a further 20 minutes.

Rub the soup through a sieve or blend in a liquidiser. Heat the soup through, season with salt and pepper; if necessary adjust consistency with milk before serving.

Crubeen Pea Soup (12 portions) F Ireland

A typical Irish country-style soup, cooked on pig trotters known in Ireland as Crubeens, and thickened with dried peas and lentils.

1 lb green or yellow dried peas
2 oz lentils
2½ lb pig trotters
1 oz chopped celery
6 oz chopped onions
6—7 pt white stock
Salt and pepper
1 lb cooked sliced sausage (optional)

Soak the peas and lentils in water overnight. Soak the trotters in cold water for 1 hour, then drain. Put the celery, onions, lentils, peas and stock in a large pan. Bring to the boil. Add the trotters and simmer for 2 hours, skimming when necessary.

Remove the trotters and rub the soup through a sieve or blend in a liquidiser. Reheat the soup, season with salt and pepper and add any meat picked off the trotters. Cooked sliced sausage may be added to the soup before serving.

Green Pea Soup (8 portions) F

The combination of dried peas and salted cured ham dates back to the Middle Ages when these ingredients were part of the staple winter diet. This soup was also known as "The London Particular" being as thick as the dense fogs that once enveloped London and were colloquially termed "pea soupers". Thick pea soup was one of the most popular hot meals sold from street-barrows.

2 oz diced bacon
4 oz diced carrots
2 oz diced celery
4 oz chopped onions
1 oz butter
1 lb split dried peas
4 pt ham stock
Salt and pepper
Garnish: cooked, diced meat (optional)
Accompaniment: sippets or pulled bread

Cook the bacon, carrots, celery and onions in the butter, under cover, for 5—10 minutes. Add the peas and cook for a further 2—3 minutes. Pour over the stock, add salt and pepper and bring to the boil; skim and simmer for 2—3 hours, skimming when necessary.

Rub the soup through a coarse sieve or blend in a liquidiser. Return the soup to the pan and heat through; correct seasoning. Serve with sippets of bread; diced meat may be added to the soup, but this is not traditional.

Haricot Bean Soup (8 portions) F

Overlong soaking of dried haricot beans may spoil the flavour, and leaving them to swell in cold water for a couple of hours is usually sufficient.

1 lb haricot beans, soaked
1 oz dripping
4 oz roughly chopped carrots
2 oz roughly chopped turnips
4 oz roughly chopped onions
4 oz roughly chopped potatoes
4 pt ham stock
Faggot of herbs
Salt and pepper
Garnish: diced ham
Accompaniment: sippets

Melt the dripping in a large pan and cook the vegetables, under cover, for 5—10 minutes. Add the drained beans and stock, with the faggot of herbs, salt and pepper; bring to the boil and simmer gently for 2—2½ hours, skimming when necessary.

Rub the soup through a sieve or blend in a liquidiser. Return the soup to the heat and bring slowly back to boiling point; correct seasoning. Chopped ham may be added to the soup just before serving.

Lentil Soup (8—10 portions) F

This is a golden lentil soup, but green lentils, available from health shops, may be substituted. The green colour can be enhanced by replacing the turnips with chopped spinach.

½ lb golden lentils
2 oz dripping
6 oz finely diced carrots
4 oz finely diced turnips
¾ lb finely diced potatoes
4 oz finely chopped onions
1 teaspoon tomato paste
4 pt white stock
1 ham bone
Faggot of herbs
Salt and pepper
Garnish: chopped parsley
Accompaniment: sippets or pulled bread

Wash and drain the lentils. Melt the dripping and cook the vegetables, under cover, for 5—10 minutes without colouring. Add the lentils and cook for a further 2—3 minutes. Stir in the tomato paste, add the stock, ham bone, herbs, salt and pepper. Cover and simmer gently for 2 hours, skimming when necessary.

Lift out the faggot of herbs and ham bone; cut off any meat, dice and return to the soup. Correct seasoning and serve the soup garnished with finely chopped parsley, and accompanied with fried sippets.

Red Pottage (8—12 portions) F

An unusual flavour and colour is given to this lentil soup by the inclusion of beetroot and tomatoes. A garnish of finely chopped, raw white of leeks makes a good contrast.

1 lb soaked lentils
2 oz butter or dripping
¾ lb skinned and chopped tomatoes
3 oz chopped beetroot
6 pt white stock
Salt and pepper
Garnish: chopped white of leek

Melt the butter and cook the tomatoes and beetroot, under cover, for 5 minutes; add the drained lentils and cook for a further 2—3 minutes. Add the stock, salt and pepper; bring to the boil. Simmer for 2—2½ hours or until the lentils are tender, skimming when necessary.

Rub the soup through a sieve or blend in a liquidiser. Return the soup to the heat; correct seasoning and serve garnished with white of leek.

White Lentil Soup (8 portions) F

This was once the traditional soup for Good Friday and was followed by boiled salt cod in egg and parsley sauce, with mashed potatoes.

½ lb golden lentils
3 pt water
2 oz chopped celery
½ lb chopped onions
Faggot of herbs
Salt and pepper
1½ oz butter
1½ oz flour
½ pt milk
5 fl oz double cream
Garnish: chopped parsley
Accompaniment: sippets or pulled bread

Wash and soak the lentils; put in a pan with the water, bring to the boil and skim as necessary. Add the celery, onions, herbs, salt and pepper; simmer for 1½ hours. Rub through a sieve or blend in a liquidiser.

Make a white roux from the butter and flour; gradually stir in the milk and the lentil pulp. Bring the soup to boiling point; correct seasoning and blend in the cream. Garnish with parsley and serve with sippets or pulled bread.

MISCELLANEOUS SOUPS

Almost any edible ingredient, fresh or cooked, can be made into a soup. An old English recipe, for example, recommends Rose Hip Soup, flavoured with cinnamon, thicked with cornflour and served with dumplings. The Irish Wattle Soup — milk and chicken stock with rice — is so called from its garnish of sieved, hardboiled egg yolks.

Almond Soup (8 portions) H

Dating back to medieval days, this thick white soup was used in invalid and building-up diets. A variation, known as Hedge Hog Soup, is garnished with small, soft rolls studded with almonds; the Westerfield White Almond Soup omits any garnish but includes 2 oz vermicelli.

1 lb ground almonds
4 oz diced ham
4 oz chopped celery
4 pt clear meat or chicken stock
2 cloves
Blade of mace
1 bay leaf, chopped basil
Salt and pepper
5 fl oz sherry
Almond essence
Garnish: blanched almonds, whipped cream

Put the ham, celery and stock in a pan with the
cloves, mace, bay leaf, basil, salt and pepper;
bring slowly to the boil and simmer over gentle
heat for 30 minutes.

Strain the soup and return to the pan; stir in
the almonds and simmer for another 15 minutes.
Add the sherry and a few drops of almond
essence. Serve the soup garnished with blanched
almonds and whipped cream.

Chestnut Soup (8 portions) H

An unusual, rich and velvety soup, ideal for cool
autumn days when chestnuts are readily available.

3 lb blanched and skinned chestnuts
4 pt white stock
Salt and pepper
½ pt milk
2 egg yolks
5 fl oz double cream

Put the chestnuts in a pan with the stock and
salt and pepper; simmer until tender after about
1½ hours. Rub the soup through a sieve or blend
in a liquidiser.

Reheat the soup and adjust to the required
consistency with milk. Blend the egg yolks and
cream and add this liaison to the soup; heat
through without boiling. Correct seasoning and
serve at once.

Herb Soup (10 portions) H and F

The chief flavouring in this creamy soup comes
from the slightly bitter sorrel leaves which blend
well with spinach.

1 lb shredded spinach
7 oz shredded sorrel leaves or green peas
1½ lb shredded cos lettuce
4 oz sliced carrots
4 oz butter

4 pt white stock
Grated nutmeg
Salt and pepper
2 egg yolks
5 fl oz double cream
Garnish: chervil or parsley

Put the spinach, sorrel leaves, lettuce and carrots in
a pan with the butter; cook over low heat,
covered, for 20 minutes without colouring. Add
the stock and simmer for 20 minutes.

Rub the soup through a sieve or blend in a
liquidiser. Return the soup to the pan, season to
taste with nutmeg, salt and pepper and heat
through. Beat the egg yolks with the cream and add
this liaison to the soup. Adjust seasoning and serve
the soup garnished with chopped chervil or parsley.

Methley Soup (8 portions) F

Possibly a corruption of medley, this is a soup
made from a mixture of ingredients readily at
hand in most households.

¾ lb chopped onions
1½ lb chopped potatoes
2 oz dripping ·
1 oz oatmeal
3 pt white stock
Salt, pepper, caster sugar
Accompaniment: sippets

Sweat the onions and potatoes in the dripping,
under cover, until golden. Stir in the oatmeal, add
the stock, salt, sugar and pepper; simmer for
25—30 minutes.

Rub the soup through a sieve or blend in a
liquidiser. Heat the soup through; adjust seasoning
and serve with sippets.

Mock Turtle Soup, Clear (8 portions) H

Less well-known than thick mock turtle soup, this
Madeira-flavoured bouillon makes a good first
course. Turtle herbs are sold ready-mixed and
consist of basil, bay, marjoram and thyme.

4 pt brown meat stock
4 egg whites
Juice and rind of 1 lemon
1 oz turtle herbs in muslin bag
6 peppercorns
4 oz roughly chopped carrots
4 oz roughly chopped celery
4 oz roughly chopped onions

1 oz arrowroot
Salt
5 fl oz Madeira or sherry
Accompaniment: hot cheese straws

Put all the ingredients, except the salt and wine in a
large pan. Boil up the mixture two or three times;
leave the pan in warm place for the stock to infuse
for at least 15 minutes. Strain the bouillon two or
three times through a double layer of muslin
when it should be perfectly clear.

Reheat the bouillon without boiling, season to
taste with salt and add the wine. Serve with hot
cheese straws.

Mock Turtle Soup, Thick (16 portions) H

This was a popular 19th-century soup for special
occasions. It should ideally be made with calf's
head, but a sheep's head may also be used; the
traditional garnish is small forcemeat balls.

1 sheep's or ½ calf's head
4 oz beef fat
4 oz flour
8 pt water or brown meat stock
½ lb roughly chopped onions
4 oz roughly chopped celery
4 oz roughly chopped leeks
2 oz butter
1 oz turtle herbs in muslin bag
6 crushed peppercorns
Juice of ½ lemon
1 glass sherry

Forcemeat Balls
½ lb sheep or calf brains
½ lb fresh breadcrumbs
1 tablespoon chopped parsley
Grated rind of ½ lemon
Salt and pepper
1 egg

Split the head and wash thoroughly; discard the
eyes and set the tongue and brains aside. Chop
the head into pieces and brown lightly in the oven.
Make a brown roux from the beef fat and flour;
gradually stir in the water or stock and bring to
the boil. Fry the vegetables in the butter until
brown. Add the vegetables, head, tongue, herbs
and peppercorns to the soup and allow to simmer
for at least 2 hours, removing the scum as it rises.

Strain the soup, heat through and add the
lemon juice and sherry. Adjust seasoning and

consistency. Dice the tongue and any flesh from
the head and stir into the soup.

While the soup is cooking, make the forcemeat
balls: Chop the brains finely and mix with the
breadcrumbs, parsley, lemon rind, salt and pepper.
Bind the mixture with the lightly beaten egg and
shape into small balls (16−32); fry in hot fat,
drain and serve hot with the soup.

Oatmeal Soup (8 portions) F

An everyday but nourishing soup made from
chicken stock and thickened with fine oatmeal.

4 oz oatmeal
2 oz butter
¾ lb finely sliced onions
Salt and pepper
2 pt chicken stock
1 pt milk
½ pt double cream
Garnish: chopped parsley

Melt the butter in a pan and cook the onions,
under cover, until soft but not coloured. Stir in
the oatmeal, salt and pepper and cook for 5
minutes. Gradually stir in the stock, bring to
the boil and simmer, covered, for 30 minutes.

Rub the soup through a sieve or blend in a
liquidiser. Return the soup to the pan, blend
in the milk and heat through. Blend in the cream,
but do not let the soup reach boiling point. Serve
garnished with parsley.

Saffron Soup (8 portions) F

Saffron was highly rated in medieval cookery,
possibly for its colour rather than its flavour. This
soup is one of the oldest known, having survived
for more than six hundred years.

½ teaspoon saffron, steeped in warm water
1 lb roughly chopped onions
1 lb roughly chopped potatoes
3 pt chicken stock
½ pt double cream
Salt and pepper
Garnish: lemon slices, whipped cream

Cook the onions and potatoes in the stock for 25
minutes or until soft. Rub the soup through a
sieve or blend in a liquidiser. Stir in the saffron
water and add the cream.

Heat through without boiling and season with
salt and pepper. Serve the soup garnished with
thin lemon slices and whipped cream.

Sauces and Dressings

In its widest sense, a sauce is any liquid or soft preparation of several ingredients intended as an appetising accompaniment to food.

Sauces, in one form or another, have been used for at least nine centuries; mackerel with gooseberry sauce, for example, was a Norman speciality. Returning crusaders in the 11th and 12th centuries brought with them hitherto unknown spices and condiments which were used, seldom discreetly, in sauces to camouflage the flavour of meat and fish which were often tainted, heavily salted or plain unpalatable.

Herbs and spices added not only flavour, but also colour: saffron imparted yellow, parsley or mint juice green, marigold flowers orange and violets purple. Gervase Markham, who in 1615 published *The English Housewife*, admonished: "The first step to skill in cooking is to have knowledge of all sorts of Herbes belonging to the kitchen, whether they be for the Pot, for Sallets, for Sauces, or for any other seasoning or adorning".

White flour was an expensive luxury in the Middle Ages, and sauces were thickened with breadcrumbs, almonds, blood and liaisons of eggs and cream. In contrast to these medieval concoctions, sauces became simplified during the following centuries, and far from masking the flavour of food, sauces today are intended to complement and enhance the main flavour or to add moisture to otherwise dry foods. Even so, the origin of mint and bread sauce, for instance, can easily be traced back to the medieval *Verde Sawse* (green sauce) which was a compound assortment of flavours including mint, parsley, garlic, wild thyme, sage, cinnamon, ginger, pepper, salt, bread, wine and vinegar.

Sauces differ according to texture, consistency and flavour as well as in the method of preparation. The following sauce recipes have been classified according to type.

1. Brown Sauces
2. White Sauces
3. Butter Sauces
4. Butter Garnishes
5. Cream Sauces
6. Purée Sauces
7. Wine and Savoury Sauces
8. Salad Dressings and Creams
9. Dessert Sauces

Woe to the Cook whose Sauce has no Sting (Chaucer)

BROWN SAUCES

Most of these have as the main ingredient a basic sauce made from a brown roux and brown stock. Various flavourings are added according to the type of meat, poultry or game the sauce is intended to accompany.

Caper Sauce H and F

Serve with roast mutton or lamb.

2 pt brown sauce
4–6 oz capers
2 tablespoons chilli vinegar or caper liquid
Salt and pepper

Add the capers, which may be chopped or left whole, and vinegar to the sauce. Heat through and season with salt and pepper.

Chicken Liver Sauce H and F

As accompaniment to roast chicken.

4 oz finely chopped chicken livers
1½ oz butter
2½ fl oz dry white wine
2 pt brown sauce
Juice of 2 lemons
Salt and pepper

Fry the livers in the butter for 5 minutes, add the wine and boil rapidly until reduced by half. Stir in the brown sauce and add the lemon juice. Heat through and season with salt and pepper.

Cider Sauce H and F Herefordshire

Particularly good with hot, boiled bacon.

1 pt dry cider
3 cloves
2 bay leaves
Salt and pepper
2 pt brown sauce

Put the cider, cloves, bay leaves and seasoning in a pan, bring to the boil and reduce by half. Stir in the brown sauce and simmer until reduced by one-third. Strain the sauce and correct seasoning.

Curry Sauce H and F

A spicy sauce to accompany meat, poultry, fish, prawns and hardboiled eggs.

1–2 oz curry powder
2 oz dripping
6 oz finely chopped onions
4 oz chopped apples
2 oz flour
1 oz tomato purée
2 pt brown stock
2 oz sultanas
2 oz chutney
Salt and pepper

Melt the dripping and fry the onions and apples until lightly brown. Stir in the flour and curry powder. Mix in the tomato purée. Gradually add the stock; bring the sauce to the boil and add the sultanas and chutney. Season to taste with salt and pepper, simmer for 45 minutes and strain. Before serving, correct seasoning and adjust consistency, adding more stock if necessary.

Devil Sauce H and F

Used not as an accompanying sauce, but brushed over poultry joints prior to grilling.

4 oz softened butter
¾ oz flour
Pinch mustard powder
1 teaspoon French mustard
2 oz chutney
Worcestershire sauce

Beat the butter, flour and mustard powder to-

gether until they form a paste. Blend in French mustard, chutney and Worcestershire sauce to taste. Spread over chicken joints before grilling; repeat when the joints are turned.

Gravy H and F

The most often used brown sauce is gravy, made from the sediments in the pan after the roast has been removed and the fat poured or skimmed off. For a thin gravy, traditional with roast beef, brown stock is added to the pan residues, brought to the boil and reduced slightly. For a thick gravy, flour is stirred into the pan sediments and brown stock added to the required consistency. Season with salt and pepper and strain before serving.

Additional flavours may be used in gravies: chopped capers for roast mutton and lamb, lemon and vinegar for venison gravy, red wine and red currant jelly with roast haunch of hare or deer. Thick chicken gravy can be flavoured with orange juice, or with claret boiled with chopped onion, strained and added to the gravy with nutmeg and thin orange slices. Chestnut purée and dry white wine can be added to thin chicken gravy and thickened with kneaded butter and flour.

Ham Sauce H and F

Serve with roast or braised veal, duck and game.

½ lb diced lean ham
1 oz butter
1 oz chopped parsley
2 pt brown sauce
Juice of 1 lemon
Salt and pepper

Melt the butter and lightly cook the ham for a few minutes; add the parsley and stir in the brown sauce. Simmer for a few minutes. Bring the sauce to the boil and skim. Sharpen with lemon juice to taste and season with salt and pepper.

Kidney Sauce H and F

Ideal with grilled steak, kidneys and liver.

4 oz ox kidney
2 oz butter
2 pt brown sauce
Salt and pepper

Cut the kidney into small pieces and fry in the

butter until lightly brown. Add the kidney to the brown sauce, bring to the boil and simmer over very low heat for about 45 minutes. Season with salt and pepper.

Laver Sauce F Wales

Traditional with roast mutton.

1 lb laver bread
2 oz butter
2 pt thickened mutton gravy
Salt and pepper

Laver is usually bought as a ready-cooked pulp; if it is collected fresh it should be thoroughly washed and simmered to a pulp for several hours. Put the cooked laver bread into a pan with the butter and gravy. Heat and stir until bubbling hot; season with salt and pepper.

Madeira Sauce H

A piquant sauce for grilled chicken portions, kidneys and ham.

5 fl oz Madeira
2 pt brown sauce
Salt and pepper
1 oz butter

Add Madeira to the brown sauce; simmer until slightly reduced. Season with salt and pepper and stir in the butter.

Mushroom Sauce H and F

Serve with grilled or braised steak, grilled or fried lamb chops or cutlets, and poultry joints.

6 oz sliced mushrooms
1 oz butter
4 fl oz white wine
2 pt brown sauce
Salt and pepper

Fry the mushrooms in the butter for 5 minutes; add the wine and reduce by half. Blend into the brown sauce; bring to the boil and simmer for 10 minutes. Season to taste with salt and pepper.

Orange Sauce H

A rich sauce, ideal with roast duck, goose and game.

4—5 oranges
2 oz caster sugar
1 teaspoon lemon juice
5 fl oz Madeira
5 fl oz brandy
2 pt brown sauce
Salt and pepper
2 oz butter

Peel the orange rind thinly, without any pith; squeeze the juice from the oranges and set both juice and orange pulp aside. Cut the rind into match-size strips, blanch in boiling water for a few minutes and refresh in cold water.

Stir the sugar into the mixed orange and lemon juice; bring to the boil, then reduce to a very light brown syrup. Cool slightly before blending in the Madeira and brandy. Add the orange pulp and brown sauce. Bring to the boil and simmer to reduce by one third. Season the sauce with salt and pepper; strain. Blend in the butter; add the orange strips and heat the sauce through.

Reform Club Sauce H London

Created by Alexis Soyer, the famous French chef of the Reform Club in Victorian days, as an accompanying sauce to lamb cutlets.

3 oz finely chopped onions
2 oz butter
3 oz thinly sliced mushrooms
3 oz wafer-thin, finely chopped ham or tongue
1 small glass sherry
2 thinly sliced hardboiled egg whites
3 oz cooked, finely diced beetroot
3 oz thinly sliced gherkins
2 pt brown sauce
Salt, sugar and crushed black pepper
Red currant jelly

Fry the onions in half the butter until soft, but not coloured; add the mushrooms and cook for a few more minutes. Stir in the ham or tongue, first soaked in the sherry. Add the egg whites, beetroot and gherkins, together with the brown sauce; heat through. Blend in the remaining butter and season with salt, sugar, pepper and red currant jelly.

Sharp Sauce H and F

Serve with grilled meat and chicken.

2 oz finely sliced gherkins
2 oz chopped capers

4 fl oz Harvey's Sauce
2 pt brown sauce
Salt and pepper
Pinch nutmeg

Mix the gherkins, capers and Harvey's sauce into the brown sauce. Heat through and season with salt, pepper and nutmeg.

Wow-Wow Sauce H and F London

Pickled walnuts were a popular accompaniment to grilled mutton chops in the early 19th century, and many chop houses also served a pickled walnut sauce, known as Wow-Wow, with boiled beef.

2 fl oz mushroom ketchup
5 fl oz Beaujolais
2 pt brown sauce
1 tablespoon chopped parsley
2 oz diced pickled walnuts
1 oz made mustard
1 oz butter
Salt and pepper

Stir the mushroom ketchup and Beaujolais into the brown sauce and leave to simmer for 5 minutes or until slightly thickened. Add the parsley, walnuts and mustard; stir in the butter. Heat the sauce through and season with salt and pepper.

Yorkshire Sauce H and F Yorkshire

A port and orange sauce, slightly thickened with brown sauce, to serve with hot boiled bacon and ham.

Juice and rind of 3 oranges
¾ pt port
½ teaspoon cinnamon
6 oz red currant jelly
1½ fl oz brown sauce
Salt and pepper

Cut the orange rind, without any pith, into narrow strips; heat with the port for 5 minutes. Strain and add the cinnamon, red currant jelly and brown sauce to the port. Heat through and add the orange juice. Season with salt and pepper before serving.

WHITE SAUCES

The basic for most white sauces, also known as béchamel sauces, is white roux, white stock, herbs and spicing. Cream is an optional extra. Numerous sauces can be made from the basic white sauce, depending on the kind of main dish they will complement.

Albert Sauce H

Serve with braised or grilled beef.

5 fl oz basic white sauce
3 oz grated horseradish
½ pt white stock
½ pt double cream
1 teaspoon made mustard
1 dessertspoon wine vinegar
1 tablespoon finely chopped parsley
2 egg yolks

Simmer the horseradish in the stock, under cover, for 30 minutes. Stir in the white sauce and cream; pass the mixture through a sieve. Put the sauce in a double saucepan to heat through; just before serving beat in the mustard, vinegar, parsley and egg yolks.

Almond Sauce H and F

A delicately flavoured sauce to accompany roast turkey.

2 pt basic white sauce
6 oz blanched and chopped almonds
1 oz butter
Salt and sugar
Juice of ½ lemon

Fry the almonds in the butter until golden; stir into the white sauce and simmer for 10 minutes. Season with salt, sugar and lemon juice.

Anchovy Sauce H and F

Suitable with poached and baked firm white fish.

2 pt basic white sauce
2 oz butter
5 fl oz double cream
2 tablespoons anchovy essence
Salt and pepper

Add butter, cream and anchovy essence to the white sauce; simmer for 5—10 minutes, without boiling, to allow the flavours to penetrate. Correct seasoning with salt and pepper if necessary.

Asparagus Sauce H

A delicate, creamy sauce, excellent with chicken
and fowl, sweetbreads, poached salmon and egg
dishes.

2 pt basic white sauce
1½ lb asparagus
Juice of ½ lemon
2 egg yolks
5 fl oz double cream
2 oz butter
Salt and pepper

Clean the asparagus and cook lightly in the butter
for 3—4 minutes. Cut into pieces, reserving some
of the asparagus tips for garnish. Add the
remaining asparagus to the sauce and cook until
tender, stirring frequently to prevent burning.

Put the sauce through a sieve or blend in a
liquidiser. Stir in the lemon juice and heat the
sauce through. Blend the egg yolks with the
cream and add to the sauce, without letting it
boil. Correct seasoning with salt and pepper. Just
before serving, stir in the reserved asparagus tips.

Caper Sauce F and H

One of the earliest sauces, this has been a traditional
accompaniment to boiled mutton since the Middle
Ages. The basic white sauce should be made with
mutton stock.

2 pt basic white sauce
1½ oz capers
1 dessertspoon lemon juice
2 egg yolks
5 fl oz double cream
Salt and pepper

Add the capers and lemon juice to the white sauce
and heat through. Blend the egg yolks with the
cream and add to the sauce, stirring until it
thickens without reaching boiling point. Season to
taste with salt and pepper.

Celery Sauce F and H

Popular in Victorian days with boiled turkey.

2 pt basic white sauce
½ lb celery
Salt and pepper
2 oz butter

Wash the celery well, blanch for a few minutes,
then chop and add to the sauce. Simmer for 15—
20 minutes or until tender. Rub through a sieve
or blend in a liquidiser. Return the sauce to the
pan, correct seasoning with salt and pepper and
heat through. Stir in the butter just before serving.

Cheese Sauce F and H

Serve with poached, baked and steamed fish, with
macaroni, cauliflower and stuffed marrow.

2 pt basic white sauce
6—8 oz grated Cheddar or Cheshire cheese

Add the grated cheese to the sauce and simmer
gently for 5 minutes before serving.

Cream Sauce H and F

The traditional English sauce for white fish.

2 pt basic white sauce
½ pt double cream
Lemon juice
Salt and pepper

Stir half the cream into the white sauce and cook
until slightly reduced. Strain the sauce through a
coarse sieve, return to the pan and add the remaining cream. Heat through without boiling and season
to taste with lemon juice, salt and pepper.

Dill Sauce F and H

Serve with hot or cold boiled bacon and with
poached and baked fish.

2 pt basic white sauce
3½ fl oz wine vinegar
7 oz sugar
1 oz fresh chopped dill
2 egg yolks
5 fl oz double cream
Salt

Boil the vinegar and sugar until reduced by half.
Stir into the white sauce and add the dill; bring to
boiling point. Blend the egg yolks and cream and
add to the sauce; do not let it reach boiling point.
Add salt to taste.

Egg Sauce H and F Scotland

An 18th century sauce, served with poached
haddock and other white fish; also suitable with
cauliflower.

2 pt basic white sauce
4–5 hardboiled eggs
Salt and pepper

Chop the whites of the eggs and add to the white sauce. Season with salt and pepper. Just before serving, press the egg yolks through a sieve on to the sauce.

Fennel Sauce H and F

Served with delicately flavoured fish dishes, this sauce brings out the slightly sweet flavour of fresh fennel.

2 pt basic white sauce
1 oz chopped fennel
2 oz caster sugar
2 tablespoons lemon juice
Salt and pepper
2 egg yolks
5 fl oz double cream

Add the fennel, sugar and lemon juice to the white sauce; bring to the boil and simmer for 10 minutes, stirring frequently. Season with salt and pepper. Blend the egg yolks with the cream and add to the sauce; heat through without boiling.

Gooseberry Sauce F

Gooseberry sauce is traditional with grilled or boiled mackerel in Cornwall. It may also be served with roast goose, or the gooseberries may be substituted with chopped rhubarb which also go well with roast pork.

2 pt basic white sauce
½ lb gooseberries
Salt and pepper

Wash, top and tail the gooseberries; simmer in a little water until soft. Rub the fruit through a sieve or blend in a liquidiser. Add the gooseberry pulp to the white sauce; season with salt and pepper and serve.

Hare Liver Sauce H and F

Serve with roast haunch of hare.

2 pt basic white sauce
½ lb hare livers
5 fl oz double cream
Salt and pepper

Boil the livers for 20 minutes. Chop finely and add to the white sauce. Add the cream, salt and pepper to taste; heat the sauce through but do not boil.

Herring Roe Sauce F and H

Excellent as an accompaniment to fresh grilled herrings.

2 pt basic white sauce
1 lb soft herring roes
4 oz butter
3 tablespoons made mustard
2 fl oz lemon juice
Salt and pepper

Cook the cleaned roes over low heat in half the butter. Rub the roes through a sieve while still hot and add to the white sauce. Stir in the mustard and lemon juice; add salt and pepper to taste. Just before serving whisk in the remaining butter, cut into pieces.

Kelly's Sauce H

Named after Michael Kelly, composer and director of music at Theatre Royal in Drury Lane, London, in the early 19th century. Served with boiled tripe, cow heel, calf's foot and knuckle of veal.

2 pt basic white sauce
1 teaspoon mustard powder
1 oz brown sugar
1 teaspoon black pepper
2 fl oz garlic vinegar
Salt

Mix the mustard, brown sugar and black pepper with the vinegar. Stir this mixture into the white sauce; heat through and season with salt if necessary.

Kelly's Piquante Sauce H

Serve chilled with grilled steaks.

½ pt basic white sauce
1 oz chopped capers
6 finely chopped anchovies
3 hardboiled, mashed egg yolks
¾ oz dry mustard
2 tablespoons olive oil
1 dessertspoon white wine vinegar
1 dessertspoon shallot vinegar
1 heaped tablespoon finely chopped parsley

Cayenne pepper
4 oz butter

Mix the white sauce with capers, anchovies, egg
yolks, mustard, oil, vinegars and parsley; season to
taste with cayenne. Heat the sauce through then
add the butter, letting it melt and blend in the
sauce. Chill before serving.

Lemon Sauce F

Serve with boiled bacon and ham.

2 pt basic white sauce
Grated rind and juice of 4 lemons
Salt and pepper

Stir the lemon peel and juice into the white sauce;
simmer for 10 minutes, stirring frequently. Add
salt and pepper to taste before serving.

Mustard Sauce I F and H

Excellent with fried or grilled herrings for a light
lunch or supper dish.

2 pt basic white sauce
1 teaspoon mustard powder
1 dessertspoon chilli vinegar
1 teaspoon lemon juice
4 egg yolks
½ pt double cream
Salt and pepper

Mix the mustard with the chilli vinegar and lemon
juice and stir into the white sauce. Bring the sauce
to boiling point. Blend the egg yolks and cream
and add to the sauce; heat through without boiling.
Season to taste with salt and pepper before serving.

Mustard Sauce II F

An economical sauce, possibly originating in the
West Country, to serve with grilled herrings.

8 herring heads
1½ lb chopped onions
12 peppercorns
2 pt beer or ale
2½ oz butter
2½ oz flour
1 dessertspoon dry mustard
Anchovy essence
Salt and pepper

Put the herring heads, onions and peppercorns in a

pan with the beer or ale; boil for 15 minutes.
Strain the liquid. Make a roux from the butter and
flour and gradually stir in the strained liquid.
Bring to the boil and cook until thickened. Add
the mustard and season to taste with anchovy
essence, salt and pepper.

Onion Sauce F

Popular in the 18th century, this sauce goes well
with boiled rabbit and duck, roast stuffed lamb
and in particular with boiled tripe.

2 pt basic white sauce
½ lb finely chopped onions
2 oz butter
1 dessertspoon lemon juice
Salt and pepper
5 fl oz double cream

Cook the onions in the butter until transparent.
Rub through a sieve or blend in a liquidiser;
add to the white sauce with the lemon juice.
Bring the sauce to boiling point and simmer over
gentle heat for 10 minutes. Season to taste with
salt and pepper; add the cream just before
serving.

Oyster Sauce H

In Roman days, oysters were a favourite accompaniment to mutton; this sauce goes equally well
with roast and boiled mutton and lamb, turkey
stuffed with oysters and with baked fish. Mussels
may be substituted for the oysters.

2 pt basic white sauce
2 doz oysters
2½ oz butter
1 dessertspoon lemon juice
3–4 egg yolks
½ pt double cream
Salt and pepper

Open the oysters and remove the beards. Put the
oysters with their liquid and the butter in a pan,
cover and cook for 4 minutes without boiling.
Drain and quarter the oysters, reserving the liquid.
   Boil the oyster liquid rapidly until reduced by
half. Add the quartered oysters, reduced oyster
liquid and lemon juice to the white sauce and
bring to boiling point. Blend the egg yolks with
the cream and add to the sauce; heat through
without boiling. Season with salt and pepper.

Parsley Sauce F and H

Another traditional sauce, dating back many centuries; serve with boiled salt beef and fried and grilled herrings and mackerel. The stock for the white sauce is made from half milk and half white stock.

2 pt basic white sauce
1 tablespoon finely chopped parsley
Salt and pepper
1 dessertspoon lemon juice (optional)

Bring the white sauce to boiling point and stir in the parsley. Add salt and pepper to taste, and lemon juice if the sauce is to accompany fish.

Red Mullet Sauce H

Served with baked red mullet and any other firm fish, this white sauce is made from sherry-flavoured fish stock, thickened with kneaded butter.

1 pt fish stock
½ pt sherry
1 teaspoon anchovy essence
1½ oz butter
1½ oz flour
Cayenne pepper and salt

Bring the fish stock to the boil, with sherry and anchovy essence. Knead the butter and flour together and add gradually to the sauce, whisking all the time until the sauce thickens. Before serving, season to taste with cayenne and salt.

Roe Sauce H and F

A strongly flavoured sauce to serve with plain poached cod, haddock and halibut steaks and fillets.

1 pt basic white sauce (made with fish stock)
¾ lb cod roe
1 pt milk
3 teaspoons made mustard
3 teaspoons anchovy essence
2 tablespoons wine vinegar
Salt and pepper

Cook the cod roe in the milk until tender; strain and make up the white sauce from half fish stock and the strained milk. Pound or liquidise the cooked cod roe, mix with mustard, anchovy essence and vinegar. Stir this mixture into the white sauce and heat through. Season to taste with salt and pepper.

Shrimp Sauce H

Traditional with turbot, shrimp sauce is also most acceptable with fillets of sole and haddock.

2 pt basic white sauce
10 oz peeled shrimps
1 dessertspoon lemon juice
1 dessertspoon anchovy essence
Cayenne pepper and salt
2 oz butter
5 fl oz double cream

Stir the shrimps, lemon juice and anchovy essence into the white sauce; bring to the boil and season with cayenne and salt. Add the butter and cream and heat through without boiling.

Sour Cream Sauce H and F

A 20th century sauce, excellent with roast beef.

1½ oz butter
1½ oz flour
½ pt milk
½ pt soured cream
½ pt dry cider
2 oz grated cheese
Salt and pepper

Melt the butter in a pan, add the flour and stir in the milk. Cook over low heat until the sauce thickens. Remove the pan from the heat, stir in the soured cream, cider and grated cheese. Add salt and pepper to taste and heat through before serving.

Stilton Sauce H and F

Traditionally served with grilled plaice on the bone, this sauce is made with the famous Blue Stilton cheese.

1 pt basic white sauce
6 oz chopped Blue Stilton
5 fl oz milk
Salt and pepper
5 fl oz double cream

Bring the white sauce to the boil over low heat; add the cheese and stir continuously until melted. Blend in the milk, and add salt and pepper to taste. Add the cream and heat through without bringing to the boil.

Truffle Sauce H

Serve with wild duck; button mushrooms may replace the truffles for a less expensive sauce.

4 oz finely chopped onions
4 oz sliced truffles
4 oz butter
3 oz flour
2 pt giblet stock
Salt and pepper

Simmer the onions and truffles in the butter until soft. Blend in the flour and gradually add the stock, stirring continuously. Heat the sauce through until thick; season to taste with salt and pepper.

Watercress Sauce H and F

A fine and delicate accompaniment to freshwater fish, especially eel. The basic white sauce should be made from fish stock.

2 pt basic white sauce
4 oz watercress
Salt and pepper
5 fl oz double cream

Use the stalks of the watercress to flavour the fish stock for the white sauce. Chop the watercress leaves finely. Heat the white sauce through, add the watercress and season with salt and pepper. Stir in the cream and heat through.

BUTTER SAUCES

Also known as English Sauce, the basic butter sauce should preferably be made from unsalted butter. It consists of a white roux thinned with water and owes its velvety texture to a high proportion of butter. All the butter sauces described are suitable with fish and vegetables.

Anchovy Butter Sauce H and F

Basic butter sauce
2 tablespoons anchovy essence
1 dessertspoon lemon juice
Cayenne pepper

Add anchovy essence, lemon juice and pepper to taste to the sauce just before serving.

Black Butter F and H

Traditional with skate, and excellent with poached brains.

4 oz butter
2 tablespoons wine vinegar
1 oz capers

Melt the butter in a pan and cook until brown. Add the vinegar and capers which may be chopped or left whole. Serve at once.

Butter Sauce, Rich H

7 oz butter
2 oz flour
2 pt boiling water
6 egg yolks
5 fl oz double cream
Juice of ½ lemon
Salt and pepper

Melt 2 oz of the butter and stir in the flour to make a white roux. Gradually stir in the water; bring to the boil. Remove the pan from the heat; blend the egg yolks with the cream and add this liaison to the sauce. Add lemon juice, salt and pepper to taste. Return the pan to the heat and whisk in the remaining 5 oz of butter without letting the sauce boil.

Caper Butter Sauce H and F

Always a favourite sauce with boiled mutton, pickled nasturtium seeds were often used instead of capers.

Basic butter sauce
3 oz capers
2 fl oz wine or caper vinegar

Add the whole or chopped capers and vinegar to the butter sauce just before serving.

Crab Butter Sauce H

Basic butter sauce
6 oz cooked crab meat
Cayenne pepper, mace,
1 teaspoon anchovy essence

Separate the brown crab meat from the white and stir the brown into the butter sauce. Flake the white meat and add to the sauce, with cayenne, mace and anchovy essence to taste. Heat through and serve.

Devil Butter

This is used to spread on chops and cutlets for grilling, or the butter may be chilled and served, cut into slices, as a garnish.

½ lb butter
1½ oz dry mustard
2 teaspoons Worcestershire sauce
2 teaspoons mushroom ketchup
Salt and cayenne pepper
2 oz white breadcrumbs

Soften the butter slightly and blend in the mustard, Worcestershire sauce and mushroom ketchup; season with salt and cayenne and mix in the breadcrumbs.

Dutch Sauce H

Said to have been Queen Anne's favourite sauce with boiled fish, this 17th century butter sauce is today better known as Hollandaise. Originally, the sauce was probably made from butter only and flavoured with lemon, but English butter being thinner needed thickening with egg yolks.

1 lb clarified butter
2 tablespoons white wine or tarragon vinegar
12 crushed peppercorns
2 fl oz water
6 egg yolks
Juice of ½ lemon
Cayenne, salt, pepper

Boil the vinegar and peppercorns in a pan until reduced by two thirds. Leave to cool, then strain and add the cold water. Put the egg yolks in a double saucepan, add the vinegar and water mixture and whisk steadily until ribbon stage. Remove the pan from the heat and gradually whisk in the butter, bit by bit, until the sauce is shiny and has thickened to the texture of cream. Add lemon juice and seasoning. Strain the sauce through muslin before serving.

Fennel Butter Sauce H and F

Basic butter sauce
2 oz chopped fennel leaves
Salt and pepper
Lemon juice

Add the finely chopped fennel leaves to the sauce. Season to taste with salt, pepper and lemon juice; heat through and serve.

Lemon Sauce H and F

Basic butter sauce
5 lemons
3 oz caster sugar

Thinly peel the rind off the lemons and cut into Julienne strips; blanch in boiling water and refresh in cold water. Squeeze the lemons, strain and add the sugar; bring to the boil and reduce slightly. Add the reduced lemon juice to the sauce and heat through. Garnish with strips of lemon.

Melted Butter H and F

½ lb butter
1 pt water
½ oz flour
Salt

Bring the water to the boil; knead the flour with ½ oz of butter and add gradually to the water, whisking constantly. Bring back to the boil and add a little salt. Remove the pan from the heat and gradually blend in the remaining butter.

Mustard Butter Sauce F

Traditionally served with grilled and fried herring.

Basic butter sauce
2 oz made mustard
1 teaspoon anchovy essence

Stir the mustard and anchovy essence into the sauce just before serving.

Nut Brown Butter H and F

4 oz butter
Juice of ½ lemon
1 teaspoon finely chopped parsley (optional)

Cook the butter over gentle heat until light brown. Add the lemon juice and parsley and serve.

Parsley Butter Sauce F and H

Basic butter sauce
2 heaped tablespoons finely chopped parsley
Salt and pepper
Lemon juice

Add the blanched, chopped parsley to the sauce and heat through. Season to taste with salt, pepper and lemon juice.

White Wine Sauce H

1 pt melted butter
3 oz caster sugar
Grated lemon rind or nutmeg

Make a melted butter sauce with 1 pt dry white wine instead of water. Add sugar and season with lemon rind or nutmeg to taste. Bring to the boil and serve at once.

BUTTER GARNISHES

Served with grilled meat and fish dishes, softened butter with various flavourings and seasoning is shaped into a cylindrical roll, wrapped in grease-proof paper and left to chill in the refrigerator. When required, the hard butter is cut into fancy slices and used as garnish.

The following flavourings may be added to 4 oz softened butter:

1 teaspoon freshly chopped parsley and 1 teaspoon lemon juice *or*
2½ oz ground almonds *or*
6 finely chopped anchovies, shake anchovy essence, pinch cayenne, black pepper, nutmeg and mace *or*
2 tablespoons chilli sauce or ketchup *or*
2 oz finely chopped mushrooms and 1 teaspoon curry powder, fried together before blending with the butter *or*
1 dessertspoon chopped dill *or*
2 crushed garlic cloves *or*
4 oz soft herring roes *or*
1 tablespoon finely grated horseradish *or*
Juice and grated rind of ¼ lemon *or*
1 oz cooked lobster coral *or*
1 teaspoon dry mustard or paprika *or*
1 oz minced cooked sweet pepper *or*
2—4 oz finely chopped shallots *or*
2 oz mashed, boned and skinned sardines *or*
1 teaspoon orange juice, grated orange rind and paprika to taste.

CREAM SAUCES

Fresh cream is the basis for these rich sauces, sometimes served hot, but more often chilled as accompaniments to main courses.

Anchovy Cream H

Served chilled, this sharp sauce is excellent with fish and also goes well with cold roast beef.

6 anchovies
1 hardboiled egg yolk
Cayenne pepper
5 fl oz liquid aspic
5 fl oz stiffly whipped cream

Pound the anchovies to a fine paste with the egg yolk; add cayenne pepper to taste. Stir in the aspic. Pass through a strainer and gradually fold in the cream.

Cream Sauce H

Excellent with baked and grilled fish, such as trout. Chopped parsley or chives may be added.

1 pt double cream
4 oz butter
Salt and pepper

Bring the cream to the boil and cook over gentle heat until slightly reduced. Stir in the butter until melted and thoroughly blended. Season with salt and pepper and serve hot.

Cucumber and Horseradish Sauce H and F

Serve chilled with cold roast beef.

6 oz finely diced cucumber
Salt and black pepper
2 tablespoons vinegar
½ pt double cream
1 tablespoon grated horseradish

Sprinkle the cucumber with salt, pepper and vinegar and leave for 15 minutes. Beat the cream until slightly thickened; strain the cucumber and mix into the cream. Add the horseradish and chill before serving.

Cucumber Cream Sauce H

An ideal cold sauce with poached cold salmon.

¾ lb peeled and grated cucumber
Salt and pepper
1 dessertspoon chopped fresh tarragon or 1 dessert-spoon tarragon vinegar
5 fl oz double cream

Sprinkle the cucumber with salt and pepper and vinegar if used. Beat the cream until thick and add the cucumber and liquid. Season to taste and stir in the chopped tarragon leaves.

Dill Sauce H and F

Serve chilled with freshwater fish, with cold roast lamb and chicken.

3 oz finely chopped dill
½ pt double cream
Salt and pepper

Blend the dill into the lightly whipped cream, season to taste with salt and pepper. Chill.

Hanover Sauce H and F

A delicately flavoured sauce, ideal with roast chicken.

1 set chicken livers
Juice of ½ lemon
½ pt double cream
Salt and pepper

Clean and boil the chicken livers; pound to a paste with the lemon juice. Stir in the cream and add salt and pepper to taste. Heat the sauce through without letting it boil; serve hot.

Horseradish Sauce H and F

Also known as Benton sauce, this is served chilled with hot or cold roast beef and other meat, and with smoked trout.

3 oz grated horseradish
1 teaspoon made mustard
1 tablespoon caster sugar
2 tablespoons white wine vinegar
Salt
½ pt double cream

Mix the horseradish with mustard, sugar, vinegar and salt to taste. Whip the cream lightly and gradually beat it into the horseradish mixture. Chill for a few hours before serving.

Lord Welby's Sauce H and F

Served chilled with hot or cold roast beef.

3 oz grated parsnip
1 teaspoon dry mustard
2 tablespoons white wine vinegar
Salt
½ pt double cream

Mix the parsnip with mustard and vinegar; add salt to taste. Whip the cream lightly and gradually

beat in the parsnip. Chill before serving.

Parsley Sauce F and H

Excellent with roast chicken, grilled and fried herring, mackerel and plaice and with cauliflower.

3 oz finely chopped parsley
½ pt double cream
Salt and pepper
1 teaspoon tabasco

Whip the cream and fold in the parsley; season to taste with salt, pepper and tabasco.

Parsnip Sauce F and H London

During the reign of Queen Mary, this was traditionally served at Marlborough House on Ash Wednesday and Good Friday, with dried salt cod, boiled parsnips and mealy potatoes.

1 lb parsnips
1 oz butter
½ pt double cream
Salt, pepper and nutmeg

Clean and chop the parsnips; boil in water until tender. Liquidise or beat the parsnips to a pulp. Reheat the parsnips with the butter and blend in the cream. Heat the sauce through over gentle heat until smooth and thick. Season to taste with salt, pepper and nutmeg. Serve hot.

White Devil Sauce

Less spicy than the popular Victorian devil sauces, this goes well with cold roast poultry and game, and poached cold salmon and trout.

½ pt double cream
1 teaspoon French mustard
1 teaspoon mushroom ketchup
1 teaspoon Worcestershire Sauce
Salt and pepper

Whip the cream lightly, with mustard, ketchup and sauce flavourings. Season to taste with salt and pepper. Chill lightly before serving.

PURÉE SAUCES

The main ingredient of these savoury sauces is a fruit or vegetable pulp which acts as the thickening agent. The purée can be made by rubbing the pulp through a coarse sieve or by blending it in a liquidiser.

Apple Sauce F and H

The traditional accompaniment to roast pork, and in earlier centuries also to roast goose.

1 lb cooking apples
1 quince (optional)
1 oz butter
1–2 oz sugar (optional)
2 cloves

Peel, core and slice the apples and the quince. Put into a pan with the butter, a little water, sugar to taste and the cloves. Cook, covered, until tender, after 10–15 minutes. Pass through a sieve or liquidise. Return the pulp to the pan and reduce over gentle heat to the required consistency.

Apple Sauce, Baked F and H

Similar to Apple Sauce but more spicy from the addition of Curry Sauce. (See Brown Sauces).

1 lb cooking apples
1 oz butter
Sugar
Curry Sauce
Mixed spice
Peel of 1 lemon

Peel, core and slice the apples; put in a pie dish, cover with foil and bake with a roast of pork until the apples have reduced to a pulp. Remove from the oven and beat the apples until smooth; beat in the butter. Blend in sugar, curry sauce and mixed spice to taste. Heat through, then add the blanched lemon peel, cut into narrow strips.

Chestnut Sauce H

Serve with roast turkey and chicken and with baked or braised ham. In some variations, ½ lb finely chopped mushrooms are added to the chestnut pulp.

2 lb peeled chestnuts
4 oz whole onions
2 oz whole carrots
1 pt white stock
4 fl oz single cream
Salt and pepper

Simmer the chestnuts, onions and carrots in the stock until the chestnuts are soft. Strain, setting the cooking liquid aside and discarding the onions and carrots. Pass the chestnuts through a sieve or liquidise. Stir the chestnut pulp into the reserved stock and bring to the boil. Remove from the heat and stir in the cream. Season with salt and pepper and serve.

County Sauce F Leicestershire

Traditionally served with local pork pies; the sauce may also be bottled and stored for several months.

1 lb chopped tomatoes
1–1½ lb peeled, cored and sliced cooking apples
1 lb roughly chopped onions
1 roughly chopped lemon
½ lb sultanas
6 oz sugar
1½ oz salt
1½ oz mixed spice
2 pt white vinegar
1 oz cornflour

Put the tomatoes, apples, onions and lemon in a pan with the sultanas, sugar, salt, spice and vinegar. Bring to the boil and simmer until thoroughly cooked. Pass the mixture through a sieve or liquidise. Bring the sauce to the boil again and stir in the cornflour blended with a little water. Cook until thick, then serve or bottle.

Cranberry and Apple Sauce F and H

Serve with roast goose and turkey.

6 oz cranberries
6 oz peeled, cored and diced apples
5 fl oz water
2 oz sugar

Cook the cranberries and apples in the water until soft. Pass through a sieve or liquidise. Reheat the sauce; add the sugar and serve.

Cranberry Sauce F and H

A traditional sauce with roast turkey and also excellent with roast lamb.

6 oz cranberries
5 fl oz water
4 oz sugar
Salt

Boil the water and sugar to make a syrup; pour into a double saucepan, add the cranberries and simmer gently until tender. Season to taste with salt and serve.

Gooseberry Sauce I F Cornwall

Dating back to Norman times, this is a favourite sauce with grilled mackerel, grilled pork chops, roast goose and cold pork.

1 lb gooseberries
2 oz butter (optional)
2 oz sugar (optional)
Nutmeg
Salt

Top and tail the gooseberries and cook in a little water until tender; pass through a sieve or liquidise. Beat in the butter and sugar; reheat and season to taste with nutmeg and salt.

Gooseberry Sauce II F and H

1 lb green gooseberries
5 fl oz white wine
1 oz sugar (optional)
2 oz butter

Top and tail the gooseberries; blanch for a few minutes then drain. Put the gooseberries, wine and sugar in a pan and simmer until the gooseberries are soft. Pass through a sieve or liquidise. Reheat the pulp, blend in the butter and serve.

Pork or Goose Sauce F and H

A spicy apple sauce to serve with roast goose and loin of pork.

1 lb peeled and cored cooking apples
¾ lb finely chopped onions
4 oz caster sugar
1 pt brown ale
½ lb cranberries
1 teaspoon mustard powder

Dice the apples and put in a pan with the onions, sugar and ale; simmer, covered, until soft. Add the cranberries and continue cooking for 10–15 minutes or until the cranberries are soft. Blend to a pulp in the liquidiser. Reheat and season to taste with mustard before serving.

Prune Sauce F and H Wales

Serve with roast sucking pig, roast venison and mutton and lamb. In Wales, the sauce supplemented with ½ lb black currants is also traditional with boiled mutton.

1 lb prunes
½ pt water
1 oz moist brown sugar
1 dessertspoon rum or brandy

Boil the prunes in the water until soft. Stir in the sugar and brandy or rum. Rub through a sieve and reheat before serving.

Sorrel Sauce F

The slightly bitter leaves of wild sorrel were much used in medieval cooking. Sorrel sauce was popular with roast duck, goose, lamb and pork.

4 oz finely chopped sorrel leaves
½ lb peeled, cored and diced Cox's Orange Pippin
   apples
5 fl oz vinegar
2 oz caster sugar
1 oz butter

Put the sorrel and apples in a pan with the vinegar and sugar. Bring to the boil, covered, and cook until the apples are soft. Rub through a sieve or liquidise. Reheat the sauce and blend in the butter until melted. Serve hot or cold.

Sorrel Sauce, Green F and H

Serve with roast duck and goose, and with plain omelets.

1 lb sorrel leaves
1 oz butter
Salt, pepper, sugar
2 tablespoons double cream
Chicken stock (optional)

Cook the sorrel leaves in the butter for 5 minutes. Rub through a sieve or liquidise. Reheat the sorrel pulp and season to taste with salt, pepper and sugar. Blend in the cream and remove the pan from the heat before boiling point is reached. Thin with chicken stock if necessary; serve hot.

Tomato Sauce I F and H

Serve with pasta dishes, minced meat, collops,

baked marrow and fish.

3 lb tomatoes
½ lb chopped onions
4 oz diced ham
6 oz diced carrots
3 oz butter
1½ oz flour
2 teaspoons tomato paste
1½ pt white stock
2 oz sugar
1 bay leaf
3 cloves
1 crushed clove garlic
Salt and pepper

Fry the onions, ham and carrots in the butter until light brown. Stir in the flour and tomato paste and cook for a further 2–3 minutes. Skin the tomatoes and cut into quarters. Add the tomatoes, stock, sugar, bay leaf, cloves and garlic to the onion mixture and stir until boiling. Simmer for 30–45 minutes or until the vegetables are tender.

Remove the cloves and bay leaf and pass the sauce through a sieve or liquidise. Reheat the sauce and season with salt and pepper before serving.

Tomato Sauce II F and H

1 lb skinned tomatoes
1 oz sliced onion
1 dessertspoon oil
1 bay leaf
Sprig thyme and parsley
½ oz butter
Salt and pepper

Fry the onion in the oil until soft. Slice the tomatoes and add to the onion, with the bay leaf, herbs and butter. Cook gently, reducing slightly. Pass through a sieve or liquidise. Season with salt and pepper and serve hot with fish.

Tomato Sauce, Spiced F and H

2 lb tomatoes
¾ lb grated onions
1 dessertspoon Worcestershire Sauce
Cayenne pepper, curry powder
Salt and pepper

Skin the tomatoes and rub through a sieve. Blend the tomato pulp with the onions and blend in the Worcestershire sauce. Season to taste with cayenne, curry, salt and pepper. Serve cold.

WINE AND SAVOURY SAUCES

This group of sauces includes those which are heavily flavoured with some kind of wine and served with main courses. Also included are sauces, such as bread and mint sauces, which fall into no defined categories but have survived for centuries as national accompaniments to certain dishes.

Bread Sauce F and H

This survival from medieval days when breadcrumbs were a common thickening agent is the national and favourite accompaniment to roast game, poultry and pork.

1 onion studded with 2 cloves
Pinch each mace and nutmeg
1 bay leaf
6 peppercorns
½ pt milk
2 oz white breadcrumbs
1 oz butter
2 tablespoons double cream
Salt and pepper

Put the onion, mace, nutmeg, bay leaf and peppercorns in a pan with the milk; simmer gently for 30 minutes. Strain and sprinkle the breadcrumbs into the liquid. Leave to infuse for 15 minutes. Heat the sauce through, beat in the butter and cream; season with salt and pepper and serve hot.

Cumberland Sauce H and F

Attributed by some authorities to Ernest, Duke of Cumberland, this sauce gained popularity in Edwardian days as a cold accompaniment to ham, chicken, duck, goose and venison. A variation, known as Oxford Sauce, omits the cherries and limits the orange flavour to that of grated peel of half an orange.

Rind and juice of 2 oranges
1¼ lb red currant jelly
1 teaspoon made mustard
5 fl oz port
Juice of 1 lemon
1 oz finely chopped, blanched shallots
1½ oz fresh cherries, stoned and chopped

Peel the rind thinly from the oranges; blanch for a few minutes in boiling water; drain and refresh

and cut into narrow strips. Put the red currant
jelly in a bowl with the mustard; whisk in the port
wine and the strained orange and lemon juice. Add
the shallots to the sauce and finally blend in the
orange strips and cherries.

Granville Sauce H and F

A favourite 19th century sauce served with poached
salmon, grey mullet, hake and cod steaks.

8 anchovy fillets
6 oz chopped shallots
2 fl oz dry sherry or white port
1 dessertspoon white wine vinegar
12 black peppercorns
Ground mace, nutmeg
½ oz butter
½ oz flour
5 fl oz double cream

Put the anchovies, shallots, sherry (or port),
vinegar, peppercorns, pinch of mace and nutmeg
in a pan and cook over gentle heat until the
shallots are soft. Knead together the butter and
flour and add to the shallot mixture; boil to
thicken. Blend in the cream and heat through
without boiling. Strain the sauce through a sieve
before serving.

Hanoverian Sauce H and F

Basically consisting of the same ingredients as
Cumberland Sauce, this sauce for serving with cold
meats has similar origins.

1 oz caster sugar
Juice and rind of 1 orange or lemon
1 teaspoon dry mustard
2 tablespoons olive oil
2 tablespoons port

Put the sugar in a bowl and grate over it the
orange or lemon rind, add the strained juice,
mustard, olive oil and port wine. Mix thoroughly
and serve.

Mint Sauce H and F

The modern equivalent of the medieval Verde
Sawse, mint sauce has remained the necessary
accompaniment to young roast lamb.

3 oz fresh, chopped mint
1 dessertspoon hot water

½ tablespoon sugar
3 tablespoons white wine, white wine or malt vinegar

Wash and strip the leaves from freshly gathered
mint; chop the leaves finely. Put into a sauceboat with the hot water and sugar to taste, leave
for at least 30 minutes. Mix in the white wine or
vinegar and serve.

Port Wine Sauce

Serve with roast mutton.

½ pt port
5 fl oz thickened mutton gravy
4 oz red currant jelly

Mix all the ingredients and bring to the boil.
Simmer for 2 minutes and serve.

Red Currant Sauce

Usually served with roast venison and young
lamb.

½—¾ lb red currant jelly
2 tablespoons port
2 tablespoons lemon juice
Salt and pepper

Dissolve the red currant jelly in the port and
lemon juice and bring to the boil over gentle heat.
Season with salt and pepper before serving.

SALAD DRESSINGS AND CREAMS

The earliest known salads were simple collections
of herbs and vegetables, dressed with oil and
vinegar. More complex salads were developed in
the course of time and with them more refined
dressings; of these the salad sauce, composed of
hardboiled egg yolks pounded to a paste and
mixed with various ingredients, became the basic
for today's creams and dressings.

English Salad Sauce H and F

According to the type of salad, different and
additional ingredients may be added to the salad
cream, such as chopped capers, pimento, chopped
celery and chives, whipped cream, finely chopped
cucumber, parsley, tomato ketchup, chopped
olives, peeled and diced tomatoes, chopped spring
onions, crumbled blue cheese (Stilton or Blue
Cheshire).

8 hardboiled egg yolks
Juice of 1 lemon
4 raw egg yolks
Salt
1 oz caster sugar
Cayenne pepper
1 teaspoon English mustard
1 pt double cream
1 teaspoon tarragon vinegar

Pound the hardboiled egg yolks to a paste with a few drops of strained lemon juice. Stir in the raw egg yolks and add salt, sugar, cayenne and mustard to taste. Gradually stir in the lightly whipped cream and finally add the remaining lemon juice and the vinegar.

Asparagus Salad Sauce H

English Salad Sauce
12 oz asparagus
Lemon juice
Salt and pepper

Cook the asparagus until soft in a little water. Pass through a sieve or blend in a liquidiser. Add to the salad sauce and flavour to taste with lemon juice, salt and pepper.

Cambridge Sauce H and F

English Salad Sauce
1 teaspoon each, finely chopped tarragon, chives, chervil
1 dessertspoon chopped capers
Cayenne pepper

Mix the finely chopped herbs and capers into the salad sauce; season with cayenne. Leave for at least 30 minutes to allow the flavours to blend.

Cream Dressing H and F

2 fl oz double cream
½ teaspooon made mustard
Salt and sugar
1 dessertspoon white wine vinegar

Stir the mustard smooth with a little salt and sugar; stir in the cream and add the vinegar drop by drop.

Cucumber Salad Sauce H and F

English Salad Sauce
1 cucumber
2½ fl oz stiffly whipped cream
1 dessertspoon tarragon vinegar
Salt
1 dessertspoon liquid aspic

Peel the cucumber, cut in half lengthways and remove any seeds. Chop roughly and blend until smooth in a liquidiser. Blend the cucumber pulp into the salad sauce, add the cream and vinegar and season with salt. Stir in the aspic.

Green Sauce H and F

Very little has changed in this recipe for *Verde Sawse* since it was first published early in the 15th century; chives have replaced costmary and bread steeped in vinegar is no longer used, but otherwise this salad sauce follows the original closely.

2 tablespoons chopped parsley
1 tablespoon chopped chives
1 teaspoon chopped mint
1 crushed clove garlic
1 teaspoon chopped tarragon
1 teaspoon chopped chervil
2 fl oz olive oil
2 tablespoons wine vinegar
1 tablespoon lemon juice
Salt and pepper

Mix all the finely chopped herbs thoroughly and blend in the oil, vinegar and lemon juice. Season with salt and pepper and serve as a salad sauce with boiled meat or poultry.

Mayonnaise H and F

6 egg yolks
½ teaspoon salt
1 teaspoon ground pepper
1 teaspoon English mustard
3 fl oz white wine vinegar
2 pt salad oil
Juice of ½ lemon

Put the egg yolks in a basin with salt, pepper, mustard and half the vinegar. Whisk vigorously until thoroughly blended; add the oil, at first drop by drop, then progressing to a thin stream, whisking all the time. Stir in the lemon juice.

Oxford Brawn Sauce F and H

Serve with cold, pressed brawn.

1 oz soft brown sugar
1 teaspoon made mustard
¼ teaspoon salt
Pinch pepper
2 fl oz olive oil
2 tablespoons vinegar

Mix the sugar, mustard, salt and pepper with the oil; pour into a bottle. Add the vinegar and shake vigorously.

Salad Cream F and H

1 dessertspoon dry mustard
1 oz sugar
1 tablespoon flour
Pinch salt
2 eggs
7½ fl oz vinegar
¼–½ pt double cream

Mix the mustard with sugar, flour and salt. Blend in the eggs and the vinegar. Put the mixture in a double boiler and stir until it thickens. Leave to get quite cold, then add enough cream to give a pouring consistency.

Salad Dressing F and H

¾ pt salad oil
½ teaspoon salt
1 teaspoon mustard
Ground black pepper
1/3 pt white wine vinegar
1 crushed clove garlic

Whisk the oil with salt, mustard, pepper and vinegar until blended to a smooth emulsion. Add the garlic and use the dressing as required.

Sour Cream Dressing H and F

5 fl oz soured cream
2 tablespoons white wine vinegar
1 oz finely chopped onion
½ teaspoon sugar
Salt and pepper

Blend the soured cream with vinegar, onion and sugar. Season with salt and pepper. Chill in the refrigerator before serving.

DESSERT SAUCES

The classic British sweet sauces were probably intended to smooth the often stodgy steamed and boiled puddings and have survived because of their rich smoothness and delicate flavours. In many cases, they are also permanently associated with certain desserts, such as brandy butter with Christmas pudding and Melba sauce with vanilla ice cream. As with any other type of sauce, dessert sauces should enhance, not mask the main flavour of a dish.

Brandy or Rum Butter H and F

Traditionally served with Christmas Pudding and also used as a spread on currant bread and toast.

½ lb unsalted butter
¾ lb soft brown sugar
6 fl oz rum or brandy
Nutmeg or cinnamon

Cream the butter and sugar until smooth and fluffy; blend in the brandy or rum a little at a time. Flavour with nutmeg or cinnamon and chill before serving.

Butterscotch Sauce: see *Syrup Sauce*

Caudle Sauce H

Developed from caudle, a hot drink of gruel and wine, sweetened and spiced and used in building-up diets, this hot sauce goes well with sweet fruit pies and tarts.

1 pt white wine
3 whole eggs or 6 yolks
1 oz caster sugar
Juice of 1 lemon
Pinch cinnamon

Put the wine, eggs, sugar and strained lemon juice in the top of a double saucepan. Cook over gentle heat, whisking continuously until the sauce thickens. Flavour with cinnamon before serving.

Cherry Brandy Sauce H and F

Serve hot with vanilla ice cream.
2 pt basic sweet white sauce
8 fl oz cherry brandy
Essence of cloves

Add the cherry brandy to the white sauce; heat through and flavour to taste with essence of cloves.

Chocolate Sauce H and F

Usually served hot, with vanilla ice cream.

½ lb block plain chocolate
½ lb caster sugar
½ pt water
1 pt double cream (optional)

Grate the chocolate finely. Boil the sugar in the water until dissolved and syrupy. Stir in the grated chocolate and cook, preferably in a double saucepan, over very low heat until the chocolate has melted. Stir in the cream.

Cider Sauce H and F

Always served hot and excellent with apple pies and puddings.

2 pt cider
½ lb caster sugar
4 oz butter

Simmer the cider with the sugar to make a light syrup. Cut the butter into small pieces and whisk into the sauce.

Coconut Sauce F

Serve hot with sweet suet puddings.

2 pt basic sweet white sauce
3 oz dessicated coconut

Stir the coconut into the sweet white sauce and simmer for 10 minutes over low heat.

Cumberland Rum Butter H and F

Traditional with Christmas pudding, mince pies and steamed puddings, this butter can also be potted in small jars and stored in the refrigerator for several weeks.

½ lb butter
¾ lb soft brown sugar
4 fl oz rum
Nutmeg, cinnamon (optional)

Beat the butter until creamy, then beat in the sugar until thoroughly blended. Gradually add the rum, beating well after each addition. Season to taste with nutmeg and cinnamon. Chill for several hours before serving.

Custard Sauce H and F

This may be poured into a mould and allowed to set as a dessert on its own, or it may be served hot as a sauce with any kind of fruit dessert.

1 pt milk
Vanilla stick, orange or lemon peel (optional)
8 egg yolks
3 oz sugar

Bring the milk to the boil over gentle heat with a vanilla stick, lemon or orange peel. Beat the egg yolks and sugar until smooth, then gradually stir in the strained milk. Pour the sauce into a double saucepan and heat through, stirring continuously until it thickens enough to coat the back of a wooden spoon. The custard may also be flavoured with a few drops of liqueur just before serving.

Fairy Butter F

Serve chilled with steamed and baked sweet puddings; it will keep for 2–3 weeks in a refrigerator.

5 hardboiled egg yolks
4 oz softened butter
2 oz ground almonds
Grated rind of ½ lemon
4 oz caster sugar
Orange flower water

Pound the egg yolks to a smooth paste, then blend in the butter, almonds, lemon rind and sugar; add orange flower water to taste.

Fruit Sauce F and H

Serve cold with steamed and baked puddings.

1 lb unsweetened fruit pulp
1 lb caster sugar
½ pt water
Juice of 1 lemon

Put all the ingredients in a pan and bring to the boil over gentle heat. Remove any scum, pour into a sauceboat and leave to cool.

Gooseberry Sauce F and H

May be served hot or cold.

1 lb gooseberries
4 oz caster sugar
2 oz butter
Pinch nutmeg

Top, tail and wash the gooseberries, put in a pan with enough water to just cover and bring to the boil. Simmer over low heat until soft. Rub the gooseberries through a sieve or blend in a liquidiser. Return the pulp to the pan and stir in the sugar, butter and nutmeg. Beat the mixture until smooth.

Honey Sauce H and F Scotland

A good dessert sauce with plain steamed sponge puddings and with vanilla ice cream.

2 pt basic sweet white sauce
4 oz heather honey

Prepare the white sauce in the usual way, but omitting the sugar. Stir in the honey and heat through until thoroughly blended. Serve hot.

Jam Sauce F and H

Serve hot or cold with steamed sponge puddings or jam roly polies.

½ lb sieved jam (currants, raspberry, strawberry)
½ pt water or fruit juice
1 oz arrowroot
Juice of 1 lemon

Heat the jam and water or fruit juice; simmer for 5 minutes. Blend the arrowroot with cold water and stir in a little of the jam. Mix into the jam sauce, bring to the boil, stirring continuously until the sauce thickens and clears. Add lemon juice just before serving.

Lemon Sauce F and H

Ideal with plain steamed puddings and with fruit pies that require a slightly tart sauce.

2 oz caster sugar
1 pt water
Juice and zest of 1 lemon
2 eggs
3 oz butter

Boil the sugar and water with the lemon juice and zest until slightly reduced. Strain into a double saucepan. Beat the eggs and whisk into the lemon juice, together with the butter. Beat continuously until the sauce thickens. Serve hot.

Alternatively, make a lemon sauce from 2 pt basic sweet sauce, adding the juice and grated rind of 4 lemons. Strain the sauce before beating in 2 eggs and heating the sauce through without boiling.

Lemon Jelly Sauce F and H

Use instead of lemon sauce to accompany any type of steamed puddings.

½ lb lemon jelly marmalade
Juice and grated rind of 1 lemon

Melt the lemon jelly in a pan over low heat; stir in the strained lemon juice and the rind. Heat through and serve hot.

Melba Sauce H and F

This famous sauce was created by Auguste Escoffier, renowned chef at the Savoy Hotel, London, for Dame Nellie Melba, the opera singer in the late 19th century. It is poured over vanilla ice cream topped with a fresh poached peach.

1 lb raspberries
Caster sugar

Rub the raspberries through a sieve and sweeten the pulp to taste with sugar.

Plum Sauce F and H

Serve hot with plum puddings and tarts, or with roast pork.

1 lb red plums
¼ pt white wine vinegar
1 tablespoon chopped mint
Sugar to taste

Cook the plums in the vinegar until tender. Rub the sauce through a sieve, return the pulp to the pan and stir in the mint. Heat through. Add enough sugar to remove any excess tartness.

Punch Sauce H and F

Serve with sweet suet and baked puddings, and with sweet fritters, such as Poor Knights of Windsor.

5 fl oz sherry
Juice and grated rind of 2 lemons

4 oz sugar
2 pt basic sweet white sauce

Put the sherry, lemon rind and juice in a pan, together with the sugar and bring slowly to the boil; heat for 2—3 minutes. Strain the sherry mixture into the sweet white sauce, heat through and serve at once. For a richer version of this sauce, add 4 well-beaten eggs to the sauce, strain again and heat the sauce through over low heat before serving.

Red Currant and Raspberry Sauce F

Serve hot with any kind of plain steamed pudding.

4 oz red currant jelly
4 oz raspberry jam
½ pt water
¾ oz cornflour

Bring the jelly, jam and water to the boil over gentle heat. Blend the cornflour with a little water, stir in a little of the hot liquid and mix into the sauce. Bring back to the boil, stirring continuously until the sauce thickens.

Red Currant Sauce with Maraschino H and F

Serve hot or cold with fruit salads, pies and puddings and with ice cream.

½ lb caster sugar
½ pt water
½ lb red currant jelly
Grated rind of 1 orange and 1 lemon
2 tablespoons Maraschino liqueur

Bring the sugar and water to the boil and simmer until concentrated to a light syrup. Add the red currant jelly, orange and lemon rind. Simmer until the jelly has melted. Strain the sauce; add the Maraschino and serve.

Syrup Sauce H and F

This is a basic syrup sauce which can be flavoured with any type of fruit juice — black currant, orange, raspberry — liqueur or essence, such as almond, vanilla, or coffee. Usually served warm with steamed and baked puddings, waffles, pancakes and ice creams.

1 lb caster sugar
5 fl oz water
4 oz butter

Boil the water and sugar until concentrated to a light syrup. Remove the pan from the heat and add the butter, whisking until the sauce is smooth.

Butterscotch sauce is a variation of syrup sauce, soft brown sugar replacing the caster sugar. Just before serving add the strained juice of 1 lemon.

Forcemeats, Stuffings and Dumplings

The main purpose of a forcemeat or stuffing is to keep meat or fish moist during roasting and this is achieved by filling the hollow cavity left after the removal of bones or intestines. The flavours of the meat are also absorbed by the stuffing which at the same time flavours the meat. Meat or poultry with a distinct flavour is usually complemented with a strong stuffing while a mild flavoured meat is complemented with a milder stuffing. Game birds are the exception; as they have strong distinct flavours they are seldom stuffed, but a piece of fat or butter is put in the body cavity to prevent drying out, and the body is barded with fat pork or bacon.

Forcemeats are mixtures of a number of ingredients, the chief one being meat, highly flavoured with herbs and spices. They have since medieval days been traditional in English cooking, being used either as a stuffing or as a garnish, often in the shape of small balls. The various ingredients of forcemeats or stuffings are finely chopped, minced or liquidised and thoroughly mixed. A starchy substance, such as breadcrumbs or rice, is used to hold the ingredients together, and a binding agent is usually necessary to combine the whole. This is often fat, chopped suet being used for large cuts of meat and poultry requiring long cooking time, and butter or lard for small birds and meats; in these instances, the cooked stuffing will have a crumbly texture. Egg, milk or water are also used to bind a stuffing which will then be more compact, suitable for cutting into slices, either with the meat or separately.

Dumplings can be made from any firm force-meat mixture and shaped into walnut-sized balls. They can be fried and served as a garnish with roast meat or poultry, added to a stew or casserole, or boiled separately and mixed into the accompanying sauce.

MEAT, POULTRY, GAME AND VEGETABLE STUFFINGS

All forcemeat stuffings contain starch and swell during cooking; it is therefore important to leave enough room in the meat or poultry cavity to allow for expansion.

Apple Stuffing H and F

This stuffing of whole apples is sufficient for a 4 lb goose (prepared weight).

1 lb Golden Russet or Golden Delicious apples
1 pt water
5 fl oz white wine
4 oz chopped onions
1 tablespoon finely chopped sage
Salt and pepper
Cornflour

Stuff the goose with the washed, unpeeled, whole apples. Blend the water, wine, onions, sage and salt and pepper and use to baste the goose regularly during roasting. When the goose is cooked, remove it to a serving dish. Boil the basting liquid rapidly until reduced and thicken to the required consistency with cornflour blended with water.

Apple and Celery Stuffing H and F

Use for stuffing pork.

2 oz chopped bacon
1 oz butter
½ lb chopped onions
2 oz chopped celery
1 lb peeled, cored and chopped cooking apples
3 oz fresh white breadcrumbs
1 teaspoon chopped parsley

Sugar
Salt and pepper
½ beaten egg

Fry the bacon in the butter for 2—3 minutes;
remove from the pan. Cook the onions and celery
for 5 minutes in the same pan, add the apples and
cook for a further 2—3 minutes. Mix the bacon
with the onion, celery and apple mixture; stir in
the breadcrumbs and parsley and season to taste
with sugar, salt and pepper. Bind the stuffing
with beaten egg.

Apple and Prune Stuffing H and F

A traditional stuffing for goose or duck at
Christmas.

20 prunes
¾ lb peeled, cored and chopped cooking apples
2 oz cooked long grain rice
1 stick chopped celery
Chopped goose or duck liver
1 dessertspoon finely chopped parsley
½ lemon
Ground mace
Salt and pepper
Brown sugar
1 egg

Soak the prunes overnight, then cook until tender;
leave to cool before cutting the prunes in half and
discarding the stones. Mix the stoned prunes with
the apples, rice, celery and liver. Blend in the
parsley and the grated rind and juice of the lemon;
season to taste with mace, salt, pepper and brown
sugar. Bind the stuffing with the lightly beaten egg.

Apricot Stuffing I H and F

Use as a stuffing for chicken or for the neck end
of turkey.

3 oz dried apricots
3 oz fresh white breadcrumbs
¼ teaspoon mixed spice
¼ teaspoon each salt and pepper
1 tablespoon lemon juice
1 oz melted butter
1 small egg

Soak the apricots in water overnight; drain and
chop finely. Combine the apricots with the
breadcrumbs, mixed spice, salt, pepper and lemon
juice. Stir in the melted butter. Bind the stuffing
with the lightly beaten egg.

Apricot Stuffing II H and F

A fruity stuffing for goose or duck:

¾ lb dried apricots
3 oz butter
1 green pepper, seeded and finely chopped
4 oz peeled, cored and finely chopped cooking
    apples
4 oz finely chopped celery
4 oz fresh white breadcrumbs
Salt and pepper
2 eggs

Soak the apricots in water overnight; drain and
chop finely. Melt the butter in a pan and fry the
apricots, pepper, apples and celery for a few
minutes, until soft. Remove from the heat and
stir in the breadcrumbs; season with salt and
pepper. Bind with the lightly beaten eggs.

Apricot and Apple Stuffing H and F

Used to stuff best end of lamb or thick lamb chops.

2 oz dried, soaked apricots
4 oz peeled, cored and chopped cooking apples
2 oz finely chopped walnuts
Grated rind of 1 lemon
5 oz fresh white breadcrumbs
Salt and pepper
2 oz melted butter

Chop the apricots finely. Combine the apricots,
apples, walnuts, lemon rind and breadcrumbs.
Season with salt and pepper and bind with the
melted butter.

Bacon Stuffing F and H

This is used to stuff boned shoulder of lamb.

2 oz finely chopped bacon
3 oz chopped shallots
2 oz chopped suet
1 tablespoon finely chopped parsley
1½—2 oz fresh white breadcrumbs
½ teaspoon grated lemon rind
½ teaspoon mixed herbs
Grated nutmeg
Salt and pepper
1 egg

Mix the bacon, shallots, suet and parsley with the
breadcrumbs. Blend in lemon rind and the dried
herbs and season to taste with nutmeg, salt and
pepper. Bind with the lightly beaten egg.

Barley Stuffing H and F

Game birds are seldom stuffed, but this gives additional flavour to roast pigeon. The ingredients are sufficient for one bird.

1 oz barley, soaked overnight
Bunch sweet herbs
1 oz butter
2 drops onion juice
1 small clove garlic
1 bay leaf

Drain the barley and put in a pan with the herbs; cover with water. Bring to the boil and simmer until the barley is tender. Drain the barley and toss in the butter. Add the onion juice, crushed garlic and bay leaf; stuff the pigeon with this mixture.

Chestnut Stuffing H and F

The Christmas turkey is traditionally stuffed with chestnuts. The roasted, skinned chestnuts may be put whole into the body cavity with butter, salt and pepper and the neck end stuffed with a herb forcemeat, or the chestnuts can be sieved and bound with egg.

1 lb chestnut or ½ lb unsweetened chestnut purée
Milk
2 oz chopped bacon
1 oz butter
4 oz fresh white breadcrumbs
1 teaspoon finely chopped parsley
Grated rind of 1 lemon
Salt and pepper
1 egg

For fresh chestnuts, split the skins and place the nuts under a hot grill until the skin can easily be peeled off. Put the peeled chestnuts in a pan, cover with milk or water and boil for 40 minutes or until quite tender. Strain and sieve or blend in a liquidiser.

Fry the bacon in the butter until crisp, drain and mix with the breadcrumbs. In a large bowl blend the chestnut pulp with the bacon and breadcrumbs; add the parsley and lemon rind and season to taste with salt and pepper. Bind the stuffing with the lightly beaten egg.

Chestnut Stuffing, Victorian H and F

1½ lb chestnuts
Milk

1 chopped turkey liver
1 tablespoon finely chopped parsley
Salt and pepper
3 egg yolks

Roast, skin and cook the chestnuts in milk as described above. Sieve the chestnuts and mix with the turkey liver and parsley; season with salt and pepper. Beat the egg yolks lightly and use to bind the stuffing.

Chicken Liver Stuffing H and F

A smooth, herb-flavoured stuffing to use with chicken.

4 oz finely chopped fat bacon
2 oz butter
1 oz finely chopped onion
Sprig thyme
1 bay leaf
½ lb chicken livers
Salt and pepper

Cook the bacon over low heat in the butter; add the onion, thyme and bay leaf and cook until the onion is golden. Add the chopped liver and fry for a few minutes; season with salt and pepper. Rub the mixture through a sieve or blend in a liquidiser. Leave to cool completely before stuffing the chicken.

Cider and Ginger Stuffing F and H Kent

This stuffing and basting liquid was traditional with boned loin of lamb and originally used with Romney Marsh sheep.

1 lemon
1 lb cooking apples
2 oz sugar
3 cloves
2 cloves garlic
2 tablespoons ground ginger
Salt and pepper
2 oz butter or oil
1 pt cider or apple juice

Grate the lemon peel and extract the lemon juice; rub the meat inside and out with peel and juice. Peel and core the apples; cut into slices and place on the meat, sprinkle with sugar, stud with cloves and roll up and skewer the meat. Split the garlic cloves into slivers and insert in the meat. Mix the ground ginger with salt and pepper and rub into the skin of the meat; brush with melted butter or oil. During roasting, baste the lamb with the warmed cider or apple juice every 15 minutes. When cooked, remove the lamb to a serving dish, skim or drain off the fat and serve the pan juices as gravy.

Cockle Stuffing H and F

Possibly originating in Wales, this is used to stuff a boned leg of mutton or lamb. For special occasions, oysters may replace the cockles.

½ pt freshly cooked and shelled cockles
6 oz finely chopped shallots

Cut two of the shelled cockles into thin slices and set aside. Chop the remaining cockles finely and mix with the shallots; stuff into the bone cavity. Make cuts in the meat with a sharp knife and insert the reserved cockle slices.

Crab or Lobster Stuffing H

Use to stuff boned leg of mutton.

6 oz cooked crab or lobster meat
4 oz fresh white breadcrumbs
1 tablespoon finely chopped parsley
Grated rind of 1 lemon
Ground nutmeg and cayenne
Salt and pepper
1½ oz butter
2 egg yolks

Shred the crab or lobster meat and mix with the breadcrumbs. Add the parsley and lemon rind and season to taste with nutmeg, cayenne, salt and pepper. Melt the butter and add to the mixture with the egg yolks; mix the stuffing to a firm consistency.

Fruit and Mushroom Stuffing H and F

A sweet, fruity stuffing for any type of boned roasting meat, particularly lamb and pork.

¾ lb fresh red currants or ½ lb red currant jelly
1 tablespoon water
1 oz sugar
1½ oz finely chopped onions
1 oz butter
2 oz chopped mushroom stalks

4 oz minced belly pork
1 oz chopped parsley
2 oz fresh white breadcrumbs
½ clove garlic
Thyme
Salt and pepper
½ egg

Cook the red currants or red currant jelly with the water and sugar until soft, pass through a sieve if using fresh red currants. Cook the onions in the butter over gentle heat until soft. Add the mushroom stalks to the onions and cook for a few more minutes. In a mixing bowl, combine the onion and mushroom mixture with the belly pork, parsley and breadcrumbs. Stir in the red currant pulp and crushed garlic; season to taste with thyme, salt and pepper. Bind the stuffing with the lightly beaten egg.

Grape Stuffing H

This fruit forcemeat is sufficient to stuff one brace of pheasants which should ideally be served with a red wine gravy.

1 lb black or red grapes
2 oz butter

Separate the grapes, wash and dry well; remove the pips and stuff half the grapes and butter into each pheasant.

Ham Stuffing F

Used to stuff marrows, peppers and tomatoes.

1 oz chopped onion
½ oz dripping
2–3 oz chopped ham (or bacon)
2 chopped mushrooms
1 oz fresh white breadcrumbs
Salt and pepper
Pinch dry mustard
Worcestershire sauce
1 egg

Cook the onion gently in the dripping for 2 minutes; add the ham and mushrooms and continue cooking until the onion is soft. Remove the pan from the heat and add the breadcrumbs, salt, pepper, mustard and a few drops of Worcestershire sauce. Bind the stuffing with the lightly beaten egg.

Hare Forcemeat F and H

This forcemeat may be used to stuff a hare for roasting or it may be shaped into small balls and fried until brown or baked in the oven for 30 minutes, basting with fat.

1 hare liver
2 oz lean chopped bacon
4 oz finely chopped suet
6 oz fresh white breadcrumbs
1 tablespoon finely chopped parsley
1 tablespoon finely chopped sweet herbs
Grated rind of ½ lemon
Salt, cayenne, nutmeg
2 eggs

Clean the liver and boil for 5 minutes; mash with a fork. In a bowl, combine the hare liver, bacon, suet and breadcrumbs; stir in the parsley, herbs and lemon rind; season to taste with salt, cayenne and nutmeg. Bind the forcemeat with the lightly beaten eggs.

Herb Stuffing I H and F

The following two stuffings are both suitable for roast chicken.

6 oz fresh white breadcrumbs
4 oz shredded suet
3 oz lean chopped bacon
Grated rind of ½ lemon
1 tablespoon finely chopped parsley
1 teaspoon chopped thyme
1 teaspoon marjoram
Pinch nutmeg
Salt and pepper
2 eggs

Mix the breadcrumbs, suet and bacon. Blend in the lemon rind, parsley, thyme and marjoram and season to taste with nutmeg, salt and pepper. Bind the stuffing with the lightly beaten eggs.

Herb Stuffing II H and F

1 oz chopped onion
4 oz butter
6 oz fresh white breadcrumbs
1 oz cooked chopped ham
1 teaspoon finely chopped parsley
1 teaspoon finely chopped thyme
Grated rind of ½ lemon
Pinch mace

Salt and pepper
1 egg

Cook the onion in the butter over gentle heat until soft. Remove from the heat and combine the onion and butter with the breadcrumbs, ham, parsley, thyme, lemon rind and mace. Season with salt and pepper. Bind the stuffing with the lightly beaten egg.

Kidney and Oatmeal Stuffing F

Use as a stuffing for roast lamb.

4 lamb kidneys
1 oz chopped salad onion
2 oz butter
6 oz coarse oatmeal (par-boiled)
1 tablespoon finely chopped parsley
Pinch rosemary or thyme
Finely chopped clove garlic
Salt and pepper
1 pt brown stock

Skin the lamb kidneys; boil for about 5 minutes, drain and chop. Lightly fry the onion in the butter, remove from the heat and blend with the kidneys, oatmeal and parsley. Season with rosemary, garlic and salt and pepper. Stir in the stock until the stuffing has a firm consistency.

Liver Stuffing H and F

This stuffing can be used for chicken, goose, duck, turkey or game birds, such as partridge. The liver used should be that of the bird, and for goose and turkey increase the given quantities by half.

Chicken or game bird liver
½ lb chopped onions
2 oz butter
4 oz fresh white breadcrumbs
1 teaspoon finely chopped sage
Pinch nutmeg
Sugar
Salt and pepper
2½ fl oz port (optional)
1 egg

Boil the liver for a few minutes, then mince or chop finely. Cook the onions in the butter over gentle heat until soft. Mix the liver, onions and breadcrumbs and stir in the sage; season to taste with nutmeg, sugar, salt and pepper. Stir in the port if used. Bind the stuffing with the lightly beaten egg.

Mint Stuffing F and H

Use to stuff chicken or thick lamb chops.

1 oz chopped celery
1 oz chopped onion
1 oz butter
½ oz finely chopped mint leaves
Salt and pepper
4 oz fresh white breadcrumbs

Cook the celery and onion in half the butter for 2 minutes over gentle heat until soft. Add the mint and salt and pepper. Continue cooking until the liquid has evaporated, then mix with breadcrumbs and the remaining melted butter.

Mushroom Stuffing H and F

A delicate stuffing for young chicken.

1 lb small button mushrooms
4 oz butter
1 set chicken livers
Salt and pepper

Wipe and trim the mushrooms; cook in the butter over gentle heat, with the finely chopped livers. Season to taste with salt and pepper. Remove the pan from the heat and leave to cool before stuffing the chicken.

Oatmeal Stuffing F

Chiefly used as a stuffing for boiled fowl, but may also be used for roast chicken with added milk as the binding agent.

1 set finely chopped chicken livers
2 oz finely chopped onions
2 oz butter or suet
4 oz toasted oatmeal
1 tablespoon finely chopped parsley
Pinch mixed herbs
Salt and pepper

Fry the livers and onions in butter until quite soft; rub through a sieve or blend in a liquidiser. Mix the oatmeal and parsley into the liver and onion pulp; season with mixed herbs, salt and pepper.

Onion and Chestnut Stuffing H and F

A traditional stuffing for roast goose, dating back to the Middle Ages.

1½ lb chestnuts
1½ lb finely chopped onions
6 oz butter
1 finely chopped goose liver
1 oz boiled rice
6 finely chopped sage leaves
Salt and pepper
Nutmeg and sugar

Slit, roast and peel the chestnuts; boil in water until tender, then chop finely. Cook the onions in the butter until soft; remove from the heat. Blend together the chestnuts, onions, liver, rice and sage leaves. Season to taste with salt and pepper, nutmeg and sugar.

Orange or Lemon Stuffing H and F

Duck may be stuffed with whole or halved oranges, or with an orange forcemeat which is also suitable with roast veal and lamb.

4 oz fresh white breadcrumbs
1 tablespoon mixed herbs
Grated rind and juice of 1 small orange or lemon
Salt and pepper
½ egg

Mix the breadcrumbs with the herbs and orange or lemon rind. Add salt and pepper. Bind the stuffing with the orange or lemon juice and lightly beaten egg.

Oyster Stuffing H

A traditional stuffing in Victorian days with turkey, and always accompanied with oyster sauce.

12 oysters
4 oz fresh white breadcrumbs
Grated rind of ½ lemon
1 tablespoon finely chopped parsley
1½ oz melted butter
Cayenne and salt
1 egg yolk

Remove the oysters from the shells, reserve and strain the liquid and chop the oysters. Combine the oysters with the breadcrumbs, lemon rind and parsley; stir in the melted butter and season lightly with cayenne and salt.

　　Bind the stuffing with the lightly beaten egg yolk and, if necessary, a little of the reserved oyster liquid; use the remainder for oyster sauce.

Pickled Herring Stuffing F

An inexpensive and unusual stuffing for roast turkey.

2 pickled herrings
4 oz finely chopped suet
6 oz fresh white breadcrumbs
Nutmeg and pepper
2 eggs

Remove all bones from the herrings and chop the flesh finely. Blend with the suet and breadcrumbs and season with ground nutmeg and pepper. Blend the stuffing with the lightly beaten eggs.

Pork Forcemeat H

Used to stuff boned veal.

½ lb lean pork
½ lb veal
5 fl oz brandy
½ lb pork fat
Ground mace
Salt and pepper

Marinate the pork and veal in the brandy for 1 hour. Pass the meats and pork fat through a mincer; season to taste with mace, salt and pepper, and stir in enough of the reserved marinade to give a fine paste.

Potato Stuffing F Ireland

Use as a stuffing for goose, duck and pork.

½ lb cooked potatoes
4 oz finely chopped onions
4 oz butter
Salt and pepper

Mash the potatoes and rub through a sieve. Cook the onion in the butter over gentle heat until soft. Mix the onion into the potatoes and season with salt and pepper.

Raisin Stuffing H and F

A sweet, fruity stuffing for guinea fowl.

2 oz seedless raisins
3 oz fresh white breadcrumbs
1 teaspoon grated lemon rind
1½ oz melted butter
Grated nutmeg
1 egg

Blend the raisins with the breadcrumbs and lemon rind; stir in the butter and season with nutmeg. Bind the stuffing with lightly beaten egg.

Raisin and Almond Stuffing H and F

Suitable as a stuffing for lean, boned pork.

3 oz seedless raisins
1 oz blanched chopped almonds
Grated rind and juice of 1 lemon
4 oz fresh white breadcrumbs
2 oz shredded suet
2 tablespoons brandy or whisky
1 egg

Mix the raisins, almonds, lemon rind and juice with the breadcrumbs and suet. Blend thoroughly and add brandy or whisky. Bind the stuffing with the lightly beaten egg.

Raisin and Apple Stuffing H

The following ingredients are sufficient to stuff two pheasants.

1 lb dessert apples
2 oz seedless raisins
2 oz melted butter

Peel, core and chop the apples, mix with the raisins. Pour over the butter and blend thoroughly.

Rice Stuffing F and H

A well-flavoured stuffing for boned shoulder of lamb.

3 oz long grain rice
½ lb bacon rashers
1 lamb kidney
1 clove garlic
2 oz sultanas
½ teaspoon finely chopped rosemary
½ teaspoon grated lemon rind
Salt and pepper
1-2 egg yolks

Boil the rice for 15 minutes in lightly salted water. Remove the rind from the bacon and chop the meat and kidney finely. Cut the garlic clove in half and rub inside the mixing bowl. Mix the cooked rice, bacon and kidney with the sultanas;

add rosemary and lemon rind and season to taste with salt and pepper.

Bind the stuffing with egg yolks.

Sage and Onion Stuffing F and H

One of the first recorded and still popular stuffings for roast pork; in some versions, 4 oz stewed apples and a little shallot vinegar is added.

2 oz finely chopped onions
2 oz pork dripping or suet
4 oz fresh white breadcrumbs
1 tablespoon finely chopped sage
Salt and pepper

Cook the onions in the dripping over gentle heat until soft. Remove from the heat and mix the onions with the breadcrumbs and sage. Season the stuffing with salt and pepper.

Sage, Onion and Apple Stuffing F and H

Excellent for complementing the fatty meat of roast goose.

1 lb finely chopped onions
3 oz butter
1 lb cooking apples
1 tablespoon finely chopped sage
1 tablespoon finely chopped thyme
Boiled and mashed potatoes
Salt and pepper

Cook the onions in the butter over gentle heat until soft. Peel, core and chop the apples; add to the onions, together with the sage and thyme and continue cooking until the mixture is smooth.

Remove from the heat and mix in boiled, mashed potatoes to make a stiff paste. Season with salt and pepper.

Sausage Stuffing H and F

A traditional stuffing for the body of turkey and for chicken.

6 oz finely chopped onions
1 oz lard
1 lb pork sausage meat
1 tablespoon finely chopped parsley
1 tablespoon mixed herbs
1 oz fresh white breadcrumbs (optional)
Salt and pepper

Cook the onions in the lard over low heat until

soft and incorporate thoroughly with the sausage meat. Mix in the parsley and herbs and breadcrumbs if the stuffing appears too moist. Season to taste with salt and pepper.

Skirlie or Skirl-in-the-Pan F and H Scotland

This forcemeat is served, cut in slices, as an accompaniment to roast grouse and chicken.

2 oz finely chopped suet
½ lb finely chopped onions
2 oz oatmeal (approx.)
Salt and pepper.

Melt the suet in a very hot frying pan and cook the onions until brown. Stir in enough oatmeal to absorb all the fat. Season with salt and pepper and continue cooking for about 5-7 minutes.

Sweetbread Stuffing F and H

Use to stuff chicken or turkey for boiling.

4 oz veal sweetbread
1 oz finely chopped suet
4 oz fresh white breadcrumbs
Grated rind of ½ lemon
Chicken or turkey liver
Grated nutmeg
Salt and pepper
2 tablespoons double cream
1 egg

Boil the sweetbread lightly and chop finely; mix with the suet. Blend in the breadcrumbs, lemon rind and chopped liver. Season the stuffing with nutmeg, salt and pepper and bind to a stiff consistency with the cream and lightly beaten egg.

Tomato Stuffing F and H

Use as a stuffing for liver.

½ lb tomatoes
½ red pepper
½ crushed garlic clove
1 oz breadcrumbs
½ oz melted butter
Salt and pepper

Skin and chop the tomatoes; remove the seeds from the pepper and chop the flesh finely. Mix these two ingredients with the garlic and breadcrumbs and bind the stuffing with the butter and juice from the tomato pulp. Season to taste with salt and pepper.

Veal Forcemeat H and F

A delicate forcemeat used to stuff poultry, roasts of pork and veal and for making forcemeat balls to accompany soups, stews and casseroles.

½ lb fillet of veal
4 oz uncooked ham or gammon
4 oz fresh white breadcrumbs
2 tablespoons finely chopped parsley
Salt and pepper
1 egg

Mince the veal and chop the ham finely. Combine thoroughly with the breadcrumbs and parsley. Season the forcemeat with salt and pepper and bind with the lightly beaten egg.

Walnut Stuffing I H

Use to stuff chicken or the neck end of turkey.

½ lb minced veal
½ lb minced lean pork
4 oz chopped walnuts
1 tablespoon finely chopped parsley
Pinch mixed herbs
2 tablespoons brandy
Salt and pepper

Mix the veal and pork with the walnuts, parsley and herbs. Stir in the brandy and season with salt and pepper.

Walnut Stuffing II F

Excellent as a stuffing for lamb hearts.

½ lb finely chopped onions
4 oz butter
2 oz white breadcrumbs
2 oz chopped walnuts
2 oz chopped fat bacon
Ground mace
Salt and pepper
1 egg

Cook the onions in the butter over low heat until soft. Combine with the breadcrumbs, walnuts and bacon. Season the stuffing to taste with mace, salt and pepper; bind with the lightly beaten egg.

Watercress Stuffing H and F

An unusual, delicately flavoured stuffing for roast chicken.

1 bunch watercress
6 oz finely chopped onions
2 oz finely chopped celery
3 oz butter
4 oz fresh white breadcrumbs
Salt and pepper

Chop the watercress finely, discarding the stalks. Cook the onions and celery in the butter until soft, over gentle heat. Mix the onions and celery thoroughly with the watercress and breadcrumbs, season to taste.

Yorkshire Stuffing F and H Yorkshire

An old recipe for stuffing a joint of pork; any surplus is mixed with an egg yolk, a little cream and gravy from the pork and served as a sauce.
4 oz fresh white breadcrumbs
2 oz currants
Sage
Ground mace
Salt and pepper

Soak the breadcrumbs in water and squeeze nearly dry. Mix with the currants to a smooth consistency. Season well with sage, mace, salt and pepper.

FISH FORCEMEATS AND STUFFINGS

Whole round and flat fish can be stuffed with a savoury forcemeat to keep the flesh moist during baking and braising.

Fish Forcemeat I H

Strongly flavoured with anchovies, this forcemeat is suitable for stuffing any kind of white fish.

1 lb fresh haddock
1 oz butter
2-3 oz fresh white breadcrumbs
3-4 chopped anchovy fillets
3-4 pickled, chopped oysters
Mixed spice, finely chopped parsley, salt
1 egg or 2 egg yolks

Poach the haddock for 10 minutes; remove skin and bones. Chop the haddock finely and blend with the butter, breadcrumbs, anchovy fillets and oysters, add a pinch of spice and parsley and the beaten egg or yolks. Pound the mixture to a smooth paste; season with salt.

Fish Forcemeat II H and F

Use to stuff haddock, hake, halibut, cod, bass and freshwater bream.

1 oz finely chopped onion
2 oz sliced mushrooms
1 oz butter
4 oz cooked rice
1 oz grated Cheddar cheese
1 dessertspoonful chopped chives
1 dessertspoon chopped parsley
Grated rind of ½ lemon
2 fl oz cream
Salt, pepper, nutmeg, cayenne
1 egg

Fry the onion and mushrooms in the butter until soft and mix with the rice and cheese. Blend in the chives, parsley and lemon rind and stir smooth with the cream. Season to taste with salt and pepper, ground nutmeg and cayenne. Bind with the lightly beaten egg.

Fish Forcemeat III H

A rich forcemeat for stuffing any kind of white fish; it can also be used for forcemeat balls and served as a garnish.

2 oz cooked turbot, sole, lobster, shrimps or oyster meat
2 oz butter
1 oz fresh white breadcrumbs
1 oz finely chopped shallot
2 hardboiled egg yolks
Grated rind of 1 lemon
1 tablespoon finely chopped parsley
Salt, cayenne pepper
1 egg

Pound the fish, butter, breadcrumbs, shallot, egg yolks, lemon rind and parsley until smooth and well blended. Season with salt and cayenne and bind with the lightly beaten egg.

Lobster Forcemeat H

Crab can be used instead of lobster for this stuffing for white fish.

3 oz cooked lobster or crab meat
2 oz butter
2 hardboiled egg yolks
3 oz fresh white breadcrumbs
1 dessertspoon finely chopped parsley
Salt, pepper, nutmeg
1 egg

Pound to a smooth mixture the lobster meat, butter, egg yolks, breadcrumbs and parsley. Season with salt, pepper and nutmeg and bind the stuffing with the lightly beaten egg.

Roe Stuffing F and H

A smooth stuffing for mackerel and herring.

4 oz soft cod or herring roes
Milk
½ oz butter
1 rounded tablespoon flour
1 teaspoon lemon juice
Salt, pepper, cayenne
1½-2 oz fresh white breadcrumbs (optional)

Oven. 250°F; gas mark ½; 30 minutes

Put the washed roes in a fireproof dish and cover with milk. Add seasoning, cover with a lid or foil and cook in the oven for 30 minutes.

Melt the butter in a pan, stir in the flour and ½ pint of milk from the roes; cook until the mixture thickens. Leave the sauce to cool, then add the mashed roes and lemon juice. Season with salt, pepper and cayenne and stir in breadcrumbs to thicken the mixture if necessary.

Shrimp Forcemeat F and H

Use with freshwater fish, especially pike, eel and lamprey.

3 oz shelled shrimps
2 oz butter
3 oz fresh white breadcrumbs
Salt, pepper, ground mace
1 egg yolk

Pound the shrimps, butter and breadcrumbs to a smooth mixture. Season with salt, pepper and mace and bind with the beaten egg yolk.

Stuffing for Eels F

A strongly flavoured stuffing to counterbalance the richness of eel.

2 oz chopped mushrooms
1 oz truffles
½ oz butter
1½ oz fresh white breadcrumbs
2 chopped anchovy fillets
1 tablespoon finely chopped parsley
Pepper, nutmeg
2 fl oz cream

Cook the finely chopped mushrooms and truffles in the butter for 5 minutes. Blend thoroughly with the breadcrumbs, anchovy fillets and parsley; pound smooth. Season with pepper and nutmeg and stir in the cream.

Tomato and Cheese Stuffing H and F

Use this mildly flavoured forcemeat for any type of white fish.

6 oz skinned and chopped tomatoes
3 oz grated Cheddar cheese
2 oz fresh white breadcrumbs
1 tablespoon mixed herbs
Salt and pepper
½ egg or milk

Blend to a smooth mixture the tomatoes, cheese, breadcrumbs and herbs. Season with salt and pepper and bind with the lightly beaten egg or a little milk.

DUMPLINGS

Small dumplings, used to garnish meat, fish and poultry, are generally made from fine forcemeat mixtures. The dumplings that accompany many traditional homely dishes, such as stews and casseroles, seldom contain meat, the basic ingredient being suet; they are shaped into larger balls and are sometimes boiled in a cloth and served cut in slices.

Batter Dumplings F

Light dumplings to be served with beef stews and with thick broths.

½ pt basic batter
Salt and pepper
Melted butter

Make a thick batter (½ pt milk, 2 eggs, ½ lb flour) and season with salt and pepper. Drop spoonfuls of batter into rapidly boiling water and cook for

5-10 minutes. Serve the dumplings separately, with melted butter.

Herb and Horseradish Dumplings F

Traditional with boiled beef and stews.

4 oz self-raising flour
4 oz fresh white breadcrumbs
2 oz chopped suet
2 tablespoons mixed herbs
1½ oz grated horseradish
Salt and pepper
2 eggs

Mix together the flour, breadcrumbs, suet and herbs; add the horseradish and salt and pepper to taste. Stir in the lightly beaten eggs to form a soft dough. Divide the dough into eight large or 16 small portions and shape into balls. Cook the dumplings in the stew or with the boiling beef for the last 30 minutes of cooking time.

Norfolk Dumplings F Norfolk

Also traditional in Suffolk and Essex, these dumplings accompany meat broths and beef stews. They are sometimes served as a pudding, with butter and sugar.

½ lb plain flour
Salt
¼ oz fresh yeast
½ teaspoon caster sugar
2½ fl oz hot water mixed with 2½ fl oz milk

Sift the flour with a pinch of salt; cream the yeast with the sugar and blend in the mixed water and milk. Blend the yeast mixture into the flour and knead the dough until firm, but springy. Leave to rise until doubled in size. After rising, shape the dough into 16 small balls and leave to stand for 10 minutes. Plunge the dumplings into boiling water, broth or stew and cook for the last 20 minutes of cooking time.

Oatmeal Dumplings F

Serve with boiled fowl, or with boiled or stewed beef.

½ lb oatmeal
½ lb finely chopped suet
4 oz finely chopped onions
Salt and pepper

Toast the oatmeal lightly in the oven. Mix the suet, onions and toasted oatmeal to a firm dough; season with salt and pepper. Tie the dough securely in a pudding cloth, leaving room for expansion, or shape into 16 or 24 balls. Immerse the dumplings in boiling salted water or the cooking liquid. Allow 1½ hours for one large dumpling and 20-30 minutes for small dumplings.

Parsley Dumplings F

Use as accompaniments to veal, lamb and chicken stews. Other fresh herbs — chives, sage, thyme or a herb mixture — may replace the parsley.

6 oz fresh white breadcrumbs
3 oz shredded beef suet
2 tablespoons finely chopped parsley
Grated rind of ½ lemon
Salt and pepper
1-2 eggs

Mix the breadcrumbs, suet, parsley and lemon

rind; season with salt and pepper. Fold in the lightly beaten eggs and mix to a soft consistency, Put spoonfuls of the mixture into the boiling stew for the last 15-20 minutes.

Suet Dumplings F

These are inevitably linked with boiled beef and carrots. Additional flavourings to the basic suet dumplings include mustard, mixed spice, finely chopped mint or chopped onions with lemon rind and juice. Green suet dumplings are made by adding 4 oz chopped spinach or sorrel to the basic mixture.

½ lb plain flour
½ teaspoon baking powder
Salt
4 oz shredded suet

Sift the flour with the baking powder and a pinch of salt; mix in the suet and add enough cold water to form a stiff dough. Shape into 16 dumplings and boil in the liquid for about 20 minutes.

Egg Dishes

Eggs have been used in British cookery since the earliest Middle Ages, to thicken soups and sauces, to bind forcemeats and pastry and to enrich cakes, blancmanges, custards and other sweet puddings. Boiled, poached and fried eggs occasionally formed part of a main dish, and the 17th century collops and eggs was the forerunner of today's bacon and eggs. The Victorians made eggs and egg dishes standard fare at the breakfast table: boiled eggs coddled in hot water in a china hen, poached or scrambled eggs on toast, fried eggs and bacon, and plain omelets.

Souffles first appeared in the 19th century, introduced through French cookery and do not have any parallels in traditional British cooking.

Eggs are still breakfast favourites, and many savoury egg dishes are also suitable for light lunches, high teas, snacks and picnics.

Arnold Bennett Omelet (8 portions) F and H London

Named after Arnold Bennett (1867-1931), novelist and theatre critic, and created for him at the Savoy Hotel.

2 lb smoked filleted haddock
4 oz grated Parmesan cheese
Salt and pepper
24 eggs
4 oz butter
4 fl oz double cream

Flake the cooked haddock and mix with the cheese; season with salt and pepper. Make the omelets individually: break three eggs for each portion and melt a little butter in a pan. Pour in the egg mixture and move gently about so that all the egg mixture comes in contact with the hot pan. Divide the fish and cheese mixture into eight portions; put one portion on top of the omelet and let it warm through for a few minutes until the underside of the omelet is golden brown. Pour over a little cream and place the omelet under a hot grill for 2 minutes. Slide the omelet on to a plate and serve without folding.

Baked Eggs (1 portion) H and F

Also known as shirred eggs, probably meaning gathered or poached, these may be served on their own for a first course. For a more substantial dish, each portion can be topped with grated cheese or a little cream, or accompanied with a side plate of grilled tomatoes, bacon or kidneys. Before breaking the eggs, the ramekins can be lined with spinach, fried mushrooms or diced chicken or haddock in a cream sauce.

Butter
1 egg
Salt and pepper
Oven: 350-375°F; gas mark 4-5; 5-7 minutes

Butter individual fireproof ramekin dishes and break an egg into each. Sprinkle with salt and pepper; set the ramekins in a roasting tin with water to near the rim of the dishes, or in a *bain marie*. Cook on top of the stove for 3-5 minutes. Remove the tin or *bain marie* to the oven and bake for a further 5-7 minutes. Serve each egg in its dish.

Eggs in Bacon Rings (8 portions) F and H

Small fireproof dishes, china or pottery, are ideal for individual baked egg dishes.

16 bacon rashers
8 eggs
Salt and pepper
8 slices buttered toast
Garnish: parsley

Oven: 350°F; gas mark 4; 15 minutes

Fry or grill the bacon until lightly cooked but
not crisp. Line eight dishes with the bacon. Break
an egg into each dish, season with salt and pepper
and bake in the oven. Turn out and serve on
buttered toast; garnish with parsley.

Eggs in Black Butter (8 portions) F and H

Reminiscent of poached eggs on toast, but with
an additional sharp taste.

8 rounds white bread
6 oz butter
8 eggs
2 tablespoons Worcestershire sauce
Juice of ½ lemon
Garnish: chopped parsley

Fry the bread rounds in part of the butter; remove
from the pan and keep warm. Fry the eggs in the
remaining butter, trim and place on the bread;
keep warm. Cook the butter until it is dark brown,
then stir in the Worcestershire sauce and lemon
juice. Arrange the fried bread and eggs on individual serving plates, pour over the butter and
garnish with parsley.

Eggs in Sour Cream (8 portions) H and F

This may be baked in individual ramekin dishes or
in a large shallow, fireproof dish. Serve with
fingers of toast.

¾ lb finely chopped onions
6 oz butter
8 eggs
Salt and pepper
1 pt sour cream
4 oz fresh white breadcrumbs

Oven: 350°F; gas mark 4; 8-10 minutes

Cook the onions in butter over low heat until
soft, then spoon into fireproof dishes. Break the
eggs carefully over the onions and season with
salt and pepper. Spoon the cream on top to
cover the eggs completely; sprinkle with crumbs
and bake in the oven for 10 minutes or until
golden and crisp on top.

Highland Eggs (8 portions) F and H
Scotland

A substantial supper dish of deep-fried eggs

coated with fish; traditionally served with
mushroom sauce.

2 oz butter
2 oz flour
1 pt milk
2 lb cooked, flaked Finnan haddock
1½ oz finely chopped parsley
Salt and pepper
8 hardboiled eggs
1 egg
4 oz breadcrumbs
Oil for frying

Make a white sauce from the butter, flour and
milk; stir in the flaked haddock and the parsley.
Season with salt and pepper. Spread the fish
mixture on a flat dish and leave to cool enough
to handle. Divide into eight equal portions. Place
a hardboiled egg in the centre of each portion and
mould this round the egg. Dip in the lightly
beaten egg, then coat with breadcrumbs. Fry in
deep hot fat until golden brown; drain and serve
at once.

Mumbled Eggs (8 portions) F and H

A kind of scrambled eggs, "mumbled" having
reference to a dish suitable for toothless gums!

½ lb butter
½ pt double cream
12 eggs
Salt and pepper
8 slices hot buttered toast
Garnish: fried mushrooms, bacon rolls

Bring half the butter and half the cream to the
boil over low heat. Beat the eggs lightly with
salt and pepper; pour into the cream and cook
gently, stirring all the time until the eggs have
scrambled. Stir in the remaining butter and
cream; pile on to hot buttered toast and surround
with mushrooms and bacon rolls.

Planked Eggs (8 portions) F and H

Literally, supported by a plank, these little
potato nests with baked eggs can be arranged and
cooked on a wooden board for sending straight to
the table.

1½ lb creamed potatoes
¾ lb skinned tomatoes
8 eggs

Salt and pepper
6 oz grated cheese
1 tablespoon finely chopped chives or onion
1 tablespoon finely chopped parsley
4 oz butter
Garnish: bacon rolls, parsley sprigs

Oven: 350°F; gas mark 4; 15 minutes

Pipe the creamed potatoes into eight nest shapes on a greased baking dish or plank. Cut the tomatoes in half and arrange in the bottom of the nests; break the eggs over the tomatoes, season with salt and pepper and sprinkle with the cheese mixed with the chives (or onion) and parsley. Dot with flakes of butter. Bake in the oven for 15 minutes or until golden; serve garnished with bacon rolls and parsley.

Savoury Baked Eggs (8 portions) H and F

Baked in ramekins, these savoury eggs are un-moulded upside down and served on toast.

Butter
4 oz finely chopped ham
1 teaspoon finely chopped parsley
8 eggs
Salt and pepper
8 rounds buttered toast

Oven: 325-350°F; gas mark 3-4.

Butter eight china ramekins and line with the chopped ham mixed with parsley. Break an egg into each dish and sprinkle with salt and pepper. Bake in the oven until firm; turn out on to buttered toast and serve.

Savoury Poached Eggs (8 portions) H and F

An unusual savoury of poached eggs on anchovy-flavoured toast.

8 eggs
1 pt milk
1 bay leaf
Sprig thyme, marjoram
Mace and pepper
6 anchovy fillets
1 oz butter
1 tablespoon oil
Anchovy essence
2 tablespoons sherry
1 egg yolk
8 slices fried bread

Bring the milk to the boil, with the bay leaf, thyme and marjoram sprigs, a pinch of mace and pepper. Cover with a lid and leave to infuse for 1 hour. Mash the anchovies and add butter, oil, a few drops of anchovy essence, sherry and the egg yolk; heat through, but do not boil. Dip the fried bread in the anchovy mixture; arrange on a serving dish and keep warm. Strain the milk and bring it back to boiling point; poach the eggs in the milk and arrange on the bread slices.

Savoury Scrambled Eggs (6-8 portions) F and H

Plain scrambled eggs can be transformed into light luncheon dishes or dinner savouries, served on hot buttered toast. To every basic scrambled egg mixture of 12 eggs, add any of the following:

½ lb cooked, diced ham added with remaining butter
1 lb sliced button mushrooms, fried in butter and piled on the scrambled eggs; garnish with chopped parsley
2 tablespoons finely chopped parsley and 2 tablespoons finely chopped chives, tarragon or chervil, added with remaining butter
1½ lb tomatoes, skinned, de-seeded, chopped and fried in 2 oz butter with 2 oz finely chopped onions until all moisture has evaporated; piled on top of the scrambled eggs.

Scotch Eggs (8 portions) F

A popular snack, served hot with tomato sauce or cold with salads.

8 hardboiled eggs
Flour
1 lb sausage meat
2 eggs
Breadcrumbs
Fat or oil for frying

Dust the hardboiled eggs lightly with flour; roll out the sausage meat and divide into eight equal rounds. Wrap the sausage meat tightly round each egg, sealing the edges firmly. Beat the eggs lightly and roll the wrapped eggs in them before coating with breadcrumbs. Heat the fat or oil until smoking and fry the eggs until golden brown.

Scotch Cheese Eggs (8 portions) F

This variation of sausage-wrapped Scotch eggs can
be served hot or cold.

½ lb grated Cheddar cheese
2 eggs
White and brown breadcrumbs
Salt and pepper
8 hardboiled eggs
Fat or oil for frying

Mix the cheese with one lightly beaten egg and
enough white breadcrumbs to make a pliable
dough; season with salt and pepper and leave to
rest for 30 minutes in a cool place. Roll out the
cheese mixture and divide into eight portions;
wrap round the hardboiled eggs. Beat the remaining egg and coat the wrapped eggs in this before
coating them with brown breadcrumbs. Deep-fry
in hot fat or oil until brown.

Scottish Farmhouse Eggs (8 portions) F Scotland

A light supper or high tea dish to serve on its own
or accompanied with a green salad.

1 oz butter
3 oz white breadcrumbs
3 oz grated Dunlop cheese
8 eggs

Salt and cayenne pepper
¾ pint double cream
Oven: 350°F; gas mark 4; 20-30 minutes

Butter the base of an ovenproof dish and coat
with half the breadcrumbs and half the grated
cheese. Break the eggs carefully over the cheese,
cover with the remaining breadcrumbs and
cheese and sprinkle with salt and cayenne. Spoon
the cream on top until it is almost all absorbed;
bake in the oven and serve at once. After 20
minutes, the eggs will still be slightly runny,
another 10 minutes will set them more firmly.

Stuffed Eggs (8 portions) H and F

Serve as a first course, garnished with watercress,
or as a light luncheon dish with salad.

8 hardboiled eggs
2½ fl oz thick white sauce
3 anchovy fillets or 3 oz grated cheese
Oil and vinegar
Cayenne pepper

Cut the eggs in half lengthways and remove the
yolks. Mash the yolks and blend with the cold
white sauce. Stir in the mashed and pounded
anchovy fillets or the grated cheese; blend
thoroughly to a smooth paste.

Pipe the filling into the egg whites and
sprinkle with oil, vinegar and cayenne.

Fish

Prior to the 19th century, one single factor — that of transportation — influenced the consumption of fish in the British Isles, endowed with a large coastal area and an abundance of rivers and lakes. The perishable quality of fish makes it vital that it is used as fresh as possible, but until the advent of the railways, transportation was both slow and costly. Freshwater fish — from rivers, lakes and artificial ponds maintained at manor houses and monasteries — were fairly easy to transport at a price which only the rich could afford, but sea fish presented a much greater problem. The catches had first to be brought to the ports and then by pack horses or carts to inland markets where they usually arrived in an extreme state of decomposition. Consequently only people living in coastal areas ever tasted fresh fish, the surplus being salted or dried as long-term commodities. Non-perishable fish thus formed the major part of fish consumption and being cheaper and more plentiful than fresh fish were chiefly bought by the poor.

Another factor which affected the consumption of fish adversely was the religious fast days when no meat was permitted. Even after the Reformation in the 16th century, "fish days" continued to be compulsory as it was government policy to stimulate the fishing and hence the shipbuilding industry to maintain Britain as a seafaring nation.

The introduction of the railways in the 19th century changed the pattern of fish consumption. Transportation became faster; refrigeration, the use of ice and the first steam trawlers further improved fish sales so that the commodity was no longer a luxury or a salted and dried alternative. At the same time, pollution of rivers caused a decrease in freshwater fish. During the 20th century fresh sea fish has become readily available, partly due to improved transportation and partly due to the introduction of refrigerated trawlers and ship factories.

Despite the 19th century changes which affected the type and amount of fish eaten, firm foundations for regional eating habits had been laid in previous centuries. Coastal areas with ancient traditions of fishing are better endowed with regional sea fish dishes than inland areas. Many of the coastal towns had monopolies or exclusive rights to landing and selling fish. Yarmouth, for example, had sole rights to the herring catch, and salting, drying and smoking of herrings as well as many fresh herring dishes are associated with the area. The West Country and the South-East produced a variety of fish dishes using white oily fish and shellfish, indicating perhaps the general nature of fishing in these parts. Although Scarborough and Grimsby are mentioned in medieval times as centres of white fisheries there is little evidence of regional fish dishes in these areas.

In Wales, sea fish played a relatively minor part although some herring, mackerel and kipper recipes exist. Cockles were the most important shellfish. Almost every part of Scotland had some association with the sea, and the abundance of regional and national fish dishes is therefore not surprising. Both white and oily fish were caught all round the coast. The fact that Shetland fishermen travelled to the Faroe Islands, Iceland and Greenland and established fishing grounds in these areas long before fishermen from other parts of the country is possibly one reason why fish plays such an important part in Shetland dishes. Original and frequent recipes for fish liver, the stomach and the roe characterise dishes from these islands, and the use of salt, pickled herrings and dried salt fish is also much evident.

The fish recipes on the following pages are grouped in these sections:
1. White and Oily Fish (Saltwater)
2. Freshwater Fish
3. Shellfish
4. Fish Offal
5. Fish Pies and Puddings
6. Fish Moulds and Jellies, Cakes and Creams
7. Potted Fish and Fish Pastes
8. Pickled Fish

WHITE AND OILY FISH

This section includes saltwater fish of the flat type
— brill, flounder, halibut, plaice and sole — and
round fish like cod and haddock. These are also
classified as white fish, the flesh having a lower oil
content than round members of the herring family,
mackerel and mullet. The recipes cover fresh,
salted, dried and smoked fish.

Anchovies, Pilchards, Sprats and Whitebait

These small oily fish are all members of the
herring family; they require little preparation
before cooking.

Anchovies in Egg and Breadcrumbs (6 portions) H and F

Serve as a light first course, with brown bread and
butter.

12 anchovies
2 oz seasoned flour
1 egg
2 oz white breadcrumbs
Butter and oil for frying

Wash and dry the fish thoroughly; dip the anchovies in the seasoned flour, coat them first in
beaten egg, then in breadcrumbs. Fry in shallow
fat until crisp and golden brown. Serve at once.

Pilchard Hot-Pot (6-8 portions) F
Cornwall

Pilchards are chiefly caught off the Cornish coast,
and most catches go to the canning industry. Local
dishes with fresh pilchards include grilled
("scrowled") and pickled pilchards; the following
is suitable as a main course.

3 lb pilchards
4 oz butter
2 oz flour
1 teaspoon tomato purée
2 pt milk
Salt and pepper
1 lb par-boiled sliced potatoes
2 oz grated Cheddar cheese

Oven: 350°F; gas mark 4; 15 minutes

Clean and scale the fish, split open and remove the
bones. Lay the fish in a greased fireproof dish.

Melt 2 oz of the butter, stir in the flour and
tomato purée, then add the milk, salt and pepper.
Stir until the sauce boils and thickens. Pour the
sauce over the fish and arrange the sliced
potatoes on top; dot with the remaining butter
and sprinkle with cheese. Bake in the oven for 15
minutes. Place under a hot grill to brown just
before serving.

Sprats in Batter (6-8 portions) H and F

Aldeborough sprats were fried or potted; in this
recipe they are deep-fried and served with thin
slices of brown bread and butter.

2 lb sprats
1 portion basic egg white batter
Fat or oil for frying
Garnish: parsley sprigs, lemon quarters

Wash and dry the sprats; dip in the prepared
batter. Fry in deep fat or oil until brown and
crisp. Garnish with fried parsley sprigs and lemon
quarters before serving.

Sprats, Skewered (6-8 portions) H and F

Small fresh sardines may be grilled and served as
an appetiser in the same way as sprats, with
brown buttered bread.

2-3 lb sprats
2 oz seasoned flour
3 oz butter
Garnish: lemon slices

Wash and dry the sprats; thread on to skewers,
pushed through the eyes, and dredge with seasoned flour. Rub the grill pan with butter and
arrange the skewered sprats on the pan. Grill
under high heat until brown, turn and cook on
the other side. Serve hot, garnished with lemon.

Sprats with Anchovies (6-8 portions) H and F

Serve as a first course or as a light supper or
lunch dish with hot crusty bread.

2 lb sprats
2 oz tinned anchovy fillets
2 oz white breadcrumbs
Salt and pepper
2 oz butter
Garnish: lemon slices

Oven: 350°F; gas mark 4; 15-20 minutes

Cut off the heads of the sprats, gut and remove backbones; wash and dry well. Roll up the sprats round a piece of anchovy. Place the rolls in a buttered fireproof dish, sprinkle with breadcrumbs and seasoning and dot with butter. Bake in the oven for 15-20 minutes. Garnish with lemon slices and serve.

Whitebait, Devilled (6-8 portions) H and F Essex

Whitebait are always cooked whole and care is needed when washing and drying them to prevent damage to the tiny fish.

2 lb whitebait
2 oz seasoned flour
Fat or oil for frying
1 teaspoon cayenne pepper

Wash and carefully dry the whitebait; coat with seasoned flour. Deep-fry in hot fat or oil until crisp and sprinkle with cayenne before serving.

Whitebait in Batter (6-8 portions) H and F Essex

Fresh whitebait, caught in quantities off Southend, are at their tastiest from late winter to early summer.

2 lb whitebait
1 oz flour
½ pt plain coating batter mixture
Fat or oil for frying
Garnish: lemon wedges, parsley sprigs

Wash the whitebait carefully and pat dry with a cloth; dust with flour. Coat the fish in the batter and fry in hot deep fat until golden brown. Serve garnished with lemon wedges and parsley sprigs.

Brill

Flat saltwater fish with light, delicately flavoured flesh and yellow-grey skin with tiny scales. Dabs and lemon soles may be cooked like brill.

Brill, Baked (6-8 portions) F

Similar to, but smaller and less expensive than turbot, brill is particularly good for baking.

2 lb brill
1 oz chopped shallot
4 oz finely chopped mushrooms
5 fl oz fish stock
5 fl oz Madeira wine
Salt and pepper
½ lb white breadcrumbs
1 teaspoon chopped herbs
2 oz melted butter
Garnish: chopped parsley and sliced cucumber
Oven: 350°F; gas mark 4; 30 minutes

Clean the fish and score it across the white side. Spread the shallot and mushrooms over the base of a buttered baking dish and pour over the stock and wine. Lay the fish on top (white side up); season with salt and pepper and sprinkle with the breadcrumbs mixed with herbs. Baste with the butter and bake in the oven for 30 minutes or until the breadcrumbs have absorbed most of the moisture. Serve the brill garnished with cucumber slices and chopped parsley.

Brill with Nut-Brown Butter (8 portions) H and F

This dish may also be made with turbot or halibut steaks.

8 brill steaks (6 oz each)
2 oz seasoned flour
2 tablespoons oil
3 oz butter
2 tablespoons white wine vinegar
Garnish: chopped pickled gherkins, chopped capers, finely chopped parsley

Wipe the fish steaks, coat in seasoned flour and fry in half the oil and butter. Arrange the fish on a serving dish and keep warm. Add the remaining butter and oil to the pan and cook to a nut-brown colour. Stir in the garnish and vinegar and pour over the fish.

Cod

For centuries, this fish was one of the most popular in Britain. Salt cod was served with mashed parsnips in medieval days, and a 19th century speciality consisted of dressed cod's head and shoulders. The poached head was covered with breadcrumbs, lemon peel and parsley and grilled before being splendidly and lavishly garnished with chopped lobster meat, fried oysters and flounders. On a more moderate scale, Glasgow Cod simply consisted of cod baked in milk and served with oatmeal dumplings and mashed potatoes.

Cod Casserole (6-8 portions) F

Although available whole, cod is more often purchased filleted or cut into steaks.

3 lb cod steaks
½ lb chopped onions
¾ lb chopped carrots
3 oz sliced celery
3 oz butter
Salt and pepper
2 tablespoons lemon juice
1 tablespoon chopped parsley

Oven: 350°F; gas mark 4; 30 minutes

Put the onions, carrots and celery in a pan, cover with lightly salted boiling water and simmer, covered, over gentle heat for 20 minutes. Fry the cod in the butter, over low heat, until light brown on both sides. Lift the cod into a shallow casserole dish, add the pan juices, salt and pepper, lemon juice and parsley. Spoon over the drained vegetables and ½ pt of the vegetable stock. Cover and bake in the oven for 30 minutes. The casserole may be thickened with cornflour if necessary.

Cod in Cream Sauce (8 portions) F and H

Small new potatoes and fresh summer vegetables would be ideal accompaniments to this delicately-flavoured dish.

8 cod steaks or fillets (6 oz each)
4 oz butter
1 pt fish stock
1½ oz flour
5 fl oz cream
1 dessertspoon lemon juice
Salt and pepper
Garnish: watercress

Wash and dry the fish carefully; melt 2 oz of the butter and fry the cod quickly on both sides without browning. Add the stock, cover and simmer gently for about 12 minutes. Lift out the cod and arrange on a hot dish. Melt 1 oz of the remaining butter and stir in the flour; gradually add the stock and bring the sauce to the boil stirring continuously. Simmer for 4-5 minutes.

Add the cream, lemon juice, remaining butter and salt and pepper to taste; strain the sauce over the fish. Garnish with watercress and serve.

Cod with Bacon and Paprika (8 portions) F

Bacon and mushrooms add substance and rich flavour to this supper dish, subtly flavoured with paprika.

8 cod steaks (6 oz each)
¾ lb streaky bacon
Paprika
Salt and pepper
2 oz butter
1 lb button mushrooms
5 fl oz creamy milk
5 fl oz double cream
2 egg yolks

Oven: 350°F; gas mark 4; 35-40 minutes

Cut the bacon into strips and place half in the base of an ovenproof dish. Rub the cod steaks with paprika until bright red; arrange on top of the bacon. Sprinkle with salt and pepper and cover with the remaining bacon; dot with butter. Bake in the oven for 35-40 minutes.

Cook the mushrooms in the milk. Lift the fish on to a serving dish and keep warm. Add the mushrooms to the liquid in the casserole, blend in the egg yolks lightly beaten with the cream; heat the sauce until it thickens, but do not let it boil. Pour the sauce over the cod steaks and serve.

Golden Cod (8 portions) F and H

New flavours can be given to plain grilled cod steaks with a cheese topping, or for devilled cod steaks, a topping of 4 oz butter mixed with chutney, curry powder, dry mustard and anchovy essence to taste.

8 cod steaks (6 oz each)
3-4 oz butter
4 oz grated cheese
2½ fl oz milk
Salt and pepper
Garnish: parsley sprigs and tomato slices

Place the fish in a greased fireproof dish, brush with a little melted butter and grill for 2-3 minutes on one side. Cream 2 oz of butter with the cheese; gradually add enough milk to make a smooth paste and season to taste with salt and pepper. Turn the fish over, spread the cheese mixture over the uncooked side and return to the grill. Reduce the heat and cook gently for a further 10-12 minutes or until the coating is brown and the fish is cooked through. Serve garnished with parsley and tomato slices.

Hashed Cod (6-8 portions) F

Left-over cooked cod is the basis for this dish, attractively served in a border of mashed potatoes.

2 lb cooked cod
1½ oz butter
1½ oz flour
1 pt milk
1 tablespoon lemon juice
5 oz shelled shrimps
Salt and pepper
Mashed potatoes
Garnish: chopped parsley

Remove any skin and bone from the cooked cod; flake the flesh. Melt the butter, stir in the flour and cook for a few minutes without colouring; gradually stir in the milk and cook the sauce until thick. Bring to boiling point and add the lemon juice. Fold in the flaked fish and the shrimps; heat through and season to taste with salt and pepper.

Pipe a deep border of hot mashed potatoes around the edge of a serving dish; spoon the fish mixture into the centre and sprinkle with chopped parsley.

North Staffordshire Swallows (6 portions) F Staffordshire

These small fritters can be made with any kind of firm white fish and served as a breakfast or high-tea dish.

6 oz white fish
¾ lb potatoes
Salt and pepper
1 portion plain coating batter
Fat for frying

Slice the uncooked fish thinly and cut the peeled potatoes into slices, about 1/8 in thick. Place a slice of fish on a slice of potato; season with salt and pepper and cover with another slice of potato.

Dip the fish sandwiches in batter and fry in hot deep fat until golden brown, after 5-7 minutes.

Somerset Casserole (6-8 portions) F Somerset

A substantial lunch or supper dish, flavoured with cider from locally grown apples.

2 lb filleted cod or haddock
2½ oz butter
Salt and pepper
4 oz sliced mushrooms
4 oz skinned, sliced tomatoes
½ pt cider
1½ oz flour
1 lb creamed potatoes
Grated cheese
Garnish: tomato slices, parsley sprigs

Oven: 375°F; gas mark 5; 25 minutes

Cut the fish into small cubes and place in a shallow, buttered fireproof dish; sprinkle with salt and pepper. Add the mushrooms, tomatoes and cider and dot with butter. Cover the dish and bake for 25 minutes in the oven. Carefully strain off the cooking liquid; melt 1½ oz of butter, stir in the flour and gradually add the liquid. Bring this sauce to the boil and cook for a few minutes.

Pour the sauce over the fish; pipe a border of creamed potatoes along the inner edge of the dish. Sprinkle with grated cheese and garnish with slices of tomato. Brown in a hot oven (450°F; gas mark 8) until the cheese is bubbling; garnish with parsley and serve.

Conger Eels

The flavour of the large saltwater eel is quite different from that of the silver eel caught in fresh waters. The flesh is tough and close-textured and excellent for stews and soups. Conger eel recipes have nearly all originated in Cornwall.

Conger Eel in Cider (6-8 portions) F Cornwall

This fish stew finds its counterpart among the fishermen of Normandy and it is probable that the recipe was imported from Cornwall together with the now extinct export of boned dried conger eel.

3 lb skinned eel
½ lb chopped onions

2 oz butter
2 oz flour
2 pt cider
Salt and pepper

Oven: 350°F; gas mark 4; 1 hour

Cut the eel into 2-3 in pieces, wash and dry well.
Fry the onions in the butter until golden. Add
the eel pieces and brown lightly. Stir in the flour
and cook until brown. Gradually stir in the cider,
season with salt and pepper and cover the pan with
a lid or foil. Bake in the oven for 1 hour. Serve the
fish in the sauce thickening it further with flour if
necessary.

Conger Eel, Stuffed (6-8 portions) F
Cornwall

The thick middle cut is best for this dish,
the tail end containing a vast quantity of bones.
Halved apples are sometimes used as plugs at
either end to keep the stuffing in place.

2-3 lb skinned conger eel
½ lb veal forcemeat
4 oz butter or fat
Flour

Oven: 350°F; gas mark 4; 1 hour

Wash and dry the fish thoroughly inside and out;
stuff with forcemeat and tie the fish securely with
tape. Melt the fat or butter in a baking dish, put
in the fish and baste well. Bake in the oven for 1
hour, basting occasionally with the pan juices and
dredging with flour. Serve the eel with the gravy or
with a tomato or brown caper sauce.

Sennen Cove Conger Eel (6-8 portions)
F Cornwall

A substantial stew for autumn days; it was formerly made from salted conger eel and soaked in milk
and water before being cooked.

2 lb conger eel
2 lb sliced potatoes
Salt and pepper
1 tablespoon chopped parsley
1 pt milk
1-1½ pt acidulated stock or water
Garnish: chopped parsley

Skin and bone the eel, wash and dry thoroughly
and cut into finger sized strips. Put the eel pieces
in a pan, cover with potato slices and sprinkle with

salt, pepper and the parsley; pour over the milk
and enough acidulated stock to come above the
contents of the pan. Simmer the stew, covered,
until the eel is tender, after about 20 minutes.
Serve garnished with chopped parsley.

Flounder, Hake, John Dory and Whiting

Flounder and John Dory are flat white fish, the
flesh of John Dory especially being extremely
delicate. Hake and whiting are both round fish
with flaky flesh, and hake is popular because of
its few bones.

Flounder with Sorrel (6-8 portions)
F and H

Flounder should be used as soon as possible as
the flesh deteriorates quickly. Sole and dab fillets
are also suitable for this dish.

16 small flounder fillets
½ lb sliced onions
2½ fl oz dry white wine
2½ fl oz fish stock
1 lb sorrel or spinach
2 oz melted butter
Salt and pepper

Oven: 425°F; gas mark 7; 30 minutes

Arrange the fish fillets in a fireproof dish and
cover with onions. Sprinkle with salt, pour over
the wine and stock and cover with buttered
greaseproof paper. Bake in the oven for 30
minutes. Meanwhile, boil the sorrel or spinach;
drain and chop finely. Heat the drained sorrel
or spinach through, stir in the butter and season
to taste with salt and pepper. Spread the sorrel
mixture over the fish and serve at once.

Hake with Onions (8 portions) F

The flaky, white flesh of hake is very tender and
easily digestible. It may be cooked like cod.

8 hake steaks (6 oz each)
1 lb sliced onions
4 oz butter
Salt and pepper
5 fl oz fish stock

Oven 350°F; gas mark 4; 30 minutes

Fry the onions in 2 oz of the butter until light
brown. Place the fish on top of the onions; season

with salt and pepper. Dot the remaining butter
over the steaks, pour over the stock and cover the
pan with a lid. Bake in the oven for 30 minutes.
Serve with mashed potatoes.

John Dory, Poached (6-8 portions) H

The flesh of John Dory, an oddly-shaped, oval
flat fish, compares favourably with that of turbot
and sole; it is becoming increasingly rare and
consequently expensive. The following recipe is
for chilled John Dory, but it may also be cooked
and served as sole and turbot.

5-6 lb John Dory
White wine
Lemon juice
Olive oil
Salt and pepper

Clean the fish and remove heads and fins. Place in
a fish kettle and cover with equal parts wine and
water; simmer gently until tender. Leave the fish
to cool, then remove skin and bones. Arrange
whole or in fillets on a serving dish and chill.
Serve with a dressing made from two parts strained
lemon juice to one part oil; season with salt and
freshly milled pepper.

Whiting in the Scots Way (8 portions)
F and H

At one time, it was fashionable to serve whole
whiting, also known as marling or merling, curled
up and with the tail stuck through the eye. Today,
whiting is usually sold as fillets.

8 whiting fillets (6 oz each)
1½ oz seasoned flour
3 oz butter
½ pt fish stock
1 rounded tablespoon finely chopped parsley
1 rounded tablespoon chopped chives
Salt and pepper
2 tablespoons double cream

Coat the whiting fillets in seasoned flour. Melt the
butter and fry the fillets quickly, on both sides,
without taking colour. Lift out the fillets; arrange
on a serving dish and keep warm. Mix the stock
with parsley and chives and add to the pan; bring
to the boil then lower the heat and simmer gently
for 5 minutes. Bring to the boil and cook rapidly
until reduced by half; season with salt and pepper,
remove from the heat and stir in the cream. Pour

the sauce over the fillets and serve at once.

Gurnard

Also known as gurnet, the red gurnard can be
recognised by its large head and clumsy cone-
shaped body covered in bright red scales. It has
firm, white flesh and is inexpensive although not
often seen. One medium-sized fish will provide
2-3 portions.

Gurnard, Stuffed (6-8 portions) F
Cornwall

The heads are left on gurnards while cooking,
and traditionally the tails were curled up and
fastened through the eyes; tucking the tails
into the mouths look more appetising. Parsley
or anchovy sauce is usually served with baked
gurnards.

2-3 lb gurnards
6 oz veal forcemeat
3-4 oz melted butter
6 rashers of bacon
Oven: 350°F; gas mark 4; 35-40 minutes

Clean and wash the fish thoroughly; cut off the
fins and remove the gills and eyes from each fish.
Stuff the fish with forcemeat and sew up the
openings or secure with fine skewers. Curve the
tails round and fasten in the mouths; arrange the
gurnards in a buttered fireproof dish and pour
the remaining melted butter over. Lay the bacon
rashers over the fish; cover with a lid or foil and
bake in the oven for about 40 minutes.

Haddock

This round white fish is related to the cod, but
smaller; it is sold whole, filleted and in steaks.
Many haddock dishes feature in Scottish cookery,
such as Rizzard Haddie, made with fresh whole
haddock, dried in the open for 24 hours, then
skinned, dusted with flour and grilled. On the
Isle of Lewis, Crappit Heids — haddock heads
stuffed with haddock liver and oatmeal — is
considered a delicacy. It was in Scotland that the
smoking of haddock reached perfection and
worldwide renown with the Eyemouths, Moray
Firths, Arbroath Smokies and Finnans.

Finnan Haddock in Milk (6-8 portions) F and H

Finnan haddock takes its name from the little fishing village of Findon in Kincardineshire where the fisherwomen began the now famous cure by hanging salted and dried haddock (known as speldings) in their chimneys to smoke over the peat fires.

2 lb Finnan haddock
1 oz butter
2 teaspoons cornflour
½ pt milk

Skin the haddock and cut into pieces. Put in a pan with the butter, cover with a lid and steam for 5 minutes. Mix the cornflour with a little milk, stir in the remaining milk. Pour over the fish, bring to the boil and cook for 1 minute until thickened. Lift the fish on to a serving dish, pour over the sauce and serve. A poached egg may be served with each portion.

Haddock, Poached (8 portions) F

The full flavour of fresh fish is often best appreciated when cooked quite simply as in this recipe. Mashed potatoes and clarified butter or hardboiled egg sauce are traditional accompaniments.

8 haddock fillets (4 oz each)
Fish stock
Salt and pepper
Garnish: parsley sprigs

Wipe the fillets with a damp cloth and place in a shallow pan; pour over enough boiling fish stock to barely cover the fillets. Season with salt and pepper. Simmer gently for about 20 minutes, then drain thoroughly and place on a serving dish; garnish with parsley sprigs.

Haddock Savoy (6-8 portions) H and F London

This was created at the Savoy Hotel, London, late in the 19th century. In some versions, the haddock mixture is cooked in a pastry case and can then be served hot or cold.

2 lb cooked smoked haddock
3 oz Parmesan cheese
Salt and cayenne pepper
4 eggs

1 pt milk
½ pt cream

Oven: 350°F; gas mark 4; 40 minutes

Flake the cooked haddock and mix with cheese, salt and cayenne. Beat the eggs well; bring the milk to the boil and pour slowly over the eggs, stirring all the time. Stir in the cream and the fish and cheese mixture. Spoon into a buttered dish, place this in a pan of warm water and bake in the oven.

Haddock Strachur (6-8 portions) H and F Scotland

A local dish from Strachur in Argyllshire, rich and satisfying; fingers of buttered toast can be served with it.

2 lb Finnan haddock
1 pt double cream
Black pepper

Poach the haddock in gently boiling water for 4 minutes. Drain and flake the fish, taking care to remove all bones. Arrange in a buttered fireproof dish; pour the cream over the fish until it is completely covered. Season with freshly milled pepper; put under a hot grill until brown. Serve at once.

Haddock with Cheese (8 portions) H and F

A substantial lunch or supper dish, ideally accompanied with tiny new potatoes and a cheese sauce.

8 haddock fillets (6 oz each)
Lemon juice
Seasoned flour
2 eggs
Breadcrumbs
Grated cheese
3 oz melted butter
Garnish: parsley sprigs, lemon slices
Stuffing: ½ lb grated cheese
           4 oz fresh white breadcrumbs
           1 egg
           Salt and pepper

Oven: 350°F; gas mark 4; 20-25 minutes

Wipe the fillets, sprinkle with lemon juice and dust with seasoned flour. For the stuffing, mix the grated cheese with the breadcrumbs and parsley; bind with the lightly beaten egg and season with salt and pepper. Divide into eight equal portions.

Spread the stuffing over the fillets and roll up, securing with wooden cocktail sticks. Brush the rolls with the beaten eggs and coat with bread-crumbs mixed with grated cheese. Lay the stuffed rolls in a buttered ovenproof dish and pour the melted butter over. Bake in the oven and serve garnished with parsley and lemon.

Haddock with Tomatoes (8 portions) F

Fluffy boiled rice attractively surrounds a mix-ture of smoked haddock, tomatoes and onions. A piped border of creamed potatoes is another alternative.

3 lb smoked haddock
2 oz butter
2 oz chopped onions
4-6 small skinned tomatoes
1 dessertspoon finely chopped parsley
Salt and pepper
¾ lb rice

Poach the haddock in a little water for 10 minutes. Drain, remove the skin and bones and separate the fish into large flakes. Melt the butter and lightly fry the onions, add the sliced tomatoes and cook until soft. Blend in the fish and parsley, season to taste and cook gently over low heat, until the fish is heated through; stir frequently. Meanwhile, boil the rice and arrange in a circle on a hot dish; spoon the haddock mixture into the centre.

Ham and Haddie (6-8 portions) F and H Morayshire

A typical Scottish dish, equally popular for breakfast and high tea.

2 large smoked haddock
5 fl oz milk
1 oz butter
2 large slices ham
Black pepper
5 fl oz cream

Place the haddock in a frying pan and just cover with milk; bring to the boil and simmer for 2 minutes on each side. Lift out the fish, remove skin and bones; cut into six or eight pieces. Heat the butter in a pan and lightly fry the ham, cut into portions to fit the haddock, turning once.

Arrange the haddock on top of the ham and gently pour over the strained milk. Season with

freshly milled pepper, cover with a lid and simmer gently for about 3 minutes. Pour the cream over the haddock and brown under a hot grill.

Humberside Haddock (6-8 portions) F Yorkshire

Mushrooms and tomatoes give extra flavourings to smoked haddock; usually served with mashed potatoes.

2 lb smoked haddock fillets
¾ pt milk
Salt and pepper
¾ lb tomatoes
½ lb sliced button mushrooms
1 oz butter

Oven: 350°F; gas mark 4; 10-15 minutes

Wipe the fillets, arrange in a buttered fireproof dish, cover with milk and add seasoning. Skin the tomatoes, remove the seeds and dice the pulp. Add the mushrooms and tomatoes to the haddock, dot with butter and cover with buttered grease-proof paper. Bake in the oven and serve hot.

Kedgeree (6-8 portions) F and H

This breakfast dish is not of true British origin, but was brought from India where it was a favour-ite among the British colonials.

2 lb smoked haddock
Parsley sprig
Bay leaf
2 lemons
Peppercorns
2 oz butter
4 oz chopped onions
1 lb long grain rice
2 pt fish stock
4 hardboiled eggs
Salt and pepper
Curry powder or grated nutmeg
Garnish: chopped parsley

Put the haddock with the parsley, bay leaf, 1 lemon cut into slices and a few peppercorns into a pan; cover with water, bring to the boil and sim-mer until tender. Drain the haddock, remove skin and bones and flake the flesh. Melt the butter in a deep pan and fry the onions gently for 5 minutes. Add the rice and fish stock; bring to the boil and simmer for 20 minutes.

Stir the flaked fish into the rice with 3 sliced
eggs, salt, pepper, curry powder or nutmeg to
taste; add the juice of 1 lemon. Pile into a hot
dish and garnish with parsley and the remaining
hardboiled chopped egg.

Planked Haddock (6-8 portions) H and F

For this dish, the fish was originally placed on a
pre-heated and greased, thick piece of wood and
surrounded with mashed potatoes. During cooking, the wood would impart a burnt flavour
to the food.

2 lb haddock fillets
Salt and pepper
2 oz melted butter
Mashed potatoes
Garnish: chopped parsley

Oven: 375°F; gas mark 5; 30 minutes

Wipe the fillets with a damp cloth, sprinkle with
salt and pepper and brush with melted butter.
Arrange the fillets in a shallow, buttered fireproof
dish; pipe a border of mashed potatoes around the
edges and in a decorative pattern between and
across the fillets. Bake in the oven for 30 minutes
or until the potatoes are light brown. Serve
garnished with parsley.

Scottish Haddock (8 portions) F and H

Also known as 'haddock in brown sauce', this dish
may take on festive aspects by adding raw or tinned
oysters or cooked mussels to the sauce.

8 haddock fillets (4 oz each)
Haddock trimmings
2 pt fish stock
½ lb chopped onions
Bunch of sweet herbs
Peel of 1 lemon
5 oz butter
2 oz flour
Mixed spice
Mushroom ketchup
Salt and pepper
Garnish: chopped parsley

Put the trimmings — heads, tails and bones — from
the haddocks into a pan with the stock, the onions,
sweet herbs and lemon peel; simmer for 15
minutes. Melt 2 oz of butter and add the flour,
stir until this roux has browned, then season with

mixed spice and mushroom ketchup. Strain the
fish stock and gradually add to the roux; bring
the sauce to the boil and reduce by half, stirring
frequently.

Fry the haddock fillets in 2 oz of butter for a
few minutes, until brown on both sides. Arrange
on a serving dish. Beat the remaining butter into
the sauce, correct seasoning with salt and pepper
and add oysters or mussels if used. Pour the sauce
over the fish and garnish with parsley.

Skued Haddock (8 portions) F Shetland

"Skued" may refer to fillets originally kept in the
folded shape by wooden skewers.

8 haddock fillets (6 oz each)
1 pt fish stock
4 oz chopped onions
5 oz butter
Salt and pepper
4 oz flour
Milk

Fold the haddock fillets in half and lay in a shallow
pan; pour over the stock and add the onions, 4
oz of butter and salt and pepper. Simmer gently
for 8 minutes; lift out the fillets and place on a
warm serving dish. Blend the flour with a little
milk and add to the hot liquid; bring to the boil
and simmer for a further 5 minutes. Remove the
pan from the heat, beat in the remaining butter;
pour the sauce over the fish and serve.

Halibut

This is one of the largest flat fish, sometimes
weighing as much as 300 lb. The firm white flesh
tends to be dry and moisture of some kind should
therefore be added during cooking. Usually sold
in steaks and cutlets.

Halibut Bristol (6-8 portions) H Gloucestershire

Attractively garnished with mussels, this main
course dish may also be cooked with turbot.

2 lb halibut, middle cut
Salt and pepper
½ pt fish stock
1 oz butter
1 oz flour
5 fl oz milk

2 doz freshly cooked mussels
3 oz grated cheese

Oven: 350°F; gas mark 4; 20 minutes;
450°F; gas mark 8; 10 minutes

Place the halibut in a greased fireproof dish, season with salt and pepper and add the fish stock. Cover with buttered greaseproof paper or foil and bake in the oven for 20 minutes. Remove from the oven, strain off the liquid, and remove the centre bone and skin from the halibut.

Melt the butter, add the flour and gradually stir in the milk and cooking liquid. Season the sauce and bring to the boil; add 1 oz of cheese. Arrange the mussels round the halibut, spoon over the sauce and sprinkle with the remaining cheese. Brown in oven (450°F; gas mark 8) for 10 minutes or under a hot grill before serving.

Farmhouse Halibut (8 portions) H and F

Cream and butter add moisture to this dish which may be cooked with one piece of halibut or with individual steaks.

3 lb halibut, middle cut
2 oz melted butter
Salt and pepper
¾ pt cream
1½ oz flour
Garnish: chopped parsley

Oven: 325°F; gas mark 3; 45-60 minutes

Grease an ovenproof dish with the melted butter; remove the skin from the halibut and place in the dish. Season with salt and pepper. Pour the cream over the halibut and bake, covered, for 25 minutes.

Lift the fish on to a serving dish and keep warm. Strain the cooking liquid; blend the flour with a little of the liquid and stir back; bring this sauce to the boil, season and pour over the fish. Garnish with parsley and serve.

Halibut in Cider (8 portions) F

English tomatoes and cider are the main flavourings in this summer casserole, served with buttered new potatoes.

8 halibut cutlets (6 oz each)
Salt and pepper
2 lemons
½ lb chopped onions

2 tablespoons oil
1 clove garlic
1 pt dry cider
1 lb skinned, sliced tomatoes
1 heaped tablespoon finely chopped parsley

Oven: 350°F; gas mark 4; 20-30 minutes

Place the halibut cutlets in a greased fireproof dish; sprinkle with salt, pepper and the juice of 1 lemon. Thinly slice the remaining lemon and arrange over the fish. Cook the onions gently in the oil for 5 minutes; add the crushed garlic and cook for a further few minutes. Remove from the heat, stir in the cider and pour over the fish.

Arrange the tomatoes on top and sprinkle with chopped parsley. Cover with buttered, greaseproof paper or foil and bake in the oven for 20-30 minutes.

Herrings, Bloaters and Kippers

The small, oily, saltwater herring (average weight 6 oz) is the most versatile of all fish. Today, it is often ignored in spite of its delicately flavoured, wholesome flesh and inexpensive price, but in bygone centuries thousands of families survived years of famine and poverty on a diet of herrings and potatoes. Fresh herrings can be grilled and fried, baked and casseroled, cooked with a variety of stuffings and served with many different sauces, quite apart from the numerous pickling methods to which the herring lends itself. Until the 19th century, salted herrings were commonplace, and salt curing has survived, not so much as a means of preserving, but as a means of imparting additional flavours. Salted herrings, including red herrings which are dried-smoked after salting, still feature strongly in Scottish and Irish cooking.

While Scotland developed and improved the smoking cures for haddock, the fishing ports on the east coast of England — the centres of the herring industry — concentrated on similar but milder cures for herrings. Yarmouth produced the first mild smoke cure in 1835 and named the product bloater, possibly because the herrings, being only half-dried prior to smoking over an oak fire, remained plump and puffed-out. A few years later, another smoke cure for herring, which was to become the world-famous kipper, was invented at Seahouses on the Northumberland coast. Unlike the bloater, which is whole ungutted herring, the kipper is split open down the back. It is then immersed for a short period in a highly concentrated salt brine which settles as a sticky solution of protein on the herring flesh and dries in the subsequent smoking process to a glossy sheen.

Fresh Herrings

Cider Herrings (6-8 portions) F

Cider lightly flavoured with pickling spice imparts a subtle taste to fresh herrings.

8 herrings
Salt and pepper
1 pt cider
6 black peppercorns
6 white peppercorns
1 piece stem ginger
4 cloves
4 bay leaves
¾ lb sliced onions

Oven: 300°F; gas mark 2; 1½ hours

Clean and bone the herrings, leave them whole or divide each into two fillets; season well with salt and pepper. Roll-up the fillets, skin inwards, beginning at the tail end. Place the herring rolls close together in an ovenproof dish, cover with cider and add the black and white peppercorns, ginger and cloves. Arrange the bay leaves and onion rings over the herrings. Bake in the oven for 1½ hours.

Cumberland Shipped Herring (8 portions) F Cumberland

These stuffed, baked herrings are traditionally served with mustard sauce.

8 fresh herrings
8 herring roes
½ oz breadcrumbs
2 teaspoons anchovy essence
½ oz chopped onion
½ oz melted butter
Salt and pepper
2 oz butter

Oven: 350°F; gas mark 4; 20 minutes

Clean the herrings, cut off the heads, tails and fins and remove the backbones. Poach the herring roes gently in boiling water for a few minutes. Chop the drained roes, mix with the breadcrumbs, anchovy essence, onion, melted butter and salt

and pepper. Stuff the herrings and keep them closed with small wooden skewers. Lay the herrings in a buttered fireproof dish and dot with the remaining butter. Bake in the oven for about 20 minutes.

Glasgow Magistrates (6-8 portions) F Scotland

The herrings for this well-known dish should be Loch Fyne herrings, considered the fattest and best flavoured; because of their plumpness they were jokingly referred to as "Glasgow Magistrates" or "Glasgow Baillies". At the annual dinner of the Grand Antiquity Society of Glasgow, herrings had the place of honour on the bill of fare.

8 herrings
1 portion herb stuffing
½ pt white wine vinegar
½ pt water
6 black peppercorns
2 cloves
1 bay leaf

Oven: 350°F; gas mark 4; 50 minutes

Clean the herrings, cut off heads and fins, but not the tails. Fillet each herring, spread with herb stuffing and roll up starting from the head. Arrange the rolls in an ovenproof dish, tails on top. Pour over the vinegar and water, add the peppercorns, cloves and bay leaf. Cover the dish and bake in the oven for 30 minutes, remove the covering and bake for a further 20 minutes.

Serve hot with buttered bread or oatcakes, or cold with potato salad.

Herring Bake (6-8 portions) F and H

On really fresh herrings, the backbones come away easily if first pressed lightly along their length on the skin side.

8 herrings
2 oz butter
Salt and pepper
½ teaspoon made mustard
2 teaspoons tomato purée
1 pt single cream

Oven: 350°F; gas mark 4; 20 minutes

Clean and fillet the herrings; divide the butter equally into 16 pieces and place a piece on each fillet; roll up, skin side outwards. Stand the herring rolls upright in an ovenproof dish; season with salt and pepper. Mix the mustard, tomato purée and cream to a smooth sauce; pour over the fish and bake in the oven for 20 minutes.

Herring Casserole (8 portions) F and H
Wales

Snoper Scadan is the Welsh name for this casserole of herrings with potatoes, onions and apples.

8 herrings
Made mustard
Salt and pepper
2 lb sliced potatoes
1½ lb peeled, cored and sliced cooking apples
¾ lb sliced onions
1 teaspoon dried sage
1 pt fish stock
1 oz butter

Oven: 375°F; gas mark 5; 1½ hours

Clean, bone and divide the herrings into fillets. Spread the fillets with mustard, sprinkle with salt and pepper and roll up. Put half the potatoes into a buttered pie dish, add half the apples and half the onion rings and arrange the herring rolls on top; sprinkle with sage. Cover with the remainder of the potatoes, apples and onions; sprinkle with salt and pepper. Pour over the boiling stock and dot with butter; cover and bake for 1½ hours. Remove the lid for the last 30 minutes of cooking.

Herring and Tomato Casserole (8 portions) F

A homely fish casserole, troublefree and a complete meal.

8 herrings
8 skinned, sliced tomatoes
Salt and pepper
Vinegar or lemon juice
½ lb boiled rice
1 oz dripping

Oven: 350°F; gas mark 4; 45 minutes

Clean, bone and fillet the herrings; arrange a layer of fillets in a buttered fireproof dish. Lay half the tomato slices over the fish, sprinkle with salt and pepper and a few drops of vinegar or lemon juice. Cover with the remaining fillets, the cooked rice and tomato slices, dot with dripping. Bake in the oven for 45 minutes.

Herring Crumb Bake (8 portions) H and F

Grilled tomatoes would be a suitable accompaniment to these savoury herring fillets with a crisp crumb topping. Serve as a breakfast dish.

8 large herrings
3 oz English mustard
1 tablespoon sugar
2 tablespoons vinegar
Salt and pepper
2 tablespoons oil or melted butter
2 oz breadcrumbs

Oven: 350°F; gas mark 4; 15-20 minutes

Clean and bone the herrings and divide into 16 fillets. Mix the mustard with sugar, vinegar, salt and pepper and spread over the fillets. Fold the fillets over and arrange in a greased fireproof dish. Brush with oil or melted butter and sprinkle with breadcrumbs. Bake in the oven for 15 minutes.

Herring in the Bute Fashion (8 portions) H and F Scotland

This herring salad differs from the usual type in that the salad ingredients are used as a stuffing for baked fillets. Serve chilled with a green salad.

8 herrings
¾ oz salt
3 oz granulated sugar
¾ pt cold water
Juice of 1 lemon
1½ lb boiled new potatoes
3 chopped hardboiled eggs
Crushed herbs
Salad dressing
Garnish: parsley sprigs, diced pimento, 1 sliced
    hardboiled egg

Oven: 350°F; gas mark 4; 45-60 minutes

Clean and bone the herrings, remove the heads and lay the fish on a flat dish; sprinkle with salt and sugar. Leave for 4 hours then drain and dry thoroughly. Roll up the herrings loosely, starting at the head, skin side out; place in a fireproof dish. Pour over the water and lemon juice, cover and bake in the oven.

Dice the cooked potatoes and blend with the eggs, herbs and salad dressing to moisten. Remove the herring rolls from the oven, drain and leave to cool, then chill. Pack the potato filling into the centre of the herring rolls; garnish with parsley, diced pimento and slices of hardboiled egg.

Herring with Oatmeal (8 portions) F Scotland

A favourite way in Scotland of frying herrings and small trout. The cleaned and boned fish may be left whole or cut into fillets. Serve for breakfast, tea or supper, with bannocks and butter, boiled mealy potatoes or oatcakes and vinegar.

8-16 herrings
4 oz oatmeal
Salt and pepper
2-3 oz bacon fat

Allow one or two herrings per portion, depending on size. Season the oatmeal with salt and pepper and coat the herrings. Melt the bacon fat in a frying pan and fry the herrings over gentle heat for 6 minutes on each side. If fillets are used, fry the skin side first.

Herrings and Apples (8 portions) F

Herring enthusiasts are sharply divided in their views on when the delectable fish is at its tastiest; some maintain the lean spring herring is the choicest, others that only in the fattened fish in early autumn can the true flavour be appreciated.

8 large herrings
Salt and pepper
2 oz finely chopped onions
1 lb peeled, cored and grated dessert apples
1 oz sugar
6 oz white breadcrumbs
4 oz melted butter

Oven: 350°F; gas mark 4; 15-20 minutes

Clean and bone the herrings; season with salt and pepper. Mix the onions and grated apples with the sugar and two thirds of the breadcrumbs. Divide this mixture into eight portions and stuff into the herrings. Secure the opening. Lay the stuffed herrings in a buttered ovenproof dish; sprinkle with the remaining breadcrumbs and pour over half the melted butter. Bake in the oven for 20 minutes; pour the remaining melted butter over the herrings just before serving.

Herrings and Horseradish Sauce (6-8 portions) F and H

Chilled baked herring fillets accompanied with apples and horseradish sauce make a light refreshing luncheon dish.

8 herrings
1 pt water
5 fl oz vinegar
4 oz sliced onions
½ teaspoon mixed herbs
1 bay leaf
Salt
1¼ lb peeled and grated cooking apples
2 tablespoons horseradish sauce
Garnish: finely chopped parsley

Clean, bone and fillet the herrings. Simmer the fish trimmings with the water, vinegar, onions, herbs, bay leaf and salt for 20 minutes. Strain and return the liquid to the pan. Roll the fillets from tail to head, secure with wooden cocktail sticks and stand side by side in the pan. Simmer for 10 minutes; remove the pan from the heat and leave the fillets in the liquid until cold.

To serve, mix the grated apple with the horseradish sauce and spread on a shallow serving dish. Remove the cocktail sticks and arrange the herring rolls over the apple; sprinkle with parsley.

Herrings Stuffed with Oatmeal (8 portions) F Scotland

In some versions of this popular Scottish dish, the herring fillets are layered in a dish with a stuffing made from 6 oz mashed potatoes, 2 oz breadcrumbs, 1 oz each oatmeal and grated cheese. Serve with creamed potatoes and mustard sauce.

8 herrings
6 oz oatmeal
1 oz chopped suet
1 oz grated onion
1 tablespoon chopped fresh herbs
Milk
Salt and pepper
1 egg
1-2 oz butter
Garnish: lemon slices (optional)

Oven: 350°F; gas mark 4; 15-20 minutes

Clean, bone and fillet the herrings. Mix together the oatmeal, suet, onion and herbs; bind this stuffing with milk. Sprinkle the fillets with salt and pepper; spread the stuffing over them and roll up, securing with wooden cocktail sticks.

Lay the herring rolls in a buttered fireproof dish, sprinkle with a little extra oatmeal, brush with beaten egg and dot with butter. Bake in the oven for about 20 minutes. Serve garnished with lemon slices.

Herrings with Potatoes (8 portions) F

A stuffing of herb-flavoured mashed potatoes makes herring fillets stretch further; a creamy onion sauce would be a good accompaniment.

8 herrings
6 oz mashed potatoes
Salt and pepper
Nutmeg and mixed herbs
Butter

Oven: 350°F; gas mark 4; 15 minutes

Clean, bone and fillet the herrings. Season the potatoes with salt, pepper, nutmeg and mixed herbs. Spread the stuffing over the fillets, roll up, skin side out and secure. Wrap each roll in buttered greaseproof paper, place on a grid set in a baking tin and bake in the oven for 15 minutes.

Herrings with Roes and Tomatoes (8 portions) F

Soft herring roes, often sold separately, are considered a great delicacy and much used for savouries; the roes also make ideal stuffings for herring and other fish fillets.

8 herrings
8 herring roes
6 oz fresh white breadcrumbs
3 oz grated onions
6 oz skinned and chopped tomatoes
1 oz chopped parsley
Salt and pepper
Milk
Butter
Garnish: skinned, sliced tomatoes

Oven: 350°F; gas mark 4; 20 minutes

Clean, bone and fillet the herrings. Blanch the roes for a few minutes in boiling water; drain and chop. Mix the breadcrumbs, onions, tomatoes and parsley; season with salt and pepper and if necessary bind with a little milk. Spread the stuffing

over the fillets and roll up, starting at the head and skin side out.

Arrange the herring rolls in a buttered fireproof dish; cover with tomato slices and bake in the oven for 20 minutes.

Herrings with Sausage Meat (8 portions) F and H

A substantial family supper dish, economic and easy to prepare.

8 large herrings
½ lb sausage meat
1 oz shredded suet
1 tablespoon finely chopped parsley
4 oz fresh white breadcrumbs
1 lemon
Salt and pepper
1 egg
2 oz butter

Oven: 350°F; gas mark 4; 15-20 minutes

Cut off heads, tails and fins; clean and gut the herrings, remove the backbones leaving the fish whole. Mix the sausage meat with the suet, parsley, breadcrumbs, juice and grated rind of the lemon; season with salt and pepper and bind with the lightly beaten egg. Stuff the herrings with this mixture and secure the opening with small wooden skewers. Lay the herrings in a buttered fireproof dish; pour in a little water, dot with butter and bake for 20 minutes.

Herrings with Shrimps (8 portions) F and H

In this recipe, plain herring fillets take on a touch of luxury with a filling of chopped shrimps.

8 herrings
2 oz fresh white breadcrumbs
2½ fl oz milk
4 oz shelled shrimps
Anchovy essence
Salt and cayenne pepper
1 egg
2 oz browned breadcrumbs
1 oz butter

Oven: 350°F; gas mark 4; 20-30 minutes

Clean, bone and fillet the herrings. Soak the white breadcrumbs in the milk. Chop the shrimps finely and mix with the squeezed breadcrumbs; season to taste with anchovy essence, cayenne and salt. Spread this mixture over the fillets, roll up and fasten with skewers. Brush the herring rolls with beaten egg, coat with the browned breadcrumbs.

Arrange in a buttered fireproof dish, dot with the butter and bake for about 20 minutes.

Herrings with Tomato Chutney (8 portions) F

For a light summer lunch or supper, serve these fillets with a tomato salad, sprinkled with chopped parsley and chives.

8 herrings
½ lb tomato chutney
1 oz butter
Salt and pepper
Juice of 1 lemon

Oven: 350°F; gas mark 4; 20 minutes

Clean and gut the herrings, cut off heads, tails and fins and remove the backbones, leaving the fish whole. Stuff the herrings with the chutney and secure the opening with wooden skewers. Lay in a buttered, fireproof dish, sprinkle with salt, pepper and lemon juice and cover with buttered grease-proof paper. Bake in the oven for 20 minutes, removing the paper after 15 minutes.

Herrings with Veal Forcemeat (8 portions) F

A stuffing of mild forcemeat is here used to absorb and complement the oil in large, fatty herrings.

8 large herrings
Salt and pepper
5 oz veal forcemeat
Milk
2 oz browned breadcrumbs
1½ oz dripping

Oven: 375°F; gas mark 5; 20-30 minutes

Clean, bone and fillet the herrings, sprinkle with salt and pepper. Spread the veal forcemeat over the fillets, roll up from the head and secure with skewers. Brush the rolls with milk and coat with breadcrumbs. Lay the herring rolls in a greased fireproof dish, dot with dripping and bake in the oven for about 20 minutes.

Lowestoft Herrings (8 portions) F Suffolk

Fresh sea water is said to make the flesh of herrings firm; lacking sea water, use plain tap water salted at the rate of 2 oz salt per pint of water. Traditionally served with boiled potatoes and mustard or hot horseradish sauce.

8-16 herrings
3 pt sea water

Clean and gut the herrings; bring the water to a fast boil and put in the herrings. Continue boiling very quickly for 6 minutes. Drain and serve.

Norfolk Herrings (8 portions) F Norfolk

For this dish, the herrings may be filleted or simply boned and left whole; in the latter case, apply light pressure to the fish while frying to prevent them opening wide.

8 herrings
4 oz fine semolina
Salt and pepper
Fat for frying

Clean, gut and bone the herrings; divide into fillets or leave folded. Season the semolina with salt and pepper; coat the herrings and fry in hot fat, for 6-8 minutes on each side.

Piquant Grilled Herrings (8 portions) F and H

Due to their high oil content, herrings are ideal for grilling, plain or with a spicy topping as here. Serve with lemon quarters and a tomato salad.

8 herrings
3 oz butter
2 tablespoons wine vinegar
1 tablespoon grated onion
Pinch dry mustard
Salt and pepper

Clean, bone and fillet the herrings. Soften the butter and mix to a paste with the vinegar, onion, mustard, salt and pepper. Spread over the flesh side of the fillets. Grill under low heat for 10 minutes and serve at once.

Salted and Cured Herrings

Buchan Potatoes (6-8 portions) F
Scotland

The strong brine in which herrings are salted must
be removed before the fish can be cooked. Soak
for at least 12 hours in cold water, changing the
water once.

4 salt herrings
2½ oz margarine
¾ lb chopped onions
2½ oz flour
2½ pt milk
2½ lb cooked potatoes

Clean, bone and skin the soaked herrings; cut the
flesh up finely. Melt the margarine and fry the
onions until golden brown; add the flour to make
a roux and gradually stir in the milk. Bring this
sauce to the boil. Cut the potatoes in slices and
add to the sauce with the herrings and simmer for
5 minutes to heat through.

Cream Cheese Herrings (8 portions) H and F

Suitable as a starter or snack, this dish needs
chilling before serving with thin slices of hot
buttered toast.

4 salt herrings
2 oz chopped onions
2 oz sugar
½ pt vinegar
Pepper
6 oz peeled and grated dessert apples
2 oz soft cream cheese
2 tablespoons lemon juice
5 fl oz single cream
Garnish: chopped chives or parsley

Wash, bone and fillet the herrings, leave to soak in
cold water for 12 hours. Skin the fillets and place
in a dish. Mix the onions, sugar and vinegar with a
pinch of pepper; pour over the fillets and leave to
steep for 6 hours. Spread the grated apple over the
base of a serving dish and arrange the drained
fillets on top. Alternatively, spread the apple over
the fillets and roll up.
   Mix the cream cheese with the lemon juice;
blend in the cream and pour this dressing over the
herrings. Chill in the refrigerator and garnish with
chopped chives or parsley before serving.

Dressed Red Herrings (8 portions) F

When salted herrings were exposed to prolonged
smoking the result became a dry, red fish — the
red herring — even more thirst-provoking than
salt herring.

8 red herrings
Milk or water
2 fl oz oil
4 fl oz vinegar
Garnish: 2 hardboiled egg yolks, 2-3 oz chopped
   gherkins

Cover the herrings with cold water; drain after a
few minutes. Soak the herrings for 1 hour in
enough milk or water to cover. Skin and fillet
the herrings, cut into bite-sized pieces and dress
with oil and vinegar.
   Arrange the herrings, with the dressing, in a
serving dish and garnish with sieved egg yolks and
chopped gherkins. Alternatively, mix the herring
pieces with diced boiled potatoes and dress with
oil and vinegar.

Irish Smoked Herrings (8 portions) F and H
Ireland

A highly popular dish in artistic circles; the barely
soaked herrings induce a great thirst, heightened
by flaming the fillets in Irish whiskey.

8 red herrings
4 oz butter
Irish whiskey

Cover the herrings with boiling water and cook
for a few minutes. Cut off the heads, split the
herrings in half lengthways and remove the bones
and skin. Fry the fillets in butter over low heat,
turning once. Arrange the fried fillets in a shallow,
fireproof dish. Bring to the table, pour over
the warmed whiskey and set alight. Serve as soon
as the flames have died down.

Red Herrings, Grilled (8 portions) F and H

Red herrings, lightly soaked in beer or boiling
water, may be grilled whole, or the heads and tails
can be cut off and the herrings split along the
backbone. They can be seasoned with pepper and
cayenne, or coated in eggs and breadcrumbs before
grilling, and may be served on hot buttered toast
or with mashed potatoes, mustard, egg sauce or
pats of chilled butter.

8 red herrings
Light beer or ale
2 oz butter

Soak the herrings in beer or ale for 1 hour. Drain,
brush with butter and put under a hot grill for
5-6 minutes, turning once.

Sherry Herrings (6-8 portions) H

A delicately flavoured first course, to be served
with triangles of brown bread and butter.

4 salt herrings
2 oz sliced onions
Pepper
5 fl oz dry sherry
Garnish: watercress

Clean and bone the herrings and leave to soak in
cold water for 12 hours; change the water once.
Skin the fillets and cut into thin strips. Arrange
the herring pieces in layers with the onion rings in
a serving dish; grate with pepper and pour the
sherry over. Leave to marinate overnight. Garnish
with watercress before serving.

Spicy Salt Herrings (6-8 portions) F and H

Enthusiasts of salt herrings maintain that to appreciate the flavour to the full, the fish should not
be soaked, merely wiped in a damp cloth. For the
average taste, however, soaking removes the
excess saltiness.

4 salt herrings
1 lemon
2 oz thinly sliced onions
1 bay leaf
Pepper and nutmeg
3 tablespoons dry cider
3 tablespoons oil

Clean and bone the herrings, leave to soak in
cold water for 12 hours, changing the water once.
Skin the fillets, cut into narrow strips and
arrange in a dish with slices of lemon and onion.
Sprinkle with crushed bay leaf and plenty of
pepper and nutmeg. Blend the cider and oil and
pour over the herrings. Leave to marinate for 3
hours before serving.

Tatties and Herrings (8 portions) F
Scotland

Reflecting the extreme poverty of former days,
this is still a favourite supper dish in Scotland.
It is equally popular in Ireland where it is made
with red herrings.

8 salt herrings
3 lb potatoes
Pepper

Put the peeled potatoes in a pan and add water to
reach halfway up the potatoes. Wash the herrings
and place on top of the potatoes; sprinkle with
pepper. Cover the pan with a lid and bring to the
boil; simmer gently for about 30 minutes or until
the potatoes are cooked.

Bloaters and Herrings (6-8 portions) F

The mild-cured bloater does not keep well and
should be used as soon as possible after purchase.
Sandwiched with fresh herring, it makes an unusual breakfast or high-tea dish.

4 bloaters
4 fresh herrings
Melted butter

Remove the bones, heads and tails from the
bloaters, cut into fillets and brush the flesh side
generously with melted butter. Clean, bone and
fillet the herrings and lay on top of the bloater
fillets, flesh sides together. Brush with melted
butter and grill for 15 minutes, turning once.

Bloaters, Devilled (8 portions) F

A spicy topping gives extra flavour to breakfast
bloaters; for a supper dish they can be served with
a salad of watercress dressed with oil and vinegar.

8 bloaters
3 oz chutney
1 oz mustard
1 teaspoon lemon juice
Salt
2 teaspoons sugar
2-3 oz butter
Browned breadcrumbs

Oven: 400°F; gas mark 6; 15 minutes

Split the bloaters down the back and remove all
bones. Mix the chutney, mustard, lemon juice,

salt and sugar to a paste. Brush the flesh sides of the bloater fillets with softened butter and spread with the paste. Lay the bloaters in a buttered ovenproof dish, sprinkle with breadcrumbs and dot with the remaining butter. Bake in the oven for 15 minutes.

Bloaters in Cider (8 portions) H and F

Although bloaters are most often served grilled, they may be cooked in other ways and can, for example, be served cold with a salad of apples and potatoes.

8 bloaters
1 pt cider
1 teaspoon salt
1 teaspoon dill seeds (optional)
1 lb cooked, diced new potatoes
1 lb diced red skinned apples
4 fl oz oil
2 tablespoons lemon juice
Salt and pepper
Garnish: watercress

Oven: 375°F; gas mark 5; 15-20 minutes

Cut the heads off the bloaters; lay in an oven-proof dish and pour the cider over the bloaters. Sprinkle with salt and dill seeds, cover with a lid or foil and bake for 15-20 minutes. Remove the bloaters and cool slightly, cut down the back and remove bones and skin. Arrange two fillets on each plate.

Mix the diced potatoes and apples and blend the oil, strained cider and lemon juice; season with salt and pepper. Toss the potato salad in half this dressing and spoon the remainder over the fish. Arrange the salad around the fish and garnish with watercress.

Mustard Bloaters (8 portions) F

Breadcrumbs and mustard are used as a crisp finish to grilled bloaters.

8 bloaters
2 oz melted butter or
    2 tablespoons oil
1 oz mustard
¾ oz browned breadcrumbs

Clean and trim the bloaters and make three diagonal slashes along one side of each fish. Brush with a little melted butter or oil and grill the bloaters lightly on both sides; fill the slashes with mustard. Sprinkle with breadcrumbs and pour over the rest of the butter. Return the bloaters to the grill until cooked through and brown and crisp on top.

Craster Kippers (8 portions) F and H Northumberland

Northumberland is the cradle of the kipper industry since John Woodger at Seahouses adapted the method of kippering salmon to herring in the mid 19th century.

8 boned and skinned kippers
8 slices granary or rye bread
Unsalted butter
8 egg yolks
Lemon juice
Garnish: lemon slices

Cut the kippers into strips about 1½ in long and ¾ in wide. Butter the bread and trim into squares or rounds. Arrange the kipper pieces on each slice in the shape of a nest-like circle. Using a spoon, slip an egg yolk into the centre, sprinkle with a few drops of lemon juice and serve with lemon slices.

Alternatively, cut the kippers into thin horizontal slices, lay on the buttered bread and serve with lemon quarters.

Kippers and Tomato Bake (6-8 portions) F

An unusual, but highly tasty supper dish combining grilled kippers and tomatoes.

8 kippers
½ oz fresh white breadcrumbs
4 oz softened butter
1 oz finely chopped parsley
Lemon juice
Salt and pepper
8 skinned, sliced tomatoes
Garnish: chopped parsley

Oven: 350°F; gas mark 4; 20 minutes

Grill the kippers for a few minutes on each side, remove all skin and flake the flesh. Mix the flaked kippers and any juices from the grill pan with the breadcrumbs, butter and parsley. Add lemon juice, salt and pepper to taste. Spread the mixture in a shallow ovenproof dish, top with the sliced tomatoes and bake in the oven for about 20 minutes. Garnish with chopped parsley.

Kippers with Onions (8 portions) H and F

A quick and easy first course of marinated kippers, best served chilled with thin slices of brown bread and butter.

16 boned kipper fillets
½ lb sliced onions
1 bay leaf
4 fl oz olive oil
3 fl oz wine vinegar
1 tablespoon caster sugar
Salt and pepper

Arrange the kipper fillets in a shallow serving dish with the onion rings and bay leaf. Mix a marinade from the oil, vinegar, sugar, salt and freshly ground pepper; spoon over the kippers. Leave for several hours to marinate. Serve chilled, having first removed the bay leaf.

Ling

A saltwater fish and a member of the cod family. Sold fresh or dried salted and then often known as stockfish, once extremely popular in Ireland and Scotland. In periods of deep poverty, the Irish peasants' diet was often confined to a stew of unpeeled potatoes topped with a piece of salt ling, simmered over a low peat fire.

Ling and Bacon (6 portions) F Ireland

Ling contains little natural oil or fat, but baked with bacon the dry flesh is continuously basted. The medieval housewife traditionally cooked parsnips, fried golden, with ling partly to give a golden colour to the fish and partly to impart a touch of sweetness.

2 lb ling
Salt and pepper
½ lb streaky bacon
Garnish: chopped parsley

Oven: 350°F; gas mark 4; 30 minutes
       400°F; gas mark 6; 15 minutes

Wash the ling thoroughly and cut off the fins; wipe dry. Arrange in a buttered baking dish, sprinkle with salt and pepper and lay the bacon over the fish. Cover with greased paper and bake for 30 minutes at 350°F (gas mark 4).

Remove the paper, increase the heat to 400°F (gas mark 6) for about 15 minutes to brown the bacon. Place on a serving dish and pour the liquid round the fish. Garnish with parsley and serve.

Mackerel

This is a slender saltwater fish, with beautiful silvery-blue and green skin and oily, delicate flesh that flakes easily. It deteriorates rapidly and must be used as fresh as possible while the skin still retains its lustre. It is sometimes known as poor man's trout and may be cooked and served as trout, the flavours being somewhat alike. As haddock is associated with Scotland and herring with East Anglia, so mackerel features in many Cornish dishes.

Herby Mackerel (8 portions) F

For grilling and frying, choose small mackerel which have a better flavour than large ones.

8 mackerel
Salt and pepper
2 tablespoons finely chopped mint, parsley and
    fennel
2 oz flour
Garnish: chopped parsley

Cut off heads, tails and fins; bone and fillet the mackerel. Wipe the fillets, sprinkle with salt, pepper, mint, parsley and fennel; pat in well. Dust with flour and grill for 4-6 minutes on each side. Garnish with parsley and serve with pats of chilled fennel butter.

Mackerel, Marinated (8 portions) F Cornwall

An ideal early summer dish for lunch or supper, served with crusty bread or a cold potato salad sprinkled with chopped parsley.

8 mackerel
½ lb chopped onions
1 tablespoon chopped parsley
4 chopped bay leaves
12 cloves
Blade mace
Sprig thyme

8 peppercorns
Salt
1 pt vinegar

Oven: 350°F; gas mark 4; 40-50 minutes

Gut and clean the mackerel and place in an oven-proof dish. Sprinkle the onions, parsley and bay leaves over the fish, add the cloves, mace, thyme, peppercorns and salt. Pour over the vinegar and bake in the oven for 40-50 minutes. Lift the mackerel carefully onto a serving dish; strain the cooking liquid and pour over. Leave to marinate and cool for several hours before serving.

Mackerel, Salt (8 portions) F

Boiling fresh mackerel results in a great loss of flavour, unless this is sealed in by a brine.

8 mackerel
Salt
4 oz melted parsley butter

Cut off heads and tails and split the mackerel down the back; remove the bones and guts. Clean the fish; rub thoroughly with plenty of salt and leave in a cool place for 3 days. Rinse the mackerel thoroughly; put in a pan of boiling water and simmer gently for 20-30 minutes. Serve with melted parsley butter.

Mackerel with Fennel Sauce (8 portions) F Wales

The slight anise flavour of fresh fennel comple-ments the fatty mackerel flesh well.

8 mackerel
1 oz freshly chopped fennel
Salt and pepper
4 oz melted butter

Clean the mackerel thoroughly, leaving them whole, sprinkle with chopped fennel, salt and pepper and brush the skin side with melted butter. Lay fresh fennel leaves on the rack of the grill pan and place the fish on top. Grill the fish for 4-6 minutes on each side. Serve with fennel sauce.

Mackerel with Gooseberry Sauce (8 portions) F Cornwall

The combination of mackerel, fried, grilled or roast, and gooseberry sauce is reputed to have been brought to England at the time of the Norman conquest.

8 mackerel
Salt and pepper
3 oz butter
1 pt gooseberry sauce

Oven: 350°F; gas mark 4; 20-30 minutes

Gut and clean the fish and place in a buttered ovenproof dish; season with salt and pepper and dot with butter. Cover with buttered greaseproof paper or foil; bake in the oven for 20-30 minutes. Remove from the oven; split the mackerel and remove the backbones. Serve with hot gooseberry sauce and small new potatoes.

Mackerel with Piccalilli Sauce (8 portions) F

First known as Indian pickle from its country of origin, this mild pickle makes a good accompani-ment to most types of oily fish.

8 mackerel
4 oz butter
4 oz finely chopped onions
2 oz flour
2 pt fish stock
Salt and pepper
½-¾ lb piccalilli

Clean, bone and fillet the mackerel; fry lightly in butter on both sides and remove from the pan. Fry the onions in the butter until golden, stir in the flour and gradually add the stock. Season with salt and pepper, bring to the boil and simmer for 3-4 minutes, stirring continuously. Gradually blend in the piccalilli and return the mackerel to the sauce. Cover with a lid and simmer over low heat for 30 minutes.

Mackerel in Vinegar (8 portions) F

Vinegar helps to preserve the oil content of mackerel, but to prevent the soft flesh from breaking up, the water should barely simmer.

8 mackerel
Vinegar

Carefully gut and clean the fish through as small an incision in the belly as possible. Wipe dry. Rub the mackerel with vinegar. Bring a large pan of lightly salted water to the boil. Place the fish on a plate or rack; lower into the boiling water and simmer very gently for 15 minutes. Drain and serve with fennel or gooseberry sauce.

Mullet

Red mullet is a round saltwater fish, with rose-pink skin and white delicate flesh. It is unrelated to grey mullet, a larger estuary fish of inferior quality. Red mullets are scarce and consequently expensive; best cooked quite simply although certain sauces are traditionally associated with them. The liver is considered a delicacy and should not be discarded with the other intestines but left in the fish.

Arundel Mullets (8 portions) H Sussex

This dish dates from the 17th century and now, as then, is served in soup plates, bread being used to mop up the wine sauce.

8 mullets (6-8 oz each)
2 pt fish stock or water
1 oz butter
½ lb diced onions
1 teaspoon lemon juice
½ pt red wine
Bunch of sweet herbs
2-3 finely chopped anchovies
Salt and pepper
Nutmeg

Clean and wash the mullets; simmer gently in stock or lightly salted water for 10-15 minutes. Lift out the fish and reduce the liquid by half. Melt the butter and cook the onions without browning; add the lemon juice, wine, reduced cooking liquid, herbs, chopped anchovies and salt, pepper and nutmeg to taste. Bring to the boil and put in the mullets. Simmer for 15 minutes; serve with the sauce poured over the mullets.

Red Mullets in Cases (8 portions) H

Wrapped and baked in paper, the mullets can also be stuffed with parsley and onion or covered with a mixture of chopped parsley, herbs, shallots and mushrooms.

8 mullets (6-8 oz each)
Salt and pepper
Oil
2 tablespoons lemon juice

Garnish: lemon slices, parsley sprigs

Oven: 350°F; gas mark 4; 15-20 minutes

Clean, wash and dry the fish well. Sprinkle the insides with salt and pepper. Wrap each mullet in a piece of oiled greaseproof paper or foil, twisting the ends securely. Place in a baking tin and bake in the oven for 15-20 minutes. Loosen the paper cases carefully and set each parcel on a hot plate. Add lemon juice to the liquid which has collected in the pan; pour over the fish and serve, garnished with parsley and lemon.

Red Mullets with Mushrooms (6 portions) H

A most attractive-looking dish with the rose-pink mullets baked on a bed of mushrooms.

8 mullets (6-8 oz each)
4 oz chopped onions
2 oz butter
1 lb chopped mushrooms
4 oz white breadcrumbs
1 oz chopped parsley
Salt and pepper
Garnish: lemon quarters

Oven: 350°F; gas mark 4; 20 minutes

Scale and clean the fish but do not remove the liver. Fry the onions in the butter, mix with the mushrooms, breadcrumbs and parsley; season with salt and pepper. Spread this mixture over the base of a buttered fireproof dish, lay the mullets on top and cover with buttered paper or foil. Bake in the oven for 20 minutes and remove the covering for the last 10 minutes. Serve garnished with lemon quarters.

Red Mullets with Tomatoes (8 portions) H

Tomatoes are traditionally used to flavour mullet; combined with garlic and red wine the sauce becomes reminiscent of Provençale cooking.

8 mullets (6-8 oz each)
3 tablespoons olive oil
2 cloves garlic
½ lb sliced onions
2 lb skinned, sliced tomatoes
5 fl oz red wine
2 oz sugar

Oven: 350°F; gas mark 4; 20-30 minutes

Scale and carefully clean the mullets. Heat the oil and quickly fry the crushed garlic and onions until light brown. Add the tomatoes, red wine and sugar and simmer for 15 minutes. Spread half of this mixture over the base of a buttered fireproof dish, place the mullets on top, add the remaining tomato mixture and cover with grease-proof paper.

Bake in the oven for 20-30 minutes.

Plaice

A flat saltwater fish with characteristic orange-red spots on the upper side. It is related to sole and while it may be cooked in the same manner it lacks the subtle taste of that supreme flatfish. Plaice is, however, inexpensive, and its lesser flavour is usually compensated for with rich sauces and garnishes.

Plaice with Anchovy Cream (8 portions) F and H

Deep-fried fish is popular at all levels in Britain; here it is given luxury treatment with anchovy-flavoured cream.

8 plaice fillets (4 oz each)
½ portion plain coating batter
Deep fat for frying
½ pt double cream
Anchovy essence

Make the batter mixture and set aside while preparing the fish. Wipe and dry the fillets well; dip in the batter and fry in hot deep fat (360°F) until golden brown. Drain and keep warm. To make the sauce, whip the cream until stiff, flavour to taste with anchovy essence and serve in a separate bowl.

Sea Bream

This is a round saltwater fish with silvery and blue skin, coarsely scaled, and pink, delicate flesh which is best grilled or baked.

Sea Bream, Stuffed (6-8 portions) F

For this dish, choose whole sea bream which need careful cleaning; scaling is unnecessary as the thick skin peels off easily after cooking.

3-4 lb sea bream
6 oz veal forcemeat

Dripping
Flour
Salt and pepper

Oven: 350°F; gas mark 4; 45-50 minutes

Clean, wash and dry the bream; prepare the stuffing. Stuff the body cavity of the fish with forcemeat and lay in a fireproof dish with melted dripping. Sprinkle with flour, salt and pepper and baste with more melted dripping. Cover with foil and bake in the oven for about 45 minutes. Serve with boiled new potatoes.

Skate

A flat, ray or kite-shaped fish the wings of which are the parts seen on fish stalls. They often have a slimy skin with a smell of ammonia which disappears in cooking. The flesh is faintly pink with bones that come away easily.

Skate with Black Butter (8 portions) F and H

Black butter is the classic accompaniment to skate in many countries. Serve with buttered potatoes and a green vegetable.

3-4 lb wing of skate
2 pt fish stock
2 oz capers
Juice of 1 lemon
4 oz butter
2 tablespoons white wine vinegar
2 tablespoons finely chopped parsley

Soak the skate overnight in cold water; cut into eight equal portions and poach in the stock for 15-20 minutes. Skin the fish on both sides, arrange on a dish and keep warm. Sprinkle with chopped capers and lemon juice.

Melt the butter in a pan and cook until nut-brown; stir in the vinegar and parsley and pour over the fish.

Skate with Tomato Sauce (6-8 portions) F

Soaking skate for at least 10 hours in cold water makes removal of the slimy coating much easier. For this dish, remove the bones from the wings of skate.

3 lb wing of skate
2 eggs or
    ½ pt basic coating batter
White breadcrumbs
Fat for frying

Cut the cleaned, boned skate into six or eight
equal portions. Dry thoroughly. Beat the eggs
lightly or prepare the coating batter; coat each
portion in egg or batter, then roll in fresh breadcrumbs. Heat the fat and shallow-fry the skate
until golden, turning once. Drain the skate before
serving with tomato sauce and small new or
creamed potatoes.

Smelt

This is a very small saltwater fish that comes up
rivers to spawn; the body is covered with silvery
scales, and the white flesh has a faint smell of
cucumber on freshly caught fish. These small fish
bruise easily and need careful handling; make a
cut below the gills and press the entrails out
through this; wash and dry gently.

Smelts, Baked (6-8 portions) H

Best at spawning time in late winter and early
spring, smelts can be substituted by small trout
at other times of the year.

2-2½ doz smelts
4 oz butter
Salt and cayenne pepper
White breadcrumbs
1 tablespoon lemon juice
Garnish: chopped parsley and lemon slices

Oven: 350°F; gas mark 4; 15-20 minutes

Gut, wash and dry the smelts. Arrange in a well-
buttered fireproof dish; sprinkle with salt and
cayenne. Cover with breadcrumbs and dot with
butter. Bake for 15-20 minutes. Just before serving add lemon juice; garnish with parsley and
lemon slices.

Smelts with Cream Sauce (6-8 portions) H

Smelts are most often served grilled or fried as a
first course; eggs, cream and wine make this dish
into a rich starter for special occasions.

2-2½ doz smelts
1 pt white wine

1 pt fish stock
2 oz butter
Sprig each rosemary and thyme
Salt and 1 blade mace
2 egg yolks
5 fl oz double cream
2 oz sugar
Garnish: chopped parsley, bread sippets

Put the cleaned smelts in a large pan with the
white wine, fish stock, butter and salt; add the
rosemary, thyme and mace tied in muslin. Bring to
the boil and simmer gently for 5-8 minutes. Lift
the smelts on to a serving dish and keep warm;
remove the muslin bag from the stock.

Blend the lightly beaten eggs with the cream,
stir in a little of the cooking liquid and return it
all to the pan. Heat the sauce through until
thickened, without letting it boil. Correct seasoning. Pour the sauce over the smelts, sprinkle the
sugar on top and serve garnished with sippets and
parsley.

Smelts with Horseradish Cream (6-8 portions) H

As an appetiser, smelts can be coated with eggs
and breadcrumbs, deep-fried and served with
lemon butter; alternatively coat them with batter
before frying. For a cold or hot first course, the
poached smelts are here served with a well-flavoured cream sauce.

2-2½ doz smelts
5 fl oz dry white wine
5 fl oz water
Salt and pepper
½ pt double cream
1 dessertspoonful lemon juice
1 dessertspoonful grated horseradish

Put the cleaned smelts in a pan and cover with
wine and water; season with salt and pepper.
Bring to the boil and simmer gently for 5-8
minutes. Drain the fish thoroughly and arrange
in a serving dish. Whip the cream lightly, blend
in the lemon juice and horseradish; serve in a
separate bowl.

Sole

The sole takes pride of place among all the fish
caught in the seas around Britain. The exquisite
flavour of the Dover sole actually improves after

killing due to a chemical substance in the flesh. Sole is equally delicious fried or grilled, whole or in fillets, or served with rich sauces. Other small flat fish, related to the sole but lacking its supreme flavour, include the lemon sole and witch, also known as megrim or Aberdeen sole.

Beaufort Fillets of Sole with Oysters (8 portions) H Scotland

A rich, but delicately flavoured dish for a main course; serve with tiny potatoes and buttered broccoli.

16 fillets of sole (2 oz each)
4 oz chopped shallots
1 tablespoon mixed chopped parsley and
    thyme
Juice of ½ lemon
½ lb tomatoes
12 oysters
½ pt white wine
6 fl oz fish stock
Salt and pepper
½ lb butter
1 dessertspoon finely chopped parsley

Oven: 350°F; gas mark 4; 10 minutes

Butter a shallow ovenproof dish, cover the base with shallots, thyme, parsley and lemon juice. Skin and quarter the tomatoes; remove the seeds. Place the sole in the dish, with the cleaned oysters and tomatoes on top. Pour over the wine and stock; season with salt and pepper. Cover with buttered paper and bake in the oven.

Lift the fillets on to a serving dish and keep warm. Strain the cooking liquid and reduce almost to a glaze; remove from the heat and gradually add the butter beating well; stir in the finely chopped parsley. Pour the sauce over the fillets and serve.

Dover Sole, Grilled (8 portions) H

The favourite way in Britain with the aristocratic sole is possibly plainly grilled; small soles, also known as slips with an average weight of 6-8 oz, may be treated similarly or garnished with whipped cream instead of parsley butter.

8 soles
Seasoned flour
6 oz melted butter

Garnish: parsley butter, lemon slices

Clean and gut the soles and remove the skin from the upper dark side. Wash and dry thoroughly. Coat the soles in seasoned flour and brush with melted butter. Grill under moderate heat for 6-10 minutes depending on size, turning once and basting with butter. Serve garnished with lemon slices and parsley butter.

Fillets of Sole in the Duart Way (8 portions) H Scotland

This recipe originates in the Duart Bay district of Argyll, off the Sound of Mull.

8 fillets of sole (4-6 oz each)
1 oz butter
1 lb button mushrooms
Salt and pepper
5 fl oz water
½ pt fish stock
2 egg yolks
2 fl oz double cream

Oven: 350°F; gas mark 4; 10 minutes

Wipe the fillets; butter an ovenproof dish and cover the base with half the mushrooms, lay the fillets on top and cover with the remaining mushrooms. Season with salt and pepper. Dot with butter and add the water; cover with buttered paper and bake in the oven for about 10 minutes or until cooked.

Lift the fillets and mushrooms on to a serving dish. Reduce the cooking liquid to a glaze, add the fish stock and simmer for 3-4 minutes. Blend in the egg yolks lightly beaten with the cream; heat the sauce through without boiling. Correct seasoning and pour the sauce over the fillets.

Fillets of Sole Tullamore (8 portions) H Scotland

Now a traditional dish in Scotland, it probably arrived there from County Kerry in Ireland as evidenced in the sauce flavoured with Irish Mist.

8 fillets of sole (6 oz each)
Salt and pepper
2 oz butter
1 oz chopped shallots
1 lb button mushrooms
1 dessertspoon chopped parsley

Juice of 1 lemon
1 pt fish stock
2-3 fl oz Irish Mist liqueur (optional)
4 egg yolks
8 fl oz cream
Garnish: parsley or watercress sprigs; tomato
    quarters

Sprinkle the sole fillets with salt and pepper; fold
in two. Melt the butter in a pan and add shallots,
mushrooms, parsley and lemon juice; cook without colouring for 2-3 minutes. Add the fillets,
cover with fish stock and simmer until tender.
Lift the fillets and mushrooms on to a serving
dish and keep warm.

   Strain the cooking liquid. Boil the liquid
until reduced by half; add the Irish Mist. Blend
the egg yolks with the cream, stir into the stock
and heat through without boiling. Pour the
sauce over the fillets and garnish with parsley or
watercress sprigs and wedges of tomato.

Fillets of Sole with Cream Sauce
(8 portions) H and F Cornwall

For this dish, thin strips of fillets are used; ask
the fishmonger for the trimmings which are
excellent for fish stock. For a less rich version,
cook the whole fillets in stock flavoured with
lemon, mace, salt and cayenne; serve with a
sauce made from the reduced stock with the
addition of cream.

8 fillets of sole (4-6 oz each)
Salt and pepper
Juice of 1 lemon
4 oz butter
4 oz chopped onions
3 oz flour
1¼ pt fish stock
5 fl oz cream
Garnish: chopped parsley, lobster coral

Oven: 350°F; gas mark 4; 10 minutes

Wipe the fillets and cut each lengthways into two;
tie each strip loosely in a knot or fold the ends
over each other towards the middle. Place in a
buttered ovenproof dish, season with salt and
pepper and sprinkle with lemon juice. Cover with
buttered greaseproof paper and bake in the oven
for 10-15 minutes.

   Melt the butter in a pan, cook the onions
gently, add the flour and gradually stir in the
stock; cook until boiling, simmer for 10 minutes

and correct seasoning. Add the cream to the
sauce just before serving. Lift the fillets on to a
serving dish, pour over the sauce and garnish with
chopped parsley and lobster coral.

Fillets of Sole in Cider (8 portions)
H and F Sussex

A tangy sauce of cider, topped with cheese, adds
an extra flavour to sole fillets. Alternatively,
bake the fillets with lemon juice and butter and
serve with slices of lemon and lemon butter.

16 fillets of sole (2 oz each)
2 oz butter
1 dessertspoon chopped shallots
Salt and pepper
1 pt cider
1 oz flour
2 oz grated cheese

Oven: 350°F; gas mark 4; 15 minutes

Put the shallots in a buttered ovenproof dish,
arrange the sole fillets on top, season with salt
and pepper and pour over the cider. Cover with
buttered greaseproof paper and bake in the
oven. Lift the fillets on to a serving dish and
keep warm. Strain the liquid.

   Melt 1 oz of butter, stir in the flour and
gradually add the strained liquid. Simmer for 5
minutes and correct seasoning. Pour the sauce
over the fish, sprinkle the cheese on top and
brown under a hot grill.

Turbot

A large flat fish with black knobbly skin and
firm, white, extremely delicate flesh the flavour
of which is comparable to that of sole. It varies
from small whole turbot, known as chicken
turbot at about 2 lb, to huge fish, usually cut
up and sold as steaks and fillets.

Turbot Atlantic (6-8 portions) H

Turbot was once considered a national dish and
wealthy households would frequently use a large,
specially designed turbot-kettle for steaming the
fish. As late as Victorian days, turbot still
featured much on the bill of fare, accompanied
with shrimp or oyster sauce and garnished with
lobster coral.

2 lb filleted turbot
2 oz butter
½ lb sliced onions
½-¾ lb tomato chutney
½ pt fish stock
1 lb sliced potatoes
Salt and pepper
2-4 oz grated cheese

Oven: 400°F; gas mark 6; 45 minutes

Fry the onions in the butter until soft and golden.
Add the chutney and fish stock; simmer gently
until heated through and well combined. Place a
layer of potatoes over the base of a deep, buttered
ovenproof dish. Cube the turbot fillets, arrange a
layer over the potatoes and season with salt and
pepper. Continue with layers of potato and
turbot, seasoning each layer and finishing with a
layer of fish. Spoon over the tomato mixture,
sprinkle with cheese and bake in the oven for 45
minutes or until bubbling and brown.

Turbot with Watercress and Pickled Walnuts (8 portions) H

This dish may be served hot or cold and is ideally
best accompanied with crusty bread and butter;
vegetables may detract from the delicate taste of
the fish, complemented but not swamped by the
sauce flavourings.

8 turbot steaks (6 oz each)
4 oz sliced onions
2 oz butter
2 oz flour
12 pickled walnuts
Bunch finely chopped watercress
Salt and pepper
Garnish: 8 pickled walnuts

Put the steaks in a pan with the onions and
enough water to cover; bring to the boil and
poach gently for 20 minutes. Remove the turbot
to a serving dish and keep warm; strain the
poaching liquid. Melt the butter in a pan, stir in
the flour and gradually add ½ pint of the strained
liquid. Mash the walnuts and add to the sauce
with the chopped watercress; season with salt and
pepper. Bring the sauce to the boil and simmer for
a few minutes. Spoon the sauce over the turbot
and serve garnished with halved, pickled walnuts.

FRESHWATER FISH

This section includes edible fish that inhabit
rivers, ponds and lakes, reservoirs and gravel pits
in the British Isles. Some species, such as carp
and tench thrive in still, muddy waters while
others, like the grayling and the brown trout, are
found in swift-running rivers. Also included are
eels, salmon and shad which, although they spend
parts of their lives in the sea, are caught in inland
waters.

Bream, Baked (6-8 portions) F

Bream is caught in muddy still waters throughout
the British Isles, but is rarely offered for sale. The
large, bronze-coloured fish need careful cleaning
to remove all traces of mud.

3-4 lb bream
¾ lb chopped onions
2 chopped cloves garlic
1 lemon
Salt and pepper
2 tablespoons oil
1-2 oz white breadcrumbs

Oven: 350°F; gas mark 4; 30 minutes

Clean the bream thoroughly, remove head and
fins and score the deep sides. Arrange the onions
and garlic over the base of a fireproof dish. Slice
the lemon thinly and put one slice in each score
of the bream. Place on top of the onions and
squeeze over the remaining lemon juice; sprinkle
with salt and pepper.

Spoon the oil over the fish and cover with
breadcrumbs. Bake the bream, covered, for 30
minutes. Remove the cover and allow the breadcrumbs to brown for the last 10 minutes.

Carp with Onions and Mushrooms (8 portions) H and F

Carp was introduced to Britain in the 15th century
and reared in artificial fish ponds at monasteries.
The mirror and king carps, with prominent scales,
are the most common, from fish farms or imports.
Locally caught carp should be soaked in water and
vinegar to remove the muddy smell and taste.

Carp can be shallow-fried and served with
lemon quarters and anchovy essence, or stewed
with additional flavours as in this recipe.

3-4 lb carp
2 oz butter
¾ lb sliced onions
1 pt fish stock
½ lb button mushrooms
1 faggot of herbs
Pinch grated nutmeg
Salt and pepper
1 oz flour
Garnish: sippets

Gut, scale and clean the carp thoroughly; soak in water and vinegar for a couple of hours, then cut the fish into slices of about 3 oz. Melt just over half the butter in a pan and fry the onions without colouring; add stock, the mushrooms, herbs, nutmeg, salt and pepper. Bring to the boil, then add the carp and simmer gently for 30-40 minutes. Lift out and keep warm.

Knead together the flour and remaining butter and add to the stock; simmer, stirring continuously until the sauce has thickened. Strain the sauce over the carp and serve with sippets.

Eel

Eels are thought to spawn in the Sargasso Sea in the Atlantic from where the young, known as elvers, begin a long migratory journey in huge shoals to reach inland rivers and estuaries. In Britain, elvers are caught in quantity in the rivers of the West Country and particularly in Somerset. The elvers which escape capture grow to maturity in rivers and streams, and after a number of years the eels, now silvery, begin the journey back to the Sargasso Sea. It is on this return journey that eels are caught for consumption.

Eels and Mash (6-8 portions) F London

This was a favourite dish to be bought from London's fish stalls and barrows in the 19th century. The cut-up eels were served in a hot parsley broth with mashed potatoes.

2-3 lb eels
Juice of 1 lemon or
    1 tablespoon of vinegar
Salt

Cut the heads off the eels; soak in cold salted

water for 15 minutes, then peel off the skin. Clean the eels, remove the backbone and rinse thoroughly. Cut the eels into 1½-2 in pieces. Place in a pan and cover with salted water; add lemon juice or vinegar. Cover and simmer gently until tender, after about 30-40 minutes.

Lift out the eel pieces and use the stock to make a fairly runny parsley butter sauce. Place the eels in individual bowls, pour over the sauce and top with a spoonful of mashed potato. Serve hot.

Eel Stew (6-8 portions) F

This is reminiscent of the Cornish conger eel stew, but a touch of sophistication is added with claret in the brown stew.

2-3 lb eels
¾ lb small peeled onions
1 oz clarified butter
1½ oz flour
½ pt brown stock
2 tablespoons claret
Salt and pepper
Garnish: finely chopped parsley, sippets

Remove the heads of the eels; wash thoroughly in cold salted water. Soak in water for 15 minutes, skin, clean, bone and rinse the eels; cut into slices 1½ in thick and dry thoroughly.

Fry the onions gently in the butter until light brown. Add the flour; stir in the stock and claret and bring to the boil. Season with salt and pepper; add the eels. Cover and simmer gently until tender, after about 30 minutes. Arrange the eels and onions on a serving dish, strain the sauce over the fish and garnish with parsley and fried sippets.

Eels, Spitchcocked (8 portions) F and H Oxford

The origin of the word "spitchcocked" is obscure, but it first appears in the late 16th century with reference to eels dressed with chopped herbs and breadcrumbs before being fried.

3 lb medium-sized eels
4 oz butter
Finely chopped parsley, thyme, sage
Salt and pepper
2 oz chopped shallots
4 egg yolks

4 oz fresh white breadcrumbs
Garnish: fried parsley sprigs

Rub the eels with salt to remove any slime, wash
and cut off the heads, leave the skin on. Slit the
eels along the belly and take out bones and guts;
wash well. Cut into 3 in long pieces; wipe and dry
thoroughly. Melt the butter in a pan and stir in
parsley, sage and thyme, salt, pepper and shallots.
Heat through. Remove the pan from the heat
and leave to get cool. Stir in the egg yolks.

Dip the eel pieces in the egg mixture and coat
with breadcrumbs. Grill under high heat until
brown and crisp. Garnish with fried parsley and
serve with anchovy sauce or melted butter.

Elver Cakes in the Keynsham Way (6-8 portions) F Somerset

At spring tides in March or April, the Severn
fishermen set out at night to scoop out the shoals
of elvers streaming up the river. In former days,
these immature eels would be sold in the street
markets, but today the majority of the catch is
dispatched for breeding at fish farms. The
remainder, still regarded as delicacies, is cooked
to local traditional recipes.

2 lb elvers
Salt and pepper
¾-1 lb savoury shortcrust pastry
1 egg

Oven: 450°F; gas mark 8; 20 minutes

Wash the elvers thoroughly in hot salted water.
Season with salt and pepper and wrap in pastry.
Place on a baking tray, brush with lightly beaten
egg and bake for about 20 minutes.

Elvers in the Epney Way (6-8 portions) H and F Gloucestershire

The minute, transparent elvers are often cooked
and served as whitebait. Gloucester, Bath and
Cheltenham had their own, zealously guarded
recipes.

2 lb elvers
¾ lb streaky bacon rashers
1-2 oz butter
4 eggs
Salt and pepper
1 tablespoon vinegar

Wash the elvers several times in salted water. Fry
the bacon in butter until crisp; lift out and keep
hot. Fry the elvers in the fat; at first they become
transparent, then opaque and milky. Fry for a
few minutes only as overcooking spoils the flavour.
Beat the eggs lightly and season with salt and
pepper. Stir this mixture into the elvers and cook
as an omelet. Serve with the bacon rashers on
top and sprinkle with vinegar.

Grayling in Beer (8 portions) H and F Herefordshire

Related to the salmon and trout, grayling is
found in swift rivers and mountain streams. The
beautiful fish, silvery and pearly, is said to have
a scent of thyme and this is emphasised in the
following recipe.

8 graylings
1½-2 pt beer
1 dessertspoon grated horseradish
Thyme, winter savory sprigs
Salt and pepper
1 oz butter
Garnish: horseradish, lemon rind, ginger

Scale and clean the fish, wash thoroughly and
make three scores on one side of each fish. Place
in a pan and cover with beer; add the horseradish,
thyme, winter savory, salt and pepper. Bring to
the boil and simmer until tender. Remove and
drain the graylings; arrange on a serving dish and
keep warm.

Strain the cooking liquid and measure ½ pint
of this; add the butter, heat through and pour
over the fish. Sprinkle with grated horseradish,
grated lemon rind and ground ginger. Serve.

Lamprey, Stuffed (6-8 portions) F

The lamprey is an eel-like, parasitic fish attaching
itself to its victim by its jawless sucker mouth.
It is rarely seen today, but the delicate fatty
flesh was once considered a delicacy.

3-5 lb lamprey
¾ lb veal forcemeat
Seasoned flour
2 eggs
6 oz fresh white breadcrumbs
4 oz butter
Garnish: lemon slices

Oven: 350°F; gas mark 4; 40-45 minutes

Rub the fish thoroughly with salt to remove any slime, wash; remove the poisonous central nerve that runs down the back by cutting off the tail and pulling the nerve through a cut made below the gills. Stuff the body with the force-meat and sew it up. Wrap the fish in buttered greaseproof paper or foil, put in a pan and cover with hot water; simmer for 20 minutes. Drain, remove the skin and dry the fish.

Dust with seasoned flour, brush with the beaten eggs and coat with breadcrumbs. Place in a buttered ovenproof dish and bake for 45 minutes, turning after 20 minutes and basting frequently with melted butter. Garnish with lemon slices and serve with anchovy sauce.

Perch with Parsley Sauce (8 portions) H

This dark green fish of lakes and rivers is distinguished by the broad black stripes on the skin and the difficulty in removing the scales. It should be scaled at once after being caught; failing that, plunge the fish into boiling water for a few minutes after which the skin can be peeled off complete with scales.

8 perch (8 oz each)
4 oz butter
¾ oz chopped onion
1 pt fish stock
2 tablespoons vinegar
1 teaspoon anchovy essence
1 bay leaf
1 faggot of herbs
2 cloves
2 oz flour
1 oz chopped parsley
Juice of 1 lemon
Salt and pepper

Scale, gut and clean the fish, cut off the fins and gills. Melt half the butter in a pan and gently fry the onion until golden. Add the stock, vinegar, anchovy essence, bay leaf, faggot of herbs and cloves. Simmer for 10 minutes, then add the perch and cook gently for 10 minutes. Remove the perch to a serving dish and keep warm.

Strain the cooking liquid. Melt the remaining butter, add the flour and cook for 2-3 minutes; gradually stir in the strained liquid and bring to the boil. Add parsley, lemon juice, salt and pepper to the sauce; pour over the fish and serve.

Pike with Bacon (6-8 portions) H and F

The long-snouted, vicious pike is the largest native freshwater fish in Britain but is seldom offered for sale. It can weigh up to 35 lb, but smaller fish of about 3 lb and sufficient for 6 people are also landed. Sliced pike can be coated with egg and breadcrumbs and deep-fried; whole pike can be stuffed and baked or, like here, cooked with bacon.

3-4 lb pike
1 oz butter
½ lb bacon rashers
¾ pt fish stock
1 dessertspoon lemon juice or
    1 tablespoon vinegar
Salt and pepper

Gut, scale and clean the pike; remove fins and gills. Melt the butter in a pan and put in the pike. Top with bacon rashers, cover with a close fitting lid and cook gently for 15 minutes. Add the stock, lemon juice or vinegar and salt and pepper. Simmer gently for a further 15 minutes; lift the pike and bacon on to a dish and serve with the strained cooking liquid poured over the fish.

Salmon

For centuries the salmon has been revered as the king of fish, the flavour of its pink, close flesh considered superior to any other. The salmon spends most of its life in cool northern seas, but is caught at spawning time from May to July, in inland swift, cool rivers. The tiny young salmon, known at this stage as parrs, live for the first few years in rivers; at the age of about four years and now named smolts, they make their way down rivers and out into the sea where they stay for several years and mature into grilse. Eventually the salmon return, mysteriously, to their native rivers to spawn. After spawning, the old salmon, now known as kelts, usually die although a few return to the sea. Kelts are worn-out salmon, entirely lacking the flavour of the majestic fish that came up river to multiply.

Fresh Salmon

This is sold whole, from 8 lb upwards, and in individual steaks. The best fresh salmon comes from Scotland in the summer months; frozen salmon is imported from Canada, Norway and North America.

Salmon, Baked (8 portions) H and F

To bake salmon in a single piece or as steaks, the prepared fish is sprinkled with salt and pepper, sometimes a little mixed spice, brushed with melted butter or oil and baked in buttered foil, in water and vinegar or in butter. Allow about 20 minutes per lb. Serve hot with the strained, reduced cooking liquid or with melted butter or oyster sauce.

8 salmon steaks (6 oz each)
4 oz butter
Juice of 1 lemon
Salt and pepper

Oven: 350°F; gas mark 4; 20 minutes

Place the salmon steaks in boiling water for a few minutes; lift out and take off the skin. Drain and dry. Melt the butter; add lemon juice, salt and pepper and brush over the steaks. Wrap the steaks in buttered foil; set on a baking tray and bake for 20 minutes. Serve hot, with the pan juices or an oyster sauce.

Salmon, Fried (8 portions) H and F

In some establishments, fried salmon steaks are served as a breakfast dish. They are coated in eggs and oatmeal and shallow-fried. For a lunch or supper dish, the steaks may be coated with eggs and breadcrumbs flavoured with parsley and fennel or mace, and sprinkled with lemon juice.

8 salmon steaks (6 oz each)
Cold boiled milk
2 oz seasoned flour
3 oz butter
2½ fl oz oil
Garnish: parsley, lemon wedges

Soak the salmon for a few minutes in the milk; dust with seasoned flour. Heat the butter and oil and fry the steaks for 4-5 minutes on each side, turning once. Garnish with fried parsley and lemon wedges. Serve at once.

Salmon, Grilled (8 portions) H

Traditional garnishes with grilled salmon steaks

include lemon wedges, grated horseradish and fresh or fried parsley; thin slices of overlapping cucumber slices, sprinkled with vinegar also make an attractive garnish. As an accompaniment, serve chilled slices of butter, flavoured with lemon, anchovy essence or chopped parsley. The steaks may also be grilled in well-buttered foil, for 10 minutes, turning often.

8 salmon steaks (6 oz each)
Salt and freshly ground black pepper
6 oz melted butter

Season both sides of the steaks with salt and pepper; leave at room temperature for 15 minutes. Place the steaks on a buttered, pre-heated baking sheet and brush with half the melted butter. Grill for 3-5 minutes, about 3 in away from the hot grill. Turn the steaks, brush with the remaining butter and grill for another 3-5 minutes, basting occasionally.

Salmon in Cider (6-8 portions) H and F

Cider has a mellowing effect on the oily salmon flesh and may be substituted with claret. Serve with a tomato sauce made with the strained cooking liquid.

3-4 lb middle cut salmon
2 oz butter
Salt and pepper
Grated nutmeg
2 small chopped shallots
1 teaspoon chopped parsley
5 fl oz cider

Oven: 375°F; gas mark 5; 15-20 minutes

Clean and wash the salmon, cut into two or three equal slices and place in a well-buttered fireproof dish; season with salt, pepper and nutmeg. Sprinkle the salmon with shallots and parsley and dot with butter; moisten with cider. Bake, basting frequently, for about 20 minutes or until tender.

Salmon in Cream (8 portions) H

Nothing detracts from the flavour of fresh salmon in this dish which is given an extra touch of luxury with cream.

8 salmon steaks (6 oz each)
3 oz melted butter

Salt and pepper
5 fl oz double cream
Juice of ½ lemon

Oven: 350°F; gas mark 4; 20 minutes

Steep the salmon in boiling water for a few
minutes; lift out, remove the skin and dry. Place
the steaks in a buttered ovenproof dish; brush
with melted butter and season with salt and
pepper. Cover with foil and bake for 20 minutes.
Arrange the baked steaks on a hot serving dish,
pour over the cream and lemon juice and return to
the oven to heat through.

Salmon in a Plate (8 portions) F Wales

Tiny new potatoes, locally grown, are the ideal
accompaniment to fresh salmon. In Wales, the
two are cooked together.

8 salmon steaks (6 oz each)
½ lb butter
Salt and pepper
Juice of 1 lemon

Clean the steaks and wipe dry; place in deep
buttered plate or dish. Cover with pats of butter
and season with salt, pepper and lemon juice.
Set over a pan of boiling water, containing new
potatoes. Cover the steaks with a lid or upturned
plate; cook for 25-30 minutes, turning the fish
once. Serve the salmon steaks surrounded with
the potatoes and the cooking liquid poured over.

Salmon in Pastry (8 portions) H

Herb-flavoured salmon wrapped in light puff
pastry makes an excellent main course dish; it
can be served hot, with tiny new potatoes and
fresh aparagus and butter sauce, or cold with
a green salad.

3 lb skinned, filleted salmon
Salt and pepper
4 oz softened butter
1 tablespoon chopped parsley
1 teaspoon chopped fennel
2 tablespoons dry white wine
¾ lb puff pastry
1 egg

Oven: 425°F; gas mark 7; 20 minutes;
          375°F; gas mark 5; 30 minutes

Lay one piece of the boned salmon fillet, skinned

side down, on a wooden board; season with salt
and pepper. Blend the butter with parsley and
fennel and spread over the fillet; cover with the
other fillet, skinned side up. Sprinkle with wine
and leave to marinate for about 1 hour, turning
occasionally.

Roll out the pastry thinly and wrap round the
salmon; seal the edges carefully. Set the pastry-
wrapped salmon on a wet baking sheet, decorate
the top with pastry strips or leaves and brush with
egg, lightly beaten with a little milk. Bake at
425°F (gas mark 7) for 20 minutes, then reduce
the heat to 375°F (gas mark 5) for another 30
minutes. Serve hot or cold.

Salmon with Cream and Cucumber (6-8 portions) H

This is an ideal lunch or supper dish for a warm
summer's day; serve with tiny new potatoes and
a green salad.

4 lb whole salmon or grilse
1 bay leaf
Salt and pepper
3 oz melted butter
½ pt cream
¾-1 lb peeled, diced cucumber
Juice of 1 lemon

Oven: 350°F; gas mark 4; 50 minutes

Gut, clean and scale the salmon; wash thoroughly
and place the bay leaf in the fish. Lay the salmon
in a buttered ovenproof dish, season with salt
and pepper, brush with butter and pour the cream
over. Cover with buttered foil or greaseproof paper
and bake for 30 minutes. Remove from the oven,
add the cucumber and sprinkle with lemon juice.

Return to the oven and bake for a further 20
minutes, uncovered. Remove the salmon and peel
off the skin. Arrange the fish on a serving dish
and coat with the cucumber and cream sauce.

Salmon with Cucumber (8 portions) H Yorkshire

An attractive looking dish, the pink salmon steaks
being arranged round a dome of pale green
cucumber. In some versions, the baked salmon
steaks are served coated with cucumber sauce.

8 salmon steaks (6 oz each)
½ lb butter

Salt and pepper
2 tablespoons white wine
Juice of 1 lemon
1 lb peeled, diced cucumber
1 dessertspoon finely chopped parsley

Oven: 350°F; gas mark 4; 20 minutes

Wipe the salmon steaks clean and place in a
buttered ovenproof dish; season with salt and
pepper, add pats of butter, the wine and half
the lemon juice. Cover with buttered foil and
bake for 20 minutes.

Simmer the diced cucumber in a little water
until tender. Drain the cucumber thoroughly
and pile in the centre of a serving dish, sprinkle
with the remaining lemon juice and the parsley.
Peel the skin from the salmon steaks and arrange
them round the cucumber. Strain the cooking
liquid and pour over the salmon.

Salmon with Elderberry Sauce (8 portions) H

Also known as Salmon Trafalgar, this dish is
served with a sharpish capers sauce mellowed with
elderberries.

3 lb whole salmon grilse or
    salmon trout
4 oz melted butter
Juice of 1 lemon
Salt and pepper
1 pt white fish sauce
1 rounded tablespoon chopped parsley
1 oz chopped capers
Lobster coral (optional)
Elderberry sauce

Oven: 350°F; gas mark 4; 20 minutes

Gut, scale and clean the salmon; remove the
skin and slice the salmon into two fillets. Place
the fillets in a buttered ovenproof dish; brush
with melted butter, sprinkle with lemon juice
and seasoning. Cover with foil or a lid and bake
for 20 minutes.

Remove from the oven; arrange the salmon
on a hot serving dish and keep warm. Use the
cooking liquid to make the white sauce. Strain
the sauce, add the parsley, capers and lobster
coral if used. Heat the sauce through and add
elderberry sauce to taste. Serve with the sauce
poured over the fish.

Salmon with Mushrooms (8 portions) H and F

A topping of mushrooms beneath crisp breadcrumbs adds new flavours to baked salmon steaks.

8 salmon steaks (6 oz each)
2 oz butter
1 oz chopped parsley
½ lb chopped onions
4 oz chopped mushrooms
Salt and pepper
4 oz browned breadcrumbs
Juice of 1 lemon

Oven: 350°F; gas mark 4; 15-20 minutes

Leave the cleaned salmon steaks in boiling water
for a few minutes; drain, remove skin and pat the
steaks dry. Melt the butter in a pan and cook the
parsley, onions and mushrooms for a few minutes
without taking colour; season with salt and
freshly milled pepper.

Arrange the steaks on buttered squares of foil;
place the onion and mushroom mixture equally
on top and cover with breadcrumbs. Close the
foil parcels. Bake in the oven for 15 minutes
and open the foil to let the breadcrumbs crisp for
a further 5 minutes. Arrange on a serving dish
and sprinkle with lemon juice.

Salmon with Port Wine (6-8 portions) H

This is a rich main course which requires very
little before or after.

3 lb whole salmon grilse
6-8 oz rich forcemeat
3 oz butter
Juice of 1 lemon
1 pt rich butter sauce
2 tablespoons port wine
1 teaspoon mushroom ketchup

Oven: 350°F; gas mark 4; 1 hour

Scale and clean the fish thoroughly, stuff with the
forcemeat and sew up or secure the opening with
skewers. Dot the salmon with butter and cover
with buttered foil. Bake in the oven for 1 hour,
basting frequently and turning once. Remove
from the oven, carefully peel off the skin and
remove skewers.

Lift the salmon on to a serving dish, squeeze
over the lemon juice. Flavour the butter sauce
with port, mushroom ketchup and the strained

cooking liquid. Heat through and serve separately in a sauce boat.

Salmon Trout (6-8 portions) H

Correctly named sea trout, this river fish has moist pink flesh reminiscent of salmon and large even flakes as found in trout. Weighing from 1-4 lb salmon trout may be cooked like either salmon or trout.

3 lb salmon trout
2 slices white bread soaked in milk
2 chopped anchovies
1 chopped hardboiled egg
1 oz chopped mushrooms
Salt and pepper
½ lb butter
2½ fl oz white wine
Juice of 1 lemon

Oven: 350°F; gas mark 4; 1 hour

Squeeze the soaked bread and break into small pieces with a fork. Mix with the anchovies, hardboiled egg and mushrooms and season with salt and pepper. Gut, scale and thoroughly clean the fish; stuff with the bread mixture and sew up the opening or secure with skewers.

Put the fish in a buttered fireproof dish, cover with 2 oz of the butter and sprinkle with black pepper. Pour the wine in the dish, cover with buttered greaseproof paper and bake for 1 hour. About 10 minutes before serving, remove the greaseproof paper and pour over half the remaining butter which has been melted and mixed with the lemon juice. Arrange the salmon trout on a hot dish and serve the remaining melted butter and lemon juice in a sauce boat.

Tweed Kettle (6-8 portions) H and F
Edinburgh

A delicious salmon stew, subtly flavoured and easily made from a left-over tail piece of salmon.

3 lb piece of salmon
Salt and pepper
Ground mace
¾ pt fish stock
½ pt white wine
3 oz chopped shallots or
   1 dessertspoon chopped chives

2 oz butter
Garnish: chopped parsley

Simmer the cleaned salmon for 5 minutes in boiling water. Drain and remove skin and bones. Cut the salmon into 2 in pieces, season with salt, pepper and mace and put in a pan with the fish stock, wine and shallots or chives; simmer for 8 minutes. Carefully lift out the salmon and place in a serving dish. Reduce the cooking liquid by two thirds; stir in the butter. Pour the sauce over the fish and garnish with parsley.

Wye Baked Salmon (8 portions) H and F
Herefordshire

The exquisite taste of salmon from the Wye river is enhanced with oysters, eels and wine, cooked on a pastry base.

8 salmon steaks (6 oz each)
¾ lb savoury shortcrust pastry
2 oz fresh white breadcrumbs
2 oz chopped mushrooms
2-3 oz melted butter
4 oz cooked flaked salmon
4 oz cooked flaked eel
Salt, pepper, cloves, nutmeg
2 eggs
Milk
8 oysters
2 tablespoons red wine
Juice of 1 lemon

Oven: 350°F; gas mark 4; 45 minutes

Line a 3 pt pie dish with pastry. Leave the salmon steaks in boiling water for a few minutes; drain and remove the skin. Cook the breadcrumbs and mushrooms in 1 oz of butter; blend in the cooked flaked salmon and eel and season to taste with salt, pepper, ground cloves and nutmeg. Remove from the heat and bind this stuffing with the lightly beaten eggs and a little milk.

Arrange the salmon steaks over the pastry base, cover with the stuffing and sprinkle with a few breadcrumbs and a little melted butter. Place the cleaned oysters round the salmon. Boil the remaining butter with the wine and lemon juice and pour over the salmon. Bake in the oven for 45 minutes.

Smoked Salmon

Scotch smoked salmon is considered the finest.
The cleaned and boned whole salmon is dry
salted for a number of hours and then cold
smoked over a juniper fire. Fresh smoked salmon
command the highest prices, while imported
products are generally less expensive though
also drier and less succulent.

St Andrew's Platter (8 portions) H
Scotland

An elaborate first course suitable for hungry
golf players.

1½ pt salad dressing
8 slices smoked salmon
8 fillets smoked trout
1 doz cooked shelled mussels
2 hardboiled eggs
8 lemon wedges
1 lettuce
Watercress
3-4 lemons
Paprika

Put the salad dressing in a bowl and set in the
centre of a large round platter. Arrange the salmon,
trout, mussels, egg slices and lemon wedges on a
bed of lettuce and watercress sprigs round the
bowl; sprinkle the salmon and trout with the
strained juice of two lemons. Dust the salad dressing with paprika and arrange half lemon slices,
slit nearly through, over the edge of the bowl.
Serve with hot toast.

Devilled Smoked Salmon (6 portions) H

Connoisseurs of smoked salmon insist that it
should be served plainly, with buttered brown
bread, lemon wedges, and possibly a dusting of
cayenne pepper. This is a slightly more sophisticated version.

1 lb smoked salmon
8 slices toast
2 oz butter
Salt and pepper
4 oz curry butter
Garnish: parsley sprigs

Oven: 400°F; gas mark 6; 5 minutes

Trim the crusts off the toast, butter one side
and sprinkle with salt and pepper. Cover with

thin slices of smoked salmon, spread with curry
butter and place in a hot oven for a few
minutes. Garnish with parsley and serve at once.

Smoked Salmon Salad (6-8 portions)
H and F

This appetising salad, suitable as a cold lunch
main course, can be made with the oddments
left on a salmon skin.

½ lb smoked salmon
12 anchovy fillets
1 lb boiled cold potatoes
2 oz cheese
6 oz cored, peeled apples
2 oz celery
2 crisp lettuce hearts
2 sweet pickled gherkins
3 fl oz claret
5 fl oz salad dressing
Garnish: peeled prawns, watercress,
        2 hardboiled eggs

Dice the salmon, anchovies, potatoes, cheese,
apples and celery and mix with the shredded
lettuce and finely chopped gherkins. Put all
the ingredients into a deep bowl, pour over
the claret and marinate for 5-10 minutes. Mix in
the salad dressing, turning thoroughly. Garnish
with prawns, watercress sprigs and slices of hardboiled eggs. Serve in the bowl or arrange in
individual glasses for a first course.

Smoked Salmon with Prawns (8 portions)
H

Whole smoked salmon should be cut across the
grain, in wafer-thin slices, starting from the tail
end. Serve with buttered wholemeal bread or
hot oatcakes.

1 lb smoked salmon
½ lb peeled prawns or shrimps
Garnish: watercress sprigs or heart of lettuce,
        lemon wedges and cayenne pepper

Arrange the salmon slices in an overlapping pattern
on chilled plates. Garnish with a cluster of prawns
or shrimps, fringed with watercress or lettuce.
Place a lemon wedge on each portion and dust the
salmon with cayenne.

Shad, Grilled (6-8 portions) F

Shad is related to herring, but travels up rivers in
the spring to spawn; it is rapidly becoming extinct
due to pollution. Like the herring, shad has
numerous bones, but to compensate the roes,
and particularly the hard roes, are extremely
tasty. Baked, stuffed shad is a traditional dish; it
may also be fried or grilled and served with a
sorrel, capers or piquant sauce.

3 lb shad
3 fl oz oil
1 dessertspoon chopped onion
1 tablespoon finely chopped parsley
Salt and pepper

Wash, clean and scale the fish; dry well. Place in a
deep dish; pour over the oil and add the onion,
parsley, salt and pepper. Leave the shad in this
marinade for 2 hours, basting frequently. Drain
and dry the shad. Put under a medium hot grill for
15 minutes, turning frequently and brushing
occasionally with the oil in which the fish was
marinated.

Tench with Herbs (8 portions) H Dorset

Tench lives in shallow muddy ponds and lakes;
they need careful cleaning to remove all traces of
mud. May be cooked like perch and brown trout,
but the delicate flavour is improved by marinating
for a couple of hours.

8 tench (6-8 oz each)
4 oz sliced onions
1 finely chopped shallot
1 tablespoon finely chopped parsley
Ground thyme
Salt and pepper
Olive oil

Wash the tench, pull out the entrails and remove
the gills. Cover with boiling water for 5 minutes,
then dry and scale carefully. Lay the tench in a
deep dish, sprinkle with onions and shallot,
parsley, a pinch of thyme and salt and pepper.
Pour over enough oil to cover and leave the
tench in this marinade for 1-2 hours.

Lift out and drain the tench; wrap individually
in paper, liberally brushed with oil. Grill under
fierce heat or bake in the oven (400°F; gas mark
6) for 10-15 minutes. Remove from the paper,
arrange on a hot dish and serve with lemon,
mustard or piquant sauce.

Trout

The native trout caught in shallow rivers and
lakes is light brown to black, with an average
weight of 6-8 oz. Trout from deep, swift-running rivers are more silvery and considerably
larger. The rainbow trout was introduced from
Canada and North America in the late 19th
century to breed in reservoirs and lakes; the
experiment has not been wholly successful, and
supplies have to be maintained with trout reared
on fish farms. Frozen trout are imported in great
quantities.

Trout, Buttered (8 portions) H and F

Absolutely fresh trout require nothing but the
plainest cooking; as an extra touch, flaked
blanched almonds can be be fried golden in butter
and poured over the cooked trout.

8 trout (6 oz each)
Salt
2 oz seasoned flour
4 oz butter
Lemon juice

Clean the fish; sprinkle with salt inside and out
and leave for about 1 hour. Wipe the fish and
coat with seasoned flour. Fry the trout in hot
butter for 2-4 minutes on each side. Stir lemon
juice into the butter in the pan and pour over
the trout.

Trout Fried in Oatmeal (8 portions) F
Scotland

Equally suitable for breakfast, lunch, high tea and
supper, this dish may also be made with herrings.

8 trout (6 oz each)
Salt
5 fl oz milk
3 oz coarse oatmeal
4 oz lard
4 oz lemon butter

Gut and clean the trout; wipe thoroughly and
sprinkle the insides with salt. Dip in milk and
coat thickly with oatmeal. Fry in hot lard over
high heat for 2-3 minutes on each side. Drain
and serve with lemon butter.

Trout Montrose (8 portions) H Scotland

Locally, this rich dish is made with the brown trout freshly caught in the North Esk river near Montrose.

8 trout (6 oz each)
1 oz chopped shallot
½ pt fish stock
Juice of 1 lemon
Salt and pepper
2 oz fresh tomato pulp
½ pt double cream
4 egg yolks
5 fl oz whisky
½ lb butter
Garnish: 4 oz shelled prawns

Oven: 350°F; gas mark 4; 30 minutes

Clean and gut the trout. Sprinkle the shallot over the base of a buttered ovenproof dish; lay the trout on top. Pour over the fish stock and lemon juice; season with salt and pepper and bake for 30 minutes. Remove the trout from the oven; drain and skin on both sides.

Arrange the trout on a serving dish and keep warm. Add the tomato pulp to the cooking liquid, reduce by half and add half the cream; bring to just below boiling point. Beat the egg yolks with the remaining cream and the whisky, add to the reduced cooking liquid and heat through to thicken; blend in pats of butter and adjust seasoning.

Coat the trout with the sauce and garnish with the prawns heated in a little butter.

Trout Rob Roy (8 portions) H Scotland

It is possible that fresh river trout was a favourite dish of Robert McGregor (1671-1734), nick-named Rob Roy, but it is doubtful that asparagus and tomatoes came readily to hand in the High-lands where he lived as an outlaw.

8 trout (6 oz each)
2 oz seasoned flour
4 oz butter
4 oz white breadcrumbs
4 oz fine oatmeal
5 fl oz oil
Garnish: 24 cooked asparagus tips, 1 lb quartered
tomatoes, 2 sliced lemons, parsley sprigs

Clean and bone the trout, cut each into two

fillets. Coat the trout with seasoned flour, then pass first through half the melted butter, then through the mixed breadcrumbs and oatmeal. Fry the trout in the hot oil and remaining butter for 5 minutes, turning once. Serve garnished with asparagus tips, tomatoes, lemon and parsley.

Trout Usquebaugh (8 portions) H Stirling

This dish is known in Ireland as well as in Scot-land; the word *usquebaugh* comes from the Gaelic and literally translated means water of life, obviously synonymous with whisky!

8 trout (6 oz each)
2 oz seasoned flour
4 oz butter
5 fl oz whisky
1½ lb skinned, chopped tomatoes
1 lb sliced mushrooms
¾ lb finely sliced onions
1 teaspoon chopped dill
Capers
½ pt double cream
Garnish: chopped parsley

Clean the trout and coat with seasoned flour. Fry the trout in the butter over gentle heat, turning once. Lift on to a serving dish and keep warm. Add the whisky, tomatoes, mushrooms, onions, dill and a few capers to the pan. Cook gently until thoroughly heated through, then stir in the cream. Pour the sauce over the fish and garnish with parsley.

Trout, Stuffed (8 portions) H and F

A delicate stuffing, such as veal or herb-flavoured breadcrumbs with butter, goes well with trout and makes a more substantial dish.

8 trout (6 oz each)
½ lb veal forcemeat
4 oz butter
6 fl oz white wine
1 oz flour
1 oz capers
1 teaspoon lemon juice
Anchovy essence
Salt and pepper

Oven: 350°F; gas mark 4; 30 minutes

Gut and clean the trout. Stuff with the forcemeat and close the openings with skewers. Place in a buttered ovenproof dish, add 3 oz of butter and the wine. Cover with a lid or foil and bake for 30 minutes, basting frequently. Lift out the trout, remove skewers and arrange the fish on a serving dish; keep warm.

Melt the remaining butter, stir in the flour and gradually add the strained cooking liquid. Stir until boiling, then add the capers, lemon juice, anchovy essence, salt and pepper to taste. Simmer for 2-3 minutes, pour the sauce over the trout and serve.

SHELLFISH

Shellfish have been an important food in the British Isles since time immemorable. Our earliest forefathers probably gathered cockles and whelks, limpets and mussels at low tide to supplement their sparse diet long before the most primitive fishing craft was developed. Excavations of Roman sites have revealed quantities of oyster shells, and lobsters and mussels featured prominently at early medieval banquets. Today, shellfish chiefly refers to crabs and lobsters, mussels and prawns, oysters and scallops, all highly expensive delicacies. The stalls with cockles, whelks and winkles so beloved in Victorian and Edwardian days and a highlight on the annual pilgrimage to the seaside are now fading memories of a bygone age.

Crab

A grey-brown crustacean which turns reddish-brown when boiled. A crab should feel heavy for its size and have both claws attached; the body shell contains the brown meat, together with the entrails, and the white flaky meat is found in the claws. One medium-sized crab, about 3 lb in weight, will serve two persons.

Crab, Buttered (6-8 portions) H and F

This may be served as a first course or as a light luncheon dish.

2 large boiled crabs
2 anchovy fillets
½ pt white wine
3 oz breadcrumbs
Salt and pepper
Grated nutmeg
3 oz melted butter

Remove the brown and white crab meat from the shell and claws. Mash the anchovy fillets with wine and breadcrumbs. Season to taste with salt, pepper and nutmeg; put the mixture in a pan, bring to the boil and simmer for 5 minutes. Mix the flaked crab meat with the butter and add to the pan, cook for a further 4 minutes. Serve on hot buttered toast.

Crab, Devilled (6-8 portions) H and F

Made in small individual dishes, this makes a good first course, with fingers of hot buttered toast.

½ lb crab meat
2 oz finely chopped onions
½ diced green pepper
1 oz butter
1 oz flour
½ pt milk
2-3 oz fresh white breadcrumbs
1 tablespoon Worcestershire sauce
1 tablespoon made mustard
4 oz grated cheese
Salt and pepper
Garnish: chopped parsley

Oven: 375°F; gas mark 5; 15-20 minutes

Fry the onions and green pepper gently in the butter for 10 minutes, without taking colour. Add the flour and cook for 2-3 minutes, gradually stir in the milk and bring to the boil. Add the crab meat, breadcrumbs, Worcestershire sauce, mustard and 2 oz of cheese, season with salt and pepper and spoon into individual dishes. Sprinkle with the remaining cheese and bake in the oven for 20 minutes or until lightly brown. Garnish with finely chopped parsley and serve.

Crab, Dressed (4 portions) H and F

One of the most popular ways of serving crab, usually with buttered brown bread and a green salad.

2 medium-sized boiled crabs
3-4 oz fresh white breadcrumbs
Salt and pepper
Lemon juice
1 tablespoon salad oil
2 tablespoons white wine vinegar
Garnish: 2 hardboiled eggs, chopped parsley

Remove the brown meat from the shells and the white meat from the large claws. Clean the shells thoroughly. Mix the dark meat with breadcrumbs, salt, pepper and lemon juice to taste. Arrange this mixture against the outer shorter sides of the shells. Flake the white meat and mix with oil and vinegar. Season and arrange in the centre of the shells. Garnish with sieved egg yolk, chopped egg white and parsley and sieved crab coral if available; decorate with the small claws.

Dorset Scalloped Crab (6 portions) H and F Dorset

An attractive starter served in well-scrubbed scallop shells arranged round a crab shell and garnished with small parsley sprigs.

2 medium-sized boiled crabs
2-3 chopped anchovies
6 scallop shells
2½ tablespoons white wine vinegar
2 oz butter
4 oz breadcrumbs
Salt and cayenne pepper
Garnish: parsley sprigs
Oven: 350°F; gas mark 4; 10 minutes

Remove the crab meat from shells and claws. Mix with the anchovies and put in a pan with the vinegar, butter and 3 oz of the breadcrumbs; season with salt and cayenne. Heat through for a few minutes. Fill one cleaned crab shell with part of the mixture and fill the scallop shells with the remainder; sprinkle with breadcrumbs and brown in the oven for 10 minutes.

Partan Pies (8 portions) H and F Scotland

Young crabs with soft shells are known as partans in Scotland; they are usually returned to the sea, but are occasionally used in cooking, coated with egg and breadcrumbs, deep-fried and served with lemon wedges.

8 small boiled crabs
Salt, pepper, grated nutmeg
4 oz fresh white breadcrumbs
4 oz softened butter
5 fl oz vinegar

Pick out the meat from the claws and shells; scrub the shells well. Season the meat with salt, pepper and nutmeg and mix in the breadcrumbs and butter, cut into small pieces. Add the vinegar

which may be mixed and heated with a little made mustard. Return the mixture to the shells and brown under a hot grill.

Crayfish

A freshwater crustacean, resembling a small lobster and cooked as such. Once prolific in inland streams, crayfish have become practically extinct in Britain due to pollution.

Crayfish with Butter and Lemon (6 portions) H and F Yorkshire

Crayfish were formerly fished in the streams of the Yorkshire dales in August; they were traditionally cooked on an open fire and eaten with butter and lemon juice.

3 doz crayfish
4 oz melted butter
Lemon juice

Plunge the crayfish into rapidly boiling salted water and boil for 10-15 minutes or until bright red. Rinse in cold water and remove the shells. Serve cold with lemon, brown bread and butter like fresh prawns, or put the crayfish under the grill to heat through. Serve with melted butter and lemon juice.

Limpet

A small mollusc with a conical grooved shell. Limpets are found clinging to rocks off the seashore at the Isle of Man and off Scotland; they must be prised off at low tide.

Limpet Stovies (8 portions) F Scotland

The term "stovie" is said to be a Scottish corruption of the French estuvier meaning to shut up; another more logical interpretation of the word is "cooked on the stove".

4 pt limpets
Peeled potatoes
Salt and pepper
½ lb butter

Put the fresh limpets in a deep pan, cover with water and bring to the boil. Rinse the limpets in cold water, pick them out of the shells and remove the eyes and sandy trails.

Weigh the shelled limpets and take three times

the amount of peeled potatoes; put a layer of
sliced potatoes in a large fireproof pot, add a
layer of limpets and season with salt and pepper.
Continue with these layers, finishing with potatoes.
Pour over two cups of the strained liquid in which
the limpets were scalded; top with pieces of butter.
Cover with a tightly fitting lid, bring to the boil
and simmer very slowly for at least 1 hour.

Lobster

This crustacean is one of the most highly priced
and appreciated of all shellfish. It should ideally
be bought fresh, at the height of the season during
the summer months; the shell is then bluish-
black but turns bright red during boiling. The male
is smaller than the female, but with larger claws;
the female, however, contains eggs known as the
coral considered a great delicacy and used for
garnishing and in lobster sauces and butter.

Lobster Arbroath Style (8 portions) H
Scotland

A rich main course dish for a special occasion and
ideally arranged, with the elaborate garnishes, on a
silver salver.

4 boiled lobsters
½ lb butter
32 boiled mussels
½ lb shelled shrimps
8 large mushrooms
1 pt fish stock
1 pt red wine
2 oz flour
Salt and pepper
Juice of 1 lemon
2½ fl oz cream
2-3 oz grated cheese
Garnish: ½ lb turned mushrooms, 8 anchovy
    fillets, parsley sprigs

Split the lobsters in half and remove the flesh
from the body and claws. Slice the lobster meat
into thick pieces and cook in 2 oz of butter
together with the mussels and shrimps. Slice the
mushrooms and cook lightly in a little butter;
line the cleaned lobster shells with the mushrooms.
Bring the stock and red wine to the boil; cook
rapidly until reduced by about half; knead 2 oz
of butter with the flour and use to thicken the
liquid. Season with salt and pepper, add the
lemon juice and cream.

Bind the lobster mixture with a little of the
sauce and pile into the lobster shells. Coat with
the remaining sauce, sprinkle with cheese and
put under a hot grill to glaze. Meanwhile, cook
the turned mushrooms in a little butter and split
the anchovies in half. Arrange the glazed lobsters
on a serving dish and garnish each with turned
mushrooms and anchovy fillets in a lattice pattern.
Arrange parsley sprigs between the shells.

Lobster, Buttered (8 portions) H

Many people consider the delicious lobster at its
best when cooked and served quite plain, without any trimmings. For a cold course, the boiled
lobster meat can be simply dressed with oil and
vinegar, salt and pepper and returned to the
shells with capers and slices of hardboiled egg.

4 boiled lobsters
3 oz butter
3 tablespoons double cream
Browned breadcrumbs

Split the lobsters in half, remove the meat from
shells and claws and cut into chunky pieces.
Scrub the shells. Melt the butter in a pan and
toss the lobster meat until heated. Spoon into
the warmed shells. Stir the cream into the pan
juices, pour over the lobsters and serve at once,
sprinkled with browned crumbs.

Lobster, Devilled (8 portions) H

Any coral in the lobsters can be sieved and added
to the finished sauce. Arrange the lobster shells on
a bed of crisp lettuce.

4 boiled lobsters
6 oz butter
4 oz white breadcrumbs
5 fl oz white sauce or cream
Cayenne pepper
Browned breadcrumbs

Oven: 350°F; gas mark 4; 20 minutes

Cut the lobsters in half lengthways, remove the
meat from the shells and claws and cut into dice.
Melt 2 oz of the butter, pour over the lobster
meat and add the white breadcrumbs and the
sauce. Season highly with cayenne and mix well.
Divide the mixture between the cleaned shells,
cover with browned breadcrumbs. Top with the
remaining butter, cut into slices, and bake in the
oven. Serve hot.

Lobster in Speyside Sauce (8 portions) H Scotland

This is a substantial main course dish, attractive also to the eye with saffron-coloured rice arranged in a circle round the rich lobster mixture.

4 boiled lobsters
3 oz butter
4 oz sliced shallots
5 oz sliced mushrooms
2 oz sliced onions
4 oz rice
8 fl oz white stock
1 bay leaf
Salt and pepper
Pinch saffron
5 fl oz whisky
Ground cloves
½ pt double cream
10 oz skinned, diced tomatoes

Oven: 325°F; gas mark 3; 15-20 minutes

Remove the meat from the lobsters and cut into pieces. Melt 2 oz of the butter and fry the shallots until soft, add the mushrooms and lobster meat, mixing well. Cover and cook over very gentle heat for 3 minutes. Sweat the onions and rice in the remaining butter without colouring, add the stock, bay leaf, salt and pepper and saffron. Bring to the boil, cover and cook in the oven for about 15 minutes.

Warm the whisky, set it alight and when the flames have died down pour over the lobster meat. Season with black pepper and cloves; add the cream. Shake gently over the heat until well mixed, cover and keep hot without boiling for 5 minutes. Add the tomatoes immediately before serving. Arrange the lobster mixture in the centre of a serving dish and surround with the boiled rice.

Lobster Hebridean (8 portions) H Scotland

Turned mushrooms usually garnish grilled meat, but they also go surprisingly well with grilled lobster. They should first be cooked in a little butter. Hebridean lobsters are traditionally served on napkins.

4 boiled lobsters
2 oz butter
3 tablespoons Drambuie

½ pt double cream
2 pt cheese sauce
8-16 turned mushrooms
2 oz grated Parmesan cheese
Garnish: parsley sprigs

Split the lobsters in half, remove the meat from the shells and claws and cut into ½ in thick pieces. Clean the shells. Melt the butter in a pan and toss the lobster meat; flame the Drambuie and pour over; add the cream. Remove from the heat and bind the mixture with warm cheese sauce.

Spoon the lobster mixture into the warmed shells and decorate with turned mushrooms. Sprinkle with Parmesan cheese and brown under a hot grill. Garnish with parsley and serve at once.

Mussel

One of the most underrated of shellfish, in spite of being abundant and relatively inexpensive. The blue-black shell of this mollusc encloses an orange coloured morsel of sweet and tender flesh. In season from September to April, mussels can be served as a first or a main course; allow 1½ pt to each person.

Mussel and Onion Stew (6 portions) H and F Scotland

Certainly known in the early Middle Ages, this mussel stew makes a satisfying main course. The mussels must be thoroughly scrubbed and any that are broken or refuse to close when tapped should be discarded.

9 pt mussels
12½ fl oz dry white wine
¾ lb chopped onions
4 oz butter
2 oz flour
1 pt warm milk
Salt and pepper
1½ oz chopped parsley
½ pt cream

Wash and scrub the mussels in several lots of water to remove sand and grit; discard any that are broken or remain open. Scrape away the beards and any barnacles with a sharp knife. Put the mussels in a large pan, add the wine and bring to the boil. Simmer gently for 5-10 minutes or until the mussels have all opened. Lift out the mussels, strain the liquid through fine muslin and set aside. Remove the mussels from the shells.

Cook the onions in half the butter until soft and translucent. Melt the remaining butter, stir in the flour and gradually add the mussel liquid, stirring all the time. Stir in the milk and the cooked onions; simmer for a few minutes. Season with salt and pepper; add the parsley, mussels and cream; heat through over gentle heat without boiling. Serve in soup plates.

Ormer

The ormer is a mollusc also known as the sea ear from its ear-like shape. It is yellow-white in colour with brown-mottled, yellow flesh that is rubbery and needs prolonged cooking. Found only around the coasts of the Channel Islands.

Ormer Casserole (6-8 portions) H and F Channel Islands

This is a 19th century speciality of Guernsey and considered a great delicacy. Ormers can by law only be caught at certain "ormering tides" during the winter; after removal from the shells, the ormers are cut into slices and beaten repeatedly with a kitchen mallet to break down the fibres and tenderise the flesh. Unbeaten ormers are too tough to be eaten.

16 ormers
5 oz butter
Faggot of herbs
½ pt white wine
5 fl oz water
3 oz chopped shallots
4 oz sliced mushrooms
1 oz flour
4 oz skinned and chopped tomatoes
2 tablespoons cream
3 oz grated cheese

Fry the sliced and thoroughly beaten ormers in 3 oz of butter to seal; add the herbs, cover with wine and water and simmer for at least 2 hours or until tender. Melt the remaining butter in a pan, add the shallots and mushrooms and cook gently for 2 minutes. Stir the flour into the shallot mixture; gradually add the cooking liquid from the ormers and bring to the boil, stirring continuously.

Draw the pan from the heat and add the tomatoes, cream, ormers and half the grated cheese. Transfer to a shallow fireproof serving dish, sprinkle with the remaining cheese and grill until brown. Serve hot with a green salad.

Oyster

Until the middle of the 19th century, oysters were everyday fare, and the oyster stalls did thriving business on Saturday nights serving huge portions of oysters seasoned with pepper and vinegar. The oyster beds have never recovered from the then indiscriminate depletion, and more than a century later the oyster in Britain is reserved for upper income brackets.

Oyster Attelets (6 portions) H

The luxury oyster is traditionally served raw in its flat shell, set on a bed of ice and accompanied with brown bread and butter. When cooked, they are usually grilled; the oyster liquid can be used to flavour any accompanying sauce.

32 large oysters
4 sweetbreads
½ lb bacon rashers
1 dessertspoon finely chopped parsley
4 oz finely chopped shallots
Ground thyme
Salt and pepper
1 egg
2 oz white breadcrumbs
Fat for frying

Remove the oysters from the shells, saving the liquid for a white sauce. Cut the sweetbreads into small chunks and the bacon into narrow strips. Sprinkle the oysters, bacon and sweetbreads with parsley, shallots, thyme, pepper and salt.

Thread the oysters on to skewers, alternating with bacon and sweetbreads; coat in beaten egg and breadcrumbs and fry in shallow fat until light brown. Arrange the skewers on a dish; offer crusty bread and an oyster flavoured sauce.

Prawns and Shrimps

Prawn and the related shrimp are small crustaceans, the prawn being the larger of the two, about 4 in long; it is grey when caught and pink when boiled. Shrimps come in two varieties, the brown which turns even browner during boiling and the grey variety which turns pink. Both prawns and shrimps are sold cooked, prawns shelled or unshelled, shrimps in their shells.

Dublin Bay Prawns (6-8 portions) H

Freshly cooked and shelled prawns and shrimps are chiefly used for garnishing, although large prawns can also be served as a first course with brown bread and butter and lemon wedges. The true Dublin Bay prawn is the largest native prawn, but Norwegian lobsters and Pacific prawns are often sold as Dublin Bay prawns.

2 lb Dublin Bay prawns
3 oz butter
Salt
Juice of 1 lemon

If alive, steam the prawns over boiling water for 20 minutes, leave to cool and shell. Melt the butter in a pan and gently toss the prawns in the hot butter. Sprinkle with salt and lemon juice. Serve hot, with brown bread and butter.

Scallop

A mollusc enclosed by a ribbed, pinkish-brown, hinged shell, one part of which is flat and the other curved. The highly nutritious flesh is white with a prominent orange roe. The rounded shells make excellent individual serving dishes.

Scallops, Baked (6-8 portions) H

For a main course, allow four scallops per person and serve with a green salad and brown bread and butter.

24-32 scallops
½ lb fresh white breadcrumbs
1 dessertspoon finely chopped parsley
1 oz chopped shallot
Salt and pepper
Juice of 2 lemons
4 oz melted butter
Paprika

Oven: 425°F; gas mark 7; 20 minutes

Remove the scallops from the opened shells; scrub the rounded shells well, and cut the beards and black threads from the scallops. Mix half the breadcrumbs with parsley, shallot, salt and pepper. Line the scallop shells with this mixture.
  Put the scallops back into the shells and sprinkle with the remaining breadcrumbs. Moisten with lemon juice and melted butter and bake in the oven. Dust with paprika and serve.

Scallops, Fried (6-8 portions) H Huntingdon

For this starter, the scallops may be left whole or cut into thick slices.

8 large scallops
1 tablespoon olive oil
Juice of 1 lemon
Salt and pepper
1 dessertspoon chopped parsley
4 oz minced ham
4 oz fresh white breadcrumbs
1 oz grated Parmesan cheese
2 oz chopped onions
Seasoned flour
2 eggs
Oil for frying
Garnish: lemon wedges

Mix the olive oil and lemon juice with salt and pepper; stir in the parsley. Marinate the cleaned scallops in this mixture for 30 minutes. Mix the ham with the breadcrumbs, cheese and onions.
  Drain the scallops, coat in seasoned flour and dip in the lightly beaten eggs. Coat with the ham mixture, pressing it in firmly. Heat the oil in a deep-frier and fry the scallops in the hot fat until brown and crisp. Drain and serve hot, garnished with wedges of lemon.

Scallops, Sherried (6-8 portions) H

Scallops are often sold already opened and cleaned. To open the closed shells of live scallops place them, rounded shell up, in a low oven for about 5 minutes or until the shells open. The following recipe is for a main course, to be served with buttered cauliflower.

24-32 scallops
½ pt medium dry sherry
½ pt water
2 oz butter
Salt and pepper
Garnish: chopped parsley

Remove the scallops from the shells and take off the beards and black threads. Cut the white flesh into cubes about 1 in across, leaving the corals whole. Put the white and orange scallop flesh in a pan with sherry and water, cover and bring to the boil. Simmer gently for about 30 minutes. Lift out and drain.

Melt the butter in a pan, add the scallops and season with salt and pepper. Cook over low heat until heated through. Put the scallops in a serving dish to keep warm. Raise the heat and pour the fish and sherry liquid into the hot butter; boil rapidly until reduced by half. Pour over the scallops; garnish with parsley and serve.

Scallops on Skewers (8 portions) H

This is intended for a first course, to be served with crusty bread and a tomato sauce. For a main course, allow two skewers per person and serve with rice instead of bread.

12 scallops
8 thinly sliced long rashers of bacon
Salt and pepper
Lemon juice
1 egg (optional)
Breadcrumbs (optional)
16 button mushrooms
2 oz melted butter

Clean the scallops, remove the coral and cut the white part of each scallop into two or three pieces. Cut the bacon, rind removed, into an equal number of pieces. Season the white scallop meat with salt and pepper and sprinkle with lemon juice; wrap in a piece of bacon. Cut the corals in half and dip in beaten egg and breadcrumbs.

Thread the corals, bacon-wrapped scallops and mushrooms on to skewers; brush with melted butter and grill for 8-10 minutes or until the bacon is crisp, turning several times.

FISH OFFAL

Today, the roes of cod and herring are the only internal organs commonly used, but in former days many other parts and fish trimmings were everyday fare, stuffed and dressed cod and haddock heads, for example, being considered delicacies. A number of dishes indigenous to Shetland were known outside the isles; Pepys mentions having dined on cod sounds — the swimming bladder of cod — in a white sauce. *Muggies* were another popular dish in Shetland

and could be made with either ling or cod liver, stuffed with oatmeal into a fish stomach bag (muggie) and boiled. Fish liver in general featured strongly in the islanders' diet: *krappen* consisted of cod or haddock heads stuffed with oatmeal and fish liver; *krolls* was the local name for small oatmeal and water cakes filled with sillock livers; *koggs* were similar, hollowed-out potatoes enclosing the liver.

Cod Roe (8 portions) F Ireland

The soft male roe and the hard, pinkish female roe are usually sold already boiled. The female roe is also sold smoked. Fried cod roe with bacon is a favourite breakfast dish in many parts of the British Isles, notably Cornwall and Ireland; in other areas, cod roe with parsley sauce is a popular high-tea dish.

2 lb boiled cod roe
4 oz seasoned flour
8 slices bacon
Fat for frying

Skin the roe and cut into ½-1 in thick slices; coat in seasoned flour. Fry the bacon in hot fat and keep warm. Fry the roe until golden brown, for about 6 minutes, turning once. Serve the roe and bacon together.

Cropadeu (6 portions) F Hebrides

This dish is a Hebridean version of the Scottish *Crappit Heids* — haddock or whiting heads stuffed with a coarse forcemeat of oatmeal, suet, onions, salt and pepper. In Shetland, the same dish is known as *Liver Krus*.

½ lb oatmeal
Haddock liver
Salt and pepper

Make a large dumpling with oatmeal and water. Put a haddock liver in the centre, season with salt and pepper. Tie the dumpling securely in a cloth, leaving room for the oatmeal to expand. Cook in boiling, salted water for about 1½ hours. Serve hot.

Herring Roes (6 portions) F

Soft and hard herring roes are sold, the soft, creamy roes being the most popular. They are used for stuffings or pastes, but may also be baked as below and served as a high-tea dish, with wedges of lemon.

1½ lb herring roes
4-6 oz browned breadcrumbs
Salt and pepper
3 fl oz vinegar
6 oz melted butter

Oven: 350°F; gas mark 4; 15-20 minutes

Blanch the roes in boiling water for a few minutes, refresh in cold water and simmer in gently boiling water for 10 minutes. Butter an ovenproof dish, arrange a layer of breadcrumbs over the base and cover with roes; sprinkle with salt and pepper. Repeat these layers, finishing with breadcrumbs. Pour over the vinegar and brush with butter. Bake in the oven for about 20 minutes.

Roe Cakes (8 portions) F Shetland

Fried herring roes make a nourishing breakfast or high-tea dish on a cold winter's day.

2½ lb herring roes
½ lb flour
Pinch cream of tartar
½ teaspoon baking powder
½ teaspoon bicarbonate of soda
Salt and pepper
4 eggs
½ pt milk
Dripping or butter

Boil the roes gently for about 10 minutes; drain, leave to cool, then mash with a fork. Blend the flour, cream of tartar, baking powder and soda into the roes, season with salt and pepper. Add the beaten eggs and milk, mixing thoroughly.

Melt dripping or butter in a pan until smoking hot; put spoonfuls of the roe mixture in the fat and fry until golden brown, after 5-7 minutes. Drain and serve at once.

Slot (8 portions) F Shetland

Traditional to Shetland, individual recipes for this supper dish still vary, but all have in common the dominant flavour of cod roe over that of fish liver.

2 lb cod roe
1 ling liver (optional)
4 oz seasoned flour
3-4 pt fish stock or water

Skin and mash the roe, add the liver and enough seasoned flour to bind; beat until thoroughly mixed. Have ready a pan of boiling fish stock or boiled salted water. Dip a dessertspoon in boiling liquid; scoop out a portion of the roe mixture and drop into the liquid; simmer gently for 20-25 minutes. Lift out the small dumplings as they rise to the surface; drain and serve at once.

Alternatively, shape the roe mixture into balls, simmer in boiling water for 20-25 minutes, drain and leave to cool. Cut the balls into ½ in slices and fry in hot fat or butter. Serve hot.

FISH PIES AND PUDDINGS

Pies and puddings were probably developed among the poorer population as economy measures. Apart from the obvious advantage of sealing in the flavour, a pastry covering would not only stretch a given ingredient further, but would also provide a complete meal in one cooking operation. Savoury shortcrust and puff pastries were most commonly used, but mashed potatoes also appeared as pie covers. Suet pastry has almost completely disappeared in the making of fish puddings; boiled mussel and Hastings boiled gurnet puddings, for example, are now merely historic curiosities. Gloucester's Royal Pie, a lamprey pie gloriously decorated with truffles and crayfish, was sent annually to the King by the Corporation of Gloucester — a tradition maintained from the time of Henry I until 1835.

Conger Eel Pie (6-8 portions) F

This pie is covered with puff pastry; in the Cornish version, beaten eggs, butter and milk are poured over the chopped eel and topped with browned breadcrumbs.

3 lb skinned and boned conger eel
½ oz butter
2 oz finely chopped onions
2 teaspoons chopped parsley
½ teaspoon mixed herbs
Salt and pepper
1 tablespoon vinegar
½-¾ pt fish stock
½ lb puff pastry
1 egg

Oven: 450°F; gas mark 8; 15 minutes;
      350°F; gas mark 4; 30-45 minutes

Cut the eel into 1 in pieces. Butter a 2½ pt pie dish and layer the eel pieces with onions; sprinkle each layer with parsley, mixed herbs, salt and pepper. Add the vinegar and enough fish stock to come three quarters up the side of the dish.

Cover the pie dish with pastry and brush with beaten egg mixed with a little water or milk; bake in the oven at 450°F (gas mark 8) for 15 minutes, then reduce the heat to 350°F (gas mark 4) for a further 30-45 minutes.

East Ham Eel Pie (6-8 portions) F and H London

In the 19th century, eel, mussel and oyster stalls abounded in London's East End. Jellied eels, eels with mashed potatoes and parsley sauce, and individual eel pies were favourite standbys. In Cornwall, a similar eel pie was flavoured with currants and covered with suet paste.

3 lb skinned eels
½ pt fish stock
Salt and pepper
Pinch mixed herbs
4 oz sliced onions
1 tablespoon lemon juice
½ lb savoury shortcrust pastry
1 egg

Oven: 425°F; gas mark 7; 45 minutes

Cut the eels into small pieces and place in a pan with the eel trimmings. Add the stock, salt and pepper, herbs and onions; simmer gently until the eel pieces are tender enough for the bones to be removed. Strain the stock, arrange the boned eel in a 2½ pt pie dish and add lemon juice and enough stock to cover the eels.

Cover with pastry; brush with beaten egg and bake in the oven. A little extra stock may be poured through the centre hole of the pie just before serving.

Eel-Pie Island Pie (6-8 portions) F and H Surrey

Eel-Pie Island near Richmond on the Thames achieved its name from the famous pies that for nearly two centuries drew visitors from far afield, there to savour eels from the river and to argue whether the pies were better hot or cold.

3 lb skinned eels
2 chopped shallots
4 oz butter
1 dessertspoon chopped parsley
Salt, pepper and nutmeg
½ pt dry sherry or white wine
4 oz flour
Juice of 1 lemon
3 sliced hardboiled eggs
1¼ lb puff pastry
1 egg

Oven: 450°F; gas mark 8; 15 minutes
       350°F; gas mark 4; 45 minutes

Cut the eels into pieces and leave whole or remove the bones. Cook the shallots in half the butter for a few minutes without colouring, add the parsley, nutmeg, salt, pepper and the sherry or white wine. Put the eels into this mixture, with enough water to cover; bring slowly to the boil. When boiling point is reached, remove the eels and arrange in a 2½ pt pie dish.

Melt the remaining butter; stir in the flour and gradually add the strained cooking liquid. Bring to the boil. Add the lemon juice, correct seasoning and pour the sauce over the fish. Arrange slices of hardboiled eggs on top, cover with puff pastry and brush with beaten egg mixed with a little water or milk. Bake in the oven, at 450°F (gas mark 8) for 15 minutes, then reduce the heat to 350°F (gas mark 4) for 45 minutes.

Finnan Haddock Pie (6-8 portions) Scotland

A creamy pie, covered with a cheese-flavoured crumb topping.

1½ lb Finnan haddock
¾ pt milk
4 oz butter
4 oz finely chopped onions
6 oz flour
1 dessertspoon lemon juice
3 chopped, poached eggs
Salt and pepper
½ teaspoon dry mustard
3 oz finely grated cheese
Garnish: chopped chives or parsley

Oven: 400°F; gas mark 6; 20 minutes

Poach the haddock in milk for a few minutes; remove the fish and flake it. Strain the milk and set aside. Melt 2 oz of the butter in a pan, fry the onions until light brown, stir in 2 oz of flour and cook for 2 minutes. Remove from the heat and stir in the milk. Return to the heat and cook, stirring continuously until the sauce thickens. Stir in the lemon juice, eggs, flaked fish, salt, pepper and mustard.

Spoon the mixture into an ovenproof dish. Rub the last 2 oz of butter into the remaining flour for the crumb top, mix in the grated cheese and seasoning. Sprinkle over the fish mixture and bake for 20 minutes. Garnish with chives.

Fish Pie (6 portions) F

For this family-type fish pie, any type of white fish can be used — haddock, cod, whiting, etc. — and a pastry crust or mixed breadcrumbs and grated cheese can replace the mashed potatoes.

1 lb cooked fish
1 pt parsley sauce
Salt and pepper
2 oz butter
¾ lb mashed potatoes
1 egg

Oven: 350°F; gas mark 4; 20 minutes

Flake the cooked fish and stir into the parsley sauce. Season with salt and pepper and spoon into a well-buttered 2½ pt pie dish. Cover with mashed potatoes, brush with beaten egg and dot with the remaining butter. Bake in the oven for 20 minutes or until brown on top.

Haddock Patties (6-8 portions) F

These small, individual fish patties are served hot with a thick tomato sauce and potatoes.

2 lb smoked haddock
2 oz oatmeal
1 lb chopped onions
Juice of 1 lemon
2 oz butter
Salt and pepper
Flour

Oven: 350°F; gas mark 4; 20 minutes

Flake the haddock and put in a pan, with the oatmeal, onions, lemon juice and the butter. Simmer gently for about 20 minutes or until cooked through; season to taste with salt and

pepper. Pack the mixture into buttered patty tins, dust with flour and bake for 20 minutes.

Kipper and Capers Pie (6 portions) F and H

A well-flavoured kipper mixture enclosed in crisp puff pastry. Use the pastry trimmings for leaves with which to decorate the pie.

1 lb kipper fillets
2 oz butter
2 oz flour
1 pt milk
Salt and pepper
1½ oz capers
1 lb puff pastry
2 hardboiled eggs
1 egg

Oven: 425°F; gas mark 7; 30 minutes

Simmer the fish for about 7 minutes in boiling water; drain and flake. Melt the butter in a pan, add the flour and cook through; add the milk, bring to the boil and allow to thicken, stirring all the time. Season with salt and pepper; stir in the flaked fish and the capers. Leave to cool.

Roll out the pastry to a square 8 in by 8 in. Place the kipper mixture in the centre and cover with slices of hardboiled eggs. Brush the edges of the pastry with beaten egg, bring the four points to the centre in an envelope shape; pinch the edges together. Decorate with pastry leaves, set on a baking sheet and brush the pastry with egg; bake for about 30 minutes.

Kipper Cheese Puffs (8 portions) H

Suitable for a first course, these small pasties can be garnished with lemon wedges or pats of fish butter.

10 oz kipper fillets
1 oz butter
1 oz flour
½ pt milk
2 oz grated Lancashire cheese
Salt and pepper
¾ lb puff pastry
1 egg

Oven: 425°F; gas mark 7; 20-30 minutes

Poach the kipper fillets gently in water for 5-7

minutes; drain and chop into small pieces. Melt
the butter, stir in the flour and cook for 2-3
minutes without colouring, then add the fish stock
and gradually add the milk, stirring continuously.
Bring to the boil, stir in the grated cheese and
kipper pieces; season with salt and pepper.
Leave to cool.

Roll out the pastry to a rectangle 10 in by
20 in; trim the edges and cut into eight squares
5 in by 5 in. Place on a damp baking sheet;
spoon the kipper mixture on to the pastry
squares. Dampen the edges, fold over into triangles and seal firmly. Brush with beaten egg and
bake for 20-30 minutes or until golden.

Kipper Cream Pie (6 portions) H and F

For this creamy pie, which can be served hot or
cold, the pastry case is first baked blind for 15-20
minutes at 375°F, gas mark 5.

¾ lb kipper fillets
½ lb savoury shortcrust pastry
3 eggs
7½ fl oz double cream
Salt and pepper
1½ teaspoons made mustard
Garnish: lemon slices, chopped parsley

Oven: 350°F; gas mark 4; 30-35 minutes

Cut the kipper fillets into ½ in wide strips; line
an 8 in flan ring with the pastry and bake blind.
Arrange the kippers in the flan case; beat the
eggs with the cream, and season with salt, pepper
and mustard and pour over the fish. Bake
until set; garnish with lemon and parsley.

Kipper Patties (6-8 portions) H and F

Smoked haddock may be used instead of kippers
for these patties, suitable as a snack, savoury or a
first course.

1 lb whole kippers
¾ pt milk or milk and water
4 oz sliced onions
1½ oz butter
1½ oz flour
2-3 oz boiled rice
Salt and pepper

Bring the milk to the boil, add the kippers and
bring back to the boil. Remove from the heat

and leave for 5 minutes, turning the kippers over
once. Lift out the kippers and take off skin and
bones. Put the skin and bones back into the milk
and simmer with the onions for 10 minutes.

Melt the butter, add the flour and cook for 2-3
minutes without browning; gradually stir in the
strained milk and bring to the boil. Add the
flaked kippers and boiled rice. Season with salt
and pepper and serve in cooked pastry cases, on
hot toast or fried bread.

Ling Pie (6 portions) F Yorkshire

This pie, traditional in West Riding, is usually
served with parsley or tomato sauce. In other
parts of the country, salted ling is used and
bacon and onion are omitted. The top is sometimes made of shortcrust.

1 lb ling
1 oz seasoned flour
4 oz chopped bacon
2 sliced hardboiled eggs
2 oz chopped onions
Salt and pepper
½ pt milk
¾ lb puff pastry
1 egg

Oven: 425°F; gas mark 7; 20 minutes

Cut the fish into portions, coat with seasoned flour
and place the fish in a buttered 2½ pt pie dish. Layer
with the bacon, hardboiled eggs and onions and
season with salt and pepper. Pour the milk over the
mixture; cover with pastry and brush with beaten
egg; bake for 10 minutes at 425°F, (gas mark 7)
and then at 350°F, (gas mark 4) for about 20 minutes or until cooked through and the pastry golden.

Lobster Patties (8 portions) H

Suitable for a first course or as part of a buffet
table, these little puff pastry cases, about 2 in
wide, can also be filled with a crab meat, shrimp,
prawn or salmon mixture.

½ lb diced lobster meat
1½ oz butter
½ oz flour
5 fl oz fish stock
2-3 tablespoons cream
3 egg yolks
½ teaspoon lemon juice

Salt and cayenne
2-3 drops anchovy essence
8 puff pastry cases
Garnish: parsley sprigs

Melt the butter and add the flour, cook for a few minutes without colouring; gradually add the fish stock and simmer the sauce until thick. Add the cream, lightly beaten egg yolks and lemon juice; season to taste with salt, cayenne and anchovy essence. Heat the mixture through without boiling.

Add the diced lobster meat and spoon into warmed pastry cases; cover with pastry lids. Garnish with parsley and serve.

Lobster Pie (6-8 portions) H London

A luxury fish pie, suitable for a chilly summer's day, with fresh home-grown asparagus.

2 lb cooked lobster meat
Salt and pepper
1 teaspoon mixed chopped parsley and thyme
5 fl oz double cream
3 tablespoons white wine vinegar
½ lb melted butter
1 oz white breadcrumbs
½ lb savoury shortcrust pastry

Oven: 350°F; gas mark 4; 1 hour

Chop up the cooked lobster and season with salt, pepper and herbs; mix in the cream. Stir in vinegar and the melted butter. Spoon the lobster mixture into a buttered 2½ pt pie dish, sprinkle breadcrumbs over the top and cover with pastry. Bake in the oven for 1 hour; serve hot.

Parson's Hat (6 portions) F

These pasties filled with cheese-flavoured fish, such as haddock or salmon, take their name from the shape of a parson's three-cornered hat.

¾ lb cooked fish
5 fl oz white sauce
2 oz grated cheese
Salt and cayenne pepper
¾ lb puff pastry
1 egg

Oven: 425°F; gas mark 7; 20-30 minutes

Flake the fish and mix with the sauce, cheese and salt and cayenne to taste. Roll the pastry out

thinly and cut into 3½ in rounds. Brush the rounds of pastry with egg lightly beaten with a little milk or water; divide the filling over the rounds. Bring the edges of the pastry together to make a three-cornered shape with the filling showing slightly at the top. Place on a baking sheet, brush with egg and bake for 20-30 minutes.

Pastai Gocos (6-8 portions) F Wales

A traditional Welsh cockle pie, served hot with new potatoes or, equally delicious, cold with a dressed mixed salad.

2½ lb cockles
¾ lb savoury shortcrust pastry
4 oz chopped chives or young salad onions
½ lb diced bacon
Pepper
1 egg

Oven: 400°F; gas mark 6; 30-40 minutes

Cook the cockles in ½ pt water for 15 minutes. Drain and set the cooking liquid aside. Remove the cockles from the shells. Roll the pastry out fairly thick and use to line the sides and base of a 4 pt pie dish. Put a layer of cockles over the base, sprinkle with chives or onions, add a layer of bacon and continue these layers until all is used up. Pour in the strained cooking liquid and season with pepper.

Make a lattice pattern of the remaining pastry over the top; brush with lightly beaten egg and bake until set and golden.

Pulborough Eels (6-8 portions) F Sussex

Pulborough on the River Arun is popular for its freshwater fishing; it is also the birthplace of this steamed eel pudding.

2 lb skinned and boned eels
2 lb savoury suet pastry
5 oz chopped pickled pork
1 tablespoon chopped onions
4 hardboiled eggs
2 tablespoons chopped parsley
Salt and pepper

Cut the eels into 1 in pieces. Put the trimmings into a pan with water and bring to the boil, simmer for 10-15 minutes. Line a 3 pt greased pudding basin with three-quarters of the suet pastry. Fill the basin with the eels, pork, onions and chopped eggs; sprinkle the layers with parsley mixed with salt and pepper.

Strain the fish stock and pour 5 fl oz over the eels; cover the basin with the remaining pastry. Tie down and steam for 1½ hours.

Salmon Pie (6-8 portions) H

In this recipe, the puff pastry cover hides cooked salmon layered with shrimp sauce. In Shropshire, the same kind of pie is made with a creamy onion sauce, and in yet other parts of the country, the Shropshire salmon pie is covered with mashed potatoes instead of pastry.

2 lb cooked salmon
1¼ lb puff pastry
2 pt shrimp sauce
Salt, pepper, sugar
2 oz breadcrumbs
½ teaspoon chopped thyme

Oven: 450°F; gas mark 8; 15 minutes
        350°F; gas mark 4; 25 minutes

Line a 3 pt pie dish with two-thirds of the pastry. Arrange a layer of flaked salmon over the base, add shrimp sauce and season with salt, pepper and sugar. Continue with these layers and top with the breadcrumbs mixed with thyme. Cover with the remaining pastry and bake, reducing the heat after 15 minutes. Serve hot or cold.

Scallop and Mushroom Pie (6-8 portions) H

Mushrooms and scallops complement each other well; this pie, covered with creamed potatoes, makes a complete meal, accompanied at the most with a green side salad.

16 cleaned scallops
½ pt milk
Salt and pepper
2 oz butter
½ oz flour
5 oz sliced mushrooms
5 fl oz dry white wine
1 lb creamed potatoes

Oven: 350°F; gas mark 4; 20-25 minutes

Cut each scallop into three or four pieces, simmer in the milk with salt and pepper for 5 minutes. Strain and set the milk aside. Melt ½ oz butter in

a pan, add the flour and cook through; gradually stir in the milk and bring to the boil. Add the sliced mushrooms, scallops and wine. Put in an ovenproof dish, cover with piped potatoes and top with pats of butter. Bake until golden.

Sole Pie (6-8 portions) H

A rich, but delicately-flavoured pie of oysters and sole fillets in a thick cream sauce under a light cover of puff pastry.

1 lb filleted sole
1 doz fresh or tinned oysters
Salt, pepper and mace
2 oz butter
¾ pt cream sauce
¾ lb puff pastry
1 egg

Oven: 400°F; gas mark 6; 20-30 minutes

Butter a 2½ pt pie dish and arrange the sole fillets and oysters in layers. Season with salt, pepper and powdered mace. Dot with butter. Spoon over the oyster liquid and the warm cream sauce. Leave to cool. Cover with pastry and brush with egg lightly beaten with a little milk. Bake in the oven for about 30 minutes; serve hot.

Star-Gazey Pie (6-8 portions) F Cornwall

Rarely seen today, the star-gazey pie of Cornwall for centuries epitomised the flourishing pilchard industry. The name is derived from the manner in which the pilchards are arranged under the pastry cover: the heads, overlapping the edge of the plate dish, point heavenwards. There was more common than artistic sense in this arrangement for while the heads themselves are inedible they contain a rich oil which drains back into the pastry during cooking.

8 pilchards
4 oz white breadcrumbs
2 fl oz milk
1 tablespoon chopped parsley
Juice and grated rind of 1 lemon
4 oz chopped onions
Salt and pepper
2 chopped hardboiled eggs
4 oz chopped bacon
5 fl oz cider

½ lb savoury shortcrust pastry
1 egg

Oven: 400°F; gas mark 6; 40-50 minutes

Gut, clean and bone the pilchards, leaving the heads on. Soak the breadcrumbs in the milk; squeeze out. Add the parsley, lemon juice and rind and half the onions to the soaked bread-crumbs; season with salt and pepper. Stuff the fish with this mixture and spread any remaining filling over the base of a 9 in pie plate. Arrange the fish on top with the heads sticking up towards the edges. In the spaces between arrange the hardboiled eggs, bacon and remaining onions; season and pour over the cider.

Roll out the pastry, place over the pilchards so that the heads stick out and point upwards. Brush with egg beaten with a little water. Bake for 40-50 minutes.

Star-gazing pasties are small variations of the pie, but made with whole, cleaned and boned herrings. These are stuffed with veal forcemeat, individually wrapped in Cornish pastry, with head and tail sticking out at either end.

FISH MOULDS AND JELLIES, CAKES AND CREAMS

Fish puddings, steamed or baked in one large or several small moulds are light in texture, and being easily digestible are excellent for invalids and convalescents. Moulds and creams also make a small amount of fish go further, like jellies and the more mundane fish cakes.

Fish Mould (6-8 portions) F

Fish mould can be served as a main course dish, hot with anchovy or tomato sauce, or cold with a dressed salad.

1 lb white fish fillets
3 oz fresh white breadcrumbs
2 oz melted butter
Grated rind of 1 lemon
Salt and pepper
2 eggs

Oven: 350°F; gas mark 4; 1 hour

Chop the skinned fish roughly, mix with the breadcrumbs, butter, lemon rind and salt and pepper. Bind with the lightly beaten eggs. Put

the mixture in a 1 pt buttered pudding basin or a loaf tin double-lined with buttered greaseproof paper. Steam on top of the stove until firm or bake in the oven for about 1 hour. Turn the mould out before serving.

Finnan Castles (8 portions) H and F

These individual fish puddings are steamed in small dariole moulds; they make a good first course and can be served hot coated with parsley sauce or cold with a salad dressing.

1 lb boiled flaked Finnan haddock
3 oz day-old breadcrumbs
3 oz melted butter
2 tablespoons finely chopped parsley
2 oz finely chopped, cooked mushrooms
Mixed herbs
Salt and pepper
3 eggs

Blend the flaked haddock with breadcrumbs, melted butter, parsley and mushrooms; season to taste with a pinch of herbs, salt and pepper. Bind the mixture with the lightly beaten eggs. Grease eight individual moulds and divide the mixture between them. Cover with buttered greaseproof paper and steam for 30 minutes.

Sole and Shrimp Pudding (6-8 portions) H

A luxury, but light and fluffy fish mould, its filling of shrimps complemented with a shrimp sauce.

1½ lb sole fillets
2 lb cooked potatoes
6 oz grated cheese
1 oz butter
2 egg yolks
Salt and pepper
1 teaspoon chopped parsley
1¼ lb shelled shrimps
Garnish: parsley sprigs

Oven: 350°F; gas mark 4; 40 minutes

Butter a pudding basin and line with sole fillets, skinned side inwards. Mash the potatoes and heat through, gradually adding the cheese, butter and egg yolks; season with salt and pepper and add the parsley.

Fill the lined mould alternately with layers of

potato and shrimps. Fold the remaining sole fillets over the top and cover with buttered grease-proof paper, place in a roasting tin with water and bake for 40 minutes. Turn out, decorate with parsley sprigs and serve at once.

Jellied Herring Mould (8 portions) H and F

This may be served as an appetiser or as a main course with a salad. The colourful mould looks most appetising provided the jelly is quite clear.

8 filleted herrings
1 oz gelatine
5 fl oz vinegar
½ teaspoon salt
2 oz sugar
2 bay leaves
4 peppercorns
8 small gherkins
2 hardboiled eggs
4 oz cooked sliced carrots

Dissolve the gelatine, using 1 pt boiling water; add the vinegar, salt and sugar. Pour half the gelatine mixture into a round 2-2½ pt dish and leave to set.

Roll up the herring fillets and secure with wooden skewers; put in a pan with the bay leaves and peppercorns and simmer in boiling water for about 5 minutes. Lift out the herrings and leave to cool completely. Remove the skewers.

Arrange the herring rolls, gherkins, sliced eggs and carrots in an attractive pattern over the set gelatine; carefully spoon a little more gelatine over this mixture, enough to hold the various ingredients in place. When set, spoon over the remaining gelatine and leave until quite firm. The mould can be turned out before serving.

Jellied Trout Mould (8 portions) H

Deliciously cool and tempting on a hot summer's day; serve with horseradish cream sauce and thin brown bread and butter.

8 trout (6-8 oz each)
¾ pt water
1 tablespoon white wine vinegar
2 oz sliced onions
1 bay leaf
2 sprigs each, thyme and parsley
½ teaspoon salt
½ oz gelatine

Bring the water and wine vinegar to the boil, add the onions, herbs and salt. Simmer for 30 minutes. Put the cleaned and filleted trout in a pan and cover with the strained liquid. Bring to the boil and simmer for 10 minutes or until the fish is just cooked.

Leave the trout to cool, then place in a deep-sided serving dish. Strain the liquid again, reduce by half and dissolve the gelatine in it. Pour over the fish and leave to set and chill in the refrigerator. The mould can be turned out or served straight from the dish.

Fish Cakes (8 portions) F

Fish cakes can be made from equal amounts of cooked white fish and mashed potatoes, but their flavour is infinitely better when made from fresh fish. Tomato or apple chutney is an unusual, but tasty accompaniment.

1 lb whole fish including 1 kipper
4 oz sliced onions
Salt and pepper
½ lb mashed potatoes
1 oz butter
1 oz flour
Seasoned flour
1-2 eggs
Breadcrumbs
Fat for frying

Fillet, skin and bone the fish except for the kipper. Put the trimmings in a pan with ¾ pt water, the onions, salt and pepper; simmer gently for about 20 minutes. Add the kipper to the pan for 2-3 minutes; lift out. Strain the fish stock and pour over the fish fillets; simmer for about 10 minutes or until quite tender. Drain. Remove the skin and bone from the kipper and add to the other trimmings.

Mash the fish and kipper meat and blend thoroughly with the potatoes. Melt the butter in a pan, stir in the flour and cook for 2-3 minutes without colouring. Remove from the heat and add the strained fish stock. Return to the heat until the sauce has thickened. Season. Add enough of the sauce to the potato and fish mixture to give it a stiff consistency. Leave to cool.

Shape the mixture into eight or sixteen round cakes; dust with seasoned flour, dip in the lightly beaten eggs, then coat thoroughly with fine breadcrumbs. Fry the fish cakes in shallow hot fat until crisp and golden, turning once.

Cutlets Victoria (6-8 portions) F and H

These are a kind of fish cake, given a touch of sophistication with the addition of mushrooms and cream — and shaped like cutlets.

1 lb cooked, flaked fish
2 oz butter
2 oz flour
½ pt cream
4 oz sliced mushrooms
2 oz grated onions
1 dessertspoon chopped parsley
Salt and pepper
Seasoned flour
1 egg
Breadcrumbs
Fat for frying

Melt the butter in a pan, stir in the flour and cook through; gradually stir in the cream. Add the fish, mushrooms, onions and parsley and season with salt and pepper. Heat the mixture through, then remove from the pan and leave to cool.

Shape the mixture into eight cutlets. Dust with seasoned flour, pass through the lightly beaten egg and coat in fine breadcrumbs. Shallow-fry in hot fat until golden brown.

Kipper Fish Cakes (2-4 portions) F
Wales

This dish has superseded the once popular cockles cakes in Wales. Cooked shelled cockles were mixed to a dropping consistency with eggs, cream and breadcrumbs and fried in spoonfuls.

¾ lb cooked filleted kippers
½ lb mashed potatoes
1 oz melted butter
1 chopped hardboiled egg
Pepper
Oil for frying

Flake the flesh from the kippers and mix with the potatoes; add the melted butter, hardboiled egg and pepper to taste. Heat the oil in a frying pan and spread the mixture like a pancake. Fry gently until brown underneath. Fold in half and serve at once.

Twice Laid (6-8 portions) F Kent

The local name for these cod fish cakes presumably refers to the fact that left-over cooked cod is used.

½ lb cooked, flaked cod
1 lb mashed potatoes
Salt and pepper
Milk
1 egg
Breadcrumbs
Fat for frying

Mix the cod with the potatoes; season with salt and pepper and bind with a little milk. Shape the mixture into balls, dip in beaten egg and coat with breadcrumbs. Heat the fat and deep-fry the balls until golden brown. Drain and serve.

Fish Cream (6 portions) H and F

This is a delicate, but nourishing type of fish mould, eminently suitable for people recovering from an illness. Colour is added by coating the mould with hot parsley sauce.

12 oz skinned, filleted fish
1½ oz butter
1½ oz flour
¾ pt fish stock
Lemon juice
Salt and pepper
4 eggs
5 fl oz double cream

Melt the butter in a pan, stir in the flour and cook through; gradually blend in the stock and cook for 2-3 minutes, stirring continuously. Chop the fish finely and add to the sauce; season to taste with lemon juice, salt and pepper. Beat the eggs and cream lightly and add to the fish mixture.

Spoon into a greased pudding basin or mould and cover with buttered paper. Steam until firm, after 1 hour. Turn out, coat with parsley sauce and serve at once.

Fish Custard (6-8 portions) F and H

Fish custard is similar to fish cream, but of a more solid texture.

1½ lb skinned, filleted fish
1½ oz seasoned flour
1 oz butter
1½ pt milk

5 eggs
Salt and pepper

Oven: 350°F; gas mark 4; 1½-2 hours

Cut the fish into 1 in pieces and coat with
seasoned flour. Place in a buttered ovenproof
dish. Heat the milk slightly and pour over the
beaten eggs. Season with salt and pepper and
strain over the fish. Place in a roasting tin with
water and bake until brown and set.

Lobster Cream (6-8 portions) H

Suitable for a patient on a building-up diet, but
with a discerning palate.

1½ lb cooked lobster
½ lb whiting
1 oz butter
2 oz flour
5 fl oz fish stock
2 eggs
Salt
Paprika and cayenne pepper
2½ fl oz cream

Skin and fillet the whiting; use the trimmings for
fish stock. Chop up the fish. Remove the meat
from the lobster, cut into pieces and put through
the mincer together with the whiting. Melt the
butter, add the flour and gradually stir in the
fish stock; cook through. Beat in the fish mixture,
followed by the eggs. Season with salt, paprika
and cayenne.

    Beat the cream stiff and fold into the mixture.
Spoon into a well greased charlotte mould or
pudding basin and cover with buttered greaseproof paper. Steam gently for ¾-1 hour and serve
hot with a cream sauce.

Newhaven Cream (6-8 portions) H and F
Scotland

This is a popular dish in the central Lowlands
and is usually served hot with parsley, egg or
mushroom sauce. In other areas, a similar
salmon cream is found; it is made with salmon
pounded to a paste, mixed with beaten egg whites
and cream, steamed in individual moulds and
served with parsley sauce, buttered green peas
and toast.

1 lb smoked, cooked and boned haddock
4 oz white breadcrumbs

Salt and pepper
4 oz butter
¾ pt milk or single cream
3 eggs

Flake and mash the fish, add breadcrumbs, salt
and pepper. Melt the butter in the milk and pour
over the mixture; fold in the beaten eggs. Spoon
into a well buttered large pudding basin. Cover
with foil and steam gently for 1 hour. Remove
the foil, turn out the mould and serve.

Oyster and Sole Custard (6 portions) H

A savoury fish custard with luxury qualities,
certain to revive jaded taste buds.

2 doz oysters
1 oz butter
1 oz white breadcrumbs
½ lb sole fillets
1 dessertspoon lemon juice
Salt and cayenne
2 eggs
½ pt milk

Oven: 350°F; gas mark 4; 15-20 minutes

Butter a shallow ovenproof dish and sprinkle
with half the breadcrumbs. Lay the sole fillets
over the base and add lemon juice. Cut the oysters
in half and lay over the sole, with salt and cayenne
to taste. Beat the eggs with the milk and pour
over the fish. Sprinkle with the remaining breadcrumbs and bake in the oven. Serve hot.

Sefton of Salmon (6 portions) H and F

The Earl of Sefton, a 19th century gourmet, gave
his name not only to several dishes, including
the following as well as to certain savouries and
sandwiches, but also to a particular type of landau.

1 lb cooked salmon
Salt, pepper, grated nutmeg
1 teaspoon anchovy essence
1 dessertspoon finely chopped parsley
1 pt milk
6 eggs

Oven: 350°F; gas mark 4; 30 minutes

Flake the salmon and season with salt, pepper,
nutmeg, anchovy and parsley. Place in a
buttered ovenproof dish. Heat the milk and
pour over the beaten eggs; strain and pour over

the salmon. Place in a roasting tin with water and bake in the oven. Serve hot or cold.

POTTED FISH AND FISH PASTES

Potting of both fish and meat is one of the oldest known preservation methods. Originally, the ingredients were cooked in a pot, left to cool and then made airtight with a thick layer of suet. By Tudor times, butter had replaced suet as the covering. Until medieval days, many fish dishes were served as a fairly liquid paste, the flesh being minced fine and mixed with seasonings, milk and sometimes rice; preserving of this type of paste in the same manner as potted fish was a logical consequence.

The texture of potted preserve varies according to the treatment of the fish, from filleted or flaked fish to a paste-like consistency. Most potted fish and pastes will keep for several weeks if stored, covered, in the refrigerator and even longer in a freezer.

Potted Fish

Generous use of spices is one of the characteristics of potted fish. Whole or filleted fish for immediate use can be cooked in ordinary ovenproof dishes, while finely flaked fish preserves are packed tightly into small earthenware pots and covered with a layer of clarified butter.

Potted Crab or Lobster (6-8 portions) H

Potted fish is ideal as a starter to a meal, with breakfasts and teas, for snacks and savouries. Serve with hot buttered toast.

3 cooked crabs or 2 lobsters
Juice of 1 lemon
¼ teaspoon ground mace
4 oz clarified butter
Salt and pepper

Remove the flesh from the crabs or lobsters, keeping the meat and any coral separate. Pound the meat in a mortar until reduced to a fine texture, not a paste. Mix in the lemon juice, mace, 1 oz clarified butter, salt and pepper. Layer the coral and meat in small pots. Cover with clarified butter and leave to set.

Potted Herrings I (6-8 portions) F

For clarified butter, melt lightly salted butter over gentle heat, stirring all the time until the butter foams; continue cooking without browning, until the bubbling ceases. Leave for a few minutes, then carefully strain the clear liquid through fine muslin.

1½ lb herring or mackerel
½ pt white wine vinegar (or white wine and
    vinegar mixed)
5 fl oz water
2 bay leaves
10 peppercorns
2 blades mace
¼ teaspoon ground nutmeg
Salt and pepper
4 oz clarified butter

Oven: 350°F; gas mark 4; 45 minutes

Clean, bone and fillet the herrings or mackerel; roll up and arrange in an ovenproof dish. Cover with the vinegar and water, add the herbs, spices and salt and pepper. Bake in the oven. Drain the fish thoroughly and pack into an earthenware pot or mould; cover with clarified butter.

Potted Herrings II (8 portions) F Ireland

In this Irish version of potted herrings, the fish is served as soon as it has cooled.

16 herrings
Salt and pepper
6 cloves
2 blades mace
1 bay leaf
12 peppercorns
3 cayenne pods
½ pt vinegar
5 fl oz water
1 oz butter

Oven: 425°F; gas mark 7; 30 minutes
        250°F; gas mark 1; 4 hours

Clean and scale the herrings, cut off heads and fins but do not bone the fish; wash and dry thoroughly. Sprinkle the herrings inside with salt and pepper. Lay the fish heads to tails in an ovenproof dish with the spices between. Pour the vinegar and water over the fish and dot with butter. Cover and bake at 425°F (gas mark 7) for 30 minutes; reduce the temperature and continue baking for 4 hours. Cool before serving.

Potted Herrings in Small Beer (6-8 portions) F

Serve hot or cold, as an appetiser with buttered brown bread.

8 herrings
Salt and pepper
Allspice, ground cloves
4 oz sliced onions
2 bay leaves
5 fl oz vinegar
¾ pt light ale

Oven: 350°F; gas mark 4; 30-45 minutes

Clean and scale the herrings, remove heads, tails and fins, leaving the fish whole. Sprinkle the herrings inside with salt, allspice and cloves. Lay the fish in an ovenproof dish and cover with plenty of pepper, onions and the bay leaves. Add vinegar and ale. Bake in the oven until tender and the bones are soft.

Potted Salmon I (8 portions) H
Herefordshire

This recipe for potting Wye salmon dates from the 18th century. Newcastle potted salmon consists of cooked, pounded salmon seasoned simply with mace, pepper and cloves; the Scottish version, which includes pounded anchovies, is made into a smooth paste with the addition of softened butter.

8 salmon steaks (6 oz each)
1 oz mixed nutmeg, mace, cloves and white pepper
4 oz butter
4 oz finely chopped onions
6 bay leaves
6 chopped anchovy fillets (optional)
4 oz clarified butter

Oven: 350°F; gas mark 4; 30-40 minutes

Wipe the salmon steaks clean and season with the spices. Arrange the steaks in a well-greased baking dish with butter between the layers; sprinkle with the onions and lay the bay leaves and anchovies, if used, on top. Dot with butter, cover with foil and bake for 30-40 minutes.

Lift out and drain the salmon, remove skin and bones and pound or flake the flesh. Pack tightly in pots, pour over clarified butter and leave to set.

Potted Salmon II (12-16 portions) H

Potted salmon can be stretched to serve a large gathering by layering it with white fish. Serve chilled, with hot buttered toast.

2 lb salmon
5 fl oz sherry
1 bay leaf
Salt and pepper
1½ lb cod, haddock or bass
2 oz white breadcrumbs
2 egg yolks
4 oz melted butter

Oven: 350°F; gas mark 4; 1¼ hours

Skin the salmon, wipe and cut into 2 in slices. Marinate for 1½ hours in the sherry with the bay leaf, salt and pepper; turn occasionally. Pound the filleted white fish, add breadcrumbs, egg yolks, butter and salt and pepper; bind the mixture with a little of the marinade.

Butter an ovenproof dish and put in a layer of the white fish mixture, then a layer of salmon pieces and so on until all is used up. Bake in a roasting tin with water in the oven for 1¼ hours. Cool and chill before serving.

Potted Shrimps (6-8 portions) H and F
Lancashire

Since the 18th century, shrimps from Morecambe Bay have been rated a great delicacy. Local housewives used to pot the surplus in clarified butter, a regional recipe which has since achieved national acclaim. Prawns may be used instead of shrimps.

1 lb fresh shrimps
5 oz clarified butter
2 teaspoons anchovy essence
¼ teaspoon mace
¼ teaspoon cayenne pepper
Salt

Oven: 350°F; gas mark 4; 30 minutes

Put the shrimps in boiling water and cook for 2 minutes. Cool and remove from the shells. Melt 3 oz clarified butter with anchovy essence, mace, cayenne and salt. Put the shrimps in an ovenproof dish and pour over the seasoned butter. Bake for 30 minutes. Remove from the oven, drain and leave to cool.

Pack the shrimps into small jars, pour over the strained butter in which the shrimps were cooked.

Leave to set, then cover with the remaining clarified butter, about ¼ in thick.

Potted Sprats (8-10 portions) H and F

Excellent as a first course, with hot toast; reminiscent of potted herrings but with a more pronounced flavour.

2 lb sprats
½ pt white wine vinegar (or white wine and
  vinegar)
5 fl oz water
¼ teaspoon ground nutmeg
Salt and pepper
2 bay leaves
10 peppercorns
2 blades mace
4 oz clarified butter

Oven: 350°F; gas mark 4; 45 minutes

Wipe the sprats thoroughly, cut off the heads and draw through the gills. Lay the sprats in an oven-proof dish, pour over the mixed vinegar and water, season with nutmeg, salt and pepper and add the bay leaves, peppercorns and mace. Bake in the oven for 45 minutes; lift out and drain the sprats.

Pack tightly into small pots, leave to cool, then cover with clarified butter.

Potted Trout (12 portions) H
Northumberland

Richly preserved in butter, these potted trout are suitable for a substantial first course.

12 trout (6 oz each)
Salt and pepper
5 fl oz white wine vinegar
½ lb butter
½ lb clarified butter
Pinch mace, nutmeg and ground cloves

Oven: 325°F; gas mark 3; 45 minutes

Scale the trout, remove gills, eyes and fins; clean thoroughly. Slit the trout down the back, remove the backbones and sprinkle the fish, inside and out with salt and pepper. Leave for several hours to absorb the seasoning.

Arrange the trout head to tail in an ovenproof dish; cover with the vinegar and add the butter, cut into pieces. Cover and bake for 45 minutes. Remove the trout from the liquid and drain. Arrange in a serving dish and leave to cool. Cover

with the clarified butter heated with mace, nutmeg and cloves and strained. Serve chilled.

Fish Pastes

These are similar to potted fish, but of a perfectly smooth and creamy consistency, best obtained in a liquidiser. Fish pastes make excellent spreads on hot toast for breakfast or high tea, as a base for many savouries and as sandwich fillings.

Anchovy Paste (4-6 portions) F and H

A strongly-flavoured paste, to be used sparingly.

4 oz whole salted anchovies
½ lb unsalted butter (approx.)
¼ teaspoon each cayenne, pepper, nutmeg and
  mace
2 oz clarified butter

Scrape the salt from the anchovies and remove bones. Pound to a paste in a mortar and rub through a fine sieve or blend in a liquidiser. Weigh the anchovies and pound to a smooth mixture with double the weight of unsalted butter. Mix in spices to taste. Pack into pots and cover with clarified butter.

Bloater Paste (8-10 portions) F and H
Norfolk

One of the best loved fish spreads for breakfast toast, bloater paste has many local variations. In some, the cooked bloater flesh is merely pounded with butter, in others the paste is flavoured with anchovy essence, cayenne, mace and cloves, and a Yorkshire recipe adds chopped hardboiled eggs. An economy bloater paste is made by incorporating cooked butter beans.

8 bloaters
1 tablespoon lemon juice
8-10 oz butter
White pepper
3 oz clarified butter

Put the bloaters in a pan, cover with boiling water and cook for a few minutes. Lift out and drain, remove heads, skins and bones and weigh the flesh. Allow half that amount of butter. Put the bloater flesh through a fine mincer two or three times and add lemon juice.

Pound in a mortar with the butter and pepper

to a smooth paste. Pot in individual dishes and cover with clarified butter.

Buckling Paste (6-8 portions) F and H

Hot-smoked herring, known as buckling, needs no cooking and is easily made into a short-time fish spread.

2 large buckling
½ lb softened butter
2 tablespoons lemon juice
2 cloves garlic
Pepper
3 oz clarified butter

Pound the skinned and boned buckling (approx. 10 oz) and blend with the softened butter. Add lemon juice and crushed garlic and season to taste with freshly ground pepper. Cover with clarified butter.

Cod Roe Paste (8-10 portions) H and F

The smoked hard roe of the cod makes an excellent if sharp fish spread; serve with hot toast and lemon wedges.

1 lb smoked cod roe
4 oz finely chopped shallots
4 oz butter
2 tablespoons vinegar or lemon juice
½ oz dry mustard
Salt and pepper
4 oz clarified butter

Scrape the cod roe from the skin; fry the shallots in the butter until soft, but not coloured. Pound the cod roe and shallots with the vinegar and mustard or blend in the liquidiser until smooth and creamy. Season with salt and pepper.

Pack the paste into small pots and cover with clarified butter.

Herring Roe Butter (8 portions) H and F

This is a short-time spread of soft and hard herring roes, excellent on biscuits and toast.

½ lb hard herring roes
½ lb soft herring roes
2½ fl oz white wine
4 oz butter
Cayenne pepper and curry powder
Salt

Place the soft and hard roes in a pan with the wine and butter; cook for 10 minutes over gentle heat. Remove from the heat; cool slightly then blend in a liquidiser until quite smooth. Season to taste with cayenne, curry powder and salt. Cool before using.

Kipper Cheese Paste (5-8 portions) F

Excellent as a spread on hot toast beneath plain scrambled eggs.

½ lb kipper fillets
½ lb grated cheese
4 oz softened butter
Cayenne pepper
3 oz clarified butter

Put the kippers in a jug of boiling water and leave for about 5 minutes. Pound the kippers with the cheese, add the butter and cayenne to taste. Rub through a sieve or blend in a liquidiser to a smooth paste. Pack in small pots or moulds and cover with clarified butter.

Kipper Paste (8 portions) F

The smoked flavour is less pronounced in the kipper than in its relation, the bloater, but like the latter it is used in many local variations of fish spreads. The basic flavourings are lemon juice and cayenne, but in one version the usual softened butter is replaced with thick cream and a little olive oil, and in another white wine substitutes lemon juice. Yorkshire kipper paste is made from kippers pounded with only butter and hard-boiled eggs.

2 large kippers
10 oz unsalted butter
1 tablespoon lemon juice
Salt, pepper, cayenne pepper
4 oz clarified butter

Stand the kippers, heads down, in a jug of water for 10 minutes. Drain, remove skin and bones. Cut the butter into pieces, set over low heat until half melted, remove from the heat and stir until completely melted. Blend the butter and chopped kippers in a liquidiser to a smooth paste. Season with lemon juice, salt, pepper and cayenne. Pack into small pots and cool; cover with clarified butter.

Lobster Paste (8 portions) H

More expensive than other fish pastes, it can be made when lobsters are offered at a reasonable price and stored for a couple of months in a freezer. Crab paste can be made by the same method.

2 small boiled lobsters
¾ lb butter
¼ teaspoon mace
Juice of 1 lemon
Salt and pepper
4 oz clarified butter

Remove the meat from the lobsters and pound to a smooth paste; alternatively, blend in a liquidiser. Blend thoroughly with the softened butter, adding mace and lemon juice and seasoning to taste with salt and pepper. Pack into pots and cover with clarified butter.

Oyster Paste (6-8 portions) H

A few oysters, the finest of which are reputed to come from Colchester and Whitstable, are sufficient to provide an ample first course, with hot buttered toast.

6 oysters
1 anchovy fillet
6 oz butter
2 teaspoons lemon juice
White pepper
2 oz clarified butter

Open and trim the oysters, chop finely and pound to a smooth paste with the anchovy fillet. Pound the oyster mixture with the butter and blend in lemon juice and pepper to taste. Pack into individual pots and cover with clarified butter. Leave to set.

Salmon Cheese Paste (6-8 portions) F and H

Left-over salmon is ideal for this spread which has a limited storage life and should be used within a few days of making.

½ lb cooked salmon
½ lb grated Cheshire cheese
2 oz butter
2 tablespoons double cream
Salt and cayenne pepper
3 oz clarified butter

Pound the boned, skinned and flaked salmon with the cheese; add the butter and cream and season to taste with salt and cayenne. Rub through a sieve or blend to a smooth paste in a liquidiser. Pack tightly in small pots and cover with clarified butter.

Salmon Paste (8-10 portions) H and F

Odd slices of smoked salmon and trimmings from salmon skins can be transformed into a smooth paste to serve with hot crackers and toast.

10 oz smoked salmon
10 oz butter
1 dessertspoon lemon juice
White pepper
3 oz clarified butter

Put the salmon through a mincer two or three times; pound to a smooth paste with the butter. Blend in lemon juice and pepper to taste. Pot and cover with clarified butter.

Shrimp Paste (12-16 portions) H and F

In many country districts and particularly in the North, home of many fine fish pastes, no high tea is complete without shrimp paste. Prawns can also be used.

¾ lb fresh shrimps
½ lb cod or haddock fillets
2 anchovy fillets
1 teaspoon anchovy essence
Cayenne, ground mace, salt
5 oz butter
3 oz clarified butter

Boil the shrimps for 2-3 minutes, cool and shell; chop the shrimps roughly and set aside. Wash the shells and put in a pan with sufficient water to cover; boil for 20 minutes. Strain the liquid and simmer the cod or haddock in it until cooked. Lift out and drain the fish; reduce the liquid to 2 tablespoons.

Pound the fish with the reduced liquid to a smooth paste, adding the anchovy fillets and essence, mace, salt and cayenne. Alternatively, blend in a liquidiser. Add the butter and continue to pound until smooth. Blend in the chopped shrimps. Pack into small pots and cover with clarified butter.

Trout Paste (8-10 portions) H

Smoked rainbow trout is popular as a first course
and can also be used for a creamy paste, spread
thickly on buttered toast fingers.

10 oz smoked trout
10 oz butter
1 dessertspoon white wine vinegar
White pepper
3 oz clarified butter

Remove skin and bones from the trout and put
the flesh two or three times through a fine mincer.
Pound to a smooth paste; gradually add the
butter and vinegar and continue pounding until
thoroughly blended. Season to taste with pepper.
Pack tightly into individual pots and cover with
clarified butter.

PICKLED FISH

Soused and pickled fish were common in medieval
days, the pickling liquid being highly seasoned to
counteract the extreme saltiness of the common
herring. Sousing as a preserving method, however,
dates back to pre-Christian times and was brought
to Britain by the Romans who had adopted it
from the classical Greek kitchen. Whole or partly
cooked fish were covered with a salty brine,
vinegar and oil.

Today, the preserving medium does not require
such a potent strength, thanks to refrigeration;
fish are now usually cooked in the pickling liquid
and served within a short time of being prepared.
Herring, mackerel and other strongly flavoured
fish are the most suitable for pickling and sousing.

Fish Roes, Soused (6-8 portions) F and H

Sousing implies a preparation or cooking method
whereby food is completely immersed in a pickle
liquid, usually vinegar. For this dish, use herring or
cod roes and serve with a potato salad.

1 lb fish roes
1 oz butter
2 oz sliced carrots
4 oz sliced onions
1 oz diced celery
1 bay leaf
2 sprigs parsley

6 black peppercorns
2 cloves
1 blade mace
¾-1 pt vinegar or white wine and water
Garnish: watercress

Oven: 350°F; gas mark 4; 30-45 minutes

Clean and wash the roes; butter an ovenproof
dish and arrange the carrots, onions, celery, bay
leaf, parsley, peppercorns, cloves and mace over
the base. Set the fish roes on top. Pour over the
vinegar or white wine and water, cover with foil
and bake in the oven.

Leave to chill; remove the roes from the
sousing liquid and serve garnished with watercress.

Pickled Herrings I (6-8 portions) F and H

A favourite fish course, served with brown or rye
bread and butter. The uncooked herrings are
steeped in pickle for several days before use.

8 herrings
1 pt water
2 oz salt
¾ oz pickling spice
2 oz sliced onions
2 bay leaves
1 pt white vinegar

Clean, bone and fillet the herrings; soak for 2
hours in a brine of water and salt. For the pickle,
boil the remaining ingredients in vinegar for 3-4
minutes. Remove from the heat and allow to infuse for 30 minutes. Roll up the herrings, skin
side out, pack into a wide-necked jar and pour
over the spiced vinegar; cover the jar and leave for
5-6 days

Pickled Herrings II (6-8 portions) F and H

These lightly salted herrings are prepared in a
sweet pickling liquid and left for 7-8 hours. They
will keep in a refrigerator for about one week.

8 herrings
1½ lb thinly sliced onions
Salt and pepper
3 oz Demerara sugar
White wine vinegar

Clean, bone and fillet the herrings and soak for
about 2 hours in a brine of 1 pt water and 2 oz
salt. Drain and wipe dry. Place the herrings in a
large serving dish in layers with the onions;

sprinkle each layer with salt, pepper and sugar.
Pour over enough vinegar to cover. Serve chilled,
after 7-8 hours.

Herrings and Mushroom Salad (6-8 portions) H and F

For this dish, served as a first course with brown
bread and butter or as a light lunch with potato
salad, use sharp-pickled herrings.

8 pickled herrings
½ lb thinly sliced button mushrooms
1 tablespoon water
2 tablespoons salad oil
½ teaspoon each salt, sugar, pepper and dry
    mustard
Garnish: chopped parsley, onion rings

Toss the sliced mushrooms in a dressing made
from the water, oil, salt, sugar, pepper and
mustard. Arrange between the herrings on a
serving dish. Garnish with chopped parsley and
onion rings either fresh or taken from the pickle.

Herrings and Orange Salad (6-8 portions) H and F

A refreshing salad of sharp-pickled rolled herrings
in an orange-flavoured dressing.

8 pickled herrings
2 lettuce hearts
2 oranges
3 fl oz olive oil
2 tablespoons vinegar
Salt, pepper, sugar, dry mustard

Drain the herrings and arrange on a bed of lettuce.
Thinly peel the zest from the oranges and shred
into fine strips. Blanch in boiling water and
refresh in cold water.
    Cut one orange in half and extract the juice.
Remove the pith from the other half and slice
thinly across the segments. Cut each slice into
quarters. Mix the oil, vinegar and orange juice and
season to taste. Add the orange peel and segments
and spoon the mixture over the herrings.

Herring Appetiser Salad (8 portions) H and F

Smooth-textured and served in small individual
ramekin dishes, this appetiser is best made with
sweet-pickled herrings.

8 pickled herrings
2 peeled and cored eating apples
2 hardboiled eggs
6 oz breadcrumbs
Salt and pepper
Garnish: olives or gherkins

Put the herrings, apples and eggs through the
mincer and blend with the breadcrumbs. Season
with salt and freshly ground pepper. Press the
mixture into small pots and garnish with slices
of olives or gherkins.

Herring Salad, Green (6-8 portions) F

Deliciously cool for a summer's day, sweet-pickled
herrings are here mixed with cucumber and peas.
Serve with thin bread and butter.

8 pickled herrings
3 fl oz salad sauce
2 fl oz double cream
½ thinly sliced cucumber
½ lb cooked peas
Salt and pepper
Garnish: watercress

Cut the herrings into ½ in slices. Blend the salad
sauce with the cream; mix in the cucumber and
peas and season with salt and pepper. Carefully
fold in the herring slices. Pile the mixture into a
serving dish and garnish with watercress.

Herring Salad, Piquant (8 portions) F and H

Pleasingly sharp, this appetiser is made with
sweet-pickled herrings and sour cream; serve in
small individual dishes.

8 pickled herrings
6 oz cored and thinly sliced eating apples
1 tablespoon lemon juice
2 oz finely chopped onions
½ pt sour cream
Salt and pepper
Garnish: watercress

Drain the herrings; cut each in half lengthways
and then cut into narrow strips. Arrange in serving
dishes. Sprinkle the apple slices with lemon juice
and reserve a few for garnish. Chop the remainder
and blend with the onions and cream; season with
salt and pepper. Spoon the cream mixture over
the herrings and garnish with apple and sprigs of
watercress.

Soused Herrings (6-8 portions) F and H
Scotland

Mackerel may be soused in the same way as these herrings. Hot crusty bread goes well with the fish for a first course or a snack.

8 Loch Fyne herrings
Salt and pepper
1 pt basic fish pickle

Oven: 300°F; gas mark 2; 1½ hours

Clean, bone and fillet the herrings; season well with salt and pepper. Roll up the fillets, skin side out, from the tail end and place close together in an ovenproof dish. Pour over the pickle, cover with foil and bake for 1½ hours. Leave to cool in the pickle; drain before serving.

Norfolk Soused Herrings (6-8 portions) F
Norfolk

Subtly seasoned herring fillets, reminiscent of the German roll-mops, can be served chilled, with thin slices of buttered bread.

8 herrings
1-2 oz flour
Salt and black pepper
1 teaspoon powdered mace
2 oz butter
1 dessertspoon chopped parsley
2 bay leaves
½ pt water
½ pt white wine vinegar

Oven: 375°F; gas mark 5; 1 hour

Clean, bone and fillet the herrings; dust with flour and season with salt, pepper and powdered mace. Place a small piece of butter in the centre of each fillet, sprinkle with parsley and roll up, from the tail end and skin side out. Put the herrings in a fireproof dish with the bay leaves and pour over the water and vinegar; cover. Bake for 1 hour and leave to cool before serving.

Sweet-Sharp Soused Herrings (6-8 portions) F

Herring fillets in a sharp, yet sweet pickle to tickle the taste-buds. Serve cold, on a bed of lettuce hearts.

8 herrings
½ pt water
½ pt malt vinegar
2 tablespoons tomato ketchup
1 dessertspoon chopped chervil or parsley
6 bay leaves
6 peppercorns
4 oz Demerara sugar
1 teaspoon turmeric or mustard

Oven: 350°F; gas mark 4; 1 hour

Clean, bone and fillet the herrings; place in an ovenproof dish. Mix the water with vinegar, tomato ketchup, chervil, bay leaves and peppercorns; pour over the herrings. Cover with a lid or foil and bake for 45 minutes.

Mix the sugar and turmeric and sprinkle over the herrings; cover the dish and replace in the oven for 15 minutes. Remove from the oven and leave the herrings to cool in the liquid. Drain before serving.

Kippers, Preserved (6-8 portions) F and H

Kippers are interchangeable with pickled herrings for most appetisers. They must, however, first be steeped in a pickling or marinating liquid for 4-5 days before use.

8 filleted kippers
3 bay leaves
8 peppercorns
½ pt olive oil
1 tablespoon vinegar

Lay the kipper fillets in a glass or stoneware jar, with bay leaves and peppercorns. Mix the olive oil and vinegar, pour over the kippers, cover and store for several days before using.

Kippers and Dill Salad (6-8 portions) H and F

This can be served as a substantial first course or a light luncheon dish. Arrange the preserved kipper fillets, the potatoes, beetroot, mixed apple and onions in separate small bowls and serve chilled, with buttered brown bread.

16 preserved kipper fillets
¾ lb cooked, diced potatoes
9 oz cooked, diced beetroot
¾ lb diced cooking apples
4 oz chopped onions
½ pt salad oil

Salt, pepper, sugar, dry mustard
1 tablespoon chopped dill

Cut the preserved kipper fillets into narrow strips and put into a small bowl. Arrange the diced potatoes in a second bowl, the beetroot in a third and the apples mixed with onions in a fourth. Make a dressing from the oil and vinegar, seasoning to taste with salt, pepper, sugar, mustard and dill. Spoon the dressing over the contents of the four bowls, mix well and leave to marinate in the refrigerator for about 30 minutes.

Before serving, drain the kippers and other ingredients from the dressing and arrange in serving dishes.

Kippers and Potato Salad (6-8 portions) H and F

A well-flavoured potato salad, with chives and shallots, happily complements preserved kipper fillets.

16 preserved kipper fillets
3 fl oz olive oil
3 tablespoons red wine vinegar
1½ teaspoon French or German mustard
1 teaspoon sugar
Salt and black pepper
1½ lb cooked, diced potatoes
1 oz chopped shallots or onions
1 tablespoon chopped chives

Slice the kipper fillets into diamond-shaped wedges. Blend the oil and vinegar, mustard and sugar, salt and pepper in a bowl; add potatoes, shallot and chives; chill. Arrange the potato salad on a serving dish, decorate with the kipper pieces and serve.

Soused Kippers (8 portions) F

Suitable for a high tea as well as a first course, these kipper fillets are baked and cooled in pickle. Serve cold with a green salad and bread and butter.

16 kipper fillets
Pepper
½ pt vinegar
½ pt water
1½ oz pickling spice
4 bay leaves
4 oz sliced onions

Oven: 300°F; gas mark 2; 1 hour

Season the kipper fillets with pepper, roll up and secure with cocktail sticks; place close together in an ovenproof dish. Cover the kippers with vinegar and water and add pickling spice, bay leaves and onions. Cover with a lid or foil and bake in the oven for 1 hour. Leave to cool in the pickling liquid; drain before serving.

Caveach Mackerel (8 portions) F

The word "caveach" is an English corruption of the Spanish *escabeche* describing a particular pickling liquid for fish. The preserved mackerel will keep for several weeks in a refrigerator.

8 large mackerel
Salt, pepper, mace, nutmeg
½ pt olive oil
½ pt vinegar

Gut and clean the mackerel thoroughly. Mix a good amount of salt, pepper, mace and nutmeg. Score each mackerel three times, press in the seasoning and rub over the skin. Fry the fish in oil until brown; remove from the heat and leave to cool.

Skin and bone the mackerel. Place in a wide-necked pickling jar, pour over the vinegar and cover with oil. Cover the jar and leave for at least 2-3 days in a cool place before use.

Caveach Salmon (8 portions) H

Caveach or pickling of fish that has first been fried seems to have first appeared in the 18th century. Other fish to be preserved for short-term storage in this manner include mackerel, sole and haddock.

8 salmon steaks (6 oz each)
½ pt vinegar
½ pt water
3 sliced shallots
2 blades mace
Salt
½ oz whole peppercorns
3 cloves
Oil

Bring the vinegar and water to the boil with shallots, mace, salt, peppercorns and cloves; leave to cool. Grill or fry the cleaned salmon steaks in oil until light brown on both sides.

When cool pack the steaks tightly into a deep jar and cover with the pickling liquid. Pour enough oil on top to cover the vinegar.

Salmon, Collared (16 portions) H

The term "collared" was originally applied to a neck piece of meat rolled up for cooking; by extension it now indicates any rolled piece of fish or meat.

7-8 lb salmon
1 teaspoon salt
½ teaspoon pepper
Pinch cayenne
Large pinch mace
1 pt water
5 fl oz vinegar
12 peppercorns
2 cloves
½ teaspoon allspice
2 bay leaves
Garnish: fennel

Clean the salmon and cut into two long fillets along the backbone. Skin the salmon and remove all bones. Mix together the salt, pepper, cayenne and mace and rub over the flesh side of both fillets. Roll up the fillets starting at the tail end; bind firmly with string or a piece of cloth. Bring the water and vinegar to the boil, add the peppercorns, cloves, allspice, bay leaves and salt to taste. Put in the fish and simmer gently for 1-1½ hours.

When cooked, place in an earthenware container, pour over the pickling liquid to cover, adding more vinegar if necessary. To serve, drain the salmon from the pickle, garnish with fresh fennel and serve with anchovy sauce or a melted butter sauce.

Salmon, Pickled I (6 portions) H

Suitable for a cold first course, with thin slices of brown bread and butter.

2 lb filleted salmon
½ pt white wine vinegar
2 oz sliced onions
4 oz sliced carrots
1 sprig each parsley, thyme, tarragon
Salt and pepper

Put the salmon in a pan with the vinegar, onions, carrots and chopped parsley, thyme and tarragon, salt and pepper; bring to the boil and simmer for 10 minutes. Leave the salmon in the pickling liquid for a few days, turning the fish twice a day. To serve, lift the salmon from the pickle, strain the liquid and pour over the fish.

Salmon, Pickled II (8 portions) H Northumberland

This dish is served hot in its pickling liquid, with boiled new potatoes.

8 salmon steaks (6 oz each)
½ pt vinegar
½ pt white wine
½ teaspoon pepper
½ teaspoon ground mace
2 cloves

Place the salmon steaks in a pan and just cover with water; poach gently for 10 minutes. Remove the steaks, drain on a clean cloth until cold; remove skin and bones.

Arrange the salmon in a baking dish, pour over the pickling liquid made from the remaining ingredients with ½ pt of the poaching liquid added. Leave for 24 hours. Heat through the next day and serve hot.

Salmon, Spiced (8 portions) H

This potted, pickled salmon dish will keep for several weeks in a cool place and can be used as required, to serve with hot buttered toast.

3 lb middle cut salmon
1 pt vinegar
⅓ pt water
1 teaspoon salt
1 oz whole black peppercorns
1 oz cinnamon stick

For the pickle liquid, mix the vinegar with the water and add salt, peppercorns and cinnamon. Clean the salmon thoroughly, cut into 1-2 in pieces and put into the pickling liquid. Bring slowly to boiling point and simmer for 12-15 minutes. Leave the fish to cool in the liquid.

When cool, pack the salmon into a large dish, pour over the liquid and cover the dish tightly to exclude air.

Pickled Smelts (6-8 portions) F

A short-term fish preserve, pickled in wine. It may be served, drained, on its own with bread and butter or as part of a herring or kipper salad.

2½ doz smelts
½ teaspoon pepper
2 oz coarse salt
½ teaspoon nutmeg
Pinch mace
½ teaspoon saltpetre
4 bay leaves
1½-2 pt red wine

Wash and gut the smelts through the gills, leaving the fish whole. Lay the smelts in an earthenware jar, seasoning each layer with mixed pepper, salt, nutmeg, mace and saltpetre; put a bay leaf between each layer. Boil the red wine and pour over the smelts. Cover with a plate; when cold tie down the jar and leave for 14 days.

Soused Sprats (6-8 portions) H and F

Smelts and pilchards may be soused in the same manner as sprats. They are all left to cool in the sousing liquid and drained before serving, preferably chilled, with a salad or bread and butter.

2 lb sprats
1 pt basic fish pickle

Oven: 300°F; gas mark 2; 45 minutes

Wash the sprats carefully; scale and cut off fins, heads and tails; draw out the guts. Place close together in an ovenproof dish, pour over the pickle, cover with foil and bake for 45 minutes. Serve chilled.

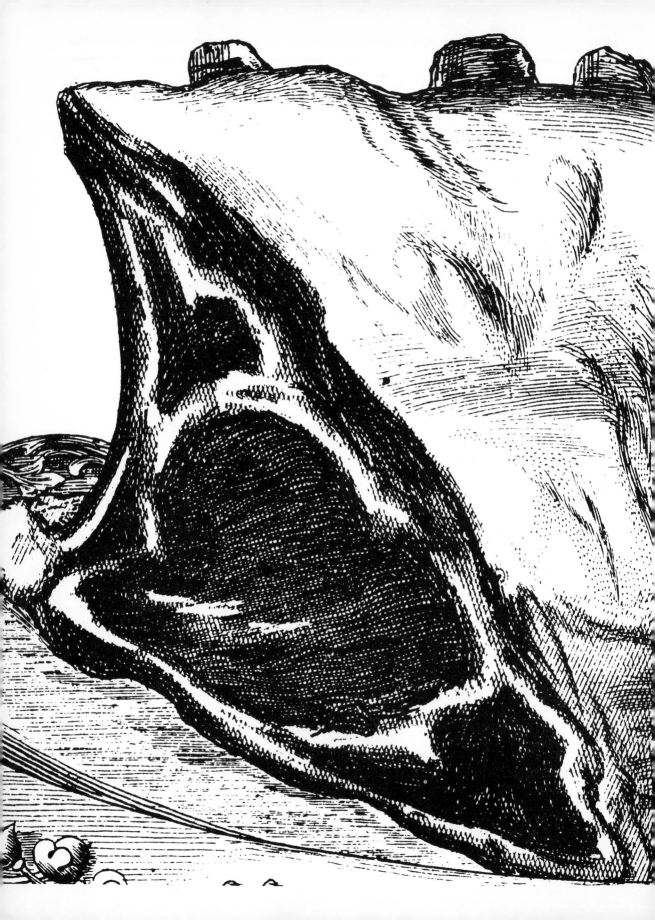

Meat, Poultry and Game

The diet of our hunting ancestors consisted for a large part of meat, first raw and then, with the discovery of fire, roasted. As the hunters settled in small ordered communities, meat supplies had to be augmented with other foods, such as grains, root vegetables and berries, and gradually meat became a luxury item available only to the noble rich. By the Middle Ages, the only meat known to the poor and the peasants was salt bacon, usually in combination with beans or eggs; occasionally a rabbit or game bird would be trapped in spite of poaching being a punishable offence. The yeoman farmer fared somewhat better, enjoying fresh meat, usually beef, in summer, mutton and pork, goose and capon at Christmas time. But royalty and nobility feasted to the extent of gluttony on beavers and squirrels, cormorants, herons and cranes, larks and curlews apart from the plain meats of beef, pork, veal and poultry. No feast was complete without its bedecked peacock or roast swan.

Any gastronomic feats which were achieved on a national or regional level in the Middle Ages were almost totally destroyed by Cromwell's puritanical regime which inhibited any interest in culinary affairs. The nobility after Cromwell adopted the French and Dutch modes of cooking introduced by succeeding monarchs and their queens while the population at large reverted to the trusted dishes of bacon and beans, bacon and eggs and savoury pies and puddings of medieval days. Relief from this monotonous diet could, however, be found at the local fairs, in urban cookshops, in taverns and inns and at the street traders' stalls. In London, roast pig was traditional at St. Bartholomew's Fair, roast goose was associated with the Stourbridge Fair in Cambridge, and in the West Country lamb pies were washed down with Devonshire cider. Cookshops, apart from catering for their guests, would also cook customers' meat for a small fee. It is probable that dishes that provided a complete meal for cooking in one pot, such as boiled pork with pease pudding, originated at this time.

During the 17th century, agricultural improvements resulted in better quality foods, and the poor man's diet of black bread and salt bacon was gradually replaced by wheaten bread and fresh meat. Prosperity was now determined by the amount of meat in the daily diet, and manliness and meat-eating became synonymous as evidenced in the fictitious English character, John Bull. Better quality meat contributed to improved roasting techniques, beef being the most popular.

The Industrial Revolution in the 18th century wrought yet another upheaval in British traditional cooking, for the worse on some levels and for the better on others. Rural life suffered most at the expense of the machine age — the general exodus to towns where workers were crowded together in tenement houses lacking proper cooking facilities meant a permanent loss of old eating and cooking traditions. At the same time, the middle classes began their ascent and encouraged an increase in ready-made and imported foods. For the working families, the daily diet became one of bread and butter (or margarine) and tea, with a Sunday treat at one of the flourishing cookshops, ale houses or taverns which expanded their business to include hot eels and pea soups, fried fish, pies and puddings, baked potatoes, sheep and lamb trotters. By the mid 19th century, tripe shops were springing up in competition with pork butchers specialising in local delicacies such as faggots, black puddings, brawns and haslet.

Among the upper classes, scarcity in good food was unknown, and quantities usually erred on the generous side. It was in this section of the population that the experimentation and development of old cooking traditions occurred which were to last through the Victorian and Edwardian eras until the early 20th century. The refinements and foreign influences which have characterised cooking since the mid 20th century have not shaken the sound basis for British culinary traditions that roast beef should be cooked to taste of roast beef only, lamb hot-pot of lamb and chicken pie of chicken.

The following recipes for meat, poultry and game have for ease of reference been divided into these categories:
1. Beef
2. Veal
3. Lamb and Mutton
4. Pork
5. Bacon, Gammon and Ham
6. Offal
7. Poultry
8. Game
9. Savoury Meat and Game Pies and Puddings
10. Potted and Pickled Meat and Game
11. Brawns, Galantines and Jellies

BEEF

It was not until the end of the Middle ages that beef began to appear regularly in British cooking: huge spit-roasts on the tables of the rich, with pot stews in numerous regional variations for ordinary people. The main cattle-rearing areas of Wales and Scotland show a marked difference from those of the West Country, the Midlands and the North West. In Wales, and Scotland, cattle were rarely killed for meat consumption, and few beef dishes occur in these areas, dairy produce featuring more strongly as by-products. In the Midlands and the North West there was less reluctance to kill beef, and from these parts come the highest proportions of traditional beef dishes, with a strong emphasis on utilising every scrap of the animals.

Aberdeen Sausage (6 portions) F Scotland

An economical dish made with uncooked minced beef, shaped into a sausage and boiled. Served cold, cut into slices, with salads or pickles.

1½ lb minced beef
¾ lb fat bacon
6 oz fine oatmeal
½ teaspoon ground mace
½ teaspoon ground nutmeg
Salt and pepper
Brown meat stock

Mince the bacon and mix with oatmeal and beef, season to taste with mace, nutmeg, salt and pepper. Grease a pudding cloth; lay the meat on it shaping it into a sausage about 3 in by 7 in. Wrap the pudding cloth around it and secure it firmly. Boil the sausage in stock until cooked through, after 2—3 hours. Re-tie the cloth to take up any shrinkage and leave the sausage to cool. Cover the sausage with a meat glaze or browned breadcrumbs. Serve cold.

Beef and Pigeon Stew (4 portions) F

A wholesome, slow-cooked winter stew which could be transformed into a pie by adding a lid of mashed potatoes or shortcrust pastry.

1 lb mixed steak and kidney
Seasoned flour
2 pigeons
4 bacon rashers
4 oz sliced onions
Dripping
½ pt stout
2 tablespoons cider vinegar
1 faggot of herbs
Salt and pepper

Oven: 325°F; gas mark 3; 3½ hours

Cut the meat and kidney into 1 in cubes and toss in seasoned flour. Cut the cleaned pigeons in half and wrap a bacon rasher round each half. Fry the onions lightly in dripping, add the meat and let it brown. Stir in the stout and vinegar and simmer for 15 minutes.
   Arrange half the meat and onion mixture in a deep ovenproof dish, lay the pigeons on top, cover with the rest of the meat and onion and pour over the pan juices. Add the herbs and a sprinkling of salt and pepper. Cover the dish with two thicknesses of greaseproof paper and a lid; bake in the oven for about 3 hours.

Beef Burgers (8 portions) H

This is the British version of the ubiquitous beef burger, but made with finest fillet steak and omitting the bread roll.

8 fillet steaks (4—6 oz each)
4 oz butter
8 slices bread

16 bacon rashers
8 slices Lancashire cheese
1 pt basic brown sauce
2½ fl oz brown stock
5 fl oz sherry
Salt and pepper
5 fl oz double cream
Garnish: parsley and watercress

Melt the butter in a pan and brown the steaks on
both sides. Cut the bread into circles to fit the
steaks; fry until golden brown. Fry the bacon
rashers; arrange two rashers on each piece of
bread, top with a steak and cover with cheese.
Heat under the grill until the cheese bubbles.

Make up the brown sauce; add the stock and
sherry and reduce slightly. Season to taste with
salt and pepper, stir in the cream and heat the
sauce through. Serve in a sauce boat. Garnish the
beef burgers with parsley and watercress.

Beef Cecils (8 portions) F

Cookery writers of the early 19th century,
including Mrs. Rundell and Eliza Acton, exhorted
their readers to use only under-cooked beef for
mince and hash dishes. Local variations of these
beef cecils include Claversham Rissoles which are
further flavoured with marjoram, thyme and
chopped celery leaves and shaped into flat rounds.
Durham cutlets have pieces of macaroni representing the bones decorated with cutlet frills.

2 lb cooked minced beef
4 oz finely chopped onions
1 oz butter
6 oz white breadcrumbs
Grated rind of 1 lemon
4 chopped anchovy fillets
1 dessertspoon chopped parsley
Pinch nutmeg, salt and pepper
1 dessertspoon Worcestershire sauce
1 egg
Egg and breadcrumbs for coating
Fat for frying

Fry the onions in butter until soft; mix with the
minced beef, breadcrumbs, lemon rind, anchovies,
parsley, nutmeg and salt and pepper to taste. Add
the Worcestershire sauce and bind the mixture
with the lightly beaten egg. Shape into 16 balls.
Coat each ball in beaten egg and breadcrumbs and
fry in deep fat until golden brown.

Beef Collops (6—8 portions) F

Also known as "scotched beef", many dishes of
minced beef have been erroneously attributed to
Scotland; the term "scotch" in culinary terms
means cutting up small. Yorkshire beef collops are
made with barley instead of oatmeal or white
breadcrumbs.

2 lb minced beef
½ lb finely chopped onions
2 oz dripping
Salt and pepper
Pinch nutmeg
¾ pt brown stock or ½ pt stock and ¼ pt Guinness
1 faggot of herbs
2 tablespoons mushroom ketchup
¾ lb white breadcrumbs or oatmeal
Garnish: hardboiled eggs, toast sippets

Fry the onions and mince in the dripping until
lightly brown; season with salt, pepper and nutmeg
and add the stock and herbs. Simmer for 40
minutes, add the ketchup, breadcrumbs or oatmeal;
mix well and cook for a further 5—10 minutes.
Serve on a hot dish surrounded by a border of
mashed potatoes and garnish with slices of hardboiled egg and toast sippets.

Beef Curry (6 portions) F and H

The British colonials of India and Malaysia took
so enthusiastically to the national dishes of these
countries that they brought the recipes back and
integrated hot spicy stews of beef, lamb and
chicken in British cooking traditions.

2 lb stewing beef
1½ oz seasoned flour
2 oz dripping
1 oz curry powder
4 oz chopped onions
4 oz chopped apples
1 crushed clove garlic
1 oz tomato purée
2 oz chutney
1 oz sultanas
2 pt brown stock
Salt and pepper

Cut the meat into 1 in cubes and dust with
seasoned flour. Melt the dripping, stir in the curry
powder and cook for a few minutes, stirring
constantly; add the onions and apples, fry for a
few minutes before putting in the cubed beef to

brown. Mix in the garlic, tomato purée, chutney and sultanas. Blend in the stock, bring the mixture to the boil; cover and simmer for 1½–2 hours. Correct seasoning.

Serve with boiled rice and the traditional curry accompaniments, such as poppadums, Bombay duck, mango or Indian chutney, diced apples, onions, cucumber, sliced bananas, tomatoes, quartered lemons and grated coconut.

Beef Dumplings with Cream Sauce (6–8 portions) F

Floury potatoes or rice would be ideal for mopping up the rich sauce with these dumplings.

1½ lb minced, uncooked beef
1½ oz softened butter
3 oz white breadcrumbs
3 fl oz double cream
Brown stock
Salt and pepper
6 oz chopped onions
1 lb finely chopped suet
3 oz finely chopped shallots
1 teaspoon lemon juice
Garnish: watercress or chopped parsley

Mix the beef in a bowl with butter until smoothly blended. Moisten the breadcrumbs with a little cream and add enough stock to give the consistency of a thick soup. Gradually beat in the meat and season with salt and pepper. Stir in the onions and suet and shape the mixture into small balls. Put in boiling stock, cover and simmer for 45 minutes.

Lift out the balls and keep them warm; reduce the liquid by half. Fry the shallots in a little butter, add the reduced stock and boil for a further 10–15 minutes; stir in the lemon juice and remaining cream. Pour the sauce over the dumplings and serve garnished with watercress or parsley.

Beefsteak Elizabetta (6–8 portions) F

This beef stew, made from shoulder or chuck steak, is traditionally served with suet dumplings flavoured with mustard.

2 lb stewing steak
1 oz seasoned flour
1 oz dripping
½ lb chopped onions
6 oz sliced carrots

1½ pt brown stock
1 tablespoon vinegar
½ teaspoon dry mustard
8 dumplings

Cut the meat into 1 in cubes and dust with seasoned flour. Melt the dripping and brown the onions and meat. Add the carrots and stock, vinegar and mustard and bring to the boil. Reduce the heat, cover and simmer gently for 2 hours. Cook the mustard dumplings in a pan of boiling water for the last 30 minutes of cooking time.

Beef Olives (8 portions) H and F

Olives have featured in British cooking since the 17th century and probably even earlier when they were known as 'aloes'. The name for these thin slices rolled round a forcemeat stuffing may derive from the elongated oval forms of the olive shellfish. Victoria steaks are a type of beef olives, anchovy fillets being added to the forcemeat, and the piece of steak cooked whole.

2 lb rump steak
½ lb veal forcemeat
2 oz dripping
½ lb sliced onions
1½ pt brown stock
Salt and pepper
1 oz butter
1 oz flour

Cut the beef into eight thin slices. Make up the forcemeat and divide equally over the steaks. Roll up the meat and tie with string. Melt the dripping and fry the onions until golden; add the meat and brown lightly. Add the stock, salt and pepper to taste and bring to the boil. Simmer gently for 1½ hours. Knead the butter and flour and stir into the stock. Bring to the boil, stirring all the time. Remove the string from the olives, place them on a serving dish and strain the sauce over the meat.

Salt beef olives from Devon differ from traditional olives only in the forcemeat which is made up from ½ lb breadcrumbs with 2 oz each of chopped, fried bacon and onions and bound with the juice and grated rind of 1 lemon. The stock is enriched with 5 fl oz red wine and 1 teaspoon of tomato purée.

Beef Royal (6 portions) H

An Elizabethan dish, the flavour of which is best

appreciated if cooked a day in advance and served cold when the sauce will have set to a jelly.

2 lb sirloin or rump of beef
1 pig trotter
5 fl oz white wine
Salt and pepper
Pinch clove, mace and nutmeg
½ teaspoon marjoram
Grated rind of ½ lemon
2 gammon rashers (2 oz each)
½ oz butter
1 bay leaf
2½ fl oz port wine
1 pounded anchovy fillet
2 oz chopped pickled walnuts

Bone the meat if necessary and cook the bones with the trotter, the white wine and just enough water to cover; add salt and pepper and simmer gently for at least 30 minutes to give a good broth. Leave to cool before straining.

Cut the meat into two slices and beat them. Sprinkle one slice with clove, mace, nutmeg, marjoram, lemon rind, salt and pepper, cover with the gammon rashers and top with the other slice of beef. Tie the meat securely with string. Melt the butter and brown the meat on all sides. Place in a large pan and add the bay leaf and strained broth. Cook, covered with a lid, over low heat for 3 hours; leave the meat to cool in the cooking liquid.

Put the meat on a serving dish. Skim the stock, add the port and the anchovy and bring to the boil; simmer for 10 minutes. When slightly cool, add the pickled walnuts and pour the sauce over and around the beef.

Beef Stew (6 portions) H

The hearty, sustaining beef stew has numerous local variations, but common to them all is the main ingredient of chuck or shoulder steak. Various flavours can be added to the basic stew, such as herbs, juice and grated rind of 1 lemon, 2½ fl oz port or 1 tablespoon of Harvey's or Worcestershire sauce.

Vegetables may also be added for different flavours, for example 2–3 oz of the following: Jerusalem artichokes, globe artichoke bottoms, celery, celeriac, parsnips, chestnuts, soaked split peas or haricot beans, pickled walnuts. Fried forcemeat balls may also be served with the stew.

2 lb stewing steak
Seasoned flour
½ lb sliced onions
2 oz dripping
1½ pt brown stock
Salt and pepper
½ lb thinly sliced carrots
½ lb thinly sliced turnips

Oven: 325°F; gas mark 3; 2–2½ hours

Cut the meat into 1 in cubes and dust with seasoned flour. Fry the onions in dripping until golden brown, add and brown the meat. Pour over the stock, add salt and pepper and bring to the boil. Put in the carrots and turnips and simmer, covered, for 2–2½ hours or until the meat is tender. Alternatively, bake in the oven for the same length of time.

The following variations are examples of local beef stews:

Cider Stew, use a stock of ½ pt cider, ½ pt tomato sauce and ½ pt brown stock; replace carrots and turnips with ½ lb soaked haricot beans.

Devilled Stew, stir 1 dessertspoon vinegar and 1 teaspoon made mustard into the onions and meat before adding stock; omit carrots and turnips.

Durham Beef Stew, cook in the oven; add suet dumplings for the last hour of cooking.

Exeter Stew, add parsley dumplings for the last 30 minutes of cooking.

Hertfordshire Stew, add herb and onion dumplings for the last 30 minutes.

Mushroom Ketchup Stew, fry 4 oz chopped mushrooms with the onions and add 2 tablespoons mushroom ketchup to the brown stock.

Steak and Anchovy Stew, add 4 chopped anchovy fillets with the stock; omit salt from seasoning.

Steak and Kidney Stew, replace ½ lb stewing steak with ½ lb skinned, cored and chopped ox or lamb kidney; garnish with chopped parsley.

Steak and Liver Stew, add ½ lb chopped pig liver to the onions, together with the meat.

Steak and Oyster Stew, omit carrots and turnips, add 12 cleaned oysters for the last 10 minutes of cooking.

Steak and Pickled Walnuts Stew, use 2½ lb steak, 6 oz onions, 2 crushed cloves of garlic and stock

made up of 1 pt brown stock and ½ pt red wine,
flavoured with marjoram and chopped parsley; add
8 chopped pickled walnuts for the last 30 minutes.
An old English dish, more popular in Australia
where it was introduced by English settlers.

Steak and Stuffed Prunes Stew, replace 2 oz of
the onions with 1 crushed clove of garlic; for
stock use ½ pt dark beer or Guinness and 5 fl oz
brown stock; 15 minutes before the end of cooking
add ½ lb soaked, stoned prunes stuffed with 4 oz
toasted hazelnuts.

Welsh Stew (Cawl Biff), replace the carrots with
1 lb chopped leeks.

Beef Stew, Pickled (8 portions) F Scotland

A Scottish method of cooking shoulder or chuck
steak which is too tough for grilling. The meat is
tenderised by steeping it in a marinade.

2 lb stewing steak
2½ fl oz olive oil
2½ fl oz vinegar
6 cloves
12 black peppercorns
1 sprig each, thyme and parsley
1 teaspoon marjoram
¾ lb sliced onions
2 bay leaves
2 oz butter
1 pt brown stock
1 oz arrowroot

Cut the meat into eight equal pieces; mix the
marinade by blending the oil with the vinegar and
adding cloves, peppercorns, thyme, parsley and
marjoram. Lay the meat in a dish, with the onion
rings and bay leaves, and pour over the marinade;
steep for 12 hours, turning the meat occasionally.

Drain and dry the meat; fry lightly on both
sides in butter and add 5 fl oz of the strained
marinade and the stock. Simmer the steak until
tender, after about 45 minutes; thicken the liquid
with arrowroot.

Beef Stew, Spicy (8 portions) H

A rich stew, elevated above the everyday family
type by the addition of red wine and brandy; ½ pt
draught cider flavoured with 1 oz black treacle
may replace the wine and brandy.

3 lb topside of beef

4 oz bacon rashers
½ oz butter
¾ lb sliced onions
6 oz sliced carrots
¾ lb skinned, chopped tomatoes
1 faggot of herbs
1 clove garlic
Salt and pepper
Nutmeg
3 fl oz red wine
1 tablespoon brandy
1–1½ pt brown stock
1 oz flour

Oven: 325°F; gas mark 3; 3 hours

Cut the meat into 1 in cubes and chop the bacon.
Fry the bacon in the butter with the onions and
carrots. Put the meat in a casserole dish with the
tomatoes and the bacon and onion mixture. Add
the herbs, crushed garlic, salt, pepper and nutmeg,
wine and brandy. Pour over the stock, cover and
cook in the oven for 3 hours. Ten minutes before
the end of cooking, thicken the sauce with the
flour mixed with a little stock; return to the oven.

Beef Stew with Walnuts and Celery (8 portions) H and F

Luxury touches are added to this stew of shoulder
or chuck steak with button mushrooms and onions,
chopped walnuts and a garnish of orange peel.

2 lb stewing steak
Seasoned flour
2 oz dripping or oil
2 oz button onions
5 fl oz red wine
1½ pt brown stock
1 sprig each, thyme and parsley
2 cloves garlic
Salt and pepper
4 oz button mushrooms
3–4 oz chopped walnuts
4 oz chopped celery
1 oz butter
Garnish: grated orange peel

Cut the meat into 2 in cubes and coat with
seasoned flour. Fry the meat in dripping until
brown, remove from the pan and fry the onions
until golden. Return the meat to the pan, add the
wine, stock, herbs and crushed garlic. Season with
salt and pepper, cover and simmer for 1½–2 hours.

After 1 hour of cooking, add the mushrooms, walnuts and celery which have been fried in the butter until crisp. Serve the stew sprinkled with orange peel.

Beef with Anchovies (6—8 portions) H and F

Salt fish was used in old traditional cooking to add flavour to fresh meat. In this adaptation, anchovy fillets lard the joint which is pot-roasted with vegetables.

2 lb boned beef
6 anchovy fillets
1 oz butter
Vegetable base
¾ pt brown stock

Mash half the anchovies and blend with the butter; brown the beef in this anchovy butter. Lard the meat with the remaining anchovies and pot-roast on a vegetable base of diced carrots, onions and celery; pour over the stock and cook gently for about 2½—2¾ hours.

Bubble and Squeak (6—8 portions) F

Early in the 19th century, cookery writers of the day suddenly turned their attention to this old method of using up cooked beef. All, however, agreed that salt boiled, underdone beef was preferable and that it should only be lightly fried, with plenty of pepper.

1½ lb cooked, thinly sliced beef
1½ lb cabbage
6 oz butter
Salt and pepper

Boil the cabbage, drain thoroughly and cut it up small. Sauté the meat gently for a few minutes in the butter; sprinkle with freshly ground pepper. Remove the meat from the pan and place in a serving dish. Fry the cabbage in the remaining butter for a few minutes. Season and pile on top of the meat.

Serve with pickled cucumber or walnuts, Wow-Wow sauce or melted butter sauce flavoured with mustard, chopped pickled cucumber and pickled onions.

Chiddingly Hot-Pot (6 portions) F Sussex

An all-in-one family stew of shoulder or chuck steak with vegetables and spicy flavours.

2 lb stewing steak
Seasoned flour
2 oz dripping
2 oz chopped celery
½ lb chopped onions
Allspice, salt and pepper
½ lb sliced potatoes
3 cloves
1 dessertspoon tarragon vinegar
1 oz melted butter
¾ pt brown stock

Oven: 325°F; gas mark 3; 2½ hours

Cut the meat into 1 in cubes and dust with seasoned flour. Brown the meat in the dripping, remove from the pan and fry the celery and onions lightly. Put a layer of onions and celery in a casserole dish, sprinkle with allspice, salt and pepper; cover with a layer of meat and a thin layer of potatoes. Repeat these layers, adding seasoning and the cloves and vinegar. Finish with a layer of potatoes and brush with melted butter.

Add enough stock to come just below the potatoes; cover with a lid. Cook in the oven for 1½ hours. Remove the lid and continue cooking to brown the potatoes for another hour.

Collared Beef (6—10 portions) F

An economical dish of spiced rolled (collared) beef, sometimes served hot with a dill or horse-radish sauce, but most often pressed between weighted boards and served cold with pickles and salads.

2—4 lb pickled or salted flank or boned rib of beef
2 tablespoons chopped parsley
½ teaspoon each, sage, mixed herbs and powdered allspice
Cayenne pepper, nutmeg, salt and pepper

Remove any gristle and bone from the meat. Mix the parsley with sage, herbs, allspice, cayenne, nutmeg, salt and pepper. Coat the meat with this mixture, roll up tightly, secure with string or tape and tie in a muslin cloth. Cover with cold water and bring to the boil; simmer for 4—6 hours.

Remove from the pan, put a heavy weight over the meat without removing the cloth and press until cold.

Collops in the Pan (6—8 portions) F

Originally, a collop meant a slice of bacon, but now refers to a thin slice of any kind of meat.

2 lb rump of beef
3 oz butter
½ lb sliced onions
Salt and pepper
½ pt brown meat stock
Oyster pickle
Walnut ketchup

Cut the beef into thin slices and fry lightly in the butter; add the onions and fry until light brown. Cover the pan and cook gently for 10—15 minutes. Season with salt and pepper. Remove the meat from the pan; stir in the stock, bring to the boil and flavour to taste with oyster pickle and walnut ketchup. Strain over the collops and serve.

Culloden Collops (8 portions) F Scotland

Originally, this was probably made with collops or slices of steak; now mince is used, but whisky and oatmeal remain as integral parts. Traditionally served with sippets, boiled potatoes and leeks in a cream sauce.

2 lb minced steak
2 oz dripping
6 oz chopped onions
4 oz chopped mushrooms
5 fl oz white stock
Salt and pepper
2 oz oatmeal
Salt and pepper
2 tablespoons whisky

Oven: 350°F; gas mark 4; 1¼ hours

Melt the dripping and fry the onions until soft. Add the meat and continue frying for 5 minutes, stirring well to break down the mince; stir in the mushrooms. Add the stock, whisky, salt and pepper.

Transfer to an ovenproof dish, cover and cook in the oven for 1 hour; add the oatmeal and cook for 10 minutes or until the fat is absorbed.

Farmer's Brew (6—8 portions) F

Probably Scottish in origin, this stew is cooked in beer.

1½ lb stewing steak
1 oz seasoned flour
4 oz sliced onions

2 oz butter
1 tablespoon sugar
Pinch mustard
Sprig thyme
1 bay leaf
Salt and pepper
½ pt Scots ale
5 fl oz brown stock
8 beef sausages

Oven: 325°F; gas mark 3; 1½ hours

Cut the meat into thin slices, toss in seasoned flour and brown with the onion rings in butter. Add the sugar, mustard, thyme and bay leaf; season with salt and pepper. Cover with a lid and put in the oven at 400°F, gas mark 6, for 10 minutes. Remove from the oven, add ale and stock, bring to the boil. Return to the oven, at 325°F, gas mark 3, for 1½ hours.

Serve the stew with the grilled sausages on a mound of mashed potatoes.

Farmhouse Brisket (6—8 portions) F and H

Brisket is one of the most suitable joints for slow pot-roasting and braising; sweetened ale imparts a subtle flavour.

2 lb boned and rolled brisket
Seasoned flour
1 oz dripping
4 oz chopped streaky bacon
1 lb diced onions
½ lb diced carrots
4 oz diced celery
½ pt brown ale
1 dessertspoon brown sugar
Salt and pepper

Dredge the meat with seasoned flour, brown in the dripping and remove from the pan. Fry the bacon with the onions, carrots and celery until soft. Pour the ale over the vegetables, add sugar, salt and pepper and put the meat on top. Cover and cook over low heat for 2½ hours. Remove the meat and vegetables to a serving dish; reduce the cooking liquid and pour round the meat.

Highland Beef Balls (6—8 portions) F Scotland

These deep-fried beef dumplings are served with a tomato sauce and floury or mashed potatoes.

2 lb minced shoulder steak
¾ lb finely chopped suet
3 oz finely chopped onions
Salt and pepper
½ teaspoon each, ground cloves, ginger, mace
2 eggs
Medium oatmeal
Fat for frying

Mix the minced meat with suet and onions, flavour to taste with salt, pepper, cloves, ginger and mace; bind the mixture with the lightly beaten eggs and shape into egg-shaped balls. Roll the balls in oatmeal and deep-fry in hot fat for 7—8 minutes or until brown. Drain before serving.

Hunting Beef (6—8 portions) F

This dish is traditionally served with boiled onions, carrots and turnips which can be cooked in the beer, boiled potatoes and suet dumplings.

2 lb salted, boned and rolled brisket
1½ pt light ale
1 bay leaf
Nutmeg, ground cloves, mixed herbs

Soak the brisket overnight in cold water. Put the meat in a pan with the ale, bay leaf and spices. Bring to the boil and simmer for 2½—3 hours. Remove from the pan and leave to cool before serving with the traditional hot accompaniments.

Inky Pinky (6—8 portions) F Scotland

A curious name for a dish of left-over beef, possibly from the colour of the underdone meat, and sliced carrots and dark brown gravy.

2 lb cold roast beef
¾ lb small whole onions
1 pt brown stock
1 lb boiled sliced carrots
1 tablespoon vinegar
Salt and pepper
1 oz cornflour
Accompaniment: sippets

Slice the beef thinly, trimming away any skin. Simmer the onions in the stock for 30 minutes, add the beef and carrots and heat through. Add vinegar, salt and pepper to taste, and thicken the stock with cornflour blended with a little cold water. Bring to the boil and serve at once with toast sippets.

Mixed Grill (8 portions) H and F

This dish has become popular in the 20th century and is habitually served with chipped potatoes or potato crisps. Some versions include liver, black pudding, veal or pork chops and fried eggs.

8 fillet steaks (4 oz each)
4 oz melted butter or dripping
8 sausages
8 lamb kidneys
1 lb mushrooms
8 tomatoes
8 bacon rashers
Garnish: watercress, parsley butter

Heat the grill and brush all ingredients with melted butter. Grill the sausages, kidneys and mushrooms; transfer to the bottom of the pan while grilling the steaks, tomatoes and bacon. Arrange the mixed grill on a serving dish and garnish with parsley butter and watercress.

Royal Brisket (6—8 portions) H London

Dating from the latter part of the 18th century, this recipe is credited to John Farley, chef at the London Tavern in Bishopsgate and included in his book *The London Art of Cookery,* published in 1783.

2 lb boned brisket
4 oz chopped streaky bacon
4 chopped oysters
2 tablespoons chopped parsley
Salt, pepper and nutmeg
2 oz flour
2 oz butter
1 pt red wine
¾ pt brown stock

Oven: 350°F; gas mark 4; 3 hours

Make slits all round the meat, about 1 in apart. Stuff the slits alternately with bacon, oysters and parsley. Season the joint and the slits with nutmeg, pepper and salt, dredge with flour and brown the meat in the butter. Put the joint into a large pan or casserole dish with the wine and stock and bring to the boil. Put on a tightly fitting lid and cook gently for 3 hours in a moderate oven or on top of the stove.

Lift the brisket on to a serving dish; skim the fat from the cooking liquid and pour the pan juices over the meat. Serve with sweet pickles and fresh, crisp vegetables.

Saunders (6 portions) F

A useful family dish for left-over beef, somewhat reminiscent of cottage pie. Serve with hot gravy and pickles.

1 lb cooked beef
Dripping
2 lb cold mashed potatoes
2 oz butter
2 egg yolks
Salt and pepper
2 oz flour
½ lb chopped onions
Pinch grated nutmeg, mixed herbs
2 tablespoons brown stock

Oven 400°F; gas mark 6; 30—40 minutes

Brush a deep loaf or cake tin with melted dripping. Mix the mashed potatoes with butter, egg yolks, salt, pepper and flour to make a pliable paste; line the base and sides of the tin with two thirds of this mixture.

Chop the meat finely and mix with onions, nutmeg, herbs and seasoning and moisten with stock. Place the meat mixture on the potato base and cover with the remaining potatoes. Bake in the oven for 30—40 minutes.

Cottage Pie (6 portions) F

As traditional as roast beef in British cookery is cottage pie, which, when made with lamb is known as shepherd's pie. Ideally it should be made with fresh minced beef but most often uses up left-over roast meat. The numerous regional variations include a sprinkling of grated cheese over the topping of potatoes or pickle mixed with the mince.

1 lb minced beef
1 tablespoon oil
1 small finely chopped onion
¾ oz flour
5 fl oz brown stock
1 teaspoon chopped parsley
Pinch marjoram or lovage
Salt and pepper
1 teaspoon Worcestershire sauce
1 lb mashed potatoes

Oven: 350°F; gas mark 4; 45 minutes

Heat the oil and fry the onion and meat until brown. If using left-over beef do not fry this. Stir in the flour and stock. Add the parsley, marjoram and salt and pepper to taste. Blend in the Worcestershire sauce and left-over beef. Put this mixture in an ovenproof dish, smooth the mashed potatoes over the top and riffle the surface with a fork. Bake in the oven for about 45 minutes or until the top is golden brown.

Spiced Beef (8—12 portions) H and F
Wales and Ireland

This is a traditional dish at the cold Christmas buffet in Wales, Ireland, parts of Yorkshire and Leicestershire. It is usually made with brisket or silverside, but skirt and flank are also suitable.

3 lb silverside or brisket
½ lb coarse salt
2 oz brown sugar
½ teaspoon each, allspice, ground cloves and nutmeg
Pinch thyme and pepper
1 crushed bay leaf
1 tablespoon (¾ oz) saltpetre
2 oz black treacle
½ lb sliced carrots
2 oz finely chopped onions

Have the beef boned but not rolled, rub it thoroughly with the salt and leave overnight. The following day, mix together the sugar, allspice, cloves, nutmeg, thyme, pepper and bay leaf; add the saltpetre.

Drain the beef from the salt and wipe dry; rub the meat thoroughly on both sides with the spice mixture and leave, covered, in a cool place for 2 days. Pour the warmed treacle over the meat, and rub the spices well into the meat every day for a week.

Roll the spiced beef up and tie firmly with string; put in a pan of boiling water with the sliced carrots and onions. Simmer gently for about 3 hours. Leave the meat to cool in the liquid, then remove and place between two boards. Press under a heavy weight for 8 hours before serving.

Spiced Brisket (8—12 portions) H and F

This probably dates back to medieval times when most meat was salted and flavoured with spices before cooking to disguise the excess saltiness. Excellent as a cold buffet dish.

2–4 lb pickled or salted brisket
Black pepper, ground ginger, cloves
½ pt claret or brown stock

Oven: 325°F; gas mark 3; 4 hours

Drain the brisket from the pickle; wipe and spread
out flat. Mix enough pepper, ginger and cloves to
sprinkle over the meat. Roll up and secure with
string or skewers.

Put the meat in an earthenware pot that will
just fit the joint. Pour over the claret or stock,
cover with two thicknesses of greaseproof paper
and press the lid on firmly. Cook in the oven for 4
hours; remove and press the joint between two
weighted plates or boards until cold.

Staffordshire Beefsteaks (8 portions) F and H Staffordshire

At the beginning of the 19th century Mrs. Rundell
published *Domestic Cookery,* one of the greatest
best-sellers of that century. It included many
regional recipes from the West Country, as well as
this recipe for steaks from Staffordshire.

2–3 lb stewing steak
Salt and pepper
1 oz flour
2 oz dripping
½ lb sliced onions
1½ pt brown stock
2 tablespoons walnut ketchup

Cut the steak into eight equal pieces, flatten with
a rolling pin and season with pepper; dust with
flour. Melt the dripping, fry the onions until light
brown, then add the steaks and brown. Pour over
the stock, cover and simmer for 1½–2 hours.
Correct seasoning. Stir the walnut ketchup into
the stock and serve the steaks with the gravy
poured over them.

STEAKS

Inherited from the bygone days of huge spit-roasts
of beef is the Englishman's love of plain grilled
steak. Fillet, rump or sirloin are the prime cuts for
grilling; the steak, brushed with melted butter and
sprinkled with pepper, but *never* salt should first
be grilled under high heat for 1 minute on each
side, then finished cooking under lowered heat
according to preference, 6 minutes on each side
for well-done steak, 4–5 minutes for medium and

3 minutes for rare steak. Serve with the juices in
the grill pan and garnish with watercress.

Minor variations of grilled steaks include
rubbing them with garlic or shallot or brushing
with anchovy, parsley, devil or shallot butter
before grilling. The following recipes for grilled and
fried steaks include old and new versions.

Steak Balmoral (8 portions) H Scotland

A modern recipe with fillet steaks cut and shaped
like tournedos.

8 fillet steaks (6 oz each)
2 oz butter
2 tablespoons oil
5 fl oz whisky
1½ pt rich brown sauce
Salt and pepper
½ lb chopped, fried mushrooms
8 fried bread rounds
Garnish: asparagus tips

Heat half the butter and all the oil; fry the steaks
as required — rare, medium or well-done. Remove
the steaks from the pan and keep warm. Add the
warmed whisky to the pan juices and flame. Stir
in the brown sauce, bring to the boil and reduce
by about half; season with salt and pepper and
blend in the remaining butter. Spread the
mushrooms over the warm bread rounds, top with
a steak and coat with the sauce. Serve garnished
with asparagus tips.

Carpet Bag Steaks (8 portions) H

This renowned Australian steak recipe is very likely
an adaptation of the beef and oyster stew brought to
Australia by the first English settlers. Ideally, the
beef should be cut from the thick or middle part
of the fillet.

2 fillets of beef (2½ lb each)
16 oysters
4 oz butter
Salt and pepper
Garnish: watercress

Leave each fillet in one piece and make a slit in
the side of each with a sharp knife; stuff 8 freshly
opened oysters into the pocket. Sew up the slit
with string. Fry the fillets in hot butter, for about
10 minutes on each side. Remove the string;
arrange the two fillets on a warm serving dish,

sprinkle with salt and pepper and garnish with sprigs of watercress.

To serve, cut each fillet into four portions, each with two oysters.

Dufftown Fillet Steaks (8 portions) H Scotland

Pepper steaks are a well-known French dish, but the Scots have improved on this with the addition of fine whisky. This is added to the sauce, or it may be set alight and spooned flaming over the fried steaks.

8 fillet steaks (6 oz each)
Black peppercorns
2 oz butter
Salt
Scotch whisky

Coat the steaks on both sides with freshly ground black pepper. Melt the butter in a heavy pan and fry the steaks over moderate heat until cooked as required; sprinkle with salt. Draw the steaks to the side of the pan and pour over enough whisky to make a sauce with the pan juices.

Serve the steaks coated with the sauce.

Steak MacFarlane (8 portions) H Scotland

Yet another favourite ingredient in Scottish cooking — oatmeal — is used to give a distinctive flavour to thick sirloin steaks.

8 sirloin steaks (6—8 oz each)
Salt and pepper
3 teaspoons made mustard
2 oz flour
2 eggs
4 oz rolled oats
3 oz butter
1 pt tomato sauce
5 fl oz claret
Garnish: chopped parsley, lemon slices

Flatten the steaks lightly, season with pepper and smear with the mustard. Dust the steaks with flour, dip in the lightly beaten eggs and coat with oats. Melt the butter and fry the steaks over low heat until cooked to the required degree.

Remove the steaks from the pan and keep warm on a serving dish. Heat the tomato sauce through with the claret, pour round the steaks and serve garnished with lemon slices and chopped parsley.

Planked Steak (8 portions) H Wales

Cooking meat or fish on a "plank" was commonly used in Wales. The plank was a thick piece of oak, about 18 in square, with a shallow depression in the centre; this was filled with hot dripping and fresh aromatic herbs over which the meat was placed. It was cooked in the oven where the wood charred slightly, imparting a smokey flavour to the meat. Modern planks are available, with grooves and channels for catching the juices.

8 rump or fillet steaks (6 oz each)
3—4 oz butter
1 bay leaf
1 faggot of herbs
Pepper
Garnish: parsley

Oven 425°F; gas mark 7; 20 minutes

Grill the steaks lightly on both sides; transfer them to the hot plank liberally smeared with butter. Lay the bay leaf and herbs on the plank beneath the steaks. Sprinkle the steaks with pepper and dot with butter. Put the plank in a hot oven until the meat is cooked, after about 20 minutes. A border of mashed potatoes is sometimes put round the board and browned with the steaks in the oven. Garnish with chopped parsley.

Steak Stella (8 portions) H and F

Beer is a marvellous tenderiser for beef as well as a flavoursome addition. Good quality braising steak can also be used for this dish.

8 sirloin or rump steaks (6 oz each)
1 pt pale ale
Pinch thyme
1 bay leaf
½ chopped chilli
8 black peppercorns
5 oz butter
3 oz chopped onions
1 teaspoon chopped parsley
2 teaspoons Worcestershire sauce

Beat the steaks flat until they are twice their original size; steep in the ale overnight with the thyme, bay leaf, chilli and peppercorns tied in a muslin bag. Half an hour before cooking, drain the steaks from the ale and wipe dry.

Mix 3 oz softened butter to a paste with the onions, parsley and Worcestershire sauce. Spread over the steaks. Heat the remaining butter and fry the steaks quickly on both sides. Remove the steaks to a serving dish; pour off excess fat from the pan juices. Add the strained ale to the pan and reduce to a glaze; pour over the steaks.

Stuffed Skirt of Beef (6—8 portions) F

An economical but nourishing dish, suitable for a family supper on a winter's night.

2 lb skirt of beef
½ lb medium oatmeal
4 oz chopped suet
1 dessertspoon chopped parsley
2 oz finely chopped onions
Salt and pepper
Milk
2 oz dripping
½ lb chopped onions
2 pt brown stock
4 oz sliced carrots
4 oz chopped turnips
2 oz cornflour

Buy the skirt in one piece, remove the skin from one side only and loosen the skin on the other side to form a pocket. Make up a forcemeat stuffing from the oatmeal and suet, mix with parsley and finely chopped onions; season with salt and pepper and bind with a little milk. Stuff into the prepared pocket and sew up the opening.

Melt the dripping in a pan and brown the meat and the onions. Add stock and seasoning; bring to the boil and simmer slowly for 2½—3 hours. About 45 minutes before the end of cooking, add the carrots and turnips. Blend the cornflour with a little water and add to the stock to thicken. Lift out the meat and remove the sewing thread; serve the meat surrounded by carrots and turnips.

VEAL

There is a scarcity of veal dishes in traditional British cooking. The Norman overlords greatly favoured veal, but the English resented the killing of young calves for food and considered it an economic wastage, preferring for centuries to breed cattle to augment their stock herds. In addition, there was a general suspicion that only if a calf was diseased would a farmer kill it. The few traditional veal dishes that do occur are generally for invalid diets, such as calf's foot jelly and the early blancmanges of tender veal cooked in milk. Not until the 18th century with farmers beginning to specialise in dairy herds and with the growing popularity of French cooking, does veal appear regularly, and then mainly on the tables of the rich.

Breast of Veal, Stuffed (6—8 portions) H and F

Breast of veal is one of the most economical cuts of a generally expensive meat. Boned and stuffed, it can be served hot with tomato, onion or parsley sauce; alternatively, press the meat between boards until cold and serve with salads and chutneys.

2½ lb boned breast of veal
4 oz veal forcemeat
2—3 pt white stock
1 faggot of herbs
Salt and pepper

Stuff the breast with forcemeat, roll up and tie firmly with string. Put in a pan with sufficient stock barely to cover the meat. Add the herbs, salt and pepper; bring to the boil and simmer until tender — allowing 20 minutes to every 1 lb. Lift out and carve the veal; use the strained cooked liquid as the basis for a sauce.

Brumbrays (8 portions) H London

As veal is a dry meat, containing no or little natural fat, it is often stuffed to impart moisture. These little rolled fillet slices are usually served with a brown sauce.

2 lb fillet of veal
4 oz blanched, diced sweetbread
2 diced artichoke bottoms
½ lb finely chopped pie veal
2 lb fat from marrow bones
4 oz white breadcrumbs
Salt and mace
2 eggs
4 oz butter
1—2 pt brown sauce

Oven: 325°F; gas mark 3; 2 hours

Cut the fillet into 16 equal pieces and beat into thin slices. Make a stuffing with the sweetbread, artichokes, pie veal and marrow fat; mix with half the breadcrumbs, season with salt and mace and bind with one egg yolk. Divide this stuffing equally over the veal slices, roll up and tie or secure with small skewers.

Dip the rolls in lightly beaten egg, coat with the remaining breadcrumbs and fry in hot butter until golden brown. Transfer the fried rolls to an ovenproof dish, cover with brown sauce and cook in the oven for 2 hours.

Cornish Cutlets (8 portions) H Cambridge University

In spite of its name, this dish originated in the late 18th century at one of the Cambridge colleges. Traditionally served with tomato sauce.

8 veal loin cutlets (6 oz each)
4 oz diced streaky bacon
1 oz lard
½ lb chopped onions
6 oz chopped carrots
6 oz chopped celery
Salt and pepper
1¼ pt white stock
1½ lb creamed potatoes

Oven: 450°F; gas mark 8; 15 minutes

Lard the cutlets with strips of fat, cut from the bacon. Melt the lard and fry the cutlets gently until light brown. Add the onions, carrots, celery and bacon and fry without browning. Sprinkle with salt and pepper. Add the stock, cover with a lid and simmer the cutlets and vegetables for 25–30 minutes.

Transfer to an ovenproof dish. Spread the creamed potatoes over the top and bake in the oven until well browned.

Dowlet Pie (6–8 portions) F London

This sweet, fruity dish is made with left-over cooked veal and served with a sweet wine and butter sauce.

1½ lb cooked minced veal
6 oz shredded beef suet
8 plums or soaked prunes or 6 oz raisins
8 dates
5 fl oz white wine
3 oz sugar
Pinch sweet herbs
Pinch nutmeg, cinnamon
1 egg (optional)
3 oz butter

Oven: 350°F; gas mark 4; 30–45 minutes

Arrange the veal, suet and plums and dates in an ovenproof dish; moisten with a little of the wine and sprinkle each layer with a little sugar mixed with sweet herbs, nutmeg and cinnamon.

Alternatively, mix the veal, suet, sugar, herbs and spices together and bind with beaten egg. Roll into balls with a date in the middle of each. Put these in a pie dish with the plums and bake. Brush with melted butter and bake for 30–40 minutes. Boil the remaining wine, sugar and butter together and pour over the veal dish just before serving.

Dunelm of Veal (6–8 portions) F

Suitable for a quick lunch snack or a high-tea dish; serve on sippets of buttered toast.

1 lb cooked minced veal
1 oz butter
½ lb finely chopped mushrooms
1½ tablespoons flour
2½ fl oz double cream
Salt and pepper

Cook the veal in the butter until light brown, add the mushrooms and fry lightly. Stir in the flour, add the cream and season with salt and pepper; simmer for 3–4 minutes and serve.

Savoury Veal (6–8 portions) H and F Shropshire

In Shrewsbury, this is a traditional way of cooking whole fillet of veal; it is always served with a creamy white sauce.

2 lb fillet of veal
2 oz flour
1 teaspoon salt
½ teaspoon each, pepper, sage, marjoram
2 pt veal stock
2 oz butter
Garnish: lemon slices

Oven: 450°F; gas mark 8; 15 minutes

Scald a pudding cloth and wring it out; dust with a little flour and sprinkle with salt, pepper and herbs. Wrap the meat in the cloth and tie securely. Poach in the veal stock over gentle heat for about 1½ hours or until tender.

Remove the cloth, brush the veal with butter, dust with the remaining flour and brown in a hot oven. Reduce the poaching liquid to 1–1½ pt and use to make a rich white sauce. Serve the carved meat garnished with lemon slices.

Scotch Collops (8 portions) H and F

The word "collop" refers to a slice of boned meat, cut across the grain like a steak.

2 lb fillet of veal
2 oz seasoned flour
1 egg
Breadcrumbs
4 oz butter
¾ pt white stock
Juice of 1 lemon
3 teaspoons mushroom ketchup
Pinch powdered mace
Salt and pepper
½ oz butter
½ oz flour
Garnish: bacon rashers, mushrooms, lemon slices

Cut the fillets into eight slices or collops and flatten them slightly; coat in seasoned flour, beaten egg and breadcrumbs. Fry the collops in the butter until golden brown; remove from the pan and keep hot.

Stir the veal stock, lemon juice, mushroom ketchup, mace, salt and pepper into the pan juices and bring to the boil. Knead the butter and flour, add to the stock and stir until it thickens. Offer the sauce separately; serve the collops garnished with crisp bacon rashers, whole fried mushrooms and lemon slices

Veal Cutlets with Lemon (8 portions) H London

Like Royal Brisket, this dish was created by John Farley as the principal cook at the London Tavern in 1783.

8 single loin veal cutlets (6 oz each)
2 oz seasoned flour
1 egg
Breadcrumbs
Grated lemon peel
Pinch sweet herbs, grated nutmeg
2–3 oz butter
1 oz flour
1 pt white stock
Juice of 1 lemon
Garnish: lemon slices

Dust the cutlets with seasoned flour; dip in beaten egg and coat with breadcrumbs mixed with lemon peel, sweet herbs and nutmeg. Fry the cutlets in the butter until golden brown on both sides; remove from the pan.

Stir the flour into the pan juices, add the stock gradually, stirring continuously. Add lemon juice, salt and pepper to taste; pour the sauce over the cutlets and garnish with lemon slices.

Veal Goose (8–12 portions) H London

The "goose" in this dish refers partly to the shape of the boned loin or fillet of veal, partly to the traditional stuffing and partly to the usual goose accompaniments of thickened brown gravy and apple sauce.

4 lb boned loin or fillet of veal
1 lb sage and onion stuffing
4 oz melted butter

Oven: 325–350°F; gas mark 3–4; 3¼–3½ hours

Spread the sage and onion stuffing over the boned meat, roll up and tie firmly with string or secure with skewers. Weigh the stuffed meat and calculate the cooking time allowing 40 minutes for every lb.

Brush the meat with butter and roast, basting frequently. Add more butter if necessary, to prevent the meat drying out. Thicken the pan juices and serve with the carved meat.

Veal Olives (8 portions) H

The concept of an olive as a thin slice of meat rolled up round a stuffing has persisted for centuries; the cooking methods have varied since the original roasting of the 16th century gave way to frying, baking and stewing.

2 lb fillet of veal
8 rashers streaky bacon
½ lb veal forcemeat
½ lb chopped onions
1½ oz butter or dripping
1½ oz flour
1½ pt white stock
Salt and pepper

Cut the veal into eight slices and beat them flat. Lay a rasher of bacon on each piece and spread over this a spoonful of the stuffing. Roll up and tie with string or secure with skewers. Fry the onions in the butter until soft; fry the olives until lightly browned. Stir in the flour. Gradually add the stock and bring to the boil; season with salt and pepper and simmer gently for 1½ hours.

Before serving the olives, remove string or skewers, place on a hot serving dish and pour the gravy over the meat.

Veal Stew (6—8 portions) F

For this family stew, inexpensive breast or shoulder of veal is ideal; to make the stew go further, serve it with veal forcemeat balls or bacon rolls and sippets of toast.

2 lb stewing veal
2 onions stuck with cloves
1 faggot of herbs
1 pt white stock
Salt and pepper
3 oz butter
1½ oz flour
1 pt milk

Cut the veal into 1 in cubes; put in a pan with the onions, faggot of herbs and stock. Bring to the boil, skim and season with salt and pepper, simmer gently for 1½ hours. Strain and keep the meat warm.

Make a white roux from 2 oz of butter and the flour; gradually blend in the heated milk and enough of the veal stock to give a sauce consistency. Beat the remaining 1 oz of butter into the sauce; add the meat and serve.

Yorkshire Veal and Oysters (8 portions) H
Yorkshire

Today, this is an expensive luxury dish, but well into the 19th century oysters were very common fare and used as additional flavouring for many homely dishes. In some versions, the stuffed veal is coated with batter and deep-fried.

2 lb fillet of veal
16 oysters
Seasoned flour
1 egg
Breadcrumbs
2 oz butter
Garnish: lemon slices

Cut the veal into eight equal slices, each about ½ in thick. Remove the oysters from their shells and reserve the liquid. Cut a slit in each piece of veal with the point of a sharp knife and stuff with two oysters. Dust with seasoned flour, brush with beaten egg and coat with breadcrumbs. Fry in butter until the meat is tender and the outside golden brown.

Make a gravy with the pan juices and the reserved oyster liquid; pour over the veal and garnish with lemon slices.

LAMB AND MUTTON

Until the 19th century, sheep were valued principally for their fleece, their food value being of secondary importance. When a sheep ceased to produce good fleece it was slaughtered and salted down. Lamb was available chiefly by accident and was thus an occasional luxury. Only in the mid-18th century, when Robert Bakewell began experiments aimed at increased yield of meat per animal, did the general demand for lamb and mutton begin to grow. Distinct breeds of sheep date from this time and include lowland breeds, such as the Romney Marsh and Southdown, the Devon, Mendip and the famous Leicestershire sheep. The less fatty, but tender mountain breeds come from Wales, the Kerry Hills and the Pennines. The introduction of the Blackfaced sheep, now common in the Scottish Highlands, caused much bitterness among crofters deprived of their land.

Today, the greater part of lamb and mutton consumed in Britain is imported; although of good quality, it does not compare in flavour and sweetness with English and Welsh lamb.

Alderman's Walk (8 portions) H and F
London

The "Alderman's Walk" was said to be the largest, longest and best cut from a haunch of mutton or venison. At City dinners in the late 19th century it is alleged to have been reserved for the alderman.

8 slices roast saddle of mutton (3 oz each)
8 slices bread
4 oz butter
1 heaped tablespoon chopped chives
2 tablespoon Worcestershire sauce
½ oz made mustard
Salt, pepper and tabasco

Cut the slices of bread to fit the roast mutton; place the meat, which should be cut from a fresh roast, on the bread and leave until cold. Soften the butter and mix in the chives, Worcestershire sauce, mustard, salt, pepper and tabasco to taste; stir until smooth.

Melt the butter mixture in a pan; remove the meat from the bread which should have absorbed the juice. Cut the bread into strips and toast them lightly. Cook the meat gently in the butter for 8 minutes, turning once; lift on to a serving dish, pour over the butter and arrange the crisp toast round the meat.

Bolton Hot-Pot: see Lancashire Hot-Pot

China Chilo (6—8 portions) F and H

This is of Anglo-Indian origin, popular because of its attractive green and white colouring. Serve on a bed of fluffy boiled rice.

3 lb best end of lamb cutlets
2 finely shredded lettuce
1 lb green peas
4 oz chopped salad onions or shallots
½ pt brown stock
2 oz butter
½ tablespoon sugar
Salt and pepper
¾ lb peeled, diced cucumber
2 oz button mushrooms (optional)

Trim off the fat and remove the bones from the cutlets; cut the meat into 1 in cubes. Put the meat, lettuce, peas and onions in a pan with the stock, butter, sugar, salt and pepper; cover and cook gently for 2 hours.

Half an hour before the end of cooking, add the cucumber and mushrooms.

Devilled Cutlets (8 portions) H and F

Devilled dishes were extremely popular in Victorian days, devilling referring to any spicy mixture used to flavour meat and game.

8 lamb or mutton cutlets (6 oz each)
½ lb softened butter
1 tablespoon Worcestershire sauce
1 tablespoon mushroom ketchup
1½ oz dry mustard
Salt, white pepper, cayenne

Trim the cutlets; put under a hot grill and cook for 10—15 minutes, turning once. Remove to a warm serving dish. Meanwhile, mix the butter with Worcestershire sauce, mushroom ketchup, mustard and salt, pepper and cayenne to taste. Spread this mixture over the cutlets just before serving.

Exmoor Lamb Stew (8 portions) F and H Devon

A rich stew of English lamb chops, fresh young vegetables and herbs, subtly flavoured with wine and thickened with cream.

8 lamb chops (4 oz each)
2 oz butter
1½ lb small potatoes
4 oz small button onions
½ lb chopped mushrooms
5 fl oz white wine
½ pt white stock
2 oz white breadcrumbs (optional)
5 fl oz double cream
Salt and pepper
1 bay leaf
Sprig thyme, parsley and lovage
Garnish: chopped parsley

Trim any fat off the chops and fry them gently in butter; remove from the pan. Put the potatoes, cut in half, the onions and mushrooms in the pan and cook for 5 minutes. Lift out the vegetables; drain the fat from the pan, then add the wine, stock, breadcrumbs and cream. Stir thoroughly and season with salt and pepper.

Return the potatoes, vegetables and chops to the pan with the bay leaf and chopped thyme, parsley and lovage. Cover and simmer for about 1 hour or until tender. Remove the bay leaf, garnish with chopped parsley and serve at once.

Grilled Lamb Cutlets (8 portions) H and F

Lamb or mutton chops are usually grilled and served plainly with the pan juices. There are, however, numerous flavourings that lift grilled cutlets and chops into the luxury class; these include chops stuffed with wafer-thin slices of garlic; chops or cutlets coated with chopped fresh herbs or lemon rind and juice blended with melted butter. Finely chopped onions can be sprinkled over the chops before grilling, or spread with chopped pickled mushrooms halfway through grilling. Alternatively, mix the melted butter with 1 teaspoon anchovy essence and garnish with anchovy fillets, lemon slices and watercress sprigs.

8 cutlets or chops (6 oz each)
Salt and pepper
Juice of ½ lemon
2 tablespoons melted butter

Trim off excess fat and remove the spinal cord; wipe the cutlets and flatten slightly. Season with salt, pepper and a little lemon juice. Place the cutlets on a greased hot grill pan, brush with butter or oil and grill quickly on both sides; lower the heat and continue cooking for 12–15 minutes according to thickness. Turn the cutlets during cooking. Add any remaining lemon juice to the pan juices and pour over the meat.

Irish Stew (8 portions) F Ireland

Although this famous, savoury winter stew is truly Irish in origin and typical of a county stricken by poverty, the English enthusiastically adopted it. It was fashionable at hunt luncheons, and in the 19th century, beef and ham became acceptable substitutes for the traditional mutton.

3 lb middle neck of mutton, scrag, breast or gigot chops
2 lb potatoes
1 lb thinly sliced onions
1 faggot of herbs
Salt and pepper
½ pt water or white stock
Garnish: 1 tablespoon chopped parsley

Trim the meat of excess fat, remove bones and cut the meat into 1 in cubes. Slice the potatoes. Put the meat, onions and potatoes in layers in a deep pan with the faggot of herbs in the middle; season each layer with salt and pepper.

Add the stock and simmer gently until tender, after about 2½ hours. Spoon the stew into a serving dish and sprinkle liberally with chopped parsley. Carrots, turnips or pearl barley are sometimes added, but they are not traditional.

Lamb, Boiled and Stuffed (6–8 portions) F and H

A typical summer dish, made with lamb or mutton, this was originally served with a sorrel sauce and fresh young peas. Today, cucumber sauce has replaced the sorrel.

2–3 lb boned shoulder of lamb
Bacon stuffing
½ lb bacon rashers
½ lb sliced onions
5 oz chopped celery
1 faggot of herbs
2 pt brown stock
Salt and pepper

Stuff the shoulder of lamb with the prepared bacon stuffing and sew up firmly. Place half the bacon over the base of a pan, top with the joint and cover with the remaining bacon. Add the onions, celery, herbs, meat bones and stock to the pan; bring to the boil and skim. Season with salt and pepper.

Cover with a well-fitting lid and simmer for about 2½ hours or until the meat is tender, allowing 20 minutes per lb of the stuffed joint plus an extra 20 minutes. Before serving, strain the stock, skim off the fat and reduce the stock to a gravy to serve with the meat.

Lamb Casserole (8 portions) F

Farmhouse casseroles and stews have for centuries belonged to British traditional cooking, lamb and mutton being favoured rather than beef. As well as distinctive regional variations, such as Irish stew, hot-pots and lobscouse from Lancashire and Prosen hot-pots from Scotland, minor variations of the basic lamb or mutton stew also occur.

2 lb stewing lamb or 8 middle neck cutlets, scrag end, breast or gigot chops
1 oz seasoned flour
1 oz dripping
½ lb sliced onions
¾ pt brown stock
Salt and pepper

Oven: 350°F; gas mark 4; 2 hours

Remove excess fat and bones; cut the meat into 1 in cubes, but leave chops and cutlets whole. Coat the meat in seasoned flour and fry in the melted dripping together with the onions. Put the meat and onion in a casserole dish or stew pan; pour over the stock. Cover and simmer on top of the stove or in the oven for about 2 hours or until the meat is tender; correct seasoning before serving.

Barley or Mushroom Lamb Stew, add 1 faggot of herbs, 2 oz capers and 2 oz pearl barley or ½ lb sliced mushrooms.

Cider Lamb Stew, use cutlets or chops and replace 5 fl oz of the stock with dry cider, 1 tablespoon Worcestershire sauce and a crushed garlic clove.

Devilled Neck of Lamb Stew, simmer in ½ pt brown stock and 5 fl oz vinegar mixed with 1 teaspoon Worcestershire sauce, mustard and extra pepper; add 2 oz chopped celery and 4 oz skinned, sliced tomatoes to the stew.

Jugged Lamb Stew, add ½ lb skinned, sliced tomatoes, the juice of 1 lemon and 2½ fl oz port wine; 10 minutes before the end of cooking, stir in 1 tablespoon red currant jelly and serve the stew garnished with chopped parsley and bread sippets.

Minted Lamb Stew, omit the onions and add ½ lb peas and 1 oz finely chopped mint for the last 30 minutes of cooking.

Poor Man's Goose, add 6 oz sliced carrots.

Lamb or Mutton Chops, Fried (8 portions) F and H

Fried chops can be given a crisp finish by coating them in egg and breadcrumbs before frying, or with separate coats of egg, chopped parsley and breadcrumbs.

8 loin or gigot chops or best end of neck cutlets
   (6 oz each)
Salt and pepper
4 oz dripping

Wipe the chops, trim off excess fat and remove spinal cords. Sprinkle with salt and pepper. Fry the chops quickly in hot dripping to brown them, turning once. Lower the heat and continue frying the chops, turning them every 2 minutes for 10–12 minutes, according to thickness. Serve the chops with a little of the fat poured over them.

Lamb Chops, Stuffed (8 portions) H and F

Chops for stuffing should be at least 1½ in thick, as in double chops. Bacon, ham, sage and onion stuffing can be used as well as the forcemeat used here, and the chops can be grilled or fried, plain or coated with egg and breadcrumbs.

8 double lamb chops
4 oz chopped chicken livers
4 oz chopped mushrooms
3 oz butter
Salt and pepper

Split the lean part of each chop in half, cutting through to the bone. Fry the chicken livers and mushrooms in 1 oz of butter and season with salt and pepper. Stuff this mixture into the incisions in the chops and sew or skewer the chops together firmly. Brush with butter and put under a hot grill for 15–20 minutes, turning frequently.

Lamb Rosettes (6–8 portions) F

Also known as lamb noisettes, this dish of stuffed lamb is sometimes made with loin of lamb, but inexpensive breast is equally suitable.

2 boned breasts of lamb
9 oz cored and chopped lamb kidneys
¾ lb sausage meat
1½ oz butter
Salt and pepper
1½ eggs
2 lb thinly sliced potatoes
6 oz chopped onions
½ lb skinned, thinly sliced tomatoes
1 tablespoon flour
½ pt brown stock

Oven: 350°F; gas mark 4; 1½–3 hours

For the stuffing, lightly fry the kidneys and sausage meat in half the butter; season with salt and pepper. Remove from the heat and bind with the lightly beaten eggs. Spread the stuffing over the breasts of lamb; roll up, tie securely and seal quickly in its own fat; remove from the pan and cut into 1 in thick slices. Fry the potatoes, onions and tomatoes in the fat, adding extra butter if necessary, for a few minutes.

Spread the vegetable mixture over the base of an ovenproof dish, arrange the lamb slices on top. Stir the flour into the fat in the pan, add the stock and bring to the boil, stirring continuously. Pour the sauce over the meat, cover and cook in the oven for 1½–3 hours or until tender. Skim off any surface fat before serving.

Lamb with Parsley Dumplings (6–8 portions) F

Boiled leg of mutton with capers sauce was a

popular 19th century dish; leg of lamb is less fatty
and dumplings absorb any excess fat. Dried peas
or beans or barley (6 oz) may be used instead of
dumplings.

2 lb leg of lamb
1 lb carrots
½ lb sliced onions
2 oz butter
1 pt brown stock
Salt, mixed herbs
1 bay leaf
Parsley dumplings
Cornflour

Wipe and trim the lamb. Cut the carrots into
narrow, 1 in long pieces. Fry the carrots and
onions in butter for 10 minutes; arrange over the
base of a large pan and place the joint on top. Add
the stock, salt, mixed herbs and the bay leaf.
Cover with a lid and simmer very gently, allowing
20 minutes per lb and 20 minutes extra. Add the
dumplings for the last 15 minutes.

Lift the meat, vegetables and dumplings on to
a serving dish. Strain the gravy into a pan, stir in
cornflour blended with a little water; bring to
the boil, stirring until thickened. Check seasoning
and serve with the joint.

Lancashire Hot-Pot (8 portions) F
Lancashire

This stew of lean lamb or mutton chops takes its
name from the deep, brown or white pottery dish
in which the stew is cooked and served. Lancashire
Hot-Pot is traditionally served with pickled red
cabbage. The Bolton Hot-Pot in addition contains
mushrooms, and fresh oysters were formerly
included for the last 30 minutes. Some Lancashire
cooks add curry powder to the stew, and in
Cumberland a small amount of stewing beef is also
part of the hot-pot. The Prosen hot-pot from
Scotland omits the potatoes and uses instead 6 oz
chopped carrots and 1 lb skinned and sliced
tomatoes.

8 middle neck lamb chops (6 oz each)
4 lamb kidneys, cored and sliced
2 lb sliced potatoes
½ lb sliced onions
Salt and pepper
½ pt white stock
1 oz lard or dripping

Oven: 350°F; gas mark 4; 2 hours
         425°F; gas mark 7; 30 minutes

Trim any excess fat from the chops. Fry the chops
and kidneys over high heat in their own fat for
3—4 minutes. Put a layer of potatoes in a deep
ovenproof dish, lay some of the chops on top,
cover with a layer of kidneys and onions; continue
with these layers, seasoning each with salt and
pepper. Finish with a layer of potatoes, pour over
the stock and brush the potatoes with melted lard
or dripping.

Cover with a lid and cook in the oven for 2
hours at a temperature of 350°F (gas mark 4).
Remove the lid; increase the heat and place the
dish near the top of the oven and cook for 30
minutes to brown the potatoes.

Lobscouse (6—8 portions) F
Lancashire, Wales

This is a regional variation of the nautical concoction
of salt pork or mutton, water and vinegar known
only too well by every sailor of whatever nationality
in the days of sailing ships. Served with rock-hard
ship's biscuits, lobscouse constituted a monotonous
diet for months on end.

1½ lb middle or scrag end of neck of mutton
½—¾ lb shin of beef
½ pt brown stock
Salt and pepper, thyme
4—6 oz diced carrots
10 oz diced swedes
6 oz diced onions
1 lb potatoes

Trim off any excess fat, remove bones and cut the
meat into 1 in cubes. Put the meat in a large pan,
with the stock, salt, pepper and a pinch of thyme;
bring to the boil and simmer for 1½ hours. Add
the carrots, swedes, onions and whole potatoes to
the meat; continue simmering for another hour or
until tender. To serve, ladle the stew into soup
plates. Usually eaten with a spoon and fork.

Mutton, Boiled (6—8 portions) F and H

Leg, shoulder, tough flank and best end of neck of
mutton are all suitable for boiling provided they
are fairly lean. Vegetables cooked with the meat
help to absorb the fat, and many traditional
accompaniments serve the same purpose, such as
mashed beans, boiled carrots, mashed potatoes

or mashed turnips as in Scotland. Capers sauce is traditional, but apple or cucumber cream sauce can also be served. In Derbyshire, peppercorns are added to the water, and ½ lb pearl barley and ½ lb potatoes are included with the vegetables. Sometimes, fresh dill sprigs replace the faggot of herbs and a dill sauce is then customary.

3 lb mutton
1 faggot of sweet herbs
Salt
½ lb onions, stuck with cloves
4 oz diced carrots
4 oz diced turnips

Wipe the meat and trim off any surplus fat; if necessary tie the meat into shape. Weigh the joint and allow 20–25 minutes per lb, plus an extra 20–25 minutes. Put the mutton in a pan, cover with boiling water and add the faggot of herbs; bring to the boil and skim thoroughly. Boil for 5 minutes to harden the outside of the meat; reduce the heat and simmer gently. Season with salt when the mutton is half-cooked.

Thirty minutes before the end of cooking time, add the onions, carrots and turnips. Place the meat on a serving dish surrounded with the vegetables. Use the cooking liquid as the basis for the accompanying sauce.

Mutton Chops, Baked (8 portions) F

Ale-flavoured batter over mutton chops absorbs and integrates the fat from the meat.

8 best end of neck chops (6 oz each)
Salt and pepper
3 eggs
2 oz flour
1 pt milk
¼ teaspoon ground ginger
2 tablespoons ale

Oven: 325°F; gas mark 3; 1½–2 hours

Trim the chops, sprinkle with salt and pepper and put in a lightly buttered dish. Mix the eggs, flour and milk to a batter, blend in ginger and the ale. Pour the batter over the chops and cook in the oven until tender and the batter has set and is beginning to brown.

Mutton, Devilled (8 portions) F and H

Thick slices of cold roast mutton were greatly relished by the Edwardians, especially with a devilled topping and were often served as a breakfast dish.

8 slices cold mutton
Salt, pepper and cayenne
Juice of ½ lemon
2 oz melted butter
4 oz browned breadcrumbs
Garnish: Watercress

Oven: 375°F; gas mark 5; 10–15 minutes

Season the mutton slices with salt, pepper and cayenne and sprinkle with lemon juice. Leave the slices to marinate for 30 minutes, then brush with melted butter and coat with breadcrumbs. Bake in the oven until well heated through. Serve within a circle of watercress.

Mutton Dormers (6–8 portions) F

Possibly a corruption of dormouse and referring to the sausage shapes of preferably underdone, cooked mutton or lamb. Serve with gravy or fried parsley and tomato sauce.

1–1¼ lb cooked mutton
4 oz finely chopped onions
6 oz finely chopped suet
½ lb boiled long grain rice
Salt and pepper
3 eggs
3–4 oz breadcrumbs
Dripping or lard
Garnish: fried parsley

Chop the meat finely and mix with the onions, suet, rice and salt and pepper. Bind with 2 beaten eggs and mould into small sausage shapes, about 2 oz each. Coat with beaten egg and breadcrumbs; shallow fry in hot fat for 10 minutes or until golden brown. Drain and serve.

Haricot Mutton (6–8 portions) F

A very old English recipe dating back at least to the 17th century. In those days, the word "haricot" simply meant a mutton stew, haricot beans not being introduced to Britain until the 19th century. A more elaborate version uses whole pickled onions and chestnuts, and the stew is flavoured with blades of mace, a faggot of herbs and 5 fl oz red wine, and garnished with shredded lettuce leaves.

2 lb best end of neck or breast of mutton
1 oz lard
4 oz haricot beans, soaked overnight
1 lb sliced onions
4 oz sliced turnips
Salt and pepper
1 tablespoon Worcestershire sauce

Oven: 325°F; gas mark 3; 2½–3 hours

Cut the meat into portion pieces, trimming off
any excess fat. Brown in the lard. Pour on enough
boiling water to cover the meat and add the drained
beans, onions and turnips. Season with salt and
pepper. Cover with a lid and simmer on top of the
cooker or in the oven for 2½–3 hours. Stir in the
Worcestershire sauce just before serving.

Mutton Hash (6–8 portions) F

Possibly of Scottish origin, mutton hash being
included in Mrs. Glasse's *The Art of Cookery
Made Plain and Easy* (1747) and Mrs. MacIver's
Cookery and Pastry (1787), both published in
Edinburgh. Both ladies recommend serving the
hash on thin toasted sippets with a garnish of
pickles and horseradish.

1½–2 lb cooked mutton
Salt, pepper and nutmeg
½ lb chopped onions
1 oz butter
2 oz red currant jelly
2½ fl oz port wine
1 oz flour
½ pt brown stock

Oven: 350°F; gas mark 4; 15–20 minutes

Slice the meat thinly and sprinkle each slice with
salt and pepper. Fry the onions gently in the butter
without colouring. Add the mutton, nutmeg, red
currant jelly and port. Transfer to an ovenproof
dish. Blend the flour with a little of the stock,
mix in the rest of the stock and add to the meat.
Heat through in the oven for 15–20 minutes.

Mutton, Spiced (8–12 portions) H and F

This old dish originated in the Middle Ages when
the mutton in all likelihood was salted and spices
were needed to disguise the fact. Well-hung loin,
leg, shoulder or saddle of mutton are suitable
joints, all of which except the saddle should be
boned. Traditionally served with a watercress
salad and red currant jelly.

4 lb mutton
3 oz fine oatmeal
½ teaspoon powdered thyme
½ teaspoon ground pepper
Pinch ground mace
Dripping
Cabbage leaves
¾ pt cider or apple juice
5 fl oz red wine

Oven: 350°F; gas mark 4; 2–2½ hours

Rub the boned joint with a mixture of oatmeal,
thyme, pepper and mace. Work the spices well in,
tie up the joint and cover with pats of dripping.
Wrap in layers of cabbage leaves to keep the spices
in and to prevent browning of the meat.

Roast in the oven allowing 30 minutes per lb;
baste with cider or apple juice. Pour off the surplus
fat and remove the cabbage leaves 40 minutes
before the end of cooking time; spoon over the
red wine, baste well and continue cooking. Serve
the carved meat with the pan juices.

Oxford John (8 portions) F and H

A quick, herb-flavoured dish made with fresh
slices cut from a leg of mutton or lamb and
served in a lemon sauce.

8 mutton or lamb slices (4 oz each)
Pinch mace, thyme, parsley
Salt and pepper
4 oz finely chopped onions or shallots
2 oz butter
1 oz flour
¾ pt brown stock
Juice of 1 lemon

Mix the herbs, salt and pepper with the onions and
coat the meat slices roughly with this mixture. Fry
the meat in the butter for about 10 minutes. Stir
in the flour, gradually add the stock and lemon
juice. Bring to the boil and simmer for about 5
minutes. Correct seasoning and serve garnished
with bread sippets.

Panjotheram (8 portions) F Co. Durham

A local name for a casserole of mutton chops and
potatoes, traditionally served at sheep-killing time.

8 mutton chops (4 oz each)
2 lb sliced potatoes
¾ lb sliced onions

Salt and pepper
1 pt brown stock

Oven: 325°F; gas mark 3; 2 hours

Arrange layers of potatoes and onions in a deep
casserole dish; season with salt and pepper and pour
over enough hot stock to half cover the vegetables.
Place the mutton chops on top, cover with a lid
and cook in the oven until tender, adding more
hot stock if necessary.

Prosen Hot-Pot: see Lancashire Hot-Pot

Reform Club Cutlets (8 portions) H London

One of the now classic dishes created by Alexis
Soyer, famous chef at the Reform Club in the
19th century.

16 lamb cutlets (3 oz each)
½ oz chopped ham
½ oz chopped tongue
1 tablespoon finely chopped parsley
1 lb white breadcrumbs
2 oz seasoned flour
1–2 eggs
5 fl oz oil
4 oz butter
1 pt Reform Club sauce
Garnish: 1 oz cooked ham, tongue, gherkins, egg
white, beetroot, truffles

Mix the ham, tongue and parsley with the breadcrumbs. Trim the cutlets and flatten slightly. Coat
the cutlets with seasoned flour, brush with beaten
egg and coat with the breadcrumb mixture. Heat
the oil and fry the cutlets until golden brown on
both sides.

Arrange the cutlets on a serving dish in the
form of a crown; keep warm. Toss the garnish in a
little butter, arrange round the cutlets and set a
frill on each. Melt the butter and cook to a nut-
brown colour; spoon over the cutlets. Serve with
Reform Club sauce in a separate sauce boat.

Regent Lamb Chops (8 portions) H and F

An excellent summer dish, incorporating the
traditional flavourings for lamb: aromatic
rosemary and red currants.

8 loin chops (6 oz each)
8 button onions
8 rashers of streaky bacon

Salt and pepper
½ teaspoon rosemary
Lard
½ lb red currants
2–3 oz caster sugar

Carefully remove the bone from each chop so that
the meat remains in one piece. Shape into circles,
set an onion in the centre and wrap a rasher of
bacon round each chop. Secure with skewers if
necessary. Sprinkle with salt, pepper and rosemary,
brush with lard and grill for about 15 minutes,
turning often.

Cook the red currants with sugar and a little
water until soft. Serve the chops with the fruit
poured over them.

Tattie Pot (8 portions) F Border Counties

Although this is also known as mutton and potato
pie, it is in fact a stew in the tradition of the
Lancashire Hot-Pot with the addition of black
puddings.

8 middle neck lamb chops (6 oz each)
4 lamb kidneys, cored and sliced
2 lb sliced potatoes
2 small black puddings
½ lb sliced onions
6 oz sliced carrots
Salt and pepper
½ pt white stock
1 oz lard or dripping

Oven: 350°F; gas mark 4; 2 hours
425°F; gas mark 7; 30 minutes

Trim any surplus fat from the chops and fry them,
with the kidneys, in their own fat for 3–4 minutes
over high heat. Put a layer of potatoes in an ovenproof dish, cover with half the chops and kidneys,
one black pudding and a layer of onions and
carrots; sprinkle with salt and pepper. Continue
with these layers, ending up with a topping of
sliced potatoes.

Pour the stock over the meat and vegetables,
brush the potato layer with melted lard and cover
with a lid. Cook in the oven for 2 hours, then
remove the lid and increase the temperature to
425°F (gas mark 7) for another 30 minutes.

Tatws A Cig Yn Y Popty (6–8 portions) F Wales

Roughly translated, the English name for this dish

is potatoes and meat in the oven. It originates in North Wales and is a favourite in Anglesey, usually served with creamed carrots or swedes or a mixture of these.

2–3 lb lean boned breast of lamb
2 lb thickly sliced potatoes
Salt and pepper
1 oz flour
½ lb sliced onions
1 pt brown stock

Oven: 375°F; gas mark 5; 1½–2 hours

Roll up the breasts of lamb; put in a roasting tin in the oven until brown. Remove the breasts from the tin, and pour off all but about 1 tablespoon of the fat. Put half the potatoes in the tin and sprinkle with salt, pepper and flour. Lay the onions over the potatoes and top with the remaining potatoes; season. Pour over the stock until just below the top layer of potatoes; place the meat on top and cover. Cook in the oven until the potatoes and the meat are tender and have browned.

Warwickshire Chops and Chestnuts (8 portions) H and F Warwickshire

These oven-baked chops with chestnuts and onions are equally delicious when made with pork chops.

8 lamb chops (4 oz each)
2 oz dripping
¾ lb finely chopped onions
1 oz flour
1 pt brown stock
1¼ lb boiled and peeled chestnuts
Salt and pepper

Oven: 350°F; gas mark 4; 1 hour

Fry the chops lightly in the dripping until sealed. Remove and arrange in an ovenproof dish. Add the onions to the dripping and fry until soft. Stir in the flour and cook for a few minutes; gradually blend in the stock and bring to the boil. Add the chestnuts, heat through and season to taste with salt and pepper.

Pour the sauce over the chops, cover with a tightly fitting lid and bake in the oven for 1 hour.

Welsh Venison (8–10 portions) H Cambridge

This dish, traditional at one of the Cambridge

colleges, takes its name partly from the mutton, which should be tender Welsh mountain mutton with its characteristic thyme flavour, and partly from the roasting method usually employed for a haunch of venison.

5 lb loin of mutton
½ teaspoon mixed herbs
Salt and pepper
2 oz dripping
Bacon trimmings
½ lb diced carrots
6 oz diced onions
4 oz diced celery
1 faggot of herbs
4 pt brown stock
½ pt port wine
1 oz cornflour

Oven: 300°F; gas mark 2; 2½ hours

Bone the mutton and season with herbs, salt and pepper. Skewer and tie up firmly. Melt the dripping and lightly brown the meat. Remove from the pan. Fry the bacon trimmings, carrots, onions and celery until golden. Transfer to a deep roasting tin, with the faggot of herbs and set the meat on top. Add the stock, cover with a lid or foil and cook for 2½ hours or until tender. Remove the meat and keep it warm.

Strain the cooking liquid and reserve the vegetables to serve with the meat. Add the port wine, reduce the liquid and thicken with blended cornflour. Correct seasoning. Pour the gravy over the mutton and serve with red currant jelly.

PORK

The sleek, purpose-bred pigs of the 20th century bear little resemblance to their wild ancestors that once roamed the forests providing sports for royal hunts. Until the end of the Middle Ages, farm-workers and cottagers kept a pig near their houses, to be slaughtered in autumn and provide meat, sausages, black puddings, hams and salted joints for the winter; the final moment of triumph was the decorated boar's head for Christmas dinner. How-ever, with mounting pressure for improved hygienic conditions, the pig was eventually outlawed from private dwellings.

The pig is probably the most useful of all our food animals, every part of it being utilised in some way — the flesh, entrails, feet, head and blood, even the trimmings that make up the once popular flead. Traditional pork dishes are chiefly found in England and Wales; in Scotland prejudice existed against pork, and there are few local specialities.

Pig-breeding is now highly specialised but falls broadly within two main categories: porkers and bacon pigs. Porkers are generally killed young to meet the demand for lean pork.

Chine of Pork, Stuffed (6—8 portions) F
Warwickshire

The bony cavity, which adjoins the loin of pork, is known as sheep-sharing chine in Warwickshire. It is traditionally served on Mothering Sunday in March, accompanied with boiled broccoli and spinach.

5—6 lb chine of pork
Parsley sprigs
1 egg yolk
6—8 oz white breadcrumbs
Lard
Garnish: parsley

Oven: 425°F; gas mark 7; 20 minutes
      350°F; gas mark 4; 3—3½ hours

Boil the chine in water for 30 minutes; make a number of incisions in the lean part of the meat, 1 in apart. With a skewer, stuff sprigs of parsley, stalk ends first, into the incisions. Brush the meat with egg yolk and coat with breadcrumbs, patting them in firmly. Baste with melted lard and roast in the oven at 425°F (gas mark 7) for 20 minutes to settle the topping.

Reduce the heat to 350°F (gas mark 4) and continue roasting, allowing 30 minutes per lb, plus an extra 30 minutes. Serve the roast garnished with fresh parsley.

Doucettes (6—8 portions) F

The word "doucet" in medieval England meant a sweet-tasting dish; sugar was then uncommon, and honey was used for sweetening.

2 lb minced lean shoulder of pork
2 eggs
Salt and pepper
4 oz honey
Milk

2 oz pork fat

Oven: 350°F; gas mark 4; 45 minutes

Beat the eggs, season with salt and pepper, mix in the honey and blend thoroughly. Mix the egg mixture with the pork; add milk to soften if necessary and shape into small balls. Melt the pork fat in a roasting tin, add the meat balls and bake in the oven for 45 minutes or until brown and cooked through.

Elizabethan Pork Stew (10—12 portions) H

The common flavourings for roast pork — apple and sage — were usual even in Elizabethan days. Other fruits, often dried, and especially oranges, were used in those days to flavour meat that perhaps was not always of prime quality.

4 lb boned shoulder of pork
2 tablespoons cooking oil or fat
¾ lb sliced onions
9 oz sliced apples
Salt and pepper
¾ oz flour
4 oz seedless grapes
6 dates
Sprig sage and parsley
1 head chopped celery
1 orange
¾ pt red wine
Brown stock

Oven: 325°F; gas mark 3; 2½ hours

Heat the oil in a pan and brown the pork on all sides over high heat. Remove the joint and fry the onions in oil until light brown. Put the onions in an ovenproof dish, cover with apple slices and season with salt and pepper. Dust the pork with flour, salt and pepper and place on top of the apples. Add the grapes, dates, chopped sage, parsley and celery. Peel the orange thinly, cut the peel into narrow strips and add to the other fruits; remove pith and pips from the orange, cut into quarters and place round the meat.

Pour the wine into the dish, adding a little stock if necessary so that the liquid is level with the top of the meat. Cover and cook in the oven for 2½ hours. Lift out the meat, carve and arrange on a serving dish; strain the cooking liquid and serve as a separate sauce.

Loin of Pork with Prunes (6—8 portions) H and F

This dish may have developed from the ancient custom of stuffing sucking pig with a type of plum pudding. To obtain crisp crackling on pork, the scored rind should never come in contact with the fat in the pan. Good accompaniments to roast pork include peeled apple halves filled with sultanas or sage and onion stuffing and roasted with the meat for the last 30 minutes, and peach halves with chutney which need only 15 minutes in the oven.

3 lb loin of pork
6—8 prunes
Dripping
Juice of 1 lemon

Oven: 425°F; gas mark 7; 20 minutes
350°F; gas mark 4; 1¾ hours

Par-boil the prunes, drain and reserve the liquid; remove the stones and quarter the prunes. Make a number of incisions in the meat and stuff with a piece of prune. Place the meat in a roasting tin with melted dripping; roast at 425°F (gas mark 7) for 20 minutes, then lower the heat to 350°F (gas mark 4) and continue roasting, allowing 25 minutes per lb, with an extra 25 minutes. Baste frequently with the reserved prune juice mixed with lemon juice.

Mock Goose (6—8 portions) F

Prunes and apples are traditional stuffings for roast goose; they are here used as a filling for lean pork fillets.

2 pork fillets (about 1 lb each)
2 teaspoons salt
½ teaspoon white pepper
½ teaspoon ground ginger
1 lb peeled and sliced cooking apples
10 stoned prunes
2 oz butter
1½ pt brown stock
1 oz flour

Trim the pork fillets of sinews and skin, beat them quite flat and sprinkle with salt mixed with pepper and ginger. Lay the apple slices and halved prunes over the fillets, roll up and tie firmly with fine string. Melt the butter and brown the meat on all sides; add the stock; cover and cook gently for

about 30 minutes or until tender, turning the meat occasionally.

Lift out the fillets, remove the string and cut the meat into thick slices; arrange on a serving dish. Thicken the gravy with flour and pour a little over the meat; serve the rest of the gravy separately.

Pickled Belly Pork, Roast (6—8 portions) F

In former days, belly, neck or shank of pork were home-pickled with thyme, bay leaves and unrefined salt; sometimes saltpetre, brown sugar, allspice, ale and stout were added to the pickling liquid. Today, pickled pork is prepared by butchers. It should be soaked in cold water for 8 hours before cooking.

2½ lb pickled belly pork
1 dessertspoon olive oil
4 fl oz water

Oven: 400°F; gas mark 6; 1½—2 hours

Wipe the soaked pork and score the rind at ½ in intervals along the grain of the meat. Rub the skin with oil which helps to crisp the crackling. Place the meat in the roasting tin with the water and roast in the oven for 2 hours. Serve with mashed turnips, strongly flavoured with pepper.

Pork and Beans (6—8 portions) F

This is one of the oldest known dishes in British cooking, occurring throughout the centuries as the farmworker's mainstay during the winter months. He would have a barrel of salted or pickled pork and a barrel of dried beans. Originally, the two ingredients were boiled separately, probably because of the excessive saltiness of the meat. Parsley sauce was and is the traditional accompaniment.

2—3 lb pickled shoulder of pork
2 oz sliced carrots
4 oz sliced onions
4 oz sliced turnips
10 peppercorns
½ lb broad beans

Soak the pork for 8 hours in cold water. Put in a pan with the carrots, onions and turnips and enough water to cover. Bring to the boil, add the peppercorns and cover. Simmer for 2—2½ hours, allowing 25—30 minutes per lb. Add the beans to the pork for the last 30 minutes of cooking. Lift out the pork, carve and arrange on a dish; serve the beans separately, dressed with parsley sauce made from the strained cooking liquid.

Pork and Caraway Pot Roast (6—8 portions) F

Caraway was a popular flavouring in Elizabethan cooking; the chopped leaves were used in sauces and salads and the seeds with roast pork, fruit dishes and cakes.

2—3 lb hand (forehough) of pork
2 oz lard
1 lb quartered onions
1 lb chopped parsnips
1 lb chopped carrots
½ teaspoon caraway seeds
¼ teaspoon powdered mace
Salt and pepper
5 fl oz brown stock

Melt the lard in a heavy-based pan, brown the meat on all sides and remove. Fry the onions, parsnips and carrots until golden. Place the joint on top of the vegetables, press down into the mixture and season with caraway seeds, mace, salt and pepper. Pour the stock over the vegetables and cover tightly. Simmer gently for about 2 hours, allowing 30 minutes per lb, plus an extra 30 minutes.

Pork and Kidney Stew (8 portions) F

A tasty hot-pot of chops, vegetables and apples, flavoured with the traditional sage.

8 pork chops (6 oz each)
1½ oz dripping
½ lb diced turnips
¾ lb chopped onions
1½ lb diced potatoes
¾ lb skinned and sliced pig kidney
2 oz seasoned flour
6 oz chopped cooking apples
Salt and pepper
Pinch powdered sage
1 bay leaf
1½ pt brown stock

Melt the dripping and lightly fry the turnips, onions and potatoes until golden; dust the chops and kidney slices with seasoned flour and brown in the dripping. Add the apples. Season with salt, pepper and sage, add the bay leaf and pour over

the stock Cover tightly with a lid and simmer gently for about 1¼ hours or until the chops and vegetables are tender.

Pork and Oatmeal Scrapple (6—8 portions) F

A scrapple describes both scraps of meat and mince; this is a meat loaf made from lean pork cooked on the bone and thickened with oatmeal.

2 lb lean shoulder of pork
¾ lb oatmeal
Salt and pepper
½ teaspoon mixed herbs
3 oz minced or finely chopped onions

Put the pork in a saucepan with enough water to just cover. Simmer until tender; cut the meat from the bone and put through a mincer. Return the mince to the liquid, bring to the boil and stir in the oatmeal, salt, pepper, herbs and onions; simmer slowly for 1 hour or until the mixture has reduced to a thick consistency. Pour the pork and oatmeal mixture into a greased loaf tin and set aside to cool. When required, cut the loaf into thin slices and fry in hot fat until crisp and brown.

Pork and Parsnips (6—8 portions) F

Belly pork is an inexpensive roasting joint with a good amount of crisp crackling; have the rind scored at ½ in intervals.

2½—3 lb belly pork
2 lb potatoes
2 lb parsnips
Salt and pepper
1 oz dripping
2 tablespoons red currant jelly
½ pt brown stock

Oven: 400°F; gas mark 6; 2 hours

Peel and halve the potatoes and parsnips. Boil in lightly salted water for 5 minutes, then drain. Rub the rind of the pork with salt and pepper and set in a roasting tin with the dripping, arranging the potatoes and parsnips round the meat. Stir the red currant jelly into the stock and pour over the vegetables. Roast in the oven for 2 hours. Arrange the meat and vegetables on a dish and serve the thin gravy separately.

Pork and Pease Pudding (8—10 portions) F and H

The combination of boiled salted or pickled pork and pease pudding, or porridge as it was originally called, goes back to the Middle Ages. Hot pease pudding was sold by street vendors well into the 19th century. Boiled cabbage and parsnips are traditionally served with the dish.

2—3 lb hand (forehough) pickled pork
4 oz sliced onions
2 oz sliced carrots
½ lb sliced turnips
4 oz chopped celery
12 peppercorns
Pease pudding;
2½ lb split peas (soaked)
1 oz butter
2 egg yolks
Salt and pepper

Put the pork in a large pan of cold water, bring to the boil and skim well. Simmer for 10 minutes, then add the onions, carrots, turnips and celery. Add the peppercorns and simmer gently for about 2½ hours.

For the pease pudding, tie the soaked peas loosely in a cloth and boil in the pan with the pork for about 1½ hours. Remove from the pan and rub the swollen peas through a sieve; dry over gentle heat until thick, then stir in the butter, egg yolks, salt and pepper to taste. Serve the boiled pork with the vegetables, boiled quartered cabbage and parsnips; offer the pease pudding separately.

Pork and Rabbit (6—8 portions) F Co. Durham

A tasty hot-pot with more rabbit than pork.

1 rabbit
1 lb diced pork fillet
1 oz seasoned flour
1 lb finely chopped onions
1 head finely chopped celery
Salt and pepper
5 fl oz brown stock
½ pt milk

Oven: 325°F; gas mark 3; 2½—3 hours

Wash the rabbit thoroughly in salted water, cut into joints and blanch in boiling water for 2—3 minutes. Coat the rabbit pieces and pork with seasoned flour. Place a layer of onions and celery in a greased casserole dish, season with salt and pepper, cover with a layer of pork and a layer of rabbit. Continue with these layers, finishing with onions and celery. Pour in the stock and milk, cover with a lid and cook in the oven for 2½—3 hours.

Pork Chops in Beer Sauce (8 portions) F and H

Plain fried pork chops are traditionally served with fried apple rings sprinkled with brown sugar. The chops can also be garnished with pineapple rings or apricot halves or they can, as here, be cooked in beer and served with a thick sauce.

8 pork chops (6 oz each)
Salt and pepper
2 oz lard or dripping
1 pt ale
1½ oz capers
4 egg yolks
Pinch nutmeg
Garnish: lemon slices, parsley

Season the chops with salt and pepper; fry quickly in hot lard to seal in the juices. Drain off the fat, add the ale and more seasoning to the chops and simmer gently until the chops are tender, after 30—45 minutes. Remove the chops and place on a warm serving dish.

Pour the hot ale into a basin, add the capers, egg yolks and nutmeg; beat thoroughly, adding a little of the drained off fat. Return the sauce to the pan and stir until it thickens, but do not boil. Pour over the chops and garnish with lemon slices and parsley.

Pork Chops Savoy (8 portions) H and F

Cutlets or chops for grilling can be quite plain or they may be coated with egg and breadcrumbs, on their own or mixed with sage, with ground nutmeg, cinnamon and cloves or with mustard and brown sugar. In this recipe, the chops are cooked in Madeira wine, with sultanas as a sweetening agent.

8 thick pork chops
2 oz butter
½ lb diced cooking apples
4 oz sultanas
2 teaspoons grated lemon peel

½ pt brown stock
5 fl oz Madeira or sherry
Salt and pepper
1 oz flour or cornflour

Oven: 350°F; gas mark 4; 1–1½ hours

Melt the butter and brown the chops on both sides over high heat. Add the apples, sultanas and lemon peel; pour over the stock mixed with Madeira and season with salt and pepper. Cover and simmer gently on top of the stove or in the oven for 1–1½ hours. Remove the chops to a serving dish. Thicken the sauce with blended flour or cornflour and pour over the chops.

Pork Cutlets with Turnips (8 portions) F and H

Turnips have the finest flavour when quite small and young; sprinkling with a little sugar helps to brown them.

8 pork cutlets (6 oz each)
2 oz butter
3 turnips
Salt, pepper and caster sugar
1½ pt brown stock

Brown the cutlets in a little butter in a pan, lift out and in the same pan brown the turnips, cut in halves or quarters and sprinkle with caster sugar. Put the cutlets back in the pan, season with salt and pepper and add sufficient stock to just cover them. Cover with a lid and simmer gently for 1 hour or until the meat is tender.

Pork Hot-Pot (8 portions) F

Prunes and apples are classic accompaniments with pork; both are used here in a stew, and that third classic — sage — comes to the fore if the hot-pot is served with dumplings made from sage and onion stuffing.

8 pork chops (6 oz each)
6 oz soaked prunes
6 oz peeled, cored and sliced cooking apples
1½ lb sliced potatoes
¾ lb chopped onions
Salt and pepper
1 bay leaf
1½ pt brown stock

Oven: 350°F; gas mark 4; 1¼ hours

Place the stoned prunes and the chops in a casserole dish and arrange the apples, potatoes and onions on top. Season with salt and pepper, add the bay leaf and pour over the stock. Cover and cook in the oven for 1 hour. Remove the lid and continue cooking until the top has browned.

Pork in Red Wine (8 portions) F

A quick supper dish, using up cold roast pork in a sweet jelly and wine sauce.

8 slices cold roast pork
¾ lb apple jelly
3 oz butter
5 fl oz red wine
6 cloves

Oven: 350°F; gas mark 4; 25–30 minutes

Put the jelly, butter, wine and cloves in an oven-proof dish; set in a pre-heated oven until the mixture has melted. Skim the mixture and remove the cloves; lay the pork slices in the sauce and return to the oven for 25–30 minutes or until heated through.

Pork Oaties (8 portions) F Scotland

Outside Scotland this dish, locally known as pan-fried pork, is made with sage and onion stuffing instead of oatmeal.

8 pork fillet steaks
1 oz seasoned flour
2 eggs
4 oz medium oatmeal
2 oz lard

Trim the steaks and beat them flat. Dust the steaks with seasoned flour, brush with the lightly beaten eggs and coat thickly with oatmeal. Fry in hot lard for 5 minutes, turning once, then lower the heat and continue cooking until brown and tender, after about 10 minutes.

Pork Olives (8 portions) F and H

The pork fillet, also known as tenderloin, is a sweet meat, but being dry usually needs a stuffing to keep it moist during cooking.

2 lb pork fillet
½ lb sage and onion stuffing
Seasoned flour
2 oz butter

4 oz chopped onions
1 pt brown stock

Oven: 350°F; gas mark 4; 2 hours

Trim the outer skin and sinews from the pork fillets, cut into eight equal pieces and beat them flat. Spread the slices with sage and onion stuffing, roll up and tie or secure with skewers. Roll in seasoned flour and fry in butter until brown; add the onions. Pour over the stock, cover with a lid and simmer until the meat is tender, either on top of the stove for about 1½ hours or in the oven for 2 hours.

Pork with Apples and Beer (8 portions) F

This pork stew with apples is cooked in strong beer, but dry cider may be substituted for a lighter sauce. As a variation, replace the onions and apples with ½ lb chopped leeks and 4 oz small whole mushrooms.

8 pork chops (6 oz each)
2 oz butter
10 oz sliced onions
1 lb peeled, cored and sliced apples
1 oz flour
1¼ pt strong ale
Salt and pepper
1 bay leaf
3 cloves
Rind of 1 lemon

Oven: 350°F; gas mark 4; 35−40 minutes

Trim the chops and brown in butter on both sides. Place in an ovenproof dish. Fry the onions and apples in the butter until golden, stir in the flour and cook through. Gradually add the ale and bring to the boil, stirring all the time. Season with salt and pepper.

Pour the sauce over the chops, tie the bay leaf, cloves and lemon rind in a muslin bag and add to the chops. Cover with a tightly fitting lid and cook in the oven for 35−40 minutes.

Pork with Apricots (6−8 portions) H and F

In Elizabethan times, apricots were commonly used to flavour ham; they go equally well with roast pork, and tinned or dried fruit may be used outside the season for fresh apricots.

3 lb leg or loin of pork
10 oz stoned apricots

2 oz melted lard
Salt

Oven: 425°F; gas mark 7; 20 minutes
350°F; gas mark 4; 1 hour, 40 minutes

Score the rind at narrow intervals to obtain crisp crackling. Make a number of incisions in the meat and insert half an apricot in each. Brush the joint with the lard, rub salt into the rind and roast in the oven, basting frequently with the pan juices. Roast for 20 minutes at 425°F (gas mark 7) to crisp the crackling, then lower the heat to 350°F (gas mark 4) and continue roasting, allowing 25 minutes per lb and an extra 25 minutes.

Pork with Dumplings (8 portions) F

This hearty winter stew, complete with vegetables, is made more substantial with the addition of suet dumplings.

8 pork chops (6 oz each)
1 oz dripping
¾ lb chopped onions
1½ lb diced potatoes
½ lb diced turnips
4 oz chopped celery
1 oz seasoned flour
1½ pt brown stock
1 bay leaf
Salt and pepper
½ lb suet dumpling mixture

Melt the dripping and fry the onions, potatoes, turnips and celery until light brown. Dust the chops with seasoned flour and brown in the pan. Pour over the stock, add the bay leaf and salt and pepper to taste; bring to the boil and skim. Cover with a tight-fitting lid.

Simmer until the chops and vegetables are tender, after about 1¼ hours. Make up the suet dumplings and add to the stew for the last 15 minutes of cooking.

Pork with Oranges (8−10 portions) H and F

Oranges give a tangy flavour to roast pork, and the accompanying sauce is less cloying than sweetened apple sauce.

4 lb leg or loin of pork
½ teaspoon powdered sage
Salt and pepper

5 fl oz water
2 oranges
1 oz red currant jelly
5 fl oz sherry

Oven: 350°F; gas mark 4; 2¼ hours

Sprinkle the joint with sage, salt and black pepper; put in a roasting tin with the water. Roast for 25 minutes per lb and 35–40 minutes extra. About 40 minutes before the end of cooking, remove the tin from the oven and pour off the fat. Grate the peel of one orange over the top of the meat and add the orange juice to the pan with the red currant jelly, sherry and salt and pepper.

Cut the other orange into four or six segments, complete with peel, and put round the joint. Return the joint to the oven and continue cooking. Carve the joint and arrange on a dish, garnished with the orange segments. Serve with a gravy made from the pan juices.

Pressed Spiced Pork (6–8 portions) F and H

Delicately spiced pork, pressed and cut into slices when cold, is best accompanied with salads, such as apple and celery, potatoes in lemon mayonnaise and lettuce and cucumber.

2 lb boned hand or shoulder of pork
½ teaspoon paprika
½ teaspoon cinnamon
Salt and pepper
½ teaspoon ginger
½ teaspoon crushed peppercorns
1 pt white stock
¾ lb chopped onions
2 bay leaves
½ oz powdered gelatine

Cut the meat into 1 in cubes and toss in a spicy mixture made up of paprika, cinnamon, salt, pepper, ginger and peppercorns. Put the meat in a pan, pour over the stock and add the onions and bay leaves. Simmer until tender, after 1½–2 hours.

Remove the bay leaves; dissolve the gelatine in a little water and add the meat mixture. Turn into a basin and when cool place a weighted plate on top to press the jellied meat. Turn out and serve cold, cut into thick slices.

BACON, GAMMON AND HAM

Throughout the history of civilisation, a variety of processes have developed aimed at making meat more palatable, especially when it had to be stored for winter supplies. The use of salt was one of the earliest methods, simultaneously with smoking which dried out the flesh and also gave it a delicate aroma from the peat fire. The flesh of the pig was most commonly used for these preserving procedures; pig meat was originally known as bacon and this name was retained for salted, dried and cured flesh taken from the back and sides of the pig. The leg, cured separately, was known as ham; over the centuries regional curing methods occurred which have survived into the 20th century as Wiltshire, Suffolk, Bradenham and York hams.

Refined curing methods resulted in the gammon. Like ham, this comes from the hind leg, but it is salted in one piece with the bacon joints and then cut from the carcass for smoking or for immediate consumption.

BACON

Alnwick Stew (6-8 portions) F
Northumberland

For a bacon stew, top or prime streaky flank, prime or end collar can be used as well as forehock. Local variations include the Somerset stew which is composed of forehock, chopped onions and mixed, chopped carrots and turnips. It is cooked in half cider and half water and apple rings are added towards the end of cooking. Bacon Stovies from Scotland is similar to the Alnwick Stew, but is made with milk rather than water.

2½ lb forehock
1 lb chopped onions
2 lb sliced potatoes
Pepper and mustard
1 bay leaf

Cut the bacon into 1 in cubes and arrange with the onions and potatoes in alternate layers in a pan finishing with a layer of overlapping potatoes. Sprinkle each layer with pepper and a little mustard; lay the bay leaf on top of the potatoes and pour over enough water to come just level with the top layer of potatoes. Cover with a lid and simmer gently for 1½-2 hours.

Bacon and Beans (6-8 portions) F

This homely dish is a great deal tastier than the bacon and bean stew that was standard winter fare in poor households four and five centuries back. Then the bacon was probably so salt as to be near inedible and the so-called gronden beans were tough from being dried in the kiln.

2½ lb forehock
1 lb chopped onions
½ lb soaked haricot beans
Pepper and mustard
1 bay leaf

Dice the bacon and put in a pan, layered with the onions and the soaked, drained beans. Season with pepper and mustard, add the bay leaf and pour over enough water to cover. Put a lid on the pan and simmer gently until the bacon and beans are tender, after 1½-2 hours.

Bacon Olives (4-8 portions) F

Bacon rolls stuffed with a little left-over meat, such as chicken, pork or ham, make a quick snack. Served with fried eggs and fried potatoes they become a complete meal.

8 rashers smoked back bacon
4 oz minced cooked meat
2 oz breadcrumbs
1 tablespoon finely chopped onions
1 dessertspoon chopped parsley
Salt, pepper and mixed herbs
1 egg

Oven: 350°F; gas mark 4; 15-20 minutes

Blend the minced meat with breadcrumbs, onions and parsley; season to taste with salt, pepper and herbs and bind with the lightly beaten egg. Spread this mixture over the bacon rashers, roll up and tie with string. Set the olives in a shallow baking tin and bake in the oven for 15 minutes.

Bacon Ribs with Onions (6 portions) F Lancashire

For this dish, allow four lean bacon ribs per person; floury boiled or mashed potatoes would be suitable as an accompaniment.

24 ribs of green bacon
2 lb finely sliced onions

3 oz butter
Salt and pepper

Wash and dry the ribs well, put in a pan and cover with water; bring to the boil. Drain the ribs, cover with fresh water, bring slowly to the boil and simmer for 2 hours.

Put the onions in a separate pan, bring to the boil and simmer until tender; drain, add the butter and season with salt and pepper. Serve the ribs on a bed of onions.

Bacon Stew (6-8 portions) F

Whole bacon joints, whether forehock, flank or collar should be soaked in cold water for at least 2 hours and preferably longer to remove the excess salt.

2½ lb forehock
1 bay leaf
½ teaspoon pepper
1 oz lard
½ lb chopped onions
4 diced carrots
4 oz diced turnips or parsnips
English mustard

Put the soaked bacon in a pan, cover with water and bring to the boil. Drain the bacon and cover with fresh water, add the bay leaf and pepper and bring to the boil; simmer, covered, for 30 minutes. Meanwhile melt the lard and fry the onions, carrots, turnips or parsnips until golden brown in a heavy-based, deep pan.

Set the bacon on top of the vegetables; add 1¾ pt of the bacon liquid and simmer for 1½-2 hours. Season to taste with mustard. Arrange the bacon on a serving dish with the vegetables.

Bacon with Oatmeal Dumplings (6-8 portions) F Scotland

Bacon should be simmered over gentle heat otherwise the meat will harden as well as shrink. In Scotland, this dish is often served with a sharp capers sauce.

4 lb forehock
1 bay leaf
6 peppercorns
½ lb oatmeal dumpling mixture

Soak the bacon overnight. Put in a large pan, with the bay leaf and peppercorns; bring to the boil and simmer for 1 hour and 40 minutes allowing 20 minutes per lb plus 20 minutes.

Peel the skin off the bacon, carve the meat into slices and serve with the dumplings. Make up the dumplings and cook with the bacon for the last 15 minutes.

Collar or Forehock with Cabbage (6-8 portions) F Ireland

This favourite farmhouse dish of boiled bacon is traditionally served with potatoes boiled in their skins, with good dollops of butter.

4 lb collar or forehock
1 bay leaf
6 peppercorns
Breadcrumbs
Brown sugar
1 large cabbage

Oven: 450°F; gas mark 8; 15 minutes

Boil the soaked bacon, with the bay leaf and peppercorns for 1 hour and 40 minutes. Strip off the bacon rind and coat the top of the joint with breadcrumbs and brown sugar, patting them in firmly. Bake in the oven until crisp.

Meanwhile boil the cabbage in the bacon stock and mash thoroughly. Serve the bacon and cabbage together in a large dish.

Chine, Stuffed (6-8 portions) F Lincolnshire

A chine or neck of chine bacon is a Lincolnshire local cut from the back of a fat pig; in some areas it can be bought already cooked. The joint is usually served cold, cut into slices and sprinkled with vinegar, but on Mothering Sunday it is sprinkled with breadcrumbs for the last 30 minutes of cooking and served hot with boiled broccoli or spinach. In Clee, chine is eaten with Clee cheesecakes on Trinity Sunday.

1 chine of bacon (3-4 lb)
Finely chopped thyme, marjoram, salad onions, lettuce and raspberry leaves or finely chopped parsley, leeks and ground mace

Oven: 350°F; gas mark 4; 1¼-1¾ hours

Soak the chine for 12 hours in cold water; wipe, dry and weigh. Score the meat deeply and stuff with the mixed herbs, salad onions and leaves,

pressing the filling well down into the cuts. Tie lightly in a cloth as for a suet roll and boil, allowing 20 minutes per pound.

Alternatively, cover the joint with huff paste or kitchen foil and bake in the oven, allowing 20 minutes per lb plus 20 minutes extra. Remove the huff paste or foil before serving.

Dublin Coddle (8 portions) F Ireland

This dish of bacon, sausages and potatoes, typical to Ireland, has been a favourite since the 17th century. Soda bread is invariably served with it; proper "coddling", meaning slow cooking, should result in a thickish stew.

2½ lb forehock
8 pork sausages
1 lb chopped onions
2 lb diced potatoes
½ teaspoon pepper
Pinch mustard
2 tablespoons chopped parsley
1 bay leaf

Cut the bacon into 2 in chunks. Layer the bacon, sausages, onions and potatoes in a deep pan; season with pepper and mustard and sprinkle each layer with parsley. Add the bay leaf and pour over enough water to come level with the top layer. Cover with a lid and simmer gently for 1½-2 hours or until the meat is tender.

Ginger Collar (6-8 portions) F

Sweet yet spicy ginger marmalade is used as a glaze for this bacon joint. Have the collar boned, rolled and tied firmly. Serve hot with Brussels sprouts or cold with salads.

4 lb piece of collar bacon
1 pt ginger beer
2 tablespoons ginger marmalade

Oven: 450°F; gas mark 8; 15 minutes

Soak the bacon overnight; put in a pan and add the ginger beer. Cover with a lid, bring to the boil and simmer for 1¾ hours, turning the meat occasionally. Remove from the pan and strip off the skin.

Place in a roasting tin and coat the top with ginger marmalade; roast for 15 minutes or until the marmalade settles to a glaze.

Panackelty (8 portions) F Co. Durham

This family-type dish made with left-over cooked bacon is brought to the table in the pan in which it was cooked.

8 slices cooked bacon
1 lb sliced onions
1 pt brown stock
2 lb sliced potatoes
1 oz melted butter
Garnish: chopped parsley

Dice the bacon and put in a deep frying pan with the onions; add the stock and arrange the potatoes in an overlapping pattern. Cover and cook until the potatoes are tender, after 25-35 minutes.

Brush the top with butter and put the pan under the grill for a few minutes to brown the potatoes. Serve garnished with parsley.

Welsh Hot-Pot (Tatws Reost) (6-8 portions) F Wales

Designed for days of austerity, this stew is still more generous than the Miser's Feast (Ffest y Cybydd) at which the potatoes mashed with the bacon liquid provided one meal, and the bacon rashers served with plain boiled potatoes made up dinner the following day.

1 lb lean back rashers
1 lb streaky back rashers
1 lb chopped onions
2 lb diced potatoes
½ teaspoon pepper
Pinch mustard
1 bay leaf

Put the bacon rashers, onions and potatoes in layers in a deep pan, finishing with a layer of potatoes. Sprinkle with pepper and mustard, add the bay leaf and pour in enough water to just reach the top layer of potatoes. Cover tightly with a lid, bring to the boil and simmer gently for about 1½ hours.

GAMMON AND HAM

Gammon and Apricot Pie (8 portions) F Buckinghamshire

Gammon rashers and steaks are cut from the tender, lean middle part of the whole leg. The association of ham and gammon with apricots is centuries old.

8 gammon rashers (1 in thick)
2 oz butter
½ lb dried, soaked apricots
Pepper
1 oz sultanas
½ pt brown stock
2 lb sliced potatoes

Oven: 350°F; gas mark 4; 1½ hours

Lightly fry the gammon rashers on both sides in half the butter; arrange in a 3 pt pie dish and cover with the apricots. Sprinkle with pepper and sultanas. Pour the stock over the gammon and cover with overlapping slices of potatoes. Brush with melted butter.

Cover with foil and bake in the oven for 1 hour; remove the foil and continue baking for a further 30 minutes to brown the potatoes.

Gammon Steaks (8 portions) H and F

Bacon chops, gammon rashers and steaks are suitable for frying after trimming away the surplus fat. They can be grilled and served as a breakfast, lunch, high tea or supper dish with grilled tomatoes, mushrooms and chipped potatoes.

8 gammon steaks (6 oz each)
4 oz softened butter
Salt and pepper
Juice of ½ lemon
Garnish: chopped parsley

Snip the outer fatty edge of the steaks with scissors; if necessary use skewers to keep the steaks in shape while cooking. Rub butter over one side of the steaks and grease the bars of the grill pan with a little butter. Lay the steaks on the heated bars, buttered side up and put under the heated grill for 2-3 minutes. Lower the heat and grill gently for 5 minutes on each side.

Melt the remaining butter in the grill pan, add salt, pepper and lemon juice, pour the liquid over the gammon steaks and serve garnished with finely chopped parsley.

Baked Ham and Gammon (8-10 portions) H and F

The Elizabethan custom in Oxfordshire of stuffing whole hams with apricots for the annual wool fairs is thought to have been brought to America by the English Pilgrim settlers. The favourite fruit, juicy Moor Park apricots from the Cotswolds, were unobtainable, but the now classic American method of garnishing baked ham with fresh or tinned fruit derives from the English custom.

For a 20th century adaptation of Oxfordshire stuffed ham, bone a 4 lb piece of gammon or ham and stuff the cavity with ½ lb stoned and chopped apricots mixed with the same amount of fresh white breadcrumbs, seasoned and bound with a little water.

Baked ham or gammon, to be served hot or cold, can be par-boiled on top of the stove for half the cooking time. Allow 20 minutes per lb and an extra 20 minutes for boiling and baking a piece of ham or gammon; for a whole ham (10-16 lb) allow 20 minutes per lb only. It is finished off with any of a variety of glazes.

4 lb piece of gammon
Glazing

Oven: 375°F; gas mark 5; 1¾ hours

Soak the ham or gammon in cold water for at least 24 hours. Wipe the joint dry, weigh and wrap in foil. Put in a tin and bake in the oven for about 1 hour and 40 minutes, according to the weight of the soaked joint. About 15 minutes before the end of cooking time, remove the foil and skin the joint.

The fat surface can be scored into a diamond pattern before being coated with any of the following glazes. Return the joint to the oven for 15 minutes or until the glaze is crisp and brown.

Glazes for Hams and Gammons

Spread with ½ lb honey, ½ teaspoon dry mustard and 1 oz ham fat.

Coat with 4 oz honey, 4 oz brown sugar and 5 fl oz orange juice.

Brush with 2 oz clear honey and 2 tablespoons vinegar; dredge with 4 oz brown sugar and breadcrumbs to give a crisp finish.

Stud with cloves and sprinkle with 4 oz brown sugar; baste with sherry, cider or beer.

Stud with stem ginger and cloves and sprinkle with 4 oz brown sugar; baste with 5 fl oz ginger syrup.

Cover with 6 oz dark Oxford or thick ginger marmalade.

Baste with 4 oz black treacle mixed with dry cider or beer; serve the pan juices as an unthickened gravy.

Dredge with 6 oz mixed oatmeal and brown sugar or oatmeal; baste with melted butter.

Baste with 1 teaspoon dry mustard, ½ teaspoon cinnamon, 4 oz brown sugar and 5 fl oz fresh orange juice.

Spread with 1½ oz ground coffee, pinch mustard, 4 oz brown sugar and a little water (thought to be of Edwardian origin).

Bake for the last 15 minutes with a garnish of apple rings, peach or apricot halves, pineapple rings or cherries; baste with the fruit juice and glaze with cloves and brown sugar.

Ham 'Beresford' (8 portions) H West Country

A quick and attractive looking lunch or supper dish to be served with a green salad.

16 thin slices cooked ham
16 asparagus spears
1 oz butter
8 hardboiled eggs
Salt and pepper
1½ pt cheese sauce
8 skinned and sliced tomatoes

Oven: 325°F; gas mark 3; 20 minutes

Wrap each piece of ham round an asparagus spear and arrange in a buttered ovenproof dish. Quarter the eggs and place between the ham rolls; season with salt and pepper. Cover with cheese sauce and arrange the tomato slices on top. Bake in the oven for 20 minutes.

Ham in Huff Paste (8-10 portions) H and F

Huff paste was once a popular covering for baked ham and poultry. The paste, which is not meant for eating, seals in the juices and aromas of the meat. Break off the paste before serving the ham but leave it on until just before carving if the ham is to be served cold.

4 lb gammon or ham
1 lb plain flour

Oven: 375°F; gas mark 5; 2-2½ hours

Soak the ham or gammon in cold water for at least 24 hours. Wipe dry and weigh the joint. Make the huff paste by mixing the flour with enough cold water to give an elastic dough; roll out ½ in thick and wrap round the ham, sealing the edges well. Bake in the oven for 20 minutes per lb plus an extra 35 minutes.

Minced Ham (8 portions) F Isle of Wight

This version of baked eggs with ham is made in one dish rather than individual small ramekins. Serve with crisp, buttered toast.

¾ lb lean ham
6 oz cream cracker crumbs
Salt and pepper
5 fl oz white stock
1 oz butter
8 eggs

Oven: 350°F; gas mark 4; 15-20 minutes

Mince the crumbs with the meat, season with salt and pepper and blend in enough stock to give the mixture a fairly stiff consistency. Spoon into a buttered ovenproof dish, level the surface and make eight holes. Break an egg into each.

Bake in the oven until the eggs are set.

OFFAL

No country outside Britain has a comparable wealth of dishes made from every conceivable item of a food animal's extremities and entrails. The survival of many of these dishes is living proof of the resourcefulness of the British house-wife in days of austerity and scarcity of food, and of her thrift even in prosperous times. The North West of England in particular displays a reluctance to discard any part of an animal slaughtered for food, and many of these original dishes persist today

Many types of offal common until the 19th century are no longer commercially available while others have been priced, by their scarcity, into the luxury class.

Brains

Calf brains are considered the most delicate, but are often in short supply. Lamb's brains are more often seen and occasionally pig's brains; they should all be soaked for several hours in cold water to remove all traces of blood.

Pig's Brains and Kidneys (6-8 portions) F Cheshire

Before cooking, prepare the soaked brains by removing the outer membrane and cutting away any fibres and bone splinters.

1 pig's brain
2 pig's kidneys
1 hardboiled egg
1 teaspoon chopped parsley
¾ pt brown stock
Salt and pepper
1 oz flour

Cut the cleaned kidneys into slices and chop the brain finely. Chop the egg and mix with the kidneys, brain and parsley. Put this mixture in a pan, add the stock and salt and pepper; simmer gently for 30 minutes.

Blend the flour with water and stir into the brain mixture to thicken. Adjust seasoning.

Brains, Stewed (8 portions) F and H

Prepared brains may be cut into thin slices, coated with egg and breadcrumbs and fried or they may be chopped finely, mixed with crumbs, mace, parsley and lemon peel and shaped into cakes for frying. In this recipe, they are cooked in a creamy, thick sauce.

8 sets lamb's or 4 sets calf's brains
1 oz seasoned flour
½ pt white stock
Salt, pepper and nutmeg
2 egg yolks
5 fl oz single cream
Garnish: chopped parsley

Cut the brains into serving portions, coat with seasoned flour and put in a pan with the stock, salt, pepper and nutmeg. Bring to the boil, cover and simmer gently for 1 hour. Beat the egg yolks and cream lightly, add to the brains, stirring all the time; heat through but do not allow to boil. Serve garnished with parsley.

Feet and Trotters

Pig's and occasionally sheep trotters are most often seen, either fresh or pickled. Calf's foot, from which the finest gelatine is obtained, is becoming a rarity, and cow heel is seldom offered for sale. This was once a favourite dish, served boiled with parsley sauce or in a brown stew with vegetables.

Calf's Feet, Stewed (6-8 portions) H and F

An extremely nourishing stew, needing little thickening; veal forcemeat balls may be cooked with the stew for the last 20 minutes.

4-6 calf's feet, depending on size
1½ pt white stock
2 oz chopped lean ham or bacon
½ lb sliced onions
4 oz sliced carrots
1 oz diced celery
Salt
1 blade mace
6 cloves
10 peppercorns
1 oz butter
1 oz flour
Juice of 1 lemon
Mushroom ketchup

Put the thoroughly cleaned calf's feet in a pan with the stock and ham; add the onions, carrots, celery, salt, and the mace, cloves and peppercorns tied in muslin. Bring to the boil; cover and simmer gently for 2½-3 hours. Remove the spices.

Allow the feet to cool slightly, then remove the meat from the bones and cut it up finely.

Make a white roux from the butter and flour, gradually add the strained cooking liquid and boil to thicken. Return the meat to the white sauce, adjust seasoning and add lemon juice and mushroom ketchup to taste.

Crubins (8 portions) F Ireland

Also known as "crubeens", this is the Irish term for pig's trotters. They are often served whole, straight from the pot, with fresh soda bread and jugs of stout, or the meat may be removed, fried in bacon fat and served with Kelly's Sauce.

16 pickled pig's trotters
½ lb chopped onions
4 oz sliced carrots
2 bay leaves
Bunch parsley and thyme
Salt and pepper
2 eggs
Pinch mustard

Breadcrumbs
Bacon fat

Put the trotters in a large pan with the onions, carrots, bay leaves, parsley and thyme, salt and pepper and enough water to cover. Bring to the boil, skim and cover with a lid. Simmer for 2-2½ hours or until the trotters are tender.

Remove the trotters from the pan, split them down the middle and remove the meat. Dip the meat in beaten eggs mixed with mustard; coat with breadcrumbs and fry in hot bacon fat until brown and crisp.

Trotters, Battered (8 portions) F

Floury potatoes or chunks of bread to mop up the sauce would go well with this dish.

16 sheep trotters
2 oz sliced onions
2 oz sliced carrot
2 oz diced celery
12 peppercorns
Salt
½ pt basic coating batter
Beef fat
1½ oz flour

Clean the trotters thoroughly; put in a pan with the onions, carrot, celery, peppercorns and salt. Bring to the boil, remove scum, cover and simmer for 2-3 hours or until tender. Lift out the trotters, leave to cool slightly, then remove the meat from the bones.

Coat the meat with batter and fry in beef fat until golden brown. Strain the cooking liquid, reduce by half and thicken with flour blended with a little water. Serve the trotters and sauce separately.

Trotters, Boiled (8 portions) F Lancashire

Pig's ears may be cooked and served in the same way as these Lancashire trotters.

8 pig's trotters
1 lb sliced onions
Salt and pepper
Pinch nutmeg
Strip lemon peel
2 pt white stock
1 pt parsley sauce

Scrub the trotters, split through the middle and put in a pan with the onions, salt, pepper, nutmeg and lemon peel. Add the stock and bring to the boil; remove scum, cover with a lid and simmer gently for 2½ hours.

Strip the meat from the trotters and keep warm. Make up the parsley sauce with ¼ pt stock and ½ pt milk. Pour the sauce over the meat and serve.

Trotters, Fried (8 portions) F

Also known as pig's petitoes, these fried trotters are served with butter, mustard and vinegar.

8 pig's trotters
2 pt white stock
1 tablespoon vinegar
Salt
½ pt basic coating batter or
   2 oz seasoned flour
Lard or dripping

Clean the trotters and soak for 2-3 hours in cold water. Drain. Put in a pan with the stock, vinegar and a little salt. Bring to the boil, skim and cover; simmer for 2½-3 hours or until tender.

Remove the trotters, drain and cut in half. Coat with batter or seasoned flour and shallow fry in hot lard for 10-15 minutes. Drain and serve.

Trotters with Oatmeal (8 portions) F
Lancashire

This dish is reputed to be a ceremonial part of dinners for a Lancashire football team. It is traditionally served with hot buttered toast.

16 sheep trotters
2 pt brown stock
Salt and pepper
½ lb fine oatmeal

Scrub the trotters thoroughly, put in a pan with the stock and seasoning and bring to the boil. Remove any scum, cover and simmer gently for 2-3 hours or until tender. Lift out the trotters, split and remove and cut up the meat.

Mix the oatmeal to a paste with a little water, add the strained stock and stir thoroughly. Season well, add the meat and simmer for 10 minutes.

Fry

Fry and pluck are both terms used to describe a mixture of internal organs, fry usually containing liver, kidney and skirt or belly, heart and brain, while pluck is the liver, heart and lungs. Pig's fry and pluck are the most common.

Chitterling Dumplings (6-8 portions) F

Colloquially known as Down Derry dumplings, these are potato balls stuffed with pig's pluck.

1½ lb pig's pluck
Salt and pepper
6 oz finely chopped onions
2-3 lb mashed potatoes
3 oz grated cheese
2 oz breadcrumbs

Oven: 350°F; gas mark 4; 15-20 minutes

Chop or mince the cleaned and prepared pluck finely, season with salt and pepper and mix with the onions. Mould the potatoes into balls about the size of an apple.

Put the chitterlings (pluck mixture) in the centre of each ball and roll in grated cheese mixed with breadcrumbs. Place in a greased roasting tin and bake until the cheese has melted and the balls are golden brown.

Faggots (6-8 portions) F

In the 19th century, faggots jokingly called savoury duck or poor man's goose, were on sale in most pork butchers' shops. In cooking, the term describes pig's fry bound together with a pig's caul. Usually served cold, but may also be shallow-fried and served hot with fried eggs as a breakfast dish.

2 lb prepared pig's fry
1 lb pig's caul or veil
1½ lb finely chopped onions
6 oz breadcrumbs or boiled potatoes
Sage, mixed herbs and pepper
2 oz butter or lard

Oven: 425°F; gas mark 7; 20-30 minutes

Soak the caul in tepid water for 2-3 hours. Boil the onions for 30 minutes and drain; put the prepared fry and the onions through the mincer. Add a little boiling water to the breadcrumbs to moisten them.

Mix the minced fry and onions with the bread-crumbs, add sage, herbs and pepper to taste and beat until smooth. Cut the caul into 4 in squares and divide the fry mixture equally over the squares. Shape into balls and pack closely into a well-greased roasting tin. Bake in the oven for 20-30 minutes.

Haslet (6-8 portions) F

Still found in many country butchers' shops, cooked to local recipes and popular cold with salads and as sandwich fillings, or shallow-fried and served hot.

1 lb prepared pig's pluck
1 lb minced fat and lean pork
1½ lb finely chopped onions
½ teaspoon chopped sage
Salt and pepper
1 pig's caul or veil
2 oz lard

Oven: 400°F; gas mark 6; 45-60 minutes

Chop or mince the pluck and mix with the pork; add the onions, sage, salt and pepper and wrap in the caul. Put in a greased roasting tin and dot liberally with lard. Bake until well browned.

Pig's Fry (6-8 portions) F Norfolk and Lincolnshire

In Norfolk, this dish of pig's fry is served with "floaters", the local name for Norfolk dumplings. Mashed potatoes, greens, onions and sage are traditional in Lincolnshire.

2 lb pig's fry
2 oz seasoned flour
2 oz dripping
½ oz cornflour (optional)

Oven: 350°F; gas mark 4; 1 hour

Cut the prepared fry into small pieces and roll in seasoned flour. Put in a greased roasting tin, with enough water to come just below the top of the meat; dot with dripping. Bake in the oven; if necessary, thicken the pan juices with cornflour blended with a little water. Serve.

Haggis

The earliest form of an edible pudding was a collection of miscellaneous ingredients stuffed into the stomach bag of an animal and boiled. From the 15th to the 18th century, pudding recipes were connected with "haggus" or "haggas" pudd-ings which indicate the use of a stomach bag and a filling of entrails with additional ingredients.

The earliest recipes use the liver and blood of sheep, but by the 17th century "haggas pudding in sheep's paunch" also included parsley, savory, thyme, cloves, mace, seasoning, onions, beef, suet and oatmeal; it was served with a hole cut in the top and filled with butter and a couple of eggs. Other recipes used calf paunch and minced entrails mixed with breadcrumbs, egg yolks, cream, spices, dried fruit, sherry and herbs; it was served as a sweet course with sugar and almonds.

Haggis (6-8 portions) F and H Scotland

Gervase Markham in *The English Housewife* (1615) described haggas as "that pudding of whose goodness it is vain to boast because there is hardly to be found a man that doth not affect them". The Scottish haggis of today is largely based on a recipe published in Edinburgh in 1787 by Mrs MacIver, professor of the culinary arts.

1 sheep's bag
Sheep's pluck (lungs, heart, liver)
4 oz suet
1 lb blanched onions
½ lb pinhead oatmeal
1 oz salt
Black pepper, cayenne pepper
½ teaspoon powdered herbs
Juice and grated rind of 1 lemon (optional)

Wash the bag in cold water, scrape and clean it thoroughly. Leave overnight in cold water. Wash the pluck, put in a large pan of boiling water and boil for 2 hours, with the windpipe hanging out; have a small basin below to catch any drips. Leave the pluck in the cooking liquid overnight.

Cut off the windpipe; grate the liver, chop the heart, lights, suet and onions. Toast the oatmeal lightly and mix with the pluck, suet and onions; add salt and pepper, cayenne, herbs and lemon juice and rind if used. Blend in the strained liquid in which the pluck was cooked.

Mix thoroughly and fill the bag just over half full, or make several smaller ones. Sew up and prick with a fork. Place in boiling water and simmer for 3 hours, pricking occasionally to prevent bursting. Serve with creamed potatoes and mashed turnips.

Pan Haggis (6-8 portions) F Scotland

This is a type of haggis, made with liver and hearts and steamed in a pudding basin rather than a stomach bag. Served, like haggis proper, with creamed potatoes and mashed turnips.

1 lb lamb liver
2 sheep hearts
¾ lb onions
3 oz oatmeal
4 oz finely chopped suet
Salt and black pepper

Clean the liver and hearts thoroughly; boil with the onions for 30-40 minutes or until tender. Drain and set the cooking liquid aside; mince the meat and onions. Put the oatmeal in a heavy pan and stir over low heat until lightly brown.

Mix the liver, hearts, onions, suet and oatmeal with enough cooking liquid to give a soft dropping consistency; season with salt and pepper. Steam for 2½-3 hours in a greased basin covered with foil.

Pig's Haggis (6 portions) F Ireland

At the annual pig slaughtering, this dish was made for the farm labourers and served with gravy and apple sauce.

1 pig's stomach
2-3 lb mashed potatoes
½ lb sage and onion stuffing
Salt and pepper
6 oz lard

Oven: 350°F; gas mark 4; 1-1½ hours

Clean the stomach bag thoroughly and soak for several hours in cold water. Stuff with the potatoes and sage and onion stuffing, mixed with plenty of seasoning. Sew up the opening with strong thread. Cover with lard and roast in the oven, basting frequently.

Heads

Pig's heads, used for brawns, are most often seen for sale, but occasionally sheep and calf heads are available. Of the ox head, the cheek is used for stews and brawns. Regional dishes using the heads of animals range from Irish boiled and grilled pig's head with boiled cabbage to the Sussex dish, known as Southdown Savoury Lamb Heads, made with cubed sheep head meat, scrag end of neck and vegetables served in a brown parsley sauce.

Hashed Calf's Head (10 portions) F

Boiled calf's head can be served with parsley sauce flavoured with lemon and chopped, cooked calf's brains; it may also be coated with egg and breadcrumbs and baked, or it may be boned and stuffed with ham, hardboiled eggs and spices, boiled, pressed and served cold.

1 boiled calf's head and tongue
½ lb chopped onions
4 oz diced carrots
½ lb diced turnips
Faggot of herbs
12 peppercorns
Salt and pepper
1 oz butter
1 oz flour
Grated rind of 1 lemon
Worcestershire sauce or mushroom ketchup
Pinch ground mace
Garnish: veal forcemeat balls, bacon rolls

Scrub and clean the head thoroughly, blanch in boiling water. Put the head and tongue in a large pan with the onions, carrots, turnips, herbs, peppercorns and salt. Cover with cold water, bring to the boil and skim; cover and simmer gently for 2-2½ hours or until the meat comes easily away from the bones. Lift out the head and tongue, strain the cooking liquid and set aside.

Bone the head and cut the meat into 1 in cubes; skin and slice the tongue. Melt the butter, stir in the flour and gradually add 1 pt of the reserved stock; flavour with lemon peel, Worcestershire sauce or mushroom ketchup and season to taste with mace, salt and pepper. Add the meat to the sauce and heat through. Serve garnished with forcemeat balls and bacon rolls or with the chopped and fried brains.

Oxcheek, Stuffed and Baked (6-8 portions) F

Oxcheek is an economical, nourishing cut, often used in stews. Here it is stuffed with veal force-meat, which may be substituted with a mushroom, ham or oyster stuffing.

2-2½ lb oxcheek
Salt
½ lb veal forcemeat
Garnish: lemon slices, cayenne pepper

Oven: 375°F; gas mark 5; 1 hour

Wash and scrape the oxcheek thoroughly to remove any blood. Put in a pan, cover with warm water, add salt and bring to the boil. Skim, cover and simmer gently for 1 hour or until tender.

Leave the cheek to cool in the liquid, then lift out and drain. Remove the bones and fill with forcemeat; tie with string and secure with skewers. Bake in the oven for 1 hour. Serve garnished with lemon slices sprinkled with cayenne and offer a gravy made from the pan juices and stock.

Thick Oxcheek Stew (6-8 portions) F

This thick, well-flavoured stew is traditionally served with suet dumplings.

2½ lb oxcheek
2 pt brown stock
¾ lb sliced onions
½ lb sliced carrots
4 oz sliced turnips
3 oz chopped celery
3½ oz butter
2½ oz flour
Salt, pepper and bay leaf
1 tablespoon chilli vinegar
1 tablespoon Harvey's sauce
2 tablespoons port
1 tablespoon mushroom ketchup

Wash the oxcheek and cut into 1 in cubes; put in a pan with the stock, bring to the boil and remove the scum as it rises. Fry the onions, carrots, turnips and celery in 2 oz of the butter until soft; add 1 oz of flour and cook until brown. Add a little of the cooking liquid, blend and stir into the meat. Add salt, pepper and bay leaf and simmer until tender, after 4-5 hours.

Thicken the stew with the remaining butter kneaded with the flour. Add vinegar, Harvey's sauce, port and ketchup. Heat the stew through and serve with suet dumplings cooked with the stew for the last 15 minutes.

Pig's Head Pudding (6 portions) F

Salted, boiled pig's head is often served with pease pudding, or the meat may be carefully removed from the bones, seasoned with pepper and cayenne, rolled up (collared) and boiled in a pudding cloth.

½ salted pig's head
1 lb cooked beef
Pepper, grated nutmeg
½ lb white breadcrumbs
3 eggs

Soak the head in cold water for at least 2 hours. Put in a pan, cover with water and bring to the boil. Remove scum and simmer for 2½ hours.

Strip the flesh from the bones and put through a mincer together with the cooked beef. Add grated nutmeg and pepper to taste, blend in the bread-crumbs and mix with beaten eggs to a firm paste. Tie the mixture in a floured pudding cloth and boil for 2 hours. Leave to cool before serving.

Hearts

Calf hearts are extremely tender, but rarely seen and can easily be replaced by the smaller but sweet lamb hearts. Pig heart is larger and less tender, and the large ox heart is coarse and stringy. All hearts require long and slow cooking.

Heart, Roast (8 portions) F

Hearts can be stuffed, as here, with sage and onion or with veal forcemeat or an anchovy stuffing. Serve with apple sauce to complement the sage, or with rowan, red currant or goose-berry jelly if veal forcemeat is used.

8 lamb hearts (2½-3 lb)
½ lb sage and onion stuffing
4 oz bacon strips
2 oz dripping

Oven: 350°F; gas mark 4; 1 hour

Rinse the hearts in cold water to remove any blood; cut away the thick muscular arteries and veins. Soak in cold salted water for 2 hours, wash again and soak for 30 minutes in fresh water. Blanch and refresh. Fill the heart cavities with the stuffing and sew up the openings with fine string.

Lard the hearts with bacon strips and put in a roasting tin with the dripping. Cover and roast for 1 hour, basting every 15 minutes. Remove the string before serving, with thickened gravy made from the pan juices.

Hearts, Stewed (8 portions) F

Creamed potatoes would go well with this satisfying stew of hearts and vegetables.

8 lamb or 4 calf hearts
2 oz seasoned flour
½ lb chopped onions
½ lb sliced carrots
4 oz sliced turnips or swedes
2 oz beef dripping
¾ pt brown stock
Salt and pepper
1 oz butter

Cut the hearts into ½ in slices, removing tubes and membranes. Soak in salt water for 1 hour, wash and dry well. Toss the slices in seasoned flour, lightly fry, with the vegetables, in melted dripping until light brown.

Add the stock, bring to the boil and simmer until tender, after 1-1½ hours. Season with salt and pepper; if necessary, thicken with the remaining seasoned flour kneaded with butter.

Love In Disguise (6-8 portions) F and H Herefordshire

This dish of baked stuffed calf hearts was popular in the 18th century. A coating of vermicelli and breadcrumbs hides the hearts.

4 calf hearts
½ lb veal forcemeat
10-12 rashers fat bacon
4 oz vermicelli
2 oz fresh breadcrumbs
1 egg
2 oz lard

Oven: 350°F; gas mark 4; 2 hours

Cut flaps, gristle and tubes from the hearts and snip out the membranes which divide the hearts inside. Soak in cold water for 2 hours, wash and soak in fresh water for 30 minutes. Stuff with veal forcemeat and sew up the opening with fine string. Wrap the bacon round the hearts and secure with wooden skewers. Wrap in foil and bake for 1½ hours in the oven.

Break the vermicelli into small pieces and boil until soft in salted water. Drain, cool and mix with breadcrumbs. Remove the hearts from the oven, cool slightly and brush with beaten egg. Coat the hearts with the vermicelli and breadcrumb mixture. Return the hearts, without foil, to the roasting tin, add the lard and bake for a further 30 minutes or until the coating is crisp and brown.

Kidneys

Ox kidney is large, up to 1½ lb, and coarse and chiefly used to flavour meat stews and puddings. Pig kidney is smaller and flat, with no suet, while lamb kidney is the smallest and considered as having the best flavour; it is covered with a thick layer of suet. Kidneys are popular for breakfast dishes and savouries (see that section); lamb kidneys baked in their own suet and served split on hot toast was a favourite Edwardian breakfast.

Kidney and Onion Stew (6-8 portions) F and H

Apart from their uses as breakfast and savoury dishes, kidneys make a good main course, fried or grilled, in stews and puddings. They may also be cooked in a curry sauce and served on a bed of fluffy rice. In Scotland, this stew is known as kidney collops.

1 ox kidney or 6 pig kidneys
1 oz seasoned flour
¾ lb sliced onions
2 oz kidney suet or lard
1 tablespoon mixed chopped parsley and marjoram
¾ pt brown stock
Salt and pepper

Oven: 350°F; gas mark 4; 2 hours

Remove the thin film of skin round the kidneys; cut into slices, snipping out the gristly core. Dust with seasoned flour and fry with the onions in the suet or lard until light brown. Add the herbs and stock and cook in the oven for 2 hours or on top of the stove for 1 hour. Season with salt and pepper before serving.

Kidneys in Onions (8 portions) F
Isle of Wight

For this dish of onions stuffed with kidneys, choose large well-shaped onions with a level base so that they will stand upright.

8 large onions (6 oz each)
8 lamb kidneys
¾-1 pt brown stock
5 fl oz red wine
1 oz cornflour

Oven: 350°F; gas mark 4; 1½ hours

Peel the onions, trim the base and cut off the top for a lid; hollow out each onion until a kidney, stripped of its suet, will fit into the centre. Replace the onion lid and place the onions in an oven-proof dish; pour stock into the dish until it reaches half way up the onions.

Cover and bake for 1 hour in the oven. Add the red wine and bake for a further 30 minutes. Drain off the liquid, reduce slightly and thicken with blended cornflour. Serve in individual bowls with the sauce poured over.

Liver

Among the many types of offal still in use, liver is one of the most nourishing, rich in necessary vitamins and minerals. Calf's liver is considered the finest and this coupled with short supplies also makes it the most expensive. Ox, on the other hand, is the cheapest, strongest and toughest and is not suitable for grilling or frying. Lamb's and pig's liver both have fine flavours, the latter softer in texture than lamb's liver.

Liver and Bacon (6-8 portions) F and H

This is one of the most popular English dishes, at its most succulent when the liver has been grilled or fried for only a few minutes.

2 lb calf's or lamb's liver
8-12 bacon rashers
2 oz seasoned flour
2 tablespoons cooking oil
½ pt brown stock
Juice of ½ lemon (optional)
Salt and pepper
Garnish: forcemeat balls, lemon slices
Cut away any gristly parts from the liver and

snip out the central cores; wash and dry well, then cut into ¼ in thick slices. Trim the rind from the bacon. For grilling, dust the liver lightly with seasoned flour; brush with oil and place in the bottom of the grill pan.

Cook the bacon on the grid above, turning once; remove and keep warm. Continue to grill the liver gently, turning once. It is cooked when small beads of blood appear on the surface, after about 8 minutes in all.

Alternatively, fry the liver in the bacon fat until lightly browned. Remove from the pan and keep hot. Pour off excess fat and make a gravy by adding stock and lemon juice to the pan juices; correct seasoning with salt and pepper. Reduce and pour over the liver or serve the gravy separately. Serve the liver and bacon garnished with veal forcemeat balls, fried in bacon fat, and lemon.

Liver and Bacon, Devilled (6-8 portions) H and F

A touch of spicing to liver makes a good hearty breakfast dish, with hot buttered toast.

2 lb calf's or lamb's liver
12 bacon rashers
4 oz mustard butter
Garnish: fried mushrooms

Grill or fry the liver and bacon as above. Just before serving, put pats of mustard butter on the hot liver; alternatively spread the butter on the liver before cooking. Garnish with fried mushrooms and serve.

Liver and Bacon, Stewed (6 portions) F

This dish is known as Cousin Jim in Co. Durham. It can be made with any kind of liver, even ox and then becomes Yorkshireman's Goose which omits the bacon, but adds sage to the seasoning.

1½ lb liver
1 oz seasoned flour
½ lb bacon rashers
1 lb sliced onions
Salt and pepper
¾ pt brown stock
Melted butter
1 lb sliced potatoes

Oven: 350°F; gas mark 4; 1 hour

Prepare and clean the liver. Wipe dry. Cut into

narrow slices and coat with seasoned flour. Fry the bacon; remove from the pan and lightly fry the liver and onions.

Put the liver, onions and bacon in layers in an ovenproof dish, sprinkle each layer with salt and pepper. Pour over the stock, top with sliced potatoes and cover with a lid or foil. Bake in the oven; remove the lid for the last 20 minutes and brush the potatoes with melted butter to brown.

Liver and Onions (6-8 portions) F
North Wales

The Welsh name for this liver and onion stew is *Stwns Rwdan*, a name which infers that a "stwns" (mashed potatoes) is mixed with another vegetable, in this case turnips.

2 lb liver
1 oz seasoned flour
1 lb sliced onions
2 oz dripping or lard
Salt and pepper
¾ pt brown stock

Oven: 350°F; gas mark 4; 1 hour

Prepare and clean the liver, cut into thin slices and coat with seasoned flour. Fry the liver and onions in the dripping until lightly browned.

Place in an ovenproof dish, season with salt and pepper and pour over the stock. Cover and bake in the oven. Serve with mashed potatoes and turnips mixed together with buttermilk.

Liver, Stuffed (6-8 portions) H and F
Hampshire

Liver dumpling is a plain steamed pudding of boiled, minced liver with suet, oatmeal and onions, contrasting with this luxury dish of calf's liver with sage and onion stuffing.

1½-2 lb calf's liver (in one piece)
1 lb sage and onion stuffing
3 oz dripping
½ pt brown stock

Oven: 375°F; gas mark 5; 1-1¼ hours

Trim the liver, wash and dry thoroughly; make an incision through half the depth, fill with the stuffing and secure with fine wooden skewers. Put the liver in a well-greased roasting tin and pour over the stock.

Cover with foil or a lid and bake in the oven for 1-1¼ hours. Lift the liver on to a serving dish; reduce the cooking liquid and serve separately.

Oxtail

Oxtail is both tasty and nourishing and relatively inexpensive. Animals store their surplus fat in the tails, and these are exceptionally meaty in winter; oxtails are usually sold already skinned and jointed, use the thick pieces from near the rump for stews and grills, and the thinner end pieces for soups and stock.

Oxtail, Glazed (6-8 portions) F

Good thick oxtail joints are covered in a layer of grey-white fat which should be trimmed off.

4 lb thick oxtail joints
2 oz butter
2 pt brown stock
12 peppercorns
Salt
1 lb green peas

Wash the joints and trim off all excess fat; fry in butter until brown. Add the stock, peppercorns and salt; bring to the boil and remove any scum. Cover with a lid and simmer for 2½-3 hours or until the meat comes easily away. Remove the oxtail from the pan and keep warm.

Strain the stock and reduce to a clear glaze by fast boiling. Cook the peas and place in the centre of a serving dish with the oxtail joints around them. Pour the glaze over the meat.

Oxtail, Grilled (6-8 portions) F

For this dish, thick stewed oxtail joints are finished off under a grill. It makes a good main course, and the stock can be used for a sauce.

3-4 lb thick jointed oxtail
1½ pt brown stock
12 peppercorns
Salt and cayenne pepper
1 egg
6 oz breadcrumbs

Wash the joints and brown in their own fat in a pan; add the stock, peppercorns, salt and cayenne. Bring to the boil, cover and simmer for 2½-3 hours. Remove the joints and drain.

Brush with beaten egg and coat with bread-crumbs, then grill gently for about 5 minutes on each side. Serve with a brown sauce.

Haricot Oxtail (6 portions) F

The fat that settles on top of stewed oxtail is easiest removed from the stock if it can be allowed to cool first.

2½ lb oxtail joints
1 lb onions
12 peppercorns
6 cloves
1 tablespoon chopped parsley
Salt
4 oz diced turnips
½ lb sliced carrots
1 lb soaked haricot beans
2 oz butter
1 oz flour
Garnish: chopped parsley

Wash the oxtail and remove excess fat; cover with water, bring to the boil and add ½ lb chopped onions, the peppercorns, cloves, parsley and salt. Simmer gently for 1 hour. Skim off all fat and strain the stock.

Add the turnips, carrots, remaining sliced onions and soaked, drained beans to the meat; pour over the strained stock and simmer for about 2 hours or until tender. Melt the butter and stir in the flour; blend in a little stock and stir until it thickens, then pour into the oxtail and vegetable stew. Heat through until thick and serve garnished with chopped parsley.

Oxtail in Stout (6 portions) F

The full flavour of oxtail is released through long slow cooking. Ideally this stew should be cooked at low temperature (275°F; gas mark 1) overnight. Serve with suet dumplings or mashed potatoes.

2½ lb oxtail joints
½ lb ox kidney
1 oz flour
2 oz butter or beef dripping
4 oz sliced carrots
½ lb sliced onions
Salt and pepper
½ teaspoon mixed herbs
1 pt each stout and brown stock

Oven: 325°F; gas mark 3; 3-4 hours

Wash the oxtail joints and trim off excess fat; slice the kidney and dust with flour. Fry the oxtail in butter or dripping, and add the carrots, onions and kidney. Sprinkle with salt, pepper and herbs and pour over the stout and stock.

Cover with a tightly fitting lid and cook in a low oven overnight, or at a slightly higher temperature for 3-4 hours. Spoon off excess fat before serving.

Oxtail Stew (6-8 portions) F and H

A thick stew suitable for a cold winter's day, for lunch or supper. A glass of port or a few pickled walnuts with a little juice can be added for extra flavour just before serving, and suet dumplings, forcemeat balls or toast sippets may complement the dish.

3 lb jointed oxtail
Salt and pepper
2 oz beef dripping
½ lb sliced onions
Faggot of herbs
2½ pt brown stock
2 oz diced carrots
4 oz diced turnips
2 oz chopped celery
¾ oz cornflour
Juice of 1 lemon
1 tablespoon Worcestershire sauce
Garnish: chopped parsley

Wash the oxtail, trim off excess fat and sprinkle with salt and pepper. Melt the dripping and fry the oxtail joints and onions until brown. Put the oxtail, onions, herbs and stock in a pan; simmer for 1½-2 hours.

Add the carrots, turnips and celery and cook for a further 2 hours. Skim off surplus fat. Blend the cornflour with lemon juice and Worcestershire sauce, add to the stew and stir until thickened.

Alternatively, cook the stew in a pressure cooker at 15 lb pressure for 45 minutes and for a further 15 minutes without pressure, after the cornflour mixture has been added. Garnish with parsley and serve.

Puddings

This section includes types of puddings contained in sausage and tripe skins or the stomach bags of sheep (see also Haggis). The filling may be pig's blood and cereals with suet (black pudding) or oatmeal and suet (white pudding). Both black and white puddings, like haggis, are surviving remnants of the original pudding concept of medieval days.

An old Sussex recipe for Ifield Vicarage Hog's Pudding is made with diced belly pork mixed with lard, flour, spices, currants and sugar, stuffed in sausage skins to the size of eggs and boiled.

Black Pudding (6-8 portions) F

These puddings are known throughout the British Isles, but are especially popular in the Midlands and the North. The chief ingredient, pig's blood, must be drawn immediately the animal is killed and stirred constantly to remove fibres and to prevent clotting. Scalded pig intestines are used for the sausage skins.

1 pt fresh pig's blood
4 oz pearl barley, rice or groats
4 oz fine oatmeal
1 oz salt
¼ level teaspoon pepper
½ lb diced beef suet or pork fat
2 oz finely chopped or minced onions

Oven: 350°F; gas mark 4; 45 minutes

Cook the barley, rice or groats in four times its volume of water until just soft. Mix the oatmeal with salt and pepper and stir to a paste with a little strained blood. Add the cereal, suet or fat, onions and the remaining strained blood to the mixture. Put into the skins through a funnel, stirring the mixture frequently to prevent the fat from separating out.

Alternatively, put the mixture into a greased baking tin and bake in the oven for 45 minutes.

Tie the sausage skins loosely and drop into hot, but not boiling water; the addition of black pudding dye will ensure an attractive dark finish. Boil for 20 minutes or until no blood comes out when a pudding is pricked with a needle. To serve, heat the puddings through in hot water for 10-15 minutes, or score at intervals and grill for 4 minutes on each side.

Alternatively, cut into rounds and grill or fry in lard. Serve with eggs for breakfast or with a mixed grill for lunch or high tea. In Derbyshire and Staffordshire, black pudding slices are served on oatcakes with fried eggs on top.

Warwick Pig's Pudding (6-8 portions) F Warwickshire

This local variation of black pudding includes minced pork and a rich flavouring of fresh herbs.

2 pt pig's blood
2 lb groats
1 lb breadcrumbs
1 teaspoon chopped leek, penny royal, sage or parsley
Pinch thyme and marjoram
2 oz salt
1 teaspoon pepper
¾ lb lean diced pork
1½ lb diced pork fat

Follow the method for black pudding, mixing the breadcrumbs with chopped leek, thyme, marjoram, salt, pepper and a little blood. Mix with the boiled groats, minced raw pork, pork fat and remaining blood. Proceed as opposite.

White Pudding (8-12 portions) F Scotland

This pudding, also known as mealie pudding, differs from black pudding in having no blood in the stuffing. It is usually stuffed in pig intestines, but thoroughly cleaned tripe skins may also be used. Fill the skins through a funnel and fasten each securely.

2 lb oatmeal
½-¾ lb chopped beef suet
1 lb finely chopped onions
½ teaspoon each salt and black pepper
Pig intestines

Toast the oatmeal lightly and mix with suet, onions, salt and pepper. Stuff the mixture into the prepared skins and prick with a fork. Boil for 2 hours, pricking the puddings occasionally to allow air to escape. The puddings can be stored for several weeks, hung up in a dry place.

Boil the puddings for 15-20 minutes or cut into slices and fry; serve as a main course or with stews.

Fitless Cock

Fitless Cock — or Dry Goose in southern Scotland — is a mealie pudding mixture bound with 2 lightly beaten eggs and moulded roughly into the shape of a chicken. It is wrapped in a floured pudding cloth and boiled for 2 hours. It was originally known as "festy cook" and baked in the ashes of the fire to be eaten on "festern eve", the night before Lent.

Sweet Marag (6 portions) F Isle of Lewis

This is a version of Scottish white or mealie pudding, but often cooked in a sheep stomach bag. A similar black pudding made with sheep's blood and without raisins and sugar is known as Savoury Marag. Another island speciality is Greiseagen, made from crisp fried suet mixed with oatmeal and currants.

½ lb flour
½ lb oatmeal
4 oz chopped suet
2 oz sugar
2 oz chopped onions
2 oz raisins
1 sheep's stomach bag

Mix all the ingredients together and stuff into the cleaned stomach bag; sew up, prick with a fork and cook in boiling water for 2-3 hours. Alternatively, tie the mixture in a floured pudding cloth or put in a greased pudding basin and boil. Serve cut into slices or fry and serve with fried potatoes and crisp bacon.

Sausages

Sausages are as popular now as when they first appeared in the 16th century. Cleaned skins are stuffed with minced pork, beef or mutton, mixed with cereals and seasonings which often give sausages their regional characteristics. Bath polonies were small, delicately flavoured sausages with a thin layer of fat next to the bright red skin. Scottish sausages, made from minced salt beef, suet and onions and highly seasoned with salt and pepper, were formerly hung up in the chimney to smoke.

The versatile sausages are used in breakfast dishes, snacks, as sandwich and pastry fillings, as main courses for lunch, high teas and suppers; they may be boiled or baked, grilled or fried.

An Elizabethan recipe is for fried sausages stewed with shallots, draught beer, white wine and lemon juice; in Lincolnshire and Yorkshire, boiled sausages are served with creamed potatoes or buttered toast, while the Glamorgan sausages contain no meat, but are made from grated cheese, breadcrumbs, chopped leeks, herbs and mustard and shaped and fried like sausages.

Beef Sausages (6-8 portions) F Yorkshire and Lancashire

In the North, beef sausages are traditionally made longer and thinner than pork sausages.

2 lb lean beef
1 lb beef suet
½ lb breadcrumbs
Salt and black pepper
Sausage skins
Dripping

Mince the beef and the suet and mix thoroughly with breadcrumbs, salt and pepper. Stuff this mixture into the prepared sausage·skins and twist to secure the ends. Fry in beef dripping until very crisp. Serve with Yorkshire pudding and mashed potatoes.

Epping Sausages (6-8 portions) F London

These pork sausages are highly favoured with spicing and fresh herbs, lemon rind giving a distinctive taste. The skins of cleaned pig intestine should be soaked in water for 3 days.

1 lb pork
1 lb beef suet
Grated rind of 1 lemon
Pinch each, thyme, marjoram and savory
I teaspoon chopped sage
Grated nutmeg
Salt and pepper
1 egg

Put the pork and suet through the fine mincer twice, add lemon rind, herbs, nutmeg, salt and pepper. Bind with beaten egg to a workable consistency and stuff into the sausage skins. Twist the skins at regular intervals. Cook in boiling water for 15-20 minutes.

Cumberland Sausages (8 portions) F Cumberland

Traditionally, this pork sausage is made into a 12 in long link, twisted into a spiral and cut into serving portions after cooking.

2 lb lean shoulder of pork
¾ lb pork fat

½ lb breadcrumbs
½ teaspoon each nutmeg and mace
Salt and pepper

Chop the pork and fat finely and mix with
breadcrumbs, nutmeg, mace, salt and pepper to
taste. Stuff into skins and tie off the ends at
12 in lengths. Serve boiled, fried or grilled.

Highland Bake (8 portions) F and H
Scotland

Suitable as a luncheon dish, this is a baked mixture of bacon, oatmeal and vegetables topped
with sausages.

2 lb skinned pork or beef sausages
1 lb bacon rashers
2 oz dripping
½ lb chopped onions
½ lb skinned and chopped tomatoes
4 oz fresh breadcrumbs
2 oz oatmeal
Salt and pepper
2 eggs
3 tablespoons milk

Oven: 350°F; gas mark 4; 30-35 minutes

Cut the rind off the bacon and chop the rashers
into small pieces; fry in the dripping over low
heat together with the onions for 4 minutes,
then add the tomatoes and cook for 1 further
minute. Remove from the pan and mix in the
breadcrumbs, oatmeal and salt and pepper.

Beat the eggs, add the milk and stir into the
mixture. Spoon into a greased shallow ovenproof
dish and arrange the sausages on top. Bake in the
oven for 30-35 minutes or until the sausages are
cooked through.

Mutton Sausages (6 portions) F

A speciality of regions with a prevalence of mountain sheep over pork. Ideally, the mutton mixture
should be augmented with a little cold boiled
bacon or ham.

1 lb lean mutton
½ lb mutton suet
½ lb breadcrumbs
Salt and black pepper
Pinch each, marjoram and thyme, finely chopped
Sausage skins

Chop or mince the mutton and suet finely, with

ham and bacon if available. Mix with breadcrumbs,
salt, pepper and herbs to taste. Press into prepared
sausage skins and boil in water for 15-20 minutes.

Mutton sausages can be baked in the oven and
are traditionally served with mashed potatoes and
mint sauce.

Oxford Sausages (8 portions) F and H
Oxford

Dating from the 18th century, Oxford sausages
are made from equal amounts of veal and pork;
they are not stuffed into skins, but shaped as
sausages and fried.

1 lb lean shoulder of pork
1 lb lean shoulder of veal
1 lb beef suet
½ lb white breadcrumbs
Grated rind of ½ lemon
1 grated nutmeg
1 teaspoon chopped sage
Pinch each, thyme, savory and marjoram, finely
    chopped
Salt and pepper
2 egg yolks
2-3 oz butter

Mince or finely chop the pork, veal and beef
suet, add the breadcrumbs, lemon rind, nutmeg,
sage, thyme, savory, marjoram, salt and pepper.
Bind the mixture with egg yolks. Mix thoroughly
and roll into sausage shapes between floured
hands. Fry in butter for about 10 minutes, turning
two or three times.

Pork Sausages with Apples (8 portions) F

Opinions differ on the necessity to prick the
skins of sausages before frying or grilling; some
authorities maintain this should be done to
prevent the sausages from bursting their skins,
others that cooked over gentle heat the skins
will remain intact.

Apple rings are a favourite accompaniment to
sausages, but banana slices or pineapple rings
lightly fried in butter can also be served.

2 lb pork sausages
2 lb cooked apples
1 oz flour
2½ fl oz milk
Pinch powdered sage

Wipe the sausages and prick the skins lightly.

Put in a cold frying pan or under a just warm grill and cook slowly until the fat begins to flow. Turn the sausages several times until brown all over, after about 20 minutes.

Meanwhile, core the apples but do not peel; cut into ½ in thick slices. Beat the flour and milk to a batter, and dip the apple rings in this mixture. Fry in the sausage fat for about 3 minutes and serve, spinkled with sage, as a garnish.

Sausages and Red Cabbage (8 portions) F

Red cabbage, particularly good with pork, needs long slow cooking and both acid and sweet seasonings to bring out its flavour.

2 lb pork or beef sausages
1½ lb red cabbage
2 oz sliced ham
2 oz butter
2 tablespoons vinegar
½ pt brown stock
1 oz sugar
Salt and pepper

Shred the cabbage and put in a pan, covered, with the ham and butter, vinegar and stock. Simmer over gentle heat until the cabbage has softened; add sugar, salt and pepper to taste and a little more stock if necessary to prevent the cabbage from burning. Simmer until most of the liquid has been absorbed and the cabbage is tender, after about 1 hour.

Prick the sausages and fry in their own fat for 20 minutes, turning frequently. Arrange the cooked sausages on the cabbage and serve hot.

Wiltshire Porkies (8 portions) F
Wiltshire

This is a dish of sausage meat, deep-fried in batter and served garnished with fried apple rings and parsley sprigs.

2 lb pork sausage meat
1 pt coating batter
Seasoned flour
¾ lb cored and sliced cooking apples
Lard or oil
Parsley sprigs

Make up the batter leaving out the whisked egg white and allow to stand for 30 minutes. Divide the sausage meat into 16 pieces and shape into small balls. Coat with seasoned flour. Beat the egg white into the batter. Dip the balls in the batter and fry in hot, deep fat until golden brown after 5-10 minutes. Dip the apple rings and parsley sprigs in the remaining batter and deep-fry for a few minutes. Drain and serve with the porkies.

Sweetbreads

Calf and lamb sweetbreads are in general the only ones sold; they come in pairs and consist of one thymus gland situated in the throat and one found in the chest cavity. To prepare sweetbreads for cooking, they should first be soaked in cold water for a couple of hours, then brought to the boil in a pan of fresh cold water. Drain at once and cover with salted, cold water; bring slowly to the boil again, lift out and refresh. Remove the thin covering and the black veins running through the sweetbreads.

Sweetbreads, Fried (6 portions) H and F

Fried mushrooms and hot buttered toast would be suitable with this light luncheon dish.

3 pairs sweetbreads (about 2 lb)
1 egg
4 oz breadcrumbs
4 oz butter
½ oz flour
½ pt white stock
2 teaspoons lemon juice
Salt and pepper
Garnish: lemon wedges, chopped parsley

Cut the sweetbreads into thin slices; coat with beaten egg and breadcrumbs. Melt the butter and fry the sweetbreads until golden brown. Lift out and keep warm.

Stir the flour into the pan juices and gradually add the stock; blend in the lemon juice and boil for a few minutes. Season to taste with salt and pepper. Pour the sauce over the sweetbreads and serve garnished with lemon wedges and parsley.

Sweetbreads in the English Style (6 portions) H and F

Calf sweetbreads are ideal for this dish, but the much less expensive lamb sweetbreads make an acceptable substitute. They are served grilled on skewers, accompanied with a bowl of bread sauce.

3 pairs sweetbreads
¾ lb smoked streaky bacon rashers
4 oz breadcrumbs
3 oz butter

Cut the prepared sweetbreads into six thick slices. Remove the rind from the bacon, stretch the rashers with the blade of a knife and wrap the rashers around the sweetbreads; thread on to skewers. Put the sweetbreads and bacon under a medium hot grill for 15-20 minutes, turning occasionally.

Fry the breadcrumbs in butter until brown and coat the sweetbreads with them. Arrange the sweetbreads on a bed of the remaining crumbs; serve immediately with bread sauce.

Sweetbreads, Stewed (6 portions) H

A creamy stew, suitable in a building-up diet, and complemented with fluffy boiled rice.

3 pairs sweetbreads
1 oz seasoned flour
½ pt white stock
Pinch nutmeg, white pepper
Salt
2 egg yolks
5 fl oz single cream
1 dessertspoon chopped parsley
Garnish: green peas

Coat the prepared sweetbreads with seasoned flour; put in a pan with the stock, nutmeg, pepper and salt. Bring to the boil, cover, and simmer for 1 hour. Beat the egg yolks with the cream and chopped parsley.

Let the sweetbreads cool slightly, add the egg and cream mixture; reheat the stew until it has thickened, but do not allow it to boil. Adjust seasoning and serve with cooked green peas.

Tongues

Lamb and ox tongue are easily bought, but calf tongue is rare and pig's tongue is always sold with the head. Ox tongue is the largest, weighing 4-6 lb, and is available fresh or salted; it should be cooked slowly for several hours so that the rough skin can be peeled off.

Ox Tongue (10-12 portions) H and F

Boiled ox tongue is not served on its own, but after cooking is prepared with additional ingredients, usually pressed and served cold with salads and pickles, or it may be served hot with a breadcrumb coating and a sauce.

1 ox tongue
6 oz sliced onions
4 oz diced carrots
Faggot of herbs
1 bay leaf
8 peppercorns
Salt

If the tongue is salted, soak it overnight in cold water. The next day, drain and put in a large pan with cold water to cover. Boil for 5 minutes and drain. Cover with fresh water and add the onions, carrots, herbs, bay leaf, peppercorns and salt if the tongue is fresh. Bring to the boil and simmer, under a lid, until tender, allowing 30 minutes per lb for salted tongue and 45 minutes for fresh tongue. Plunge into cold water, peel off the skin beginning at the tip and trim off bones and gristle from the root end.

Hot tongue: cover the tongue while still hot with browned breadcrumbs and garnish with parsley and lemon slices; serve with parsley sauce (made with half milk and half stock from the tongue), tomato sauce or a sweet cherry sauce.

Pressed tongue: twist the skinned tongue into a circle and set it in a round cake tin just large enough to hold it. Spoon over some of the strained stock to come just above the top of the tongue; cover with a weighted board and leave to press until cold and set.

Ox Tongue, Roast (10 portions) H and F

This is an impressive dish, a whole boiled tongue stuffed with a spicy filling and served with orange sauce. Ideally the tongue should be covered with fatty calf caul while roasting, but as this is seldom available use a thick piece of foil.

1 boiled ox tongue
3 oz fat bacon
2 oz lean minced bacon
6 oz peeled, grated dessert apples
1 oz chopped suet
2 hardboiled egg yolks
½ teaspoon mixed herbs

Pinch ground ginger
Salt
Garnish: lemon peel, barberries

Oven: 350°F; gas mark 4; 1 hour

Skin the boiled tongue, cut away the bone and
gristle from the root end and trim neatly. Cut
a slit lengthways in the root end and make a
cavity by scooping out part of the meat. Chop
the meat and set aside. Lard the tongue
with the bacon fat cut into strips.

Mix the tongue meat (about 6 oz) and
minced bacon with the apples, suet and egg
yolks; season with herbs, ginger and salt. Stuff
this mixture into the tongue and sew the open
edges together. Cover with caul or foil and roast
in the oven for 45-60 minutes. Remove the foil
for the last 20 minutes. Garnish with lemon
peel and barberries and serve.

Lamb Tongues, Stewed (6 portions) F

A lamb tongue is quite small, weighing on
average ½ lb. Soak for 1-2 hours in lightly salted
water and blanch twice in boiling water.

6 lamb tongues
4 oz streaky bacon
1-2 oz dripping
4 oz sliced carrots
½ lb sliced onions
Faggot of herbs
Black pepper
1 pt brown stock

Fry half the bacon in the dripping, add the carrots
and onions and continue frying until light brown.
Add the tongues and herbs, sprinkle with black
pepper and put the remaining bacon on top.
Pour over the stock, bring to the boil and simmer
gently for about 2-2½ hours.

Remove the tongues, plunge into cold water and
peel off the skin; trim all bone and gristle from the
root end. Cut each tongue in half lengthways and
return to the pan; heat through and serve. The
gravy may be strained and thickened before the
tongues are added.

Tripe

There are two types of tripe — the stomach
lining of the ox — blanket tripe which comes
from the first stomach and honeycomb tripe
from the second stomach. Most tripe is sold
dressed, that is par-boiled and blanched, and
cooking time depends on the amount of boiling
the tripe has already undergone. It is most often
boiled in milk or stock for stews, but may also
be fried. Cut the tripe into 2-3 in strips and fry
with bacon rashers and onions in bacon fat, or
coat the strips in batter mixed with chopped
parsley and onions and flavoured with ginger;
fry in hot dripping.

Tripe and Onions (6-8 portions) F
Lancashire

Tripe and onions is associated with the tripe
parlours of the Midlands and the North, the
forerunners of today's fish and chip shops. It is
traditionally served with mashed potatoes.

2 lb dressed tripe
¾ lb sliced onions
1½ pt milk
2 oz butter
1 oz flour
Pinch nutmeg
Salt and pepper
Garnish: sippets

Cut the dressed tripe into narrow strips, about 2
in long. Simmer the tripe and onions in milk for
about 1 hour or until tender. Melt the butter in a
pan, stir in the flour and cook for a few minutes
without colour. Gradually add the milk from the
tripe to make a thick sauce.

Bring to the boil and season with nutmeg, salt
and pepper to taste. Add the tripe and onions,
heat through and serve. Garnish with sippets of
hot toast.

In Ireland, nutmeg is replaced by mustard and
lemon juice; lemon slices and barberries are used
for garnishing.

Balmoral Tripe (6-8 portions) F and H
Scotland

The Normans are said to have introduced tripe
as a food to England; tripe dishes in Scotland
show a distinct, if later, French influence.

2 lb dressed tripe
1 lb lean unsmoked bacon or cooked ham
6 oz finely diced onions
2 oz seasoned flour

1 oz lard
4 oz finely diced carrots
2 pt white stock
1 oz butter
Salt and pepper
5 fl oz single cream
Garnish: chopped parsley

Cut the tripe into 4 in squares and cover with
slices of bacon or ham cut into shape. Spread
half the onions over the bacon slices, roll up
and secure with skewers or fine string. Dip each
roll in seasoned flour and fry in lard until lightly
brown; drain thoroughly.

 Put the remaining onions and carrots in a pan
with the tripe rolls and stock; simmer, covered,
for 1-1½ hours over gentle heat. Remove
the tripe rolls and keep hot. Add the butter to
the pan and the seasoned flour blended with a
little milk; boil until the sauce has thickened.
Adjust seasoning with salt and pepper. Add the
cream, return the tripe to the sauce and heat
through without boiling. Garnish with parsley.

Derbyshire Tripe (6 portions) F
Derbyshire

Based on the traditional tripe and onion recipe,
this dish includes pork sausages and split cow
heel, rich in protein.

1 lb dressed tripe
1 cow heel
¾ lb chopped onions
1 pt milk
¾ lb pork sausages
½ oz flour
Salt and pepper

Split the cow heel into two or four pieces, leave
the tripe whole and wash both thoroughly. Put the
cow heel in a large pan with enough water to
cover; bring to the boil and simmer for 15 minutes.
Drain and return to the pan with fresh water;
simmer covered for 2 hours, then drain and set the
water aside.

 Put the tripe, cow heel pieces and onions in a
pan with the milk and enough of the strained
water to cover; bring to the boil and simmer for 1
hour. Prick the sausages, add to the pan and
simmer for a further 30 minutes.

 Lift out the cow heel pieces and the tripe;
trim any meat from the heel and cut the tripe

into small squares. Blend the flour with a little
milk and add to the stew; bring to the boil and
simmer gently until thickened. Add the meat
and tripe, season with salt and pepper and heat
through before serving.

Dressmaker Tripe (6-8 portions) F
East Anglia

The strange title of this dish probably refers to a
large piece of tripe carefully sewn up round an
onion and breadcrumb stuffing. It is traditionally
served with a brown sauce.

2 lb dressed tripe
½ lb onions
½ lb white breadcrumbs
½ teaspoon each chopped parsley and thyme
Salt and pepper
1 egg
4 oz streaky bacon

Oven: 350°F; gas mark 4; 1 hour

For the stuffing, boil the onions until soft, then
chop them finely; mix with breadcrumbs, herbs,
salt and pepper and bind with beaten egg. Spread
this stuffing over half the piece of tripe, fold the
other half over and sew up the edges. Place the
tripe in a greased roasting tin and arrange the
bacon rashers over it. Bake for 1 hour and serve.

POULTRY

Chicken, duck and geese were birds of the
farmyard from the earliest days onwards, chicken
or hen being favoured for its reliable supply of
eggs. Capons — fatted, castrated cocks — might
be bred for the tables of noblemen, but for the
ordinary man poultry was far too valuable to be
eaten; not until a hen became stringy, old and
past egg-laying would it end its life in the cook
pot. Poultry was generally boiled or made into
pies and puddings, but in the 17th century
chicken and geese became status symbols and
appeared in elaborately prepared dishes. Goose
remained the traditional Christmas bird until the
early 20th century.

 Pigeons were rated as poultry and housed in
dovecots, so fashionable in the 16th and 17th
centuries, but are now classified as game birds.
In contrast, the guinea fowl was originally a game

bird, but is now bred on poultry farms for domestic consumption.

Poultry dishes do not show any regional characteristics; Norfolk turkey and Aylesbury ducklings are not indicative of particular cooking methods but refer to areas suitable for rearing table poultry.

One of the few local poultry recipes to have survived is "Hindle Wakes Fowl" which has changed little in concept since it was brought to England by Flemish spinners when they settled near Bolton in the 12th century. It became a traditional "Hen de la Wake" dish for serving during the annual Wakes Week and consisted of a boiling fowl stuffed with prunes, herb-flavoured breadcrumbs, suet and vinegar; it was served cold coated with a thick lemon sauce and garnished with lemon wedges and stoned prunes.

Chicken, Devilled (8 portions) H and F

Left-over chicken joints or slices of cold roast turkey take on interesting aspects with a devil sauce. Alternatively, blend the devil spicing into ½ pt double cream and heat the poultry carefully in this, or fold it into the same quantity whipped cream and serve with the grilled poultry.

8 chicken joints
4 oz softened butter
1½ oz flour
Pinch dry mustard
2 oz fruit chutney
1 tablespoon Worcestershire sauce
French mustard
6-7 fl oz poultry gravy

Skin the poultry joints; blend the butter, flour and dry mustard thoroughly to a paste. Add the chutney, Worcestershire sauce and French mustard to taste. Work the paste until smooth, adding a little more flour if it appears thin.

Spread most of the paste over the poultry and put under a low grill. Heat the gravy and add the remaining devil paste; heat through and serve poured round the joints.

Devonshire Chicken (8 portions) H and F
Devon

For this dish, bought chicken joints may be used, but it is more economical to purchase whole

chickens as the odds and ends can be used for stocks or broths.

2 oven-ready chicken (2½ lb each)
Seasoned flour
6½ oz butter
1¼ lb dessert apples
½ lb chopped onions
1 oz flour
¾ pt cider
7½ fl oz white stock
7½ fl oz double cream or evaporated milk
Garnish: 1 tablespoon chopped parsley

Oven: 350°F; gas mark 4; 15 minutes

Cut the chicken into four leg and four breast joints; dust each with seasoned flour. Melt 4 oz of the butter and fry the chicken joints until just golden; lift out. Peel, core and chop half the apples and fry with the onions in the butter for 2-3 minutes without colour. Stir in the flour, add the cider and stock and replace the chicken. Cover with a lid and cook in the oven for 15 minutes.

Arrange the chicken on a serving dish. Reduce the sauce and add the cream, blend in 1 oz butter and heat through without boiling. Brown the remaining, sliced apples in butter and arrange on top of the chicken. Pour over the sauce, sprinkle with parsley and serve.

Jugged Fowl with Oysters (8 portions) H and F

This is an old country dish dating from the days when oysters were everyday fare and consumed in huge quantities by the poor. Mussels or cockles are more likely to replace the oysters today.

2 boiling fowls (3 lb each)
1-2 dozen fresh oysters
2 egg yolks
2 tablespoons double cream
Salt and pepper
Pinch ground mace

Oven: 350°F; gas mark 4; 2-2½ hours

Truss the fowl, stuffing the body cavities with oysters and reserving a few for the sauce. Put the fowl in a large earthenware jar and cover with greaseproof paper, tied on lightly. Set the jar in a pan of water, coming half way up the jar or place on the stove or in the oven.

Simmer slowly on top of the stove or in the oven for about 2 hours or until the fowl are quite tender. Lift out and thicken the gravy with the blended egg yolks and cream, add the reserved oysters and season to taste with salt, pepper and mace. Serve the sauce poured over the fowl.

Spring Chicken, Grilled (8 portions) H

Poussins, also known as baby or spring chicken, weigh about 1½ lb each. In the 19th century, grilled spring chicken was a popular dish in taverns and chop houses.

4 poussins
Salt and pepper
Juice of 4 lemons
½ lb melted butter
Garnish: watercress

Split the birds in half along the soft backbones; sprinkle with salt, pepper and lemon juice. Brush with melted butter and grill the chicken for approximately 5 minutes on each side until lightly browned. Reduce the heat and continue grilling until cooked through.

Serve hot, seasoned with salt and pepper, garnished with watercress and accompanied with a sharp or mustard sauce.

Stoved Chicken (8 portions) F Scotland

A homely chicken casserole with potatoes and onions. The term "stoved" is possibly a corruption of the French *estuvier* or may simply mean "enclosed"

2 chicken (2½ lb each)
2 oz butter
½ lb sliced onions
2½ lb sliced potatoes
Salt and pepper
1 pt chicken stock
Garnish: chopped parsley

Oven: 275°F; gas mark 1; 2½ hours

Joint each chicken into four pieces; melt 1 oz of butter and lightly brown the joints. Lift out. Mix the onions and thinly sliced potatoes together and sprinkle with salt and pepper. Place a layer of onions and potatoes in a deep ovenproof dish. Add the chicken joints and cover with the remaining potatoes and onions. Pour over the stock and

cover with buttered paper and a lid. Bring to the boil on top of the stove.

Cook in the oven for 2 hours, then remove the lid and paper. Brush the potatoes with the remaining butter and cook in the oven for a further 30 minutes or until brown on top. Sprinkle with parsley and serve.

Stoved Howtowdie with Drappit Eggs (8 portions) F and H Scotland

This is reminiscent of the old Kentish Farmhouse Chicken which was baked in the oven with milk and brown rice and served garnished with hardboiled eggs. Howtowdie is a young hen, and "drappit eggs" are eggs dropped for poaching in boiling liquid. Spinach is traditional with this dish, and the sauce made with the reserved chicken livers may be enriched with mushrooms, oysters, celery or small forcemeat balls.

2 young chicken (2½ lb each)
Salt and pepper
2 lb herb forcemeat
4 oz butter
½ lb button onions
1 faggot of herbs
½ teaspoon rosemary
1½ pt white stock
8 eggs

Wipe the chicken inside and out; sprinkle with salt and pepper and stuff with the forcemeat. Truss the birds. Melt the butter in a pan large enough to hold the birds. Add the onions, herbs and rosemary, and brown the chicken. Pour over the stock, cover with a tight fitting lid and simmer for 1 hour. When the chickens are tender, poach the eggs in a little of the cooking liquid.

Arrange the eggs on flattened balls of spinach set on a serving dish with the chicken in the centre. Rub the chicken livers through a sieve and mix with the cooking liquid; thicken if necessary and pour over the birds before serving.

Duck in Honey Sauce (8 portions) H

The breast is the most succulent part of the duck, plump and a little fatty. Although usually roasted, duck portions are here cooked in a rich creamy sauce, flavoured with honey and fresh thyme.

8 duck breasts
6 oz butter
2 fl oz olive oil
4 oz finely chopped onions
4 fl oz white wine
4 oz honey
2 sprigs thyme
Juice of 1 lemon
Salt and pepper
1 pt double cream
Garnish: thyme

Cut each duck breast into two pieces. Heat 4 oz of butter and the oil in a pan and fry the meat without colour. Add the onions and continue cooking until the onions are soft. Remove the meat from the pan and keep warm; pour off any excess fat.

Add the wine to the pan and boil to reduce slightly; mix in the honey and thyme. Add lemon juice, salt, pepper and cream; replace the duck in the pan. Cover and cook gently for 5 minutes or until tender.

Remove the duck to a serving dish, discard the thyme and whisk the remaining butter into the sauce. Pour over the duck and garnish with fresh thyme.

Duck with Onion Sauce (8-10 portions) H and F

This is a modified version of the Hermit of Gower's Salt Duck from Wales; the latter is a 19th century recipe, the duck being rubbed with coarse salt for several days before being boiled and served with onion sauce.

2 duck (3 lb each)
1 faggot of herbs
2 onions studded with cloves
2 oz chopped celery
½ lb carrots
4 oz butter
1 lb finely chopped onions
3 oz flour
2 pt milk
Salt and pepper
3 fl oz double cream

Put the prepared, trussed duck in a large pan with the herbs, studded onions, celery and carrots; cover with water and bring to the boil. Simmer the ducks covered, for 1½-2 hours or

until tender; skim frequently. Lift out the ducks and keep warm; strain the liquid.

Melt the butter in a pan and cook the onions gently until soft. Stir in the flour and gradually add the milk, stirring constantly until the sauce boils and thickens. The consistency of the sauce can be adjusted by adding a little of the strained duck liquid. Season the sauce with salt and pepper and blend in the cream. Lay the carved or jointed duck on a serving dish and pour over the sauce.

Duckling with Peas (6-8 portions) H

A popular dish in the 17th and 18th centuries and traditional at Whitsun, with small new potatoes and fresh garden peas and mint.

2 ducklings
2 oz seasoned flour
2 oz butter
2 pt game stock
Salt and pepper
1¼ lb shelled peas
2 finely chopped lettuce
1 bunch sweet herbs
½ grated nutmeg
2 egg yolks
5 fl oz double cream
Garnish: chopped mint

Oven: 350°F; gas mark 4; 30 minutes

Dust the trussed ducklings with seasoned flour and brown in the butter; roast in the oven for 30 minutes. Pour off the surplus fat, add stock, salt and pepper to the pan. Bring slowly to the boil and simmer for 15-20 minutes. Add the peas, lettuce and herbs. Cover and simmer for 40 minutes or until the ducks are tender. Remove the sweet herbs.

Lift out the ducklings and keep warm on a serving dish. Rub the cooking liquid through a sieve or liquidise; add the nutmeg and blend in the egg yolks beaten with the cream. Heat the sauce through to thicken but do not boil. Season; pour over the ducklings and serve garnished with mint.

Goose

The goose has always been England's festive bird, traditional at the end of harvest time, Michaelmas, and at Christmas; in the North, the turkey has never replaced the goose in popularity. Roast goose, probably cooked under a cover of huff paste, was certainly known as early as the 13th century. Goose was valued not only for its rich meat, its downs and feathers, but also for its fat. Country people spread goose grease on their bread, with salt and pepper, used it as a poultice to ease tight chests, rubbed it on to cows' udders and dairymaids' hands to prevent chapping, and smeared it on to harnesses and straps to keep the leather supple.

Roast goose is traditionally stuffed with sage and onion or with prunes and apples and is served with apple and bread sauce, boiled potatoes and a green vegetable. The tradition of Michaelmas goose is dying out, but a Royal decree by Queen Elizabeth I ordained that roast goose be served on Michaelmas Day to commemorate the English victory over the Spanish Armada, news of which she is said to have received while feasting on roast goose. The harvest or Michaelmas goose was fattened on gleanings left by the harvesters and was often roasted together with fat young rabbits. This tradition survived for many centuries, often as an economy measure, the goose being stuffed with rabbit joints which were given to the children of the household while the adults enjoyed the goose.

Gosling, also known as green goose, was killed at about 6 months old and, being less fatty, was stuffed with butter and served with sorrel or green gooseberry sauce.

Goose pie was a traditional Christmas dish, made from two boned geese, one stuffed inside the other and baked in a raised pie crust.

Guinea Fowl, Fried (6-8 portions) F
Norfolk

Large guinea fowl, up to 3 lb, are suitable for braising and casseroles; here the fowl are jointed and fried in butter.

2 large guinea fowl
2 pig trotters
Salt and pepper
4 oz butter
½ lb minced onions
4 oz finely chopped streaky bacon
½ lb button mushrooms
½ pt white wine

Joint the guinea fowl neatly. Chop up the remaining carcasses and the trotters, place in a pan,

cover with water and simmer for about 1 hour to make stock. Strain the stock and reduce to ½ pt.

Season the joints liberally with salt and pepper, fry in 2 oz of butter until lightly brown. Cover the pan and simmer for 30 minutes or until the guinea fowl is tender. Remove to a serving dish and keep the joints warm.

Fry the onions in the pan until brown, adding more butter as necessary, then add the bacon and cook until crisp; add the mushrooms and cook for a few more minutes, stirring constantly. Stir in the wine and stock; reduce this sauce until it thickens. Adjust seasoning, pour over the joints and serve.

Guinea Fowl, Pan-Fried (8 portions) H

Creamy onion sauce with breast of guinea fowl provides a quick main course; the remainder of the birds can be used for a casserole.

4 guinea fowl
Juice of 1 lemon
1 oz seasoned flour
4 oz butter
4 oz finely chopped shallots
½ pt single cream
1 dessertspoon chopped chives or parsley
Salt and pepper

Oven: 350°F; gas mark 4; 15 minutes

Cut two breasts from each guinea fowl, remove the skin and brush the meat with lemon juice; dust with seasoned flour. Melt the butter in a pan and fry the fowl gently on both sides, without colouring. Cover the pan and cook in the oven for 15 minutes. Remove the guinea fowl to a serving dish and keep hot.

Add the shallots to the pan and fry gently until soft but not brown; stir in the cream and simmer until the sauce thickens slightly. Blend in the chives or parsley, season with salt and pepper and pour the sauce over the guinea fowl.

Guinea Fowl, Roast (8 portions) H

For roasting, choose young guinea fowl at about 1½ lb each. The flesh, somewhat reminiscent of pheasant, improves by hanging the unplucked birds for a few days.

4 guinea fowl
1 faggot of herbs

Sprigs of tarragon or parsley
½ lb butter
1½ lb streaky bacon rashers or pork fat
3 oz flour
1 pt dry white wine
5 fl oz sherry
¾ lb skinned and seeded green grapes
Salt and pepper
Juice of 1 lemon

Oven: 350°F; gas mark 4; 1½ hours

Put the giblets in a pan with the faggot of herbs, cover with water and bring to the boil; simmer for 1 hour to make stock.

Put 1 oz of butter and a sprig of tarragon or parsley inside each guinea fowl; melt 2 oz of butter and brush liberally over the birds; cover the breasts with streaky bacon and roast in the oven for 1 hour. Baste frequently and remove the bacon for the last 20 minutes to allow the meat to brown.

Remove the guinea fowl, and carve into joints. Pour off most of the fat in the roasting tin, stir in the flour, scraping up all the residues. When the roux is well coloured, add the wine, sherry and 1 pt of strained giblet stock; boil through, then add the guinea fowl and ½ lb of the prepared grapes. Season to taste with salt, pepper and lemon juice.

Cover and cook for 20-25 minutes in the oven. Remove the joints from the sauce and place on a serving dish. Strain the sauce and finish with 2 oz butter; pour over the birds and serve garnished with the remaining grapes.

Guinea Fowl, Stuffed (8 portions) H
Suffolk

The delicate stuffing for small guinea fowl is intended for flavouring only and does not form part of the finished dish.

4 guinea fowl (1½ lb each)
2 oz chopped celery
5 chopped sprigs of watercress
Salt and pepper
2 crushed cloves garlic
½ lb butter
2 lemons
4 oz bacon or pork fat
5 fl oz dry white wine
1 pt game stock
4 egg yolks
Garnish: sippets, lemon slices

Mix the celery and watercress, season with salt, pepper and garlic to taste and bind with 2 oz of the butter. Put this mixture into the birds, but do not tie them up. Grate the rind from the lemons, mix with salt and pepper and rub over the skin of the birds; cover with bacon or pork fat. Brown the birds in 4 oz of butter, pour in the wine and boil until slightly reduced; add the stock. Cover and simmer for 45 minutes. Lift out the guinea fowl and drain; remove the stuffing, joint the birds and place on a hot dish.

Squeeze the lemons and beat the juice with the egg yolks, add a little of the hot stock and pour into the pan. Blend in the remaining butter and heat the sauce without boiling until thickened. Pour over the joints and garnish with sippets of fried bread and lemon slices.

Boiled Turkey with Celery Sauce
(6-8 portions) H and F

This was a popular Victorian sideboard dish, usually served together with boiled ham, tongue or pickled pork for a large gathering. The traditional accompaniment was celery sauce, but sometimes the turkey was stuffed with oysters and an oyster sauce replaced the celery.

1 turkey (approx. 8 lb)
1-2 lb veal forcemeat or sausage meat
1 faggot of herbs
1 onion studded with cloves
1 oz chopped celery
4 oz carrots
Salt and pepper

Stuff the cleaned turkey with forcemeat and truss. Put in a large, heavy-based pan with the herbs, onion, celery, whole carrots and salt and pepper. Cover with cold water, bring to the boil and skim. Cover with a lid and simmer for 1½-2 hours or until the turkey is tender.

Lift out and drain the turkey; carve and keep warm on a serving dish. Strain the cooking liquid and use as a base for celery sauce.

GAME

Poultry was considered to be the woman's domain while game for the table was essentially a man's prerogative that he might display his skill, patience and cunning. The vast variety of game hunted and trapped by our forefathers has greatly diminished and is today limited to furred game, such as deer, rabbits and hares; few game birds, apart from grouse, partridge, pheasants, pigeons and the occasional wild duck appear on a commercial scale. Snipe and woodcock, considered great game delicacies well into the 20th century, are now rarely seen.

Swans and peacocks — which are neither game nor poultry birds and probably enjoyed more for their spectacular appearance at grandiose banquets than for their dry stringy flesh — were supplemented with game birds such as blackbirds, larks, starlings, sparrows — and rooks for the poor — wild duck and geese, curlews, plovers, redshanks, herons and bitterns.

The reduction of game for consumption has been due to two factors, one of which was the near extinction of many birds with subsequent conservation laws and close seasons, and a radical change in taste coupled with a ready supply of fresh meat and poultry.

Hanging for both furred animals and game birds is necessary to develop their flavours and soften their flesh before cooking. The length of hanging, from two days to a week or longer, depends on several factors, but most game lovers will insist on game being "high".

Game Birds

Wild Duck with Port Wine Sauce (6-8 portions) H

The mallard is the largest of the wild duck, giving about three portions. It is in season from 1 September until the end of February.

2 wild ducks
2 oz melted butter
½ lb streaky bacon rashers
Salt, cayenne, black pepper
Juice of 1 lemon
4 oz orange marmalade
4 fl oz port wine
½ pt rich brown sauce
1 teaspoon mushroom ketchup or relish

Oven: 325° F; gas mark 3; 45 minutes;
400° F; gas mark 6; 10 minutes

Truss the ducks, brush the breasts with melted

butter and cover with the bacon. Roast in the oven for 45 minutes. Remove the bacon, score the breasts and sprinkle with salt, pepper and cayenne; pour over the lemon juice and return to the oven for 10 minutes at high temperature.

Remove and carve up the birds and arrange on a serving dish. Boil the pan juices and reduce to a sauce with the marmalade, port wine, brown sauce and mushroom ketchup. Finish the sauce with a little butter and serve with the duck.

Buttered Grouse (6-8 portions) H Yorkshire

The glorious Twelfth of August sees the opening of the grouse season which lasts for four months. Young grouse from the Yorkshire Moors are considered the finest game delicacy.

2 brace of grouse
Blades of mace
4 oz pork or bacon fat
Salt, pepper and cayenne
½ lb butter

Oven: 400° F; gas mark 6; 10 minutes;
350° F; gas mark 4; 20-30 minutes

Place a piece of mace over the breast of each trussed grouse, bard with strips of fat and tie in place. Set the grouse in a greased roasting tin and cook for 10 minutes at high temperature to seal. Sprinkle with salt and pepper and reduce the heat. Continue roasting for 20-30 minutes depending on the age of the birds.

Cut the grouse into portions and place in a pie dish. Add the butter to the dripping in the roasting tin, season with salt, pepper and cayenne and pour over the birds. Serve cold.

Autumn Partridge Pot (6 portions) F and H Norfolk

Young partridges are usually roasted and served whole, one per person; older and tougher birds are ideal for a well-flavoured casserole which will also serve more people.

3 partridges
2 oz seasoned oatmeal
2 oz diced fat ham or bacon
3 cloves
1 bay leaf, 1 spring of thyme
Salt and pepper

4 oz sliced mushrooms
4 oz finely chopped onions
½ lb skinned, seeded and chopped tomatoes
5 fl oz red wine or port

Oven: 350°F; gas mark 4; 2½ hours

Joint the partridges, using the necks and other trimmings to make stock. Coat the joints with oatmeal. Put the ham or bacon in a 3-4 pt casserole dish and lay the joints on top. Add cloves, bay leaf, thyme and salt and pepper. Lay the mushrooms, onions and tomatoes on top, pour over ¾ pt of the prepared stock and enough wine to cover the joints.

Cover the casserole with a close fitting lid and cook in the oven for 2½ hours or overnight at the lowest possible temperature.

Partridge with Cabbage (6-8 portions) F and H Leicestershire

Many old country recipes for tough grouse birds include cabbage with the casserole dish. Some versions add a glass of sherry to the stock, in others it is thickened with cream, and the cabbage may be omitted, the casseroled birds being served with an onion pulp.

4 partridges
4 shallots
Salt and pepper
1 lb bacon rashers
4 oz diced carrots
1 lb sliced onions
Sprig of thyme
1 cabbage
2 pt game stock
Garnish: chopped parsley

Oven: 375°F; gas mark 5; 30 minutes ;
300°F; gas mark 2; 2-3 hours

Put one shallot inside each partridge and season, inside and out, with salt and pepper. Truss the partridge and tie a bacon rasher over the breast of each. Place in a casserole dish with the carrots, onions and remaining diced bacon. Add the necks, giblets and thyme and brown in the oven for 30 minutes turning frequently.

Par-boil the cabbage, cut in four and pack round the birds. Cover with boiling stock, replace the lid of the casserole and cook slowly in the oven for 2-3 hours. Serve the casserole garnished with parsley.

Pheasant Casserole (8 portions) H and F Lincolnshire

Ideally, the breast pieces only should be used for this dish, the remainder being used in a game pie or for potting.

2 brace jointed pheasants
½ lb butter
½ lb diced onions
4 oz diced carrots
½ lb sliced mushrooms
2 oz flour
5 fl oz light red wine (optional)
3 pt game stock
1 lb skinned, seeded and chopped tomatoes
Salt and pepper
Garnish: 1 dessertspoon chopped parsley

Brown the pheasant joints lightly in butter, then lift out. Fry the onions and carrots for 5 minutes, add the mushrooms and cook for another few minutes. Blend in the flour and cook for a few minutes, then stir in the wine and gradually add the stock.

Blend in the tomatoes, season to taste with salt and pepper and return the pheasants to the pan. Simmer, covered, for 30 minutes or until tender. Serve garnished with parsley.

Boiled Pigeons and Bacon (8 portions) F

The combination of poultry or game birds with meat goes back to the Middle Ages when boiling was the usual cooking method. The flavours blend and complement each other and the fat of the meat is absorbed by the dry game flesh.

8 young pigeons
2 lb piece of bacon forehock or shoulder
1 faggot of herbs
1 onion studded with cloves
1 oz chopped celery
4 oz carrots
Salt and pepper
Garnish: spinach

Put the trussed pigeons and bacon in a large pan with the herbs, onion, celery and whole carrots; season with salt and pepper and pour over enough cold water to cover. Bring to the boil, remove scum, cover with a lid and simmer gently for 1-1½ hours or until tender.

Arrange the bacon in the centre of a serving dish, surround with the pigeons and garnish with

spinach. Melted butter and parsley butter sauce
are the usual accompaniments.

Pigeons in Pimlico (8 portions) F and H London

This is similar to another pigeon dish, popular
in London in the 19th century — the pigeon pie.
This was a layered pie of sausage meat, pigeons,
mushrooms and ham, the whole covered with puff
pastry. In this recipe, roasted pigeons are garnished with small puff pastry cases containing the
remaining stuffing.

8 pigeons
6 oz melted butter
1½ lb diced ham
¾ lb chopped mushrooms
1 oz chopped parsley
Pinch sweet herbs, mace
Salt and pepper
3-4 egg yolks
8 slices veal
8 bacon rashers
24 small puff pastry cases

Oven: 350°F; gas mark 4; 1 hour

For the stuffing, par-boil the pigeon livers, then
fry lightly in 2 oz butter with the ham, mushrooms and parsley. Blend thoroughly and season
with herbs, mace, salt and pepper; bind with the
lightly beaten egg yolks.

Stuff the pigeons, keeping enough mixture
over to fill the pastry cases. Roll each bird in a
slice of veal and a slice of bacon; tie with fine
string. Roast in the oven, basting frequently with
the remaining melted butter. Serve garnished
with the small hot pastry cases, filled with the
left-over stuffing.

Furred Game

Baron of Hare (6-8 portions) H and F

The baron of hare or a young leveret consists of
the back and hind legs in one piece. Old hares
are not suitable for roasting, but the meat of a
leveret is extremely tender. Serve with rowan or
red currant jelly, boiled potatoes and green peas.

1 hare or leveret
½ lb veal forcemeat
4 oz fat bacon

Butter
2½ fl oz beef stock
1 teaspoon lemon juice
1 glass sherry or Madeira
5 fl oz double cream
Salt and pepper
Garnish: bacon rolls, forcemeat balls

Oven: 425°F; gas mark 7; 45 minutes

Trim the ribs of the hare and stuff the cavity
with forcemeat; tie in place with fine string and
lard the back with bacon. Roast in the oven for
45 minutes, basting with melted butter every
10 minutes; remove the bacon for the last 15
minutes.

Transfer the hare to a serving dish and pour
off the fat in the tin. Stir the stock into the
pan residues, add lemon juice and sherry and
bring to the boil; remove from the heat, stir in
the cream and season with salt and pepper. Pour
the sauce over the hare and serve garnished with
bacon rolls and forcemeat balls.

Jugged Hare (8 portions) F

One of the oldest and best loved English dishes,
taking its name from the deep, lidded stoneware
jug in which it was originally cooked. The rich
gravy is thickened with blood which must not
be allowed to boil or it may curdle.

1 well-hung hare
1 teaspoon vinegar
Seasoned flour
Oil for frying
Brown stock
1 onion studded with cloves
Bunch of sweet herbs
Pinch mace, nutmeg
2 oz red currant jelly
5 fl oz port or claret
Salt and pepper
Garnish: heart-shaped sippets, forcemeat balls

Oven: 350°F; gas mark 4; about 3 hours

Have the hare skinned, cleaned and neatly jointed,
reserving the blood and liver. Mix the blood with
the vinegar to prevent it curdling and keep in a
cool place.

Dust the joints with seasoned flour and fry in
oil until golden brown; transfer to a deep ovenproof dish, pour over enough stock to cover, add

the onion, herbs, mace and nutmeg. Cover
the dish with a tight-fitting lid, bring to the boil
and place in the oven for about 3 hours. When the
meat is tender, transfer to a serving dish and
garnish with the diced, fried liver.

Strain the cooking liquid into a pan and reboil, add the red currant jelly and pour a little
liquid into the blood, stirring until smooth. Blend
the blood into the gravy and heat through to
thicken, but do not boil; add the port or claret,
season to taste with salt and pepper and pour
over the meat. If blood is not available, thicken
the gravy with 1 oz butter and 1 oz flour
kneaded together. Garnish with sippets and
forcemeat balls and serve with jacket potatoes
and a green vegetable.

Hare Stew (8 portions) F

This is a more modern version of jugged hare and
is also suitable for rabbit, venison or older tough
game birds.

1 jointed hare
1 oz flour
Salt and paprika
3 oz streaky bacon
2 oz butter
½ lb chopped onions
2 oz chopped celery
½ teaspoon each dried thyme and mint
½ teaspoon ground cloves
1 dessertspoon Worcestershire sauce
5 fl oz whisky
½ pt brown stock

Oven: 375°F; gas mark 5; 2 hours

Set the best and meatiest joints aside and put the
remainder in a pan, cover with 1½ pt of water
and simmer for 30 minutes. Strain and use for
stock. Season the flour with paprika and salt
and coat the joints carefully with this. Fry the
bacon in the butter, draw to one side and fry the
hare joints until brown. Transfer to a 3 pt
casserole dish.

Fry the onions until brown, add the celery,
herbs and cloves and fry lightly. Stir in the
Worcestershire sauce, whisky and 1 pt stock made
up of ½ pt hare and ½ pt brown stock; bring to
the boil and pour over the hare. Cover with a lid
and cook in the oven. Serve with pickled peaches
and baked potatoes.

Boiled Rabbit (8 portions) F

Most rabbits on sale are of the domesticated
type and lack the gamey taste of wild rabbits.
Rabbits are prepared like hares but are not hung
first. Boiled rabbit is served with a rich onion
sauce and potatoes cooked in their skins, but in
some versions the rabbit joints are arranged on a
bed of spinach and served with a capers sauce.

2 young rabbits
Salt and pepper
1 faggot of herbs
2 pt rabbit stock
1½ lb minced onions
4 oz butter
½ pt double cream

Soak the paunched and skinned rabbits in cold
water for several hours. Drain and place in a pan
of hot water with salt, pepper and the herbs; bring
to the boil. Skim, cover with a lid and simmer for
45 minutes. Joint the rabbits and keep warm.

For the sauce, boil the rabbit stock until
reduced by half. Fry the onions in butter until
soft, but not brown, add the reduced stock and
cream. Season and heat through but do not boil.
Place the rabbits on a serving dish and pour over
the sauce.

Elizabethan Rabbit (8 portions) F

This old recipe illustrates the Elizabethan
preference for mixing sweet flavours with savoury.
Hares may be used as well as rabbits.

2 jointed rabbits
1 oz flour
2 oz lard or dripping
3 sliced Jerusalem artichokes
6 oz finely chopped onions
2 oz sliced mushrooms
2 oz diced carrots
½ pt red wine
1 faggot of herbs
4 oz finely diced, peeled apples
4 oz halved, seeded grapes
2 oz raisins
Rind of ½ orange
1 crushed clove garlic
Salt and pepper
5 fl oz brown stock

Oven: 350°F; gas mark 4; 2 hours

Dust the joints with flour and fry in lard until

brown. Lift out and fry the artichokes, onions, mushrooms and carrots for a few minutes. Pour over the wine and reduce slightly.

Transfer the contents of the pan to a 4 pt casserole dish, add the herbs, apples, grapes, raisins, strips of orange rind, garlic and salt and pepper. Pour over the stock, cover and simmer in the oven for 2 hours.

Rabbit in the Dairy (8 portions) F

The tender white meat of young rabbit, resembling chicken in taste, should not be overpowered by strong herbs. The dairy allusion is to the milk in which the rabbit joints are cooked.

2 jointed rabbits
2 oz chopped bacon rashers
½ lb chopped onions
Salt, pepper and mace
2 pt milk
1 oz cornflour

Oven: 350°F; gas mark 4; 1¾-2 hours

Wash and dry the rabbit joints; place in an oven-proof dish. Add the bacon, onions, salt, pepper and mace; pour over the milk, cover and cook in the oven for about 2 hours. Remove the rabbit joints and keep warm.

Blend the cornflour with a little milk, add to the cooking liquid and bring to the boil. Pour the thickened sauce over the rabbit joints and serve with boiled carrots and green cabbage.

Mustard Rabbit (8-12 portions) F

An old hot-pot recipe of rabbit with pork, served with boiled potatoes and a thick, mustard-flavoured sauce. In some versions, the rabbit joints are smeared with mustard and left to steep in this overnight.

2 jointed rabbits
1½ lb skinned, boned and sliced belly pork
¾ lb diced carrots
1 lb finely chopped onions
1 tablespoon each, chopped thyme and parsley
1 crushed clove garlic
Salt and pepper
1 bay leaf
5 fl oz dry white wine
5 fl oz chicken stock
1 tablespoon wine vinegar
4 egg yolks

½ pt double cream
1 dessertspoon English mustard
Garnish: chopped parsley

Oven: 350°F; gas mark 4; 2½-3 hours

Arrange half the pork slices in a 4 pt dish, cover with half the carrots and onions, sprinkle with thyme, parsley and garlic; add salt, pepper, and bay leaf. Put the rabbit joints on top and cover with the remaining vegetables and pork. Place the skin from the belly pork on top.

Fill up with wine, chicken stock and vinegar; cover with a lid and cook in the oven. Discard the pork skin, lift out the rabbit joints and strain the cooking liquid. Remove excess fat and reduce the liquid. Beat the egg yolks with cream and mustard, add to the sauce and heat through to thicken but do not boil.

Pour the sauce over the rabbit and sprinkle with finely chopped parsley.

Wakefield Rabbit (8-10 portions) F
Yorkshire

Jointed rabbit with a crisp finish of herb-flavoured crumbs can be served with a thickened gravy or a sharp sauce.

2 jointed rabbits
Seasoned flour
2 eggs
4 oz dry breadcrumbs
1 dessertspoon mixed herbs
Cayenne pepper and salt
Lard or dripping

Oven: 350°F; gas mark 4; 1½-2 hours

Coat the washed and dried joints with seasoned flour. Dip in the beaten eggs and coat with breadcrumbs mixed with herbs. Place the prepared joints in a greased roasting tin and sprinkle with cayenne and salt. Roast in the oven, basting occasionally with lard or dripping, for 1½-2 hours.

Blair Atholl Venison Chops (8 portions) H
Scotland

The best-flavoured venison comes from the Highlands of Scotland, from the Borders and the North East. These venison chops are garnished with butter laced with Blair Athol whisky.

8 venison loin chops
4 oz butter
1 tablespoon Blair Atholl whisky
1 dessertspoon blanched, finely chopped parsley
Salt, cayenne and black pepper
1½ oz melted butter
Garnish: watercress

Blend the 4 oz of butter with whisky and parsley; season to taste with salt, pepper and cayenne. Shape the butter into a roll and leave in the refrigerator to chill.

Brush the chops on both sides with melted butter. Grill under a moderate heat for 20-25 minutes, turning several times; season with salt and pepper.

Arrange the chops in a crown on a heated dish and top with pats of Blair Athol butter. Fill the centre with green peas or fried mushrooms, and garnish with sprigs of watercress.

Cider Venison (6-8 portions) H and F
West Country

Watercress is a traditional garnish with game, and the usual accompaniments consist of game chips and rowan or red currant jelly, as well as brown gravy. Venison from the Forest of Dean was often marinated and cooked in local cider.

2-3 lb haunch of venison
1 pt cider
2 oz flour
Salt and pepper
2 oz melted butter
½ teaspoon allspice
1 faggot of herbs
½ lb finely chopped onions
4 oz diced carrots
2½ fl oz venison stock
Garnish: mushroom caps, watercress

Oven: 350°F; gas mark 4; 2 hours

Marinate the venison for 8 hours in the cider. Drain and dry; dust with flour, seasoning well with salt and pepper. Brown the venison in the butter; sprinkle with allspice and add the faggot of herbs, onions, carrots, cider and stock.

Cover with a close-fitting lid and cook in the oven for 2 hours. Serve garnished with mushrooms, tossed in butter, and sprigs of watercress.

Flank of Venison, Rolled (6-8 portions) F and H

Flank is one of the less expensive cuts of venison, excellent for braising and for stuffing to keep the slightly dry meat moist. Use the bones to make venison stock or soup.

3 lb boned flank of venison
½ lb veal forcemeat
2 oz dripping
2 pt brown venison stock
1 oz butter
1 oz flour
Salt and pepper

Oven: 350°F; gas mark 4; 2 hours

Flatten the venison with a rolling pin and spread with the forcemeat. Roll up and tie securely with string. Brown and seal the venison in the dripping, then transfer to a casserole dish; pour over the stock. Cover and cook in the oven until tender, turning occasionally.

Remove the lid from the casserole and thicken the gravy with the kneaded butter and flour; season with salt and pepper. Serve the venison cut into slices and coated with gravy; stewed red cabbage is a suitable vegetable.

Game Stew (6-8 portions) F and H

This is made with the slightly tough meat from venison shoulder or neck and older grouse and hare not tender enough for roasting. Any kind of game can be used for a rich stew which may be further flavoured with brandy or port.

¾ lb venison
¾ lb grouse meat
¾ lb hare meat
2 oz seasoned flour
3-4 oz butter
4 oz chopped onions
2 oz chopped carrots
4 oz chopped celery
4 oz diced ham
1½ pt game stock
5 fl oz red wine
Salt and pepper
Garnish: chopped parsley

Cut the venison, grouse and hare meat into cubes and dust with seasoned flour. Melt the butter and fry the onions, carrots and celery until soft; add the cubed meat and ham and continue frying until browned. Pour over the game stock, made from bones and carcasses, and the wine.

Cover with a lid and simmer gently for 1-2 hours, skimming occasionally. Season with salt and pepper, garnish with parsley and serve with mashed potatoes and rowan jelly.

Haunch of Venison (8 portions) H Scotland

This dish of marinated haunch of red deer is reputed to have been a favourite of Mary of Guise and is said to have been created for her by the master of the kitchen at Holyrood Palace.

5 lb haunch of venison
Salt, pepper and mixed spice
1 pt claret
Juice of 3 lemons
10 oz butter
Flour
½ pt venison stock
1 teaspoon walnut ketchup

Oven: 425°F; gas mark 7; 20 minutes;
       350°F; gas mark 4; about 1½ hours

Rub the haunch with salt, pepper and spice; leave to marinate in the claret and lemon juice for 6 hours, basting frequently. Place the venison in a roasting tin, with 6 oz melted butter. Strain the marinade and pour over the venison; cover the tin with foil.

Roast at high heat for 15-20 minutes to seal the meat, then reduce the heat to 350°F (gas mark 4) and continue roasting, allowing 15 minutes for every lb and 15 minutes extra. Baste often. Remove the foil for the last 15 minutes, cover the haunch with butter and dredge with flour. Remove the venison from the roasting tin and keep hot on a serving dish.

Add the stock to the pan juices and boil up, skim and season with walnut ketchup; pour the gravy round the roast venison and serve.

Venison Collops (8 portions) H and F

Steaks cut from the haunch or loin chops are equally suitable. Serve with a red wine sauce and mashed potatoes.

8 venison steaks (6 oz each)
Salt, pepper, cayenne and nutmeg
3 fl oz cooking oil
5 fl oz claret
Juice of ½ lemon
1 pt venison stock
1 oz butter
1 oz flour

Season the steaks with salt, pepper, cayenne and nutmeg. Fry the steaks quickly in the hot oil to seal and brown the meat; lower the heat and continue frying for about 15 minutes or until tender. Lift on to a serving dish and keep warm.

Add the claret, lemon juice and stock to the pan and bring to the boil. Thicken the sauce with the butter kneaded with flour. Adjust seasoning and consistency and pour over the steaks.

Venison Steaks (8 portions) H and F

Steaks cut from the saddle or cutlets from the loin are tender enough for quick cooking. Serve with grilled mushrooms, game chips and rowan or red currant jelly.

8 venison steaks or cutlets (6 oz each)
2 oz seasoned flour
2 eggs
½ lb dry white breadcrumbs
4 oz butter
Nut-brown butter

Wipe the steaks and dust with seasoned flour. Coat in beaten eggs and breadcrumbs, pressing them well in to the meat. Fry in hot butter for 5-6 minutes on each side. Arrange on a dish and serve with nut-brown butter.

SAVOURY MEAT AND
GAME PIES AND PUDDINGS

A great number of traditional meat and game pies have been developed over the centuries. The original concept of the pie was a collection of ingredients, sometimes of dubious character, and usually a mixture of sweet and savoury items hidden under a pastry crust. The first pies were probably raised pies or "coffins" which were a practical way of eating cold meat in gravy with the fingers before forks were introduced. By the early 18th century, pies had become firmly divided into sweet and savoury; at the same time there came a move towards more fillings and less pastry. The raised pie lost in popularity against the lighter shortcrust, flaky and puff pastries which sometimes became a top cover only. Later still, while the pie concept remained the same, the crust was often replaced by a potato, scone mix or batter covering. Huff paste remained in general use, but now as then was removed and discarded after cooking.

The pudding, like the pie, was originally a number of ingredients boiled in the stomach bag of an animal. In the 15th and 16th centuries, entrails were commonly referred to as "puddings". Pudding Lane in London is thought to have derived its name from the fact that the butchers of Eastcheap carted "animal puddings and other filth of beasts" through that lane down to the dung boats on the Thames.

A natural development when "puddings" were not available was to use a cloth to hold the ingredients together. Later, basins and/or suet crust replaced cloths, and the puddings were steamed rather than boiled. Today the term pudding is somewhat indefinite and may be applied to any savoury — or sweet — mixture, boiled, steamed, baked or even fried, with or without a lining or covering of pastry. The following puddings are all of a savoury nature as in the original pudding concept.

MEAT PIES AND PUDDINGS

Bacon and Cow Heel Pudding
(6—8 portions) F

This is a true savoury pie, possibly developed from the earlier Medley Pie which as the name implies was a combination of ingredients. The Leicestershire Medley Pie contained boiled bacon, roast pork, apples, ginger and ale, while the Derbyshire Medley Pie also included onions and sage and was served with a jug of hot vinegar.

¾ lb lean bacon rashers
1 cow heel, dressed
1 onion studded with cloves
1 pt brown stock
Salt and pepper
½ lb savoury shortcrust pastry
1 egg

Oven: 350°F; gas mark 4; 1 hour

Put the cow heel in a large pan, add the onion and cover with stock; season with salt and pepper. Bring to the boil, cover and simmer for about 3 hours or until tender. Remove the cow heel, strip off the meat and cut into cubes. Wrap the meat in the bacon rashers, place in a 2 pt pie dish and cover with pastry. Brush with beaten egg and bake in the oven for 1 hour.

Bacon Badger (6—8 portions) F
Buckinghamshire

A suet pudding which may be steamed in a pudding basin or boiled in a cloth.

1½ lb lean bacon rashers
1 lb suet pastry
½ lb finely chopped onions
1 teaspoon chopped sage
Pinch chopped parsley
Pepper
6 oz thinly sliced potatoes

Roll out the suet pastry to a rectangle, lay the bacon rashers over it and sprinkle with onions, sage and parsley; season with pepper and cover with the potato slices. Fold the pastry in three and seal the edges firmly. Wrap in a pudding cloth and boil for 2½–3 hours or steam in a basin for the same length of time.

Bacon Cake (8–10 portions) F
Co. Durham

A cross between a pie and pudding, this is made with a scone mix and filled with cold, left-over bacon.

1 lb boiled, sliced bacon
1 lb flour
1 teaspoon baking powder
½ lb lard

Oven: 400°F; gas mark 6; 25–30 minutes

Sift the flour and baking powder, rub in the lard and mix to a scone consistency with water. Roll out to two rounds, each 7 in across. Put the sliced bacon on one round, cover with the other round and press down to release any air trapped inside; prick all over with a fork and pinch the edges together. Place on a baking sheet and bake until golden brown. Serve hot.

Beef Cobbler (6–8 portions) F and H

The term "cobbler" was originally applied to a type of pie with a thick dough lining for a filling. In the modern version, a scone mixture is used instead of paste and is placed on top of the pie.

1½ lb shoulder or chuck steak
1½ oz seasoned flour
¾ lb sliced onions
½ lb sliced carrots
2 oz chopped celery
2 oz dripping
1¼ pt brown stock
5 fl oz brown ale
½ lb savoury scone mixture

Oven: 350°F; gas mark 4; 2½ hours

Cut the meat into ½ in cubes and toss in seasoned flour. Fry the meat, onions, carrots and celery in the dripping until light brown. Stir in any remaining flour and gradually add the stock and brown ale; bring to the boil. Pour into a deep ovenproof dish and cook for 2 hours in the oven.

Shape the scone mixture into eight rounds and place on top of the meat; return to the oven for a further 20–25 minutes.

Bacon Froise (6–8 portions) F

A "froise" or "fraise" is a kind of pancake batter cooked with bacon rashers or slices.

1½ lb streaky bacon rashers
1½ pt Yorkshire pudding batter

Oven: 450°F; gas mark 8; 15–20 minutes

Remove rind and gristle from the rashers and cut the bacon into narrow strips; fry without any additional fat in a heavy-based pan. Pour the pudding batter over the bacon strips. Place in the oven and bake until the batter is well risen and light brown. Serve immediately.

Bacon Pudding (6 portions) F Berkshire

This makes a hearty supper dish for a cold day. Boil the pudding in a cloth and serve with boiled potatoes and turnips.

¾ lb lean bacon rashers
1 lb suet pastry
½ lb chopped onions
1 teaspoon chopped sage
Chopped parsley
Pepper

Roll out the suet pastry, about ½ in thick, to a 6 in square. Lay the bacon rashers over the pastry, cover with the onions and sprinkle with sage, parsley and pepper. Roll up the pastry, wrap in a pudding cloth and boil for 2½–3 hours.

Beef and Cow Heel Tart (6–8 portions) F

A tart usually consists of a pastry base with the filling on top; this dish, however, in spite of its name, is correctly a pie, being enclosed in pastry.

¾ lb shin of beef
½ cow heel, dressed
1 clove-studded onion
1 pt brown stock
Salt and pepper
1 lb savoury shortcrust pastry
1 egg

Oven: 375°F; gas mark 5; 45 minutes

Put the beef and cow heel in a pan with the onion, pour over the stock and season with salt and pepper. Simmer for about 3 hours. Lift out the beef and cow heel, strip off the meat and cut into 1 in pieces.

Line an 8 in flan ring, set on a baking sheet, with half the pastry; spoon the meat over the pastry and add a little of the stock. Cover with the remaining pastry, brush with beaten egg and bake until golden.

Beef Pudding (8 portions) F

To modern tastes, this steamed suet pudding is probably more acceptable than the older Bedfordshire Clanger which basically consisted of the same ingredients but also contained chopped onions – and jam!

1½ lb shoulder (stewing) steak
1 oz chopped suet
1 egg
2 tablespoons cream
Salt and pepper
2 lb savoury suet pastry
½–¾ pt brown stock

Mince the beef and suet and mix with the egg and cream; season with salt and pepper. Line a 3 pt pudding basin with three quarters of the pastry, spoon in the meat and add sufficient stock to just cover the meat. Cover with a pastry lid and tie down with greaseproof paper and a pudding cloth. Steam for 2–2½ hours.

Buckinghamshire Dumplings (6–8 portions) F Buckinghamshire

A suet roly poly enclosing liver and bacon. Serve with floury boiled potatoes and gravy or brown sauce.

¾ lb lean bacon rashers
¾ lb sliced pig's liver
1 lb savoury suet pastry
½ lb chopped onions
1 teaspoon each, chopped sage and parsley
Pepper

Roll the suet pastry out to a square, ¼ in thick. Lay the bacon rashers on top, cover with liver and onions and season with sage, parsley and pepper. Roll up the pastry, wrap and secure in a pudding cloth and boil for 2½–3 hours.

Calf's Foot Pie (6–8 portions) H and F

This is one of the oldest English pies to survive the tradition of mixing savoury and sweet ingredients. After cooking, it is flavoured with a rich wine caudle, and the pie can be served hot or cold. A Scots Bride's Pie is entirely similar, although it also contains chopped apples, but it differs in the elaborate pastry decorations. These were set on the pastry lid and shaped as cupids, turtle doves, torch flames and darts; a gold ring was sometimes concealed in the lid.

1 calf's foot
1 lb stewing veal (breast)
Salt and pepper
4 oz currants
Grated peel of ½ lemon and ½ orange
3 oz shredded suet
¼ teaspoon each mace, nutmeg
½ lb quince or red currant jelly
¾ lb savoury shortcrust or 1¼ lb flaky pastry
Caudle: 1 pt white wine
         2 egg yolks
         Pinch cinnamon
         1 tablespoon sugar

Oven: 350°F; gas mark 4; 30–45 minutes

Split the calf's foot down the middle and put it in a pan with the veal; cover with water, add salt and pepper and boil for 2½ hours. Leave the meat to cool in the liquid which should set to a jelly. Remove the veal and calf's foot and cut the meat into 1 in cubes.

Put a layer of meat in a 3 pt pie dish, cover with a layer of currants, grated lemon and orange peel, suet, mace, nutmeg, salt and pepper. Repeat these layers and cover with the quince jelly. Put on the pastry lid and bake until golden.

For the caudle, beat together the wine, egg yolks, cinnamon and sugar; heat in a double saucepan until thick but do not allow to boil. Remove the pie from the oven and pour the caudle through the hole in the pastry lid.

Cornish Pasty (8 portions) F and H Cornwall

The Cornish pasty for centuries constituted the working man's midday meal. The classic pasty shape contained a filling of diced vegetables, and meat when times were favourable. Hot or cold it still provides an excellent lunch or supper dish and is ideal for packed lunches or as snacks.

The Cornish pasty is sometimes known as a "hoggan" which contains no potatoes, or as a "tiddy oggy", the local name for potato. In the North of England a similar pasty, known as Lancashire Foot, is made. It is elliptical in shape but much higher than the Cornish pasty, and the filling is not always meat, but may be fish, chicken, bacon or vegetables.

2 lb topside or rump of beef
½ lb diced potatoes
½ lb diced onions
¾ oz chopped mixed herbs
Salt and pepper
2 lb savoury shortcrust pastry
1 egg

Oven: 350°F; gas mark 4; 45–60 minutes

Finely dice or mince the beef, mix with potatoes, onions and herbs and season with salt and pepper.

Roll out the pastry, ¼ in thick, and cut into rounds about 6 in wide. Divide the filling equally between the pastry rounds, dampen the edges and draw up to meet on top of the filling. Crimp the edges firmly together and make a small slit in the top to allow the steam to escape. Brush with beaten egg and bake until golden.

Cow Heel and Butter Bean Pie (6–8 portions) F

A substantial and nourishing family type of pie. Have the cow heel prepared and par-boiled by the butcher.

1 cow heel, dressed
1 onion studded with cloves
1 pt brown stock
Salt and pepper
½ lb butter beans (soaked overnight)
½ lb savoury shortcrust or ½ lb savoury suet pastry
1 egg

Oven: 350°F; gas mark 4; 1 hour

Put the cow heel in a pan with the onion, pour over the stock, add salt and pepper and bring to the boil. Simmer for about 3 hours. Remove the meat from the cow heel, cut into small chunks and arrange in a 2½ pt pie dish with enough stock to barely cover.

Add the soaked and drained beans and cover with pastry. Brush the top with beaten egg and bake in the oven until golden brown, after about 1 hour.

Cow Heel Pasty (6–8 portions) F

A pasty is properly a complete covering of pastry, usually in individual portions as in Cornish pasties and Lancashire Foot. This pasty is correctly a double crust large pie.

3 cow heels, dressed
¾ lb shin of beef
1 pt brown stock
Salt and pepper
¾ lb savoury shortcrust pastry
1 egg

Oven: 400°F; gas mark 6; 45 minutes

Have the cow heels split by the butcher; put the heels and the shin of beef in a pan, cover with stock, add salt and pepper and simmer for about 3 hours. Strip the meat from the heels and cut this and the beef into 1 in cubes.

Line an 8 in pie plate with half the pastry, spoon over the meat filling and cover with the remaining pastry. Brush with beaten egg and bake for about 45 minutes.

Devizes Pie (6–8 portions) H and F Wiltshire

Dating from the early 19th century, this pie is cooked under a huff paste covering which merely serves to seal in all the different flavours. The huff paste is left on while the pie cools, but is removed before serving.

1 calf's head
½ lb chopped onions
4 oz diced carrots
½ lb diced turnips
Faggot of herbs
Salt and pepper
1 set calf brains
1 set calf sweetbreads
½ pt vinegar
6 oz pickled tongue
4 sliced hardboiled eggs
4 oz sliced bacon
Cayenne and allspice
¾ pt reduced jellied stock
¾ lb flour and water paste (huff paste)
Garnish: parsley sprigs, pickled eggs

Oven: 325°F; gas mark 3; 1½–2 hours

Scrub the calf's head thoroughly clean and blanch in boiling water. Drain and refresh. Put the head in a large pan, with the onions, carrots, turnips and faggot of herbs; season with salt and pepper and cover with water. Simmer for 2—2½ hours or until the bones can be pulled out.

Lift out the head, strain the stock and boil until reduced to about ¾ pt; set aside to cool and jellify. Remove the bones and cut the meat into thin slices. Wash the brains and sweetbreads in vinegar and cold water; boil separately for 10 minutes in water, drain and chop.

Arrange layers of calf's head, sweetbreads, pickled tongue, brains, eggs and bacon in a 3 pt pie dish; season each layer with cayenne, allspice, white pepper and salt. Spoon over the jellied stock and cover the pie with huff paste. Make a hole in the centre and bake in the oven for about 1½ hours.

Leave the pie to cool. To serve, take off the huff paste, turn the pie out on to a serving dish and garnish with parsley sprigs and slices of pickled eggs.

Egg and Bacon Pie (6—8 portions) F and H

An excellent lunch dish, hot with small buttered potatoes and peas, or cold with salads.

1 lb thin lean bacon rashers
6—8 eggs
¾ lb puff pastry
Salt and pepper
1 beaten egg

Oven: 425°F; gas mark 7; 10 minutes
350°F; gas mark 4; 15—20 minutes

Roll out the pastry and use half to line a 7 in pie plate. Dice the bacon and spread half over the pastry base; break the eggs over it and cover with the remaining bacon. Season with salt and pepper.

Cover with the remaining pastry, brush with egg and bake for 30 minutes or until golden and risen, reducing the heat after 10 minutes.

Elizabeth Pasty (6—8 portions) F

This is a modern version of the medieval pasty used to enclose the innards of a newly killed pig; originally "scratchings" — crumbs of meat left after the fat had been rendered down for lard — were also included in the filling. It resembles the Cornish Muggity Pie which had a filling of sheep pluck, currants and parsley.

½ lb pig liver
6—8 oz pork tongue

4 oz pig heart
2 oz breadcrumbs
1 dessertspoon chopped mixed herbs
1 teaspoon Demerara sugar
4 oz currants
4 oz sliced onions
2 hardboiled eggs
¾ lb savoury shortcrust pastry
1 egg

Oven: 350°F; gas mark 4; 1½ hours

Par-boil the liver, tongue and heart for 1 hour; lift out and drain and set the cooking liquid aside. Cut the liver, heart and tongue into slices and arrange in a 3 pt pie dish. Top with the breadcrumbs mixed with the herbs, sugar and currants. Add a little of the reserved liquid and spread the mixture smoothly. Place the onion rings and halved hard-boiled eggs on top. Cover with pastry, brush with beaten egg and bake.

Farmhouse Pudding (6—8 portions) F and H Northamptonshire

This steamed pudding of layers of meat and suet pastry is also known as Hough and Dough Flake, indicating that the minced beef is hough or shin of beef.

1½ lb raw minced beef
¾ lb chopped onions
2 oz dripping
6 oz grated carrots
1½ oz chopped parsley
1½ oz flour
1½ pt brown stock
Salt and pepper
1 lb savoury suet pastry

Fry the beef and onions in the dripping until light brown. Add the carrots and parsley, stir in the flour and gradually add the stock; stir until thick and boiling. Season with salt and pepper.

Grease a 2—2½ pt pudding basin and put a layer of pastry over the base. Place a layer of meat over the suet pastry and continue filling the basin with alternate layers of meat and pastry, finishing with a layer of pastry. Cover with greaseproof paper and a pudding cloth and steam for 1½ hours.

Fidget Pie (6—8 portions) F Shropshire

Also known as figet or fitchet pie, the term is

thought to have derived from "fitched", meaning five-sided and related to the original shape of the pie. In some Shropshire versions, thinly sliced potatoes are added to the filling, and in others the pie is covered with potato pastry rather than shortcrust.

1½ lb green back bacon or gammon
½ lb sliced onions
1 lb peeled, cored and sliced cooking apples
1 oz butter
Salt, pepper and nutmeg
Sugar
2 tablespoons brown stock
½ lb savoury shortcrust pastry
1 egg

Oven: 350°F; gas mark 4; 40–45 minutes

Cut the bacon into small pieces, discarding the rind. Fry the onions and apples in butter without colouring. Layer the bacon, apples and onions in a 2 pt pie dish, seasoning well with salt, pepper and nutmeg; add a little sugar if the apples are sour.
   Spoon over the stock, cover with pastry and brush with beaten egg. Bake in the oven until the pastry is golden brown.

Forfar Bridies (8 portions) F and H Angus

A bridie in its original form was made with best steak which cooked quickly so that a simple flour and water paste was adequate. Today, a variety of pastries are used depending on the type of meat, and bridies are the equivalent of the Cornish Pasties; pork bridies are similar to these except that the meat filling is diced pork instead of beef.

2 lb topside or rump steak
2 lb shortcrust pastry
6 oz shredded suet
2 oz chopped onions
Salt and black pepper
Brown stock
1 egg

Oven: 350°F; gas mark 4; 1 hour

Roll the pastry out thinly and cut into four large or eight small ovals. Cut the meat into thin strips and mix with the suet, onions, seasoning and a little stock to moisten.
   Cover half of each pastry with a portion of meat, fold over the other half to make a half-moon shape and seal the edges. Brush with beaten

egg. Make a hole in the top of each bridie to allow the steam to escape. Bake until golden.

Heart and Kidney Pudding (6 portions) F Shropshire

Shropshire is the home of a great many traditional puddings and pies, frequently with an offal filling.

1 pig heart
2 pig kidneys
Seasoned flour
½ lb savoury suet pastry
Salt and pepper
½ pt brown stock

Cut the prepared heart and kidneys into small pieces and coat in seasoned flour. Line a 2–2½ pt pudding basin with two thirds of the pastry, add the meat, season with salt and pepper and pour over the stock. Cover the pudding with the remaining pastry, tie down with foil or greaseproof paper and a cloth and steam for 3 hours.

Herby Pie (6–8 portions) F and H Cornwall

A light summery pie, delicately flavoured with fresh vegetables and herbs.

1 lb lean green bacon rashers
1 lb finely chopped leeks
½ lb finely chopped spinach
1 oz finely chopped watercress
3 sprigs finely chopped parsley
3 eggs
Salt and pepper
5 fl oz brown stock
½ lb savoury shortcrust pastry

Oven: 350°F; gas mark 4; 40–45 minutes

Line a 2½ pt pie dish with half the bacon rashers and top with the leeks mixed with the spinach, watercress and parsley. Beat 2 eggs and pour over the vegetable mixture; season with salt and pepper and add the stock.
   Lay the remaining bacon rashers on top and cover with pastry. Brush with beaten egg and bake until the pastry is golden brown.

Hunter's Pie (8 portions) F Ireland

This pie is lined and covered with mashed potatoes, often used in Ireland in preference to pastry.

8 mutton chops (4–6 oz each)

1 oz butter
3 lb mashed potatoes
Salt and pepper
½—¾ pt gravy

Oven: 350°F; gas mark 4; 30 minutes

Braise the mutton chops on a bed of diced carrots, onions and celery, with added brown stock. When cooked, lift out the chops, strain the gravy and skim off the fat. Set the chops aside to cool, and reserve the gravy.

Butter a large pie dish and line with two thirds of the mashed potatoes, place the chops on top and sprinkle with salt and pepper. Cover with the remaining potatotes and bake in the oven until golden brown. Make a hole in the top of the pie, pour in the hot gravy and serve.

Kidney Pudding (6—8 portions) F

Ox kidney is too strongly flavoured for frying or grilling, but ideal as a filling for a steamed suet pudding.

1½ lb ox kidney
1 oz seasoned flour
6 oz chopped onions
1 oz suet
¾ lb savoury suet pastry
Salt and pepper
½ pt brown stock

Cut the cleaned kidney into slices and toss in seasoned flour; fry the onions and kidney in the suet until light brown. Line a 2½ pt pudding basin with two thirds of the suet pastry, spoon in the kidney and onions, season with salt and pepper and add enough stock to just cover the filling.

Cover with a lid of suet pastry and tie down with a pudding cloth or foil. Steam for 1½—2 hours.

Lamb Ciste (8 portions) F and H

The word "ciste" is derived from the Welsh, meaning a coffin, the original name for a pie. Some cistes are made with pork chops, and 2 oz sultanas are sometimes added to the filling. The kidney may be substituted with liver.

8 lamb chops (4 oz each)
10 oz lamb kidney or liver
¾ lb sliced onions
4 oz sliced carrots
2 oz butter

1 teaspoon chopped parsley
½ teaspoon chopped thyme
1 bay leaf
Salt and pepper
1¼ pt brown stock
½ lb savoury suet pastry

Trim the chops, leaving the ends of the bones clean of fat and gristle. Fry the chops, sliced kidneys, onions and carrots in the butter until light brown. Put the prepared chops around the inside edge of a medium sized saucepan with the bone ends sticking up; arrange kidneys or liver, carrots, onions and herbs in the centre. Season with salt and pepper and add enough stock to barely cover the vegetables in the centre.

Cook with a lid on and simmer for 30 minutes; adjust seasoning. Roll out the pastry to fit the size of the saucepan. Lift on to the top of the pan and press down over the stew so that the bones of the chops protrude through the ciste lid. Cover with a tightly fitting lid, leaving space for the ciste to rise. Simmer for about 1 hour.

To serve, loosen the ciste with a knife, divide it into eight wedges and place them round a deep serving dish; spoon the stew into the centre.

Lamb Pie (8 portions) F and H

In Surrey, this pie is made with mutton chops and the covering is ½ lb sliced mushrooms instead of puff pastry.

8 lamb cutlets (3—4 oz each) or 2 lb loin, neck or breast of lamb
1 oz seasoned flour
1 oz butter
1 lb sliced onions
2 lamb kidneys
Salt and pepper
2 sprigs rosemary or ½ teaspoon dried rosemary
½—¾ pt brown stock
1¼ lb puff pastry
1 egg

Oven: 350°F; gas mark 4; 1½ hours

Trim the cutlets or cut the meat from the bone of loin, neck or breast of lamb and divide the pieces into suitable sizes. Coat the meat in seasoned flour and fry in butter until light brown.

Put the meat in a 3—4 pt pie dish and arrange the onions on top. Add the sliced kidneys and sprinkle with salt, pepper and rosemary; pour over the stock. Cover with puff pastry, brush with beaten egg and bake for 1½ hours or until the pastry is golden and well-risen.

Leek and Potato Pie (6—8 portions) F
Cornwall

In Cornwall as in Wales, leeks and potatoes in varying combinations are favourite pie and pudding fillings. The Cornish Likky Pie has layers of chopped leeks and bacon rashers under a shortcrust pastry lid and is richly flavoured with eggs mixed with clotted cream poured beneath the pastry half-way through cooking.

1½ lb stewing steak
1 oz seasoned flour
2 oz dripping
½—¾ pt brown stock
½ lb chopped potatoes
¾ lb chopped leeks
Salt and pepper
½ lb savoury suet pastry

Oven: 375°F; gas mark 5; 1 hour

Cut the meat into small cubes and toss in seasoned flour. Melt the dripping and brown the meat for 2—3 minutes; add the stock, cover and simmer gently for 1 hour.

Add the potatoes and leeks to the meat, season with salt and pepper and spoon into a 3—4 pt pie dish; cover with a suet pastry lid. Bake for 1 hour or until the pie is well risen and brown.

London Double Crust Pie (8 portions)
F and H London

A double crust pie has a lining as well as a covering of pastry. Some versions of the London beef pie are flavoured with herbs or orange peel and cooked with wine instead of stock.

2 lb minced beef
4 oz sliced onions
2 oz dripping
4 oz sliced mushrooms
½ teaspoon curry powder
1 oz flour
¾ pt brown stock
Salt and pepper
1 lb savoury shortcrust pastry
1 egg

Oven: 425°F; gas mark 7; 30 minutes
            350°F; gas mark 4; 15—20 minutes

Fry the beef and onions in the dripping for 5 minutes, add the mushrooms; stir in the curry powder and flour and cook for 2—3 minutes. Add the stock and season with salt and pepper; bring to the boil and simmer for 15 minutes.

Line a 2 pt pie dish with two thirds of the pastry; put in the meat, cover with the rest of the pastry and brush with beaten egg. Bake in a hot oven until the pastry is golden brown, after about 30 minutes; reduce the temperature and bake for a further 15—20 minutes.

Monkton Milnes Mutton Pie (6—8 portions)
H and F

Named after a Victorian gourmet, Monkton Milnes, this steamed pudding originated in the days when oysters were everyday fare. A mutton pudding proper omits the oysters, replacing them with ¾ lb finely chopped onions.

1½ lb loin of mutton
2 lb savoury suet pastry
1 doz oysters
1 oz seasoned flour
1 oz butter
½ pt brown stock
Salt and pepper

Line a 2 pt pudding basin with two thirds of the pastry. Cut the meat off the bone, trim away any excess fat and cut the mutton into 1 in cubes. Shell and beard the oysters; simmer the beards in the oyster liquid to bring out the flavour.

Roll the meat in seasoned flour, fry in butter until brown and place in the pudding basin; leave a hollow in the centre for the oysters. Add the prepared oysters, stock and strained oyster liquid; season with salt and pepper. Cover the basin with the remaining pastry; tie down with a cloth and steam for 2 hours.

Mutton Pies (6 portions) F and H
Cumberland

Cumberland mutton pies differ from those of neighbouring Westmorland which are sweet and savoury. They are sometimes made with lamb, but the main difference is the sweet filling which consists of ½ lb each of currants, raisins and sultanas, 1 lb grated cooking apples, 4 oz blanched, chopped almonds, orange juice, lemon juice and peel, ½ lb brown sugar seasoned with mace, cinnamon and nutmeg; the stock is made up of rum and ale, and the pie is baked in a pie dish.

1 lb cooked, minced mutton
¾ lb savoury shortcrust pastry
2 oz chopped onions
1 teaspoon chopped parsley
½ pt brown sauce
Salt and pepper
½ beaten egg

Oven: 350°F; gas mark 4; 40 minutes

Roll out the pastry and use two thirds to line small patty tins. Mix the mutton with the finely chopped onions and parsley, blend in the brown sauce and season to taste with salt and pepper.

Divide the mixture between the patties, cover with lids made from the remaining pastry and brush with beaten egg. Bake in the oven for 40 minutes or until golden brown.

Oxcheek Pie (6—8 portions) F and H

The low cost of oxcheek is heavily outweighed by the addition of truffles and morels in this pie.

2—2½ lb oxcheek
¾ pt brown stock
4 oz veal forcemeat balls
½ oz truffles (optional)
½ oz morels (optional)
5 oz pickled mushrooms or ½ lb fresh, chopped
    mushrooms
Salt and pepper
1 lb puff pastry
1 egg

Oven: 400°F; gas mark 6; 45 minutes

Clean and scrape the oxcheek and simmer in the stock for at least 3 hours or until quite tender. Cut all the meat off the bones and chop into 1 in cubes.

Put the meat in a 2 pt pie dish with the strained stock, forcemeat balls, truffles, morels and mushrooms and pickling liquid. Season with salt and pepper, cover with pastry and brush with beaten egg. Bake for 45 minutes or until the pastry is golden brown.

Oxford Pudding (6—8 portions) F

A substantial steamed pudding with a filling of pork, liver, bacon, onions, chestnuts and baked beans. Serve with boiled floury potatoes.

1 lb diced pork shoulder
2 lb savoury suet pastry
4 oz sliced pig liver
4 oz diced bacon
Seasoned flour
4 oz chopped onions
6 oz baked beans
6 oz boiled chestnuts
1 dessertspoon chopped parsley
Salt and pepper
½ pt brown stock
Worcestershire sauce

Line a 3 pt pudding basin with three quarters of the pastry. Toss the pork, liver and bacon in seasoned flour. Mix the meat, liver, bacon, onions, baked beans and chestnuts broken into small pieces. Blend in the parsley, season with salt and pepper and put the mixture in the pudding basin.

Pour over the stock seasoned with a little Worcestershire sauce and cover with the remaining pastry. Tie down with foil or greased paper and steam for 2½—3 hours.

Parsley Pie (6—8 portions) F and H

A light summery pie of delicate veal cooked in white stock and cream and flavoured with parsley.

2 lb breast of veal
1 oz finely chopped parsley
Salt and pepper
½ pt white stock
¾ lb savoury shortcrust pastry
1 egg
5 fl oz double cream
1 oz flour
1 oz butter

Oven: 350°F; gas mark 4; 2 hours

Cut the meat into 1 in cubes and arrange in a 3 pt pie dish, sprinkling with parsley and salt and pepper. Add the stock and cover with the pastry. Brush with beaten egg and bake for 1½ hours.

Mix the cream with flour and butter, lift the lid of the pie carefully at one corner and pour in the cream mixture, shaking gently to mix it with the stock. Return to the oven and cook for a further 20—30 minutes.

Pork Cobbler (6—8 portions) F

The thick dough lining of medieval cobbler pies is replaced in modern recipes with a lighter scone mix used for covering only.

1 lb diced shoulder of pork
Seasoned flour
4 oz diced carrots
4 oz diced onions
4 oz diced turnips
4 oz chopped leeks
½ pt brown stock or cider
½ teaspoon salt
Black pepper
½ teaspoon mixed herbs
½ lb savoury scone mix
1 egg

Oven: 325°F; gas mark 3; 1¼ hours
       425°F; gas mark 7; 10–15 minutes

Toss the meat in seasoned flour, mix with the vegetables and put in a 3 pt pie dish, add stock, salt, pepper and herbs. Cover with foil and bake in the oven for 1¼ hours at 325°F (gas mark 3).

Make up the scone mix and roll out a little larger than the pie dish, cut into 2 in squares, brush with beaten egg and arrange over the meat. Return the pie to the oven and continue baking at 425°F (gas mark 7) for a further 15 minutes or until the scone mixture is well-risen and brown.

Pork Crumble (4–6 portions)

A cheese-flavoured breadcrumb topping replaces a pastry lid in this pork and potato pie.

1½ lb boned belly pork
2 oz seasoned flour
1 oz lard
1 lb sliced potatoes
½ lb sliced onions
½ pt stock or cider
½ teaspoon marjoram
Salt and pepper
½ cup breadcrumbs
½ cup finely grated Cheddar cheese
Cayenne pepper

Oven: 350°F; gas mark 4; 1½ hours

Cut the pork into 1 in cubes and toss in seasoned flour. Fry in lard for a few minutes and arrange in a casserole dish with the potatoes and onions. Add stock and marjoram and season with pepper and salt. Cover with a lid or foil and bake in the oven for 1 hour.

For the crumble, mix the breadcrumbs with the

cheese and season with cayenne. Remove the foil from the casserole, sprinkle the crumble on top and return to the oven, uncovered; bake for a further 30 minutes or until the crumble is golden brown.

Pork Pie (6–8 portions) F and H Cheshire

This sweet and savoury pork pie from the early 18th century has hardly altered in concept since first published by Mrs. Glasse in Edinburgh in 1747.

2 lb pork fillets
1 oz butter
1 lb peeled, cored and sliced cooking apples
Salt and pepper
Nutmeg
2 oz sugar
1 pt white wine or cider
½ lb savoury shortcrust pastry
1 egg

Oven: 350°F; gas mark 4; 1½ hours

Trim the pork fillets of membranes and sinews and cut into 1 in cubes. Butter a 3½ pt pie dish and arrange layers of pork with layers of sliced apples, sprinkling each layer with salt, pepper, nutmeg and sugar. Pour over the wine and dot with the remaining butter. Cover with the pastry, brush with beaten egg and bake until firm and well brown.

Pork Pudding (6–8 portions) F

Also known as pork toad-in-the-hole, this is a batter-type pudding, versions of which occur all over the country; in Norfolk it is made with minced shoulder of pork, and in other areas the batter mixture covers pork chops topped with mushroom stuffing.

2 lb chopped salt pork
¾ lb stoned raisins
1 oz pork fat
Pepper
1 pt Yorkshire pudding batter

Oven: 375°F; gas mark 5; 30 minutes
       425°F; gas mark 7; 30 minutes

Put the raisins and pork in an ovenproof dish with the pork fat; sprinkle with pepper and bake for 30 minutes at 375°F (gas mark 5). Make up the batter and pour over the meat; return to the oven and bake at 425°F (gas mark 7) for 30 minutes or until the batter is well-risen and brown.

Pork and Onion Pudding (6—8 portions) F and H Northamptonshire and Huntingdonshire

There are several regional recipes for pork suet pudding, onions sometimes being replaced by that traditional accompaniment with pork — apples. In the February Pork Pudding, ¾ lb potatoes only are used, but 1 lb chopped leeks are also added and ale takes the place of stock.

2 lb diced shoulder of pork
2 lb savoury suet pastry
1 lb sliced onions
Salt and pepper
Pinch sage
5 fl oz brown stock

Line a 2½—3 pt pudding basin with two thirds of the suet pastry. Put alternate layers of meat and onions in the basin, seasoning each layer with salt, pepper and sage. Pour in the stock and cover with a lid of the remaining pastry. Cover with foil or greased paper and steam for 2½ hours.

Pot Pie (6—8 portions) F and H Durham

This is a local type of steak and kidney pudding, but differs from the traditional dish in not being entirely lined with pastry. Rabbit may be substituted for steak and kidney, and leeks for onions.

1½ lb stewing steak
½ lb ox or lamb kidney
4 oz chopped onions
1 tablespoon chopped parsley
Salt and pepper
½ lb savoury suet pastry
½—¾ pt brown stock

Cut the steak and kidney into 1 in pieces and layer with the onions in a 3 pt pudding basin. Season each layer with parsley, salt and pepper.

Roll out the suet pastry, and fit in a 2 in deep band of pastry inside the top of the basin. Continue with the meat and onion layers and pour over the stock. Cover the basin with a pastry lid and tie down with buttered foil or greaseproof paper and a pudding cloth. Steam for 4 hours.

Potato Pie (6—8 portions) F Lancashire

A homely type of savoury pie, the potato filling given a meaty flavour with shoulder or chuck beef.

1 lb stewing steak
1 oz seasoned flour
4 oz chopped onions
1 oz dripping
¾ pt brown stock
1 dessertspoon chopped parsley
Salt and pepper
2 lb sliced potatoes
1 lb savoury suet pastry

Oven: 375°F; gas mark 5; 1 hour

Chop the meat into cubes, coat with seasoned flour and fry, with the onions, in the dripping until sealed and light brown. Add the stock, parsley, salt and pepper and simmer, covered, for 1—1½ hours or until the meat is tender.

Spoon the mixture into a 3 pt pie dish, cover first with the sliced potatoes and then the pastry. Bake until well-risen and brown.

Priddy Oggies (8 portions) F and H Somerset

The depression that followed the closure of tin mines in Cornwall inspired the "tiddy oggie", literally potato pasty. This was adopted in nearby comfortable Somerset where local Cheddar cheese and pork were incorporated in the "oggie". The following recipe originated at the Miner's Arms at Priddy.

1¼ lb pork fillet
¾ lb cheese pastry
2 oz thinly sliced smoked pork or bacon
6 oz grated mature Cheddar
1 teaspoon chopped parsley
Salt, cayenne or black pepper
1 large egg
Fat for frying

Oven: 350°F; gas mark 4; 10 minutes

Make the cheese pastry and divide it into eight equal portions; roll each out to a rectangle 6 in by 3 in. Trim the pork fillet of fat, membranes and sinews and cut each fillet lengthways into two; beat them flat to a thickness of ¼ in. Cut the smoked pork or bacon into eight strips. Make a stuffing by mixing together the cheese and parsley; season with salt and cayenne and bind with half the beaten egg. Spread the cheese stuffing evenly over the pork fillets, roll up firmly and put in the refrigerator to set.

To assemble the oggies, cut the fillets into eight pieces. Wrap each piece in a strip of smoked pork or bacon, lay on a cheese pastry portion and moisten the edges with the remaining egg. Draw the short edges of pastry together, seal and crimp to give a scalloped crest effect. Brush with beaten egg and bake in the oven for 10 minutes.

Deep-fry the baked oggies in hot fat for about 10 minutes or until golden brown. Drain and serve at once.

Quorn Bacon Roll (6–8 portions) F Leicestershire

This suet roly poly was probably served after a hunt meeting, more likely to the cold and hungry beaters than to their lordly masters.

1½ lb lean collar of bacon rashers
1 lb savoury suet pastry
½ lb finely chopped onions
1 teaspoon chopped sage
Pepper
Garnish: chopped parsley

Roll out the suet pastry to a 10–12 in square, about ¼ in thick. Lay the bacon rashers over the pastry, add the onions and sprinkle with sage and pepper. Roll up and wrap in a pudding cloth.

Boil for 2½–3 hours, turn out and garnish with chopped parsley; surround with potatoes, turnips and carrots and serve.

Sage Cobbler of Lamb (6–8 portions) F

Shoulder, neck or breast of lamb can be used for this casserole with a sage-flavoured scone topping.

2 lb boned lamb
1 oz seasoned flour
1 oz cooking fat, dripping or lard
½ lb thinly sliced onions
2 oz dried peas (soaked overnight)
1 pt brown stock
Salt and pepper
½ lb flour
1½ teaspoons baking powder
Salt
2 oz butter
½ teaspoon sage
1 egg

2 tablespoons milk

Oven: 425°F; gas mark 7; 20–30 minutes

Cut the meat into 1 in pieces and dust in seasoned flour. Melt the fat and fry first the onions and then the drained peas. Add the meat and brown; transfer the contents of the pan to a 2–3 pt casserole dish, add the stock, salt and pepper. Cover with a lid and cook in the oven (325°F; gas mark 3) or on top of the stove for 2 hours.

Make the scone topping by sifting the flour, baking powder and a pinch of salt into a bowl; rub in the butter and add the sage. Mix to a soft dough with the beaten egg and the milk. Knead on a floured board and roll out ½ in thick; cut into eight triangles or rounds. Arrange these on top of the meat in the casserole and brush with milk.

Return the casserole to the oven without the lid and bake until the scone topping is risen and golden brown.

Sea Pie (6–8 portions) F and H

Also known as sailor pie, possibly because this was the nearest sailors at sea came to a traditional beef suet pudding.

1½ lb stewing steak
1 oz seasoned flour
6 oz sliced onions
2 oz dripping
6 oz sliced carrots
Salt and pepper
1¼ pt brown stock
¾ lb savoury suet pastry

Cut the meat into 1 in cubes and coat with seasoned flour. Fry the onions and meat in the dripping until light brown. Put in a deep saucepan, add the carrots, salt and pepper and sufficient stock to cover the meat; simmer for 1 hour.

Roll out the pastry to a circle to fit the saucepan; place the pastry on top of the stew and make a hole in the centre of the pastry. Replace the lid which should be deep enough to allow the pastry to rise. Simmer for a further 30 minutes when the pastry should be cooked and well risen.

A Sefton of Veal Custard (6–8 portions) H and F

A light, delicately flavoured flan, suitable for convalescents' diets. It may also be made as individual patties. Serve with a green salad.

1 pt rich veal stock, reduced from 2 pt
4 eggs
Grated rind of 1 lemon
Salt and cayenne pepper
¼ teaspoon mace
½ lb savoury shortcrust pastry
2 oz melted butter

Oven: 325°F; gas mark 3; 40–45 minutes

Beat and strain the eggs, pour the warm stock over them, whisking all the time. Add the lemon peel, salt, cayenne and mace to taste.

Line an 8 in flan ring set on a baking sheet with the pastry and bake blind for 15 minutes. Pour the melted butter into the flan, add the veal custard and bake in the oven for 40 minutes or until set.

Sheep Head Pie (6–8 portions) F

Sheep heads can sometimes be obtained from local slaughterhouses; cleaned, boiled and skinned they can be used for brawns or as fillings for savoury pies.

2 boiled sheep heads
1 dessertspoon chopped parsley
½ teaspoon mixed herbs
Salt and pepper
4 hardboiled eggs
½ lb chopped bacon
½ pt stock
¾ lb savoury shortcrust pastry
1 egg

Oven: 425°F; gas mark 7; 30 minutes

Trim all meat from the bones and skin the tongues. Put a layer of meat in a 3½ pt pie dish, sprinkle with parsley and herbs, salt and pepper and cover with slices of egg and chopped bacon. Repeat these layers and pour over strained stock from the heads.

Cover with pastry, brush with beaten egg and bake until the pastry is golden brown.

Sparerib Pie (6–8 portions) F Cumberland

This pie is traditionally served cold, accompanied with pickled beetroot.

2 lb pork spareribs
Salt and pepper
1 teaspoon chopped parsley
¾ pt brown stock

½ lb savoury shortcrust pastry
1 egg

Oven: 350°F; gas mark 4; 1½–2 hours

Strip the meat off the bones and cut into 1 in pieces; arrange in a 2 pt pie dish and season with salt and pepper; sprinkle with parsley. Pour over the stock and cover the top with pastry. Decorate with pastry leaves and brush with beaten egg. Bake in the oven until golden brown.

Steak and Cow Heel Pie (6–8 portions) F Lancashire and North Cheshire

The Midlands are well known for their economical use of all parts of food animals. Cow heels were formerly great favourites for pie fillings and should still be obtainable from family butchers.

½ cow heel, dressed
¾ lb shin of beef
1 onion studded with cloves
1 pt brown stock
Salt and pepper
½ lb savoury shortcrust or savoury suet pastry
1 egg

Oven: 350°F; gas mark 4; 1 hour

Have the cow heel dressed and cooked by the butcher. Put the heel in a large pan with the shin of beef, add the onion and stock and season with salt and pepper. Simmer for 3 hours or until tender.

Remove the meat from the pan, chop into 1 in cubes and put in a 2½ pt pie dish adding part of the strained stock and extra seasoning. Cover with pastry, brush with beaten egg and bake in the oven for 1 hour.

Steak and Kidney Pie (6–8 portions) F and H

Almost as popular as the related Steak and Kidney Pudding, this pie appears with numerous regional differences. In the West Country, ½ pt clotted or double cream is poured into the pie through the pastry hole just before serving. The Ormidale Steak Pie from the Highlands is flavoured with 1 teaspoon each of Worcestershire sauce, vinegar and tomato sauce. In East Yorkshire, the pie becomes Meat and Pot Pie, sliced potatoes being substituted for kidneys.

Yet other versions add sliced mushrooms to

the stewed filling, beneath the pastry covering. Some authorities maintain that the meat and pastry should be cooked together so as to impart all the meat flavours to the pastry; the pie should then be baked at 450°F (gas mark 8) for 20 minutes and thereafter for just under 2 hours at 350°F (gas mark 4).

1½ lb stewing steak
½ lb ox or lamb kidney
1 oz seasoned flour
1 tablespoon chopped parsley
1 oz dripping
4 oz chopped onions
¾ pt brown stock
Salt and pepper
¾ lb savoury shortcrust, flaky or puff pastry
1 egg

Oven: 400°F; gas mark 6; 1 hour

Cut the steak and kidney into small cubes, dust with seasoned flour and mix with the chopped parsley. Melt the dripping and fry the onions and meat in the fat until light brown. Cover with stock, bring to the boil and simmer gently for 1—1½ hours. Correct seasoning with salt and pepper.

Put the meat in a 3 pt pie dish, cover with pastry and brush with beaten egg. Bake in the oven until golden brown.

Steak, Kidney and Oyster Pie

This is yet another version of Steak and Kidney Pie, extremely popular throughout the Midlands and the North. In Scotland, it is known as Musselburgh Pie. One dozen chopped oysters, with their liquid, are added to the steak and kidney stew before the pastry lid is put on; sometimes 4 oz sliced mushrooms are also added.

Steak and Kidney Pudding (6—8 portions) F and H

This is one of the oldest puddings, the pride and joy of British classic cooking and traditionally served in its basin, tied round with a freshly starched, white napkin. Serve with boiled potatoes, Brussels sprouts and a jug of hot water with which to thin down the rich thick gravy in the pudding after the pastry has been cut.

Steak and oyster pudding is a classic version, incorporating 1 doz chopped oysters — and sometimes 4 oz sliced mushrooms — with the layers of

beef and kidney; half the stock can be replaced with sherry and a dash of mushroom ketchup.

John Bull Pudding is a steak and kidney pudding without kidneys, 4 oz chopped mushrooms taking their place. In some recipes, ½ lb chopped ham is mixed with the beef.

1½ lb stewing steak
½ lb ox or lamb kidney
1 oz seasoned flour
2 lb savoury suet pastry
4 oz chopped onions
1 dessertspoon chopped parsley
Salt and pepper
½—¾ pt brown stock

Cut the beef and kidney into cubes, toss in seasoned flour. Line a 3—4 pt pudding basin with three quarters of the pastry and fill the basin with alternate layers of beef, kidney and onions; sprinkle each layer with parsley and a little salt and pepper. Add sufficient stock to just cover the meat, cover with the pastry lid and tie down with buttered foil or greaseproof paper and a pudding cloth. Steam for 4 hours.

Stockenchurch Pie (6—8 portions) F Buckinghamshire

Cold roast beef or lamb can be used, with cooked macaroni, as a filling for a savoury quick pie. Serve with a jug of hot, thickened gravy.

1½ lb cooked meat
Brown stock
4 oz cooked macaroni
1 lb savoury shortcrust pastry
3 quartered hardboiled eggs
Salt and pepper
1 egg

Oven: 425°F; gas mark 7; 30 minutes

Mince the meat, moisten with stock and add the finely chopped macaroni. Line an 8 in flan ring, set on a baking sheet, with three quarters of the pastry; arrange the meat and eggs in layers over the pastry, seasoning each layer with salt and pepper. Cover with the remaining pastry, brush with beaten egg and bake until golden brown.

Teviotdale Pie (8 portions) F Roxburghshire

The main ingredient in this Scottish pie is freshly

minced beef or lamb; it is covered with a thick batter and should be served as soon as it comes out of the oven.

2 lb minced beef or lamb
1 oz dripping
½ pt brown stock
Salt and pepper
Worcestershire sauce
1 lb flour
1½ oz cornflour
6 oz chopped suet
1¼ pt milk

Oven: 350°F; gas mark 4; 30—40 minutes

Fry the mince lightly in dripping for 5—10 minutes, add the stock, cover and simmer for 1 hour. Season with salt, pepper and Worcestershire sauce to taste and spoon into a 2½—3 pt pie dish.

Mix the flour and cornflour with suet and a pinch of salt; gradually stir in the milk and beat to a thick smooth batter. Pour over the mince and bake in the oven for 30—40 minutes.

Toad-in-the-Hole (6—8 portions) F

Although this well loved batter pudding is often made with pork and beef sausages, cooked with the batter, the classic toad-in-the-hole contains slices of prime rump steak. The Cornish toad-in-the-hole, however, resembles neither of these, the batter being replaced with mashed potatoes mixed with flour and suet, beaten eggs and milk to a paste-like consistency; it is used to line a baking tin and sausages are thrust into the potato mixture and baked.

1¼ lb rump or frying steak
2 oz dripping
¾ lb ox kidney
Salt and pepper
1½ pt Yorkshire pudding batter

Oven: 400°F; gas mark 6; 40 minutes

Cut the steak into 2 in long slices and fry for a few minutes in half the dripping. Cut the kidney into small pieces and season with salt and pepper.

Make up the batter; heat the remaining dripping in a 3 pt pie dish until smoking. Pour in half the batter and bake until set. Place the fried steak and the kidney on top of the batter, pour over the remaining batter and bake until well risen.

Tripe Pie (8 portions) F

The Lancashire dish of tripe and onions (see recipe) is sometimes used as a filling for a pie. It is usually covered with mashed potatoes, but in Scotland the pie lid is shortcrust pastry, and the pie has a base of sliced ham.

2 lb tripe and onions
3 hardboiled eggs
Salt and pepper
2 lb mashed potatoes

Oven: 425°F; gas mark 7; 20 minutes

Prepare and cook the tripe and onions, arrange in a 3½ pt pie dish and cover with sliced, hardboiled eggs; sprinkle with salt and pepper. Cover the eggs with mashed potatoes and bake in the oven until light brown on top.

Veal Olive Pie (8 portions) H and F

This veal and bacon pie is a 20th century version of the medieval Ham Olive Pye. In this, the ham olives contained a sweet-savoury stuffing of finely chopped eggs, dates, currants, gooseberries and mushrooms, spiced with nutmeg, salt, pepper, cinnamon, sugar, parsley and lovage, the whole being moistened with cider. The pie, which was covered with puff pastry was, like this veal olive pie, served cold.

2 lb fillet of veal
½ lb veal forcemeat
4 oz diced bacon
2 sliced hardboiled eggs
Salt and pepper
Pinch marjoram or tarragon
½ pt white stock
¾ lb savoury shortcrust pastry
1 egg
5 fl oz jellied white stock

Oven: 350°F; gas mark 4; 1½—2 hours

Cut the veal into thin slices, spread each piece with forcemeat, roll up and arrange in a 3 pt pie dish. Add the chopped bacon and hardboiled eggs; sprinkle with salt, pepper and marjoram and pour over the stock.

Cover with the pastry, brush with beaten egg and bake until golden brown. Make a small hole in the cooked pastry, pour the warmed jelly through and leave to set before serving.

Veal Flory (8 portions) F and H Scotland

Thought to be of Italian origin and brought to
Scotland via France, this pie is known in England
as Florentine Pie. Flory, however, may simply be
a corruption of *fleury,* indicating pastry trimmings
shaped as *fleurs-de-lis.*

2 lb best end of neck or single loin veal chops
Salt and pepper
½ teaspoon mixed herbs
½ lb lean bacon rashers
½ lb veal forcemeat balls
2 oz sliced mushrooms
¾ pt veal stock
¾ lb savoury shortcrust pastry
1 egg

Oven: 350°F; gas mark 4; 1½ hours

Trim the meat from the bones, season with salt,
pepper and herbs and arrange in a 3 pt pie dish
with the bacon, forcemeat balls and mushrooms.
Add the stock and cover the pie with pastry. Brush
with beaten egg and bake in the oven until golden.

Veal Kidney Pie (8 portions) H and F Hertfordshire

A light, gently flavoured pie, perfect for a summer
day's luncheon, served with a green salad and a
well chilled, dry white wine.

8 veal kidneys
4 oz chopped celery
4 sliced hardboiled eggs
4 oz white breadcrumbs
½ teaspoon each, ground nutmeg, cloves
Salt and pepper
Bunch of sweet herbs
1 pt stock
½ pt white wine
½ lb savoury shortcrust pastry
1 egg

Oven: 350°F; gas mark 4; 1½ hours

Dice the kidneys and fry them lightly in their own
suet. Mix the kidneys with the celery and arrange
in a 2½ pt pie dish with layers of sliced eggs and
breadcrumbs. Season each layer with nutmeg,
cloves, salt and pepper.

    Add the herbs and pour over the stock and
wine. Cover with pastry, brush with beaten egg
and bake until golden.

Veal Pot Pie (6—8 portions) F

The pastry lids of savoury pies are usually decorated
with leaf shapes or more elaborate cut-outs made
from pastry trimmings. The top is glazed with
beaten egg, mixed with milk or water to give a glossy
finish.

1¼ lb breast or shoulder of veal
½ lb pickled pork
Salt and pepper
1 teaspoon chopped parsley
¾ pt white stock
6 oz sliced onions
½ lb par-boiled thickly sliced potatoes
½ lb savoury shortcrust pastry
1 egg

Oven: 350°F; gas mark 4; 45 minutes

Cut the veal into 1 in cubes and the pork into thin
slices. Put the veal in a pan with salt, pepper,
parsley and stock. Simmer gently for 1 hour.
Transfer to a 2½ pt pie dish, add the pork and
onions and cover with the sliced potatoes. Put on
the pastry lid, brush with beaten egg and bake in
the oven until golden brown.

Welsh Lamb Pie (6—8 portions) F and H Wales

This is an old Welsh recipe, made with young hill
lamb and small new carrots; it may be served hot
or cold.

1½—2 lb neck of lamb
6 oz sliced carrots
Salt and pepper
1 teaspoon finely chopped parsley
1 lb savoury shortcrust pastry
1 egg
4 oz roughly chopped onions

Oven: 350°F; gas mark 4; 2 hours

Bone the meat and cut into dice. Line a pie dish
with the carrots, cover with meat and sprinkle
with salt, pepper and parsley. Cover with the
pastry, brush with beaten egg and bake until
golden brown.

    Meanwhile boil the bones with the onions, salt
and pepper for 1½ hours or until it has reduced to
¾ pint. Strain the stock and pour into the cooked
pie through the hole in the pastry lid just before
serving.

Yorkshire Sausage Roll (6—8 portions) F
Yorkshire

This is a boiled or steamed pudding made from pork and ham, and always served cold with salads and pickles. Veal or chicken may take the place of pork.

1 lb lean pork
1 lb ham or bacon
1 lb fresh white breadcrumbs
Salt and pepper
Pinch mace and cayenne
3 eggs

Mince the pork and ham finely, mix with the breadcrumbs and season to taste with salt, pepper, mace and cayenne. Bind the mixture with the lightly beaten eggs. Shape the mixture into a roll and tie in a floured pudding cloth, boil for 3 hours or steam in a pudding basin for 5 hours. Serve cold.

POULTRY AND GAME PIES AND PUDDINGS

Ashdown Partridge Pudding (6—8 portions) H and F Sussex

The combination of game and meat is found in the earliest known records. The medieval cook probably discovered that old game birds, too tough for roasting and grilling, became tender and succulent when cooked for hours under a pastry covering. Rabbit and pigeon are equally suitable for this type of steamed game pudding.

1 brace partridge
4 oz sliced rump steak
2 lb savoury suet pastry
4 oz sliced mushrooms
½ teaspoon finely chopped mixed herbs
½ teaspoon finely chopped parsley
Salt and pepper
5 fl oz claret
1 pt beef or game stock

Joint each partridge into four or six portions and dice the beef. Line a 3—4 pt pudding basin with two thirds of the suet pastry. Put the partridge joints and meat in the basin, add the mushrooms, herbs and parsley and season with salt and pepper. Pour over the claret and enough stock to cover the contents.

Cover with the remaining pastry and tie down with buttered greaseproof paper and a pudding cloth. Steam for 3 hours.

Aylesbury Game Pie (20 portions) H
Buckinghamshire

In Victorian and Edwardian days, this dish would form one of the centrepieces of the cold buffet at fashionable balls. It is not truly a pie, but rather a terrine which may be served hot from the dish in which it is cooked or it may be turned out when cold and served with green salads and Cumberland sauce.

1 boned hare (approx. 2 lb flesh)
3 lb oven-ready chicken
1 pheasant (optional)
1 lb pork fat
Hare liver
Salt and pepper
1 lb lean veal or pork
2 fl oz brandy
1 sprig thyme
1 bay leaf
1 lb thinly sliced bacon

Oven: 325°F; gas mark 3; 3 hours

Make a forcemeat by mincing the pork fat with the meat from the chicken and pheasant legs and any meaty trimmings from the hare, including the liver. Season with salt and pepper and mix thoroughly.

Cut the remaining meat from the hare, chicken, pheasant and veal or pork into rough dice; place in a basin with the brandy, seasoning, thyme and bay leaf, cover and leave to marinate for at least 3 hours in a cool place.

Line the base and sides of a 4 pt casserole dish with bacon and cover with a ½ in layer of forcemeat. Top with a layer of diced meat and continue with alternate layers of forcemeat and diced meat, finishing with forcemeat. Cover with the remaining bacon and pour over the marinade. Place the casserole, covered with a lid, in the oven in a roasting tin with hot water and cook for 3 hours.

Cornish Chicken Pie (8 portions) H and F Cornwall

Reminiscent of the medieval dish known as Chicken Pie with a Caudle; chicken joints and hardboiled eggs were cooked in butter under a puff pastry cover, and a caudle of egg yolks, white wine, cream, sugar and nutmeg was poured into the pie when cooked. In this modern version, stewing veal may be substituted for chicken, and sliced leeks for parsley as in the Welsh recipe.

8 chicken joints
2 oz butter
8 slices chopped gammon or ham
1 oz chopped parsley
6 oz chopped onions
1 tablespoon caster sugar
Pinch mace and nutmeg
½ pt chicken or veal stock
Salt and pepper
¾ lb savoury shortcrust pastry
1 egg
½ pt double or Cornish cream

Oven: 350°F; gas mark 4; 1 hour

Lightly fry the chicken joints in butter for 5—10 minutes without colouring. Place a layer of gammon or ham over the base of a 3 pt greased pie dish, sprinkle with parsley and put the chicken on top. Cover with onions, sugar, mace and nutmeg. Repeat these layers, ending with a layer of ham. Add the stock, season with salt and pepper and cover with pastry. Brush with beaten egg and bake for 1 hour.

Open the hole in the top of the pastry, pour in the hot cream and serve.

Grampian Grouse Pudding (6 portions) H and F Scotland

From the Scottish Highlands comes this steamed game pudding of grouse and rump steak. Serve with mealy boiled or creamed potatoes.

1 grouse
1 lb rump steak
1 oz seasoned flour
2 lb savoury suet pastry
1 chopped onion or a few mushrooms
Salt and pepper
1—2 tablespoons Madeira or port
½ pt stock

Strip the meat from the grouse and chop this and the beef into small pieces; coat in seasoned flour. Line a greased 3—4 pt pudding basin with two thirds of the pastry, fill with grouse and steak, onion or mushroom and season with salt and pepper; add Madeira or port and enough stock to cover the meat. Cover with the remaining pastry, make a hole in the centre and tie down with greaseproof paper and a pudding cloth.

Steam for 4—6 hours or until the grouse is quite tender; after 2—3 hours, pour more stock into the pudding through the hole in the pastry lid.

Grouse and Hare Pie (6—8 portions) H and F

This is a true game pie, containing not only grouse and hare, but also venison and pigeon. May be served hot with potatoes and vegetables, but is more often served cold with salads.

1 pigeon
1 grouse
½ hare
½ lb shoulder of venison
Salt and pepper
1 sliced lamb kidney
2 oz sliced mushrooms
2 oz diced bacon
½ lb veal forcemeat balls
2½ fl oz port
¾ lb savoury shortcrust pastry
1 egg

Oven: 350°F; gas mark 4; 2½ hours

Joint the pigeon and grouse and remove the best meaty parts from the hare. Slice the hare and venison meat into large pieces; put the bones and trimmings in a pan with water, bring to the boil and simmer gently for 1 hour.

Sprinkle the venison with pepper and salt and put in a 3—4 pt pie dish; arrange the pigeon and grouse, hare, kidney and mushrooms in the dish and place the bacon and forcemeat balls on top. Strain the game stock and mix ½—¾ pt with the port; pour over the meat. Cover with the pastry, brush with beaten egg and bake for 2½ hours.

Kentish Chicken Pudding (8 portions) F and H Kent

In medieval days, farmyard fowl were kept strictly for egg-laying, and not until they became old and scraggy were they killed. By then they were so tough that only by prolonged boiling in a suet pastry could they become edible. The Sussex Goose or Chicken Pudding is a survival from those days, but is superseded by this recipe for young, tender chicken.

2 oven-ready chicken (2½ lb each)
1 lb diced salted belly pork
2 lb savoury suet pastry
Salt and pepper
½ lb chopped onions
1 dessertspoon finely chopped parsley

Cut each chicken into four leg joints and four breast joints. Use the carcass, trimmings and giblets to make stock. Blanch, refresh and drain the diced pork. Line a 3–4 pt greased pudding basin with three quarters of the suet pastry and put in the chicken pieces, seasoned with salt and pepper. Mix in the pork and onions and sprinkle with parsley. Pour over ½ pt of the strained chicken stock and cover with the remaining pastry.

Tie down with buttered greaseproof paper or foil and a pudding cloth. Steam for 2 hours, turn the pudding out on to a serving dish and serve with parsley sauce.

Kingdom of Fife Pie (8 portions) F and H Scotland

This has been developed from the 18th century Shropshire Pie which was made with rabbit, diced pork and forcemeat balls made from the rabbit livers, fat bacon and sweet herbs. Half a dozen oysters, chopped onions, apples, currants and artichoke bottoms were also included in the pie which was moistened with equal amounts of red wine and stock. For the forcemeat balls in this dish use the par-boiled rabbit livers as part of the mixture.

2 rabbits
1 lb pickled belly pork
Salt, pepper, grated nutmeg
½ lb veal forcemeat balls
½ pt brown stock
3 tablespoons white wine
1¼ lb puff pastry
1 egg

Oven: 425°F; gas mark 7; 15 minutes
350°F; gas mark 4; 1 hour

Strip the meat from the rabbits and cut into 1 in cubes; slice the pickled pork thinly and season both meats with salt, pepper and grated nutmeg. Layer the two meats in a greased 4 pt pie dish and pack the forcemeat balls in between the meat.

Add the stock and white wine; cover with pastry, brush with beaten egg and bake for 15 minutes at 425°F (gas mark 7), then reduce the heat to 350°F (gas mark 4) and continue baking until the pie is well-risen and golden.

Lowland Game Pie (8 portions) H and F Scotland

Older game birds — grouse, partridge or pheasant — can be used for this game pie; they should be cooked until quite tender before being covered with pastry.

1 brace grouse
1 lb rump or topside of beef
2 oz diced bacon
2 hardboiled eggs
Salt, cayenne pepper, mace and nutmeg
1 pt game stock
1 tablespoon sherry
1¼ lb puff pastry
1 egg

Oven: 325°F; gas mark 3; about 1½ hours
425°F; gas mark 7; 30 minutes

Joint the grouse into four leg pieces and four breast pieces; place in a greased 3 pt pie dish. Cut the steak into 1 in cubes and put in the spaces between the grouse joints. Sprinkle the bacon over the meat and game and add the sliced eggs. Season with salt, cayenne, mace and grated nutmeg and pour over enough stock to cover. Cover with a lid and bake in the oven for 1½ hours or until tender.

Remove from the oven and leave until cool. Add the sherry, adjust seasoning and cover with pastry. Brush with beaten egg and bake in a hot oven for 30 minutes.

Pigeon Pie (6–8 portions) F

This traditional pie is first cooked with a suet crust which is later broken up and pushed in with the meat and then covered with puff pastry. The suet crust was originally known as dumpling crust and takes the place of potatoes or bread for mopping up the gravy.

4 pigeons
2 cloves
1½ lb shoulder steak of beef
1 bay leaf
1 crushed clove garlic (optional)
4 oz sliced shallots or onions
Salt and pepper
6 oz small mushrooms
½ lb diced bacon trimmings
¾ lb savoury suet pastry
1¼ lb puff pastry
1 egg

Oven: 350°F; gas mark 4; about 1½ hours

Joint the cleaned pigeons and put the trimmings in a pan with water and cloves to make stock. Cut the beef into 1 in cubes, mix with the bay leaf, garlic and shallots and put in a greased 3—4 pt pie dish. Put the pigeon joints on top of the beef, season with salt and pepper and top with mushrooms and bacon. Pour over enough strained pigeon stock to come halfway up the dish.

Cover with the suet pastry, pressing it down flat over the meat inside the pie dish; put on a lid and bake for 1 hour. Remove from the oven, cut the suet crust into squares and pack down amongst the pigeon meat.

Fill up the dish with stock and cover the pie with puff pastry; brush with beaten egg and bake until well-risen and brown, after 20—30 minutes.

A Queen's Pie (6—8 portions) H and F

A dainty chicken pie with tiny forcemeat balls under a covering of featherlight puff pastry.

2 oven-ready chickens (2½ lb each)
Salt, pepper and mace
4 oz diced bacon
4 oz butter
2 pt white stock
½ lb veal forcemeat
1¼ lb puff pastry
1 egg

Oven: 350°F; gas mark 4; 1½ hours

Cut each chicken into four leg and four breast joints. Season with salt, pepper and mace and fry with the bacon in butter for a few minutes without colouring. Put the chicken and bacon in a deep 3—4 pt pie dish; add stock and season.

Make 16 small balls from the forcemeat and put in the spaces between the chicken. Cover with pastry, brush with beaten egg and bake for 1½ hours or until golden.

Rabbit Pie (6—8 portions) F and H

At harvest time there used to be a glut of rabbits as the animals bolted from the stubble fields. Young tender rabbits would be roasted or grilled, the not so young became pie fillings, and elderly rabbits ended up in suet puddings. In Staffordshire, the rabbit pie also contained veal forcemeat balls, but omitted both ham and onions.

2 rabbits, jointed
½ lb diced ham or bacon
2 oz minced onion

1 teaspoon chopped parsley
Pinch ground mace
Game stock
1¼ lb puff pastry
1 egg

Oven: 425°F; gas mark 7; 15 minutes
       375°F; gas mark 5; 15—30 minutes

Put the rabbit joints, ham, onion, parsley and mace in an earthenware jar, pour over the stock, cover and simmer for 1 hour. Turn the contents into a 3 pt pie dish, correct seasoning and allow to cool.

Cover with the pastry, brush with beaten egg and bake for about 45 minutes reducing the temperature after 15 minutes.

Rabbit and Mushroom Pudding (6—8 portions) F and H Rutland

This is usually served with boiled potatoes and a rich thick brown sauce made with stock from the rabbit heads and ribs.

2 rabbits, jointed
2 lb savoury suet pastry
4 oz chopped onions
½ lb sliced mushrooms
½ lb diced bacon
Salt and pepper
Pinch sage
5 fl oz stock or water

Line a 3½—4 pt pudding basin with three quarters of the pastry. Layer the rabbit joints, onions, mushrooms and bacon in the basin, seasoning each layer with salt, pepper and sage. Pour over the stock, add the pastry lid and seal the edges firmly. Cover the pudding with buttered greaseproof paper or foil and steam for 2 hours.

Rook Pie

Rooks are not commercially available, but rook pie was once a much prized speciality in farming communities, especially in May when the farmers thinned out the population in large rookeries. For an average size pie, 16 rooks would be needed; only the breast meat was used, the carcasses being made into stock which was poured over the meat in a deep pie dish. The covering was usually flaky pastry, although Welsh Rook Pie used shortcrust pastry and flavoured the rook meat with bacon, chives and thyme.

There was also a rook pudding, in which rook breasts and fat bacon were steamed in a so-called figgy pastry. This was made from flour and butter (with salt and pepper), currants and raisins and used as a suet crust. The pudding was traditionally served with gooseberry jelly.

Squab Pie (6—8 portions) F and H Cornwall

Squab is an old name for pigeon and many regions have a local recipe for squab pie. It appears to have originated in Devon where, in the 18th century, squab had taken on the meaning of lamb or mutton chop. The Devonshire Squab Pie, with prunes, cinnamon and brown sugar, was traditionally eaten with clotted cream.

4 young squabs (pigeons)
1 lb lean mutton
Brown stock
1 lb sliced onions
2 lb Bramley Seedling apples, peeled, cored and sliced
2 oz caster sugar
¾ lb savoury shortcrust pastry
Salt and pepper
1 egg

Oven: 350°F; gas mark 4; 2 hours

Cut the mutton into dice and simmer in the stock for 1 hour. Clean the squabs thoroughly and cut in half. Lay the squabs, mutton, onions and apples in a buttered 3—4 pt pie dish, pour over ½ pt of strained mutton stock; sprinkle with sugar and season to taste with salt and pepper.

Cover the pie with pastry, brush with beaten egg and bake for 2 hours.

Venison Pasty (6—8 portions) F and H

Professional pastry cooks used to decorate this venison pie with dogs and deer made from the pastry trimmings.

2 lb neck, breast, flank or shoulder of venison
Salt and pepper
2 oz seasoned flour
2 oz butter
5 fl oz port
Juice of ½ lemon or 1 teaspoon vinegar
½ pt venison stock
Mixed herbs, nutmeg
6 oz lamb suet or fat

1¼ lb puff pastry
1 egg

Oven: 425°F; gas mark 7; 15 minutes
      350°F; gas mark 4; 1¾ hours

Cut the venison meat into small steaks, season with salt and pepper and dust with seasoned flour; fry quickly in butter to seal in the juices. Put the steaks in a 3—4 pt pie dish, add the port, lemon juice and stock and season with mixed herbs and grated nutmeg. Lay the lamb suet or fat on top and cover with the pastry.

Brush with beaten egg and bake for 2 hours, reducing the heat after the first 15 minutes. Add more stock near the end of cooking if necessary.

RAISED PIES

Beef and Egg Pie, Raised (6—8 portions) F and H Devon

Originally, the hot water crust pastry for a raised pie was moulded and raised up the sides of the meat filling by hand. This requires great skill as the hot pastry cools quickly and is then liable to crack.

1½ lb hot water crust pastry
2 lb lean shoulder or chuck steak
4 oz beef suet
1 teaspoon salt
½ teaspoon pepper
3 hardboiled eggs
1 egg
5 fl oz stock or aspic

Oven: 425°F; gas mark 7; 30 minutes
      325°F; gas mark 3; 2 hours

Raise three quarters of the hot water crust round a mould; mince the beef and mix with the shredded suet, put into the pie. Season with salt and pepper and push the whole eggs among the meat mixture.

Cover the pie with the remaining hot water crust and decorate the lid; brush with beaten egg and bake for 2½ hours, reducing the temperature after the first 30 minutes.

When the pie has cooled, pour the stock through the hole in the lid and leave to settle and jellify. Serve cold.

Cumberland Raised Pie, Original (16—20 portions) F and H Cumberland

This pie is the forerunner of the modern mince

pie. In isolated districts of Cumberland, often cut off during the winter months, large numbers of these pies were made in one session and would be stored for several months.

1½ lb lean mutton
2 lb stoned raisins
2 lb currants
4 oz candied peel
Pinch each, nutmeg and mixed spice
2 lb soft brown sugar
Salt and pepper
4 fl oz rum
4 lb hot water crust pastry
1 egg

Oven: 425°F; gas mark 7; 30 minutes
         325°F; gas mark 3; 2 hours

Put the mutton, raisins, currants and candied peel through the mincer and mix with the spices, sugar, salt and pepper. Stir in the rum and leave the mixture overnight.

Make up the pastry and use to line two large oval raised-pie moulds, setting part of the pastry aside for the lids. Fill the pies with the mince mixture, cover with pastry lids and make a hole in the tops. Brush with beaten egg and bake for 2½ hours, reducing the temperature after 30 minutes. Serve hot or cold.

Game Pie, Raised (6—8 portions) F and H

Game pies, always served cold with pickles and salads, may contain any kind of game bird. For a 1½ lb hot water crust, allow four pigeons, partridge, grouse, woodcocks or ptarmigans, three teal, two wild duck or one capercaillie.

A raised pheasant pie can be made from two young pheasants, 1 lb pork forcemeat, three sliced hardboiled eggs and two mushrooms; follow the recipe below and fill the cooked, cool pie with jellied stock made from the pheasant carcasses.

1½ lb hot water crust pastry
4 pigeons
1 lb herb forcemeat
6 oz streaky bacon
4 oz thinly sliced fillet or rump steak
4 oz sliced mushrooms
Pinch each, cayenne and mace
Salt and pepper
1 egg
Aspic jelly

Oven: 375°F; gas mark 5; 2½—3 hours

Roll out the hot water crust and use three quarters to line a greased pie mould. Bone the pigeons, mince the legs and livers and mix with the forcemeat. Cut the breasts into thin slices. Place a layer of bacon over the base of the pie, add a layer of forcemeat, beef, pigeon breasts and mushrooms; repeat these layers until the mould is filled, sprinkling each layer with cayenne, mace, salt and pepper.

Cover with the pastry lid, brush with beaten egg and bake. Aspic jelly may be poured into the cold pie to fill up any spaces caused by shrinkage.

Hare Pie, Raised (12—14 portions) H and F

The stock which settles to a jelly in a raised pie is not cooked with the pie, but added when the pie has cooled. It is usually made from a carcass and reduced until well concentrated; it sometimes has added gelatine. This raised pie may also be made with rabbit; both should be served cold, garnished with parsley.

2 lb hot water crust pastry
2½ lb hare meat
6 oz white breadcrumbs
Hare liver, chopped
Grated rind of ½ lemon
4 fl oz port
3 oz melted butter
Salt and pepper
2 eggs
Pinch nutmeg
3 oz butter
1 bay leaf
½ pt hare stock
½ oz gelatine
Garnish: parsley

Oven: 425°F; gas mark 7; 30 minutes
         325°F; gas mark 3; 2 hours

Make up the pie crust and while still warm line a large raised-pie mould, reserving enough pastry for the lid. Slice the meat from the hare and put the bones in a pan of water to make stock.

Make up a forcemeat by mixing the breadcrumbs with the finely chopped hare liver and lemon rind; moisten with 2½ fl oz port and the melted butter, season with salt and pepper and bind with 1 egg.

Line the sides and base of the pie crust with forcemeat. Arrange the hare meat in the pie, season with salt, pepper and nutmeg and add knobs of butter and the bay leaf. Cover with a pastry lid, make a hole in the centre and brush with beaten egg; bake for 2½ hours.

Reduce the stock to ½ pt, strain and adjust seasoning; mix with the gelatine and the remaining port, pour into the cooled pie and leave to set. Serve cold, garnished with parsley sprigs.

Lamb Pies, Raised (8 portions) F and H

These small raised pies each contain a lamb cutlet and forcemeat; they are served hot and make an economical luncheon dish.

8 lamb cutlets (4 oz each)
Salt and pepper
1 dessertspoon lemon juice
2 oz butter
1½ lb hot water crust pastry
1 lb veal forcemeat
1 egg
½ pt brown sauce

Oven: 350°F; gas mark 4; 40–45 minutes

Trim the cutlets, taking off most of the fat. Sprinkle with salt, pepper and lemon juice. Fry the cutlets in butter until light brown on both sides. Leave to cool.

Make up the hot water crust pastry and mould into eight pie shells wide enough to hold a cutlet. Line the base of each pie shell with forcemeat, top with a cutlet and fill the remaining spaces round the meat with more forcemeat. Cover each pie with a pastry lid, make a small hole in each and brush with beaten egg. Bake for 45 minutes; allow the pies to cool slightly before pouring the brown sauce into the pies.

Mutton Pies (6 portions) F Scotland

These small raised pies are known in Glasgow as "Tuppenny Struggles"; they bear little resemblance to the much older Pembrokeshire Pies which apart from mutton also contained an equal amount each of currants and sugar and sometimes red currant jelly beneath the pastry lid.

1 lb cooked minced mutton
¾ lb hot water crust pastry
½ pt brown sauce
Salt and pepper
Pinch nutmeg
1 egg

Oven: 350°F; gas mark 4; 40 minutes

Mould the warm pie pastry into six individual shapes, about 3½ in wide and 1½ in high. Moisten the meat with part of the brown sauce, season with salt, pepper and nutmeg and divide equally between the pie shells.

Cover with pastry lids, make a hole in each and brush with egg. Bake for 40 minutes. Pour warmed brown sauce into the cooked pies before serving them hot.

Pork Pies, Raised (8 portions) F and H
Leicestershire

The great majority of the famous raised pork pies originated in Leicestershire, but within that county are found several local variations, the Melton Mowbray Pork Pie being the best known.

Raised pork pies, which can be eaten hot or cold are the oldest known English pies; the pie crust moulded by hand or round a wooden shape was known as a *coffyn*. Today, Leicestershire pork pies are sometimes made in long, greased bread tins, with hardboiled eggs and pickled walnuts laid along the length. The pork should be in proportions of two thirds lean to one third fat pork.

3 lb sparerib of pork
1 tablespoon salt
Pepper
1½ lb hot water crust pastry
Pinch each, dry mustard and allspice
1 egg
¼ oz gelatine

Oven: 425°F; gas mark 7; 30 minutes
325°F; gas mark 3; 2 hours

Trim the meat from the bones and chop into small pieces. Put the bones and gristle into a pan with salt and pepper, cover with water and simmer for 2–3 hours to make stock.

Shape the pie crust from three quarters of the pastry and fill with the chopped meat, seasoned with salt, pepper, mustard and allspice. Cover with the pie lid and brush the top with beaten egg, making a hole in the centre of the pastry.

Bake for 2½ hours, reducing the heat after 30 minutes. Remove from the oven and allow to cool. Strain the stock, mix with the gelatine dissolved in 1 tablespoon hot water and pour into the pie. Serve hot or cold.

Lincolnshire Pork Pie is similar to Leicestershire

pork pies, but is made from chopped shoulder of pork and jellied stock from pig trotters. The chief difference is in the shape of the raised pie, the sides sloping inwards towards the top so that this is about a quarter the size of the base.

Market Harborough Pork Pie is also made with 2 lb chopped or minced shoulder of pork, seasoned with sage and salt; the pork is layered in the pie crust with 2 lb cooking apples and ½ lb chopped onions, sprinkled with 4 oz of sugar.

Melton Mowbray Pork Pie is traditionally moulded and raised by hand and the pastry is made up from 2 lb flour, 6 oz each lard and butter, ½ pt milk and 1 egg. The filling of 3 lb chopped shoulder of pork is seasoned with salt, pepper and cayenne.

Yorkshire Pork Pie differs little from other pork pies, the meat being seasoned with fresh sage or grated nutmeg; the pie crust is enriched with 1 egg. In the Derbyshire variation of this pork pie, the meat is cooked with the bones for about 1½ hours before being filled into the pie crust; this is baked for 1 hour only.

Tongue Pie, Raised (8 portions) H and F

For this raised pie, mould the pie crust to a round shape that will fit the tongue. Make the jellied stock from pig trotters, season well and reduce, and if necessary mix with a little dissolved gelatine. Serve the pie cold with salads.

2 lb ox tongue
1½ lb hot water crust pastry
½ lb veal forcemeat
Pinch each mace and cayenne
6 oz streaky bacon rashers
1 egg
½ pt jellied stock

Oven: 425°F; gas mark 7; 30 minutes
      325°F; gas mark 3; 2 hours

Boil the soaked and prepared tongue until tender, strip off the skin and cut off the root end with gristle and bone. Use three quarters of the warm pastry to raise the pie round a mould. Leave to set, then roll up the tongue and put into the crust. Fill the spaces with forcemeat, sprinkle with spices and cover with the bacon rashers.

Put on the pastry lid, brush with beaten egg and bake for 2½ hours. Remove the pie from the oven, leave to cool slightly, then pour the warmed stock through the hole in the pastry lid. Leave the

pie to cool completely and the stock to set to jelly before serving.

Veal and Ham Pie, Raised (8—10 portions) H and F

This is another classic English pie, as popular and esteemed as raised pork pies. Commercially, veal and ham pies are usually made in bread-tin moulds, but they are a great deal more attractive when shaped in a traditional decorative pie mould and decorated with pastry leaves and cut-outs on the lid. Serve cold with salads and pickles.

There are several variations of the classic veal and ham pie; 2 oz chopped mushrooms or 4 oz whole pickled walnuts may be layered with the meat filling or 1—2 oz pistachio nuts may be distributed in the veal for colour effect. Veal forcemeat may substitute ½ lb of the veal and used in alternate layers.

Veal and Chicken pie is made like a veal and ham pie, the ingredients consisting of 1 lb veal, ½ lb white chicken meat, 1 calf sweetbread and 4 oz of ham. A few chopped mushrooms may also be added.

1½ lb veal
1½ lb hot water crust pastry
½ lb ham, uncooked gammon or bacon
Salt and pepper
½ teaspoon each, finely grated lemon rind and
    chopped parsley
3 hardboiled eggs
1 egg
½ pt rich stock

Oven: 425°F; gas mark 7; 30 minutes
      325°F; gas mark 3; 2 hours

Prepare the pie crust and use three quarters of the pastry to line the mould. Cut the veal and ham into dice and place a layer of veal in the base of the pie; sprinkle with lemon rind, pepper, salt and parsley. Add a layer of chopped ham, arrange the whole hardboiled eggs amongst the meat; repeat with alternate layers of veal, seasoning and ham until the pie is filled.

Cover with the pastry lid and decorate with pastry trimmings; brush with beaten egg and leave a small hole in the centre of the lid. Bake for 2½ hours; remove from the oven and leave to cool.

Pour the warm stock through the hole in the centre of the pie to fill the spaces inside; leave until the stock has set to a jelly.

Venison Pie, Raised (8 portions) H and F

This game pie, which is flavoured with red currant jelly can be served hot or cold; it may also be made as individual pies (see Mutton Pies). Venison pie is often garnished with sprigs of watercress or bog myrtle to distinguish it from other types of raised pies.

2 lb breast or shoulder of venison
Salt and pepper
Pinch nutmeg or clove
1 pt water
1½ lb hot water crust pastry
3 oz butter
½ oz gelatine
5 fl oz red wine or 4 oz red currant jelly
1 egg

Oven: 350°F; gas mark 4; 1—1½ hours

Cut the venison into small pieces, put in a pan with salt, pepper, spices and the water. Simmer gently for 1 hour. Raise the pie crust round a mould and fill it with the strained venison and enough of the stock to moisten the meat. Add the butter, cut into small pieces; cover with the pastry lid, decorate and brush with beaten egg.

Bake for 1—1½ hours. Reduce the strained stock to ½ pt and mix with the dissolved gelatine and wine or red currant jelly; pour into the pie when it has cooled slightly.

Yorkshire Christmas Pie

This was a traditional "standing dish" at Christmas in the homes of hospitable Yorkshire squires, and many of the pies were of tremendous size. It is recorded that one, sent from Sheffield in 1832 as a present to the then Lord Chancellor, broke down on account of its weight. It is doubtful if these pies are made now, except as a curiosity. The following recipe, dating from 1860, admonishes:

"Bone a fowl and goose; fill the fowl with veal forcemeat and put the fowl inside the goose which is then trussed and sewn up. Line a pie mould with hot water pastry. Cover the pie with a layer of forcemeat and lay the goose upon it, and place around it slices of pigeons, boned hare, tongue, etc. Fill the spaces with forcemeat and when the meat is closely packed in the crust, put over it a layer of clarified butter. Place the pastry cover on the top and brush with egg wash, ornament if wished.

Cover with buttered paper and bake for 4 hours. Make a stock by boiling the bones and trimmings with seasonings and pour this into the pie after it is baked. When the pie is to be served, place it on a dish covered with a napkin, remove the pastry top whole and cut the meat into thin slices".

The pastry was not intended to be eaten, but was merely a case in which to preserve and serve the meat.

POTTED AND PICKLED MEAT AND GAME

Potting is an old method of preserving meat and fish. It involved packing meat so tightly into a pot that air was completely excluded and for that reason the meat had to be pounded to an extremely fine texture. Only the best meat was used, and potting was essentially used for convenience foods. An old potting recipe suitable for ships' provisions was the so-called beef cheese, cooked in an earthenware pot lined with bacon and filled with a mixture of lean, minced beef, bacon and beef suet, flavoured with salt, pepper, cloves and thyme and moistened with brandy.

Potted meat was originally covered with a flour and water paste or a thick layer of suet. Today, potted meat is made on the same principle and for the same uses as the French pâtés and terrines, the consistency being either paste-like or coarse. Clarified butter is used for the airtight covering.

Mitton of Pork (6—8 portions) F Northumberland

This is a coarse-textured pork mould and can be served hot with grilled mushrooms and brown gravy, or cold with salads.

1½ lb lean, thinly sliced pork fillet
½ lb streaky bacon rashers
6 oz sage and onion stuffing
Salt and pepper
½ teaspoon ground mace
Oven: 350°F; gas mark 4; 1 hour

Line a round, 7 in wide pot or pudding basin with bacon rashers, put in a layer of pork and a layer or sage and onion stuffing; season with salt, pepper and mace. Continue with these layers until the pot is full, finishing with a layer of pork or bacon. Press the meat down well and cover the pot with a close-fitting lid.

Stand the pot in a baking tin to catch any fat which might drip down; bake in the oven until golden brown. For serving cold, place a weighted board over the meat and leave until completely cold; turn out and serve the mould cut into slices.

Manchester Collared Pork (6—8 portions) F Lancashire

The term "collared" is applied to a piece of meat, originally the neck piece, coiled or tied up in a roll. This dish is served cold after being immersed for 24 hours in a pickle solution.

2 lb pickled belly pork
1 cow heel, dressed
½ teaspoon ground nutmeg
¼ teaspoon cayenne
½ pt vinegar
½ pt water
1 oz sugar
1 oz salt
6 cloves

Put the belly pork and cow heel in a saucepan, cover with cold water, bring to the boil and simmer for 1 hour. Remove from the pan; cut off and dice any edible meat from the cow heel. Sprinkle both the cow heel meat and belly pork with nutmeg and cayenne; spread out the belly pork and cover with the diced cow heel, roll up and tie in a floured pudding cloth. Bind the cloth with tape, replace in the pan and simmer for a further 2 hours.

Remove the meat from the pan and tighten the cloth; return to the pan and leave the meat to cool in the stock. Meanwhile, make the pickle by mixing the vinegar with the water and adding sugar, salt and cloves. When cold, remove the meat from the cloth and immerse in the pickle for 24 hours. Serve cold, cut into slices.

Potted Beef I (6—8 portions) H and F

This is of coarse texture and made with flank of beef like Manchester Collared Pork, but not immersed in pickle; it is served cold, with pickles and salads.

2 lb diced rump or shoulder of beef
6 cloves
Salt and pepper
½ teaspoon anchovy essence

½ pt beef stock
3 oz clarified butter

Oven: 325°F; gas mark 3; 2 hours

Trim away any bone, gristle and fat and cut the meat into small pieces, no more than 1½ in. Put the meat in a potting dish in layers sprinkled with cloves, salt, pepper and anchovy essence; pour over the stock. Cover the dish with foil and bake in the oven until the meat is quite tender.

Remove from the oven; press the meat under a heavy weight for 2—3 hours or until cool and the cooking liquid has set. Cover with clarified butter.

Potted Beef II (6—8 portions) H and F

Minced to a paste-like texture, this potted beef will store for several weeks in the refrigerator if adequately covered with clarified butter. Serve with thin, hot toast.

2 lb rump or shoulder of beef
½ pt beef stock
6 cloves
½ teaspoon anchovy essence
Salt and pepper
6 oz clarified butter

Oven: 325°F; gas mark 3; 2 hours

Put the meat in an ovenproof dish with the stock, cloves, anchovy essence, salt and pepper; cover with foil and bake in the oven until the meat is tender. It should be ready when the fat coming from the meat is no longer cloudy. Remove and discard the cloves; strain the cooking liquid and set aside.

Pass the meat through the fine blade of a mincer two or three times or reduce the meat in the liquidiser. Pound to a smooth paste, add half the clarified butter and adjust consistency with the cooking liquid.

Correct seasoning and put the meat paste in a potting dish. Leave until cold, then cover with the remaining clarified butter.

Potted Chicken and Ham (10—12 portions) H and F

A delicately flavoured paste, excellent as a starter with hot toast.

¾ lb cooked chicken
¾ lb cooked ham

½ lb fresh pork fat
¼ teaspoon each, ground mace, nutmeg and pepper
2 tablespoons brandy
4 oz clarified butter

Mince or pound the ham with the pork fat and mix with the spices; mince or pound the chicken and arrange the ham and chicken in layers in a potting dish. Spoon over the brandy and cover with the clarified butter. Serve when set.

Potted Chicken Liver Paste (10 portions) H and F

Pack this fine paste into small individual pots and serve when set with thin slices of toast. Goose and duck livers may be treated similarly, but being fatty need only half the amount of butter in the mixture.

1 lb chicken livers
4 oz butter
1 crushed clove garlic
¾ teaspoon ground black pepper
¼ teaspoon dried thyme
Salt
2 tablespoons brandy
2 tablespoons port or Madeira
2 oz clarified butter

Clean the livers carefully, cutting away any discoloured parts. Fry the livers in the butter for 10 minutes, then pass twice through the fine blades of the mincer. Blend the paste with the crushed garlic and add pepper, thyme and salt to taste. Moisten with brandy and port and pack into small pots. Cover with clarified butter.

Potted Goose (8—10 portions) H and F

Duck, chicken and turkey may be potted in the same way as goose, adding 2 oz of softened butter to chicken and turkey when layering it.

1 lb diced goose meat
1 lb diced belly pork
2 sage leaves
1 sprig thyme
¼ teaspoon ground mace
Salt and pepper
5 fl oz claret
4 oz clarified butter

Oven: 325°F; gas mark 3; 2 hours

Pack the goose meat and belly pork in layers into a potting dish, with the herbs, mace, salt and pepper; pour over the claret and cover the dish with foil. Bake in the oven until tender.

Remove from the oven and press the meat under a heavy weight until cold. Cover with clarified butter and serve cold.

Potted Grouse (8 portions) H

This is a delicious game paste, to be served with hot buttered toast as a first course, in small individual pots or one large dish. The grouse, which should be young, may be replaced by pheasants, partridges, wild duck or woodcock.

4 grouse
Cayenne and black pepper
Salt
½ pt brown game stock
½ lb butter
1 tablespoon brandy or port
4 oz clarified butter

Oven: 325°F; gas mark 3; 2 hours

Pluck and draw the grouse, reserving the necks, livers and giblets. Cut the birds in half along the spine. Mix cayenne, black pepper and salt together and rub thoroughly into the flesh side of the grouse. Place the giblets, necks and livers in a fireproof dish and set the birds on top. Moisten with stock, cover with a well-fitting lid and bake until the flesh falls away from the bones.

Leave the grouse to cool slightly, then remove all bones. Mix the butter with the grouse meat and strained cooking liquid, blending thoroughly with a fork; add the brandy. Press the mixture into pots, cover with clarified butter and leave until the butter has set.

Potted Ham (8—10 portions) H and F

Use this paste-like meat with hot toast as a breakfast dish, a first course or as a spread for sandwiches.

1½ lb lean ham
½ lb fresh pork fat
¼ teaspoon each, ground mace, nutmeg and pepper
½ pt white stock
2 tablespoons brandy
4 oz clarified butter

Oven: 325°F; gas mark 3; 2 hours

Mince the ham and pork fat twice and blend with the spices; add the stock. Put in an ovenproof dish, cover with foil and bake in the oven for 2 hours.

Strain off the liquid and pound the meat to a smooth paste, moisten with brandy and enough of the liquid to give a soft consistency. Correct seasoning and spoon into a potting dish. Cover with clarified butter and use when set.

Potted Ham and Game (8—10 portions) H and F

A quickly made, smooth paste packed into individual pots and equally suitable as a breakfast dish and a starter to luncheon or dinner.

½ lb cooked ham
½ lb cooked game meat
2 teaspoons sugar
Pinch cayenne, allspice, ground mace
Salt and pepper
2 tablespoons beer
6 oz butter

Mince the ham and game meat finely and pound to a smooth paste. Add the sugar, spices, salt and pepper and moisten with beer. Blend in 4 oz softened butter and pack the mixture into pots. Clarify the remaining butter and pour over the paste to cover.

Potted Hare (12—16 portions) H and F

This well-flavoured, smooth paste cooked with red wine can also be made with rabbit. Pack into a large pot and serve as a first course, garnished with watercress and accompanied with hot buttered toast.

1½ lb hare meat, including the liver
½ lb pork or bacon fat
½ teaspoon finely chopped sweet herbs
Pinch nutmeg
Salt and pepper
5 fl oz red wine
4 oz clarified butter

Oven: 325°F; gas mark 3; 2 hours

Cut the hare carcass into joints and strip the meat from the bones. Chop the hare meat, liver and pork or bacon fat and put through the mincer twice; add the herbs, nutmeg, salt and pepper to taste, and the wine.

Put the mixture in a pot and cover closely with a lid or foil. Bake in the oven for 2 hours, remove and cool slightly before covering with clarified butter; leave to cool and set.

Potted Head (Heid) (40 portions) H Scotland

This dish, set in moulds and served with salads or hot toast and lemon is suitable for a banquet or large buffet; for smaller occasions, use 2—3 lb ox cheek, with 1 cow heel or 2 pig trotters to provide the jellied stock and reduce the spices to one quarter of the amounts given here.

1 ox head, split
3 oz salt
4 oz chopped onions
½ oz whole peppercorns
8 cloves
4 blades mace
25 allspice berries
4 sprigs each, thyme, marjoram and parsley
4 bay leaves

Soak the split ox head for 2—3 hours. Scald the head and when cool scrape it thoroughly. Place the head in a large pan, cover with cold water and add the salt; bring to the boil slowly and skim. Simmer for 5—6 hours. Remove the head and cut the meat from the bones.

Replace the bones in the cooking liquid, add the onions and the spices and herbs tied in muslin; if necessary add more water to cover the bones. Simmer for 2 hours, then remove the lid and boil rapidly to reduce the stock slightly; strain into a basin and set aside until cold.

Remove the fat from the top of the stock which should have set to a jelly. Cut the meat into small pieces and arrange in wetted moulds or basins, Warm the stock to melt it, leave to cool, then pour over the meat in the moulds, stirring to distribute the meat. Turn out the moulds when cold and set.

Potted Hough (6—8 portions) F Scotland

Similar to potted head and jellied ox cheek and served in the same manner, with hot toast and a small bowl of fresh lemon juice.

2 lb hough (shin of beef)
1 cow heel or 2 pig trotters
¾ oz salt
1 faggot of herbs
4 whole allspice berries

12 peppercorns
4 cloves
1 blade mace

Cut the hough into small pieces; split the cow heel or trotters down the middle, scald and chop them into pieces. Put the hough and cow heel in a pan with sufficient cold water to cover. Add the salt and herbs and the spices tied in a muslin bag. Bring the water to the boil, cover and simmer gently for 3 hours or until the meat falls off the bones.

Remove the meat and muslin bag, adjust seasoning of the stock and continue to boil until it has reduced and begins to jelly. Chop the meat finely and arrange in a wet mould or basin. Strain the jellied stock over the meat, stirring with a fork to distribute the meat. Leave to set, and turn out before serving.

Potted Lamb Liver (10 portions) H and F

A lightly flavoured paste, packed into small pots and served as a starter or with high tea, accompanied with toast.

1 lb lamb liver
1 finely chopped onion
1 crushed clove garlic
4 oz bacon fat
5 fl oz red wine
2½ fl oz cream
¼ teaspoon each, ground black pepper and rosemary
Salt
2 oz clarified butter

Clean the liver carefully, cutting away any gristle and sinew. Fry the liver, onion and garlic in the bacon fat for 10 minutes, remove from the pan and pass twice through a fine mincer. Put the wine in the frying pan and boil to reduce by about half. Set aside to cool.

Mix the liver with the cream and reduced wine; season with pepper, rosemary and salt and pot in individual dishes. Press until cold, then cover with clarified butter.

Potted Marbled Veal (8—10 portions) F and H

The marbled effect in this paste is achieved by setting small knobs of minced smoked ox tongue against layers of minced veal. Serve with hot toast.

1½ lb stewing veal
½ lb smoked ox tongue

4 oz butter
½ teaspoon each ground mace and nutmeg
Salt and pepper
½ pt white stock
4 oz clarified butter

Oven: 325°F; gas mark 3; 1½—2 hours

Soak the ox tongue overnight, drain and boil until tender. Skin the tongue and remove any bone and gristle, cut it into thin slices and pound or mince to a paste with half the butter. Mince the veal and pound with the remaining butter; mix in mace, nutmeg and salt and pepper to taste.

Put a layer of veal in a potting dish; roll small knobs of the tongue paste and set on the veal; cover with another layer of veal and continue with these layers finishing with veal. Pour over the stock and bake in the oven for about 2 hours.

Remove from the oven, cover with a weighted board and leave to press for about 8 hours. Remove any fat from the surface of the veal and cover with clarified butter.

Potted Ox Tongue

A smooth, piquant paste of pickled ox tongue, packed in small pots and served as a first course with hot toast.

2 lb pickled ox tongue
½ teaspoon ground mace
¼ teaspoon each, ground nutmeg, cloves and
    cayenne
Salt
5 fl oz red wine
4 oz clarified butter

Soak the tongue for 2—3 hours, drain and put in a pan; cover with water and boil gently for 2 hours. Skin the tongue, trim the root and remove any gristle. Mince the meat finely two or three times; blend in mace, nutmeg, cloves, cayenne and salt to taste. Moisten with wine and pack into pots; cover with clarified butter.

Potted Pigeons (6—8 portions) H and F

Made of pigeon meat and flavoured with port and brandy, this coarse paste makes a good luncheon dish, with a green salad and chunks of fresh wholemeal bread.

3 pigeons
1 lb fat pork

1 crushed clove garlic
Pinch thyme or marjoram
6 juniper berries
Salt and pepper
2 tablespoons port
2 tablespoons brandy
4 oz clarified butter

Oven: 300°F; gas mark 2; 1½—2½ hours

Clean and joint the pigeons, put in a pan and cover
with water. Bring to the boil and simmer gently for
20—30 minutes; strip the pigeon meat from the
bones and cut into thin slices. Mince the pork
fat and mix with the garlic, thyme, juniper berries
and salt and pepper to taste. Stir in the brandy and
port.

   Put layers of pork and pigeon in a potting dish,
repeating the layers and finishing with pigeon.
Cover with foil and bake for 1½—2½ hours or until
the pigeon is tender. Remove the foil, cover with
clarified butter and leave to cool.

Potted Pork (6 portions) F and H

Crusty bread and a watercress salad are the usual
accompaniments with this inexpensive, coarse-
textured paste, potted in small dishes. Suitable
for a first course or for high tea.

1 lb lean pork shoulder
1 lb belly pork
¼ teaspoon each, ground mace and pepper
Salt
1 crushed clove garlic
6—8 juniper berries
5 fl oz white wine
4 oz clarified butter

Oven: 325°F; gas mark 3; 1½ hours

Chop the boned shoulder of pork into small pieces;
remove bones, rind and fat from the belly pork
and chop up the meat. Mix the pork and belly
pork and pack tightly into small pots, seasoning
with mace, pepper, salt, garlic and juniper berries.

   Pour over the wine, cover with foil and bake in
the oven for about 1½ hours. Remove from the
oven and press the meat under a heavy weight until
cold. Cover with clarified butter.

Potted Rabbit (6—8 portions) F and H

Made with diced, cooked rabbit and belly pork,
this potted meat is of coarse consistency. The

meat is easiest removed from the bones if the
cleaned rabbit is wrapped in foil and cooked in
the oven at 350°F, gas mark 4, for 30 minutes.
Reserve the liquid from the roasting tin.

1½ lb rabbit meat
1 lb belly pork
1 crushed clove garlic
¼ teaspoon each, ground allspice, mace and
   cayenne
Salt and pepper
1 sprig thyme
2 tablespoons brandy
4 oz clarified butter

Oven: 325°F; gas mark 3; 2 hours

Dice the rabbit meat and trim the belly pork of
bones, rind and gristle; cut the meat into small
pieces. Layer the rabbit meat and belly pork in a
potting dish and season each layer with garlic,
allspice, mace, cayenne, salt and pepper. Add the
thyme and pour the reserved liquid and brandy
over the meat. Cover with foil and bake in the
oven until tender.

   Press the meat under a heavy weight before
covering with clarified butter. Serve when cold
and set.

Potted Veal and Ham (6—8 portions) H and F

Light and smooth in flavour and texture and
excellent for a starter with hot toast or as a
sandwich filling.

¾ lb veal
¾ lb lean ham
½ lb pork fat
¼ teaspoon each, ground mace, nutmeg and pepper
Salt
½ pt white stock
2 tablespoons brandy
4 oz clarified butter

Oven: 325°F; gas mark 3; 2 hours

Put the veal, ham and pork fat through the fine
blade of a mincer two or three times. Season with
mace, nutmeg, pepper and salt and pound the
meat mixture to a smooth paste before blending
in the stock and brandy.

   Pack into one large or several small potting
dishes and bake in the oven for 2 hours. Remove
and leave to cool, then cover with clarified butter.

Venison Paste (8—10 portions) F and H

A strongly flavoured smooth game paste, packed
in individual pots and served as a first course with
toast and a watercress and orange salad.

1 lb shoulder of venison
½ lb gammon or ham
4 oz butter
8 fl oz claret
1 crushed clove garlic
Mace, salt, pepper, ground thyme and marjoram
4 oz clarified butter

Oven: 300°F; gas mark 2; 2—3 hours

Remove bones and gristle from the venison and
chop the meat and gammon roughly. Put in an
ovenproof dish with half the butter and half the
wine; cook in the oven for 2—3 hours or until the
venison is quite tender.

Mince the venison and gammon mixture twice;
pound until smooth with spices, herbs and seasoning to taste. Blend in the remaining wine and
softened butter to give a smooth, dropping
consistency. Pack into pots and cover with
clarified butter.

Potted Venison (6—8 portions) F and H

This is similar to venison paste, but has a coarser
texture; use breast or shoulder of well-hung
venison to bring out the gamey flavour.

1½ lb venison
½ lb belly pork
1 crushed clove garlic
¼ teaspoon each, ground mace and pepper
Salt
Sprig thyme and marjoram
5 fl oz claret
4 oz clarified butter

Oven. 325°F; gas mark 3; 2 hours

Cut the boned venison and belly pork into dice
and pack in layers into a potting dish; sprinkle
each layer with garlic, mace, pepper and salt and
lay the herb sprigs on top. Pour the claret over the
meat, cover closely with foil and bake in the oven
for at least 2 hours or until tender.

Remove the foil and herb sprigs and set a
weighted board over the potted meat, leaving it to
press for 2—3 hours. Cover with clarified butter
and serve when cold and set.

BRAWNS, GALANTINES AND JELLIES

Brawns are extensions of the potted meat concept,
but packed into moulds, turned out and often, in
former days, richly decorated and garnished. The
texture varies according to the preparation of the
ingredients, from whole joints of poultry and
game, to roughly chopped or finely minced meat.
In addition, some brawn dishes have a jelly-like
texture when they are made with bones of a high
gelatinous content.

Galantines or galyntynes, possibly Roman in
origin, belong to the oldest known dishes in the
British Isles. They were originally flavoured with
the spice galingale (a species of sedge) and were
popular at medieval banquets and feasts. Basically,
a galantine consists of whole poultry or game bird
carefully boned in such a way that the skin remains
unbroken and the bird retains its shape. The
galantine is stuffed with seasoned meat, eggs,
truffles, nuts, etc., cooked and usually served cold,
decorated with aspic. Meat is sometimes used for
fake galantines, the mixture being shaped as a roll.

Ayrshire Galantine (6—8 portions) F and H Scotland

This is a meat galantine of bacon and beef; it is
covered with aspic and served cold as a main
course with salads.

1 lb Ayrshire bacon
1 lb lean shoulder of beef
½ lb breadcrumbs
½ teaspoon each, ground nutmeg and mace
Salt and pepper
2 eggs
White stock
1 chopped onion
2 chopped carrots
2 small chopped turnips
2 parsley sprigs
Aspic

Remove any gristle and rind from the bacon and
beef and put both through the mincer. Blend
the minced meat thoroughly with breadcrumbs
and season with nutmeg and mace, salt and pepper
to taste. Beat the eggs and add to the mixture with
sufficient stock to moisten. Turn on to a floured
board and shape into a roll. Tie securely in a
floured pudding cloth.

Place the roll in a pan with boiling water and add the vegetables and parsley. Cover and simmer gently for 2 hours; remove from the pan and untie the cloth. Press the galantine overnight beneath a heavy weight. Glaze the galantine with well-flavoured aspic and serve when set.

Brawn (8–12 portions) F and H

Brawn, which correctly means a fleshy muscle, was originally made from a pig's head and trotters; in the Middle Ages brawns were made from boars' heads and frequently used as centrepieces, heavily decorated with piped creams, glazes and gilding. During the following centuries, other types of meat were used for brawns; in Wales and North England, cow heel brawn, sometimes with tripe, was a popular dish and used to be sold from market stalls. The Tonbridge Brawn, made with pig's head, trotters and ears, was particularly heavily spiced and more solid in texture than ordinary brawn.

Sheep or calf's head may also be used for brawns, the trotters being replaced by diced bacon in a sheep head brawn and omitted completely in a calf's head brawn.

1 pig's head
2 trotters
12 peppercorns
1–2 blades mace
1 bay leaf
4 cloves
Sprig each, parsley, thyme and sage
Salt and pepper
6 oz roughly chopped onions
2 hardboiled eggs

Split the head in half, remove the brains and clean the nostrils and teeth by brushing with salt; rinse, blanch and refresh the head. Soak the head in brine for 3–5 days, using 2 oz salt to 1 pt water.

Clean the head and trotters thoroughly, cover with cold water and bring to the boil; tie the peppercorns, mace, bay leaf, cloves and herbs in muslin and add to the pan with salt and pepper. Simmer, covered, until tender, after about 4 hours. Lift out the head and trotters, remove the tongue and slice. Remove all the meat from the bones and cut into dice. Place the bones in a pan with 2 pt of the cooking liquid, the onions and seasoning and simmer for 1 hour.

Strain this stock and reduce to 1 pint. Wet a mould and line with slices of tongue and hard-boiled eggs; fill the mould with diced meat. Pour the reduced stock into the mould and leave to cool and set. When cool put a weight over the mould and leave in a cold place for about 24 hours.

To serve, turn out from the mould, cut into slices and accompany with Oxford Brawn Sauce.

Chicken Brawn (6–8 portions) H and F
Cheshire

Brawns were served as a breakfast dish in Victorian days, but even this light delicate chicken brawn would today be more acceptable as a first course or a main dish for a cold luncheon.

3½ lb boiling fowl or chicken
2 pig trotters
Salt and pepper
Mixed herbs
Scrumpy or dry bottled cider
2 hardboiled eggs
Garnish: Watercress

Oven: 300°F; gas mark 2; 4 hours

Place the trussed fowl in a pan with the trotters, salt, pepper and mixed herbs. Cover with cider or water and bring to the boil. Remove to the oven, cover and cook for 4 hours. Strain the stock and leave the chicken and trotters to cool.

Strip the meat from the chicken and trotters, chop finely and correct seasoning if necessary. Return the meat to the liquid and heat through. Line a wetted mould with sliced hardboiled eggs, pour in the meat and stock, pressing down well. Leave to cool, then press under a weight for several hours. Turn out when set and garnish with sprigs of watercress.

Jellied Chitterlings (6 portions) F
Warwickshire

The small intestines and other parts of pig entrails are known as chitterlings. They are here set in a mould with jellied and aspic stock, turned out and served with a jug of vinegar. In County Durham, onions accompany the chitterlings.

1½ lb pig's fry
Salt and pepper
Fresh sage
1 oz aspic

Place the prepared pig's fry in a pan, cover with water and add salt, pepper and a few sage leaves.

When the fry is thoroughly cooked, remove from the pan, cut up finely and arrange in a mould.

Strain the stock and reduce to 1 pint. Mix the aspic with a little stock, blend into the stock and pour over the meat. Leave to set.

Jellied Pigeons (6—8 portions) F and H

This is an unusual, highly tasty dish of cold pigeons, set in a rich game jelly. It is served cold, complete with the top seal of butter.

3 young pigeons
Salt and pepper
Sprigs of tarragon
4 oz butter
5 fl oz red wine or sherry
Game stock
Garnish: parsley sprigs

Oven: 325°F; gas mark 3; 2 hours

Clean the pigeons thoroughly, sprinkle inside with salt and pepper and stuff with a sprig of tarragon and a few knobs of butter. Pack the pigeons into an ovenproof dish, add wine, the rest of the butter and enough game stock to cover.

Cover the dish tightly with foil and a lid and cook in the oven for 2 hours or until the birds are tender. If necessary, top up with more stock so that the pigeons are completely covered in liquid throughout cooking. Leave the pigeons until cold and the butter has risen and formed a seal. Garnish with parsley before serving.

Jellied Pig's Tongue (6—8 portions) F

Pig's ears as well as tongue can be used for a jellied mould and flavoured with thyme instead of ginger.

2 lb salted pig's tongues
2 pig trotters
6 oz roughly chopped onions
Juice of 1 lemon
1 bay leaf
8 crushed peppercorns
Pinch ginger

Wash the tongues and trotters thoroughly, place in a pan with cold water and bring to the boil; skim and simmer for 1½ hours; after the first 30 minutes, drain off the water and replace with fresh boiling water. Add the onions, lemon juice, bay leaf, peppercorns and ginger; simmer for a further

30 minutes or until the tongues are tender.

Remove the tongues and trotters, leave to cool; skin and trim the tongues removing all small bones and muscles from the root end of the tongues. Strip the meat from the trotters.

Pack the tongues and trotter meat into a wetted mould or basin. Skim the liquid and strain over the tongues to cover. Place a plate slightly smaller than the mould on top and press under a heavy weight until cold.

Oxtail Brawn (6—8 portions) F and H

Serve this rich brawn as a cold luncheon dish with salad, or with hot toast as a first course.

2 jointed oxtails
Salt
6 oz roughly chopped onions
1 sprig each, thyme and parsley
12 peppercorns
2 blades mace
4 cloves

Soak the jointed oxtails in warm water for 1 hour; drain, cover with fresh water and add salt, the onions, thyme, parsley, and the peppercorns, mace and cloves tied in muslin. Bring to the boil, skim and simmer gently for 5 hours or until the meat falls from the bones. Strain off the liquid and reduce to 1 pint.

Remove all the meat from the bones and cut into small pieces. Arrange in a large or several small wetted moulds. Cool the reduced stock and remove the fat from the surface. Pour the stock over the meat in the mould and leave to set before turning out.

Rabbit Brawn (8—12 portions) F and H Gloucestershire

This brawn may also be made with hare; have both animals cleaned and jointed before cooking, and serve the brawn turned out of its mould, accompanied with lettuce, cucumber and pickles.

2½—3 lb rabbit
4 oz sliced carrots
½ lb sliced onions
Salt and pepper
Pinch each ground nutmeg and cloves
Sprig thyme
2 hardboiled eggs
2 oz gelatine

Cover the jointed rabbit with water, add the carrots, onions, salt, pepper, nutmeg, cloves and thyme. **Bring to the boil and simmer until the meat is tender, after about 2 hours.** Remove the meat from the bones and cut into small pieces; arrange in a wetted mould with slices of hard-boiled eggs as decoration.

Reduce the strained cooking liquid to 2 pints by rapid boiling; season to taste and mix with the gelatine. Strain over the meat and leave to set.

Veal and Ham Mould (8 portions) F and H

This veal and ham loaf is probably a development of a much earlier Ham Cake, traditional to Ongar in Essex. This consisted of minced ham thickened with bread soaked in ale, the seasoned mixture being bound with eggs.

1 lb stewing veal
1 lb ham or bacon
1 teaspoon roughly chopped parsley
Grated rind of ½ lemon
¼ teaspoon ground mace
Salt and pepper
4 hardboiled eggs
½ pt white stock

Oven: 325°F; gas mark 3; 2 hours

Chop the veal and ham roughly and mix with the parsley, lemon rind, mace and salt and pepper. Arrange alternate layers of meat and sliced hard-boiled eggs in a greased 1 lb loaf tin. Fill up with stock, cover with foil and bake in a pan of water in the oven for 2 hours.

Leave to get completely cold; turn out the following day and serve the mould cut into slices.

Venison and Pork Galantine (8—10 portions) H and F

A type of mould rather than a true galantine; the origin of this dish goes back to the 14th century when the venison meat would probably be supplemented with meat from wild boar.

2 lb thick flank of venison
4 oz gammon or ham
½ lb pork sausage meat or minced pork
1 large clove garlic
Sprig each, thyme and marjoram
2 black peppercorns
Salt and pepper
2 hardboiled eggs

Bone the venison and cut away any gristle. Cube the gammon and mix with the sausage meat and crushed garlic. Put the venison bones in a pan, cover with 2 pt of water and add thyme and marjoram, peppercorns and salt.

Place the boned venison on a board and spread over it half the sausage meat mixture, top with the sliced hardboiled eggs, season with salt and pepper and lay the remaining sausage meat over the egg slices. Roll the venison up carefully and tie in a floured pudding cloth. Place in the strained venison stock and simmer gently for 3—4 hours.

Leave the roll to cool in the liquid, then remove from the stock, take off the cloth and put the galantine in a dish that just fits it. Place a heavy weight on top of the galantine and press for several hours.

Vegetables

Wealthy barons of medieval days often consumed meat and game at the rate of 2—3 lb a day while the poor had to rely on vegetables to eke out expensive and scarce flesh foods. Onions, leeks, garlic and cabbage were then the most common vegetables, dried peas, beans and other lentils also being popular. With the passage of time, the variety of vegetables grew as they were introduced from other countries, but almost the opposite is true of herbs. The herb garden was an essential feature of early religious houses, and the number of varieties grown far exceeded the few that are common today. Herbs were vital to the cook, and a working knowledge of their uses was a pre-requisite of his or her ability.

Market gardening as such did not develop until towns began to expand in the 18th and 19th centuries and was then mainly confined to South England. Distinct regional vegetable dishes rarely developed, possibly due to a prejudice against fresh vegetables. They were regarded as additions to homely broths and stews, and the habit of subjecting fresh vegetables to prolonged boiling in water is largely responsible for the shortage of memorable vegetable dishes.

The few exceptions to the lack of regional vegetable dishes include potatoes, leeks and sea-weeds. The long social and economic history of the potato dates back to the 16th century when it began to achieve its position as a staple item of diet. There is substantial evidence in the patterns of potato dishes throughout the country to show to what extent it was accepted or rejected. In Ireland, where the potato was first grown, dependence on this vital food developed to such a degree that when the potato famine struck in 1846—47 its catastrophic consequences resulted in widespread death from starvation. The North of England, Lancashire, Scotland and Wales readily adopted the potato although these regions never placed as heavy a dependence on it as did the Irish. It was nearly a hundred years after the introduction of the potato before it was generally accepted in South England where it was long considered fit only for animal fodder.

Leeks and onions, which were the original vegetables, have become integrated in the national diet, but leeks also appear frequently in some regional dishes. There seems to be some correlation between this strongly flavoured vegetable and mining areas, leek dishes being particular to such areas as Tyne Tees, South Wales and Cornwall.

Seaweed dishes also illustrate regional uses, but principally pinpoint a shortage of fertile land and a need for utilising all edible types of food. They occur in the poorer areas of Britain, along the coastal stretches of Wales, Ireland, Scotland and the Highland Islands.

ASPARAGUS

In season only from May to early July, there are two types of English asparagus: the fat green asparagus from Norfolk, Sussex and Essex, and the thinner stems from the Vale of Evesham.

The dish, known as Tod Heatley's Asparagus consists of cooked, iced asparagus arranged in small bunches, wrapped with strips of fresh lettuce and covered with green mayonnaise or with double cream mixed with a little aspic jelly.

Asparagus Points or Pease (6—8 portions) H

1½ lb asparagus
2 oz melted butter
2 oz caster sugar
Salt and pepper

Wash the points and tender green parts of the asparagus; put into a pan of lightly salted boiling water and cook gently for 5—8 minutes or until almost cooked. Drain well and put in a clean pan with melted butter, sugar and pepper. Fry gently for a few minutes before serving.

BEANS, BROAD

Best when quite young and pale green when the
whole pods may be sliced and boiled with mint or
parsley for about 8 minutes. Broad beans were
sometimes known as Windsor beans.

Windsor Bean Pudding (6—8 portions)

1 lb boiled broad beans
Salt and pepper
2 egg yolks
1 oz butter
2 oz white breadcrumbs
2 tablespoons single cream

Pound the boiled beans to a paste in a mortar or
blend in a liquidiser. Season to taste with salt and
pepper, add the egg yolks, softened butter and the
breadcrumbs soaked in the cream. Tie the mixture
in a floured cloth, place in boiling water and boil
for 30 minutes. Squeeze out the water by pressing
the cloth, and serve.

Alternatively, bake the pudding for 30 minutes
in the oven at 350°F (gas mark 4).

BEETROOT

Small globe varieties, in season during early
summer are the tastiest. Wash carefully so as not
to break the skin, causing the beetroot to bleed.

Baked Beetroot (8 portions) F

8 beetroot (4—6 oz each)

Oven: 350°F; gas mark 4; 1—3 hours

Wrap the cleaned beetroots in greaseproof paper or
foil. Set on a baking tray and bake in the centre of
the oven for 1—3 hours according to size and age
of the beetroot. To test for tenderness, press the
beetroot with a finger, and if the skin pulls off
easily they are ready.

Fried Beetroot (6—8 portions) F

1½—2 lb cooked beetroot
3—4 oz butter
Salt and pepper
2 tablespoons vinegar

Peel the cooked beetroot and cut into ¼ in thick
slices. Fry in the butter for 5—10 minutes, turning
the slices several times. Sprinkle with salt and
pepper and arrange on a serving dish. Add the
vinegar and the same amount of water to the
frying pan, stir up the residues, bring to the boil
and pour over the beetroot.

BROCCOLI

Introduced to Britain in the 17th century, the
sprouting form has achieved popularity only
during the second half of the 20th century.

Broccoli Pasty (8 portions) F and H

2 lb sprouting broccoli
1 lb savoury shortcrust pastry
Salt and pepper

Oven: 375°F; gas mark 5; 30—45 minutes

Divide the broccoli into sprigs and cook in lightly
salted water for 4—5 minutes or until still slightly
hard. Roll out the pastry and cut into eight
rounds. Arrange the cooled broccoli sprigs over
the pastry, sprinkle with pepper and draw up the
pastry to small pasties. Bake in the oven and serve
hot or cold.

CABBAGES

There are several types of cabbages; winter
cabbages include varieties of green cabbage, round
and firm and in season from September to
February. Drumhead winter cabbages are large
and white, hard and excellent shredded in
winter salads; season August to November. Bright
green, crinkled Savoy cabbage is available from
December onwards and a good accompaniment to
boiled bacon. Spring cabbage or spring greens
continue until July and have bright green loose
leaves. The firm red cabbage is in season chiefly
from November to February and goes particularly
well with all rich meats, such as pork, duck, goose
and hare.

Spiced Cabbage (8 portions) F

2 lb winter cabbage
4 oz grated onions

4 oz grated cooked apples
1 oz butter
½ teaspoon ground cinnamon

Prepare and shred the cabbage, boil in a little salted water for 7 minutes, or until still crisp. Drain thoroughly and keep hot. Fry the onions and apples in the butter until soft, sprinkle with cinnamon and blend into the cabbage. Toss over the heat and serve hot.

Stewed Cabbage (8 portions) F

1 medium-sized winter cabbage
½ pt white stock
1 oz butter
1 quartered onion
4 allspice berries

Shred the cabbage and put in a pan with the boiling stock, butter, onion and allspice tied in muslin. Simmer until the cabbage is tender and nearly all the liquid has evaporated. Drain thoroughly, remove the onion and spices and serve at once.

Stuffed Cabbage (8 portions) F

1 medium-sized winter cabbage
½ lb bacon or ham forcemeat
2 oz melted butter

Oven: 350°F; gas mark 4; 35 minutes

Remove the outer large leaves of the cleaned cabbage without breaking them. Divide the forcemeat into eight portions and wrap in the leaves; secure with skewers or tie with string.

Arrange the cabbage rolls in a well-buttered ovenproof dish; brush with butter, cover with foil and bake in the oven.

Cabbage with Milk (6—8 portions) F

1 medium-sized white cabbage
½ pt milk
4 oz butter
Salt and pepper
1 egg

Prepare and shred the cabbage; put in a pan with the milk, half the butter and salt and pepper to taste. Simmer slowly, covered with a lid, for 15 minutes, being careful not to let it burn. Drain the cabbage and set the milk aside. Toss the cabbage in the remaining butter and keep warm.

Beat the egg and place in a double saucepan with the milk; stir until it thickens. Pour over the cabbage and serve immediately.

Devonshire Stew (8 portions) F Devon

2 lb mashed potatoes
1 lb shredded boiled cabbage
1 lb boiled chopped onions
Salt and pepper
3 oz butter

Mix the potatoes, cabbage and onions and season thoroughly with salt and pepper. Melt the butter in a large frying pan, add the vegetable mixture and brown well, turning frequently until the mixture is heated through.

Stewed Red Cabbage (6—8 portions) F and H

Firm red cabbage may be cooked like winter cabbage in lightly salted boiling water (add lemon juice or vinegar to the water to prevent staining of the pan), or boiled in bacon stock to be served with a boiled bacon joint. May also be cooked as spiced white cabbage.

1 medium-sized red cabbage
1 oz butter
½ pt white stock
2½ fl oz white wine vinegar
¾ lb finely chopped or grated cooking apples
1—2 tablespoons brown sugar

Oven: 350°F; gas mark 4; 1 hour

Place the finely shredded cabbage in an earthenware dish, with the butter, stock and vinegar. Cover with a lid and cook in the oven until tender and soft; stir in the apples and sugar halfway through cooking. Serve with rich, roast meats.

CARROTS

One of the most commonly used vegetables, carrots are added to stocks, soups and stews for flavouring and also served as a separate vegetable dish. Young carrots, available June to August, are sold in bundles with leaves attached while the larger maincrop carrots are sold loose.

Carrots and Turnips in Brown Sauce (6—8 portions) Lancashire

1 lb carrots
1 lb turnip
Pepper
Brown sauce

Prepare the carrots and turnips and boil in lightly salted water for 20 minutes. Drain and use the water to make a brown sauce. Season the vegetables with pepper; dice and arrange in a hot dish; pour over the sauce and serve with buttered toast.

Fried Carrots (6 portions) H and F

1½ lb young carrots
1 oz seasoned flour
1 egg
2 oz white breadcrumbs
2—3 oz butter

Cut off the green tops and scrape the skin off the carrots, leaving them whole. Par-boil for about 10 minutes, drain and dry on a cloth. Coat the carrots with seasoned flour, dip in the beaten egg and coat with breadcrumbs. Fry in hot butter until golden.

CAULIFLOWER

Good quality cauliflower should be creamy-white and have a firm head of tight unblemished florets. Clean in acidulated water to preserve the white colour.

Cauliflower in Batter (6 portions) H and F

1 medium-sized cauliflower
½ pt yeast batter
Fat for frying

Clean the cauliflower and divide into sprigs. Boil in lightly salted water for about 3 minutes; drain on a cloth. Dip the sprigs in coating batter and deep-fry in hot fat until crisp and golden-brown; drain and serve immediately.

CELERIAC

Also known as turnip-rooted celery, this root vegetable is in fact larger than turnip and has a distinct celery flavour. It is a winter vegetable and may be used raw, finely chopped in winter salads, or served as a cooked vegetable dish. The leaves may be used to flavour stocks and soups in place of celery.

Celeriac Purée (6—8 portions) H and F

1½ lb celeriac
½ lb potatoes
2 oz butter
Double cream
Salt and pepper

Peel the celeriac and cut into slices; simmer in lightly salted water until almost tender; add the potatoes and finish cooking together. Drain off the liquid and rub the vegetables through a sieve.

Put the pulp in a pan with the butter and stir well; add enough cream to give a smooth texture. Heat through, season with salt and pepper and serve hot, with venison, pheasant; partridge or hare. Gravy from the meat may be added to the pulp with the cream.

CELERY

Available most of the year from either homegrown or imported crops. The crisp stems are used raw or cooked, and leaves and seeds can flavour stocks, soups, sauces and chutneys.

Braised Celery with Apple (6—8 portions) H and F

2 heads celery
1 lb cooking apples
8 cloves
2 oz sugar
2 lb streaky bacon (16 rashers)
Salt and pepper

Oven: 350°F; gas mark 4; 1½ hours

Wash the apples, leave whole and cook to a pulp in a little water. Add the cloves and sugar, stir well and rub the pulp through a sieve. Cover the base of a deep casserole dish with half the bacon and top with the apple pulp.

Cut the cleaned celery into 3—4 in lengths and arrange them upright in the apples. Sprinkle with salt and pepper. Arrange the remaining bacon on top, cover with a lid and bake in the oven for 1½ hours.

Celery Cheese (6 portions) Northumberland

2 heads celery
Milk
Salt and pepper
6 oz grated Cheddar cheese
2 eggs
1—2 oz white breadcrumbs

Oven: 350°F; gas mark 4; 10—15 minutes

Clean the celery and grate the sticks finely, put in a pan with enough milk to barely cover. Add salt and pepper and simmer until tender, after about 10—15 minutes. Leave to cool, then mix in the cheese and beaten eggs. Place in a greased pie dish, cover with breadcrumbs and bake until brown.

CUCUMBERS

Introduced in the 16th century and originally known as cowcumbers, cucumbers reached their height of popularity in Victorian times. Today, cucumbers are chiefly used as a raw salad vegetable, but they can also be served as a vegetable dish with steaks and roast lamb.

Dressed Cucumber (6—8 portions) H and F

1 lb peeled, diced or thinly sliced cucumber
½ lb finely chopped onions
Pinch cayenne
1 tablespoon chilli vinegar
5 fl oz sherry or Madeira
Grated rind and juice of 1 lemon

Arrange the sliced or diced cucumber mixed with the onions in a serving dish. Sprinkle with cayenne and lemon rind; mix well. Blend the vinegar with the sherry and lemon juice and pour over the cucumber; leave to steep for at least 10 minutes before serving with roast meat, cold salmon or pickled fish.

Stuffed Cucumbers (8 portions) H and F·

2 lb cucumbers
½ lb bacon or ham stuffing
½ pt white stock

Oven: 350°F; gas mark 4; 30—40 minutes

Peel the cucumbers and cut into 2½—3 in lengths. Remove the seeds with the handle of a spoon and fill the cavities with stuffing. Stand the stuffed cucumber pieces upright in a baking tin, pour the stock round and cover the tin with foil or grease-proof paper; bake in the oven for 30—40 minutes.

GLOBE ARTICHOKES

Until the 20th century, globe artichokes were a common vegetable, the bases or fonds in particular being used to flavour stews and pies. Today, globe artichokes are usually served as a separate first course, hot or cold, either the whole artichoke with the central choke removed or the fond only.

Globe Artichoke Tart (8 portions) H and F

8 artichoke bottoms
½ lb savoury shortcrust pastry
½ lb chopped onions
¼ teaspoon sweet herbs
1 tablespoon tarragon vinegar
Salt and pepper
Pinch nutmeg
½ pt white sauce
2 egg yolks

Oven: 400°F; gas mark 6; 30 minutes

Clean the artichokes, boil and remove all leaves and the choke, leaving the fonds whole. Line an 8 in flan ring set on a baking sheet with three quarters of the pastry. Arrange the artichoke fonds and the onions over the pastry and sprinkle with the chopped herbs.

Add the vinegar, salt, pepper and nutmeg to the white sauce; cool and beat in the egg yolks. Pour this sauce into the pie, cover with a pastry lid and bake until well browned. Serve with beef.

JERUSALEM ARTICHOKES

This root vegetable is a member of the Sunflower family and takes its name from the Italian word for this plant, *Girasole*. The knobbly white variety is the one most frequently seen, from October to April.

Buttered Jerusalem Artichokes (6—8 portions) H and F

2 lb Jerusalem artichokes
3 oz butter

Salt and pepper
Garnish: 1 tablespoon chopped parsley

Peel and blanch the artichokes. Melt the butter in
a pan, add the artichokes and toss well. Cover the
pan with a lid and cook over low heat for 15
minutes, shaking the pan occasionally. Sprinkle
with salt and pepper and garnish with parsley.

Jerusalem Artichoke Hot-Pot (6—8 portions) F and H

2 lb Jerusalem artichokes
1¼ lb streaky bacon rashers
½ lb chopped leeks
½ pt white stock
Salt and pepper
1 oz butter
¾ oz flour

Oven: 400°F; gas mark 6; 1 hour

Peel the artichokes and leave in acidulated water.
Fry half the bacon it its own fat until crisp, cut
in half and arrange over the base of a casserole
dish. Fill up the dish with the drained, sliced
artichokes and chopped leeks, including the fresh
green parts. Add the stock, season with salt and
pepper; cover and bake in the oven for 1 hour.

Drain off the stock. Melt the butter in a pan
and stir in the flour; gradually add the stock and
bring to the boil. Roll up the remaining bacon
rashers and fry or grill. Pour the thickened stock
over the vegetables and garnish with bacon rolls.

KALE

This hardy winter vegetable with crisp curly leaves
is little grown and used outside Ireland and
Scotland where it is known as kail and a popular
vegetable with strongly flavoured and salted meats.

Colcannon (6—8 portions) F Ireland

This is a traditional dish at Hallowe'en in Ireland
and left-overs may be fried and served again. In
England, Colcannon is sometimes known as Bubble
and Squeak, but this dish properly contains meat.
In the Scottish Highlands, Colcannon sometimes
includes cooked carrots and turnips, and the cream
is omitted. In Aberdeenshire and North-East
Scotland, Colcannon is known as "Kailkenny",
and in the Border areas as "Rumbledethumps"

when cream is excluded but the amount of butter
increased; it is sometimes covered with grated
cheese and baked in the oven.

1 lb kale (or cabbage)
1 lb potatoes
2 finely chopped leeks or onion tops
5 fl oz milk or cream
Salt, pepper and pinch mace
4 oz melted butter

Wash and shred the kale or cabbage; boil in salted
water for 15—20 minutes, drain, chop finely and
keep warm. Boil the prepared potatoes and leeks
in the milk; mash and season with salt, pepper and
mace. Mix in the kale, heat thoroughly and put
into a deep dish.

Make a well in the centre and pour in the
butter. When serving, a spoonful of the butter is
served with each portion of colcannon.

Kale Brose (6 portions) F Scotland

There are several versions of this dish which used
to be served as a complete meal. Basically, they all
consist of kale cooked in stock and thickened
with oatmeal, barley or rice. "Tartan Purry" is
another name for kale brose and is a corruption of
the French *Tarte en purée*.

1 lb kale
1 oz oatmeal, barley or rice
3 pt stock (brown or game)
Salt and pepper
2 oz chopped onions, carrots and turnips (optional)

Cook the oatmeal, barley or rice in the stock for
30 minutes; season with salt and pepper and add
the kale, the onions, carrots and turnips if used.
Simmer for a further 30 minutes. Serve with hot
oatcakes as an accompaniment to meat dishes.

LAVER

This is an edible seaweed, now mainly restricted to
Wales, the South West and the Cumberland coasts.
The purple or true laver is known as Sloke in
Ireland and Scotland. Laver is available already
cooked, boiled down to a pulp; fresh laver should
be gathered at low tide and washed thoroughly in
sea water. Other edible seaweeds include Irish Sea
Moss (Carageen Moss in Scotland) and dulce
which is found mainly on the Scottish coasts.

Laver Bread (6—8 portions) F Wales

Laver bread and bacon (*Bara Lawr*) is a popular breakfast dish; laver cakes can also be served with grilled meat.

1 lb fresh laver
1 lb oatmeal
Salt and pepper
3—4 oz bacon fat

Soak the laver in sea water for a few hours to remove salt and sand. Simmer in hot water for several hours, until tender, breaking the laver up with a wooden spoon. Mix the pulp with oatmeal, salt and pepper to taste. Shape into small cakes, ½ in thick, dust with oatmeal and fry in bacon fat.

Laver Salad (6 portions) F Ireland

1 lb cooked laver
Salt and pepper
Olive oil
White wine vinegar

Season the cold cooked laver with salt and pepper; blend in oil and vinegar to taste. Serve as an appetiser with hot buttered toast.

Laver with Mashed Potatoes (6—8 portions) F

1 lb cooked laver
1 lb mashed potatoes
1 oz butter
Salt and pepper

Oven: 425°F; gas mark 7; 15—20 minutes

Butter a fireproof dish thoroughly; put a layer of potatoes over the base and cover with a layer of laver. Repeat these layers, sprinkling with salt and pepper, and finish with a layer of potatoes. Heat through in the oven until brown on top.

LEEKS

This vegetable has been cultivated for thousands of years; it is closely related to the onion but with a milder flavour. It is the national emblem of Wales and the traditional vegetable, and is also popular in Cornwall and the North-East.

Leek Porridge (6—8 portions) F Wales

12—18 even-sized leeks
Salt and pepper

Clean the leeks and boil in a small quantity of lightly salted water for 10—15 minutes or until tender, depending on size. Drain thoroughly and set the liquid aside.

Cut the leeks into thin slices, sprinkle with pepper and arrange in porridge plates; pour over a little of the cooking liquid and serve with fingers of hot toast.

Leek Pudding (8 portions) F Northumbria

3 lb leeks
2 lb savoury suet pastry
6 oz butter
Salt and pepper

Clean the leeks thoroughly and chop into small pieces. Line a 3 pt pudding basin with three quarters of the pastry, fill with leeks, dot with the butter and season with salt and pepper. Cover with the remaining pastry and tie down with buttered greaseproof paper or foil. Steam for 2 hours and serve with stews.

Leeky Stew with a Nackerjack (6—8 portions) F Devon

In South Devon, the local name for a dumpling is nackerjack; in the North it is spelled naggerjack.

1½ lb leeks
½ lb potatoes
½ lb streaky bacon (or pickled pork)
4 pt white stock
Salt and pepper
2 lb savoury suet pastry

Wash the leeks thoroughly, halve or quarter and cut into 3 in lengths. Put the leeks, diced potatoes, bacon and stock in a pan; season with salt and pepper. Bring to the boil and simmer for 1 hour.

Shape the suet pastry into one large dumpling or eight smaller ones. Place on top of the vegetables and simmer for another 30 minutes. To serve, place the vegetable stew in the centre of a dish and the dumplings round the edge.

LETTUCE: see Salad Vegetables

MARROW

Good marrows should be harvested when 9—12 in long and 3—4 in thick, before the seeds have had time to develop. Marrows are used as a vegetable, cooked in butter, for jams and chutneys and often stuffed and served as a complete dish.

Baked Stuffed Marrow (6—8 portions) F and H

1 marrow
6 oz forcemeat: cheese and tomato, ham or bacon, sausage meat or minced beef
1 oz melted butter

Oven: 350°F; gas mark 4; 1—1½ hours

Peel the marrow, cut in half lengthways and remove the seeds. Put the forcemeat into the two halves and put the halves together again. Place in a baking dish, brush with butter and cover with foil. Bake in the oven and serve with a tomato or brown sauce.

MUSHROOMS

These edible fungi are extensively used in cooking. Types include button, cup and flat mushrooms all of which should be used as soon as possible after gathering. The small young button mushrooms are attractive for garnishes, but lack the full flavour of the larger and darker flat mushrooms.

Mushrooms in Cream Sauce (6 portions) H and F

1 lb mushrooms
1 oz butter
½ oz flour
5 fl oz cream
Salt and pepper
Garnish: chopped parsley

Clean and trim the mushrooms and fry lightly in the butter. Stir in the flour and gradually add the cream. Season to taste with salt and pepper. Simmer for 5 minutes and serve with grilled meat or as a savoury on toast, sprinkled with finely chopped parsley.

Mushroom Pudding (6 portions) F

1 lb mushrooms

1 oz butter
1 teaspoon lemon juice
½ lb savoury suet pastry
Salt and pepper

Clean and trim the mushrooms and fry them gently in the butter; stir in the lemon juice. Line a 1½ pt pudding basin with three quarters of the suet pastry; fill the basin with mushrooms. Season with salt and pepper and cover with the remaining pastry. Tie down with greaseproof paper or foil and steam for 1½ hours. Serve with beef stews.

Stuffed Mushrooms (6 portions) H and F

1 lb large cup mushrooms
4 oz ham forcemeat
3 oz butter
Salt and pepper

Oven: 350°F; gas mark 4; 20 minutes

Clean the mushrooms, remove the stalks and set the cups, hollow side up, in a greased fireproof dish. Arrange the forcemeat equally in the mushrooms, dot with butter and season with salt and pepper. Bake in the oven until tender.

ONIONS

This root vegetable has a long history of culinary uses, as a flavouring and a separate vegetable dish. English maincrop onions vary from round bulbs with red-brown or pale skins to flat bulbs with light brown skins; there is little difference in the taste between these two while the large Spanish onions are milder. In addition to these main types, there are salad or spring onions, chiefly used in salads, small onions for pickling and the small shallots which have a slight garlic taste and are used for flavouring.

Baked Onions (8 portions) F and H

8 Spanish onions (6 oz each)
Salt and pepper
2 oz butter

Oven: 350°F; gas mark 4; 1—1½ hours

Place the onions, unpeeled, on a baking tray on a bed of coarse salt and bake for 1—1½ hours or until tender. Carefully peel off the outer skin, open up the top, sprinkle with salt and pepper and dot with butter. Serve at once.

Alternatively, peel and par-boil the onions, arrange round a roasting joint for the last hour of cooking and baste well.

In Devon, baked onions are eaten at tea or supper with bread and cheese.

Onion Cake (6—8 portions) F Wales

A traditional Welsh dish, known as *Teisen Nionod,* and served with hot or cold meats.

2 lb sliced potatoes
½ lb finely chopped onions
3 oz melted butter
Salt and pepper

Oven: 375°F; gas mark 5; 1 hour

Place a layer of potatoes over the base of a well greased 7 in cake tin. Sprinkle a layer of onions over the potatoes, brush with melted butter and season with salt and pepper. Continue with these layers, finishing with a layer of potatoes. Brush the top with butter, bake in the oven and turn out to serve.

Stuffed Onions (8 portions) F and H

8 medium-sized Spanish onions
½ lb forcemeat: veal, ham, sausage meat or cheese
Salt and pepper
Dripping

Oven: 350°F; gas mark 4; 1 hour

Par-boil the unpeeled onions for about 15 minutes; remove the skins and cut out the centre of each onion. Chop the removed onion finely and mix with the forcemeat; season with salt and pepper. Stuff the onions and set in a roasting tin with melted dripping. Bake for about 1 hour and serve.

PARSNIPS

This root vegetable is native to Britain and has been cultivated and eaten since earliest times. It was the traditional accompaniment to roast beef before the potato was introduced and was equally traditional with boiled salt cod on Ash Wednesday.

Parsnip Cakes (6—8 portions) F

2 lb boiled mashed parsnips

2 oz flour (approx.)
Salt and pepper
Pinch mace
2 oz melted butter
1—2 eggs
2 oz white breadcrumbs
Fat or dripping

Blend the flour into the mashed parsnips to make a workable dough; season with salt, pepper and mace and stir in the butter. Shape into round cakes, about ½ in thick; brush with beaten egg and coat firmly with breadcrumbs. Shallow-fry in hot fat until golden brown, turning once.

Parsnips, Potato and Bacon (6—8 portions) F

1 lb parsnips
1 lb potatoes
½ lb streaky bacon rashers
½ pt white stock
Salt and pepper

Oven: 350°F; gas mark 4; 1 hour

Peel the parsnips and potatoes; dice the parsnips and slice the potatoes thickly; chop the bacon. Arrange these ingredients in a buttered ovenproof dish, pour over enough stock to cover and season with salt and pepper. Cover the dish and bake in the oven until the vegetables are tender.

Equal quantities of mashed parsnips and potatoes can be mixed, creamed with butter or cream and heated through before serving with grilled or roast meat.

Parsnip Salad (6 portions) F and H

12—18 young parsnips
Lettuce leaves
½ pt salad sauce

Peel the parsnips thinly and cut into rings. Boil in lightly salted water until tender but still slightly crisp. Drain and leave to cool.

To serve, arrange lettuce leaves on a dish, coat the parsnip rings with salad sauce and set on the bed of lettuce.

POTATOES

This highly versatile root crop was introduced to Britain from South America in the 16th century.

It is a valuable source of starch and protein and a
staple food item in the national diet. Numerous
regional potato dishes have developed over the
centuries, notably in Ireland.

Angus Potatoes (8 portions) F and H Scotland

8 jacket baked potatoes
2 Arbroath smokies
Salt and pepper
6 oz butter
Milk

Flake the fish and remove any bones and skin.
Cut a slice from the top of each hot baked potato,
spoon out the flesh and mix with the fish, salt
and pepper to taste and 2 oz of the butter. Add
enough milk to give a consistency of mashed
potatoes. Fill the potato cases with the mixture,
sprinkle with pepper, top with a pat of butter
and heat through in the oven.

Banffshire Potatoes (8 portions) F and H Scotland

8 jacket baked potatoes
1 oz butter
¼ teaspoon each, chopped parsley and dried sweet
    herbs
Salt and pepper
3 oz fine white breadcrumbs
½ beaten egg
5 fl oz milk

Oven: 425°F; gas mark 7; 20–30 minutes

Slice the top off each potato and scoop out most
of the flesh. Mash the potato flesh and mix with
butter, parsley and herbs; season to taste with salt
and pepper, add the breadcrumbs and egg and
blend in the milk.
    Return this mixture to the potato skins, replace
the lids and bake in the oven.

Champ (6–8 portions) F Ireland

Champ, which is known as Stelk in Scotland, can
also be made with chives or onions, chopped
parsley or nettles, green peas or a mixture of peas
and onions. Red Champ is made with cooked
mashed beetroot and garnished with pieces of
beetroot; traditional in the Borders of Scotland.

1½ lb hot mashed potatoes
½ lb salad onions or leeks
5 fl oz milk
Salt and pepper
4 oz melted butter

Chop the onions and cook in the milk until tender.
Drain, setting aside the milk. Add salt and pepper
and the onions to the potatoes with enough milk to
give a creamy consistency. Spoon into a deep
warm serving dish; make a well in the centre and
pour in the melted butter.

Cheshire Potato Cakes (6 portions) F Cheshire

1 lb mashed potatoes
6 oz flour
½ oz butter
Buttermilk
Salt and pepper
Bacon fat

Mix the warm potatoes with the flour and butter,
add enough buttermilk to give a smooth, firm
consistency. Season with salt and pepper and shape
into small rounds, about ¾ in thick. Fry in hot
bacon fat and serve with fried bacon for breakfast.

Cornish Potato Cakes (8 portions) F Cornwall

2 lb boiled potatoes
2 oz butter
2 oz flour
Salt and pepper

Mash the potatoes while still hot and add the
butter, flour and salt and pepper to taste. Roll
the mixture out thinly on a floured board and cut
into rounds of about 6 in wide. Prick with a fork
and cook on a hot griddle or greased frying pan for
about 3 minutes on each side; serve hot.

Crowdie Potato Cakes (6 portions) F Scotland

1 lb hot mashed potatoes
1 egg yolk
2 oz Crowdie cheese
3–4 oz butter
1 tablespoon chopped chives
Salt and pepper

Mix the egg yolk and cheese into the hot
potatoes, with 1 oz of butter and the chives;
season with salt and pepper. Shape into small
rounds, ¾ in thick, and fry in hot butter until
golden brown on both sides.

Lenten Pie (6—8 portions) H and F

1½ lb par-boiled, sliced potatoes
1 lb par-boiled, sliced onions
1 lb peeled, cored and sliced apples
2 teaspoons salt
1 teaspoon paprika
4 oz butter
4 hardboiled eggs
½ pt white stock
10—14 oz puff pastry or ½ lb savoury shortcrust
   pastry
1 egg

Oven: 400—425°F; gas mark 6—7; 20 minutes
        350°F; gas mark 4; 20—25 minutes

Arrange the potatoes, onions and apples in layers
in a 5 pt pie dish, seasoning each layer with salt and
paprika; dot with butter. Tuck in the whole eggs.
These may also be sliced and added in layers with
the other ingredients but sliced tend to turn brown
during cooking.

   Pour in the stock and cover with the pastry;
brush with beaten egg and bake until golden,
reducing the heat after 20 minutes.

Pan Haggarty (6—8 portions) F
Northumberland

1 lb thinly sliced potatoes
2 oz dripping
½ lb thinly sliced onions
4 oz grated cheese
Salt and pepper

Heat the dripping in a frying pan and add a layer
of potatoes, the onions and the grated cheese; top
with another layer of potatoes. Season with salt
and pepper and fry gently until almost cooked
through. Brown under the grill and serve straight
from the pan as a high tea or supper dish.

Poor Man's Goose (6—8 portions) F

2 lb potatoes
1 lb sliced onions
4 oz dripping

1 lb thinly sliced lamb's liver
1 oz seasoned flour
¼ teaspoon sage
Salt and pepper
½ pt brown meat stock

Oven: 350°F; gas mark 4; 1 hour

Boil the potatoes in lightly salted water for 10
minutes. Fry the onions in the dripping until light
brown; lift out. Coat the liver with seasoned flour
and fry in the pan until brown and sealed.

   Butter a 4 pt pie dish and place the sliced
potatoes, liver and onions in layers, seasoning with
sage, salt and pepper and finishing with a layer of
potatoes. Pour over the stock, brush the potatoes
with dripping and bake in the oven for about 1
hour. Serve with apple sauce.

Potato Floddies (6 portions) F

1 lb grated potatoes
½ lb finely chopped onions
2 oz flour
1 egg
Milk
Salt and pepper
2 oz dripping

Mix the potatoes and onions; blend with the flour
and egg and beat with enough milk to give a stiff
batter. Season with salt and pepper; fry tablespoons
of the mixture in shallow hot fat until golden.

   Grated cheese, sausage meat or chopped herbs
may be added to the batter mixture, and the
floddies served as a complete supper dish.

Potato Pudding (6 portions) F Ireland

1 lb mashed potatoes
2 oz flour
2 oz melted butter
2 eggs
¼—½ pt milk
Salt and sugar

Oven: 225°F; gas mark ¼; 6 hours

Blend the flour and butter into the mashed
potatoes, add the eggs and enough milk to give a
dropping consistency. Season to taste with salt and
sugar. Turn into a greased ovenproof dish and
bake, covered, for 6 hours in a very low oven.

Pratie Oaten (Potato Oat Cakes)
(6—8 portions) F and H N. Ireland

1 lb mashed potatoes
½ lb fine oatmeal
Salt and pepper
Milk

Mix the oatmeal with the mashed potatoes, salt
and pepper to taste. Add enough milk to give a
dough-like consistency. Roll the mixture out on a
board floured with oatmeal, cut into small triangles
or rounds and bake on a hot griddle. Serve hot with
butter.

Punchnep (6—8 portions) F Wales

1 lb mashed potatoes
1 lb young mashed turnips
3 oz butter
Salt and pepper
2½ fl oz cream

Beat the potatoes and turnips to a pulp with the
butter; season with salt and pepper and heat
through. Spoon into a serving dish, press down
and make several holes in the top; pour the cream
into the holes and serve at once.

Scots Potato Pie (8 portions) F and H
Scotland

8 partly baked potatoes
4 oz chopped cooked meat
4 oz finely chopped onions
Salt and pepper
Stock
1 oz dripping

Oven: 425°F; gas mark 7; 1 hour

Cut a lid off each potato, scoop out most of the
flesh and mix with the meat and onions. Season
with salt and pepper and moisten with stock. Fill
this mixture back into the potato skins, replace
the lids and set the potatoes in a baking tin; bake
for 1 hour, basting occasionally with dripping.

Stovies (6—8 portions) F Scotland

2 lb potatoes
¾ lb sliced onions
1 oz butter
Salt and pepper
½ pt white stock

Fry the onions in the butter in a pan, add the
thickly sliced potatoes, with salt and pepper and
stock. Brush the top of the potatoes with butter
to prevent them drying out. Bring to the boil,
cover and simmer gently for 1 hour.

Small quantities of cooked meat, such as bacon,
chicken or mutton, may be added to the pan for
the last 15 minutes.

Welsh Potato Pie (6—8 portions) F Wales

1½ lb mashed potatoes
5 fl oz milk
4 oz grated Cheddar cheese
Salt and pepper
2 oz butter
4 oz white breadcrumbs

Oven: 425°F; gas mark 7; 20-30 minutes

Blend the milk and cheese into the mashed
potatoes; season with salt and pepper. Butter a
2 pt pie dish and sprinkle with breadcrumbs.
Spoon the potato mixture into the dish and brush
with melted butter. Bake until brown and serve
with pickled beetroot or pickled red cabbage.

PULSES

This is the name given to dried leguminous
vegetables such as beans, lentils and peas. Dried
beans include the small white haricot beans, the
red or kidney beans, green or flageolet beans and
the large yellow butter beans. There are two
varieties of lentils, the German lentil, purple green
and flat, and the Egyptian lentil, yellow-red and
resembling a small split pea. Dried green peas are
sold whole or split. All pulses except lentils should
be soaked in cold water for 24 hours before
cooking.

Baked Beans and Bacon (6—8 portions) F

1 lb white haricot beans
1 lb hock or collar bacon
2 oz honey
Pinch white pepper
1 bay leaf

Oven: 300°F; gas mark 2; 8—10 hours

Put the beans, unsoaked, into an ovenproof dish
with the bacon, honey, pepper, bay leaf and 3 pt
of water. The dish should be large enough to allow

the beans room for swelling. Cover with a tightly fitting lid and bake in a low oven.

Alternatively, soak the beans first and cook in the oven with the bacon, other ingredients and a little stock for 2–3 hours.

Green Pea Cakes (6–8 portions) F

¾ lb cooked dried peas
¼ oz butter
½ pt milk
Salt and pepper
2 eggs
4 oz flour
½ teaspoon baking powder
2 oz dripping or lard

Rub the cooked drained peas through a sieve or blend in a liquidiser while still warm. Mix with butter, milk, salt and pepper to taste and the well-beaten eggs. Stir in the flour sifted with the baking powder and shape the mixture into small rounds; shallow-fry in hot fat until golden brown on both sides.

Serve hot with sausages as a breakfast dish.

SALAD VEGETABLES

The combination of uncooked edible leaf vegetables and herbs with dressings was introduced to Britain as early as Roman times. This constituted the so-called "Simple Salad" while the more complicated "Grand Salad" which developed later included a mixture of meat, fish, nuts, raisins, olives, oranges, lemons and other suitable ingredients arranged in a decorative mound and dressed with oil and vinegar. This came to be known as Salamagundy, Solomon Gundy or Salamongundi.

The following vegetables are all suitable for fresh salads, on their own or mixed with other ingredients. Preparation and dressing should be done just before serving; a cut clove of garlic may be rubbed over the inside of the salad bowl before making up the salad.

Sliced or diced cooked and pickled beetroot, broccoli florets, finely shredded white cabbage, whole young or grated maincrop carrots, cauliflower florets, grated celeriac, chopped celery, halved, quartered or sliced chicory, thinly sliced cucumber.

The feathery leaves of endive may be used to replace lettuce; dry the leaves thoroughly. Young peeled marrow, cut into narrow strips, finely chopped onions, whole salad onions and sliced and whole radishes can also be added to salads, as well as shredded sea kale and spinach, grated young turnips and sprigs of watercress.

Tomatoes may be added to mixed salads or dressed on their own, peeled and sliced, halved or quartered.

English Salad F and H

1 lettuce
1 bunch watercress
Tomatoes
Hardboiled eggs

Separate the lettuce leaves, wash and dry thoroughly; divide the watercress into sprigs, discarding yellow leaves and tough stalks. Skin and slice the tomatoes and slice the eggs. Arrange all these ingredients in a salad bowl and serve with English salad sauce.

Salamagundy H and F

This salad, also known as Grand Salad, consists of a selection of salad vegetables, cooked vegetables and fresh fruit mixed with diced cooked meat, poultry, game or fish. Blend all the ingredients in a salad bowl and offer separately a bowl of dressing, mayonnaise or salad sauce and various pickles.

In contrast, a Simple or Green Salad is made up of green salad vegetables only, sprinkled with oil and vinegar dressing, tossed and served.

Winter Salad H and F

Dice a selection of vegetables, cooked or raw, such as potatoes, carrots, beetroot, cauliflowers, French beans, garden peas, celery etc. Mix the ingredients and add enough dressing or mayonnaise to coat thoroughly. Pile into a salad bowl and garnish with chopped parsley or mint.

TOMATOES

The tomato is correctly a fruit, not a vegetable, but is mainly used in savoury dishes, for flavouring, as a salad ingredient and for garnish. Available throughout the year, the home grown English tomatoes are superior to imported crops, being firm and well shaped.

Baked Stuffed Tomatoes (8 portions) H and F

8 large tomatoes
6 oz forcemeat: ham, bacon, cheese or sausage
   meat
Salt and pepper
Melted butter

Oven: 350°F; gas mark 4; 15—20 minutes

Wash and dry the tomatoes; cut a slice from the rounded end and scoop out the tomato flesh and mix into the forcemeat. Sprinkle the inside of the tomatoes with salt and leave them to drain upside down for 30 minutes.

Season the forcemeat with salt and pepper and pack loosely into the tomatoes. Replace the tops and set the tomatoes in a baking dish, brush with butter and bake for 20 minutes.

Skirlie Tomatoes (8 portions) F Scotland

Traditional in Aberdeenshire and Moray, these large tomatoes are stuffed with the oatmeal, onion and suet forcemeat known as Skirlie.

8 large firm tomatoes
Skirlie

Oven: 350°F; gas mark 4; 10—15 minutes

Slice the tops off the washed tomatoes, scoop out the flesh and mix into the prepared skirlie. Drain the tomatoes before stuffing them loosely; replace the tomato lids and bake in the oven for about 15 minutes.

Stilton Stuffed Tomatoes (8 portions) H and F

8 large tomatoes
Salt and pepper
6—8 oz Stilton cheese
2 oz butter
1 dessertspoon chopped chives
Cayenne pepper

Skin the tomatoes, cut off the tops and scoop out the flesh; discard the pips. Drain the tomatoes upside down, then sprinkle the insides with salt and pepper. Crumble the cheese into a bowl and

work in the butter, finely chopped chives, tomato flesh and cayenne pepper.

Pile the mixture into the tomatoes, replace the lids and chill before serving.

TURNIPS

This root vegetable is available all year round; the taste of young turnips, usually sold in bunches with the foliage attached, differs greatly from that of maincrop turnips.

Baked Turnips (6—8 portions) F and H

2 lb young turnips
2 oz butter
½ pt milk or white stock
Salt and pepper
1½ oz breadcrumbs

Oven: 350°F; gas mark 4; 30—45 minutes

Prepare and par-boil the turnips for about 15 minutes; drain well and cut into slices. Butter a 2 pt pie dish and arrange the sliced turnips in the dish; pour over the milk and season with salt and pepper. Cover with breadcrumbs and bake until the top is brown.

Clapshot (6—8 portions) F Orkney Islands

1 lb mashed potatoes
1 lb mashed turnips
1 dessertspoon chopped chives
2 oz dripping
Salt and pepper

Mix together the hot mashed potatoes and turnips; blend in the chives and dripping. Season to taste with salt and pepper, heat through and serve.

Glazed Turnips (6—8 portions) F and H

2 lb young turnips
2 oz butter
2 oz caster sugar
½ pt white stock
Salt and pepper

Put the cleaned turnips in a pan with the butter, sugar, stock, salt and pepper. Cover with a lid and simmer slowly for about 40 minutes. When almost cooked, increase the heat and reduce the sauce to a glaze, shaking the pan to prevent burning and ensuring that all the turnips are coated.

Welsh Stwns (6—8 portions) F Wales

It is a custom in Wales to mix mashed potatoes with other cooked vegetables to make a *stwn*. Peas, broad beans and swedes as well as turnips are used and served with fried liver and onions. See also Punchnep.

1 lb mashed potatoes
1 lb young mashed turnips
3 oz butter
Salt and pepper
Buttermilk

Mix the potatoes and turnips with the butter, salt and pepper. Add enough buttermilk to give a creamy consistency. Heat through and serve.

WATERCRESS

A herb cultivated in running, shallow streams and much used fresh for garnishing and salads. Also used in summer soups or as a vegetable side dish.

Stewed Watercress (6—8 portions) F and H Cornwall

2 bunches watercress
2 oz butter
Salt and pepper
1 tablespoon white wine vinegar

Wash the watercress thoroughly in cold salted water. Drain and cook in boiling water for 10 minutes. Strain and chop finely. Return the chopped watercress to the pan, with the butter, salt and pepper and simmer gently until tender.

Just before serving, stir in the vinegar; serve with sippets of fried bread as an accompaniment to boiled chicken or ham.

Savouries

The original meaning of the word "savoury" in culinary terms simply meant a savoury dish as distinct from one that was sweet; in the 17th century this might equally well be served at the beginning of a meal as at the end. By Victorian days, however, the savoury, always served in small portions, had become established as the last course of a dinner, before the dessert and was the exact opposite of an appetiser. It was supposed to aid the digestion — highly necessary after the huge dinners in Mrs. Beeton's days — but it is a fair assumption that a savoury also offered an opportunity for the gentlemen to finish off the dinner wines before the dessert and the sweet wines.

Today, the cheeseboard, correctly served *before* the dessert has largely replaced the savoury except at formal banquets; it is still a logical extension of the original concept as a large proportion of savouries are based on cheese. Smoked and other cured fish, oysters and shellfish, caviar, devilled liver and kidneys, grilled mushrooms and bacon were other favourite savouries. Most savouries are, of course, also suitable as quick snacks or light luncheons or as part of high teas.

Aberdeen Nips (8 portions) H and F
Scotland

A quick savoury made with left-over smoked haddock.

¾ lb cooked smoked haddock
4 egg yolks
½ pt thick white sauce
Salt, pepper and paprika
8 slices fried bread or toast
Garnish: parsley

Remove any skin and bone from the fish and flake the flesh finely. Blend the haddock and egg yolks into the sauce and season with salt and pepper. Heat the mixture through over low heat, pile on to rounds of fried bread or buttered toast, sprinkle with paprika and garnish with parsley.

Angels on Horseback (8 portions) H

Victorian in origin and sometimes made with scallops instead of oysters, when the "angels" become "archangels".

16 large oysters
16 bacon rashers
Buttered toast

Shell and clean the oysters and trim the bacon. Wrap each oyster in a rasher and secure with a small skewer. Grill until the bacon is crisp; arrange on rounds of hot buttered toast.

Buttered Bloaters (8 portions) F

This savoury can be made into a substantial snack by serving scrambled eggs with the bloaters.

8 bloaters
4 oz butter
Juice of 1 lemon
Salt and pepper
8 slices buttered toast

Oven: 350°F; gas mark 4; 10 minutes

Cut the heads, tails and fins from the bloaters and remove the skin and bones; put into a greased oven-proof dish, dot with butter, sprinkle with lemon juice and season with salt and pepper. Cover with foil and bake for 10 minutes. Serve piled on hot buttered toast.

Bloater Sandwich (8 portions) F

Suitable for a quick lunch-time snack, the filling of

grilled bloaters may be supplemented with hot mashed potatoes or scrambled eggs.

8 bloaters
4 oz butter
16 thin slices toast

Cut the bloaters down the back and place in a pan of boiling water; leave for 5 minutes. Remove the bloaters from the water, dry well and brush with melted butter. Grill slowly for 4—5 minutes, turning once. Remove skin and bones. Butter the toast and cover eight slices with bloater fillets, top with the remaining toast and serve hot.

Bloater Toast (8 portions) F

Serve as a small savoury or with drinks as a change from the usual accompaniments to drinks.

4 bloaters
2 oz softened butter
1 dessertspoon Worcestershire sauce
Cayenne pepper
2 egg yolks
8 thick slices bread

Grill the bloaters lightly on both sides, remove skin and bones and flake the flesh. Pound smooth with the butter, sauce and cayenne pepper and bind with the egg yolks. Rub through a coarse sieve or blend in a liquidiser.

   Cut the bread into 1 in squares, fry in butter and keep hot. Heat the bloater mixture through, pile on to the bread squares and serve.

Cheese Pudding (6—8 portions) F Wales

A savoury dish, suitable for lunch or high tea, on its own or with a green salad.

¾ lb grated Cheddar cheese
8 slices bread
2 oz butter
1 teaspoon dry mustard
Salt, nutmeg, cayenne pepper
2 eggs
1½ pt warm milk

Oven: 350°F; gas mark 4; 30 minutes

Toast the bread on one side, cut off the crusts and butter the untoasted side, cut into fingers and place a layer, toasted side down, in a greased oven-proof dish; cover with cheese. Top with toast, buttered side up, and continue with these layers,

seasoning with mustard, salt, nutmeg and cayenne. Finish with a layer of cheese.

   Beat the eggs, add the milk and pour over the cheese and toast. Bake in the oven for 30 minutes and serve hot.

Cheese Ramekins (8 portions) H and F

A light and fluffy savoury baked in small ramekin dishes.

½ lb grated Cheshire cheese
¾ pt milk
4 oz white breadcrumbs
6 eggs
4 oz butter
Mace, salt and pepper

Oven: 425°F; gas mark 7; 10—15 minutes

Pour the milk over the breadcrumbs and leave for 10 minutes. Separate the eggs. Blend the cheese, butter, egg yolks and seasoning with the bread-crumbs and blend to a smooth mixture. Whisk the egg whites until stiff and fold into the cheese mixture. Spoon into eight china or pottery ramekins and bake in the oven until set.

Cheese Tartlets (6—8 portions) H and F

May be served as a savoury or appetiser, and with drinks, mulled beer and wine.

4 oz grated cheese
10—12 oz puff pastry
2—3 eggs
1 oz butter
1 oz flour
½ pt milk
Salt and cayenne pepper

Oven: 425°F; gas mark 7; 15 minutes

Roll the pastry out thinly and cut into 18—24 rounds, 3—3½ in wide, and place in patty tins. Separate the eggs. Melt the butter in a pan, stir in the flour and gradually add the milk, stirring all the time; boil for 2—3 minutes.

   Let this sauce cool slightly, then beat in the egg yolks and heat gently, but do not boil. Add the cheese, season to taste with salt and cayenne and fold in the stiffly beaten egg whites. Spoon the mixture into the patty cases and bake in the oven for 10—15 minutes; serve hot.

Cheese with Ale (8 portions) F
Gloucestershire

Traditionally, this hot snack is accompanied with pickles and mulled ale.

½ lb grated Gloucestershire cheese
1 teaspoon made mustard
2½ fl oz strong ale
8 slices toasted brown bread

Put the grated cheese in an ovenproof dish with the mustard and ale and melt in a hot oven. Toast the bread, arrange on individual plates and pour over the melted cheese.

Chicken Livers, Devilled (8 portions) H and F

Serve this delicate savoury on fried bread or toast cut into fluted rounds with a pastry cutter.

8 sets chicken livers
3–4 oz finely chopped shallots
1 teaspoon chopped parsley
Salt and cayenne pepper
16 thin slices streaky bacon
8 slices toast

Oven: 375°F; gas mark 5; 8 minutes

Wash and dry and divide the chicken livers into sixteen pieces. Sprinkle with shallots, parsley, cayenne and salt. Wrap a bacon slice round each piece of liver and fasten with wooden skewers.

Bake in the oven, remove the cocktail sticks and serve the chicken rolls on fried bread or toast.

Crayfish and Bacon Savoury (8 portions) H
Warwickshire

Fresh, boiled crayfish are rarely seen, but frozen tails are generally available.

16 crayfish tails
1 lb bacon rashers
Salt and pepper
8 slices toast

Dice the bacon and fry gently, without any extra fat, in a pan. Remove the meat from the tails of the crayfish and cut into small pieces; add to the bacon when the fat in the pan is running freely. Cook for a few minutes to heat through; season with salt and pepper and spoon the mixture over hot buttered toast.

Devils on Horseback (8 portions) H and F

A favourite savoury in Victorian days, the "devils" do not denote the opposite of Angels on Horseback, but refer to the hot stuffing of chutney and the mustard which is smeared over the devils.

16 soaked prunes
2 oz chutney or 2–3 oz blanched almonds
16 bacon rashers
2 oz butter
Hot cream
8 rounds toast
Made mustard

Remove the stones from the prunes and stuff with chutney or blanched almonds. Wrap a bacon rasher round each prune and secure with a wooden cocktail stick. Fry in butter or grill until crisp. Arrange two devils on each round of toast and serve at once with hot cream and mustard.

Herring Roes, Devilled (8 portions) H and F

Devilled or spiced dishes were extremely popular with the Victorians and Edwardians, both for breakfast and dinner savouries. Herring roes may also be devilled with mushroom ketchup, lemon juice and cayenne pepper.

1 lb soft herring roes
4 oz butter
1 dessertspoon made English mustard
2 dessertspoons Harvey's sauce
Salt and pepper
8 slices toast

Mix the butter, mustard, Harvey's sauce, salt and pepper together and heat in a pan. Place the cleaned herring roes carefully in the pan and cook gently for 5 minutes. Lift the roes on to hot buttered toast, pour over the sauce and serve very hot.

Kidneys, Devilled (8 portions) H and F

To prevent kidneys from curling up during grilling, thread them on to skewers.

16 lamb or 8 pig kidneys
Melted butter
8 rounds toast
Lemon juice
1 dessertspoon chopped parsley
Garnish: mustard butter

Clean and trim the kidneys and thread them on to
skewers. Brush with melted butter and grill for
3–4 minutes on each side. Set hot buttered toast
on individual plates, top with the kidneys and
sprinkle with lemon juice and parsley. Garnish
with pats of mustard butter.

Kidneys, Grilled (8 portions) H and F

The grilled kidneys served for breakfast can be
transformed to a savoury by first coating them
with egg and breadcrumbs or by flaming them with
whisky as they are being served.

16 lamb or 8 pig kidneys
2–3 oz melted lard or kidney suet
Salt and pepper
8 rounds toast

Place the prepared kidneys on a grill pan, cut side
up, or thread them on to skewers; brush with
melted lard or suet. Grill gently for 3–4 minutes
on each side until cooked but still pink and
tender at the centre. Sprinkle with salt and pepper
and serve at once on hot buttered toast.

Kidneys and Oysters (8 portions) H

A luxury savoury, surviving from the 19th century
when oysters were inexpensive fare. Other oyster
savouries were oyster and bacon fritters, oyster
and ham toasts and oysters on fried bread spread
with anchovy paste.

8 lamb kidneys
16 oysters
8 slices toast
Salt and pepper

Trim the kidneys, cut in half lengthways, and grill
gently for about 8 minutes, turning once. Meanwhile, slide the oysters from their shells and blanch
them in their own liquid for a few minutes only.
Arrange the kidneys on the toast, place two
oysters on each portion, season with salt and
pepper and serve at once.

Kipper Rarebit (8 portions) F and H

Masculine palates in particular would appreciate
this strongly flavoured savoury.

2–4 kippers
1 pt milk
2 crushed cloves garlic

2 oz butter
2 oz flour
4 oz grated cheese
2 chopped hardboiled eggs (optional)
Paprika
8 slices fried bread or toast

Put the kippers in a pan with the milk; bring to
the boil, then remove from the heat and leave for
5 minutes. Lift out the kippers, remove the skin
and bones and flake the flesh. Return the skin and
bones to the milk and simmer with the garlic for
10 minutes; strain.

Melt the butter, stir in the flour and gradually
add the flavoured milk; bring to the boil, stirring
constantly. Fold in the cheese and flaked kippers.
Heat the mixture through, colour with paprika
and add the eggs, if used. Spoon on to fried bread
or hot buttered toast and serve.

Kipper Savoury on Toast (8 portions) H and F

This may be served as a dinner savoury and would
also make a good luncheon snack.

1 lb cooked kipper fillets
2 tablespoons single cream
4 hardboiled eggs
Salt and pepper
1 tablespoon lemon juice
8 slices hot toast
Garnish: 8 cucumber slices, 4 pickled walnuts or 8
    stoned olives

Remove the skin from the kippers and flake the
flesh; mix with the cream and blend in the roughly
chopped eggs. Season to taste with salt, pepper
and lemon juice. Pile the mixture on to slices of
toast and put under a hot grill for 2 minutes to
heat through.

Garnish each portion with a twist of cucumber
and a stoned olive or half a pickled walnut.

Loch Fyne Toasts (8 portions) F and H Scotland

Mushrooms are used to garnish this kipper savoury,
served on small rounds of toast.

4 Loch Fyne kippers
16 large mushrooms
3–4 oz butter
Pepper and paprika

16 slices toast
Lemon juice

Peel if necessary and trim the stalks of the mushrooms; fry gently in butter. Grill the kippers for about 6 minutes; remove skin and bones and mash the flesh with 2 oz of butter and pepper to taste.

Cut the toast into 2½–3 in rounds, butter and top with a mushroom. Sprinkle with lemon juice, dust with paprika and place under a hot grill for 1–2 minutes before serving.

Marrow Bones (8 portions) H and F

Marrow bones are considered a great delicacy; it is said that Queen Victoria was so fond of marrow toasts that they were served at dinner every single day.

8 marrow bones
Salt and pepper
Dry toast
Chopped parsley

Have the marrow bones sawn into 5–6 in lengths; cover the open ends with foil. Stand the bones upright in a large pan of boiling salted water; simmer gently for 3 hours. Remove the foil, wrap the bones in white napkins and serve upright with salt, pepper and dry toast.

For marrow toasts, scoop the marrow out of the bones and spread on thin slices of hot toast. Sprinkle with salt, pepper and chopped parsley.

Mushrooms on Toast (8 portions) H and F

It is often the simplest dishes that achieve the greatest popularity. As a savoury, fried or grilled mushrooms remain one of the great favourites. Towards the end of the 19th century, the traditional mushroom savoury was daringly embellished with anchovy-flavoured whipped cream at one of the Cambridge colleges.

1 lb button mushrooms
2 oz butter
Salt and pepper
8 slices toast

Trim the mushrooms and fry gently in the butter. Season with salt and pepper and arrange on small rounds of hot buttered toast.

RAREBITS

The best known of rabbits or rarebits is the Welsh Rarebit. The controversy as to the correct name has gone on since the 18th century, the Welsh themselves insisting on rabbit or *Caws Pobi*, but rarebit in the sense of rare meaning soft appears more probable. However, rarebit — or rabbit — was credited to the Welsh as far back as the 14th century and later immortalised by Boorde in his tale of *Toasted Cheese and St. Peter*. It is reasonable to assume that other rarebits are but imitations of the Welsh, using local cheeses and adding bits of embellishments.

Welsh Rarebit (8 portions) F and H

1 lb grated Cheddar cheese
1 oz butter
5 fl oz milk or ale
2 teaspoons made mustard
Salt and pepper

Melt the butter in a pan, add the grated cheese and stir over gentle heat until melted. Add milk or ale, mustard and salt and pepper to taste. Pour the mixture piping hot over hot buttered toast, brown under the grill until bubbling and serve.

Welsh Rarebit with Chutney (8 portions) F and H Wales

Welsh rarebit mixture
8 slices toast
2 sliced tomatoes
1 oz chutney
8 grilled bacon rolls
Garnish: parsley sprigs

Prepare the Welsh Rarebit mixture as above and pour over the toast. Top each rarebit with a slice of tomato, a little chutney and a bacon roll. Place under a hot grill for a few minutes, garnish with parsley and serve.

Irish Rarebit (8 portions) F and H Ireland

1 lb grated Irish Cheddar cheese
½ oz butter
5 fl oz milk
1 tablespoon vinegar
1 teaspoon made mustard
Salt and pepper
1 oz coarsley chopped pickled gherkin

Put the cheese in a pan with butter and milk and stir until creamy. Add the vinegar, mustard, salt and pepper to taste and the gherkins.

Pile the rarebit mixture on to buttered toast, brown under the grill and serve immediately.

Scotch Rarebit (8 portions) F and H

1 lb grated Dunlop cheese
3–4 oz butter
6–7 fl oz brown stout (porter)
1 teaspoon made mustard
Pepper
8 slices toast

Melt the cheese with the butter in a double sauce-pan; add the stout, mustard and pepper to taste. Stir the mixture until thoroughly blended. Spoon the rarebit into a dish and serve with slices or fingers of toast to dip into the cheese mixture.

Yorkshire or Buck Rabbit (8 portions) F and H Yorkshire

1 lb grated Cheshire or Cheddar cheese
2 oz butter
5 fl oz milk or ale
Worcestershire sauce or vinegar
½ teaspoon made mustard
Salt and pepper
8 poached eggs
8 slices toast

Put the grated cheese in a pan with butter, milk, a few drops of Worcestershire sauce, mustard and salt and pepper to taste. Stir over low heat until the mixture has the consistency of thick cream.

Poach the eggs, toast the bread and remove the crusts. Pour the cheese mixture over the toasts, brown under a hot grill and top with poached eggs; serve immediately.

Scotch Woodcock (8 portions) F and H

Much relished by Victorian gentlemen, this savoury has one thing in common with woodcock: both are served on toast.

8 egg yolks
1 pt single cream
Salt and pepper
Butter
8 slices toast

16 anchovy fillets
1 dessertspoon capers

Beat the egg yolks with the cream and season with salt and pepper; scramble the eggs with a little butter in a pan or a double saucepan. Toast the bread, remove the crusts and butter generously.

Spoon the scrambled eggs over the toasts, arrange two anchovy fillets on top in the shape of a cross and fill the spaces with capers.

Scrambled Egg Kippers (8 portions) F and H

Most savouries are served piping hot, but this egg and kipper dish can be served with cold strips of kippers laid in a pattern over hot scrambled eggs.

4 cooked kippers
12 eggs
1 large crushed clove garlic
Salt and pepper
6 oz butter
8 slices toast

Flake the kipper flesh roughly. Beat the eggs, add garlic, salt and pepper. Melt the butter in a thick pan over low heat, pour in the eggs and scramble. When the eggs are beginning to set, fold in the kipper flakes and stir until cooked. Pile on hot buttered toast and serve.

A Sefton of Herring Roes (6–8 portions) H and F

A creamy savoury, ideal for hot summer days, as it is served chilled on thin savoury or water biscuits, garnished with cayenne and watercress.

½ lb soft herring roes
Salt and pepper
1 tablespoon lemon juice
1 oz butter
3 anchovy fillets
2 fl oz double cream
1 teaspoon capers
8 water biscuits
Cayenne pepper
Garnish: watercress

Season the herring roes with salt, pepper and lemon juice and fry in the butter. Rub the roes, with the chopped anchovies, through a sieve or blend in a liquidiser to a smooth pulp. Whip the cream and blend into the roe pulp, together with the capers. Chill in the refrigerator before serving.

SAVOURY PUDDINGS

These batter puddings are specialities of North England where they are cooked and served with roast meat. Yorkshire pudding is the most famous and was traditionally cooked in a pan set beneath the meat being roasted over the open fire so that the fat from the meat dripped down into the pudding.

Savoury Pudding I (6—8 portions) F and H Derbyshire

Serve with any kind of roast meat.

1 pt milk
6 oz white breadcrumbs
4 oz fine oatmeal
2 eggs
½ lb plain flour
1 teaspoon chopped sage
Salt and pepper
1 lb finely chopped onions
4 oz finely chopped suet

Oven: 400°F; gas mark 6; 1 hour

Heat the milk and pour over the breadcrumbs and oatmeal; leave for 10 minutes, then beat in the eggs. Mix the flour with sage, salt and pepper, add the onions and mix thoroughly with the suet. Stir this into the egg and milk mixture.

Put in a greased pudding mould, cover with buttered greaseproof paper and bake for 1 hour. Turn out and serve.

Savoury Pudding II (6—8 portions) F Yorkshire

This savoury pudding, to be served with roast meat, is baked in a pudding basin.

3 oz flour
½ lb white breadcrumbs
¾ oz chopped sage
Salt and pepper
¾ lb boiled, finely chopped onions
½ pt milk
1 egg

Oven: 400°F; gas mark 6; 30 minutes

Mix the flour, breadcrumbs, sage, salt, and pepper, add the onions, milk and lightly beaten egg. The mixture should be fairly stiff. Spoon into a greased pudding basin, cover with greaseproof paper and bake. Turn out to serve.

Yorkshire Pudding (6—8 portions) F and H

The original Yorkshire Pudding, cooked beneath a spit roast, was usually about 1 in thick; it was turned once during cooking, cut into squares and served as an individual course with gravy before the roast meat. Today, the pudding, cooked in a Yorkshire Pudding tin or individual round patty tins, is the traditional accompaniment to beef.

½ lb plain flour
Pinch salt
3 eggs
¾ pt milk
Dripping

Oven: 400°F; gas mark 6; 20 minutes

Sift the flour and salt together, make a well in the centre and drop in the eggs with one third of the milk. Stir to a smooth paste, beating thoroughly and gradually adding the remaining milk. Leave the batter to rest for 1 hour before use.

Heat the dripping until smoking hot in a Yorkshire Pudding tin or in individual patty tins. Pour in the batter and bake until well-risen.

A Rich Yorkshire Pudding (6—8 portions) H and F London

This version of the Yorkshire Pudding used to be served with the huge joints of roast beef at Simpson's in the Strand, London.

4 eggs
½ lb plain flour

½ pt water and milk mixed
Salt and pepper
Fat or dripping

Oven: 400°F; gas mark 6; 20—30 minutes

Separate the eggs and whip the whites until stiff; beat the yolks thoroughly. Gradually add the flour to the yolks and thin the mixture down little by little with the milk and water; season with salt and pepper. When all the milk and water has been added and the batter has the consistency of thick cream, carefully fold in the egg whites.

Pour the batter into a tin with hot fat and bake for 20—30 minutes or until well-risen and brown.

Puddings, Sweets and Desserts

The contents of puddings and pies were until the 17th century generally savoury although sweet ingredients, spices and dried fruit were included, and puddings were sometimes served with sugar and almonds. As sugar became more readily available and fruit production increased, the sweet version began to develop. The fashion for sweet puddings was set by "the pudding-eating monarch", George I, who delighted in heavy, rich and often indigestible puddings.

As the pudding concept widened to include steamed, boiled and baked items, of a sweet or savoury nature, the English in particular earned for themselves the nickname of "pudding-eaters". Endless varieties of sweet and steamed heavy puddings developed, many of which are now extinct, and "pudding" became synonymous with a sweet dish or course.

Until the 19th century, each course of a meal consisted of a collection of dishes, savoury and sweet, arranged on the table for people to help themselves. This meant that all types of puddings were eaten along with meat and fish and were often designed specifically to accompany them. During the second half of the 19th century, meal courses gradually became more defined, and soups, fish and meat dishes emerged as distinct courses. The dessert, derived from the French *desservir* meaning to clear the table, was a collection of elaborate sweet dishes, fresh fruits, ices, fancy cakes and preserves; it became the natural place for the sweet puddings and pies now excluded from the other courses. Thus in the 20th century, the three terms, pudding, sweet and dessert all apply to the course served at the end of the meal.

Puddings, sweets and desserts have been divided into a number of sub-sections, some of which by necessity overlap as they are nearly all developments and versions of the basic pie and pudding concepts.

1. Sweet Pies
2. Sweet Puddings
3. Rice and Cereal Puddings
4. Pancakes, Fritters and Sweet Batter Puddings
5. Cake Mixture Puddings
6. Fruit Desserts
7. Custards and Trifles
8. Fools, Syllabubs and Junkets
9. Jellies, Moulds and Other Cream Sweets
10. Ice creams

SWEET PIES

The original pie was a miscellany of ingredients under a pie crust. The term "pie" has no foreign connections in its history and is unique to Britain thus lending credence to the theory claimed by some etymologists that it is derived from magpie, with the implied connection between the contents of a pie and the collection of articles in a magpie's nest. This analogy is further supported by an unproven theory that an early name for the magpie was "maggot-pie" or "Margaret-pie", often simply abbreviated to "pie".

The early pie was savoury, but gradually received sweet additions in the form of spices and dried fruit. These were brought back from the Holy Land by returning Crusaders, and it was natural that the Lord's Nativity should be celebrated with a pie containing the fruits of His native land. In order to satisfy the medieval obsession with analogy it was shaped as an oblong or square to represent the manger. During the 17th century, this Christmas Pie was denounced by the Puritans as "popish". When it returned to favour after the

Restoration it acquired the title of "superstitious" or "minced", the latter finally being adopted as the correct name. The minced meat content was common well into the 19th century, but was eventually omitted towards the end of the Victorian era.

Apple and pear pies were the earliest forms of sweet pies, well established by the 16th century and popular Elizabethan dishes. Although pies, tarts, pastries and pudding pies are all true British specialities, a certain amount of confusion exists over their correct terminology. This is possibly due to the fact that the names are, to some extent, interchangeable. In England, for example, a tart was and still is a pastry base with an open filling, while in Ireland and Scotland the same term was applied to a sweet pie with a pastry top; in Scotland today, a tart often refers to a pie having both a pastry base and a pastry top.

FRUIT PIES

These may be covered or open, or topped with meringue; a few are raised, and many of the small fruit pies, commonly known as pastries or turn-overs have regional connections.

A jug of custard or cream is usually served with fruit pies today, but in earlier days the custard was poured into the pie just before the end of cooking, and the pie was known as a creamed fruit pie. In the West Country, clotted cream is spread over the fruit, and in Yorkshire and Lancashire cheese is often served with apple pie — Wensleydale cheese in Yorkshire and Lancashire cheese in Lancashire. Sometimes, the cheese is cooked with the apples, approximately 6 oz cheese to 2 lb of apples.

Covered pies, which include deep dish pies, plate pies and flan pies, are traditionally left plain without any pastry decorations. They were formerly finished with a glaze or icing the sweetness of which contrasted with the flavour of the pie filling. The following are a few of the traditional glazes:

Clear glaze
Pour liquid caramel over the pastry when it is removed from the oven; alternatively, sift icing sugar over the finished pie and put under a hot grill to brown the sugar.

Icing
Sift 4 oz icing sugar into 1 egg white and beat until smooth and stiff enough to stand in peaks. Remove the pie from the oven 10 minutes before it is done

and let it cool slightly. Cover the pie crust thickly with the icing and return the pie to the oven at reduced temperature until lightly brown on top.

Jam or Jelly glaze
Melt 4 oz jam or jelly and brush over the pie when baked and slightly cool.

Sugar glaze
Before the pie goes into the oven, moisten the pastry with cold water and sprinkle thickly with caster sugar, pressing it in lightly. The sugar browns slightly during baking; alternatively, sprinkle with sugar after baking.

DEEP DISH PIES

Covered fruit pies, made in a 2–2½ pt dish, the fruit being covered with shortcrust or puff pastry. Any kind of fresh fruit is suitable, on its own or in combinations.

Apple Pie

This may be made with all apples or with apples and quinces.

1½ lb peeled, cored and sliced apples
6 oz sugar
2 cloves
2 fl oz water
1 lb puff pastry or ½ lb savoury, sweet or rich
    shortcrust pastry

Oven: 425°F; gas mark 7; 10–15 minutes
       350°F; gas mark 4; 30 minutes

Butter the dish and fill with layers of apple, sprinkling with the sugar. Add the cloves and water. Roll out the pastry and cover the dish; trim and seal the edges and make a slit in the pastry. Bake for 45 minutes, reducing the temperature after 15 minutes. Dredge the pie with sugar and serve hot.

As a variation, use only ¾ lb apples and augment with ½ lb prepared quinces cooked until tender with 1 oz each of honey and butter and 2½ fl oz water.

For a gooseberry pie, use 1½ lb ripe goose-berries, with ½ lb Demerara sugar and 5 fl oz ale.

Apple Florentine Pie (6–8 portions) F and H Bedfordshire

Traditionally the apples in this pie were left whole and the pastry was cut into triangular portions after baking, then replaced. It was served in a large pewter dish.

1 lb cooking apples
4 oz sugar
Grated rind of 1 lemon
½ pt ale
Pinch grated nutmeg and cinnamon
1 clove
1 lb puff pastry or ½ lb savoury, sweet or rich
  shortcrust pastry

Oven: 425°F; gas mark 7; 10–15 minutes
  350°F; gas mark 4; 30 minutes

Wash, core and quarter the apples or cut into rings and place in the pie dish with 3 oz sugar and the lemon rind. Heat the ale with nutmeg, cinnamon, clove and the remaining sugar; leave to infuse for 15 minutes, then strain over the apples.
  Cover with pastry and bake for 45 minutes.

Banbury Apple Pie (6–8 portions) F and H Oxfordshire

¾ lb peeled, cored and sliced cooking apples
2 oz sugar
1 oz currants
½ lb chopped candied peel
Pinch ground ginger and cinnamon
2 fl oz water
1 lb puff pastry or ½ lb savoury, sweet or rich
  shortcrust pastry

Oven: 425°F; gas mark 7; 10–15 minutes
  350°F; gas mark 4; 30 minutes

Arrange the apples in a buttered pie dish, mixing thoroughly with the sugar, currants and peel and sprinkling with the spices; add the water. Cover with the pastry and bake for 45 minutes.

Bilberry Pie (6–8 portions) F and H Derbyshire and Yorkshire

1½ lb prepared bilberries
6–8 oz sugar
½ oz chopped mint
2 fl oz water
¾ lb peeled, cored and sliced cooking apples
1 lb puff pastry or ½ lb savoury, sweet or rich
  shortcrust pastry

Oven: 425°F; gas mark 7; 10–15 minutes
  350°F; gas mark 4; 30 minutes

Put the bilberries in a buttered pie dish and sprinkle with the sugar mixed with mint; add water. For the Yorkshire bilberry pie, use half the amount of berries and substitute with apples; omit the mint.
  Roll out the pastry and cover the dish; bake for 45 minutes.

Pippin Tart (6–8 portions) F

A survival from the custom of serving tomatoes as a sweet when they were first introduced to Britain.

1 lb stewed Cox's Orange Pippin apples
½ lb skinned tomatoes
2 oz sugar
5 fl oz double cream
1 lb puff pastry or ½ lb savoury, sweet or rich
  shortcrust pastry

Oven: 425°F; gas mark 7; 10–15 minutes
  350°F; gas mark 4; 30 minutes

Liquidise the tomatoes and add to the apples with the sugar. Spoon the mixture into a buttered pie dish and pour over the cream.
  Cover with the rolled out pastry, taking care it does not touch the cream. Bake for 45 minutes.

Pumpkin Pie (6–8 portions) F

½ lb prepared pumpkin (peeled and seeded)
½ lb peeled, cored and diced cooking apples
4 oz currants
1 oz mixed peel
1 teaspoon mixed spice
1 lb puff pastry or ½ lb savoury, sweet or rich
  shortcrust pastry

Oven: 425°F; gas mark 7; 10–15 minutes
  350°F; gas mark 4; 30 minutes

Cut the pumpkin into ½ in cubes and mix with the apples, currants, peel and spice. Arrange in a buttered pie dish; roll out the pastry and cover.
  Bake in the oven for 45 minutes and coat with a sweet glaze.

PLATE PIES

The saucer pie is the original type of these pies, made in an 8—9 in pie plate or dish. The pie consists of a pastry base and top crust, with a fruit filling.

Apple or Pear Plate Pie (6—8 portions) F and H

½ lb peeled, cored and thickly sliced apples or pears
2 oz sugar
12 oz sweet, savoury or rich shortcrust pastry

Oven: 425°F; gas mark 7; 10—15 minutes
        350°F; gas mark 4; 30 minutes

Butter the pie plate; divide the pastry in two and roll out to fit. Line the plate with one pastry circle, cover with the fruit and sprinkle with sugar. Cover with the remaining pastry, trim and seal the edges and make a slit in the top.

Bake for 45 minutes, lowering the heat after the first 15 minutes. When baked, dredge with sugar and serve hot or cold.

Many other fruits can be used for plate pies, including:
Blackberry and Apple pie, 4 oz each black-berries and apples.
Cherry Pie, ½ lb stoned cherries.
Damson and Apple Pie, 4 oz each stoned damsons and apples.
Gooseberry Pie, ½ lb gooseberries, 2—3 oz sugar.
Plum Pie, ½ lb stoned plums.
Rhubarb Pie, ½ lb diced rhubarb, 3 oz sugar.

Cumberland Rum Nicky (6—8 portions) F and H Cumberland

¾ lb sweet, savoury or rich shortcrust pastry
4 oz chopped dates
2 oz chopped preserved ginger
2 oz butter
1 oz caster sugar
2 tablespoons rum

Oven: 425°F; gas mark 7; 10—15 minutes
        350°F; gas mark 4; 30 minutes

Line the buttered pie plate with half the pastry and cover with the mixed dates and ginger. Beat the butter, sugar and rum and spread over the filling; cover with the remaining pastry and bake in the oven for 45 minutes.

Devonshire Tart (6—8 portions) F and H Devon

6 oz peeled, cored and sliced apples
¾ lb sweet, savoury or rich shortcrust pastry
1 oz currants or sultanas
1 oz brown sugar
1 teaspoon mixed spice
1 oz butter

Oven: 425°F; gas mark 7; 10—15 minutes
        350°F; gas mark 4; 30 minutes

Roll out the pastry and use half to line a buttered pie plate. Arrange the filling in layers of apples and currants, sprinkling with the sugar and spice. Dot with butter and cover with the remaining pastry. Bake for 45 minutes.

Mince Pie (6—8 portions) F and H

Early recipes for the old Christmas Pie used enormous quantities of suet, apples, dried fruit, peel and spices; the moisturing agent varied from claret and sack to brandy and sweet wine. Meat was an essential ingredient and might be veal, beef, tongue or tripe; the pies were plate pies, Mrs. Acton first recommending the use of patty tins in her *Modern Cookery* (1863).

6 oz mincemeat
¾ lb sweet, savoury or rich shortcrust pastry

Oven: 425°F; gas mark 7; 10—15 minutes
        350°F; gas mark 4; 30 minutes

Line the pie plate with half the pastry and cover with the mincemeat; roll out the remaining pastry, lay over the mincemeat and seal and trim the edges. Bake for 45 minutes and spread the pie with glacé icing when cool.

Treacle Tart (6—8 portions) F and H

6 oz sweet shortcrust pastry
6 oz fresh white breadcrumbs
1 lb golden syrup
6 oz rich shortcrust pastry

Oven: 425°F; gas mark 7; 10—15 minutes
        350°F; gas mark 4; 30 minutes

Line a deep pie plate with the sweet shortcrust pastry; mix the breadcrumbs with the syrup and fill the pastry case. Cover with rich shortcrust pastry and bake for 45 minutes.

Westmorland Cake (6—8 portions)
F and H Westmorland

¾ lb sweet, savoury or rich shortcrust pastry
4—6 oz currants
2 oz caster sugar
2 oz butter
1 egg white

Oven: 425°F; gas mark 7; 10—15 minutes
      350°F; gas mark 4; 30 minutes

Roll out half the pastry and use to line an 8—9 in
pie plate. Fill with the currants, sugar and butter
cut into flakes. Cover with the remaining pastry
and brush with beaten egg white; sprinkle with
sugar and bake for 45 minutes.

Yorkshire Treacle Tart (6—8 portions)
F and H Yorkshire

¾ lb sweet, savoury or rich shortcrust pastry
6 oz mixed dried fruit
2 oz grated apples
Grated rind and juice of ½ lemon
3 oz golden syrup
1½ oz brown breadcrumbs

Oven: 425°F; gas mark 7; 10—15 minutes
      350°F; gas mark 4; 30 minutes

Line an 8 in buttered pie plate with half the pastry;
mix the dried fruit with the apples, lemon juice
and rind, syrup and breadcrumbs. Spread this
mixture over the pastry base and cover with the
remaining pastry.

    Bake for 45 minutes, lowering the heat after
the first 15 minutes.

FLAN PIES

Similar to plate pies, but the pastry is used to line
and cover an 8—9 in flan ring. Set the ring on a
baking sheet before assembling the pie.

Apple or Pear Flan Pie (6—8 portions)
F and H

¾ lb peeled, cored and sliced apples or pears
3 oz sugar
1 lb savoury, sweet, rich or spiced shortcrust pastry

Oven: 425°F; gas mark 7; 10—15 minutes
      350°F; gas mark 4; 30 minutes

Set the greased flan ring on a baking sheet, roll out
two thirds of the pastry and line the ring. Lay the
prepared fruit over the pastry base, sprinkle with
sugar and cover with the remaining pastry. Trim
and seal the edges and make a slit in the top for the
steam to escape.

    Bake for 45 minutes, reducing the temperature
after 15 minutes. Ice or glaze the pie and serve
warm or cold.

    The following are variations of flan pies:
Blackberry and Apple Pie, 6 oz each brambles and
apples.
Cherry Pie, ¾ lb stoned cherries.
Cumberland Rum Nicky, 6 oz dates, 3 oz preserved
ginger, 4 oz butter, 2 oz sugar and 2 tablespoons
rum; see also Plate Pies.
Damson and Apple Pie, 6 oz each stoned damsons
and prepared apples.
Devonshire Tart, ¾ lb apples, 2 oz currants, 2 oz
butter, 2 oz brown sugar and 1 teaspoon mixed
spice; see also Plate Pie.
Gooseberry Pie, ¾ lb ripe gooseberries and 3—4 oz
sugar.
Mince Pie, ¾ lb mincemeat.
Plum Pie, ¾ lb stoned plums.
Rhubarb Pie, ¾ lb chopped rhubarb, 4 oz sugar.

Fig Pie (6—8 portions) F and H Midlands

½ lb dried figs, soaked overnight
½ teaspoon mixed spice
2 oz golden syrup
1 dessertspoon cornflour
1 oz currants
1 lb rich shortcrust pastry

Oven: 425°F; gas mark 7; 10—15 minutes
      350°F; gas mark 4; 30 minutes

Put the soaked figs in a pan with the spice and
syrup and enough water to cover; simmer until
tender. Thicken the liquid with the cornflour
blended with a little water; add the currants and
mix well.

    Line an 8 in flan ring with two thirds of the
pastry, spoon in the cooled filling and cover with
the remaining pastry. Bake for 45 minutes.

Prune Flory (6—8 portions) F and H

¾ lb dried prunes, soaked overnight
2 tablespoons port

Juice of ½ lemon
Pinch cinnamon
4 oz sugar
1 dessertspoon cornflour
5 fl oz prune liquid
1 lb rich shortcrust pastry

Oven: 425°F; gas mark 7; 10—15 minutes
     350°F; gas mark 4; 30 minutes

Simmer the prunes in water until soft. Drain, reserve
5 fl oz of the liquid and remove the stones. Add
the port, lemon juice, cinnamon and sugar to the
prune juice; thicken with cornflour blended with
water and leave to cool.

   Roll out two thirds of the pastry and use to
line a flan ring. Arrange the prunes on the pastry,
spoon over the thickened liquid and cover with the
remaining pastry. Trim and seal the edges and bake
the pie for 45 minutes.

Spiced Apple Pie (6—8 portions) F and H

10 oz peeled, cored and sliced cooking apples
4 oz stoned prunes or dates
1 teaspoon ground cinnamon
4 oz sugar
1 lb spiced shortcrust pastry

Oven: 425°F; gas mark 7; 10—15 minutes
     350°F; gas mark 4; 30 minutes

Soak the prunes overnight, strain and remove the
stones. Simmer the prunes for 10 minutes with
cinnamon and sugar and enough of the strained
liquid to cover. Mix the prunes with the apples
and leave to cool.

   Line a flan ring with two thirds of the rolled
out pastry; spoon in the apple and prune filling
and cover with the remaining pastry. Bake for 45
minutes.

   Dust the pie thickly with icing sugar and serve
warm or cold.

Sussex Apple Pie (6—8 portions)
F and H Sussex

½ lb peeled, cored and sliced cooking apples
1 lb spiced shortcrust pastry
2 oz currants
2 oz raisins
2 oz sugar
1 teaspoon ground cinnamon
1 teaspoon mixed spice
2 tablespoons water

Oven: 425°F; gas mark 7; 10—15 minutes
     350°F; gas mark 4; 30 minutes

Roll out two thirds of the pastry and line an 8 in
flan ring set on a baking sheet.

   Arrange layers of apples, currants and raisins
over the pastry base, sprinkling each with sugar
mixed with cinnamon and spice. Spoon over the
water, cover with the remaining pastry and bake
for 45 minutes.

TARTS

These open pies are reminiscent of the old English
Pudding Pies which were made in a shallow mould
and left uncovered. The fillings may be fruit but
are just as often jam, custard or treacle.

PLATE TARTS

These are made in 8—9 in shallow pie plates, a
pastry strip being fitted to the rim of the buttered
plate and the remainder used to line the plate,
up over the rim.

   Many open tarts are decorated with strips of
pastry in attractive patterns; in the North of
England, traditional designs are used for jam
tarts and up to eight different jams may sometimes
be incorporated in one tart, each separated with a
pastry bar. These traditional designs were often
associated with certain fillings, treacle tarts, for
example, are usually decorated with a pastry lattice
pattern.

Apple Tart After the Pig (6—8 portions) F

½ lb peeled, cored and chopped apples
2 oz soft brown sugar
4 cloves
½ lb savoury, sweet or rich shortcrust pastry
2 oz pork fat

Oven: 425°F; gas mark 7; 30 minutes

Simmer the apples over low heat with the sugar and
cloves until soft and light brown in colour. Discard
the cloves. Line a buttered pie plate with pastry,
setting the trimmings aside for decoration.

   Spread a thin layer of melted pork fat over the
pastry to form a waterproof base. Spoon the
apples over the pastry and decorate with four ½ in
wide strips in a lattice design; secure the pastry
strips on the rim with cloves. Bake for 30 minutes.

Fruit Tart (6—8 portions) F and H

½ lb prepared fruit
½ lb savoury, sweet or rich shortcrust pastry
2—4 oz sugar
4 oz melted jam or jelly

Oven: 425°F; gas mark 7; 30 minutes

Prepare the fruit according to type, leaving soft fruits fresh and cooking harder fruits, such as apples and pears, in a little water until tender but still retaining the shape. Cool before use.

Line an 8—9 in pie plate with the pastry and arrange the fruit on the base in alternate layers with the sugar, starting and finishing with a layer of fruit. Coat the top with jam or jelly and bake for 30 minutes or until firm

Jam Tart (6—8 portions) F and H

3—4 oz jam, marmalade, curd or mincemeat
½ lb savoury, sweet or rich shortcrust pastry

Oven: 425°F; gas mark 7; 30 minutes

Butter an 8 in pie plate, cover the rim with a strip of pastry and fit most of the remaining pastry over the base and sides.

Spread the filling over the base and use the pastry trimmings to decorate the tart. Bake for 30 minutes or until the pastry is firm.

North Country Tart (6—8 portions) F and H

½ lb savoury, sweet or rich shortcrust pastry
4 oz raspberry jam
2 oz butter
1 oz caster sugar
1 oz golden syrup
4 oz desiccated coconut
1 egg

Line an 8 in pie plate with the pastry and spread with raspberry jam.

Melt the butter, sugar and syrup in a pan over low heat, add the coconut and beaten egg. Mix thoroughly and spoon over the jam. Bake for 30 minutes or until the pastry is firm.

Treacle Custard Tart (6—8 portions) F and H Suffolk

2 eggs
6 oz golden syrup
½ lb savoury, sweet or rich shortcrust pastry

Oven: 375°F; gas mark 5; 30—40 minutes

Beat the eggs and mix with the warmed syrup. Leave to cool while lining an 8 in pie plate with the pastry; spoon the filling over the pastry base and bake until golden brown.

Serve cold when the filling will have set to a jelly-like consistency.

Treacle Tart (6—8 portions) F and H

½ lb golden syrup
½ lb savoury, sweet or rich shortcrust pastry
1½—2 oz white breadcrumbs
Grated rind and juice of 1 lemon
Pinch ginger or cinnamon

Oven: 375°F; gas mark 5; 20—30 minutes

Use about two thirds of the pastry to line an 8 in pie plate. Spread the syrup over the pastry base and sprinkle over the breadcrumbs mixed with lemon rind and juice, ginger or cinnamon. Decorate with narrow pastry strips in a woven lattice pattern.

Bake until golden brown and serve warm or cold with whipped cream flavoured with rum.

FLAN TARTS

These are entirely similar to plate tarts, but are baked in 8 in buttered flan rings set on a baking sheet.

Apple and Orange Tart (6—8 portions) F and H

1¼—1½ lb peeled, cored and sliced cooking apples
4 oranges
½ lb savoury, sweet or rich shortcrust pastry
2 oz sugar
½ teaspoon cinnamon
¾ oz flour
4 oz melted orange marmalade

Oven: 375°F; gas mark 5; 30—40 minutes

Poach the apple slices in a little water until soft but still retaining their shape. Peel the oranges, remove pith and cut the flesh into segments.

Roll out the pastry and line an 8 in flan ring. Mix the sugar, cinnamon and flour; arrange the fruits in layers on the pastry base, dusting each layer with the sugar mixture. Finish with a layer of orange. Brush with melted marmalade and bake until firm and golden.

Baked Apple Pudding (6—8 portions)
F and H Worcestershire

½ lb peeled, cored and sliced apples
4 oz sugar
Grated rind and juice of 1 lemon
½ lb creamed butter
2 eggs
2 egg yolks
½ lb savoury, sweet or rich shortcrust pastry
Candied lemon and orange peel

Oven: 375°F; gas mark 5; 30—40 minutes

Simmer the apples gently with the sugar; sieve to a
pulp and add the lemon juice and rind and the
butter. Beat the eggs and yolks and mix.

Line an 8 in flan ring with the rolled out pastry,
fill with the apple mixture and decorate with
candied peel. Bake for about 40 minutes or until
set and firm.

Baked Apricot Pudding (6—8 portions)
F and H

1 lb apricots
4 oz sugar
3 eggs
2½ fl oz double cream
½ lb savoury, sweet or rich shortcrust pastry

Oven: 400°F; gas mark 6; 15 minutes
        350°F; gas mark 4; 30 minutes

Cook the apricots until tender, remove skins and
stones, dice the flesh and mix with sugar to taste.
Beat the eggs with the cream and fold into the
apricots.

Line an 8 in flan ring with the pastry and spoon
in the filling. Bake in the oven for 45 minutes,
reducing the temperature after 15 minutes;
continue baking until the filling is set.

Bakewell Tart or Pudding (6—8 portions)
F and H Derbyshire

In some versions of this famous tart, the jam is
replaced with 3 oz mixed dried fruit soaked in
cider or wine.

Bakewell Pudding or Tart is reputed to have
originated at the Rutland Arms in Bakewell; one
legend maintains that it was created by an Italian
cook, another that it came about by accident
when an inexperienced cook omitted the flour
in an almond sponge pudding.

½ lb savoury, sweet or rich shortcrust pastry
1 oz raspberry jam
4 eggs
4 oz sugar
4 oz butter
4 oz ground almonds

Oven: 400°F; gas mark 6; 30—40 minutes

Line an 8 in flan ring with the pastry or use the
traditional Bakewell pudding tins which are oval
with sloping sides, about 2½ in deep, 6 in long
and 4 in wide.

Cover the pastry base with raspberry jam; beat
the eggs and sugar until pale and thick; melt the
butter and pour it slowly into the eggs, stirring
all the time. Fold in the ground almonds. Pour
this mixture into the pastry case and bake until
the filling is set.

Custard Tart (6—8 portions) F and H

½ lb savoury, sweet or rich shortcrust pastry
½ pt milk
3 egg yolks
1½ oz caster sugar
Grated nutmeg

Oven: 400°F; gas mark 6; 15 minutes
        350°F; gas mark 4; 30 minutes

Roll out the pastry and use to line an 8 in flan
ring. Heat the milk to blood heat, beat the egg
yolks with the sugar and pour the milk over them
beating all the time. Strain this custard and pour
into the pastry case; sprinkle with nutmeg.

Bake for 45 minutes, lowering the heat after 15
minutes and continue baking until the custard has
set golden and firm.

Edinburgh Tart (6—8 portions)
F and H Scotland

½ lb savoury, sweet or rich shortcrust pastry
2 oz butter
2 oz caster sugar
2 oz chopped candied peel
½ oz sultanas
2 oz flour
2 eggs

Oven: 375°F; gas mark 5; 30—40 minutes

Line an 8 in flan ring, set on a baking sheet, with
the pastry.

Melt the butter and add the sugar, peel, sultanas and flour; remove from the heat and stir in the beaten eggs. Pour the mixture into the pastry case and bake for about 40 minutes.

Fruit Tart (6—8 portions) F and H

14 oz prepared fruit
½ lb savoury, sweet or rich shortcrust pastry
4 oz sugar
4 oz melted jam or jelly

Oven: 375°F; gas mark 5; 30—40 minutes

Line an 8 in flan ring with the rolled out pastry. Prepare the fruit leaving soft fruits fresh, but stewing hard fruits in a little water and cooling before use.

Arrange the fruit in the pastry case, sprinkling with sugar, beginning and finishing with a layer of fruit. Coat the top with jam or jelly and bake until firm and set.

Kent Lent or Pudding Pies (6—8 portions) F Kent

The Pudden Pies, traditional at the Deddington or Pudding Pie Fair, Oxfordshire, on 22nd November, were identical to the Kent Lent Pies.

½ pt milk
¾ oz ground rice
2 oz butter
2 oz caster sugar
Grated rind of ½ lemon
Pinch salt
2 eggs
½ lb savoury, sweet or rich shortcrust pastry
½ oz currants

Oven: 375°F; gas mark 5; 20—30 minutes

Boil the milk, stir in the rice and add the butter, sugar, lemon rind and salt; leave to cool, then stir in the beaten eggs.

Line an 8 in flan ring with the pastry, pour the mixture into the pastry case and sprinkle with the currants. Bake for 20—30 minutes or until the filling has risen. Serve hot or cold.

Lemon Pie (6—8 portions) F and H

½ lb savoury, sweet or rich shortcrust pastry
2 eggs
2 yolks

5 oz caster sugar
6 oz melted butter or cream
Grated rind and juice of 2 lemons

Oven: 325°F; gas mark 3; 40 minutes

Roll out the pastry and line an 8 in flan ring. Lightly beat the eggs and egg yolks, add the sugar and continue whisking while adding the butter or cream. Fold in the lemon juice and rind. Pour the mixture into the pastry case and bake.

Madeira Pudding (6—8 portions) F and H

½ lb savoury, sweet or rich shortcrust pastry
1 oz raspberry jam
4 oz butter
4 oz caster sugar
1 teaspoon vanilla essence
2 eggs
4 oz flour
Pinch baking powder

Oven: 400°F; gas mark 6; 10 minutes
        350°F; gas mark 4; 30—35 minutes

Line an 8 in flan ring with the pastry and spread the jam over the base. Cream the butter and sugar, add vanilla essence and beat in the eggs.

Fold the flour and baking powder into the mixture; spoon into the pastry case and bake for about 40 minutes, reducing the heat after the first 10 minutes.

MERINGUE TOPPED FLANS

These flans are made like ordinary open flans in 8 in flan rings, but are topped with whipped meringue about halfway through baking. Served hot or cold.

Apple Amber Pudding (6—8 portions) F and H

¾ lb peeled, cored and sliced apples
4 oz sugar
Juice and rind of 1 lemon
2 eggs, separated
1½ oz butter
3 oz caster sugar
½ lb savoury, sweet or rich shortcrust pastry

Oven: 375°F; gas mark 5; 30 minutes
       300°F; gas mark 2; 15—20 minutes

Simmer the prepared apples with the sugar; sieve
to a pulp and add the lemon rind and juice; beat
in the egg yolks and butter. Line a flan ring with
the pastry and fill with the apple mixture.

    Bake for 30 minutes and meanwhile whisk the
egg whites and caster sugar to make a meringue;
pipe this on top of the flan and bake in the oven,
at reduced heat, for 15—20 minutes or until the
topping is pale brown.

Butterscotch Tart (6—8 portions) F and H

½ lb savoury, sweet or rich shortcrust pastry
½ lb soft brown sugar
4 oz flour
5 fl oz water
5 fl oz warmed milk
3 oz butter
1 teaspoon vanilla essence
3 eggs, separated
3 oz caster sugar

Oven: 375°F; gas mark 5; 30 minutes
       300°F; gas mark 2; 15—20 minutes

Line an 8 in flan ring with the pastry and bake blind
in the oven (375°F; gas mark 5) for 30 minutes.

    Mix the brown sugar and flour and blend with
the water; pour the milk over. Return this
mixture to the pan and cook until it thickens.
Remove from the heat, blend in the butter,
vanilla essence and egg yolks. Pour into the flan.

    Whisk the egg whites with the caster sugar to a
firm meringue, pipe on top of the flan and bake
for 15—20 minutes or until light brown.

Chocolate Meringue Pie (6—8 portions) F and H

½ lb savoury, sweet or rich shortcrust pastry
1 oz cornflour
¾ oz cocoa powder
5 oz sugar
¾ pt warmed milk
2 oz butter
3 eggs, separated
Vanilla essence
3 oz caster sugar

Oven: 375°F; gas mark 5; 30 minutes
       300°F; gas mark 2; 15—20 minutes

Roll out the pastry and use to line an 8 in flan
ring; bake blind for 30 minutes.

    Blend the cornflour, cocoa powder and sugar
and stir in the milk; cook this mixture over
gentle heat until thick. Remove from the heat, stir
in the butter and egg yolks and flavour to taste with
vanilla essence. Spoon into the baked flan, and
pipe over the meringue made from the egg whites
and caster sugar. Bake for 15—20 minutes or until
golden brown.

Lemon Meringue Pie (6—8 portions) F and H

½ lb savoury, sweet or rich shortcrust pastry
1 oz cornflour
½ pt boiling water
4 oz sugar
Grated rind and juice of 3 lemons
2 oz butter
3 eggs, separated
3 oz caster sugar

Oven: 400°F; gas mark 6; 15 minutes
       350°F; gas mark 4; 20 minutes

Line an 8 in flan ring with the pastry and bake
blind for 15 minutes at 400°F, gas mark 6.

    Blend the cornflour with a little cold water and
stir into the boiling water; add sugar, lemon juice
and rind and cook until thick. Set aside to cool,
then stir in the butter and egg yolks; pour into
the pastry case.

    Make up the meringue from the egg whites and
caster sugar and pipe it over the lemon filling.
Bake for 20 minutes or until the meringue is
golden brown.

Oxford and Cambridge Pudding (6— 8 portions) F and H

1 lb apricots
4 oz sugar
3 eggs, separated
2½ fl oz double cream
½ lb savoury, sweet or rich shortcrust pastry
3 oz caster sugar

Oven: 350°F; gas mark 4; 35 minutes
       300°F; gas mark 2; 15 minutes

Cook the apricots until tender; remove the skins
and stones, dice the flesh and mix with the sugar.
Beat the egg yolks with the cream and stir into
the apricots.

Line an 8 in flan ring with the pastry and spoon the apricot filling into the case. Bake for 35 minutes or until set at 350°F, gas mark 4.

Meanwhile, whisk the egg whites and caster sugar to a stiff meringue; pipe on to the baked flan and return to the oven for 15 minutes, at reduced heat. Serve hot or cold.

Welsh Border Tart or Chester Pudding (6—8 portions) F and H

1 oz butter
4 oz sugar
4 oz raisins
4 oz sultanas
3 eggs, separated
½ lb savoury, sweet or rich shortcrust pastry
3 oz caster sugar

Oven: 350°F; gas mark 4; 30 minutes
300°F; gas mark 2; 10—15 minutes

Melt the butter and cool; add the sugar, raisins, sultanas and egg yolks.

Line an 8 in flan ring with the pastry, spoon in the filling and bake at 350°F (gas mark 4) for 30 minutes. Make up a meringue from the egg whites and caster sugar, pipe on to the baked flan and return to the oven, at 300°F, gas mark 2.

Bake for 10—15 minutes or until the meringue is pale brown. Serve hot or cold.

RAISED FRUIT PIES

These are made with hot water crust pastry, slightly sweetened with a little sugar. They appear to have been less popular than shortcrust and puff pastry fruit pies and chiefly had a filling of soft fresh fruit.

Raised Fruit Pies (6—8 portions) F Nottinghamshire

1 lb hot water crust pastry
1½ lb prepared gooseberries
6 oz sugar
6 oz melted apple jelly

Oven: 425°F; gas mark 7; 15 minutes
325°F; gas mark 3; 45 minutes

Make up the pastry and mould two thirds into one large pie, 6 in wide and 3 in deep or into eight small pies. Put the gooseberries in the pie shell, layered with the sugar. Cover the pie or pies with the remaining pastry, sprinkle lightly with sugar and make a hole in the centre.

Bake for 1 hour or until the pastry is well browned, reducing the temperature after 15 minutes. When baked, pour the melted apple jelly into the pie; leave to set and serve cold, cut into slices, with whipped cream.

Oldbury Tarts (6—8 portions) F Gloucestershire

1 lb hot water crust pastry
1½ lb prepared gooseberries
6 oz Demerara sugar

Oven: 400°F; gas mark 6; 30—40 minutes

Prepare the pastry and use two thirds to make up eight small pie shells. Fill these with the gooseberries, sprinkle with the sugar and fit on the lids.

Bake until golden brown and serve warm or cold, with a jug of cream.

PASTIES, TURNOVERS AND BAKED DUMPLINGS

This is a collection of individual, sweet pies, mainly with regional connotations.

Ashburton Open Pastie (6—8 portions) Devon

1 lb puff pastry
¾ lb stewed fresh or dried fruit, mincemeat or jam

Oven: 425°F; gas mark 7; 20 minutes

Roll out the pastry, ½ in thick, to a rectangle twice as long as it is wide. Spread the filling over the pastry, to within 1 in of the edges. Fold the edges towards the centre of the pastie and bake for about 20 minutes.

Baked Apple Dumplings (8 portions) F

In Gloucestershire, these are known as Newent Apple Cobs.

8 large cooking apples
4 oz butter
½ lb brown sugar
Pinch cinnamon or cloves

Grated rind of 2 lemons
1¼ lb sweet shortcrust pastry
Caster sugar

Oven: 350°F; gas mark 4; 1 hour

Peel and core the apples. Mix the butter with the
sugar, cinnamon and lemon rind and stuff this
mixture into the apples. Roll out the pastry and cut
into eight circles, each large enough to enclose an
apple. Wrap each apple in pastry, sealing the
moistened edges firmly.

Set the apples on a baking tray, sealed edges
down, and bake until the apples are soft when
tested with a skewer and the pastry is cooked.
Serve warm, dusted with sugar and accompanied
with whipped cream.

Cherry Bumpers (8 portions) F Buckinghamshire

Traditional at the end of cherry picking in
August.

1 lb puff pastry or ¾ lb savoury, sweet or rich
  shortcrust pastry
¾ lb stoned black cherries
2 oz sugar
Milk

Oven: 425°F; gas mark 7; 30 minutes

Roll out the pastry, ¼ in thick, and cut into eight
rounds. Top each pastry round with a cold
filling of the cherries simmered until soft with
the sugar.

Draw the pastry edges up over the top, moisten
and crimp together to seal. Brush with milk or
water, sprinkle with a little sugar and bake until
golden brown.

Cumberland Scrap and Currant Pasty (8 portions) F Cumberland

¾ lb savoury, sweet or rich shortcrust pastry
3 oz lard
3 oz currants
4 oz peeled, cored and chopped apples
4 oz brown sugar
½ teaspoon cinnamon

Oven: 425°F; gas mark 7; 30 minutes

Roll the pastry out thinly and cut into eight rounds;
brush with melted lard. Mix the currants and
apples with the sugar and cinnamon and divide

this filling equally over the pastry rounds. Draw up
the pastry edges and seal; brush with water or milk
and sprinkle with a little sugar. Bake for 30
minutes.

Fruit Turnovers (8 portions) F

Fresh fruit for turnovers should be prepared in
advance, currants stripped and strawberries hulled;
apples and pears should be peeled, cored and
sliced, plums and cherries should be stoned.

1 lb puff pastry of ¾ lb savoury, sweet or rich
  shortcrust pastry
1 lb cleaned fresh fruit or ½ lb dried fruit or
  mincemeat or 4—6 oz jam
Milk
Caster sugar

Oven: 425°F; gas mark 7; 30 minutes

Roll the pastry out, ¼ in thick, and cut into
eight rounds. Spoon the filling into the centre
of each pastry round, fold over the moistened
edges and seal. Brush with milk or water and
sprinkle with sugar. Bake for 30 minutes or until
golden brown.

Plum Shuttles (8 portions) F Rutland

1 lb puff pastry or ¾ lb savoury, sweet or rich
  shortcrust pastry
¾ lb stoned chopped plums
4 oz sugar
1 egg
Caster sugar

Oven: 425°F; gas mark 7; 30 minutes

Roll out the pastry, ¼ in thick, and cut into eight
oblongs. Mix the chopped plums with the sugar
and spoon this filling along the pasties. Join the
oblongs along the edges so that they resemble
weavers' shuttles. Brush with beaten egg or milk
and sprinkle with sugar. Bake.

Sorrel Turnovers (8 portions) F Lancashire

These are known in Cornwall as Sour Sauce
Pasties and are served with sugar and cream.

1 lb roughly chopped sorrel
6 oz brown sugar
1 lb puff pastry or ¾ lb savoury, sweet or rich
  shortcrust pastry

Milk

Oven: 425°F; gas mark 7; 30 minutes

Mix the sorrel with the sugar and use as a filling
on eight rounds of the pastry, rolled out ¼ in
thick. Moisten the edges and fold over, crimping
to seal. Brush with milk and bake for 30 minutes
or until golden brown.

Teisen Planc Afalan (6—8 portions) F Wales

1 lb savoury shortcrust pastry
¾ lb stewed sweetened apples
Caster sugar

Roll the pastry out thinly and cut into two even-
sized rounds. Spread the apple mixture on one
round and place the other round on top; moisten
the edges and seal thoroughly.

Bake gently on a bakestone (griddle) or in a heavy
frying pan, turning the pasty once. Sprinkle with
sugar and serve hot.

Westmorland Pasty (8 portions) F Westmorland

In one version of these pasties apples are topped
with a few elderberries beneath the pastry.

3 oz chopped suet
3 oz brown sugar
1 level teaspoon ground nutmeg
1 lb puff pastry or ¾ lb savoury, sweet or rich
    shortcrust pastry
Milk
Caster sugar

Oven: 425°F; gas mark 7; 30 minutes

Mix the suet with the sugar and nutmeg and divide
equally over eight pastry rounds. Fold over the
moistened pastry edges, seal and brush with milk.
Sprinkle with a little sugar, and bake until golden.

Yorkshire Mint Pasty (8 portions) F Yorkshire

1 lb puff pastry or ¾ lb savoury, sweet or rich
    shortcrust pastry
2 oz currants
2 oz raisins
1 oz candied peel
1½ oz brown sugar
Pinch grated nutmeg or mixed spice

1 tablespoon freshly chopped mint
1½ oz butter
Milk
Caster sugar

Oven: 425°F; gas mark 7; 30 minutes

Roll out the pastry, ¼ in thick, and cut into eight
rounds. Mix the currants and raisins with candied
peel, sugar, nutmeg and mint and bind with the
butter. Divide this filling equally over the pastry
rounds, fold over and seal the edges.

Brush with milk, sprinkle with sugar and bake
until golden brown.

Wholemeal or Great Pasty (8 portions) F Cornwall

This, as the name implies, is a meal-in-one pasty,
containing a savoury as well as a sweet filling; the
meat portion is eaten first.

1½ lb shortcrust pastry
1½ lb sweet filling
1½ lb meat and vegetable filling
1 egg

Oven: 375°F; gas mark 5; 30 minutes

Cut a small piece from the pastry, roll the remainder out thinly and cut into eight large rounds.
Roll the small piece into a 1 in wide strip and
place across the large rounds to divide them into
two equal halves.

Place the sweet filling in one half and the meat
in the other. Close the pasties towards the centre
and crimp the edges. Mark the sweet filling with
an "S" and the meat filling with an "M"; brush
with beaten egg. Bake for 30 minutes.

SWEET PUDDINGS

Originally an extension of the savoury pudding
concept, steamed and boiled sweet puddings are
more closely connected with traditional British
cooking than any other type of dish. The great
majority of dessert dishes have developed from the
sweet pudding, and while the connection may
sometimes seem obscure it is evident from early
cookery writings that custards and milk and batter
puddings, for example, were originally boiled in a
cloth.

Although many of the steamed and boiled
suet puddings have disappeared, a surprising

number, mainly from the 19th century, have survived and are often named after a particular town or district. The obsessive dread of carbohydrates and animal fats in the second half of the 20th century is endangering the perpetuity of such famous puddings as Plum Duff and Spotted Dick, despite the fact that such puddings apart from being extremely tasty and energy-giving are also easy and inexpensive to make.

STEAMED SUET PUDDINGS

These are all based on the simple method of mixing suet with dry ingredients and adding milk to give a soft consistency. The mixture is steamed, turned out and served hot, usually with a sauce that complements the filling.

Sweet Suet Pudding (6—8 portions) F

This is the basic suet pudding from which other variations have evolved. A beaten egg may be added to the mixture for a richer pudding. Cumberland Pudding, which is served with rum sauce, includes ½ lb grated apples, grated rind of 1 lemon and 2 oz treacle.

½ lb plain flour
4 oz finely chopped suet
3 oz caster sugar
3 teaspoons baking powder
$^{1}/_{3}$ pt milk

Blend the dry ingredients and mix to a soft consistency with the milk. Put the pudding mixture in a scalded and floured pudding cloth and tie securely, leaving room for expansion.

Alternatively, put the mixture into a 1½ pt well-greased pudding bowl or basin and cover with foil or greaseproof paper. Steam for 2½—3 hours. Turn out the pudding and serve with a sweet sauce.

A number of flavourings may be added to the basic pudding mixture, such as a pinch of ground ginger or mixed spice; serve with ginger sauce. Add 6—8 oz currants, dates or raisins, sultanas or figs or other dried fruit and the grated rind of 1 lemon; serve with lemon sauce.

Spoon 3 oz black treacle, golden syrup, jam or marmalade over the base of the basin before putting in the mixture; serve with custard, syrup or jam sauce. Add ½ lb finely chopped cooking apples; serve with a sweet white sauce flavoured with nutmeg.

Apple "In and Out" (6—8 portions) F West Country

1 lb peeled, cored and diced cooking apples
1 lb self-raising flour
1 teaspoon salt
½ lb chopped suet
4 oz sugar

Sif the flour and salt, add suet, sugar and the apples with enough cold water to make a soft, elastic dough. Put the mixture in a 2½ pt greased pudding basin and steam for 2½ hours. Serve with custard or treacle.

Brown George Pudding (6—8 portions) F Isle of Wight

6 oz white breadcrumbs
2 oz plain flour
1 teaspoon bicarbonate of soda
3 oz brown sugar
4 oz finely chopped suet
1 egg
Milk
½ lb black treacle

Mix the breadcrumbs, flour and bicarbonate of soda with the sugar and suet; mix to a dough with the lightly beaten egg, milk and treacle to give a soft dropping consistency.

Steam for 2½—3 hours in a 2½ pt greased pudding basin tied down with foil or greaseproof paper. Serve with jam or treacle.

Chester Pudding (6—8 portions) F Cheshire

4 oz self-raising flour
4 oz shredded suet
4 oz white breadcrumbs
4 oz black currant jam
2 oz caster sugar
1 egg
Milk

Mix all the dry ingredients thoroughly with the jam. Mix to a dough with the lightly beaten egg and milk. Spoon the pudding mixture into a greased 2 pt pudding basin and steam for 3 hours. Serve with black currant jam.

Christmas Pudding F and H

The most famous of all suet puddings, — Christmas Pudding — also has the longest recorded history.

It has undergone numerous changes since it first appeared as a traditional dish on Christmas Eve in the form of a frumenty of hulled wheat and milk. By early medieval days, the Christmas frumenty, now made with beef or mutton broth, thickened with oatmeal and flavoured with eggs, currants, dried plums, mace and ginger, had become plum porridge. The Elizabethans made few changes, except for substituting oatmeal with breadcrumbs and adding suet and ale or wine; plum porridge was still semi-liquid, but by 1675 the meat broth disappeared, plum porridge changed to plum pudding and as such was boiled in a cloth.

Since then, the plum pudding has remained virtually unchanged, its present name being adopted in the 19th century when dried plums were replaced by raisins, currants, sultanas and candied peel. The Christmas pudding reached its fullest glory in the Victorian era when huge puddings were the order of the day; they were round as cannon balls and boiled in cloths; the present pudding-basin shape did not become popular until well into the 20th century.

1 lb white breadcrumbs
1 teaspoon ground ginger
1 teaspoon mixed spice
2 teaspoons salt
½ lb shredded or finely chopped suet
½ lb brown sugar
4 oz chopped mixed peel
4 oz currants
4 oz sultanas
1 lb seedless raisins
3 oz grated carrots
3 tablespoons brandy
2 tablespoons milk
4 oz golden syrup

Mix the breadcrumbs, spices, salt, suet, sugar, mixed peel, fruits and carrots together in a large bowl. Blend the brandy, milk and syrup and stir thoroughly into the dry ingredients; let the mixture stand for at least 1 hour. Spoon into 1½– 2 pt greased pudding basins, cover with grease-proof paper and cloth or foil and steam.

Christmas puddings may be steamed in various sized basins; for 1 pt puddings allow 5 hours; for 1½ pt puddings 7 hours and for 2 pt puddings

9 hours. When cooked, remove from the steamer and allow to cool. Cover with fresh paper and store in a cool place; they will keep for 12–18 months and improve and mature during this time. On the day of serving, renew the covering and steam the pudding as follows:

1 pt puddings for 2 hours; 1½ pt and 2 pt puddings for 3 hours. Turn out on to a hot dish, decorate with holly and flame with warmed brandy; serve with brandy or rum butter or a sweet white sauce flavoured with rum.

King George's Christmas Pudding H and F

Numerous traditions surround the making and serving of Christmas puddings, such as Stir-up Sunday (November 30) when every member of the household took turns in stirring the pudding, in an east-west direction as a tribute to the Three Kings. Silver coins and charms were incorporated for luck; the prickly holly sprig in the steamed pudding is said to represent Christ's suffering on the cross.

The following Christmas pudding (4 puddings, 2 lb each) is similar to the one served for George I at his first Christmas in England.

1½ lb finely chopped or shredded suet
1 lb Demerara sugar
1 lb white breadcrumbs
1 lb plain flour
1 lb raisins
1 lb stoned prunes
4 oz chopped candied lemon peel
4 oz chopped candied orange peel
1 teaspoon mixed spice
1 teaspoon ground nutmeg
1 tablespoon salt
5 fl oz brandy
8 eggs
½ pt milk

In a large bowl mix together the suet, sugar, breadcrumbs, flour, dried fruits and spices. Mix the brandy with the beaten eggs and add to the dry ingredients with enough milk to give a soft dropping consistency.

Cover the mixture and leave for 12 hours, stir thoroughly and spoon into well-greased basins; cover with buttered greaseproof paper and clean pudding cloths.

For steaming and serving, see opposite.

Cloutie Dumpling (12—16 portions)
Scotland

"Cloute" (pronounced "cloot") is the Scottish term
for a cloth.

1 lb flour
4—6 oz breadcrumbs
½ lb sugar
½ lb finely chopped suet
½ lb sultanas
½ lb currants
4 oz muscatel raisins
4 oz chopped peel
2 grated apples or carrots
1 teaspoon baking powder
½ teaspoon salt
2 teaspoons each, cinnamon, spice and ginger
2 eggs
½ lb black treacle
Milk

Mix together the flour, breadcrumbs, sugar, suet,
dried fruits, apples, baking powder, salt and spices.
Blend the beaten eggs with the treacle and stir into
the dry mixture, with enough milk to give a soft
dough.
   Put the mixture in a floured pudding cloth and
tie the ends; alternatively, spoon into a 2½ pt
greased pudding basin and tie down with buttered
greaseproof paper and foil or cloth. Steam for
2½—3 hours.

Helston Pudding (6—8 portions)
F Cornwall

4 oz plain flour
4 oz ground rice
1 teaspoon bicarbonate of soda
3 oz caster sugar
4 oz finely chopped or shredded suet
4 oz currants
4 oz sultanas
2 oz raisins
2 oz candied peel
Salt
1 teaspoon mixed spice
1 tablespoon lemon juice
½ pt milk

In a large bowl, mix together the flour, rice,
bicarbonate of soda, sugar, suet, dried fruit and
spice. Blend thoroughly, then stir in the lemon
juice and milk, mixing to a dropping consistency.

Spoon the mixture into a greased 2½ pt pudding
basin; cover with greaseproof paper and a cloth
or foil and steam for 2½—3 hours.

Huntingdon Pudding (6—8 portions)
F Huntingdon

This suet and gooseberry pudding is also known
in Hertfordshire and Essex.

½ lb plain flour
½ oz baking powder
4 oz finely chopped or shredded suet
3 oz caster sugar
$^1/_3$ pt milk
1 lb topped and tailed green gooseberries
3 oz brown sugar

Mix together the flour, baking powder, suet and
caster sugar; stir in enough milk to give a soft
dropping consistency.
   Grease a 2½ pt pudding basin and arrange
layers of the pudding mixture and the prepared
gooseberries; sprinkle the fruit with brown sugar
and begin and finish with a layer of pudding
mixture. Cover with greaseproof paper and tie
down with a pudding cloth or foil; steam for
2½—3 hours.

New College Pudding (6—8 portions)
F and H Oxford

Traditional at New College, Oxford, since the
early 19th century, these small suet puddings
are fried in butter.

4 oz shredded suet
4 oz white breadcrumbs
2 oz sugar
½ oz baking powder
Pinch salt
4 oz currants
1 oz candied peel
3 eggs
1 tablespoon brandy
Butter

Mix the suet, breadcrumbs, sugar, baking powder
and salt with the currants and candied peel; blend
thoroughly and stir in the beaten eggs mixed with
the brandy. The mixture should have a soft,
dropping consistency.
   Fry the pudding mixture in spoonfuls in hot
butter for about 6 minutes or until brown,
turning once. Serve hot, sprinkled with sugar.

Northamptonshire Pudding (8—10 portions)
F and H Northamptonshire

1 lb plain flour
1 oz baking powder
2 teaspoons salt
¾ lb finely chopped or shredded suet
1 egg
1 egg yolk
5 fl oz single cream

Sift the flour, baking powder and salt into a bowl and mix in the suet, egg and egg yolk. Stir in the cream until the mixture has a soft consistency.

Spoon into a greased 2 pt pudding basin and cover with greaseproof paper; tie down with a cloth or foil. Steam for 2½—3 hours, turn out and serve with a sweet sauce.

Plum Duff (6—8 portions) F and H Sussex

This dates from the first half of the 19th century and describes a boiled suet pudding with raisins or currants; "duff" is a colloquial corruption of dough. In Sussex, Plum Duff is also known as Hunt Pudding.

½ lb plain flour
2 teaspoons baking powder
1 teaspoon mixed spice
3 oz caster sugar
4 oz finely chopped or shredded suet
6 oz raisins
⅓ pt milk
½ lb red currant jelly (optional)

Sift the flour and baking powder and mix in the spice, sugar, suet and raisins; stir in the milk and blend thoroughly. Put the pudding mixture in a floured cloth; tie the ends securely, leaving room for expansion and boil for 2½—3 hours.

Serve with the melted red currant jelly poured over the plum duff.

Sweet Haggis (6—8 portions) F Scotland

This is a sweet-savoury pudding served as a main course and sometimes sliced, fried or grilled. It is similar to Gold Belly which is oatmeal soaked in buttermilk and mixed with shredded mutton fat, raisins, peel and prunes and shaped into a ball with butter and brown sugar in the centre. Traditionally served with melted butter and brown sugar.

½ lb chopped suet
¾ lb coarse oatmeal
2 oz plain flour
4 oz raisins
4 oz currants
4 oz sugar
½ tablespoon salt
¼ teaspoon pepper
3 fl oz water

Blend all the dry ingredients thoroughly and mix to a stiff consistency with the water. Put the mixture into a sheep's stomach bag, sew it up and prick with a fork.

Alternatively, tie in a pudding cloth and boil for 3 hours or spoon the mixture into a 2½ pt pudding basin and steam for 3—4 hours.

Treacle Roll (6—8 portions) F and H

½ lb plain flour
2 teaspoons baking powder
4 oz finely chopped or shredded suet
3 oz caster sugar
1 egg
⅓ pt milk (approx)
2 oz white breadcrumbs
½ lb golden syrup

Sift the flour and baking powder and mix with the suet and sugar; stir in the beaten egg and milk to give an elastic dough. Roll out on a floured board to a square, ¾ in thick.

Warm the syrup and pour half on the dough, leaving a 1 in margin at one edge. Sprinkle the breadcrumbs over the syrup, turn in the side edges and wet them. Roll up the dough from the 1 in margin and seal the edges.

Roll in buttered paper and a pudding cloth and tie the ends securely, allowing room for expansion. Steam for 2 hours and serve the remaining syrup as a sauce.

ROLY POLY PUDDINGS

These consist of a sweet suet pastry rolled up round a sweet filling. They are generally steamed or boiled in a pudding cloth or a special metal pudding "sleeve", but may also be baked in a large greased pie dish for about 30 minutes at 400°F, gas mark 6. Occasionally a roly poly is made as a suet layer pudding and steamed in a basin. The Sussex

Blanket Pudding, which now is of historical interest only, was folded like a blanket, not rolled, and was made with either savoury or sweet suet pastry according to the filling.

Black Treacle Roll (6—8 portions) F Leicestershire

10 oz sweet suet pastry
6 oz black treacle (approx)
3 oz dried chopped fruit
1 teaspoon ground ginger

Oven: 400°F; gas mark 6; 25-30 minutes

Mix the treacle with the chopped fruit and ground ginger. Roll out the pastry, about ¼ in thick, to a 10—12 in long strip; spread the treacle filling over this to within 1 in of the edges. Moisten the edges, fold over to hold the filling in place and roll up the pastry. Seal firmly.

Arrange join-side down in a large greased pie dish and bake. Serve hot with warmed treacle.

Jam Roly Poly (6—8 portions) F and H

This may also be made as a suet layer pudding in which case the pastry is divided into four uneven portions and rolled out to fit a 1½ pt greased pudding basin. The pastry and jam filling are layered in the basin, beginning with jam and finishing with pastry, and the layer pudding is steamed for 2½ hours.

10 oz sweet suet pastry
½ lb jam, lemon curd, mincemeat or marmalade

Roll out the pastry to a 10 in strip, about ¼ in thick, and moisten the edges; spread the pastry with the softened jam, leaving at least ½ in clear all round. Fold over and roll up, sealing the edges well.

Tie in a floured pudding cloth, allowing room for expansion; tie the ends securely and boil for 1½ hours. A pudding cloth should first be dipped into boiling water, wrung out, and then sprinkled, on the inside, with flour before the pudding is laid on it.

Plain Bolster Pudding (6—8 portions) F

10 oz sweet suet pastry
4 oz brown sugar
1 teaspoon ground cinnamon

Roll out the pastry as for Jam Roly Poly; mix the sugar and cinnamon and spread over the pastry,

pressing it in lightly. Roll up and tie in a floured pudding cloth and steam for 1½ hours. Serve with butter and brown sugar and a fruit sauce.

Spotted Dog (6—8 portions) F and H

This well-known roly poly pudding, named after the raisins in the suet dough, is also called Spotted Dick or Plum Bolster.

10 oz sweet suet pastry
4 oz raisins or currants (dates or figs)
Grated rind of 1 lemon

Roll out the pastry to a strip, about 10 in long and ¼ in thick. Lay the raisins over the pastry, leaving a clear ½ in margin all round; press the raisins in lightly and sprinkle with lemon rind. Moisten the edges and roll up from one of the long sides; seal the edges firmly and roll in a floured pudding cloth.

Make a pleat in the cloth to allow the pastry to expand and tie the ends firmly. Boil or steam for 1½ hours, remove from the cloth and serve at once with red currant and raspberry sauce, butter and brown sugar or a sweet white sauce.

Syrup Roll (6—8 portions) F and H Hampshire

10 oz sweet suet pastry
6 oz golden syrup
1 teaspoon ground ginger or grated rind of 1 lemon

Roll out the pastry, ¼ in thick, into a strip 10—12 in long. Spread with syrup to within 1 in of the edges and sprinkle with ginger or lemon peel. Roll up the pudding, sealing the edges carefully to prevent the syrup seeping out.

Tie securely in a floured pudding cloth, leaving room for the pastry to swell. Steam for 1½ hours. Serve with warm syrup.

Vectis Pudding (6—8 portions) F and H Isle of Wight

10 oz sweet suet pastry
6 oz black treacle
3 oz currants
½ lb peeled, cored and chopped apples
Grated rind of ½ lemon
1 teaspoon mixed spice

Roll the pastry out, ¼ in thick, to a 10—12 in long

strip; spread the treacle over the pastry leaving a clear 1 in margin all round. Arrange the currants and apples over the treacle and sprinkle with lemon rind mixed with spice.

Roll up carefully from the long sides and seal the edges well. Tie securely in a floured pudding cloth and steam for 2 hours.

Wet Nelly (6—8 portions) F Lancashire

This was originally made with crusts of bread, left over from bread sauce.

½ lb white breadcrumbs
5 fl oz water
2 teaspoons mixed spice
4 oz chopped suet
4 oz sugar

Oven: 350°F; gas mark 4; 1½ hours

Soak the breadcrumbs in water for 30 minutes, add the spice, suet and sugar. Spoon the mixture into a greased, rectangular bread tin and bake for 1½ hours until firm. Serve hot or cold, cut into squares.

Steamed Fruit Pudding (6—8 portions) F and H

This is really a combination of a steamed suet pudding and a roly poly and known in Scotland as a fruit dumpling. It may be filled with any kind of berry fruit — bilberries, black or red currants — or with apples, quinces, apricots, damsons, cherries, nectarines, plums or peaches.

Midsummer Pudding has a filling of equal amounts of red currants and raspberries and is served with a cider sauce. In Herefordshire, the pudding is filled with whortleberries and crowberries.

10 oz sweet suet pastry
1½—2 lb prepared fruit
6 oz sugar (approx.)

Prepare the fruit according to type, peeling, coring and chopping apples, stoning damsons, cherries, plums, peaches, etc. and stripping currants from the stalks.

Roll out the pastry and use three quarters to line a greased 2 pt pudding basin. Put in half the fruit, add the sugar according to taste, and the remaining fruit; spoon over a little water with hard non-juicy fruits.

Roll out the remaining pastry to fit the top of the basin and cover the pudding; seal the edges and press the lid down firmly. Cover with foil or greaseproof paper and steam for 2—2½ hours. Serve with custard.

Soft fruits take the shorter time to cook.

RICE AND CEREAL PUDDINGS

Often considered nursery-type puddings as they are easily digestible, many of these traditional milk puddings are in fact quite rich desserts. Most have developed from the frumenty of the 14th century; this, as so many of our sweet dishes, was originally a savoury, semi-liquid dish of hulled wheat cooked in milk and flavoured with spices. It was served as an accompaniment to meat and other savoury dishes.

Barley Pudding (6—8 portions) F The Lothians of Scotland

6 oz barley
2 pt water
4 oz currants

Oven: 300°F; gas mark 2; 3 hours

Wash the barley and put in an ovenproof dish with the water. Bake for 3 hours, stirring in the currants for the last 20 minutes. Serve with sugar and single cream or milk.

Buxton Pudding (6—8 portions) F Derbyshire

6 oz butter
3 oz flour
2 pt warm milk
Grated rind of 2 lemons
6 egg yolks
4 oz caster sugar

Oven: 350°F; gas mark 4; 30—40 minutes

Melt half the butter in a pan, stir in the flour and gradually add the warm milk mixed with lemon rind. Stir continuously until the mixture has thickened; heat through and cool slightly. Beat in the egg yolks one by one.

Pour the mixture into a 3 pt greased ovenproof dish, dot with the remaining butter and sprinkle with the sugar. Bake in the oven until well risen and golden brown.

Clipping Time Pudding (6—8 portions) F Cumberland

3 oz long grain rice
2 pt milk
Pinch cinnamon
3 oz sugar
1 egg
4 oz currants
4 oz raisins
4 oz chopped beef marrow

Oven: 350°F; gas mark 4; 20 minutes

Blanch the rice in a little salted water and drain.
Put in a pan with the milk, cinnamon and sugar
and cook slowly until tender. Beat the egg and
stir into the rice, with the currants and raisins. Add
the beef marrow.
   Spoon the pudding mixture into a 3 pt greased
pie dish and bake.

Colchester Pudding (6—8 portions) F and H Essex

1¾ pt milk
1½ oz tapioca
Salt
Grated rind of 1 lemon
Vanilla essence
1 lb stewed fruit
6 egg yolks
½ lb caster sugar
5 fl oz double cream
3 egg whites

Oven: 400°F; gas mark 6; 10—15 minutes

Heat 1 pt of the milk in a pan, sprinkle in the
tapioca with a pinch of salt, stirring continuously.
Bring to the boil over gentle heat and simmer until
soft after about 10 minutes. Add the lemon rind
and flavour with a few drops of vanilla essence.
   Put a layer of stewed fruit in an ovenproof dish,
cover with the tapioca mixture. Make up a rich
custard from the egg yolks, 3 oz caster sugar and
the remaining ¾ pt milk and the cream; cook in a
double saucepan and pour over the tapioca.
   Whisk the egg whites stiffly and fold in the last
5 oz caster sugar to make a meringue. Pipe the
meringue over the custard and bake the pudding
until the top is pale brown. Serve cold.

Cornflour Pudding (6—8 portions) F

This pudding may also be made in a mould and
served cold: omit the eggs and pour the mixture
into a wet mould to set; turn out and serve with
fruit or jam sauce. Cornflour pudding can be
flavoured with chocolate — 1½ oz cocoa blended
with the cornflour or 4 oz melted chocolate stirred
into the cooked mixture — or coffee, ¼ oz instant
coffee or 1 tablespoon coffee essence added to
the blended cornflour.

3 oz cornflour
2 pt milk
Pinch salt
2 oz sugar
Flavouring
2 eggs

Oven: 375°F; gas mark 5; 20 minutes

Blend the cornflour with a little milk and salt.
Heat the rest of the milk and pour on to the blended flour. Return to the pan and stir until boiling;
simmer, stirring for about 2 minutes. Remove
from the heat. Add the sugar and the chosen
flavouring.
   Separate the eggs and beat the yolks into the
mixture; beat the whites until stiff and fold in.
Pour the mixture into a greased 2½—3 pt pie dish
and bake for 20 minutes or until set.

Crail Pudding (6—8 portions) F Scotland

6 oz butter
3 oz flour
2 pt warm milk
½ teaspoon cinnamon
4 eggs
4 oz caster sugar
Garnish: ground cinnamon

Oven: 350°F; gas mark 4; 45 minutes

Melt half the butter, stir in the flour and gradually
add the milk, stirring all the time; add the cinnamon
and heat through. Leave to cool slightly, stirring
occasionally to prevent a skin forming.
   Separate the eggs and add the yolks to the
cooled mixture. Whisk the whites stiffly with the
sugar and fold in carefully. Spoon into a 3 pt
greased pie dish, dot with the remaining butter and
bake until well browned and risen. Sprinkle with
cinnamon just before serving.

Frumenty (6—8 portions) F

For this ancient dish of early medieval days, use fresh wheat with the husks removed or failing this barley. Dried fruit — currants, raisins — may be included for additional flavouring and honey can be used as a sweetener instead of sugar. A richer frumenty is made by thickening it with egg yolks instead of flour.

10 oz wheat
1½ pt water
2 pt milk
Sugar, nutmeg, cinnamon
Grated rind of 1 lemon
1 oz flour

Wash the wheat and put in a pan or earthenware jar with a cover; add the water and cover with a lid. Put the jar in a cool oven or stand it in a double saucepan over slow heat on top of the cooker for about 24 hours. The wheat should then have formed a thick gelatinous mass and is now known as creed wheat, ready for making the frumenty. It will keep for up to 3 days before using.

Add the milk to the creed wheat and boil together. When it begins to thicken, add sugar, spices, lemon rind and dried fruits to taste. Blend the flour with a little milk and stir into the mixture; boil until the frumenty has thickened.

George Pudding (10—12 portions) F and H

Dating from the 18th century, this is probably another favourite of the "pudding-eating monarch".

1 pt milk
Strip lemon peel
3 cloves
1½ oz long grain rice
1 oz caster sugar
2½—3 lb stewed apples
5 fl oz white wine
1 oz butter
2 oz candied lemon and orange peel
5 eggs, separated
2 baked puff pastry cases, each 8 in wide

Oven: 350°F; gas mark 4; 35—45 minutes

Bring the milk to the boil with the lemon peel and cloves, add the rice and simmer over gentle heat until tender, after about 40 minutes. Remove the cloves and lemon peel, sweeten with the sugar and add the stewed apples, wine, butter, candied peel and lastly the egg yolks.

Whisk the egg whites until stiff and fold into the mixture; spoon into the baked pastry shells. Bake in the oven until golden brown and the filling is set; serve with a wine sauce.

Ground Rice Pudding (20 portions) Bath, Somerset

This pudding may also be made in individual patty cases; the given ingredients are sufficient to fill about 20 cases.

1 pt single cream
1½ oz ground rice
Pinch salt
Grated nutmeg
2 tablespoons sherry
¾ lb butter
6 eggs
4 oz caster sugar
3 sweet shortcrust pastry cases, each 8 in wide

Oven: 350°F; gas mark 4; 30—35 minutes

Heat the cream and sprinkle in the ground rice, stirring all the time; simmer for 10 minutes without letting the mixture boil. Remove from the heat and leave to cool slightly; season with salt and add nutmeg to taste.

Stir in the sherry, the butter cut into pieces and the eggs; sweeten to taste with the sugar. Blend thoroughly and spoon into the baked flan cases. Bake in the oven for about 30 minutes or until set and golden brown.

Hasty Pudding (6—8 portions) F

As the name implies, this is a pudding that can be made from available ingredients at a few moments' notice.

6 oz butter
3 oz flour
2 pt warm milk
2 teaspoons cinnamon or nutmeg
Pinch mace or 1 bay leaf
2 eggs (optional)
4 oz caster sugar

Melt half the butter in a pan and stir in the flour; gradually add the warm milk, stirring all the time until the mixture is smooth; add cinnamon and mace and simmer for a few minutes. Remove from the heat and cool slightly before beating in the eggs if used.

Pour the mixture into a well greased 3 pt pie dish, dot with the remaining butter and cover thickly with the sugar. Sprinkle with a little extra cinnamon or nutmeg and put under a hot grill until the surface is well browned. Serve at once.

Malvern Pudding (6—8 portions) Worcestershire

3 oz butter
1½ oz flour
1 pt warm milk
1 lb stewed apples
2 oz caster sugar
Ground cinnamon

Oven: 350°F; gas mark 4; 20 minutes

Melt half the butter, stir in the flour and gradually add the milk, stirring until thick and smooth. Put layers of apples and this hasty pudding alternately into a 2½ pt greased pie dish, finishing with a layer of hasty pudding. Dot with the remaining butter and sprinkle with the sugar and cinnamon.

Bake in the oven for 20 minutes and finish off under a hot grill to brown the top.

Marquis Pudding (6—8 portions) F and H

1 pt milk
1½ oz long grain rice
4 oz caster sugar
5 fl oz double cream
4 oz apricot jam
1 lb stewed cooking apples
3 oz ground almonds
1 egg

Oven: 350°F; gas mark 4; 35 minutes

Bring the milk to the boil, stir in the rice and simmer gently until cooked, after about 40 minutes; sweeten with 1 oz sugar. Cool slightly.

Half whip the cream and fold into the rice. Put a layer of jam in the bottom of a deep pie dish, then a layer of stewed apples and a layer of rice. Repeat until the dish is two thirds full. Mix the ground almonds with the remaining sugar and the egg and spoon in small peaks over the top. Bake for 35 minutes and serve with apricot jam sauce flavoured with brandy.

Porridge (6—8 portions) F

2 pt water

4 oz oatmeal
Salt

Bring the water to the boil, rain in the oatmeal, stirring with a porridge stick, the so-called spurtle. When the porridge is boiling steadily, reduce the heat, cover with a lid and simmer for 30—40 minutes. Add salt to taste towards the end of cooking time.

Serve in porridge bowls or soup plates with small individual bowls of fresh cream, milk or buttermilk. Each spoonful of porridge is dipped in the cream or milk.

Pwdin Reis Mamgu (6—8 portions) F Wales

A Welsh type of baked rice pudding, lightened with stiffly beaten egg whites.

2 pt milk
Salt
Pinch grated nutmeg
1 bay leaf
3 oz long grain rice
4 egg yolks
4 egg whites

Oven: 425°F; gas mark 7; 10—15 minutes

Bring the milk to the boil with salt, nutmeg and the bay leaf; stir in the rice and simmer gently for 45—60 minutes or until cooked and the milk absorbed. Remove from the heat, discard the bay leaf and cool the rice slightly.

Mix in the egg yolks and fold in the stiffly beaten egg whites. Bake in the oven until the top has browned. Serve with jam, honey or fruit.

Rice Pudding, Baked (6—8 portions) F

In Yorkshire, 1—1½ oz finely chopped suet is added to this rice pudding before baking. Barley and tapioca puddings are baked as rice pudding.

3 oz short grain rice
Pinch salt (optional)
2 oz caster sugar
1 oz butter
2 pt milk
Grated nutmeg or cinnamon

Oven: 300°F; gas mark 2; 2 hours

Wash the rice and put in a 2½—3 pt buttered pie dish, with salt, sugar and stir in milk. Sprinkle nutmeg over and dot with butter. Bake in the centre or towards bottom of the oven for 2 hours. Stir in the skin at least once during cooking.

Rice Pudding, Boiled (6—8 portions) F

Barley and tapioca may be boiled as rice. Sultanas or raisins can be added for the last 20 minutes or an egg may be beaten into the cooked rice and the pudding baked in the oven until brown on top.

2 pt milk
3 oz Carolina rice
2—3 oz caster sugar

Bring the milk to boil, rain in the rice and simmer over gentle heat until tender, after 45—60 minutes. Add sugar to taste and serve hot or cold.

Semolina Pudding (6—8 portions) F

Ground rice, seed pearl tapioca and sago puddings are all cooked like semolina pudding; sago should be boiled until transparent, after 20 minutes. Dried fruit, chocolate and caramel may be added to any of these puddings for extra flavouring.

2 pt milk
3 oz semolina
2 oz sugar
2 eggs

Oven: 350°F; gas mark 4; 20—30 minutes

Heat the milk and sprinkle in the semolina, stirring continuously. Bring slowly to the boil, stirring frequently; simmer until thickened, cook, stirring over low heat for 3—5 minutes. Remove from the heat, blend in the sugar. Cool a little then add the beaten eggs, stirring thoroughly, or beat in the egg yolks and carefully fold in the stiffly beaten whites.

Pour into a greased ovenproof dish and bake until set. Serve hot with jam, rose hip syrup, golden syrup, honey, grated nutmeg or stewed fruit.

If eggs are not used, once sugar has been added pour into a greased dish, sprinkle the top with nutmeg and bake in the centre of the oven for 30 minutes, or until lightly browned on top.

Welbeck Pudding (6—8 portions) F and H
Nottinghamshire

4 oz apricot jam
2 lb peeled, cored and sliced cooking apples
5 fl oz milk

¾ oz cornflour or arrowroot
1 egg
1 oz caster sugar

Oven: 350°F; gas mark 4; 30 minutes

Place the jam and apples in layers in a 3 pt greased pie dish. Blend the milk with the arrowroot or cornflour and bring to the boil. Cool slightly. Separate the egg and add the yolk.

Beat the egg white until stiff, blend in the sugar and fold into the thickened milk. Pour this mixture over the apples and bake in the oven until golden brown.

White Pit (6—8 portions) F
Gloucestershire, Somerset

½ lb butter
3 oz flour
2 pt warm milk
½ lb black treacle
4 eggs
Ground cinnamon

Oven: 350°F; gas mark 4; 1 hour

Melt half the butter, stir in the flour and gradually add the milk; stir continuously until the mixture has thickened and is smooth. Bring to the boil, simmer for a few minutes and remove from the heat. Stir in the treacle and add the eggs.

The mixture should now be curdled and when baked it will separate into a jelly at the base and a custard at the top. Pour the mixture into a 4½ pt greased pie dish, dot with the remaining butter and sprinkle with cinnamon. Bake in the oven and serve cold.

PANCAKES, FRITTERS AND SWEET BATTER PUDDINGS

Common to these sweets is a batter mixture of flour, milk or water and eggs. This mixture is beaten thoroughly so as to incorporate air, and the subsequent cooking is done over high heat and in hot fat which causes the beaten-in air to expand and give a light texture.

It is a mistaken belief that batters should rest before use; they may well be left for up to 24 hours, in a cool place, but this does in no way improve them, and they generally have to be beaten lightly again, often with extra liquid.

PANCAKES

Pancakes are fried in hot fat and should be very thin, enough batter being poured into the pan to just cover it when tilted. The fried pancakes may be filled and rolled up or left plain and folded in four. Always served hot.

The filling may simply consist of a sprinkling of sugar and a squeeze of lemon juice, as in the pancakes traditional on Shrove Tuesday or they may be filled with jam, marmalade, syrup, treacle or honey. Fruits, sieved, stewed or fresh soaked in brandy or liqueur are other alternative fillings, as are chopped dried fruits, candied peel or butter mixed with spices, chopped nuts and sugar.

Pancakes (16—20) F and H

½ lb plain flour
Pinch salt
3 eggs
¾ pt milk
1—2 oz fat or lard

Prepare the batter by mixing the sifted flour with the salt; make a well in the centre, drop in the eggs and beat to a smooth paste with a little of the milk. Continue beating thoroughly, gradually adding all the milk.

Melt the fat in a 7 in shallow frying pan and when hot pour in just enough batter to cover the base in a thin layer. When the batter is cooked on the underside, loosen with a palette knife, toss or turn and brown on the other side. Turn out on to sugared paper and keep warm in the oven while cooking the remaining batter. Spread with a filling and roll up or fold in four and serve hot.

Mrs. Briscoe's Quire Pancakes are piled flat on top of each other; 2 tablespoons dry sherry with a pinch of grated nutmeg are added to the batter.

Cream Pancakes (16—20) H and F

3 oz plain flour
1 pt single cream
4 oz butter
8 egg yolks
1 oz sugar
Pinch grated nutmeg
3 tablespoons sherry
1 teaspoon orange flower water
6 egg whites
Fat for frying

Blend the flour with a little cream, soften the butter and add to the remaining cream. Beat in the egg yolks, sugar and nutmeg and gradually beat in the cream, sherry and orange flower water.

Whisk the egg whites very stiff and carefully fold into the batter mixture just before using. Fry the pancakes at once in hot fat and serve folded and sprinkled with sugar.

Kentish Cherry Pancakes (16) H and F Kent

½ lb plain flour
Pinch salt
3 eggs
¾ pt milk
Fat for frying
1 lb stewed, stoned cherries
4 oz sugar
½ pt water
½ oz cornflour
4 oz raspberry jam
Cherry brandy
Whipped cream

Make up the pancake batter from the flour, salt, eggs and milk and beat until smooth. Bake 16 thin pancakes and fill with two thirds of the cooked cherries, roll up and keep warm in the oven.

Boil the sugar and water until it has reduced to a syrup. Blend the cornflour with a little water, add the raspberry jam and stir this mixture into the syrup; bring to the boil. Flavour with cherry brandy and simmer the sauce for 10 minutes.

Pour the sauce over the pancakes, pipe on whipped cream and decorate with the remaining cooked cherries.

Welsh Pancakes or Crempog (8 portions) F Wales

1 oz butter
½ lb plain flour
½ pt buttermilk
1 egg
½ teaspoon bicarbonate of soda
Few drops lemon juice or vinegar
Fat for frying

Rub the butter into the flour and stir in the buttermilk until the mixture is a smooth batter. Beat the egg well and mix it into the batter; leave to rest for at least 1 hour.

Just before frying, beat the batter well, adding

the bicarbonate blended with lemon juice or
vinegar. Fry the pancakes in hot fat, drain on
kitchen paper and fill as desired, piling three or
four pancakes on top of one another with filling
in between.

Cut each pile of pancakes into quarters,
serving one quarter as a portion.

FRITTERS

These basically consist of a batter used to coat
pieces of fruit, or the batter may be deep-fried on
its own in very hot fat and served with sugar and
fruit. Fritter comes from the French *friture*,
meaning deep-frying.

Fritters, Plain (6—8 portions) F and H

½ lb plain flour
Pinch salt
2 eggs
½ pt milk
Fat or oil for frying
Lemon or orange juice and slices
Sugar

Sift the flour into a bowl, make a well in the
centre and add the salt and eggs; pour in half the
milk. Beat thoroughly until smooth and gradually
beat in the remaining milk.

Heat the fat or oil in a deep-frier to 345°F.
Put spoonfuls of batter into the fat and cook
until golden brown. Drain well on kitchen paper
and serve the fritters sprinkled with sugar and
lemon or orange juice and decorated with sliced
orange or lemon.

Apple Fritters (6—8 portions) F and H

Small halved bananas, tinned pineapple rings,
orange segments and tinned apricot halves are all
suitable for coating with batter and frying as
fritters. Serve with the appropriate fruit sauce.

2 lb cooking apples
½ pt coating batter
Caster sugar mixed with cinnamon
Fat or oil for frying

Peel and core the apples and cut into ¼ in thick
rings. Dip each ring in the batter and deep-fry in
fat heated to 345°F.

Drain well and serve the fritters with sugar and

cinnamon or, as in the North of England, with
wedges of cheese.

Yorkshire Fritters (6—8 portions) F and H Yorkshire

1 lb plain flour
2 teaspoons salt
½ tablespoon sugar
2 oz fat
1 egg
½ oz fresh yeast
4 tablespoons milk and water
3 oz currants
3 oz raisins
4 oz grated apples
Fat or oil for frying
Caster sugar
5 fl oz sherry

Make an enriched bread dough: sift the flour and
blend in salt and sugar, rub in the fat and mix in
the beaten egg and the yeast dissolved in the milk
and water. Knead, leave to rise and knock back.
Work in the currants, raisins and apples.

Divide the mixture into 24 pieces and shape
into round balls. Leave to prove on greaseproof
paper and then deep-fry in fat or oil heated to
345°F, until golden brown. Drain and toss in
caster sugar, sprinkle with the warmed sherry and
serve at once.

BATTER PUDDINGS

The original batter pudding consisted of a sweet
batter mixture, steamed or sometimes baked, and
served plainly with butter and brown sugar. Today,
the batter mixture is usually flavoured in various
ways and often served with a sweet sauce.

The batter mixture may also be poured over
any type of fruit and baked in the oven, and the
batter may be spiced with ginger or ground spice.
Kentish fruit batter is made with stoned cherries
covered with batter and steamed.

Batter Pudding, Steamed (6—8 portions) F Duffield, Derbyshire

6 eggs
6 oz plain flour
2 pt milk
2 oz butter

Separate the eggs; sift the flour into a bowl and mix in the egg yolks; beat thoroughly and gradually incorporate the milk, beating until the batter is smooth and free of lumps. Fold in the stiffly beaten egg whites.

Spoon the batter into a well buttered 3 pt pudding basin, cover with greaseproof paper and foil and steam for 1½–2 hours. Turn out and serve hot with a fruit, jam or wine sauce.

Gotham Pudding (8–10 portions)
F Nottinghamshire

8 eggs
¾ lb plain flour
Pinch salt
4 oz sugar
2 pt milk
½ lb chopped candied peel

Separate the eggs and sift the flour; blend the flour with the salt and sugar, make a well in the centre and add the egg yolks and part of the milk. Beat thoroughly until free from lumps and gradually beat in all the milk. When perfectly smooth, beat in the candied peel and fold in the stiff egg whites.

Grease a 3 pt pudding basin well, pour in the batter mixture and cover with greaseproof paper or foil. Steam the pudding for 1½ hours; turn out and serve sprinkled with sugar.

Marmalade Batter Pudding (8–10 portions)
F Scotland

¾ lb plain flour
Pinch salt
4 oz sugar
1 teaspoon ground ginger
Grated rind of 1 lemon and 1 orange
8 eggs (separated)
2 pt milk
4–6 oz orange marmalade

Oven: 400°F; gas mark 6; 20 minutes

Sift the flour and mix with salt, sugar, ginger and lemon and orange rind; beat to a smooth batter with the egg yolks and milk and carefully fold in the stiffly beaten egg whites.

Line a baking tin or basin with the marmalade and pour in the batter. Bake in the oven and turn out on a plate; serve with marmalade sauce.

Muffin Pudding (6–8 portions)
F and H North England

6 oz plain flour
Pinch salt
2 oz sugar
1 pt milk
4 egg whites
6 muffins
½ lb honey
1 teaspoon mixed spice

Sift the flour and blend with salt and sugar; gradually add the milk, beating thoroughly until the batter is smooth and free of lumps. Carefully fold in the stiffly beaten egg whites. Spread the muffins thickly with the honey, blended with the mixed spice.

Grease a 3 pt pudding basin and arrange the muffins in the basin. Pour the batter over them and cover with greaseproof paper or foil. Steam for 1–1½ hours, turn out gently and serve sprinkled with sugar.

Nottingham Batter Pudding (6–8 portions)
F and H Nottingham

5 eggs
7½ oz plain flour
Pinch salt
1¼ pt milk
1½ oz butter
1½ oz Demerara sugar
Pinch ground nutmeg and cinnamon
8 even-sized cooking apples, peeled and cored

Oven: 350°F; gas mark 4; 1 hour

Separate the eggs and sift the flour with salt; beat the egg yolks into the flour, add the milk and continue beating until the batter is quite smooth.

Blend the butter, sugar, cinnamon and nutmeg to a smooth paste and stuff into the whole apples. Set the apples in a buttered pie dish. Fold the stiffly beaten egg whites carefully into the batter and pour this over the apples.

Bake in the oven until the apples are soft and the batter is well risen and lightly browned.

Poor Knights of Windsor (8 portions)
F and H Berkshire

8–12 thin slices white bread
5 fl oz sherry

1 oz sugar
3 egg yolks
3 tablespoons milk
3 oz butter
4–6 oz jam

Soak the bread in the sherry mixed with the sugar. Beat the egg yolks with the milk and coat the bread in this. Melt the butter and fry the bread until crisp and lightly brown on both sides. Spread each slice with jam, roll up and secure with a wooden cocktail stick.

Alternatively, spread the bread with a mixture of cinnamon and sugar. Serve with jam sauce or a sauce made from the butter, sugar and sherry.

Tewkesbury Saucer Batter (6–8 portions) F Gloucestershire

This is occasionally known as Malvern Pudding although this correctly refers to a Hasty Pudding with stewed apples.

4 eggs
6 oz plain flour
Pinch salt
2 oz sugar
1 pt milk
2 lb cooked soft fruit

Oven: 400°F; gas mark 6; 20 minutes

Separate the eggs; sift the flour with salt and mix with the sugar. Beat to a smooth batter with the egg yolks and milk and fold in the stiffly beaten egg whites.

Grease two large ovenproof saucers or plates and pour in the batter. Bake in the oven for 20 minutes. Place one layer of cooked batter on a serving dish and then spread with cooked soft fruit. Cover with the other layer of batter, sprinkle with sugar and serve hot.

CAKE MIXTURE PUDDINGS

The origin of these is almost as old as the suet puddings which they resemble and like these, cake mixture puddings are steamed in pudding basins. They are, however, of a much lighter texture as the lining is composed of a plain or rich cake mixture of butter, sugar, eggs and flour. The steamed puddings are turned out and served hot with a sweet sauce or custard.

Apple and Honey Pudding (6-8 portions) F and H Yorkshire

4 oz sugar
4 oz butter
2 beaten eggs
4 oz plain flour
Pinch salt and grated nutmeg
2 oz brown sugar
½ lb peeled, cored and chopped apples
4 oz honey

Cream the sugar and butter until light and fluffy, gradually beat in the eggs and fold in the flour sifted with the salt.

Sprinkle the inside of a 2½ pt greased pudding basin with brown sugar, put the chopped apples mixed with nutmeg and honey in the basin and pour over the creamed mixture. Cover with grease-proof paper, tie down and steam for 1½-2 hours.

Turn out and serve the pudding with warmed honey or custard.

Castle Pudding (8 portions) F and H

Castle is an English corruption of the German *Kassel*, and this recipe can be traced back to the Hanoverian Royal House.

4 oz sugar
4 oz butter
2 beaten eggs
4 oz plain flour
Pinch salt
Grated rind of 1 lemon

Beat the sugar and butter until creamy; add the eggs and continue beating until fluffy; fold in the sifted flour, salt and lemon rind.

Divide the mixture between eight dariole moulds. Cover with greaseproof paper and steam for 30-40 minutes. Turn out and serve with lemon sauce.

Cherry Pudding (6-8 portions) F and H

4 oz sugar
4 oz butter
2 beaten eggs
4 oz plain flour
Pinch salt
3 oz halved glacé cherries

Oven: 375°F; gas mark 5; 30 minutes

Beat the sugar and butter until creamy, add the

eggs and fold in the sifted flour and salt. Add the cherries or place in a greased 2 pt pudding basin. Pour the mixture into the basin, cover with grease-proof paper and steam for 1½-2 hours.

Alternatively, put the mixture in a greased pie dish and bake for 30 minutes.

Chocolate Pudding (6-8 portions) F and H

4 oz sugar
4 oz butter
2 beaten eggs
4 oz plain flour
Pinch salt
2 oz cocoa
2 tablespoons milk

Cream the sugar and butter until fluffy, add the beaten eggs, flour and salt and beat thoroughly. Fold in the cocoa and add enough milk to give a dropping consistency.

Pour into a 2 pt greased pudding basin; cover with greaseproof paper and steam for 1½-2 hours. Serve with chocolate or rum sauce.

Coffee and Walnut Pudding (6-8 portions) H and F

4 oz sugar
4 oz butter
2 beaten eggs
4 oz plain flour
Pinch salt
1 tablespoon coffee essence
2 oz chopped walnuts

Beat the sugar, butter and eggs until fluffy and creamy. Fold in the flour sifted with the salt and add the coffee essence and chopped walnuts.

Spoon into a 2 pt greased pudding basin, cover with greaseproof paper and steam for 1½-2 hours. Serve with butterscotch sauce.

Eve's Pudding (6-8 portions) F and H

This is known as Dunfillan Pudding in Scotland. It is sometimes made with other fruits, but a true Eve's Pudding is made with apples.

4 oz caster sugar
4 oz butter
2 beaten eggs
4 oz plain flour

Pinch salt
1½ lb peeled, cored and thinly sliced apples
4 oz sugar
2 cloves

Oven: 375°F; gas mark 5; 45 minutes

Cream the sugar and butter until light; beat in the eggs and add the sifted flour and salt. Grease a 2 pt ovenproof dish and place half the apples over the base; add the sugar and cloves and cover with the remaining apples. Spoon over the creamed mixture and bake until set.

Ginger Pudding (6-8 portions) F and H

As a variation of ginger pudding, place a layer of 4 oz chopped rhubarb in the basin before covering with the creamed mixture.

4 oz sugar
4 oz butter
2 beaten eggs
4 oz plain flour
Pinch salt
2 oz preserved ginger or
    1 teaspoon ground ginger
3 tablespoons preserved ginger syrup

Cream the sugar, butter and eggs until fluffy, fold in the sifted flour and a little salt and add the chopped or ground ginger.

Line a 2 pt pudding basin with the ginger syrup and pour in the creamed mixture; cover with greaseproof paper and steam for 1½-2 hours. Serve with a syrup sauce.

Glister Pudding (6-8 portions) F and H Dundee

This is a steamed marmalade pudding, known in England as Sandhurst Pudding.

4 oz sugar
4 oz butter
2 beaten eggs
4 oz plain flour
Pinch salt
½ teaspoon ground ginger (optional)
6 oz orange marmalade

Beat the sugar and butter until creamy, beat in the eggs and fold in the flour, salt and ground ginger if used.

Line a 2 pt greased pudding basin with the marmalade, spoon over the creamed mixture and cover with greaseproof paper. Steam for 1½-2 hours and serve with custard or marmalade sauce.

Hampshire Roll (6-8 portions) H and F
Hampshire

4 oz sugar
4 oz butter
2 beaten eggs
4 oz plain flour
Pinch salt
1 lb peeled, cored and sliced cooking apples
3 oz apricot jam

Oven: 350°F; gas mark 4; 45 minutes

Cream the sugar and butter, beat in the eggs and fold in the sifted flour and salt. Spoon half this mixture into a 2 pt greased pie dish. Arrange the apples and jam on top and cover with the remaining mixture.

Bake and serve hot with a sweet sauce.

Leicester Pudding (6-8 portions) H
Leicestershire

6 oz self-raising flour
3 oz butter
3 oz sugar
Pinch salt
1 beaten egg
2-3 tablespoons milk
6 oz jam

Sift the flour and rub in the butter to a crumbly texture; blend in the sugar and salt and mix to a dropping consistency with the egg and milk.

Line a 3 pt buttered pudding basin with the jam and spoon in the mixture. Cover with greaseproof paper and steam for 1½-2 hours. Turn out and serve with melted jam or jam sauce.

Malvern Apple Pudding (6-8 portions)
F and H Worcestershire

4 oz sugar
4 oz butter
2 beaten eggs
4 oz plain flour
Pinch salt
½ lb Russet apples
Grated rind of 1 lemon
1½ oz currants
2-3 tablespoons brandy

Beat the sugar and butter until creamy, beat in the eggs and fold in the sifted flour and salt. Peel, core and finely chop the apples and fold into the mixture with the lemon rind, currants and brandy.

Spoon into a greased 2½-3 pt pudding basin, cover with greaseproof paper and steam for 1½ hours. Turn out and serve warm with custard or a wine sauce.

Mattress Pudding (6-8 portions) F
Co. Durham

6 oz self-raising flour
3 oz butter
3 oz sugar
Pinch salt
1 beaten egg
2-3 tablespoons milk
6-8 oz warmed jam

Oven: 375°F; gas mark 5; 30 minutes

Sift the flour and rub in the butter to a crumbly mixture; add the sugar and salt and beat to a soft dropping consistency with the egg and milk.

Spoon this mixture into a 6-8 in square, shallow cake tin and bake. Turn out while still warm. Spread the pudding with warm jam and serve with custard.

Prince Albert's Pudding (6-8 portions)
F and H

4 oz sugar
4 oz butter
2 beaten eggs
4 oz plain flour
Pinch salt
6 oz seedless raisins
1 oz chopped candied peel
½ teaspoon ground mace

Cream the sugar and butter until fluffy; beat in the eggs and fold in the sifted flour and salt. Add the raisins, candied peel and mace.

Grease a 2 pt pudding basin and spoon in the mixture; cover with greaseproof paper and steam for 1½-2 hours. Turn out the pudding and serve with custard.

Speechhouse Pudding (6-8 portions)
H and F Gloucestershire

This was a speciality in the Forest of Dean and

named after one of the lodges where the Forest Law Courts were held in times long gone by.

4 oz butter
4 oz sugar
2 eggs
4 oz plain flour
Pinch salt
6 oz jam

Beat the butter and sugar until light and creamy; separate the eggs and gradually beat in the yolks. Sift the flour and salt and fold in lightly. Beat the egg whites stiff and carefully fold into the mixture. Blend in the jam to give a marbled effect.

Spoon the mixture into a greased 2 pt pudding basin, cover with greaseproof paper and steam for 1½-2 hours. Turn out and serve with jam sauce.

Syrup Pudding (6-8 portions) F Kent

Variously known as Rochester, Patriotic and Treacle Pudding.

6 oz self-raising flour
3 oz butter
3 oz sugar
Pinch salt
1 beaten egg
2-3 tablespoons milk
6 oz golden syrup or black treacle

Sift the flour and rub in the butter to a crumbly mixture, add the sugar and salt and mix to a soft dropping consistency with the egg and milk.

Line a greased 2 pt pudding basin with syrup or treacle, pour over the mixture and cover with greaseproof paper. Steam for 1½-2 hours; turn out and serve with warmed syrup or custard.

Urney Pudding (6-8 portions) F and H Scotland

4 oz sugar
4 oz butter
2 beaten eggs
4 oz plain flour
Pinch salt
6 oz red jam

Beat the sugar and butter until light and creamy, beat in the eggs and fold in the sifted flour and salt. Mix the jam lightly into this mixture to give a marbled effect.

Grease a 2 pt pudding basin and pour in the mixture; cover with greaseproof paper and steam for 1½-2 hours. Turn out and serve with jam sauce.

FRUIT DESSERTS

The Romans established what was later to become known as "The Garden of England". They introduced the first cultivated cherry trees to Kent, and the orchards there were further enlarged during the reign of Henry VIII. Apples, too, and soft fruits flourished in Kent as in most other parts of Southern England and in East Anglia. Somerset and Devon built a brisk trade on their orchards of cider apples, and apricots ripened in sheltered Cotswold gardens. In spite of these benign factors, there is little evidence of regional fruit dishes outside Kent, and as with vegetables fruits were generally considered unwholesome unless cooked.

Apple Charlotte (6-8 portions) F and H

Also known as Brown Betty, Apple Charlotte is sometimes made with apples and blackberries in equal quantities.

2 lb peeled, cored and sliced cooking apples
½ teaspoon ground cinnamon
6-8 oz sugar
Rind and juice of ½ lemon
White bread slices
2 oz melted butter
1 oz breadcrumbs or cake crumbs

Oven: 375°F; gas mark 5; 1 hour

Simmer the apples with the cinnamon, sugar and lemon rind in a little water until pulpy. Cut the crusts off the bread and trim the slices to fit a 5-6 in cake tin. Brush the tin with melted butter, dip the bread slices in this and use to line the base and sides of the tin.

Add the breadcrumbs and lemon juice to the apples and spoon this filling into the lined tin. Top with bread, cut to fit the tin, and bake for 1 hour. When baked, turn out and serve with custard or fresh cream.

Apple Dice, Buttered (6-8 portions) F

1½ lb peeled, cored and sliced cooking apples
½ lb sugar
6 oz butter

4 thick slices stale bread

Toss the apple slices in the sugar until completely covered. Melt half the butter in a pan and fry the apples until soft and brown. Remove the apples and keep warm in a hot serving dish.

Add the remaining butter to the pan and fry the bread, cut into ½ in dice, until brown and crisp. Toss the bread with the apples, sprinkle with sugar and serve with hot cider sauce or cream.

Apple Hedgehog, Victorian (6-8 portions) H

1¼ lb even-sized, peeled and cored dessert apples
2 lb peeled, cored and sliced cooking apples
½ lb granulated sugar
Grated rind of 1 lemon
½ pt water
3 egg whites
3 oz caster sugar
24 blanched almonds

Oven: 350°F; gas mark 4; 10-15 minutes

Put the granulated sugar, lemon rind and water in a pan and bring to the boil; simmer for 2-3 minutes, then add the whole dessert apples and cook until tender but not broken. Lift out the apples and strain off the syrup. Cook the sliced apples in the syrup until reduced to a thick pulp.

Arrange the whole apples in a pyramid on a serving dish, using the apple pulp between the apples to make a smooth mound. Whisk the egg whites stiff and mix in the caster sugar; spread this meringue over the apples, covering them entirely. Sprinkle with more caster sugar. Split the blanched almonds and stick into the meringue. Brown in the oven for 10-15 minutes.

Apples and Elderberries (6-8 portions) F
Lothians of Scotland

2 lb apple pulp
Elderberries
½ lb sugar
6 cloves (optional)
2 oz cornflour or arrowroot

Strip the elderberries from the stalks, simmer in water with the sugar and cloves until the berries burst. Strain the berries and measure off 1 pt of juice. Blend with the cornflour or arrowroot and simmer for 5-10 minutes or until thick.

Spoon the elderberry jelly into a dish and cover with apple pulp. Serve with whipped cream.

Apples, Baked (8 portions) F and H

Baked apples may also be stuffed with mincemeat or with currants, sultanas, raisins, chopped dates or walnuts mixed with sugar. Brandy butter can be used for the topping.

8 cooking apples (6 oz each)
4 fl oz water
½ lb Demerara sugar
4 oz butter

Oven: 400°F; gas mark 6; 45-60 minutes

Wipe and core the apples; make a shallow cut through the skin round the middle of each. Place in an ovenproof dish. Pour the water round them, fill each apple with sugar and top with ½ oz butter. Bake in the centre of the oven until the apples are soft.

Apples, Stewed (6-8 portions) F

2 lb prepared apples or
    1½ lb apples and ½ lb quinces
½ lb sugar
½ pt cider
2 cloves or 1 in cinnamon stick
Juice of ½ lemon
Strip lemon or orange peel
1 oz heather honey

Peel, core and chop or slice the apples; put in a pan with the sugar, cider, cloves, lemon juice and peel. Simmer gently until soft, remove the cloves and peel and sweeten to taste with honey. Spoon into a dish and serve warm or cold with cream.

Black Caps (8 portions) F Norfolk

Beefings or Biffins were hard sweet apples which had been slowly dried in bread ovens and packed down in layers as they dried so that they were round and wrinkled. They are still available in some market towns in Norfolk.

8 Norfolk Biffins
Lemon rind, thinly peeled and cut into strips
2 oz candied peel
½ lb soft brown sugar
½ pt sweet wine

Oven: 450°F; gas mark 8; 10-15 minutes
        350°F; gas mark 4; 30-45 minutes

Cut the apples in half lengthways without peeling and scoop out the cores. Fill the cavities with mixed strips of lemon rind and candied peel.

     Cover the base of an ovenproof dish with the sugar, press the two halves of each apple together and tie with string if necessary; pack close together in the dish on top of the sugar. Pour the wine over them, making sure the tops of the apples are moistened. Sprinkle with a little sugar and put in a hot oven for 10-15 minutes until the outsides of the apples go dark brown. Cover with foil. Reduce the temperature and continue baking until the apples are soft.

Cherries in Kirsch (6-8 portions) H

2 lb stoned black cherries
4 oz blanched almonds
¾ pt water
4 oz granulated sugar
3 tablespoons Kirsch or Maraschino
½ pt double cream

Stuff the cherries with almonds in place of the stones and arrange in serving dishes. Boil the water and sugar until it has reduced to about 5 fl oz syrup; cool and blend in the Kirsch. Pour the syrup over the cherries and chill.

     Whip the cream and pipe on top of the cherries; serve with macaroons or shortbread fingers.

Cherries in Red Wine (6-8 portions) H

2 lb stoned red cherries
½ pt red wine
½ lb red currant jelly
Arrowroot
5 fl oz double cream

Put the cherries in a pan with sufficient wine to cover; add the red currant jelly and simmer gently until the cherries are soft but not broken up. Drain carefully through a colander; return the juice to the pan and thicken with blended arrowroot.

     Arrange the cherries in individual serving dishes and pour over the thickened juice. Chill before serving and decorate with piped cream.

Cherries, Poached (6-8 portions) H and F

2 lb stoned cherries
Juice of 1 lemon
½ lb Demerara sugar

Put the cherries in a double saucepan with the lemon juice and sugar; simmer until the cherries are tender but not broken. Serve hot or cold, with fresh cream.

Fig Sue (6 portions) F Westmorland

1 lb dried figs
½ pt ale
½ lb Demerara sugar

Wash the figs and leave in 1 pt of water to soak for at least 12 hours. Simmer gently in the soaking water until tender, then rub through a sieve.

     Heat the ale and add the fig pulp and sugar; bring to the boil, stirring continuously. Simmer until thick and serve.

Friar's Omelet (6-8 portions) F and H

2 lb peeled, cored and sliced cooking apples
2 cloves
Pinch mace
½ lb brown sugar
½ lb butter
Juice of 1 lemon
4 eggs
½ lb fresh white breadcrumbs

Oven: 325°F; gas mark 3; 1½ hours

Simmer the apple slices with the cloves, mace, sugar and a little water until soft. Add the butter and lemon juice and beat to a pulp. Leave to cool, then add the beaten eggs.

     Butter an ovenproof dish and sprinkle the sides and base with breadcrumbs. Spoon the apple mixture into the dish and cover the top with the remaining breadcrumbs. Bake in the oven until brown; serve hot or cold, sprinkled with sugar. If served cold, decorate with whipped cream.

Fruit Cobbler (6-8 portions) F

"Cobbler" originally referred to a type of pie with a thick dough lining as a filling.

1 lb prepared fruit (berry or hard)
4 oz sugar

½ lb self-raising flour
Pinch salt
2 oz caster sugar
2 oz butter
1 egg
2½ fl oz milk

Oven: 400°F; gas mark 6; 15-20 minutes
375°F; gas mark 5; 15-20 minutes

Prepare the fruit and put into a 1½ pt pie dish with the sugar and enough water to bring the fruit juices out. Sift the flour and add salt and caster sugar; rub in the butter and stir to a scone dough with the beaten egg and the milk.

Roll the dough out, ½ in thick, and cut into eight rounds with a 2 in cutter. Place these scones on top of the fruit, brush with milk and sprinkle with a little granulated sugar. Bake for 40 minutes, reducing the temperature after 15-20 minutes.

Fruit Crumble (6-8 portions) F and H

1 lb prepared fruit (berry or hard)
7 oz caster sugar
4 oz butter
½ lb plain flour

Oven: 375°F; gas mark 5; 15 minutes
350°F; gas mark 4; 20-25 minutes

Prepare the fruit according to type and place in a 1½ pt greased ovenproof dish, layered with 4 oz sugar. Rub the butter into the flour until it resembles fine breadcrumbs; blend in the remaining caster sugar.

Sprinkle this mixture over the fruit and press down well. Bake for 35-40 minutes until the topping is lightly brown, reducing the heat slightly after 15 minutes. Serve with custard or cream.

Fruit Salad (6-8 portions) H and F

For a fresh fruit salad, use any kind of dessert fruit — firm apples, oranges, tangerines, pineapples, peaches, nectarines, apricots, grapes, bananas. Cinnamon or nutmeg or brandy, rum or any sweet liqueur may be added to the syrup for extra flavour.

½ lb sugar
1 pt water
Juice of 1 lemon
2 lb prepared fruit
1 oz blanched, split almonds

Make a syrup by dissolving the sugar in the water over a gentle heat. Boil for 5 minutes, cool and add the lemon juice. Prepare the fresh fruits according to type and put in the syrup. Mix carefully and add the almonds.

Leave the salad for 2-3 hours in a cool place before serving to allow the flavours to blend. Serve with fresh cream or egg custard.

Ginger Apples (8 portions) F and H
Berkshire

1 oz root ginger
5 fl oz whisky
2 lb peeled, cored and sliced cooking apples
1½ lb sugar
Juice of 2 lemons

Bruise the ginger and put in a jar with the whisky; cover and leave for 3 days. Strain off the whisky.

Put the apple slices, sugar, lemon juice, whisky and ½ pt water in a pan; simmer gently until the apples are soft and transparent, but not broken.

Gooseberries, Stewed (6-8 portions) F

2 lb gooseberries
½ lb sugar
½ pt ale
1 or 2 elderflower heads
2½ fl oz elderberry wine (optional)

Make a syrup from the sugar and ale and add the elderflowers tied in muslin. Bring to the boil and simmer for a few minutes; add the topped and tailed gooseberries and simmer until tender. Remove the elderflowers; flavour with wine if used.

Serve warm or cold, with cream or custard.

Old Yorkshire Apple Cake (6-8 portions) F and H Yorkshire

This is a traditional side dish at Christmas; damson cheese is served in the same way.

1 lb apple butter or apple cheese
Chopped almonds
Whipped cream

Turn the apple cheese or butter out on to a serving dish and decorate with chopped almonds and cream.

Pear and Orange Caramel (6-8 portions) H and F Gloucestershire

Poached in a light syrup and chilled before serving, this elegant dish may be given extra flavour by adding a few drops of Cointreau to the syrup.

2 lb peeled, cored and quartered cooking pears
½ pt water
5 oz sugar
4 large oranges

Poach the pears in a syrup of the water and 3 oz sugar until tender, but not broken. Place in a serving dish. Thinly peel the rind from two oranges and cut into thin strips. Cook until tender in a little water. Drain and set aside. Remove peel and pith from all the oranges, divide the flesh into segments and mix with the pears. Chill in the refrigerator.

Boil the remaining 2 oz sugar with 1 table-spoon water to make a caramel; allow to set on an oiled plate or tin. When set, crush into small pieces and sprinkle over the fruit. Garnish with orange peel and serve with cream.

Pears, Stewed (6-8 portions) F and H Devon

Stewed pears used to be sold from market stalls at the annual Barnstaple Fair.

2 lb peeled pears
Blanched almonds
½ pt red wine
½ lb sugar
2 cloves or 1 in cinnamon stick

Insert the almonds in the peeled pears; simmer gently in a syrup made from the wine and sugar, flavoured with cloves. When the pears are tender, lift out and arrange in a serving dish.

Serve warm or cold with clotted cream.

Perthshire Bramble Mist (6-8 portions) H and F Scotland

1½ lb blackberries
2 tablespoons Kirsch
½ pt double cream
2 oz Demerara sugar

Rinse the berries and drain well. Arrange in individual serving glasses and spoon over the Kirsch. Whip the cream and spoon over the black-berries; sprinkle lightly with sugar. Heat a metal skewer glowing hot and draw across the sugar until it caramelises slightly. Serve at once.

Port and Pippins (6-8 portions) H and F

A traditional cold sweet at Christmas.

2 lb peeled and cored Cox's Orange pippins
½ lb sugar
1 pt water
1 in cinnamon stick
1 oz root ginger
Thinly peeled rind of 1 lemon
5 fl oz port
Red colouring (optional)

Put the sugar, water, cinnamon and ginger in a pan with the lemon rind; boil for 10 minutes. Strain and cool; pour this syrup over the apples and leave to soak overnight.

The following day, transfer the apples and syrup to a pan and simmer until tender. Lift the apples on to a serving dish, add the port to the syrup and a little red colouring if liked; strain and pour over the apples. Serve chilled with whipped cream.

Quince and Raisins, Stewed (6-8 portions) F

2 lb peeled, cored and sliced quinces
4 oz butter
½ lb stoned raisins
4 oz sugar
½ pt sweet sherry

Melt the butter and simmer the quinces in this until soft. Add the raisins, sugar and sherry and simmer for 5 minutes or until the sugar has dissolved. Serve warm or cold with cream.

Quinces, Baked (8 portions) F and H

8 even-sized quinces
6 oz sugar
1 teaspoon ground ginger
5 fl oz double cream

Oven: 400°F; gas mark 6; 45 minutes

Wipe the quinces and bake whole, without peeling or coring, until quite soft. Scrape the quince flesh from the skins and beat to a pulp with the sugar, ginger and cream.

Serve hot or cold.

Raspberry Lockets (6-8 portions) H
Lockets Club, London

1½ lb raspberries
2 tablespoons Kirsch or Cointreau
½ pt whipped cream
2 oz Demerara sugar

Wash the fruit carefully and drain; arrange in
individual serving dishes and sprinkle the liqueur
over the berries. Cover with whipped cream and
sprinkle a thin layer of Demerara sugar on top.
Heat a skewer until it glows hot and draw it
through the sugar to caramelise it.

Rhubarb, Stewed (6-8 portions) F

2 lb rhubarb
½ lb sugar
5 fl oz water
1 oz root ginger
1 in stick cinnamon
Strip lemon rind

Wash the rhubarb and cut into 1 in lengths. Make
a syrup from the sugar and water, with the bruised
ginger, cinnamon and lemon rind. Bring to the boil,
simmer for a few minutes then remove from the
heat and cover with a lid.

Leave the syrup to infuse for 10 minutes, strain
and put in a pan with the rhubarb. Simmer gently
until tender and serve warm or cold.

Strawberries in Syrup (6 portions) H

1 lb strawberries
1 lb double refined sugar
1 pt red currant juice

Hull, rinse and drain the strawberries; sprinkle
with half the sugar and leave overnight. Make a
syrup from the remainder of the sugar and the
red currant juice. Add the strawberries and simmer
gently until the syrup thickens. Do not let the
berries break up.

Spoon into individual glasses and serve with
fresh cream.

Strawberry Sweet (6-8 portions) H and F
Aberdeenshire

1 lb strawberries
1 lb sugar
½ lb red currants

Sprinkle half the sugar over the hulled and rinsed
strawberries; leave overnight. Simmer the red
currants in water for 10 minutes or until the
juices run freely. Strain.

Make a syrup with the red currant juice and
remaining sugar, add the strawberries and simmer
for a few minutes. Spoon into individual dishes
and serve with cream.

Summer Pudding (6-8 portions) H and F

Also known as Hydropathic Pudding, this sweet
was designed in the 18th century for patients not
allowed the then fashionably rich pastry desserts.
Any kind of ripe berry fruits can be used, preferably in a mixture.

2 lb soft red fruits
    (cherries, strawberries, black and red currants,
    loganberries, raspberries, bilberries)
4 oz sugar
Juice and finely grated rind of 1 lemon
8-10 thin slices white bread

Clean the fruits and simmer for a few minutes with
the sugar, lemon rind and juice. Butter the sides
and base of a 2 pt pudding basin. Remove the
crusts from the bread and arrange the slices
round the sides and base of the basin. Fill with
the cooked fruit and arrange the remaining bread
on top. Cover with a saucer and set a heavy
weight on top; chill in the refrigerator overnight.

Turn out the pudding and serve garnished with
fresh fruit and accompanied with thick cream.

CUSTARDS AND TRIFLES

Originally known as "crustades", custards have
developed from the medieval open pie filled with
fruit and covered with sweetened, spiced milk
thickened with eggs. Several examples of the
original concept have survived in the form of
custard tarts indicating the contents rather than
the pie crust.

Custards as we know them to day were popular
already in the 17th century, and the traditional
little custard cups date from this time. During the
18th century they developed into a number of
different sweet dishes. The Bread and Butter
Pudding is one example, while the Trifle is of a
richer and more elaborate nature. It at first consisted of cooked custard poured over wine-soaked

almond biscuits, covered with a syllabub. Firmly established by the 18th century, a variation of the trifle occurs in the form of Tipsy Cake; by later amalgamation the trifle finally perpetuated itself as a mixture of the original recipe and the tipsy cake. The syllabub disappeared and was replaced by cream.

Burnt Cream is yet another variation of the custard, a top layer of sugar being burnt to a caramelised crust.

Almond Custard (8 portions) H and F

¾ pt milk
5 fl oz cream
4 eggs
3 oz sugar
4 oz ground almonds
1 dessertspoon rose or orange flower water

Oven: 325°F; gas mark 3; 45 minutes

Heat the milk and cream. Pour this over the eggs beaten with the sugar; blend thoroughly and strain. Add the ground almonds and rose or orange flower water to the custard, pour into dariole moulds and set in a baking tin of hot water. Bake for about 45 minutes or until set, turn out and serve hot or cold with cream.

Ben Rhydding Pudding (6-8 portions) H and F West Riding of Yorkshire

2 lb juicy berry fruits
Sugar
2 round sponge cakes
¾ pt milk
5 fl oz double cream
8 egg yolks
3 oz sugar
5 fl oz whipped cream
Garnish: glacé cherries

Prepare the fruit, simmer to a pulp and sweeten to taste. Cut a round of sponge cake to fit the top of a 2½ pt plain mould and set aside; cut the remaining sponge into thin slices and use to line the base and sides of the mould.

Put the fruit into the mould, with any scraps of sponge cake, until the basin is filled; cover with the sponge round. Set a plate with a weight on top and leave until the cake has soaked up the fruit juices and is cold.

Make a rich custard sauce by heating the milk and the cream and pouring it over the egg yolks beaten with the sugar. Strain and heat through in a double saucepan until thickened. Leave to cool and then fold in the whipped cream. Turn out the sponge and fruit mould, pour over the custard cream and decorate with cherries.

Bread and Butter Pudding (6-8 portions) F

Dating from the early 18th century this is also known as Nursery Pudding.

1½ pt warm milk
Grated rind of 1 lemon.
4 eggs
2 oz sugar
2 tablespoons brandy, 1 tablespoon rose water or
   1 teaspoon vanilla essence (optional)
4 slices white bread
2 oz butter
½ oz currants
½ oz sultanas
½ oz chopped mixed peel
Grated nutmeg or cinnamon

Oven: 350°F; gas mark 4; 45 minutes

Heat the milk with the lemon rind and leave to steep for 10 minutes. Beat the eggs with the sugar and brandy; pour the strained milk over and mix well. Butter the bread, remove crusts and cut the slices into triangles. Place half the mixed currants, sultanas and peel over the base of a greased pie dish. Arrange half the bread on top and sprinkle with the remaining fruit.

Strain half the egg and milk custard over the bread and leave to soak for 5 minutes. Place the remaining bread on top and strain over the rest of the custard. Dust with grated nutmeg or cinnamon. Bake in a roasting tin of hot water for 45 minutes. Serve with cream.

Brown Bread Pudding (6-8 portions) H and F

¾ pt milk
5 fl oz double cream
8 egg yolks
3 oz sugar
1 tablespoon brandy or sherry

3 oz fresh brown breadcrumbs
½ pt whipped cream

Heat the milk and cream and pour over the eggs beaten with the sugar; mix and strain. Cook in a double saucepan until thick, then add the brandy, breadcrumbs and whipped cream. Pour into a serving dish and chill in the refrigerator.

Burnt Cream (6-8 portions) H

¾ pt milk
5 fl oz double cream
8 egg yolks
3 oz sugar
1 tablespoon brandy or a few drops vanilla essence
2 oz caster sugar

Heat the milk and cream, pour over the eggs beaten with the sugar; blend and strain and add the brandy or vanilla essence. Heat through in a double saucepan until thick, then pour the custard into small dishes or cups.

When set sprinkle with caster sugar and brown under a hot grill.

Cornish Burnt Cream (6-8 portions) H Cornwall

¾ pt milk
5 fl oz double cream
8 egg yolks
3 oz sugar
½ pt clotted cream
2 oz caster sugar

Heat the milk and cream; pour over the eggs beaten with the sugar and blend. Strain the custard and cook in a double saucepan until thick. Let the custard set in the pan, then spoon it into small dishes or cups in alternate layers with the clotted cream. Sprinkle with the caster sugar and brown under a hot grill.

Cabinet Pudding (8 portions) H

1 pt milk
1 vanilla pod
1 oz chopped glacé cherries
1 oz sultanas
1 oz chopped angelica
1 oz currants
2 oz diced sponge cake
2 oz ratafia biscuits

4 eggs
3 oz sugar

Oven: 325°F; gas mark 3; 45 minutes

Warm the milk and steep with the vanilla pod for 15 minutes. Butter one charlotte mould or eight dariole moulds; half fill with the mixture of cherries, sultanas, angelica, currants, sponge cake and ratafia biscuits. Pour the milk over the eggs beaten with the sugar, blend and strain.

Pour half the custard into the mould and leave for 5 minutes to soak. Add the remaining custard and bake in a tin of hot water until set. Turn out and serve hot with a jam sauce.

Chichester Pudding (6-8 portions) H and F Sussex

The Deptford Pudding from London is entirely similar to this custard pudding with the exception of the egg whites being thoroughly folded in to give a smooth rather than a rough texture.

1 pt milk
6 egg yolks
3 oz sugar
6 egg whites
6 oz fresh white breadcrumbs
Cinnamon or ratafia flavouring

Oven: 350°F; gas mark 4; 30-40 minutes

Warm the milk to blood heat and pour over the egg yolks beaten with the sugar; mix and strain. Beat the whites until stiff. Blend the breadcrumbs and flavouring into the custard and fold the egg whites in roughly so that the mixture has a marbled effect.

Pour into a 2 pt buttered pie dish and bake in a pan of hot water until set.

Chocolate Custard (8 portions) H and F

¾ pt milk
5 fl oz double cream
2 oz grated dark chocolate
8 egg yolks
3 oz sugar

Heat the milk and cream, pour about one quarter over the grated chocolate and stir until melted; add the remaining milk and cream. Pour this mixture over the beaten eggs and sugar; blend and strain. Cook in a double saucepan until thickened.

Pour into small custard cups or dishes and leave to set.

Cream Darioles (8 portions) H Cambridge

3 oz ground almonds
3 oz plain flour
3 oz caster sugar
3 egg yolks
¾ pt milk
5 fl oz double cream
4 eggs
3 oz sugar
Garnish: ½ lb red currant jelly

Oven: 350°F; gas mark 4; 20-25 minutes

Mix the ground almonds, flour and caster sugar with the egg yolks to make a stiff dough; roll out ¼ in thick, and use to line eight dariole moulds. Bake these blind.

Heat the milk and cream and pour over the eggs beaten with the sugar; blend thoroughly and strain into the dariole moulds. Place in a roasting tin of hot water and bake until set. When cold turn out and decorate with chopped red currant jelly.

Custard Dish, Old Scots Style (8 portions) H Scotland

¾ pt milk
5 fl oz double cream
8 egg yolks
3 oz sugar
½ pt whipped cream
Garnish: glacé cherries and angelica or
    red and green crystallised fruits

Heat the milk and cream together, pour over the beaten eggs and sugar; blend and strain.

Cook the custard in a double saucepan until thickened, and pour into a glass serving dish. Leave to set. Decorate with piped cream, cherries and strips of angelica.

Diplomatic Pudding (8 portions) H

1 oz chopped glacé cherries
½ oz chopped angelica
1 oz currants
1 oz sultanas
8 sponge biscuits
2½ fl oz golden syrup
1½ tablespoons brandy
½ pt milk
3 egg yolks
3 oz sugar
½ oz gelatine
2 fl oz water
½ pt double cream
Garnish: whipped cream

Lightly butter one charlotte mould or eight dariole moulds and decorate the base with cherries and angelica. Soak the currants, sultanas and biscuits in the mixed syrup and brandy.

Warm the milk to blood heat and pour over the egg yolks, beaten with the sugar; mix and cook in a double saucepan until thickened. Dissolve the gelatine in the water and add to the custard; strain. Leave the custard to cool and just before setting, fold in the stiffly beaten cream.

Fill the mould with alternate layers of soaked fruit and custard, beginning and finishing with custard. Leave to set in the refrigerator, turn out and decorate with piped cream.

Drambuie Cream (8 portions) H Scotland

¾ pt milk
5 fl oz double cream
8 egg yolks
3 oz sugar
1 small glass Drambuie
Garnish: toasted almonds

Heat the milk and cream and pour over the eggs beaten with the sugar; blend and strain. Stir in the Drambuie and cook in a double saucepan until thickened.

Pour the custard into small dishes and leave to set. Decorate with toasted almonds and serve with extra cream.

Ginger Custard (8 portions) H and F

¾ pt milk
5 fl oz double cream
8 egg yolks
3 oz sugar
2 fl oz ginger syrup
1½ oz preserved ginger

Heat the milk and cream. Pour this over the beaten eggs, sugar and ginger syrup; mix thoroughly and strain. Cook this custard in a double saucepan until thickened.

Chop the ginger finely and arrange over the base of small cups or dishes. Half fill the cups with custard; leave to set, then pour over the remaining custard. Serve chilled.

Her Majesty's Pudding (8 portions) H

¾ pt milk
5 fl oz double cream
½ vanilla pod
8 egg yolks
3 oz sugar
Garnish: crystallised fruit

Heat the milk and cream; add the vanilla pod and leave to steep for 30 minutes. Pour the milk over the eggs beaten with the sugar; blend thoroughly and strain, then cook in a double saucepan until thick.

Pour into small dishes and leave to set. Decorate with crystallised fruit.

Ipswich Almond Pudding (6-8 portions) H and F Suffolk

The original Ipswich Almond Pudding from the 18th century was a rich custard filling over a base of puff pastry.

¾ pt milk
5 fl oz double cream
2 oz white breadcrumbs
3 oz sugar
6 oz ground almonds
1 teaspoon rose or orange flower water
3 eggs
1 oz butter

Oven: 350°F; gas mark 4; 30 minutes

Warm the milk and cream and pour over the breadcrumbs; stir in the sugar, ground almonds and rose water; leave to soak for 15 minutes.

Pour this mixture over the beaten eggs; blend thoroughly and pour into a buttered 2 pt pie dish. Dot with butter and bake in a tin of hot water until set.

Newcastle Pudding (6-8 portions) F and H Northumberland

1 pt milk
Grated rind of 1 lemon

4 eggs
3 oz sugar
4-6 thin slices bread, thickly buttered

Heat the milk, add the lemon rind and leave, covered, to steep for 1 hour. Pour over the beaten eggs and sugar; mix and strain. Remove the crusts from the bread and line a greased 2½ pt pudding basin with the bread slices; pour over the custard and leave to soak for 1 hour.

Cover the basin with greaseproof paper and steam for about 45 minutes. Turn out and serve with lemon sauce.

Orange Custard (8 portions) H

¾ pt milk
5 fl oz double cream
8 egg yolks
3 oz sugar
1 Seville orange
1 oz caster sugar
1 dessertspoon brandy

Heat the milk and cream, pour over the beaten eggs and the sugar; mix and strain. Peel half the orange, remove pith and cut the peel into fine strips; blanch in boiling water and refresh.

Pound three quarters of the peel with caster sugar, stir in the brandy and the strained juice from the orange. Stir this mixture into the custard and cook in a double saucepan until beginning to thicken.

Pour into small cups or dishes and leave to set. Garnish with the remaining orange rind.

Osborne Pudding (6-8 portions) H Isle of Wight

Osborne was one of Queen Victoria's favourite residences.

4 thin slices brown bread
2 oz orange marmalade
¾ pt milk
5 fl oz double cream
8 egg yolks
3 oz sugar
1 tablespoon sherry or brandy
½ pt whipped cream

Remove the crusts from the bread, spread with marmalade and cut into tiny strips. Heat the milk and cream, pour over the egg yolks beaten with the sugar, blend and strain.

Cook this custard in a double saucepan until thick, then carefully fold in the bread, sherry and whipped cream. Spoon into a glass serving dish and chill before serving.

Queen of Puddings (6-8 portions) H

Manchester Pudding is made like the rich Queen of Puddings, but the meringue topping is piped straight on to the custard and baked with the pudding so that it becomes hard and crisp. It is always served cold.

1½ pt milk
2 oz butter
6 oz white breadcrumbs
Grated rind of 1 lemon
Grated nutmeg
1½ oz sugar
6 egg yolks
3 egg whites
2 oz melted raspberry jam
Meringue: 3 egg whites and
     4 oz caster sugar

Oven: 350°F; gas mark 4; 30-40 minutes
         300°F; gas mark 2; 15-20 minutes

Heat the milk with the butter and pour over the breadcrumbs; soak for a few minutes, then add the lemon rind, a pinch of nutmeg, the sugar and the egg yolks beaten with the whites.

Pour this mixture into a 3 pt buttered pie dish, place in a roasting tin of hot water and bake until set, at a temperature of 350°F, gas mark 4.

Remove from the oven and spread the pudding with jam. For the meringue, beat the egg whites stiffly and add the sugar, pipe on top of the pudding and dredge with a little more caster sugar. Bake in the oven until the meringue is pale brown; serve the pudding warm.

Ratafia Cream (8 portions) H

For an unusual flavouring to this custard, steep clean fresh laurel leaves in the milk and cream for 15 minutes.

¾ pt milk
5 fl oz double cream
8 egg yolks
3 oz sugar
5 fl oz brandy
Few drops ratafia essence

Heat the milk and cream, pour over the beaten eggs and sugar; mix and strain. Add the brandy and ratafia essence to the custard mixture and cook in a double saucepan until thickened.

Pour the custard into small dishes and leave to set before serving.

Rout Cream (8 portions) H and F

¾ pt milk
1 vanilla pod
3 tablespoons sherry
8 egg yolks
3 oz sugar
5 fl oz whipped cream

Heat the milk, add the vanilla pod and leave to steep for 15 minutes. Stir in the sherry and pour over the beaten eggs and sugar; mix and strain.

Cook in a double saucepan until thick; remove from the heat and continue stirring until cold, then fold in the whipped cream. Spoon the custard into small custard cups and leave to set.

Sack Cream (8 portions) H and F

¾ pt milk
5 fl oz double cream
Grated peel of 1 lemon
8 egg yolks
3 oz sugar
2 fl oz sherry

Heat the milk and cream, add the lemon peel and steep, covered, for 15-20 minutes. Pour the milk over the beaten eggs and sugar; blend thoroughly and strain.

Add the sherry and cook the custard in a double saucepan until thickened. Spoon into small cups or dishes. Serve the custard when set with sponge fingers.

Scots Flummery (8 portions) H and F
Scotland

2 oz currants
5 fl oz dry sherry or white wine
¾ pt milk
5 fl oz double cream
8 egg yolks
3 oz sugar
1 dessertspoon rose water
Pinch grated nutmeg

Soak the currants in the sherry for at least 1 hour. Heat the milk and cream; pour this over the beaten eggs and sugar; mix and strain. Add the rose water and nutmeg and cook in a double saucepan until thickened.

Stir in the soaked currants and sherry and spoon the custard into small dishes to set.

Spinach Cream (8 portions) H

An unusual custard, illustrating the former preference for a mixture of savoury and sweet flavours.

¾ pt milk
5 fl oz double cream
½ cinnamon stick
4 spinach leaves
8 egg yolks
3 oz sugar
Garnish: crystallised fruit

Heat the milk and cream, add the cinnamon stick and steep, covered, for 1 hour. Boil the spinach in 2 tablespoons water, squeeze out the resulting liquid and set aside.

Pour the strained milk over the beaten eggs and sugar; mix and strain. Cook until thickened in a double saucepan; add the spinach juice and pour the custard into small cups or dishes. When set, decorate with strips of crystallised fruit.

Tansy Custard Pudding (6-8 portions) F and H

Tansy is a wild herb with bright green, bitter leaves; tansy juice was much used as a flavouring in medieval cooking and was thought to have therapeutic properties. In modern cookery, tansy describes a fruit pulp of, for example, buttered gooseberries or apples.

4 spinach leaves
1 oz tansy leaves
¾ pt milk
4 fl oz cream double
3 eggs
3 oz sugar
6 oz sponge cake crumbs
2½ fl oz brandy
Pinch nutmeg

Oven: 325°F; gas mark 3; 45 minutes

Simmer the spinach and tansy leaves in 3 tablespoons water; squeeze out the juice and set aside.

Heat the milk and cream and pour over the beaten eggs and sugar; mix and strain. Put the cake crumbs, brandy and nutmeg in a buttered 2 pt pie dish, add the tansy and spinach juice and pour the custard over.

Bake until set in a tin of hot water and serve at once without turning out.

Tipsy Cake (6-8 portions) H and F

This 19th century custard sweet is the forerunner of the modern trifle. It was often decorated with flowers or chips of currant jelly.

2 round sponge cakes (6 in each)
Jam
2½ fl oz brandy (approx.)
2-3 oz blanched almonds
¾ pt milk
5 fl oz double cream
8 egg yolks
3 oz sugar

Sandwich the sponge cakes with jam, set in a serving dish and pour the brandy over it. Cut the almonds into long slivers and push into the sponge sandwich.

Heat the milk and cream and pour over the egg yolks beaten with the sugar; blend and strain. Cook the custard in a double saucepan until thick, then pour over and round the cake. Leave to set. Serve cold.

Trifle (8 portions) H and F

Mrs. Glasse's 18th century trifle differs little from that served two centuries later. It was covered with a syllabub rather than cream and decorated with flowers or jelly.

In Scotland, the trifle sponge is soaked in equal parts fruit syrup and Drambuie and the cream for decoration is flavoured with the same liqueur.

8 trifle sponges or 2 sponge cakes
½ lb raspberry or apricot jam
Ratafia or macaroon biscuits
2 fl oz brandy
6 fl oz sherry
¾ pt milk
5 fl oz double cream
8 egg yolks
3 oz sugar

½ pt whipped cream
Garnish: ratafia biscuits; split, blanched almonds,
    glacé cherries or angelica

Slice the sponge cakes and spread with jam;
arrange over the base of a glass serving dish. Lay a
few ratafia biscuits or macaroons over the sponge;
pour over the brandy and sherry and leave to soak
for at least 30 minutes.

Heat the milk and cream and pour over the egg
yolks beaten with the sugar; blend and strain.
Heat in a double saucepan until thick, cool slightly
then pour over the sponge cakes. Leave the trifle
to set, and when cold pipe on the whipped cream
and decorate with biscuits, almonds, cherries or
angelica.

Welsh Egg Whey (6-8 portions) F Wales

Also known as *Maidd yr Iar*, this steamed egg
custard is similar to Newcastle Pudding.

1 pt milk
1 teaspoon ground ginger
Grated nutmeg or cinnamon
Grated rind of 1 lemon
4 eggs
3 oz sugar
4-6 thin slices bread, thickly buttered

Heat the milk with the ginger and a pinch of
nutmeg; add the lemon rind and leave to steep
for 1 hour. Pour the milk over the eggs beaten
with the sugar; blend and strain.

Remove the crusts from the bread and line a
2½ pt buttered pudding basin with the bread
slices. Pour in the custard, leave to soak for 1
hour, then cover with greaseproof paper.

Steam for 45-60 minutes, turn out and serve
with a sweet lemon sauce.

White Ladies Pudding (6-8 portions) F Worcestershire

4 oz desiccated coconut
6 thin slices white bread thickly buttered
1 pt milk
Vanilla essence
Pinch salt
3 eggs
3 oz sugar

Oven: 350°F; gas mark 4; 30-40 minutes

Butter a 2½ pt pie dish and sprinkle with

desiccated coconut. Remove the crusts and cut
the buttered bread into triangles or squares
and arrange in the pie dish.

Heat the milk, add a few drops of vanilla
essence and a pinch of salt; pour this over the
eggs beaten with the sugar, mix and strain over
the bread. Leave to soak for 30 minutes, then
place in a tin of hot water and bake until set.

Yorkshire Wine Pudding (6-8 portions) H and F Yorkshire

1 pt sherry
Pinch cinnamon
Grated rind of 1 lemon
4 oz sponge cake crumbs
6 eggs
Orange flower water
Pinch salt
1 oz sugar
1 oz butter
1 oz currants

Oven: 350°F; gas mark 4; 30 minutes

Heat the sherry, add cinnamon, lemon rind, cake
crumbs and leave to soak for 15 minutes. Beat the
eggs and add a little orange flower water and salt,
the sugar, butter and currants.

Add the sherry mixture to the eggs; put into a
2-2½ pt buttered dish set in a baking tin of hot
water. Bake until set.

FOOLS, SYLLABUBS AND JUNKETS

There is no clear distinction between custards
and fools; both are based on cream, but while the
original custard had a pie crust foundation, the
16th century fool consisted of cooked or crushed
fruit mixed with cream.

Syllabubs have changed little since they first
became popular in the 17th century; in its simplest
form a syllabub consisted of a bowl of sweetened
wine into which was milked fresh milk straight
from a cow thus creating a rich froth on top of
the wine. Sometimes a syllabub was whipped and
left for several hours, so that the curds would
separate out from the wine.

Junket was originally a term applied to the
rush mat on which cream cheeses were served,
but as early as the Middle Ages it became identical
with a dish of sweetened curds and scalded cream.

FOOLS

These light creamy concoctions are always served chilled, usually arranged in tall individual glass dishes and often elaborately garnished.

Boodle's Orange Fool (6-8 portions) H London

A speciality at Boodle's Club in St. James's Street, founded in 1763.

Sponge cakes
Grated rind and juice of 4 oranges and 2 lemons
3 oz caster sugar
1 pt double cream
Garnish: crystallised orange slices

Cut the sponge cakes into ½ in thick strips and use to line the base and sides of a 2½ pt serving dish. Mix the rind and juice of the oranges and lemons with the caster sugar and stir until this has completely dissolved.

Whip half the cream until thick but not stiff; beat the mixed juice slowly into the cream. Spoon this mixture over the sponge cakes and chill thoroughly until the juice has penetrated the sponge cakes and the cream has set.

Whip the remaining cream stiff and pipe on top of the fools. Garnish with orange slices.

Caledonian Cream (6-8 portions) F and H Scotland

6 oz finely cut orange marmalade
5 fl oz brandy
Juice of 3 lemons
6 oz caster sugar
1½ pt double cream
Garnish: crystallised orange slices

Mix the marmalade with the brandy, lemon juice and sugar; whisk the cream and fold in the marmalade mixture. Beat the mixture thoroughly until stiff enough to stand in soft peaks.

Spoon into individual dishes; decorate with crystallised oranges and chill before serving.

Cranachan or Cream Crowdie (6-8 portions) F and H Scotland

This dish used to be traditional at Hallowe'en, and charms would be folded into the cream mixture; each charm had a particular significance: a ring indicated marriage, a button bachelorhood, a thimble spinsterhood, a coin wealth and a horse shoe good luck.

6-8 oz oatmeal
1 pt double cream
4 oz caster sugar
2½ fl oz rum or a few drops vanilla essence
Garnish: ripe, soft berries

Toast the oatmeal lightly under the grill or in a thick frying pan and leave to cool completely. Whip the cream until stiff, sweeten to taste with sugar and add the rum or vanilla essence.

Stir in the oatmeal and spoon the cream into serving dishes. Decorate with fresh berries. Chill and serve.

The Dean's Cream (6-8 portions) H and F Cambridge Colleges

8 small sponge cakes
2 oz raspberry jam
2 oz orange marmalade
Ratafia biscuits
5 fl oz sherry
2½ oz sugar
Grated rind and juice of 1 lemon
2½ fl oz wine
2 fl oz brandy
7½ fl oz double cream
Garnish: glacé cherries, angelica and candied pineapple

Spread half the sponge cakes with raspberry jam and the remainder with marmalade; arrange alternately in a deep dish. Cover with ratafia biscuits and pour over the sherry.

Dissolve the sugar in the lemon juice, add the lemon rind, wine and brandy; warm through and fold in the whipped cream. Spoon this syllabub over the sponge cakes.

Chill for several hours. Decorate with cherries, angelica and candied pineapple before serving.

Edinburgh Fog (6-8 portions) H and F Scotland

1 pt double cream
1 tablespoon caster sugar
Vanilla essence
4 oz ratafia biscuits
2 oz blanched chopped almonds

Sweeten the cream with sugar and vanilla essence to taste. Beat until stiff and fold in the biscuits and almonds. Spoon into glasses and serve chilled.

Gooseberry Fool (6-8 portions) H and F

Gooseberry Fool was established as early as the 15th century. Any kind of fresh fruit, such as apricots, blackberries, damsons, plums, raspberries and rhubarb can be made into a pulp and used as a base for a fool. A Scottish version uses equal amounts of brambles and apples.

2 lb gooseberries
5 fl oz water
6-8 oz sugar
2 sprigs of elderflower, 2 tablespoons orange
    flower water or elderberry wine
½ pt double cream
½ pt milk
3 egg yolks
1½ oz caster sugar
Garnish: chopped nuts

Top and tail the gooseberries, simmer in the water until soft and then sweeten to taste with sugar. Flavour with elderflowers, orange water or elderberry wine. Pass the mixture through a sieve and leave the fruit pulp to cool. Whip the cream lightly.

Make a custard from the milk, egg yolks and caster sugar and leave to cool. Mix the gooseberry pulp with the custard, correct flavourings if necessary and fold in the cream, setting a little aside for decoration.

Spoon into small dishes or glasses and decorate with cream and chopped nuts. Serve with shortbread or sponge fingers.

Kentish Fruit and Cream (6-8 portions) F and H Kent

1 lb preserving sugar
2 oz stoned cherries
4 oz red currants
2 oz white currants
4 oz raspberries
4 oz strawberries
1 pt double cream

Put the sugar, cherries and red and white currants in a pan and bring to the boil. Simmer for 10 minutes, stirring continuously. Add the raspberries and strawberries and simmer for a further 2-3 minutes.

Press the fruit through a sieve and leave to cool. Stir in the cream, whisking quickly until it thickens. Spoon into individual dishes and chill before serving.

Lemon Posset (6-8 portions) F and H

½ pt double cream
½ pt single cream
Grated rind and juice of 2 large lemons
3-4 fl oz dry white wine
2 egg whites
4 oz caster sugar
Garnish: crystallised lemon slices

Whisk the two creams (or use all double cream) until thick; add the grated lemon rind and juice, a little at a time. Gradually add the white wine, being careful not to beat too much.

Whisk the egg whites with the sugar until stiff and gently fold into the cream mixture. Spoon into individual dishes and decorate with crystallised lemon slices.

Orange Blossom Dessert (6-8 portions) H and F

4 eggs
2 oz caster sugar
Juice and grated rind of 2 oranges
¾ lb sieved cottage cheese
½ pt double cream
Garnish: crystallised orange slices, whipped cream

Separate the eggs, and blend the egg yolks, sugar, orange juice and rind in a bowl over a pan of simmering water; whisk until the mixture is thick enough to coat the back of a wooden spoon. Remove from the heat and cool.

Blend the cheese and cream into the cooled mixture and whisk until thick. Fold in the whisked egg whites and spoon into serving glasses; chill.

Serve decorated with whipped cream and crystallised orange slices.

Seville Cream (6-8 portions) H

2 Seville oranges
4 oz caster sugar
2 tablespoons sweet orange juice
2 tablespoons Grand Marnier Aurium or other
    orange-flavoured liqueur or brandy
4 egg yolks

½ pt double cream

Pare the orange rind thinly and blanch for 10
minutes in boiling water. Drain and refresh; cut
into strips and pound to a paste with the sugar
and strained Seville orange juice.

Alternatively, blend in the liquidiser. Add the
sweet orange juice and the liqueur; Stir in the
beaten egg yolks and whisk until thick and fluffy.
Bring the cream to the boil and pour slowly over
the orange and egg mixture. Whisk until cold.
Serve chilled in custard cups.

Tansy Cream (6-8 portions) H and F

This is more a custard pudding than a fool; for
preparation of tansy juice see Tansy Custard
Pudding.

4 eggs
1 pt double cream
2 oz caster sugar
Pinch grated nutmeg
5 fl oz strained tansy and spinach juice

Oven: 350°F; gas mark 4; 20-30 minutes

Beat the eggs and cream and add the sugar and
nutmeg; beat in the tansy juice.

Pour the mixture into a buttered 2½ pt pie
dish and bake until set and brown on top.

Whim-Wham (6-8 portions) H and F Scotland

1½ pt double cream
5 fl oz white wine
3 oz caster sugar
Grated rind of 1 lemon
Sponge fingers
½ lb red currant jelly
Garnish: crystallised orange or lemon slices

Mix the cream with the wine, sugar and lemon
rind and beat until frothy. Spoon one third of
this mixture into individual serving dishes, put a
few sponge fingers over the cream and cover with
a layer of jelly.

Arrange another layer of cream, sponge and
jelly and finish with the remaining cream. Decorate with orange or lemon slices and chill.

Yellow Milk (6 portions) F and H Scotland

1 pt sweetened cream

6 egg yolks
Caster sugar
Ground cinnamon

Beat the cream and egg yolks over low heat
until thick; do not allow to boil. Pour into serving
dishes and sprinkle with sugar and cinnamon.

SYLLABUBS

Modern syllabubs are made with an infusion of
sherry or wine mixed with whipped cream. They
are served in tall glasses and should ideally be left
in a cool place for 8 hours to let the wine and
cream separate. The wine is spooned up or drunk
through the creamy froth in the manner of Irish
Coffee.

Syllabub (8 portions) H

10 oz caster sugar
Rind and juice of 3 lemons
½ pt sherry or wine
5 fl oz brandy
1½ pt double cream

Mix the sugar with the lemon juice; add the rind,
sherry and brandy. Warm slightly to dissolve the
sugar and blend the flavours. Whip the cream
and fold into the wine. Pour into tall glasses and
serve when separated.

There are numerous variations of syllabubs,
all made by the same method, but differing in
flavouring ingredients.

Farmhouse Syllabub

6 oz caster sugar
¼ teaspoon grated nutmeg
5 fl oz cider
5 fl oz beer
1½ pt double cream
1 oz currants

Simmer the sugar and nutmeg in cider and beer
and leave to cool completely. Blend with the
whipped cream and let the syllabub stand for
1 hour. Sprinkle the currants on top.

Fruit Syllabub

Sprig rosemary
5 fl oz red fruit juice or sieved pulp

5 fl oz white wine
Grated rind and juice of 2 lemons
¼ teaspoon grated nutmeg
6 oz caster sugar
1½ pt double cream

Steep the rosemary with the fruit juice, wine,
lemon juice and rind, nutmeg and sugar for several
hours, preferably overnight. Strain and mix with
the whipped cream.

Hampshire Syllabub

6 oz caster sugar
¼ teaspoon grated nutmeg
½ pt strong beer
2½ fl oz brandy
1½ pt double cream

Infuse the sugar and nutmeg with the beer and
brandy. Blend with the whipped cream.

London Syllabub

6 oz caster sugar
¼ teaspoon grated nutmeg
½ pt port
1½ pt double cream

Infuse the sugar and nutmeg in the wine; blend
with the whipped cream.

Devonshire Syllabub is similar to London
Syllabub, but is topped with clotted cream for
serving.

Punch Syllabub

6 oz caster sugar
¼ teaspoon grated nutmeg
Grated rind of 1 lemon
½ pt lemon juice, rum and brandy
1½ pt double cream

Infuse the sugar, nutmeg and lemon rind in equal
measures of lemon juice, rum and brandy, making
a total of ½ pint. Blend with the whipped cream.

Somerset Syllabub

6 oz caster sugar
¼ teaspoon grated nutmeg
5 fl oz port
5 fl oz sherry
1½ pt double cream
Clotted cream

Infuse the sugar and nutmeg in port and sherry;
blend with the whipped cream. Top with clotted
cream for serving.

Alternatively, infuse in 1 pt port or sherry,
blend with 1½ pt milk and top with double
cream.

Staffordshire Syllabub

6 oz caster sugar
¼ teaspoon grated nutmeg
½ pt cider
2½ fl oz brandy
1½ pt double cream

Infuse sugar and nutmeg in cider and brandy and
blend with whipped cream.

JUNKETS

Also known as Curds and Cream, junket is made
with fresh, flavoured milk and set with rennet.
Double the quantities of rennet shown in individual
recipes if pasteurised milk is used and follow the
instructions on the bottle of rennet. To serve,
junkets are usually sprinkled with grated nutmeg
and single cream is offered separately.

Junket (6-8 portions) F

2 pt milk
1 oz sugar
1 tablespoon rennet

Warm the milk to blood heat and add the sugar;
pour into a glass dish. Stir in the rennet and
allow to set at room temperature, for approximately 30 minutes.

Various flavourings, such as 1 dessertspoon
fruit syrup, 1 dessertspoon coffee essence or
1 teaspoon cocoa dissolved in warm milk may be
stirred into the junket after the rennet.

A beaten egg may be added with the rennet
and broken-up ginger biscuits can be put over the
base of the serving bowl before the junket is
poured in.

Cornish Junket (6-8 portions) F Cornwall

2 pt milk
1 tablespoon sugar
3-4 sugar lumps rubbed on lemon

5 fl oz brandy
1 tablespoon rennet
Cornish clotted cream

Warm the milk to blood heat and add the sugar. Stir in the sugar lumps; pour the brandy into a serving dish, add the junket and stir in the rennet. Use 2 tablespoons of rennet if pasteurised milk is used. Leave to set at room temperature.

Cover with clotted cream when set.

Devonshire Junket (6-8 portions) F Devon

2 pt milk
5 fl oz brandy
2 oz sugar
1 tablespoon rennet
Devonshire clotted cream
Grated cinnamon
Sugar

Warm the milk and brandy to blood heat, add the sugar and pour the junket into a serving bowl. Stir in the rennet, doubling the quantity with pasteurised milk.

Leave to set, then cover with clotted cream and sprinkle with cinnamon and sugar. The junket may be decorated with apricot or strawberry jam.

Junket with Wine (6-8 portions) F

2 pt milk
2 oz sugar
1 tablespoon rennet
5 fl oz brandy
5 fl oz white wine
½ pt double cream
Clotted cream

Heat the milk to blood heat, add the sugar and pour the junket into a serving dish. Stir in the rennet, using 2 tablespoons with pasteurised milk. Leave to set at room temperature.

Mix the brandy, wine and double cream and pour gently over the junket without breaking the curd. Cover with clotted cream and serve.

Clotted Cream
Devon and Cornwall

3 pt fresh milk

Pour the milk into a large pan and leave to stand for 24 hours in winter, or 12 hours in summer, in order to let the cream rise. Scald the milk by setting the pan over a low heat (maximum temperature 180°F) until the cream begins to show a raised ring round the edge. Watch the cream until it forms a thick layer on top of the milk.

The exact timing for scalding depends on the size of the pan and the heat, but the slower it is done the better. Remove the pan from the heat and leave in a cool place, being careful not to break up the layer of cream. Leave until the next day and then skim the cream off in layers and store in a cool place. Chill and serve with fruit, junkets, scones, cakes, etc.

Clotted cream will keep for 2-3 days in summer, 3-4 days in winter or if stored in a refrigerator. Devonshire Clotted Cream is more solid and smooth than Cornish Clotted Cream which has a pronounced flavour of scalded cream.

JELLIES, MOULDS AND OTHER CREAM SWEETS

All these desserts are set with gelatine in the case of clear jellies, and with gelatine and cream for creamy moulds. The jellies and blancmanges, on which cream moulds are based, developed side by side over several centuries.

A number of curious spellings for blancmange, including such peculiarities as *Blomanger* and *Blamanageree*, illustrate the transition of this dish from the savoury to the sweet. Adopted from the French *blanc-manger*, meaning white food, the 14th century dish was a soft mess of capon meat minced with almonds, sugar and rice, and cooked in broth.

The almond flavouring, setting agent, milk or cream and sugar have persisted over the centuries, but by the 17th century, meat and rice had disappeared from the blancmange.

Both jellies and blancmanges were originally set with calf's foot or hartshorn, later with isinglass and later still with commercially produced gelatine.

JELLIES

The 15th and 16th century jellies were splendid affairs, set in intricate moulds and castles and elaborately decorated with coloured piped creams.

Ale Jelly (8-12 portions) F

1½ pt ale
1½ oz gelatine
1 lb sugar
½ pt lemon juice
2 sticks cinnamon or 1 oz root ginger
3 egg whites

Dissolve the gelatine in a little of the ale, which has been heated almost to boiling point. Put the ale, sugar, lemon juice, cinnamon sticks and egg whites in a pan and bring to the boil, stirring continuously; boil for 15 minutes. Strain through a jelly bag until perfectly clear. Add the gelatine.

Pour the jelly into a wetted mould and leave to set. Turn out and serve with whipped cream and sponge fingers.

Fruit Jelly (8 portions) F and H

Rind of 4 lemons
½ lb caster sugar
2 cloves
2 egg whites
1¼ pt water
½ pt lemon juice
2 oz gelatine
5 fl oz sherry

Place the thinly cut lemon rind, the sugar, cloves, egg whites, water and lemon juice in a pan and bring slowly to the boil. Strain through a jelly bag and whisk in the gelatine dissolved in a little water. Simmer gently for 10 minutes, then add the sherry.

Leave to cool and pour into a wetted mould. When set, dip the mould quickly in hot water and turn out.

Other flavourings can be used for fruit jellies. The Yorkshire Orange Jelly is made as above, half the lemon rind and half the lemon juice being replaced with orange.

Bilberries, blackberries, black currants, grapes, loganberries, raspberries and strawberries all make good fruit jellies; press 1 lb fresh berries through a cloth to give 1 pt juice and make up the liquid to 2 pt with 5 fl oz lemon juice and ¾ pt water.

Apricots, apples, gooseberries, rhubarb and quinces for jellies must be first stewed in 5 fl oz of water to each lb of fruit; squeeze the juice through a cloth and make up to 2 pt of juice as for soft fruits.

Fruit in Jelly (8 portions) F and H

½ portion fruit jelly
1 lb fruit

Make up half a portion of fruit jelly (see opposite), using the same flavouring as the fruit to be set. Pour ½ inch of jelly in the base of a wetted mould and leave to set. Prepare the fruit and if necessary cut into pieces.

Put a layer of fruit in the mould, cover with jelly and leave to set. When set, pour in more jelly to a depth of ½ in. Put in another layer of fruit and continue until the mould is filled, finishing with a layer of jelly and leaving each layer to set before adding the next.

Pass the set mould through hot water and turn out on to a cold dish. It may be decorated with fruits or whipped cream.

Fruit suitable for setting in jelly include strawberries, raspberries, blackberries, black currants, grapes, oranges and tangerines in segments; bananas can be set in lemon or lime jelly. Tinned and thawed frozen fruits may also be used.

Port or Claret Jelly (8-10 portions) H

1 pt port or claret
1 pt water
½ lb sugar
4 oz red currant jelly
2 inch piece cinnamon
6 cloves
Rind and juice of 2 lemons
2 oz gelatine

Put the water, sugar, red currant jelly, cinnamon and cloves in an enamelled pan; add the thinly peeled rind and juice of the lemons.

Dissolve the gelatine in a little boiling water and add to the pan. Stir the mixture over low heat until the gelatine has completely dissolved and mixed in; simmer for a few minutes, then add the port or claret, but do not allow to boil again.

Strain the jelly through muslin and stir until almost cold and just beginning to set. Pour into a wetted mould and leave to set. Turn out and serve with whipped cream.

Strawberries in Wine Jelly (8-10 portions) H

1 lb strawberries
5 fl oz brandy

1 portion claret jelly

Soak the strawberries in the brandy for 1 hour. Make up the jelly (see opposite).

Arrange the soaked strawberries and jelly in layers in a wetted mould. Turn out when set and decorate with fresh strawberries and cream.

BLANCMANGES AND MOULDS

These are made with cream and flavourings, or with custards or fruit pulps. They should be allowed to set completely for several hours in the moulds before being turned out.

Blairgowrie Foam (6-8 portions) H Scotland

½ lb sieved raspberry pulp
3 eggs
½ oz gelatine
Juice of 1 lemon
½ lb sugar
½ pt double cream
Toasted nuts

Prepare a soufflé dish with a paper collar. Separate the eggs. Dissolve the gelatine in the lemon juice and whisk the egg yolks and sugar to ribbon stage over a pan of warm water. Add the dissolved gelatine and fruit pulp and leave to cool completely.

Whisk the egg whites until stiff and whisk the cream separately. When the gelatine mixture is cold, fold in the whipped cream and the egg whites. Pour the mixture into the soufflé dish and leave to set.

Remove the paper collar when the mixture has set and coat the exposed sides with toasted nuts; decorate with whipped cream.

Blancmange (6-8 portions) F and H

Thinly peeled rind of 1 lemon
1 pt milk
1½ oz gelatine
4-6 oz caster sugar
1 pt single cream
3 oz ground almonds
2 fl oz brandy

Infuse the lemon peel in the warmed milk for 1 hour; strain and dissolve the gelatine in a little of the milk. Add the gelatine to the milk and stir in the sugar.

Blend in the cream and ground almonds and stir until almost cold. Finally stir in the brandy, pour into a wetted mould and leave to set.

Custard Cream (6-8 portions) H and F

This custard cream may be flavoured with 1 dessertspoon vanilla essence, 2 tablespoons coffee essence, a few drops of almond essence and green colouring or a caramel cream made by dissolving 6 oz granulated sugar in the milk for the custard; 2 tablespoons brandy may also be added.

1 pt milk
3 eggs or 6 yolks
3 oz sugar
1 pt double cream
1½ oz gelatine
2½ fl oz water

Heat the milk and pour over the eggs beaten with the sugar; cook in a double saucepan, stirring continuously until the custard thickens. Whip the cream.

Cool the custard, and add any flavouring and the lightly whipped cream. Dissolve the gelatine in the water and add to the custard when cool enough. Stir until the mixture shows signs of setting, then pour into a wetted mould and leave to set.

Crystal Palace Pudding (6-8 portions) H and F London

5 fl oz lemon jelly
3 oz candied peel, chopped angelica and
    chopped glacé cherries
1 pt milk
3 eggs or 6 egg yolks
3 oz sugar
1 dessertspoon vanilla essence
1 pt double cream, whipped
1½ oz gelatine
2½ fl oz water

Line a plain mould with half the lemon jelly and decorate with the candied fruits. Leave to set in a cool place.

Prepare a custard from the milk, eggs and sugar, cooking it in a double saucepan until it thickens. Leave to cool, then stir in the vanilla essence and the lightly whipped cream. Dissolve the gelatine in the water and stir into the custard.

Pour the custard cream into the mould and cover with the remaining lemon jelly. Leave to set. Turn the mould out and serve.

Flummery (6-8 portions) H

Thinly peeled rind of 1 lemon
¾ pt water
½ lb caster sugar
2 oz gelatine
Juice of 4 lemons
1 pt wine or sherry
8 egg yolks
5 fl oz brandy

Put the lemon rind, water and sugar in a pan; bring to the boil and simmer for 5-10 minutes or until it has formed a light syrup. Dissolve the gelatine in a little of the syrup and add to the pan with the lemon juice, sherry and the well beaten egg yolks. Strain.

Cook in a double saucepan until thick, stirring constantly to prevent it from curdling. Stir in the brandy and pour the mixture into a wetted mould. Leave to set completely before turning it out.

Fruit Cream (6-8 portions) H and F

Suitable fruits for fruit creams include strawberries, raspberries and apricots. Use 1 lb strawberries to give 1 pt fresh pulp and the same for raspberries with the addition of a little red currant jelly and carmine colouring. Simmer 1 lb apricots in 1 pt water to obtain 1 pt pulp and flavour with a few drops of almond essence.

1 pt fruit pulp
6 oz sugar
1 pt double cream
Colouring (optional)
1½ oz gelatine
5 fl oz water

Stir the sugar into the fruit pulp and sieve; fold in the lightly whipped cream. Add colouring if necessary.

Dissolve the gelatine in the water and blend into the fruit and cream mixture stirring until it is beginning to set. Pour into a wetted mould and leave to set completely.

Fruit Mould (6-8 portions) F

This fruit mould is made with rhubarb, but gooseberries, raspberries, plums or damsons can also be used.

2 lb rhubarb
2 tablespoons water
Juice of 1 lemon
1 oz gelatine
6 oz sugar
Colouring (optional)

Wash and cut up the rhubarb, add the water and simmer to a pulp. Add the lemon juice, measure and make the pulp up to 1 pt.

Dissolve the gelatine in a little water and mix in with the rhubarb. Stir in the sugar thoroughly, add colouring if necessary and pour into a mould. Leave to set; turn out and serve with custard or whipped cream.

Fruit Sponge (6-8 portions) F

1 oz gelatine
6 oz sugar
1 pt water
Rind and juice of 2 lemons
2 egg whites

Put the gelatine, sugar, water and lemon rind in a pan, stir until the gelatine is dissolved. Bring to the boil and infuse, covered, for 5-10 minutes; add the lemon juice, strain and cool.

Beat the egg whites until very stiff, add a third of the lemon mixture at a time, beating between each addition until a stiff white froth is obtained. Pour this mixture into a scalded and rinsed mould.

Leave the mould to set until quite firm, turn out and serve with a rich custard.

Other fruits can be used for this sponge mould. For an orange sponge, use grated rind and juice of 1 lemon and 1 orange instead of 2 lemons; for damson or plum sponge, simmer 1 lb damsons or plums in 1 pt water and sieve to make 1 pt pulp; dissolve the gelatine in this.

For apricot sponge, cook 1 lb fresh or ½ lb dried soaked apricots in 1 pt water and sieve to make 1 pt pulp.

Grassy Corner Pudding (8 portions) H
Oxford and Cambridge Colleges

A 19th century cream mould composed of alternate layers of strawberry fruit cream and vanilla custard cream.

Strawberry Fruit Cream:
5 fl oz lemon jelly
Pistachio nuts
½ pt strawberry pulp
3 oz sugar
½ pt double cream
¾ oz gelatine

Vanilla Custard Cream:
½ pt milk
3 egg yolks
1½ oz sugar
Vanilla essence
½ pt double cream
¾ oz gelatine

Line a mould with half the lemon jelly and sprinkle thickly with pistachio nuts; leave to set.

For the strawberry fruit cream, mix the pulp with the sugar and rub through a sieve; stir in the lightly whipped cream. Dissolve the gelatine in a little water and stir into the fruit cream until almost set.

Prepare the vanilla custard cream by making a plain custard from the milk, egg yolks and sugar; cool, flavour to taste with vanilla essence and fold in the lightly whipped cream. Dissolve the gelatine and stir into the custard cream.

Arrange alternate layers of strawberry cream and vanilla custard cream in the mould; cover with the remaining lemon jelly and leave to set. Turn out and serve.

Stone Cream (8 portions) H

Glacé cherries, angelica and candied peel
Grated rind and juice of 1 lemon
1½ oz gelatine
5 fl oz white wine
4 oz caster sugar
1¾ pt double cream

Arrange the candied fruit over the base of a mould, pour over the lemon juice with the grated rind. Dissolve the gelatine in a little water, add the wine, sugar and lightly whipped cream and pour over the fruit in the mould. Leave to set before turning out.

SWEETS MADE WITH CARAGEEN SEAWEED

Carageen, Sea Moss or Irish Moss (L. *Chondrus crispus*) is a seaweed found below high water mark on many coasts of Europe, among them Ireland, the West Coast of Scotland and the Western Isles.

Owing to its gelatinous quality it is used as a vegetable gelatine and makes excellent jellies and beverages, although its use is limited to Ireland and remote parts of Scotland. It is rich in minerals and vitamins and for this reason has become more easily available in health food shops and chemists.

In its natural state, carageen is dark purple or green, but it is usually sold dried and bleached.

Carageen Mould (6-8 portions) F
Hebrides, West Scotland, Ireland

½ oz dried carageen
1½ pt milk
Grated rind of 1 lemon
1 oz sugar

Wash the carageen and soak in water for 10 minutes; drain. Warm the milk and infuse with the lemon rind and sugar for 10 minutes. Mix with the carageen, return to the pan and simmer for 20 minutes.

Strain into a wetted mould and leave until set. Turn out and serve with cream or fruit.

In the Hebrides, it is common to eat the mould without any additional flavouring, but the following additions are used elsewhere: 1 well beaten egg added to the mixture before pouring it into the mould. Alternatively, omit lemon rind and add instead the strained juice of two Seville oranges, or omit lemon rind and infuse 1 bay leaf, 1 stick cinnamon or a pinch of dried elder flowers.

Tea Cream (8 portions) H and F

1 pt milk
2 oz tea leaves
1 pt double cream
1 oz gelatine
4-6 oz sugar

Bring the milk to the boil and pour over the tea leaves; leave to infuse, covered, for 20 minutes.

Strain and fold the lightly whipped cream into
the flavoured milk.

Dissolve the gelatine in a little boiling water
and stir into the cream. Sweeten the mixture to
taste and pour into a wetted mould. Leave to set
before turning out.

ICE CREAMS

Cream ices and water ices do not feature in British
cookery until the 19th century. They are Italian
in origin and were introduced via France; the
Victorians and Edwardians set great store by ice
creams, and in particular by water ices or
sorbets which were served between courses at
grand dinners to cleanse and refresh the palate.

Cream Ices (8 portions) H and F

These are made from rich custard and cream,
with a chosen flavouring. They are frozen for
several hours, and the freezing compartment
of the refrigerator should be set to its coldest
temperature at least 1 hour in advance.

1 pt single cream
8 egg yolks
3 oz sugar
Flavouring
1 pt double cream
10-12 oz caster sugar

For the custard, beat the single cream and pour
over the egg yolks beaten with the sugar. Strain
and cook in a double saucepan, stirring all the
time, until the custard begins to thicken. Leave
to cool.

Add the chosen flavouring, the softly whipped
double cream and the caster sugar. Pour the cream
mixture into clean and dry freezing trays or
plastic boxes. Cover.

When half frozen and ice crystals begin to
form, spoon the cream into a bowl and whisk
until smooth. Return the cream to the trays and
continue freezing for several hours.

Flavourings for Cream Ices:

Banana, add ¾ lb mashed or sieved bananas to the
ice cream just before freezing.

Brown Bread, add ¾ lb wholemeal breadcrumbs to vanilla ice cream just before serving;
this was a favourite Edwardian ice cream.

Caledonian Ice Cream (Iced Stapeg), add 6 oz
coarse oatmeal, lightly toasted, just before
freezing.

Chocolate, add 3 oz melted chocolate to the
custard; alternatively, chop the chocolate roughly
and mix with the ice cream before freezing.

Coffee, add 1 tablespoon coffee essence to the
ice cream just before freezing.

Ginger, add 3 oz finely chopped preserved
ginger and 2 tablespoons ginger syrup just before
freezing.

Rum and Raisin, add ½ lb raisins and flavour
with rum, up to 5 fl oz.

Rum and Walnut, add ½ lb finely chopped
walnuts and up to 5 fl oz rum just before
freezing.

Vanilla, heat the cream with a vanilla pod or
use vanilla sugar with the eggs.

McCallum (8 portions) F and H Glasgow

Popular sayings maintain that this favourite
Glaswegian sweet originated early in the 20th
century, the red and white colours representing
the Clyde football team.

Vanilla ice cream
Raspberry syrup

Arrange the ice cream in individual dishes and
cover with raspberry syrup.

Peach Melba (8 portions) H and F

This sweet was created late in the 19th century by
Escoffier at the Savoy Hotel, London, as a tribute
to Dame Nellie Melba, then appearing at the
Royal Opera House.

4 fresh peaches
4 oz vanilla sugar
¾ pt water
Vanilla ice cream
½ pt sieved raspberry pulp
Caster sugar

Blanch and skin the peaches and poach them
lightly in a syrup made from the vanilla sugar
and water. Drain, cut in half and remove the
stones; cool.

Arrange a portion of ice cream in each of
eight individual glasses and place half a peach on

top. Sweeten the fresh raspberry pulp to taste and spoon over the peaches; serve.

Fruit Ices (6 portions) H and F

These are made like cream ices with the addition of fruit pulp. Any fruit, fresh, tinned or frozen may be used; soft fruit can be freshly sieved, but hard fruit should be cooked and cooled. With frozen or tinned fruit, reduce the amount of sugar if they are in a heavy syrup.

½ pt single cream
3 egg yolks
1½ oz sugar
½-¾ pt fruit pulp
Squeeze lemon juice
½ pt double cream
6-8 oz caster sugar
Food colouring (optional)

Heat the single cream and pour over the egg yolks beaten with the sugar; strain and cook in a double saucepan until thick. Cool.

Beat the fruit pulp, lemon juice and the lightly whipped double cream into the custard; add caster sugar to taste and any colouring if used. Pour the mixture into ice trays and freeze until crystals begin to form.

Transfer the mixture to a bowl and beat until broken up but not soft. Return the mixture to the trays and freeze until firm.

Water Ices or Sorbets (6-8 portions) H

1 pt water
5 fl oz lemon juice and grated rind of 2 lemons
½ lb caster sugar
2 egg whites

Put the water, lemon rind and sugar in a pan and boil for 10 minutes. Leave to cool. Strain the lemon juice which should measure 5 fl oz.

Strain the syrup, add the lemon juice and freeze until nearly firm. Remove the near-frozen mixture, break down thoroughly and beat in the stiff egg whites. Continue freezing until firm.

For orange water ice, use the juice of 3 oranges and 1 lemon, with the finely grated rind; reduce the sugar to 6 oz.

Yeast Baking

A complex collection of items has developed from the basic concept of bread. The original term for the product was loaf, restricted today to whole bread, while the original meaning of bread — bit piece, morsel of food — developed through a piece of bread or to break bread, into the concept of bread as a substance.

A loaf or piece of bread in its original form was cereal mixed with water to a porridge which was then heated and dried. The grinding process was important to this method since the result depended on the texture of the grain. The early Egyptian, Greek and Roman civilisations concentrated their efforts on reducing cereal to its finest form so that the finished product might hold together better and have a smoother texture.

The Egyptians are given credit for discovering the process which transformed a hard, heavy, dried product into a softer and lighter one by means of aeration. An Egyptian baker is said to have accidentally missed a piece out of his daily batch of bread. Left lying in the sun for the rest of the day the dough began to ferment so that when he discovered it the following day and mixed it in with the new batch of bread, the fermenting dough leavened the rest of the dough, and the result was a light aerated bread. This was the method used for centuries until it was discovered that the thick scum strained from fermenting wine and beer could also be used as leaven for bread. Bakers usually obtained their leaven from brewers and it became known as brewers' yeast or barm. Today, compressed yeast is prepared from grain or molasses.

Leavening and grinding led to new developments in the variety of bread, but there had already been in existence from earliest times an inherent variety due to the available type of grain. In Britain, this ranged from wheat (soft or strong) barley, oats, maize, rye, beans, peas and even acorns. People baked their bread with whatever happened to be available and in whatever proportions they found practicable.

There were basically three types of bread, white, brown and black. White was made from wheat which had been finely ground and sifted. The grinding and sifting processes were much less sophisticated than today, and the loaf had a brownish yellow colour rather than pure white. Below this the decreasing order depended on the shade of brown which in turn depended on the amount of bran or rye or other dark cereal included: the lowest standard of bread consisted of all bran or all rye or a mixture of the two and was known as black bread. Rich people demanded the whitest bread which became a symbol of social class, initiated, it is thought, by the Romans who introduced the art of grinding cereal and making leavened bread to Britain.

The bannock was a slight modification of the cereal-and-water concept; it was usually unleavened, large, oval or round in shape, thicker and softer than a biscuit, but eaten as bread. Barley bannocks were the most common, but peasemeal, oatmeal and sometimes wheat flour were also used.

In the late 17th century there emerged another type of bread or cake which brought new connotations — the crumpet. Referred to originally as a crompid cake this apparently meant a griddle-baked cake which was so thin that it curled up or bent into a curve. It seems to have been made originally with buckwheat.

Earlier the Welsh were making soft cakes of fine flour which they called "Barrapyclids", later known as 'Barra-picklets' and finally shortened to "Pikelet". The term is now used in the West of England, the Midlands as well as Wales for a small round tea cake made of fine flour, a crumpet or in some districts a muffin. The origin of the muffin is obscure though it is thought to have connection with the old French word *moufflet* meaning soft.

A later term which to some extent confused the cake development was the bun. The original concept is doubtful though it is possible that it may have developed from the fritter. In the early 17th century, this type of baked bread was referred to as "bunne" or "Lenten loaf" or "little round loaf" or "lump made of the meale, oyle or butter and reasons".

The use of the term bun today differs greatly according to the locality. In England, it generally denotes an item akin to the original form of cake, sweetened and flavoured. Scotland has another meaning as the richest form for fancy bread, composed almost entirely of fruit and spice and known as black bun. In other places, and particularly in Northern Ireland, the round shape and composition of the original cake of bread and the original plain bread concept is preserved in bun-bread; in Lancashire and Yorkshire, currant bun-loaf is in between the rich Scottish bun and the plain Irish one.

The Hot Cross Bun is another development which probably originated as a type of round bread, its origin being pagan rather than Christian. The shape was important since originally the round was representative of the sun, and the cross divided the circle into four sections, representing the four seasons.

Bread with a cross was commonly made for festivals in Rome and Greece many centuries before Christ. The custom persisted into the Middle Ages, and when loaves, cakes and buns were marked with a cross before baking, the reason was to confound any evil spirit.

Superstitious people had great faith in bread as a cure for diseases; toasted bread steeped in cider was regarded as a certain cure for headaches and colds, but the strongest medicine of all was bread baked on Good Friday. Housewives in the West Country usually kept back one of the batch of loaves baked on this day; it was suspended on a string from the ceiling and left there as protection against evil until the following Good Friday. It is presumably from a perpetuation of this custom that the cross was put on the bun, and the bun came to be associated with Good Friday.

YEAST BREAD, ROLLS AND BUNS

In the following recipes for mainly regional types of yeast breads, rolls, buns and cakes, the common methods of bread-making are referred to only briefly. For full details of the method for making white, brown and enriched dough, see the section on Basic Cookery.

Apple Bread Derbyshire

2 lb plain flour
1 oz salt
1 oz lard
1 oz fresh yeast
1 pt sweetened apple pulp

Oven: 350°F; gas mark 4; 1—1¼ hours

Sift the flour and salt, rub in the lard and crumble the yeast finely into this mixture. Add the apple pulp and knead to a smooth dough.

Shape the dough to fit two greased, long loaf tins and leave to rise for 3—4 hours or until the dough has almost doubled in size. Bake for about 1 hour.

Bara Brith Wales

Meaning "speckled bread", this was originally made with fresh currants or blackberries.

¾ lb dried fruit
4 oz candied peel
1 pt warm water
½ teaspoon mixed spice
2 lb plain flour
2 teaspoons salt
6 oz lard
1 oz fresh yeast
½ lb Demerara sugar
2 eggs

Oven: 450°F; gas mark 8; 15 minutes
        375°F; gas mark 5; 45 minutes

Soak the fruit and candied peel in the water with the spice. Leave to steep in a warm place and use the warm spicy, strained water to mix the dough.

Sift the flour and salt and rub in the lard; cream the yeast with the sugar and a little of the spiced water; mix this into the flour, together with the eggs, and use enough of the water to give a firm, yet elastic dough. Knead well, leave to rise and knock back; blend in the drained fruit and knead again.

Shape the dough into loaves and set in greased

1 lb tins in a warm place to prove; bake, reducing the temperature after the first 15 minutes.

Baps Scotland

Also known as Scottish breakfast rolls and always served warm.

1 lb plain flour
½ tablespoon salt
2 oz lard
1 oz fresh yeast
½ tablespoon sugar
½ pt milk and water
Milk
Flour (optional)

Oven: 425°F; gas mark 7; 20—30 minutes

Sift the flour and salt and rub in the lard; cream the yeast with the sugar and half the milk. Add the yeast mixture and remaining milk to the flour and mix the dough thoroughly.

Knead well, leave to rise until doubled in size, then knock back. Divide the dough into equal oval shapes about 3 in long and 2 in wide. Brush with milk and water to give a glaze; for floury baps, dust with flour after brushing and again just before baking.

Place on greased floured baking sheets and set to prove. To prevent blisters, press a finger into the centre of each bap before they are placed in the oven; bake for 20—30 minutes.

Barm Brack Ireland

Meaning speckled cake, this was originally served at Hallowe'en, a ring or other charm being hidden in the dough.

3 lb plain flour
½ tablespoon salt
1 oz fresh yeast
½ tablespoon caster sugar
1 pt water
4 eggs
4 oz melted butter
6 oz sugar
2 oz caraway seeds

Oven: 425°F; gas mark 7; 45 minutes

Sift the flour and salt, make a well in the centre and add the yeast creamed with the sugar and half the water; break in the eggs and the remaining water and mix the dough. Knead thoroughly, rise until doubled in size, then knock back.

Knead the dough again with the butter, sugar and caraway seeds. Shape into a round loaf or set in a large round cake tin. Prove in a warm place and bake.

Bath Buns Somerset

1 lb plain flour
2 teaspoons salt
½ oz yeast
½ tablespoon sugar
6 oz butter
2½ fl oz milk and water
3 eggs
4 oz chopped candied peel
2 oz sultanas
1 beaten egg
2 oz crushed lump sugar
Caraway comfits
Lemon or orange peel

Oven: 425°F; gas mark 7; 10—15 minutes

For this enriched dough sift the flour and salt, cream the yeast and sugar and add to the flour. Melt the butter in the warm milk and water, blend into the flour together with the three beaten eggs, candied peel and sultanas.

Knead and set aside to rise until doubled in size. Knock back and shape into 12 rough buns; brush with egg and sprinkle with the lump sugar. Top with five or six caraway comfits and lemon or orange peel. Prove in a warm place and bake.

Belvoir Castle Buns Nottinghamshire, Rutland

1 lb plain flour
2 teaspoons salt
2 oz butter
½ oz fresh yeast
4 oz sugar
4 fl oz water and milk
4 oz chopped mixed dried fruit and peel
Milk

Oven: 425°F; gas mark 7; 10 minutes

Sift the flour and salt and rub in the butter; cream the yeast with the sugar and warm water and milk. Blend the yeast mixture into the flour, together with half the dried fruit. Knead on a floured surface until the dough is smooth and elastic, then set aside to rise and double in size. Knock back.

Roll the dough out to a ½ in thick square; sprinkle the remaining fruit on top and roll up to a sausage shape. Cut into 12 pieces, 1 in thick, and set, cut side up, on greased baking sheets to prove. Brush with a little milk and bake.

Birstall Buns

1 lb plain flour
2 teaspoons salt
½ oz fresh yeast
½ tablespoon sugar
4 fl oz milk and water
2 oz fat
1 egg
3 oz currants
3 oz sultanas
½ oz chopped candied peel

Oven: 425°F; gas mark 7; 10—15 minutes

Sift the flour and salt; cream the yeast with the sugar and the warm milk heated with the fat until melted; add the yeast mixture and the beaten egg to the flour and mix to a smooth dough. Knead and set to rise.

Knock back the dough, work in the dried fruits and knead the mixture well. Divide into 12 round buns, place on a greased baking sheet and prove. Bake for 10—15 minutes.

Brotherly Love Suffolk

1 lb plain flour
1 teaspoon salt
1 oz lard
½ oz fresh yeast
½ tablespoon caster sugar
½ pt water
1 oz flaked lard
2 oz sugar

Oven: 425°F; gas mark 7; 30 minutes

Sift the flour and salt, rub in the lard and blend in the yeast creamed with the sugar and warm water. Mix to a smooth dough, knead and leave to rise.

Knock back the dough and roll out into a rectangle ½ in thick. Cover with small pieces of lard and sprinkle with the sugar. Roll up to a sausage shape from the short side and prove. Bake for about 30 minutes.

Bun Loaf Lancashire

3 lb plain flour
1 tablespoon salt
1 oz lard
1 oz fresh yeast
½ tablespoon sugar
1½ pt warm water
¾ lb raisins
¾ lb currants
3 oz chopped orange peel
2 teaspoons mixed spice
6 oz melted butter

Oven: 450°F; gas mark 8; 15 minutes
375°F; gas mark 5; 45 minutes

Sift the flour and salt and rub in the lard; cream the yeast with the sugar and 5 fl oz of the warm water. Add the yeast mixture and the remaining water and mix the dough until it comes away clean from the sides of the bowl.

Knead thoroughly on a floured surface and leave to rise in a warm place. Knock the dough back and work in the dried fruits, spice and melted butter. Knead thoroughly until well blended and smooth.

Shape the dough and put into greased loaf tins. Prove until doubled in size and bake for 1 hour, reducing the heat after the first 15 minutes.

Buttery Rowies or Butteries Aberdeenshire

3 lb plain flour
1 oz salt
1 oz lard
1 oz fresh yeast
½ tablespoon sugar
1½ pt warm water
2½ lb flaked lard

Oven: 425°F; gas mark 7; 20—30 minutes

Sift the flour and salt, rub in the lard and add the yeast creamed with the sugar and warm water. Mix to a smooth dough, knead and leave to rise until doubled in size.

Knock back the dough, roll out into a rectangle and mark into three equal sections. Dot one third of the flaked lard over two thirds of the dough as for flaky pastry. Fold up the bottom third and fold down the top third; seal the edges and roll out. Repeat this twice more until all the fat is used up.

Cut the dough roughly into oval shapes, set on greased and floured baking sheets and prove until twice the size. Bake for 20–30 minutes.

Carmarthen Yeast Cake Wales

½ lb plain flour
1 teaspoon mixed spice
Pinch salt
½ lb mixed dried fruit
1½ oz butter
1½ oz lard
3 oz caster sugar
½ oz golden syrup
1 egg
5 fl oz milk
½ oz fresh yeast
½ teaspoon bicarbonate of soda

Oven: 425°F; gas mark 7; 1½–2 hours

Sift the flour, spice and salt and add the dried fruit. Beat the butter, lard, sugar and syrup to a cream, add the egg and beat well. Warm the milk and dissolve the yeast in half the milk, the bicarbonate of soda in the other half. Add both mixtures to the creamed butter and beat thoroughly; fold this into the flour and mix to a soft dough.

Put the dough in a 1 lb greased loaf tin and prove until doubled in size. Bake for 1½–2 hours.

Cattern Cakes (St. Catherine Cakes) Bedfordshire

St. Catherine was the patron saint of spinsters, lace makers and spinners; young women used to bake these cakes to celebrate her feast day on 25th November.

2 lb plain flour
½ tablespoon salt
3 oz butter or lard
½ oz fresh yeast
2 oz sugar
1 egg
1 oz caraway seeds

Oven: 350°F; gas mark 4; 1½–2 hours

Sift the flour and salt, rub in the butter and add the yeast creamed with the sugar; blend in the beaten egg and the caraway seeds and mix to a firm dough.

Knead well on a floured surface; leave to rise, then knock back. Shape the dough and place in a

1 lb greased and floured loaf tin. Prove and bake.

Chelsea Buns London

The Chelsea Bun, sometimes baked in one large round circle as a tea cake, was a speciality of the popular Chelsea Bun House.

1 lb plain flour
2 teaspoons salt
½ oz fresh yeast
½ tablespoon sugar
2 oz butter
4 fl oz warm water and milk
1 egg
3 oz caster sugar
3 oz currants
1 beaten egg
Glacé icing

Oven: 425°F; gas mark 7; 15 minutes

Mix an enriched dough by sifting the flour and salt and adding to it the creamed yeast and sugar, the butter melted in the water and milk, and the beaten egg. Mix to a smooth dough, knead well and set to rise until doubled in size.

Knock the dough back and roll out to a square, ½ in thick. Sprinkle with caster sugar and currants, roll up to a sausage shape and cut into pieces about 1 in thick.

Set the buns, cut side up, on greased baking sheets, in a circle with one bun in the centre, leaving room for proving. Prove, brush with egg and bake, While still warm, brush the buns with a thin white glace icing.

Chester Buns Cheshire

1 lb strong plain flour
2 teaspoons salt
2 oz butter
½ oz fresh yeast
1 teaspoon sugar
2½ tablespoons warm milk
1 egg
5 fl oz condensed milk

Oven: 425°F; gas mark 7; 10–15 minutes

Sift the flour and salt and rub in the butter. Cream the yeast with the sugar and warm milk. Make a well in the centre of the flour, add the beaten egg mixed with the condensed milk, and the yeast mixture; blend to a smooth dough.

Knead on a floured surface until elastic, then set aside to rise in a warm place. Knock the risen dough back, shape into about 12 round buns and set on greased baking sheets to prove. Bake for 15 minutes and brush with a sugar and water glaze while still warm.

Coconut Bread

1 fresh grated coconut
1½ pt coconut milk and fresh milk
3 lb plain flour
½ tablespoon salt
1 oz lard
1 oz fresh yeast
2 oz sugar

Oven: 450°F; gas mark 8; 15 minutes
375°F; gas mark 5; 45 minutes

Cook the grated coconut in milk until tender. Strain and set aside. Sift the flour and salt, rub in the lard and add the yeast creamed with the sugar and a little of the warm coconut milk. Add the coconut and the remaining milk and mix to a smooth dough. Knead thoroughly and leave to rise until doubled in size.

Knock the dough back and shape into loaves; set in three greased 1 lb loaf tins and prove. Bake for 1 hour, reducing the temperature after the first 15 minutes.

Cookies Scotland

1 lb plain flour
2 teaspoons salt
½ oz fresh yeast
3 oz sugar
4 oz butter
2½ fl oz milk
3 eggs
1 beaten egg

Oven: 425°F; gas mark 7; 10 minutes

Sift the flour and salt, add the yeast creamed with the sugar, and the butter melted in the warm milk; blend in the three beaten eggs and mix to a soft dough. Knead on a floured surface and set aside to rise and double in size.

Knock the dough back and divide it into 2 oz pieces shaping them into rounds. Set on a greased baking tray and prove. Brush with egg and bake.

Cornish Splits Cornwall

"Thunder and Lightening" is the name given to these little yeast cakes when served with cream and black treacle.

1 lb plain flour
2 teaspoons salt
2 oz fat
½ oz fresh yeast
½ tablespoon sugar
4 fl oz milk

Oven: 425°F; gas mark 7; 15—20 minutes

Mix all the ingredients to a soft enriched dough, knead and leave to rise until doubled in size.

Knock back and shape the dough into small round cakes. Prove and bake. Split and butter the cakes and serve hot, or leave until cold, then split and butter them and serve with jam.

Crumpets or Pikelets

A crumpet is a round flat sweet scone with holes in it. The traditional crumpet rings are 3½ in wide and 1 in deep.

1¼ lb flour
½ oz yeast
1 pt warm water
1 oz salt

Dissolve the creamed yeast in a little of the warm water; sift the flour and salt and mix in the remaining water. Add the creamed yeast to the mixture and cover with a cloth; keep in a warm place until the dough is well risen.

Thin the dough to a batter consistency with a little warm water, and leave for 5 minutes. Bake in greased crumpet rings on a hot plate or griddle, filling the rings halfway up with batter and turning when dry on top and slightly browned underneath; remove the crumpet rings.

It is advisable to test one crumpet first; if the batter is too thick the holes will not form and more warm water should be added.

Devonshire Yeast Cake Devon

1 lb plain flour
2 teaspoons salt
2 oz fat
½ oz fresh yeast
½ tablespoon sugar

1 beaten egg
4 fl oz warm water and milk
4 oz currants
2 oz chopped candied lemon peel
½ grated nutmeg

Oven: 450°F; gas mark 8; 15 minutes
      375°F; gas mark 5; 45 minutes

Mix all the ingredients except the dried fruits and spice to an enriched dough; knead thoroughly and set to rise.

Knock the dough back, add the currants, peel and nutmeg and knead again. Shape the dough and place in a greased cake tin. Prove and bake for 1 hour, reducing the temperature after the first 15 minutes.

Doughnuts

Isle of Wight doughnuts are shaped into small round balls; a hole is made in each and a little red jam is dropped into it. The hole is closed securely, sealed with egg and the doughnuts deep-fried in fat after proving.

1 lb plain flour
2 teaspoons salt
4 oz butter
4 fl oz warm milk
½ oz fresh yeast
2 oz sugar
2 eggs
Fat or lard for frying
Caster sugar
Ground cinnamon

Make an enriched dough from the flour and salt, butter and milk, sugar and yeast and the beaten eggs. Mix to a soft consistency, knead the dough well and leave to rise.

Knock the dough back and knead; roll out, 2 in thick; cut into round shapes using a cutter with a hole in the middle. Prove until well-risen, then deep-fry in fat heated to 345°F, for 5—6 minutes or until golden brown, turning once. Drain, toss in caster sugar and cinnamon and serve.

Fourses Cake Suffolk

A traditional bread served to harvesters in the afternoon, together with sweetened beer.

3 lb plain flour
1 tablespoon salt

2 teaspoons mixed spice
¾ lb lard
1 oz yeast
½ tablespoon sugar
1½ pt warm water
¾ lb currants

Oven: 400°F; gas mark 6; 45 minutes

Sift the flour, salt and spice, rub in the lard and add the yeast creamed with the sugar and a little warm water; add the remaining water and mix to an elastic dough.

Knead thoroughly, set aside to rise until doubled in size. Knock the dough back and knead in the currants. Shape into loaves and set in greased 1 lb loaf tins. Prove and bake.

Guernsey Gache Guernsey

3 lb plain flour
½ tablespoon salt
1 oz yeast
1 tablespoon sugar
1 lb butter
1 pt warm water
2 eggs
1 lb currants

Oven: 450°F; gas mark 8; 15 minutes
      375°F; gas mark 5; 45 minutes

Make an enriched dough from the sifted flour and salt, the yeast creamed with sugar, and the butter melted in the warm water; drop in the eggs and mix, gradually adding the currants. Mix to a soft dough, knead and leave to rise until doubled.

Knock the dough back, shape into loaves and set in greased 2 lb tins. Prove and bake for 1 hour, reducing the temperature after the first 15 minutes.

Hot Cross Buns London

Like Chelsea Buns, Hot Cross Buns were a speciality of the Chelsea Bun House, and both King George II and George III with their queens honoured the proprietress with their patronage.

1 lb plain flour
2 teaspoons salt
Pinch each, cinnamon and mixed spice
½ oz fresh yeast
2 oz sugar
2 oz butter
4 fl oz milk

1 egg
2 oz currants
2 oz sweet shortcrust pastry
Milk
Sugar

Oven: 425°F; gas mark 7; 10–15 minutes

Sift the flour and salt, add the cinnamon and spice, the yeast creamed with the sugar and the butter melted in the milk. Add the beaten egg and the currants and mix until the dough leaves the bowl clean. Knead thoroughly and set to rise until doubled in size.

Knock the dough back and shape into small round buns; place on greased baking sheets, leaving 2 in spaces between them. Prove and when risen, make a cross with thin strips of pastry across the top of each. Bake and glaze with milk and sugar while still hot.

Huffkins Kent

1 lb plain flour
½ tablespoon salt
½ oz fresh yeast
½ tablespoon sugar
½ pint milk and water
2 oz lard

Oven: 425°F; gas mark 7; 15–20 minutes

Sift the flour and salt; cream the yeast with the sugar and half the warmed milk and water. Rub the lard into the flour, add the yeast mixture and work in the flour, adding the remaining milk and water.

Knead the dough until smooth and elastic; leave to rise in a warm place until doubled in size. Knock back and divide the dough into three oval cakes, ½ in thick; make a hole in the centre of each. Place on greased baking trays to prove.

Bake for 20 minutes and wrap the cakes in a warm cloth to cool, this will keep the crust soft.

Kensington Rolls London

1 lb plain flour
2 teaspoons salt
½ oz yeast
2 oz sugar
4 oz butter
5 fl oz milk
3 eggs

½ lb almond paste
Glacé icing
Chopped almonds

Oven: 425°F; gas mark 7; 10–15 minutes

Make an enriched dough from the sifted flour and salt, the creamed yeast and sugar and the butter melted in the warm milk; add the beaten eggs. Mix to a smooth soft dough, knead well and leave to rise until doubled in size.

Knock the dough back and roll it to a rectangle, ½ in thick. Roll out the almond paste to a square and place in the centre of the dough. Roll up to a sausage shape, prove and bake.

When cold, coat with white glacé icing and decorate with blanched chopped almonds.

Lancashire Cakes Lancashire

1 lb plain flour
1 teaspoon salt
½ oz lard
½ oz fresh yeast
½ tablespoon sugar
½ pt water
4–6 oz currants
Nutmeg
Sugar
2 oz candied peel

Oven: 425°F; gas mark 7; 15 minutes

Sift the flour and salt, rub in the lard and add the yeast creamed with the sugar and a little warm water; mix to a smooth dough with the remaining water and knead well. Leave the dough to rise and double in size. Knock back.

Roll the dough out to circles the size of a tea plate and sprinkle the centre of each with currants, nutmeg, sugar and peel. Bring in the edges and seal. Turn the rounds over, join underneath, and roll out re-shaping into rounds. Prick well on top, prove and bake.

Lancashire Plum Cake Lancashire

1 lb plain flour
½ teaspoon baking powder
½ teaspoon bicarbonate of soda
2 oz butter
6 oz lard
2 oz yeast
Milk

½ lb brown sugar
½ grated nutmeg
½ lb currants
4 oz raisins
2 oz chopped peel

Oven: 350°F; gas mark 4; 1½–2 hours

Sift the flour, baking powder and bicarbonate of soda and rub in the butter and lard; cream the yeast in a little warm milk. Mix the flour with the sugar, nutmeg, currants, raisins and chopped peel; add the yeast mixture and more milk until the dough is soft and smooth.

Knead lightly and place the dough in a double-lined tin. Bake for about 1½ hours or until well-risen and brown.

Lardy Cake Wiltshire, Oxfordshire, Cambridgeshire

Also known as Shaley or Sharley Cake, this was traditionally served at tea time on Saturdays and Sundays.

1 lb plain flour
½ tablespoon salt
½ oz fresh yeast
½ tablespoon sugar
½ pt warm water
12–14 oz lard
2 oz crushed lump sugar
¼ teaspoon each, nutmeg, cinnamon and allspice
1 oz currants and sultanas

Oven: 425°F; gas mark 7; 15–20 minutes

Make a plain dough by mixing the sifted flour and salt with the yeast creamed with sugar and water. Knead until smooth, then set aside until doubled in size. Knock back.

Roll the dough out to a rectangular shape, ½ in thick. Dot with one third of the lard, 1½ in apart, and sprinkle with a third of the sugar. Fold the dough in three as for flaky pastry; fold once more from the side, turn and roll out from the open end.

Repeat the process of dotting with lard and sugar twice more and at the last rolling out, sprinkle with sugar, spices, currants and sultanas.

Roll out to the size of a square baking tin. Mark the top into squares along which the baked bread will be broken, never cut. Bake.

London Buns London

1 lb plain flour
2 teaspoons salt
¼ teaspoon ground nutmeg
½ oz fresh yeast
2 oz caster sugar
2 oz butter
4 fl oz milk
½ oz candied orange peel
½ teaspoon caraway seeds (optional)
1 egg
Sugar glaze

Oven: 425°F; gas mark 7; 10–15 minutes

Sift the flour and salt, add the nutmeg, creamed yeast and sugar and the butter melted in the warm milk. Mix to a smooth dough with the orange peel, and caraway seeds if used. Knead thoroughly and leave to rise until doubled in size.

Knock the dough back and shape into 12 round or oval buns. Prove and bake. Brush with beaten egg and sugar glaze while still hot.

Muffins

3 lb strong plain flour
1 oz salt
1 oz fresh yeast
½ tablespoon sugar
1½ pt warm water

Oven: 425°F; gas mark 7; 15–20 minutes

Sift the flour and salt and mix in the yeast creamed with the sugar and a little of the warm water; add the remaining water, knead well and leave to rise until doubled in size.

Knock back and divide the dough into pieces of 2½ oz each; shape into rounds, ½ in thick, on a floured surface to prevent sticking. Bake on greased heated oven plates of iron or steel; turn when half baked to cook evenly on both sides.

Nottingham Coffee Biscuits Nottingham

2 oz butter
5 fl oz milk
½ oz fresh yeast
4 oz caster sugar
¾ lb plain flour
1 coffeespoon salt
Caraway seeds
1 egg

Oven: 325°F; gas mark 3; 30 minutes

Warm the butter in the milk, pour into a bowl and add the yeast, creamed with the sugar; work in the flour, salt and a few caraway seeds. Leave, covered with a damp cloth, in a warm place until double the size.

Knock the dough back, roll out and cut into round biscuits; brush with beaten egg. Place on a baking sheet, prick with a fork and leave to prove. Bake for about 30 minutes.

Oven Bottom Cake Yorkshire

Originally made with a piece of leftover dough from a previous bread mix. Served cut into irregular pieces and eaten hot with butter and jam.

1½ lb plain flour
½ tablespoon salt
½ oz fresh yeast
½ tablespoon sugar
¾ pt warm water
4 oz lard

Oven: 425°F; gas mark 7; 10 minutes
375°F; gas mark 5; 35 minutes

Sift the flour and salt and add the yeast creamed with the sugar and a little of the warm water. Mix to a smooth dough with the remaining water, knead and leave to rise.

Knock the dough back, cut off a handful and stick the lard, cut into pieces into the dough. Replace the dough and with the knuckles of one hand press it into a cake, giving it a lumpy appearance which it will retain in baking. Place the cake on a greased baking sheet and prove. Bake until golden brown, reducing the temperature after 10 minutes.

Pitchy Cake Cornwall

The name arises from "pitching" fat, currants and sugar into the bread dough.

1½ lb plain flour
½ tablespoon salt
½ oz fresh yeast
½ tablespoon sugar
¾ pt warm water
½ lb fat
4 oz currants
4 oz sugar

Oven: 425°F; gas mark 7; 1–1½ hours

Make a plain bread dough by sifting the flour with salt and mixing it until smooth with the creamed yeast and sugar, and the warm water. Knead well and leave to rise.

Knock the dough back, work in (pitch in) the fat, cut into small pieces, the currants and sugar. Knead again, shape into a loaf and set in a greased baking tin to prove. Bake for 1½ hours.

Plank Bread Wales

The plank or baking iron of Wales was originally made of wood; it was heated slowly over moderate heat so that the bread baked through without scorching.

2 lb plain flour
½ tablespoon salt
1 oz lard
½ oz fresh yeast
½ tablespoon sugar
1 pt warm milk and water

Oven: 350°F; gas mark 4; 40 minutes

Sift the flour and salt, rub in the lard and cream the yeast with the sugar and a little of the warm liquid. Mix to a smooth dough, adding the milk and water; knead well. Leave to rise, then knock the dough back.

Mould the dough into a large flat cake, 1–1¼ in thick. Set to prove; bake for 20 minutes on one side, turn over and bake for a further 20 minutes on the other side.

Revel Buns Devon

Traditionally made for village festivals, the buns were baked wrapped in sycamore leaves or sometimes shaped and baked as loaves.

1 lb plain flour
2 teaspoons salt
Pinch cinnamon
½ oz fresh yeast
½ tablespoon sugar
2 oz fat
2–3 tablespoons saffron milk
5 fl oz Devon cream
1 egg
6 oz currants
Icing sugar

Oven: 375°F; gas mark 5; 35–45 minutes

For the saffron milk, dissolve a pinch of saffron

in a little milk and leave to soak overnight.

Sift the flour, salt and cinnamon, add the creamed yeast and sugar, and the fat melted in the saffron milk; mix in the cream. Add the beaten egg and mix to a smooth dough.

Knead thoroughly, leave to rise until doubled in size, knock back and add the currants. Shape into small buns and, if possible, bake the buns wrapped in sycamore leaves for about 35 minutes. Sprinkle the cooled buns with icing sugar.

Ruthven Cake Scotland

1 lb plain flour
2 teaspoons salt
½ teaspoon ground cinnamon
½ oz fresh yeast
3 oz caster sugar
Grated rind of 1 lemon
4 oz butter
2½ fl oz milk
2 eggs

Oven: 400°F; gas mark 6; 1 hour

Sift the flour, salt and cinnamon, add the yeast creamed with the sugar and blend in the lemon rind. Mix to a smooth dough with the butter melted in the warm milk and adding the beaten eggs. Knead lightly and leave to rise.

Knock the dough back, set in a greased cake tin and prove before baking.

Saffron Cakes West Country

The original saffron cakes were not sweetened, but made from a basic white bread dough with the addition of saffron water. This is made by snipping a pinch of saffron and leaving it to steep overnight in warm water.

3 lb plain flour
1 oz salt
1 teaspoon grated nutmeg
1 oz yeast
4 oz soft brown sugar
1 lb butter and lard
1 pt saffron water
3 eggs
1 lb currants
4 oz chopped peel

Oven: 400°F; gas mark 6; 1½ hours

Make an enriched dough from the flour sifted with

salt and nutmeg. Add the creamed yeast and sugar mixture, the butter and lard melted in the saffron water, and the beaten eggs. Fold in the currants and chopped peel, knead lightly and leave to rise until doubled in size.

Knock the dough back, shape into loaves and set in greased 2 lb tins to prove. Bake for about 1½ hours.

Saffron Wigs London

For the preparation of saffron water, see Saffron Cakes.

1 lb plain flour
2 teaspoons salt
½ oz fresh yeast
6 oz sugar
6 oz fat
2½ fl oz saffron water
2 eggs
½ oz caraway seeds
1 beaten egg

Oven: 425°F; gas mark 7; 10−15 minutes

Sift the flour and salt and cream the yeast with the sugar. Blend the yeast mixture, the fat melted in the warm saffron water, the two beaten eggs and caraway seeds into the flour. Mix to a smooth dough and set aside to rise until doubled in size.

Knock back and shape the dough into buns, set on a greased baking sheet to prove and brush with beaten egg before baking for about 15 minutes.

Sally Lunn Buns Somerset

Named after Sally Lunn who lived in Bath and used to "cry" the buns in the streets; legend goes that the cry − in West Country French − was really *Solet Lune* or *Soleilume* with reference to the sun represented on top of the bun and the moon underneath, substantiated in earlier spellings of *Soli Lune, Solielume* or *Sollyluma*.

1 lb plain flour
2 teaspoons salt
½ oz fresh yeast
½ tablespoon sugar
2 oz fat
4 fl oz milk
2 beaten eggs

Oven: 425°F; gas mark 7; 15−20 minutes

Sift the flour and salt and add the yeast creamed

with the sugar, the fat melted in the warm milk and one beaten egg. Mix to a smooth dough of dropping consistency and leave to rise and double in size.

Knock the dough back and shape to fit greased round baking rings about 6 in wide; leave to rise until the rings are full, then bake. Brush with beaten egg halfway through baking. Serve hot, filled with whipped cream and sprinkled with crushed sugar.

Selkirk Bannocks Borders

3 lb plain flour
1 tablespoon salt
1 oz fresh yeast
¾ lb sugar
1½ pt water
¾ lb melted butter and lard
1¼ lb sultanas or 1 lb sultanas and 4 oz currants
6 oz finely chopped orange peel

Oven: 425°F; gas mark 7; 1½ hours

Sift the flour and salt and add the yeast, creamed with a little sugar and a little of the warm water; mix to a dough with the remaining water. Knead thoroughly and set to rise and double.

Knock the dough back, knead and work in the butter and lard, sugar, dried fruit and peel. Shape, put into large round greased tins and set to prove. Bake for about 1½ hours.

Softies or Soft Biscuits Aberdeen

9 oz melted butter
3 lb plain flour
1 tablespoon salt
1 oz fresh yeast
3 oz caster sugar
1½ pt water

Oven: 425°F; gas mark 7; 20–30 minutes

Work the melted butter into the sifted flour and salt, add the yeast creamed with sugar and a little warm water. Mix to a dough with the remaining water, knead until elastic and leave to rise until doubled in size.

Knock the dough back and shape into rounds like flattened buns and 3–4 inches in diameter. Prove and bake.

South Tyne Yeast Cake Co. Durham

½ lb butter
½ lb caster sugar
2 eggs
½ lb currants
½ lb sultanas
4 oz chopped mixed peel
1 lb plain flour
1 oz fresh yeast or ½ oz dried yeast (dissolved in 5 fl oz sour milk)
½ teaspoon bicarbonate of soda (dissolved in 5 fl oz cold milk)

Oven: 350°F; gas mark 4; 2–2½ hours

Cream the butter and sugar, beat in the eggs and add the dried fruits. Fold in the flour alternately with the yeast and bicarbonate of soda mixtures.

Knead to a smooth, soft dough, and put into two 1 lb greased loaf tins. Prove until doubled in size and bake for about 2 hours. Keep for at least 1 week before eating.

Suffolk Rusks Suffolk

These small yeast cakes, which after baking are dried in the oven, are sweetened. They can also be served as a kind of bread roll in which case the sugar should be omitted.

1 lb plain flour
2 teaspoons salt
½ oz fresh yeast
½ tablespoon sugar
2 oz fat
4 fl oz milk and water
2 eggs

Oven: 425°F; gas mark 7; 20–30 minutes

Sift the flour and salt and add the yeast creamed with the sugar, the fat melted in the warm milk and water, and the beaten eggs. Work to a smooth dough and knead lightly. Rise until doubled in size, then knock the dough back.

Divide into 16 pieces and roll out to 3 in long rectangular shapes; prove on greased baking sheets and bake for 10 minutes.

Remove from oven and pull the rusks in half lengthways; return to the oven, uneven sides up to brown and crisp for 10–20 minutes.

Sultana Cake, Plain Cornwall

3 lb plain flour

1 tablespoon salt
¾ lb lard or butter
1 oz fresh yeast
½ tablespoon sugar
1½ pt warm water
½ lb sultanas
Chopped lemon peel (optional)

Oven: 400°F; gas mark 6; 1½−2 hours

Sift the flour and salt, rub in the lard and add the yeast creamed with the sugar and a little warm water. Blend in the remaining warm water and mix to a smooth dough that leaves the sides of the bowl clean.

Knead on a floured surface and leave to rise. Knock back, knead in the sultanas and peel, shape and put into greased loaf tins and prove. Bake for at least 1½ hours.

Tandra Cake Bedfordshire

Also known as St. Andrew's Cake.

1 lb plain flour
1 teaspoon salt
½ oz fresh yeast
½ tablespoon caster sugar
½ pt water
4 oz currants
4 oz sugar
1 oz diced lemon peel
1 egg
4 oz melted lard

Oven: 350°F; gas mark 4; 1−1½ hours

Sift the flour and salt; cream the yeast with the sugar and blend in the warmed water. Add the yeast mixture to the flour, mixing until the dough is smooth and leaves the bowl clean. Knead on a floured board, set to rise, then knock back.

Knead the currants, sugar, lemon peel, beaten egg and melted lard into the dough. Shape the dough and set in greased loaf tins and prove. Bake for 1−1½ hours.

Valentine Buns or Plum Shuttles Rutland

Shaped to represent shuttles, these buns were baked for St. Valentine's Day.

1 lb plain flour
2 teaspoons salt
½ oz fresh yeast
½ tablespoon sugar

2 oz fat
4 fl oz warm water and milk
1 egg
½ lb currants or 1 oz caraway seeds

Oven: 425°F; gas mark 7; 10−15 minutes

Make an enriched dough by adding to the sifted flour and salt the creamed yeast and sugar, the fat melted in the water and milk and the beaten egg. Mix to a smooth dough, knead and leave to rise until doubled.

Knock the dough back, work in the currants or caraway seeds and knead again. Divide the dough and shape into small ovals resembling shuttles. Prove and bake.

Wigs

A "wig" is thought to be a medieval corruption of the word wedge or wigge.

1 lb plain flour
2 teaspoons salt
½ teaspoon each, nutmeg, mace and cloves
½ oz fresh yeast
4 oz sugar
½ lb butter
2½ fl oz cream
1 egg
4 oz caraway seeds
Sugar glaze

Oven: 425°F; gas mark 7; 10−15 minutes

Sift the flour and salt and add the spices and the yeast creamed with ½ tablespoon of the sugar. Melt the butter in the warm cream and beat into the flour mixture, together with the beaten egg. Mix to a smooth dough, knead lightly and set to rise and double.

Knock the dough back, sprinkle with the remaining sugar and the caraway seeds and knead again until smooth. Roll the dough out thinly and place on greased saucers or small plates; mark the surface of each lightly in a cross. Prove and bake; while still warm brush with a sugar and water glaze.

Yorkshire Tea Cakes Yorkshire

2 lb plain flour
2 teaspoons salt
1 oz fresh yeast
1 tablespoon sugar
4 oz fat

¾ pt milk and water
2 eggs
1 oz currants
1 oz candied peel

Oven: 350°F; gas mark 4; 20–30 minutes

Sift the flour and salt into a large bowl, add the
yeast creamed with the sugar, the fat melted in
the warm milk and the beaten eggs. Mix thoroughly
then add the currants and peel, beating the dough
until it leaves the sides of the bowl clean.

Knead on a floured surface and leave to rise at
room temperature. Knock the dough back and
divide into 12 pieces; shape into round flat cakes
and set on greased baking sheets to prove. Bake
and leave to cool; serve toasted, with butter.

Yorkshire Yule or Spice Cake Yorkshire

Made for Christmas and offered to callers, with
cheese and wine or beer.

4 lb plain flour
1 tablespoon salt
1 lb lard
¾ lb butter
1¼ oz fresh yeast
1½ pt warm water
1½ lb soft brown sugar
1 teaspoon each, mixed spice and grated nutmeg
3 lb currants
4 eggs

Oven: 400°F; gas mark 6; 50–60 minutes

Sift the flour and salt, rub in the lard and butter to
a crumbly texture, and add the yeast creamed with
a little of the warm water. Blend in the sugar and
remaining water and beat to a smooth dough. Knead
thoroughly and leave to rise.

Knock the dough back, work in the spice and
nutmeg, currants and beaten eggs. Knead again,
divide the dough into three and shape to fit
greased cake tins. Prove and bake.

Cakes and Biscuits

An original term for bread made in small regular shapes was "kaak of bread". In Scotland, Wales and the North of England "bread" was eventually dropped, and "kaak" came to define a small type of bread, usually made from oats. Sweet breads or loaves, today generally referred to as teabreads, are variations on the plain "cake-bread" theme; buns, crumpets, pancakes, pikelets and scones are developed from the same concept.

Throughout the country, a bun describes a type of plain cake-bread shaped into a small round, except in Scotland where a plain bun is called a cookie and where bun is synonymous with currant bread. Pancakes, although made on the same principle, also have different meanings; in England, they are served as a type of pudding, but in other regions, notably Scotland, Ireland and Wales, pancakes are cooked and eaten as a type of sweet bread; like crumpets and pikelets, they are made with a rich batter mixture.

The scone was originally any type of sweet bread and could be plain or rich, the point of similarity being the shape which was either three or four-angled. Today, the scone may be round, oval, triangular or square, sometimes baked in the oven and sometimes cooked on a griddle. The hot stones used for baking were known as "greadeal" by the Gaelics and were the fore-runners of the griddle iron. The griddle — or girdle as it is known in the North of England and Scotland — is traditional to many types of small teabreads, especially scones and crumpets. It should be prepared in advance of cooking, being set over low heat for at least 30 minutes and greased with a piece of suet. To test for correct heat, hold the palm of the hand about 1 in above the griddle plate which should give off a bearable heat, not be burning hot. Alternatively, dust with a little flour which should turn brown in a few minutes, not immediately.

TEABREADS AND SCONES

Bakestone Cakes Monmouthshire

2 oz butter
½ lb flour
½ oz baking powder
Cream

Rub the butter into the flour sifted with the baking powder; work to a stiff paste with cream. Roll out very thinly, cut into small round cakes and bake on a hot griddle. Split and serve hot with butter.

Ballywindland Rolls Ireland

4 oz butter
1 lb flour
2 teaspoons baking powder
Pinch salt
Milk

Oven: 375–400°F; gas mark 5–6; 20 minutes

Rub the butter into the flour sifted with baking powder and salt. Mix to an elastic dough with a little sweetened milk. Roll out and fold over as for rough puff pastry. Roll out the dough again and cut into small rounds with a cutter. Fold each round over and bake until golden brown.

Boxty Bread Ireland

Boxty dumplings are made from boxty bread mixture, using suet or lard instead of butter; they are shaped into small dumplings, boiled in water for 45 minutes and served as savoury puddings with meat.

1 lb peeled potatoes
1 lb mashed potatoes
1 lb plain flour

1 oz baking powder
Salt and pepper
4 oz melted butter or bacon fat (optional)

Oven: 350°F; gas mark 4; 40 minutes

Grate the peeled potatoes into a clean cloth and wring lightly over a basin in which to catch the liquid. Mix the grated potatoes with the cooked mashed potatoes.

Leave the starch liquid in the basin to settle, then pour off the water and scrape the starch into the potatoes. Mix thoroughly, adding the flour, baking powder, salt, pepper and melted butter.

Roll the mixture out into four flat round cakes and mark each round into quarters. Set on greased baking sheets and bake for about 40 minutes. Serve hot, broken into quarters and split in half, with butter.

Boxty Pancakes Ireland

These potato pancakes may be made with buttermilk instead of bicarbonate of soda and milk.

Boxty bread mixture
1 teaspoon bicarbonate of soda
Milk

Follow the above method for Boxty Bread, mixing the flour with bicarbonate of soda and adding milk to give a dropping consistency.

Drop the mixture in spoonfuls on a heated griddle and cook for about 4 minutes on each side or until golden brown. Serve with butter and sprinkled with sugar.

Brides Bonn Shetland

1 lb plain flour
1 oz baking powder
½ lb butter
4 oz caster sugar
½ oz caraway seeds
Milk

Sift the flour and baking powder, rub in the butter and add the sugar and caraway seeds. Mix in enough milk to give a smooth elastic dough.

Roll out, ¼ in thick, and cut into 2 in rounds; bake on a hot griddle until golden on both sides.

Buns, Plain

These buns are variations of plain cakes, but made from a stiffer mixture and shaped into small rounds. A number of other ingredients can be added to the basic mixture, before the eggs and milk.

1 lb plain flour
1 oz baking powder
Pinch salt
6 oz butter
6 oz caster sugar
2 eggs
½ pt milk (approx.)
Beaten egg

Oven: 425°F; gas mark 7; 15–20 minutes

Sift the flour, baking powder and salt. Rub in the butter until the mixture is crumbly, mix in the sugar and add the beaten eggs and enough milk to give a fairly stiff consistency.

Shape into small rounds, brush with beaten egg or milk; place on a greased baking sheet and bake until golden.

Cherry Buns, chop ½ lb glacé cherries, setting some aside for decoration; add to the dry ingredients and top each bun with a whole cherry.

Coconut Buns, mix 4 oz desiccated coconut with the dry ingredients; shape the mixture in rough spoonfuls and sprinkle with more coconut.

Coffee Buns, sift the flour with 1 oz mixed spice, add 6 oz currants to the dry mix and 2 fl oz coffee essence to the liquid.

Marmalade and Raisin Buns, add ½ lb marmalade and ½ lb seedless raisins, sultanas, chopped dates or prunes to the mixture; dredge with caster sugar before baking.

Orange or Lemon Buns, mix in the grated rind of 2 oranges or lemons; soak lumps of sugar in the juice for a few minutes and press two lumps into each bun before baking.

Pineapple Buns, blend 3 oz crushed pineapple into the dry mix and add 2 tablespoons pineapple syrup to the liquid.

Raspberry Buns, shape the finished mixture into balls, make a hole in the centre of each and add a teaspoon of raspberry (or strawberry) jam. Leave the hole open or close it, then turn over and press the ball down to a bun shape; brush with beaten egg and sprinkle with sugar.

Rock Buns, add 2 oz chopped mixed peel and 4 oz currants to the basic mixture; shape into rough heaps, brush with egg, sprinkle with coarse sugar and decorate each bun with half a glacé cherry.

Suffolk Buns, blend 3 oz currants and ½ oz caraway seeds into the dry mix; roll the dough out, 1 in thick, and cut into rounds.

York Buns, mix 6 oz currants and 2 oz chopped mixed peel into the ingredients before adding eggs and milk.

Buttermilk Bread

This is more commonly known as soda loaf.

1 lb plain flour
2 teaspoons bicarbonate of soda
2 teaspoons cream of tartar
1 teaspoon salt
3 oz lard
¾ pt buttermilk

Oven: 350°F; gas mark 4; 1—1½ hours

Sift the flour with bicarbonate of soda, cream of tartar and salt; rub in the lard to a crumbly mixture and pour the buttermilk into the centre. Mix thoroughly until blended and soft.

Put the dough in a greased loaf tin and bake until golden brown.

Buttermilk Scones: see Scones, savoury

Cheese and Apple Loaf

4 oz butter
6 oz caster sugar
2 eggs
½ lb unpeeled, grated apples and juice
4 oz grated Cheddar cheese
2 oz chopped nuts
1 lb plain flour
½ oz baking powder
½ teaspoon bicarbonate of soda
½ tablespoon salt

Oven: 350°F; gas mark 4; 1½—2 hours

Cream the butter and sugar, add the beaten eggs, the apples, cheese and nuts. Stir in the flour, sifted with the baking powder, bicarbonate of soda and salt, and mix well. Spoon the mixture into a greased loaf tin and bake.

Crumpets, Scottish

These are different from the English crumpets which are made with a yeast batter and baked in crumpet rings.

1 pt milk
2 eggs
10 oz caster sugar
2 oz melted butter or oil
1 lb plain flour
1 oz baking powder
1 teaspoon salt

Blend the milk, eggs, sugar and butter in a bowl, add the flour sifted with the baking powder and salt and mix to a pouring consistency.

Drop spoonfuls of the batter on to a heated griddle, leaving room for spreading, about 6 in for each. When bubbles appear on the surface, turn and brown on the other side. Cool wrapped in a towel, or roll the crumpets up and serve hot with butter and jam.

Currant Bread

1 lb plain flour
3 teaspoons baking powder
½ teaspoon bicarbonate of soda
4 oz butter
6 oz caster sugar
6 oz currants
6 oz raisins
1 oz candied peel
2 oz black treacle
2 eggs
½ pt buttermilk

Oven: 350°F; gas mark 4; 1—1½ hours

Sift the flour; add the baking powder and bicarbonate of soda and rub in the butter. Blend in the sugar, currants, raisins and candied peel and mix to a smooth dropping dough with the treacle, beaten eggs and buttermilk.

Spoon this mixture into two greased 1 lb loaf tins and bake for about 1½ hours.

Derwentwater Cakes Cumberland

½ lb butter
½ lb caster sugar
4 eggs
1 lb plain flour
½ lb currants

Oven: 350°F; gas mark 4; 15 minutes

Cream the butter and sugar, separate the eggs and beat in the yolks. Stir in the sifted flour and the currants.

Beat the egg whites stiffly, fold into the mixture and shape into a round, 1 in thick. Bake.

Devon Potato Cake Devonshire

6 oz plain flour
½ teaspoon mixed spice
1 teaspoon baking powder
2 oz butter
6 oz mashed potatoes
4 oz brown sugar
½ lb currants
½ oz caraway seeds
2 eggs

Oven: 400°F; gas mark 6; 30 minutes

Sift the flour with the mixed spice and baking powder; rub in the butter and add the potatoes, sugar, currants and caraway seeds.

Add the beaten eggs and mix well; pour into a well greased shallow cake tin and bake. Serve hot, cut into squares.

Durham Pikelets Co. Durham

Pikelet is a regional name, originating in Wales, for a crumpet.

½ lb plain flour
1 teaspoon bicarbonate of soda
1 teaspoon cream of tartar
½ tablespoon salt
1½ oz lard
8–10 fl oz buttermilk

Sift the flour, bicarbonate of soda, cream of tartar and salt; rub in the lard until the mixture resembles breadcrumbs. Make a well in the centre, pour in the buttermilk, beating lightly to give a dropping consistency.

Drop the mixture in spoonfuls on to a hot greased griddle or frying pan and cook for about 4 minutes on each side or until golden brown. Spread with butter and serve hot.

Durham Popovers Co. Durham

½ lb plain flour
1 oz butter

4 eggs
Pinch salt
Milk

Oven: 425°F; gas mark 7; 30 minutes

Rub the butter into the flour, add the salt and mix to a smooth batter with the beaten eggs and a little milk.

Spoon the mixture into well greased patty tins to half fill them; bake for 30 minutes.

Felton Spice Loaf Northumberland

4 oz butter
4 oz caster sugar
2 eggs
2 oz ground almonds
4 oz plain flour
4 oz self-raising flour
2 oz shredded peel
½ lb currants
Milk

Oven: 375°F; gas mark 5; 30 minutes

Cream the butter and sugar and beat in the eggs, one by one. Fold in the almonds and the two flours, and add the peel and currants, with enough milk to give a soft dropping dough.

Put the mixture in a well-greased dripping tin, level the mixture with a knife and bake for 30 minutes.

Gipsy Bread Hampshire

½ lb plain flour
1 teaspoon each, bicarbonate of soda, baking powder and ground ginger
4 oz soft brown sugar
4 oz sultanas
2 oz chopped candied peel
1 egg
4 oz black treacle
5 fl oz milk

Oven: 350°F; gas mark 4; 1–1½ hours

Sift the flour with the bicarbonate of soda, baking powder and ginger; mix in the sugar, sultanas and peel and add the beaten egg.

Dissolve the treacle in the milk and mix into the dry ingredients until the dough has a soft dropping consistency. Place the dough in a greased 2 lb loaf tin or in two 1 lb tins. Bake until risen and firm.

Girdle Sponges Scotland

1 oz butter
2 oz caster sugar
3 eggs
½ lb plain flour
½ teaspoon salt
¼ teaspoon bicarbonate of soda
½ teaspoon cream of tartar
Milk

Cream the butter and sugar, separate the eggs
and beat in the yolks. Sift the flour, salt,
bicarbonate of soda and cream of tartar and beat
into the mixture. Add enough milk to make a
thick batter.

Beat the egg whites until stiff and fold into
the batter. Drop in spoonfuls on a hot griddle and
cook until bubbles appear on the surface; turn
over and brown the other side. Serve the girdle
sponges hot, with butter.

Highland Slim Cakes Scotland

1 lb plain flour
4 oz butter
2 eggs
Hot milk

Sift the flour, rub in the butter and add the
beaten eggs. Mix with milk to give an elastic
dough. Roll out, ½ in thick, and cut into rounds;
bake on a hot griddle, cooking each side for 4—5
minutes.

Irish Currant Soda Scones Ireland

1 lb plain flour
2 teaspoons bicarbonate of soda
2 teaspoons cream of tartar
1 teaspoon salt
3 oz lard
2 oz caster sugar
3 oz currants
3 oz sultanas
2 oz chopped mixed peel
¾ pt buttermilk

Oven: 425°F; gas mark 7; 8—10 minutes

Sift the flour, bicarbonate of soda, cream of
tartar and salt; rub in the lard to a crumbly
mixture and add the sugar, currants, sultanas and
chopped peel. Mix in the buttermilk, stirring with
a knife until the dough is smooth.

Shape the dough into 2 in rounds, about ½ in
thick; set on greased baking sheets and bake until
risen and golden.

Irish Treacle Loaf Ireland

2 oz butter
2½ fl oz water
2 oz black treacle
2 oz soft brown sugar
1 egg
½ lb plain flour
½ teaspoon mixed spice
½ teaspoon ground ginger
1 teaspoon bicarbonate of soda
2 oz currants
2 oz raisins

Oven: 350°F; gas mark 4; 1½—2 hours

Melt the butter in the water and set aside. Cream
the treacle with the sugar and the egg, add the
flour sifted with the spice, ginger and bicarbonate
of soda. Fold in the currants and raisins and mix
thoroughly.

Add the butter and water mixture and spoon
the dough into one greased 2 lb or two 1 lb loaf
tins and bake.

Kirrie Loaf Angus

1 lb sultanas
½ lb caster sugar
½ pt strong hot tea
3 eggs
4 oz butter
4 oz golden syrup
1 lb plain flour
1 teaspoon baking powder
½ teaspoon each, ground ginger and mixed spice
1 teaspoon salt

Oven: 350°F; gas mark 4; 1½—2 hours

Put the sultanas and sugar in a bowl and cover
with tea; leave overnight.

Beat the eggs; melt the butter and syrup and
stir into the eggs. Fold in the flour sifted with
baking powder, ginger, spice and salt; add the
sultana mixture and mix thoroughly. Spoon the
dough into greased loaf tins and bake.

Lancaster Spice Loaf Lancashire

¾ lb plain flour
½ oz baking powder
1 teaspoon each, grated nutmeg, cinnamon and
    ginger
Pinch salt
½ lb butter
½ lb brown sugar
½ lb currants
½ lb sultanas
2 oz chopped mixed peel
4 oz chopped glacé cherries
2 oz blanched chopped almonds
3 eggs
Milk

Oven: 350°F; gas mark 4; 1½–2 hours

Sift the flour with baking powder, the spices and
salt; rub in the butter to a crumbly texture and
blend in the sugar, currants, sultanas, peel, glacé
cherries and almonds. Beat the eggs and use to
gather the dough, adding a little milk if necessary
until the mixture is smooth and dropping.

    Spoon the dough into one 2 lb greased loaf tin
or two 1 lb tins and bake for 1½–2 hours.

Malt Nut Bread

1 lb plain flour
1 oz baking powder
2 oz soft brown sugar
4 oz seedless raisins
2 oz finely chopped walnuts
2 oz black treacle
4 oz malt extract
½ pt milk

Oven: 350°F; gas mark 4; 1–1½ hours

Sift the flour and baking powder and mix in the
sugar, raisins and walnuts.

    Blend the treacle and malt extract with the
milk, stir into the flour and beat to a smooth
dough. Spoon into greased loaf tins and bake for
about 1½ hours.

Northumbrian Girdle Cakes
Northumberland

Also known as Gosforth Gridies.

1 lb self-raising flour
1 teaspoon salt

½ lb butter
4 oz sugar
4 oz currants
2 eggs
5 fl oz milk

Sift the flour and salt, rub in the butter to a
crumbly mixture and add the sugar and currants.
Make a well in the centre, add the lightly beaten
eggs and the milk and stir with a round-bladed
knife until well blended and smooth.

    Knead the dough lightly and roll it out, ½ in
thick, on a floured board; cut into small rounds
and bake on a hot greased griddle for about 4
minutes on each side, until golden brown.

Oaten Bread Ireland

½ lb rolled oats
½ pt sour milk or buttermilk
10 oz plain flour
½ teaspoon bicarbonate of soda
½ tablespoon salt

Oven: 350°F; gas mark 4; 40 minutes

Soak the oats in the milk overnight. Add the flour
sifted with bicarbonate of soda and salt, mix to a
stiff dough and knead until smooth.

    Divide the mixture into four and shape into
rounds, 2–2½ in thick; place on greased baking
sheets and bake until risen and golden brown.

Pancakes, Scottish

These are known as Drop Scones in England and
are similar to Welsh Pikelets except that the batter
includes 4 oz currants and an extra 6 oz butter.

¾ pt milk
2 eggs
5 oz sugar
2 oz oil or melted butter
1 lb plain flour
1 oz baking powder
Pinch salt

Beat together the milk, eggs, sugar, oil or melted
butter; fold in the flour sifted with baking powder
and salt. Mix to a soft dropping consistency.

    Drop the batter in spoonfuls on to a heated
griddle and cook until bubbles appear on top, then
turn and cook on the other side. Serve hot or cold,
with butter and jam.

Potato Apple Cakes Ireland

These were once traditional at Hallowe'en when a ring was hidden in one of the cakes.

1 lb cold cooked potatoes
1 oz melted butter
1 teaspoon salt
4 oz flour or fine oatmeal
1 teaspoon baking powder
1 lb peeled, cored and sliced apples
4 oz sugar
1 oz butter

Oven: 350°F; gas mark 4; 5–10 minutes

Mash the potatoes and blend in the melted butter and salt; sift the flour with the baking powder and work into the potatoes to make a pliable dough.

Roll the mixture out to a large round, about ½ in thick; cut into quarters and pile the apple slices over two of the sections. Top with the other two potato portions and pinch round the edges to seal firmly.

Bake on a hot griddle until brown on both sides. Slit each cake along the rounded edge and turn the top back; cover the apples with thin slices of butter and sprinkle with sugar. Replace the top and bake in the oven until the butter and sugar have melted. Cut into pieces and serve.

Potato Scones Ireland

The Potato Oaten Cakes or Pratie Oaten from Antrim are similar to these potato scones, but oatmeal is used instead of flour.

½ lb cooked, cold potatoes
½ oz melted butter
½ teaspoon salt
2 oz white flour or fine oatmeal
½ teaspoon baking powder

Mash the potatoes and add the melted butter and salt. Work into the potato mixture as much sifted flour and baking powder or oatmeal as will make a pliable dough.

Roll the mixture out thinly and prick with a fork. Cut into circles round a plate, then cut into quarters and bake on a hot griddle for 3 minutes on each side. Serve hot or cold, with butter.

Scones, Savoury

These buttermilk scones, known in Ireland as Girdle Scones, are served hot with butter. Various ingredients may be added to the basic savoury mixture. Elcho Scones are identical, but are shaped into four rounds, each marked into four quarters and baked.

1 lb plain flour
1 teaspoon bicarbonate of soda
1 teaspoon cream of tartar
1 tablespoon salt
3 oz lard
¾ pt buttermilk

Oven: 425–450°F; gas mark 7–8; 8–10 minutes

Sift the flour, bicarbonate, cream of tartar and salt; rub in the lard and stir to a smooth dough with the buttermilk.

Knead lightly and shape into small, flat rounds, about ½ in thick. Cook on a hot griddle for about 4 minutes on each side until golden brown, or bake in the oven for about 10 minutes.

For Treacle Scones, add 1 teaspoon ground cinnamon and 1 teaspoon mixed spice to the flour and dissolve 4 oz black treacle in the milk.

Scones, Sweet

These scones may be made with plain flour rather than self-raising in which case 1 oz baking powder or 1 teaspoon bicarbonate of soda and 2 teaspoons cream of tartar should be added to 1 lb flour; a little more milk may also be necessary. Serve hot or cold, with butter and jam.

1 lb self-raising flour
1 teaspoon salt
4 oz butter
4 oz sugar
2 eggs
5 fl oz milk
1 beaten egg

Oven: 425–450°F; gas mark 7–8; 8–10 minutes

Sift the flour and salt, rub in the butter until the mixture resembles breadcrumbs. Stir in the sugar and make a well in the centre, drop in the eggs and gradually add the milk, working in the flour from the sides until the dough is quite smooth and elastic.

Handle the dough lightly, shaping it into small rounds rather than rolling it out, and flattening it with the knuckles to a thickness of ½–¾ in. Brush with milk or beaten egg or dust with flour.

Place the scones on greased baking sheets and bake for about 10 minutes.

The following are variations of the basic sweet scones:

Cheese Scones, add ½ lb finely grated Cheddar cheese, ½ teaspoon dry mustard and a pinch of pepper to the dry mixture; cut the dough into finger-wide strips, brush with egg and bake.

Devonshire Scones, use an extra 6 oz butter in the scone mixture, roll out ½ in thick and cut into 2½ in rounds; brush with beaten egg and bake. Serve cold, split and filled with jam and Devonshire cream.

Walnut and Cinnamon Scones, mix 2 oz finely chopped walnuts and 1 teaspoon ground cinnamon into the dry ingredients.

Walnut and Honey Scones, add 2 oz finely chopped walnuts to the dry ingredients and 4 oz clear honey to the eggs.

Welsh Scones, use an extra 4 oz butter and add ½ lb currants before the eggs and milk.

Yorkshire Scones, made from the basic mixture, but rolled out, 1 in thick, and cut into rounds.

Singin' Hinnies Northumberland

1 lb self-raising flour
1 teaspoon salt
4 oz lard
4 oz sugar
6 oz currants
2 eggs
5 fl oz milk

Sift the flour and salt and rub in the fat. Mix in the sugar and currants, make a well in the centre and drop in the eggs and milk. Stir in the flour towards the centre, mixing well until the dough is soft and elastic.

Roll the dough out, ½ in thick, on a floured board and cut into two rounds. Cook on a hot greased griddle for about 10 minutes, turning once only until the cakes are golden brown on both sides.

Cut the rounds into wedges, split in half and butter. Sandwich together again and serve while still warm.

Sour Skons Orkney Islands

½ lb fine oatmeal

1 pt buttermilk
½ lb plain white flour
½ teaspoon bicarbonate of soda
Pinch salt
2 oz caster sugar
1 oz caraway seeds

Soak the oatmeal in the buttermilk for 2 days. Beat the flour sifted with bicarbonate of soda and salt, the sugar and caraway seeds into the oatmeal and mix well.

Roll the mixture out thinly, cut into small rounds or quarters and bake on a hot griddle until golden brown on both sides.

Sussex Heavies

2 oz lard
½ lb plain flour
1 oz caster sugar
2 oz currants
Juice of ½ lemon
6–7 fl oz milk

Oven: 350°F; gas mark 4; 15 minutes

Rub the lard into the flour and add the sugar and currants; mix in the lemon juice and milk to make a stiff dough.

Roll the mixture out, on a floured board, to 1 in thick and cut into 3 in rounds; brush with milk and bake for about 15 minutes.

Teabreads

These sweet loaves or breads have a fairly coarse texture and should be eaten within a short time of baking as they do not keep well. They are usually baked in loaf or round cake tins.

1 lb plain flour
1 oz baking powder
4 oz butter
4 oz caster sugar
2 eggs (optional)
½ pt milk (approx.)

Oven: 350°F; gas mark 4; 1–1½ hours

Sift the flour and baking powder, rub in the butter to a crumbly mixture and add the sugar. Make a well in the centre, drop in the eggs if used and gradually add the milk, stirring with a round-bladed knife until the dough has a soft dropping consistency.

Spoon into one greased 2 lb or two 1 lb loaf tins and bake.

A number of ingredients, especially fruits, can be added to the basic sweet loaf mixture.

Banana Loaf, add 2 lb mashed bananas before the milk.

Date and Apricot Loaf, add 4 oz soaked and chopped apricots and 4 oz chopped dates to the dry ingredients.

Date and Banana Loaf, blend 4 oz chopped dates and ½−¾ lb mashed bananas into the dry mix.

Date and Walnut Loaf, add 2 oz chopped walnuts, 4 oz chopped dates and ½ teaspoon mixed spice to the dry ingredients.

Orange Loaf, blend 4 oz thick orange marmalade and the grated rind of 1 orange into the mixture before adding the milk.

Spice Loaf, add 2 oz sultanas, 2 oz currants and 1 teaspoon mixed spice into the dry mix.

Syrup and Nut Loaf, blend 3 oz chopped nuts and 6 oz chopped dates into the dry ingredients; blend 4 oz syrup or clear honey with the milk.

Walnut Loaf, add 4 oz finely chopped walnuts to the dry ingredients.

Teisen Dinca Wales

These griddle scones (*Teisen* meaning cake) are served hot with sugar and butter or syrup.

1 lb plain flour
2 teaspoons baking powder
½ lb butter
6 oz sugar
¾ lb peeled, cored and grated cooking apples
Milk

Sift the flour and baking powder, rub in the butter and add the sugar and grated apples; gradually mix in milk to give a dough of smooth consistency. Roll the mixture out, ¼ in thick, and cut into 2 in rounds.

Cook on a hot griddle for 4 minutes on each side, until golden brown.

Welsh Cakes Wales

½ lb plain flour
½ teaspoon baking powder

¼ teaspoon mixed spice
2 oz margarine
2 oz lard
3 oz caster sugar
2 oz currants
1 egg
Milk

Sift the flour, baking powder and mixed spice; rub in the margarine and lard, add the sugar, currants and beaten egg. Mix in milk to make a stiff dough and roll out ¼ in thick.

Cut into 2 in rounds and bake on a hot griddle until golden brown, after about 4 minutes on each side.

Wholemeal Scones

For Wholemeal and Date Scones, add ½ lb finely chopped dates to the mixture before the milk.

½ lb wholemeal flour
½ lb plain flour
1 oz baking powder
4 oz butter
4 oz caster sugar
2 eggs
5 fl oz milk

Oven: 425−450°F; gas mark 7−8; 8−10 minutes

Sift the two flours and baking powder, rub in the butter to a crumbly mixture and add the sugar. Make a well in the centre and drop in the eggs; add the milk gradually until the dough is smooth.

Knead lightly and shape into small flat rounds. Set on greased baking sheets and bake until golden brown. Serve hot or cold, with butter.

CAKES

The cake concept, as a sweet or fancy item of
food, developed from the custom in medieval days
of adding sweet ingredients, such as honey and
dried fruits, together with spices and butter, to a
basic bread dough. Bread was defined by its
ingredients and retained the term "bread" for
several centuries, being substituted with "cake"
only in the 18th century. This type of enriched
bread was reserved for special occasions as both
fine flour and imported ingredients were scarce
and expensive. As late as 1784, bakers were pro-
hibited by law from baking these types of bread
for any other occasions but Christmas, Easter,
weddings, christenings and funerals.

The first break with the bread tradition was the
abandonment of the kneading, rising and proving
of the mixture although some form of leaven was
still used in the form of ale yeast or barm. Later
came the discovery that a high proportion of eggs
beaten with butter and sugar incorporated enough
air for a cake to rise without leaven. With chemical
raising agents, such as ammonium carbonate,
bicarbonate of soda and tartaric acid, the yeast-
raised dough concept was entirely abandoned
although in general terms enriched dough cakes
still rank as cakes.

LARGE PLAIN CAKES

These have a small proportion of eggs, sugar and
butter to flour and therefore need a raising agent,
usually in the form of baking powder. As the
amount of fat is small this is rubbed in rather than
creamed, resulting in a coarse-textured cake with
short keeping qualities.

Batley Cake Yorkshire

This is also known as Courting Cake.

¾ lb plain flour
¾ oz baking powder
½ tablespoon salt
6 oz butter
6 oz caster sugar
1 egg
Milk
2 oz jam
1 beaten egg

Oven: 350°F; gas mark 4; 30-35 minutes

Sift the flour, baking powder and salt, rub in the
butter and add the sugar; mix to a stiff consistency
with beaten egg and a little milk if necessary.

Divide the mixture into two equal parts. Roll
out to two rounds, ½ in thick, and spread one with
the warmed jam; cover with the other half and
pinch the edges together. Brush with beaten egg,
place on a greased baking tray and bake for 30-
35 minutes.

Bristol Cake Gloucestershire

1 lb plain flour
1½ teaspoons baking powder
6 oz butter
6 oz caster sugar
½ lb sultanas
3 eggs

Oven: 350°F; gas mark 4; 1½-2 hours

Sift the flour and baking powder, rub in the
butter and add the sugar and sultanas.

Mix to a dropping consistency with the lightly
beaten eggs, spoon into a greased 6-7 in cake tin
and bake.

Buttermilk Cake

1 lb plain flour
½ teaspoon bicarbonate of soda
½ teaspoon each, mixed spice, ground ginger and
    ground cinnamon
½ lb butter
½ lb soft brown sugar
1 lb mixed dried fruit
2 oz black treacle
2 eggs
½ pt buttermilk or sour milk

Oven: 350°F; gas mark 4; 2 hours

Sift the flour, bicarbonate of soda and the spices;
rub in the butter and add the sugar and dried
fruit. Mix with the treacle, lightly beaten eggs and
the buttermilk.

Spoon the mixture into a 9-10 in greased cake
tin and bake for about 2 hours.

Carstairs Sultana Cake Scotland

4 oz butter
9 oz plain flour
¾ teaspoon baking powder
4 oz sugar

6 oz sultanas
2 oz chopped mixed peel
3 eggs

Oven: 350°F; gas mark 4; 1½-2 hours

Rub the butter into the sifted flour and baking
powder, add the sugar, sultanas and mixed peel;
mix to a dropping consistency with the lightly
beaten eggs.

Spoon the mixture into a greased 7 in cake tin
and bake for up to 2 hours.

Devonshire Apple Cake Devon

The Dorset Apple Cake is similar, but also
includes 2 oz currants and 1 oz mixed peel; the
top is sprinkled with brown sugar rather than
granulated.

½ lb self-raising flour
1 teaspoon salt
4 oz butter
4 oz caster sugar
1 lb peeled, cored and sliced cooking apples
2 eggs
1 oz granulated sugar

Oven: 400°F; gas mark 6; 30-40 minutes

Mix the flour and salt, rub in the butter, and
add the caster sugar and apples. Gather the
mixture with the lightly beaten eggs and spoon
into two greased 8-9 in sandwich tins; sprinkle
with granulated sugar and bake.

Dripping Cake West Country

1 lb plain flour
1 teaspoon grated nutmeg
1 teaspoon bicarbonate of soda
½ lb dripping
½ lb soft brown sugar
4 oz each currants and sultanas
2 oz mixed peel
4 eggs
2-3 tablespoons milk

Oven: 350°F; gas mark 4; 1½-1¾ hours

Sift the flour, nutmeg and bicarbonate of soda;
rub in the dripping and add the sugar, currants,
sultanas and peel.

Mix to a dropping consistency with the beaten
eggs and milk; spoon into a 9-10 in cake tin lined
with buttered greaseproof paper. Bake until firm.

Durham Lunch Cake Co. Durham

1 lb plain flour
¼ teaspoon salt
¾ oz baking powder
6 oz mixed lard and margarine
6 oz caster sugar
½ lb currants
½ lb sultanas and raisins
2 oz mixed peel
Grated rind of 1 lemon
2 teaspoons each, nutmeg, cinnamon and mixed
    spice
½ level teaspoon ground cloves
2 eggs
6 fl oz milk

Oven: 350°F; gas mark 4; 2 hours

Sift the flour, salt and baking powder, rub in the
lard and margarine and add the sugar fruits, mixed
peel, lemon rind and spices. Mix to a dropping
consistency with the lightly beaten eggs and the
milk, spoon into a greased 9-10 in cake tin and
bake.

Gloucestershire Boiled Cake Gloucestershire

3 oz caster sugar
2 oz butter
2 oz golden syrup
3 eggs
3 oz dried fruit
11 oz plain flour
½ teaspoon bicarbonate of soda
1 teaspoon mixed spice

Oven: 350°F; gas mark 4; 1½-2 hours

Boil the sugar, butter and syrup in a pan; remove
from the heat and leave to cool. Beat in the eggs;
add the fruit and the flour sifted with bicarbonate of soda and spice. Spoon the mixture into a
greased 6-7 in cake tin and bake.

Guard's Cake

1 lb plain flour
2 teaspoons mixed spice
1 teaspoon bicarbonate of soda
½ lb butter
½ lb Demerara sugar
4 oz mixed peel
4 oz sultanas
5 eggs

Oven: 350°F; gas mark 4; 2 hours

Sift the flour, spice and bicarbonate of soda; rub in the butter and add the sugar, mixed peel and sultanas. Mix to a dropping consistency with the beaten eggs; spoon into a greased 9-10 in cake tin and bake for about 2 hours.

Harrier Cake

½ lb plain flour
½ teaspoon bicarbonate of soda
¾ teaspoon baking powder
1 teaspoon mixed spice
4 oz butter
4 oz caster sugar
½ lb chopped dates
2 oz chopped walnuts
1 oz treacle or syrup
1 egg
½ pt milk

Oven: 350°F; gas mark 4; 1½-2 hours

Sift the flour, bicarbonate of soda, baking powder and spice; rub in the butter and add the sugar. Fold in the dates and walnuts and mix with the treacle, beaten egg and milk.

Spoon the mixture into a greased 6-7 in cake tin and bake for 1½-2 hours.

Ilkley Cake Yorkshire

1 lb plain flour
½ teaspoon salt
¾ oz baking powder
1 teaspoon each, mixed spice and grated nutmeg
4 oz dripping
¾ lb brown sugar
½ lb currants
4 oz raisins
2 oz candied peel

Oven: 350°F; gas mark 4; 2 hours

Sift the flour, salt, baking powder and spices; rub in the dripping and add the sugar, currants, raisins and candied peel. Mix to a dropping consistency with water, spoon into a greased 9-10 in cake tin and bake for 2 hours.

Irish Boiled Cake Ireland

The Nottinghamshire Boiled Cake omits the spices and syrup as does the Lincolnshire Boiled

Cake in which the butter is rubbed in, not boiled.

3 oz golden syrup
4-5 fl oz water
4-5 oz caster sugar
4 oz currants
4 oz sultanas
4 oz butter
½ lb plain flour
¾ teaspoon baking powder
1 teaspoon mixed spice
1 teaspoon ground ginger
1 egg

Oven: 350°F; gas mark 4; 1½-2 hours

Boil the syrup, water, sugar, currants, sultanas and butter for 7 minutes, stirring occasionally; set aside to cool.

Fold in the flour sifted with baking powder, spice and ginger and mix to a soft consistency with the beaten egg. Spoon into a greased 6-7 in cake tin and bake.

Irish Rink Cake Ireland

4 oz plain flour
¾ teaspoon baking powder
2 oz butter
4 oz caster sugar
2 eggs
2 oz blanched, chopped almonds
1 oz currants

Oven: 350°F; gas mark 4; 20 minutes

Sift the flour and baking powder; rub in the butter and add the sugar. Mix to a dropping consistency with the beaten eggs and spoon into a greased 8 in sandwich tin.

Sprinkle the top with almonds and currants and bake for 20 minutes.

Lancashire Poor Man's Cake Lancashire

¾ lb plain flour
1½ teaspoons baking powder
1 oz butter
6 oz soft brown sugar
Milk
1 egg

Oven: 350°F; gas mark 4; 30-40 minutes

Sift the flour and baking powder; rub in the

butter and add the sugar. Mix to a stiff consistency with milk and shape on a floured board into a round tea cake. Place on a greased baking tray, brush with beaten egg and bake.

Lemon Kali Cake

2 oz lard
½ lb plain flour
2 oz caster sugar
1 oz candied peel
½ oz lemon kali (sherbert)
1 beaten egg

Oven: 350°F; gas mark 4; 30-40 minutes

Rub the lard into the sifted flour, add the sugar, candied chopped peel and lemon kali. Mix to a dropping consistency with the beaten egg and water.

Spoon into a greased 6 in cake tin and bake for 30-40 minutes.

Ovington Fruit Cake

½ lb plain flour
¾ teaspoon baking powder
½ lb ground rice
7 oz butter
½ lb caster sugar
Grated rind of 2 lemons
¾ lb currants
3 eggs
Milk

Oven: 350°F; gas mark 4; 1½-2 hours

Mix the sifted flour, baking powder and ground rice; rub in the butter and add the sugar, lemon rind and currants. Mix to a dropping consistency with the beaten eggs and a little milk.

Spoon into a greased 9-10 in cake tin and bake for about 1½ hours.

A Penzance Cake Cornwall

1 lb plain flour
½ teaspoon bicarbonate of soda
4 oz butter
6 oz caster sugar
2 teaspoons cinnamon
1 lb currants
½ lb chopped crystallised ginger
4 oz mixed chopped peel
2 eggs
5 fl oz warm milk

Oven: 350°F; gas mark 4; 2 hours

Sift the flour and bicarbonate of soda, rub in the butter and add the sugar, cinnamon, currants, crystallised ginger and peel. Mix to a soft dough with the beaten eggs and the milk.

Spoon into a greased 9-10 in cake tin and bake.

Pope Lady Cake Hertfordshire

4 oz butter
4 oz caster sugar
1 teaspoon lemon, almond essence or rose water
4 oz plain flour
¼ teaspoon baking powder
½ oz cornflour
2 egg whites

Oven: 400°F; gas mark 6; 15-20 minutes

Cream the butter and sugar and add the lemon essence. Add the sifted flour, baking powder and cornflour and mix well.

Fold in the stiffly beaten egg whites and spoon the mixture into two 6 in sandwich tins. Bake for about 20 minutes.

Portree Plum Cake Isle of Skye

This cake improves with keeping and can be stored in an airtight tin for at least one week.

1 lb plain flour
1 oz baking powder
½ lb butter
1 teaspoon each, ground cinnamon and grated nutmeg
½ lb Demerara sugar
4 oz chopped candied peel
1 lb currants
3 eggs
½ pt stout

Oven: 350°F; gas mark 4; 2 hours

Sift the flour and baking powder; rub in the butter and add the spices, sugar, peel and currants. Mix to a dropping consistency with the beaten eggs and the stout.

Spoon into a greased 9-10 in cake tin and bake.

Somerset Apple Sauce Cake Somserset

4 oz butter
½ lb brown sugar

1 egg
6 oz unsweetened apple sauce
½ lb self-raising flour
½ teaspoon each, cinnamon, cloves, nutmeg and
    salt
4 oz raisins
Vanilla butter icing

Oven: 350°F; gas mark 4; 1 hour

Cream the butter and sugar until light and fluffy;
gradually beat in the beaten egg and add the apple
sauce. Stir in the sifted flour, spices and salt and
finally the raisins. Spoon into a greased 8 in cake
tin and bake.

When cool cover with vanilla butter icing.

Spiced Oxford Cake Oxfordshire

10 oz plain flour
½ teaspoon mixed spice
¾ teaspoon baking powder
6 oz butter
6 oz soft brown sugar
½ lb raisins
3 oz chopped mixed peel
2½ oz black treacle
5 fl oz milk

Oven: 350°F; gas mark 4; 1½-2 hours

Sift the flour, spice and baking powder; rub in
the butter and add the sugar, raisins and peel.
Mix to a dropping consistency with treacle and
milk.

Spoon into a greased 8 in round cake tin and
bake for about 2 hours.

Teisen Lap Wales

1 lb plain flour
½ oz baking powder
4 oz lard
4 oz margarine
7 oz caster sugar
½ lb currants
Pinch grated nutmeg
3 eggs
5 fl oz buttermilk or milk (approx.)

Oven: 350°F; gas mark 4; 45-60 minutes

Sift the flour and baking powder; rub in the
lard and margarine and add the sugar, currants
and nutmeg. Mix with the beaten eggs and
enough milk to give a soft consistency.

Spoon into a greased, shallow 9-10 in
cake tin and bake.

Wimbledon Cake London

1 lb plain flour
½ lb butter
½ lb caster sugar
½ lb currants
2 oz chopped candied peel
½ pt sour milk
2 oz syrup
1 teaspoon mixed spice
½ teaspoon bicarbonate of soda

Oven: 350°F; gas mark 4; 2 hours

Sift the flour and rub in the butter; add the
sugar, currants and candied peel. Mix the milk
with syrup, spice and bicarbonate of soda and
blend into the flour mixture.

Spoon into a shallow, 8 in square, greased
cake tin and bake for 2 hours.

Windsor Castle Cake Berkshire

4 oz plain flour
¾ teaspoon baking powder
6 oz ground rice
½ lb butter
½ lb caster sugar
Grated rind of 1 lemon
2 eggs
½ pt milk

Oven: 350°F; gas mark 4; 2 hours

Sift the flour and baking powder, mix in the
ground rice and rub in the butter. Add the
sugar and lemon rind and mix to a dropping
consistency with the beaten eggs and the milk.

Spoon into a greased 6-7 in cake tin and bake.

LARGE RICH CAKES

These have a high proportion of eggs, sugar and
butter to flour. No chemical raising agent is
needed as air is beaten in by creaming the sugar
and butter and whisking in the eggs. Rich cakes
have a light crumbly texture and keep better than
plain cakes. The original plum cake was a basic
rich cake mixture with the addition of powdered
spices and dried plums (prunes); today prunes
are seldom used, but the name has persisted.

Rich cakes are always baked in lined tins to prevent sticking and burning; the tins should be prepared before the cake mixture.

Almond Cake

1 lb butter
1 lb caster sugar
9 eggs
1 lb plain flour
4 oz ground almonds
1 teaspoon almond essence
1 oz blanched flaked almonds

Oven: 350°F; gas mark 4; 2 hours

Cream the butter, cut into pieces, with the sugar until light and fluffy. Beat the eggs in a bowl set over a pan of hot water and gradually whisk into the creamed mixture. Fold in the sifted flour, add the ground almonds and the almond essence and mix to a soft dropping consistency without beating the mixture.

Turn into a lined and greased 9-10 in cake tin; level the top and decorate with the flaked almonds. Bake for 2 hours.

Auld Reekie Plum Cake Edinburgh

1 lb butter
1 lb caster sugar
10 eggs
2½ fl oz whisky
1 lb plain flour
4 oz currants
4 oz raisins
2 oz chopped preserved ginger

Oven: 350°F; gas mark 4; 2 hours

Cream the cut-up butter and sugar until light and fluffy. Beat the eggs and whisky in a bowl over a pan of hot water and add to the creamed mixture alternately with the sifted flour. Fold in the currants, raisins and ginger and turn the mixture into a lined and greased, 9-10 in cake tin.

Level the top and bake for 2 hours.

Battenburg Cake

4 eggs
½ lb butter
½ lb caster sugar
½ lb plain flour
2 teaspoons baking powder
1 teaspoon vanilla essence
Food colouring
2-4 oz warmed jam
½ lb almond paste

Oven: 375°F; gas mark 5; 20 minutes

Beat the eggs over a pan of warm water; cream the butter and sugar until light and fluffy and gradually beat in the eggs. Fold in the flour sifted with the baking powder and add the vanilla essence.

Divide the cake mixture into two equal portions and colour one portion pink with a few drops of food colouring.

Line a swiss-roll tin with greaseproof paper and lay a twist of greaseproof paper lengthways in the tin, dividing it into two sections. Fill one section of the tin with the pink mixture and the other with the plain cake mixture. Bake for about 20 minutes and cool on a cake rack.

Trim the sides of the two sections to the same size. Cut each section in half lengthways and brush the sides of each strip with warmed jam; lay a pink strip next to a plain-coloured strip and press together. Brush the top with jam and cover with the two strips, setting a plain above a pink strip and a pink above a plain.

Roll the almond paste out thinly on a surface sprinkled with sugar, cut to a shape that will fit the whole cake. Brush the cake all over with warm jam, then wrap the almond paste round it, leaving the short ends of the cake uncovered. Seal the join neatly.

Beadle Plum Cake Yorkshire

1 lb butter
1 lb caster sugar
9 eggs
18 oz plain flour
2 teaspoons mixed spice
1½ teaspoons baking powder
½ lb raisins
½ lb currants
½ lb sultanas
4 oz chopped mixed peel
Grated rind and juice of 1 lemon

Oven: 350°F; gas mark 4; 2 hours

Cream the butter and sugar until light and fluffy;

beat the eggs in a bowl set over a pan of hot water
and whisk into the creamed mixture. Fold in the
flour sifted with the spice and baking powder.
Add the raisins, currants, sultanas, peel, lemon
rind and juice, mixing to a soft consistency.

Turn into a greased and lined, 9-10 in cake tin;
smooth the top level and bake the cake for 2 hours.

Beer Cake Westmorland

4 oz butter
4 oz moist brown sugar
1 egg
½ lb plain flour
½ teaspoon bicarbonate of soda
3 oz currants
5 fl oz beer

Oven: 350°F; gas mark 4; 1½-2 hours

Cream the butter and sugar until fluffy, whisk in
the well-beaten egg and fold in the flour sifted
with bicarbonate of soda. Add the currants and
mix to a soft dropping consistency with the beer.

Spoon into a lined and greased, 6-7 in cake tin;
smooth the top and bake for about 1½ hours or
until firm.

Cherry Cake

1 lb butter
1 lb caster sugar
9 eggs
1 lb plain flour
½-¾ lb chopped glacé cherries

Oven: 350°F; gas mark 4; 2 hours

Cut the butter into small pieces and beat with
the sugar until light and fluffy. Beat the eggs in a
large bowl set over a pan of hot water; whisk into
the butter and sugar mixture and fold in the sifted
flour. Add the chopped cherries and turn the
mixture into a lined and greased, 9-10 in cake tin.

Smooth the top level and bake for 2 hours.

Instead of cherries, add any of the following
ingredients after folding in the flour: 10 oz
topped and tailed fresh black currants; 6 oz
desiccated coconut; ½ lb chopped preserved
ginger and 1 teaspoon ground ginger; 1 lb chopped
glacé cherries and 4 oz chopped preserved ginger;
½ lb finely chopped walnuts and grated rind of 1
lemon (this cake may be coated with a lemon
syrup made from the juice of 1 lemon and 3 oz
sugar spooned over the baked warm cake).

Hallowe'en cake, traditional in Scotland and
Ireland, is made from the basic rich cake mixture,
half of which is poured into a lined tin, covered
with charms — rings, buttons, thimbles, coins,
wishbones and horse shoes — wrapped in greaseproof paper. The remaining cake mixture is
spooned over and the baked cake is covered with
orange glacé icing and decorated with silhouettes
of witches on broomsticks, cats, owls and bats in
chocolate icing.

Chocolate Sandwich Ireland

4 oz butter
6 oz caster sugar
3 oz mashed potatoes
2 oz plain melted chocolate or 1½ oz cocoa
      powder
2 eggs
6 oz self-raising flour
2 fl oz milk

Oven: 350°F; gas mark 4; 25-30 minutes

Cream the butter and sugar with the mashed potatoes, add the melted chocolate or cocoa powder.
Whisk in the beaten eggs, add the flour and milk
and mix to a soft dropping consistency.

Spoon into two greased 8 in sandwich tins,
level the tops and bake. When cool, sandwich
together with whipped cream.

Christmas Cake

1 lb butter
1 lb soft brown sugar
9 eggs
1¼ lb plain flour
½ teaspoon salt
¾ oz mixed spice or cinnamon
1 lb currants
4 oz chopped raisins
1 lb sultanas
4 oz chopped citron peel
4 oz chopped mixed peel
4 oz blanched chopped almonds
½ lb chopped glacé cherries
Grated rind of ½ lemon
2 oz black treacle
5 fl oz rum
Vanilla, almond or ratafia essence

Oven: 325°F; gas mark 3; 4½-5 hours

Cut the butter into small pieces and cream

with the sugar until light and fluffy; beat the eggs in a large bowl set over a pan of hot water and whisk into the creamed mixture. Fold in the flour sifted with salt and mixed spice, alternately with the dried fruits, citron and mixed peel, almonds, cherries and lemon rind. Finally, add the treacle, rum and a few drops of essence.

Turn the cake mixture into a double-lined and greased, 12 in cake tin and level the top making sure no air pockets are left. Tie a couple of layers of brown paper round the sides of the tin and stand it on a double layer of newspaper in the oven and bake for 4½-5 hours. If the cake browns on top before the end of cooking time, cover the top with a double layer of greaseproof or brown paper.

Leave the cake to cool completely before decorating it; it will keep for several weeks if stored in foil and an airtight tin. Cover the cake, top and sides, with almond paste or marzipan and leave to set. Spread Royal Icing over the marzipan and pipe on decorations in plain or coloured Royal Icing.

Cornish Black Cake Cornwall

¾ lb butter
¾ lb caster sugar
12 eggs
½ lb plain flour
¾ teaspoon baking powder
½ teaspoon bicarbonate of soda
1 teaspoon mixed spice
1 teaspoon grated nutmeg
2 teaspoons ground cinnamon
½ lb rice flour
2 lb currants
4 oz chopped raisins
¾ lb chopped sultanas
½ lb candied orange peel
½ lb candied lemon peel
½ lb blanched chopped almonds
2 tablespoons brandy

Oven: 350°F; gas mark 4; 3 hours

Cream the butter and sugar until fluffy; beat the eggs in a large bowl over a pan of hot water until creamy. Whisk the eggs into creamed mixture, fold in the sieved flour, baking powder, bicarbonate of soda, mixed spice, nutmeg, cinnamon and rice flour. Add the currants, raisins, sultanas, orange and lemon peel, almonds and lastly the brandy.

Turn into double-lined and greased 9 in cake tins, level the tops and bake. One cake is tradi-

tionally stored for a whole year and eaten on the anniversary of being baked.

Cover the cake completely with marzipan and decorate with glacé or Royal icing.

The North Devon Black Cake is similar, but also includes 6 oz black treacle.

Cuddieston Cake, Scotland

¾ lb butter
¾ lb caster sugar
6 eggs
1½ lb plain flour
¾ teaspoon baking powder
1 lb sultanas
1 lb currants
½ lb chopped glacé cherries
½ lb chopped mixed peel
4 oz ground almonds
2 oz golden syrup
5 fl oz milk

Oven: 325°F; gas mark 3; 4 hours

Cut the butter into small pieces and beat with the sugar until light and creamy. Whisk the eggs in a bowl over a pan of hot water and beat into the butter and sugar: fold in the flour sifted with the baking powder, adding this alternately with the sultanas, currants, cherries and peel. Stir in the almonds, syrup and enough milk to give a dropping consistency.

Spoon the cake mixture into a double-lined and greased 9-10 in cake tin; smooth the top and tie brown paper round the tin before baking.

Cumberland Sand Cake Cumberland

2 eggs
½ lb butter
½ lb caster sugar
½ lb cornflour
2 oz plain flour
1 teaspoon baking powder
Lemon essence
Milk

Oven: 350°F; gas mark 4; 2 hours

Double-line a 6-7 in cake tin with greaseproof paper. Whisk the eggs in a bowl set over a pan of warm water; cream the butter and sugar until fluffy and beat in the eggs. Gradually fold in the cornflour and plain flour sifted with the baking powder.

Mix in a little lemon essence and enough milk to give a soft dropping consistency. Spoon the mixture into the prepared tin, level the top and bake.

Druids Cake

6 oz butter
6 oz caster sugar
3 eggs
½ lb plain flour
3 teaspoons baking powder
Glacé icing
Glacé cherries, hazel nuts, candied angelica

Oven: 350°F; gas mark 4; 30 minutes

Cream the butter and sugar until fluffy; whisk in the beaten eggs and fold in the flour sifted with the baking powder until the mixture is soft and dropping.

Spoon into a lined and greased, 8 in square cake tin; smooth the top level and bake.

Cover the cooled cake with glacé icing and decorate with halved glacé cherries, nuts and strips of angelica.

Dundee Cake Scotland

1 lb butter
1 lb caster sugar
9 eggs
1 lb plain flour
6 oz currants
6 oz raisins
6 oz sultanas
4 oz chopped mixed peel
Grated rind of 1 orange
2 oz blanched, split almonds

Oven: 350°F; gas mark 4; 2 hours

Cut the butter into small pieces and cream with the sugar until light and fluffy; beat the eggs in a bowl set over a pan of hot water and whisk into the creamed mixture. Fold in the sifted flour, alternately with the currants, raisins, sultanas, mixed peel and orange rind.

Turn into a double-lined, greased 9-10 in cake tin and arrange the almonds over the top in circular patterns. Bake in the oven for 2 hours.

Fruit Cake

1 lb butter
1 lb caster sugar
9 eggs
1 lb plain flour
½ lb currants
½ lb sultanas
½ lb raisins
4 oz chopped candied peel
4 oz chopped glacé cherries

Oven: 350°F; gas mark 4; 2 hours

Cream the butter, cut into small pieces, with the sugar until light and fluffy; whisk the eggs in a bowl set over a pan of hot water and beat into the butter and sugar mixture. Fold in the sifted flour, alternately with the currants, sultanas, raisins, candied peel and glacé cherries.

Spoon the mixture into a double-lined, greased 9-10 in cake tin; level the top and bake for 2 hours.

Grettleston Cake

½ pt milk
½ lb syrup
¾ lb butter
¾ lb caster sugar
6 eggs
1½ lb plain flour
1 lb sultanas
1 lb currants
½ lb citron peel

Oven: 350°F; gas mark 4; 2½ hours

Heat the milk and syrup lightly until well blended; cream the butter and sugar and beat in the eggs, one at a time. Fold in the sifted flour and add the sultanas, currants and peel; mix to a dropping consistency with the warm milk.

Turn into a lined and greased 8 in cake tin, smooth the top and bake.

Hereford Cider Cake Herefordshire

The Oxford Cider Cake is identical to that from Herefordshire.

4 oz butter
4 oz caster sugar
2 eggs
½ lb plain flour
½ grated nutmeg
½ teaspoon bicarbonate of soda
5 fl oz cider

Oven: 375°F; gas mark 5; 45-60 minutes

Beat the butter and sugar until light and creamy; mix in the eggs, one at a time, whisking well after each addition. Fold in the flour, sifted with the nutmeg and bicarbonate of soda, alternately with the cider.

Mix well and turn into a lined and greased 7-8 in cake tin; level the top and bake for 1 hour.

Kentish Cake Kent

4 oz butter
4 oz caster sugar
3 eggs, separated
4 oz self-raising flour
1 oz desiccated coconut
1 oz cocoa powder
1 oz ground almonds
¼ teaspoon vanilla essence

Oven: 375°F; gas mark 5; 25 minutes

Cream the butter and sugar until fluffy; beat in the egg yolks, one at a time, then fold in the flour, coconut, cocoa, almonds and vanilla essence. Whisk the egg whites until stiff and carefully fold them into the cake mixture.

Spoon into a lined and greased, 6 in round cake tin, smooth the surface level and bake for 25 minutes.

Madeira Cake

In the 19th century, Madeira wine was traditionally served with this cake, hence the name.

1 lb butter
1 lb caster sugar
9 eggs
1 lb plain flour
1 teaspoon grated lemon rind
2 strips citron peel

Oven: 350°F; gas mark 4; 2 hours

Cut the butter into small pieces and cream with the sugar until light and fluffy; beat the eggs in a large bowl set over a pan of hot water. Whisk the eggs into the creamed mixture and fold in the sifted flour and the grated lemon rind.

Turn the cake mixture into a lined and greased, 9-10 in cake tin, smooth the top level and bake in the oven for 30 minutes; arrange the citron peel,

cut into narrow strips, over the top and continue baking for another 1½ hours.

Old English Cider Cake

2 eggs
4 oz butter
4 oz caster sugar
½ lb plain flour
1 teaspoon baking powder
½ grated nutmeg
5 fl oz cider

Oven: 375°F; gas mark 5; 20 minutes

Beat the eggs over a pan of warm water; cream the butter and sugar until fluffy and gradually beat in eggs. Fold in the flour sifted with the baking powder and add the nutmeg and cider.

Spoon the cake mixture in a 9 in sandwich tin lined with greaseproof paper and bake.

Plum Cake Ireland

1 lb butter
1 lb caster sugar
8 eggs
1 lb plain flour
1 teaspoon each, ground cinnamon and ground ginger
3 oz ground almonds
1 lb raisins
1 lb currants
2 oz chopped mixed peel
3 oz flaked almonds

Oven: 350°F; gas mark 4; 2 hours

Cut the butter up and beat with the sugar until creamy and light; whisk the eggs in a large bowl over a pan of hot water and beat into the butter and sugar. Fold in the sifted flour, cinnamon, ginger and ground almonds. Add the raisins, currants, peel and flaked almonds.

Spoon the mixture into three lined and greased 7 in cake tins and bake.

Pound Cake

8 eggs
1 lb butter
1 lb caster sugar
1 lb plain flour
1 lb mixed dried fruit
4 oz chopped mixed peel

Grated rind of 1 lemon
2 fl oz brandy

Oven: 350°F; gas mark 4; 2 hours

Beat the eggs in a deep bowl above a pan of hot water; cream the butter and sugar until fluffy, gradually beat in the eggs and fold in the flour.

Mix in the fruit, peel, lemon rind and brandy and spoon the mixture into a 9 in square lined tin. Level the top and bake. A few halved walnuts may be placed on the top before baking.

Rice Cake

1 lb butter
1 lb caster sugar
9 eggs
½ lb ground rice flour
6 oz plain flour
2 oz self-raising flour
1 teaspoon lemon essence

Oven: 350°F; gas mark 4; 2 hours

Cut the butter up small and cream with the sugar until light and fluffy; beat the eggs in a bowl over a pan of hot water and whisk into the creamed mixture. Fold in the rice flour, plain flour and self-raising flour and finally the lemon essence.

Spoon the mixture into a lined and greased, 9-10 in cake tin, level the top and bake for about 2 hours.

Scottish Seed Cake, Scotland

1 lb butter
1 lb caster sugar
9 eggs
1 lb plain flour
½ teaspoon each, ground cinnamon and grated
    nutmeg
4 oz chopped citron peel
2 oz chopped candied orange peel
2 oz chopped candied lemon peel
4 oz blanched chopped almonds
1 oz caraway comfits

Oven: 350°F; gas mark 4; 2 hours

Cream the butter and sugar until light and fluffy; beat the eggs in a large bowl set over a pan of hot water and whisk into the creamed mixture; fold in the flour sifted with the spices, alternately with the citron, orange and lemon peel and the chopped almonds.

Turn the cake mixture into a lined and greased, 9-10 in cake tin, sprinkle the caraway comfits on top and bake for 2 hours.

Scottish Snow Cake Scotland

3 eggs
3 egg whites
½ lb unsalted butter
10 oz caster sugar
18 oz arrowroot
2 fl oz cream
½ teaspoon almond essence

Oven: 350°F; gas mark 4; 1-1¼ hours

Separate the three whole eggs and beat the six whites until stiff. Cream the butter and sugar and beat in the egg yolks alternately with the arrowroot. Stir in the cream and almond essence and finally fold in the egg whites.

Spoon the cake mixture into a lined and greased, 9-10 in cake tin and bake.

Seed Cake

1 lb butter
1 lb caster sugar
9 eggs
1 lb plain flour
1 teaspoon ground cloves
1 teaspoon cinnamon
2 oz caraway seeds

Oven: 350°F; gas mark 4; 2 hours

Cut the butter into small pieces and cream with the sugar until fluffy; beat the eggs in a bowl set over a pan of hot water and whisk into the butter and sugar mixture. Fold in the flour sifted with the cloves and cinnamon and add the caraway seeds.

Turn the mixture into a lined and greased, 9-10 in cake tin; smooth the top and bake in the oven for 2 hours.

The Northamptonshire Seed Cake is similar, but uses one grated nutmeg instead of cloves and cinnamon.

Simnel Cake

4-5 eggs
½ lb butter

½ lb caster sugar
½ lb plain flour
1 teaspoon each, grated nutmeg, cinnamon and
  allspice
¾ teaspoon salt
½-¾ lb sultanas
4 oz chopped candied peel
1 lb currants
2 oz black treacle
1½ lb marzipan
Apricot jam
1 egg yolk
Olive oil

Oven: 325°F; gas mark 3; 3½ hours

Beat the eggs in a bowl over a pan of warm water;
cream the butter and sugar until fluffy and light;
gradually beat in the eggs and fold in the flour,
spices and salt. Add the sultanas, peel, currants
and treacle and mix well.

Line an 8 in round cake tin with greaseproof
paper. Roll a third of the marzipan into a circle
to fit the tin. Put half the cake mixture in the tin,
level and cover with the marzipan circle. Cover
with the remaining cake mixture, level the top
and bake.

When cool, roll out the remaining marzipan to
fit the top of the cake. Brush the top with jam
and cover with the marzipan, press down and mark
the top into 1 in squares. Make small balls from
the marzipan trimmings and place round the
edges.

Brush the top with egg yolk beaten with a
little oil and put under a medium hot grill to
brown lightly.

Staffordshire Fruit Cake Staffordshire

¾ lb butter
¾ lb caster sugar
8 eggs
1 lb plain flour
1 teaspoon ground mace
¾ teaspoon baking powder
4 oz black treacle
4 oz ground almonds
1 lb currants
4 oz chopped glacé cherries
4 oz chopped mixed peel
1 tablespoon brandy
1 tablespoon lemon juice

Oven: 350°F; gas mark 4; 2 hours

Cream the butter and sugar until light; whisk the
eggs in a large bowl over a pan of hot water and
then beat into the creamed mixture. Fold in the
flour sifted with mace and baking powder, alternately with the treacle and ground almonds.

Add the currants, cherries and peel and finally
mix in the brandy and lemon juice. Turn the
mixture into two greased and lined 8 in cake tins;
level the tops and bake for 2 hours.

Stanhope Nut and Date Cake Co. Durham

½ lb butter
½ lb caster sugar
3 eggs
1 lb plain flour
¾ teaspoon baking powder
4 oz chopped walnuts
4 oz chopped dates
5 oz raisins
5 oz sultanas
5 fl oz milk
1 oz black treacle

Oven: 350°F; gas mark 4; 2 hours

Cut up the butter and cream with the sugar until
fluffy; whisk in the eggs, one at a time, and fold
in the flour sifted with the baking powder. Add
the walnuts, dates, raisins and sultanas, alternately
with the milk; mix to a soft consistency with the
treacle. Spoon into a lined and greased, 9-10 in
cake tin, smooth the top and bake.

Sultana Cake

1 lb butter
1 lb caster sugar
9 eggs
1 lb plain flour
1-1½ lb sultanas
4 oz chopped candied peel
2 oz chopped glacé cherries
Grated rind of 1 lemon

Oven: 350°F; gas mark 4; 2 hours

Cream the softened butter and sugar; whisk
the eggs in a bowl set over a pan of hot water
and beat into the creamed mixture. Fold in the
sifted flour, the sultanas, peel, cherries and lemon
rind and mix gently to a soft dropping consistency.

Turn the cake mixture into a lined and greased
9-10 in cake tin, level the top and bake for 2 hours.

Twelfth Night Cake London

Once traditional on Twelfth Night or 6th January,
a whole dried bean was inserted in the cake
for luck; the person who was served the slice
containing the bean was proclaimed "King Bean"
for the night.

4 eggs
½ lb butter
½ lb caster sugar
½ lb plain flour
1 lb currants
3 oz chopped candied peel
2 oz blanched chopped almonds
½ teaspoon grated nutmeg
2½ fl oz brandy
Garnish: Royal icing, crystallised fruits

Oven: 350°F; gas mark 4; 2 hours

Beat the eggs thoroughly over a pan of warm water;
cream the butter and sugar until light and fluffy
and gradually beat in the eggs. Carefully fold in
the sifted flour and blend well before adding the
currants, peel, almonds and nutmeg; blend in the
brandy to give a soft dropping consistency.

Spoon the cake mixture into a 9-10 in cake tin,
double-lined with greaseproof paper; level the top
and bake.

Turn out and leave the cake to cool; cover
with Royal icing and before this sets, decorate
with pieces of crystallised fruit.

SPONGE CAKES

These consist of a light cake mixture of eggs and
sugar vigorously beaten to incorporate air. An
equal amount of flour is folded in and the
mixture is baked for a short length of time.
The light mixture is unable to hold any type
of filling, but is usually sandwiched with a
jam or cream filling after baking. Sponge cakes
date from the 19th century before the introduction of chemical raising agents.

Sponge Cake

4 eggs
4 oz caster sugar
4 oz plain flour
Red jam
Icing sugar

Oven: 375°F; gas mark 5; 20 minutes

Grease two sandwich tins, 6-7 in wide, and dust
with flour. Put the eggs and sugar in a warm bowl,
set over a pan of hot water and whisk the mixture
until light and creamy; it should be stiff enough
to leave a trail from the whisk.

Remove the bowl from the heat, sift in half the
flour and fold in lightly with a metal spoon. Add
the remaining flour in the same way. Spoon the
cake mixture immediately into the prepared tins
and bake in the oven.

When cool, sandwich with jam and dust the top
with sifted icing sugar.

Diet Loaf Scotland

8 eggs
1 lb caster sugar
¼ oz caraway seeds
2 teaspoons ground ginger or finely grated rind
    of 1 orange and 1 lemon
¾ lb plain flour

Oven: 375°F; gas mark 5; 45 minutes

Grease an 8 in round cake tin and line the base
with greaseproof, buttered paper. Dust lightly
with flour. Whisk the eggs and sugar in a bowl
over a pan of hot water until thick and creamy.
Remove from the hot water and fold in the
caraway seeds and ginger or grated rind.

Sift the flour and carefully fold half into the
creamed mixture with a metal spoon. Fold in the
remaining flour, then spoon the cake mixture into
the prepared tin. Bake for 45 minutes, sprinkling
with sugar before baking or covering with a glacé
icing when cold.

Harrogate Sponge Yorkshire

4 eggs
4 oz caster sugar
2 tablespoons boiling water
4 oz plain flour
¾ teaspoon baking powder

Oven: 375°F; gas mark 5; 20 minutes

Grease two 8 in sandwich tins and dust lightly
with flour. Beat the eggs and sugar in a bowl set
over hot water. When the mixture is thick and
creamy, add the boiling water and continue
whisking for 5 minutes.

Fold in half the sifted flour and baking powder,
then add the remaining flour. Spoon into the cake
tins and bake for 20 minutes.

Sandwich the cold sponge cakes with jam, butter icing or fresh cream; dust the top with sifted icing sugar.

Marlborough Cake Wiltshire

4 eggs
½ lb caster sugar
6 oz plain flour
1 oz caraway seeds

Oven: 425°F; gas mark 7; 10 minutes

Grease and flour an 8-9 in round cake tin. Put the eggs and sugar in a warm bowl and set over a pan of hot water. Whisk steadily until creamy and thick enough for the whisk to leave a trail.

Remove the bowl from the heat, fold in half the sifted flour and the caraway seeds; fold in the remaining flour, using a metal spoon in both instances.

Spoon the mixture into the prepared cake tin and bake for 10 minutes. When cold, cover the top with sifted icing sugar.

Swiss Roll

3 eggs
3 oz caster sugar
3 oz plain flour
1-2 oz sugar
2 oz melted jam

Oven: 425°F; gas mark 7; 10 minutes

Grease and line a 7 by 11 inch swiss-roll tin with greaseproof paper. Beat the eggs and caster sugar in a bowl over a pan of hot water, whisking until the mixture is light-coloured and thick enough to leave a trail.

Remove the bowl and sift in half the flour; fold it in carefully with a metal spoon and repeat with the remaining flour. Spoon quickly into the prepared tin, tilting to cover it evenly with the sponge mixture.

Bake until light golden and springy and turn out on to a sheet of greaseproof paper, sprinkled with sugar and placed on a damp tea towel. Trim the edges and cut a slit ½ in from one of the narrow edges, cutting halfway through the sponge. Spread the sponge with warm jam almost to the edges. Roll up tightly using the slit to start the roll and pulling on the greaseproof paper to keep the roll in shape. Place, seam downwards, on a cake rack to cool.

Other fillings, such as butter cream icing or cream may be used, but not until the sponge has cooled. For such variations, roll the sponge up loosely in the greaseproof paper and unroll when cold. Spread with the chosen filling and roll up.

Victoria Sandwich

There are numerous variations of this light layer cake, named after Queen Victoria.

2 eggs
4 oz butter
4 oz caster sugar
4 oz plain flour
1 teaspoon baking powder
½ teaspoon vanilla essence
Jam or butter icing
Icing sugar

Oven: 375°F; gas mark 5; 20 minutes

Beat the eggs in a bowl set over a pan of warm water; cream the butter and sugar until white and fluffy and gradually beat in the eggs. Carefully fold in the flour sifted with the baking powder; stir in the vanilla essence.

Pour the mixture into two lined sandwich tins, 6-7 in wide; level the top and bake until golden and firm, yet springy.

Leave to cool on a cake rack, then sandwich the two layers with jam or butter cream icing and dust the top with sifted icing sugar.

Brunswick Cake, similar to Victoria Sandwich, ½ teaspoon ground cinnamon being added with the flour; sandwich with a butter or cinnamon butter cream and coat with cinnamon glacé icing.

Chocolate Sandwich, melt 2 oz chocolate or 1 oz cocoa powder in a little milk and add before the flour which should be reduced to 3 oz; fill with chocolate butter cream and coat with chocolate glacé icing.

Douglas Honey Cake, a Scottish sandwich which adds 1 oz ground almonds to the flour; fill with 1 oz ground almonds mixed with 2 oz honey, and dust with icing sugar.

Orange or Lemon Sandwich, add the grated rind of 1 orange or lemon after folding in the flour; coat with orange or lemon icing and decorate with crystallised orange or lemon slices.

GINGERBREAD

Gingerbread was, according to early recipes, a mixture of grated bread, ginger, liquorice, aniseeds and pepper, sweetened with honey and made into a stiff paste with old ale or claret. It was formed into thin flat cakes, often in the shape of men or letters or numbers and dried gently until hard and brittle. Thus it was a development from the hard primitive type of unleavened bread and akin to the biscuit in texture though in form and composition more like a cake. Later grated bread was omitted and substituted with flour, eggs and fat. Sugar and treacle displaced the honey and the new form of gingerbread was in general more refined but still baked hard, with no leaven. During the 18th century a type of gingerbread emerged, thicker and moister than the previous types and baked in cake tins.

In the 19th century, bicarbonate of soda was added for aeration. This new gingerbread was called thick light gingerbread and was quite different in form and texture to the hard thin type which was made into small gingerbreads or nuts (see Biscuits). In the North of England and Scotland, where oatmeal was common, the parkin, perkin or parken described a certain type of gingerbread or cake made of oatmeal and treacle. The origin of the word parkin is unknown though it may have developed from a proper name. In Scotland, the parkin followed the original form as a fairly hard, small, thin, round biscuit whereas in the North of England it was thicker, softer and baked as a cake in a square tin.

Gingerbread can be made by any one of the three methods described: melting, creaming or rubbing in, depending on the composition of the ingredients. Gingerbread is best when kept for a few days before cutting.

½ lb butter or lard
½ lb caster sugar
6 oz black treacle
1 lb plain flour
3 teaspoons ground ginger
2 teaspoons bicarbonate of soda
4 eggs
Milk

Oven: 375°F; gas mark 5; 1½-2 hours

Line a 9 in, square cake tin, about 2 in deep, with buttered greaseproof paper. Make up the gingerbread by any of the following methods:

Melting Method:
Melt the butter, sugar and treacle over gentle heat. Sift the flour, ginger and bicarbonate of soda, pour in the treacle mixture and stir well. Add the beaten eggs and mix with enough milk to give a soft consistency. Spoon into the prepared tin and bake.

Creaming Method:
Cream the butter and sugar until light and fluffy; beat in the eggs. Dissolve the treacle in milk and stir in the sifted dry ingredients, mixing to a soft consistency with the treacle and milk. Blend into the butter and sugar mixture; pour into the prepared tin and bake.

Rubbing-In Method:
Rub the butter into the flour until mixture has reached "breadcrumb" stage, add sugar, ginger and bicarbonate of soda, lightly beat the eggs. Dissolve the treacle in milk, and add with the eggs to the butter and flour mixture to give a soft consistency. Pour the mixture into the greased tin and bake.

Apple Gingerbread

2 oz butter or lard
2 oz caster sugar
1½ oz golden syrup
4 oz plain flour
1 teaspoon ground ginger
½ teaspoon bicarbonate of soda
½ teaspoon ground cloves
Milk
¾ lb peeled, cored and finely chopped cooking
   apples

Oven: 350°F; gas mark 4; 1½ hours

Line and butter a shallow, 8 in cake tin. Melt the butter, sugar and syrup over gentle heat. Remove from the heat and blend in the sifted flour, ginger, bicarbonate of soda and cloves. Mix with milk and the apples until the mixture has a soft dropping consistency.

Spoon into the prepared tin and bake. Cover with cinnamon icing when cool.

Bedfordshire Wigs Bedfordshire

The name of this gingerbread cake is derived from the thick curl over the edge of the shallow tin as the cake rises during baking.

1 lb black treacle
¾ lb butter
1 lb plain flour
½ teaspoon bicarbonate of soda
2 teaspoons ground ginger
1 teaspoon caraway seeds
4 oz caster sugar
5 fl oz milk

Oven: 350°F; gas mark 4; 30-40 minutes

Grease a 9 in square cake tin, about 2 in deep. Melt the treacle and butter, add the sifted flour, bicarbonate of soda, ginger, caraway seeds, sugar and milk, stirring well until throughly mixed.

Pour into the prepared tin to fill it by three-quarters so that the mixture will rise over the edge of the tin when baked. Set on a baking sheet and bake for about 45 minutes.

Edinburgh Gingerbread Scotland

4 oz butter
2 oz caster sugar
4 oz black treacle
½ lb plain flour
1 teaspoon each, ground cinnamon, cloves and ginger
2 eggs
2 oz blanched split almonds

Oven: 350°F; gas mark 4; 1½-2 hours

Line and grease a 1 lb loaf tin and dust lightly with flour. Melt the butter, sugar and treacle over gentle heat, fold in the flour sifted with the spices and add the beaten eggs and the almonds.

Spoon into the prepared tin and bake until firm after about 2 hours.

Flapjacks

4 oz margarine
2 oz brown sugar
5 oz golden syrup
½ lb rolled oats
Pinch salt
6 oz caster sugar
½ lb plain flour
1 oz baking powder
4 oz oatmeal
3 eggs
1 pt milk

Oven: 375°F; gas mark 5; 30-40 minutes

Grease and flour a shallow, 8 in square tin. Melt the margarine, brown sugar and syrup over gentle heat; pour over the rolled oats mixed with a pinch of salt and add the caster sugar. Blend thoroughly, then fold in the flour sifted with the baking powder, and the oatmeal. Mix to a soft dropping consistency with the beaten eggs and the milk.

Spoon the mixture into the prepared tin and bake for about 40 minutes or until risen and firm. Serve cut into squares or fingers.

Fochabers Gingerbread Scotland

½ lb butter
4 oz caster sugar
½ lb black treacle
1 pt beer
1 lb plain flour
½ teaspoon bicarbonate of soda
2 teaspoons each, ground ginger and mixed spice
1 teaspoon each, ground cinnamon and cloves
4 oz sultanas
4 oz currants
3 oz finely chopped candied peel
3 oz ground almonds

Oven: 350°F; gas mark 3; 3 hours

Line and grease a round, 10 in wide, shallow cake tin; sprinkle lightly with flour.

Cream the butter and sugar until light and fluffy; dissolve the treacle in the beer and sift the flour, bicarbonate of soda and the spices. Fold the flour into the creamed mixture, alternately with the treacle and beer; add the sultanas, currants, candied peel and ground almonds.

Pour into the prepared tin and bake for about 3 hours.

Gloucestershire Ginger Cake

3½ oz margarine
3 oz brown sugar
4 oz golden syrup
2 oz black treacle
10 oz plain flour
½ teaspoon bicarbonate of soda
2 teaspoons each, mixed spice and ground ginger
1 egg
½ pt milk

Oven: 375°F; gas mark 5; 1½-2 hours

Line and grease a 1 lb loaf tin; dust with flour.

Melt the margarine, brown sugar, syrup and treacle over gentle heat. Sift the flour, bicarbonate of soda and mixed spice and ginger and stir into the syrup mixture; add the beaten egg and milk to give a dough of soft dropping consistency.

Pour into the prepared tin and bake for 1½-2 hours or until risen and firm.

Grantham Gingerbread Lincolnshire

4 oz butter
4 oz caster sugar
3 eggs
½ lb plain flour
¾ oz ground ginger
1½ teaspoon baking powder
Milk

Oven: 350°F; gas mark 4; 1½ hours

Cream the butter and sugar until light and fluffy and beat in the eggs. Sift in the flour, ginger and baking powder and stir to a soft consistency, adding milk if necessary.

Spoon into a well greased 1 lb loaf tin and bake until firm.

Grasmere Gingerbread Westmorland

4 oz butter
2 egg yolks
3 oz golden syrup
½ lb self-raising flour
1 teaspoon ground ginger
4 oz soft brown sugar
2 oz chopped almonds
1 beaten egg or milk
2 oz chopped preserved ginger
Chopped almonds
Brown sugar

Oven: 350°F; gas mark 4; 35-45 minutes

Warm the butter slightly and mix with the egg yolks and syrup. Blend in the flour and ground ginger, the sugar and almonds; mix to a stiff paste. Roll out half the mixture, ¼-½ in thick, and place on a greased baking tray. Brush with egg or milk and sprinkle with the chopped ginger.

Roll out the remaining mixture to the same size and place over the filling.

Brush with egg or milk and sprinkle with chopped almonds and sugar. Bake for about 45 minutes.

Grasmere Shortcake Westmorland

4 oz butter
½ lb plain flour
4 oz moist brown sugar
¼ teaspoon baking powder
½ teaspoon ground ginger
Filling: 2 oz butter
          4 oz icing sugar
          ½ teaspoon ground ginger
          2 oz finely chopped preserved ginger
          1 teaspoon ginger syrup

Oven: 350°F; gas mark 4; 30 minutes

Rub the butter into the flour and add the sugar, baking powder and ginger. Mix thoroughly and turn the mixture into a shallow baking tin, lined with greaseproof paper. Press evenly into the tin and bake.

Turn out the cake, trim the edges and slice in half horizontally while still hot. For the filling, cream the butter until light and fluffy, and gradually work in the sifted icing sugar and ginger. Beat in the preserved ginger and enough syrup to make a smooth paste. Spread this evenly over one half of the cake and press the other half on top. Mark and cut into fingers with a sharp knife.

Rhubarb Gingerbread

2 oz butter or lard
2 oz caster sugar
1½ oz black treacle
4 oz plain flour
½ teaspoon bicarbonate of soda
3 teaspoons ground ginger
1 egg
Milk
1¼ lb cleaned and chopped rhubarb
6 oz chopped crystallised ginger

Oven: 350°F; gas mark 4; 1½ hours

Line and grease a shallow, square 8 in cake tin; sprinkle lightly with flour. Melt the butter, sugar and treacle over low heat; add the flour sifted with bicarbonate of soda and 1 teaspoon ground ginger. Stir in the beaten egg and enough milk to give a soft consistency.

Spoon half the gingerbread mixture into the prepared tin, top with the rhubarb and crystallised ginger and sprinkle with the remaining 2 teaspoons of ground ginger. Spoon in the remaining cake mixture and bake for 1½ hours.

Startforth Gingerbread Yorkshire

4 oz butter
2 oz brown sugar
½ lb black treacle
½ lb plain flour
½ teaspoon bicarbonate of soda
1 teaspoon mixed spice
Pinch ground ginger
2 eggs
2 fl oz sour milk

Oven: 375°F; gas mark 5; 1½-2 hours

Line and grease a 1 lb loaf tin and dust lightly with flour. Melt the butter, sugar and treacle over gentle heat. Remove from the stove and stir in the flour sifted with bicarbonate of soda, spice and ginger. Add the beaten eggs and the sour milk. Mix thoroughly, pour into the prepared tin and bake for about 2 hours.

Wakefield Gingerbread Yorkshire

5 oz butter
11 oz self-raising flour
5 oz caster sugar
2 teaspoons ground ginger
1½ oz chopped mixed peel
4 oz golden syrup
1 dessertspoon brandy

Oven: 350°F; gas mark 4; 1½-2 hours

Line and grease a shallow, square 8 in cake tin; sprinkle with flour.

Rub the butter into the sifted flour, add the sugar, ginger and mixed peel; dissolve the syrup in the brandy and work into the dough until it has a soft consistency.

Spoon into the prepared tin and bake.

PARKINS

These types of gingerbread are indigenous to the North of England and Scotland, with oatmeal being used instead of white flour. A great many varieties developed, but essentially most English Parkins are baked as large cakes while in Scotland they are baked as small cakes (see also Biscuits).

Parkin (Leeds Parkin) Yorkshire

½ lb butter
½ lb plain flour
½ lb caster sugar
4 teaspoons ground ginger
½ teaspoon bicarbonate of soda
2 lb medium oatmeal
2 lb golden syrup
2½ fl oz milk

Oven: 350°F; gas mark 4; 45-60 minutes

Grease a 2 in deep and 8 in wide square cake tin and dust with flour. Rub the butter into the sifted flour, add the sugar, ginger, bicarbonate of soda and oatmeal. Melt the syrup, with the milk, over gentle heat and mix into the dry ingredients to a fairly stiff consistency. Spoon into the prepared tin and bake.

When cold cut with a fork through the cake to divide it into small squares; the squares are then pulled apart along these perforations.

Fig Parkin includes ½ lb dried, cooked and chopped figs, added to the cake mixture before the syrup and milk.

Broomie Orkney Islands

2 oz butter
6 oz plain flour
3 oz brown sugar
6 oz medium oatmeal
½ teaspoon bicarbonate of soda
1 teaspoon ground ginger
1 egg
2 oz black treacle
½ pt buttermilk

Oven: 350°F; gas mark 4; 1 hour

Grease an 8 in square cake tin, 4 in deep, and dust with flour. Rub the butter into the sifted flour, add the sugar, oatmeal, bicarbonate of soda and ginger; mix in the beaten egg and the treacle to give a stiff dough, then add sufficient buttermilk for a soft dropping consistency.

Spoon into the prepared tin and bake for about 1 hour.

Oldham Parkin Lancashire

4 oz butter
7 oz plain flour
½ teaspoon bicarbonate of soda
4 oz caster sugar
4 oz fine oatmeal
2 teaspoons each, ground ginger and nutmeg
1 teaspoon ground mace

¾ oz chopped candied peel
4 oz black treacle
1 tablespoon cream

Oven: 350°F; gas mark 4; 45-60 minutes

Rub the butter into the flour sifted with bicarbonate of soda, then add the sugar, oatmeal, ginger, nutmeg, mace and candied peel. Melt the treacle over gentle heat and mix with the cream; stir into the parkin mixture, cover and leave overnight.

The next day, grease and flour a shallow, round or square, 8 in cake tin; spoon in the parkin mixture and bake for about 1 hour.

Preston Parkin Lancashire

2 oz butter
2 oz lard
½ lb plain flour
½ teaspoon bicarbonate of soda
4 oz brown sugar
1 teaspoon each, ground ginger, mixed spice and
    grated nutmeg
½ lb fine oatmeal
½ lb black treacle
Milk

Oven: 350°F; gas mark 4; 45-60 minutes

Grease a shallow, square 8 in cake tin and dust with flour. Rub the butter and lard into the flour sifted with bicarbonate of soda; add the sugar, spices and oatmeal. Melt the treacle gently in a little milk and work into the mixture, adding more milk as necessary until the dough has a soft dropping consistency.

Spoon into the prepared tin and bake for about 1 hour. Serve cold, cut into squares.

Yorkshire Parkin Yorkshire

3 oz butter
3 oz lard
½ lb plain flour
1 teaspoon bicarbonate of soda
4 oz fine oatmeal
4 oz medium oatmeal
2 teaspoons ground ginger
1 egg
1 lb black treacle
½ pt beer

Oven: 350°F; gas mark 4; 45-60 minutes

Grease and flour a shallow, square 8 in cake tin. Rub the butter and lard into the flour sifted with bicarbonate of soda; add the two types of oatmeal and the ginger. Mix with the beaten egg to a fairly stiff consistency, then gently melt the treacle in the beer and work into the parkin until it has a soft dropping consistency.

Spoon into the prepared tin and bake. Cut into squares when cold.

CUP CAKES

These are made from a plain or rich cake mixture but baked as individual cakes in small patty tins. The tins can be lined with small fluted paper cups or simply greased well with butter. Test for readiness by pressing the risen, golden cakes gently with the fingertips; if the cakes rise again immediately, leaving no impression, they are ready. Small cakes do not store as well as large cakes and should be eaten within a short time of baking.

As well as cup cakes, this section also covers small sponge cakes, cheesecakes and pastry tarlets.

Brighton Rocks Sussex

½ lb butter
3 eggs
4 oz ground almonds
1 teaspoon rose water
4 oz currants
½ lb caster sugar
1 lb plain flour
1 beaten egg (optional)

Oven: 425°F; gas mark 7; 10 minutes

Cream the butter until soft, then beat in the eggs. Fold in the almonds, rose water, currants, sugar and sifted flour.

Work the mixture until smooth and shape into small buns. Set on a greased baking tray, brush with beaten egg and bake.

Cable Cakes Yorkshire

2 oz caster sugar
4 oz lard
1 lb mincemeat
1 lb plain flour
1 oz baking powder

2 eggs
5 fl oz milk (approx.)

Oven: 450°F; gas mark 8; 15 minutes

Cream the sugar and the lard until fluffy, add the mincemeat, sifted flour and baking powder. Beat the eggs with the milk and stir into the flour mixture; mix to a stiff dough.

Spoon into lined or greased patty tins and bake for 15 minutes.

Coburg Cakes

2 oz butter
2 oz caster sugar
1½ oz black treacle
4 oz plain flour
1 teaspoon ground ginger
½ teaspoon bicarbonate of soda
1 egg
Milk
2 oz blanched halved almonds

Oven: 350°F; gas mark 4; 15 minutes

Melt the butter, sugar and treacle over gentle heat; sift the flour, ginger and bicarbonate of soda and fold into the treacle mixture. Add the beaten egg and enough milk to give a mixture of soft dropping consistency.

Put half a blanched almond in each greased patty tin, spoon over the gingerbread mixture and bake for 15 minutes. Serve the baked, cooled cakes upside down, with the almonds on top.

Crulla Scotland

The word *Crule* is derived from the Gaelic *Kirl* meaning a small cake; it also defines a *Cruller* from the Dutch *Krullen*, which translated means to curl. These deep-fried cakes are thought to have been introduced to Scotland from the Low Countries.

2 oz butter
2 oz caster sugar
2 eggs
¾ lb self-raising flour

Cream the butter and sugar together until light and fluffy. Beat the eggs and whisk into the creamed mixture; add the sifted flour and mix to a soft dough.

Roll the mixture out, ¼ in thick, and cut into lengths, 5 in long and ½ in wide; cut each piece

into three strips; plait together and deep-fry in hot fat at 325°F until light brown, turning once. Drain on absorbent paper and dredge with sugar.

Deer Horns Scotland

¾ lb plain flour
1 oz ground almonds
5 oz caster sugar
Grated rind of 1 lemon
6 egg yolks
5 fl oz cream
1 egg white

Blend the sifted flour, ground almonds, sugar and lemon rind; beat in the egg yolks and the cream and work to a dough of fairly stiff consistency with the egg white.

Roll the dough out as thinly as possible and cut into narrow strips. Wrap the strips round greased cornets or "horn tins", overlapping the edges. Leave to set on the tins in a cool place, carefully ease out the tins and deep-fry the "horns" in hot fat (325°F) until golden brown, turning once. Drain and leave to cool.

Serve filled with whipped cream.

Honey Cakes

6 oz butter
4 oz caster sugar
4 oz honey
Grated rind of 1 lemon
6 eggs
¾ lb plain or self-raising flour
1 oz ground cinnamon
1 oz honey
4 oz mixed peel

Oven: 350°F; gas mark 4; 20 minutes

Cream the butter, sugar and honey until light and fluffy; add the finely grated lemon rind and beat in the eggs, one at a time. Fold in the sifted flour. Mix the last three ingredients together, spread this over the base of greased patty tins and spoon the cake mixture over. Bake in the oven for 20 minutes and turn out, with the spicy mixture on top.

Alternatively, make up the cake mixture and spoon into a lined and greased 7-8 in cake tin. Bake at 325°F; gas mark 3; for 1-1½ hours.

Huish Cakes

4 oz butter
½ lb caster sugar
4 oz plain flour
4 oz ground rice
½ oz caraway seeds
4 eggs

Oven: 350°F; gas mark 4; 1 hour

Beat the butter and sugar until creamy and light;
add the sifted flour, ground rice and caraway
seeds. Separate the eggs and beat in the egg yolks,
one at a time, mixing thoroughly.

Whisk the egg whites stiff and carefully fold
into the cake mixture. Spoon into a lined and
greased, square 8 in cake tin and bake for 1 hour.
Cut into squares when cold.

Hurlington Cake

1 egg
5 fl oz milk
6 oz orange marmalade
6 oz plain flour
¼ teaspoon cream of tartar
½ teaspoon bicarbonate of soda
6 oz caster sugar
Milk
Desiccated coconut
Chopped orange peel

Oven: 425°F; gas mark 7; 20 minutes

Beat the egg, milk and marmalade together;
gradually mix in the flour sifted with cream of
tartar and bicarbonate of soda, add the sugar and
sufficient milk to give a texture of thick batter.

Pour into a greased, square 7-8 in cake tin and
bake. After 15 minutes, brush the top with milk
and sprinkle with desiccated coconut and orange
peel. Continue baking for another 5 minutes. Cut
into diamond shapes when cold.

Montrose Cakes Angus

1 lb butter
1 lb caster sugar
12 eggs
1 lb plain flour
1 oz baking powder
½ whole grated nutmeg
2 tablespoons brandy
¾ lb currants

Rose water

Oven: 350°F; gas mark 4; 20-25 minutes

Cream the butter and sugar until light and fluffy;
beat the eggs in a bowl over a pan of hot water
and gradually whisk into the creamed mixture.
Fold in the sifted flour and baking powder, using
a metal spoon.

Add the nutmeg, brandy and currants and
flavour with a few drops of rose water. Spoon the
rich cake mixture into lined or greased patty tins
and bake for about 20 minutes.

Oast Cakes Kent

1 lb plain flour
¾ teaspoon salt
¾ teaspoon baking powder
4 oz lard
3 oz caster sugar
6 oz currants
Fat for frying

Sift the flour with the salt and baking powder,
rub in the lard to a crumbly mixture and add the
sugar and currants. Mix to a light dough with
water and divide into small pieces; roll out lightly
to ½ in thick rounds.

Fry in shallow fat until golden brown, turning
once. Serve hot.

Rout Cakes Middlesex

1 lb plain flour
1 oz butter
4 oz caster sugar
4 oz mixed candied orange and lemon peel
2 oz currants
4 fl oz brandy
1 teaspoon orange flower water
3 eggs

Oven: 425°F; gas mark 7; 10 minutes

Sift the flour and rub in the butter; blend in the
sugar, chopped peel, currants, brandy and orange
flower water. Mix to a soft dropping consistency
with the beaten eggs.

Drop teaspoons of the mixture on to greased
baking sheets and bake until golden.

Seventeenth Century Small Cakes

½ lb butter

1 lb plain flour
1 oz baking powder
4 oz caster sugar
½ lb currants
3 eggs
Grated nutmeg
Rose water

Oven: 375°F; gas mark 5; 20-25 minutes

Rub the butter into the sifted flour and baking powder; add sugar and currants. Separate the eggs and blend the yolks and two whites into the mixture. Knead to a paste, adding nutmeg and a few drops of rose water.

Roll the mixture out thinly and cut into 3 in rounds. Set on greased baking trays and bake for about 20 minutes. Brush with the remaining egg white and sprinkle with caster sugar; return to the oven for 2-3 minutes.

Spion Kops (Coconut Pyramids)

½ lb desiccated coconut
4 oz caster sugar
2 eggs
Glacé cherries

Oven: 350°F; gas mark 4; 15 minutes

Mix the coconut and sugar and blend in the eggs. Work to a moist dropping consistency; mould in an egg cup and turn out on a baking tray lined with buttered greaseproof paper. Top each coconut mould with half a glacé cherry and bake for about 15 minutes.

Victoria Sandwich Cup Cakes

These little cup cakes are basically made from a Victoria Sandwich cake mixture. Additional ingredients give rise to a number of varieties.

2 eggs
4 oz butter
4 oz caster sugar
4 oz plain flour
1 teaspoon baking powder

Oven: 375°F; gas mark 5; 15 minutes

Beat the eggs in a bowl set over a pan of warm water; cream the butter and sugar and gradually beat in the eggs. Carefully fold in the flour sifted with the baking powder. Spoon the cake mixture into lined or greased patty tins and bake for 15

minutes. The cakes may be iced with plain or coloured glacé icing when cool.

From this basic recipe, any of the following versions can be made, adding the additional ingredients after folding in the flour.

Aberffrau Cakes (Wales), spoon the mixture into greased deep scallop shells; sprinkle with sugar after baking for 15 minutes.

Adelaide Cakes, add 2 oz cornflour to the plain flour and fold in 2 oz chopped glacé cherries and 1 oz blanched chopped almonds.

Buckingham Cakes, mix in 1 teaspoon ground ginger and 1½ oz chopped preserved ginger.

Golden Bettys, fold in 2 teaspoons ground ginger and 2 oz golden melted syrup.

Hazelnut Cakes, add 4 oz finely chopped hazelnuts and a few drops of vanilla essence.

Leamingtons, bake the cake mixture in a square 2 in deep, 8 in wide cake tin; after baking, cut into squares, cover with chocolate glacé icing and coat with desiccated coconut.

Louise Cakes, add 1 teaspoon lemon essence to the cake mixture.

Madelines, bake the cake mixture in greased dariole moulds; coat when cool with melted red jam and roll in desiccated coconut.

Queen Cakes, fold in 1½ oz currants, grated rind of 1 lemon and 1 teaspoon brandy.

St. Patrick's Cakes (Ireland), traditionally baked in three-cornered tins; after baking, coat with white glacé icing and pipe on small shamrocks of green icing.

CHEESECAKES

These were originally a farmhouse speciality made with warm milk from the cow, and rennet to make the curd (or cheese); lemon, sugar, eggs and brandy were added, and the mixture was baked in small patty tins lined with shortcrust pastry. During the 18th and 19th centuries, curd — or cheese — was often omitted or substituted, but the term "cheesecake" persisted.

Curds

Fresh curd should be used for proper cheesecakes; it is prepared and made by several methods, always from fresh new milk.

4 pt milk
Rennet (approx. 4 teaspoons)

Heat the milk to blood heat, add rennet and stir until curds form and the liquid turns pale green. Remove from the heat and leave to cool, then strain through butter muslin to separate the curds from whey. Approximate yield, ½ lb curds.

Alternatively, heat 2 pt fresh milk until scalding hot, mix in 4 pt fresh, cold buttermilk and let the mixture stand until cold and firm. Skim the top and strain off the whey. Approximate yield, ½-¾ lb curds.

A third method is to use 1 pt sour milk, or 1 pt fresh milk soured with 1 dessertspoon lemon juice or vinegar. Boil the milk until it curdles, leave it to cool, then strain through muslin. Yield, about 4 oz curds.

Beestings Curd

Beestings or beastlyns or firstings is the first milking from a cow after calving. It is yellow and thick as cream and fed to the newborn calf; the surplus is used in country districts for puddings — thinned down with four times the quantity of ordinary milk, sweetened and variously flavoured it will set to a rich custard. Beestings are also turned into curds.

2 pt fresh new milk
½ pt water
½ pt beestings

Heat the milk, water and beestings to blood heat; set aside to cool and set, then strain. Approximate yield, ½ lb curds.

Almond Cheesecakes I

½ lb rich shortcrust pastry
4 oz ground almonds
4 oz caster sugar
4 oz softened butter
Grated rind of 1 lemon
1 dessertspoon lemon juice
1 tablespoon brandy or sherry
4 egg yolks
2 egg whites

Oven: 350°F; gas mark 4; 20-25 minutes

Roll out the pastry and use to line 16-20 patty tins. Beat together the almonds, sugar, butter, lemon rind, juice and brandy; mix in the beaten egg yolks.

Whisk the egg whites until stiff and fold into

the mixture. Spoon into the patty tins and bake until set.

Almond Cheesecakes II Ireland

½ lb rich shortcrust pastry
2 oz butter
3 oz caster sugar
3 eggs
4 oz blanched chopped almonds
1 dessertspoon rose water
Juice and rind of ½ lemon

Oven: 350°F; gas mark 4; 20-25 minutes

Line 16-20 patty tins with the pastry. Cream the butter and sugar until light and fluffy and gradually add the beaten eggs.

Fold in the almonds, rose water, lemon rind and juice; spoon into the patty cases to three-quarters fill them. Bake for about 20 minutes or until set.

Balmoral Cheesecakes Scotland

½ lb rich shortcrust pastry
4 oz butter
½ lb caster sugar
2 eggs
1 oz stale cake crumbs
½ teaspoon cornflour
1 oz chopped glacé cherries
1 oz chopped candied peel
1 teaspoon brandy
1 stiffly beaten egg white

Oven: 350°F; gas mark 4; 25 minutes

Roll out the pastry and line 16 patty tins. Heat the butter until soft and gradually add the sugar, beaten eggs, crumbs and cornflour. Stir the cherries, peel and brandy into the mixture, fold in the egg white and spoon the filling into the lined tins. Bake for 25 minutes.

Bread Cheesecakes Bedfordshire

½ lb rich shortcrust pastry
3 oz butter
½ pt milk
½ lb white breadcrumbs
3 oz currants
3 oz caster sugar
2 teaspoons grated nutmeg
4 eggs

2 fl oz brandy

Oven: 350°F; gas mark 4; 25 minutes

Line 16-20 patty tins with the rolled out pastry. Melt the butter in the milk and pour over the breadcrumbs. Leave until cold, then add the currants, sugar, nutmeg, beaten eggs and the brandy. Spoon into the lined patty tins and bake.

Cheesecakes Yorkshire

These small cheesecakes and jam tarts are traditional in Ripon during Wilfra or Wilfred Week, the first week in August, when the town commemorates St. Wilfred.

½ lb rich shortcrust pastry
½ pt milk
1 oz white breadcrumbs
4 oz butter
2 oz ground almonds
1 oz caster sugar
Grated rind of 1 lemon
3 eggs

Oven: 350°F; gas mark 4; 20-25 minutes

Roll out the pastry and line 16 patty tins. Boil the milk and stir in the breadcrumbs; leave for 10 minutes. Add the butter, ground almonds, sugar and lemon rind to the milk and beat in the eggs, one at a time.

Fill the patty tins and bake until set.

Clee Saucer Cheesecakes Lincolnshire

Served with stuffed chine of bacon on Trinity Sunday in Clee.

1 lb rich shortcrust pastry
½ lb curds
6 oz caster sugar
Pinch salt and nutmeg
Grated rind of ½ lemon
6 egg yolks
2 oz chopped citron peel

Oven: 350°F; gas mark 4; 45 minutes

Roll out the pastry and use to line eight well buttered ovenproof saucers. Mix the curds, sugar, salt, nutmeg and lemon rind with the egg yolks and beat to a stiff paste. Spread this mixture over the pastry and decorate with chopped citron peel.

Bake in the oven until golden and serve at once.

Coconut Cheesecakes

½ lb rich shortcrust pastry
6 oz fresh grated coconut and coconut milk or
    6 oz desiccated coconut and 5 fl oz water
6 oz caster sugar
5 eggs
Grated rind of 1 lemon
1 tablespoon brandy (optional)

Oven: 350°F; gas mark 4; 20-25 minutes

Roll out the pastry and use to line 16 patty tins. If using fresh grated coconut put this, with the coconut milk and sugar, in a pan and simmer over low heat until the coconut is tender. Leave to cool.

Alternatively, mix desiccated coconut with the water and sugar.

Mix the beaten eggs, lemon rind and brandy into the coconut mixture; spoon this filling into the pastry cases and bake for about 20 minutes.

Country Cheesecakes

½ lb rich shortcrust pastry
Fresh curds from 3 pt milk
1 oz butter
1 tablespoon cream
6 oz caster sugar
2 teaspoons grated nutmeg
2½ oz currants
2 eggs
2½ fl oz brandy or wine

Oven: 350°F; gas mark 4; 25-30 minutes

Line 16 patty tins with the rolled out pastry, setting the trimmings aside for strips to lay over the cakes.

Rub the curds through a sieve, beat with the butter and cream until smooth, then add the sugar, nutmeg and currants. Blend in the beaten eggs and the brandy and spoon the mixture into the lined patty tins.

Top each cake with two narrow pastry strips in the form of a cross. Bake for about 25 minutes.

Curd Cheesecakes

¾ lb rich shortcrust pastry
¾ lb fresh curds
6 oz butter
4 oz caster sugar
2 oz ground almonds
4 oz currants

2 tablespoons double cream
½ teaspoon grated nutmeg
2 teaspoons ground cinnamon
4 eggs
5 fl oz sherry or Madeira

Oven: 350°F; gas mark 4; 20-25 minutes

Roll out the pastry and line 24 patty tins. Rub the curds through a sieve and beat with the butter until smooth; add the sugar, almonds, currants, cream, nutmeg and cinnamon, beating thoroughly.

Stir in the beaten eggs and the sherry; spoon the mixture into the patty cases and bake for about 20 minutes.

Curd Tarts I Yorkshire

½ lb rich shortcrust pastry
½ lb curds
4 oz caster sugar
2 oz currants
2 eggs
Grated nutmeg

Oven: 350°F; gas mark 4; 25-30 minutes

Roll out the pastry and use to line 16-18 patty tins. Mix the curds with the sugar, currants and beaten eggs; spoon into the patty cases and sprinkle with nutmeg. Bake until set and golden.

Curd Tarts II Yorkshire

½ lb rich shortcrust pastry
½ lb curds
2½ fl oz cream
2 eggs
2 oz caster sugar
Vanilla essence
Juice and rind of 1 lemon

Oven: 350°F; gas mark 4; 25-30 minutes

Line 16-18 patty cases with shortcrust pastry. Rub the curds through a coarse sieve and beat in the cream, egg yolks, sugar, a few drops of vanilla essence and the lemon juice and rind. Beat the egg whites stiffly and fold into the mixture.

Fill into the patty cases and bake.

Farmhouse Cheesecakes

½ lb rich shortcrust pastry

Fresh curds from 1 pt warm milk and 1 teaspoon rennet
4 oz butter
4 oz caster sugar
3 eggs
2-4 tablespoons brandy
Juice and grated rind of 1 lemon
1-2 oz currants
Grated nutmeg

Oven: 350°F; gas mark 4; 25-30 minutes

Line 16 patty tins with rolled out pastry. Rub the fresh curds through a coarse sieve and blend to a smooth mixture with the butter, sugar, eggs beaten with the brandy, and the lemon juice and rind.

Fill the patty cases with this mixture and sprinkle the tops with currants and nutmeg. Bake for about 25 minutes.

Ground Rice Cheesecakes

½ lb rich shortcrust pastry
3 oz ground rice
5 fl oz cold milk
1 pt boiling milk
3 oz butter
3 oz caster sugar
Grated rind of 1 lemon
½ teaspoon ground cinnamon
5 eggs
1 tablespoon brandy

Oven: 350°F; gas mark 5; 20-25 minutes

Roll out the pastry and line 16-20 patty tins. Mix the rice with the cold milk until smooth, gradually add the boiling milk stirring well. Simmer over gentle heat for 10 minutes, then add the butter, sugar, lemon rind and cinnamon.

Set aside to cool before mixing in the eggs beaten with brandy. Spoon the filling into the pastry cases and bake for about 20 minutes.

Hot Apple Cheesecakes

¾ lb rich shortcrust pastry
½ lb caster sugar
½ oz rice flour
4 oz ground almonds
3 egg whites
½ teaspoon vanilla essence
9 oz sieved apple pulp
4½ oz cake crumbs

Icing sugar

Oven: 350°F; gas mark 4; 25 minutes

Line 24 patty tins with the rolled out pastry.
Make a macaroon mixture by mixing the caster
sugar with rice flour and ground almonds and
working this to a smooth blend with the unbeaten
egg whites and vanilla essence. Set aside.

Mix the apple pulp with the cake crumbs and
half fill the pastry cases with this mixture; cover
with the macaroon topping and bake. Serve hot,
dredged with icing sugar.

Lemon Cheesecakes

½ lb rich shortcrust pastry
4 oz ground almonds
1½ oz melted butter
3 egg yolks
2 oz caster sugar
Juice and rind of 1 lemon
5 fl oz double cream

Oven: 350°F; gas mark 4; 20-25 minutes

Roll out the pastry and use to line 16 patty tins.
Mix the ground almonds, butter, egg yolks and
sugar with the lemon juice and finely grated rind;
stir in the cream. Spoon the lemon mixture into
the lined patty tins and bake.

Lemon or Orange Cheesecakes

½ lb rich shortcrust pastry
Juice and rind of 1½ lemons or oranges
5½ oz melted butter
2½ oz ground almonds
2½ oz caster sugar
4 egg yolks
7½ fl oz cream

Oven: 350°F; gas mark 4; 25-30 minutes

Line 16 patty tins with the rolled out pastry.
Grate the lemon or orange rind finely, extract the
juice and mix peel and juice with the butter,
ground almonds, sugar and egg yolks. Blend in the
cream and spoon the filling into the pastry cases.

Bake for about 25 minutes or until the filling
has set.

Northamptonshire Cheesecakes
Northamptonshire

½ lb rich shortcrust pastry

Fresh curds made from 2 pt sour milk
2 oz butter
2 eggs
3 oz caster sugar
4 oz currants
Grated rind of 2 lemons
Almond essence
Pinch grated nutmeg

Oven: 350°F; gas mark 4; 25-30 minutes

Roll out the pastry and line 16 patty tins. Press
the freshly made curds smooth; put the butter,
eggs and sugar in a pan and heat gently, until
thickened. Do not allow to boil. Remove from
the heat; add the curds, currants and lemon rind
and flavour with a few drops of almond essence.

Fill the patty cases with the mixture, sprinkle
with grated nutmeg and bake.

Orange Cheesecakes

½ lb rich shortcrust pastry
3 tablespoons cream
4 oz sponge biscuits or cakes
4 oz butter
4 oz icing sugar
1 teaspoon grated nutmeg
Grated rind of 1 Seville orange
3 eggs
1 tablespoon brandy

Oven: 350°F; gas mark 4; 20-25 minutes

Line 16-20 patty tins with the rolled out pastry.
Spoon the cream over the diced sponge cakes or
biscuits and beat to a smooth texture with the
butter and sugar, nutmeg and orange rind.

Beat the eggs thoroughly with the brandy and
mix into the orange mixture; fill into the lined
patty tins and bake.

Potato Cheesecakes

½ lb rich shortcrust pastry
4 oz thinly peeled lemon rind
4 oz icing sugar
6 oz mashed potatoes
4 oz clarified butter
4 egg yolks
2 egg whites

Oven: 350°F; gas mark 4; 20-25 minutes

Roll out the pastry and use to line 16-20 patty
tins. Simmer the lemon peel in a little water until

tender, strain and chop finely. Mix the peel
with the icing sugar and stir in the mashed potatoes, creamed with the butter.

Stir to a smooth mixture, then add the lightly
beaten egg yolks and whites. Spoon the filling into
the pastry cases and bake for about 20 minutes or
until set.

Richmond Maids of Honour I Surrey

There are several recipes for these classic little
curd cakes which, according to one tradition,
derived their name from the Maids of Honour
attending Queen Elizabeth I at the Palace of
Richmond; yet another tradition claims that
the cakes were a favourite delicacy of Anne
Boleyn's and her entourage and were given their
nickname by Henry VIII.

½ lb rich shortcrust pastry
4 oz dry curds
3 oz butter
2 eggs
2½ fl oz brandy
3 oz caster sugar
3 oz floury baked potatoes
1 oz ground almonds
¼ teaspoon grated nutmeg
Grated rind of 1½ lemons
Juice of ½ lemon

Oven: 350°F; gas mark 4; 20-25 minutes

Roll the pastry out thinly and use to line 16 patty
tins; sieve the curds and mix with the softened
butter; beat the eggs with the brandy and sugar
and blend into the curd mixture.

Mix the potatoes with the almonds, nutmeg,
lemon rind and juice; stir into the curds, mixing
well. Fill the lined patty tins and bake until set.

Richmond Maids of Honour II

The fresh curds in this version are made from 2 pt
fresh milk, 2 pt boiling water, lemon juice and 2
beaten eggs.

¾ lb rich shortcrust pastry
½ lb fresh curds
4 egg yolks
7-8 fl oz clotted cream
Grated rind of 1 lemon
Pinch cinnamon and nutmeg
6 oz currants
2 oz caster sugar

5 fl oz brandy

Oven: 350°F; gas mark 4; 20-25 minutes

Roll out the pastry and line 24 patty tins. Mix the
fresh curds with the beaten egg yolks, clotted
cream, lemon rind, cinnamon, nutmeg, currants,
sugar and brandy. Blend thoroughly, spoon into
the patty tins and bake.

Richmond Maids of Honour III

In this variation, the fresh curds are made from
new milk and rennet.

10 oz rich shortcrust pastry
½ lb fresh curds
4 oz butter
3 eggs
1 tablespoon brandy
4 oz caster sugar
Pinch cinnamon
½ oz chopped blanched almonds
Juice and rind of 1 lemon
2 tablespoons orange flower water
2 oz currants

Oven: 350°F; gas mark 4; 20-25 minutes

Line 16-20 patty tins with the rolled out pastry.
Rub the fresh curds through a coarse sieve and
blend with the softened butter. Beat the eggs with
the brandy and add to the curds with the sugar,
cinnamon, almonds, lemon rind and juice and
orange flower water; mix well. Fill the lined
patty tins, sprinkle with currants and bake.

Seventeenth Century Cheesecakes

½ lb rich shortcrust pastry
1 pt double cream
4 eggs
4 oz butter
4 oz caster sugar
4 oz currants
Nutmeg and cinnamon
2 tablespoons brandy

Oven: 350°F; gas mark 4; 25-30 minutes

Line 16-18 patty tins with the pastry. Boil the
cream and eggs until the mixture curdles; strain
the curds in muslin until all the liquid has dripped
through. Soften the butter and beat with the
sugar, currants, pinch each of nutmeg and cinnamon and the brandy.

Fold in the cream curds and spoon the mixture into the patty tins. Bake for about 25 minutes.

Welsh Cheesecakes

½ lb rich shortcrust pastry
Raspberry jam
2 eggs
2 oz caster sugar
2 oz plain flour

Oven: 375°F; gas mark 5; 20-25 minutes

Roll out the pastry and use to line 16-20 patty tins. Put half a teaspoon of raspberry jam over the base of each case; whisk the eggs in a bowl set over a pan of hot water and gradually beat in the sugar. Whisk until thick and pale, then carefully fold in the sifted flour.

Place this sponge mixture equally over the jam and bake the cakes for about 20 minutes or until well-risen and golden.

PASTRY CAKES

These are small variations of large sweet pies and may be made with shortcrust, flaky or puff pastry, with a variety of fillings, often with regional connections. These range from the rich Banbury Cakes from Oxfordshire to the plainer than plain Flead Cakes from Kent which consisted of thin rounds of flead pastry brushed with beaten egg.

Banbury Cakes Oxfordshire

The traditional shape of these little puff pastry cakes is an elongated oval with the pastry crust rising in a dome over the filling of mincemeat.

½ lb butter
½ lb finely chopped lemon and orange peel
1 lb currants
2-3 teaspoons cinnamon
2½ oz allspice
1 lb puff pastry
Egg white
Sugar

Oven: 425°F; gas mark 7; 15 minutes

Make up the mincemeat mixture by creaming the butter until soft and fluffy, then blending in the peel and currants and flavouring with cinnamon and allspice.

Roll the pastry out thinly and cut into 4 in rounds or squares. Spread a layer of mincemeat over half the pastry rounds, moisten the edges and cover with the other pastry rounds. Press and seal the edges firmly and make a small slit in each pastry for the steam to escape. Brush the tops with beaten egg white and sprinkle with coarse sugar.

Bake in a hot oven for about 15 minutes and serve hot or cold.

Belem Tarts Ireland

½ lb flaky pastry
10 egg yolks
½ lb caster sugar
Salt
1 pt double cream
Cinnamon

Oven: 400°F; gas mark 6; 20 minutes

Roll out the pastry and use to line 16 patty tins. Beat the egg yolks with the sugar, a pinch of salt and the cream until smooth. Spoon this filling into the pastry cases, sprinkle with ground cinnamon and bake for about 20 minutes.

Chester Cakes Cheshire

½ lb rich shortcrust pastry
4 oz plain flour
1 teaspoon ground ginger
4 oz stale cake crumbs
½ oz currants
3 oz black treacle or syrup

Oven: 400°F; gas mark 6; 30-40 minutes

Roll out the pastry and line a greased, 8 in square and 2 in deep cake tin with two thirds of the pastry.

Mix the flour with the ginger, cake crumbs and currants and bind to a stiff mixture with the treacle. Spread this over the pastry base and cover with the remaining pastry; seal the edges and mark the top into small squares with a knife.

Bake for 30-40 minutes and leave to cool before cutting the pastry into the marked squares.

Chorley Cakes Lancashire

1 lb rich shortcrust pastry
4 oz currants
Icing sugar

Oven: 350°F; gas mark 4; 25-30 minutes

Roll the pastry out, ¼ in thick, and cut into four rounds, the size of a dinner plate. Place the currants in the centre of the circles, bring the moistened edges together and press to seal; roll out the cakes until the currants show through, keeping to the round shapes. Bake for 30 minutes and sprinkle with icing sugar when cool.

Cornish Heavy Cake Cornwall

1 lb plain flour
Pinch salt
1 lb butter
6 oz currants
Milk

Oven: 450°F; gas mark 8; 10 minutes
       400°F; gas mark 6; 20 minutes

Sift the flour and salt; divide the butter into four equal parts and rub one quarter into the flour until the mixture has a crumbly texture. Add the currants and enough cold water to give an elastic dough. Knead lightly and roll out to an oblong shape.

Dot two thirds of the pastry with another quarter of butter; fold in the pastry, turn and roll out again. Repeat the process of dotting with butter, folding, turning and rolling out twice more until all the butter is used up.

Roll the pastry out to a rectangle, 1 in thick, score the surface in a diamond pattern and brush with milk. Bake for 30 minutes, reducing the temperature after 10 minutes.

Coventry God Cakes Warwickshire

1 lb rough puff or flaky pastry
½ lb mincemeat
1 egg white
Caster sugar

Oven: 425°F; gas mark 7; 20-25 minutes

Roll the pastry out, very thinly, and cut into triangles. Place a little mincemeat in the centre of half the triangles. Moisten the edges and cover with the other triangles. Press well together and make two slits in the centre.

Bake for 20 minutes. Brush with egg white, sprinkle with sugar and return to the oven for 5 minutes to settle the glaze.

Eccles Cakes Lancashire

1 lb puff pastry or shortcrust pastry
4 oz currants
2 oz butter
2 oz brown sugar
1 egg white
Caster sugar

Oven: 425°F; gas mark 7; 20-25 minutes

Roll the pastry out, ¼ in thick, and cut into 4-6 in rounds. Mix the currants with the butter and sugar and place a heaped teaspoonful in the centre of each round. Moisten the edges with water, gather together and pinch to seal. Turn each round over and roll out until the fruit is just showing through.

Score across the top in a diamond pattern, brush with egg white and sprinkle with caster sugar. Bake until golden and risen.

Fig Sly Cake

½ lb rich shortcrust pastry
3 oz chopped cooked figs
1½ oz chopped walnuts
1 oz currants
¾ oz raisins
1 oz caster sugar

Oven: 425°F; gas mark 7; 20 minutes

Roll the pastry out into two thin rounds. Mix the figs, walnuts, currants and raisins with the sugar and arrange this mixture over one pastry round. Moisten the edges, cover with the other pastry round and seal the edges firmly.

Set on a greased baking tray; brush the top with a sugar and water glaze and bake for about 20 minutes.

Kentish Cheese Pasties Kent

½ lb flaky pastry
4 oz grated cheese
Salt, cayenne pepper
1 egg

Oven: 425°F; gas mark 7; 15-20 minutes

Roll out the pastry, very thinly, and cut into rounds the size of a saucer. Divide the cheese equally between the pastry rounds and sprinkle with salt and cayenne.

Fold up the edges and seal; brush the pasties with beaten egg and bake until golden brown.

Lancashire Sly Cake Lancashire

Cumberland Currant Cakes are similar to Lancashire Sly Cake, but the filling consists of 6 oz currants, 2 oz chopped mixed peel and 2 teaspoons mixed spice.

¾ lb plain flour
1½ oz caster sugar
½ teaspoon mixed spice
6 oz butter
6 fl oz cold water
½ lb currants
5 fl oz rum

Oven: 425°F; gas mark 7; 20 minutes

Sift the flour and mix in the sugar and spice. Divide the butter into four portions and rub one quarter into the flour to give a crumbly texture; mix with the water to give an elastic dough. Knead lightly and roll out to a long rectangle.

Dot two thirds of the dough with another quarter of the butter; fold up as for flaky pastry, turn and roll out. Dot with another quarter of butter, fold, turn and roll out. Repeat with the remaining butter and leave the pastry to rest for at least 10 minutes before using. Steep the currants in rum.

Divide the pastry in half, and roll each half out to a round or square. Spread the rum-soaked currants on one pastry round, cover with the other round and seal the edges. Brush the top with a sugar and water glaze and bake for about 20 minutes.

Teisen Planc or Plank Pastry Wales

¾ lb sweet shortcrust pastry
4-6 oz jam
Caster sugar

Roll out the pastry, ¼ in thick, and cut into two rounds, each the size of a dinner plate. Spread one pastry round with jam to within 1 in of the edge; place the other round on top and seal the edges. Bake on a bakestone (griddle) until golden brown; turn and bake on the other side.

Serve hot, sprinkled with sugar.

Three Deckers Westmorland

¾ lb sweet shortcrust pastry
1 lb prepared fruit (apple, rhubarb, black currants, etc.)
6 oz caster sugar

Oven: 350°F; gas mark 4; 1 hour

Roll out the pastry and cut into three rounds the size of a 7 in round cake tin. Place one pastry round in the tin, spread with half the prepared fruit and sprinkle with sugar. Cover with another pastry round and the remaining fruit and sugar.

Top with the last pastry round and bake for about 1 hour. Serve hot, sprinkled with sugar.

BISCUITS

The plain biscuit is a direct descendant of the original hard and flat bread. Until the middle of the 16th century, bread was synonymous with bisket or biscuit, made from flour and water, without salt or leaven; the biskets were generally baked twice in order to reduce the water content and improve the keeping qualities.

This type of bread was commonly used on long sea voyages and was referred to as sea biscuit. Today, the original concept of the plain biscuit is perpetuated in water biscuits and other types consisting merely of cereal and water, such as the Scottish oatcakes, which are dried and hardened although not necessarily baked twice.

The Biddenden Biscuits were probably of the plain type in their original form; they commemorate the Siamese twins, Eliza and Mary Chulkhurst, born around 1100 in the little village of Biddenden in Kent. On their death, at the age of 34, they left the village a large plot of land to be used for charity for the poor; their generosity is remembered in the annual distribution, on Easter Monday, of small cakes or biscuits stamped with an imprint of the sisters' figures.

Today, most biscuits are of the sweet enriched type, sometimes incorporating a raising agent or eggs as well as butter, sugar and various flavourings. They do, however, resemble the original hard biscuit in having a low moisture content. They are in general made either by the creaming or the rubbing-in methods.

Abernethy Biscuits Scotland

The original Abernethy Biscuit was a hard, un-leavened biscuit flavoured with caraway seeds.

2-4 tablespoons milk
4 oz caster sugar
2 oz margarine
2 oz lard
½ lb plain flour
¾ teaspoon baking powder

Oven: 325°F; gas mark 3; 30 minutes

Bring the milk and sugar to the boil and set aside. Rub the margarine and lard into the sifted flour, add the baking powder and milk and knead the dough. Roll out, ¼ in thick, and cut into rounds with a 2½ in cutter.

Set the biscuits on greased baking trays; prick the centres with a fork and bake.

Bath Olivers

These are thought to be the original digestive biscuits and were made from white flour, milk, butter, malt and hops. They were devised by a Doctor Oliver of Bath for medicinal purposes and recommended to any overweight patient.

Blackburn Cracknels Lancashire

1 lb plain flour
4 oz lard
1 oz baking powder
½ pt warm milk

Oven: 325°F; gas mark 3; 30 minutes

Sift the flour, rub in the lard and add the baking powder. Work in the milk to a smooth dough and knead thoroughly.

Roll out, 1/8 in thick, and cut into 3 in rounds; set on greased baking sheets, prick with a fork and bake.

Blackness Porcupines

4 oz chopped walnuts
4 oz chopped dates
4 oz caster sugar
1 egg
1 teaspoon lemon juice
2 oz melted butter
4 oz desiccated coconut (optional)

Oven: 350°F; gas mark 4; 20-25 minutes

Mix the walnuts, dates and sugar and gather to a soft mixture with the beaten egg, lemon juice and melted butter. Divide into walnut-sized pieces, roll in coconut and set on greased baking sheets. Bake until brown.

Bosworth Jumbles Leicestershire

The recipe for those biscuits is said to have been picked up on the battlefield of Bosworth where King Richard III's cook had dropped it.

6 oz butter
1 lb caster sugar
1 egg
½ lb plain flour

Oven: 350°F; gas mark 4; 25 minutes

Cream the butter and sugar until light and fluffy, then beat in the egg; add the flour and mix to a stiff consistency. Shape the dough into small "S" forms and place on greased baking trays. Bake for 25 minutes.

Chester Fingers Cheshire

4 oz butter
4 oz caster sugar
3 eggs
6 oz plain flour
½ teaspoon baking powder
4 oz ground almonds
4-6 oz jam
Glacé icing

Oven: 350°F; gas mark 4; 25-30 minutes

Cream the butter and sugar until light and fluffy; beat in the eggs and add the sifted flour, baking powder and ground almonds. Gather to a smooth dough and spread over a greased, flat cake tin.

Prick with a fork and bake for about 30 minutes; cut the cake into fingers while still warm. Leave to cool, then sandwich together with jam and cover with glacé icing.

Cream Crackers

4 oz butter or lard
1 lb plain flour
¾ teaspoon baking powder
Pinch salt
Milk

Oven: 375°F; gas mark 5; 30 minutes

Rub the fat into the flour, sifted with baking powder and salt. Mix with milk to a stiff dough and knead thoroughly.

Roll the dough out as thinly as possible and cut into 2 in squares. Prick well. Place on greased baking trays, and bake until crisp, turning the crackers over half way through baking.

Derby Cakes Derbyshire

1 lb plain flour
½ lb butter
½ lb soft brown sugar
½ lb currants
1 egg
5 fl oz milk

Oven: 350°F; gas mark 4; 10 minutes

Sift the flour, rub in the butter to a crumbly mixture; add the sugar and currants and mix to a stiff consistency with the beaten egg and the milk.

Knead the dough thoroughly and roll it out, ¼ in thick; cut into small round cakes, about 36, and set on greased baking sheets.

Prick with a fork and bake for 10 minutes.

Derbyshire Oatcakes Derbyshire

1 lb fine oatmeal
¼ oz fresh yeast
½ tablespoon caster sugar
1 pt warm water
½ tablespoon salt

Cream the yeast with the sugar and add the water. Mix this into the oatmeal with the salt; stir until smooth, then leave the mixture to rest for 2 hours.

Pour one cupful at a time on to a hot greased griddle; turn when brown and cook on the other side. Serve cold, split and buttered.

Devon Flats Devonshire

1 lb plain flour
½ pt Devonshire cream
½ lb caster sugar
1 egg
Milk

Oven: 425°F; gas mark 7; 10 minutes

Sift the flour. Mix into the cream and add the sugar, beaten egg and enough milk to give a smooth, stiff dough.

Roll the mixture out very thinly and cut into 2 in rounds. Set on greased baking trays and bake.

Devonshire Biscuits Devon

½ lb plain flour
4 oz butter
4 oz caster sugar
1 oz ground almonds
2 egg yolks
5 fl oz milk (optional)

Oven: 350°F; gas mark 4; 15 minutes

Sift the flour and rub in the butter; add the sugar and ground almonds. Mix to a stiff paste with the egg yolks, adding milk if necessary.

Roll the dough out, ¼ in thick, and cut into 2½ in rounds. Set on greased baking trays, prick and bake.

Dundee Biscuits Scotland

4 oz butter
½ lb plain flour
2 oz caster sugar
1 egg white
2 oz blanched, toasted and roughly chopped almonds

Oven: 325°F; gas mark 3; 30 minutes

Rub the butter into the sifted flour, add the sugar and gather to a stiff dough, using a beaten egg yolk if necessary.

Knead thoroughly and roll out ¼ in thick; cut into rounds with a 2 in cutter and set on greased baking trays. Brush the biscuits with beaten egg white and sprinkle with the toasted, chopped almonds. Bake for about 30 minutes.

Fat Rascals I Yorkshire

There are two types of these, one made from a biscuit dough and one from a scone mixture.

½ lb butter
1 lb plain flour
½ teaspoon salt
4 oz currants
1 oz soft brown sugar
Milk and water
Caster sugar

Oven: 425°F; gas mark 7; 10-15 minutes

Rub the butter into the flour sifted with the salt; add the currants and brown sugar.

Mix to a stiff dough with milk and water; roll out, ½ in thick, and cut into small rounds. Dust with caster sugar and bake until golden brown.

Fat Rascals II

1 lb self-raising flour
1 teaspoon salt
½ lb lard
3 oz caster sugar
2 oz currants
1 oz sultanas
2 eggs
5 fl oz milk

Oven: 425°F; gas mark 7; 10 minutes

Sift the flour and salt, rub in the lard until the mixture in evenly crumbly, then add the sugar, currants and sultanas; mix to a soft dough with the beaten eggs and the milk.

Roll the dough out, ½ in thick, on a floured surface and cut into small rounds; set on greased baking trays and bake until golden.

Fife Bannocks Scotland

6 oz plain flour
½ oz butter
4 oz fine oatmeal
½ teaspoon bicarbonate of soda
¾ teaspoon cream of tartar
½ tablespoon sugar
Pinch salt
Milk or buttermilk

Oven: 425°F; gas mark 7; 10 minutes

Sift the flour and rub in the butter; add the oatmeal, bicarbonate of soda, cream of tartar, sugar and a pinch of salt. Mix to a stiff dough with a little milk or buttermilk.

Knead the dough lightly and roll out; ¼-½ in thick, and shape into rounds, squares or triangles. Cook until brown on both sides on a greased griddle or bake in a hot oven for 10 minutes.

Figgie Hobbin Cornwall

½ lb plain flour
¾ teaspoon baking powder

2 oz chopped suet
2 oz lard
½ lb dried chopped figs
2-3 fl oz milk

Oven: 400°F; gas mark 6; 30 minutes

Sift the flour and baking powder, rub in the suet and lard and mix with the chopped figs. Blend in enough milk to give a stiff dough.

Roll the dough out, ½ in thick, on a floured surface and cut into 4 in squares. Set on greased baking trays, score the surfaces lightly and bake.

Gipsy Creams

2 oz margarine
2 oz lard
2 oz sugar
4 oz plain flour
1 teaspoon bicarbonate of soda
4 oz porridge oats
3 tablespoons water
1 teaspoon syrup or jam
Chocolate butter icing

Oven: 350°F; gas mark 4; 30 minutes

Cream the margarine and lard with the sugar until fluffy; mix in the flour, bicarbonate of soda and oats and gather to a stiff dough with the water and syrup.

Knead the dough lightly and shape into small balls; set on greased baking trays, allowing room for spreading, and bake. When cold, sandwich with chocolate butter icing.

Goosenargh Cakes Lancashire

¾ lb butter
1 lb plain flour
2 oz caster sugar
Caraway seeds and coriander seeds

Oven: 350°F; gas mark 4; 20 minutes

Rub the butter into the sifted flour; knead to a smooth dough and roll out into a square, ½ in thick. Set on a baking tray, sprinkle with sugar and caraway seeds and leave to rest in a cool place for 8 hours.

Bake for about 20 minutes and cut into small squares while still warm.

Hampshire Drops Hampshire

4 oz butter
4 oz caster sugar
2 eggs
4 oz cornflour
4 oz plain flour
½ teaspoon baking powder
Jam

Oven: 325°F; gas mark 3; 30 minutes

Cream the butter with the sugar until fluffy, beat
in the eggs and mix in the cornflour and flour
sifted with the baking powder. Mix to a fairly
stiff consistency.

Drop teaspoons of the mixture on to greased
baking trays and bake. Leave the biscuits to cool,
then sandwich together with jam.

Imperial Biscuits

½ lb butter
½ lb caster sugar
1 egg
1 lb plain flour
1½ teaspoons baking powder
2 teaspoons ground cinnamon (optional)
Jam
Glacé icing
Glacé cherries

Oven: 325°F; gas mark 3; 30 minutes

Cream the butter and sugar until light and fluffy;
beat in the egg and fold in the sifted flour and
baking powder, with the cinnamon if used. Knead
the dough lightly and roll out, ¼ in thick.

Cut into 3 in rounds, set on greased baking
trays and prick with a fork. Bake and cool.

Sandwich the biscuits together with jam, cover
with glacé icing and decorate each biscuit with
half a cherry.

Irish Shortcakes Ireland

1 lb plain flour
4 oz bacon fat or lard
4 oz caster sugar
6 oz currants
1½ teaspoons baking powder
1 egg
Milk

Oven: 350°F; gas mark 4; 30 minutes·

Sift the flour and rub in the fat; add the sugar,
currants and baking powder and mix to a stiff
dough with the lightly beaten egg and a little
milk if necessary.

Roll out, ½ in thick, and cut into 2½-3 in rounds
or squares, set on greased baking sheets. Prick
closely with a fork and bake for 30 minutes.

Jumbles

4 oz butter
6 oz caster sugar
1 egg
Grated rind of 1 lemon
6 oz plain flour

Oven: 325°F; gas mark 3; 30 minutes

Cream the butter and sugar until light and fluffy,
beat in the egg and lemon rind and fold in the
sifted flour.

Divide the mixture into three portions and
roll each into a long sausage shape, about ½ in
wide; cut these into 3-4 in pieces and set in the
form of an "S" on greased baking trays. Bake
until light brown.

Lancashire Nuts Lancashire

4 oz butter
4 oz caster sugar
1 egg
4 oz plain flour
½ teaspoon baking powder
4 oz cornflour

Filling:
4 oz softened butter
½ lb icing sugar
1-2 tablespoons warm water or milk

Oven: 325°F; gas mark 3; 30 minutes

Cream the butter and sugar until light and
fluffy, beat in the egg and mix in the flour sifted
with the baking powder and the cornflour. Mix to
a smooth dough of stiff consistency.

Roll the mixture into balls the size of a walnut,
using a little flour to prevent sticking. Place on
greased baking trays and bake.

Make up a butter cream filling from the softened butter beaten until fluffy; gradually beat in the
icing sugar and add water or milk to give a spreading consistency. When the biscuits have cooled,
sandwich with the butter cream filling.

Macaroons

3 egg whites
½ lb caster sugar
4 oz ground almonds
½ oz rice flour
½ teaspoon vanilla essence
Rice paper
Blanched chopped almonds

Oven: 350°F; gas mark 4; 20 minutes

Beat the egg whites stiff, fold in the sugar, ground almonds, rice flour and vanilla essence. Using a plain nozzle, pipe the mixture in 1 inch rounds on to rice paper, setting them well apart on baking sheets. Sprinkle with finely chopped almonds and bake.

Mazarins

2 oz butter
1 tablespoon caster sugar
1 egg yolk
4 oz plain flour
1 oz ground almonds
Raspberry jam
1 egg white
4 oz granulated sugar
½ oz grated chocolate
2 oz blanched, roughly chopped almonds

Oven: 350°F; gas mark 4; 10-15 minutes
        325°F; gas mark 3; 15-20 minutes

Cream the butter and caster sugar until light; beat in the egg yolk and blend in the flour and ground almonds. Knead to a stiff dough, roll out and cut into two strips 4 in wide and 10 in long. Cut a ¼ in strip from each long side and place on top of the pastry edges to form a raised edge; set on a greased baking tray and bake in the oven for 10-15 minutes.

Remove from the oven and spread each strip with jam. Beat the egg white until frothy and fold in the sugar, chocolate and almonds. Stir this mixture over gentle heat until boiling, then spoon over the two pastry strips.

Return to the oven, and bake for 15-20 minutes or until the topping is firm and glossy. Cut into fingers while still hot.

Melting Moments

½ lb butter

6 oz plain flour
2 oz cornflour
2 oz icing sugar
Glacé cherries

Oven: 350°F; gas mark 4; 20-30 minutes

Melt the butter in a pan; remove from the heat and fold in the sifted flour, cornflour and sugar. Work to a smooth paste and shape into small balls.

Set on greased baking trays, flattening the balls slightly. Decorate with halved cherries and bake for about 20 minutes.

Oatcakes Scotland

½ tablespoon melted fat
¼ teaspoon salt
½ teaspoon bicarbonate of soda
½ lb fine oatmeal
Lukewarm water

Add the fat, salt and bicarbonate of soda to the oatmeal, mix with enough lukewarm water to make a stiff but pliable dough. Roll out in oatmeal, 1/8 in thick.

Cut the dough round a dinner plate to make one large round and cut this into quarters; alternatively, cut the rolled out mixture into small rounds or triangles.

Bake on a fairly hot griddle, for 5 minutes, turning once; finish off in a hot oven for a few minutes.

Petticoat Tails

These little biscuits are cut like a full, hooped petticoat, the centre of the dough being cut out to avoid points on the brittle biscuits.

½ lb butter
6 oz icing sugar
¾ lb plain flour
Water
Caster sugar

Oven: 325°F; gas mark 3; 30-40 minutes

Cream the butter and sifted icing sugar, fold in the flour and mix to a stiff dough with water. Roll out to a round, ¼ in thick. Cut out a small circle from the centre with a tumbler and remove; cut the outer circle into eight wedges, bake for 30-40 minutes and dust with caster sugar.

Pitcaithly Bannock Scotland

4 oz butter
3 oz caster sugar
5 oz plain flour
1 oz rice flour
1 oz blanched chopped almonds
1 oz chopped candied citron peel
Caraway seeds
Chopped candied orange peel

Oven: 350°F; gas mark 4; 1 hour

Knead the butter and sugar until thoroughly
blended on a marble or wooden slab; sift over
the flour and rice flour and work gradually into
the butter; mix in the almonds and citron peel.

Shape the mixture into a round, ¾ in thick,
and sprinkle caraway seeds and orange peel over
the top. Tie a narrow band of greaseproof paper
round the cake to prevent it spreading and to
keep the edges from becoming burnt. Bake for
1 hour; cool before serving.

Reay Biscuits

6 oz butter or margarine
½ lb plain flour
¾ teaspoon baking powder
½ lb caster sugar
Ground rice

Oven: 325°F; gas mark 3; 30 minutes

Rub the butter into the sifted flour, add the
baking powder and sugar and mix to a stiff dough.
Knead thoroughly; sprinkle the board with
ground rice and roll out the dough, ¼ in thick.
Cut into small rounds, squares, triangles or fancy
shapes.

Set on greased baking sheets, prick with a
fork and bake for about 30 minutes.

Shortbread Scotland

½ lb butter
4 oz caster sugar
½ lb plain flour
4 oz rice flour
Pinch salt

Oven: 425°F; gas mark 7; 5 minutes
       325°F; gas mark 3; 30-40 minutes

Place the butter and sugar on a board and knead
until thoroughly blended. Sift the flour and rice
flour with a pinch of salt over the board and
gradually work these into the butter and sugar.
Keep the butter cool by ideally working the mixture on a marble slab.

When all the flour is incorporated, shape the
dough into ½ in thick and 8 in wide rounds with
the hand or a shortbread mould. Pinch the edges
neatly all round with the finger and thumb; set
on greased baking trays and prick closely with a
fork. The mixture may also be shaped into strips
and cut into fingers.

Bake in a hot oven, reducing the temperature after 5 minutes. Leave to cool before removing from the trays or tins; sprinkle with sugar.

Ayrshire Shortbread Scotland

4 oz butter
4 oz plain flour
4 oz rice flour
2 oz caster sugar
1 egg
1 tablespoon cream

Oven: 350°F; gas mark 4; 30 minutes

Rub the butter into the sifted flour; add the rice
flour and sugar and mix to a stiff dough with the
egg and cream. Knead well and turn out on a
floured board; roll out, ¾ in thick, and cut into
rounds with a 2½ in cutter.

Set on greased baking trays, prick with a fork
and bake. Sprinkle with sugar while still hot.

Shrewsbury Biscuits Shropshire

½ lb butter
½ lb caster sugar
1 egg
2½ fl oz double cream
1 dessertspoon sherry or rose water
Caraway seeds
½ lb plain flour

Oven: 325°F; gas mark 3; 30 minutes

Cream the butter and sugar until light and fluffy,
beat in the egg and mix in the cream and sherry
with a few caraway seeds. Fold in the sifted flour
and mix to a stiff consistency.

Roll the mixture out thinly and cut into
rounds 1½ in wide. Place on a baking tray and
rest in the refrigerator for 15 minutes before
baking for about 30 minutes.

Shrewsbury Cakes Shropshire

½ lb butter
½ lb caster sugar
1 egg
¾ lb flour
Rind and juice of ½ lemon
2½ fl oz cream

Oven: 375°F; gas mark 5; 15-20 minutes

Cream the butter and sugar until light and fluffy;
beat in the egg and add the sifted flour, lemon
rind and juice. Mix to a smooth dough with the
cream. Knead thoroughly and leave the dough to
rest for 30 minutes in a cool place.

Roll the dough out, ¼ in thick, and cut into
rounds with a fluted or plain 2½ in cutter. Set
on greased trays and bake.

Somerset Easter Cakes Somerset

½ lb plain flour
4 oz butter
4 oz caster sugar
4 oz currants
½ teaspoon each, ground cinnamon and mixed
    spice
1 egg
2 tablespoons brandy

Oven: 350°F; gas mark 4; 20 minutes

Sift the flour and rub in the butter; add the
sugar, currants, cinnamon and spice. Beat the
egg and brandy and blend into the flour, mixing
the dough to a stiff consistency.

Knead the mixture; roll out ½ in thick and cut
into 2½-3 in rounds. Set on greased baking sheets
and bake.

Souling Cakes

½ lb butter
1 lb plain flour
½ lb caster sugar
Pinch nutmeg
1 teaspoon each, cinnamon and mixed spice
2 eggs
1 dessertspoon malt vinegar

Oven: 350°F; gas mark 4; 20-25 minutes

Rub the butter into the sifted flour; fold in the
sugar, nutmeg, cinnamon and spice and mix to a
stiff dough with the beaten eggs and vinegar.

Knead thoroughly and roll out, ¼ in thick;
cut into 3 in rounds and set on greased baking
trays. Prick with a fork and bake; sprinkle with
sugar while still warm.

Stanhope Firelighters Co. Durham

½ lb rolled oats
½ lb melted margarine
½ lb brown sugar or mixed white and brown

Oven: 350°F; gas mark 4; 30 minutes

Blend the oats, margarine and sugar thoroughly;
press the mixture into a well-greased swiss-roll
tin and bake for 30 minutes. Cut into squares
when cool.

Tantallion Biscuits Scotland

4 oz butter
4 oz caster sugar
2 eggs
4 oz plain flour
¼ teaspoon bicarbonate of soda
4 oz rice flour

Oven: 325°F; gas mark 3; 30 minutes

Cream the butter and sugar until light and fluffy;
beat the eggs lightly and add to the creamed
mixture, alternately with the sifted flour and
bicarbonate of soda and the rice flour.

Roll the dough out thinly and cut into small
rounds with a 2½ in fluted cutter. Set on
greased baking trays, prick with a fork and bake.
Dust with icing sugar when cool.

Tunbridge Wells Cakes Kent

1 lb plain flour
4 oz butter
½ lb caster sugar
4 oz caraway seeds
Milk

Oven: 325°F; gas mark 3; 30 minutes

Sift the flour, rub in the butter and add the
sugar and caraway seeds. Mix to a stiff dough
with a little milk.

Knead the dough thoroughly and roll out as
thinly as possible; cut into 1½ in rounds. Set on
greased baking trays, prick with a fork and bake.

Water Biscuits

These biscuits most closely resemble the original hard plain biscuits. Blister Biscuits are made like Water Biscuits, but are cut into 1-1½ in rounds and not pricked before baking.

3 oz margarine
5 fl oz warm water or milk
½ lb plain flour
½ teaspoon salt

Oven: 375°F; gas mark 5; 20 minutes

Melt the margarine in the water or milk and heat to blood heat. Stir in the flour and salt with a knife; knead the mixture until smooth and roll out paper-thin on a floured board.

Cut into 2½ in rounds or squares; set on baking trays. Prick with a fork and bake.

Whetstone Cakes Leicestershire

4 oz butter
½ lb caster sugar
2 eggs
1 teaspoon caraway seeds
1 teaspoon rose water
¾ lb self-raising flour

Oven: 325°F; gas mark 3; 20 minutes

Cream the butter and sugar until light and fluffy; beat in the eggs, add the caraway seeds and rose water and lastly fold in the flour. Mix and knead thoroughly.

Roll the dough out as thinly as possible and cut into 2 in rounds. Set on greased baking trays, prick with a fork and bake.

York Biscuits Yorkshire

6 oz butter
6 oz caster sugar
1 lb plain flour
1½ teaspoons baking powder
5 fl oz milk

Oven: 325°F; gas mark 3; 30 minutes

Beat the butter and sugar until fluffy, fold in the sifted flour and baking powder and mix to a stiff dough with the milk. Knead well.

Roll the mixture out, no more than 1/8 in thick, and cut into 2 in rounds. Set on greased trays and bake for about 30 minutes.

GINGERBREAD AND PARKIN BISCUITS

The original gingerbread was a hard thin biscuit, heavily flavoured with spices and usually shaped into letters, numbers, animal and human figures. Numerous local variations developed and most fairs had their particular gingerbread biscuits, baked to traditional recipes and shapes.

Parkins are a type of gingerbread biscuit with oatmeal replacing all or part of the white flour; they are traditional in the North of England and Scotland. See also Cakes, Large.

Brandy Snaps

These traditional biscuits are know as Mothering Sunday Wafers in Hampshire, where they are made with orange flower water instead of brandy and served with jelly. In Devon and other parts of the West Country, brandy snaps are known as Honiton or West Country Fairings and in Yorkshire as Ormskirk Gingerbread.

4 oz plain flour
4 oz butter
4 oz caster sugar
4 oz golden syrup
1 teaspoon ground ginger
1 dessertspoon brandy
Grated rind of ½ lemon

Oven: 350°F; gas mark 4; 10 minutes

Place all the ingredients in a pan and heat through to melt, stirring all the time. Put teaspoons of the mixture on greased baking sheets, setting them 6 in apart. Bake until golden brown.

Roll the soft biscuits while still hot round the greased handle of a wooden spoon. Store in an airtight tin and fill the centres with whipped cream just before serving.

Fairings Cornwall

Fairing was originally a gift bought at a fair, but later came to mean a cake or sweet sold at a fair; as the gingerbread stall was a major feature of the fairs, gingerbread in Cornwall became known as fairings.

1 lb flour
½ teaspoon mixed spice
1 teaspoon ground ginger

5 oz butter
2 oz lard
½ lb Demerara sugar
4 oz candied citron peel
½ lb golden syrup
4 level teaspoons bicarbonate of soda
4 level teaspoons cream of tartar

Oven: 350°F; gas mark 4; 30-40 minutes

Sift the flour and add the mixed spice and ginger; rub in the butter and lard and mix in the sugar and peel.

Blend the syrup with the bicarbonate of soda and cream of tartar, add to the flour mixture and mix to a soft paste. Roll out, 1 in thick, cut into 1 in wide strips and cut these into 1 in pieces. Lift on to baking trays allowing room for spreading. Bake until risen and firm.

Ginger Snaps I

½ lb plain flour
1½ teaspoons baking powder
1 dessertspoon ground ginger
3 oz caster sugar
4 oz lard
4 oz golden syrup
½ beaten egg

Oven: 350°F; gas mark 4; 15 minutes

Sift the flour, baking powder and ginger and add the sugar. Melt the lard and syrup and add to the flour; mix to a stiff paste with the egg. Roll into walnut-sized balls and place well apart on a greased baking tray and bake.

Leave the biscuits to cool or shape them while still warm round the buttered handle of a wooden spoon; serve cold filled with whipped cream.

Ginger Snaps II

4 oz plain flour
½ teaspoon bicarbonate of soda
½ teaspoon each, ground ginger and mixed spice
1½ oz margarine
2 oz golden syrup
1 oz caster sugar

Oven: 350°F; gas mark 4; 15 minutes

Sift the flour, bicarbonate of soda, ginger and spice. Melt the margarine, syrup and sugar over gentle heat, mix into the flour and work to a paste.

Drop the mixture on to greased baking trays with the aid of two teaspoons and bake for 15 minutes or until golden brown.

Honey Biscuits

1½ lb plain flour
1 oz baking powder
1 dessertspoon mixed ground ginger and cinnamon
½ lb caster sugar
½ lb butter
¾ lb honey
4 oz chopped citron peel
½ oz chopped orange peel
2 eggs

Oven: 375°F; gas mark 5; 15-20 minutes

Sift the flour, baking powder and ground ginger and cinnamon; add the sugar. Melt the butter and honey, pour into the flour and blend in the citron and orange peel.

Gather the mixture with the beaten eggs; roll out, ¼ in thick, on a floured board and cut into 2½ in rounds. Bake for about 15 minutes.

Hunters Buts Scotland

1½ oz butter
3 oz golden syrup
½ teaspoon bicarbonate of soda
2 oz medium oatmeal
2 oz wheat flour
2 oz plain flour
1 teaspoon each, ground ginger and allspice
1 oz soft brown sugar
1 egg
Garnish: blanched, halved almonds

Oven: 350°F; gas mark 4; 20 minutes

Melt the butter and syrup in a pan; dissolve the bicarbonate of soda in a little water and add to the syrup. Mix the oatmeal, wheat and white flour with the ginger, allspice and sugar; add the syrup mixture and work to a stiff dough, kneading until smooth.

Divide the mixture into 10-12 pieces and shape into small balls. Place on greased baking trays, brush with beaten egg and decorate with half almonds. Bake for 20 minutes.

Inverness Ginger Nuts Scotland

7 oz plain flour
2 oz lard or dripping
½ teaspoon bicarbonate of soda
2 teaspoons ground ginger
½ teaspoon mixed spice
3 oz caster sugar
4 oz fine oatmeal
6 oz black treacle
Milk

Oven: 325°F; gas mark 3; 30 minutes

Sift the flour and rub in the lard; add bicarbonate of soda, ginger, spice, sugar and oatmeal. Melt the treacle, mix into the dry ingredients and gather to a smooth dough; knead well.

Roll the dough out, 1/8 in thick, prick with a fork and cut into 2½ in rounds. Brush with milk; set well apart on greased baking trays and bake.

Market Gingerbread

½ lb plain flour
½ teaspoon bicarbonate of soda
1 teaspoon ground ginger
10 oz golden syrup
3 oz lard

Oven: 350°F; gas mark 4; 8-10 minutes

Sift the flour, bicarbonate of soda and ginger; melt the syrup and lard gently and work into the flour. Knead the mixture lightly, roll it out thinly and cut into traditional gingerbread men or horse shapes.

Set on greased baking trays and bake until golden brown. When cold, decorate with coloured, piped icing.

Moggy

These may be made also with black treacle and ground ginger instead of golden syrup.

¾ ib plain flour
Pinch salt
1½ teaspoons baking powder
2 oz lard
4 oz margarine
4 oz caster sugar
4 oz golden syrup
Milk

Oven: 350°F; gas mark 4; 20-30 minutes

Sift the flour with a pinch of salt and the baking powder; rub in the lard and margarine and add the sugar. Melt the syrup and add to the flour, kneading until smooth and adding milk if necessary.

Knead the dough on a floured surface; roll out, ½ in thick, and placed in a greased baking tin. Bake for about 30 minutes and cut into squares while still warm.

Ormskirk Gingerbread Yorkshire

This is the Yorkshire equivalent of brandy snaps.

5 oz plain flour
1 teaspoon each, ground cinnamon, ginger and mace
Grated rind of ½ lemon
6 oz butter
½ lb golden syrup
½ lb caster sugar

Oven: 375°F; gas mark 5; 10 minutes

Sift the flour, cinnamon, ginger and mace and add the lemon rind. Melt the butter, syrup and sugar, pour into the flour mixture and blend to a soft dropping consistency.

Drop the mixture in teaspoons on to greased baking trays, setting them well apart to leave room for spreading. Bake for about 10 minutes or until golden brown; while still warm wrap each biscuit quickly round the buttered handle of a wooden spoon. Ease off and leave to cool. Serve filled with whipped cream.

Parkins Scotland

4 oz plain flour
½ teaspoon mixed spice
1 teaspoon each, cinnamon and ground ginger
1 teaspoon bicarbonate of soda
2 oz lard
4 oz medium oatmeal
3 oz caster sugar
½ beaten egg
3 oz syrup
Blanched, halved almonds

Oven: 350°F; gas mark 4; 20 minutes

Sift the flour and mix with the spice, cinnamon, ginger and bicarbonate of soda; rub in the lard and blend in the oatmeal and sugar. Mix the egg and syrup, add to the flour and knead to a stiff dough.

Roll into small balls and set well apart on greased baking trays. Press half an almond on top of each ball and bake.

Parlies (Scottish Parliament Cakes) Scotland

4 oz black treacle
4 oz butter
½ lb plain flour
2 teaspoons ground ginger
4 oz soft brown sugar

Oven: 325°F; gas mark 3; 30-35 minutes

Melt the treacle and butter over gentle heat, fold in the sifted flour and ginger and add the sugar.

Mix to a stiff dough and roll out very thinly. Set on greased baking trays, mark in squares and bake. Separate the squares while still warm.

Shah Biscuits

½ lb plain flour
2 teaspoons ground ginger
½ teaspoon ground cinnamon
½ teaspoon bicarbonate of soda
4 oz margarine
½ lb caster sugar
1 egg
2 oz chopped citron peel

Oven: 350°F; gas mark 4; 20-30 minutes

Sift the flour, ginger, cinnamon and bicarbonate of soda; rub in the margarine and add the sugar. Gather to a stiff dough with the beaten egg and knead lightly.

Shape the dough into small balls the size of walnuts. Set on greased baking trays, leaving room for the biscuits to spread; press a piece of citron peel into each ball and bake.

Westmorland Parkins Westmorland

4 oz lard
4 oz dripping
½ lb black treacle
¾ lb plain flour
3 teaspoons ground ginger

1 teaspoon mixed spice
½ teaspoon bicarbonate of soda
¾ lb medium oatmeal
½ lb brown sugar
Milk

Oven: 325°F; gas mark 3; 30-40 minutes

Melt the lard, dripping and treacle together, blend in the flour sifted with the ginger, spice and bicarbonate of soda and add the oatmeal and sugar.

Mix to a stiff consistency with a little milk and roll out the mixture, ¼ in thick; prick with a fork and cut into 2½ in rounds. Set on greased baking trays and bake.

Widecombe Fair Gingerbreads Devon

6 oz plain flour
1 teaspoon ground ginger
5 oz butter
6 oz caster sugar
6 oz black treacle

Oven: 350°F; gas mark 4; 30-40 minutes

Sift the flour, add the ginger and rub in the butter; blend in the sugar. Dissolve the treacle and mix into the flour, blending to a soft consistency.

Drop the mixture in spoonfuls on to greased baking trays and bake until firm, yet springy to the touch.

CAKE FILLINGS AND ICINGS

These are used not only as a decorative finish to cakes and biscuits, but also serve a practical purpose in keeping cakes moister for a longer period.

Butter creams which can be flavoured with different ingredients are used for fillings in sandwich cakes as well as for toppings. Glacé icings and the more elaborate Royal icing are used for covering only.

Butter Cream

4 oz butter
½ lb icing sugar
1-2 tablespoons warm water or milk

Beat the butter until creamy and light; gradually beat in the sifted icing sugar, adding water or milk until the mixture is soft and spreading.

To this basic butter cream, add any of the following:

Almond, blend in a few drops of almond essence and 2 oz finely chopped toasted almonds.

Chocolate, add 2 oz melted chocolate or 1 oz cocoa powder.

Coffee, use 1-2 tablespoons coffee essence instead of the water.

Mocha, add 2 teaspoons cocoa and 2 teaspoons instant coffee dissolved in a little water.

Orange or Lemon, blend in the finely grated rind of 1 orange or lemon, use 1-2 tablespoons orange or lemon juice and a few drops of colouring instead of water.

Vanilla, add 2-3 drops vanilla essence.

Walnut, fold in 2 oz finely chopped walnuts.

Glacé Icing

½ lb icing sugar
3 tablespoons warm water

Sift the icing sugar into a bowl. Add the water and any flavouring little by little; the icing should be thick enough to coat the back of a wooden spoon. If necessary add more sifted icing sugar or water to adjust the consistency.

Flavour and colour plain glacé icing with any of the following:

Chocolate, add 2-3 oz melted chocolate or 1 oz cocoa with a few drops of vanilla essence.

Coffee, blend in 2 teaspoons instance coffee or 1 teaspoon coffee essence.

Lemon, replace part of the water with 2 tablespoons strained lemon juice and 2-3 drops of lemon colouring.

Mocha, add 1 teaspoon each of cocoa and instant coffee.

Orange, substitute 2 tablespoons of the water with orange juice and add 2-3 drops of orange colouring.

Royal Icing

Used to coat and decorate large celebration cakes. It should ideally be made at least 24 hours before use and kept, covered with a damp cloth in the refrigerator. Re-work the icing and let the coating set before piping on decorations.

1 lb icing sugar
2 egg whites
1 teaspoon lemon juice

Sift the icing sugar two or three times. Whisk the egg whites until fluffy and gradually stir in the sugar, beating well between each addition. Beat in the strained lemon juice after half the sugar has been incorporated.

Continue adding the sugar until the icing is smooth and stands up in soft peaks.

Preservation

This section includes a wide range of dishes which have derived from original preservation techniques as well as some miscellaneous items which are not classified in other sections.

Salting was one of the earliest preservation methods. Mixed with water to form a brine or used dry, it permeated food, thus delaying the action of harmful bacteria. Vinegar had the same effect and the two were often combined. The term, adopted from the Dutch, to describe brine, vinegar, or any other acid liquid in which flesh or vegetables were preserved was "peckel", now known as pickle which describes not only the liquid but also the items preserved in this way. In order to obtain a non-perishable product which would keep for many months, or for years, after the pickling process, it was often subjected to a further period of smoking and drying so that the result was not only very salt but also blackened and hardened by smoke.

Young scarlet runner or French beans may be salted, using 1 lb cooking salt to 3 lb beans. Wash, dry and string the beans and slice them finely. Put a 1 in deep layer of salt in an earthenware pot, press in a layer of beans, another layer of salt and so on until the pot is full, finishing with a 1 in layer of salt. Cover with cloth or paper, never foil, and tie down with string. To cook salted beans, wash them well in warm water, put in a pan of cold water and bring to the boil. Boil for 3 minutes, drain and then boil the beans in fresh water until tender.

Meat and fish hung up inside the chimney of a peat fire were permeated with the delicate aroma from the smoke. During the process they were dried out, and in pre-eighteenth century times supplied a type of food which could be used during the winter months when food was scarce. Lamb and pork were the meats most commonly smoked; bacon survives from this practice.

In those days, fish presented more preservation problems than any other commodity. It is not surprising, therefore, that a greater variety of techniques developed as a result. Sea fish were particularly difficult to deal with as not only did the catch have to be transported from the fishing grounds to the port, but it also had to be taken by pack horse or cart to inland markets. Slow sailing ships and poor roads prevented the fast transport of sea fish, and only people near the coast saw much fresh fish. The excess was salted and dried to a non-perishable commodity which became an important feature of fish consumption.

Smoke-curing, pickling, sousing and potting were other preservation methods; for recipes using these products see the sections on Fish and Meat.

Honey was the earliest, most readily available sweetening agent up to the eighteenth century, and fruits preserved in a sweet liquid were fairly common among the rich and were mentioned in 1420 as "Wardonys (pears) in Syrup".

Another popular medieval fruit which was also preserved in syrup was the quince. This is now much less common, but significant in that the Portuguese name was *marmelo* from which the Portuguese word *marmelada* and the French word *marmalade* were formed. The term, adopted in this country in the sixteenth century, is applied to a variety of confections made by boiling fruit with sugar to produce a thick mass. Although quinces were the original fruit, cherries, plums, dates and apricots are also mentioned in early recipes, while the use of Seville oranges came much later.

In the eighteenth century sugar became more readily available and as a result new sweet confections developed. At least one new name appeared for what was an extension of the marmalade concept, based on bruising, crushing or jamming the fruit with sugar. Shortened to "jam", this term came to be applied to all confections not already classified as marmalades and excluding those which derived their names from the finished texture, such as fruit jelly, curd, cheese and butter.

JAMS

These are made from any kind of fresh or dried fruit, sometimes with additional flavourings. They are cooked with water until soft, then sugar is added and the mixture boiled to make a syrup which will set depending on the pectin content of the fruit. Lemon juice is added to help set fruit low in pectin. The mixture is poured into jars, covered and allowed to cool and set.

Basic Preparation and Cooking Method

1 lb fruit
1 lb sugar
Water

Prepare the fruit according to kind; put in a preserving pan and add water and any other liquid if indicated.

Simmer gently until quite tender; the time varies according to the type of fruit used. Remove the pan from the heat, add the sugar, stir until dissolved and return the pan to the heat.

Boil rapidly, stirring frequently to prevent sticking. Skim when necessary. Test for setting; pot, cover and store.

Testing for Setting

Temperature test. Using a sugar thermometer, a set will be obtained when the temperature reaches between 200° and 222°F. This depends on pectin, acid and sugar content.

Saucer test. Put a little jam on a cold saucer and allow to cool. Push the finger across the top of the jam, and the surface will wrinkle when a set has been obtained.

Potting

Jars must be clean and warm. Jelly should be potted at once, jam should be cooled and stirred to prevent the fruit from rising to the top. Fill the pots to the rim as the jam shrinks a little on cooling.

Covering

Wipe the pots, cover the jam with a waxed disc, wax side down, and make sure that it lies flat and no air bubbles are trapped beneath. Cover with damped cellophane, held in place with a rubber band; label when cold with the name and the date.

Storage

Store in a cool, dry place away from light.

RECIPES

The following jam recipes list ingredients in correct proportions; they are all made according to the basic jam method unless otherwise stated.

Apple and Ginger Jam

4 lb peeled, cored and sliced cooking apples
Rind and juice of 2 lemons
4 oz finely chopped crystallised ginger
1 pt water
3 lb preserving sugar

Follow the basic jam method.

Apple and Pineapple Jam

6 lb peeled, cored and sliced cooking apples
6 lb preserving sugar
Juice of 2 lemons
1 tin pineapple chunks
2 pt tinned pineapple juice

Follow the basic jam method.

Apricot Jam (Fresh)

6 lb fresh, stoned apricots
6 lb preserving sugar
1 pt water

Follow the basic jam method, placing the stones in a muslin bag and cooking them with the fruit; remove the bag before adding the sugar.

Apricot Jam (Dried)

2 lb finely chopped, dried apricots
6 lb preserving sugar
6 pt water

Follow the basic jam method, soaking the apricots in water overnight before chopping them.

Apricot and Tangerine Jam

2 lb soaked, finely chopped, dried apricots
7 lb preserving sugar
Juice and finely shredded rind of 12 tangerines

Follow the basic jam method, adding the
tangerine pips in a muslin bag for the preliminary
boiling process.

Bilberry Jam

3 lb bilberries
3 lb preserving sugar
1 tablespoon water
Juice of ½ lb rhubarb or 1 lemon

Follow the basic jam method, adding the lemon
or rhubard juice with the sugar.

Bilberry and Cranberry Jam

2 lb bilberries
2 lb cranberries
4 lb preserving sugar
½ pt water

Follow the basic jam method.

Blackberry or Bramble Jam

2 lb blackberries
2 lb preserving sugar
2 tablespoons water
Juice of 1 small lemon

Follow the basic jam method.

Blackberry and Apple Jam

4 lb cooked and sieved blackberries
1½ lb peeled, cored and sliced acid apples
½ pt water
1 lb preserving sugar to 1 pt pulp

Follow the basic jam method, measuring the
pulp after the apples have been cooked in the
water and mixed with the blackberries.

Blackberry and Elderberry Jam

2 lb blackberries
2 lb elderberries
3 lb preserving sugar

Follow the basic jam method, stripping the elderberries from the stalks.

Black Currant Jam

4 lb stripped black currants
6 lb preserving sugar
3 pt water

Follow the basic jam method.

Cherry Jam

3 lb stoned cherries
3 lb preserving sugar
8 fl oz raspberry juice
16 fl oz red currant juice

Tie the stones in a muslin bag and boil with the
cherries and juices before adding the sugar. Follow
the basic jam method.

Cherry and Gooseberry Jam

3 lb stoned cherries
1½ lb topped and tailed gooseberries
¼ oz cream of tartar
4 lb preserving sugar

Follow the basic jam method; tie the stones in a
muslin bag and simmer with the fruit.

Cherry and Red Currant Jam

2 lb stoned dark cherries
1 lb stripped red currants
5 fl oz water
3 lb preserving sugar

Follow the basic jam method; tie the stones in a
muslin bag and simmer with the fruit.

Morello Cherry Jam Kent

1 lb stoned Morello cherries
1 pt gooseberry or apple juice
1½ lb preserving sugar

Tie the stones in a muslin bag and simmer with
the fruit; follow the basic jam method, adding the
fruit juice at the beginning.

Chestnut Jam Cambridge

1½ lb sweet cooked chestnuts
1½ lb preserving sugar
½ pt water
2 tablespoons vanilla essence

Rub the cooked chestnuts through a sieve or blend to a pulp in the liquidiser. Make a syrup from the sugar and water and flavour with vanilla; when boiling, stir in the chestnuts and blend thoroughly. Pot and seal.

Cranberry Jam

3 lb cranberries
3 lb preserving sugar
½ pt water

Follow the basic jam method.

Cranberry and Apple Jam

2 lb cranberries
2 lb peeled, cored and sliced cooking apples
4½ lb preserving sugar
½ pt water

Follow the basic jam method.

Damson Jam

5 lb stoned damsons
6 lb preserving sugar
1½ pt water

Follow the basic jam method, simmering the stones in a muslin bag with the fruit.

Fig and Lemon Preserve

2 lb dried figs
2 pt water
3 lb preserving sugar
Juice and grated rind of 4 lemons

Cut up the figs and soak for 24 hours. Follow the basic jam method.

Glencar Jam

1 lb chopped dried figs
4 lb chopped rhubarb
6 oz candied lemon peel, or rind and juice of
    1 lemon
3 lb preserving sugar

Soak the prepared figs and rhubarb in the sugar overnight. Follow the basic jam method.

Gooseberry Jam

6 lb slightly unripe gooseberries
6 lb preserving sugar
2 pt water

Follow the basic jam method. For additional flavour, tie 3-4 elderflower heads per 1 lb fruit in muslin and boil with the fruit.

Greengage Jam

6 lb stoned greengages
6 lb preserving sugar
1 pt water

Follow the basic jam method, simmering the stones in a muslin bag with the fruit. Remove the stones just before potting.

Marrow and Pineapple Jam

4 lb peeled marrow
3 lb preserving sugar
1 large tin of chopped pineapple chunks

Cut the marrow into 1 in cubes and soak overnight in the sugar; follow the basic jam method, adding the pineapple chunks and juice.

Mulberry Jam

3 lb just ripe mulberries
1 lb peeled, cored and sliced apples
3½ lb preserving sugar
1 pt water

Follow the basic jam method.

Pear and Ginger Jam

4 lb hard, peeled, cored and finely chopped pears
3 lb preserving sugar
2 oz chopped crystallised ginger
Juice of 2 lemons

Soak the prepared pears with the sugar and lemon juice overnight. Continue as for the basic jam method, adding the ginger.

Pear and Peach Jam

1½ lb firm, ripe pears, peeled, cored and cubed
1½ lb peaches, skinned, stoned and sliced
Grated rind and juice of 3 lemons

3 lb preserving sugar
5 fl oz water

Follow the basic jam method.

Pear, Apple and Quince Jam

2 lb peeled, cored and sliced cooking apples
2 lb peeled, cored and sliced cooking pears
1½ lb peeled, cored and sliced quinces
Juice and rind of 1 lemon
6 lb preserving sugar
1 pt water

Put the peel and cores of the fruit in a muslin
bag with the lemon rind and add when boiling up
the fruit. Continue as for the basic jam method.

Plum Jam

4 lb stoned plums
4 lb preserving sugar
½ pt water

Follow the basic jam method, adding the stones in
a muslin bag when boiling the fruit.

Plum and Raisin Jam

3 lb stoned plums
3 lb preserving sugar
6 oz stoned raisins
4 oz blanched chopped almonds

Follow the basic jam method, adding the stones in
a muslin bag when boiling the fruit. Add the
raisins and chopped almonds just before setting
point is reached.

Raspberry Jam

6 lb raspberries
6 lb preserving sugar

Use very dry, under-ripe rather than over-ripe
fruit; dry the sugar in a cool oven and then follow
the basic jam method.

Raspberry and Red Currant Jam

1½ lb raspberries
1½ lb stripped red currants
3 lb preserving sugar
1 pt water

Follow the basic jam method.

Raspberry Preserve

3 lb raspberries
3 lb preserving sugar

Place the fruit and sugar in the oven in separate
dishes and heat through at 300°F, gas mark 2.
When warm, beat them together in a bowl for 15
minutes, pot and cover as for basic jam method.

Rhubarb Jam

8 lb finely chopped rhubarb
Juice of 4 lemons or 1¼ pt red currant or goose-
     berry juice
6 lb preserving sugar

Follow the basic jam method.

Rhubarb and Ginger Jam

6 lb finely chopped rhubarb
¾ lb finely chopped, crystallised ginger
Rind of 1 lemon
5 lb preserving sugar

Soak the prepared rhubarb in the sugar for 24
hours. Boil the ginger and lemon in the strained
rhubarb syrup for 30 minutes. Add the rhubarb
and finish as for basic jam method. Leave for 30
minutes before potting.

Rhubarb and Blackberry Jam

8 lb blackberries
4 lb chopped rhubarb
1½ pt water
12 lb preserving sugar

Simmer the rhubarb in the water for 30 minutes
before adding the blackberries and sugar. Continue
as for the basic jam method.

Rhubarb and Mixed Peel Jam

6 lb chopped rhubarb
1 piece root ginger
6 oz mixed, chopped peel
6 lb preserving sugar

Soak the rhubarb in the sugar for 24 hours;
strain off the juice, boil for 10 minutes and pour
over the rhubarb, bruised ginger and chopped peel;
leave for another 24 hours. Bring to the boil and
boil rapidly until the jam sets. Remove the ginger
and pot as for the basic jam method.

Rhubarb and Rose Petal Jam

1 lb chopped rhubarb
Juice of 1 lemon
2 handfuls scented chopped rose petals
1 lb preserving sugar

Let the prepared rhubarb layered with the
sugar stand overnight. Follow the basic jam
method, adding the rose petals just before
potting.

Rose Hip Jam

1 lb rose hips
1 lb peeled, cored and sliced apples
¾ lb preserving sugar
1½ pt water

Scoop out the seeds from the hips; simmer the
hips in water for 2 hours and strain the juice
through muslin. Continue as for the basic jam
method, simmering the apples, rose hip juice and
sugar together until setting point is reached.

Red Rose Petal Jam

1 lb rose petals
2 tablespoons water
1 dessertspoon orange flower water or rose water
1 lb preserving sugar

Boil the sugar and water to make a syrup. Wash
and dry the petals, add with the flavouring and
simmer until thick.

Strawberry Jam

7 lb strawberries
Juice of 4 lemons
6 lb preserving sugar

Follow the basic jam method.

Wild Strawberry Jam

1 lb wild strawberries
¾ lb preserving sugar

Soak the berries in half the sugar overnight.
Strain off the juice and boil with the remainder
of the sugar. Boil to reduce slightly. Add the
fruit and simmer for 20 minutes. Pot as for the
basic jam method.

This jam is never thick, and no amount of
boiling will make it set; the less it is boiled the
better the flavour.

Green Tomato Jam

4 lb roughly chopped green tomatoes
Cloves or 1 oz whole ginger or rind of 1 lemon
3 lb preserving sugar

Follow the basic jam method.

JELLIES

Fresh or dried fruit, often with additional flavourings, is cooked in water to a soft pulp. The mixture
is strained through a jelly bag or muslin to extract
the juice which is then boiled with sugar to make a
syrup. This sets on cooling, depending on the
pectin content of the fruit. Jellies are poured into
small jars, covered and allowed to set. A wide
variety of fruits may be used although fruits
with a low pectin content are not recommended
for jellies.

Basic Preparation and Cooking Method

Fruit
Water
1 lb preserving sugar to each pint of juice extract

Prepare the fruit according to type. Put into a
preserving pan and add water if indicated; simmer
until quite tender. The time varies according to
the fruit. Remove the fruit from the pan and
strain through a scalded jelly bag or muslin; leave
until the dripping has stopped, ideally overnight.
Do not squeeze or poke the bag or the finished
jelly will be cloudy.

Measure the juice and add the correct amount
of sugar. Stir over a low heat until the sugar has
dissolved. Boil rapidly, stirring frequently to
prevent sticking and skimming when necessary.
Test for setting, pot, cover and store as for jams.

RECIPES

The following jellies are all made according to the
basic method unless otherwise indicated.

Apple Jelly

6 lb quartered cooking apples
Juice of 1 lemon
3½ pt water
1 lb preserving sugar to 1 pt juice

Follow the basic jelly method; green-skinned apples give the best colour.

Barberry Jelly

2 lb barberries
2 lb preserving sugar
½ pt water

Follow the basic jelly method, simmering the berries until just soft and no more.

Blackberry or Bramble Jelly

2 lb blackberries
Juice of 1 small lemon
1 lb preserving sugar to 1 pt juice
2 tablespoons water

Follow the basic jelly method.

Blackberry and Apple Jelly

4 lb blackberries
2 lb quartered cooking apples
1 lb preserving sugar to 1 pt juice
1 pt water

Follow the basic jelly method.

Blackberry and Sloe Jelly

2 lb blackberries
½ lb sloes
1 lb preserving sugar to 1 pt juice

Follow the basic jelly method, pricking the sloes with a fork to aid the release of the juice.

Spiced Blackberry Jelly

1 lb blackberries
5 fl oz water
1 in cinnamon stick
½ small bay leaf
2 cloves
5 fl oz malt vinegar

1 lb preserving sugar

Cook the blackberries in the water with the spices tied in muslin until tender and pass through a sieve. Add the vinegar and sugar to the pulp, and dissolve the sugar over low heat.

Bring to the boil and simmer for about 20 minutes. Pot and cover as for jam.

Blackberry and Chilli Jelly

3 lb ripe blackberries
4 small dried red chillies
1 dessertspoon lemon juice
1 lb preserving sugar to 1 pt juice

Put the blackberries, lemon juice and broken chillies in a pan set on a warm stove. Crush the fruit and leave for several hours to draw the juice. Strain and finish as for jelly.

Black Currant Jelly

4 lb black currants
3 pt water
1 lb preserving sugar to 1 pt juice

Follow the basic jelly method.

Cranberry Jelly

2 lb cranberries
1 pt water
1 lb preserving sugar to 1 pt juice

Follow the basic jelly method.

Cranberry and Apple Jelly

2 lb cranberries
3 lb quartered cooking apples
1 lb preserving sugar to 1 pt juice
Water to cover

Follow the basic jelly method.

Damson Jelly

6 lb stoned damsons
1 lb preserving sugar to 1 pt juice
3 pt water

Follow the basic jelly method, simmering the stones in a muslin bag with the fruit.

Damson and Apple Jelly

3 lb stoned damsons
6 lb peeled, roughly chopped cooking apples
1 lb preserving sugar to 1 pt juice
4 pt water

Follow the basic jelly method, adding the stones in a muslin bag to the fruit.

Elderberry and Blackberry Jelly

1 lb elderberries
1 lb blackberries
¾ lb preserving sugar to 1 pt juice

Follow the basic jelly method; strip the elderberries from the stalks.

Follow the basic jelly method, simmering the apples and elderberries separately, each in 1 pt of water, as the elderberries require less cooking. Mix the juices.

Gooseberry Jelly

4 lb gooseberries
Elderflower heads
1 lb preserving sugar to 1 pt juice
Water to cover

Follow the basic jelly method, simmering the elderflowers in muslin with the juice and sugar.

Gooseberry Mint Jelly

2 lb green gooseberries
6 stalks fresh green mint
1 lb preserving sugar to 1 pt juice
Water to cover

Follow the basic jelly method; tie the mint in a bundle and boil it with the juice and sugar. Remove before potting.

Green Grape Jelly

3 lb small green unripe grapes
1 lb preserving sugar to 1 pt juice
Water to cover

Follow the basic jelly method.

Hawthorn Jelly

4 lb picked and stalked red haws

1 lb preserving sugar to 1 pt juice
2 pt water

Follow the basic jelly method. Simmer the haws for 10-15 minutes; additional cooking develops a bitter flavour.

Haw and Crab Apple Jelly

2 lb picked and stalked haws
2 lb crab apples
1/8 oz ground ginger and cloves
1 lb preserving sugar to 1 pt juice
1 pt water

Follow the basic jelly method. Do not simmer the haws for longer than 10-15 minutes.

Japonica Jelly

2 lb japonicas
1 lb preserving sugar to 1 pt juice
5 fl oz water

Follow the basic jelly method. Wash the japonicas, but leave them whole.

Lemon Jelly

4 lb large lemons
3 Seville oranges
5 lb preserving sugar
6 pt cold water

Peel a thin rind from the lemons and cut into thin strips. Tie in a muslin bag. Chop the fruit roughly and put in a pan with the water and muslin bag; simmer for 2½ hours. Remove the strips of lemon after 1 hour.

Strain, add the sugar and the finely shredded peel. Bring to the boil and finish as for the basic jelly method.

Medlar Jelly

3 lb ripe, roughly chopped medlars
Juice of 1 lemon
¾ lb preserving sugar to 1 pt juice
1½ pt water

Follow the basic jelly method.

Mint Jelly

6 lb quartered cooking apples

2 oz chopped mint
1 lb preserving sugar to 1 pt juice
2¼ pt water
2¼ pt vinegar

Put the apples in a pan with the mint, water and vinegar. Simmer until tender and pulpy; strain. Follow the basic jelly method, potting when cold Serve with roast lamb.

Mulberry Jelly

6 lb just ripe mulberries
Juice of 2 lemons
¾ lb preserving sugar to 1 pt juice

Follow the basic jelly method, simmering the fruit with the lemon juice for 2 hours.

Orange Jelly

2 lb Seville oranges
Juice of 2 lemons
3 lb preserving sugar
4½ pt water

Follow the method for Lemon Jelly, but add 4 oz finely shredded orange zest to the sugar before simmering the fruit with the water.

Parsley Jelly

6 oz parsley stalks
6 oz preserving sugar to 1 pt liquid
2 tablespoons vinegar
½ oz powdered gelatine
Water to cover

Boil the parsley in water until the parsley is pale yellow; add sugar and vinegar; boil for 15 minutes and strain. Dissolve the gelatine in liquid and add before potting. Serve with poultry, veal or lamb.

Quince Jelly

4 lb quartered quinces
1 lb preserving sugar to 1 pt juice
6 pt water

Follow the basic jelly method. Serve with cold meats, hot roast pork, game or lamb.

Raspberry and Apple Jelly

4 lb raspberries

2 lb quartered cooking apples
1 lb preserving sugar to 1 pt juice
2 pt water

Follow the basic jelly method.

Red Currant Jelly

6 lb stripped red currants
1 lb preserving sugar to 1 pt juice
2½ pt water

Follow the basic jelly method.

Rhubarb and Mint Jelly

6 lb chopped rhubarb
2 oz chopped mint
2¼ pt vinegar
1 lb preserving sugar to 1 pt juice
2¼ pt water

Follow the basic jelly method, cutting the rhubarb into 1 in pieces. Leave the jelly to cool before potting. Serve with lamb instead of mint sauce.

Rose Hip Jelly

2 lb rose hips
4 lb roughly chopped apples
Water
14 oz preserving sugar to 1 pt juice

Remove seeds from the hips and mince the fruit; place with the roughly chopped apples in a pan, cover with water and simmer until soft. Continue as for the basic jelly method.

Rose Petal Jelly

2 lb gooseberries or apples
Dried rose petals
1 lb preserving sugar to 1 pt juice
½ pt water

Proceed as for gooseberry or apple jelly and add as many rose petals as the mixture will take just before setting.

Rowan Jelly

4 lb almost ripe rowan berries
1 lb preserving sugar to 1 pt juice
2 pt water

Follow the basic jelly method. Strip the berries from the stalks and do not boil for more than 10-15 minutes as a bitter flavour develops if cooked too long.

Rowan and Apple Jelly

2 lb almost ripe rowan berries
2 lb unpeeled apples, cut into thick slices
1 lb preserving sugar to 1 pt juice
1½ pt water

Follow the basic jelly method. Do not cook the berries for longer than 10-15 minutes.

Spiced Rowan Berry Jelly

2 lb rowan berries
Juice and rind of 1 lemon
2 lb diced green apples
¼ oz cloves
1 lb preserving sugar to 1 pt juice
1½ pt water

Follow the basic jelly method. Do not simmer the rowans for more than 10-15 minutes. Serve with hare, rabbit, mutton and grouse.

Sloe Jelly

3 lb sloes
1 lb quartered apples
1½ lb preserving sugar to 1 pt juice
Water to cover

Prick the sloes with a fork or needle; simmer in the water for 2 hours, adding the apples 45 minutes before the end of cooking. Continue as for the basic jelly method. Serve with game and meat.

Sloe and Crab Apple Jelly

1-2 lb sloes
Water
1 lb quartered crab apples
1 lb preserving sugar to 1 pt juice

Prick the sloes and simmer in enough water to cover for 2 hours; add the crab apples after 1¼ hours. Continue as for the basic jelly method.

Tangerine Jelly

2 lb tangerines

1 large grapefruit
2 large lemons
1 lb preserving sugar to 1 pt juice
5 pt cold water

Follow the recipe for Lemon Jelly.

FRUIT BUTTERS AND FRUIT CHEESES

Fresh fruit is cooked in water until soft, then sieved. The pulp is mixed with sugar and boiled until thick. Butters are cooked until they have the consistency of thick cream, while cheeses should be so thick that when a wooden spoon is drawn across the bottom of the pan it leaves a clear line.

They are traditionally potted in straight-sided jars and should be stored for at least a year to allow the flavours to develop. Fruit butters and cheeses are classic country preserves usually made only when there is a glut of fruit as a large quantity gives only a comparatively small amount of finished preserve.

Fruit Butter

1 lb pulp
¾ lb preserving sugar

Fruit Cheese

1 lb pulp
¾ lb preserving sugar

Basic Preparation and Cooking Method

Wash the fruit, put into a pan with just enough water to cover; simmer until soft. Pass the fruit pulp through a nylon sieve. Measure and add sugar accordingly.

Return the pulp and sugar to the pan and stir until the sugar has dissolved. Boil gently to the required consistency.

Stir frequently to prevent sticking. Pot and cover butters as for jams. For cheeses, brush the inside of small sterilised pots or jars with olive oil; this enables the preserve to be turned out. Pour in the cheese and cover. Store for at least 3-4 months before using as the flavours develop with age.

Apple Butter I

3 lb quartered windfall apples
5 fl oz water or cider
½ teaspoon each, ground cloves and cinnamon
¾ lb preserving sugar to 1 lb pulp

Follow the basic butter method, rubbing the apples through a sieve after cooking.

This butter improves on keeping for up to 1 year. It is traditionally served at Christmas, garnished with hazelnuts and fresh cream

Apple Butter II

8 lb quartered apples
6 pt sweet cider, reduced by half
¼ oz ground cinnamon
1/8 oz salt
1-1½ lb brown sugar to 1 lb pulp

Follow the basic butter method.

Sweet Spiced Apple Cheese

8 lb quartered windfall apples cooked to a
    pulp and sieved
12 cloves (tied in a muslin bag)
½ pt vinegar
5 lb preserving sugar
½ pt water

Prepare and cook the apples and sieve to a pulp. Soak all the ingredients for 24 hours. Boil for 45 minutes and pot as for basic cheese.

Cranberry Cheese

1 lb cranberries
½ lb preserving sugar to each 1 lb pulp
5 fl oz water

Follow the basic cheese method.

Damson Cheese

3 lb damsons
1 lb preserving sugar to each 1 lb pulp

Bake the damsons in the oven at 300°F, gas mark 2, until soft. Add a few kernels to the pulp. Follow the basic cheese method.

Store for at least 6 months; it improves for up to 2 years. It is turned out on to a plate, stuck with split almonds and served as a dessert with port wine poured over.

Plum and Apple Cheese

1 lb plums
3 lb roughly chopped apples
¾ lb preserving sugar to 1 lb pulp

Follow the basic cheese method, rubbing the fruit through a sieve when cooked.

Quince Cheese

3 lb quartered quinces
1 chopped orange
Water
1 lb preserving sugar to 1 lb pulp

Soak the orange and quinces overnight in enough water to cover; cook until soft and then pass through a sieve. Follow the basic cheese method.

Sloe Cheese

3 lb sloes
1 lb apples
1 lb sugar to 1 lb pulp
Water to cover

Prick the sloes and simmer in water for 2 hours; add the apples after 1¼ hours cooking. Pass the fruit through a sieve and continue as for the basic cheese method.

FRUIT CURDS

These are mixtures of sugar and butter thickened with eggs. The most common flavouring is lemon, though there are other variations.

Basic Preparation and Cooking Method

4 lemons
¾ lb loaf sugar
4 oz butter
8 egg yolks or 4 whole eggs

Rasp the sugar on the rind of the washed lemons, or use granulated sugar, and mix with the finely grated or thinly peeled rind; in the latter case strain before potting to remove the peel.

Place the sugar in a double saucepan with butter, lemon juice and the beaten egg yolks. Mix and stir until the sugar has dissolved. Continue cooking, stirring until the curd thickens.

Pot as for jam; curds should be made in small quantities only because of poor keeping qualities.

Apple Curd

2 lb boiled, pulped and sieved apples
½ lb butter
½ lb sugar
2 eggs
Juice and rind of 1 lemon

Follow the basic curd method.

Apricot Curd

½ lb cooked and sieved fresh apricots
½ lb caster sugar
2 eggs
2 oz butter
Rind and juice of 1 lemon

Follow the basic curd method.

Blackberry Curd

1 lb blackberries
4 oz green apples
2 eggs
½ lb caster sugar
Juice and rind of 1 lemon
4 oz butter

Follow the basic curd method, cooking and sieving the blackberries separately and mixing with the apple pulp.

MARMALADES

Marmalades are usually made with citrus fruits which require a certain amount of softening before cooking. The juice is extracted and the remaining rind and pith are chopped, shredded or minced into small pieces. Cooked in water until soft then mixed with sugar and boiled to make a syrup which sets on cooling.

Basic Preparation and Cooking Method

2 lb bitter oranges

2 lemons
3 pt water to 1 lb fruit
1 lb sugar to 1 pt pulp

The peel of citrus fruits is tougher than that of fruits used for jam making, and the preparation of citrus fruits is more protracted. Wash and weigh the fruit, measure the water and put in a bowl. Squeeze out the fruit juice, tie the pips in a muslin bag, shred or mince the peel and add to the measured water. Soak overnight to soften the peel.

Place the contents of the bowl in a preserving pan and bring to the boil. Boil until tender and the liquid has reduced by half, after about 1 hour. Measure the liquid pulp and allow 1 lb sugar to 1 pt pulp. Bring to the boil, stir in the sugar, dissolve and boil rapidly.

Test for setting, pot, cover and store as for jams.

Grapefruit Marmalade

1½ lb grapefruit
3 lemons
¼ oz tartaric acid
3¼ lb preserving sugar
6 pt water

Follow the basic marmalade method.

Lemon Marmalade

3 lb lemons
6 lb preserving sugar
6 pt water

Follow the basic marmalade method.

Oxford Orange Marmalade

2 lb Seville oranges
1 small lemon
1 oz black treacle
½ lb chopped crystallised ginger
6 lb preserving sugar
6 pt water

Follow the basic marmalade method, adding the chopped ginger just before potting.

Quince Marmalade I

4 lb quinces

1½ lb sugar to 2 pt pulp
Water to cover

Peel and chop the quinces, cover with water and cook until soft. Add the sugar and boil until set. Pot and cover as for jams.

Quince Marmalade II

1 lb quinces
1½ lb preserving sugar
½ pt water

Scald the quinces, peel, core and pulp the flesh. Boil the sugar in the water to a thick syrup, removing any scum as necessary. Add the quince pulp and boil for 10 minutes. Pot and cover as for jams.

Three-Fruit Marmalade

2 grapefruit
4 lemons
2 sweet oranges
6 lb preserving sugar
6 pt water

Follow the basic marmalade method; the mixed fruits should have a total weight of 3 lb.

MINCEMEAT

This is a mixture of spices, dried fruits and suet. The ingredients are chopped finely when necessary so that they can be thoroughly mixed and the variety of flavours distributed. It is left for a few days before potting.

Basic Preparation and Cooking Method for Mincemeat

4 oz currants
4 oz sultanas
4 oz raisins
4 oz finely chopped suet
4 oz finely chopped mixed peel
4 oz finely chopped apples
4 oz Demerara sugar
¼ oz mixed spice
Grated rind and juice of 1 lemon and 1 orange
2½ fl oz rum
2½ fl oz brandy

Mince the currants, sultanas and raisins and blend with all the other ingredients. Put in a bowl, cover and leave for 2 days. Pot, cover and store as for jam.

Apricot Mincemeat

1 lb dried apricots
1 lb shredded suet
1 lb dates
1 lb currants
1 lb apples
1 lb raisins
1 lb brown sugar
2 oz chopped almonds
½ oz nutmeg
Rind of 1 large lemon

Follow the basic mincemeat method, soaking the apricots overnight and then chopping them finely.

Raspberry Mincemeat

1 lb raisins
1 lb sultanas
1 lb currants
1 lb caster sugar
¾ lb chopped suet
Grated rind of 2 lemons
Juice of 3 lemons
2 lb peeled, cored and chopped cooking apples
¾ lb mixed peel
1 lb raspberry jam
1 grated nutmeg

Follow the basic mincemeat method.

Russet Mincemeat

½ lb apricots, soaked overnight and chopped
½ lb peeled, cored and finely chopped cooking apples
½ lb large prunes, soaked overnight and chopped
½ lb sultanas
½ lb chopped suet
1 tablespoon golden syrup
1 teaspoon ground cinnamon
½ teaspoon ground cloves
Rind and juice of 1 lemon
Rind and juice of 1 orange
½ pt ginger wine
4 oz glacé cherries
4 oz mixed peel
4 oz soft brown sugar
2 oz chopped almonds

Follow the basic mincemeat method and use within three weeks.

CANDIED FRUIT

These may be made with cooked fresh or tinned fruit. The fruit is allowed to soak in a syrup for a period of about 14 days during which time the syrup solution is strained off and reduced at regular intervals. The candied fruit is dried slowly and may then be coated with sugar to give a crystallised finish, or it may be dipped in syrup to give a glacé finish. Stored in airtight containers. Flowers may also be candied using gum arabic crystals and rose water.

Candied Fresh Fruit

1 lb prepared fruit
½ pt cooking liquid
1¼ lb granulated sugar

The fruit should be ripe, but firm and free from any blemishes. Small whole apricots, plums and crab apples should be pricked all over, cherries should be stoned, peaches and pears peeled and halved or cut into quarters.

Place the fruit in sufficient boiling water to cover and cook gently until just tender. Drain the fruit and measure ½ pt of the cooking liquid; add 6 oz sugar, dissolve and bring to the boil. Pour the syrup over the fruit and leave, covered, for 24 hours.

Drain off the syrup and add 2 oz sugar; dissolve, bring to the boil and pour over the fruit. Leave for 24 hours and repeat this procedure six times, adding 2 oz sugar to the syrup every day.

On the 7th day, add 3 oz sugar and leave the fruit to soak for 48 hours. Repeat again with 3 oz sugar and leave in the syrup for 4 days.

Dry off the fruit in the oven at the lowest setting or in a warm place for 2-3 days, turning occasionally. When the fruits are thoroughly dried, pack them in cardboard or wooden boxes between layers of waxed paper.

Candied Tinned Fruit

1 lb tinned fruit (pineapple chunks or rings, plums, peaches and apricots are all suitable)
5 fl oz tinned syrup
1¼ lb granulated sugar

Use good quality tinned fruit. Dissolve ½ lb sugar in the tinned syrup, bring to the boil and pour over the fruit; leave for 24 hours. Drain off the syrup and add 2 oz sugar, dissolve, bring to the the boil and pour over the fruit.

Leave for 24 hours and repeat this procedure three times more. On the 4th day, add 3 oz sugar and leave the fruit to soak for 48 hours. Repeat once more, adding 3 oz sugar and leave for 4 days.

Dry off in the oven at the lowest setting or in a warm place for 2-3 days, turning occasionally. When the fruits are thoroughly dried, pack them in cardboard boxes, between layers of waxed paper.

Crystallised Finish to Candied Fruit

Dip the pieces of candied fruit quickly into boiling water; drain off excess moisture and roll each piece in caster sugar.

Glacé Finish to Candied Fruit

Dissolve 1 lb caster sugar in 5 fl oz water and bring to the boil for 1 minute. Pour a little syrup into a cup. Dip the candied fruit, one piece at a time, in boiling water for 20 seconds and then dip into the syrup using a skewer. Place on a wire rack to dry.

Keep the syrup slightly warm and replace the syrup in the cup as it becomes cloudy. Dry the fruit as before, turning from time to time.

Candied Flowers

¼ oz gum arabic crystals
1 dessertspoon rose water
Caster sugar

Primroses, violets, cowslips, anchusa, japonica, marigold, rose petals, lilac, leaves and flowers of nasturtiums, pansy, sage flowers, sweet peas, plum and apple blossom, wild crab apple, hawthorn, violet and mint leaves are all edible and suitable for candying.

Place the gum arabic and rose water in a small wide-necked jar with a screw top. Leave overnight, when it will have dissolved into a sticky glue; this will keep indefinitely if well covered.

Gather small amounts of fresh flowers, free from dew, rain or dust. They preserve best when quite fresh. Using a small paint brush with soft bristles, cover the petals, calyx and as much of the stem as possible with the solution; do not leave any area uncovered.

Large flowers are best broken into single

petals, small flowers may be held with a pair of tweezers. Dredge lightly but thoroughly with caster sugar until the flower is coated. Shake off any surplus and place the flowers on strips of sugared greaseproof paper on a wire rack to dry.

Place in a cool oven with the door open or in a warm place and leave until the flowers are quite crisp; this may take 24 hours. Store on greaseproof paper in an airtight tin; they will keep indefinitely.

PICKLES

These consist of fruits and vegetables preserved in spiced vinegar. Vegetables are usually brined in salt, rinsed and preserved without cooking in spiced vinegar while fruits, also pickled in spiced vinegar, are cooked in a sugar syrup before potting.

Vegetable Pickle

It is essential to use young, perfect vegetables and under-ripe fruit.

Spiced Vinegar
2 pt vinegar
2 oz pickling spice or
    ¼ oz blade mace
    ¼ oz whole allspice
    ¼ oz cloves
    ¼ oz cinnamon stick
    6 peppercorns

Bring the ingredients to the boil, cool and cover. Leave for 2 hours or longer for a stronger flavour. Strain and use the vinegar as required.

Prepare the vegetables according to type and immerse in a dry or wet brine.
Dry brining. Layer the prepared vegetables in a bowl with salt, allowing one level tablespoon salt to 1 lb vegetables. Cover and leave overnight.

Wet brining. Place the prepared vegetables in a bowl. Cover with a brine solution, allowing 2 oz salt to 1 pt water to each 1 lb vegetables. Put a plate over the top to keep the vegetables immersed.

Pack the brined, rinsed and drained vegetables into jars to within 1 in of the top. Pour spiced vinegar over, covering the vegetables by ½ in and leaving ½ in between vinegar and cover.

Cover with one of the following: metal or bakelite caps with a vinegar-proof lining, grease-proof paper and a round of muslin dipped in melted paraffin wax or fat, preserving skins or

boiled corks covered with greaseproof paper; tie down with string.

Store in a cool, dry, dark place; mature for 2-3 months before using.

Fruit Pickle

Sweet Vinegar
2 pt vinegar
¼ oz cloves
2 lb sugar

Bring the ingredients to the boil, dissolve the sugar, cover and leave for 2 hours or longer for a stronger flavour.

Pack the prepared fruit into jars, cover and seal as for vegetable pickles.

Sweet Pickled Apples

3 lb peeled, cored and quartered apples
3 lb Demerara sugar
3 sticks cinnamon
Cloves
2 pt vinegar

Put one or two cloves in each apple quarter and boil with the other ingredients until cooked. Pot and cover immediately, leaving the cinnamon sticks in the pickle.

Apricot Pickle

4 lb stoned, halved apricots
1 pt spiced vinegar

Cover the fruit with the vinegar and pot immediately; store for 3 months before use.

Pickled Beetroot

1 lb beetroot
1 pt vinegar

Oven: 350°F; gas mark 4; 1½ hours

Wash the beetroot, wrap in foil and bake in the oven or place in boiling salted water (1 oz salt to 1 pt water) and simmer for 1½-2 hours, depending on size. Cool the beetroot, skin and thinly slice or dice. Add ½ oz salt if the beetroot was baked and pour over the vinegar. A sweet pickle vinegar can also be used.

Sweet Pickled Bilberries

3 lb bilberries
¾ pt sweet vinegar

Follow the basic method for sweet pickled fruits.
Store for at least three months, 1 year is
recommended.

Sweet Pickled Blackberries

2½ lb blackberries
1 pt white vinegar
2 lb sugar
½ oz ground ginger
1½ oz allspice

Soak the blackberries in the vinegar and ginger
for 12 hours. Add the sugar and boil for 30
minutes. Allow to cool and add the allspice.
Pot and cover.

Spiced Cranberries

1 lb cranberries
½ oz each, root ginger, allspice and cinnamon
    stick
4 cloves
½ pt cider vinegar
½ lb Demerara sugar

Put the cranberries in a pan with the spices tied
in muslin, and the vinegar. Simmer until the fruit
is soft. Add the sugar, bring to the boil, and
simmer for 20 minutes or until thick.
    Pot and seal as for jam.

Cucumber Pickle

4½ lb cucumber
6 oz onions
5 oz salt
2 pt white wine vinegar
¼ oz mace
12 white peppercorns
¼ oz whole ginger

Wipe and clean the cucumber and slice 1/8 in
thick. Chop the onions finely and dry brine the
cucumber and onion in the salt for 24 hours.
    Drain from the brine; place in a jar and cover
with the vinegar. Leave for 4 hours.
    Drain off the vinegar and boil up with the
spices tied in a muslin bag.
    Strain the liquid and pour over the cucumber.
Pot and seal.

Sweet Pickled Damsons

3½ lb damsons
4 pt sweet vinegar

Wash and prick the fruit. Follow the basic sweet
pickle method, but leave the fruit to steep in the
syrup for 24 hours.
    Drain off the syrup and boil to reduce slightly,
then pour over the fruit. Repeat this every 24
hours for 4 days. Pot and cover.

Sweet Pickled Elderberries

1 lb elderberries
½ pt sweet pickle vinegar

Follow the basic sweet pickling method.

Pickled Gherkins

1 lb whole or sliced gherkins
1 pt spiced vinegar (omit the cinnamon) or sweet
    vinegar

Blanch the gherkins and refresh. Make up the vinegar pickle and marinate the gherkins overnight. Pot
and seal.

Sweet Pickled Gooseberries

3 lb gooseberries
1¼ lb sugar
½ pt vinegar
¼ oz ground cloves

Put all the ingredients in a pan and boil to the
consistency of jam. Pot and cover as for basic
pickles.

Sweet Pickled Melon

4 lb melon
1 pt sweet vinegar

Peel the melon, remove the seeds and cut the flesh
into 1 in cubes. Soak in wet brine for 24 hours.
Drain and simmer in the sweet vinegar for 3-5
minutes. Pot and cover.

Sweet Pickled Mint

1½-2 oz fresh mint leaves
½ lb small quartered tomatoes
6 oz small sliced onions

1 lb peeled and cored apples
1½ oz sultanas
¾ lb sugar
½ oz salt
¼ oz dry mustard
2 in piece of cinnamon stick
¼ oz peppercorns
1 blade of mace
1 pt vinegar

Put the sugar, salt, spices and vinegar in a pan and
boil up as for a sweet pickle.

Put the tomatoes, onions, apples and sultanas
in a wide-necked jar with mint leaves between each
layer. Pour the strained vinegar over the fruit
and vegetables and seal.

Pickled Mushrooms

1 lb peeled button mushrooms
¼ oz salt
½ pt malt vinegar

Place the mushrooms in a pan and sprinkle with
salt. Toss over gentle heat for a few minutes to
dry off. Cover with vinegar and simmer gently
for 5-10 minutes. Pot and cover.

Pickled Onions

2 lb small pickling onions
4 oz salt
1½ pt malt vinegar
4 oz sugar
1 oz pickling spice
10 cloves
10 black peppercorns

Boil the onions in water for a few minutes to
soften the skins. Drain and peel. Put in dry brine
for 24 hours. Drain and wash the onions.

Make an infusion of the vinegar, sugar and
spices; add the onions. Boil gently until the onions
are par-cooked; they should still be hard in the
centre. Pot and cover with vinegar and spices.
Leave for two weeks before use.

Sweet Pickled Peaches

1 lb peaches
½ lb granulated sugar
¼ oz each, ground cinnamon, allspice, ground
   coriander and ground cloves
½ grated nutmeg
3 fl oz cider

Mix the sugar and spices thoroughly. Blanch,
refresh and skin the peaches, cut in half and remove the stones; place in a pan and add the sugar,
spices and cider. Heat slowly until all the sugar has
dissolved and boiling point is reached. Simmer for
3 minutes, then transfer the fruit to a wide-necked
preserving jar, using a slotted spoon so that the
liquid is left behind.

Continue boiling the liquid and reduce until
thick, after 7-10 minutes. Pour over the peaches
and seal the jars as for jam. Serve with hot or cold
duck or pheasant.

Sweet Pickled Pears

2 lb peeled, cored and quartered hard pears
Sweet vinegar: 2 lb sugar, 1½ pt vinegar, 2 cloves

Follow the basic sweet pickle method.

Sweet Pickled Plums

2 lb hard plums
Sweet vinegar: 2 lb sugar, 1½ pt vinegar, 2 cloves

Follow the basic method of sweet pickling.

Sweet Pickled Quinces

4 lb peeled, cored and halved quinces
1 pt sweet pickle vinegar

Follow the basic sweet pickling method; keep for
at least 3 months before using.

Pickled Red Cabbage

2 lb shredded red cabbage
¾ lb sliced Spanish onions (optional)
2 oz cooking salt
2 pt cold spiced vinegar

Dry brine the cabbage and onions in a cool place
for 24 hours. Drain and pack into pots; pour over
the cold spiced vinegar and cover. Use after 2-3
weeks.

Pickled Samphire

Young samphire leaves
Spiced vinegar

Put the cleaned leaves in wet brine for 24 hours.
Rinse and follow basic pickle method. Store for
at least 3 weeks before using with roast mutton.

Green Tomato Pickle

3 lb sliced green tomatoes
1 lb peeled and sliced cucumber or marrow
1 seeded and chopped large red pepper
1 pt malt vinegar
½ oz garlic
1/8 oz dry mustard
½ teaspoon each, turmeric, allspice and celery
    seeds
½ oz salt

Dry brine the prepared tomatoes, cucumber and
red pepper for 24 hours; drain. Place all the
ingredients in a pan, bring to the boil and simmer
for about 1 hour. Pot and seal. Store for 3 months
before use.

Pickled Walnuts

4 lb green walnuts
1 pt spiced vinegar
1 lb salt
8 pt water

Test the walnuts with a needle at the opposite
end from the stalk, ¼ in from the end, for any
shell formation. Discard any that have shells.

Wet brine the walnuts for 7 days; change the
brine and continue soaking for a further 14 days.

Wash and dry and expose the walnuts to the
air until they blacken, after about 1 day. Bottle
and pour over the hot spiced vinegar and cover.
Store for at least 5-6 weeks before using.

Mixed Pickle

2 lb prepared mixed vegetables:
    ¾ lb cauliflower florets
    ½ lb sliced cucumber
    6 oz peeled whole shallots
    6 oz sliced French beans
1½ pt cold spiced vinegar

Wet brine the vegetables for 24 hours. Put them
in jars and add the spiced vinegar. Cover as
for pickles.

Mixed Sweet Pickle

1½-2 lb chopped cucumber
2 lb seeded and coarsely minced tomatoes
3 lb peeled, seeded and roughly chopped marrow
Sweet pickle:

1½ pt malt vinegar
½ pt white vinegar
1 oz salt
½ teaspoon each, powdered mace, celery seed,
    and mixed spice
½ oz bruised root ginger
¾ lb Demerara sugar
½ oz turmeric

Put the prepared vegetables in a pan with the
vinegar, salt, sugar and the spices tied in a muslin
bag; bring to the boil. Simmer for 3 minutes.
Remove the spices and pot as for basic pickles.
Store for at least 2 months before using.

Bread and Butter Pickle

2½ lb sliced cucumber
1 lb sliced onions
Pickle:
    1 pt vinegar
    6 oz sugar
    ¼ oz celery seed
    ¼ oz mustard seed

Dry brine the onions and cucumber for 1 hour.
Put the vegetables in a pot. Heat the vinegar and
other pickle ingredients until the sugar has dissolved. Boil until slightly reduced. Strain the
pickle over the vegetables and cover immediately.

Pickled Eggs

16 hardboiled eggs
2 pt spiced vinegar

Remove the shells and place the eggs in a wide-
necked jar. Boil the pickle ingredients for 10
minutes, cool and pour over the eggs. When cold,
cover and store for 3 weeks before use. Use within
1-2 months.

Piccalilli

6 lb prepared mixed vegetables:
    cauliflower florets, diced marrow and
    cucumber, topped, tailed and sliced beans,
    small button onions
¾ lb cooking salt
6 pt water
9 oz sugar
½ oz dry mustard
¼ teaspoon ground ginger
3 pt white vinegar

1½ oz flour
1½ oz turmeric

Place the prepared vegetables in a large bowl and wet brine for 24 hours. Blend the sugar, mustard and ginger with 2½ pt vinegar in a large pan; add the drained and rinsed vegetables, bring to the boil and simmer for 20 minutes.

Blend the flour and turmeric with the remaining vinegar and stir into the vegetables. Bring to the boil and cook through. Pot and cover. Store for at least 2 months before using.

CHUTNEYS

These are strong hot relishes or condiments composed of a variety of ripe fresh fruits, dried fruits, vegetables, herbs and spices. Usually simmered in vinegar or other acid liquid until thick, potted and stored as for pickles. Used as accompaniments or sauces to meat and fish. Pot and seal as for pickles.

Apple Chutney

3 lb peeled, cored and sliced cooking apples
3 lb peeled and chopped onions
1 lb sultanas or stoned raisins
Juice and rind of 2 lemons
1½ lb Demerara sugar
1 pt malt vinegar

Put the prepared apples, onions and sultanas in a pan. Add the lemon juice and rind, sugar and vinegar. Bring to the boil, reduce the heat and simmer until thick and no liquid remains.
Pot and seal.

Apple and Marrow Chutney

1½ lb peeled, sliced and cubed marrow
1½ lb peeled, cored, sliced and chopped apples
Dry brine (1½ oz salt)
½ lb chopped onions
¾ pt vinegar
¼ oz salt
¼ oz mustard seed
¾ lb brown sugar
¼ oz white peppercorns
½ oz whole ginger

Put the prepared marrow in a bowl, sprinkle with salt and leave for 12 hours. Strain the marrow.

Put the marrow, apples, onions, vinegar, salt and brown sugar in a pan with the spices tied in a muslin bag. Bring to the boil and simmer gently until all the vegetables are tender, and reduced to a thick consistency. Remove the muslin bag. Pot and seal.

Runner Bean Chutney

2 lb runner beans
1½ lb chopped onions
1 lb Demerara sugar
1 lb soft brown sugar
1½ pt vinegar
1 oz cornflour
¾ oz turmeric
¾ oz dry mustard

Top and tail the runner beans and cut into 1 in lengths. Cook the chopped onions in ½ pt vinegar until soft. Mix the dry ingredients to a smooth paste with the remaining vinegar.

Blend the beans into the vinegar; cook for 10 minutes. Add the sugar and onions and simmer until reduced to a thick consistency. Pot and seal.

Beetroot Chutney

3 lb beetroot
1½ lb prepared apples
1 lb onions
½ lb Demerara sugar
½ teaspoon ground ginger
1 pt vinegar
Juice of 1 lemon
1 oz salt

Boil the beetroot for 1½ hours, cool and peel. Pass the beetroot, apples and onion through a mincer; place all the ingredients in a pan and boil until soft, stirring frequently. Pot and seal.

Bengal Chutney

3 lb peeled, cored and chopped apples
1½ lb skinned and chopped tomatoes
½ lb sultanas
½ lb raisins
½ lb finely chopped onions
2 pt malt vinegar
4 oz salt
3 lb sugar
¼ oz cayenne

1 oz ground ginger
1 oz crushed garlic
2 oz mustard seed

Put the vinegar in a pan with the apples and tomatoes and add the raisins, sultanas, onions and other ingredients. Boil together until the apples are reduced to a pulp, and the chutney is thick. Pot and seal.

Blackberry Chutney

6 lb blackberries
2 lb cooking apples
2 lb onions
2 lb brown sugar
1 oz salt
2 oz mustard
2 oz ground ginger
2 teaspoons powdered mace
1 teaspoon cayenne
2 pt malt vinegar

Peel and chop the apples and onions, put them in a pan with the blackberries, spices and vinegar. Cook for about 1 hour. Rub through a sieve to remove pips; add sugar and cook until thick. Pot and seal.

Cranberry Chutney

2 lb cranberries
1¾ lb white sugar
½ lb coarsely chopped stoned raisins
Juice and rind of 2 oranges
½ lb chopped onions
5 fl oz wine or white vinegar
¼ oz mustard seed
½ teaspoon each, ground ginger, powdered cloves
    and cinnamon
Salt and pepper

Put the cranberries in a preserving pan with the sugar, raisins, rind of oranges and onions. Add the vinegar, strained orange juice and other ingredients. Bring to the boil and cook gently, stirring from time to time until the chutney thickens after about 1½ hours.
    Pot and seal.

Cruachan Chutney

2 lb peeled and chopped green tomatoes
2 lb peeled, cored and chopped cooking apples

2 lb chopped onions
1/8 oz grated nutmeg
4 oz sultanas
1 lb dark brown sugar
1 pt vinegar
1/8 oz cloves
Pinch cayenne
4 oz raisins

Put the tomatoes, apples and onions in a bowl and leave overnight. The next day put all the ingredients in a pan and boil for 2 hours, stirring often. Pot and seal.

Date and Banana Chutney

4 lb unpeeled bananas
2 lb chopped onions
1 lb chopped dates
1 lb black treacle
1 pt vinegar
¼ oz curry powder (optional)
½ lb chopped crystallised ginger
¼ oz salt

Peel and slice the bananas. Put the bananas, onions and dates in a pan with the vinegar and cook until tender. Beat the mixture to a pulp and add the curry powder, ginger, salt and treacle. Cook the mixture until a rich brown colour. Pot and seal.

Dower House Chutney

1½ lb stoned halved plums
2 lb peeled and sliced tomatoes
1½ pt malt vinegar
½ oz garlic
¾ lb peeled onions
2½ lb peeled and cored apples
½ lb mixed dried fruit
1 lb Demerara sugar
2 oz salt
1 oz pickling spice (tied in muslin)

Place the plums, tomatoes and vinegar in a large pan. Mince the garlic with the onions, apples and dried fruit and add to the plums with the sugar, salt and pickling spice. Simmer until tender and reduced. Remove the muslin bag; pot and seal.

Gooseberry Chutney

5 lb soft gooseberries
1 pt vinegar

2 lb sugar
¾ oz mixed black pepper, spice and cinnamon
½ lb sultanas
½ lb raisins

Boil the gooseberries and vinegar to a pulp. Add
the sugar and other ingredients and boil until a
thick consistency is obtained. Pot and seal.

Indian Chutney

3 lb apples
¾ lb large onions
2 pt malt vinegar
2 lb brown sugar
1 teaspoon salt
1 lb stoned, chopped raisins
6 oz chopped crystallised ginger
½ teaspoon cayenne
1 dessertspoon dry mustard

Peel, core and chop the apples and onions. Add the
vinegar and simmer for 10 minutes; add the other
ingredients and boil for 20 minutes, stirring occasionally. Pot and seal.

Pear Chutney

3 lb peeled, cored and sliced pears
1 lb chopped onions
1 lb skinned and sliced green tomatoes
2 pt malt vinegar
½ lb chopped stoned raisins
½ lb chopped celery
1½ lb Demerara sugar
¼ teaspoon each, cayenne pepper and ground
    ginger
½ oz salt
6 peppercorns (tied in muslin)

Put the prepared vegetables and pears in a pan
with the vinegar; simmer until tender. Add the
remaining ingredients and simmer to a thick
consistency. Remove muslin bag; pot and seal.

Plum and Apple Chutney

1 lb sugar
2 pt malt vinegar
1 lb peeled, cored and chopped apples
3 lb stoned and quartered plums
1 lb chopped onions
½ lb stoned chopped raisins
½ lb sliced carrots

¼ oz each, ground cloves, cinnamon, ginger
    and allspice
2 oz salt

Put the sugar and most of the vinegar in a pan and
bring slowly to the boil; add the fruit and vegetables. Blend the spices and salt with the remaining
vinegar and stir into the ingredients in the pan.
Bring to the boil, reduce the heat and simmer to a
thick consistency. Pot and seal.

Pumpkin Chutney

2½ lb pumpkin
2 lb preserving or moist sugar
½ lb seedless raisins
1 pt vinegar
4 oz chopped onions
¼ teaspoon ground nutmeg
1 oz salt
4 bay leaves
1/8 oz each, ground ginger and pepper
Juice of 1 lemon
2 tablespoons grape juice

Put all the ingredients in a large bowl and mix;
cover and leave for 3 hours. Simmer gently until
cooked, then boil until the juices have reduced
and a firm texture is obtained. Pot and seal.

Quince and Lemon Chutney

1½ lb quinces
½ lemon
1 oz chopped shallot
1 clove garlic
4 oz raisins
2 oz chopped stem ginger
½ pt white wine vinegar
½ teaspoon each, coriander, ground
    cinnamon and black pepper
1/8 oz salt
¼ teaspoon ground cloves
½ lb granulated sugar
½ lb Demerara sugar

Peel, core and chop the quinces; mix with the
lemon and shallot. Put all the ingredients in a
pan, bring to the boil and simmer slowly, stirring
from time to time until the fruit is cooked and
the mixture is thick. This will take approximately
45 minutes. Pot and seal.

Rhubarb Chutney

2 lb rhubarb
4 oz chopped onions
Rind and juice of 2 lemons
1 oz salt
1/8 oz ground ginger
1 lb brown sugar
1 lb sultanas
1 pt spiced vinegar

Cut the rhubarb into ½ in cubes and mix with
the onions and other ingredients. Put in a pan,
cover and boil until soft and thick. Pot and seal.

Rhubarb and Orange Chutney

2½ lb rhubarb
Grated rind and juice of 2 oranges
¾ lb peeled and chopped onions
1½ pt malt vinegar
2 lb Demerara sugar
1 lb raisins
¾ oz mustard seed
¾ oz peppercorns
1/8 oz allspice

Place the orange rind and juice, rhubarb, cut into
1 in cubes, onions, raisins, sugar, vinegar and the
spices tied in muslin, in a pan. Bring to the boil
and simmer until a thick pulp. Remove the muslin
bag; pot and seal.

Green Tomato Chutney

3 lb green tomatoes
1½ lb peeled, cored and sliced cooking apples
1 lb sliced onions
1 lb sultanas
1 head diced celery
1 oz salt
¾ lb brown sugar
1½ oz dry mustard
1/8 oz each ground ginger and cayenne pepper
1¼ pt vinegar

Remove the stalks from the tomatoes, blanch,
peel and cut into quarters. Put all the ingredients
in a pan, bring to the boil and simmer for 2-3
hours, until soft, stirring from time to time. Pot
and seal.

Red Tomato Chutney

2½ lb ripe tomatoes

½ lb chopped onions
Salt
½ pt vinegar
1 lb Demerara sugar
8 cloves
1/8 oz cayenne pepper
¼ oz salt

Blanch and peel the tomatoes. Put them with
the onions in a bowl, sprinkle with salt and leave
for 12 hours.

Drain off the brine and mix the tomatoes and
onions with the other ingredients. Boil the mixture
until tender. Pot and seal.

BOTTLED SAUCES

These are infusions, usually in vinegar, of a variety
of spices and herbs to a give a very strong relish.
Vegetables or fruits may be added, and the mixture
is strained, bottled and stored for use as an
accompanying sauce.

Anchovy Ketchup

1 pt ale
2 oz anchovy fillets
1½ oz finely chopped shallots
1½ tablespoons mushroom ketchup
¼ teaspoon each, caster sugar and ground ginger
Pinch ground mace
1 clove

Put all the ingredients in a pan and simmer for 1
hour, strain and when cold pour into bottles, cover
and store.

Spiced Cranberry Sauce

2½ lb cranberries
½ pt water
1/8 oz mixed spice
6 cloves
12 allspice berries
10 oz brown sugar
1 dessertspoon lemon juice or vinegar

Put the fruit, spices and water in a pan and simmer
until soft. Pass through a sieve. Stir in the sugar
and when dissolved, simmer for 2 minutes; add the
lemon juice or vinegar. Pot, cover and store.

Harvey's Sauce

3 anchovies
2 pt vinegar
1 tablespoon soy sauce
5 fl oz walnut ketchup
2 oz finely chopped shallots
1 crushed clove garlic
½ teaspoon cayenne pepper
Cochineal

Chop each anchovy into three pieces and place them in a wide-necked bottle; add all the ingredients with a few drops of cochineal and cover closely. Leave the bottle to stand for about 14 days, shaking vigorously once a day. Strain the sauce into small bottles, cork securely and store in a cool dry place.

Herb Sauce

1 root horseradish
2 oz finely chopped shallots
Sprigs basil, marjoram and thyme
6 cloves
Juice and grated rind of 1 lemon
½ pt string vinegar
1 pt water

Wash and scrape the horseradish. Put all the ingredients in a pan and simmer for about 20 minutes; strain. When cold, pour into small bottles and seal carefully.

Use the sauce to flavour stews and gravies.

Leamington Sauce Warwickshire

¾ pt vinegar
5 fl oz walnut pickle or ketchup
5 fl oz soy sauce
2 tablespoons port wine
½ oz chopped shallot
1 crushed clove garlic
½ teaspoon cayenne pepper

Mix all the ingredients, cover and store for 3 weeks. Strain and re-bottle. Serve with cold meat or fish.

Pontac Sauce Leicestershire

1¼ lb ripe elderberries
¾ pt vinegar
¼ oz salt
Mace and root ginger to taste

40 peppercorns (2 oz)
12 cloves
4 oz chopped shallots

Pour the boiling vinegar over the elderberries; let the jar stand overnight in a cool oven. Strain and boil the liquid for 5 minutes with the salt, root ginger, mace, peppercorns, cloves and shallots. Bottle with the spices when cold.

Quinn's Sauce

5 fl oz mushroom ketchup
2½ fl oz walnut pickle
2½ fl oz port wine
3 finely chopped anchovies
2 finely chopped shallots
1 tablespoon soy sauce
Pinch cayenne pepper

Put all the ingredients in a pan and simmer for 15 minutes. When cold, bottle and store with sealed corks. Serve with fish.

Rhubarb Sauce

3 lb rhubarb
½ lb chopped onions
1 lb sugar
¾ pt vinegar
1 oz salt
6 cloves
Pinch cayenne
¼ oz each, turmeric and dry mustard

Cut the rhubarb into 1 in pieces and place in a pan with the onions and half the sugar. Put in a little of the vinegar and add the salt, cloves and cayenne; boil gently for about 1 hour.

Pass the mixture through a sieve; return it to the pan and add the remains of the sugar and vinegar; bring to the boil and add the turmeric and mustard mixed with a little vinegar. Boil gently for about 45 minutes or until thick. Cool, bottle and cork tightly. Serve with cold meats.

A Sauce for Cold Meat

3 lemons
1½ oz salt
1 oz allspice
1 oz mustard seed
1 oz white pepper
1 oz grated horseradish

½ oz each, mace, cayenne and cloves
2 pt vinegar

Slice the lemons, remove the pips and rub salt into the slices. Mix the allspice, mustard seed, pepper, horseradish, cayenne, mace and cloves. Put the lemon slices in layers in a jar and sprinkle with the mixed spices between each layer. Pour over the vinegar at boiling point. Set aside for 24 hours, squeeze, strain and bottle.

Worcestershire Sauce

1 pt malt vinegar
3 tablespoons walnut ketchup
3 tablespoons anchovy essence
2 tablespoons soy sauce
¼ teaspoon cayenne pepper
2 oz finely chopped shallots
Salt

Put all the ingredients in a bottle and cork it tightly. Leave for about 2 weeks, shaking the bottle several times a day. Strain into small bottles, cork tightly and store in a cool, dry and dark place.

SYRUPS AND CORDIALS

The two terms are identical and are applied to drinks that do not contain any alcohol. The yeasts naturally present in the raw materials must be killed or their growth prevented otherwise the syrups will ferment in the bottle which may explode. Syrups may be diluted with hot or cold water or milk, or used as flavouring for puddings, jellies and ice creams.

There are two basic methods of preparing syrups and cordials.

Hot Method

This involves sterilising the syrup to kill the yeasts present.

Fruit, over-ripe, but free from mould; washed
    clean
Water
¾-1 lb white sugar to 1 pt pulp

Place the fruit in a basin and bruise with a wooden spoon. Add 1 dessertspoon of water and stand the basin in a saucepan half full of water. Cover with a lid or use a double boiler. Simmer gently until the juices flow freely; pulp again.

Squeeze the pulp in a jelly bag or through a thick cloth; add sugar and stir until the sugar dissolves. If necessary, strain through muslin again. Bottle syrup to 1½-2 in below the base of the cork or screw stopper. If corks are used, wire or tie them down firmly or they will be forced out during heating. Sterilise corks or stoppers by immersing them in boiling water for 15 minutes.

Put the bottles in a deep pan with a false bottom such as a fish kettle. Add sufficient water to come to the bases of the corks; heat the water to simmering point and maintain for 20 minutes. Take the bottles out and stand on a wooden table to cool.

Cold Method

This method gives a fresher flavoured syrup, but is slightly more difficult.

Fruit, over-ripe, but free from mould
Pectoenzyme (a commercial pectin-destroying
    enzyme that may be purchased from most
    winemakers' sundriesmen)
¾-1 lb white sugar to 1 pt pulp

Crush the fruit in a bowl and mix with ¼ oz Pectoenzyme for each 8 lb fruit. Cover with a clean cloth and leave overnight. Squeeze the pulp in a jelly bag or through a thick cloth. Add sugar, bottle, cork and sterilise as for the hot method.

Storing

Keep syrups in a dark cool place to retain colour and flavour. The sediment may be used, but if a clear product is required, the syrup can be decanted from the bottle as necessary. No syrup should be kept for more than one year as the flavour slowly deteriorates.

Apricot

6 lb apricots
3 lb sugar
6 pt water

Make up a syrup with water and sugar, add the apricots and boil until tender. Finish as for hot method.

Blackberry

6 lb blackberries
½ pt water
1 lb sugar to 1 pt juice
8 cloves
3 oz root ginger (tied in muslin)

Follow the hot method. After adding sugar, boil
for 10 minutes with the spices in the liquid.
Remove spices before bottling.

Black Cherry

Follow either of the basic methods.

Black Currant

Follow the hot method, using 1 pt water to 3 lb
fruit; or follow the cold method using ¼ oz
Pectoenzyme to each 5 lb fruit. Leave for two to
three days, mixing daily.

Damson

Follow either of the basic methods.

Elderberry

Follow either method. A muslin bag with 6
cloves and 1 oz root ginger may be added to each
quart of unsweetened juice and simmered for 10-
15 minutes.

Ginger

1 lb white or Demerara sugar
1 pt water
2 oz honey
30 drops ginger essence

Simmer the sugar and water to dissolve,
add the honey and stir until this also dissolves.
Allow to cool, add the essence, bottle and cork.

Dilute 2 tablespoons in one tumbler of hot
water.

Lemon

6 lemons
4 lb white sugar
2 pt water
½ oz citric acid

Dissolve the sugar in the slightly warmed water,
add the lemon juice, finely grated rind and citric
acid. Stir vigorously, leave for 12 hours; strain,
bottle and sterilise as in the hot method.

Loganberry

Follow either method.

Mulberry

Follow either method.

Orange

6 oranges
4 lb white sugar
3 pt water
1 oz citric acid

Boil the sugar, water and grated orange peel in
a pan for 10 minutes. Leave overnight, then add
the citric acid and orange juice; strain, bottle
and cork. Sterilise as for the hot method.

Peppermint

Follow the recipe for Ginger Cordial, substituting
peppermint essence for ginger essence.

Raspberry

Follow either method.

Rose Hip

2 lb ripe rose hips
4½ pt water
1 lb white sugar

Mince the cleaned rose hips and place in a pan
with 3 pt boiling water. Bring to the boil, remove
from the heat and leave for 15 minutes. Pour
through a scalded jelly bag and allow to drip.

Return the pulp to the pan, add the remaining 1½ pt water, boil and allow to stand without
further heating for another 10 minutes. Drain
through a jelly bag and combine the two extracts
in a clean enamelled pan; simmer until reduced
to 1½ pt, add the sugar and boil for 5 minutes.

Cork and sterilise as for the hot method.

Strawberry

Follow either method.

Mixed Fruit

Use equal quantities of black currants, strawberries and raspberries and follow either of the methods.

CONFECTIONERY

This includes all products made with a high sugar content. Generally, the sugar is dissolved in liquid and brought to the boil. As the temperature begins to rise, water evaporates and the resulting syrup thickens and eventually darkens in colour when the caramel stage is reached. In order to produce a variety of textures in the finished product, the stages through which the syrup passes are classified so that the boiling process can be stopped at any of these stages: smooth (when the mixture begins to look syrupy); firm or hard ball (when it forms a harder ball); small crack (when a thread of syrup breaks sharply); hard crack (when the thread of syrup is harder to crack); and caramel (when the syrup begins to turn a dark brown).

The following are the basic types of confectionery: fondant (fudge and tablet); caramel; toffee; marzipan (boiled and unboiled).

Equipment

Sugar boiling thermometer, necessary for measuring temperature accurately, graduated from 60-450°F and preferably with a sliding clip that fits on to the side of the pan.

Place the thermometer in cold water, bring to the boil and check for accuracy; the temperature should read 212°F at boiling point. Leave in water to cool.

To use, shake the thermometer well so that the mercury thread is unbroken. Place in the mixture and ensure that the bulb is completely immersed. Stand it in hot water when not in the sweet mixture. Do not leave too long in the confectionery without moving it around as the syrup will adhere to the ball and cause a faulty reading. Clean thoroughly after use as crystals left might spoil the next boiling.

Saucepan, use a strong, heavy-based pan to prevent sticking; enamel is not suitable.

Wooden spatula, for beating fondants and fudges.

Flexible palette knife, with a stainless-steel blade; useful for lifting and shaping sweets.

Marble slab, not absolutely essential as an enamelled surface can be used instead. Certain plastic surfaces will also withstand temperatures up to 280°F, but usually not beyond this.

Stages in Sugar Boiling

After the sugar has been dissolved in the liquid and brought to the boil, the temperature continues to rise as the water evaporates and the syrup thickens, darkening in colour. The stages through which the sugar passes are classified as follows:

Smooth (230°F), for crystallising purposes. The mixture begins to look syrupy. To test, dip finger in water and then very quickly into the syrup, the thumb will slide smoothly over the fingers, but the sugar will cling.

Soft ball (240°F), for Fondants and Fudges. To test, drop a little syrup into cold water and leave for a few minutes. Pick up between the finger and thumb when it should roll into a small soft ball.

Firm or hard ball (250°F), for caramels, marshmallows, nougat and soft toffee. Test as above, when the syrup should roll into a hard ball.

Small crack (280°F), for toffees. Test as above, when a thread of syrup should break lightly.

Hard crack (290°F), for hard toffees and rock. Test as above, when the thread of syrup should break sharply.

Caramel (310°F, upwards), when the syrup begins to turn a darker brown colour, caramel stage is reached. If allowed to become too dark, the taste will be bitter.

Basic Sugar Boiling Process

1 lb sugar
¼-½ pt liquid
Pinch cream of tartar or 1 oz glucose or
   a few drops lemon juice (to prevent
   granulation)

Ensure that all equipment is absolutely clean. Dissolve the sugar over low heat in the liquid, stirring with a wooden spoon until no particles of sugar are left. To test, examine the back of the spoon for any sugar crystals.

Brush the sides of a pan with water to remove any crystals. When the sugar is completely dissolved, the syrup may be brought to the boil and cream of tartar added to prevent granulation. Skim if necessary and allow to simmer gently; do not stir unless the recipe states so.

When the required temperature has been reached (see Stages in Sugar Boiling), remove immediately from the heat so that the temperature does not rise any higher.

Fondant

1 lb granulated sugar
5 fl oz water
1 oz glucose or pinch cream of tartar

Follow the basic sugar boiling process until the soft ball stage at 240°F.

Remove from the heat and allow to cool for 5 minutes, pour into a bowl and leave for 15 minutes. Work the mixture in the bowl until thick. Knead on greaseproof paper to an even texture throughout.

Divide the mixture into portions and flavour and colour as required. Store in an airtight tin.

The mixture may be worked on a marble slab or other suitable surface. Sprinkle the surface with water and pour on the mixture; leave for a few minutes to cool until a skin forms round the edges. Take a wooden spatula and collect the mixture together, then work it backwards and forwards in a figure of eight movement. Continue to work the syrup, collecting it into as small a mass as possible, until it changes character and becomes opaque white and plastic.

Fondant creams. Flavour and colour the basic mixture with any of the following: tangerine juice or essence, orange juice or orange flower water (both orange yellow); lemon juice or essence, pineapple juice or essence (both lemon yellow); banana, apricot or pear essence (warm yellow); peach, strawberry, raspberry or cherry essence, rose water (shades of pink); violet or lilac essence (violet); powdered ginger and coffee essence (brown); peppermint oil (green).

Roll the fondant out to the required thickness, using a little icing sugar on the board and cut out with a small cutter or model by hand. A rubber mat may be used to make more elaborate shapes, in which case the fondant must be melted and poured into the moulds.

Fondant fruits. Cubes of crystallised fruit may be dipped in liquid fondant, coloured and flavoured to suit the fruit.

Fondant nuts. Flavour the liquid fondant with coffee essence; dip halved walnuts and brazil nuts in it.

Fudge

1 lb granulated sugar
2 oz butter
3 fl oz evaporated milk
Flavouring

Follow the basic sugar boiling process until soft ball stage at 240°F. Stir occasionally to prevent sticking. Remove the pan from the heat, place on a cool surface and add flavouring or any other additional ingredients.

Beat the mixture until it becomes thick and creamy and "grains" when minute sugar crystals form. Pour the mixture into a well-greased tin; leave to cool and then mark with a sharp knife using a sawing movement.

Tablet

1 lb granulated sugar
9 fl oz thin cream
Flavouring

Follow the basic sugar boiling process until soft ball stage is reached, at 240°F. Remove from the heat, place the pan on a cool surface and beat until it "grains" slightly. It should not be too highly grained, but must pour out flat into a buttered tin. Mark as above just before setting.

Flavourings and Colourings for Fudge and Tablet

Orange or lemon, add grated rind of half an orange or whole lemon and 2 tablespoons juice with a little sugar.

Chocolate, add 4 oz grated plain chocolate and 2 oz honey when dissolving the sugar.

Vanilla, mix in 2-3 drops of vanilla essence and 2 oz finely chopped walnuts and vanilla.

Coffee, add ¾ oz instant coffee and 2 oz finely chopped walnuts (coffee and walnut).

Coconut, add 2 oz desiccated coconut.

Cinnamon, add 2-3 drops cinnamon oil.

Ginger, dissolve 1/8 oz ground ginger in a little

water and add 2 oz chopped preserved ginger.

Peppermint, add 2-3 drops peppermint oil.

Nut, add 2-4 oz finely chopped nuts.

Fruit and nut, blend in 2 oz finely chopped nuts and 2 oz seedless raisins.

Date, add 3 oz finely chopped dates.

Fig, mix 2 oz chopped, cooked, dried and soaked figs.

Marshmallow, ½ lb chopped marshmallows before beating.

Caramel

1 lb granulated sugar
5 fl oz water
5 fl oz cream
4 oz glucose
1 oz butter
1 teaspoon rose water
1 teaspoon orange flower water

Follow the sugar boiling process, adding the glucose when boiling point is reached, and boil to 240°F or soft ball. Add the cream, butter and waters, boil to 250°F or hard ball, stirring continuously. Pour the mixture into a buttered tin and mark just before it sets.

Toffee

1 lb granulated sugar
1 oz butter
5 fl oz water
1/8 oz cream of tartar

Follow the sugar boiling process to 250°F or hard ball. Do not stir the mixture. Remove from the heat and pour into greased tins. Mark into small squares just before setting.

Angus Toffee Scotland

1½ lb granulated sugar
2 oz ground almonds
1 oz butter
5 fl oz milk

Follow the basic sugar boiling process to hard ball, at 250°F. Boil for about 7 minutes, stirring all the time. Remove from the heat and beat until it thickens. Pour into well greased tins and mark just before setting.

Barley Sugar

1 lb granulated sugar
1 pt barley water
½ oz butter

Follow the basic sugar boiling process to hard crack, at 290°F. Pour on to an oiled slab; double the mixture over and cut into strips as quickly as possible with scissors. Twist lightly as it is cut.

To make barley water, place 1 oz barley in a pan; cover with water and bring to the boil; pour off the water. Add 1¼ pt fresh water and ½ oz liquorice stick. Boil until all the strength is out of the liquorice. Remove from the heat, pour into a bowl and leave to settle, then pour off the clear liquid.

Black Man (or Treacle Candy)

1 lb Demerara sugar
5 oz black treacle
1/8 oz cream of tartar
2½ fl oz water
Peppermint, almond or lemon essence

Follow the basic sugar boiling process to small crack, at 280°F. Remove from the heat and add the essence. Pour into greased tins. When it is cool enough to handle, remove from the tin with buttered hands.

Pull rapidly with both hands as long as this is possible (confectioners use an iron hook upon the wall to assist them in pulling). When it is too hard to work, cut sticks to the desired lengths with scissors.

Bulls Eyes

2 lb loaf sugar
¼ teaspoon cream of tartar
1 cup cold water
Yellow colouring
¼ teaspoon each, tartaric acid and lemon essence

Dissolve the sugar and cream of tartar in water. Boil until hard crack, at 290°F. Pour a small portion on to a buttered slab and pull until creamy white. Add yellow colouring, tartaric acid and lemon essence to the remaining portion and pull again.

Lay strips of the white portions on the coloured one, 1 in apart. Fold in two with the stripes outside and cut into convenient strips to shape into balls.

Butterscotch

1 lb Demerara sugar
4 oz butter
¼ oz ground ginger dissolved in a little water or
    lemon juice

Follow the basic sugar boiling process to small
crack, at 280°F. Remove from the heat and shake
in the ginger mixture. Pour the mixture into well
greased tins and mark just before setting.

Doncaster Butterscotch Yorkshire

1 lb Demerara sugar
½ pt milk
6 oz butter
1/8 oz cream of tartar

Follow the butterscotch method.

Edinburgh Rock Scotland

1 lb granulated sugar
½ pt cold water
Colouring and flavouring (peppermint, white;
    ginger, brown; cinnamon, pink; lemon,
    yellow)
Icing sugar
Pinch cream of tartar

Follow the basic sugar boiling process to hard
ball, at 250°F. Remove from the heat and add
colouring and flavouring. Pour on to a buttered
marble slab.
　　As the mixture begins to cool, turn the ends
and edges towards the middle with a buttered
knife. When cool enough to handle, dust with
icing sugar and pull gently until dull. Do not
twist. Cut into pieces with scissors. Place in a
warm room and leave for 24 hours or until the
granulation process is complete and the rock
powdery and soft.

Everton Toffee   Lancashire

1 lb granulated sugar
4 oz butter
5 fl oz water
Pinch cream of tartar

Follow the basic sugar boiling process to hard
crack, at 290°F. Pour into well-greased tins and
mark just before setting.

Glasgow Toffee Scotland

4 oz granulated sugar
4 oz Demerara sugar
2 oz unsalted butter
2 oz salted butter
1½ oz grated chocolate
½ teaspoon vanilla essence
5 oz golden syrup
5 fl oz cream

Follow the basic sugar boiling process, adding the
butters and chocolate, to hard ball, at 250°F,
stirring all the time. Blend in the vanilla, syrup and
cream and pour into well greased tins; mark just
before it sets.

Glessie

½ lb soft brown sugar
1 oz butter
1 dessertspoon water
1/8 oz cream of tartar
1½ lb golden syrup

Boil the sugar, tartar, butter and water for 5
minutes. Add the syrup and follow the basic sugar
boiling process to hard crack, at 290°F, without
stirring. Pour out very thinly into well-greased
tins and chop up when cold.

Gunday Scotland

1 lb Demerara sugar
½ oz golden syrup or black treacle
2 oz butter
Aniseed or cinnamon flavouring

Follow the basic sugar boiling process to hard
crack, at 290°F. Remove from the heat and pour
into well-greased tins and mark just before setting.

Helensburgh Toffee Dunbartonshire

2 lb granulated sugar
4 oz butter
7½ fl oz condensed milk
5 fl oz water
Few drops vanilla essence
Walnut halves (optional)

Follow the basic sugar boiling process, boiling for
10 minutes before adding the condensed milk,
butter and flavouring; boil to soft ball, at 240°F,
stirring occasionally to prevent sticking.

Remove from the heat and beat for 1 minute. Pour the mixture into well-greased tins and mark before it sets. Half a walnut may be pressed into each square.

Mansfield Toffee Nottinghamshire

2 lb Demerara sugar
1 oz butter
½ teaspoon vanilla essence
2 oz chopped nuts

Follow the basic sugar boiling process to hard ball, at 250°F, stirring occasionally to prevent sticking. Add the vanilla and nuts and pour into well-greased tins; mark just before setting.

Treacle Toffee

1 lb Demerara sugar
4 oz butter
½ lb black treacle
1 tablespoon vinegar

Follow the basic sugar boiling process cooking the sugar with butter, treacle and vinegar to soft crack stage, at 280°F. Pour the mixture into well-greased tins and leave to set, marking it just before setting.

Toffee Apples

Boil the treacle toffee (see above) to hard crack stage, at 290°F; push sticks into the cores of apples and dip the apples in the toffee, twirl round for a few seconds and leave to cool on a greased baking tray or waxed paper.

Yellow Man Ireland

1 lb golden syrup
½ lb brown sugar
1 oz butter
1 dessertspoon water
1/8 oz bicarbonate of soda

Melt the butter and add the sugar, syrup and water; boil until hard crack stage, at 290°F. Stir in the soda and pour on to a greased marble slab. Turn the edges into the centre and pull when cool enough, until pale in colour.

Usually brought to the fair in one large lump and chipped off as required.

Marzipan (Boiled)

2 lb caster sugar
½ pt water
2 oz glucose
¾ lb ground almonds
Icing sugar

Dissolve the sugar in water and add glucose. Bring to the boil and boil to soft ball, at 240°F. Add the almonds and beat until stiff. Cover with a damp cloth and leave to cool. Work to a smooth paste with as much icing sugar as the mixture will absorb.

Marzipan (Unboiled)

1 lb icing sugar
1 lb ground almonds
5-6 egg yolks
1 teaspoon vanilla essence
1 teaspoon lemon juice

Sift the icing sugar and mix with the almonds; make a well in the centre and add the egg yolks, essence and lemon juice. Mix gradually to a stiff dough.

Remove from the bowl and form into a ball; knead lightly on a board until all the cracks have disappeared. Use as required; may be stored in plastic containers in the refrigerator.

This is a quicker method than boiled marzipan, but needs careful handling to prevent cracking or oiling.

Marzipan Fruits

Orange, colour with orange-yellow. Shape and roll on a fine grater to give a pitted effect; place a clove, flower side out at one end.

Peach, colour pale orange-pink. Roll to a smooth ball, mark lightly with blunt knife edge to make a dent in one side

Apple, colour green. Shape and paint red areas on sides; stick clove in top end, stalk side out.

Pear, colour green. Shape and place clove in top end, stalk side out.

Strawberry, colour red. Shape and roll on fine grater to give a pitted effect. Stick clove, flower side out at one end.

Banana, colour pale yellow. Shape and mark with fine paint brush, using chocolate-brown colouring.

Marzipan walnuts, roll marzipan into small balls and press a halved walnut into the top of each.

Marzipan dates, remove stones from dessert dates and fill cavities with plain or coloured marzipan; roll in caster sugar and place in paper cases.

MISCELLANEOUS SWEETMEATS

Coconut Ice

1 lb granulated sugar
5 fl oz milk
5 oz desiccated coconut
Pink colouring

Dissolve the sugar in milk over low heat; bring to the boil and boil gently to soft ball stage, at 240°F. Remove from the heat and stir in the coconut.

Pour half the mixture into a well-greased tin, colour the other half and pour quickly into the tin on top of the white mixture. Leave until half set; mark into bars.

Fruit Jellies

½ lb thick jam
2½ fl oz water
4 oz granulated sugar
1½ oz dissolved gelatine
Colouring

Boil the jam, sugar and water. Rub through a fine sieve. Return the mixture to the pan and slowly add the gelatine and colouring to suit the jam. Remove from the heat and pour into a wetted tin.

Turn out when cold and cut up into diamonds, oblongs or cubes.

Crystallise or glacé (see Candying Fruits).

Marshmallows

10 oz granulated sugar
¾ oz gelatine dissolved in 5 fl oz water and orange flower water
5 fl oz water
1 oz glucose
1 egg white

Grease a tin and dust with icing sugar. Melt the gelatine in the water and orange flower water in a large pan. Dissolve the sugar, water and glucose in another pan and boil to 280°F or small crack stage.

Pour this mixture on to the gelatine, beating briskly with a whisk. Fold in the stiffly beaten egg white and pour the mixture into the prepared tin. When set, rub over with icing sugar and cut into squares with scissors. Toss the squares in icing sugar.

BEVERAGES

SOFT DRINKS

Barley Tonic Drink

2 oz pearl barley
5 pt boiling water
½ oz liquorice root
2 oz sliced figs
2 oz stoned raisins

Wash and blanch the barley, add 4 pt water and cook until reduced by half. Strain and add the raisins, figs and remaining water. Simmer and reduce to 2 pt. Add liquorice before cooking is completed and strain.

Use diluted for drinks or mixed with plain barley water or given in small quantities without being diluted.

Barley Water

2 oz pearl barley
1 oz sugar
1 pt boiling water
Rind and juice of 1 lemon

Pour the boiling water over the other ingredients. Cover with a clean towel and leave until cold.

Boston Cream

6 pt water
2 oz tartaric acid
1½ lb sugar
2 lemons
3 egg whites

Wash and dry the lemons, peel thinly and place the peel and lemon juice in a basin. Add water, acid and sugar and stir until the sugar has dissolved. When quite cold, stir in the beaten egg whites. Bottle.

When required, dilute to taste with chilled soda water or with an equal quantity of water and a pinch of bicarbonate of soda.

Lemonade

3 lemons
1 pt boiling water
2 lb sugar
2 oz citric acid

Peel the lemon rind thinly and cover with part of the measured water. Pour the remaining water on the sugar and citric acid. Stir to dissolve the sugar. When cold add the lemon juice and combine with the strained liquid from the rind.

Bottle and cork, dilute as required.

Orangeade is made in the same way, using only 1½ lb sugar.

PUNCH BOWLS

Made by combining alcoholic and non-alcoholic drinks, sugar and fruit to suit individual taste. Usually served in large deep china bowl, and ladled out with a small silver mounted scoop.

Punch

Juice of 10 lemons
Rind of 3 lemons, cut into fine strips
Juice of 4 oranges
Rind of 2 oranges, cut into fine strips
4 pt boiling water
1 pt brandy
1 pt white wine
¼-½ pt Jamaica Rum
4 oz sugar

Put the lemon and orange juice with the peel and boiling water into a hot jug. Stir and leave to cool completely.

Put the brandy, wine, rum and sugar in a punch bowl, pour over the jug of lemon and orange water and stir.

Brixton Punch Devon

4 oz loaf sugar
1 large lemon
1½ pt boiling water
½ pt sherry
½ pt brandy

Put the sugar in a bowl and add the very thinly sliced lemon. Pour over boiling water, brandy and sherry. Leave to stand for 15 minutes, remove the lemon and leave the punch to cool.

Cambridge Hot Milk Punch Cambridge

2 lemons
½ lb loaf sugar
4 pt milk
3 eggs
1 pt rum
½ pt brandy

Rub the rind of the lemons on the sugar and put into 3½ pt of milk. Simmer for 10 minutes over low heat; remove from the heat. Beat the eggs in the remaining cold milk, strain and stir gradually into the hot milk. Add the rum and brandy, return to the heat and beat until frothy.

Serve immediately.

Cornish Punch I Cornwall

(Dated 1849)

9 lemons
4 pt rum
1½ lb sugar
2 pt boiling milk
5 pt boiling water

Steep the peel of the lemons in 1 pt rum for 3 days, keeping it well covered. On the second day squeeze the juice of the lemons over the sugar, and on the third day combine lemon peel and rum, lemon juice and sugar with rum, milk and water. Stir while pouring in the milk. Cover and leave for 2 hours. Strain through a jelly bag and bottle.

Cornish Punch II Cornwall

2-4 lb sugar to taste
Grated rind of ½ lemon
½ pt lemon juice
½ bottle brandy
1 bottle Jamaica rum

1 tablespoon Benedictine

Put the sugar in the bowl, add lemon juice and rind, brandy, rum and Benedictine. Fill up to 1 gallon with boiling water, poured from a height.

Glasgow Punch Scotland

3½ pt cold water
½ lb sugar
12 lemons
½ pt rum
2-3 limes

Dissolve the sugar in a little water, squeeze the lemons and place in a punch bowl with sugar and water. Add the rum and squeezed lime juice.

FLIPS AND TODDIES

Ale Flip

4 pt ale
1 blade mace
2 cloves
1 oz butter
2 eggs

Put the ale in a pan with mace, cloves and butter. Beat the egg yolks with a little cold ale and beat the whites until stiff. Place the eggs in a very large jug and pour the hot ale over them. Pour the ale back and forth in two jugs until cool enough to drink.

Ale Gruel or Ale Berry

2 oz rolled oats
2 pt water
½ oz grated root ginger
2 pt ale
Nutmeg, cinnamon and sugar to taste

Boil the oats in the water until thick, adding the root ginger. Strain into the ale heated almost to boiling point, adding sugar, cinnamon and nutmeg to taste.
   Drink as hot as possible.

Beer Flip

2 pt strong beer
8 egg yolks beaten with sugar, orange juice and spices to taste

8 egg whites beaten until stiff

Heat the beer until fairly hot and pour into a jug with the egg yolks and other ingredients; pour back and forth in two jugs, add the egg whites and serve hot.

Brown Betty Oxford

An early 19th century Oxford nightcap.

3 oz brown sugar
1 pt hot water
1 slice lemon
Cloves, cinnamon
Brandy
2 pt strong ale
Brown toast
Nutmeg, ground ginger

Dissolve the sugar in the water, add the lemon slice, cloves, cinnamon and brandy to taste. Heat in a pan with the ale, without bringing to the boil. Serve hot, with a slice of brown toast floating on top of each glass and sprinkled with grated nutmeg and ginger.

Bumpo

Rum
Nutmeg
Sugar to taste
Hot water

Follow the method for Toddy, using rum instead of whisky.

Cambridge Ale Cup Cambridge

3 pt water
1 oz cloves
1 oz cinnamon
1 oz mace
3 oz sugar
1 lemon rind
3 pt brown ale
½ pt sherry
Garnish: thin slices of toast seasoned with nutmeg

Boil the spices in the water for 1 hour and strain. Add the sugar, lemon rind, ale and sherry. Heat just before serving and add thin slices of fresh toast sprinkled with nutmeg.

Irish Coffee Ireland

Cream, rich as an Irish brogue
Coffee, strong as a friendly hand
Sugar, sweet as the tongue of a rogue
Whiskey, smooth as the wit of the land

Heat a stemmed whisky goblet and pour in one third of a glass of whiskey. Add 3 coffeespoons of caster sugar.

Fill up the goblet with strong black coffee to within 1 in of the brim; stir to dissolve the sugar and top up to the brim with cream lightly aerated. Do not stir after adding the cream as the true flavour is obtained by drinking the hot coffee and Irish whiskey through the cream.

Lamb's Wool or Brasenose Ale Oxford

8 baked apples
2 pt brown beer
Nutmeg, ground ginger and sugar to taste

Peel and mash the apples and add the beer. Rub through a sieve and add nutmeg, sugar and ginger to taste. Heat through and serve hot.

Alternatively, leave the apples whole and float in the hot spiced beer.

Negus Cornwall

1 dessertspoon black currant jam
1 tumbler boiling water

Place the jam in boiling water and stir well. Leave to cool and serve for sore throats.

Eggiot or Eggy'ot Cornwall

1 egg
1 teaspoon sugar
½ pt milk

Beat the egg with sugar in a tumbler. Heat the milk and before it reaches boiling point pour it over the beaten egg.

Rum Booze Cambridge

½ bottle sherry
Rind of ½ lemon
½ grated nutmeg
Piece cinnamon stick
Sugar
1 glass rum

4 beaten eggs

Put the sherry, lemon rind, nutmeg and cinnamon with sugar to taste in a pan over low heat. Remove as soon as it boils, pour into a large jug and add the rum, gradually pouring the mixture on to the beaten eggs. Beat to a white froth before serving hot.

Toddy Scotland

1 glass whisky
Hot water
Sugar to taste

Pour boiling water slowly into a tumbler until half full. Let the water remain until the crystal is thoroughly heated, then pour it out.

Put in loaf sugar to taste with boiling water. When melted, put in half a glass of whisky and stir with a silver spoon. Add more boiling water and finally top up with whisky. Stir and serve hot.

MULLED WINES

Mulled Red Wine

1 bottle red wine
½ pt water
2 fl oz brandy
2 sugar lumps
Stick cinnamon or grated nutmeg
1 slice lemon per glass
12 cloves
Pinch mace

Warm all the ingredients together and serve strained with a slice of lemon in each glass.

Mulled White Wine

1 bottle dry white wine
2 glasses brandy
Juice of 1 lemon
6 oz honey

Warm all the ingredients together and serve.

Mulled Madeira

1 bottle Madeira
½ tablespoon brandy

Pinch cinnamon and ginger
Sugar to taste

Bring all the ingredients almost to the boil and
serve warm.

Mulled Cider

2 pt cider
4 oz sugar
12 cloves
4 sticks cinnamon
9 whole allspice

Heat all the ingredients until the sugar has
dissolved; strain and serve hot.

Mulled Wine

½ bottle claret
6 cloves
Pinch each, grated nutmeg, mace and pepper
½ cinnamon stick

Boil the spices in the wine; simmer for 10-15
minutes; strain and serve.

Bishop

1 bottle port wine
1 orange or lemon
Cloves
½ pt water
½ teaspoon each, cinnamon, cloves and allspice
Blade mace
½ oz root ginger
1 lemon
3 oz loaf sugar
Nutmeg

Bake the orange or lemon stuck with cloves in a
cool oven. Boil the spices in the water until
reduced by half. Heat the port until almost at the
boil, add the strained spiced water, orange or
lemon and leave over a very low heat for 10
minutes.

   Meanwhile, rub the sugar lumps on the lemon
skin and put with the lemon juice into a serving
bowl. Pour the wine over, grate nutmeg on top
and serve hot.

   Cardinal is made with claret, and Pope with
champagne.

Rumfustian

12 egg yolks
2 pt strong beer
Cinnamon, nutmeg, sugar and ginger to taste
1 bottle wine
1 pt gin

Beat all the ingredients together, heat in a pan
but do not boil or the egg yolks will curdle. Serve
warm; it should be opaque rather than thick.

POSSETS

A posset was taken instead of a meal by invalids;
it was usually served in a specially made china
posset dish, with a cover to it. Possets could vary
however, from a simple cold cure to an elaborate
concoction.

Almond Posset

1 pt milk
2 oz white breadcrumbs
4 oz ground almonds
1 teaspoon rose water
2 pt cream
4 eggs
Caster sugar
6-8 macaroons

Pour the milk over the breadcrumbs and leave to
steep for 2-3 hours. Beat thoroughly, adding the
ground almonds, rose water and cream. Simmer
gently for 15 minutes without letting the mixture come to the boil. Cool and beat in the eggs.

   Sweeten to taste and heat through to thicken,
but do not boil. Pour into a serving bowl and
float the macaroons on top.

Oatmeal Posset

2 oz oatmeal flour
1 pt milk
1½ tablespoon sherry
1½ tablespoon ale
1 oz sugar
Grated nutmeg
1 in cinnamon stick
6 oz grated apple (optional)

Boil the milk with nutmeg and cinnamon and add
the oatmeal; simmer until the oatmeal is cooked.

Heat the sherry, ale and sugar in another pan until scalding hot. Pour into the milk and stir once; add the apple if used. Leave over the heat for a minute or two, then pour into a posset bowl. Cover and leave for a few minutes before serving.

Pope's Posset

¾ lb ground almonds
½ pt water
1 pt sherry
Sugar

Add the almonds to the water and heat through. Heat the sherry with sugar to taste until boiling. Mix the two liquids together and serve hot.

Sack Posset

3-4 eggs
½ pt milk
5 fl oz sherry
3 oz sugar

Beat the eggs. Put the other ingredients in a pan and bring to the boil, skimming if necessary. Add to the beaten eggs, stirring well and return to the heat. Heat very gently until the eggs thicken without curdling. Pour into a posset bowl and serve hot.

Simple Posset

1 pt milk
5 fl oz white wine
2 oz sugar lumps
1 lemon
1/8 oz ginger
Grating of nutmeg

Heat the milk in a pan and when it froths up, add the white wine. Strain out the curds and rub the sugar lumps on the lemon rind. Add the sugar, ginger and nutmeg to the strained milk and wine and serve hot.

TRADITIONAL CUPS AND LIQUEURS

Athole Brose Scotland

The original Athole Brose consisted of oatmeal and whisky, in the proportions of ½ lb oatmeal to 2 pt whisky.

1 lb heather honey
5 fl oz water
1½ pt whisky

Dissolve the honey in the cold water, stirring well. Add the whisky gradually, beating until a froth begins to rise.

Bottle and cork tightly. Store for two days before use, as a cure for colds or as a luxury celebration drink.

Caledonian Liqueur

1 pt whisky
5 oz loaf sugar
1 dessertspoon cinnamon oil

Add the cinnamon oil to the crushed sugar. Pour the whisky over and stir to dissolve the sugar. Filter and bottle.

Damson Gin

1 lb ripe damsons
1 lb sugar
1 bottle gin

Prick the damsons and place in a jar, add the sugar and pour over the gin.

Cork and seal tightly; shake the jar gently daily for a fortnight. Leave for 6-12 months, then strain the liqueur through fine muslin; bottle, cork and store.

Live Long

6 eggs
Juice of 6 lemons
5 fl oz rum
½ lb brown sugar

Put the eggs and the shells in a jar with the lemon juice. Leave for 3 days and 3 nights, stirring daily. Strain through a sieve, add sugar and rum and shake well. Bottle and store.

Loving Cup | London

The Loving Cup was traditionally served at the annual City of London banquets. A communal cup was passed to each member who stood up to drink, together with his immediate neighbours on either side. As the drinker had to use both hands to lift the cup and would be unable to draw his sword in an emergency, his neighbours acted as temporary bodyguards.

Toasted bread squares
6 oz lump sugar
Orange flower water
½ grated nutmeg
½ teaspoon each, cinnamon and ginger
2 pt ale
1 bottle sherry
1 bottle soda water

Place the small toasted bread squares in a bowl, with the lump sugar soaked in orange flower water, the nutmeg, spices, ale and sherry.

For a cool cup, shake this mixture vigorously with crushed ice, strain and add soda water just before serving.

For a hot cup, heat the mixture very slowly, covered with a lid so that the spirit does not evaporate and the fine flavours are not destroyed. Serve warm, mixed with soda water.

Loving Cup II

2 lemons
4 oz lump sugar
Balm leaves
2-3 borage sprigs
1½ pt water
½ bottle Madeira wine
5 fl oz brandy
1 bottle champagne

Rub the peel of one lemon with lumps of sugar; slice off the peel and remove pith; slice the remaining lemon thinly, discarding all peel and pith. Put the balm, borage, sliced lemons and sugar-rubbed peel, together with the sugar, in a large jar; add the water.

Stir in the Madeira and brandy, cover and surround with crushed ice; leave for about 1 hour. Chill the champagne and add to the cup when ready to serve.

Nectar Ireland

4 lemons
16 pt water
2 lb sugar
1 lb seeded raisins

Slice the lemons thinly and boil in water for 30

minutes. Bring the 16 pt of water to the boil, add the sugar, raisins and strained lemon slices and boil for 10 minutes. Cover and leave for 4 days, stirring daily. Strain and bottle. Leave for 14 days before using; serve chilled.

Old Sowerby Pick-Me-Up

1 pt brown ale
1 pt stout
½ pt rum
½ pt strong beer
½ lb soft brown sugar

Mix all the ingredients and take 1 wine glass of the mixture three times a day.

Samson Cornwall

1 pt cider
½ pt rum
Honey

Boil the cider for 1 hour; add the rum, and bottle when cold. Sweeten to taste with honey and serve in wine glasses.

Scots Noyau

2 pt whisky
¾ pt water
¾ lb golden syrup
5 oz blanched and chopped almonds

Place all the ingredients in a bottle and infuse for a fortnight, shaking the compound occasionally; filter before use.

Sloe Gin

Sloes
Gin
Barley sugar
Essence of almonds

Half fill clean, dry wine bottles with the mashed and pricked sloes. Add to each bottle 1 oz crushed barley sugar and a few drops of almond essence. Fill the bottles with dry gin, cork securely and leave in a moderately warm place for 3 months. Strain the liqueur through fine muslin, bottle, cork and store.

Spruce

1 lb loaf sugar
Water
2 teaspoons tartaric acid
1/8 oz ground ginger
15 drops lemon essence

Dissolve the sugar in boiling water, add tartaric
acid, ginger and lemon essence. Fill up with water
to make 1 gallon.
　　This was an old Cornish harvest drink.

Stokos

4 oz fine oatmeal
½ sliced lemon
6 oz sugar

Put the ingredients in a pan, add a little warm
water and mix. Stir in 1 gallon of boiling water;
mix thoroughly and serve cold.

Vanilla Liqueur

3 pt brandy or gin
2 vanilla pods
1 lb loaf sugar
1 pt water

Break the vanilla pods into short lengths, put them
in the spirit, cork closely and leave to infuse for
14 days.
　　On the last day boil the sugar and water to a
thick syrup, strain the spirit into this and when
quite cold bottle and store.

A Scientific Approach To Professional Cookery

Inherent in the ability to cook any commodity, even one that nobody has yet attempted to cook, are two major related abilities, that of recognising in any raw commodity its potential as a cooked finished product and that of identifying in any cooked product the processes that have produced its particular characteristics.

This chapter is an attempt to analyse recipes so as to identify the factors that are involved in the production of any dish. An approach cannot prescribe what should be done with a raw commodity in order to obtain a finished dish which is acceptable as food. Food as such exists only when it is eaten, in the same way that it has no nutritive value until it has been consumed. The decision as to which process to employ on a raw material in order to obtain a finished dish can be arrived at in part by an examination of the relevant factors in the situation. It is with these relevant factors that this chapter is concerned.

The starting point lies in the definition of cooking. Cooking is concerned with producing controlled changes in food commodities to obtain acceptable quality in the finished product. Therefore the first part is concerned with the meaning of quality in food products, together with certain principles related to their assessment for acceptability and presentation. Following this, is a second part dealing with the use of recipes in cooking. Because of the many operations involved in controlling the changes in commodities, a selected number of skills and their nature are described.

An examination of food commodities in general and how various cooking processes affect their major constituents leads to a more detailed consideration of groups of specific commodities, such as meat, fish, vegetables and fruit. The linkage between raw materials, cooking process and finished characteristics is discussed in detail and the chapter closes with a series of charts classifying food products in general use in British cookery.

THE DIFFERENT QUALITIES IN FOOD

Food is inexorably linked with man's life, much more than any other of his products for it provides him not only with life-giving nutrients, but also with life-sustaining pleasure. It is part of his symbolic view of life. The words he uses to express his reactions to food pass into his language and are used to communicate depths of feeling in other spheres. It has been said that not only do men produce their foods, but foods produce their men.

Because food is part of human culture, part of the sum total of the arts, sciences, social customs and educational aims of a people as a whole it is difficult to examine the subject other than subjectively.

Quality

The term quality is used to denote a degree of excellence, or the relative nature of a given product. It implies a judgement of characteristics of cooked food involving pleasure, nutritional value and safety.

Pleasure

Pleasure is dynamic and is particular to the individual. It changes with the time of day, the day of the week, and even hour by hour. Pleasure is basically an attitude to a food or dish and attitude is not constant. Groups of consumers will not all express pleasure, at the same time and to the same degree.

Consumers can be regarded as a statistical concept, as in American and British Army studies on food preferences, or they can be regarded as individuals. As an individual the consumer has dynamic moods — for example, while he can generally be expected to like a particular dish there will be certain occasions when he dislikes it.

The factors that may influence the consumers' pleasure or satisfaction are the dish itself and the eating environment. The consumer as a unique individual, tempered by the environment in which he is eating, obtains information via his senses about the dish. His reaction to this information is modified by the price charged and if he knows the price in advance this also influences his expectations. Does the dish match up to his experience of similar dishes in the past, at the particular price? It is interesting to note that in respect of food many consumers have some idea of the cost of the raw materials, and this again affects acceptance or rejection. The more elaborate the dish, the less likely rejection is to occur.

All these relationships can be illustrated diagrammatically as follows:

Consumer is influenced by age, sex and background in terms of social experience, education and training and nationality. His religion and economic circumstances, hunger and appetite often play an equally important part.

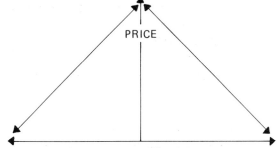

PRICE

The dish: temperature, colour, shape, viscosity, texture, flavour.

The eating environment: other diners, waiters, decor, heating, lighting, ventilation, furniture, fittings, cutlery and crockery.

Each of these factors can be modified by the others; for example, what is perceived in terms of colour in the food is affected by lighting in the environment. Whether the consumer feels cold or too warm will influence his reaction to the temperature of the food. As previously indicated the relationships are dynamic and change continuously with time and place. Because of the time dimension the assessment of quality is a process that has to be constantly repeated. This means that the creator of a dish may be required to make adjustments in his product to ensure that the consumers obtain maximum pleasure over a long period.

Nutritional Value

The estimated potential nutritional value of a dish can be assessed. The nutrients it contains can be calculated and from this some indication can be obtained of its use in maintaining health and promoting growth.

Its potential for doing this is dependent upon the ability of the body to digest and absorb the nutrients as well as the willingness of the consumer to eat the dish. Nutrients are classified into proteins, fats, carbohydrates, vitamins, mineral salts and water. These nutrients have the potential for performing various functions in the body, some of them quite specific.

From the point of view of professional cooking an outline knowledge of where these nutrients are to be found and their relative stability in processing will provide added argument for choosing to process foods in a particular way. For example, if it is known that ascorbic acid, vitamin C, is found in green vegetables and fruit and that it is easily destroyed by over-cooking or reheating, then action can be taken to avoid its destruction, consistent with maintaining other qualities that are required in the end product.

The following lists indicate the main sources of the more common nutrients and their stability in cooking.

Proteins: meat, offal, poultry, game, fish, cheese, beans, eggs, nuts, milk.

Fats: butter, lard, margarine, meat fats, oil, cream, nuts, cheese.

Carbohydrates: sugars, starches, syrups, jams, flour and flour products, breads, crackers, cereals, potatoes and other starchy vegetables.

Vitamins:

A (Carotene):	liver, kidney, green and yellow vegetables, butter, cream, eggs, milk.
B^1 (Thiamine):	offal, bacon, pork, cod roes, pulses, peanuts, potatoes.
B^2 (Riboflavine):	offal, milk, eggs, yeast, tea.
C (Ascorbic acid):	fruit and vegetables.
D^3 (Cholecalciferol):	liver, butter, margarine, eggs, salmon, herring, mackerel.
Nicotinic acid:	peanuts, bread, yeast, pulses, liver, coffee.

Minerals:

Calcium:	milk, cheese, sardines, pilchards, wholewheat bread.
Phosphorus:	meat, offal, poultry, game, fish, cheese, beans, peas, eggs, milk.
Iron:	meat, offal, fish, pulses, wholewheat bread

Stability of Nutrients in Cooking

Proteins, fats, carbohydrates and minerals are all relatively stable in cooking. Vitamins vary in their stability as follows: Carotene A is fat-soluble, but relatively stable in most cooking processes. Some loss occurs if the fat is exposed to light, warmth and air, to the point of rancidity. Thiamine B^1 is water-soluble and is damaged by heat and alkalis. Riboflavine B^2 is destroyed by sunlight. Nicotinic acid is stable to heat and light, but can be leached out of food into the cooking liquid. Ascorbic acid C, soluble in water, is destroyed by heat, air, sodium bicarbonate and copper utensils. Cholecalciferol D^3 is relatively stable in most cooking processes.

The object of showing these factors is to provide a background against which the professional cook can make decisions when processing or producing a finished dish. It is not intended here to discuss dietetics — the scientific planning of meals with a specific nutritional value.

Safety

Safety refers to the degree of harm that food may cause when it is eaten and involves a consideration of the structure of the food and in particular the extent to which inedible parts have been removed. It is also concerned with the conditions of production and service and whether the risk of foreign bodies getting into the food has been eliminated. Safety also concerns food as being bacteriologically safe. For example, contamination of food by bacteria that may cause food poisoning is minimised if the temperature of processing is below $50°F$ ($10°C$) or above $140°F$ ($60°C$) and is carried out in clean surroundings.

Assessing the Quality of a Dish

From an operational point of view quality can be defined as a composite response obtained from the properties that we sense in a specific dish and which cause us to judge it superior because as users we have been exposed to random selections of the dish over a period of time. The professional cook uses his experience of a wide variety of examples of a particular dish to try to make a valid assessment of its particular qualities. In practice the validity of his judgement can be increased by the knowledge of the number of consumers that repeatedly chose a particular dish, assuming that on each occasion there was a minimum variation in cost and quality.

More sophisticated assessment techniques involve groups of trained people. They are required to carry out one or more tests on costed food samples submitted to them. These assessments may be involved with ranking samples in order of intensity of the characteristics, e.g. colour, flavour, or with awarding marks for specific characteristics in each sample, e.g. tenderness, flavour. Again they may be asked to express likes or dislikes of samples on a scale attempt to assess thresholds of flavour, taste or smell by progressively weakening the strength of the sample; or they may be required to give descriptions of the samples that are being assessed, e.g. meatiness or chewiness.

Whichever method of assessment is used, the following five suggestions may help to make the assessment more effective.

1. The assessor or producer of the dish should try to see the food as the consumer will see it, e.g. visual examination should take place under similar lighting conditions.
2. An assessment of shape and form should be carried out with the food arranged in the way it is to be served.
3. As the temperature of both food and environment affects taste and acceptability, the assessment of these qualities should take place under identical conditions.
4. Individual consumers' preferences should be considered when assessing flavour, e.g. in general, younger people have a greater sensitivity to flavours than older people — tenderness may be more important to people with dentures.
5. Consideration should be given to accompanying foods, in respect of contrasting or complementary colours, flavours and textures.

These five points mean, in practice, that the producer of a dish should sample the food under the same conditions as the consumer. This may mean after it has been prepared for service some time in advance.

When setting a quality standard, the producer of a dish needs to determine how far he, personally, should allow consumer preference to dictate the extent of changes made in the characteristics of a product. For example, if customers prefer soft cabbage, with consequent loss of colour and taste, should the cook classify this as "good quality"? It may be argued that raw food materials have an intrinsic merit related to their potential eating qualities and that the producer as a professional has a moral obligation to take these into account when producing a dish and set a standard of quality higher than the average minimum requirements demanded by popularity, legislation or acceptability. This obligation involves decisions on the part of the professional cook in respect of the name he gives to the particular dish in relation to materials used and the process. It also involves decisions as to what additives he ought to use to achieve particular results.

On the question of quality standards, the cook must take the responsibility for deciding on the type of sole to be used for "fried fillet of sole" — megrim, lemon or dover sole — and whether in the absence of these another type of fish can be used without changing the name of the dish. He determines whether roast potatoes are potatoes cooked in the oven or par-boiled and then finished off in the oven. The professional cook must be able to judge what percentage of vegetable protein can be added to a "brown beef stew" before this ceases to be a "beef stew", or if the colour of the stew is to be obtained by browning the meat and vegetables or by means of gravy browning. He should also be knowledgeable enough to determine which of certain additives may be used to achieve particular textures and flavours in the baking of pastry products.

Obviously the cost of producing a particular dish may be affected by these decisions; however, the obligation remains on the professional cook to set a quality standard after taking all these factors into account. The quality standard is itself dynamic because it is affected by varying consumer tastes, commodities and costs. To satisfy the quality/cost requirements of a dish in relation to the environment, consumer and price charged a continuous monitoring needs to take place. The degree of sophistication involved in this monitoring and controlling of quality is obviously dependent upon volume and rate of production. The larger the volume and greater the rate, the more sophisticated are the controls. Sampling and statistical techniques can be employed, together with scientific analyses of the food, to ensure that it falls within the limits of tolerance set for pleasure and nutritional value and safety. Continuous checking on costs both of raw materials and production are necessary. These need to be related to yield, volume, rate of production and the demand by the consumer at the price charged. The information obtained will help in future decisions in respect of purchasing, preparing, cooking and serving.

Food Presentation

Food presentation is concerned with the display or orderly arrangement of food for service to a consumer. In maintaining a high standard of quality in food, food presentation also involves a knowledge of portioning. Account must be taken of the plates, dishes or containers on which the food is to be presented and of the interrelated factors, such as the type or method of service, time and temperature, food portions and aesthetic considerations.

Type or Method of Service

This refers to the way in which a customer is provided with the food. Whatever method of service is used, there should be standardisation of plates, dishes or containers according to the type, size and number of portions of food being served. For this purpose, food can be classified according to its main characteristics, i.e. whether it is liquid or solid, crisp or soft. Containers and plates should be deep for foods that are predominantly liquid, such as soups, stews and certain milk puddings — rice, semolina; the dimensions should correspond to the amount. Crisp foods, such as fried fish, chipped potatoes, fritters and apple turnovers, should be presented on shallow containers.

Time and Temperature

These are critical factors in the period between having the food ready and it being presented to a consumer. It is possibly during this interval that most food spoilage occurs, increasing the food costs and the risk of food poisoning. This waiting period, as it were, should, where possible, be reduced to a minimum and the temperature in the interim should be adjusted to suit the type of food. Ice creams and water ices, for example, should be kept at below freezing temperature, cold dishes between 32° (0°C and 50°F (10°C) hot dishes above 140°F (60°C).

In order to reduce the period between cooking and presenting of food to a minimum, the professional cook will consider the possibility of cooking the food to order, and presenting it immediately, e.g. omelets, bacon and eggs, steaks and small cuts of meat, fish and poultry. Alternatively, it may be possible to portion the food before processing, in individual steamed puddings and pies, or the food presentation – containers and service equipment – can be prepared in advance so that they are at the appropriate temperature.

It is important to remember that the temperature of foods presented for eating should be below 50°F (10°C) if cold or above 140°F (60°C) if hot. Between these temperatures food poisoning bacteria multiply at their maximum rates. Bearing these temperatures in mind, food presentation (waiting) is also related to the type of food and the maintenance of its important qualities such as proteins in eggs, meat, poultry and game. Colour in green vegetables is also critical. The preference of consumers for hot and cold foods are relative to body temperatures, the temperature of the dining area, consumer expectations and the effect that temperature has on other food qualities and their acceptability.

Food portions

The division and subsequent control of the size and shape of each item of food is a major factor in relation to a high standard of quality. This is concerned with maintaining portion size, controlling food costs and assisting service.

Without some standardisation of portion size and shape the orderly arrangement of presented food is difficult to achieve. Standardisation involves a consideration of plate size, because the consumer's reaction to food is partially tempered by its visual appearance on the plate. The plate is the starting point in determining portion size; for example in the case of soups, any one of three types of plate could be used: 5 in diameter without a rim; 7 in diameter with a 1 in rim; or 9 in diameter with a 1¼ in rim. Each of these will take, without over-filling, 7 fluid ounces of soup, an adequately sized portion. The visual appearance of quantity differs in each case: in the 9 in diameter 7 fluid ounces appear greater in volume; the maintenance of portion size is easier to achieve in the 5 in diameter dish, because in actual capacity it is the smallest. Filled, it will hold 8 fluid ounces whereas the 9 in diameter plate will hold 14 fluid ounces.

Plates for main course fish and meat also vary in size and shape, round plates being 6½ in diameter with a 1 in rim, 8 in diameter with a 1 in rim or 9½ in diameter with a 1¼ in rim, while oval plates may be 10 in long and 6 in wide with no rim. The visual appearance of meat, fish and to some extent vegetables is affected not only by how far they cover the particular plate used but also by the number of pieces. For example, two pieces of fish or meat cut thinly will cover a larger area than one piece cut thickly. The actual weight of raw meat or fish to achieve this may not be related to visual size – 5 oz raw fillet steak cooked and presented on a plate will appear smaller than two fillet steaks each of 2 ounces.

The relationship between visually satisfactory portion size, size of plate, amount of uncooked food, relating to plate portion cost and purchase price of raw materials (usually expressed per pound) is a complicated one. It is made even more difficult, because the size of the cooked portion and its cost per portion is dependent upon losses during processing. The important loss is volume loss, not necessarily weight loss. For example, a great deal of water can be extracted from a piece of meat, thereby decreasing its weight, without reducing its volume. Commercially this is carried out by accelerated freezing-drying. Conversely, some leaf vegetables when overcooked will pick up cooking water thereby increasing in weight, but the volume and hence number of portions obtainable will usually be less.

Losses vary with the cooking process and type of food. To standardise portion size and control food costs it is necessary to standardise all the procedures associated with the production, viz. purchasing, preparing, cooking, holding and service. The standardisation is primarily based on what is required on the consumer's plate. Other considerations are the limiting factors imposed by the range of sizes and the physical structure of the raw food materials that are available, coupled with the facilities and equipment used for processing.

Portioning before processing makes standardisation of portion size easier, because it can be carried out without the pressure of time that is inherent in holding. If pre-portioning is not possible then some preparation for subsequent portioning can be done; for example, the size and shape of a cut or joint of meat should in part be dictated by the size of slice that is required for presentation and service. The decoration of a pie or cake can also be used to dictate portion size. It is important when presenting food that portions should be equal; one customer should not be served with 1½ portions and another with half a portion. Aids to control portioning and thereby food presentation should always be used in the form of standard sized scoops, ladles, measures and perhaps a periodic weight check.

Aesthetic Considerations

In relation to food presentation, aesthetics are a question of arranging food so that it appears attractive and in good taste.

This involves consideration of layout, garnishing, decorating, colour, form and finish. From an aesthetic point of view a particular layout and garnishes are matters of personal opinion, stemming from a particular culture and culinary tradition. It also varies within each culture, due to changing eating habits and food fashions. However, within Great Britain some general rules may be suggested to produce a classic style that translates into harmonious, proportioned and finished dishes. To achieve this, food should be placed in an orderly fashion on or in the plate or container; pan-fried fillets of fish, for example, should be placed rounded side up, slightly overlapping and all pointing in the same direction. If presented on an oval plate they should be slightly on the slant and off centre. The same rule may apply to grilled flat fish, thin steaks and carved slices of hot or cold meat or poultry. Over-regimentation in arrangement and shape is to be avoided, however, as much as disorderly arrangement and lack of uniformity.

The garnishing and decorating of foods should be carried out quickly for reasons of time and temperature; this means that in general garnishes and decorations should be simple. Due consideration should be given to contrasting and complementing the natural colours and textures of the food so that they all contribute to a combination of harmonious simplicity.

Grilled steaks, tomatoes and watercress are a typical example. It is more practical to group the tomatoes on one side of the arranged steaks and finish with one small trimmed bunch of watercress than to dot the cress and tomatoes all round the dish. It is undesirable on the grounds of hygiene to serve hot food in close contact with fresh food for any length of time. Parsley sprigs as a garnish to dishes that have been covered in a sauce can be aesthetically displeasing and are certainly impractical when the parsley is scraped up with the sauce during service.

The finish of a dish often relates to the degree in which it reflects light – if food is left for any length of time it skins over and reflects less light. For a shiny finish, leave the presentation to the last possible moment before serving; this applies particularly to any item of food that is topped with a sauce, whether fish, meat dishes or desserts, such as apple pie and custard.

THE USE OF RECIPES IN COOKING

A recipe is a statement of ingredients and a procedure for preparing a dish. It is a descriptive norm, acting as a guide to the control of the many variables inherent in the cooking process. The latter is specifically concerned with producing controlled changes in shape, colour, consistency, texture, flavour and temperature in food to obtain an acceptable finished dish. These changes are controlled throughout one or more processes involving handling, mixing, heating or cooling. Because the characteristics of a finished dish vary according to the preferences of the customer, tradition and economic circumstances, these variables are reflected in the procedures for producing the dish and hence in the recipe. Furthermore, other variables arise when we consider variety in the characteristics of the ingredients and the variety in equipment and machinery used in cooking. A person wishing to prepare a dish reads the recipe and, using his abilities, interprets it according to his circumstances and for purposes of his own. This adds perhaps the greatest variable of all to the usefulness of a recipe — the variability of people's ability.

Each of the variables are interdependent in the sense that a change in one will affect another, as will adjustments made to try to obtain a satisfactory finished dish.

A basic recipe for cooking winter cabbage could involve the following elements of preparation, cooking and presentation.

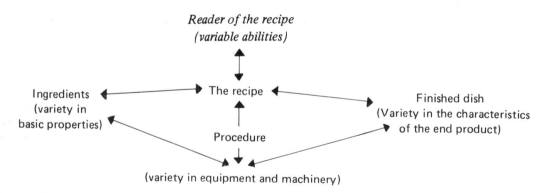

Preparation   Remove coarse outer leaves, cut the cabbage into quarters and remove the stalk. Wash thoroughly under running water, soak for 5-10 minutes to remove any grit or insects. Shred finely.
Cooking   Put in a little boiling, salted water and boil rapidly, 20 minutes (Savoy), 7-10 minutes (Drumhead or white Dutch); drain thoroughly.

In an attempt to find out the variables which have not been taken into account in the recipe, list the factors inherent in the actual procedure of making the dish, thus highlighting those that are not included in the recipe as it is written.

1. Finished dish of cabbage: colour, consistency, texture, flavour, temperature, quantity.
2. Ingredients: type, quantity and quality of cabbage.
3. Equipment: as used in preparing, cooking, holding and serving, e.g. type, size, shape of cooking utensils, covered or open.
4. Water: hard or soft; volume in relation to 2 and 3; temperature.
5. Salt: amount in relation to 2, 3 and 4.
6. Heat: source and amount in relation to 2, 3 and 4.
7. Time: preparation, cooking, holding and serving.

Questioning the Recipe

In order to utilise a recipe for the effective production of a dish it is worthwhile asking a series of questions about it in regard to the stated procedures and proportions of ingredients. Answers should be obtained from trying the recipe out in practice or from authoritative sources.

For example, in the cabbage recipe, the following questions could be asked:

Q *What other effects can soaking in cold water have on the finished product?*

A Soaking in cold water will enable the cabbage to pick up water which, if not adequately drained before shredding, will lower the temperature of the cooking water, therefore taking longer to bring it back to the boil and therefore producing greater colour change (leaching out Vitamin C).

Q *What is implied by "shred finely"? How "fine" is "fine", in what direction should the cabbage be shredded and does this affect the finished texture and colour?*

A Shredding can be across the fibres of the leaves or in the same direction; the direction affects the finished texture and length of cooking. In this case, shredding means across the fibres, thereby reducing cooking time and helping to retain the colour. The degree of "fineness" has the same effect as the finer the cabbage is shredded the less time it will take to cook.

Q *How much is a "little" water? What happens if a "lot" of water is used?*

A With little water, the flavour of the cooked cabbage will be stronger and its texture may be firmer due to the increased acidity of the cooking medium; this may also change the colour. If the volume of water to cabbage is increased, the flavour will be weaker.

Q *"Boil rapidly" – what is implied here in terms of the finished result? Which sources of heat can be used?*

A The implication of boiling rapidly is that it should be kept at $212°F$ ($100°C$) from the moment it is added to the boiling water until it is cooked. If it is not kept at this temperature, colour and flavour changes will occur due to the reduced temperature and the consequent increase in cooking time that is necessary to produce the same degree of tenderness. The question of what source of heat to employ has a bearing on the finished result, particularly if a larger volume of cabbage is being cooked. If colour and flavour changes are the result of slowly bringing the cabbage to the boil and cooking for a longer period, then for larger volumes of cabbage to obtain minimum colour and flavour change a better source of heat is desirable, such as a steam boiler at 15 lb pressure.

Q *Will the procedure, as stated in the recipe, produce the same end product if the volume of cabbage is increased?*

A No. See above.

Q *How accurate is the timing? What effect will it have if the time is reduced or increased?*

A The timing for a given end result can never be completely accurate as indicated in the answers to previous questions.

Q *What effect does shredding well in advance of cooking have on the product?*

A It increases the leaching out of Vitamin C. However, the amount of Vitamin C retained in cooked cabbage is minimal and the most important effect is on colour change. These changes are also affected by the temperature at which the cabbage has been stored.

Q *What happens to colour, flavour, nutritional value if the cabbage is not eaten immediately it is cooked?*

A These can all change, depending on the length and conditions of storage after cooking. A strong smell of sulphur compounds develops as a result of long cooking and holding at temperatures above approximately 50°F (10°C).

Abilities needed to Produce a Finished Dish

Perhaps the most important of the variables is the abilities of the person making use of and reading the recipe. To produce a finished dish with the aid of a recipe, one should have the ability to identify the characteristics of the finished product. This identification may be a mental picture involving smell, taste, tactile and visual memories, ideally supplemented by a coloured picture or an example of the actual article. It is necessary to be able to recognise the raw foods and equipments and identify them with the items written into the recipe. Having identified them in this way, one should have an ability to make adjustments to the recipe to suit the particular situation in which the dish is to be prepared. For example, decisions must be taken and implemented in respect of the quantities of ingredients used to give the desired number of portions and also in changes to the procedures to suit the time and equipment at one's disposal.

Using a recipe requires the ability to select equipment in addition to those items mentioned in the recipe. For example, most items of equipment for preparing, arranging and serving are only implicit in the recipe. Furthermore, it is important that the person using the recipe should have developed the necessary manual and perceptual skills to carry out and control the process effectively. Finally, a decision-making ability is required to obtain a finished product that satisfies the customers. These decisions are based on the variables outlined above; while variables can be discussed in general, many of them are often specifically important only to one dish.

How far these abilities have been developed will be the main decisive element in the usefulness of a recipe and the effective preparation of a dish. The more abilities that have been developed the more use can be made of recipes, both as a source of reference for a named dish and as a basis for variations.

SKILLS AND METHODS

In order to understand the skills and methods involved in the production of dishes, it is useful to consider each recipe as a job that can be analysed. This analysis will demonstrate that the job is composed of a logically related set of actions or tasks. Further breakdown of the tasks show that they are themselves composed of a number of separate steps, and from this analysis one can recognise that there are many skills and methods common to the production of recipe dishes.

The task of producing roast beef, for example, may involve the following steps: (1) selection and purchase of the beef; (2) preparation of the beef for roasting; (3) lighting or switching on the oven; (4) placing beef in the oven; (5) removing the beef from the oven; and (6) carving the beef on a dish. These tasks are logically related in that the sequence is not arbitrarily decided and each task must be completed to a standard in order to obtain a pre-determined standard product. Looked at in another way, the tasks form a sequence, and the tasks and their sequence constitute the method.

To understand the tasks and hence the method in greater detail, take each of the tasks and examine which steps are involved in their completion. In the case of the fifth task, the steps in completing the moving of beef from the oven may include opening the oven door, checking that the beef is cooked, turning off the oven, preparing a place for the meat, removing the meat from the oven and putting into place for "carry-over" cooking, closing the oven door. It is obvious that the individual steps are logically related, and the sequence constitutes the method of carrying out the task. When each of these steps and tasks are performed smoothly and evenly in a comparatively short space of time and well within the performer's reserves of energy they are recognisable as skill.

The definition of a skill may be expertise, practised ability, facility in doing something or dexterity. However, these definitions do not really explain the nature of skills in cookery. To do this requires an explanation of which abilities require practice in order to obtain dexterity in a given task.

Considering the six steps involved in removing the beef from the oven, several abilities can be identified that require practice. For example, the perceptual ability to sense the characteristics of cooked beef may involve sight (degree of brownness), touch (degree of coagulation of protein, i.e. firmness), taste (degree of flavour, aroma, tenderness and juiciness). Equipment can be used to help assess these, such as a thermometer, fork, knife or slicing machine. Perceptual abilities on their own are not adequate to carry out skills; other abilities are required, such as the need to know what "brownness" is; in terms of attitude, willingness to carry out the assessment is necessary as well as the physical ability to lift and carry the cooked beef. When these abilities have been acquired and practised so that the performance becomes skilful, there is little realisation of the abilities or skills being applied.

Generalisation of Skills and Methods Inherent in Recipes

From the example of roast beef, one can turn to similar recipes for roasting meat, poultry or game and observe that certain skills and methods are common to all of these. This also applies to the equipment being used. From an analysis of recipes one can identify those skills that appear to involve predominantly physical or manual ability and list them, together with their associated equipment, and examples of the foods or dishes on which they are carried out.

Physical Actions Becoming Skills with Practice

Action/Skill	Associated Equipment	Food or Dish
Peeling/scraping	Hand or machine peelers/scrapers	Apples, pears, carrots, potatoes, etc
Shredding	Knife, machine or mandolin hand-slicer	Leaf vegetables, onions, zest of orange, potatoes
Slicing/carving	Knife, machine or mandolin slicer	Apples, pears, cucumber, potatoes, meat
Chopping	Knife or machine bowl chopper	Parsley, nuts, onions, vegetables for broths

Shaping/rolling out	Moulding by hand or on a table, machine moulding or shaping by means of a knife	Fish cakes, cutting out pastry, turning and dicing vegetables
Ladling	Ladle, measure or jug	Soups, stocks, gravies, sauces
Mixing/blending, creaming, rubbing-in, stirring	Hand mixing in a basin or on a table, using a spatula, spoon or a machine	Suet pastry (mixing), shortcrust pastry (rubbing-in), Victoria sandwich cake (creaming), sauces (stirring)
Whisking/beating	Hand or machine whisk	Meringues (egg whites), sponge cakes
Kneading	Hand kneading on table or in a basin, or by machine	Bread-making to develop gluten or holding protein together as in sausage meats
Lifting and carrying	Plates, pots, pans, trays, containers, hot or cold	All foods, liquid or solid
Cleaning, washing, polishing	All equipment and the area in which skills are performed	All foods

The method adopted will usually be a compromise to suit the quantity of food, the equipment being used, the time available and the standard of finished product acceptable.

Peeling and Scraping

Peeling involves the distinct cutting off of the outside skin of a food; it implies the use of a blade, which may be a hand tool (peeler or knife) or a machine, such as for peeling apples. The method of peeling often involves previous softening of the immediate outside layer of the fruit or vegetable, e.g. blanching peaches or tomatoes prior to pulling off the skin. Potatoes and carrots can be treated in this way prior to scraping. Scraping implies rubbing off the outer skin with the scraping action of a knife or of a machine; potatoes or carrots are particular examples.

The method involves selection of the appropriate tool and equipment for the removal of the peelings and a receptacle to take the food once it is peeled. It may also involve the prior cleaning and washing of the food and always the cleaning of the area in which the skill has been carried out. It is important to decide on the depth of the skin to remove, which varies with the type of food, and cost factors.

Shredding

Shredding involves cutting a food into strips using a knife or blade or a hand machine, such as a mandolin, or using a power operated machine with a rotary blade and a safety guard. The considerations as to method are similar as for peeling or scraping. The important decision is in respect of the fineness of the shredding, the direction of shredding and the length of each of the shreds. This again is decided by the structure of a particular food and the effect one requires; cabbage, for example, is shredded about 1/8 in thick across the grain and its length is approximately equal to one quarter of the diameter of the whole cabbage. Onions on the other hand are cut in half and shredded very finely in the same direction as the fibres to give a more equal length when cooked.

Slicing and Carving

These terms are used for the action of cutting a joint into thin pieces, usually across the grain or fibres. The term slicing is also used for cutting root vegetables into thin pieces. Again, with regard to methods, equipment has to be selected and the thickness of the slice decided upon. The important factors in respect of methods for carving meat are the thickness and size in relation to the size of the plate. A thin slice, for example, that covers the plate will give an impression of a larger portion than a thick slice that covers half the plate, even though the former may weigh less or be using less meat than the latter.

Chopping

Chopping refers to cutting any raw or cooked food into small pieces. The size, shape and evenness of the piece varies with the food and its purpose; chopped bones and vegetables used for flavourings are coarsely chopped and uneven in size, whereas parsley is so finely chopped that its shape is not apparent. Similar considerations apply to vegetables used for broths, although small dice are preferable (see Shaping).

Shaping

Shaping involves moulding by hand as when producing forcemeat balls or fish cakes. The method may involve the use of a piping bag or palette knife for greater effectiveness and to avoid too much handling. Shaping also involves cutting out rounds from pastry which has been previously rolled out. This again may be carried out with a hand cutter or by a machine.

Finally shaping can refer to cutting vegetables into dice, batons, even strips, or turning them into barrel or olive shapes. The important factor is that the size is related to the purpose, e.g. a dice of vegetable for broths is roughly a 1/8 in cube as opposed to the ¼ in cube of vegetables to serve on their own. The next consideration is that the method should be carried out in the correct order of cutting the vegetables into the length required, then the width and finally the thickness. This order will produce greater evenness of shape throughout the whole batch.

Ladling

Transferring liquids by means of a ladle, measure or jug is a skill which requires some consideration as to method in order to avoid spillage. Of chief importance is the handling of the ladle so as to obtain control over the leverage necessary when pouring out the contents. An unskilled person should use a drip tray, plate or container for catching drips when ladling large quantities.

Mixing

In this group of skills, five terms are used to denote different degrees of carrying out the actions of stirring, mixing, rubbing-in, blending and creaming.

Stirring refers to the action taken to keep a food moving without the excessive agitation involved in whisking. It is used predominantly with viscous foods such as soups, sauces, jams and mashed vegetables that are being heated; the purpose is to minimise the risk of burning. Stirring is also sometimes used to speed up the cooling of a food. Use equipment that will not scratch metal pans and pots. The amount of stirring depends on the viscosity and temperature of the food. Stirring to prevent burning can be overcome by controlling the amount of heat applied.

Mixing, rubbing-in, blending and creaming involve similar actions, but the length of time that the action is carried on varies according to the required result. The aim is to disperse two or more foods within each other; this can be done by hand or with an electrically operated mixer.

In mixing suet pastry, the suet is dispersed in the flour, i.e. mixed for a short time. In rubbing-in for shortcrust pastry, the butter is dispersed in flour until the grains of flour are coated with butter, i.e. mixed over a longer period. Blending is usually applied to the mixing of foods of similar consistency and involves complete dispersal of each food with the other, such as sauces and cream. Creaming is similar to blending, but involves mixing to produce an end result which has the consistency and texture of whipped cream and has an increased volume, e.g. butter and sugar in creamed cakes.

Whisking

This is a skill which can be considered with those of mixing as it may involve more than one food, such as whisking eggs and sugar for a sponge. However, as whisking generally involves the incorporation of air bubbles in a food, either by the use of a hand or machine whisk, it is defined separately. It is important to note that discoloration can occur if whisking takes place in a soft metal bowl (aluminium), and the whisk comes in contact with the metal. Earthenware or plastic bowls and basins are therefore preferable if hand whisking with a balloon whisk.

Kneading

This implies the working up into a dough and is particularly applied to a skill in bread making, its purpose being to develop and stretch the gluten in the flour. It can be carried out by hand or by using dough-hooks on an electric mixer.

Lifting and Carrying

Lifting and carrying actions are involved in batch production of all dishes. Posture and stance are important in lifting and carrying as they are all physical skills. Because of the variety in sizes and shapes of articles to be lifted and carried, these methods are summarised as follows: use a dry cloth for hot dishes, a wet cloth will not give sufficient insulation against heat. Clear a place for the article prior to moving it. If two hands are required, the article should be gripped, with the hands as widely spaced as possible, at either end of the tray, pan or container. Avoid letting the equipment and food act as a lever which may cause spillage during carrying.

Cleaning and Washing

The actions of cleaning and washing are involved in the production of most dishes and can be divided into two categories: (1) cleaning, washing and polishing the area and equipment in which production is taking place; and (2) cleaning and washing vegetables, fruit, fish, poultry and game prior to processing. Adequate cleaning, washing and polishing of the kitchen area and equipment is an essential condition for effective production of food.

In considering the method of cleaning and washing of vegetables, fruit, fish, poultry and game several rules apply: (1) consider the shape and structure of the food to be cleaned — lettuce, leeks and cabbage, for example, must be opened to remove dirt; (2) all leaf vegetables, including parsley, cress and edible fungi should be plunged into large amounts of water so that soil and sand can sink to the bottom and the clean foods lifted out, as opposed to draining the water away or using a colander to wash them. Root vegetables require hand or mechanical scrubbing.

The Learning of Basic Skills

In order to acquire certain skills with the minimum amount of trial and error, steps are taken in a pre-determined sequence that mainly involves muscular activity spaced over a sufficient period of time that will prevent fatigue with subsequent loss of attention, yet allow the muscles used to develop sufficient strength.

A tentative classification has been produced to define and illustrate the order of steps taken to acquire a skill, using a knife as an example.

1. Perception. The application of a person's senses before he can begin to perform any skill. In the use of a knife, the three main senses are kinaesthetic, tactile and visual. The feel and touch of the knife is perhaps more important in the first learning step. The recognition of the relative importance of each of these in respect of the task to be performed is essential, and following this the realisation of what the task is about.

2. Set. This step involves the preparation to carry out the task, mentally, physically and emotionally. Mentally by knowing which type of knife and which steps to take and physically by adopting the correct stance and position of the hands in relation to the knife and the food; emotional preparation can be translated as being willing or wanting to carry out the task.

3. Guided response. This concerns imitation and trial and error. Some guidance is required, perhaps the degree of pressure needed to exert or the extent of the cutting movement of the knife.

4. Mechanism. This describes the stage where the learner can perform a task as a habit, but the performance is not yet smooth and skilful.

5. Complex overt response. A performance that is skilful, uncertainties having been overcome.

6. Adapting and originating. At this stage, the learner is able to adapt a skill to suit the situation and the demands of different food materials that require shredding, slicing, chopping and shaping with a knife.

7. Selection of equipment for basic skills. The factors that decide which piece of equipment is required to carry out a skill include purpose, availability, labour and cost.

In order to determine the purpose factor, the raw food, in terms of type, size and structure must be considered in relation to the size and shape of the end product, or the particular skill to be carried out. Then match up in terms of functions the requirements inherent in this with the requirements of the equipment, in this case the knife. Consider the length and metal composition (e.g. stainless steel) of the blade, width, depth, thickness and sharpness of blade as well as the size, shape and construction of the handle. Also take into consideration the person who is carrying out the skill in terms of any physical limitation, and any factors regarding safety and hygiene.

A similar approach can be adopted when performing any operation in cooking by substituting items of equipment for the knife. The choice between two different types of equipment that will perform the same operation is determined primarily by the time available, volume of food and the end product characteristics.

CHARACTERISTICS OF FOOD COMMODITIES AND COOKING PROCESSES

The following pages examine the general composition of food and the effect that cooking processes have on the main food constituents. Also taken into account is the fact that food is subject to the normal processes of change, brought about by air, light and micro organisms. Food characteristics, cooking processes and agencies of change are linked with time and quality in the cooked food; these factors can be illustrated as follows:

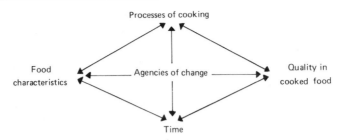

The producer of a dish needs to adjust the relationships between these factors in order to satisfy cost restraints and consumer needs. For example, the quality in the dish may have to be changed, and consequent changes may be required in the characteristics of the raw food. On the other hand, the raw food characteristic may change resulting in the possible necessity for adjusting both process of cooking and time to maintain the dish quality.

Water

Water is the most common constituent of all foods and in terms of controlling the changes in food it is also the most significant. Water is not only important in food, but it is also important as an outside commodity, in both cases as a medium for heat transfer. Water contains dissolved substances which may affect the characteristics of the food. Terms such as hard and soft water, for example, temporarily refer to the effect of substances dissolved in water; calcium and magnesium sulphates, for example, give permanently hard water, calcium carbonate temporarily hard water — the less there are of these substances the softer the water will be. Water boils, vapourised, at 212°F (100°C) under normal atmospheric pressure (14 lb per sq in approx.); if temporarily hard water is boiled, the calcium carbonate precipitates and is deposited in the sides of the utensil.

Water may be more or less acid. This acidity is expressed numerically as a pH value. A pH of 7 is neutral (distilled water), pH values of 6, 5, 4 indicate relatively more acidic content, figures above 7 less. The pH value and the relative hardness of water are considered further in relation to other food constituents, because it is only then that it assumes significance in obtaining the desired characteristics in a finished dish. However, where water is regarded as part of the food itself its effect is generally beneficial, in that it gives crispness and relative rigidity to food plants, and is responsible for much of the juiciness of meat. Where water is external to food, being used either as a medium for heat transfer or evaporated out of the food, its effects are not usually beneficial in that it will remove a considerable amount of flavour or juiciness from the food and may consequently reduce yield.

Protein

Protein is a term used for a class of structurally complicated substances that are relatively easy to change in the course of processing food. Handling, mixing and heating alters their physical characteristics quite dramatically.

Carbohydrates

These embrace both starches and sugars because the substances are complexes of carbon, hydrogen and oxygen. The simplest carbohydrate formed by food plants is the sugar, glucose; this is built into more complicated sugars such as the sugar we eat, sucrose. These simple sugars are in turn built up to form starch and cellulose. The important characteristics of sugars as far as cooking is concerned are their flavour, readiness to absorb or dissolve in water, and, when heated, to burn.

Starches occur in food as grains of various sizes and shapes. They absorb water and swell on heating. The differences in size and shape are responsible for some of the differences in texture and consistency in finished dishes which contain food with relatively large amounts of starch. Starch grains are enclosed in cellulose skins. Cellulose is the most complicated of the carbohydrates and on heating in water will soften and stretch. This softening and stretching is limited if the water has a low pH value, and increases to the point of complete breakdown if an excess of alkali, such as sodium bicarbonate, is added to the water.

Fats and Oils

Many foods, such as animal tissues, fruits and seeds, contain fats and oils. These fats and oils are extracted to form a series of substances: butter, margarine, lard, dripping and vegetable oils. Their characteristics, from the point of view of cooking, are that they possess a melting point and a smoke point, and that fats are more or less solid at normal temperature (approx. 60°F, 16°C) whereas oils are liquid. Furthermore, the various fats are more or less plastic. The melting point, smoke point and plasticity vary with the type of fat or oil.

The specific characteristics are important when cooking food in fat or heating food containing fat, and in obtaining specific characteristics in bakery and pastry products. The technology in respect of fats and oils is such that a fat or oil can be produced with quite specific melting or smoke points, and with flavour and plasticity characteristics that match up to specific purposes in cooking.

Types of Food

The proportion of water to protein, carbohydrates or fat varies in each food. However, to avoid examining each food in turn, foods can be grouped according to their principle constituents, for example separating those of a relatively high water content from those low in water.

Foods with a high water content are meat, fish, poultry, game, eggs, milk, cream, fruit and vegetables. These foods are known as perishables and have a short shelf life because unless otherwise processed or preserved they are easily subject to undesirable changes. Foods with a low water content, while still perishable to some extent, are known as non-perishables or dry goods. These include cereals and starches such as rice, semolina, flour and oatmeal, fats and oils.

Foods can also be grouped according to the proportion of protein, carbohydrates or fat they contain: meat, fish, poultry, game, eggs and milk contain varying proportions of protein and little or no carbohydrates while most vegetables and fruits contain carbohydrates and little protein.

The figures in this table are approximate percentages to illustrate the variety in composition.

Food	Water	Protein	Carbohydrates	Fat/oil
Meat	60	20	—	15
Potatoes	80	2	17	—
Cabbage	90	2	7	—
Flour	13	13	70	2

Agencies of Change

Raw food is alive and in common with other organic matter is subject to the process of decay leading to food spoilage. Changes that result in food spoilage are caused by one or more components, some of which, however, may also be beneficial. The changes do not occur naturally in isolation, but in combination with each other.

Enzymes

This term describes a large group of proteins produced by living cells. Their function is to produce changes in the cells and hence in the food, reactions upon which life depends. From a food processing or cooking point of view these changes may be beneficial, but when uncontrolled will result in food spoilage. Enzymes are proteins and their activity can be arrested or stopped altogether by certain cooking processes.

The particular enzymic changes that occur are specific to the type of food, and their acceptability therefore varies. In meat, for example, enzymic changes occur on hanging or ageing meat, which result in meat with more flavour and greater tenderness; up to a point this is beneficial. In cabbage, on the other hand, enzyme activity brings about colour change which is considered undesirable.

Micro Organisms

There are two main groups of organisms, bacteria, and yeasts and moulds, that produce changes in food. Both occur as the result of their introduction to the food from outside and there are thousands of different types. They may be beneficial, undesirable or harmful in terms of producing acceptable food.

Bacteria are minute single-celled plants that cannot be seen with the naked eye. They multiply rapidly by each cell dividing in two under suitable conditions specific to the type of bacteria. If conditions are unfavourable, bacteria can form spores that lie dormant and are difficult to destroy.

Yeasts are similar to bacteria, slightly larger and their method of reproduction is by budding. The buds grow out of the single cell and split off as a separate yeast cell. Moulds on the other hand are simple plants that under favourable conditions will grow a network of threads throughout the food.

Bacteria, yeasts and moulds will attack food constituents. Some will ferment sugars and change starches and cellulose, others digest protein or induce rancidity in fat. Others will manufacture acid so that the food turns sour, or in fermentation make food foam. Discoloration in food can be caused by bacteria and some bacteria will produce deadly poisons. Given food, warmth and moisture, bacteria, yeasts and moulds will grow. The optimum temperatures for growth are between $50°F$ ($10°C$) and $140°F$ ($60°C$), although some bacteria will grow at temperatures as low as $32°F$ ($0°C$) and as high as $158°F$ ($70°C$).

Insects, Parasites and Rodents

The spoilage of food by certain groups of insects, parasites and rodents can take many forms. Not only do many of them consume vast quantities of food, but they also contaminate food with micro organisms or damage food in such a way that it is exposed to bacterial contamination and other agencies of change.

Heat or Cold

Exposure to uncontrolled heat or cold leads to food spoilage, quite apart from the effect heat or cold may have on bacterial growth and enzymic action. Heat may de-nature the protein or evaporate water from foods; cold may freeze water thereby causing structural damage.

Moisture and Dryness

The effects, in terms of food spoilage, of exposing dry goods to uncontrolled moisture, or conversely foods with a high water content to uncontrolled dryness, are obvious, particularly if considered in relation to bacterial contamination and growth of moulds.

Oxygen

Oxygen in the air accelerates changes in food; fat for example may go rancid more quickly if left exposed to air. Browning of prepared foods, such as apples and pears, occurs as a result of exposure to air and enzymic action.

Light

Sunlight indicates changes in food leading to a deterioration in colour, undesirable changes in protein foods and rancidity in fats.

Cooking Processes

The fundamental processes of cooking in logical sequence involve handling, mixing, heating or cooling. The cooking of foods as regards heat transfer is a combination of methods. It is a complicated process involving more than one heat transfer method. Unless food is uniform in physical and chemical properties, the understanding of heat transfer will remain a fundamental problem.

Handling

This process covers any manual operation carried out on food. It includes all the physical skills such as cutting, slicing, chopping, mincing, whisking and beating.

Any handling process affects the water content of foods by damaging the cell structure in foods with high water content. It is also through handling and the water content that foods become contaminated with micro organisms. Handling can generate heat which, transferred by the water in food, speeds up many of the undesirable changes. Proteins are structurally altered by handling; the whisking of egg white or the mincing and beating of meat produces, for example, a more cohesive mass. This type of handling exposes more surface area and increases the risk of contamination by micro organisms and subsequent food spoilage.

Foods with a high carbohydrate content are little changed by handling other than increasing the possibility of contamination. Sugars absorb moisture, and handling increases the likelihood of this happening. Flour and water when handled become rubbery; this, however, is due to the protein and water rather than the starch. Handling may contaminate fats and oils with micro organisms. However, because fat and oil on their own are not good media for bacterial growth, contamination does not lead to rapid food spoilage. The exceptions to this are fats that have water dispersed through them, such as butter, margarine and untreated animal fat. The softening and melting of fats through heat engendered in handling can occur; depending upon the purchase this may be desirable or not.

Mixing

All the changes in food that are referred to under handling apply equally to mixing, with the additional factor that mixing specifically refers to the vast range of cooking processes concerned with incorporating one food ingredient with others (salting, smoking, pickling, preserving), as well as the preparatory blending of foods, such as creaming butter and sugar for cakes, incorporating onions with meat, or folding a salad dressing into salads.

Ignoring water, the two most common ingredients mixed into foods are salt and sugar. Not only are they used for flavour, but are also used to preserve foods in order to delay or inhibit actions of change. The effect of large quantities of salt or sugar on the water content of food is similar because they will both extract water through the semi-permeable cell membranes. The extent to which this happens depends on the strength of the sugar or salt solution inside. This movement of water is known as *osmosis* and can occur in either direction, water passing from an area with a lower concentration of solution to one with a higher. The action is particularly noticeable if any protein food, meat or fish, is salted before cooking. Given time the surface of the food will become moist as water is drawn out by the salt. For this reason it may be desirable to salt or season foods of this nature after they have been cooked.

With high concentrations of salt or sugar — and acid — harmful bacteria action is inhibited and foods alter in their texture characteristics. In meat and fish the flesh firms up, giving a rigid structure. Colour changes occur on the surface. In meat, the pink colour that characterises salted cured meats is achieved through the addition of sodium nitrate to the salt or brine. This chemically changes the colour pigments from red to pink, and the meat remains this colour even after it is cooked. Exposure of the cooked meat to light and air will, however, cause loss of surface colour.

Heating and Cooling

Conventionally the concept of "cooking" is most closely identified with the application of heat to food, the heat processes being known as roasting, boiling, baking, stewing, steaming, frying, braising or grilling. These terms are difficult to define clearly, because the processes associated with them vary according to circumstances, but they can be taken as descriptions of finished dishes to give some indication of the characteristics of the product. For example, there is a common notion of what constitutes roast meat in terms of colour, texture and flavour; it may vary in detail but in general there would be agreement. However, the process of producing roast meat in terms of time, temperature and equipment may vary considerably.

Another limitation imposed by the adoption of conventional names for cooking processes is that there are methods of applying heat that do not readily fall into any category. For example, meat placed in a sealed plastic bag and immersed in water at 176°F (80°C) until it is cooked will not bear much resemblance to boiled meat, but will be closer to the characteristics of roast meat.

Heating and cooling are relative terms referring to the effect of an energy transfer to or within a substance that is sensed hot or cold. Heat is the most common form of energy. It is a property that all matter possesses as a result of the motion of its molecules, a rapid motion giving rise to a sensation of warmth, greatly reduced movement being sensed as cold. Because the assessment of heat via the senses is relative to personal body warmth it is an inaccurate measure. A better measure is obtained by using a thermometer. This registers heat and cold in terms of temperature in degrees Fahrenheit or Celsius. Temperatures that have significance in heating or cooling foods expressed in degrees Fahrenheit and Celcius include:

	Degrees (Fahrenheit)	Degrees (Celcius)	
Steam at 15 lb per sq in	248	121	
Steam at 5 lb per sq in	228	109	
Boiling point (water) at atmospheric pressure	212	100	
Freezing point (water)	32	0	
Protein coagulation	140—188	60—87	
Cessation of enzyme action	176	80	and above
Carbohydrates —			
starch thickens or gelatinises	203—206	95—98	
sugar caramelises	302—347	150—175	
Vegetable shortening	350—363	177—185	
Lard	361—450	183—232	
Smoking point for frying oil	329—450	165—232	
Micro organisms inactivated	180	82	and above
multiply	50—140	10—60	
lie dormant	Below 50	Below 10	

The temperatures listed for proteins, enzymes and micro organisms are approximations and depend on the length of time each is held at a particular temperature, as well as the tolerances that are set up for a particular degree of change. For example, a food held at a temperature of 161°F (72°C) for 15 seconds will have a similar number of micro organisms destroyed as one held at 148°F (62°C) for 30 minutes, so that a high temperature for a short time has a similar effect as a lower temperature for a longer time.

A transfer of heat energy does not always give rise to a change in the temperature of food. When steam changes back into water, or when water freezes, a great deal of energy is released or absorbed without a change in temperature. This is called latent heat, and its significance in cooking is that with frozen food, a great deal of time and heat energy is required in thawing it out before there is any rise in temperature. This can be illustrated graphically as below.

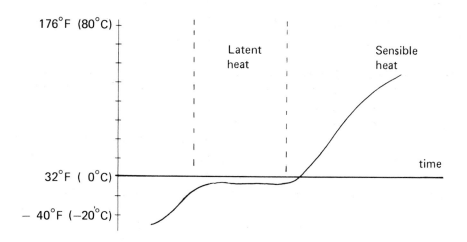

Heat Transfer by Conduction

This is the process of transferring heat from one place to another by direct contact. It occurs because the smallest particles of a substance, known as molecules, can be made to vibrate faster and this energy is transmitted to molecules that have less vibration. Examples of conduction of heat to food are shallow-frying or heating on a griddle where the food is in direct contact with a hot pan or plate. Conduction occurs in cooling down where relatively warm food is in direct contact with cold metal. Conduction of heat takes place inside food, either from the relatively hot outside to the cooler inside when heating or the reverse when cooling.

Different materials conduct heat at different rates. For example, copper is a better conductor of heat than aluminium; in food, meat muscle conducts heat better than fat. The less dense the material the slower it will conduct heat.

Heat Transfer by Convection

When the heat is transferred through the actual movement of a liquid or a gas this is known as convection. If one part of a liquid or gas is heated, it tends to expand and move upwards leaving room for cooler parts to take its place. These movements are known as convection currents. It is chiefly by convection currents that the whole of a liquid becomes hot; the thickness or viscosity of the liquid will affect the rate of movement of convection currents, a thick liquid conveying heat more slowly than a thin liquid. The conventional terms for transferring heat to food using convection currents are boiling, poaching, simmering, deep-frying, steaming and roasting in an oven. Some conduction is also involved in these processes because the article to be cooked must rest on or come in contact with a part of the utensil being used. In the case of roasting, some radiation may also take place, particularly where the oven has exposed elements that glow red.

Heat Transfer by Radiation

Radiation refers to the transfer of energy by rays or waves directly to the food. The rays or waves travel in straight lines from the heat source in much the same way as light. They are reflected by bright shiny, white surfaces and absorbed by dark surfaces. The difference between rays for heating and rays for light lies in the wave-length, frequency and penetrating power. A heat source, such as a grill, generates waves in what is known as the infra-red wave band. These are shorter in wave-length than micro-waves (generated in a micro-wave oven), but both are longer than waves in the light spectrum.

Infra-red and micro-waves can penetrate into food. The depth of penetration depends upon the wave-length and the type of food being heated. For example, a piece of meat with high water content will be penetrated to a depth of some 3 inches by micro-waves and by infra-red to a depth of about 1/8 inch. Because of the penetration of 3 inches and the heat generated to this depth, micro-wave cooking is carried out in a relatively short time.

The relative effectiveness of each method of heat transfer in terms of the time required to heat or cool a food can be illustrated by considering the cooking time of an egg. An egg will cook to hard-boil — total coagulation of egg proteins — in water at 176-212°F (80-100°C) in approximately 10 minutes. The same effect will be achieved in steam in approximately 7 minutes. If placed in an oven at 350°F (177°C) the egg will be only soft-boiled — partial coagulation of egg proteins — after 40 minutes. In a micro-wave oven, the egg will explode and the proteins will be coagulated in a matter of seconds.

The effect of latent heat accounts for the differences in the first two examples. Steam, condensing on the egg, gives up its latent heat so providing a more effective heat transfer to the egg than the water. In the case of the egg in the oven, evaporation of surface moisture on the outside of the egg will give a cooling effect, thereby slowing down the effectiveness of heat transfer to the egg. The exploding of the egg in the micro-wave oven is caused by too effective a generation of heat inside the egg; the water in the egg turns to steam, expands and blows up the egg.

Transfer of Cold

The cooling of foods occurs through cool air convection currents absorbing heat from relatively warm food. The air itself is cooled, for example, in a refrigerator, by causing a liquid with a low boiling point to turn into a gas round the freezing compartment, latent heat or evaporation causing the cooling.

In both an oven and in a refrigerator or freezer the rate of heat transfer can be increased by introducing a fan to speed up the convection currents. Whether an increased rate of heat transfer is desirable or not depends upon the food characteristics and the end product required. In general it is desirable to cool foods so as to reduce the rate at which any harmful micro organisms may multiply. In speeding up the heating of some foods, shrinkage and toughening will occur if the foods get hot too quickly. In both heating and cooling by convection currents in air, some drying out of the surface moisture occurs which in itself will affect the rate at which foods attain the desired internal temperatures.

Whether solid frozen food is boiled, poached, steamed, fried, roasted or grilled it is chiefly by conduction of heat — from the outside to the centre or from the centre to the outside — that it attains the desired temperature. The rate at which heat is transferred is specific to the type of food.

MEAT AND MEAT PRODUCTS

This part deals with the general nature of meat in terms of structure and composition, the factors that affect potential tenderness in the cooked product, and cooked qualities, such as flavour, juiciness, colour and yield. It also discusses meat products such as those used in stews, hot-pots and pies, sausage-type fillings with regard to controlling the quality in the end product.

The term meat is here restricted to mean the muscle of morbid animals used for human consumption. The chief meats in British cookery are beef, veal, mutton, lamb, pork, poultry and game. The bone content and internal organs known as offal are therefore not included although the heart, from a cooking point of view, has a muscular structure that is similar to other muscles.

Muscle Structure and Composition

Muscle structure can be considered as consisting of fibres of varying lengths and thicknesses, held together in bundles by connective tissues. This is a semi-transparent, polythene-like material of which the principal constituent is collagen. Muscle primarily consist of water (approximately 60-70 per cent); of the remaining solids some 20 per cent is protein and 10 per cent is fat. Protein is found in the muscle fibres and in the connective tissues, the fat being dispersed between the fibres. A non-fatty looking meat still has fat within its structure.

Quality in Cooked Meat

Some of the qualities in cooked meat that are deemed to be important are tenderness, flavour, juiciness, colour and yield. Tenderness is a relative term associated in the case of meat with chewiness or ease of slicing with a knife. Age, type of cut, storage, tenderisers, time and temperature of heating all influence tenderness.

Age and Tenderness

The younger the animal and the less work it has done, the more tender the meat, be it lamb, mutton, veal, pork, beef, poultry or game. The age of an animal is indicated by the colour in the fat and muscle, and by the colour and hardness of the bones. A combination of pale to white fat, pale pink or white muscle with a bluish tinge, coupled with relative pliability in rib bones, indicates that the meat is from a young animal and will therefore have potentially more tender eating qualities. Yellow fat, dark muscle, hard white bones with very little pliability indicate older animals and tougher meat.

Cuts and Tenderness

Whatever the age of the animal, certain cuts or joints from a carcass are tougher than others; in some cases an increased toughness is difficult to detect. Toughness is concentrated in the connective tissues, not in the fibres. Tough cuts are those muscles that, in the animal's life, have had to do the most work. The leg, neck and shoulder muscles and, excluding poultry and game, the chest and stomach are tougher than those on the loin or rump. The breast muscles of poultry and game are more tender than the leg.

Storage and Tenderness

The length of time that a cut or carcass has been stored prior to cooking and the conditions under which it has been stored will affect potential tenderness. Freshly killed animals or poultry will be tougher than those which have been stored. The reasons for this are connected with the changes that occur in meat after slaughter and these again are dependent upon the state of the animal prior to slaughter and the time and temperature after slaughter.

The two main changes are, firstly, a condition of rigidity known as *rigor mortis*, and secondly, a change due to the action of enzymes on the muscle protein, enzymes being specialised proteins that produce changes without themselves being changed. In *rigor mortis*, the muscle fibres tighten or bunch up and become rubbery shortly after slaughter. After a day or two, depending on conditions, they relax again and become appreciably softer. If cooked during *rigor mortis*, meat and poultry of any age will be tough.

The action of enzymes on muscle protein can increase the potential tenderness of meat and occurs in a similar way to the action of commercial added tenderisers. The extent of this activity is influenced by the pH value of the muscle, the storage temperature and time. If the animal is rested before slaughter, then the pH of the muscle will be lower due to an increased amount of lactic acid being formed. This in turn will increase the action of the enzymes so giving a potentially more tender product.

Enzyme activity is also influenced by temperature. Up to a point a rise in temperature speeds up the action, and while an optimum temperature is difficult to give because any increase in temperature and humidity during storage increases the risk of food spoilage, temperatures of up to 35°F (2°C), together with adequate ventilation and low humidity for some ten days, will give beef cuts considerably greater potential tenderness. For this reason the purchaser of meat should enquire when it was killed.

Tenderisers

An increase in tenderness can be achieved by the pre-slaughter injection of an enzyme which spreads throughout the body, or by the application of an enzyme to the cut surfaces of the muscle. Unfortunately, the resulting tenderness can be increased by these methods to the point where the meat is so tender that it loses all chewiness and appears dry and powdery when cooked. Furthermore, the application of the enzyme to cut surfaces is generally only suitable for small cuts of meat, such as steaks, because the penetration of larger cuts appears to be minimal. Difficulty is experienced in obtaining the necessary even distribution of the enzyme over the cut surface.

A further method for increasing apparent tenderness is by mechanical means, such as by grinding, beating, chopping or mincing. This in effect makes the collagenous fibres shorter and so gives the effect of increased tenderness. There is also some evidence that tenderness can be increased with freezing due to enzyme action and the formation of ice crystals; this change, however, is of minimal importance.

Heating and Tenderness

Heat is a relative term used to indicate temperature which we measure through our senses as warmth or absence of cold. Foods are changed in their physical composition, and these changes can be speeded up or controlled by transferring heat to them or removing heat from them.

Most food is semi-solid, always containing water, and it is this water that is important in transferring heat from the environment to the centre of the food or vice versa. Just as there are convection currents and conduction of heat in a pan of water on a stove, so there are in semi-solid food. In scientific terms, heat transfer is brought about by a difference in temperature; the molecules of water in heating vibrate faster, transferring energy from one to another, so heat travels inwards to the centre of food. In cooling, the greatest vibration is inside so that the heat travels from the inside to the outside.

The most important factors in the composition of meat are fibre and connective tissue which are combinations of water, protein and fat. When muscle fibre and connective tissue are heated they react in different ways. The protein in the muscle fibre sets or coagulates in much the same way as eggs. Complete internal coagulation of muscle protein occurs at 171°F (77°C). Suggested internal temperatures for general use are 140°F (60°C), 158°F (71°C) and 171°F (77°C) to obtain under-coagulation (rare, blue/red), partial coagulation (medium, pink), full coagulation (well-done, brown) of protein in the muscle fibre of beef. Up to a point all muscle fibres of animals and poultry will become tougher the longer they are heated above 171°F (77°C). For example, a well-done steak is generally tougher than rare or medium.

Under certain conditions of heat and timing, the water and connective tissue convert to the tender product gelatine. This conversion is a function of the rate of heat penetration in the muscle and is independent of the vehicle of heat transfer. Thus it is possible to roast shin beef by controlling the rate of heat penetration. In practice this can be achieved by subjecting a 4 lb piece of shin to a temperature of 248°F (120°C) for some 5 hours on the bars of an oven. The problem of obtaining maximum tenderness by converting connective tissues to gelatine only occurs in those animals, poultry and game that are old; and even then generally only those whose muscles have done the most work.

Heat is transferred from an outside source to the muscle; it is then conducted to the centre of the muscle. If the internal temperature exceeds 171°F (77°C) for long periods then the cooked meat will be tough regardless of the amount of connective tissue. In cuts with a large amount of connective tissue, tenderness will be most easily achieved by a slow rate of heat penetration to an internal temperature of between 140-171°F (60-77°C).

Methods of Heat Transfer and their Effect on Tenderness

Every method of transferring heat can produce tenderness in cooked meat, provided that the temperature can be regulated. The lower the temperature of the heat source, the easier it is to control the rate of heat penetration.

Heat is transferred to the surface of meat by convection or conduction via air, water (or stock or sauce), fat or steam or by direct radiation from a grill. To obtain some idea of the comparative effectiveness of these ways of transferring heat, imagine the sensations of heat that would be experienced if the hand was placed in either of these mediums or close to a grill at various temperatures.

Heat Transfer via Air

Warm air passing over and round meat has a drying effect; the extent of drying and the amount of heat transferred depends on time and temperature. At external temperatures over 212°F (100°C) it will become more apparent that the surface moisture is being evaporated from the meat because the surface can be seen to be drier. This has a cooling effect on meat, thereby slowing down the rate of heat penetration. It is a similar effect to that of evaporation of petrol or methylated spirits from the skin, and it is because of this type of cooling effect that the heat of an oven at 302°F (150°C) is more bearable for longer periods than water, stock, sauce or fat at 167°F (75°C).

In general it takes very much longer to heat the centre of meat to 140-171°F (60-77°C) in air than it will in water, stock, sauce or fat at a temperature of 140-212°F (60-100°C). Because of the slower rate of heat penetration, all meat can therefore be made more tender by air heat transfer, and however much connective tissue is present in the meat, it can be converted to gelatine and made tender.

It is difficult to give specific temperatures because the effectiveness of the air circulation in equipment used for cooking meat varies, as does the amount of connective tissue in the various cuts. Furthermore, if a large number of cuts are being cooked at any one time then the environment in which the meat is being heated will change due to the increase in water vapour from the meat. The time or temperature may have to be varied; for cuts with much connective tissue, as in shin of beef, the external temperature should be nearer 176°F (80°C) for maximum tenderness. However, if meat is placed so that the air can circulate round it, then 176-325°F (80-163°C) is a suitable temperature range.

The practice of heating meat by air, that is by roasting, requires further qualification. For example, in conventional roasting the cut is usually placed in a roasting tin which impedes air circulation, but may transfer heat directly by conduction through the tin. Again, the practice of pouring hot fat over the meat (basting) may be in conflict with the aim of obtaining tenderness. Depending upon the temperature of the fat, this practice may change the rate of heat penetration by evaporating so much of the surface moisture that the joint becomes surrounded by a layer of over-coagulated protein which acts as an insulator. This would suggest that the practice of basting is not necessary.

Because fat and bone are poor conductors of heat compared with the muscle itself, joints with a layer of fat on the outside and cooked on the bone will take longer to reach the required internal temperature. This again will increase the tenderness.

Heat Transfer via Water, Stocks and Sauces

The transfer of heat by convection currents in water, stocks and sauces, a method which also involves some conduction of heat, is a more direct way of transferring heat than by air, mainly because of the lack of surface evaporation. To achieve the same tenderness than results from roasting a piece of meat at 325°F (163°C) in air, a water, stock or sauce temperature of approximately 176°F (80°C) is required.

Because of the increased viscosity of a sauce, meat cooked in it will take longer to reach the required internal temperature (slower convection currents). The end product may therefore be more tender.

Heating in Fat or Oil

The same principles of producing tender cooked meat by heating in water, stocks or sauces apply to immersion in fat or oil. Fat temperatures between 176-212°F (80-100°C) will produce a tender end product, as will temperatures up to 248°F (120°C). Due to the high cost of fat or oil this practice is not often employed.

Shallow-frying is a misleading term for cooking food in a pan or on a griddle with temperature control. It is misleading because the heat is mainly transferred by conduction through the pan or griddle and not via the small amount of fat, oil or butter being used; the purpose of the fat is to provide preliminary coagulation of the surface protein thus reducing the likelihood of food sticking to the pan.

Small cuts of meat, poultry or game, low in connective tissue and therefore already tender, may be cooked in this way. The temperature of the pan or griddle need not be low, but should be varied according to the thickness of the cut of meat. As a guide 347-437°F (177-225°C) is a suitable temperature range; very thick cuts, such as mutton chops, requiring a lower temperature, and very thin cuts, such as minute steaks, requiring a higher temperature.

Heat Transfer by Steam

Steam is water vapour which can be produced by boiling water in a ventilated chamber. This steam will be at atmospheric pressure which can be raised by decreasing the ventilation. This effectively increases the temperature from 212°F (100°C) at atmospheric pressure to 259°F (126°C) at a pressure of 20 lb per square inch. Steam condenses on the surface of the meat and gives up its latent heat. This release of energy plus increased temperature accounts for the faster rate of heat penetration than if the meat were immersed in water at 212°F (100°C). However, to some extent depending on the pressure, steam is also created on the surface of the meat; this steam absorbs heat and causes some evaporative cooling. Consequently meat cooked in steam will in general be more tender than if cooked in water at 212°F (100°C), but tougher than if cooked in an oven to the same internal temperature.

Heat Transfer by Radiation

Radiation is a direct method of transferring heat that involves subjecting meat almost instantaneously to energy waves. These waves travel in straight lines from the heat source and have various wave-lengths, the most effective being within the region 1.4 to 5 millionths of a metre long. They are effective in so far as they will penetrate the water vapour which surrounds the meat when it is heated.

A further factor that influences the effectiveness of radiation as a means of heat transfer is the temperature of the heat source and the distance between that and the meat. This distance is proportional to the amount of energy that reaches the food. Halving the distance will increase the amount of energy fourfold.

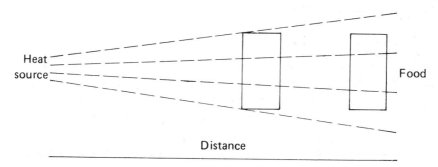

With this degree of control over heat this process could be used to achieve tenderness. However, in general it is used mainly for small cuts of meat and poultry and whole small game birds, such as teal, woodcock, snipe and grouse, that are already potentially tender.

Carry-Over Cooking

This term refers to what happens within a cut of meat when it is removed from a heat source and the temperature at the centre of the thickest part is less than the temperature at the surface. Some of the heat on the surface will be absorbed by the air round the meat, but some will continue to be conducted to the centre of the meat. The principle of carry-over cooking is important, particularly in roasting, grilling and shallow-frying, because meat, particularly small cuts, could be subjected to a high temperature — 527°F (265°C) — for a short period of time and rely on carry-over cooking to attain the desired internal temperature, i.e. degree of coagulation of the muscle protein.

Flavour and Juiciness

These qualities are important in cooked meat and therefore need consideration in respect of their control. Flavour, which denotes sensations obtained through taste, smell and aroma, is developed in meat by hanging and by the amount of intra-muscular fat which is more predominant in older animals.

Juiciness in cooked meat is dependent on water and fat retention in the meat during cooking. The most important factor influencing this is the cooking procedure. In general, cooking methods that result in the most tender product without over-coagulation of muscle fibre will have the most flavour and greatest juiciness.

The degree of shrinkage during cooking is directly correlated with loss of juiciness to the palate. Greater shrinkage occurs at high temperatures coupled with fast rate of heat penetration. More fat will be melted and squeezed out of the meat along with other juices as a result of the rapid coagulation and contraction of the muscle fibres and connective tissue.

Flavour varies according to the process of cooking. Duration and temperature also influence the nature and intensity of aroma and taste. The conflict of the dry environment of an oven producing a less juicy meat can be overcome by sealing the meat in a polythene bag and cooking it in water at a temperature of about 176°F (80°C).

Colour Changes

Colour changes occur in meat processing most noticeably in meats that are bright red, e.g. beef, mutton and some game. The colour changes from red or blue at 140°F (60°C) to pink at approximately 158°F (70°C) and greyish-brown at 171°F (77°C) internal temperatures.

Surface browning has importance both in terms of colour and flavour. This aspect of appearance is particularly connected with roasting and grilling. A feature of grilled meats is the dark brown lattice work produced either in the course of the process by the grill bars or simulated with a hot iron rod or poker.

Browning in roasts occurs as a result of a time and temperature relationship, low temperatures for a long time producing the same effect as high temperatures for a short time. The advantage of the former is that the point at which adequate browning has occurred is not critical and control is therefore easier.

Yield

This defines the amount of cooked food produced in relation to a given amount of raw food. Assuming that the cooked food is equally acceptable in its other qualities to the consumer, yield is probably the most important quality.

Because of the comparatively high cost of meat in relation to other foods, it is important to obtain the highest yield possible and therefore adopt a process which is consistent with this aim. This object is usually to obtain the maximum volume from a given cut of meat, not necessarily the maximum weight, because it is the size of the piece or pieces of meat on a plate that determines whether the portion is large enough. It is only after this has been decided that the portion is weighed to give some form of measure.

Maximum volume will be obtained from a given piece of meat if the rate of heat penetration is slow and the final internal temperature is not held above 171°F (77°C) for any appreciable length of time. Two factors that influence yield are the physical shrinkage that occurs due to rapid coagulation of connective tissue, and the skill and method used for portioning. If the meat is cooked to the point where all the connective tissue is converted to gelatine, portioning becomes difficult as the meat will fall apart.

Meat Products

This part is concerned with meat products used for stews, hot-pots and pies that contain mixtures of meat or meat and vegetables in stock, gravy or sauce. It also deals with products prepared from chopped seasoned meat that are sold in casings as pork or beef sausages, and with minced or chopped raw meat.

The distinction between the two types arises largely as a consequence of certain differences in the qualities of the end products, and thus differences in respect of control factors. For example, the juicy moist eating quality of a sausage, meat loaf or meat roll requires more consideration than the juiciness inevitably resulting from added stock, sauce or gravy in a stew, hot-pot or pie. Conversely, the tender quality of the meat in the latter products requires control, whereas tenderness in the filling for sausages and meat rolls is usually the inevitable result of chopping or mincing (mechanical tenderising).

The component parts of a stew are meat, vegetables and flavourings, stock, gravy or sauce, and each requires individual consideration in respect of its qualities in relation to the other components and to the total qualities in the finished dish.

The Meat

The type and particular cut of meat for a stew may be indicated in the name of the dish, e.g. lamb stew. Otherwise decisions must be made to the type and cut to be used; these decisions are primarily based on the cost of the cuts available and their potential yield, and the intrinsic properties of each cut and their potential in obtaining the characteristics required in the end product.

For example, one cut of meat may cost more than another, but it may also yield a larger number of portions and may therefore be the more economical of the two. However, the structure and composition may be such that it will not readily produce the tenderness required, and consequently, a compromise must be reached. A decision may be taken to adjust the process of production to compensate either for the lack of tenderness or lower yield, in the first case by extending the cooking period, and in the second case by increasing the volume of vegetables and the viscosity of the sauce to obtain an appearance of greater yield. The shape and size of the pieces of meat must also be determined in general, the smaller the pieces the greater the apparent yield in giving more pieces of meat per portion.

The size and shape of the meat pieces can be an important quality factor. Its importance decreases with the size, so that if the meat is minced the size and shape are less important. Where necessary, a process should be adopted that will retain the size and shape; frying the meat beforehand or blanching will help to retain shape because of the rapid coagulation of the protein and consequent tightening and shrinkage of the connective tissue. This, however, greatly reduces the size of each piece, which can best be maintained by a cooking process not exceeding 185°F (85°C).

The Vegetables

The vegetables in a stew can be considered as flavourings alone or as flavouring and a visibly integral part of the dish. For example, in a steak pie the onions are added for flavour whereas in braised steak and onions they are seen as an integral part of the dish as well as giving it flavour.

The functional aspects therefore determine the size and shape of the prepared vegetables and to some extent the quantities. In general, the quantity by weight of onions to meat varies from 50 to 25 per cent, or by volume from 100 to 50 per cent although this is influenced by the strength of flavouring in the stock, sauce or gravy.

The shape of the vegetables and the colour are of importance if they are to be seen in the finished dish. It may be desirable to cook the vegetables separately and add them when the meat is cooked, partly to control shape and colour and partly to overcome the differences in times for producing tender meat and soft vegetables.

Stocks, Gravies and Sauces

The type of stock, gravy or sauce is determined by the type of meat and is sometimes indicated by the name of the dish; brown beef stew, for example, requires brown beef stock. Nevertheless, it is possible to produce all stews using only water, the colour and viscosity being obtained as a result of the natural colour of the ingredients, browning, caramelisation or added colour, length of cooking period or a type of thickening agent. For example, if diced beef is placed in water and held at approximately 176°F (80°C) until tender, the resulting liquid will be a light amber colour. One of the colour components in carrots is water-soluble, but the major colour component, a carotenoid pigment, is soluble in fat. Thus if the carrots are cut in small pieces and browned in fat, two sources of colour are available, one the surface browning and the other the fat which may be dispersed in the sauce.

Thickening of the liquid in a stew may result from the vegetables used, such as potatoes or finely chopped onion, or from a thickening agent. It is interesting to note that if finely chopped onion is mixed with an equal volume of diced or minced meat and cooked until the meat is tender without any added liquid, it will naturally produce a thickened sauce due to the over-softening of the onions, the liquid protein from the meat coagulating to give an appearance of viscosity to the water from both the onions and the meat.

Sausages, Meat Loaves and Rolls

An understanding of these products and their eating qualities can be obtained by considering chopped or minced meat on its own, then examining the effect of adding other ingredients.

When finely chopped or minced meat is heated without mixing until all the protein is coagulated it will be seen to lose water and thereby juiciness and to cohere in a lump. This tendency to bind can be increased if the minced meat is vigorously beaten and moulded into shape before cooking. Loss of water occurs due to the damage caused by chopping or mincing; the binding together during cooking arises from coagulation of surface protein.

Water and Fat Retention

Control of juiciness in sausages, meat loaves and meat rolls lies in water and fat retention, or in the addition of extra fat and water. The retention of water and fat within minced meat during cooking depends on the age of the meat, the proportions of fat and water added, the amount of salt, the extent of mixing and the temperature during mixing, and the time and temperature of cooking.

The age or condition of the meat, the proportions of fat, water and amount of salt that are added are interdependent. For example, the amount of fat and water that can be held in minced meat increases with conditioning or age and with the addition of salt. The amount of salt is affected by the flavour required in the end product. However, as a general rule 1.4 per cent salt to total content is adequate. If the minced meat is produced from a muscle having a high content of intra-muscular fat it will tend to have a high water-holding capacity.

Meat Proportions

The following mixture is suggested for pork sausages: 72 per cent lean pork, 26 per cent fat and 2 per cent flavouring of which 1.4 per cent is salt. This basic mixture can be varied at the expense of meat and to a limited extent fat, by the addition of bread or rusks soaked in water. Acceptable proportions could then be composed of 50 per cent lean meat, 22 per cent fat, 26 per cent soaked bread and 2 per cent salt and flavouring.

Fundamental to the production of an even texture is a stable emulsion. This is a factor common to many other food products, e.g. sauces, soups and to the batters for bakery, pastry and confectionery products. If the proportion of fat in the mixture is greater than the water, the emulsion is known as a water-in-fat emulsion, the water being dispersed in small globules and held throughout the fat or oil, such as in mayonnaise. In minced products the opposite is the case, the fat being dispersed and held throughout the water protein base.

The stability of an emulsion can be increased by the use of egg yolks which in themselves are an emulsion; commercially certain chemicals are used to achieve stability, certain phosphates for example, being added to sausage mixes. In order to produce an even-textured product the ingredients must be mixed and blended. However, temperature affects the extent to which this is possible, and it is advisable to keep the temperature of mixing below 60°F (16°C) from the point of view of hygiene as well as helping to stop the moisture and fat from separating out during mixing. Heat is generated during mincing and mixing, and the temperature can rise by 14°F by the end of the operation; to avoid over-heating the mixture, ice is sometimes used instead of water.

Cooking Processes

The same principles for cooking of meat apply to the cooking of meat products. High cooking temperatures over a long period will cause undue over-coagulation of the protein and thereby lower its water-holding capacity and cause shrinkage. Considerably less shrinkage occurs in meat products if they are heated in water at temperatures of 176-194°F (80-90°C) than if cooked in fat or under a grill.

Finally, perhaps the most important point in respect of all meat products is that the number of operations involved in their processing greatly increases the risk of contamination by harmful bacteria.

Consequently it is vitally important that the area in which these processes are carried out and the equipment are scrupulously clean. If possible devise a method of production which will reduce the number of processes and the time taken to carry them out to a minimum.

The following diagram indicates some of the relationships described under meat and some of the factors that influence the utilisation of various meat commodities.

Basic type of meat   *Initial*
                                                                                                                                              cost

Quality
Degree of *rigor mortis* change
Composition of meat
Added ingredients which

influence the type of dish   Wages

Operatives:

number available
skill available
which

influence uses of the basic commodity   Capital expenditure
                                                                                                                                    overheads

Equipment available
which

influence cooking operation

Cooking process:
Length of time in preparation.
Degree to which meat is cooked.
Internal temperature.
External temperature.
Surface area.
Thickness which

influences starting and finishing
times and therefore service
which   influences
                                                                                                                                    Selling price

Percentage loss in cooking

Cooking finished
Quality acceptable

This diagram shows many inter-related factors that influence the decision regarding the compromise that is inherent in cooking any food. Inevitably the number of acceptable portions is the ultimate criterion of what constitutes yield; this is discussed in the section on Food Presentation.

This outline of technical information related to meat, poultry and game recipes demonstrates that the qualities of tenderness, flavour, colour and yield in cooked meat can only be achieved as the result of a compromise. This must be made between the choice of the particular cut of meat and the process, the qualities required and their relative importance, together with nutritional and hygienic considerations.

FISH

Marine, river and lake fish are used for human consumption. They are classified according to type of flesh and shape, with a separate class that includes edible shellfish, i.e. crustaceans and molluscs.

The muscle structure consist of short fibres arranged in blocks separated by connective tissue. These blocks form the flakes in cooked fish. The flakes are curved and run from the backbone to the skin, being arranged in fillet-like groups. The number of main fillets varies with the shape of the fish, flat fish having four and round fish having two, in both cases running from head to tail on either side of the backbone. The size of the flakes also varies according to the stage of development and the type of fish. Young fish have small flakes and a fine texture; older fish have large flakes and a coarse texture.

Flat fish generally have smaller flakes than round fish and less fat content. Because of its structure and the shortness of the fibres together with the relatively fine connective tissue, fish has a much more delicate and tender flesh than other meat animals. The colour of fish muscle varies; those with a high fat content have a dark coloured, oily muscle. The fat distribution is uneven, the area with the highest fat concentration lying under the skin beneath the lateral line on round fish.

The composition of fish muscle varies according to the type of fish, state of growth and time of year. In general, it consists of 60-92 per cent water, 6.9-23 per cent protein and 0.2-24 per cent fat.

Qualities in Cooked Fish

The most important qualities in cooked fish are flavour, juiciness and shape and colour (appearance). Tenderness does not present major control difficulties because the amount of connective tissue in fish is relatively small and of a tender gelatinous nature.

Flavour

Apart from the flavour imparted to fish as a result of a particular recipe, added ingredients and process of cooking, the most significant aspect of flavour in cooked fish is related to the freshness of the raw product. This refers to qualities in the fish when it was caught and how well these qualities have been maintained in transit and storage.

Fish is an extremely perishable food due to the fact that it is not possible to stop fish struggling before they die; consequently there is a lowering of the amount of lactic acid and an increase of pH. Bacterial action is not inhibited and this leads to a breakdown of certain substances that produce the characteristic smell of bad fish. Freshly caught fish is firm to the touch, slimy and with red gills. There is no unpleasant smell, and the eyes are bright. Shellfish should be live, molluscs tightly closed and both crustaceans and molluscs relatively heavy for their size. Fresh fish landed at a port may have been caught for anything from 1 to 17 days.

Fillets of fish are fresh if they feel firm and springy to the touch and the flakes are firmly attached to each other. Colour is also an indication, a bright translucent appearance indicating a fresher fillet than a matt pink-white colour. To maintain fish in as fresh a condition as possible it should be held at a controlled temperature and in a controlled environment. The temperature, environment and keeping quality varies with the type of fish.

Soft textured and some small fish, such as witch and grey soles, deteriorate more rapidly than firmer fleshed and larger fish like turbot and salmon. However, to maintain maximum freshness in all fish, it should ideally be packed in ice which will keep it at around 32°F (0°C) without the drying out that may occur if stored in a refrigerator. If the temperature falls to 28°F (−2°C) the flesh is physically damaged by the formation of large ice crystals.

Storage temperatures for white fish (cod and haddock)

Days in ice at 32°F (0°C)	Flavour	Days at 50°F (10°C)
0	Fresh	0
3	Sweet	
6	Less sweet	2
9	No sweetness	
12	Slightly stale	4
15	Sour	
18	Bitter	6
21	Putrid	7

Freezing and Flavour

Provided that freezing, storage and subsequent thawing are carried out under controlled conditions, the fresh condition and flavour of fish can be maintained by quick freezing. Quick freezing is defined in Britain as a process whereby the whole of the fish is reduced in temperature from 32°F (0°C) to 23°F (−5°C) in not more than two hours and the fish is retained in the freezer until the temperature of the warmest part is reduced to 5°F (−15°C) or lower.

Thawing of fish should take place at temperatures no higher than 68°F (20°C) or spoilage of the outside may occur before the inside is thawed. The conditions of thawing are important. If fish is thawed in water and not removed after thawing, it is likely to become waterlogged. It is more satisfactory if it is thawed in a refrigerator at a temperature of 33-39°F (1·4°C) because the thawed part stays cool while the centre is defrosting.

Juiciness

As far as taste is concerned juiciness has two components, one related to water (fluid in the food) and one related to fat content. The water content of fish is high, but its fat content in the form of oil is low. Among some sixty fish listed, including shellfish, only eight − eel, herring, mackerel, pilchard, salmon, sprat, trout and witch − have a potential fat content of over 10 per cent. The potential juiciness of fish is therefore much lower than that of most meat. However, there is also a much greater difference in composition, flavour and texture between herring, haddock, halibut, salmon, etc., than there is between meats and this range is even wider when shellfish are considered.

Compensation for lack of potential juiciness through shortage of fat is created by cooking fish in shallow or deep fat or by serving it with sauces of a high fat content.

Shape, Appearance and Colour

The maintenance of an acceptable appearance and shape of fish is difficult to achieve because of their relatively delicate or tender nature. Coatings of flour, batter or egg and crumbs help to form a more rigid structure on the outside of the fish, thus aiding in the retention of shape and, incidentally, giving a texture difference to the product.

It is usual to wash fish fillets that are to be cooked in water, stock or steam in order to remove the surface liquid protein and then cook the fish in a liquid that has already been heated; this helps to retain the natural colour and the shape of the fillets. However, large whole fish, such as salmon, should be immersed in a cold liquid in order to avoid structural damage to the skin before the heat has penetrated.

Temperatures for Cooking Fish

When heating fish in either water or stock the minimum temperature should be 162°F (72°C) and the centre of the thickest part of the fish should be held at that temperature for at least 2 minutes. In order to maintain the qualities in cooked fish, the internal temperature should not exceed 176°F (80°C) for any appreciable length of time so as to avoid over-coagulation of protein and a consequent lack of juiciness.

Time is a major factor in relation to temperature and quality control. For example, higher temperatures are used for cooking fish in fat or butter, but the time is short since the coating of flour or batter acts as a barrier against hot fat penetrating between the flakes of fish.

FOOD PLANTS

The term food plants refers to vegetable matter that is used for human consumption. It covers a very wide variety of seemingly different items (see chart on page 595). This variety can in part be simplified by considering (a) the general characteristics of structure, colour and flavour, and (b) the characteristics of the particular part of a plant that is used for food.

General Characteristics

Structure, colour and flavour changes occur in all food plants during storage. These changes can be retarded by storing away from sunlight, under controlled temperature and humidity conditions. The structure of food plants can be understood by examining the individual plant cells, their contents of starches, sugars, acids, colour compounds and hence plant tissue. Plant cells are small, water-filled cellulose containers and their crispness and juiciness is largely related to the amount of water they contain and the type and amount of cellulose. The cells are cemented together into plant tissue by pectic materials, air spaces occurring between the cells.

The cells vary in their size, the thickness of the cell wall and their composition. These variations depend on the part of the plant in which the cell is situated; for example, larger cells occur in the fleshy part of most fruits. Other factors include the stage of development, because the older the plant the thicker the cell wall with more lignum (woodiness). Storage conditions are also important in maintaining freshness. Plants are still living when harvested; their metabolism is slowed down and the original composition is maintained by storing them away from sunlight, at controlled temperatures and humidity.

In addition to the general concept of plant cells, other cells help to make up the structure of food plants, such as the tube-like structures that conduct water and salts throughout the plant. They produce tough fibrous structures containing cellulose, lignum and pectic substances. An important structural feature of all plants is the protective tissues, formed by surface cells into a water-impermeable skin which in some cases is extremely tough.

One other factor that influences structure is the starch content of the cells that form peas; potatoes and some beans also contain a high percentage of starch. This substance is a carbohydrate, a complex of carbon, hydrogen and oxygen, more complex than the sugars that are also contained in the cells.

Colour

Within the cell walls are various complex chemicals which, coupled with its structure and light refraction, give the food plant its characteristic colour. The most important of these colours are green (chlorophyll), yellow/orange (carotenoids), red/purple/blue (anthocyanins), white/colourless/pale yellow(anthoxanthins) and tannin that affects both colour and flavour.

Flavour

Like the chemicals associated with colour, the flavour constituents of food plants are extremely complex. The characteristic flavour of fruit and vegetables is related to the sugar and acid contents of the cells, sweet and sour being the tastes most readily recognised.

The sugar/acid content varies with the type of plant, its maturity, conditions of storage and processing. For example, during ripening, fruits decrease in acid and increase in sugar whereas cereals, peas and maize decrease in sweetness because the sugars change to starch. The acids contained within the plant cells vary, several acids being present in once cell, e.g. malic and citric acids in apples and oranges. Some sulphur compounds and the changes that occur in them may be responsible for the main flavour and aromas of, for example, cabbages, onions and Brussels sprouts.

In processing, the structure of food plants changes from crisp and firm to a soft and wilted or mushy texture. These structural changes occur as a result of softening of cellulose, collapsing of cell walls and release of water, and the dissolution of pectin and the release of air.

The degree of softening of the cellulose is governed by time, temperature, storage environment and the cooking medium. For example, the cellulose of most food plants will soften in under 10 minutes at a temperature of 208°F (98°C). The main problem is the cooking medium; if cellulose is in contact with water of a low pH or in permanently hard water it tends to remain firm. In the presence of alkaline water — water with bicarbonate of soda — the cellulose will break down and a slimy texture result.

The gelatinisation of any starch in plant cells occurs on heating at 208°F (98°C) in water, causing a swelling of the cells sometimes to the point where the cells burst and the whole structure is broken down. Over-cooking of potatoes or peas, for example, results in a product that resembles thick soup. Some of the causes of changes in colour on processing are illustrated in the following chart which shows that the green, red, purple and blue colours are the least stable and also, that in common with the structure, changes occur as a result of contact with an acid or alkaline cooking medium. The colour change from green to olive-green caused by enzymic action occurs at temperatures of 151-174°F (66-79°C).

Apart from the effect of adding salt, butter, sugar and other ingredients to food plants during processing to affect their flavour, the most characteristic flavour change occurs in those food plants that contain quantities of sulphur compounds. Prolonged storage or holding of these food plants at temperatures above 50°F (10°C) will break down the sulphur compounds to produce the unpleasant smell of cooked cabbage.

Food Plant Pigments and their Stability in Cooking

GREEN	YELLOW/ORANGE	RED/PURPLE/ BLUE	WHITE/PALE YELLOW	TANNIN
Chlorophyll	Carotenoids	Anthocyanins	Anthoxanthins	
Unstable; not soluble in water and changes to	Stable (fat-soluble)	Unstable (soluble in water)	Relatively stable changes to	Causes foods to turn brown after cutting, e.g. bananas
(a) brown-green (olive-green) caused by acid or enzyme or by storing for long periods, either cooked or raw or at temperatures above 50°F (10°C)		(a) red becomes redder in presence of acid	(a) bright yellow caused by alkali	Also responsible for astringent tastes, e.g. tea and unripe bananas
or		or	or	
(b) bright unnatural green (soluble in water), caused by excess of alkali, e.g. sodium bicarbonate		(b) purple-blue become bluer in presence of alkali or metallic salts	(b) brownish, caused by iron salts or whiter in presence of acid	

Characteristics of Food Plants

Plants that are used as food can be classified according to the part of the plant that is deemed edible, such as roots, tubers and bulbs; stems, shoots and leaves; flowers; fruits, pods and seeds (legumes, pulses).

Roots, Tubers and Bulbs

Roots may be long and tapering or bulbous, but are generally firm in texture; when old they develop thick fibres with a high lignum content making them tough and woody. They have good keeping qualities if stored at 32-34°F (0-1°C) with a humidity of approximately 90 per cent. In general, colour, texture and structure of root vegetables are relatively easy to control during cooking.

Tubers also develop below ground and are bulbous growths on roots of certain plants, such as potato and Jerusalem artichokes. Structurally less firm and fibrous than roots, they require greater control during cooking. Both examples are susceptible to browning when the flesh is exposed to air. Keeping qualities are generally good if kept in the dark (potato storage temperature 37-50°F (3-10°C), artichokes 32-34°F (0-1°C) with a humidity of 85-90 per cent).

Bulbs have a layered structure held together at the base where the roots develop. Examples of these are onions and leeks. Keeping qualities are generally good at 32°F (0°C) with a humidity of 72 per cent for onions and 90 per cent for leeks.

Stems, Shoots and Leaves

This class has a much less rigid structure than roots, is more susceptible to damage and requires greater control in cooking. Storage temperature of 32°F (0°C) and a humidity of 90 per cent will maintain their qualities for some 2-3 weeks. Stems of good eating quality, such as rhubarb and cardoons, will be crisp and moist when broken and have no thick fibres.

Shoots have similar characteristics to stems, but they are young and fleshy as in asparagus and sea kale. Keeping qualities and conditions of storage are similar to stems.

Examples of leaf vegetables include spinach and cabbage. Their life in storage is similar to stems and shoots. Leaf vegetables are more susceptible to colour and structure change, and more easily damaged during cooking. They become fibrous when old, and the colour changes from green or red to yellow.

Flowers

The storage life of flower vegetables — broccoli and cauliflower — is comparatively short, their structure is relatively delicate and therefore easily damaged in processing. A general rule for storage is difficult because of the difference in size and structure, but broccoli kept at 32°F (0°C) and a humidity of 90-95 per cent would generally have a storage life of one week, cauliflower at the same temperature and slightly less humidity could keep for two or three weeks.

Fruits, Pods and Seeds

The variety in fruits is so great that they are divided into those that are extremely perishable, e.g. soft fruits such as strawberries, raspberries and currants, and those firmer-fleshed fruits, such as apples, pears and peaches with better keeping qualities. Because of the variety in colour and flavour and the consequent changes during processing no generalisations can be made. For details see tables on pages 595-605.

Pods, often referred to as legumes, include peas and several varieties of beans. They are the immature seeds enclosed in a pod that varies in length from 3-24 inches depending upon type and age. Sometimes the seeds alone are eaten and the pod is discarded, in others pod and bean are eaten together as in French beans, runner beans and sugar peas (mange tout).

The matured dried seeds of these plants are known as pulses. Other seeds used in cookery — wheat, oats and rye — are classed as cereals.

Some seeds are primarily used for their flavour, for example fennel and coriander, and herbs serve the same purpose. Other edible plants that do not fall readily into any category are fungi and seaweeds.

The Use of Food Plants

The different ways in which food plants are used reflect their extraordinary variety. They are used to give contrast in texture, colour and flavour to both individual dishes and meals, or they can form the main constituent of a dish in their own right. Apples, for example, can be used as an appetiser (apple and cheese salad), an accompaniment (apple sauce), sweets or puddings (apple fritters, Eve's pudding), and as a drink (cider).

The particular variety of apple must suit the particular purpose, in the same way as some varieties of potato are more suitable for chips than others; Russet apples, for example, are more suitable for desserts than Bramleys which are better for savoury purposes.

BASIC PREPARATIONS

This part deals with the factors that affect the qualities of viscosity, texture, colour, flavour and finish in a group considered as basic preparations and which includes stocks, soups, gravies, sauces, custards, jellies and preserves. They are basic in the sense that they can be the foundation of many finished dishes and their control is fundamental to much of professional cookery. The apparently diverse food products of stocks, soups, gravies, sauces, custards, jellies and jams have been classified together because they are thickened, flavoured liquids. The qualities of thickness or viscosity and hence texture, colour, flavour and finish are inter-related and depend upon the ingredients used, their proportions and the purpose for which the product was made. The terms thickness and viscosity signify the relative appearance of solidity or the pouring and coating quality of the product. This quality is achieved by using one or more thickening agents, such as gelatine, sugar, pectin, starch, pulp, eggs and liquid protein or butter, fat and cream.

Viscosity

Stock will be viscous to the extent that bones used for the stock are of a gelatinous nature. Bones from young animals and poultry will provide more viscous stock depending on the length of cooking time and the amount of water used. When fish bones are used, turbot bones give a more viscous stock than most other fish. Powdered or leaf gelatine can be used to make a liquid viscous, in varying quantities up to the point when it will set to a jelly when cold. Gelatinous thickening is unstable and is affected by temperature, sugar content, the pH of the liquid and some enzymes.

Syrup will have a viscosity in proportion to its sugar content and to its temperature. The greater the sugar content, the more viscous the syrup. Control can be achieved by adding more sugar or evaporating the water. However, sugar added to any liquid thickened with any other agent will reduce viscosity.

Pectin is the name given to a substance that is capable of forming a jelly in the presence of acid and sugar. It is contained in varying proportions in fruits, it is relatively unstable and the proportions of acid, sugar and pectin are critical. In general, between 1½-1 per cent pectin to 55-70 per cent sugar with an acidic pH value of 3 will produce a gel.

Butter or fat in emulsion in a liquid will give an appearance of thickening; this is unstable and changes in temperature will affect it. Mechanical agitation, e.g. whisking, will sometimes keep the butter in temporary suspension in the product.

Starches used for thickening include flour, cornflour, arrowroot, potato starch, rice flour and cereals. The proportions are dependent on the effect required and the thickening properties of the starch. For example, 2 oz of plain flour per pint of unthickened liquid will produce a sauce of fairly thick coating consistency. To achieve a similar consistency with cornflour or arrowroot approximately half this amount of starch is required.

Starch gels, as they are called, have some instability; they begin to thicken at around 147°F (64°C); the final temperature of thickening varies with the starch used but in general they must all be cooked to at least 205°F (96°C). Prolonged heating or stirring has a tendency to make the product thinner.

Starches for thickening should be evenly dispersed throughout the liquid. If the starch is finely ground it is mixed into a paste with some cold liquid and added to the hot liquid, stirring continuously. The practice of making a flour paste has certain disadvantages because of the development of gluten. It is for this reason that the flour is mixed with melted butter or fat to form a roux or kneaded into softened butter to form a paste in the proportions of equal amounts of flour and butter.

In order to obtain an even dispersal of the starch throughout the liquid before the starch gelatinises, a medium must be available in which to disperse the starch; the temperature of the liquid and the time taken to add the starch should be controlled and stirring should be vigorous. Starches are heavier than water and fall to the bottom of the pan unless stirred; they have a tendency to burn easily unless the cooking heat is controlled, best achieved in a double saucepan.

Pulps can give an appearance of thickening through the dispersal of small particles of food in a liquid. The size of the particles and the amount in relation to the liquid is important in that large particles have a tendency to sink to the bottom of the liquid and burn. They can be held in suspension by the addition of another thickening agent.

Whole eggs as used in baked egg custard or egg yolks in a custard sauce are used for thickening. The proportions are three whole eggs per pint of custard not to be turned out. For a turned-out custard, use four whole eggs per pint, while eight egg yolks per pint will give a sauce of coating consistency. The object of thickening with eggs is to obtain partial coagulation of the protein.

Depending on the length of cooking time the following temperatures can be used as a guide:

	Degrees Fahrenheit	Degrees Celcius
Coagulation temperature of egg white:	140 — 149	60 — 65
Coagulation temperature of egg yolk:	149 — 158	65 — 70
Coagulation temperature of whole egg and egg mixture:	158 — 176	70 — 80
Maximum temperature for egg mixture without coagulation:	176 — 188	80 — 87

Coagulation temperature is affected by the addition of sugar. High concentration of sugar makes thickening with yolks difficult if not impossible to control. When thickening with eggs the eggs should not be added to the hot liquid, but the hot liquid should be poured gradually on to the whisked eggs while stirring continuously. If the volume of liquid and the speed of adding is insufficient to partially coagulate the eggs the mixture should be returned to a low controlled source of heat and stirred until it thickens without boiling.

In order to achieve greater control over the heat applied to baked egg custards, the containers are placed in water during cooking, and the water is not allowed to boil. The conductivity of the container in which the custard is cooked helps in the control, glass or earthenware containers being preferable.

Similar rules are applicable to the use of liquid albumen (blood) as a thickener.

Cream can give an appearance of greater viscosity to a liquid either on its own or with egg yolks as in liaisons. It is fairly stable although the casein in the cream can be made more sensitive to heat, coagulation depending upon other ingredients in the liquid, e.g. acids, which could produce a curdled effect.

When butter is used in conjunction with egg yolks, the yolks act as an emulsifier and help to keep the butter in suspension in the liquid, thereby ensuring viscosity. Temperature variations should be avoided because of the unstable nature of the product. Butter in a starch gel will rise to the surface depending on the viscosity of the liquid, the proportion of butter used and length of time that the product stands without any stirring or whisking.

Texture

Texture — smoothness — control begins with the initial liquid and what has been cooked in that liquid. For example, some roughness of texture will occur on products made from stocks if all the particles of coagulated protein from the bones are not strained out with a fine enough strainer. The same applies to jellies if any particles of cellulose from the fruit are not removed.

The next stage in control of texture is to consider the relative smoothness of the thickening agents themselves. Gelatine, pectin, butter and cream will produce a smoother texture than eggs, starches or pulps. In some soups and jams a deliberate variation in texture is desirable, pieces of meat, vegetables or fruit being dispersed within a different textured product; the size and even shapes of the pieces as well as the amount in relation to the whole are critical in terms of texture appearance. The degree to which these pieces are cooked will affect the finished texture result.

When considering finished texture in a vegetable soup that is thickened with a pulp and flour, all the cellulose can be removed by straining to achieve a smooth texture; a purée soup is left unstrained. Sometimes vegetables in soups are softened in fat or butter prior to the liquid being added; this appears to affect the finished texture. It is probably due to the fact that in a liquid with a low pH the cellulose in the vegetables remains firmer.

Texture in egg-thickened products depends on the degree of partial coagulation of the egg and on the particular recipe. The higher the temperature, the greater the degree of coagulation and the rougher the texture. Varying the ingredients in the recipe will vary the texture; for example, in a baked egg custard 3 eggs, 8 yolks and 2 pints of milk will produce a slightly different texture from 8 whole eggs to 2 pints of milk, the former appearing rougher than the latter.

Colour

The extent of colour change and the actions taken to control it depend on the particular colour of the raw food. Changes occur in the green colour of vegetables during cooking because of the presence of acid and alkalis, and if the vegetables are cooked for a long period. Colour change will also occur due to the action of an enzyme in the vegetable itself.

Less colour change will occur by either cooking in large quantities of water at a pH of 7-8.5 as large quantities of water will neutralise the effect of acid in the vegetables, or by ensuring that the pH does not rise too high. Alternatively, adopt short cooking periods and inactivate the enzyme by plunging the vegetables into a large quantity of boiling water.

Other colours in vegetables and fruit are relatively stable at least in terms of appearance in the end product. The exception is red cabbage which turns blue if cooked in water of a high pH, whereas acid will turn the cabbage a brighter red. Soft water will turn many colourless vegetables, such as onions, yellow. Colour changes may occur dur to browning. This is caused by leaving vegetables and fruit, e.g. potatoes and apples, exposed to air, or by caramelising in cooking. Browning through exposure to air can be prevented by keeping the prepared product in cold water, rubbing it with lemon, blanching or by the use of a chemical, such as sulphur dioxide.

Caramelising is often desirable in brown stocks and is controlled by the length of cooking time and the temperature, both during the initial browning and during the cooking period after water is added. The extent to which water is evaporated again determines the degree of brownness.

Extraction of colour into the liquid is often important, as some colours are fat-soluble and others water-soluble; sweating carrots in fat will, for example, extract fat-soluble colour. The main colour in most fruits and in red cabbage and beetroot is water-soluble.

A thickening agent may have some effect on the colour in the end product; those with least effect are gelatine, pectin, cornflour, arrowroot and potato starch, whereas flour, cereals, butter, cream, eggs and pulps affect more colour changes.

Flavour

Many of the main flavours in foods have been isolated, examined and much is known in some cases about the changes that take place in them during cooking. Some flavours disappear quite rapidly in cooking; mustard, for example, contains extremely volatile oils which produce a characteristic flavour which will, however, be lost unless the mustard is added at the end of the cooking process. Because of the many chemical changes that take place during the cooking process only an approach to the control of flavour can be indicated. It is helpful to consider the relative strengths in flavour of various ingredients used, such as sugar to fruit or onions to carrots in order to determine the proportions of ingredients and thereby control the flavour. Account should also be taken of changes that occur in the flavour of individual items; the flavour of onions, for example, is milder when cooked than when raw and particularly if the onions are in a large volume of liquid.

Vegetables such as cabbage, sprouts, broccoli and cauliflower produce strong sulphur flavours if cooked for long periods. This can be noticeable in some vegetable soups.

Finished Appearance

Finish refers to the degree to which a product reflects light thus giving a shiny or matt appearance. This characteristic can be controlled by identifying the conditions under which an otherwise shiny product turns into a product with a dull finish. All liquids thickened with any of the previously mentioned agents, with the possible exception of sugar, will, if left, skin over and give a matt finish. The extent to which this occurs depends on the type of thickening used and the conditions of time, temperature and humidity. In general, butter, gelatine and sugar produce a more persistently shiny finish than any of the other thickening agents. To avoid skinning over, the product should be used immediately or covered over with a lid or a film of butter.

Ices and Ice Creams

As ices and ice creams are basically coloured, flavoured liquids, this section would be incomplete without a consideration of their control. The ingredients used in the mixtures for ices vary, but they can be put into two groups, one of which contains milk or milk products and another that is basically flavoured syrups. They can also be categorised according to the method of production in that some ice creams are aerated before freezing and others during the freezing process.

The technology of ice cream production has been well developed and regulations exist in respect of its hygienic production. The purpose here is to consider basic factors that relate to the structure and texture of the finished product.

Thickness/viscosity and texture in these products depend on five inter-related variables: ingredients, temperature of the refrigeration and the length of time and temperature of freezing, degree of aeration, size of the ice crystals and storage conditions.

Ingredients affect the freezing point in that the higher the sugar content, the lower the freezing point becomes; 40 per cent sugar in water will reduce freezing point by several degrees. Addition of spirits or liqueurs also lowers freezing point.

In order to prevent the formation of large ice crystals which would inhibit an acceptable texture, the temperature in the freezer should be as low as possible. The shorter the time needed to freeze the mixture, the smaller the ice crystals will be. A freezing temperature of $5°F$ ($-15°C$) is recommended.

The degree of aeration also affects the size of ice crystals. The greater the aeration and the finer the structure, the smaller the ice crystals; ingredients and methods used to aerate the mixture will influence this. Ice creams form large ice crystals during storage if the temperature fluctuates; recommended storage temperature is $11 \cdot 2°F$ (-12 to $-17°C$).

BAKING, PASTRY AND CONFECTIONERY PRODUCTS

The characteristics of these products vary from crisp, crumbly and apparently dry as in shortbread, to soft, moist and tender as in sponge cakes. Some cakes are light and soft with a close even structure and others may be coarse and heavy for a given volume with a less even structure. These products exemplify better than any other group the fundamental principle that a wide variety of seemingly different foods can be produced from very similar ingredients.

Because of this almost endless variety any attempt at a logical classification of the products becomes difficult, and a more useful approach would seem to lie in examining the factors that produce the varieties. The primary concern here is with providing an outline of technical knowledge to assist in small batch production. The factors under consideration for this purpose are concerned with (a) the type of proportions of basic ingredients; (b) the process employed to combine and shape them; (c) the time and temperature of cooking; and (d) any added ingredients or finishes.

Variations in one or more of these factors produce variety in the finished characteristics as illustrated below:

Sequential Nature of Production

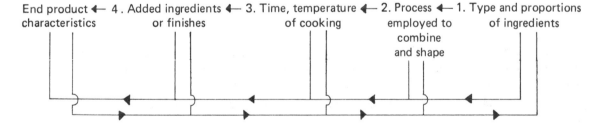

End product ← 4 . Added ingredients ← 3. Time, temperature ← 2. Process ← 1. Type and proportions
characteristics   or finishes   of cooking   employed to   of ingredients
                                                                           combine
                                                                           and shape

In order to show the interdependence of each stage in the above flow diagram three pastries with particular types and proportions of ingredients will be considered: suet, shortcrust and puff pastry.

Type and Proportion of Ingredients

Suet pastry	1 lb plain flour	½ lb suet	½ lb water	= 9 fl oz (approx.)
Shortcrust pastry:	1 lb plain flour	½ lb butter	4 oz water	= 4 fl oz (approx.)
Puff pastry:	1 lb strong plain flour	1 lb butter	½ lb water	= 9 fl oz (approx.)

The structure of these end products is largely dependent upon the flour, its properties when mixed with fat and water, and the effect of the heat.

Flour

Flour is a product obtained by milling or grinding certain cereals, such as wheat, rice and corn. However, unless otherwise stated flour refers to that obtained from wheat. It is composed of 70 per cent starch, 13 per cent water, 13 per cent protein, 1 per cent fat, 2.5 per cent sugars and 0.5 per cent mineral matter.

From the point of view of flour providing structure in the end product, protein is the most significant constituent in its composition. When mixed with water in the right proportions, flour will hold together to form a dough. This is due to certain insoluble proteins forming the elastic cohesive mass of gluten, within which the starch granules are dispersed. Rice and cornflour do not have this property, and they will not form a cohesive dough when mixed with water. The elasticity or strength of the dough varies with the type of flour and with the extent of mixing and the amount of water, together with the length of time the dough is rested after mixing.

Types of Flour

Flour can be classified into three main types: hard, general purpose and soft. Hard flour, normally called strong flour, has the highest protein content and will potentially give a dough with the most elasticity.

General purpose flour is suitable for many products and can be used for most baking products that require flour, in sauces, soups, stews, and as a coating. Its protein content is lower than hard flour and higher than soft. Soft, weak, "winters" or patent flour develops a much less elastic dough, its protein and gluten content being low.

Mixing with Water

The amount of water to mix into the flour depends on two factors, one of which is the water absorbing quality of the flour and the other the effect required. The resulting mixture, i.e. the dough, should not stick to a table nor break up when it is rolled out. This is achieved as a result of the flour absorbing half its weight of water, in that 1 lb flour will take approximately ½ lb water to form a dough. Once the water is added, gluten is formed and is insoluble; adding more water after this will cause a lumpy uneven texture. Looking at it another way, it is possible to add more flour to a dough that is too sticky to roll out, but not possible to add more water to a dry dough and still retain an even texture. Therefore the general rule for making an even-textured dough is never to add water or any liquid a little at a time.

Another important principle is that the more the mixture is worked or kneaded, the smoother, more elastic the dough becomes.

To understand the part played by flour in the final structure and texture of the end product it is useful to take some of the dough and wash the starch out in water, retaining the gluten. The gluten, a greyish rubbery substance, can then be placed in an oven at a temperature of approximately 400°F (200°C) and will be seen to increase in volume; this is due to the formation and expansion of steam within the rubbery structure causing it to swell and stretch and so producing a structure full of large holes. The colour on the outside changes to a golden-brown and the aroma is similar to that of any protein that is being heated at a comparatively high temperature.

On the other hand if the dough is put in the oven without washing out the starch, the expansion will be comparatively slight, its structure upon removal from the oven will be tight and there will be fewer holes; the dough will be relatively heavy for the volume and unacceptable in flavour and texture.

Adding Fat

The effect that fat has on the structure and texture depends upon the type and proportion of fat to flour and the method used to incorporate it. For example, in suet pastry, the suet is the fat from round the beef kidney. It is freed from connective tissue and chopped, grated or minced into small pieces and mixed with flour. Its melting point is higher than butter and has very little plasticity so that small pieces will retain their size and shape when mixed with flour and cold water. If the resulting dough is then placed in boiling water until all the starch in the flour has gelatinised (this can be identified by cutting open the product and examining the centre to ensure that all the milky whiteness that characterises gelatinised starch and water has disappeared), it will be seen that the dough has increased in volume and has a loose texture with small holes where the suet has melted, and steam formed to cause expansion. The less suet, the tighter the mixture, the more suet the looser the mixture. The extent of mixing — the degree at which the elasticity/rubberiness of the dough or development of the gluten has occurred — again affects texture and structure.

The more a dough is kneaded the more rubbery it becomes and the suet breaks up into even smaller pieces causing a heavier, tighter end product. The more gently it is mixed the lighter the product. The flavour has changed and is characterised by that of beef fat and the feel in the mouth is affected because of the melting point of the suet. Suet melts at 104-122°F (40-50°C), slightly higher than normal body temperature, causing a clinging sensation in the mouth.

In shortcrust pastry by contrast, the fat introduced is butter which has a comparatively low melting point and good plasticity. The method of introducing it is by rubbing in, the objective being to coat the flour. Tenderness or crumbliness in the dough and hence in the cooked end product is dependent on the temperature of the ingredients, the extent to which the fat is rubbed in and the amount of water and degree to which it is incorporated.

Ingredients at temperatures of 69-75°F (21-24°C) produce a more tender product than 39-44°F (4-7°C) (refrigeration temperatures) because more complete and easier coating of the flour occurs at higher temperature. The more vigorously the butter is rubbed in, the more flour is coated.

The amount of water that the flour and fat mixture will take to produce a dough or paste is dependent on temperature and rubbing in. The more evenly and thoroughly the fat is rubbed in and the higher the temperature, the less water can physically be incorporated to achieve a structure for rolling out without sticking.

To understand why shortcrust pastry is called short and why it is so different in structure and texture from other pastes, the original concept of gluten development (gluten being the thin elastic membraneous substance) must be considered. When the fat is rubbed in thoroughly, the strands or layers of gluten are "shortened" because they cannot develop properly or fully when water is added so a rubbery texture in the dough is less likely to occur.

Uneven Fat and Water Distribution

If the paste has uneven fat distribution, white streaks (gluten streaks) will appear when the water is added. These will manifest themselves in the end cooked product as bubbles or blisters as steam will make them expand, rise and distort the pastry. Distortion also occurs if the pastry is put in the oven immediately it is made; resting allows the gluten to relax and become less rubbery.

Effects of Types of Fats

The type of fat used, e.g. lard instead of butter, affects the crumbliness and tenderness of the end product. Lard has a greater shortening effect than butter, margarine generally has less shortening effect than both. Flavour and cost are further factors that decide which fat to use.

Insufficient water and a high fat content will make the pastry tender, but difficult to roll out and handle, and the end cooked product may not have sufficient structure to retain its shape. A large amount of water and low fat content will produce a hard, tough and dry pastry.

All these elements are inter-related with time, temperature and environment of cooking. Crumbliness, crispness and tenderness are greater if the pastry is dried out, that is if water is evaporated off in the oven at low temperature: at 275-325°F (140-160°C) rather than 400°F (200°). If, however, the pastry is used as a covering for a fruit or meat pie, then some compromise is needed, and a higher temperature may be preferred for the pastry to form an adequate structure before it sinks into or absorbs the liquid in the pie.

Puff pastry is the last of the three examples chosen to illustrate the sequential nature and inter-dependence of the stages in production and the effect on finished characteristics of these products. Puff pastry is crisp, light and flaky and this effect is achieved with very thin layers of dough with equally thin layers of fat between them. In the oven, the layers of fat melt, and if the temperature is high enough, 375-425°F (190-220°C) depending on the size and shape of the puff pastry product, steam will be formed between the layers. This expands, and the pastry rises in layers; structure is formed by coagulation of the flour proteins and gelatinisation of the starch; because of this the shape created by the steam is retained.

A strong flour is required to produce the initial unbroken elasticity of the pastry and a plastic fat that will stretch and spread out when rolled and folded between the layers. Consistent with melting point in the mouth, the fat must have a high enough melting point to avoid becoming too soft during handling. To achieve this effect, the fat should have the same consistency as the dough into which it is being incorporated. Again, the flavour and cost of the fat are major factors in deciding which fat to use.

Recipe Balance

From the fundamental background of basic recipes arises the concept of recipe balance. If any change is introduced in the type or quantity or if any single ingredient is changed, or if there is a change in the method or process of combining or cooking the ingredients, a compensatory change must take place in another ingredient or method. The opposite is also true; for example, if a sweet-flavoured shortcrust or suet pastry is wanted and 4 oz sugar is added per 1 lb of flour to change the flavour, then the water content should be reduced from 5 oz to approximately 2 oz in order to obtain a similar texture and structure.

Carrying this concept to its logical conclusion recipes can be developed to achieve a variety of products. A biscuit recipe, for example, of 1 part sugar, 2 parts butter and 3 parts flour, gives a very short-textured product, little or no gluten being developed during the mixing because there is no added water other than that present in the butter.

Characteristics of Scones, Bread, Cakes, Sponges and Batters

These products have a more or less open texture achieved by introducing and dispersing air or gas bubbles into a flour and liquid mixture and retaining these through coagulation of protein and gelatinisation of starch. The process used to obtain the characteristic structure and texture known as aeration are chemical, biochemical or physical.

Chemical Aeration

Various chemicals will, when moistened and heated, produce a gas and consequently aerate the product. The chemicals vary in the rate of gas production and the amount produced, bicarbonate of soda producing less volume of gas than if the flour is mixed with an acid such as cream of tartar in the proportions of 2 parts bicarbonate to 4 parts cream of tartar.

Used in the wrong proportions the chemicals can produce discoloration of the crumb and the characteristic flavour of soda. The darker the product and the stronger the flavour, the less noticeable is this effect. For example, gingerbread and parkin recipes often have bicarbonate of soda as the sole chemical aerating agent.

Brands of flour, known as self-raising flour, are sold with a chemical aerating agent already mixed in.

Biochemical Aeration

A commercially prepared yeast is used for this method of aeration. The yeast is a single-celled micro-organism that under certain conditions will grow and in the course of growth produce a gas, carbon dioxide.

The control of yeast growth in baking products is relatively critical. To grow, it requires moisture, food and warmth. The process of growth and gas production is known as fermentation. In the presence of moisture and at themperatures of 77-82°F (25-28°C) yeast cells with the aid of enzymes will break the fermentable sugars in flour down into alcohol and carbon dioxide. Cane sugar on its own is inadequate for yeast cell growth because the yeast requires materials containing protein to make new cells. If mixed solely with cane sugar it will eventually die. Temperatures above 82°F (28°C) will endanger the life of the yeast cell and temperatures above 140°F (60°C) will kill it. Yeast will grow slowly, given food, at below 77°F (25°C).

Physical Aeration

This process of incorporating air into a product involves beating or working the ingredients; air is incorporated when butter and sugar are creamed for cakes, and the beating in of eggs, a little at a time, introduces more air, making the mixture light.

Whisked egg or whole eggs can have the capacity of forming a structure that holds large amounts of air in small bubbles. The stability of the foam can be increased by warming and also by incorporating sugar. It is advisable to ensure that an adequate structure has been formed before any fat or flour is folded in. There is an observable difference between a froth of whisked egg that on standing will lose the air, and the necessary firm foam required for the light, loose, spongy texture in a cake. Butter can be added, without endangering the foam if it is melted and boiled first.

The type of flour is related to the method of aeration: yeast as an aerating agent requires a flour that will produce a strong elastic gluten in order to expand, stretch and hold in the gas that is produced. The gluten content of flours in products containing a chemical aerating agent is less important, and a general purpose or soft flour can be used. On the other hand, air incorporated by beating or whisking would be released or forced out by the physical incorporation of strong flours, and soft flours are therefore preferable for cakes and sponges. Another factor that should determine the type of flour to use is the tenderness of the product – the more tender the end product, the softer the flour.

In puff pastry, aeration is achieved through the production of steam between layers of dough; this can be considered as physical aeration, as can Yorkshire pudding batter.

Batters of pouring consistency are used for pancakes and for Yorkshire puddings. They consist of flour, eggs, milk or milk and water in varying proportions. When cooked in the oven, structural changes occur due to protein coagulation and starch gelatinisation and at the same time steam within the structure expands giving lightness and aeration. Tenderness and aeration are generally greatest in batters with a high egg content; greater crispness on the outside occurs when part of the milk is replaced with water.

Recipe Balance in Cakes

The basic mixture for cakes is referred to as a cake batter; the balance of ingredients in these batters deserves some consideration in order to help interpret a recipe and control production.

In principle, 1 lb butter and 1 lb sugar creamed together with 1 lb eggs gradually beaten in and 1 lb soft flour folded in will produce a cake batter consistency. This will give an end product with a structure and texture that is characteristic of a cake. In order to balance this recipe so as to produce a less expensive product, consider the relative cost of the ingredients – butter and eggs are more expensive than flour. To lower the cost, increase the proportion of flour. However, unless the increased flour is compensated for it will change the cake batter's structure and texture in the end product to such a degree that it would scarcely be accepted as a cake. Compensation for increasing the flour by, for instance, 1 lb can be achieved by adding more liquid (milk) or by adding an aerating agent (baking powder) to aerate the extra flour plus milk.

The ingredients in the recipe now become 1 lb butter, 1 lb sugar, 1 lb eggs, ¾ lb milk, 2 lb flour and 1 oz baking powder. The end product will be less sweet and the colour will be paler; it will, nevertheless, have a cake texture and structure.

The basic recipe can be balanced and used for a rich cake in that the mixture will carry approximately its own weight (4 lb) of dried fruit. Therefore up to 4 lb of dried fruit can be added according to preferences in flavour and appearance. If 4 lb of fruit are actually incorporated, the amount of flour should be increased by 4 oz to provide the greater structure required to hold the fruit.

Times and Temperatures of Cooking

Cooking times and oven temperatures for various products are based on the end characteristics required, the distance from the outside to the centre and the surface area and the type of dough, batter or pastry, (conductivity), and the number of cakes, loaves or pastries in the oven at the same time.

The end characteristics and conductivity are considered together; for example, a soft, moist, fatless sponge needs cooking at a higher temperature for a shorter time than a cake with a high fat content. This is because the conductivity of a fatless sponge is relatively better, fat being a poorer conductor of heat than water when subjected to heat in an oven. Breads low in fat require a high temperature for a short time to remain moist.

If a large number of items are cooked at the same time, the steam created will change the cooking conditions; an oven full of rich fruit cakes will stand a higher temperature without undue surface caramelisation than a single cake.

The following figures may be used as a guide:

Temperature	Products
275-325°F (140-160°C) gas mark 1-3	Shortbreads, biscuits that require drying out, rich cakes
325-375°F (160-190°C) gas mark 3-5	Shortcrust pastry, small cakes, plain cakes, sponges, Victoria sandwich
400-450°F (200-230°C) gas mark 6-8	Breads, scones, puff pastry, Yorkshire pudding

The last part of a cake to cook — the part that forms the characteristic structure and texture — is just below the crust at the top centre, not the centre of the cake. This is due to flow and convection currents before the protein coagulates and the starch gelatinises.

Added Ingredients and Finishes

These terms apply to the variety of foods that can be introduced either into or on to the top of a basic product. The simplest finish is the one produced naturally on the crust of bread by the condensed steam that has dried out on the surface of the bread. This is the golden-brown, shiny and crisp crust typical of some bread rolls. A shiny finish can be obtained by brushing syrup over the product when it is removed from the oven, particularly in sweet yeast buns.

Granulated or caster sugar is sometimes used to give a finish to fruit pies by brushing them with water and sprinkling with sugar prior to cooking in the oven. The water may be replaced with egg white; milk and beaten egg (egg wash) is also used to produce a degree of shine, and to increase the golden-brown colour.

Small and large cakes are often finished with icing that may be coloured and flavoured as desired, water icing, Royal icing and fondant being the most popular.

Pulverised sugar (icing sugar) can be used in conjunction with water to produce a white finish on some types of cakes and buns. As icing sugar is generally more expensive than ordinary sugar, stock syrup may be used instead of water to give a similar effect. When warm icing is applied to hot buns, a more glossy finish due to the recrystallisation of the powdered sugar is obtained.

Royal icing is basically a meringue with a high icing sugar content; it is particularly used for icing and decoration of large cakes. Fondant icing is obtained by boiling sugar and water to 240°F (115°C) and working it to a smooth mass. When using it for icing, a shiny white finish will only be achieved if the temperature at which it is used does not exceed 104°F (40°C).

Other ingredients, such as marzipan or almond paste, glacé cherries, angelica and nuts are used to give a characteristic finish to a variety of cakes.

CLASSIFICATION OF FOODS

The following tables classify the foods most commonly used in British cookery, under the following headings of Meat (including poultry, game and offal); Fish; Food Plants (vegetables and fruits); Cheeses; and Milk and Cream (dairy products).

Naming of Cuts and Joints

The names of meat cuts and joints are not standardised throughout Britain. This lack of uniformity leads to an apparent increased variety when compiling a bill of fare, but this positive feature is offset by the difficulty in accurately describing the cut required when purchasing the raw material.

Not only are names not standardised, but there are also variations in the shape of joints and cuts because of different methods of dissecting carcasses. For example, a leg of lamb or mutton, referred to as a gigot in Scotland, may be removed from the carcass in the so-called "Cumberland style" by cutting in a curve leaving the hips or aitch bone and muscle, or it may be cut square off the carcass and the leg include the hip or aitch bone and muscle. Many similar examples could be cited for most meat cuts.

Meat, Poultry and Game, Offal

A carcass of meat is the whole body by dissection of which specific cuts and joints are obtained. The way in which a carcass is dissected is determined by the skeletal structure of the animal and the direction of muscle fibres, the size of muscle and the distribution of fat.

The skeletal structure of beef, veal, mutton, lamb and pork are basically the same, the main variations being in size of bone and muscle, the amount of fat and hence weight of carcass. The weight relationship can be expressed to a standard at which the weight of a lamb carcass is equivalent to 1; mutton will then be 1½, veal and pork 2 to 3 and beef 15 to 20 times as heavy.

In general, the most convenient place for dividing up a carcass is where the bones meet. However, in some cases this will produce joints that are too large and further sub-division is necessary. The direction in which this is carried out is in part decided by the situation of the muscles, direction of muscle fibres and the amount and distribution of the fat. It is desirable for cooking purposes, subsequent portioning and also palatability that the direction of the primary division is along and around the main muscle seams, and that further cutting takes place across the muscle fibres.

Small Cuts of Beef

Steaks

A steak is a slice across the fibres of a muscle. It varies in shape, size and thickness, from 4 oz to 2½ lb and may be from a cut of any animal, though more usually from beef, with or without bone.

Steaks may be described according to cooking process, e.g. grilling, stewing or braising steaks. This can be an indication of the amount of connective tissue they possess, and therefore toughness. Stewing and braising steaks have more connective tissue than grilling steaks, being cut from the muscles in the hind leg (topside, silverside, thick flank) or from the shoulder.

The following types of steaks are usually tender; because of demand and relative scarcity in terms of size and amount on the carcass they are more expensive than stewing and braising steaks.

Fillet.   Sometimes known as undercut steak. Fillet can apply to the whole round, tapering muscles that run from the hip or aitch bone, under the sirloins; a slice across this muscle is a fillet steak.

Point.   A steak from across the pointed end of the rump.

Porterhouse.   A sirloin and fillet steak on the bone. Cut across the unboned sirloin, it may be known as a T-bone steak (equivalent to a chop).

Sirloin.   A slice across the eye muscle of a boned-out sirloin.

Baron.   This is a large cut, consisting of two rumps and two sirloins in one piece.

Rump.   A slice across the muscle on the outside of the aitch bone; may be divided into steaks.

Small Cuts of Veal

The following small cuts of veal are all relatively tender because of the age of the animal.

Chop.   Equivalent to the T-bone steak in beef, cut from the loin through the eye muscle and fillet.

Collop.   A slice of muscle; collops may come from the fillet or from the boned muscles in the leg, particularly the cushion.

Cutlet.   Cut from the best-end, each side of the carcass yielding six or seven cutlets. They consist of a slice across one of the eye muscles that run on either side of the back bone plus one third of a rib bone. The first six or seven rib bones, counting from the loin end, are those that provide cutlets.

Fillet.   In veal, this refers to the same muscle as in beef, i.e. the long tapering muscle running inside the loin, the thick end being under the aitch bone. However, the term can also be applied to a cut across the thick end of the leg, including the bone.

Leg-chop.   A cut across the thick end of the leg, including bone. It is, however, usually a somewhat thin slice.

Small Cuts of Lamb and Mutton

Small cuts of these animals are known by the same terms, distinguished only by reference to the carcass, such as lamb or mutton cutlets. The large saddle of lamb or mutton is equivalent to a baron of beef and consists of two rumps and two loins in one piece, often including the tail in smaller animals. A baron of lamb or mutton, however, would include both legs as well as the chump and saddle.

Small cuts — cutlets, chops, fillet, leg-chop and collops — are cut in the same way as those from veal. A double loin chop — a cut across both loins including bone and two eye muscles — is also known as crown chop.

Some confusion exists in that the words chop and cutlet are often used indiscriminately for cuts from either the loin or the best end. Strictly speaking, loins provide chops and best ends provide cutlets. Again, a double loin chop may refer to an exceptionally large single chop rather than a crown chop. In Scotland, the single loin is referred to as a double loin distinguishing it from the best end; a chop cut from this joint is referred to as a double loin chop.

Small Cuts of Pork

The small cuts from a carcass of pork are chops, cutlets and fillet and the fillet is sometimes known as tenderloin although this occasionally refers to breast of pork cut into strips, including the bone, a cut which is less tender than the fillet.

Poultry and Game

The cuts from poultry and game birds of similar size, such as pheasant and guinea fowl, are drumstick, thigh, wing, winglet and breast. Cuts of hare and venison are the saddle and haunch, saddle being the hind without the legs, and the haunch the saddle including the legs.

Offal

The dissection and dressing of animals afford other edible by-products termed offal. These include the heart, liver, kidneys, brain, stomach (tripe), sweetbreads, testicles and udder of certain animals. Also included are those parts of the intestines that are used for pudding casings.

CLASSIFICATION OF MEAT, POULTRY AND GAME
(Many birds are protected by preservation laws and others are rarely, if ever, offered for sale)

NAME	DISTINGUISHING CHARACTERISTICS AND REMARKS
BACON	Side of pork, partly boned, usually salted, cured and smoked. May be bought unsmoked (green). Weight of a side approximately 60 lb, but usually dissected into about 18 cuts.
BEEF	Characteristics vary with the type of animal, age, condition of rearing, slaughter and hanging. Beef from younger animals ranges from white of veal to deep purple-red of old cow beef. Colour of the fat varies from the pink/white of veal to the deep, bright yellow of old beef. Bones have a pinkish colour with bluish cartilaginous tissue at the joints in young animals, whitish-grey in old animals.

	BULL CALF	Immature male up to 1 year old
	YEARLING BULL	1 year old
	BULL	Adult male over 1 year old
	OX STEER	Male (castrated) over 1 year old
	BULLOCK	Male not used for service before castration
	HEIFER CALF	Immature female up to 1 year old
	YEARLING HEIFER	Female 1 year old
	HEIFER	Adult female that has not calved
	COW	Adult female that has calved
	STIRK	Young lean beast, generally used for sausage manufacture

NAME	DISTINGUISHING CHARACTERISTICS AND REMARKS
BLACK GAME (Game)	Also known as blackcock; related to capercaillie and red grouse; up to 4 lb in weight. Glossy black feathers with white wing patches
BOILING FOWL	See chicken
CAPON	See chicken
CAPERCAILLIE (Game)	Also known as wood grouse; up to 4 lb in weight; similar in colour to grouse. Cook as for grouse

CHICKEN (Poultry)		
	BABY CHICKEN	Also termed spring chicken or poussin; weight up to approximately 1 lb; soft pliable breast bone; very tender white flesh
	CAPON	Castrated chicken inducing greater meat to bone ratio; weight up to approximately 8 lb; tip of breast bone pliable; tender white flesh
	CHICKEN	Various weights up to approximately 5 lb; tip of breast bone pliable; tender white flesh
	FOWL	Term applied to older birds; weight up to approximately 6 lb; hard brittle breast bone, flesh darker than chicken. Requires prolonged/moist cooking

NAME	DISTINGUISHING CHARACTERISTICS AND REMARKS
COOT (Game)	Water-bird up to 18 in. in length, weighing up to 2 lb. Black plumage; should be skinned rather than plucked; lacks flavour, with coarse flesh
DEER (Game)	See venison
DUCK (Poultry)	Weight up to approximately 6 lb; flesh light brown in colour. Roasted or braised. DUCKLING: Bird up to 6 months old; weight up to approximately 4 lb
GOOSE (Poultry)	Weight up to 12 lb. Flesh almost pink in colour, skin white, feet and beak yellow. Birds under 12 months considered more tender. Usually roasted GOSLING: Bird up to six months old, weight up to 6 lb. Also known as green goose

NAME	DISTINGUISHING CHARACTERISTICS AND REMARKS

GROUSE
(Game)

Soft downy plumes on breast and wings. Young birds can be recognised by pointed wings, rounded soft spurs; greyish-white feathered legs; dark flesh; weight up to 1 lb. Roasted or braised

GUINEA FOWL
(Poultry)

Purple-grey plumage evenly dotted with white; flesh dark brown in colour. Game-flavoured. Now domestically reared and classified as poultry; up to 3½ lb in weight. Roasted or braised

GULL
(Sea bird)

Gulls to be eaten should be caught, fed in captivity for a period to reduce the strong fishy flavour; flesh firm, creamy in colour

HARE
(Game)

Fur brown, white underneath; hind legs longer than fore; flesh dark red. Gamey flavour; 5—6 lb in weight. Other species, e.g. mountain hare or blue hare change to white during winter

LAMB AND MUTTON

Colour of flesh varies from pale pink in young new season's lamb to dark blue-red of old mutton. Relative coarseness of fibres vary, the older the animal the coarser they are. Bones have a pinkish colour with blue cartilaginous tissue at the joints in young animals; whitish-grey in an old ram or ewe.

RAM TUP	Uncastrated male after second shearing
SHEARLING TUP	Uncastrated male between first and second shearing
TUP HOG	Uncastrated male between weaning and first shearing; under 1 year old
TUP LAMB	Male, 2 — 3 months old
WETHER	Castrated male after second shearing
EWE	Female after lambing; over 1½ years old
THEAVE	Female between first and second shearing; over 1 year old
EWE HOG	Female between weaning and first shearing; 2 — 3 months old
EWE LAMB	Female up to 3 months old
TEG	Young sheep of either sex

MOORHEN
(Game)

Water-bird similar in size to grouse; dark olive brown in colour, grey underneath with a scarlet front. Lacking in flavour and coarse flesh

MUTTON

See lamb

ORTOLAN
(Game)

Very small bird, fairly rare; black wings, greyish-green head. Also known as garden bunting. Considered a delicacy

PARTRIDGE
(Game)

Small game bird, off white to fawn-coloured flesh when cooked; weight approximately ½ — 1 lb

PIGEON
(Game)

May be wild or domesticated; dark flesh; young pigeons known as squabs; over 1 year old requires prolonged cooking to become tender

PHEASANT
(Game)

Young birds have pliable breast bones, soft pliable feet, light plumage and the last large feather on the wing pointed. The cock bird has extended tail feathers, brightly coloured breast and head; hen has same colouring brown dappled coloured plumage; weight up to 4 lb

PORK

The flesh from young pigs

SUCKING PIGS	Up to approximately 10 lb dressed weight
PORK PIGS	Pigs reared for pork purposes; lighter in weight than bacon pigs, less fat, soft skin (rind)
BACON PIGS	Pigs reared for bacon purposes
BREEDING PIGS	After its usefulness as a breeding pig, may be used for manufactured products

NAME	DISTINGUISHING CHARACTERISTICS AND REMARKS
POUSSIN	See chicken
PTARMIGAN (Game)	Member of the grouse family; feathers light brown and white; during winter colour changes to white, and then sometimes referred to as white grouse. Approximately 8 – 12 oz; whitish-brown flesh when cooked
QUAIL (Game)	Similar to partridge; now reared on poultry farms; greyish-brown soft feathers streaked with white; grey-white flesh when cooked
RABBIT (Game)	Distinguished from the hare by shorter ears and feet, absence of black on the ears and shorter body. Young rabbits distinguished by size, ears tear easily. Whitish flesh when cooked; approximate weight 2 – 4 lb
RED GROUSE (Game)	Young birds have soft downy plumes on breast and under wings; pointed wings and rounded soft spurs which become scaly and hard in older birds. See also grouse
ROOK (Game)	Distinguished from the crow by the lack of feathers on its face, which are lost at an early age, leaving a bare, scabrous and greyish-white skin. Black plumage with rich purple gloss on head and neck. Weight up to 12 oz
SNIPE (Game)	The name given to a large class of small game birds with long beaks, including jack snipe, pin-tailed snipe, great snipe, red-breasted snipe. Weights vary from 2 to 10 oz. Best roasted
SPRING CHICKEN	See chicken
SQUAB (Game)	Young pigeon or guinea fowl
TEAL (Game)	Species of wild duck; very colourful. Apply recipes given for wild duck; requires less cooking time; young birds distinguished by small pinkish legs and downiness under the wings. Approximate weight 1 – 1½ lb
TURKEY (Poultry)	Weight ranges up to approximately 30 lb. Birds of good quality between 15 – 22 lb most economical. When young the legs are black and smooth, eyes bright, feet supple, the tom spur should be short. As the bird matures the legs turn grey-reddish in colour and become scaly, eyes dull, feet hard
VEAL	Flesh of beef calf whitish when cooked. Good quality carcasses should be broad, compact and evenly fleshed with relatively short shanks; legs, loins, ribs and shoulders should have good muscular development; lack of flesh on these parts indicates poor development. Three basic types: SLINK, BOBBY and MILK FED VEAL
VENISON (Game)	Flesh of the deer, improved by moderate hanging. Indications of old and stale meat are offensive smell under kidney and neck vein green or yellow instead of a bluish hue. Dark flesh when cooked
WILD DUCK (Game)	Many varieties, e.g. mallard, muscovy, teal, widgeon; vary in sizes up to 3 lb; young birds pliable beak, flexible pinions. Dark flesh inclined to have strong, fishy flavour
WILD GOOSE (Game)	Illegal to buy or sell, but may be shot and eaten domestically
WOODCOCK (Game)	Resembles snipe, but larger; long beak, brown mottled plumage; approx. weight 12 oz
WOOD PIGEON (Game)	As pigeon

OFFALS OF MEAT, POULTRY, GAME

TYPE	SOURCE	CULINARY PURPOSE	DISTINGUISHING CHARACTERISTICS AND REMARKS
BLOOD	Cattle Pigs Sheep	Black puddings and blood flour. Blood sausages	Vinegar added to blood to prevent coagulation before cooking; all blood coagulates like eggs on heating and then scrambles
	Hare	Used as thickening agent for hare stews	
BRAINS	Cattle Sheep Pigs Deer	As a savoury, a dish on its own or eaten with other parts of the head	A mass of soft pulpy substance corrugated in form and covered with slimy membrane, white-pink-grey in colour
BONES	All animals, birds and game used as food	Flavour in stocks, gravies and sauces	Gelatinous nature of bones varies with age and type of animal, young animals producing the most gelatinous gravies and sauces. Hard white bones = old animals, cartilaginous pink-bluish bones = young animals
CAUL VEIL FLEAD	Pig Lamb Veal	Wrapping around meat to increase fat content and protect it during cooking	Fatty veil which covers some of the abdominal organs; used as covering on legs and shoulders of lamb to compensate for any deficiency of fat. Also used as a casing, e.g. savoury duck
DRIPPING	Beef Mutton	Any cooking process involving fat	Clarified or rendered down fat from cattle and sheep
EARS	Pigs	Boiled and used in appetisers	
FEET	Cattle Sheep Pigs	High gelatinous content, used for jellies. Can be eaten on their own or with stews	Feet referred to as calves' feet; cow heels; pig trotters, in Ireland known as crubins.
GIBLETS	Poultry and game birds	Used like bones for stocks, sauces, gravies. Giblets from larger birds, e.g. turkey, eaten in puddings and pies	Giblets consist of neck, heart, gizzard and liver (liver not usually used in stocks and sauces)
HEART	Cattle Sheep Pigs	Eaten stuffed or sliced in sauces; usually requires long slow cooking to tenderise	Arterial tubes need removal. Vary in weight from ½ − 2½ lb
KIDNEYS	Cattle Sheep Pigs	Stewing, grilling and frying, braising. Used in pies and puddings	Vary in size, structure, shape and tenderness (most tender from young animals). Ox kidney, weight approx. 1 lb. Calf kidney approx. ½ lb weight. Lamb kidney, weight 2− 4 oz. Pig's kidney, approx. weight 6 oz

TYPE	SOURCE	CULINARY PURPOSE	DISTINGUISHING CHARACTERISTICS AND REMARKS
LIVER	Cattle Sheep Pigs Poultry and Game	Grilling, frying, stewing, braising	Single important organ, involved in regulating metabolism. Varies in size, structure and shape and relative tenderness. In common with kidneys, possesses little connective tissue in younger animals; toughness is caused by over coagulation of the protein due to prolonged cooking. Membrane covering the liver should be removed. Livers from chicken, duck, geese, pheasant, grouse, etc. also used for flavouring sauces
LARD	Pigs	Any cooking process involving fat	The rendered down fat from pigs
LEAF/FLARE FAT OR FLEAD	Pigs	Used in the making of lard or recipes where pork fat is required	The lining fat of the belly which continues up to the kidneys. Greasy-white layered fat generally preferred for preparation of leaf lard
MARROW	Cattle	Used as garnish, savouries	Fatty substance found inside shin and leg bones
PLUCK	Sheep	Used in haggis	One internal unit containing lungs, heart, spleen, liver and windpipe
SPLEEN	Cattle	Pies and flavouring for soups	Oblong in shape with rounded extremities; colour dull reddish-brown to greyish-blue
	Sheep	Blanched and used for stews	Round oyster shape
	Pigs	As sheep	Oblong in shape with rounded tongue-shaped extremities; colour bright red
SWEET BREADS	Calf Lamb	Used as dish in its own, or as garnish	The thymus gland of calves and lamb; lambs fry, often referred to as sweetbread, are the testes
SUET	Cattle Mutton	Used in puddings, pastries. Also rendered down for dripping	Kidney knob fat usually from beef cattle, but may be the kidney fat from sheep, i.e. mutton suet
TAIL	Ox	Used in soups or stews	Extension of spine, high proportion of bone and collagen, resulting in relatively gelatinous stock or sauce when cooked
TONGUE	Ox Calf Sheep	Ox tongue eaten hot or cold as a dish in its own; others as an accompaniment to calf's or sheep's head	Elongated muscle, with thick fibrous coating removed after cooking
TRIPE	Cattle and Sheep	Cooked and usually eaten hot as dish on its own	Stomach lining; often bought ready cooked and bleached
TROTTERS			See feet
UDDER	Cows	Eaten boiled, salted, smoked and fried	Can be bought cooked ready for use

AVAILABILITY OF MEAT, POULTRY AND GAME

(- - Periods of availability)

TYPE	CLOSE SEASON	JAN.	FEB.	MAR.	APR.	MAY	JUN.	JUL.	AUG.	SEP.	OCT.	NOV.	DEC.
BABY CHICKEN		--	--	--	--	--	--	--	--	--	--	--	--
BACON		--	--	--	--	--	--	--	--	--	--	--	--
BEEF		--	--	--	--	--	--	--	--	--	--	--	--
BLACK GAME	11 Dec. — 19 Aug.								-	--	--	--	-
BOILING FOWL		--	--	--	--	--	--	--	--	--	--	--	--
CAPON		--	--	--	--	--	--	--	--	--	--	--	--
CAPERCAILLIE	1 Feb. — 30 Sep.	--									--	--	--
COOT	Limited supply, little demand									--	--	--	--
DEER	See separate table												
DUCK AND DUCKLING		--	--	--	--	--	--	--	--	--	--	--	--
GOOSE AND GOSLING		--	--	--	--	--	--	--	--	--	--	--	--
GROUSE	11 Dec. — 11 Aug.								-	--	--	--	-
GUINEA FOWL		--	--	--	--	--	--	--	--	--	--	--	--
GULL	Limited supply, little demand	--									--	--	--
HARE	No close season but may not be sold March to July inclusive	--	--							--	--	--	--
LAMB		--	--	--	--	--	--	--	--	--	--	--	--
MALLARD	See wild duck												
MOORHEN	Limited supply, little demand									--	--	--	--
MUTTON		--	--	--	--	--	--	--	--	--	--	--	--
ORTOLAN	Limited supply, little demand	--									--	--	--

TYPE	CLOSE SEASON	JAN.	FEB.	MAR.	APR.	MAY	JUN.	JUL.	AUG.	SEP.	OCT.	NOV.	DEC.
PARTRIDGE	2 Feb. — 31 Aug.	- -								- -	- -	- -	- -
PIGEON		- -	- -	- -	- -	- -	- -	- -	- -	- -	- -	- -	- -
PHEASANT	2 Feb. — 30 Sep.	- -									- -	- -	- -
PORK		- -	- -	- -	- -	- -	- -	- -	- -	- -	- -	- -	- -
POUSSIN		- -	- -	- -	- -	- -	- -	- -	- -	- -	- -	- -	- -
PTARMIGAN	11 Dec. — 11 Aug. Limited supply								-	- -	- -	- -	-
QUAIL		- -	- -	- -	- -	- -	- -	- -	- -	- -	- -	- -	- -
RABBIT		- -	- -							- -	- -	- -	- -
RED GROUSE	See grouse												
ROOK PIGEON	See pigeon Good supply, little demand in some regions												
ROOK	No commercial supply			- -	- -	- -							
SNIPE	1 Feb. — 11 Aug.	- -							-	- -	- -	- -	- -
SPRING CHICKEN		- -	- -	- -	- -	- -	- -	- -	- -	- -	- -	- -	- -
SQUAB		- -	- -	- -	- -	- -	- -	- -	- -	- -	- -	- -	- -
TEAL	See wild duck												
TURKEY		- -	- -	- -	- -	- -	- -	- -	- -	- -	- -	- -	- -
VEAL		- -	- -	- -	- -	- -	- -	- -	- -	- -	- -	- -	- -
VENISON	See separate table												
WADERS	1 Feb. — 31 Aug.	- -								- -	- -	- -	- -
WIGEON	See wild duck												
WILD DUCK	1 Feb. — 31 Aug.	- -								- -	- -	- -	- -

Season extends to 20 Feb. in areas below high-water-mark of ordinary spring tide.

TYPE	CLOSE SEASON	JAN.	FEB.	MAR.	APR.	MAY	JUN.	JUL.	AUG.	SEP.	OCT.	NOV.	DEC.
WILD GOOSE	1 Feb. — 31 Aug. Illegal to shoot	- -								- -	- -	- -	- -
WOODCOCK	1 Feb. — 30 Sept. Poor supply	- -									- -	- -	- -
WOOD PIGEON		- -	- -	- -	- -	- -	- -	- -	- -	- -	- -	- -	- -

AVAILABILITY OF DEER

(- - Periods of Availability)

TYPE	CLOSE SEASON	JAN.	FEB.	MAR.	APR.	MAY	JUN.	JUL.	AUG.	SEP.	OCT.	NOV.	DEC.
ENGLAND AND WALES													
RED STAG	1 May — 31 July	- -	- -	- -	- -				- -	- -	- -	- -	- -
RED HIND	1 May — 31 Oct.	- -	- -									- -	- -
FALLOW BUCK	1 May — 31 July	- -	- -	- -	- -				- -	- -	- -	- -	- -
FALLOW DOE	1 Mar. — 31 Oct.	- -	- -									- -	- -
ROE BUCK	No close season	- -	- -	- -	- -	- -	- -	- -	- -	- -	- -	- -	- -
ROE DOE	1 Mar. — 31 Oct.	- -	- -									- -	- -
SIKA STAG	1 May — 31 July	- -	- -	- -	- -				- -	- -	- -	- -	- -
SIKA HIND	1 Mar. — 31 Oct.	- -	- -									- -	- -
SCOTLAND													
RED STAG	21 Oct. — 30 June							- -	- -	- -	-		
RED HIND	16 Feb. — 20 Oct.	- -	-								-	- -	- -
FALLOW BUCK	1 May — 31 July	- -	- -	- -	- -				- -	- -	- -	- -	- -

TYPE	CLOSE SEASON	JAN.	FEB.	MAR.	APR.	MAY	JUN.	JUL.	AUG.	SEP.	OCT.	NOV.	DEC.
FALLOW DOE	16 Feb. — 20 Oct.	- -	-								-	- -	- -
ROE BUCK	21 Oct. — 30 Apr.					- -	- -	- -	- -	- -	-		
ROE DOE	1 Mar. — 20 Oct.	- -	- -								-	- -	- -
SIKA STAG.	1 May — 31 July	- -	- -	- -	- -				- -	- -	-	- -	- -
SIKA HIND	16 Feb. — 20 Oct.	- -	-								-	- -	- -

CUTS OF FISH

The structure of fish makes portioning much simpler than meat because both bones and flesh are delicate. There are a greater number of different types, and a great variation in the size and weight of the different types of fish; halibut can be any weight up to 300 lb, and Dover sole varies from 6 oz to about 2 lb. Most fish can be obtained and cooked whole or portioned before or after cooking. Portioning may be inclusive of bones and skin although this can present safety problems where the consumer may have to remove small sharp bones.

Cuts of fish on the bone are referred to as tail, middle and head or shoulder cut, depending on the part of the fish from which they are taken. Other cuts are cutlets or steaks, usually slices cut across the whole of a fish, thickness varying with the diameter and shape and the required portion size. Fish can be removed from the bone in the form of fillets; these may require further portioning by cutting on a slant across the fillet — if cut square the resulting portion can appear too symmetrical.

Sizes of portion vary with the circumstances. As a guide, raw portion weight from 6 oz to 1¼ lb on the bone, and 2½ oz to 10 oz of filleted fish will prove adequate. These relatively wide weight ranges are partially due to the role that the portion of fish plays in the meal, that is whether it is the main or first course on the bill of fare, and partially on the method of preparation and cooking. If the portion of fish is to be coated with batter and deep-fried, the satisfactory initial portion size may be smaller than if it were to be steamed or baked.

CLASSIFICATION OF FISH AND SHELLFISH

NAME	EXTERNAL FEATURES AND MAIN CHARACTERISTICS	INTERNAL AND COOKED CHARACTERISTICS AND COOKING METHODS	AVAILABILITY
ANCHOVY Salt water	Greenish-blue back, silvery belly. Small, approximately 6 in long, slender, head long and sharp-pointed	Oily, brown flesh, usually salted. Fillets preserved in oil and used in savoury dishes, for garnishing and flavouring. Also available as an essence	Mainly available as a tinned product
ANGELFISH Salt water	Blotchy greyish-brown body with wing-like fins, up to 8 ft long and approximately 100 lb in weight	Flesh white, very firm, remains firm when cooked; cut in fillets and fingers. Normal cooking methods	All year round. Best latter part of the year

NAME	EXTERNAL FEATURES AND MAIN CHARACTERISTICS	INTERNAL AND COOKED CHARACTERISTICS AND COOKING METHODS	AVAILABILITY
ANGLER Salt water	Dirty brown colour, darker network pattern. Very large head, body short and tapering. Length up to 7 ft and weight up to 80 lb. Also known as monkfish, sea devil and fighting frog from its ugly appearance	Flesh white, firm, remains firm when cooked. Best baked, braised, deep-fried	All year round. Best during summer months
BASS Salt water	Long flat silvery body, silvery scales, pink at base of fins; up to 20 lb. Also known as salmon dace, sea salmon and white salmon	Firm flesh remains firm when cooked. Delicate flavour, keeps texture well in cooking. Apply salmon recipes and methods	May to September
BLUE LING Salt water	Elongated body, greenish-blue, white belly. Length up to 3 ft	Flesh firm and white; cut in fillets; liver rich in oil. Cook as for cod	November to April
BREAM Fresh water	Olive or yellowish-green, lighter on sides; fins reddish-brown, tinged scarlet. Length up to 16 in; approx weight ½ – 4 lb. Also known as carp bream	Poor quality flesh, insipid flavour. Normally grilled, not recommended for boiling	June to March
BRILL Salt water	Flat fish, closely resembling turbot. Body oval, brown-mottled, white belly; distinguished from turbot by lesser breadth to length. Weight up to 8 lb approx.	Flesh firm, slightly off white; remains firm and white when cooked. Prepare and cook as for turbot or any white fish	All year round. Best June to March
BRISLING	See Sprat		
BROWN TROUT Fresh water	Greenish-brown with dark speckles; body round and long. May be mistaken for salmon parr. Weight ½ – 3 lb approx.	Very delicate flavour, flesh soft, firmer when cooked; creamy colour. Normal cooking methods	Best April to July
CARP BREAM	See Bream		
CALAMARY	See Squid		
CARP Fresh water	Golden brown upper side, paler on belly; large round scales; two barbules on each side of mouth. Length up to 3 ft; weight up to 18 lb approx.	Flesh soft, firmer when cooked. Cooked whole or cut into fillets. Roe is used as a cheap grade caviar. Normal cooking methods	June to March
CATFISH (See also Dogfish) Salt water	Bluish-grey elongated body; ferocious appearance; dorsal fin extends from behind head to tail. Also called rock salmon, rock turbot, spotted cat and sea wolf	Firm texture; slightly pink. Cut in fillets. Cook as for any strongly flavoured white fish	All year round. Best March to December
CHAR Fresh water	Same shape as trout; bluish-black on back, orange or crimson below. Found in the lakes of Cumberland. Up to 15 in. long	Flesh is similar to trout. Normal cooking methods as for trout	June to March

NAME	EXTERNAL FEATURES AND MAIN CHARACTERISTICS	INTERNAL AND COOKED CHARACTERISTICS AND COOKING METHODS	AVAILABILITY
CLAMS Salt water (Mollusc)	Similar in shape to oysters, but smaller and with a smoother shell	Similar to the oyster and can be eaten raw. Also used in soups and stews	Mainly available tinned
COALFISH Salt water	Bluish-black, silvery belly; large scales and protruding jaw. Member of the cod fish family. Also known as green cod, saithe, sillock, coley	Flesh slightly pink and of coarse texture, cooks lighter; firm and dry, breaks easily in cooking	All year round. Best September to May
COCKLES Salt water (Mollusc)	Shellfish with double concave shell, hinged by a ligament; shell dirty white. Inside yellowish-white with bright red part	Flesh opalescent white, goes firm on cooking. May be roasted, boiled, used in sauces, soups and garnishes.	All year round
COD Salt water	Olive-grey to greenish-brown in colour; round and long. Barbule under lower jaw. Market weights up to 10 lb approx. Length up to 5 ft	White firm, flaky flesh; cut in fillets or steaks. Liver rich in oil. Normal cooking methods	All year round. Best September to March
COLEY	See Coalfish		
CONGER EEL Salt water	Long serpentine body, flattening towards the tail; dark grey on top, lighter on the belly. Up to 9 ft long	Flesh white, firm, of good flavour when cooked; cut in steaks or fillets Larger fish coarse in texture. Used in soups and stews; recipes for cod and hake also suitable	All year round. Best September to May
CRAB Salt water (Crustacean)	Shellfish, reddish-brown, tinted with purple, legs reddish, claws black. Legal minimum size 4½ in. Size across back up to 12 in	Boiled. Brown soft meat from body; firm white flesh from claws. Used as appetisers, soups or main fish course	All year round. Best April to September
CRAWFISH Salt water (Crustacean)	Shellfish (spiny lobster), reddish-brown, legs brown, brick-red when boiled; entirely covered with spines and lacking claws. Up to 18 in long	Flesh opalescent white, goes pink-white when cooked. Treat as lobster	All year round. More plentiful during summer months
CRAYFISH Fresh water (Crustacean)	Shellfish, dull greenish-grey or brown; fore legs are heavy claws. Up to 4 in long	Flesh opalescent, on cooking turns white and firms. Used in soups, shellfish dishes and garnishes	October to March, supply limited
DAB Salt water	Flat fish, colour light brown with or without dark spots, light colour belly. Distinguishable from flounder by the arch on the lateral line. Length up to 17 in	Similar to flounder, flesh off-white and fairly firm, retains colour and texture when cooked. Cook as white fish	April to January
DOGFISH Salt water	Name also applied to catfish and rock salmon; a species of the shark family. Grows to a length of 5 ft	Flesh white, lacks delicacy. Normally cooked by moist methods	All year round

NAME	EXTERNAL FEATURES AND MAIN CHARACTERISTICS	INTERNAL AND COOKED CHARACTERISTICS AND COOKING METHODS	AVAILABILITY
DOVER SOLE Salt water	Flat fish, colour brown with black blotches, white underneath. Up to 18 in long and 6 oz to 2 lb in weight. Small sizes known as slip soles	Flesh firm, white; upper and lower skin can be pulled off. Expensive compared with other sole, but held in high esteem. Normal cooking methods	All year round. Best September to May
DUBLIN BAY PRAWNS	See Scampi		
EEL Fresh water	Colour dark olive-green above, white or yellow below; scales small and embedded in the skin; surface smooth and slimy. Serpentine body; up to 3 ft long	Flesh firm and oily; cooked, firm, white. Normal cooking methods	All year round. Best in autumn
FIGHTING FROG	See Angler		
FLOUNDER Salt water	Flat, dark brown to black, white below; found in sea rivers and estuaries around the coasts. Approximately 12 in long. Also known as fluke	Flesh white and firm, remains firm when cooked as other flat fish. Normal cooking as for white fish	All year round. Best August to November
FLUKE	See Flounder		
GRAYLING Fresh water	Greenish-brown to purple, white belly; large scales, small mouth, long dorsal fin. Length up to 16 in. Approximate weight ½-4 lb	Flesh white and soft, firming when cooked. Normal cooking methods as for trout	June to March
GREEN COD	See Coalfish		
GREY MULLET Salt water	Silvery-grey coarse scales, dark lines running longitudinally, pair of fins protrude from head like ears of a donkey. Approx. length up to 18 in, weight ½-5 lb approx.	Flesh white and soft, remains soft in cooking; less well flavoured than red mullet. Normal cooking methods	All year round. Best June to October
GRILSE	See Salmon		
HADDOCK Salt water	Greyish-bronze top, lighter on sides and belly. Similar in shape to cod; easily distinguished by finger-and-thumb marks near the head	Flesh white opalescent, firm and flaky when cooked. Normal cooking methods	All year round. Best March to December
HAKE Salt water	Brownish-grey on back, white belly. More slender than cod; head large and not unlike pike. Up to 4 ft in length	White firm flesh, finer than cod, ideal for invalids and infants; backbone easily detached, flesh free from bones, easily digested. Normal cooking methods	All year round. Best May to February

NAME	EXTERNAL FEATURES AND MAIN CHARACTERISTICS	INTERNAL AND COOKED CHARACTERISTICS AND COOKING METHODS	AVAILABILITY
HALIBUT Salt water	Dark olive, marbled with lighter olive, white belly; body long and narrow but deep. Up to 5 lb called baby halibut or chicken halibut. May reach over 300 lb in weight	Flesh firm, white, remains firm and white when cooked, inclined to become woolly if not cooked with care. Cut in fillets or steaks. Normal cooking methods as for any white fish	All year round. Best May to September
HERRING Salt water	Steely blue-green, silvery belly. Length 8-15 in. Look for firm flesh, gleaming scales, bright red gills, and full bright eyes. Young called fry or whitebait	Flesh soft and oily; brown in colour; firms up in cooking. High in protein and other nutrients. Smoked, pickled, salted. (See table on preserved fish)	Best June to March
JOHN DORY Salt water	Brown with yellow wavy bands; large ugly head. Compressed body nearly oval, two-thirds in height as length. Weight up to 12 lb	Flesh firm and white, very delicate, resembles lobster meat. Cut into steaks or fillets. Cook as for brill, turbot or sole	All year round. Best September to March
LAMPREY Salt water	Eel-like, scaleless fish, averaging 30 in long; no jaws, but sucker mouth with horny projections simulating teeth	Flesh soft, glutinous, delicate, but difficult to digest; the reputation of being dangerous as two filaments on the back are poisonous and must be removed before cooking. Normal cooking methods	Best April to May
LEMON SOLE Salt water	Shape regular oval, skin smooth and slimy; rich yellow-brown, marbled with round and oval blotches of darker or lighter colour; white below. Approx. length up to 18 in	Flesh white, fairly soft, on cooking firms up to delicate texture and mild flavour. Normal cooking process as for any white fish	All year round. Best June to October
LIMPET Salt water (Mollusc)	Conical, tent-like shellfish with grooved shell. Found clinging to rocks around coasts	Firm flesh, inclined to be rubbery. Normally boiled	All year round
LING Salt water	Greenish brown-grey on back, white below; cod-like in appearance. Up to 7 ft in length	Flesh white, firm, fine; liver rich in oil. Cook as for cod; boiled is inclined to be insipid	Best November to April
LOBSTER Salt water (Crustacean)	Shellfish with a bluish-black shell, thick round body and two large forward claws. Length up to 18 in, weight varies ¾-2¼ lb	Flesh opalescent grey. Boiled, flesh firms up and turns whiter colour, shell turns bright red. Boiled, baked, grilled or fried	All year round. Best and most plentiful during summer
LONG FLOUNDER	See Witch		
MACKEREL Salt water	Colour green, shot with blue, silvery and iridescent; elongated streamlined body; white belly. Length up to 16 in	Flesh firm, oily and dark, similar to herring. Cooks well, apply as for herring. Tendency to become stale very quickly. Excellent smoked	All year round. Best April to November
MONKFISH	See Angler		

NAME	EXTERNAL FEATURES AND MAIN CHARACTERISTICS	INTERNAL AND COOKED CHARACTERISTICS AND COOKING METHODS	AVAILABILITY
MUSSEL Salt water (Mollusc)	Shellfish with almond shaped blue-black shells, concave, long and curved, hinged by ligaments. Good specimen approx. 2 in long	May be eaten raw, usually cooked; orange in colour, firm in texture. All recipes for oysters suitable. Also available smoked and pickled	September to March
NORWEGIAN LOBSTERS	See Scampi		
ORMER Salt water (Mollusc)	Shellfish common around the coast of Channel Isles; shaped like human ear; yellowish-white or white	Flesh yellow mottled with brown; texture similar to whelks and rubbery. Requires long cooking	At special "ormering tides" in winter
OYSTER Salt water (Mollusc)	Shellfish, enclosed in two shells one flat, the other concave; roughly circular and joined with a ligament. Growth rings apparent on shell	Flesh opalescent white, eaten raw. Cooks out white and firm and used as garnish, also in soups, stews and fried	September to April
PERCH Fresh water	Olive-green top, dark vertical bands, yellowish on sides and belly, fins and tail tinged with pink or red. Length up to 17 in	Flesh white, firm good flavour, easily digested. Normal cooking methods	June to March
PERIWINKLE Salt water (Mollusc)	Shellfish, distinguished from whelks, by black shell, smaller size. Also known as winkle	Flesh black or greyish-black. Treat as whelks	All year round
PIKE Fresh water	Elongated body, greenish-grey with yellow blotches, belly white; back straight from head to dorsal fin; mouth large, almost flat. Up to 3 ft in length, weight 30 lb	Flesh white; cooked, rather coarse and firm. Normal cooking methods	June to March
PILCHARD Salt water	Greenish, white belly, similar to herring. Up to 9 in. long. Sardine is smaller and younger	Characteristics as herring. Used as appetiser, fish course or savoury	Mainly available tinned
PLAICE Salt water	Flat, greyish-brown, orange and red spots, bony knob on head behind eyes, white belly. Up to 2 lb in weight	Flesh white, firm; cooked flesh remains firm and white. Cook as for sole	All year round. Best May to December
PRAWN Salt water (Crustacean)	Shellfish, bright grey shell, lined with dark purplish-grey. Length up to 4 in	Normally boiled before they reach market; pink flesh, quite firm. Used as appetiser, garnish	All year round
QUEEN SCALLOP Salt water (Mollusc)	Shellfish, both shells concave, smaller than a scallop; red, pink or brown. Inside white with orange-coloured part	Flesh opalescent white, on cooking it becomes firm. Used in fish dishes, soups, stews	October to March

NAME	EXTERNAL FEATURES AND MAIN CHARACTERISTICS	INTERNAL AND COOKED CHARACTERISTICS AND COOKING METHODS	AVAILABILITY
RAINBOW TROUT Fresh water	Olive-green, darker above lateral line, numerous spots along whole length of the body, reddish iridescent. Up to 12 in long	Treat as brown trout	Best April to September
RED MULLET Salt water	Red or pink with yellow band along sides; two long stiff barbules protruding from lower jaw. Length up to 17 in	Flesh white and firm, good flavour. Baked or grilled, rarely boiled or steamed to avoid loss of flavour	April to October
ROACH Fresh water	Dark blue to greenish on back, silvery on sides and belly, fins tinged with red. Length up to 15 in	Flesh white, turns pink when boiled, firm and bony, good for fish soups. Normal cooking methods	September to March
ROCK SALMON, ROCK TURBOT	See Catfish, Dogfish		
SAITHE	See Coalfish		
SALMON Fresh and salt water	In prime condition, steel-blue on back and sides, silvery on lower sides and belly, round black spots on head and back. Length up to 5 ft and up to 60 lb in weight. Best weights for prime salmon 3-10 lb. Salmon parr and smolt, the young of salmon, under legal minimum size and not allowed to be marketed. Grilse name of a young salmon which has not yet spawned; approx. 3 years old, weight 3-8 lb	Flesh pink, firm, in definite flakes, keeps colour and firmness in cooking. Normal cooking methods	Close season varies; England and Wales: Feb. - Oct. Scotland: mid-Feb.- Oct. Ireland: Jan. - Sep.
SALMON DACE	See Bass		
SARDINE Salt water	See Pilchard	Used as appetiser or savoury, hot or cold	Normally only available tinned
SCALLOP Salt water (Mollusc)	Shellfish with top shell concave, bottom flat, both broadly ribbed, hinged by a ligament. Colour shades of red, pink and brown	Flesh opalescent white with one orange red part; firms on cooking. Used as fish dish, soups, stews	September to March Best November to March
SCAMPI Salt water (Crustacean)	Shellfish with flesh-coloured shell, patches of brown or pink. Two foreward claws, long slender, rough; body cylindrical, broad tail. Up to 8 in. long. Also known as Norwegian lobsters and Dublin Bay prawns	Flesh opalescent-grey, firm; cooks white and firm. Avoid overcooking as flesh becomes pulpy and tasteless. Normal methods of cooking	All year round
SEA BREAM Salt water	Deep plump body, large scales; brownish-scarlet shading to red and silvery on sides and below; black spot at origin of lateral line. Length up to 15 in	Firm white flesh, a little coarse in texture. Best grilled	All year round. Best February to November

NAME	EXTERNAL FEATURES AND MAIN CHARACTERISTICS	INTERNAL AND COOKED CHARACTERISTICS AND COOKING METHODS	AVAILABILITY
SEA DEVIL	See Angler		
SEA SALMON	See Bass		
SEA TROUT Salt water	Colour bluish-black, with purple-silver sides and black spots; whitish belly. Length up to 4 ft. May be mistaken for salmon smolts which are illegal	Pink fleshed, similar to salmon; firm and keeps colour and firmness when cooked. Treat as for salmon	March to August. Best in May
SEA WOLF	See Catfish		
SHRIMP Salt water (Crustacean)	Shellfish of which two kinds are popular. Brown variety larger, turns browner when cooked. Pink variety grey when caught, turns pink when cooked. Up to 2½ in long	Pink variety cooked immediately on catching, usually at sea. Both types used in soups, fish dishes, potted, appetisers, garnishes	All year round
SILLOCK	See Coalfish		
SKATE Salt water	Brownish-grey top, blackish-grey belly, skin smooth with row of spines down centre of back. Usually purchased as wings of skate	Creamy colour, heavy in bones. Cooked, white, firm, tasty. Normal cooking methods; usually served on the bone	All year round. Best August to April
SLIP SOLE	See Dover Sole		
SMELT Salt water	Light olive-green on back, silvery below with iridescent colours on sides. Length up to 10 in; average weight 2-3½ oz	Flesh fairly soft, firms on cooking. Usually cooked whole with head intact but intestines removed. Deep-fried or grilled	Best early autumn and winter months
SPINY LOBSTER	See Crawfish		
SPOTTED CAT	See Catfish		
SPRAT Salt water	Greenish-blue above, silvery and iridescent on sides and below. The young known as brisling, whitebait (see herring) and fry	Similar to herring, soft oily brown flesh which firms on cooking. Treat as herring	November to March
SQUID Salt water	Known as calamary, elongated cap-like body with tentacles. Similar to octopus but smaller	Specialised recipes and treatment but can be deep-fried, poached.	All year round. Best April to October
TENCH Fresh water	Blackish-brown to grey, round; scales embedded in skin. Length up to 2 ft	Flesh white, firm, slightly unpleasant flavour. Normal cooking methods	June to March
TORBAY SOLE	See Witch		

NAME	EXTERNAL FEATURES AND MAIN CHARACTERISTICS	INTERNAL AND COOKED CHARACTERISTICS AND COOKING METHODS	AVAILABILITY
TUNNY Salt water	Also known as tuna, member of the mackerel family, grows to a great size. Body dark blue, lower white, fins yellowish, tipped with black	Flesh brown red, rich in flavour, firm and flaky. Remains firm when cooked. Normal cooking methods	May to October, unless tinned
TURBOT Salt water	Diamond-shaped body, no scales but bony tubercles; colour mottled and speckled brown with off-white belly. Flat fish, distinguishable from brill by greater breadth to length. Up to 3 ft long; called chicken turbot when young	Flesh creamy-white, firm; retains colour and texture in cooking, meaty texture and flavour; cut in steaks or fillets. Normal cooking methods	All year round. Best April to December
WHELK Salt water (Mollusc)	Shellfish, common around the coasts. Spirally coiled shell, creamy in colour	Flesh yellow, mottled with brown or black; texture rubbery. Boiled in the shell	All year round
WHITEBAIT Salt water	The "young" of herring and sprat; small silvery fish, approx. 1-2 in long	Delicate flavour, eaten as caught including head. Normally floured and deep-fried	October to July
WHITE SALMON	See Bass		
WHITING Salt water	Greyish-yellow with yellow stripes along sides; sides and belly silvery. Length up to 16 in	Fragile flesh, soft and white; handled carefully in cooking, flesh retains colour and texture; inclined to be flaky. Normal cooking methods	All year round. Best May to February
WINKLE	See Periwinkle		
WITCH Salt water	Flat fish, body long, oval and thin; pale brown top, white belly. Length up to 17 in. Also known as witchsole, long flounder and torbay sole	Flesh opalescent grey, soft. Cooked, flesh is white and firm, poor flavour. Cook as for sole	All year round. Best September to May

PRESERVED FISH

SMOKED, DRIED, SALTED, PICKLED FISH	NATURE AND TYPE OF FISH	PROCESS
Arbroath Smokies, "Smokies"	Whole gutted haddock or whiting	Hot smoked without excessive drying
Bloater	Whole ungutted herring	Salted, smoke-dried
Buckling	Whole ungutted herring	Salted, hot-smoked
Eyemouth Pales	Split haddock, paler than "Finnans"	Brined; cold-smoked for a shorter time than "Finnans"

Finnan Haddock, "Finnans"	Split haddock or codling	Brined, cold-smoked
Glasgow Pales	Same as Eyemouth Pales	
Golden Cutlets	Split and boned whiting	Brined, dyed, smoked
Kippers	Split herring	Brined, cold-smoked
Morue	Filleted cod	Salted, dried
Pale Cure, "Pales"	Split haddock	Brined, cold-smoked for a shorter time than "Finnans"
Red Herring	Herring, pilchard, sprat, whole ungutted	Salted, cold-smoked
Roll Mops	Filleted herring	Boiled, vinegar-pickled

These do not include every type of smoked, dried, salted and pickled fish since these processes may be applied to a number of fish which are described by the appropriate term, e.g. smoked salmon, pickled herring, salted anchovies etc. The table, therefore applies only to those items with particular names which do not indicate the nature of the fish or the preserving process.

FISH OFFAL

NAME	SOURCE	REMARKS
BONES	White fish	Used in the preparation of stocks and sauces
HEADS	White fish	May be used for main course dishes
LIVER	Various fish	Used in the preparation of fish dishes and for extraction of oil
MUGGIE	Ling	Stomach bag, usually stuffed, used for main courses
OIL	Liver	Extracted from various fish, e.g. cod, halibut
ROE	Various fish	Herring and cod widely used for appetisers, salads, potted

CLASSIFICATION OF FOOD PLANTS
(Fruit and vegetables, herbs and spices, home grown and imported)

NAME/SEASON	PART OF PLANT USED	CULINARY PURPOSES	DISTINGUISHING CHARACTERISTICS AND REMARKS
ALLSPICE (all year)	Fruit (unripe berries)	Flavouring and pickling	Reddish-brown, hard, dried berries, combined flavour of cinnamon, nutmeg, cloves. Available whole or ground
ALMOND (all year)	Nut	Oil, cakes, biscuits, garnishes	White to cream, oval and flat. Available whole, in nibs, flaked, ground; also essence
ANGELICA (all year)	Stem	Flavouring, decoration in sweet dishes	Bright green colour; usually preserved candied
ANISE (all year)	Seed	Flavouring, liqueurs, soups, cakes, sweets	Greyish-brown fruit, size of a pea, liquorice flavour. Available whole or ground
APPLE (all year)	Fruit	Cooking and dessert, acid or sweet; desserts, puddings, stuffings, sauces, preserves, cider. D = dessert apple, C = cooking apple	

ALLINGTON PIPPIN (D) Lemon coloured skin, faintly touched with red; pale sharp flesh. Available from Oct.-Nov.

BLENHEIM ORANGE (D/C) Dual-purpose, russet and orange skin; crisp, yellow, juicy flesh. Available from Nov.

BRAMLEY'S SEEDLING (C) Large, greenish-yellow skin, slight orange-red flush; flesh white, firm, juicy tart flavour. Available Oct. onwards

CHARLES ROSS (D) Well-flavoured, lime-yellow skin touched with red; sweet soft flesh. Available Oct.-Nov. onwards

COX'S ORANGE PIPPIN (D) One of the finest flavoured apples; pale green orange to red flushed skin; yellow, crisp, juicy and scented flesh. Available from Sept.

EGREMONT RUSSET (D) Russet-brown skin, orange blush; crisp, creamy, nutty flesh. Available from Oct.

ELLISON'S ORANGE (D) Greenish-yellow skin with orange-red flecks; juicy, slightly acid flesh, with aromatic, aniseed flavour. Available from Nov.

GRANNY SMITH (D) Green skin, firm, white flesh, sweetly flavoured. Home grown and imported

GRENADIER (C) Yellowish-green skin; flesh white, firm and tart. Available from Aug.

JAMES GRIEVE (D) Pale yellow, red-streaked skin; creamy, sweet, juicy flesh with a fine flavour. Available Aug.-Oct.

NAME/SEASON	PART OF PLANT USED	CULINARY PURPOSES	DISTINGUISHING CHARACTERISTICS AND REMARKS
			LAXTON'S EXQUISITE (D) Golden skin, striped scarlet; faintly spicy, very juicy flesh. Available from Sept.-Oct.
			LAXTON'S FORTUNE (D) Light green skin, red flush and stripes; sweet and well-flavoured. Available from Sep.-Oct.
			LAXTON'S SUPERB (D) Similar to a Cox's Orange Pippin, but sweeter. Red russet skin streaked with bronze; crisp, white, juicy, sweet flesh. Available from Nov.
			LORD DERBY (C) Ribbed skin, green turning yellow. Available from Oct.
			MILLER'S SEEDLING (D) Pale yellow skin, scarlet dots and stripes; crisp, juicy, sharp flavoured flesh. Available from Aug.
			PRINCE ALBERT (C) Pale green skin; soft, white, juicy flesh. Available from Nov.
			RIBSTON PIPPIN (D) Brownish skin merging to dull red; firm, creamy, sweet flesh, strongly scented. Available from Nov.
			RIVAL (D) Brilliantly striped primrose skin, flushed with scarlet; flesh white and juicy. Available from Oct.
			STIRLING CASTLE (C) Pale green skin; flesh white, tender and juicy. Available from Sep.
			TYDEMAN'S EARLY (D) Rich red skin streaked with green; white, crisp, juicy and sweet flesh. Available from Aug.
			WORCESTER PEARMAIN (D) Rich red, pale green streaks; flesh white, crisp and juicy. Available from Sep.
APRICOT (Dec.-Feb., May-Aug.)	Fruit	Desserts, salads, appetisers, stuffings, sauces	Yellow-orange skin and flesh, sweet and acid. Available fresh, tinned or dried
ARROWROOT (all year)	Root (rhizome)	Thickening agent in soups, stews, sauces, baked goods	Fine, white, silky powder. Imported
ARTICHOKE, GLOBE (U.K., May-Sep.)	Flower, leaves	Appetisers, vegetables and salads	Fibrous green leaves that do not soften appreciably in cooking. Fonds tender when young; brown easily when exposed to air. Available fresh (whole) or tinned (fonds)
ARTICHOKE, JERUSALEM (Oct.-Mar.)	Tuber	Vegetable, soups, cooked in salads	Rough, brown appearance; white, firm, sweet flesh; browns when exposed to air. Available fresh
ASPARAGUS (home/grown May-June)	Stem	Appetisers, soups, vegetable, garnish, salads, savouries	Green or purple tips, white stems, fibrous at base. Available fresh, tinned or frozen

NAME/SEASON	PART OF PLANT USED	CULINARY PURPOSES	DISTINGUISHING CHARACTERISTICS AND REMARKS
AUBERGINE (all year)	Fruit	Vegetable	Large purple, glossy skin, firm flesh. Also known as egg plant. Grown in U.K., also imported. Available fresh
BALM (all year)	Leaves	Herb, wine, herb tea	Green, lemon-scented leaves. Available fresh or dried
BANANA (all year)	Fruit	Salads, desserts, garnish	Long yellow fruit; cream-coloured flesh; browns when exposed to air. Imported. Available fresh
BARLEY (all year)	Grain	Beer production, soups, beverages	Seed-like; light white-brown in colour with distinct cut along one side
BASIL (all year)	Leaves	Herb, soups, meat, fish dishes	Green or purple leaves. Available fresh or dried
BAY (all year)	Leaves	Aromatic herb, soups, meat, fish dishes, garnish	Dark green leaves. Available fresh and dried
BEETROOT (all year)	Bulbous root	Salads, vegetable, soup, pickles	Dark purple-red, soluble in water, brighter in presence of acid; round or tapering flesh in concentric rings. Available fresh, pickled, tinned
BILBERRY (July-Aug.)	Berry fruit	Dessert, fruit, puddings, jams	Red-purple, soluble in water. Available fresh, tinned, frozen
BLACKBERRY (July-Oct.)	Berry fruit	Puddings, preserves	Black, juicy and acid. Available fresh, tinned or frozen
BLACK CURRANT (July-Sept.)	Berry fruit	Puddings, jams jellies	Black and juicy. Available fresh, tinned or frozen
BLUEBERRY (July-Sept.)	Berry fruit	Puddings	Blue-black, acid in flavour. Available fresh, tinned or frozen
BRAMBLE (July-Oct.)	Berry fruit	Preserves	The wild, smaller form of blackberry
BROAD BEAN (Apr.-Sept.)	Immature seed	Vegetable, soups, salads	Light green, thick skin on older bean removed before serving. Available fresh, frozen, tinned or dried
BROCCOLI, SPROUTING (all year)	Flower stem	Vegetable, soups	Dark green, purple or white, according to type; similar to small cauliflower. Available fresh or frozen
BRUSSELS SPROUT (Aug.-Mar.)	Leafy buds	Vegetable, soups	Green, small, round, cabbage-like; firm when young. Available fresh or frozen
BUTTER BEAN (all year)	Seed	Vegetable, soups	Variety of Lima bean; creamy-white. Imported. Usually available dried or tinned
CABBAGE (all year)	Leaves	Vegetable, salads, pickles	Several varieties. White, green to purple; multi-leaf, decreasing in size towards heart. Available fresh, pickled (tinned)

NAME/SEASON	PART OF PLANT USED	CULINARY PURPOSES	DISTINGUISHING CHARACTERISTICS AND REMARKS
CAPER (all year)	Flower bud	Pickles, sauces,	Dark green. Available pickled
CAPSICUM	See Peppers		
CARAWAY (all year)	Seed	Cakes, bread, cheese, soups, flavouring, Kummel liqueur	Dark brown, highly scented. Available whole and ground
CARAGEEN (summer)	Seaweed	Jellies, ice cream, salad dressing, confectionery, soups	Dark red, leathery, stalks of varying length, branching in flattened segments; Available fresh and tinned
CARROT (all year)	Root	Vegetable, salads, soup	Bright orange-red; sizes vary with type; sweet flesh. Available fresh, frozen or tinned
CAULIFLOWER (all year)	Flowers	Vegetables, salads, pickles, soups	White, multi-clustered flower; easily discoloured and damaged. Available fresh, tinned or frozen
CELERIAC (Oct.-Mar.)	Bulbous root	Vegetable, salads, soups, appetisers	White, firm texture; spongy and fibrous when old. Discolours in air. Available fresh and tinned
CELERY (all year)	Fibrous stem	Vegetable, salads, stocks, soups, appetisers	Creamy-white to green stems. Available fresh
CHERRY (home grown June-Aug.)	Stone fruit	Dessert, fruit, flavouring, garnish, preserves	Yellow, red and black, according to variety; sweet and acid. Available fresh, frozen or tinned
CHERVIL (summer)	Leaves	Herb, soups, garnish, flavouring	Pale green leaves like parsley or carrot leaves; more delicate flavour than parsley. Available fresh, dried or tinned
CHICORY (winter months)	Leaves and root	Salads, vegetable; root used with or as substitute for coffee	Leaves long and close together, white, tinged with green. Slightly bitter flavour especially when cooked. Available fresh
CHILLI	See Peppers		
CHIVE (spring-autumn)	Leaves	Flavouring, salads, garnish	Long, thin, green leaves with mild onion flavour. Available fresh or dried
CINNAMON (all year)	Bark of tree	Curries, flavouring, confectionery	Pale brown, curling into semi-tubular shape. Available whole or ground
CLOVE (all year)	Flower bud	Flavouring, meats and sweet dishes	Dark brown, nail shape with a bulbous head. Available whole or ground
COCONUT (all year)	Nut	Curries, desiccated coconut, confectionery, cakes, garnish	Ovate with fibrous husk and white flesh. Contains juice (coconut milk). Available fresh or dried (desiccated)
CORIANDER (all year)	Seed	Condiment, herb, alcoholic beverages	Similar in colour and size to peppercorn. Available whole or ground

NAME/SEASON	PART OF PLANT USED	CULINARY PURPOSES	DISTINGUISHING CHARACTERISTICS AND REMARKS
CORN	See Maize		
CRANBERRY (Oct.-Feb.)	Berry fruit	Preserves, sauces, garnish	Red and glossy. Available fresh, frozen or tinned
CRESS (all year)	Seedling	Salads, garnish	Green leaf, white stem, similar to mustard, not to be confused with water cress. Available fresh
CUCUMBER (all year)	Fruit	Vegetable, salads, garnish, pickles	Long, round green fruit, dark green; pale green flesh. Available fresh or pickled
CUMIN (all year)	Fruit	Culinary spice used for curry powder	Resembles caraway in aroma and flavour; oblong and bristly. Available whole or ground
DAMSON (Aug.-Sept.)	Fruit	Preserves, puddings, pickles	Oval, purple in colour. Available fresh or tinned
ELDER (June-Sept.)	Flowers or berries	Preserves, wine	Flowers white and open; berries purple or dark red, juicy and bitter. Available fresh
ENDIVE (winter)	Leaves	Salads, vegetable	Leaves curled and finely divided, light green; lettuce size. Available fresh
FENNEL (all year)	Seeds, leaves, stems	Fish soups, vegetable, sauces, salad dressings, herb	Bulbous base, fibrous stem. Seeds available whole or ground; stems available fresh or tinned
FIG (Aug.-Dec.)	Fruit	Dessert fruit, fresh salads, preserves	Green, brown or purple according to variety; sweet and juicy. Available fresh, dried or tinned
FRENCH BEAN (July-Sept.)	Pod and seed	Vegetable, salads, appetiser, pickles	Long thin green pod. Available fresh, frozen or tinned
GARLIC (all year)	Bulb	Flavouring	Bulbous, containing several separate cloves. Available fresh and as a flavoured salt
GHERKIN (all year)	Immature fruit	Pickles, garnish	Immature cucumber shaped, 1-3 in long. Available pickled and fresh
GINGER (all year)	Root (rhizome)	Flavour, confectionery, curry powder, beverages	Irregular, knobbly shape; pungent flavour. Available fresh or as dried pieces, ground; also preserved
GOOSEBERRY (Apr.-Sept.)	Fruit	Fruit pies, sauces, preserves	Bright green, yellow or red; hairy. Available fresh, tinned or frozen
GRAPEFRUIT (all year)	Fruit	Appetisers, jams, salads, juice	Yellow skin; juice and flesh pale yellow or pink; sharp citrus flavour. Available fresh, tinned (segments or juice)
GRAPE (all year)	Fruit	Fruit salads, desserts, garnish	Green, red or black in bunches. Available fresh or tinned
GREENGAGE (Aug.-Sept.)	Fruit	Pies and puddings, jams, sauces	Size of plum, often russet colour, firm green flesh with scented, sweet flavour. Available fresh or tinned

NAME/SEASON	PARTS OF PLANT USED	CULINARY PURPOSES	DISTINGUISHING CHARACTERISTICS AND REMARKS
HARICOT BEAN (all year)	Seed	Soups, vegetable, salads	Dried bean, brown or white. Soaked before cooking. Available dried
HORSERADISH (Sept.-Mar.)	Root	Condiment, flavouring, sauces	Yellow-fleshed, tap root. Available fresh, whole or ready grated or in preparations
JUNIPER (all year)	Berry	Flavouring, cordial	Bluish-black. Available fresh or dried
KALE (Nov.-May)	Leaves	Vegetable	Green, curly. Available fresh
KOHL RABI (Autumn & winter)	Bulbous root	Vegetable, salads	Turnip-rooted cabbage, swollen base of stem used; green and purple. Available fresh
LAVER (summer)	Seaweed	Vegetable, soups, stews, pickles	Resembling spinach when cooked; dark brown in colour. Available fresh or prepared
LEEK (Aug.-May)	Bulbous stem	Vegetable, soups, stews	Elongated white bulb, green leaves; almost whole plant used. Available fresh
LEMON (all year)	Fruit	Flavour, juice, baking, confectionery, garnish	Yellow skin; acid flesh with sharp citrus flavour. Available fresh or bottled
LENTILS (all year)	Seeds	Soups, stews, vegetable	Yellow, green and orange-red. Available dried
LETTUCE (all year)	Leaves	Salads, soups, vegetable, garnish	Round or elongated; pale green crisp leaves, lighter in colour near centre. Many varieties. Available fresh
LOGANBERRY (June-Aug.)	Berry Fruit	Dessert fruit, pies, jams	Pale red, seedless, sweet and juicy. Available fresh, frozen and tinned
MAIZE (Corn cobs July-Nov.)	Seed	Flour, vegetable, soups, cereals	Corn cob or sweet corn, individual ears attached to husk, covered by green leaves, silky hairs. Available whole fresh, and as kernels frozen, tinned or dried
MARJORAM (all year)	Leaves	Aromatic leaf for soups, sauces	Dark green leaves. Available fresh or dried
MARROW (April-Nov.)	Fruit	Vegetable, pickles	Oval-cylindrical; green striped green and yellow. Available fresh
MEDLAR (Oct.-Dec.)	Fruit	Preserves	Plum-size; chestnut colour, tart flavour. Available fresh or preserved
MELON (all year)	Fruit	Dessert fruit, appetisers, preserves	Several varieties. Cantaloup has rough, deeply grooved skin, orange coloured, aromatic flesh. Charentais, yellow-green mottled skin, deep orange flesh, strongly aromatic. Honeydew is smooth-skinned, green, yellow or near white; dark green, yellow, sweet flesh. Ogen is small, about 6 in across; bright yellow, ribbed green; sweet, yellow aromatic flesh. Home grown and imported. Available fresh and tinned

NAME/SEASON	PARTS OF PLANT USED	CULINARY PURPOSES	DISTINGUISHING CHARACTERISTICS AND REMARKS
MINT (all year)	Leaves	Flavouring, sauces, garnish	Aromatic green leaves. Available fresh or dried
MOREL (all year)	Fungus	As mushrooms	Species of mushroom, conical globe-shaped cup; black-yellow in colour, stem white. Available fresh or tinned
MORELLO	See Cherry		
MULBERRY (Aug.-Sept.)	Berry fruit	Dessert fruit, preserves	Purple, juicy, easily bruised. Available fresh
MUSHROOM (all year)	Fungus, stem and cap	Soups, sauces vegetable, salads, pickles	Brown gills; white cap and stalk; firm when fresh, softens and discolours with age. Available fresh in various sizes, buttons up to large flat caps. Also available tinned and dried
MUSTARD (CRESS) (all year)	Stem and leaves	Sandwiches, salads, garnish	Bright green leaves. Available fresh
NECTARINE (July-Sept.)	Stone fruit	Fruit salads, preserves, dessert fruit	Peach-like, smooth and shiny skin; white flesh. Available fresh and tinned
NUTMEG (all year)	Seed	Flavouring, desserts, cakes, sauces, vegetables	Walnut size; wooden texture throughout; brown. Available whole or ground
OATS (all year)	Seed	Oatmeal, porridge	Purchased in prepared form, e.g. pin-meal, rolled oats, etc.
OLIVE (all year)	Stone fruit	Pickles, appetisers, garnish. Oil for cooking and salad dressings	Green or black, cherry-size; firm flesh. Available pickled in brine, whole or stoned
ONION (all year)	Bulb	Soups, stews, vegetable, flavouring, pickles, chutneys	Bulbous, cream-white to yellow flesh, layered; highly flavoured. Available fresh, dried, frozen or tinned
ORANGE (all year)	Fruit	Salads, sauces, juices, preserves, dessert fruit, garnish	Sweet, juicy or bitter (marmalade) flesh. Available fresh and tinned, frozen and tinned as juice
PARSLEY (all year)	Leaves and stem	Flavouring, garnish	Curly or crisp, green leaves. Available fresh and dried
PARSNIP (Aug.-Apr.)	Root	Vegetable, soups, salads	Cream-white flesh, light colour skin; carrot shape. Available fresh
PEAS (May-Oct.)	Seed	Vegetable, soups, salads	Pod contains about six peas; bright green colour. Available fresh, frozen, dried or tinned
PEACH (U.K., May-Oct.)	Stone fruit	Dessert fruit, salads, preserves, pies	Rose pink to golden in colour; velvety skin; juicy pink flesh. Home grown and imported. Available fresh or tinned

NAME/SEASON	PARTS OF PLANT USED	CULINARY PURPOSES	DISTINGUISHING CHARACTERISTICS AND REMARKS
PEAR (U.K., Aug.-Mar.)	Fruit	Dessert fruit, fresh salads, puddings, preserves	Season extends from Aug. to Mar. Numerous varieties, varying in colour, shape and size. COMICE large-sized, tough yellow skin, showing slight russeting; sweet, juicy flesh with superb flavour. CONFERENCE medium-sized, also suitable for cooking; clear russet skins with pale green; flesh sweet and juicy with a pink flush when ripe
PEPPERS (all year)	Seed	Hot pungent flavouring	Unripe dried berries known as black peppercorns. Ripe dried, skinned berries known as white peppercorns, milder than black. Available whole or ground
	Fruit (chilli)	Flavouring, accompaniments, pickles	Small conical red, green or yellow, firm fruits; strong, pungent flavour. Used in manufacture of cayenne pepper. Imported. Available fresh, dried or pickled
	Capsicums (pimento or sweet pepper)	Vegetable, flavouring, appetisers, garnish	Large and bulbous, red or green; mild in flavour; red inclined to sweetness. Used in manufacture of paprika pepper. Home grown and imported. Available fresh, tinned or dried
PIMENTO	See Peppers		
PINEAPPLE (all year)	Fruit	Juice, preserves, sauces, salads, garnish	Rough brown outer skin, yellow, sweet, juicy flesh. Imported. Available fresh or tinned
PISTACHIO (all year)	Nut	Sweets, meat dishes, flavouring, garnish	Nut coated in purple skin; green inside. Available fresh
PLUM (home grown July-Oct.)	Stone fruit	Dessert fruit, pies, jams, pickles, puddings, sauces	Numerous varieties, shapes and sizes, colour from yellow, red, blue and deep purple; sweet or slightly acid, juicy flesh. Available fresh, tinned or dried (prunes)
POTATOES (all year)	Tuber	Main vegetable, soups, salads, pies, stews, garnish	Numerous varieties, early and main crop, most being suitable for general purposes, others with particular characteristics as shown

ARRAN BANNER (early main crop) large, round, skin and flesh white, slightly mealy

ARRAN CAIRN (late main crop) medium-sized, long oval, skin white, flesh white or slightly lemon.

ARRAN CONSUL (early main crop) medium-sized, oval, skin white, flesh white to pale lemon

ARRAN PILOT (first early) medium to large, kidney shape, skin and flesh white, good for frying

BALLYDOON (first early) medium-sized, oval, skin and flesh white

BEN LOMOND (second early) medium-sized, oval, skin and flesh white

BRITISH QUEEN (second early) medium-sized, oval, skin and flesh white

CRAIG'S ROYAL (second early) medium to large, round, skin partly coloured, pale cream flesh, nutty flavour

DR. McINTOSH (early main crop) medium-sized, kidney shape, skin and flesh white, close-textured, fries well

DESIRÉE (main crop) oval, red skin, pale cream flesh, mealy texture, good for boiling, mashing, roasting, jacket baking and chipping

NAME/SEASON	PARTS OF PLANT USED	CULINARY PURPOSES	DISTINGUISHING CHARACTERISTICS AND REMARKS

DUNBAR STANDARD (late main crop) medium-sized, oval to kidney shape, skin and flesh white

EPICURE (first early) irregular size, round, skin and flesh white, mealy with age.

GOLDEN WONDER (late main crop) medium-sized, oval to pear shape, russet brown, flesh white to pale lemon, mealy, good for baking

GREAT SCOT (early main crop) medium-sized, round shape, slightly flattened, skin light lemon, flesh white

HOME GUARD (first early) medium-sized, oval, skin and flesh white.

KERR'S PINK (late main crop) medium-sized, round, skin pink, flesh white, mealy, good for mashing, creaming, baking

KING EDWARD (main crop) medium-sized, oval, skin white, splashed with pink, creamy flesh, slightly mealy

MARIS PEER (second early) medium-sized, oval, skin and flesh white

MARIS PIPER (early main crop) medium to large, oval, skin and flesh white

MAJESTIC (early main crop) medium to large, oval or pear shape, white skin and flesh, good fried or baked, may discolour when boiled

NINETYFOLD (first early) medium-sized, oval, pointed, skin and flesh white

PENTLAND ACE (second early) medium-sized, oval to kidney shape, skin white, flesh pale lemon

PENTLAND CROWN (early main crop) medium to large, oval, skin and flesh white

PENTLAND DELL (early main crop) medium to large, kidney shape, skin and flesh white

RECORD (early main crop) medium to large, oval, skin white with yellow tinge, flesh yellow, mealy

RED KING (early main crop) medium-sized, oval, pink skin, creamy flesh, mealy, good for baking

REDSKIN (early main crop) medium-sized, short oval to round, skin pink, flesh pale lemon, mealy, good for baking

STORMONT DAWN (early main crop) medium-sized, oval, skin white splashed pink, flesh creamy

SUTTON'S ABUNDANCE (early main crop) medium-sized, oval to round, skin and flesh white

ULSTER CHIEFTAIN (first early) medium-sized, oval, skin and flesh white, mealy

ULSTER DALE (second early) medium to large, kidney shape, skin white, flesh white with yellow tinge, slightly mealy

ULSTER PRINCE (first early) medium to large, kidney shape, skin and flesh white, mealy

ULSTER SUPREME (late main crop) medium-sized, oval, skin and flesh white

VANGUARD (first early) medium-sized, oval to round, skin and flesh white

WITCHILL (first early) medium-sized, oval to kidney shape, skin and flesh very white

PUMPKIN (summer, autumn)	Fruit	Savouries, desserts, pies	Large, round, yellow; heavy in seeds. Available fresh or tinned
QUINCE (Oct.-Nov.)	Fruit	Preserves, confectionery	Pear-like in appearance; hard texture; acid. Available fresh
RADISH (all year)	Tuber	Salads, garnish	Bright red or white skin; white or pink flesh. Available fresh
RASPBERRY (July-Oct.)	Berry fruit	Dessert fruit, sweets, pies, jams, preserves, sauces	Bright red. Available fresh, frozen, tinned and as an essence
RED CURRANT (July-Aug.)	Berry fruit	Dessert fruit, puddings, sweets, jams, jellies	Bright red, juicy. Available fresh, frozen or tinned

NAME/SEASON	PARTS OF PLANT USED	CULINARY PURPOSES	DISTINGUISHING CHARACTERISTICS AND REMARKS
RHUBARB (Dec.-July)	Stem	Pies, puddings, sweets, sauces, jams	Long red stalks, white at base, green at leaf, acid flavour. Available fresh or tinned
RICE (all year)	Grain	Vegetable, accompaniments, sweets, garnish	Small hard grain. Long pointed, suitable for garnish and vegetable dishes; short round for sweets and puddings. Available fresh, par-boiled and cooked. Also ground (rice flour)
ROSE HIP (summer/autumn)	Fruit	Syrups, sauces, jams, soups	Fruit of wild roses, bright red to orange, centre with hairy seeds. Available fresh or preserved
ROSEMARY (all year)	Leaves	Aromatic herb, meat and poultry dishes	Sweet scented leaves. Available fresh or dried
ROSE PETAL (all year)	Flower petal	Jams, jellies, rose water	Usually purchased in crystallised form for decoration purposes
ROWAN (autumn)	Berries	Preserves, jellies	Orange-red, size as red currants; hard bitter flesh. Available fresh or preserved
SAFFRON (all year)	Flower stigmas	Flavouring, dye	Dried stigma of crocus flowers; dark red to orange colour, fine misshapen shreds. Available dried
SAGE (all year)	Leaves	Aromatic herb, soups, stews, stuffings	Greyish-green leaves. Available fresh or dried
SALSIFY (Oyster plant) (Oct.-May)	Root	Soups, salads, vegetable	Cylindrical shape, white firm flesh and dark colour skin; peeled subject to browning. Available fresh or tinned
SAMPHIRE (all year)	Leaves	Aromatic herb, pickles	Light green leaves. Available fresh or dried
SHALLOT (Sept.-Mar.)	Bulb	Flavouring, garnish	Similar in shape to onion but smaller, flavour fuller than that of onion. Available fresh
SLOE (autumn)	Stone fruit	Wines, gins, jams, jellies	Wild plum, size of large peas, almost black when ripe. Available fresh
SORRELL (summer)	Leaves	Vegetable, sauces, salads, garnish	Arrow-shaped green leaves; acid flavour. Grows wild. Available fresh
SOYA BEAN (all year)	Seed	Oil, margarine, vegetable, pickles, flour	Hairy, yellow-green pod containing three or four green, yellow brown or black beans. Available dried, fermented, fresh. Excellent source of vegetable protein
SPINACH (all year)	Leaves	Vegetable, soups, salads	Broad triangular leaf, bright green. Available fresh, frozen or tinned
STRAWBERRY (home grown May-July, autumn)	Berry fruit	Dessert fruit, jams, sauces	Bright red. Available fresh, frozen, tinned and as an essence

NAME/SEASON	PARTS OF PLANT USED	CULINARY PURPOSES	DISTINGUISHING CHARACTERISTICS AND REMARKS
SWEDE (Sept.-May)	Root	Vegetable, stews, salads	Purple top, ridged; flesh white to yellow. Available fresh
SWEET CORN (home grown July-Nov.)	See Maize		
TANGERINE (Oct.-Mar.)	Fruit	Dessert fruit, sweets, preserves	Smaller than the orange, same characteristics; sweet. Available fresh or tinned
TANSY (summer)	Leaves	Flavouring herb, puddings, omelets, cakes	Dark green, fragrant leaves. Available fresh. Rare
TAPIOCA (all year)	Root extract	Soups, thickening agent, sweets, pudding, garnish	Small white pellets. Available in bullet, pearl, crushed or flaked form
TARRAGON (summer)	Leaves	Flavouring herb, fish, pickles, French mustard	Olive green, thin and narrow leaves. Available fresh, dried or as flavoured vinegar
THYME (all year)	Leaves	Aromatic herb, soups, stews, stuffings, sauces	Small grey or green aromatic leaves. Available fresh or dried
TOMATO (all year) (U.K., Mar.-Nov.)	Fruit	Vegetable, salads, soups, appetisers, garnish	Bright red or orange-yellow skin and flesh. Available fresh or tinned
TRUFFLE (all year)	Fungus (underground)	Garnish, flavour	Irregular round shape; dark brown and warty. Rarely available fresh, imported tinned
TURMERIC (all year)	Root	Seasoning, spice, pickles	Yellow grey outside, orange inside; principal ingredient in curry powder. Available in root form or ground
TURNIP (all year)	Root	Vegetable, soups, salads	Round, flattened or cylindrical; yellow or white, may have green or purple zone near the top. Available fresh or tinned
VANILLA (all year)	Pod	Flavouring, sauces, confectionery	Elongated thin pod, black; boiled in milk or stored in sugar for flavour transfer. Available in pod form, as an essence or prepared vanilla sugar
VIOLET PETAL (all year)	Flower petal	Confectionery	Usually purchased crystallised for cake and confectionery decoration
WALNUT (all year)	Nut	Oil, confectionery, pickles, desserts, garnish	Light brown in colour; cream-white flesh. Hard outer shell. Available green (young), whole or shelled
WATERCRESS (all year)	Stalk and leaves	Soups, salads, garnish	Dark green stems and leaves; minty flavour. Available fresh
WHEAT (all year)	Grain	Flour, bread, cakes, thickening agent	White, amber, purple or blue-coloured grains; white flesh. Usually only available milled (flour)

CLASSIFICATION OF BRITISH CHEESES

NAME	REGION	DISTINGUISHING CHARACTERISTICS AND REMARKS
ARRAN	Central Lowlands	Small, rindless, Dunlop-type cheese, weighting 2¼ lb. Yellow, similar texture to Cheddar, mellow flavour. Available in tartan cartons
AYRSHIRE COTTAGE	Central Lowlands	Cottage cheese. Available in cartons and bulk form
AYRSHIRE CREAM	Central Lowlands	Cream cheese, nutty. Available in cartons and bulk form
BATH	West Country	Round of flat shape; soft, unripened white cheese, firm texture, distinguished flavour
BLAIRLIATH CREAM	Highlands	Cream cheese. Available in cartons
BLAIRLIATH CROWDIE	Highlands	Available in cartons and as a mixture of Crowdie cheese with fresh cream. See Crowdie
BLARNEY	Northern Ireland	Semi-soft cheese, mellow, smooth flavour; numerous small holes; skin red or cream, firm texture
BLUE DORSET	See Dorset Blue Vinney	
CABOC	Highlands	Small sausage-shaped rolls covered in oatmeal; soft full-cream cheese, light cream colour, mild flavour
CAERPHILLY	Wales	Large flat round cheese, creamy-white in colour, close crumbly texture; mild delicate buttermilk flavour
CAITHNESS	North East Scotland	Available in flat ½ lb rounds with removable wax skin, semi-soft cheese, smooth texture and mild flavour
CAITHNESS, SMOKED	North East Scotland	Similar to Caithness cheese, but with natural smoke flavour
CAITHNESS, SOFT	North East Scotland	Available in tubs. Full-cream, soft texture, delicate flavour; additional flavours of pineapple, chives, Drambuie liqueur
CARRICK	Central Lowlands	Available in wedges, rind-less orange coat. Full-cream, soft cheese, creamy colour, soft to firm texture and mild buttery flavour
CHEDDAR	West Country	Several sizes up to 70 lb. Close, creamy, firm texture; a full-milk cheese with rich nutty taste
CHESHIRE	North West England	Large flat round shape, available in red and white varieties, mellow, slightly salty flavour, crumbly texture. Also available blue, close texture and rich creamy flavour
COTHERSTONE	North England	Similar to Blue Wensleydale; a rich double-cream cheese, known as Yorkshire Stilton
COTTAGE CHEESE	National	Soft creamy cheese, white in colour with fine grains bound together; made from separated milk with added cream; a mild or bland flavour. Also available with additional flavours, e.g. chives
CREAM CHEESE	National	White, soft, smooth-textured cheese with mild savoury flavour. Double cream cheeses contain 40-60 per cent butter fat, other cream cheeses contain 25-35 per cent. Available with additional flavours

NAME	REGION	DISTINGUISHING CHARACTERISTICS AND REMARKS
CROWDIE CHEESE	Scotland	White, smooth-textured, crumbly cheese made from skimmed milk. Also available with the addition of full cream
DERBY	North Midlands	Large flat round cheese weighing approximately 30 lb. White-cream in colour, fairly close texture with mild flavour, developing tangy flavour with maturity. See also Sage Derby
DORSET BLUE VINNEY	West Country	Flat round shape weighing approximately 12 lb. White in colour with blue veins and open texture; strong rich flavour
DOUBLE GLOUCESTER	West Country	Large, flat, round shape weighing approximately 30 lb. Pale yellow to a deep gold, smooth texture; flavour varies from mellow to fairly pungent
DUNLOP	Central Lowlands	Similar to Cheddar, but with softer texture, moister and milder in flavour. Available in a variety of sizes and shapes
GALLOWAY CHEDDAR	Central Lowlands	Rind-less Cheddar type, available in 10 lb blocks
GLOUCESTER	See Double Gloucester	
HOWGATE	Central Lowlands	Available in small rounds and half rounds; mild, soft cream cheese, creamy and smooth texture
HOWGATE CREAM	Central Lowlands	Cream cheese; rolled in oatmeal
HRAMSA	North East Scotland	Available in cartons; soft cream cheese made from double cream, flavoured with wild garlic
IRISH BLUE	Northern Ireland	Available in large flat rounds. Creamy-white in colour with blue-green veins; strong flavour
IRISH CAERPHILLY	Northern Ireland	Hard cheese, tangy buttermilk flavour
IRISH CAMEMBERT	Northern Ireland	Available in large flat rounds; soft delicate cheese, pale creamy colour; flavour mild to strong depending on age
IRISH CHEDDAR	Northern Ireland	Available in large flat rounds and in rind-less blocks
IRISH CHESHIRE	Northern Ireland	Hard, pressed cheese with crumbly texture. Available red or white; similar to Cheshire cheese
IRISH EDAM	Northern Ireland	Available in 4-5 lb rounds, covering of red skin. Pale yellow in colour, with few small holes throughout close texture; mild milky flavour
IRISH EMMENTHAL	Northern Ireland	Available in a large flat round, traditional large round holes throughout; mild sweet flavour, firm texture
IRISH GOUDA	Northern Ireland	Available in flat rounds. Mild, creamy, semi-soft cheese, deep yellow
LAMMERMOOR	Central Lowlands	Available in 1 lb squares; soft full-fat cheese, mild flavour
LAMMERMOOR, PEAT-SMOKED	Central Lowlands	Smoked version of Lammermoor

NAME	REGION	DISTINGUISHING CHARACTERISTICS AND REMARKS
LANCASHIRE	North West England	Available in large flat rounds, weighing approximately 40 lb. Creamy-white colour, crumbly texture and creamy mild flavour
LEICESTER	North Midlands	Available in large flat rounds, weighing approximately 35 lb. Rich reddish-brown in colour, slightly flaky texture, mild mellow flavour
MORVEN	Highlands	Available in small squares; mild flavour. Also available flavoured with caraway seeds; coated with cheese wax, no rind
ORKNEY CHEDDAR	Orkney Isles	Available in 1 and 1½ lb flat rounds; white or red in colour with similar characteristics to Cheddar. A smoked version also available
PIPER	North East Scotland	Available in 1 lb flat rounds; similar to Caithness cheese; coated with cheese wax
SAGE DERBY	North Midlands	Similar to Derby cheese, but with additional flavour of sage
STILTON	East Anglia	The king of cheeses. Available in flat rounds weighing approximately 14 lb. Starts as white Stilton and matures to blue Stilton. Open crumbly texture, flavour ranging from mild and mellow to rich mellow; rind usually crusted and browny-grey
TARA	Northern Ireland	Open textured cheese, mild clean flavour
WENSLEYDALE	North Yorkshire	Available in flat rounds weighing approximately 10 lb or in 1¼ lb rounds. Double-cream, white cheese with fairly close texture and mild, slightly salty flavour. A blue variety also available with a soft, close texture and rich creamy flavour
WEXFORD	Northern Ireland	Characteristics similar to Cheshire cheese; hard, pressed cheese, bright yellow in colour with distinct sharp flavour

CLASSIFICATION OF MILK

TYPE	DISTINGUISHING CHARACTERISTICS AND REMARKS
BUTTERMILK	By-product after the manufacture of butter; may be sweet or sour; watery consistency, used in baking
CHANNEL ISLAND	Milk from Jersey or Guernsey breeds of cow with minimum butter fat content of 4 per cent, available untreated or pasteurised; relatively high cream content and rich creamy flavour
CONDENSED	Available in tins; may be derived from whole milk, partially skimmed or skimmed milk. Subjected to a process which removes a high proportion of water resulting in a thick consistency. During the process sugar is added; sometimes referred to as sweetened milk; off-white in colour and very sweet
CULTURED MILK	See Yogourt
DRIED	Sometimes referred to as milk powder and available in packaged weights. May be derived from full cream milk, skimmed milk or filled milk. Shelf life of approximately one year without refrigeration, reconstituted into liquid milk for direct consumption or cooking

EVAPORATED	Available in tins. May be derived from whole milk, partially skimmed or skimmed milk. Subjected to a process which removes a high proportion of water, no sugar added. Off-white in colour and rich creamy flavour; may be used straight from tin or diluted as required
FILLED MILK	Term applied to skimmed milk where non-milk fats have been substituted for original butter fat
HOMOGENISED	Term applied to milk which has first been pasteurised and then processed in order to break down and distribute the butter fat content. No cream line apparent. Type of milk most commonly used in "static milk dispensers"; smooth creamy flavour
LONG LIFE	See Ultra High Treated Milk
PASTEURISED	Milk which has been subjected to mild heat treatment in order to destroy bacteria. Most common type of milk available, must not contain less than 3 per cent butter fat. Cream line very apparent
SKIMMED MILK	Milk from which the cream has been removed resulting in blue milk. Also obtainable as a filled milk with added non-milk fat
SOUTH DEVON	Milk from South Devon breeds of cow with minimum butter fat content of 4 per cent; relatively high cream content, very apparent cream line and rich creamy flavour
STERILIZED	Available in bottles only. Homogenised milk heat treated after sealing in bottles producing rich creamy appearance with cooked-milk-pudding flavour. Will keep unopened for several weeks without refrigeration; especially popular in the Midlands. No apparent cream line
ULTRA HIGH TREATED (U.H.T.)	Homogenised milk subjected to ultra high temperature treatment, a milk of exceptional keeping qualities (unopened) without refrigeration. Similar flavour to homogenised milk. No apparent cream line
YOGOURT	May be made from whole, partially skimmed, evaporated or dried milk. Milk is first homogenised and partially cooled, specially prepared culture added, which with time and temperature controls produce distinctive characteristics. Available plain or flavoured. Long storage not recommended as this may increase acidity

CLASSIFICATION OF BRITISH CREAMS

TYPE	DISTINGUISHING CHARACTERISTICS AND REMARKS
CLOTTED	Made mainly in Cornwall, Devon and Somerset; applied to cream which has been separated by scalding, cooling and skimming; should contain no less than 55 per cent butter fat. Flavour full and nutty; golden yellow in colour, thick granular texture; better keeping qualities than fresh cream
CULTURED	Prepared similarly to yogourt; may be purchased or used in any recipe with sour cream
DOUBLE	Contains a minimum of 48 per cent butter fat; normally pasturised to kill harmful bacteria and improve keeping qualities. Colour varies, depending on type of cattle feed and time of year, from white to yellow; thick flowing consistency. See also whipping cream
LONG KEEPING (Longlife)	See Ultra High Treatment
SINGLE	Contains a minimum of 18 per cent butter fat, similar characteristics to double cream but of thinner consistency, unsuitable for whipping

SOUR	See Cultured cream
STERILIZED	Similar characteristics to sterilised milk, but thicker, containing a minimum of 23 per cent butter fat; not suitable as whipping cream
ULTRA HIGH TREATMENT	Homogenised cream subjected to an ultra high temperature treatment which produces a cream of exceptional keeping qualities (unopened) without refrigeration. Treatment has little effect on flavour or use; provided it has a minimum content of 35 per cent butter fat it can be whipped
WHIPPED	Contains a minimum of 35 per cent butter fat. Creams with butter fat content of less than 35 per cent are not recommended for use unless some agent such as egg white is added. Characteristics similar to double cream, but of thinner consistency. Care should be taken not to over-whip or a curdled effect will be produced. Whipping cream is more economical than double cream although lacking its stability and richness

Metric Cookery In Britain

With the proposed introduction of the Metric System by 1980 and the gradual phasing-out of the Imperial System, professional cookery schools are adopting the new weights and measures and attempting to convert existing recipes in a practical manner.

Many foodstuffs and drinks are at present already sold in the recommended metric weights and measurements. The basic unit is the kilogram (kg) divided into smaller units of 25, 50, 75, 125, 250, 375 or 500 grams (g).

The liquid metric unit is the litre (l) and its multiples of 1000 millilitres (ml).

The standard equipment of measuring which will replace the British Imperial Standard spoons are as follows:

¼ teaspoon = 1.25 ml	2 teaspoons = 10 ml
½ teaspoon = 2.5 ml	1 tablespoon = 15 ml
1 teaspoon = 5 ml	4 teaspoons = 20 ml

The 1.25 ml and the 20 ml are optional spoon sizes.

In order to avoid confusion the term "cup" has been dropped and "measure" is used instead. The range of standard measures is:

50 ml = 1/6 measure = 1¾ fl oz	150 ml = ½ measure = 5¼ fl oz
75 ml = ¼ measure = 2½ fl oz	300 ml = full measure = 10½ fl oz
100 ml = 1/3 measure = 3½ fl oz	

In addition, a 50 ml measure = 50 g sugar; 75 ml measure = 50 g flour; 100 ml measure = 100 g sugar; 150 ml measure = 100 g flour.

The capacity of measuring jugs will be marked as follows:

1 litre = 35 fl oz	125 ml (1/8 l) = 4½ fl oz
750 ml (¾ l) = 26 fl oz	100 ml (1/10 l) = 4 fl oz
500 ml (½ l) = 17½ fl oz	50 ml = 2 fl oz
250 ml (¼ l) = 9 fl oz	25 ml = 1 fl oz

Proposals for dual marked scales recommend divisions of 5 g for scales designed to take a low range of weights up to 2 kg. For larger models which would weigh up to 10 kg, divisions of 25 g are advised.

Baking tins, flan rings and all equipment measured in length will be converted to the nearest round centimetre so that a 6 inch flan ring equals a 15 cm one and pastry will be rolled out to 20 cm by 50 cm rather than 8 inches by 20 inches. (see Table I). It may be necessary to use millimetres for fine details.

Temperatures in ovens and thermometers for sugar boiling, etc. will follow the Celsius scale for electric cookers (see Table II).

METHODS OF CONVERSION

The range of equipment associated with the cooking process as well as the weight and volume of packaging are critical factors in writing and using metric recipes. Centuries of development based on these physical factors have combined to produce a system of manageable quantities in Britain based on Imperial measures. In order to replace this system with that of Metric, recipes should be easily read, be quickly measured out, using the most readily available equipment, and produce a finished article comparable in texture, flavour, consistency and quantity with the original.

In order to read easily and measure ingredients quickly, exact conversions from Imperial to Metric must be ruled out since these would produce unwieldy figures. Approximate conversions have therefore been arrived at as shown in Tables III and IV.

Table 1. Metric Length *versus* Approximate Imperial Lengths		Table II. Temperature Equivalents for Oven Thermostat Markings		
1 metre contains 100 centimetres (cm)				
I metre = 100 cm =	40 inches	°F 550 —— 290 °C		Gas Marks
95	- 38	525 —— 270		—
90	— 36	500 —— 250		—
85	- 34	475 —— 240		9 —
80	— 32	450 —— 230		8 —
75	- 30	425 —— 220		7 —
70	— 28	400 —— 200		6 —
65	- 26	375 —— 190		5 —
60	— 24	350 —— 180		4 —
55	- 22	325 —— 170		3 —
50	— 20	300 —— 150		2 —
45	- 18	275 —— 140		1 —
40	— 16	250 —— 130		½ —
35	- 14	225 —— 110		
30	— 12	200 —— 100		
25	— 10	175 —— 80		
20	— 8	150 —— 70		
15	- 6			
10	— 4			
5	- 2			

Table III. Solid. Conversions based on 1 pound to 500 grams (½ kilo) and units of 25 grams

IMPERIAL		METRIC
16 oz (1 lb)	——	450 – 500 g (½ kg)
15 oz	——	425
14 oz	——	400
13 oz	——	375
12 oz (¾ lb)	——	350 – 325
11 oz	——	300
10 oz	——	275
9 oz	——	250
8 oz	——	250 – 225
7 oz	——	200
6 oz	——	175
5 oz	——	150
4 oz	——	125 – 100
3 oz	——	75
2 oz	——	50
1 oz	——	25
½ oz	——	12
¼ oz	——	6

Table IV. Liquid. Conversions based on 2 pints to 1 litre and units of 25 millilitres

IMPERIAL		METRIC	
Fluid ounces	Pints	Litre	Millilitres
40	2	1	1000
32			800
28			700
24			600
20	1	½	500
16			400
15	¾		375
14			350
13			325
12			300
11			275
10	½	¼	250
9			225
8			200
7			175
6			150
5	¼	1/8	125
4		1/10	100
3			75
2			50
1			25

Glossary

Acidulated Applied to water to which lemon juice or vinegar has been added to prevent discoloration of vegetables or fruit.

Arrowroot A starchy substance used to thicken sauces.

Aspic A clear jelly with setting properties; made from the reduced cooking juices of fish, meat or chicken.

Bain marie A French term for a large pan of hot water in which a smaller pan or dish is placed for cooking or baking delicate-textured dishes; also applied to a double boiler, the lower half of which contains boiling water.

Bannock Originally applied to bread, this term loosely describes any large round scone or biscuit the size of a dinner plate.

Bap An oval-shaped white bread roll served warm for breakfast. A Shearer's or Harvester's Bap was the size of a dinner plate, served at the mid-day meal, accompanied with ale.

Bard To cover lean meat, especially game birds and young chicken, with thin slices of pork fat or fat bacon to keep the flesh moist during roasting.

Baste To moisten meat and poultry during roasting with pan juices to prevent the flesh from drying out.

Baton A narrow strip of, for example, carrot, turnip or other firm vegetable.

Batter A fairly liquid mixture of flour, milk or water, and eggs in which ingredients are dipped prior to deep or shallow-frying.

Beat To introduce air into a mixture with the aid of a wooden spoon, whisk or electric mixer in order to achieve a light and fluffy texture.

Bind To hold a dryish mixture, such as a stuffing, together with eggs, cream, melted butter or a thick white or brown sauce.

Blanch To immerse in hot or boiling water for a short period of time in order to loosen tough skins from nuts, such as almonds, fruits like peaches or vegetables such as tomatoes. Blanching also preserves the colour of green vegetables and removes excessively acid flavours.

Blancmange A sweet, flavoured cream mould set with gelatine.

Blend To amalgamate ingredients of different textures to a smooth texture by mixing them with a spoon, beater or liquidiser.

Blind Used of pastry which is baked in advance prior to being filled with a sweet or savoury mixture.

Boil To cook in a liquid maintained at a temperature of 212°F (100 °C).

Braise Applied to meat, game, poultry or vegetables browned in hot fat or dripping, then cooked in a covered pot with additional vegetables and a small amount of water, stock, milk or wine.

Brawn Meat or offal, frequently pickled, cooked to a soft consistency, covered with aspic (or jelly) and left to cool and press in a mould under a heavy weight. Usually turned out, upside down, before serving.

Bread, pulled Chunks, about 2 inches thick, pulled from the inside of a loaf, dried in a cool oven until creamy-yellow in colour and served with thick lentil, pea or bean soup.

Bridie A Scottish term applied to a semi-circular pasty.

Brine A solution of salt and water used in preserving and pickling of meat, fish and vegetables.

Broth The liquid in which meat or fish has been boiled, with the additional flavours of herbs, spices and vegetables. Often thickened with a starchy substance.

Brown To fry in fat over high heat in order to sear the outer surfaces of meat so as to seal in the juices.

Bumper Similar to a turnover, but slightly larger.

Carcass A slaughtered animal before it is cut up into joints.

Carotenoid Applied to any red or yellow pigment such as is found in carrots.

Carvie An abbreviation of caraway sticks made from a dough of 6 oz plain flour, salt, 3 oz butter and 3 oz cream cheese gathered with 1 tablespoon of cold water. Chilled and rolled out into 5in long strips, ½in wide, decorated with blanched almonds and baked for 10 minutes, at 400°F, gas mark 6. Served hot as an accompaniment to soups.

Casserole A stew of meat, fish or vegetables cooked over a long period in a slow oven. Also applied to the dish, usually earthenware and covered with a lid, in which the stew is cooked.

Cecil A small round ball of cooked, minced beef, breadcrumbs, lemon peel, anchovies and herbs and seasoning, coated with egg and breadcrumbs and deep-fried.

Charlotte mould A plain mould used for setting creamed sweets and puddings; the term is also applied to a fruit cream itself.

Cheeky pig Pasty shape originating in Leicestershire and made in the shape of a pig.

Chine Chiefly applied to a joint of bacon or pork and consisting of the whole loin.

Chill To cool food in a refrigerator or cool place without submitting it to freezing temperatures.

Chlorophyll The green colour pigment in plant leaves and stalks.

Chop To cut with a sharp knife blade into roughly, finely or very finely divided segments.

Clarified butter Butter melted slowly and strained through muslin to remove all traces of impurity.

Collared Referring to a piece of meat or fish tied up into a roll or coil.

Collier s foot A type of pasty taken down the coal pits by colliers in the North of England; designed to fit into the space of a miner's lunch box and having a thick pastry base and a thinner pastry cover over the filling. The name refers to the shape of the pastry when rolled out, the heel part of the "foot" being the thicker.

Collier's roast Meat, usually salted mutton, roasted over a "collier" meaning a charcoal burner, with particular reference to meat that had been poached and cooked in the woods under cover of night.

Collop A slice of boneless meat, the equivalent today of a steak.

Compôte A dessert of fresh or dried fruit stewed in a syrup of water and sugar; served chilled.

Cop loaf A hollow loaf containing an apple in the centre, the top decorated with the head of a cock or dragon made with paste. Traditional in Wiltshire and placed by a child's bedside on Christmas mornings.

Curd The semi-solid part of milk produced by souring fresh milk with the addition of rennet.

Curdle To cause fresh milk to separate into curds and liquid by heating or by the addition of an acid substance. Also applied to a sauce, soup or creamed butter and sugar that separates through overheating or faulty addition of beaten eggs.

Cure To preserve fish or meat by drying, smoking, salting or pickling.

Custard Sweetened or spiced milk or cream thickened with eggs; originally made on a pastry base.

Dariole mould Small cup-shaped mould used for making individual cream desserts and jellies.

Deep dish pie A savoury or sweet pie having one layer of pastry over the filling.

Deep-fry To immerse food, often coated in a batter or egg and crumbs, into hot fat until crisp.

Devilling A highly seasoned and spiced preparation spread on meat, poultry or fish prior to grilling or roasting.

Dice To cut into small or large cubes.

Dough The basic mixture for bread, consisting of flour, water or milk, and sometimes egg and butter. Usually made with a raising agent; kneaded, shaped and proved.

Dredge To sprinkle food with flour or sugar.

Dress To prepare poultry or game for cooking by plucking, draining and trussing; also to arrange cooked shellfish, such as lobster or crab, to be served in their shells or to decorate or garnish a cooked dish.

Dripping The fat which is melted or drips from a meat joint, poultry or game during cooking.

Drover's bread A basic fermented dough with a layer of strips of beef, rolled to a sausage and baked; it constituted the staple diet for drovers and travellers.

Dumpling A small ball, made from forcemeat or dough, usually poached or steamed and served with soups and stews. Also a whole fruit wrapped in pastry and baked.

Dust To sprinkle food lightly with flour, sugar, seasoning or spicing.

Faggot (of herbs) A small bunch of one sprig of thyme, parsley stalk, bay leaf and celery stick wrapped in leek leaves and tied with fine string. Used as a flavouring to soups and stews; also known as pot posy.

Farl One of the quarters from a large round bannock.

Flake To separate cooked fish into small slivers.

Flan pie A pie having two layers of pastry, one above and one below a savoury or sweet filling; arranged in a flan ring.

Flan tart Arranged in a flan ring like a flan pie, but having only a pastry base.

Fool A sweet of sieved fruit pulp mixed with whipped cream.

Freeze To subject food for storage to temperatures at or below $32^\circ F$ ($0^\circ C$).

Fritter A small piece of food coated with a sweet or savoury batter and deep-fried.

Galantine Boned and stuffed poultry, game or meat, covered with aspic and served cold.

Garnish Edible decorations to a finished dish.

Gelatine A transparent substance made from animal bones which sets to a jelly when cold; used to gel both savoury and sweet dishes.

Giblets The offal of poultry and game as well as the trimmings, such as neck, pinions and feet.

Girdle In North England and Scotland, the term for a griddle.

Glacé Glazed or iced.

Glaze A glossy finish to a cooked dish, achieved by brushing the hot surface with beaten egg, milk, sugar syrup or jelly; also the pan residues from roasted or fried meat, or concentrated meat stock.

Grate To reduce a food to small particles by rubbing it against a sharp, rough surface.

Griddle A flat, heavy metal baking plate used on top of the stove; it replaced the original baking stones. Also the item baked on such a plate.

Hang To suspend game by the feet, game birds by the beaks in order to tenderise the flesh.

Hoggan In the West Country, a round of pastry enclosing a savoury or sweet filling; similar to a pasty, but with the join at the top of the long thin shape.

Huff paste A flour and water dough formerly used to enclose meat, poultry or game in order to prevent the food from drying out during cooking and afterwards discarded.

Infuse To steep ingredients in a liquid, hot or cold, so as to extract the flavour.

Joint A prime roasting cut of meat; also the action of cutting up an animal carcass, poultry or game.

Jug To stew a meat dish in a covered pot.

Junket A sweet dish made with fresh milk, variously flavoured, and set with rennet.

Kedgeree Of Indian origin, a savoury dish containing rice, cooked fish, eggs, herbs and spices.

Knead An essential step in bread-making which strengthens the dough enabling it to rise.

Knock back To press out air bubbles in a risen dough before shaping and proving.

Lancashire foot A pasty made from an oval of pastry and folded over into an elliptical shape; higher in the centre than an ordinary pasty.

Lard Refined or natural pork fat.

Larding Inserting thin strips of pork fat or bacon with a larding needle into lean meat to prevent it from drying out during roasting.

Leaven A raising agent, such as yeast, which causes the air in bread dough or batter to expand and rise.

Liaison An amalgam of egg yolks and cream used to thicken and enrich soups.

Mandolin slicer A cutting tool, consisting of a sharp blade in a flat wooden surround, on which to slice food thinly.

Marinade A mixture of oil, wine or vinegar, with herbs, spices and seasoning in which meat, game or fish is steeped in order to flavour or tenderise it.

Meringue Whisked egg white and sugar baked until crisp at low oven temperature.

Mince To pass food through a hand-operated or electric mincing machine to reduce it to a fine, smooth texture.

Mousse A savoury or sweet cold dish of light fluffy texture through the incorporation of cream, whipped eggs and air trapped with gelatine.

Offal The internal edible organs of food animals.

Oggie A local Cornish name for a pasty.

Olive A thin slice of meat rolled round forcemeat to an elongated shape resembling the olive shellfish. shellfish.

Onion, studded Whole onion to which a bay leaf is attached with whole cloves.

Par-boil To cook food partially by boiling, prior to another cooking method.

Pastry A dough of flour, fat and water or milk, baked until golden brown and crisp.

Pasty A pastry circle folded over a savoury or sweet filling to a semi-circle.

Patty Small cake, savoury or sweet, or an individual pie; baked in small cases.

Pickle To preserve meat, fish, vegetables or fruit in a brine or vinegar solution. Also applied to the preserving liquid and the finished product.

Pie Any item of food, savoury or sweet, encased in or covered with pastry.

Pipe To decorate finished dishes with cream, meringue, icing, etc., through a forcing bag fitted with a plain or fluted nozzle.

Pith The white cellular lining beneath the skin of lemon, orange and other citrus fruits.

Plate pie A pie made on a plate or deep dish, having two layers of pastry, one beneath and one on top of the filling.

Plate tart Pie made on a plate, consisting of a pastry base and a sweet or savoury open filling.

Pluck Heart, liver and lungs of a food animal; also to remove feathers from poultry or game birds.

Poach To cook food at a simmer, just below boiling point.

Pot posy Faggot of herbs.

Pottage A thick broth containing chopped-up pieces of meat.

Pottager Earthenware or wooden bowl or basin for pottage.

Priddy oggie A modern version of the Cornish Tiddy Oggie; originating in Somerset the cheese pasty contains pork, Cheddar cheese, parsley and egg.

Preserve To store food in good condition by treating it with heat, refrigeration, chemicals, pickle, brine or sugar solutions.

Prove To rise bread dough a second time, after knocking back and shaping.

Pudding An alternative term for dessert or sweet; also a suet crust with a sweet or savoury filling.

Pudding Pie The old original term for what is now called a flan tart, made in a shallow mould and left uncovered.

Pulp Food reduced to a soft consistency by boiling and/or crushing; sometimes sieved to remove pips from soft fruit pulp, for example.

Purée An alternative term for pulp; usually sieved.

Raised pie Savoury or sweet pie filling completely enclosed in hot water crust.

Ramekin Small ovenproof dish, usually of earthenware.

Ratafia biscuit Small biscuit or cake, flavoured with bitter almonds; macaroon.

Reduce To concentrate a liquid by rapid boiling and evaporation.

Render To melt down fat from meat and trimmings through slow cooking or to clarify fat of impurities.

Relish Sharp sauce to accompany savoury food.

Rennet Substance used to curdle cream for junkets.

Rice paper Edible flimsy paper used as a base for macaroons.

Rissole Small cake or patty made from cooked, minced meat.

Roast To cook over an open fire, on a spit or in the oven through radiant heat.

Roe Applied to the milt of male fish and known as soft roe, while hard roes are the eggs of female fish; the roes of shellfish are known as coral, from the red colour.

Roux Basic mixture of fat and flour to which liquid is added to create a sauce; may be white or brown, depending on initial cooking and type of liquid.

Saucer pie The original name for a plate pie.

Savoury Term applied to any dish that does not constitute a sweet course. Also a separate course towards the end of a meal, before the dessert.

Scald To heat milk to just below boiling point. Also to immerse fruit or vegetables in boiling water prior to removing peel.

Scone A section from a large round bannock or a small round of bannock dough.

Score To cut through the outer covering of fat on pork, for example, to produce crackling. Also to make decorative patterns in the pastry crust on sweet pies.

Seasoned flour Flour mixed with salt and pepper and sometimes other spices; used as a coating for food to be shallow-fried.

Sear To brown meat over high heat so as to seal the surfaces and prevent the juices from escaping.

Shallow-fry To cook in a small-amount of melted fat or oil until brown, not necessarily crisp.

Shred To tear or cut thin strips from an ingredient.

Sift To press flour or sugar through a sieve to remove lumps.

Simmer To cook food in a liquid kept just below boiling point.

Skewer Wooden or metal pin of various sizes used to hold food in shape during cooking.

Skim To remove fat or scum from a boiling liquid; also to take the top layer of cream from fresh milk.

Sippet Bread dice tossed in butter or oil and fried until crisp and brown, or dried in the oven.

Slice To cut food, such as bread, meat, fish or vegetables into flat pieces, varying in thickness.

Smoke To cure fish or bacon over wood smoke for various lengths of time.

Sorbet Water ice made with sieved fruit pulp.

Souse To pickle fish in a brine or a vinegar and spice solution.

Spurtle Wooden spoon used for stirring porridge.

Stand pie A raised pie shaped without a mould; it originates in Yorkshire and describes a round pie with slightly bulging sides.

Steam To cook over the vapours arising from boiling water.

Steep To soak food in a liquid until saturated or to soak in water to remove excess flavour, such as salt.

Sterilise To destroy food germs by exposing them to heat.

Stew To simmer food slowly in a covered pan or casserole dish, on top of the stove or in the oven.

Stir To mix ingredients with a spoon or fork.

Strain To separate solids from liquids by passing them through a sieve, muslin or jelly bag.

Stuffing Forcemeat mixture used as a filling for meat, poultry, sometimes game, and fish and vegetables.

Sweet herbs Small bunch of fresh parsley, sweet marjoram, winter savory, orange and lemon thyme; tied with fine string and used for flavouring.

Syllabub Cold sweet made with wine and thick cream.

Syrup Thick solution of sugar and water or fruit juice.

Tiddy oggie Cornish term for a pasty at the time of depression after the closure of tin mines in Cornwall when meat in the pasties were substituted with potatoes.

Trifle Originally a cold dessert of thick custard over wine-soaked almond biscuits and covered with a syllabub, now replaced with cream.

Truss To tie a bird or joint of meat into shape with skewers and string prior to cooking.

Turnover In the South of England and in the Midlands, a semi-circular pasty with a sweet filling.

Unleavened Thin flat bread made from dough without any raising agent.

Vanilla sugar Sugar flavoured with vanilla, obtained by enclosing a vanilla pod with sugar in a closed jar.

Wafer Thin biscuit, usually made with rice flour.

Waffle Usually a sweet batter mixture cooked to a crisp golden biscuit in a special waffle iron.

Whip To beat ingredients, such as eggs or cream, until frothy or thick.

Whisk To beat air into a soft mixture until fluffy.

Yogourt Curdled milk treated with beneficial bacteria.

Yeast Raising agent chiefly used in bread dough which rises as the cells ferment.

Yule dough Small bread doll made at Christmas to represent the infant Jesus; also known as Yule dows or Yule babies.

Zest Piece of the outer coloured skin from lemon, orange or other citrus fruit; used peeled or grated as a flavouring or garnish.

Index